A HANDBOOK
on
THE BOOK OF JOB

The Handbooks in the **UBS Handbook Series** are detailed commentaries providing valuable exegetical, historical, cultural, and linguistic information on the books of the Bible. They are prepared primarily to assist practicing Bible translators as they carry out the important task of putting God's Word into the many languages spoken in the world today. The text is discussed verse by verse and is accompanied by running text in at least one modern English translation.

Over the years church leaders and Bible readers have found the UBS Handbooks to be useful for their own study of the Scriptures. Many of the issues Bible translators must address when trying to communicate the Bible's message to modern readers are the ones Bible students must address when approaching the Bible text as part of their own private study and devotions.

The Handbooks will continue to be prepared primarily for translators, but we are confident that they will be useful to a wider audience, helping all who use them to gain a better understanding of the Bible message.

Helps for Translators

A HANDBOOK ON

The
Book
of Job

by William D. Reyburn

UBS Handbook Series

United Bible Societies
New York

Books in the series of **UBS Helps for Translators** may be ordered from a national Bible Society or from either of the following centers:

United Bible Societies
European Production Fund
D-70520 Stuttgart 80
Postfach 81 03 40
Germany

United Bible Societies
1865 Broadway
New York, NY 10023
U. S. A.

L. C. Cataloging in Publication Data:

Reyburn, William David.
    A handbook on the book of Job / by William D. Reyburn.
      p.   cm. — (UBS handbook series)
    Includes bibliographical references and index.
    ISBN 0-8267-0117-5 (flexible)
    1. Bible. O.T. Job–Translating. 2. Bible. O.T. Job—Commentaries. I. Title. II. Series.
BS1415.2.R49   1992
223'.1077—dc20

92-12735
CIP

ABS-1/94-300-1,050-EB-2-104880

Contents

TABLE OF CONTENTS

Illustrations

Preface

This Handbook, like others in the series, concentrates on exegetical information important for translators, and it attempts to indicate possible solutions for translational problems related to language or culture. The authors do not consciously attempt to provide help that other theologians and scholars may seek but which is not directly related to the translation task. Such information is normally sought elsewhere. However, many church leaders and interested Bible readers have found these Handbooks useful and informative, and we hope that this volume will be no exception.

As translators move from their work on books of the New Testament into the Old Testament, they find that the material with which they work is quite different. This is especially true of the Book of Job, with respect both to its form and to its content. *A Handbook on the Book of Job* has been prepared with the hope that this volume in the series of Helps for Translators will clarify the content and show the significance of the forms of the discourse.

The format of this Handbook follows the general pattern of earlier volumes in the series. The RSV and TEV texts are presented in parallel columns, first in larger segments that will make possible an overview of each section of discourse, and then in bold print, normally verse by verse, followed by detailed comments and discussion. RSV serves as the base upon which the discussion takes place, and quotations from the verse under discussion are printed in **boldface**. Quotations from other verses of RSV and from other versions are printed between quotation marks and in normal typeface. TEV serves as a primary model of how a translation may take shape; however, many other versions are provided as well, especially where they offer models that may be more satisfactory than those of TEV.

Toward the end of the project the Revised English Version and the New Revised Standard Version became available, but it is to be regretted that it was too late to use them in any systematic fashion. Translators may wish to have these new versions available during the translation of the Book of Job, because they provide many good models of possible translations.

A limited bibliography is included for the benefit of those interested in further study. The glossary explains technical terms according to their usage in this volume. The translator may find it useful to read through the glossary in order to become aware of the specialized way in which certain terms are used. An index gives the location by page number of some of the important words and subjects discussed in the Handbook, especially where the Handbook provides the translator with help in rendering these concepts into the receptor language.

The original author who prepared an exegetical draft for this Handbook was the Reverend Brynmor F. Price, who served at the time on the staff of the British and Foreign Bible Society. He has since retired, and in the meantime the base and model approach to our Handbooks has changed radically, and new insights are available, not only about the content and meaning of this book, but about the forms of the Hebrew poetry that comprise the major section of the book. It was therefore necessary to begin the drafting anew. The author, however, found that the original draft did serve as a good resource, and both credit and thanks are due to Mr. Price for his work on the project.

The editor of the UBS Handbook Series continues to seek comments from translators and others who use these books, so that future volumes may benefit and may better serve the needs of the readers.

Abbreviations Used in This Volume

General Abbreviations, Bible Versions, and Other Works Cited
(For details see Bibliography.)

B.C.	before Christ	LB	Living Bible
BDB	Brown, Driver, and Briggs lexicon	Mft	Moffatt
		NAB	New American Bible
BJ	*Bible de Jérusalem*	NEB	New English Bible
FRCL	French common language version	NIV	New International Version
		NJB	New Jerusalem Bible
GECL	German common language version	NJV	New Jewish Version
		RSV	Revised Standard Version
HOTTP	Hebrew Old Testament Text Project	SPCL	Spanish common language version
K-B	Koehler-Baumgartner lexicon	TEV	Today's English Version
		TOB	*Traduction œcuménique de la Bible*
KJV	King James Version		

Books of the Bible

Gen	Genesis	Prov	Proverbs
Exo	Exodus	Isa	Isaiah
Lev	Leviticus	Jer	Jeremiah
Num	Numbers	Lam	Lamentations
Deut	Deuteronomy	Ezek	Ezekiel
Josh	Joshua	Zeph	Zephaniah
1,2 Sam	1,2 Samuel	Hag	Haggai
1,2 Kgs	1,2 Kings	Zech	Zechariah
1,2 Chr	1,2 Chronicles	Matt	Matthew
Est	Esther	1,2 Cor	1,2 Corinthians
Psa	Psalms	1,2 Thes	1,2 Thessalonians

Translating the Book of Job

The Book of Job is a story told in the form of a poem. It begins with a prose introduction describing Job as a good man who is faithful to God, wealthy, and concerned for the right relation between God and his family. In a meeting between God and Satan, God permits Satan to test Job's loyalty. These tests result in the destruction of Job's family and wealth. He is reduced to sitting in agony on a pile of ashes, where three friends find him when they arrive to bring him comfort. In his despair Job regrets that he was born and curses his origins. The friends enter into three rounds of lengthy arguments with Job, in which they maintain that Job's suffering is the result of his sin. Job argues against them, insisting stubbornly that he is innocent, and demands that God appear in court with him. These speeches make up the main body of the poem.

After the three rounds of speech arguments, there is a poem on wisdom, and then Job gives his final speech, in which he recalls his former happy days and compares them to his present suffering and shame. When Job becomes silent, a young man who has overheard the arguments, and who is unhappy with the way the three friends have confronted Job, delivers lengthy opinions about Job's tragedy. His remarks are essentially a repetition of the traditional wisdom expressed already by the friends. Finally the LORD speaks out of the storm and confronts Job with many unanswerable questions concerning creation and nature. Job confesses his ignorance, and the poem ends in prose, as it began. Job and his friends are reconciled with each other and with God, and Job is restored to even more than his former glory. In his old age Job dies.

The Book of Job may be divided into 10 major sections:

1. Prose introduction (chapters 1-2)
2. Job regrets that he was born (chapter 3)
3. First round of speeches (chapters 4-14)
4. Second round of speeches (chapters 15-21)
5. Third round of speeches (chapters 22-27)
6. A poem about wisdom (chapter 28)
7. Job's final statement (chapters 29-31)
8. Elihu's speech (chapters 32-37)
9. God's speech (chapters 38-41)
10. Prose closure (chapter 42)

It is also possible to view the outline of Job as made up of five sections which form a pattern on the order A-B-C-B'-A'. This is to be read as: A is one thing, B

1

is a different thing, and C is different again, A′ is similar to A, and B′ is similar to B. This scheme may be arranged as follows:

A *Introduction in prose* (chapters 1–2)

    B *Arguments* (three rounds of speeches, chapters 3–27; Job initiates the speeches in chapter 3, and closes them in chapters 26–27)

        C *Meditation* (a poem on wisdom, chapter 28)

    B′ *Arguments* (Job again initiates the speeches, chapters 29–31, and closes them, 42.1-6; Elihu's speech, chapters 32–37; God's speech, chapters 38–41.)

A′ *Conclusion in prose* (42.7-17)

Although somewhat forced into a mold, this patterned view of the poem has the advantage of calling attention to the structural similarities in each half of the poem, and of viewing the chapter on wisdom (chapter 28) not as foreign to the structure but rather as the bridge between the two halves. In the body of the Handbook, we will call attention to various ways in which the poet anticipates or foreshadows matters in A and B that take on their fuller meaning in B′ and A′.

Regardless of how the chapters of Job may be arranged to depict the overall structure, the translator has to work with the poem in the order it is presented, verse by verse and chapter by chapter. For this reason a guide is required that will reveal the specific content of the poem as the discourse flows from topic to topic.

Detailed Outline of the Book

The above general outline of ten section will now be revised and laid out in detail. Each major section consists of one or more divisions which may also be subdivided into smaller units. Each section, division, and subdivision is accompanied by a reference in parentheses. These ten sections serve to organize the material in the Handbook.

In order for translators to get a good grasp of the content of the Book of Job, it is recommended that they read Job by following this outline before beginning to translate. It is also recommended that translators consider using more subdivision headings than Today's English Version (TEV) does. They may also organize their own translations along the lines of this outline—mainly by the use of carefully chosen headings, as suggested below.

    1. **Prose Introduction** (1.1–2.13)
        A. The man Job (1.1-1.5)
        B. First meeting of God and Satan (1.6-12)
        C. First test of Job (1.13-19)
        D. Job praises God (1.20-22)
        E. Second meeting of God and Satan (2.1-6)
        F. Second test of Job (2.7-10)
        G. Job's three friends arrive (2.11-13)

2. Job's Opening Speech (3.1-26)
    A. Job regrets that he was born (3.1-26)
        1. Job curses his birth (3.1-10)
        2. Job's complains that his existence is unbearable (3.11-26)

3. First Round of Speeches (4.1-14.22)
    A. Eliphaz's first speech (4.1-5.27)
        1. Job should have hope (4.1-6)
        2. The righteous do not suffer from God's anger (4.7-11)
        3. Eliphaz reports a vision: no one is righteous in God's eyes
           (4.12-21)
        4. Eliphaz says Job alone is to blame (5.1-7)
        5. Eliphaz advises Job to take his case to God (5.8-16)
        6. Eliphaz assures Job that God will restore him (5.17-27)
    B. Job replies (6.1-7.21)
        1. Job is weighed down by grief (6.1-7)
        2. Job is without hope and strength (6.8-13)
        3. Job complains that his friends deceive him (6.14-23)
        4. Job insists that he is innocent (6.24-30)
        5. Job complains to God about his oppressive existence (7.1-8)
        6. Life is short and Job wishes God would leave him alone
           (7.9-16)
        7. Job asks God why he watches him so closely (7.17-21)
    C. Bildad's first speech (8.1-22)
        1. Bildad advises Job to plead with God and have his fortunes
           restored (8.1-7)
        2. The ancients knew that the godless suffer (8.8-19)
        3. God will help Job if he is faithful (8.20-22)
    D. Job replies (9.1-10.22)
        1. Job sees no way to win his case with God (9.1-4)
        2. Job cannot confront a powerful God (9.5-13)
        3. It is futile for Job to attempt to prove that he is innocent
           (9.14-24)
        4. Job recognizes there is no one to mediate between him and
           God (9.25-35)
        5. Job accuses God of being unfair to his creatures (10.1-7)
        6. Job accuses God of watching over him to destroy him (10.8-17)
        7. Job asks God to leave him alone as he is near death (10.18-22)
    E. Zophar's first speech (11.1-20)
        1. Zophar says God has not punished Job to the extent his guilt
           demands (11.1-6)
        2. God's wisdom is beyond Job's understanding (11.7-12)
        3. Zophar assures Job that God will reward him if he will re-
           nounce his evil (11.13-20)
    F. Job replies (12.1-14.22)
        1. Job claims he is just as wise as the friends (12.1-6)
        2. God has given wisdom to the animals (12.7-12)
        3. God is the divine destroyer (12.13-25)

3

4. Job's argument is with God (13.1-5)
5. Job questions the friends' worth as witnesses against him (13.6-12)
6. Job will argue his case face to face with God (13.13-16)
7. Job calls on God to appear in court with him (13.17-23)
8. Job complains again against God (13.24-28)
9. Job describes the briefness of life (14.1-6)
10. Job complains that God destroys his hope to live (14.7-22)

4. Second Round of Speeches (15.1–21.34)
  A. Eliphaz's second speech (15.1-35)
    1. Eliphaz rebukes Job for his claims of innocence (15.1-16)
    2. The fate of the wicked (15.17-35)
  B. Job replies (16.1–17.16)
    1. Job accuses Eliphaz of substituting words for comfort (16.1-5)
    2. Job accuses God of treating him with violence (16.6-17)
    3. Job hopes someone in heaven will witness for him (16.18–17.2)
    4. Job asks God to be his guarantor (17.3-5)
    5. Job complains that people think he is godless (17.6-10)
    6. Job's only hope is to die (17.11-16)
  C. Bildad's second speech (18.1-21)
    1. Bildad scolds Job for his talk (18.1-4)
    2. How God punishes the wicked (18.5-21)
  D. Job replies (19.1-29)
    1. Job accuses the friends of being arrogant (19.1-6)
    2. Job accuses God of treating him violently (19.7-12)
    3. Job accuses God of turning his family and servants against him (19.13-22)
    4. Job is sure of having one in heaven who will defend him (19.23-29)
  E. Zophar's second speech (20.1-29)
    1. Zophar is anxious to speak to Job (20.1-3)
    2. Zophar describes the fate of the wicked (20.4-11)
    3. Zophar compares evil to food eaten by the wicked (20.12-22)
    4. Zophar describes disasters that happen to the wicked (20.23-29)
  F. Job replies (21.1-34)
    1. Job asks his friends to listen to him (21.1-6)
    2. Job claims the wicked are happy (21.7-16)
    3. Job claims the wicked go unpunished (21.17-26)
    4. Job claims the wicked live well and are buried with honor (21.27-34)

5. Third Round of Speeches (22.1–27.23)
  A. Eliphaz's third speech (22.1-30)
    1. Eliphaz accuses Job of committing crimes against the poor (22.1-11)
    2. Eliphaz accuses Job of thinking God does not see his sinful deeds (22.12-14)

        3. Eliphaz accuses Job of following the ways of evil men (22.15-20)
        4. Eliphaz urges Job to give up evil, return to God, and be rewarded (22.21-30)
    B. Job replies (23.1–24.25)
        1. God would listen to Job if Job knew where to find him (23.1-7)
        2. Job has searched everywhere for God (23.8-12)
        3. Job believes God has a plan for him (23.13-17)
        4. Job complains that evil men exploit the poor (24.1-12)
        5. Job describes the crimes of evil men carried out under cover of darkness (24.13-17)
        6. The fate of the wicked and God's judgment described (24.18-25)
    C. Bildad's third speech (25.1-6)
        1. Mankind's lowly place in God's great design (25.1-6)
    D. Job interrupts (26.1-4)
        1. Job ridicules Bildad's speech (26.1-4)
    E. Bildad continues his speech (26.5-14)
        1. The greatness of God (26.5-14)
    F. Job replies (27.1-23)
        1. Job affirms that his conscience is clear (27.1-6)
        2. Job asks God to punish those who have opposed him (27.7-10)
        3. Job wishes he could instruct his opponents (27.11-12)
        4. How God punishes the wicked (27.13-23)

6. A Poem about Wisdom (28.1-28)
    A. A poem by someone not named (28.1-28)
        1. The places where precious metals are mined (28.1-6)
        2. Birds and wild animals do not know the way (28.7-8)
        3. How men mine in the earth (28.9-11)
        4. The source of wisdom is not known (28.12-14)
        5. Wisdom is more valuable than precious stones (28.15-19)
        6. The source of wisdom is not known (28.20-22)
        7. God alone knows the way to wisdom (28.23-28)

7. Job's Final Statement of His Case (29.1–31.40)
    A. The opening of Job's final speech (29.1-25)
        1. Job recalls his prosperous and honored life (29.1-10)
        2. Job recalls his fair treatment of the oppressed (29.11-17)
        3. Job recalls how people respected him (29.18-25)
    B. Job continues his final speech (30.1-31)
        1. Job considers the fathers of those who ridicule him as worthless (30.1-8)
        2. Job describes the attacks of those who mock him (30.9-15)
        3. Job accuses God of attacking him (30.16-26)
        4. Job cries for help but none comes (30.27-31)
    C. Job concludes his final speech (31.1-40)
        1. Job has sworn an oath and challenges God (31.1-6)
        2. Job swears he has avoided adultery (31.7-12)
        3. Job swears that he never wronged the unfortunate (31.13-23)

4. Job denies avarice and idolatry (31.24-28)
5. Job denies revenge, inhospitality, and hypocrisy (31.29-34)
6. Job's final challenge and final oath (31.35-40)

8. Elihu's Speeches (32.1–37.24)
  A. Prose introduction (32.1-6a)
  B. Elihu's first speech (32.6b–33.33)
    1. Elihu maintains his right to speak (32.6b-10)
    2. Elihu accuses the friends of failing to answer Job (32.11-14)
    3. Elihu says he must speak or he will burst (32.15-22)
    4. Elihu challenges Job to argue with him (33.1-7)
    5. Elihu restates Job's argument of his innocence (33.8-11)
    6. Elihu refutes Job's claim (33.12-14)
    7. Elihu says God warns men in their dreams to stop sinning (33.15-18)
    8. Elihu says God sends sickness as a warning (33.19-22)
    9. Elihu says God sends an angel to save men (33.23-30)
    10. Elihu asks Job to be silent and learn (33.31-33)
  C. Elihu's second speech (34.1-37)
    1. Elihu criticizes the friends (34.1-4)
    2. Elihu criticizes Job's claim to be innocent (34.5-9)
    3. Elihu testifies to God's justice (34.10-15)
    4. Elihu defends God's rule (34.16-30)
    5. Elihu calls on Job to repent (34.31-37)
  D. Elihu's third speech (35.1-16)
    1. Elihu challenges Job's claim to innocence (35.1-4)
    2. Elihu claims that it is not God but Job's fellow men who are affected by his sin (35.5-13)
    3. Elihu ridicules Job for being ignorant (35.14-16)
  E. Elihu's final speech (36.1–37.24)
    1. Elihu speaks the truth for God (36.1-4)
    2. God is just, and so people suffer (36.5-15)
    3. Elihu warns Job that he is being punished as he deserves (36.16-21)
    4. Elihu asks Job to remember how great God is (36.22-25)
    5. Elihu describes God's activity in the storm (36.26–37.13)
    6. Elihu challenges Job to reflect on God's greatness in nature (37.14-22)
    7. Elihu reminds Job that God ignores those who think they are wise (37.23-24)

9. The LORD Addresses Job (38.1–41.34)
  A. The LORD's speech: first part (38.1–40.2)
    1. God challenges Job to answer his questions (38.1-3)
    2. The earth and the sea (38.4-11)
    3. Dawn, darkness, and Sheol (38.12-21)
    4. The heavens (38.22-38)
    5. Wild life (38.39–39.12)

      6. The ostrich, horse, and eagle (39.13-30)

      7. God challenges Job to answer (40.1-2)

   B. Job will answer no more (40.3-5)

   C. The LORD's speech: second part (40.6–41.34)

      1. God challenges Job to punish the wicked (40.6-14)

      2. God invites Job to think about the monster Behemoth (40.15-24)

      3. God challenges Job to capture Leviathan (41.1-11)

      4. God describes the terror of Leviathan (41.12-34)

10. The LORD Restores Job (42.1-17)

   A. Job's final response is repentance (42.1-6)

   B. The LORD instructs the friends to make a sacrifice, and Job prays for them (42.7-9)

   C. The LORD gives Job twice as much as was taken from him (42.10-15)

   D. Job dies (42.16-17)

Headings

The headings in the detailed outline give the translator the possibility of providing readers with topical guides at three levels: section headings (1 to 10); division headings (A, B, C, and so on); and subdivision headings (1, 2, 3, and so on). In addition to the three levels of headings, the Handbook provides the location for each and identifies the level of heading as section, division, or subdivision. Although the Book of Job consists of 42 chapters, these chapters are not isolated units but sections or divisions in the larger outline. Most translators will want to identify the section and division headings, and many will also want to give serious consideration to the subdivision headings used in this Handbook. These headings go beyond those provided by TEV and others, but many translators will find them extremely useful, particularly in the three rounds of speeches (4.1–27.23), in which the speaker may suddenly shift his line of thought, drop it, take up a new subject, or return to a previous one. Without some help in the form of a heading, the reader may find these speeches confusing and difficult to follow.

However, translators may wish to follow the headings given in a major language translation known to their readers. In doing so the translators should be aware that many such translations use very few headings and may depend on marking subdivisions with white space only (see RSV and TEV), or white space with some special mark such as an asterisk. This method of separating paragraphs or thought units may be unknown to readers. Furthermore, this usage gives no guidance as to the meaning of the text. Some translators may feel that it is unnecessary to identify all the subdivisions according to the Handbook. In such cases translators will select those headings and places at which they think the reader needs help.

In some cases headings used in various translations and commentaries are cited in the Handbook. However, these seldom correspond fully with the subdivision headings in the Handbook. Translation suggestions are given to assist the translator in adjusting the Handbook headings into other languages. The Handbook headings are only suggestive, and translators are encouraged to use headings that reflect the content, and are clear and natural in their own languages.

Message of the Book of Job

The Book of Job is considered by many to be the most expressive poem ever written. The heart of the poem is a dispute between Job and his three friends Eliphaz, Bildad, Zophar, and a late-comer, Elihu. Fundamental to their arguments is the question of God's fairness in dealing with his creatures. Stemming from this is the question "Why do the righteous suffer?" The friends marshal a host of arguments to support the traditional view that righteousness always brings prosperity and good fortune, whereas wickedness gives rise to suffering. There is no reason to doubt that Job subscribes to this same principle; however, Job's integrity will not allow him to apply it to his own situation, because he knows in his heart that he is innocent of wrongdoing. Therefore he stubbornly resists every effort by the friends to get him to admit to being wicked and be restored to God's favor.

Neither Job nor the friends know that God considers Job to be righteous. Neither do they know that Job's suffering is the result of a wager between God and Satan. Therefore the reader, who has been told these things, watches sympathetically as Job wrestles against his friends and God. Enraged by the friends' lack of understanding of his plight, Job hurls sarcasm and insults at them. Angered by his outbursts, the friends do the same to Job. But the real target of Job's bitter complaints is God. And so he says "But I would speak to the Almighty, and I desire to argue my case with God" (13.3). In his despair Job sees God as a hunter shooting him with poison arrows (6.4). He accuses God of creating him just to turn around and destroy him (10.8). In his isolation from God he asks "Why dost thou hide thy face and count me as thy enemy?" (13.24). Job is without hope, and he compares himself unfavorably to a tree: "For there is hope for a tree, if it be cut down, that it will sprout again and that its shoots will not cease" (14.7).

In spite of his harsh accusations against God, Job clearly recognizes God's power and greatness (9.5-13; 12.7-12; 12.13-25; 23.13-17; 27.7-10). Although Job accuses God of denying him justice, of treating him cruelly, still Job longs for fellowship with God: "Oh that thou wouldest hide me in Sheol, that thou wouldest conceal me until thy wrath be past, that thou wouldest appoint me a set time, and remember me! If a man die, shall he live again? All the days of my service I would wait, till my release should come. Thou wouldest call, and I would answer thee; thou wouldest long for the work of thy hands" (14.13-15). But Job does not know where to find God; if only he could, he is confident of God's willingness to hear him out: "Oh, that I knew where I might find him, that I might come even to his seat! I would lay my case before him and fill my mouth with arguments. I would learn what he would answer me, and understand what he would say to me. Would he contend with me in the greatness of his power? No; he would give heed to me" (23.3-6).

Job gathers courage as he prepares for a court trial with God. However, Elihu, who upholds the traditional theology of the friends, disallows a trial and informs Job that God goes to court with no one. Furthermore, Job should realize that he is dealing with the invisible God, who has left his imprints clearly on his creation, and Job should see these and interpret them correctly.

No sooner has Elihu ruled out the possibility of God appearing to Job, when God speaks directly to Job out of the storm. God proceeds to challenge Job with a mass of unanswerable questions. God never mentions the wager made with Satan, nor that he considers Job a righteous hero; and he never enters into the debate with Job and the friends. He says nothing about being just or unjust, nor does he have anything to say about the suffering of the righteous. Therefore the Book of Job does not solve the questions so heatedly argued by Job and the friends. So overpowering is God to the broken and defenseless Job that it is tempting to think that Job merely collapses into repentance and submission. This is hardly the way the poet expected his readers to react. God's speech is about the mysteries of created life: the earth, the sea, dawn, darkness, the heavens, wild life, Behemoth, and Leviathan. God points to these mysteries in nature which Job cannot grasp nor control; and he leaves Job to grasp on his own, which he does, that suffering is likewise a mystery. The God whom Job could not find, and from whom he was separated in his suffering, came to him and spoke to him from the storm. Thus Job learns that suffering is not the evidence that God has abandoned him. Theological talk gives way to religious experience. And so Job can finally say "I had heard of thee by the hearing of the ear, but now my eye sees thee; therefore I despise myself, and repent in dust and ashes" (42.5-6).

Translating Poetry in Job

The translator of Job is faced with the problems inherent in transferring meaning from a poetic source to the language of the translation. In a poetic text the message is in many complex ways bound up with the form of the message. Whether the translator is translating Job as prose, as poetry, or a mixture of both, it is necessary to consider some of the poetic devices used by the author of the book, in order to prepare the translator to understand how these devices function and how they affect the meaning that is being conveyed. It is the task of the translator to seek to convey equivalent meaning sometimes through similar poetic structures, but more often through different poetic forms. In the sections that follow, only a few of the many Hebrew poetic usages that are known to cause problems in translation will be discussed. These and others are dealt with in the body of the Handbook.

1. *Parallel Lines*

The most detailed discussion of translating the poetry of Job concerns parallel lines. This is because parallelism is the very ground upon which Hebrew poetic style is built. Furthermore, the content which the translator must translate is contained within these structures. It is necessary, therefore, for the translator to have a clear picture of what parallelism is and how it functions.

There are two major linguistic features that characterize poetic discourse. The first is the way in which the poet deviates from expected linguistic regularities. The poet plays on the letters or sounds of words, grammar, and sentences, so that these deviations are made to stand out or be prominent. Or, quite the opposite, the poet may focus on certain regularities in the language and cause these features to be prominent. Parallelism is the result of concentrating on the regularity of repetition. However, it would be wrong to assume that, because repetition is made prominent, linguistic irregularities are lacking. Even where lines are parallel and much is repeated, the poet usually builds into these lines lots of irregularity. For example, patterns of sound may be created through devices such as acrostics and chiasmus (see the Glossary for the definition of these terms). A word may be selected for its sound rather than for its meaning. The poet may drop a word or add a phrase in order to get a better balanced line, or invert the usual word order to call attention to it. Most of these deviations take place at the sound or grammatical level of language, and translators cannot expect their language to be able to do the same things without distortion of both grammar and meaning. Regardless of the deviations from normal grammar, parallel lines within the discourse carry the sense of the poem, and it is this sense that the translator must understand and translate.

A word of caution is needed before considering the examples of parallel lines. These examples are given only to show some of the relationships that exist between the two or more parallel lines. Every couplet or set of lines is part of a longer discourse; that is, they fit in with all the other lines in the subdivision, division, and the entire text. Therefore it is important to keep in mind that what is said about a pair of isolated lines may have to be modified when these are analyzed in terms of the wider discourse structure.

Two lines standing next to each other and saying something very similar is the most obvious aspect of parallelism, but it is not the only one. Two such lines may be parallel in structure without having much meaning in common. In this case they say something quite different but have the same word order. Two lines may be parallel in that their consonants, vowels, or stresses are much the same. These similarities are possible due to the nature of the language—in this case Hebrew. It may be totally impossible to translate the meaning of the two lines and at the same time keep the kinds of repetitions used in Hebrew. What the translator needs to know is what poetic purpose is served by this or that poetic device, and how that same purpose may be expressed in the receptor language.

In the following discussion the examples from Job are taken from the Revised Standard Version (RSV) as representing in English the Hebrew form sufficiently well to illustrate the principles. The first of two parallel lines is referred to as the a line and the second as the b line. Most parallel lines occur in groups of only two, but there are numerous exceptions.

In 23.16 Job complains against God:

> God has made my heart faint;
> the Almighty has terrified me.

These two lines say approximately the same thing. In fact it is possible to understand Job's thought if we read only one line; it does not matter which. Not only does each line give essentially the same message, but both lines are even constructed in Hebrew on the same word order of subject plus verb plus object. Accordingly the two lines may be said to be parallel in both sense and sentence form.

In 18.5 Bildad describes the misery of the wicked:

> Yea, the light of the wicked is put out,
> and the flame of his fire does not shine.

Here again the two lines say something very similar. It is not possible to read line b in isolation from line a because of the substitution of the pronoun "his" for the noun "wicked." In line a "the light of the wicked" is matched in line b by "the flame of his fire"; and "is put out" in line a is matched in line b by "does not shine." Nothing new is said in line b that we did not learn in line a. It is only the way the thought is expressed that is different. Accordingly the two lines are parallel in meaning. Nevertheless they are not parallel or the same in their Hebrew clause structure. The poet could have made them the same, but he chose not to. Line <u>a</u> is subject plus verb, and line <u>b</u> is verb plus subject.

Not all parallel lines express the same thought. They may each express a related but different sense. In 16.10 Job complains:

> Men have gaped at me with their mouth,
>> they have struck me insolently upon the cheek,
>> they mass themselves together against me.

Although there are textual problems in this verse, each line expresses a different action Job's enemies have taken against him. The lines do not say the same thing. What is common to each line is the men who have done these things, an expression of threat or aggression, and Job as the object of their bad behavior. In Hebrew lines <u>a</u> and <u>b</u> are the same in form, while line <u>c</u> is different.

Other parallel lines do not have any kind of repetition. In contrast, a logical relation is what maintains a link between them. For example, in 16.22 Job expresses grief that his life is ending:

> For when a few years have come,
>> I shall go the way whence I shall not return.

Line <u>a</u> is a time clause and line <u>b</u> is the subsequent result. In a less poetic form Job is saying "After a few years, I shall die." The poetic force is not carried by the parallel line structure but by other poetic elements.

In 17.4 Job addresses God:

> Since thou hast closed their minds to understanding,
>> therefore thou wilt not let them triumph.

Here again these two lines stand in the relation of reason in line <u>a</u> to consequence in line <u>b</u>. They are both essential clauses of the same sentence. There is no parallel meaning involved. In Job there are numerous instances of these kinds of line structures.

It is no doubt true that in most cases of parallel lines in Hebrew poetry the two or more lines do not say the same thing twice. Instead line <u>b</u> picks up a word or phrase in line <u>a</u>, expresses it in different words, and thus gives the two lines at least something that is common to both. What is common may be based on only one or two words. For example, in 8.11-15 Bildad describes the failure of the wicked to survive, and he does so by the use of analogy:

> 11 Can papyrus grow where there is no marsh?
>> Can reeds flourish where there is no water?
> 12 While yet in flower and not cut down,
>> they wither before any other plant.
> 13 Such are the paths of all who forget God;
>> the hope of the godless man shall perish.
> 14 His confidence breaks in sunder,
>> and his trust is a spider's web.

11

> 15   He leans against his house, but it does not stand;
>   he lays hold of it, but it does not endure.

None of the pairs of lines gives a single message, although the rhetorical questions in verse 11 come the closest. Notice that the poet selects a word or phrase for each <u>b</u> line that has some association of meaning with a word or phrase in the <u>a</u> line: 11 papyrus plants grow, reeds flourish; marsh, water; 12 flower, wither; 13 who forget God, godless man; 14 confidence, trust; breaks in sunder, spider's web; 15 leans against, lays hold of; stand, endure.

The poet does not, however, select just any word which has some association in meaning, or a synonym, for the <u>b</u> line. Usually, but not always, a choice is made in both lines so that the word or phrase in the <u>b</u> line goes beyond the meaning of the element it matches in the <u>a</u> line. In other words the biblical poet tends to create a movement from one line to the next in which the second line is more specific, more concrete, more dramatic, more picturable than the more general first line. The first line suggests a broad picture, and the second line completes it by dramatizing it. Often the <u>b</u> line will be more elevated in style.

In 29.14 Job defends himself in these words:

> I put on righteousness, and it clothed me;
>   my justice was like a robe and a turban.

In this pair of parallel lines "righteousness" in line <u>a</u> is matched by "justice" in line <u>b</u>. However, the poetic movement from the general to the specific is in "clothed me" in <u>a</u>, which becomes concretely expressed in <u>b</u> in the simile "like a robe and a turban." The poet could have said "I put on righteousness and justice like a robe and a turban." In that case the model would be "<u>a</u> is so," but the common model for much of parallelism is "<u>a</u> is so and <u>b</u> is even more so," in which the <u>b</u> line goes beyond the <u>a</u> line in being more specific, more picturable. The two lines form a unit. Line <u>a</u> takes the first step and line <u>b</u> completes it. The two lines are in a dynamic relation due to the poetic movement between them. The arrangement gives the two lines an added element of meaning, which in this example is preciseness by using a particular or specific object.

In 30.10 Job describes the acts of those who hate him:

> They abhor me, they keep aloof from me;
>   they do not hesitate to spit at the sight of me.

In the first line "abhor" and "keep aloof" describe in a general sense the way Job's enemies deal with him. The second line dramatizes what it means to "abhor" and "keep aloof." Line <u>b</u> makes concrete, picturable, and specific an instance of what is suggested by the rather vague and general verbs in the first line. Line <u>b</u> goes well beyond line <u>a</u> so that we may illustrate the relation between the two lines as "They hate me and keep away from me; they even spit in disgust when they see me."

To show how the tendency in the second line is to go beyond the first line, an example of number parallelism is instructive. The model in such cases is always "<u>a</u> is so and <u>b</u> is more so." In 5.19 Eliphaz entreats Job to call on God and assures him of God's care:

> He will deliver you from six troubles;
>> in seven there shall no evil touch you.

The poet is not using two numbers to express distinct events. Rather, he is applying the principle that holds throughout Old Testament poetry, in which any number expressed in the first line is always increased in the second line. The writer could have said something like "a half dozen" in the second line, thus voiding the tendency for the second line to go beyond the first. However, this does not happen in number parallelism.

In 18.4 Bildad speaks to Job in three lines:

> You who tear yourself in anger,
>> shall the earth be forsaken for you,
>> or the rock be removed out of its place?

The first line is Bildad's manner of addressing Job. The other two lines are somewhat parallel in their meanings and are in the form of rhetorical questions. In keeping with the principle that the second line tends to be more specific, the b line often is a smaller object in association with the larger object in the a line. Here the reduction is from "earth" to "rock." The effect of reducing the size is to pinpoint an example. It has the effect of providing a more focused view, of fine tuning, in the second line.

The same principle applies to units of time. For example, 29.2:

> Oh, that I were as in the months of old,
>> as in the days when God watched over me.

Here the movement is from the larger unit "months" in the first line to the smaller unit "days" in the second line.

Another technique by which poetic movement is created between parallel lines is through the occurrence of a literal item in the first line followed by a figurative term or phrase in the second. For example, in 22.23 Eliphaz says to Job:

> If you return to the Almighty and humble yourself,
>> if you remove unrighteousness far from your tents . . . .

The first line has "return" and "humble," and these are matched by "remove unrighteousness far from your tents." It is not the tents that are unrighteous but rather the people who inhabit them. In this case the figurative expression in the second line has the effect of dramatizing the literal sense in the first line. Figurative language tends to shift the sense to the picturable and dramatic. It is one more way of making the second line go beyond the first line, thus giving the two lines a dynamic movement which carries meaning that is in addition to the words themselves.

Although the kinds of parallelism illustrated above are the most frequent ones in Job, it would be inaccurate to suggest that the principles they illustrate are hard and fast rules. The translator must be prepared to find many exceptions. For example, at the beginning of this section the text of 23.16 was quoted:

13

> God has made my heart faint;
> the Almighty has terrified me.

Here the poet has chosen to place the figurative expression in line a and the literal "terrified" in line b. Consequently the typical poetic movement from the literal in the first line to the more dramatic in the second line has been reversed. Line b restates line a without the expected poetic heightening of style.

In 28.9 the poet reverses the pattern of placing the smaller instance of the larger item in the second line, which normally serves to sharpen the picture:

> Man puts his hand to the flinty rock,
> and overturns mountains by the roots.

In the most common pattern we would expect "mountains" in the first line and the smaller instance "rock" in the second line.

In 18.3 Bildad asks Job:

> Why are we counted as cattle?
> Why are we stupid in your sight?

Again these two lines violate the more common practice of placing the metaphor in line b and the literal "stupid" in line a.

In 16.3 Job answers Eliphaz with a rhetorical question in which the expected pattern is reversed:

> Shall windy words have an end?
> Or what provokes you that you answer?

Not only may the poet choose to violate the principle of line b going beyond line a in sense, dramatic effect, or in sharpening the focus, but he may even prefer to create as little movement as possible. In this kind of arrangement we have the model "a is so and b is so," in which the two lines say about the same thing. This kind of parallelism shows very little movement between the two lines.

In 18.6 to 18.10 Bildad describes the wicked for Job in a series of parallel lines that show little movement between line a and line b:

> 6   The light is dark in his tent,
>   and his lamp above him is put out.
>   . . . .
> 8   For he is cast into a net by his own feet,
>   and he walks on a pitfall.
> 9   A trap seizes him by the heel,
>   a snare lays hold of him.
> 10 A rope is hid for him in the ground,
>   a trap for him in the path.

Chapter 28, a discourse on wisdom, concludes with a pair of parallel lines of the same kind:

> "Behold the fear of the Lord, that is wisdom;
> and to depart from evil is understanding."

In 22.5 Eliphaz asks Job a question and then comments:

> Is not your wickedness great?
> There is no end to your iniquities.

In 15.9 Eliphaz puts questions to Job in a rhetorical style that creates parallel lines with little if any movement:

> What do you know that we do not know?
> What do you understand that is not clear to us?

The translator is faced with the problem of translating Hebrew poetic forms into the receptor language. One of these structures is parallel line arrangements of the kind discussed here. Although attention has been called to the fact that the Hebrew line arrangement (as seen in RSV) often shows some kind of movement from line a to line b, it does not automatically follow that the same movement will be carried across into the translation. The reason for this is that translating frequently requires adjustments due to the differences between the source and receptor languages. For example, it is sometimes necessary to reverse the order of the parallel lines. It may be the case that a dramatic image is used in the second line in Hebrew, but the receptor language may have no equivalent expression. Therefore a nonfigurative term or expression must be used. In other cases in which Hebrew has a nonmetaphor, the receptor language may find it natural to use a vivid image. In other cases discourse considerations may require making adjustments that will change the relation between the parallel lines.

In his study of parallelism, James L. Kugel expresses the way in which the b line often goes beyond the idea in the a line and thus extends its meaning, reinforces, completes, emphasizes it. He expresses this idea by saying that in English it is possible to illustrate the relation between the two lines as follows: a, and what's more b; not only a, but b; not a, not even b. Obviously parallelism cannot be reduced to a handful of model sentences. If that were the case, the poetry of the Bible would be extremely boring. Where such examples are used in the Handbook, they illustrate a principle and are not to be taken as models to be translated. The movement between the lines may be perfectly clear from the choice of vocabulary. Some languages need no linking words to show the kind of relation between the lines. In others special particles may be employed or special constructions that show emphasis or intensification in the second line.

Translators should keep in mind that movement between parallel lines is a matter of degree—from very little to very much. Furthermore, as one examines parallel lines in their wider discourse, the movement between the lines becomes part of the more general kinds of movement that the discourse gives rise to.

Here are some questions that may help translators as they deal with parallel lines in translation:

1. What do these lines have in common: similar structures, similar meanings, both, or neither?
2. If the meanings are similar, which elements in line a are matched by which elements in line b?
3. If the relation between the lines is a logical one, what is it: reason–result, means–purpose, condition–consequence, or other?
4. If there is a number, space, object, or event word, or expression in line a, is there a larger number, a more specific, dramatic, visual, or figurative matching expression in line b? If yes, name it (them).
5. How would you describe the nature of the movement between the lines: focuses, makes more specific, makes more visual, makes more emphatic, makes more literary, other?
6. In your language, what adjustments will be required to translate parallel lines in a form that is poetic, clear, faithful, and stylistically appropriate?

Here is a small sample of the adjustments translators are often required to make when translating poetic lines:

a. Shift from a nonfigure to a figure or vice versa.
b. Shift from a noun or verb to a clause.
d. Reverse the order of lines for clarity and style.
e. Employ or avoid a linking marker to show the relation between the lines.
f. Shift from semantically parallel lines to logically related ones for clarity and style.
g. Shift from questions to statements or from statements to questions.
h. Shift from personification to nonpersonification or vice versa.

2. Rhetorical questions

Rhetorical questions are particularly important as a poetic device in Job. Their frequency raises the problem of naturalness of style for many languages. For example, in the RSV text of Job 41.1-7 there is a series of nine rhetorical questions (using the question marks as items counted); in the five verses of Job 7.17-21 there are eleven; and in the eight verses of Job 40.24–41.7 there are no less than sixteen. Not only is the rhetorical question a frequent device of the author of Job, but it is used as a discourse marker many times. For example, each of the friends begins his speech in chapters 4, 5, 7, 8, 11, 15, 18, and 22 with such questions as a dramatic way to catch Job's attention and to challenge his arguments. Translators who are sensitive to the style of language used in translating Job must give careful consideration to the frequent use of this question form and determine where it may or may not be used, and where it is best to adjust it to another form of expression.

A rhetorical question is commonly described as a question which does not ask for information. When Paul asks in Romans 8.31 "If God is for us, who is against us?" he is not asking his readers to answer a question by giving the name of someone. Rather he is making a strong statement which says "If God is for us, no one can prevail against us." It may be asked why a writer or speaker would use a question to make a statement. The answer is that all languages have many kinds of style, and to ask a question where a statement could be used is one variation of style. More importantly, questions, like commands, call on the reader or listener to react.

16

A rhetorical question is attention-getting and dramatic because it seems to demand an answer which is not provided. It challenges the reader to question something being indirectly asserted by the writer. In the Romans example, "who is against us?" suggests that someone is against us. But in the context, "If God is for us," the reader corrects the suggestion or implication and answers "No one!" In this way the reader has interacted with the writer. The writer has elevated the style, avoided monotony perhaps, and the reader has been drawn into the interpreting process.

In addition to encouraging reader involvement and providing a text with more dramatic value, rhetorical questions normally contain assumptions that are shared by writer and reader alike. This means that the implications in a rhetorical question may be specific to a given context and a given language community. For example, an individual who is asked if he is able to walk over a mountain trail may respond with "Am I sugar that I should melt?" The user of this question implies that sugar when heated melts, and that liquids are not strong elements. If the one asking the original question were not aware of these implications in the rhetorical response, it may not be clear whether the person is saying "Yes," "No," or something else. In the same way it is often necessary in translating these kinds of questions in Hebrew wisdom literature such as Job to determine what is implied in many rhetorical questions. In this way the translator will be in a better position to translate them.

In chapter 7 Job is determined to voice his complaints to God, and in 7.12 he asks:

> Am I the sea, or a sea monster,
> that thou settest a guard over me?

The reference to the sea and a sea monster being guarded will make little sense without inquiring into the cultural background. TEV and some others provide this information in a footnote. The implication is:

(1) The sea and the sea monster were believed to cause destruction.

(2) Job does not cause destruction.

(3) Therefore Job does not need a guard over him.

Without identifying these assumptions the translator runs the risk of leaving the reader to wonder what kind of question this is. It may be possible to adjust the translation of this question by saying, for example, "Do I destroy things as do the sea and the sea monster, so that you have to watch everything I do?" Even in this case a footnote may be advisable.

Consider the following example in 10.4, in which Job is complaining against God's treatment of him:

> Hast thou eyes of flesh?
> Dost thou see as man sees?

Here Job is accusing God of being unfair to his creatures. Since Job is one of these creatures, it is implied in line a that:

(1) Job has eyes of flesh.

(2) God does not have eyes of flesh.

The second line emphasizes these implications by repetition, in which "see" matches "eyes," and "man sees" matches "eyes of flesh." Through this question Job is challenging God to think about a difference between himself and his creatures, one that results in God being unfair. If necessary these two questions may be restructured as negative assertions following the implications above. "You do not have human eyes like I have. You do not see things the way humans do." It will be evident for speakers of English that shifting to a negative assertion is less dramatic, less engaging, and is more aggressive in tone. This may not be the case in other languages.

In 4.7 Eliphaz challenges Job:

> Think now, who that was innocent ever perished?
> Or where were the upright cut off?

In the context of Eliphaz's speech it is clear that Eliphaz, like the other friends, believes that a person who is not guilty of sin will not suffer disaster or be cut off from God's care. Therefore lying behind Eliphaz's question are these assumptions:

(1) Innocent people do not perish.
(2) Job is perishing.
(3) Therefore Job is not innocent.

Eliphaz is not asking Job to identify someone who was innocent and still suffered badly; he is using the question to challenge Job to admit that Job is not innocent. Job, however, also knows the innocent should not suffer, and that he is suffering—but that Job is guilty of sin is not assumed by either God or Job. It is this difference of assumption that sustains the conflict between Job and his friends throughout the poem.

In translating rhetorical questions the translator needs to ask the following questions:

(1) Is this a real question asking for information, or a rhetorical question?
(2) If it is rhetorical, what is implied or assumed in the question or questions?
(3) If it is translated as a rhetorical question, will it be natural in the context and correctly understood?

If the answer to question number 3 is "No," then what kind of adjustment is required? This may mean the question may be retained but must be answered, that the question form must be shifted to a negative statement, or that some of the implication or assumption must be built into the statement or question.

In the case of Job 4.7 above, the translator may decide:

(1) that the context makes clear that the questions may be translated as questions, and that they will be fully understood and natural in the receptor language;
(2) that the question form may be retained, but that a negative reply must be added, "No one";
(3) that the questions must be shifted to negative statements: "Think about it, Job, the innocent have never perished and the upright have never been cut off"; or
(4) that some information that is assumed or implied should be included; for example, "Think about your own innocence, Job, no one who is innocent ever perished as you are perishing, or was ever cut off by God as you have been."

3. *Irony*

All languages seem to use some means to misrepresent things. Of course an outright misrepresentation of facts is a lie. However, it is also possible to say things in a deceptive manner and yet not be lying. When, for example, a host speaks to his guest and calls his small house "my palace," the hearer is perhaps amused but certainly not deceived. If the host lives in a palace and refers to it as "my shanty," there is again no deception. Exaggeration and understatement are common ways to misrepresent things honestly. Closely related to these are irony, sarcasm, and satire. These terms do not define devices which are different in language or meaning from each other. They are all used to describe some of the ways in which Job and his friends express their bitter feelings and their contempt as they attempt to discredit each other's arguments. In order to see how they do this, we need to look at several examples. Following these examples some suggestions are made concerning their translation.

In 12.2 Job's bitter feelings against his friends have been mounting, and so he says:

> No doubt you are the people,
> and wisdom will die with you.

Although there are differences of interpretation in this passage, Job is saying "No one doubts that you are a special class of people, and when you die all wisdom will disappear." Job is accusing the friends of having a superior attitude. He is expressing a bitter reaction to what he has heard from them. His aim is to inflict a wound on the friends' emotions by making this exaggerated statement. If taken at its face value, it would be a true statement, or at least an honest opinion. The friends know that Job is honestly deceiving them, because he goes on to say immediately "But I have understanding as well as you; I am not inferior to you. Who does not know such things as these?" (12.3). Job is here like an actor or dancer wearing a mask before an audience. He creates a certain mood with the mask but then removes it, which modifies the previous mood.

In 11.12 Zophar makes a biting remark about Job's intelligence:

> But a stupid man will get understanding,
> when a wild ass's colt is born a man.

Although interpreters differ in their understanding of this verse, RSV will again be retained as adequate for illustration. It is clear that Zophar is expressing stinging sarcasm. In the context Zophar has been belittling Job's ability to understand the ways of God, and brings his speech on this subject to a climax with this proverbial saying. In the context Job would understand clearly that "a stupid man" refers to him. The two lines give a comparison: stupid man becomes wise; wild ass becomes a human. If the one can happen then the other can happen, which is to say that both are equally unlikely. There is nothing in the context that removes the comparison or suggests that it is to be understood other than as literally given. It is straightforward, stinging criticism, raw sarcasm whose only result can be to send still another barb into Job's failing flesh. However, it is exaggeration, and neither Zophar nor Job is deceived.

In his first speech Eliphaz is quite gentle with Job, but he later joins the friends in their rebukes of Job. In 15.7-9 Eliphaz asks Job:

7.   Are you the first man that was born?
        Or were you brought forth before the hills?
8.   Have you listened in the council of God?
        And do you limit wisdom to yourself?
9.   What do you know that we do not know?
        What do you understand that is not clear to us?

Here Eliphaz picks up on Job's own caustic remarks from 12.2 and throws them back at him. The scorn in the exaggerations is softened slightly by being expressed in the form of rhetorical questions. Both Eliphaz and Job know that the questions in verses 7 and 8 can only be answered with a resounding "No!" And, since neither Job nor the friends know the game plan of God and Satan, verse 9 must also be answered with a negative. By shifting his irony to a question form, Zophar challenges Job to recognize the right answer. However, the answers are so obvious that the challenge is reduced to a minimum, and the element of sarcasm or ridicule predominates.

Job can always be counted on to hand his friends whatever they dish out to him. As negotiators seeking a settlement of their differences, Job and his friends are tragically flawed in their dealings with each other. In 26.2-3 Job resorts to that form of irony in which he means the opposite of what he says:

2.   How you have helped him who has no power!
        How you have saved the arm that has no strength!
3.   How you have counseled him who has no wisdom,
        and plentifully declared sound knowledge!

In both verses Job refers to himself, as the friends would know. In Job's angry mood there is no possibility for the friends to be deceived or to congratulate themselves. By exaggerating the positive the friends will understand everything as negative and will feel the full force of Job's sarcastic complaint. Job is misrepresenting the truth he has experienced, but no one is deceived.

Throughout the Handbook attention is called to these apparent deceptions referred to as irony, sarcasm, or satire. Translators need to pay particular attention to this device in Job in order to convey the appropriate meanings to their readers. The translator should examine the context to determine: (1) if the mood of the speaker is clearly signaled; and (2) if the context makes adequately clear that the speaker is not to be taken in a literal sense.

It may be clear that the context shows that the speaker is using strong sarcasm, but a literal rendering of what he says will not be understood as sarcasm in the language of translation. Some languages have special markers to show that the usual sense is not to be understood, but that it should be reversed. Other languages require special devices before or after satirical material to warn the reader to interpret appropriately. In some cases the translator must determine the speaker's intention and make clear in the translation that the reader is dealing with irony. For example, in 26.2-3 Job scorns the friends for their failure to "help," "save"—RSV is inadequate at this point—"counsel" him. A translator may have to introduce sarcasm by saying, for example, "Job got no help from the friends, but he said to scorn them, 'You have helped this poor weak man so much.'" (The two lines are joined into one.) In verse 3 one may have to say "Job got no good advice but said mockingly 'You have given such good advice to such a dumb man as I am, and you have shown how really wise you are!'"

11.12 may have to be restructured in some languages to say "Zophar ridiculed Job and said, 'A stupid person like you, Job, is as unlikely to become wise as it is likely that a wild ass will give birth to a man.'"

It may be necessary in some languages to make clear in 12.2 that Job is using sarcasm, by saying, for example, "Job spoke words that mock: 'You probably think you are the wisest people, and when you die no one left will know anything.'"

Because irony or sarcasm is often subtle and is used in greatly different ways in different cultures, the translator must take special pains to assure that the readers understand it as intended in Job. It is advisable that translators test their readers' understanding to see if they interpret irony appropriately.

The Names of God

Five divine names in Hebrew are used in the Book of Job: *'El, 'Eloah, 'Elohim, Shaddai,* and *Yahweh.* Translators should refer to a Bible Dictionary for analysis of these and other Old Testament names for God. The purpose of the present discussion is limited to a brief look at the nature of these names, the way these names are distributed in Job, and suggestions regarding their translation.

'El was the common term to designate the deity in ancient Middle Eastern cultures. It was used as a generic term which could include many more specific divine beings. *'El* was "the god" or "God." The plural of *'el* was not used. As the Hebrews took over Canaanite religious shrines, they associated the name *'El* and the accompanying religious beliefs with the name of the Hebrew God *Yahweh.*

'Eloah is likewise a general word for the deity, and most of its occurrences are found in the Book of Job. *'Eloah* did not become a widely used name for God in Israel. The plural of *'Eloah* is *'Elohim,* which is the most common of the general words for God in the Old Testament. Although grammatically a plural formation, it functions as both a singular and plural generic name for God. It most often refers to the God of Israel, but it can be used in the plural to refer to the "gods" of the other nations (Exo 12.12; Judges 10.6).

Shaddai is the name in Exodus 6.3 by which God made himself known to Abraham, Isaac, and Jacob. Scholars have not been able to prove what the name means. It often occurs together with *'El* as *'El Shaddai.* The English "Almighty" follows the Septuagint and the Vulgate usage.

Yahweh is the approximate pronunciation of the four Hebrew letters *YHWH.* This represents the personal name of the God of the Hebrews. Later this name was written with the vowels of *'adonai* "my lord" and pronounced "adonai" to avoid uttering the personal name of their deity. The Septuagint translators rendered it by the Greek word for "lord," and English translations have followed this tradition and write it "LORD."

The author of Job appears to have a purpose in the way he puts these names on the lips of his characters. Job, with two exceptions (1.21; 12.9), the three friends, and Elihu never use the name *Yahweh.* The implication may be to show they are non-Israelites. On the other hand, aside from 1.21 and 12.9, the use of *Yahweh* is entirely restricted to the prose sections (chapters 1, 2, and 42), as if the poet reserves for himself alone the use of the name of Israel's God. However, in the prologue Yahweh himself uses *'Elohim* (1.8; 2.3), as does Job (1.5; 2.10), the messenger (1.16), Job's wife (2.9), and Satan (1.9). In the dialogues the four other names are found, but *'Elohim* is spoken only twice, and in each case it is in parallel with *'El* (5.8; 20.29).

Shaddai occurs alone in eleven verses in Job, and in combinations with *'El, 'Eloah* in seventeen other verses. RSV translates *Shaddai* as "the Almighty," whether it occurs alone or in combination with another word for God in parallel lines. TEV, on the other hand, makes little attempt to be consistent in the rendering of this term. It prefers "Almighty God" but may shift to "God" in some contexts, or if appropriate use only a pronoun. In at least one instance (15.25) TEV uses "the Almighty," where "God" is used in the previous line.

Parallel line usage of the three principal names occurring in the dialogues is found in such verses as 27.2-3, in which Job says:

> As *'El* lives, who has taken away my right,
>   and *Shaddai*, who has made my soul bitter;
>
> as long as my breath is in me,
>   and the spirit of *'Eloah* is in my nostrils;

Job continues in 27.8-11:

> For what is the hope of the godless
>   when *'Eloah* cuts him off,
>   when *'El* takes away his life?
>
> Will *'El* hear his cry,
>   when trouble comes upon him?
>
> Will he take delight in *Shaddai*?
>   Will he call upon *'El* at all times?
>
> I will teach you concerning the hand of *'El*;
>   what is with *Shaddai* I will not conceal.

The sequence *'El, 'Eloah* is found only in 12.6; *'El, 'Elohim* in 20.29; and *Shaddai, 'El* only in 13.3. The sequence *'Eloah, Shaddai* occurs in 5.17; 11.7; 31.2. *Shaddai, 'Eloah* is found in 6.4; 22.26; 27.10; 40.2. The most common sequence is *'El, Shaddai* in 8.3,5; 15.25; 22.17; 23.16; 27.2,11,13; 33.4; 34.10, 12; 35.13. No other sequences occur, and no other name for God combines with *Yahweh*.

Historically interpreters have used the distribution of divine names to argue that the prose sections and the dialogues were written by different authors. However, the opposite case can be equally made, that a single poet with a purpose in mind reserved *Yahweh* and *'Elohim* largely for the prose sections narrated by the author, and placed the other three names on the lips of the foreigners. Whatever the truth may be, the translator is faced with the task of deciding how these names are to be handled.

Words or titles for God in most languages are either general terms, specific terms, or combinations of both. The specific names associated with the exploits of a local deity are the most troublesome, because too often these specific names suggest attitudes and behavior that are contradictory to a biblical understanding of God. On the other hand, some words or titles refer to general attributes such as power, greatness, highness, ruling, creativity, care, protection, sustaining. Names associated with such qualities are usually acknowledged as more appropriate. Even so, a specific name with questionable attributes can often over a period of time become accepted, and it is usually better than a borrowed word which may have little meaning and sometimes has unfortunate foreign associations.

How to translate adequately and faithfully the words referring to God is a problem for all translators. In some cases the problems have remained long after the translation was completed. It will be helpful to consider the translation of the general words for God separately from the problems related to the translation of the Hebrew personal name of God written *YHWH*.

We may attempt to translate each of the Hebrew words referring to God by a different term. However, this is not often a practical solution, because most languages do not have a large number of words which are equally generic in their meanings. Furthermore, the impression may be given that each word, name, or title refers to a different deity.

A common practice is to translate all these general words for God by the most general word for God in the language. In languages influenced by Islam this may be some form of "Allah."

In some cases the local word for God is unsuitable for use because of its associations with local cultural practices. For example, the name may represent one of a pair of gods or one of a group; and what is said about the one applies also to the others. In some cases the local god's name refers to one whose behavior would be unsuitable to represent the God of the Bible. Nevertheless, translators have often found that an inappropriate local name for a god can and does become identified eventually with the God of scripture. It is therefore difficult to make hard and fast rules.

Another solution, particularly in languages which may have no name for God, is to adopt an honorific title which describes a major feature of God; for example, "The Creator," "The Heavenly Ruler," "The Supreme One."

The translation of the divine name poses a related but somewhat different set of problems. It is important to recognize that *YHWH* represents the name of the God of the Israelites. The Hebrew Bible does not use such expressions as "the *YHWH*," "*YHWH* of Israel," or "our *YHWH*," which confirms that *YHWH* is used as a personal name for God. It is the most frequently used term for God in the Old Testament. Although it is a name whose explanation is given in Exodus 3.13-14, scholars differ in their interpretation of the meaning. Furthermore, to translate *YHWH* as "I am who I am" is difficult and may not sound at all like a name. Furthermore, in very few of the occurrences of this name in the Old Testament is the name as such in focus. Normally it is a reference to God, the same as is the term *'elohim* and others.

Translators and particularly revisers of earlier versions are frequently faced with what to do with the name "Jehovah." This name is based on a misinformed belief by an early English translator that the Jews pronounced the consonants of *YHWH* with the vowels of *'adonai* "Lord." What they actually pronounced was the word *'adonai*. Accordingly the Handbook does not encourage translators to use "Jehovah." At the same time it recognizes that this word has often become somewhat sacred, and that translators and revisers are sometimes under great pressure from churches to retain it.

To translate the name of Israel's God there are several options open to the translator.

1. Transliterate. In this case the sacred name is written in the receptor language phonology in a form that represents the sounds of the word *Yahweh,* which is approximately the pronunciation of *YHWH.* If, of course, the transliteration already has another meaning, it cannot be used, or it must be transliterated in a different manner. Since Jews do not pronounce the name, and if they are a significant number of readers, they should be consulted before deciding to transliterate *YHWH.*

2. Translate with a term equivalent to "Lord." This is a practice begun by the translators of the Septuagint, who translated *YHWH* by the Greek word *kurios* "Lord." An equivalent term may be " Master," "Owner," "Ruler," "One who commands." *'Adonai* as a separate term for God does not occur in Job.

3. Translate the meaning of *YHWH.* It is sometimes possible to translate the sacred name by a term or expression that suggests one of the meanings usually assigned to *YHWH.* In these cases we may suggest expressions like "the Ever-Present One" or "the Eternal One."

4. Use the name of a local god. If the receptor language god has a personal name, it is sometimes possible to use that name to represent *YHWH.* As was pointed out earlier, this does not always depend on the local god being in conformity to the God of the Bible. If the receptor language has both a personal name and an honorific or descriptive title, it may be possible to use the personal name for *YHWH* and the other term to translate the general words for God.

5. Translate both *YHWH* and the general words for God by the same term. If none of the other suggestions seems advisable, and there is not an established practice to overcome, it may be best to use a single term or expression for *YHWH* and all the other terms that refer to God. An exception to this may be if the translator wishes to reserve a special name to translate *YHWH* in those passages in which attention is drawn to the name of God. None of these are in the book of Job. However, translators may wish to use a special name to translate *YHWH* in the book of Job. In doing so they will be following the practice of the author of the book, who restricts the divine name to chapters 1, 2, and 42.

Changing the Hebrew Text

For translators who may not be able to familiarize themselves with the problems in translating the Hebrew Masoretic text, a brief explanation is needed in order to understand why scholars sometimes propose changes or corrections in the Masoretic text. In some cases the differences in meaning between two or more versions is due to the different decisions made by the translators regarding a particular Hebrew word or phrase. RSV and TEV do not always explain in a note their reasons for departing from the Hebrew text. However, in many passages they do warn us. By reading their footnotes we are sometimes able to see how the words or expressions in RSV and TEV are different from those in the Hebrew text.

Many times the RSV footnote has "Heb. obscure" and TEV "Hebrew unclear." RSV often gives the names of the ancient versions which it follows, and this is followed by a comment on the Hebrew text. In similar cases TEV says "One (or some) ancient translation(s)" and gives its translation, and then adds what the Hebrew text says, or it states that the Hebrew is unclear.

An example will suffice to illustrate.

> For he draws up the drops of water,
> he^c distils his mist in rain. [Job 36.27]

The footnote says "^c Cn: Heb They distil." This note is to be read " 'He' in 'he distils' is a correction of the Masoretic text, which has 'they distil.' " The RSV translators base the change on the judgment of textual scholars. Most of the "corrections" in RSV are based on the ancient versions, which were made before the Masoretic revision.

When the Handbook says that a change has been proposed in the Hebrew text, it does not mean that the translators of a particular version or textual scholars simply did not like the Hebrew form, but that the Hebrew we have in the Masoretic text has perhaps been wrongly copied. Their concern is to represent the oldest and most authentic form of the Hebrew text.

Translators of the book of Job who are able to do so should familiarize themselves with "HOTTP," which stands for "Hebrew Old Testament Text Project." Part of the work of this committee is contained in *Preliminary and Interim Report on the Hebrew Old Testament Text Project, Volume 3: Poetical Books.* That volume presents the committee's recommendations on selected passages from every chapter in the book of Job. The most important of these are discussed in this Handbook.

Exclusive and Inclusive language

The book of Job is written largely from a male point of view, and the words translated "man," "men," "he," and "him" occur from beginning to end. However, the vast majority of these terms are not used to refer exclusively to one or more male humans. On the contrary, they are used generally to refer to anyone, male or female. However, RSV makes little if any attempt to avoid these exclusive terms. TEV shows some awareness of this kind of usage, but is far too inconsistent to serve as a model.

Some examples will illustrate the usage of exclusive language. When Eliphaz says in 5.7 "Man is born to trouble as the sparks fly upward" (TEV "Man brings trouble on himself"), he is not speaking exclusively of male humans. The New Jerusalem Bible (NJB) avoids exclusive language by translating "It is people who breed trouble for themselves."

In 5.17 we read "happy is the man whom God reproves,"which TEV translates "Happy is the person whom God corrects." In 7.1 Job asks "Has not man a hard service upon earth," which is again made inclusive by TEV "Human life is like forced army service." Unfortunately TEV does not translate consistently with inclusive language. Verse 9.2 "How can a man be just before God . . . ?" is rendered by TEV "How can a man win his case . . . ?"

The lesson we learn by comparing numerous examples from RSV and TEV is that RSV uses exclusive language almost every time. Fortunately this has been corrected in the revision of RSV, the "New Revised Standard Version." Furthermore, TEV does not give us a dependable model of inclusive language.

The Handbook does not always call attention specifically to the use of exclusive language in RSV and TEV, but it does attempt to illustrate inclusive language through its model translations. Accordingly translators should evaluate these for their suitability for use in the receptor language.

Title

The Book of Job

The Book of Job bears the name of the man whose story it tells. In this way it is similar to the titles of the books of Joshua, Samuel, Jonah, Ruth, Esther, Daniel, Ezra, and Nehemiah. Job's name in English is taken from the Greek and Latin spellings of the Hebrew *'Iyyob*. Writers in ancient times suggested that Job's name was connected with a similar sounding noun meaning "enemy" or one who is the object of enmity, and so "persecuted." Others saw in the name an Arabic word meaning "one who repents." Later studies have shown that various forms of Job's name were commonly used from ancient times in languages related to Hebrew. Accordingly the writer of Job was probably using a personal name that would be easily recognized as such by his readers.

Many translations use "Job" or "The Book of Job" as the title. These titles do not identify Job as a person. Because many readers will be unfamiliar with the name Job, it is often better to make clear in the title that Job is a man; for example, "The book about a man called Job" or "The story of a man named Job." Translators should take particular care when adapting the name Job from Hebrew or from a major language not to create a word that may be confused with an existing word in the receptor language. In Muslim areas where Job's name is well known from the Koran as *ayyub*, it is normally best to retain this form of the name, or use it as a base to adjust from.

1. Prose Introduction

(1.1–2.13)

The first two chapters of Job, as well as 32.1-5 and the conclusion (42.7-17), are in prose form. Chapters 1 and 2 provide the background for the poetic speeches or dialogues (3.2–42.6), which make up the core of the book. See the detailed outline in the introduction.

The first two chapters, sometimes called the prologue, establish that Job is a true servant of Yahweh, and that, although Job is prosperous and successful, he serves Yahweh without regard for rewards. To lay this foundation the writer uses narration, drama, and dialogues. Location of the scenes regularly alternates between Job's land on earth and the place in heaven where those who serve Yahweh gather around him.

The book opens with the writer introducing Job to his readers (1.1-5). He presents Job as a wealthy livestock owner and the father of a large and faithful family. Equally important, Job is pictured as an honest and devout man, always taking care to insure the ritual purity of his family. The writer does not mention Job's wife until chapter 2. The first action scene (1.6-12) takes place in Yahweh's presence, where Yahweh and Satan discuss the testing of Job's character. Satan is given permission to test Job's faithfulness to his God. Scene two (1.13-19) takes place on Job's property, where in one tragic day Job loses all his possessions and also all his children. The final three verses (20-22) show Job reacting with patient resignation, and the first chapter closes affirming that Job did not sin by blaming Yahweh for the crushing blows that fell on him, as Satan had predicted Job would do (1.12).

Having introduced the man Job in 1.1-5, the author opens chapter 2 in the setting of Yahweh's heavenly assembly, as in 1.6. Verses 1-5 of chapter 2 lay the groundwork for a second testing of Job, and are nearly a repetition of 1.6-12. In 2.3 Yahweh again calls Satan's attention to the blameless and upright Job, who has maintained his faithfulness through the first testing. This time the skeptical Satan replies that Job remains faithful only because the first tests did not take away his health. If this is done, Job will certainly curse Yahweh to his face. The scene ends with verse 6, in which Yahweh allows Satan to attack Job's body; he does not, however, permit Job's death.

Scene 2 (2.7-10) is again on earth, where Job breaks out with sores, and his wife urges him to end his misery by cursing God and dying. Although much more compact, this scene corresponds to 1.12b-22.

Scene 3 (2.11-13), still on earth and now in a rubbish heap, brings Job's three friends to mourn with him. This scene has no parallel in chapter 1, but serves as a transition by preparing the ground for the long disputes which will follow between Job and his friends.

Section Heading

This is the first of ten headings at the level of a section and concerns the content of 1.1–2.13. The title **Prose Introduction** indicates that the content is in prose in contrast to poetry, and that the section introduces the setting of the entire poem as well as the background of Job, the main character. Some translations call these two chapters "Prologue" or "Introduction." In some languages a heading for this opening section may be expressed "This is the beginning of the story," "The opening of the story," or "This is the way Job's story begins."

1A. THE MAN JOB (1.1-5)

REVISED STANDARD VERSION   TODAY'S ENGLISH VERSION

1 There was a man in the land of Uz, whose name was Job; and that man was blameless and upright, one who feared God, and turned away from evil. 2 There were born to him seven sons and three daughters. 3 He had seven thousand sheep, three thousand camels, five hundred yoke of oxen, and five hundred she-asses, and very many servants; so that this man was the greatest of all the people of the east. 4 His sons used to go and hold a feast in the house of each on his day; and they would send and invite their three sisters to eat and drink with them. 5 And when the days of the feast had run their course, Job would send and sanctify them, and he would rise early in the morning and offer burnt offerings according to the number of them all; for Job said, "It may be that my sons have sinned, and cursed God in their hearts." Thus Job did continually.

1 There was a man named Job, living in the land of Uz, who worshiped God and was faithful to him. He was a good man, careful not to do anything evil. 2 He had seven sons and three daughters, 3 and owned seven thousand sheep, three thousand camels, one thousand head of cattle, and five hundred donkeys. He also had a large number of servants and was the richest man in the East.

4 Job's sons used to take turns giving a feast, to which all the others would come, and they always invited their three sisters to join them. 5 The morning after each feast, Job would get up early and offer sacrifices for each of his children in order to purify them. He always did this because he thought that one of them might have sinned by insulting God unintentionally.

Division Heading

The first division within section 1 concerns the author's description of Job (1.1-5). The Handbook heading, "An introduction to Job the man," calls attention to the way in which the first five verses consider nothing other than statements about Job and what made him different from all others. Translators may have to adapt the Handbook heading by saying, for example, "The description of Job," "The author describes Job," "This tells what kind of man Job was," "A picture of Job." TEV has "Satan tests Job" as a heading for 1.1-12. However, the first test of Job takes place in verses 13-19, and it will be dealt with at that point. Translators wishing to use fewer headings may follow TEV, or adapt TEV to say, for example, "God arranges for Satan to test Job" or "God calls Satan's attention to Job."

1.1 RSV   TEV

There was a man in the land of Uz, whose name was Job; and that man

There was a man named Job, living in the land of Uz,[a] who worshiped was blameless and upright, one who feared God, and turned away from evil.

God and was faithful to him. He was a good man, careful not to do anything evil.

^a UZ: *An area whose exact location is unknown.*

There was a man: the words **There was** translate a Hebrew form which is not used to begin a historical narrative, but rather to signal the opening of a story. (For parallel usage of the story form, see 2 Sam 12.1 and Est 2.5.) "Once upon a time there was a man" is suggested by Habel as the English equivalent story opening. It should be kept in mind, however, that Job was not told as a children's tale, and it differs in many ways from a fairy tale. No English translation consulted uses "Once upon a time." The use of **There was a man** in RSV and TEV does not by itself signal that what follows is a story. However, the association of this man with the very uncertain **land of Uz** suggests that the meaning and purpose of the book are not dependent on whether its narrative elements are factual. Furthermore, the absence of any historical events, places, or persons locates Job outside history. The New English Bible (NEB) has "there lived in the land of Uz," which is more clearly a story opener in English than the RSV or TEV forms. In many languages the setting "in the land of Uz" will not mark Job as a story in contrast to history.

Some languages use specific forms at the beginning to signal the type of story that is being told. However, in languages which do, the translator must be careful not to start the story in such a way that the reader would perhaps expect a fox or rooster to begin speaking. In some languages the most natural way to open a story of this kind is to have the author say, for example, "I tell this about Job. He lived in a country called Uz." In some languages it will be necessary to make explicit whether the author is reporting observed events or ones he has learned from others. The author obviously did not participate in Yahweh's heavenly gathering, and so the facts are not first-hand experience.

It is particularly important that the translator think in terms of the discourse unit (verses 1-6) and handle this paragraph as one theme made up of related parts. In some languages this may mean presenting the whole paragraph as a single sentence, while in others the various sentences will have to be carefully linked together. The paragraph contains a great deal of information the readers may know nothing about, and accordingly, the flow of new ideas may have to be slowed down by building in more redundancy. Introductions in the story forms in each language have their own inner characteristics, including the proper order for the presentation of information about time, place, and so on. The translator must be sensitive to these if the Job story is to be properly communicated.

In some languages the location may need to be stated even before giving Job's name; for example, "In a country called Uz there lived a man . . . ." In some languages a story opener must contain some information about the time. This is lacking in the Hebrew story, or at best implied by the use of verb tenses. Especially for first-time readers unfamiliar with this story, as well as for languages which require it, it may be necessary to say "A long time ago" or an equivalent expression.

In the land of Uz: although the location of Uz is uncertain, there are three main areas which have been suggested: Hauran, east of the Sea of Galilee in present-day Syria; Edom, south of the Dead Sea; and Western Arabia (note that Pope has a full discussion). There are three references to **Uz** in Genesis, one in Lamentations, and one in Jeremiah, but none of these throws any light on the location of Job's land. Since it is impossible to provide a map showing where Job's homeland was, translators may wish to follow TEV's note: "UZ: *an area whose exact location is unknown.*"

In translation it will often be necessary to say, as TEV does, that Job "lived in the land of Uz." **Land of Uz** suggests a country rather than a city and may sometimes be rendered "in the country called Uz."

Whose name was Job: the name **Job** in English is taken from the Greek form of the Hebrew *'Iyyob*. The name occurs in Ezekiel 14.14,20, along with Noah and Danel (the TEV version of the name), as that of a man noted for his personal goodness. Job is also mentioned once in the New Testament as a model of patience (James 5.11). For a discussion of the meanings of Job's name, see the discussion under **Title** at the head of this chapter.

Job's character is described by the use of two pairs of qualities: **blameless** and **upright**, and **one who feared God** and **turned away from evil**. The first pair depicts Job as a morally good man, and the second pair as a religious person. The first word is translated in the King James Version (KJV) as "perfect," which suggests a state of sinlessness. The idea is more exactly one of "moral integrity." **Upright** translates a word having to do with "straightness" and again focuses upon Job's honesty in his dealings. This first pair of terms in Hebrew is found in Psalm 25.21, translated by RSV as "integrity and uprightness," and by TEV as "goodness and honesty"; in Psalm 37.37 they occur in parallel. In many languages the first pair of descriptions used of Job are rendered idiomatically; for example, "having one heart" or "speaking with one mouth." Also common are terms for straightness, "going on the straight road," and confidence, "man on whose word people rest."

Feared God is to say in the biblical way that Job was a religious man. He was one who **turned away from evil**, or who avoided evil as a result of his fearing God. TEV, which says "who worshiped God," has shifted this clause forward. However, there does not seem to be any advantage in doing this. This description of Job is repeated by God in 1.8 and makes it clear that Job did not bring his troubles on himself. **Feared God** may sometimes be translated "was faithful to God" or "showed respect for God." In some languages it is not natural to turn away from an abstract idea like **evil**. Accordingly we may sometimes say "did not do as evil people do," or "refused to follow the way that evil people go," or "he said 'No' to people who did bad things." Verse 1b may be rendered, for example, "Job was a good and honest man. He worshiped God and did nothing that was evil." The parallelism in structure here is good to maintain, since it serves the purpose of slowing the information in what is otherwise a tightly packed paragraph.

1.2	RSV	TEV
	There were born to him seven sons and three daughters.	**He had seven sons and three daughters,**

There were born to him expresses the Hebrew form of saying that Job was the father of his children. Some languages prefer this kind of passive construction while some require it; but many others must use an active voice, as in TEV "he had seven sons." Many languages distinguish between bearing animals and bearing children. **Seven sons and three daughters** provides the evidence for Job's goodness and his fear of God: he is rewarded with a large family (see Psa 127.3; 128.3 where children are rewarded to the faithful). Seven children was a desirable number (1 Sam 2.5), but seven sons was even more ideal (Ruth 4.15). In some languages it may appear odd that the children are left nameless and are said to be born to Job without reference to his wife. (In the conclusion Job's three new daughters have names). Readers in some languages will most likely infer from the statement that there were several wives. The author refers to Job's wife only in chapter 2, without specifying that she is the mother of his children.

In some languages a bridge may be required in moving from one subject to the next; for example, "speaking of his children . . . ," or "about Job as a father . . . ."

1.3   RSV   TEV

He had seven thousand sheep, three thousand camels, five hundred yoke of oxen, and five hundred she-asses, and very many servants; so that this man was the greatest of all the people of the east.	and owned seven thousand sheep, three thousand camels, one thousand head of cattle, and five hundred donkeys. He also had a large number of servants and was the richest man in the East.

Verse 3 is an inventory of Job's animals and servants, and concludes that having so much livestock and so many servants made him "the richest man in the East" (TEV). As with his seven sons and three daughters, he owns seven thousand sheep and three thousand camels. The Hebrew term *miqneh,* which is translated **sheep,** includes sheep, goats, and cattle, the animals of a grazing culture. **Five hundred yoke of oxen** is translated by TEV as "one thousand head of cattle." The text, however, suggests pairs of working animals and not ordinary cattle. **Five hundred she-asses** emphasizes the large number of females, which were valuable for milk and breeding, and superior to males for riding. Only a small number of males would be required for breeding.

Translators should refer to *Fauna and Flora of the Bible* (pages 36, 62, 75) for detailed descriptions of each of these animals. In areas where these animals are unknown, the translator may have to borrow terms from a major language. In such cases it is often helpful to add a classifying word or phrase; for example, "burden-carrying animals called camels" and "work animals called oxen," or "animals called oxen that pull loads." Translators are cautioned in the use of descriptive phrases such as "long-eared animal" for donkey, since the only long-eared animal the people may know is the rabbit. In most cases in which these animals are unknown, publications should contain illustrations.

Very many servants translates a term which includes both male and female workers as used in Genesis 12.16. **Servants** must often be rendered by a descriptive phrase; for example, "work-people" or "people who work for the owner."

So that in the Hebrew text marks a consequence; because of Job's great wealth and his religious character, he was known as the **greatest of all the people of the east.** In some languages the consequence will have to be more explicitly marked; for example, "because Job had so much wealth, the people knew him as the richest man."

Greatest of all: Job is called "greatest" by comparing his wealth with others. Accordingly TEV, the Spanish common language version (*Dios Habla Hoy,* or SPCL), and Pope say that he was "the richest man" (see Gen 26.13 for a similar description of Isaac). In some languages the greatest or richest man is said to be "the man with the most loads" or "the big owner man." The translation of comparatives and superlatives differs greatly from language to language. In the present superlative one must sometimes say "No person had wealth like Job's wealth," "Many people had wealth; Job surpassed all in wealth," or "Job was rich; everyone else was poor."

People of the east is literally "sons of the east" and was used to designate various ethnic groups living to the east of the Jordan valley: Arameans along the northern Euphrates (Gen 29.1); the people of Edom, Moab, and Ammon, who were Israel's enemies (Isa 11.14); the nomadic Midianites and Amalekites who raided Israel's eastern borders during the rule of the Judges (Judges 6.3,33). **The east** does not help to locate Job's country with any exactness.

The author assumes his readers know that **the east** is a general geographical area in a particular part of the world. However, a local rendering of the direction "east" may not designate for modern readers the area the author has in mind. Therefore it may be preferable to avoid speaking of "east" as a direction and say, for example, "he was the richest man in his part of the world." If the translator keeps the expression, it may be expressed as "east of Israel" or "east of where the people of Israel live." **East** may be translated in some languages in reference to local geography; for example, "where the headwaters of the river are" or "beyond the mountain." A common designation is "where the sun rises."

1.4 RSV	TEV
His sons used to go and hold a feast in the house of each on his day; and they would send and invite their three sisters to eat and drink with them.	Job's sons used to take turns giving a feast, to which all the others would come, and they always invited their three sisters to join them.

With verse 4 the author returns to Job's children, mentioned in verse 2, in order to illustrate what he meant when he said in verse 1 that Job feared God and turned away from evil. Verse 4 expands and illustrates verse 2, and verse 5 expands and illustrates 1b. TEV and many other modern translations begin a new paragraph with 1.4. Whether or not the translator will make a new paragraph here depends on the way in which the language most naturally handles the relations between verses 4 and 5 and verses 1 and 3. Verses 4 and 5 constitute a tiny episode. However, since the episode of feasting and sacrificing makes specific the content of the previous verses, in some languages it may be appropriate to preface verse 5 with something like "This is how Job was careful to do nothing evil."

His sons used to go: in the Hebrew text, as in RSV, the pronoun can only refer to Job, since no other subject has been used. Languages vary greatly in the use of pronouns. In some languages the use of a pronoun here would unduly emphasize that these were Job's sons and not the sons of someone else. In such languages it will be necessary to say "Job's sons." **Used to go** translates the verb "go," which in this context does not mean "they used to go somewhere" but rather expresses an action that continues. Therefore "Job's sons used to take turns" (TEV).

Hold a feast in the house of each on his day: the meaning of this statement, according to Rowley, is that feasts were held seven days a week throughout the year, and each brother took his turn being the host. Such excessive feasting is pictured as part of the lavish display of Job's wealth. The other view is that the feasts were annual festivals (so Pope); for example, the feast of ingathering at the end of the year (Exo 34.22) and the festival of booths, which was observed with seven days of offerings (Lev 23.36; Num 29.35; 2 Chr 7.9). Another view, held by some commentators, is that **on his day** refers to the birthday of each son, in which case there would be seven feasts a year. In any event (daily or annual feasting) **each on his day** refers to each son taking his turn to provide the feast, which is the way it is rendered by TEV, NEB, French common language version (*La Bible en français courant,* FRCL), *Traduction œcuménique de la Bible* (TOB), German common language version (*Die Gute Nachricht: Die Bibel in heutigem Deutsch,* GECL). **Hold a feast** must sometimes be rendered "to invite the others to eat at his house" or "get the food ready at his house." The whole clause may sometimes be translated "Each son took his turn to get the feast food ready to eat at his house" or "The sons of Job took turns serving the big eating meal at their houses."

Send and invite their three sisters: the two verbs translate what is literally "send and call," an expression that is used somewhat idiomatically, the focus of meaning being on the second verb. (For a similar double verb see "send and sanctify" in verse 5.) It may be implied that the sisters were unmarried and lived with their father, while each of the sons had his own house. In some languages the translator will have to decide if the sisters are younger or older in reference to the brothers. There is no way of knowing from the text. Verse 13 speaks of the "eldest brother," but this need not exclude the sisters from being older than the first born male. In some languages it will be more natural to bridge between 4a and 4b by saying, for example, "and when the feast was ready, they would invite their sisters."

To eat and drink with them: TEV shifts to the more generic "to join them," which avoids repeating the idea of "feast" (also SPCL). Translators need to be sensitive to ways in which local cultural interpretations may be given to this kind of event. The author intends to give the impression of family harmony in the midst of lavish consumption, and is not suggesting an incestuous orgy. If the latter is understood commonly, the translator should examine ways of stating the facts the author presents without favoring a misinterpretation. In some languages this may be "They would invite their sisters to come and share the food with them" or "They would ask their sisters to visit them and to have a meal together."

1.5   RSV   TEV

And when the days of the feast had run their course, Job would send and sanctify them, and he would rise early in the morning and offer burnt offerings according to the number of them all; for Job said, "It may be that my sons have sinned, and cursed God in their hearts." Thus Job did continually.	The morning after each feast, Job would get up early and offer sacrifices for each of his children in order to purify them. He always did this because he thought that one of them might have sinned by insulting God unintentionally.

At the end of each feast, Job, who apparently did not take part, made a sacrifice to purify his children, in case they had offended Yahweh. Regulations governing the sacrifice required one bull, one ram, and seven male lambs (Num 29.36). Such a sacrifice would require considerable wealth, whether it was done daily or several times a year.

When the days of the feast had run their course: TEV understands the sacrifice to take place "the morning after each feast," which could be understood to be the morning after each day of feasting, or the first morning following each festive period. NEB says "when a round of feasts was finished," making it explicit that the sacrifice took place only at the close of each series of festivities, and ruling out the "birthday" interpretation; see also RSV, SPCL, GECL.

Send and sanctify them: TEV takes this double verb to have the meaning of the second verb, as in verse 1.4. Other translations understand the two verbs as distinct (so SPCL, NEB, FRCL, GECL). The idea is that of removing any ritual impurity from his children which would prevent them from participating in the worship of Yahweh. In addition to the burning of the sacrifice, there would probably be washings and changes of clothing (Rowley). TEV has "purify them"; so SPCL, FRCL. In translation **sanctify** should not be rendered here "make holy." The act was a cleansing from possible contact with tabooed food or objects which caused the person to be defiled, as well as saying words that might be offensive to God, as in 1.5. Accordingly we may say in some languages "wash away the defilement," "remove the taboo," or "take away the effect of that which was forbidden."

Offer burnt offering according to the number of them all: it is not clear from the Hebrew whether this means seven sacrifices for the seven sons or ten for the sons and daughters. The term for **sons** can sometimes refer to "children," but since it means "sons" in verse 4, it is probably the same in verse 5. TEV understands the purpose of the sacrifice was "in order to purify them." Some interpreters understand that the purification refers to the washing of the body and change of clothing, and that this was followed by the whole burnt offerings according to Leviticus 1. In some languages the idea of burning animals as an offering to God is entirely strange. Nevertheless the idea can normally be communicated with little difficulty; for example, "burned animals offered to God" or "animals killed and burned as a gift to God." In some languages it is necessary to add that the animals were first killed, to prevent readers from thinking they were burned while still alive. Verse 5a may be rendered "After the feast was over, Job would get up early and kill the animals which he would burn as an offering to God. He would do this for each of his children."

For Job said: this statement introduces not a remark that Job made to someone, but rather his inner thinking. In other words, "Job thought to himself." In many languages it is common for a person's thoughts to appear as quoted speech. However, the form may differ; for example, " 'Maybe my sons have sinned by cursing God without thinking,' I say this." In some languages it will be more natural to follow TEV "because he thought . . ." and omit the quotation marks. If the use of quotation marks gives a meaning other than that of thinking to himself, then the quotation marks should not be used.

And cursed God in their hearts: Job was concerned that his children may have thought or said something which would offend God and therefore cause God to punish them. The Hebrew word is literally "blessed" and may be a correction made by a scribe to avoid putting the word "curse" next to "God"; some interpreters think that "blessed" (a mild word) is used by the author to avoid saying the harsh word "cursed." In any case, it is clear that the implied meaning is "cursed." For similar usages see 1.11; 2.5,9; 1 Kings 21.10; Psalm 10.3.

A curse normally involves a formula of words pronounced against someone, and calls on a supernatural being or force to bring about the results of the curse. Here the idea is more general, and in translation it may often be rendered as "saying evil words against God."

In their hearts: in the Old Testament the heart is the center of the intellect and will, more than of the affections and emotions. TEV's rendering "by insulting God unintentionally" expresses accurately in modern English the meaning of the Hebrew phrase. In many languages in which the heart is used idiomatically to refer to the center of the emotions, it will be better here to shift to something like "in their thoughts" or "in what they thought and said."

Thus Job did continually: **continually** translates Hebrew "all the days" and means "always." TEV shifts this clause forward as "He always did this" and follows with the reason "because he thought that one of them . . . ." The translator must decide where this statement most naturally fits in. In Hebrew it is not necessarily emphasized.

1B. FIRST MEETING OF GOD AND SATAN (1.6-12)

RSV	TEV
6 Now there was a day when the sons of God came to present themselves before the LORD, and Satan also came among them. 7 The LORD said to Satan, "Whence have you come?" Satan answered the LORD, "From going to and fro on the earth, and from walking up and down on it." 8 And the LORD said to Satan, "Have you considered my servant Job, that there is none like him on the earth, a blameless and upright man, who fears God and turns away from evil?" 9 Then Satan answered the LORD, "Does Job fear God for nought? 10 Hast thou not put a hedge about him and his house and all that he has, on every side? Thou hast blessed the work of his hands, and his possessions have increased in the land. 11 But	6 When the day came for the heavenly beings to appear before the LORD, Satan was there among them. 7 The LORD asked him, "What have you been doing?" Satan answered, "I have been walking here and there, roaming around the earth." 8 "Did you notice my servant Job?" the LORD asked. "There is no one on earth as faithful and good as he is. He worships me and is careful not to do anything evil." 9 Satan replied, "Would Job worship you if he got nothing out of it? 10 You have always protected him and his family and everything he owns. You bless everything he does, and you have given him enough cattle to fill the whole country.

put forth thy hand now, and touch all that he has, and he will curse thee to thy face." 12 And the LORD said to Satan, "Behold, all that he has is in your power; only upon himself do not put forth your hand." So Satan went forth from the presence of the LORD.

11 But now suppose you take away everything he has—he will curse you to your face!"
12 "All right," the LORD said to Satan, "everything he has is in your power, but you must not hurt Job himself." So Satan left.

In verse 6 the story teller shifts the scene to describe a new episode. The location is undisclosed, which is part of the author's way of separating the story from known historical events. The setting with Yahweh surrounded by his heavenly servants is similar to the one found in 1 Kings 22.19-23. The actors in this brief scene are Yahweh and Satan; Job is the subject of their conversation. In verse 7 Yahweh opens the conversation with a true question (in contrast to a rhetorical one). Satan replies by giving the information requested. In verse 8 Yahweh follows up with a second question which makes clear the reason for the first question: "Have you considered my servant Job?" From verse 9 onward Satan switches the strategy on his end of the conversation. In verses 9 and 10 he comes back with two rhetorical questions and follows these up with a statement which to him accounts for Job's goodness: Yahweh blesses him. In verse 11 Satan throws down a challenge in the form of a command, "touch all he has." Yahweh appears to have changed his strategy too, for in verse 12a he replies with a concession that is conditioned: "he is in your power . . . do not put forth your hand."

This brief drama with its dialogue between Yahweh and Satan is never disclosed to Job and his friends but serves as the background for their dispute in the main body of the poem. It has a very clear opening and closing, and the theme of Job's goodness is the single thread of the dialogue. Translators must handle it as a single discourse unit and adjust the various kinds of speech events to the most natural way of doing the same in their own languages.

Division Heading

Verses 6-12 concern the first of two encounters between Yahweh and Satan. Translators wishing to place a heading before verse 6 may adjust the Handbook heading to say, for example, "God meets with his servants and Satan," "First meeting with Satan in heaven," or "God asks Satan concerning Job." TOB has "The heavenly court," GECL "Job's integrity is doubted," Rowley "The first scene in heaven."

1.6	RSV	TEV

Now there was a day when the sons of God came to present themselves before the LORD, and Satan[a] also came among them.

[a] Heb *the adversary*

When the day came for the heavenly beings[b] to appear before the LORD, Satan[c] was there among them.

[b] HEAVENLY BEINGS: *Supernatural beings who serve God in heaven.*
[c] SATAN: *A supernatural being whose name indicates he was regarded as man's opponent.*

Now there was a day switches the scene from Job's home on earth to Yahweh's presence, presumably in heaven, though that is not stated. The Jerusalem Targum (an ancient Hebrew translation and commentary) interprets this day to be New Year's Day, and the second day's assembly in 2.1 to be on the Day of Atonement. The text itself does not imply that there was a set day on which Yahweh called his servants together. The same wording is used again in 1.13, where it shifts the scene and moves the action forward. Here the expression provides the time setting and is the equivalent of saying "one day when . . ."; that is the sense in which SPCL, FRCL, GECL take it. The Hebrew form of this scene begins with the time aspect of the setting, vague and general as it is. Languages differ considerably as to the order of time, place, and participants in a story or episode opening. In languages in which it is more natural in narrative to place the time element later, the translator should do so.

The English expression **the sons of God** gives the impression that a father-son relationship exists between Yahweh and these beings. This expression is an example of a Hebrew idiom in which members of a particular category or class are called "sons" of that group, and in this case it is a group of divine beings (see TEV footnote). The parallel expression "sons of the prophets" (see 2 Kings 2.3,5,15) is rendered by NEB as "company of prophets," by TEV, and by FRCL as "group of prophets." So here and in 2.1; 38.7 the reference is to the members of the heavenly assembly surrounding Yahweh. Normally translators should avoid any kind of expression that would imply that these are the male offspring of God. It is often possible to call them "angels," "God's servants," "God's messengers in heaven," or "gods." These heavenly servants are not actors in the scene. They are background, part of the scenery, and by implication Satan is one of them. The author is careful, however, not to stress this. In languages in which the principal characters must be presented first, it may be possible to say, for example, "One day (a long time ago) God and Satan were together. It was the place where the angels came to appear before God, and Satan was also appearing before God." In some languages the essential information needed by the reader is the relationship between the actors, and one character is normally referred to, not by his name, but by the relationship to the main character. For suggestions see comments under 6b below.

'Elohim, which is the same Hebrew word for God used in verses 1 and 5, is taken by some interpreters as a plural "sons of gods" (so Pope, Habel). Translators render the expression in various ways; for example, NEB "members of the heavenly court," SPCL "his heavenly servants," FRCL "God's angels," and TEV "heavenly beings." All translations consulted take *'Elohim* as singular, referring to God.

To present themselves has the sense of "take up their position" or "to station themselves," which is rendered more generally by TEV "to appear before." It depicts a body of servants waiting in attendance on Yahweh, who presides over the assembly. In some languages **to present themselves** is rendered, for example, "to put their eyes in the presence of" or "to place their bodies before."

This is the first occurrence of **the LORD** in the Book of Job. **The LORD** represents in English the Hebrew consonants *YHWH,* pronounced more or less *Yahweh.* Yahweh occurs twenty-nine times in the Book of Job, all but one of these (12.9) being in the prose portions of the book. Only in 1.21 and 12.9 does Job use the name Yahweh.

It is the general custom in English translations of the Bible to substitute the title "the LORD" for the Hebrew name Yahweh. In this they follow the early Greek and Latin versions, which in turn imitated the custom of the Jews, who avoided speaking the proper name Yahweh and substituted a title meaning "my Lord." Presumably the translator of Job will have solved the problem of how to render the term "Lord" in the New Testament. For a detailed discussion of the translation of *YHWH,* see the introduction to this Handbook, "Translating the Book of Job," page 21.

Satan also came among them: the word **Satan** is used in Hebrew here with the article, which designates a role or title rather than a personal name. In later biblical and postbiblical texts **Satan** occurs without the article and is understood as a personal name; for example, 1 Chronicles 21.1. The noun *satan,* which is derived from the Hebrew verb of the same root, occurs in the Hebrew Old Testament 24 times. The verbal root carries the meaning of "bear a grudge against someone" or "harbor animosity" (Holladay). A person who does this is called an "opponent or enemy." The noun form is used in 2 Samuel 19.22 with the meaning of "enemy," when David protected the life of Shimei and accused the sons of Zeruiah being "as an adversary (*satan*) to me"; see also 1 Samuel 29.4; 1 Kings 11.23. In Zechariah 3.1 Satan is found standing at the right hand of the high priest "to accuse him." In Job we see Satan as one of the "sons of God" who tests men's claims to be religious. He does not appear to be evil so much as he is skeptical of religious pretensions. The testing of Job is Satan's idea, since testing people is his job. The destruction he carries out against Job is not in opposition to God, but rather is done with divine approval. In doing so he operates within his role as God's servant. Job would, if he knew the plot hatched in heaven against him, consider Satan the worst sort of enemy.

All of this is to say that "the Satan" in the Book of Job cannot be entirely identified with "the Devil" or "Satan" in the New Testament. However, readers of the Scriptures have normally formed their idea of Satan based on the New Testament. Accordingly the translator is faced with a serious translation problem. If he is translating for people who are regular readers of the New Testament and merely transliterates the name "Satan," his readers will be misled, since they will read their New Testament meaning into it. If the translator is translating Job for people who have not read the New Testament and transliterates "Satan," those readers will attempt to read the Satan of the book of Job into the New Testament. Therefore it is better in Job to make an adjustment (regardless of the readers' background). The possibilities are the following: (1) transliteration with translation; for example, "Satan the accuser"; (2) translation only; for example, "the accuser, the tester." FRCL employs (1) on the first occurrence in verse 6 and then drops the name "Satan" in subsequent verses. SPCL and TOB use solution (2) throughout. If the translation is for readers accustomed to marginal notes, a footnote is advisable, regardless of the solution taken. For examples of footnotes see TEV, FRCL, TOB.

In some languages it will be advisable to identify Satan in his role of "tester" or "accuser" when he is first mentioned. Thereafter he may be referred to by his role, rather than his name.

The LORD said to Satan, "Whence have you come?" Satan answered the LORD, "From going to and fro on the earth, and from walking up and down on it."	The LORD asked him, "What have you been doing?" Satan answered, "I have been walking here and there, roaming around the earth."

In verse 7 Yahweh opens the conversation with Satan which will set the course for all the events to follow. **The LORD said to Satan** represents the Hebrew usage, but "asked" (so TEV and most other modern English versions) is more appropriate for a question.

The LORD asks Satan **Whence have you come?** The form of the question in TEV "What have you been doing?" is, however, a more natural way of expressing the kind of question that would prompt Satan's reply. Here the question and answer form is simply used by the story teller as an opportunity to bring Job into the situation, and is not to be understood to imply that God did not know where Satan had been; for a similar question asked by God to Moses, see Exodus 4.2. TEV uses direct address and quotation marks; likewise SPCL, FRCL, TOB, GECL, *La Bible de Jérusalem* (BJ). NEB begins direct address only with Satan's reply. TEV and others start a new paragraph with each change of speakers. Translators should not necessarily follow this, but rather use the most natural way of indicating a change of speaker.

Satan replies **From going to and fro on the earth.** Some interpreters see a play on words here in which Hebrew *shut* "roam or rove about" is suggested as the origin of the word "Satan" (so Tur-Sinai). Satan is thought of as a roving secret agent who accuses his victims and may serve as their prosecutor, as in Zechariah 3.1. The verb used here is the same one used in 2 Samuel 24.2,8, in which Joab and his assistants travel all over Israel for the taking of a census. Languages differ greatly in their ways of expressing movement, and it is important here that the expression used convey the sense of going about with a purpose.

The second half of Satan's reply, **and from walking up and down on it,** contains the common word for "walk or stroll," the same word used of David strolling on his roof in 2 Samuel 11.2, and of God walking about in the Garden of Eden in Genesis 3.8. In Proverbs 24.34 the same verb is used of poverty compared with an armed robber who "stalks" his victim. TEV has reversed the order of the two verbs, so that "roaming around the earth" is an expansion of "walking here and there." In some languages it may not be necessary to use both expressions, as both ideas are often contained in a single verb. The author is indirectly revealing characteristics of Satan in the manner of his replies to Yahweh. He is evasive and vague. In translation, terms should be carefully chosen which will reveal the same kind of avoidance of direct reply. However, the translator should weigh carefully the implication of indirectness, as the meaning in the receptor language may be quite different from that intended by the author.

1.8   RSV   TEV

And the LORD said to Satan, "Have you
considered my servant Job, that there is
none like him on the earth, a blameless
and upright man, who fears God and
turns away from evil?"

"Did you notice my servant Job?"
the LORD asked. "There is no one on
earth as faithful and good as he is. He
worships me and is careful not to do
anything evil."

In verse 8 Yahweh asks Satan a second question, **Have you considered my
servant Job . . . ?** which is literally "Have you set your heart (meaning, mind) on
my servant Job?" (For a similar usage see "consider" in Isa 41.42; Hag 1.5.) The
question means "Have you paid attention and thought about?" Yahweh's question
is directed to Satan's powers of observation and good judgment, in this case his
ability to pick out a man with such character as Job displays. Yahweh takes the
initiative in drawing Satan's attention to Job, who might otherwise have been left in
peace. TEV "Did you notice" is somewhat casual for this context. FRCL, TOB, and NJB
translate "Have you observed," and SPCL has "paid attention to." In some languages
this question will be rendered through another figure; for example, "Have you put
your good eye on my servant named Job?" Now that Job has been identified in his
role as "servant," "faithful one," or "obedient one," in some languages it will be
appropriate to refer to him by his role rather than by his name.

Yahweh calls Job **my servant**, which in the Bible is a title of respect. Others
to whom this title is given include Abraham (Psa 105.42), Moses (Num 12.7,8), and
the unnamed Servant of the LORD (Isa 42.1). Prophets are often referred to as
servants of the LORD (Amos 3.7). Assuming that Job is a non-Israelite, this seems
to be the only example of this title being given to a foreigner, aside from Nebuchad-
nezzar in Jeremiah 43.10, where the emphasis is on the foreign king who is used as
an instrument in the hand of Yahweh. In many languages the term "servant" suggests
a person who performs menial tasks for an employer. If "servant" in the present
context carries a wrong meaning, it may be better to translate with a verb phrase; for
example, "Job, the man who serves me," "Job, the one who is faithful to me," or
"Job, the man who obeys me faithfully."

The second part of verse 8 is linked with the first part (the question) by the use
of a Hebrew particle translated **that** by RSV. Here the linking word serves to
introduce a statement which is an expansion of a preceding remark or question.
Hence TEV, NEB, and New International Version (NIV) all begin the expansion as a
separate sentence.

There is none like him on the earth summarizes Yahweh's opinion of his
servant, Job, and indirectly informs Satan that Job is a unique case for Satan's secret
operations. Yahweh then repeats the pair of doublets used by the author in verse 1,
one of which Satan will take up again in verse 9. TEV maintains the order of the two
pairs of descriptions in verse 8.

1.9   RSV   TEV

Then Satan answered the LORD, "Does
Job fear God for nought?

Satan replied, "Would Job worship
you if he got nothing out of it?

Satan replies in verse 9 using a rhetorical question, one which does not seek a reply: **Does Job fear God for nought?** Satan is referring to Yahweh's observation in verse 8, "He worships me." Satan is saying "Job does not worship God for nothing," or positively, "Job worships God because he gets something in return." When addressing Yahweh Satan does not call him by this name but by *'Elohim*. In some languages this rhetorical question will require a negative response; for example, "Does Job worship God for nothing? No!" It is sometimes better to shift the question to a statement, negative or positive, as stated above. In some languages rhetorical questions are used when the speaker wants to make a certain point or create a certain atmosphere between speakers, such as doubt, rebuke, or indifference. The translator should not translate automatically using a rhetorical question until he has examined the implication this kind of device has for the speaker and hearer. If we can assume that the rhetorical questions used by Satan in verses 9 and 10 are a device used by the author to depict Satan's character as deceptive, then the translator must use the forms (implicit or explicit) which will reflect the author's intention.

In some languages Satan, or "The accuser," will say "you" instead of "God," as in TEV, thus making the question more direct. To ask the question as it is in Hebrew and RSV would in some languages refer to another god. Furthermore, in some languages it will be more natural for Satan to avoid Job's name, since he has already been identified by his role of "servant," and to say, for example, "Does that servant of yours serve you for nothing? Of course not," "Your servant serves you because you reward him for it," or "Your servant doesn't serve you for nothing."

The Hebrew word translated **for nought** occurs in 2.3 with the meaning "for no reason at all." The same word occurs in 2 Samuel 24.24, but there with the meaning "for which nothing has been paid." The common meaning element is lack of payment on one side or the other, whether of goods or actions, as the English word "gratuitous" may mean either "costing nothing" or "unjustifiable." The traditional teaching put forward by Satan here, that wealth and good fortune are the reward for piety, is supported by such passages as Leviticus 26; Deuteronomy 11.8-15; 28.1-14; Psalms 1, 37, 49, 73; Jeremiah 7.5-7; 12.14-17; Ezekiel 18.

1.10 RSV	TEV
Hast thou not put a hedge about him and his house and all that he has, on every side? Thou hast blessed the work of his hands, and his possessions have increased in the land.	You have always protected him and his family and everything he owns. You bless everything he does, and you have given him enough cattle to fill the whole country.

Satan goes on to complain in a second rhetorical question that he cannot carry out any action against Job because Yahweh has **put a hedge about him and his house and all that he has.** Hedges are used to mark boundaries between owners' properties. Thorn hedges are also used to keep intruders out. TEV has rendered Satan's question as a statement and shifts from "put a hedge" to the purpose, "you have always protected him . . . ." Other translations use different solutions; GECL avoids the metaphor and says "you have kept him from harm"; SPCL "you don't allow anyone to touch him." NJB replaces the hedge metaphor with "have you not put a wall around him?" FRCL, like TEV, states the purpose and adds a simile, "you protect him all around like in an enclosure." In many language areas hedges are used for protection, particularly to keep animals out of cultivated plots. Where hedges are not known and used, it will be best to follow the kinds of adjustments suggested by the various modern translations cited above.

This is Satan's second rhetorical question, and its force is to complain that God protects Job. In some languages the rhetorical question will not accomplish this purpose, and the translator must use a statement or other form; for example, in English one may say "The trouble is that you protect him," "I object that you protect him," or "I can do nothing because you take care of him."

His house is the Hebrew form which here means "his family" (so TEV, NEB, SPCL, FRCL, GECL). From the context of the story, this must be taken in the sense of Job's immediate family, his wife and children, although in the end his brothers and sisters come to celebrate his happy recovery.

And all that he has refers to all of Job's vast possessions; TEV "everything he owns." The final phrase **on every side** goes with the initial part of the question "Have you not put a hedge all around him?"

Blessed the work of his hands expands Satan's first question to a comment similar to the question; that is, Job worships God because God richly rewards him. The verb translated **blessed** is in the perfect tense in Hebrew, denoting past action continuing into the present. "Bless" refers to God's giving his favor to someone; such blessings give the receiver happiness and prosperity. Most modern translations keep the word "bless" here (see TEV). However, GECL is better with "you allow him to succeed in everything he undertakes," and FRCL has "you have certainly supported him in his endeavors." In some languages it may be necessary to say "you have made him rich in everything he does" or "no matter what he does, you cause him to be rich."

The work of his hands is not limited to certain activities done with the hands, but is an idiomatic way of saying "everything he does or undertakes" (so TEV, NEB, FRCL, SPCL, GECL, TOB, NJB).

His possessions: the word translated **possessions** can refer to all of one's wealth, but in Job it refers to his livestock. NJB has "flocks," which in English is appropriate for sheep but not for cattle, donkeys, and camels. NEB, FRCL, TOB use "herds." TEV, SPCL, GECL have the more restricted "cattle." In languages in which herds of animals are unknown, it may be necessary to say, for example, "all of his animals" or, in case this might suggest wild animals, "all the animals he takes care of."

Increased in the land translates a verb which literally means "break out" and is used of Jacob's sudden increase of wealth in Genesis 30.30 ("increased abundantly"); see also Genesis 38.29; Micah 2.13 ("breach"). Here it means that Job's wealth is practically limitless, or as NEB says, "beyond measure." TEV "enough to fill the whole country" expresses the idea idiomatically and well. This expression serves as the result of Yahweh's having blessed the work of his hands. In RSV the two statements appear to be coordinate. In some languages it will be preferable to place the result before the reason; for example, "He has animals throughout the country because you have made him rich in everything he does."

But put forth thy hand now, and touch all that he has, and he will curse thee to thy face."	But now suppose you take away everything he has—he will curse you to your face!"

But put forth thy hand now: Satan, who is a specialist in revealing the weakness of people's claims to be devout, suggests to Yahweh how Yahweh can prove Job a pretender. Verse 11 begins with a conjunction which contrasts this verse with Satan's previous remarks. **Put forth thy hand** is the first movement in **touch all he has**. It contributes no information but only makes Satan's suggestion more vivid. This part of the double metaphor is not translated by TEV. TEV renders the connective as "But now" and the suggestion as "suppose you take away everything he has." The author employs the idiom **touch**, but the action is far more aggressive than the word "touch" suggests. There does not seem to be an attempt on the part of the author to use the word **touch** as understatement as suggested by *The Old Testament Translated by Ronald Knox* (Knox), who attempts to retain the Hebrew idiom by saying "One little touch of thy hand assailing all that wealth of his!" and NJB "lay a finger on his possessions." The meaning of **touch** is to be taken as in TEV "take away everything he has." If the translator prefers to retain both parts of the figure, it may be translated sometimes as "Reach out your hand and take away everything Job has" or "Reach out and destroy Job's wealth." Since the following statement is a consequence resulting from taking away Job's possessions, it will be more natural in some languages to make the first statement a condition; for example, "If you reach out and take away everything Job has . . . ."

And he will curse thee to thy face: **and** translates what is literally "if not." In oaths "if" may be made negative, and the result becomes emphatically positive with the meaning of "certainly, without any doubt." TEV renders this certainty by creating a break in structure between the tentative dependent clause and the positive claim in the main clause, "suppose you take away everything he has—he will curse you . . . ." FRCL and GECL make the certainty clear through "and I wager you"; "wager" means to place a bet. **Curse** is again "bless" as in verse 5. In translation it is necessary to distinguish between a curse which means calling on a supernatural power to inflict injury on someone, and the act of saying evil words against someone. Here the latter sense is meant. In this sense **curse** may be rendered in some languages as "speak evil words against you" or "say that you are worthless." Verse 11 may sometimes be rendered "If you reach out and take away all his wealth, he will speak evil words against you." In some languages it will be more natural for the condition clause to follow the result clause.

To thy face refers to the fact that Job will curse Yahweh openly, not behind Yahweh's back; so FRCL, GECL. Variations of the same expression are found in 6.28; 21.31. In some languages this is rendered, for example, "on your head," "in your eyes," or "as if you were nothing."

1.12 RSV TEV

And the LORD said to Satan, "Behold, all that he has is in your power; only upon himself do not put forth your hand." So Satan went forth from the presence of the LORD.

"All right," the LORD said to Satan, "everything he has is in your power, but you must not hurt Job himself." So Satan left.

Behold, all that he has is in your power: Yahweh does not pursue the conversation but abruptly hands the unknowing Job over to Satan's scheme. Yahweh so completely trusts Job that he grants Satan a free hand to strike him down. In other words Yahweh is willing to bet everything that Job will remain faithful and Satan will be proved wrong. **Behold**, which is archaic in English, translates a Hebrew word which opens a sentence and directs attention to the idea to follow. TEV has "All right," and NIV "Very well, then." **Power** translates the word "hand." The same hand is not to destroy Job's person; only his possessions and family may be taken away. This concession must be restructured in some languages to say, for example, "I give you the power to destroy everything he owns" or "All right, you can take away all that he has."

Only upon himself do not put forth your hand: Yahweh uses the same expression Satan employed in 11a. Here it is used as a restriction put on Satan's power. TEV and SPCL translate "you must not hurt Job himself." "Hurt" would appear mild in terms of the manner in which Satan strikes Job, even his body. Other translations use some form of "touch" (NEB, FRCL, BJ, TOB). The reference is to taking away Job's life. If this restriction had not applied, the drama would end, and neither Yahweh nor Satan would be proved right about Job. In languages in which a metaphor such as "touch" or "strike down" can be used with the meaning of "destroy," there is no problem, but if not, then it is better to say, for example, "don't take away his life" or "you must not kill him."

Having been given permission to test Job, Satan **went forth from the presence of the LORD**. TEV makes Satan's exit short, and without pausing for details, "so Satan left," **from the presence of the LORD** being implied. Other versions retain some form of "from the LORD's presence" (SPCL, FRCL, TOB, NJB); GECL says "from the council meeting." Satan's exit from the scene marks the close of the episode. Again note that the story teller gets Satan off the stage quickly and without a reply. Satan has neither agreed nor disagreed with Yahweh's conditions. Thus silence is used to heighten the mystery of what is about to unfold on the unsuspecting Job. Translators must pay particular attention to this closing. In some languages this kind of closing is marked by various particles, or grammatical forms. In others an episode, even a short one like this, must not end without an explicit reference to the central theme; for example, "So the accuser left God's place saying 'I'll go and test his servant'" or "When God finished speaking, Satan left. He went to test the faithful servant." In such a case nothing outside the context is added.

1C. FIRST TEST OF JOB (1.13-19)

RSV   TEV

13 Now there was a day when his sons and daughters were eating and drinking wine in their eldest brother's house; 14 and there came a messenger to Job, and said, "The oxen were plowing and the asses feeding beside them; 15 and the Sabeans fell upon them and took them, and slew the servants with the edge of the sword; and I alone have escaped to tell you." 16 While he was yet speaking, there came another, and said, "The fire of God fell from heaven and burned up the sheep and the servants, and consumed them; and I alone have escaped to tell you." 17 While he was yet speaking, there came another, and said, "The Chaldeans formed three companies, and made a raid upon the camels and took them, and slew the servants with the edge of the sword; and I alone have escaped to tell you." 18 While he was yet speaking, there came another, and said, "Your sons and daughters were eating and drinking wine in their eldest brother's house; 19 and behold, a great wind came across the wilderness, and struck the four corners of the house, and it fell upon the young people, and they are dead; and I alone have escaped to tell you."

13 One day when Job's children were having a feast at the home of their oldest brother, 14 a messenger came running to Job. "We were plowing the fields with the oxen," he said, "and the donkeys were in a nearby pasture. 15 Suddenly the Sabeans attacked and stole them all. They killed every one of your servants except me. I am the only one who escaped to tell you."

16 Before he had finished speaking, another servant came and said, "Lightning struck the sheep and the shepherds and killed them all. I am the only one who escaped to tell you."

17 Before he had finished speaking, another servant came and said, "Three bands of Chaldean raiders attacked us, took away the camels, and killed all your servants except me. I am the only one who escaped to tell you."

18 Before he had finished speaking, another servant came and said, "Your children were having a feast at the home of your oldest son, 19 when a storm swept in from the desert. It blew the house down and killed them all. I am the only one who escaped to tell you."

In verse 13 a new stage is set for the next scene. As background for the events to follow, Job's children are feasting at the oldest brother's house. The focus of the action is not on them but on the reporting of the destructions to Job. In verses 14-19 the author uses repetition and quickly-paced succession of events to emphasize the speed and systematic destruction of Job's wealth. Each servant reports in essentially the same manner what he has seen, and adds that he is the only one who escaped. So rushed are the reported events, that Job is not given opportunity to react. In a sense he is breathless.

Division Heading

The Handbook uses one heading for verses 13-19 and a second one for verses 20-22. The reason is that verses 20-22 deal with Job's praise of God following his first trial. If the Handbook heading is used, it may be necessary to adapt it in translation by saying, for example, "Satan gives Job his first trial," "This is the first test of Job," or "Satan begins by destroying Job's animals and children." Many translations, like TEV, provide a single heading for verses 13-22, and translators may prefer to do the same. TOB has "The first sufferings," GECL "Satan is allowed to test Job," Habel has "The first test—on Earth," and Rowley, "Job's first trial."

1.13   RSV   TEV

Now there was a day when his sons and daughters were eating and

One day when Job's children were having a feast at the home of their

drinking wine in their eldest brother's oldest brother,
house;

Now there was a day: this expression marks a transition, as in verse 6; see also 2.1. These words serve to shift the scene from heaven back to Job's country. It is translated by TEV as a nonspecific time clause, "One day when . . . ." NEB takes it in the sense of a special day having arrived: "When the day came . . . ." It serves as the time element in the new setting.

When his sons and daughters: as the scene opens, Job's children are busy having still another banquet. The text says "his sons and his daughters." TEV and most modern translations replace the pronoun with "Job's." Whether or not we should do likewise in translation depends upon the way in which the focus may be shifted. In some languages it will be inappropriate to shift to Job's name here. In others the use of the pronoun will be confusing, since the last person mentioned was Satan. Verse 13 is backgrounding for the scene and should be handled in a manner appropriate for such in a narrative tale. Its purpose is to say that everything was proceeding according to expectations.

Were eating and drinking wine follows the Hebrew elliptical pattern meaning "eating food and drinking wine." NEB prefers "eating and drinking." SPCL avoids both eating and drinking and says "holding a banquet"; GECL has "celebrating." In each case eating and drinking are implied. In some languages there are different words used for eating and drinking, depending on what the food and drink are. In languages in which "wine" is unknown and a borrowed word is not satisfactory, the local fermented drink would be the closest equivalent. Vocabulary or constructions that call attention to themselves should be avoided here, if undue emphasis will be drawn to the wrong part of the stage.

In their eldest brother's house translates "in the house of their brother the first born." Many languages have special terms for the first-born son or daughter. In languages in which brother and sister terms differ according to whether the speaker is male or female, it is usually best to assume the male point of view. TEV makes verse 13 a dependent clause with the main clause starting with verse 14. In English and many other languages, this serves the purpose of backgrounding verse 13. In some languages, however, background must be made more conspicuous, often by using several sentences; for example, "What I will say now was happening first. Job's children were having a feast. They were feasting at the oldest brother's house. While they were doing this . . . ."

1.14	RSV	TEV

and there came a messenger to Job, and said, "The oxen were plowing and the asses feeding beside them;

a messenger came running to Job. "We were plowing the fields with the oxen," he said, "and the donkeys were in a nearby pasture.

And there came a messenger to Job: with verse 14 begins a swift succession of events, each repeated in much the same language until the end of verse 19. The word translated **messenger** can also mean "angel" (as it does in 4.18 and 33.23), but here the context makes clear that a human messenger is meant. TEV "came running to Job" translates "came to Job" (also in verses 16, 17, 18), and in the context of the rapid series of events, "running" is appropriate; it is used likewise in NEB, GECL. The author does not pause to tell where Job may be; however, in verse 20 he stands up and shaves his head. It is probably implied that he was in his house, and in languages which require locating Job, one may translate "a messenger ran to Job's house and told him . . . ," or more generally, "a messenger ran to where Job was sitting and told him . . . ."

The oxen were plowing and the asses feeding beside them: the scene reveals a normal agricultural day in the Middle Eastern winter, when plowing is done; winter in the Middle East starts in October and ends in April. This is the second time the author calls attention to the fact that life was going along in its habitual routine. Job's sons, if they ever worked, certainly did not do so when feasting was called for. Plowing was done by Job's farm hands using teams of oxen joined by a yoke. **The asses** refers to the female donkeys of verse 3. **Feeding beside them** gives a picture of these animals grazing in a freshly plowed field, which is hardly the case. The TEV rendering has the messenger report to Job as a participant in the work, "We were plowing . . . ," which is more natural and vivid than in RSV. TEV also makes it clear "the donkeys were in a nearby pasture." In languages in which "oxen" and "plowing" are unknown, some adaptations will have to be made. As suggested in verse 3, sometimes a borrowed word from a major language has to be used. It is also possible sometimes to use a generic such as "animal" joined with a limiting qualifier such as "work"; for example, "work animals" or "work animals called oxen." The same procedure may be necessary where the plow is unknown. For example, one may say "the animals were pulling the instrument called plow." It is also possible to express the idea without using "plow" by saying "the work animals were preparing the ground for planting." If the ox is unknown and another animal is used for plowing, it may be possible to substitute that animal, provided it can also be done with no conflict in verse 3. Illustrations can usually help make the picture clear. In some languages the absence of a possessor in **the oxen** and **the asses** will suggest that these animals were wild. Accordingly we should say "Job's oxen" and "Job's donkeys."

1.15 RSV	TEV
and the Sabeans fell upon them and took them, and slew the servants with the edge of the sword; and I alone have escaped to tell you."	Suddenly the Sabeans[d] attacked and stole them all. They killed every one of your servants except me. I am the only one who escaped to tell you."
	[d] SABEANS: *A tribe of wandering raiders from the south.*

The collective form **the Sabeans** translates the singular *seba'*, which refers to the Sabeans in the same way that "Israel" refers to the "Israelites." There are two groups with similar spelling mentioned in the Old Testament. Some interpreters doubt that these were the Sabeans from distant South Arabia, and find it more reasonable to believe they were from North Arabia (so Pope). In either case, their location and ethnic identity is uncertain. Moffatt (Mft) calls them "Arabs." GECL calls them "Bedouins from Saba," while other translations simply transliterate the name; and some provide a footnote (see TEV, NJB, TOB, FRCL). Translators may find it best to transliterate and identify these people in the text; for example, "some robbers who came from the people called Sabeans." To the early readers of Job, this name was familiar, but to modern day readers that will not be the case. The use of this particular group as representing the robbers was probably because of traditional reputation. However, in translation it may be preferable to avoid slowing down the narrative and simply call them "a band of robbers."

Fell upon them and took them describes the suddenness of the attack by the raiders. NEB has "swooped down." The two actions are rendered by TEV as "attacked and stole them all."

Slew the servants: the robbers not only stole the animals, they killed all but one of the workmen in the field. In each episode the writer spares one servant to report to Job. The dead farm hands were part of "very many servants" of Job mentioned in verse 3.

The edge of the sword translates the Hebrew "mouth of the sword," which is the cutting edge; but here it is used as a part which symbolizes the whole weapon. TEV, GECL, TOB do not translate the manner in which these servants were killed. NIV has "They put the servants to the sword"; also mentioning the sword are SPCL, NEB, FRCL, BJ. In languages in which the sword is unknown, other instruments such as "machete" or "long knife" will substitute. If a borrowed word is used, it is often helpful for the reader to have a known generic word to identify it; for example, "weapon called sword" or "soldier's knife called sword." However, the author had no intention of focusing upon the manner in which the robbers killed their victims, and the translator should not do so either.

And I alone have escaped to tell you: the writer emphasizes that the messenger was the only survivor of the massacre, by using a double expression which TEV renders "except me. I am the only one . . . ." For similar occurrences in which one person escapes disaster, see Genesis 44.20; Joshua 13.12; 2 Samuel 13.32; 1 Kings 18.22; Isaiah 49.21.

In the translation of verse 15, the translator needs to pay particular attention to the way the background scene (the plowing of the oxen) relates to the main event. In some languages this can be done as in TEV verse 14, where a similar structure occurs. TEV makes the plowing and the nearby donkeys part of the quoted report, and puts the action in the first person plural. Whether or not other languages can follow the TEV model will depend on a number of factors. For example, "we" may mean "I and others," but since the others have not been introduced, it may be necessary to say "the other workmen and I." It may be necessary to shift the passive donkeys forward, and in some languages more redundancy will be required; for example, "Near the pasture where your donkeys were, some of your workers and I were plowing with the oxen. As we were plowing there, robbers attacked us and stole all the animals. Those robbers killed all of your workmen except me. I am the only one who is alive to tell you this."

1.16   RSV   TEV

While he was yet speaking, there came   Before he had finished speaking,
another, and said, "The fire of God fell   another servant came and said, "Light-
from heaven and burned up the sheep   ning struck the sheep and the shep-
and the servants, and consumed them;   herds and killed them all. I am the only
and I alone have escaped to tell you."   one who escaped to tell you."

While he was yet speaking a second messenger suddenly appears. In this
manner the writer draws attention to the rapidity of the blows that are falling on Job.
Repetition is used in verses 15-19 to highlight the recurring order of events. The
concluding words of verse 15 are repeated at the end of verses 16, 17, 19; and the
opening words of verse 16 are found again at the beginning of verses 17 and 18. For
a similar repetition see Exodus 7.8–11.10, in which the king of Egypt reacts to the
plagues. The translator must know if the repetition used by the author accomplishes
the task of presenting successive events of a basically similar nature, or if there is a
different device used in his language which does this. The patterns that are effective
in Hebrew may not have the same effect in another language. It may be better in
some languages to recast this clause to say, for example, "While the first messenger
was still speaking . . . " or "Before that messenger finished telling Job what had
happened . . . ."

**The fire of God fell from heaven and burned up the sheep and the
servants, and consumed them**: robbers carried out the first attack; the second
blow is struck from heaven and destroys seven thousand sheep and all the herdsmen.

Fire of God can mean lightning. (See 1 Kgs 18.38, the contest between Yahweh
and Baal on Mount Carmel; also Gen 19.24; Num 11.1; 2 Kgs 1.12.) Thunder is the
"voice of God" in Psalm 29. NEB, TOB, GECL, NJB prefer to keep "fire," while TEV,
SPCL, FRCL have "lightning." **Fire of God** may easily be misunderstood if translated
literally. Therefore it is probably best to follow TEV.

The next two verbs in verse 16, **burned up** and **consumed**, emphasize the
total destruction. TEV, which uses "lightning struck" in 16b, has "killed them all" in
16c. **Consumed** translates the Hebrew for "ate." (See also 15.34; 20.26; 22.20; Num
16.35; 26.10.) **Consumed** is repetitive and adds no new information, and may be
handled in some languages by the techniques used for indicating the completeness
of an action.

The sheep and the servants is literally "the sheep and the young men," the
latter understood as in TEV "shepherds." In languages where sheep raising is
unknown or where people do not look after domestic animals, it will sometimes be
necessary to say, for example, "the lightning struck the sheep (using whatever term
has been used in verse 3) and the workmen who were taking care of them."

1.17   RSV   TEV

While he was yet speaking, there came   Before he had finished speaking,
another, and said, "The Chaldeans   another servant came and said, "Three
formed three companies, and made a   bands of Chaldean[e] raiders attacked us,
raid upon the camels and took them,   took away the camels, and killed all

and slew the servants with the edge of the sword; and I alone have escaped to tell you."

your servants except me. I am the only one who escaped to tell you."

e CHALDEANS: *A tribe of wandering raiders from the north.*

The pattern of verse 17 closely resembles that of verse 15: the sudden raid on the animals (this time it is the camels), which are taken away, and the herdsmen, who are all killed except the messenger who reports back to Job.

In the Old Testament **the Chaldeans** are the people who conquered Babylon in the late eighth century B.C. In Job, however, they appear to be a band of raiders, perhaps to the north of Job's land; see TEV footnote. Some interpreters believe the Job story is from a very early tradition, and that these raiders are to be identified with the Chaldeans who later conquered Babylon, but that is uncertain. The translation of these raiders should follow the same pattern as used in verse 15.

Formed three companies translates the Hebrew "put three heads," meaning they made a three-pronged attack (so Pope); for similar strategy see Judges 7.16; 9.43; 1 Samuel 11.11. This maneuver would enable the raiders to surround the fast-moving camels, which they came to steal. Again the fate of the herdsmen is the same as in verse 15. Since all three groups of attackers were of the same body, it is the same whether one translates "three groups of Chaldean robbers" or "Chaldean robbers who came in three groups."

And made a raid upon the camels and took them: camels were in great demand for transporting goods from India westward. A herd as large as Job's would be a great prize to camel raiders. In some languages it may be necessary to adjust the order of the events in verse 17 so that the killing of the servants takes place before taking away the camels; for example, "attacked us, killed your herdsmen, and stole the camels."

In one day all Job's livestock (and his herders) mentioned in verse 3 have disappeared.

1.18-19   RSV   TEV

18 While he was yet speaking, there came another, and said, "Your sons and daughters were eating and drinking wine in their eldest brother's house; 19 and behold, a great wind came across the wilderness, and struck the four corners of the house, and it fell upon the young people, and they are dead; and I alone have escaped to tell you."

18 Before he had finished speaking, another servant came and said, "Your children were having a feast at the home of your oldest son, 19 when a storm swept in from the desert. It blew the house down and killed them all. I am the only one who escaped to tell you."

Verses 18-19 form a unit on the pattern of 1.16-17. The first and third attacks were by human forces; the second and fourth are the work of nature. The fourth messenger arrives with the worst news of all: Job's children are all dead. The present episode began depicting the children feasting. Now the author returns to the celebration that has been going on during the series of tragedies. (See verse 13.)

In 1.19 **behold, a great wind came across the wilderness** begins with the same word translated "Behold" in verse 12. Here the word serves more as an attention-getter, pointing forward to a sudden action about to be reported. In some languages this is rendered "hear my two words," "listen, I say," or by particles that serve this purpose.

A great wind: TEV uses "storm," which is generic. The wind **came across the wilderness**. Winds blowing off the desert are normally hot, dry, and dusty. Jeremiah 13.24 speaks of a desert wind. Here the emphasis is on the suddenness and destructive force of the wind. NEB has "whirlwind," FRCL "hurricane," and BJ "violent wind." In language areas which experience such winds, there are usually specific terms. In such cases it may only be necessary to qualify the particular wind term as "strong," "violent," or "destructive." The author does not intend to suggest that the wind is a mysterious one, but rather that it blew in from the desert. In languages where desert areas are unknown, one must often translate "a strong wind blew from the dry, barren place." If this expression is ambiguous or too vague, it will be better to say, for example, "a strong wind blew."

Struck the four corners of the house: no part of the house escaped the violence of the storm. In languages in which houses cannot be described as having "corners" (because they are round), we may speak of the "walls"; for example, "the wind blew against the walls." In any event **the four corners** is simply a way of saying the wind struck the house, the entire building, and is a dramatic device leading up to the destruction of the building and its occupants.

And it fell upon the young people, and they are dead: the wind hit the house on all four sides, causing it to collapse on the occupants and killing them, or as TEV says with economy of words, "it blew the house down and killed them all." The word translated **the young people** is the same word translated "servants" in the other destructions. Although the word in Hebrew is masculine, it includes Job's daughters as well as the servants (male and female) working in the oldest brother's house.

Now Job has lost everything except his wife, who has been spared to echo the pitiless heart of Satan in chapter 2.

1D. JOB PRAISES GOD (1.20-22)

RSV	TEV
20 Then Job arose, and rent his robe, and shaved his head, and fell upon the ground, and worshiped. 21 And he said, "Naked I came from my mother's womb, and naked shall I return; the LORD gave, and the LORD has taken away; blessed be the name of the LORD."	20 Then Job got up and tore his clothes in grief. He shaved his head and threw himself face downward on the ground. 21 He said, "I was born with nothing, and I will die with nothing. The LORD gave, and now he has taken away. May his name be praised!"
22 In all this Job did not sin or charge God with wrong.	22 In spite of everything that had happened, Job did not sin by blaming God.

Only when everything has been taken away does the author finally focus on Job in verses 20-21, where Job now displays his grief, first in customary gesture and then in words. The author concludes the scene by affirming that "in all this Job did not sin or charge God with wrong" (verse 22).

Division Heading

If a heading is to be placed before verse 20, translators may find it necessary to modify "Job praises God" to say, for example, "Job does not blame God for his trouble," "Job still praises God," or "Job grieves, but does not blame God."

1.20 RSV TEV

Then Job arose, and rent his robe, and shaved his head, and fell upon the ground, and worshiped.

Then Job got up and tore his clothes in grief. He shaved his head and threw himself face downward on the ground.

Then Job arose, and rent his robe: Job had been seated (like Eli in 1 Sam 4.13) as he listened to the reports of the messengers. Now he "stood up and tore his clothes in grief" (TEV). David reacts to the sad news of the death of his son by standing up and tearing his clothes (2 Sam 13.31). In some languages the transition **Then** suggested by RSV and TEV may have to be recast as a clause; for example, "When Job had finished hearing the messengers" or "Job listened to the last messenger and then . . . ."

Tearing the clothing was the custom used to display grief (Gen 37.34; Josh 7.6; 1 Sam 1.11; 3.31; 13.31; Ezra 9.3,5; Est 4.1). The robe which Job tore was the outer garment. TEV makes clear the purpose of this gesture by adding "in grief"; so also SPCL. Translators should follow some such model as TEV here. It is also possible to translate the meaning of the gesture only; for example, "Job stood up full of grief" or "Job got to his feet, his heart broken." It is also possible, where there is a common local custom used to display grief, to translate the biblical custom in the text and to compare it to the local custom in a note; for example, "This is equivalent to the practice of painting the face to show that one is in mourning."

Shaved his head: shaving the head and beard were likewise signs of mourning (see Isa 22.12; Jer 7.29; 16.6; 41.5; Ezek 7.18; Amos 8.10). These mourning rites, which were commonly practiced in Middle Eastern cultures, were forbidden in the Law of Moses (Lev 19.27-28; Deut 14.1). It will be important in some languages to link the shaving of the head with the tearing of the robe as part of the same expression of sorrow. For example, "Job stood up (from sitting). He tore his clothes, then shaved his head to show how much he grieved for his children."

Fell upon the ground, and worshiped translates the Hebrew "fell on the ground and bowed down." The second verb is the same one used of Abraham, who in Genesis 23.7 bowed before the Hittites; see also Exodus 17.7; 1 Kings 2.19. The act involved lying or kneeling, and touching the forehead on the ground, very much as in Muslim prayer position. Bowing to the ground was not a gesture of despair but of reverence (2 Sam 1.2; 9.6; 14.4). Job humbly bows in submission to Yahweh. TEV "threw himself face downward on the ground" fails to express this attitude of reverence. RSV, SPCL, and TOB use some form of worship. Better is "he knelt down on the ground to honor God" or "Job bowed himself to the ground in prayer to God."

1.21   RSV   TEV

| And he said, "Naked I came from my mother's womb, and naked shall I return; the LORD gave, and the LORD has taken away; blessed be the name of the LORD." | He said, "I was born with nothing, and I will die with nothing. The LORD gave, and now he has taken away. May his name be praised!" |

Naked I came from my mother's womb: in verse 20 Job expresses his worship in poetic form. The poetic effect is gained by the contrast of "came" and "return" in the first two lines, and "gave" and "has taken away" in the second pair. In prose terms Job says "I was born with nothing, and I will die with nothing" (TEV). For a similar expression of this resignation to events, see Ecclesiastes 5.15, and in the New Testament, 1 Timothy 6.7. The main reason for not translating literally here is that it is not really possible to maintain the parallelism in the next line. If a language offers a similar metaphor for being born with no material goods, it may be possible to construct the second line in a parallel manner. Otherwise the translator is encouraged to follow something like TEV. The translation problem for some languages is that of quoted speech which is not directed to a specified listener. However, since Job has placed himself in a position of reverence before God, it is possible to say "He said to the LORD, 'I was born with nothing . . .'" or ". . . 'When I was born I owned nothing, and likewise when I die I will own nothing.'"

Naked shall I return translates what appears to be an ellipsis; that is, "return to my mother's womb." Obviously, the writer did not intend that meaning. Interpreters have sought to find the meaning in "return to the womb of the earth." However, dead people do not "return" to the grave or to Sheol. In any case, it is not the translator's responsibility to copy a poetic expression from one language into another, but to reflect the intended meaning—preferably in appropriate poetic terms. TEV renders Job's thought in prose, "and I will die with nothing." NEB, which uses "womb" in the first line, translates "return whence I came," but that leaves the reader wondering where that is supposed to be. If it is possible to retain the contrast of **came . . . return**, translators should consider doing so. This may mean translating something like "I arrived naked in this world, and I shall be naked when I leave it."

The LORD gave, and the LORD has taken away: only in this verse and in 12.9 does Job use the name Yahweh. With these words Job refuses to complain; neither does he question Yahweh's ultimate ownership of all things. In translation in many languages it will be necessary to complete the verb phrase by saying, for example, "The LORD gave me everything and the LORD has taken away everything" or "The LORD gave me family and wealth and the LORD has taken away my family and wealth." In some languages it is not natural to address someone in the third person. Hence, here Job must sometimes say "You, LORD, gave me wealth and family, and now you have taken them away from me."

Blessed be the name of the LORD: the word translated **blessed** here is the same word translated "curse" in verse 5 and 11. The form of this benediction is also found in Psalm 113.2 with "now and forever" added. This was a standard formula for praise. The meaning of **blessed be . . . the LORD** is that Yahweh should receive praise and honor from people. Accordingly TEV translates "May his name be praised." FRCL renders "blessed" in terms of gratitude and says "I have only to thank the Lord." GECL relates the final line more closely to the preceding one by saying "I will praise him no matter what he does." In some languages this benediction is expressed "Everyone should praise the LORD" or "Let all people say that God is great."

So Job praises Yahweh and does not curse him, and Satan's prediction that "he will curse you to your face" is proved wrong.

1.22	RSV	TEV

> In all this Job did not sin or charge God with wrong.

> In spite of everything that had happened, Job did not sin by blaming God.

In all this Job did not sin: Job has passed Satan's first test without sinning. Some (including the Septuagint) take **In all this** to refer to the statement Job has just made in verse 21. Others take it to refer to all the events reported by the messengers; so TEV "everything that had happened." **In all this** marks the end of the episode by way of summing up. Translators should make certain that the reader knows he has reached a point which will tie together the author's conclusion with Yahweh's confident evaluation of his servant Job. Furthermore, in some languages it will be necessary to identify the story teller as the one offering this affirmation; for example, "I tell you this, although Job lost everything he owned . . . ."

Or charge God with wrong: **wrong** translates a word meaning "insipid, empty, unsteady" (Holladay). It occurs in Jeremiah 23.13 with the meaning of "unseemly" (RSV "unsavory"). In the present verse it is used to mean that Job did not accuse Yahweh of doing something that was unworthy. TEV relates the second clause to the first as the naming of the sin: "Job did not sin by blaming God." NEB retains the separate clauses as coordinate: "Throughout all this Job did not sin; he did not charge God with unreason," meaning he did not claim that God had done something foolish. In some languages it may be better to shift here to direct address and say, for example, "Job did not sin and say to God, 'You are the one I blame.'" The author's defense of Job marks the conclusion of the episode.

1E. SECOND MEETING OF GOD AND SATAN (2.1-6)

RSV	TEV

1 Again there was a day when the sons of God came to present themselves before the LORD, and Satan also came among them to present himself before the LORD. 2 And the LORD said to Satan, "Whence have you come?" Satan answered the LORD, "From going to and

1 When the day came for the heavenly beings to appear before the LORD again, Satan was there among them. 2 The LORD asked him, "Where have you been?" Satan answered, "I have been walking here and there, roaming around the earth."

fro on the earth, and from walking up and down on it." 3 And the LORD said to Satan, "Have you considered my servant Job, that there is none like him on the earth, a blameless and upright man, who fears God and turns away from evil? He still holds fast his integrity, although you moved me against him, to destroy him without cause." 4 Then Satan answered the LORD, "Skin for skin! All that a man has he will give for his life. 5 But put forth thy hand now, and touch his bone and his flesh, and he will curse thee to thy face." 6 And the LORD said to Satan, "Behold, he is in your power; only spare his life."

3 "Did you notice my servant Job?" the LORD asked. "There is no one on earth as faithful and good as he is. He worships me and is careful not to do anything evil. You persuaded me to let you attack him for no reason at all, but Job is still as faithful as ever."

4 Satan replied, "A man will give up everything in order to stay alive. 5 But now suppose you hurt his body—he will curse you to your face!"

6 So the LORD said to Satan, "All right, he is in your power, but you are not to kill him."

Division Heading

The Handbook heading for verses 2.1-6 reflects the parallel events in 1.6-12. Translators should provide a heading that retains wording used in 1.6-12. Some translations are similar to TEV in having a single heading for 2.1-10; for example, FRCL has "Job's second test," and GECL "Job will be tried more harshly." Others include only verses 1-6, as in the Handbook. TOB has again "The heavenly court," Habel "The second assembly—in heaven," Rowley "The second scene in heaven."

2.1   RSV   TEV

Again there was a day when the sons of God came to present themselves before the LORD, and Satan also came among them to present himself before the LORD.

When the day came for the heavenly beings to appear before the LORD again, Satan was there among them.

The scene is again in the heavenly assembly. Satan, who has failed to make Job curse God, is confronted by Yahweh. **Again there was a day** serves to shift the scene to the heavenly setting, as it does in 1.6. **Again** merely makes explicit the repetition of the scene. For **sons of God** see 1.6.

And Satan also came among them to present himself before the LORD: the words **to present himself before the LORD** are not in 1.6, neither are they found in the Septuagint (see also New American Bible [NAB], NEB). Some interpreters believe these words were unintentionally written in the process of copying. However, it seems more reasonable that the author uses the expression deliberately to call attention to Satan's continuing role in the story, and to point out the involvement of Yahweh in Job's suffering. The expression **present himself before the LORD** may sometimes be recast as direct address; for example, "I am your servant, LORD," or "I am present, LORD."

2.2   RSV   TEV

And the LORD said to Satan, "Whence have you come?" Satan answered the

The LORD asked him, "Where have you been?"

LORD, "From going to and fro on the earth, and from walking up and down on it."	Satan answered, "I have been walking here and there, roaming around the earth."

Verse 2 is identical to 1.7. If the Job story was originally an oral story, these repetitive units would give listeners the opportunity to pick up slight changes that signal the direction in which the plot is going to move from that point. The same is true for the attentive reader.

2.3 RSV	TEV
And the LORD said to Satan, "Have you considered my servant Job, that there is none like him on the earth, a blameless and upright man, who fears God and turns away from evil? He still holds fast his integrity, although you moved me against him, to destroy him without cause."	"Did you notice my servant Job?" the LORD asked. "There is no one on earth as faithful and good as he is. He worships me and is careful not to do anything evil. You persuaded me to let you attack him for no reason at all, but Job is still as faithful as ever."

Verse 3 is the same as the whole of 1.8, except that Yahweh adds **He still holds fast his integrity, although you moved me against him, to destroy him without a cause.** Yahweh admits that Satan has influenced him to bring Job down, and having done so serves no good purpose. The reader catches a new vision of Yahweh as a king who may not be soundly in control of all his servants. Verse 3 contains three clauses. TEV renders them so that the contrastive conclusion is placed in final position, which is more logical and easier to follow.

Integrity in **holds fast his integrity** is the noun form of the adjective used in 1.1 and 2.3a, translated "blameless" in RSV. TEV has "faithful"; see 1.1 for translation suggestions.

Although you moved me against him: the Hebrew verb rendered **moved me** is found in 36.18, "entice." It is used in 1 Kings 21.25, where Jezebel is said to "incite" her husband, King Ahab. Translations using "incite" are NEB, TOB, Pope, and Habel; NJB has "provoked," FRCL "pushed," and SPCL says "you made me . . . ." TEV "persuaded" gives the impression that it was done by argument.

To destroy him without a cause: destroy translates the verb "swallow." It is used in 10.8, and also in Numbers 16.30, where the ground "swallowed" Korah and those who opposed Moses. Yahweh picks up "without cause" from Satan's speech in 1.9, in which Satan argued that Job did not serve Yahweh "without cause," that is, without getting something good for himself. If there was any reason, it was to prove that Satan was mistaken about Job. TEV says "to let you attack him for no reason at all." It is important in the translation of such passages to cause an equivalent response on the part of the reader. Therefore "swallow" or **destroy** may often be rendered by other metaphors; for example, "chew up," "grind to dust," "crush to pieces."

2.4

RSV	TEV
Then Satan answered the LORD, "Skin for skin! All that a man has he will give for his life.	Satan replied, "A man will give up everything in order to stay alive.

Then Satan answered the LORD: Satan is not ready to be proved wrong. **Answered** does not mean that Satan is responding to a question, but rather reacting to Yahweh's belief in Job's faithfulness; TEV "replied" is more suitable for English.

Skin for skin! All that a man has he will give for his life: with this enigmatic saying Satan throws down a new challenge, which Yahweh soon accepts. **Skin for skin** has the appearance of a proverbial saying, for which many interpretations have been given. (Gordis includes a discussion of these.) However, the second part of the saying is interpretive and restricts the meaning of the first part. Therefore the saying can be understood as "Skin covers a deeper [layer of] skin." Thus Yahweh has "put a hedge" around Job and all that he has (1.10). In the first test Satan has been allowed to penetrate the hedge, perhaps the first layer of "skin." Yahweh's hedge still limits Satan's attacks, and for this reason Satan challenges Yahweh to remove it. Translators will notice that TEV has not retained the proverbial saying, assuming that the second part makes the point unambiguously. Some modern translations keep the literal saying and offer several explanations in a note. Others rephrase the saying; for example, SPCL "Unless you touch someone in his very hide, everything goes along fine"; GECL "Thus far he has not made a bad trade," implying that he has allowed his family and wealth to be sacrificed to save his own skin, but evidence for this interpretation is weak. In some languages it will be possible to substitute another proverb for **skin for skin**, but in other languages it will be better to follow the model of TEV.

2.5

RSV	TEV
But put forth thy hand now, and touch his bone and his flesh, and he will curse thee to thy face."	But now suppose you hurt his body—he will curse you to your face!"

Satan again asks Yahweh to **put forth thy hand**, as he did in 1.11. There he challenged Yahweh to "touch all that he has." In verse 4 Satan speaks of "skin"; now, however, he goes further to speak of **bone and flesh**. His argument is that God has not allowed him to go deep enough below the surface to really injure Job. Therefore **touch his bone and his flesh** refers to striking, injuring, harming Job's body. We may translate, for example, "strike him down and make him ill," "reach out and injure his health," or "put him down and harm his body." Job, who suffers mentally and spiritually, will now suffer also physically.

He will curse thee to thy face: see comment on 1.5,11.

2.6 RSV TEV

And the LORD said to Satan, "Behold, he is in your power; only spare his life."

So the LORD said to Satan, "All right, he is in your power, but you are not to kill him."

Behold, he is in your power: without further discussion, Yahweh hands over to Satan the power to strike Job again. In place of "all that he has" in 1.12, the attack now is to be directed against Job's person. **Power** translates "hand" as in 1.12. This expression may sometimes be rendered "You can do with him as you wish," "Your power is over him," or figuratively, "He is in your hands."

Only spare his life: the word **spare** translates a Hebrew verb meaning "protect or watch over" and normally expresses the care which Yahweh gives for his own, as in Psalm 16.1. The restriction Yahweh has put on Satan's second attack is expressed variously by different translations. TEV has "he is in your power, but you are not to kill him"; SPCL "do whatever you like provided you respect his life"; GECL "I give you power over his body, but you must not attack his life."

1F. SECOND TEST OF JOB (2.7-10)

RSV TEV

7 So Satan went forth from the presence of the LORD, and afflicted Job with loathsome sores from the sole of his foot to the crown of his head. 8 And he took a potsherd with which to scrape himself, and sat among the ashes.
9 Then his wife said to him, "Do you still hold fast your integrity? Curse God, and die." 10 But he said to her, "You speak as one of the foolish women would speak. Shall we receive good at the hand of God, and shall we not receive evil?" In all this Job did not sin with his lips.

7 Then Satan left the LORD's presence and made sores break out all over Job's body. 8 Job went and sat by the garbage dump and took a piece of broken pottery to scrape his sores. 9 His wife said to him, "You are still as faithful as ever, aren't you? Why don't you curse God and die?"
10 Job answered, "You are talking nonsense! When God sends us something good, we welcome it. How can we complain when he sends us trouble?" Even in all this suffering Job said nothing against God.

Division Heading

Translators should provide a heading that is similar to that used before 1.13. TOB has "New sufferings," Habel "The second test—on earth," Rowley "Job's second trial." Many modern translations, like TEV "Satan Tests Job Again," have only a single heading for 2.1-10.

2.7 RSV TEV

So Satan went forth from the presence of the LORD, and afflicted Job with loathsome sores from the sole of his foot to the crown of his head.

Then Satan left the LORD's presence and made sores break out all over Job's body.

So in verse 7 marks the conclusion of the first scene. Satan's departure serves as a transition which brings him back to Job on earth (without saying so). In some languages such time and place movements must be very explicit; for example, "So Satan left the place where the LORD was, and went to Job's place; having arrived at Job's home, Satan caused Job to break out with bad sores."

So Satan went forth from the presence of the LORD: as in 1.12, Satan leaves immediately to undertake his new task.

Afflicted Job with loathsome sores: unlike 1.13, which opened a new scene on earth at the banqueting of Job's children, verse 7 has no defined setting. **Sores** translates a Hebrew term which is associated with skin disease in Leviticus 13.18-20. Interpreters have offered various medical identifications of Job's disease: elephantiasis, biskra button, eczema, erythema, smallpox, leprosy, malignant ulcers, and many others. The same word is used for boils in Exodus 9.9-11. The author is not concerned to identify the disease but to show the degree of suffering.

These awful sores covered Job's entire body **from the sole of his foot to the crown of his head**. TEV "all over his body" is a generic way of expressing the extent of the sores. Most modern versions consulted retain the physical extent in terms of "from head to foot"; so SPCL, FRCL, GECL, NJB, NIV, TOB, BJ, NEB, NAB. The translation of **loathsome sores** may sometimes be rendered as "painful boils," "running ulcers," or simply "a bad skin disease."

2.8 RSV	TEV
And he took a potsherd with which to scrape himself, and sat among the ashes.	Job went and sat by the garbage dump and took a piece of broken pottery to scrape his sores.

He took a potsherd with which to scrape himself: a **potsherd** is a broken piece of pottery and would be plentiful in rubbish heaps in the Middle East. The action described here was either to get relief or to cut his flesh as a sign of mourning (Lev 19.28; Deut 14.1). All translations consulted prefer "scrape" or "scratch." In language areas where pottery making is not practiced, it will be necessary to use a different object; for example, "a piece of bone" or "a sharp stone."

In order to call attention to his grief, Job **sat among the ashes**. The verse has two clauses. **Sat among the ashes** connects with what precedes. TEV puts this clause at the beginning: "Job went and sat by the garbage dump." In Hebrew this is a circumstantial clause, that is to say, one that describes the circumstances of the main clause; it can be rendered "Job, meanwhile, was sitting among the ashes," or ". . . among the ashes of the garbage heap," or ". . . ashes where people burn what they throw away." The Septuagint has "on the dung hill" and adds the words "outside the city." It is probably best to maintain a chronological order as TEV does. In many language areas there is no area designated for disposing of ashes or rubbish, and it will be necessary to make clear that Job is sitting in ashes as a sign of mourning; for example, "as was the custom while mourning for the dead, Job sat in ashes."

Then his wife said to him, "Do you still hold fast your integrity? Curse God, and die."

His wife said to him, "You are still as faithful as ever, aren't you? Why don't you curse God and die?"

Then his wife said to him: the storyteller introduces Job's wife without giving her a name. With the exception of this verse, 19.17, and 31.10, she is totally ignored. There is no reference in the story to other wives. The Septuagint adds here a long discourse by Job's wife in which she speaks of her own sufferings. Translators in Muslim languages should be familiar with Job's rebuke of his wife for urging him to curse God (Koran, *sura* 38 section 4). RSV **said** may reflect the fact that her question is rhetorical.

Do you still hold fast your integrity? The words are a sarcastic echo of Yahweh's confident comment to Satan in 2.3. The context and not the Hebrew form indicates that her words are to be taken as a rhetorical question. TEV uses a comment plus a tag question to reinforce the bitterness of the comment: "You are still as faithful as ever, aren't you?" In translation it may be necessary to make clear that this question refers to Job's holding fast after all his suffering: "After all that has happened, are you still faithful?" or "In spite of all the suffering, are you still loyal to God?"

Curse God and die: the first verb translates Hebrew "bless," as in 1.5 and 1.11. Here it is again taken in the sense of "curse." Some interpreters would prefer it to mean "bless" in the positive sense, but Job's reply does not support such an interpretation. Death was the result of cursing God (Lev 24.10-16; 1 Kings 21.10). It is difficult to interpret clearly Job's wife's intention. Did she mean for her husband to curse God and let Yahweh's anger finish his sufferings, or does she mean that he should curse God because he was so uncaring for his creature? Most translations (like TEV "Why don't you curse God and die?") leave open the question of death being caused by the cursing. FRCL, by contrast, says "curse God and die from it." In translation **Curse God** may appear strange, as God is normally the one who is invoked in a curse to bring about its results. In the present case it will often be necessary to translate something like "speak evil words against God" or "tell God that he is worthless."

But he said to her, "You speak as one of the foolish women would speak. Shall we receive good at the hand of God, and shall we not receive evil?" In all this Job did not sin with his lips.

Job answered, "You are talking nonsense! When God sends us something good, we welcome it. How can we complain when he sends us trouble?" Even in all this suffering Job said nothing against God.

Job rejects his wife's advice by saying **You speak as one of the foolish women would speak. Foolish** refers not to a person of simple mentality, but rather to one who denies the reality of God. The attitude of the fool is seen in Psalm 14.1.

TEV "you are talking nonsense" places the emphasis on the inappropriateness of his wife's suggestion. Some translations, such as GECL, focus on the wrong religious attitude, which is better: "you talk like someone who doesn't take God seriously." **Foolish women** is sometimes expressed as "women with heads made of gourds," "women with black livers," or "women whose minds have gone away." The translator should not give the impression that Job is accusing his wife of being stupid or insane. His intention is to say that she is morally and religiously off balance; for example, "You are like a person who does not trust God," or "You are like someone who does not even know who God is."

Job responds further to her with a contrastive two-part rhetorical question, **Shall we receive good at the hand of God, and shall we not receive evil?** In 1.21 Job drew the parallel between God as giver and God as taker. Here the parallel is between receiving good from God and receiving evil from God, in both cases God being the giver. **Evil** in this context is not moral evil but rather the sufferings contrasted with the blessings. Problematic for many translators is the referent of **we**. The ancient rabbis taught that Job included his wife. This is possible, but it may be an editorial type of "we" in which Job is referring to all religious people. Many languages will need to recast the rhetorical question as TEV does, with "When God sends us something good, we welcome it. How can we complain when he sends us trouble?" In a similar way it may be necessary in some languages to use two "if" clauses; for example, "If God does something good for us, we accept it. How can we reject it if God causes us to suffer?"

In all this Job did not sin with his lips: in 1.22 the storyteller gave his verdict of Job as "Job did not sin or charge God with wrong." He again brings the action to a pause and declares that Job has now undergone terrible physical suffering and still has not cursed God, contrary to Satan's prediction. **In all this** does not refer to just his conversation with his wife, but to all the preceding events. Thoughts that remained unspoken were not considered sins (see Psa 39.1-3). **Sin with his lips** must be recast in some languages to say, for example, "Job did not say a word against God," "Job did not sin by saying something against God," or TEV "Job said nothing against God."

1G. JOB'S THREE FRIENDS ARRIVE (2.11-13)

RSV	TEV
11 Now when Job's three friends heard of all this evil that had come upon him, they came each from his own place, Eliphaz the Temanite, Bildad the Shuhite, and Zophar the Naamathite. They made an appointment together to come to condole with him and comfort him. 12 And when they saw him from afar, they did not recognize him; and they raised their voices and wept; and they rent their robes and sprinkled dust upon their heads toward heaven. 13 And they sat with him on the ground seven days and seven nights, and no one spoke a word to him, for they saw that his suffering was very great.	11 Three of Job's friends were Eliphaz, from the city of Teman, Bildad, from the land of Shuah, and Zophar, from the land of Naamah. When they heard how much Job had been suffering, they decided to go and comfort him. 12 While they were still a long way off they saw Job, but did not recognize him. When they did, they began to weep and wail, tearing their clothes in grief and throwing dust into the air and on their heads. 13 Then they sat there on the ground with him for seven days and nights without saying a word, because they saw how much he was suffering.

Division Heading

Verse 11 marks the beginning of a new scene and should be indicated with a heading. Translators may wish to make the Handbook heading more full by saying, for example, "Job's friends come to give him comfort," or "Job's friends come to cheer him up." TOB has "The arrival of the three friends," GECL "Job's friends visit him," Habel "The third assembly—on earth."

2.11 RSV	TEV
Now when Job's three friends heard of all this evil that had come upon him, they came each from his own place, Eliphaz the Temanite, Bildad the Shuhite, and Zophar the Naamathite. They made an appointment together to come to condole with him and comfort him.	Three of Job's friends were Eliphaz, from the city of Teman, Bildad, from the land of Shuah, and Zophar, from the land of Naamah. When they heard how much Job had been suffering, they decided to go and comfort him.

The names of these friends and their places of origin have been the subject of much speculation. However, little can be said about them that is certain. **Eliphaz** is an Edomite name (Gen 36.4), and "Teman" occurs in Genesis 36.11 as an Edomite personal name. In Jeremiah 49.7; Ezekiel 25.13; Amos 1.12 "Teman" is represented as one of the main localities of Edom. TEV identifies "Teman" as a city and "Shuah" and "Naamah" as "the land of . . . ." The names **Bildad** and **Zophar** are not found elsewhere in the Bible. The place-name "Naamah" is found in Joshua 15.41 but may have no connection. Translators will want to transliterate these names from Hebrew or, in certain cases, borrow the form from a major language. The sentence order in Hebrew is not in accordance with the natural way of expressing this introduction in English, as the names of Job's friends are not mentioned until the end of the first half of verse 11. For this reason TEV opens with "Three of Job's friends were . . ." and names them. TEV clearly implies that these three were three among others. Some translations, like RSV, imply that Job had only three friends; others leave the question of exclusion open.

Heard of all this evil: evil refers to Job's losses and consequent sufferings, or as TEV says, "heard how much Job had been suffering."

They made an appointment together sounds somewhat businesslike. It is the storyteller's way of saying "they decided to meet," or as TEV says, "they decided to go."

To come to condole with him and comfort him: come in English suggests movement as seen from the place where Job is. As the three friends decide to leave the place where they are, it is more appropriate in English to say "go," as in TEV. Translators will have to determine what is appropriate in their own language. **Condole** translates a verb which had the meaning of "move to and fro," that is, rocking back and forth with the body in the ritual of mourning. In Job 42.11 it is used as a synonym with the word translated "to comfort." Accordingly TEV translates the two verbs as one, "they decided to go and comfort him." In some languages idiomatic expressions are used to render the verb "to comfort"; for example, "to make his heart strong" or "to make solid his innermost."

2.12   RSV   TEV

| And when they saw him from afar, they did not recognize him; and they raised their voices and wept; and they rent their robes and sprinkled dust upon their heads toward heaven. | While they were still a long way off they saw Job, but did not recognize him. When they did, they began to weep and wail, tearing their clothes in grief and throwing dust into the air and on their heads. |

And when they saw him from afar, they did not recognize him: Job's disease and sufferings had disfigured him so badly his friends did not know him, at least not until they were near.

When they do finally recognize him, they express their sympathy by three acts of mourning. First, **they raised their voices and wept,** which means they wailed, or as TEV says, "they began to weep and wail."

In their second mourning action **they rent their robes,** just as Job did in 1.20, after hearing the news of his losses.

The third action is **sprinkled dust upon their heads toward heaven,** which is confusing, as it involves two upward positions. The Septuagint omits "toward heaven." The Hebrew Old Testament Text Project committee (HOTTP) suggests that one of the two adverbial expressions is a later addition to the Masoretic text; but which of the two cannot be decided. The sprinkling of dust on the head is found in Joshua 7.6; 1 Samuel 4.12; 2 Samuel 13.19; Lamentations 2.10; Ezekiel 27.30. Habel suggests that the act of throwing dust "into the heavens" recalls the symbolic act of Moses, who did this on orders from Yahweh so that boils would break out on the Egyptians and their animals (Exo 9.10). Habel suggests that Job's three friends, in solidarity with him, would in this way produce on themselves the same disease. It seems more reasonable to consider the act as throwing the dust "into the air" and therefore on their heads. TEV and SPCL say "throwing dust into the air and on their heads." NAB follows the Septuagint; NEB and NJB have "into the air over their heads," but this would require an unusual meaning for the Hebrew preposition.

In view of the difficulty in interpreting this expression, translators may have to make a choice between: (a) putting dust on their heads, and (b) throwing dust into the air above their heads. If the former is chosen we may say, for example, "they covered their heads with dust" or "they threw dust on top of their heads." If the latter is followed we may say, for example, "they threw dust into the air above them." In either case it is advisable to include a cross reference.

In translating these acts of mourning, it may be necessary to make clear that they were expressions of grief. Accordingly we may translate the three ritual actions and then say, for example, "to show how they mourned for Job."

2.13   RSV   TEV

And they sat with him on the ground | Then they sat there on the ground with
seven days and seven nights, and no one | him for seven days and nights without
spoke a word to him, for they saw that | saying a word, because they saw how
his suffering was very great. | much he was suffering.

And they sat with him on the ground seven days and seven nights: TEV translates the connecting word with "Then," which makes a more logical transition from the expressions of mourning to their sitting silently with Job. **Seven days and nights** is the period of mourning for the dead in Genesis 50.10; 1 Samuel 31.13. Ezekiel sat "overwhelmed" for seven days with the exiles of Tel Abib (Ezek 3.15).

In translation in some languages it may be necessary to shift the reason clause ahead of the result clause; for example, "Because they saw how much Job was suffering, they sat with him on the ground for seven days and nights without saying a word" or "They sat with Job on the ground for seven days and nights; because they knew how much he was suffering, they did not say a word."

2. Job's Opening Speech

(3.1-26)

Chapter 3 marks a clear shift from the prose narrative of the first two chapters. In this section the poetic argument begins which sets down the literal and figurative terms of Job's complaint against God. Many of the key terms used in this chapter will reappear in chapters 38–41, when, finally, God will answer Job.

The first verse, which continues the prose style from chapters 1 and 2, introduces the content of the section, almost in the manner of a heading. This section contains two themes expressed by means of curses and laments. In verses 3-10 Job curses his origins, and in 11-26 he laments his sufferings. His outburst of curses and laments serves the purpose of directing his complaint against God and setting the stage for the speeches which follow.

As this is the beginning of the poetic body of the book, it is important for the translator to see how the principles on translating poetry given in the introduction, "Translating the Book of Job," are related to specific contexts. As Alter points out, the author of Job has made considerable use of poetic intensification. Poetic intensification refers most commonly to the build-up of feeling from line a to line b in semantically parallel lines, that is, lines which are parallel in meaning. However, there can also be a rising level of intensification running across larger segments of a poem. It may be thought of as a small wave which picks up momentum, grows in force, and reaches a peak. There may then be a summary, conclusion, or transition to a related image, and the process may then be repeated. This may be seen, for example, in verses 3-4, where Job begins by wishing **let the day** (of his birth) **be darkness.** In verse 5 he goes farther: **let gloom and deep darkness claim it.** Then he pushes the level still higher by including even the night he was conceived: **let thick darkness seize it.** He wants it even blotted out of the calendar: **let it not come into the number of the months.** The poet is not content to break off the upward sweep of his crescendo. He carries it forward this time by shifting to another dimension. He appeals even to the forces which control Leviathan and the morning star, asking them to cast the day of his birth into blackness.

Verse 10 comes as a transition to the next development. **Shut the doors of my mother's womb** looks back to the imagery of darkness and forward to the grave of verses 13-19. Here again this section on the peace of the grave makes specific what in verses 3-9 was more generally stated as Job's wish for death. This development in verses 13-19 relates therefore to the section in verses 3-9 as a sharpening of the focus, intensifying the poetic movement between these two parts of the chapter. Within verses 13-19 there is little rise of feeling, since the poet is concerned with dwelling on the passivity of the peace of the dead. However, the closing of the chapter again surges. Verses 20-23 speak of the general plight of mankind, but verses

24-26 refer to Job himself. This movement from the general to the specific creates the focusing effect which makes Job's confession of fear powerfully emphatic.

All of this is to say that poetic movement at the discourse level is an integral part of the meaning of a poem, and since the poem would mean something else without it, these components of intensification must find their expression in the translation.

Section Heading

In the Handbook outline chapter 3 is a section and so requires a section heading. It is "Job's Opening Speech," which begins the first series or round of arguments between Job and his friends. A section heading will often be printed in bolder or larger type. Some translations use a bold heading before chapter 3 to show that this chapter is the opening of the arguments; for example, FRCL and TOB have "Dialogue between Job and his three friends." The Handbook heading suggests that this is the beginning of the dialogues, but starts the body of the dialogues or speeches with a new section 3 in chapter 4. Translators wishing to follow the outline of the Handbook's headings may say, for example, "Job begins the arguments," "Job's speech opens the arguments," or "Job is the first to speak."

2A. JOB REGRETS THAT HE WAS BORN (3.1-26)

Division Heading

Translators may wish to use the division heading before chapter 3, in which case it may be necessary to say something like "Job wishes he had never been born" or "Job is angry that he was born."

2A-1. Job curses his birth (3.1-10)

RSV	TEV
1 After this Job opened his mouth and cursed the day of his birth. 2 And Job said:	1 Finally Job broke the silence and cursed the day on which he had been born.
3 "Let the day perish wherein I was born, and the night which said, 'A man-child is conceived.'	*Job* 2-3 O God, put a curse on the day I was born; put a curse on the night when I was conceived!
4 Let that day be darkness! May God above not seek it, nor light shine upon it.	4 Turn that day into darkness, God. Never again remember that day; never again let light shine on it.
5 Let gloom and deep darkness claim it. Let clouds dwell upon it; let the blackness of the day terrify it.	5 Make it a day of gloom and thick darkness; cover it with clouds, and blot out the sun.
6 That night—let thick darkness seize it! let it not rejoice among the days of the year, let it not come into the number of the months.	6 Blot that night out of the year, and never let it be counted again;
7 Yea, let that night be barren; let no joyful cry be heard in it.	7 make it a barren, joyless night.
8 Let those curse it who curse the day, who are skilled to rouse up Leviathan.	8 Tell the sorcerers to curse that day, those who know how to control Leviathan.

9 Let the stars of its dawn be dark;
   let it hope for light, but have none,
   nor see the eyelids of the morning;
	9 Keep the morning star from shining;
	   give that night no hope of dawn.

10 because it did not shut the doors of my
   mother's womb,
   nor hide trouble from my eyes.
	10 Curse that night for letting me be born,
	   for exposing me to trouble and grief.

The curse section falls into two parts: verses 3-7 and verses 8-10. In verses 3-7 Job curses the time related to his birth and conception. This curse covers the full range of time: day, night, month, and year. In verses 8-9 Job shifts the focus of his death wish by appealing to the forces that control the sea monster Leviathan and that control the morning star. Verse 10 summarizes through a metaphor the reason for Job's wish to have died at birth, and at the same time provides a transition to the lament section.

Subdivision Heading

The first of the subdivision headings in the Handbook covers 3.1-10. If subdivision headings are used, they should be printed in a smaller or less bold type, but they should be placed so that the reader will not miss them. This subdivision heading may need to be restated; for example, "Job cries out against his birth," "Job says bad things about his birth," or "Job uses strong words to complain that he was born."

At the beginning of many chapters the author identifies the speaker. These identifications are usually numbered as verse 1 in RSV (verses 1 and 2 in chapter 3), but they are not part of the poetic body of the text. Rather than leave them as isolated short prose lines, TEV has reduced the identification to the name of the speaker, but printed in italics. It is also possible to consider the headings as sufficient identification.

3.1 RSV	TEV
After this Job opened his mouth and cursed the day of his birth.	Finally Job broke the silence and cursed the day on which he had been born.

After this refers to the week of silence mentioned in 2.13 and may need to be translated by a transitional term showing that something new is about to take place. TEV says "Finally" (likewise SPCL, FRCL, NJB, TOB). In some languages this transition marker will need to be translated so as to show the time sequence between the end of chapter 2 and the opening of chapter 3. This is sometimes done by repeating the previous time clause; for example, "After his friends had been sitting with him silently for a week, Job began to curse . . . ."

Job opened his mouth and cursed the day of his birth: Job, who scolded his wife for suggesting he curse God and die, now erupts with curses against his origin and wishes he were dead. He is, nevertheless, careful not to curse God. The ineffective words of Job's curses should unleash the destruction he so passionately desires, but they are curses directed against the past, which cannot be undone, and therefore become even more pathetic. RSV translates the literal Hebrew "opened his mouth," which means "began to speak" or, as TEV says in this context, "broke the silence," which makes a better transition from the end of chapter 2.

Cursed translates the actual Hebrew word "curse" here and not the word "blessed." **The day of his birth** translates the Hebrew "his day," but the context makes it clear that it was the day of his birth he was cursing and not some other important day in his life. In many languages it will not be normal to invoke a curse upon a past event or a period of time, such as a day or a night. It will often be necessary to say, for example, "Job spoke evil words about the day of his birth," or ". . . against the day he was born." In some languages this may best be handled in direct address; for example, "Job said, 'I speak evil words against the day I was born'" or "'. . . the day my mother gave birth to me.'"

3.2   RSV   TEV

And Job said: *Job*

Verse 2 has only **And Job said**, which can best be merged with verse 1. Literally this is "And Job answered and said," but most languages will not use this Hebrew formula. If the translator wishes to keep verse 2 separate, it may be best to fill it out by saying, for example, "These are the words Job said when he cursed."

TEV places the speaker's name in italics at the left margin, and some other modern versions indicate the speaker's name within the margin instead of translating within the body of the text the repetitive "Then Job answered and said."

3.3   RSV   TEV

"Let the day perish wherein I   O God, put a curse on the day I
    was born,   was born;
and the night which said,   put a curse on the night when
'A man-child is conceived.'   I was conceived!

Verse 3 is the opening of the formal poetic body of the Book of Job. Job begins his curses by attacking the day of his birth and the night of his conception. The Hebrew is composed of two half-lines that are semantically parallel. The verb phrase **Let . . . perish** in **Let the day perish wherein I was born** serves double duty, since it must also be applied to line <u>b</u>. By not repeating the verb in line <u>b</u>, the poet has more line space in the Hebrew text to extend the birth image: **A man-child is conceived**. Through this technique of ellipsis the two Hebrew lines are kept compressed. **Day** followed by **night** is a commonly-used sequence in Hebrew poetry. If the parallelism were only "let the day perish" followed by "(let the) night (perish)," the parallelism would have little movement in the second line. However, the parallelism is between the commonplace statement in line <u>a</u> **I was born** and the more specific **A man-child is conceived** in the last line. There is a further dramatization of line <u>b</u> in that it is the night which is personified, that is, which speaks like a person and announces that a male child has been conceived. For instances of the personification of day and night, see Psalm 19.2-4. The poet has used this kind of dramatic parallelism to carry the idea in line a to a new pitch of intensity. Hence the last half does not merely repeat line a, but it goes beyond it and lifts it to a new poetic height. The two halves are a unit, and one cannot be dropped without causing a serious distortion of meaning. This intensification is an important feature of the poetic meaning. We may express it in English, for example, as "Cursed be the day I was born, and still more cursed the night I was conceived." However, as was pointed out in the introduction, "Translating the Book of Job," this English translation merely illustrates the way in which the b line carries the a line to a greater intensity. It may not be useful as a translation model because of its style. Furthermore, each language has to deal with the translation problems in each line. For example, in some languages it will be clearer and more natural to reverse the order of the lines so that being **conceived** occurs before being **born**. It may be necessary to recast the personification **the night which said** to say, for example, "the night people said." The passive **is conceived** allows the reference to Job's parents to be avoided. In some languages it will be necessary to shift to an active construction which will introduce "mother" or "parents." And the expression **man-child**, which in Hebrew refers specifically to a male, may have to be rendered by a term equivalent to "baby," in which no sex distinction is made.

These adjustments are often required to translate the parallel lines. As a result the translated lines may not retain the same poetic intensification and other feelings that the Hebrew lines create. However, the translator should aim to produce what will be recognized by the readers as an equally good arrangement of poetic lines.

TEV and some others assume that God is implied as the operator of the curse, and therefore Job calls on God to "put a curse on the day I was born." However, most modern versions consulted avoid explicit involvement of God in Job's curses. In some languages, however, it will be necessary to make God the one called upon to operate the curse, while in other languages it can be left implicit.

English **Let**, as used in verse 3 and the following verses, is a command addressed in the third person. It has the sense of a request or wish, "I wish that . . . ," or more directly as a command, "Do so and so." In some languages the request form in these verses must be addressed directly to God; for example, "How I wish that God would take away the day . . . ," or as a command, "God, take away the day . . . ."

The Septuagint reads "behold a man" instead of the Hebrew text "a man has been conceived," and in this way both day and night refer in the Septuagint to Job's birth. TEV keeps the parallelism and drops the personification, "put a curse on the night when I was conceived." Some modern versions avoid the night's "speaking" by using an impersonal subject, "the night when they said" (NAB), or a passive voice, "the night it was said" (NIV).

SPCL attempts to restore the order of conception and birth by saying "Cursed be the night in which I was conceived and the day I was born." As was pointed out above, this reversal of the Hebrew order may be required for reasons of style and naturalness.

3.4   RSV   TEV

Let that day be darkness!   Turn that day into darkness,
   May God above not seek it,   God.
   nor light shine upon it.   Never again remember that day;
                                                  never again let light shine on
                                                  it.

Verses 4-9 show examples of hyperbole, that is, exaggerated language which is
aimed to capture the reader's attention through overstatement. Verse 4 calls upon
day, God, and light to act against the day of Job's birth. The first is positive and the
next two are negative. Because verse 4 has three lines (as do verses 5-6), some
scholars prefer to drop the first line. However, three-line parallelism is not
uncommon, and there is no justification for omitting one line. The poetic rise of
intensity is seen in the replacement of the impersonal operator in line a to God in
line b. If **light** in line c refers to God, the movement in that line is to a metaphor.
This point is not certain.

   Let that day be darkness is almost the reversal of Genesis 1.3. **Darkness**
symbolizes mystery, awesomeness, and evil in such passages as 12.25; Exodus 20.21;
2 Samuel 22.29; Psalm 82.5; Isaiah 5.20; Matthew 6.23. TEV (so also GECL) makes
God the agent of the action, since God is mentioned in the second line. **That day**
refers to the time of Job's birth picked up from 3a. In translation it may be necessary
to make clear that **that day** refers to Job's birth; for example, "May the day I was
born be covered with darkness" or "May the day I was born be dark as night."

   May God above not seek it: **God**, which translates the Hebrew *'Eloah*, is
asked to refrain from "seeking" it. The Hebrew verb may refer to seeking an oracle
from God (1 Sam 9.9). In ancient Babylonia at the New Year's rites, each day of the
calendar year was summoned by a priest (see TOB note). Here Job calls on God to
refrain from doing this, which means therefore "to ignore, pay no attention," or as
in TEV, "never again remember." In translation we may often say, for example, "May
God who is above (in the heavens) forget that day" or "May God above never think
of the day I was born."

   Nor light shine upon it: Job wants the day cursed by being without light, which
is the negative counterpart of the first line. The Hebrew word for light found here
is not the usual word. Some take it to mean "dawn" (NEB, SPCL). In some languages
light is not said to shine. Accordingly we must adjust to something like "may that day
not dawn," "may the sun not shine on it," or "may that day have no light."

   The three lines may be rendered, for example,

> Let the day I was born be dark;
>   may God himself not even remember it,
>   and may the sun never shine on it.

In languages in which the "let" command in line a requires an agent, the translator
may follow the TEV model.

3.5   RSV   TEV

> Let gloom and deep darkness
>   claim it.
> Let clouds dwell upon it;
> let the blackness of the day
>   terrify it.

> Make it a day of gloom and thick
>   darkness;
> cover it with clouds, and blot
>   out the sun.

Verse 5 has three lines, all being positive wishes expressed against the day of Job's birth. These expand to six the number of curses Job speaks against the day he came into existence.

Let gloom and deep darkness claim it: **gloom** translates the same Hebrew noun translated "darkness" in verse 4. **Deep darkness** translates a noun which has been variously understood. Some scholars take it to be a compound word made up of "shadow" and "death" (see KJV). Dhorme understands it to mean "be dark." Others would keep the original word but read it as two words with an intensive sense meaning "very dark" or "deep darkness." Some translations make an explicit association between darkness and death; for example, NJB "shadow dark as death"; others like RSV and TEV speak of "thick" or "deep" darkness.

The verb translated **claim** is the Hebrew verb usually translated "redeem," used of a relative's right to claim the property of a next of kin who has died (see Ruth 4.4). In the use of this figure of speech, the day is to be thought of as a dead relative. The author is drawing an analogy in which darkness lays claim to what the day would have produced, namely Job. GECL personifies by saying "it was the property of darkness." Some interpreters feel this analogy is too forced. Another view is that the verb may be read as meaning "to pollute" (Dhorme, Tur-Sinai). KJV has "Let darkness . . . stain it" (similarly NEB). Others take it to mean "to protect," which may explain TEV "cover" in the following line. Modern translations are quite divided. It is not possible to advise translators with high degree of certainty. However, NJB, NAB, Mft, NIV, FRCL, GECL all prefer something meaning "to claim" or "possess." In translation, if it is possible to use the metaphor of claiming rights, one may say, for example, "Let darkness claim the day of my birth as its own property." In cases where such personalization of nonliving things is inappropriate, or where the image would not apply, we may follow TEV, which makes no attempt to use the metaphor; or we may say "May the day I was born be like a very dark night."

Let clouds dwell upon it: the second parallel line carries the thought of darkness to a more specific image, **clouds dwell**, and thus focuses the picture of darkness in a still and passive manner. TEV "cover" is applied to clouds more naturally than **dwell**. The verb is literally **dwell**, as in RSV, and this calls to mind the cloud of God's presence settling over the sacred tent in Numbers 9.15-22.

Let the blackness of the day terrify it: **blackness** translates a Hebrew word used only here in the Bible, and so its meaning is somewhat doubtful. Some interpret the Hebrew to mean "the bitterness (plural) of the day." In Amos 8.10 the expression "bitter day" is associated with the eclipse of the sun, and some translations prefer that rendering (SPCL, NEB, FRCL, GECL, TOB, NJB, BJ). Terrifying darkness is associated with the Day of the Lord in Joel 2.2 and Zephaniah 1.15. The sense of fear which Job invokes is not reflected in TEV. Here it is the day of Job's birth that is to be terrified by the eclipse. The three lines are clearly a case of stepped-up intensity, which may or may not be retained in translation. For example, "May it be a day of gloom and deep darkness; may it be covered over with clouds, and may the day I was born be terrified by that darkness." Many languages require a model with personal subjects and active verbs. For example, "I call upon God to make the day I was born to be very dark, to cover it all over with dark clouds, and to terrify that day with darkness in the same way that darkness in the day frightens people."

3.6

RSV	TEV
That night—let thick darkness seize it! let it not rejoice among the days of the year, let it not come into the number of the months.	Blot that night out of the year, and never let it be counted again;

In this verse Job turns his attention to **That night**, referred to in verse 3 as the time when he was conceived. This verse again has three lines in which a positive curse is followed by two negative ones. Typical of heightening poetic effect is the step up from a limited time, **days of the year** in 6b, to a larger unit of time, **months**. This process is similar to number parallelism, in which line b̲ always goes beyond the number in line a̲. For example, Psalm 91.7, "A thousand may fall at your side, ten thousand at your right hand." The intensification occurs in lines b̲ and c̲.

That night—let thick darkness seize it! In verse 4 Job asked that the day of his birth be darkness, and now he invokes the same upon the night he was conceived. The word "darkness" in the two passages represents two different words in Hebrew. The author uses another word of similar meaning here to enrich the poetic effect. Although the night is by its nature dark, Job calls upon it to be darker still, a thought translated by NEB, "blind darkness swallow up that night." In translation it will often be necessary to make **That night** refer explicitly to the night Job was conceived, since the last reference was in 3b. In some languages it is necessary to employ euphemisms concerning conception, particularly when the Bible is to be read in public. Sometimes we must say "make disappear the night when my mother knew she carried me in her belly" or "remove the night when my mother knew that she was pregnant with me."

Let it not rejoice among the days of the year: this rendering follows the Masoretic text. A change of vowels permits the rendering of KJV, "let it not be joined unto the days of the year." HOTTP says the verb has three meanings: "to unite or integrate," "to rejoice," or "to see," and gives no preference of one meaning over the others. However, "rejoice" and "see" could only be used metaphorically as parallel with the verb in 6c, and therefore TEV "be counted again" offers a good model (see similar renderings in SPCL, Mft, GECL, FRCL, NAB, NIV, TOB, NJB). TEV has switched "the year" to the first line and does not repeat it in the second. Only RSV among modern translations consulted has "rejoice." So Job is saying that the night of his conception should be dropped from the calendar.

In terms of the parallelism, the poet here raises the level of intensification. He is repeating 6b, but repeating it with heightening effect, which now says "Let it not be counted as one of the days of the year; don't even let it find its way into the months of the year." TEV has combined and shortened lines b and c into one. This, however, has been done on the basis of the apparent repetition, and at the expense of the poetic intensification that occurs between the two lines. As a general rule, before combining and shortening parallel lines, translators should determine if there is movement between the lines, and then seek to represent it in their translations. This may or may not permit the parallel line structures.

In languages in which an impersonal agent cannot be used, it may be necessary to address the command to God, as in TEV verses 2-3.

3.7   RSV   TEV

> Yea, let that night be barren;   make it a barren, joyless night.
>   let no joyful cry be heard[b] in
>   it.

[b] Heb *come*

This verse continues Job's curse of the night of his conception. Both lines are negative in meaning, and there is a limited degree of movement between lines a and b. Line a contains the figurative expression, which in poetic heightening is normally found in the second line.

Yea, let that night be barren: the word translated **barren** is found outside Job only in Isaiah 49.21. It is not the usual word for sterility but calls attention to stony, unproductive soil. Job wants the night responsible for his conception to be punished by never allowing another child to be born on it. In some languages it is not possible to speak of a night being barren; therefore it may be necessary to recast this expression to say, for example, "never (again) let anyone be conceived on the night I was conceived." This may be expressed in active form as "never let another woman become pregnant on the night my mother did."

Let no joyful cry be heard in it: **joyful cry** refers to the happy sounds of the adults, not to the crying of the newborn infant. In other words, each time the anniversary of Job's conception comes round, it must be greeted by silence, not any word of happy congratulations. TEV combines and shortens the two lines into one but retains the components of meaning. In languages in which the passive cannot be used here, it may be necessary to say, for example, "let no one make a joyful shout," or as in TEV, "joyless night."

3.8   RSV   TEV

> Let those curse it who curse the   Tell the sorcerers to curse that
>   day,   day,
>   who are skilled to rouse up   those who know how to control
>   Leviathan.   Leviathan.[f]

f LEVIATHAN: *Some take this to be the crocodile, others a legendary monster. Magicians were thought to be able to make him cause eclipses of the sun.*

Let those curse it who curse the day: In this verse line b merely extends the meaning of line a by defining who is meant by **those who curse the day.** The word **curse** occurs twice in RSV, representing two different Hebrew words. The first one is found infrequently in the Old Testament, except in the story of Balaam (Num 22), where it occurs nine times. Both words are different from the word for **curse** used in 3.1. **Who curse the day** may be understood to mean persons who are able to invoke a spell or put a curse on the day and thereby produce an eclipse of the sun; TEV has "Tell the sorcerers to curse that day." In contrast, the object of the curse in RSV is **it,** referring to the night of verses 6-7, and this is followed by nearly all other translations. **Those who curse the day** are understood to be associated with Leviathan in 8b. Consequently some interpreters read Hebrew *yom,* "day," as *yam,* "sea," and get "those who curse the sea," and thereby cause the sea monster in 8b to create chaos. Taking **it** to refer to the night, which Job has been cursing since verse 6, we may translate "Let the sorcerer curse the night of my conception." In some areas cursing, or putting a spell on someone, is a rather elaborate procedure, involving the making of "medicine" and chanting rituals. The translator should use general terms for "sorcerer" and "curse" so that the focus of the poem is not drained away in specific secondary details. For this reason it may be better here to say "Let the ones curse that night who practice cursing things" or ". . . who know how to do such things."

Who are skilled to rouse up Leviathan: skilled refers to those who are able, know how, are experienced. The word is used in 15.24 with the sense of prepared, or ready. **Rouse up** translates a word that is used in Isaiah 14.9, where it refers to awakening the ghosts of the dead. In our context Job calls on the ones knowing how to awaken, stir up, arouse this monster, to lend their skill in cursing the day of his birth. **Leviathan** is a name which means "coiled," as in the shape of a coiled snake. In Psalm 104.26 the psalmist says that God formed **Leviathan** as a plaything for himself. In Isaiah 27.1 **Leviathan** is the sea monster that battles with Baal. It represents the forces of chaos overcome by God in Psalm 74.13-14; 89.10-11. In chapter 41 **Leviathan** seems to be described as a crocodile. However, in 3.8 the sense seems to be that of a mythological animal that lives in the sea, and which can be stirred up to cause destruction. In some languages **Leviathan** may be translated as "great sea snake" or "big animal that lives in the sea." If possible the translator should qualify the animal as a "monster" or "dragon" so that it is not equated with a natural animal. In some languages such an animal is called "an animal people tell tales about" or "an animal people imagine." It may be necessary to place this qualification in a footnote. In areas where the sea is unknown, we must sometimes say something like "big river snake," unless, of course, such a phrase would be identified with the largest local river snake. TEV "control Leviathan" may have to be recast to say, for example, "they who know how to make the great sea snake do what they want" or ". . . obey them."

3.9 RSV	TEV
Let the stars of its dawn be dark; let it hope for light, but have none, nor see the eyelids of the morning;	Keep the morning star from shining; give that night no hope of dawn.

This verse has three lines in Hebrew. The second and third intensify the picture through the use of figurative language. **Let the stars of its dawn be dark:** the word translated **dawn** may refer to morning twilight as in 7.4; Psalm 119.147, or to evening twilight as in 24.15; Proverbs 7.9. Since the pronominal reference has been to the night of Job's conception, it is best to take it that way here. So the meaning is the dawn following the night of conception, and the stars are the planets Venus and Mercury, which can sometimes be seen as the brightest stars in the sky just before sunrise. Job wishes these stars had remained dark so that the day of his birth never would have come round. The translation of **the stars of its dawn** may be as specific as is customary when the language speaks of the stars that shine at dawn. If specific names are not used to designate these, it will be best to say, for example, "the stars that shine at dawn" or ". . . before the sun rises."

Let it hope for light, but have none, nor see the eyelids of the morning: these two lines are parallel. The personified **hope for light** is paralleled by the more dramatic figure **see the eyelids of the morning**. The heightening effect may be translated in English as "Let the morning stars of the night I was conceived not shine, let that night hope to have light, but have none, and do not let the day dawn at all." In some languages these wishes, which represent already-realized events, will need to be expressed differently to say something like "How I wish the morning star had not shone the night I was conceived." The personalization of the night hoping may have to be restructured to say, for example, "Let the night become very long without any daylight coming," "Let the night end without a sunrise," or "Let the night go on and on without a dawn." **Eyelids of the morning** suggests the streaks of light that glow on the eastern horizon as sunrise approaches. This will usually have to be changed into a different figure, or more commonly expressed as a nonfigure. TEV has combined and shortened lines b and c and makes no attempt to show the poetic intensification. And TEV has kept the poetic personalization but done away with the poetic imagery: "give the night no hope of dawn."

3.10 RSV	TEV
because it did not shut the doors of my mother's womb, nor hide trouble from my eyes.	Curse that night for letting me be born, for exposing me to trouble and grief.

Here Job ceases his curses and offers a poetically expressed reason for not wanting to be born: **because it did not shut the doors of my mother's womb.** It refers to "that night," which has been the object of his curses in verses 6-9. **My**

mother's womb translates the Hebrew "my womb." Job has been careful to avoid any direct reference to his parents. Here he refers to the womb from which he came, which RSV renders **my mother's womb.** The shutting of the womb is used in 1 Samuel 1.6 as a figure for the prevention of conception, and in Genesis 29.31-32 the opening of the womb allows conception to take place. Translations are divided between those that make the closing of the womb refer to birth (TEV, FRCL, SPCL) and those which avoid any specific reference to conception or birth (NEB, NAB, Mft, NIV, TOB, NJB, BJ).

When translating this verse it may be necessary to move away from the metaphor of the night shutting the doors of the womb, by saying, for example, "because on that night I was conceived in my mother's womb" or "because . . . nothing was done to prevent me from being conceived." We may also follow TEV, but make the sense more explicitly related to conception; for example, "curse the night for letting me be conceived," or in some languages, "curse the night for allowing me to start life in my mother's womb."

Nor hide trouble from my eyes: Jeremiah (20.18) says of his birth, "Why did I come forth from the womb, to see toil and sorrow . . . ?" The word translated **trouble** in RSV is a Hebrew term that refers to the hardships and agonies of Israel in Deuteronomy 26.7 and Isaiah 53.11 respectively. It may also refer to human wickedness in Psalm 94.20, where TEV translates "injustice." In 4.8 Eliphaz will pick up on Job's use of this word as the evil which people reap for the sins they sow. TEV has "trouble and grief," which combine well to fit the present context. The second and third lines are negatively stated and thus maintain a poetic balance. In some languages it may be better, however, to restructure the final line as a positive statement; for example, "because it let me see so much grief" or "because it allowed me to have so much trouble."

2A-2. Job complains that his existence is unbearable (3.11-26)

	RSV		TEV
11	"Why did I not die at birth, come forth from the womb and expire?	11	I wish I had died in my mother's womb or died the moment I was born.
12	Why did the knees receive me? Or why the breasts, that I should suck?	12	Why did my mother hold me on her knees? Why did she feed me at her breast?
13	For then I should have lain down and been quiet; I should have slept; then I should have been at rest,	13 / 14	If I had died then, I would be at rest now, sleeping like the kings and rulers who rebuilt ancient palaces.
14	with kings and counselors of the earth who rebuilt ruins for themselves,	15	Then I would be sleeping like princes who filled their houses with gold and silver,
15	or with princes who had gold, who filled their houses with silver.	16	or sleeping like a stillborn child.
16	Or why was I not as a hidden untimely birth, as infants that never see the light?	17	In the grave wicked men stop their evil, and tired workmen find rest at last.
17	There the wicked cease from troubling, and there the weary are at rest.	18	Even prisoners enjoy peace, free from shouts and harsh commands.
18	There the prisoners are at ease together; they hear not the voice of the taskmas-	19	Everyone is there, the famous and the unknown, and slaves at last are free.

19 The small and the great are there,
and the slave is free from his master.

20 "Why is light given to him that is in misery,
and life to the bitter in soul,
21 who long for death, but it comes not,
and dig for it more than for hid treasures;
22 who rejoice exceedingly,
and are glad, when they find the grave?
23 Why is light given to a man whose way is hid,
whom God has hedged in?
24 For my sighing comes as my bread,
and my groanings are poured out like water.
25 For the thing that I fear comes upon me,
and what I dread befalls me.
26 I am not at ease, nor am I quiet;
I have no rest; but trouble comes."

20 Why let men go on living in misery?
Why give light to men in grief?
21 They wait for death, but it never comes;
they prefer a grave to any treasure.
22 They are not happy till they are dead and buried;
23 God keeps their future hidden
and hems them in on every side.
24 Instead of eating, I mourn,
and I can never stop groaning.
25 Everything I fear and dread comes true.
26 I have no peace, no rest,
and my troubles never end.

The lament section is dominated by a series of "Why" questions in which Job asks rhetorically why he has lived to suffer. It is introduced by two of these questions (verses 11-12) and a hypothetical condition (verse 13) which opens the subtheme of the peace of the grave. The people Job would have been buried with are arranged in a hierarchy beginning with kings in verse 14 and ending with slaves in verse 19. Verses 20-23 are framed by two more "Why" questions, in which Job's queries are shifted from the personal to people in general. In the closing part of the lament (verses 24-26), Job again speaks out in the first person, as he did at the opening of the chapter, and expresses emphatically the fear he now feels.

Subdivision Heading

Translators should consider placing a heading before verse 11 which will call attention to Job's miserable condition. Some suggestions for the heading are: "Job asks 'Why do I have to go on living?'" "Job says his troubles never end," "Job asks why he has to suffer," or "Job hopes to die, but he goes on living."

3.11   RSV   TEV

"Why did I not die at birth,   I wish I had died in my mother's
come forth from the womb and   womb
expire?   or died the moment I was
                                         born.

This is the start of the second part of the chapter (verses 11-26), in which Job complains against his suffering. He begins by asking the first of five "Why" questions, which are repeated to emphasize Job's wish that he could have died. This kind of question is typical of a lament or complaint. Since Job obviously could not prevent his birth, he now wishes he had died at birth; for similar laments asking "Why," see Psalm 10.1; 22.1; Jeremiah 20.18; Lamentations 5.20.

Why did I not die at birth, come forth from the womb and expire? The first line translates "Why did I not die from the womb?" The Septuagint has "in the womb." TEV also takes it to mean "in my mother's womb," as do SPCL, TOB, NJB. TEV expresses the question as a wish. The "Why" question is not repeated in the second line, since it serves for both lines. In line a the poet uses the usual word for "die," but in line b the term in Hebrew is more literary, meaning to "breathe out a last breath" or "expire." The two lines say the same thing twice but with a difference in that the figurative expression in line b steps up the poetic pitch. If the verse is translated as a wish, it may be rendered, for example, "I wish I had died when I was born, in fact, I wish I had never even taken one breath when I came from my mother's womb." The distinction is not in wishing to die in the womb or outside the womb as in TEV, but rather in the step up of intensity between "die" and "breathe my last breath."

Translators may find the repetitive use of the "Why" questions fails to emphasize Job's desire to die, and that expressing these rhetorical questions as wishes likewise does not make his wish stronger, but only more monotonous. In such cases the translator must use devices in the receptor language that will lend such emphases. For example, it may be necessary to alternate between "Why" questions and wishes.

3.12 RSV	TEV
Why did the knees receive me? Or why the breasts, that I should suck?	Why did my mother hold me on her knees? Why did she feed me at her breast?

Why did the knees receive me? It is not clear from the Hebrew whose knees are meant. Joseph's great-grandchildren are said to have been born on his knees (Gen 50.23). Some have suggested that the knees are those of Job's father, who in this manner legitimizes or formally acknowledges his infant son as his own. However, line 12b refers to the mother's breasts, and so TEV and others are perhaps right in relating the knees to the mother. Living Bible (LB) has "why did the midwife let me live? Why did she nurse me at her breasts?" There is no justification in the text for introducing a midwife into this verse. The question in line a is literally "Why were the knees before me?" In translation it is again possible to restructure the rhetorical question **Why did the knees . . . ,** using "I wish . . . ," as done by TEV in verse 11. However, in some languages this type of repeated structure may be less satisfactory than varying them as TEV has done. In some languages it will be more natural to say "lap" or "arms"; for example, "Why did my mother hold me on her lap?" or ". . . hold me in her arms?" If the translation follows a wording similar to RSV, it may be advisable to provide a note saying, for example, "This is an act showing that the child is formally welcomed into the family."

Or why the breasts, that I should suck? RSV translates the Hebrew literally, and the result is stilted, awkward English. TEV has restructured this line so that "she feed me" is parallel with "my mother hold me" from 12a. To avoid monotony of style TEV has used the double "Why" question instead of the wish of the previous verse.

3.13   RSV   TEV

> For then I should have lain down   If I had died then, I would be at
>   and been quiet;   rest now,
> I should have slept; then I
>   should have been at rest,

For then I should have lain down and been quiet: verse 13 presupposes that, if the events of verse 12 had not occurred, then Job would have died, and 13a, which is a consequence, would have been true. Accordingly TEV supplies "If I had died then" from 13b and goes on to complete the consequence, "I would be at rest now." In 10.21-22 Job will characterize Sheol as a place of gloom, deep darkness, and chaos. Here, however, the idea of death appeals to him as a place of rest and quiet, compared with his earthly suffering.

I should have slept; then I should have been at rest: this line is parallel to 13a, and TEV reduces the two lines to one. Sleep is an image of death (Deut 31.16; Psa 13.3; 1 Cor 15.51). Both lines contain metaphors for death: "lie down" and "sleep." Here the author avoids stepping up the force of the imagery, since he is dealing with death as a quiet, restful, inactive existence. TEV shifts "sleep" to verse 14 and applies it to Job's wish to be buried with kings and rulers. NEB fills out the idiom with "asleep in death." Translators must be certain that the metaphor "sleep" is used naturally of death and dying. If there is an alternative metaphor which is appropriate for this context, it should be used; if there is no metaphor, then it will be better to say "I would have died" or "I would be dead."

3.14   RSV   TEV

> with kings and counselors of the   sleeping like the kings and
>   earth   rulers
> who rebuilt ruins for them-   who rebuilt ancient palaces.
>   selves,

With kings and counselors of the earth describes the company Job would have kept, if at birth he had gone down into the world of the dead. For a similar idea see Isaiah 14.9-11, where in Sheol the rulers of the earth rise from their thrones to mock the dead king of Babylon. The word translated **counselors** refers to the officials or ministers who carried out the king's orders. **Of the earth** simply emphasizes their realm, or as Mft says, "the kings and statesmen of the world." In some languages Job's companions in death would be "chiefs and tribal headmen" or "great chiefs and minor chiefs." In language areas where there are no persons with such authority, it may be necessary to say "with important ancestors and their helpers." TEV picks up "sleeping" from 13b, which it does not use there, and uses it metaphorically here.

Who rebuilt ruins for themselves: scholars are divided regarding what is meant by this line. RSV understands that the kings rebuilt what they found as ruins during their rule. In this sense they restored what were probably old palaces. NEB says "who built themselves palaces." NIV understands that the palaces they built are "places now lying in ruins." Another group of translations takes **for themselves** to mean that the kings built burial places or pyramids (so SPCL, GECL, NJB, BJ, Mft). TEV follows RSV and expresses the idea of **ruins** through the use of "rebuilt ancient palaces." Considering the various possibilities, RSV and TEV are adequate models for translation. "Palaces" may be rendered in some languages as "houses which chiefs live in," "big house for the rulers," or "big houses important people live in."

3.15   RSV   TEV

> or with princes who had gold,   Then I would be sleeping like
> who filled their houses with   princes
> silver.   who filled their houses with
>   gold and silver,

Or with princes who had gold again expresses a consequence which would have followed if, as in TEV verse 13, Job had died. Accordingly TEV again says "Then I would be sleeping . . . ." Hebrew lacks a verb in 15a; RSV supplies **had**. The Hebrew term translated **princes** never really refers to sons of kings but rather to some of the highest leaders in the Israelite system of government. The **princes** who had gold are said to have **filled their houses with silver**. Some understand these houses to refer to the tombs or burial places of the rich. However, 22.18a expresses nearly the same form, where it refers to the riches of the living, and most probably it does also here. TEV and others make both gold and silver the object of "filled their palaces." Very often a literal translation of **filled their houses** will mean to fill them as with a liquid. In such cases it may be necessary to say, for example, "they put great amounts of gold and silver in their houses" or, more likely, ". . . objects made from gold and silver . . . ." If the names of these metals are not familiar, they may have to be borrowed from a major language, or referred to generically as "valuable metals" or a combination of these. Alternatively we may simply say "wealth."

3.16   RSV   TEV

> Or why was I not as a hidden   or sleeping like a stillborn
> untimely birth,   child.
> as infants that never see the
> light?

This verse appears to interrupt the continuity of verses 15-17. Consequently NEB inserts it after verse 12, while NAB puts it after verse 11. Most modern translations, however, do not transpose this verse from its traditional place. It seems best to retain the order of verses as in RSV. TEV avoids transposing verse 16 by repeating "sleeping" in verses 14, 15, 16. In this way the condition "if I had died" in verse 13 is followed by three result clauses, all beginning with "sleeping." The two lines of the Hebrew of this verse are contracted into one in TEV, for which a better translation may be "I would be buried and hidden like a stillborn child."

Or why was I not as a hidden untimely birth: if Job had been an aborted fetus, he would have been buried and hidden among the dead. The second line, **as infants that never see the light**, is parallel to the first line, and TEV reduces the two to one line with "or sleeping like a stillborn child." By keeping the "Why" question the two lines may be rendered, for example, "Why was I not gotten rid of like an abortion, or buried like a baby that never lives to see the light of day?" In Hebrew only the first line contains the verb "hide." The second line omits the verb in order to have more room for the expanded noun clause. In the form of a wish, the two lines may be rendered, for example, "I wish I had been put out of sight while still a fetus, or even gotten rid of like a dead baby which never opens its eyes."

3.17   RSV   TEV

> There the wicked cease from
>   troubling,
>   and there the weary are at
>   rest.

> In the grave wicked men stop
>   their evil,
>   and tired workmen find rest at
>   last.

In verses 17-19 Job depicts those freed by death. The parallel lines in these three verses show little movement between each pair of lines. Here the lack of rising emotion is used to call attention to the subjects of each verse, who are pictured as being at rest and at peace. Job identifies himself with the workmen, prisoners, and slaves.

There the wicked cease from troubling: There is separated from its referent by verse 16; it refers to Sheol or the place of the dead and is rendered by TEV as "In the grave." NJB has "down there." The RSV rendering of 17a is ambiguous, since **troubling** may denote either causing trouble to others or being anxious. TEV "wicked men stop their evil" interprets the Hebrew to mean "doing evil deeds." In other words, Job praises the grave as the place not only where "tired workmen find rest," but also where wicked people no longer carry out their evil acts.

And there the weary are at rest: the weary translates what is literally "the exhausted of strength." Gordis takes the expression to mean "those exhausted by violence," the violence being that of the wicked in 17a. In this interpretation the meaning would be "victims of oppression." GECL understands the Hebrew to mean "forced laborers." NEB agrees with TEV "tired workmen" without relating their condition to the previous line. The two lines refer to different groups of dead persons, and the two parallel phrases **cease from troubling** and **are at rest** are without intensification.

3.18   RSV   TEV

> There the prisoners are at ease
>   together;

> Even prisoners enjoy peace,
>   free from shouts and harsh

> they hear not the voice of the
>   taskmaster.

commands.

There the prisoners are at ease together: in the context of people being shouted at by a taskmaster, the term **prisoners** is probably to be taken as "captives doing forced labor" rather than as prisoners who are locked up, doing nothing. **At ease** means they are "at peace" as in TEV, and **together** simply designates them as a group, or as NJB says, "all left in peace." In some languages it may be necessary to recast this clause to say, for example, "In the world of the dead, the people who have been captured and forced to work are all at peace."

They hear not the voice of the taskmaster: the term translated **taskmaster** is used of Egyptian "slave-drivers" who oppressed the Israelites (Exo 3.7; 5.6). TEV leaves implicit the origin of "shouts and harsh commands" directed at the prisoners. NIV, NAB, and Mft are to be preferred, with "slave-driver." In some languages the role of "slave-driver" will be unknown, and in such cases it will be best to follow TEV.

3.19   RSV   TEV

> The small and the great are
>   there,
> and the slave is free from his
>   master.

> Everyone is there, the famous
>   and the unknown,
> and slaves at last are free.

The small and the great are there: in Hebrew the word following **there** is the pronoun "he," which some interpreters take to mean "the same" or "alike." The meaning is that the small and the great are all equal in Sheol, their worldly differences having been leveled out. The Hebrew "he" is used with the meaning "same" or "like" in Psalm 102.28; Isaiah 41.4; 43.10,13; 46.4, and is translated in that way by SPCL, GECL, NAB, Mft, FRCL, TOB, BJ. TEV takes **The small and the great** to include everyone and refers to them as "Everyone is there, the famous and the unknown." RSV and TEV do not say that they have all become equal in Sheol, but this may be implicit. In some languages the distinction between **The small and the great** is rendered, for example, "People who live near the chief and those who live far," "People everyone knows and people no one knows," or "Big people and little people."

In RSV **slave** occurs only here and in 7.2. In line a a distinction is made between two social groups, the **small** and the **great** (people). in line b the **slave** is contrasted with the **master**. Also in line b the **slave** makes specific the more general **small** in line a, and the same applies to the movement from **great** in line a to **his master** in line b.

The sense of **slave** here is a person who is forced to be under the authority of another. **Master** is the one who controls the slave and keeps the slave under subjection. **Free** means the slave ceases to be under the master's control.

In languages in which slaves and masters are unknown, some adjustments are required, as was the case of "prisoners" in verse 18. In verse 19b it may be necessary to say, for example, "the one forced to labor no longer has a boss over him" or "the people who were captured to do work do not have to work anymore."

3.20	RSV	TEV
	"Why is light given to him that is in misery, and life to the bitter in soul,	Why let men go on living in misery? Why give light to men in grief?

In verses 20-23 Job continues his lament, asking again why any sufferer has to go on living when his life has lost direction. Just as Job gave a reason for his curses in verse 10, he concludes his lament in verses 24-26 by again giving a reason for it.

Why is light given to him that is in misery: Job has ended his contemplation of what death and the grave could have meant to him, and now he turns to asking about the meaning of the life of one who suffers. In Hebrew line 20a is literally "Why does he (or one) give light to the sufferer?" RSV follows the traditional rendering of the verb as a passive; however, SPCL, GECL, Mft, FRCL have supplied God as the subject of an active verb. TEV (also NJB) uses an impersonal "Why give light . . . ?" TOB, which says "why does he give . . . ," has an instructive note: " 'He' refers to God. Greek, Syriac, Vulgate, Aramaic have 'is given.' The passive perhaps shows that translators of the ancient versions desired to exonerate God." TEV, like RSV and others, avoids any explicit reference to God; however, TEV has made God explicit in the curse section, and the text itself mentions God in verse 23. Accordingly it is probable that the reader of TEV will understand God as the one being addressed. Translators will often have to choose a passive or impersonal expression, or express God as the subject; for example, "Why does God let people who suffer go on living?"

TEV has transposed "life" to the first line and "light" to the second line, and has in this case retained both lines, which are parallel.

And life to the bitter in soul: line b steps up the intensity in this verse through the use of the figurative expression **bitter in soul**. **Life** is parallel to **light** in 20a and defines it. The verb in 20a must also be understood in 20b. **Bitter in soul**, a Hebrew idiom parallel to the New Testament idiom "pure in heart" (Matt 5.8), is literally "bitternesses in soul," where the plural form refers to Job and others having such a condition; therefore TEV "men in grief." For other references see Judges 18.25 ("angry fellows"); 1 Samuel 1.10 ("deeply distressed"); 2 Samuel 17.8 ("enraged"). In some languages this may be rendered idiomatically as "people whose insides are undone," "people whose hearts are low," or "people who carry trouble on them." The build-up in the second line may be illustrated, for example, by "Why are people allowed to live in misery, or more important still, how does it happen that they can go on living when their lives have become bitter?" In languages in which impersonal subjects and passive verbs are not used, it may be necessary to say, for example, "God, why do you let people who suffer go on living; why do you allow this even when a person's heart has become bitter?"

3.21   RSV   TEV

> who long for death, but it comes   They wait for death, but it never
>   not,   comes;
> and dig for it more than for   they prefer a grave to any
>   hid treasures;   treasure.

Who long for death, but it comes not, and dig for it more than for hid treasures: like the sufferers in Revelation 9.6, "they wait for death, but it never comes." Line <u>b</u> steps up the death wish from the prosaic **long for death** to the intensely dramatic picture of digging for a buried treasure. The Hebrew verb translated **dig** can mean either "seek" (NEB) or "dig" (RSV), and either meaning fits the context. "Seek" or "search" is a better parallel to the first line, but in English "dig" fits the imagery of the treasure seeker. A similar picture is applied to the search for wisdom in Proverbs 2.4. TEV "they prefer a grave to any treasure" retains the sense but sacrifices the intensity of the poetic imagery. In translation it may be necessary to make clear in the second line that the persons referred to are those who want to die to escape their suffering. The two lines may be rendered, for example, "They are people who wish they could die, but death does not come; they want death so much that they search for it like people who hunt for treasures."

3.22   RSV   TEV

> who rejoice exceedingly,   They are not happy till they are
>   and are glad, when they find   dead and buried;
>   the grave?

Who rejoice exceedingly: the Hebrew of 22a may be read as in RSV, **exceedingly**, or with the more specific meaning of "to see the burial mound," but as Dhorme points out, a burial mound is not found by digging. NEB has "when they reach the tomb"; similar renderings are found in GECL, Mft, NJB, BJ. Line <u>b</u> repeats the meaning of line <u>a</u>, **and are glad**, and completes it with the consequence **when they find the grave**. There is little step-up of intensity in the parallel parts. TEV has condensed both lines to a somewhat toned-down "they are not happy till . . . ."

3.23   RSV   TEV

> Why is light given to a man   God keeps their future hidden
>   whose way is hid,   and hems them in on every
> whom God has hedged in?   side.

In 1.10 Satan claimed that God put a hedge of protection around Job and all he possessed. Now Job objects that God has imprisoned him with a hedge that prevents him from finding any hope in life. He expresses this thought first by asking **Why is light given to a man whose way is hid?** In Hebrew **Why is light given** is left implicit, but the question is supplied in RSV and others from line 20a. The translator may, like RSV, supply the question from verse 20 or, like TEV, avoid the question form and make a statement. **Light** here as in verse 20 refers to the "light of life," that is, physical life. Job clearly implies that God is the one who hides a man's way. Accordingly TEV supplies God as the subject and shifts from a question to a statement: "God keeps their future hidden." The word translated **way** in RSV refers in wisdom literature to a person's conduct or personal destiny (so Habel). Many modern versions retain the idea of **way,** often through the use of a verb phrase; for example, FRCL has "a man who does not know where he is going." The sense of being ignorant of where one is headed may be expressed as "God makes them go along blindly" or "God keeps them from seeing where they are going."

Whom God has hedged in: Job again mentions God by the same name as in 3.4. The object of the verb **hedge** is singular; however, TEV, which uses the impersonal "their" in the first line, must also use the plural in the second "hems them in." In this verse Job finally comes to the point of declaring God to be his adversary, the one who is causing him to suffer and despair. For translation comments see 1.10.

3.24	RSV	TEV

For my sighing comes as^c my
   bread,
and my groanings are poured
   out like water.

Instead of eating, I mourn,
   and I can never stop groaning.

^c Heb *before*

In verses 24-26 Job, still lamenting, summarizes his feelings and gives something of a reason for them, as he did at the conclusion of the series of curses in verse 10.

For my sighing comes as my bread: the word translated **as** (see RSV footnote) may also be read "before" or "instead." Interpreters have attempted various changes in the Hebrew vowels to get clearer readings, but these have not won much acceptance. A parallel example is Psalm 42.3, "Tears are my only food." TEV restructures this expression as two verb phrases, "instead of eating, I mourn."

And my groanings are poured out like water: by this figure of speech Job says that he groans continually, or as TEV says, "I can never stop groaning." The word translated **groanings** normally refers to the roaring of a lion and is used poetically here to show the intensity of Job's mourning. In fact, the two lines are parallel, with bread and water corresponding to each other. However, the stepping up of "sighing" to "roaring" in line b and **comes** in line a to **pours out** in line b exhibits a clear development of heightening poetic effect. In translation it will often be necessary to avoid the noun "groanings" and use a verb phrase, as TEV. If these figures are not in regular use in the language, the translator should be careful not to follow what appear in English to be perfectly logical ones. It is better to translate using an equivalent figure, or to render the meaning instead of the form.

3.25   RSV   TEV

> For the thing that I fear comes   Everything I fear and dread
>   upon me,   comes true.
>   and what I dread befalls me.

The poet brings the chapter to a close with a crescendo of emphasis and a personal revelation of Job's inner self. No sooner does Job fear some disaster than it happens to him. The emphatic nature of the parallel lines is accomplished by the step-up in the movement of the verb **fear** in line a followed by **dread** in line b. In some languages it may not be possible to find two verbs for fear which heighten the intensity. In such cases it is often possible to use only one verb and to reinforce it through an intensive; for example, "The things I fear are the very things that happen to me, and what I really fear most takes place."

3.26   RSV   TEV

> I am not at ease, nor am I quiet;   I have no peace, no rest,
>   I have no rest; but trouble   and my troubles never end.
>   comes."

Finally Job summarizes his tragedy. In verse 22 those who find the grave rejoice and are glad. By contrast Job in life finds just the opposite: no ease, quiet, or rest—only troubles. The verb of state translated **quiet** is the same as in verse 13, and **rest** is the same as in verse 17. These verb forms in Hebrew are in the perfect tense, which could be taken to mean they refer to Job's past experiences; accordingly KJV translates "I was not in safety, neither had I rest, neither was I quiet." In this way verse 26 links up with the prologue. However, all modern translations consulted relate verse 26 to the rest of chapter 3 through the use of the present tense, as in TEV "I have no peace, no rest . . . ."

TEV understands **ease** and **rest** as synonymous and therefore reduces them to "rest." **I am not at ease** is sometimes rendered, for example, "my heart is not cool" or "my heart does not sit in the shade."

The **trouble** Job mentions (also in verse 20) is his continuing anguish, which affects his inner self and creates his confusion. In some languages **trouble** is expressed as the subject of a transitive verb; for example, "troubles never stop taking hold of me."

Job concludes his discourse. He has cursed his birth and longed for death, but he has not cursed God, nor has he died. The friends, who have sat in silence for seven days and nights, have now heard Job's outbursts of emotions and are ready to take their turns to dispute with him.

3. First Round of Speeches

(4.1–14.22)

Section 3 contains the first of three rounds or series of speeches given by the friends, with Job responding after each speaker. The order of speakers in each round is Eliphaz, Bildad, Zophar. Eliphaz, who may be the senior friend, speaks in chapters 4 and 5, with Job replying in chapters 6 and 7. Then Bildad picks up the argument in chapter 8, with Job responding in chapters 9 and 10. Finally Zophar has his turn in chapter 11, and the first cycle of speeches closes with Job replying in chapters 12–14. The same procedure is repeated in sections 4 and 5.

Section Heading
The Handbook divides chapters 4–27 into three sections and provides a section heading for each. Translators wishing to follow the Handbook may need to reword this section heading to say, for example, "The first group of arguments," "Job and the friends now begin to argue," "The first arguments between Job and the friends." TEV has "The first dialogue," and some translations prefer to place this heading before chapter 3.

3A. ELIPHAZ'S FIRST SPEECH (4.1–5.27)

Eliphaz's speech in chapter 4 has two major themes. In verses 2-11 he explores Job's suffering, and in verses 12-21 he discusses a teaching which he says has been revealed to him. The first theme begins with verses 1 and 2, with Eliphaz making a cautious and respectful approach to Job. In verses 3 and 4 he reviews Job's past experience as one who has instructed and strengthened people in need. In verses 5-6 Eliphaz observes that, in spite of Job's helping others, he is impatient when calamity comes to him. If Job is to have hope and confidence in God, he should be able to rely on his trust in God and his own integrity. Verses 7-11 form the conclusion. Eliphaz prods Job to acknowledge that the innocent and upright are not cut off by God. On the contrary, according to Eliphaz's experience, it is the wicked who are punished (verses 8-9), no matter how powerful they may be (verses 10-11).

In the second part of chapter 4, Eliphaz seeks to justify his wisdom through a revelation he has experienced (verses 12-16). What he describes is a ghostly visit in which a voice asks if any man can be as righteous as God. The answer comes that even angels are not trustworthy in God's eyes, and the consequence is that a man is even less so (verses 17-19). Man's plight is even worse, for men die and disappear without having attained wisdom (verses 20-21).

In chapter 5 Eliphaz continues to offer wise counsel to Job. His advice is based on traditional wisdom plus his own personal experience, and is given with the intention of restoring Job to his former self. In a complex sequence of ancient sayings (5.2-5), Eliphaz argues that the foolish person comes to a tragic end. Verse 6 explains negatively the grounds for this teaching, and verse 7 completes it by stating the argument positively. Starting with verse 8 Eliphaz counsels Job to seek God, and verses 9-16 form a list of the great things God does which should provide reasonable assurance for seeking him. In the third and final section of the chapter (verses 17-27), Eliphaz offers Job assurance and restoration, and closes with a strong affirmation that the advice of Eliphaz has been investigated and found to be true. Job is advised, therefore, to accept it for his own good.

Division Heading

The Handbook heading shows that this is the first of the speeches to be given by Eliphaz. He will speak again in the next two rounds of speeches. Translators may wish to reword this heading to say, for example, "Eliphaz gives the first argument," "Eliphaz is the first to argue with Job," or "Eliphaz makes the first speech." TEV has just *"Eliphaz,"* which replaces verse 1 of the text. TOB has "First poem of Eliphaz," and Habel has "The counsel of Eliphaz the friend."

3A-1. Job should have hope (4.1-6)

RSV	TEV
1 Then Eliphaz the Temanite answered:	*Eliphaz*
2 "If one ventures a word with you, will you be offended? Yet who can keep from speaking?	1-2 Job, will you be annoyed if I speak? I can't keep quiet any longer.
3 Behold, you have instructed many, and you have strengthened the weak hands.	3 You have taught many people and given strength to feeble hands.
4 Your words have upheld him who was stumbling, and you have made firm the feeble knees.	4 When someone stumbled, weak and tired, your words encouraged him to stand.
5 But now it has come to you, and you are impatient; it touches you, and you are dismayed.	5 Now it's your turn to be in trouble, and you are too stunned to face it.
6 Is not your fear of God your confidence, and the integrity of your ways your hope?	6 You worshiped God, and your life was blameless; and so you should have confidence and hope.

Subdivision Heading

The Handbook heading applies to verses 2-6 and may have to be restructured in some languages to say, for example, "Eliphaz tells Job to have confidence in God" or "You should trust in God." Some translations have a single heading for chapters 4 and 5. For instance, NJB has "Confidence in God," and FRCL has "The mediation of Eliphaz: Happy is the man whom God corrects." Some prefer one heading for verses 2-11: Habel has "Exploration of Job's situation," Rowley has "Introduction and theory of retribution," and GECL has "The first friend: Follow your own advice."

4.1   RSV   TEV

Then Eliphaz the Temanite an-   *Eliphaz*
swered:

Then Eliphaz the Temanite answered: in Hebrew this formula is "then answered (name of speaker) and said." It is in prose form and its function is to mark the introduction of each new or next speaker. **Answered** does not mean literally that the speaker replied to a question that has been asked. In fact the new speaker may open a new line of thought that has little or nothing to do with what the previous speaker has said. Therefore the word **answered** may be inappropriate in this context. NEB has "Then Eliphaz the Temanite began: . . . ," FRCL "Then Eliphaz of Teman spoke up (*prit alors la parole*) and said to Job . . . ." NJB says "Eliphaz of Teman spoke next. He said: . . . ." TEV and others reduce this formula to nothing more than speaker identification in italics, "*Eliphaz*." Translators must consider carefully the most natural manner to signal the change of speaker and to introduce each following speaker. In some languages the use of speaker identification in the margin will be unfamiliar, and in others it may be more customary to identify the speaker by origin than by name. In some languages it may be better to place the speaker identification at the end or to repeat it at the end by saying, for example, "This is what Eliphaz from the city of Teman said when he spoke to Job," or in direct address, "I am Eliphaz, and those are the words I spoke to Job." See 2.11 for suggestions on the transliteration of proper nouns.

4.2   RSV   TEV

"If one ventures a word with you,   Job, will you be annoyed if I
    will you be offended?   speak?
Yet who can keep from speak-   I can't keep quiet any longer.
    ing?

Eliphaz speaks first, perhaps because he is the oldest of the three. His question reflects respect and caution in the context of Middle Eastern courtesy. Job has been cursing his origin, and now the poet must initiate a line of discussion in sharp contrast to the content of chapter 3. Parallelism occurs as line a **ventures a word** is matched in line b by **keep from speaking.** Like RSV most translations understand line a to be a condition. However, FRCL translates it as a negative statement followed by a reason, "I don't dare speak to you because you are so depressed," giving alternative interpretations in a footnote. The impersonal **one** must often be shifted to "I" as in TEV and others. NJB prefers an editorial "we," which would represent all three friends. **Ventures a word** translates the Hebrew "shall one try a word" and reveals Eliphaz's hesitation to open up the dialogue with the suffering Job. Many languages have idiomatic expressions for **venture a word**; for example, "Will you become sad if I say two words to you?" or ". . . if my mouth speaks a word for your ears?" Eliphaz and Job would both know a number of proverbial sayings which would apply to their situation. For example, Proverbs 10.19b "he who restrains his lips is prudent." On the other hand, "A word fitly spoken is like apples of gold in a setting of silver" (Prov 25.11).

Will you be offended translates the Hebrew "would you be weary." Some understand the verb to mean "being impatient or unable to endure." The New Jewish Version (NJV) has "Will it be too much?" and NEB "Will you lose patience?" The question is similar to the English "Would you mind if I say something now?" or "I hope you won't mind if I say something now." In some languages this thought may be expressed idiomatically: "Will it make you turn away?" or "Will it make you throw my words behind you?"

Who can keep from speaking? translates a verb meaning to refrain or hold back. It is used in Jeremiah 20.9, where the prophet describes holding God's message in himself as a burning fire in his heart. Eliphaz's compassion for Job, as well as the revelation he will describe, make it impossible for him to keep quiet. The rhetorical question may need to be shifted to a negative statement; for example, "I can't keep from speaking" or "I am not able to remain silent."

4.3   RSV   TEV

Behold, you have instructed many, and you have strengthened the weak hands.	You have taught many people and given strength to feeble hands.

The two lines of verse 3 are parallel, with the common verb **instructed** in line a, and the figurative **strengthened the weak hands** matching it and stepping up the poetic intensity in line b. Some scholars suggest changing the Hebrew verb translated **instructed** to a similar one meaning "bind or support." This is done to make the verb in line a closer in meaning to **strengthened** in line b. However, such a procedure is based on the assumption that parallel lines should say the same thing in different words, and fails to take into consideration that parallel lines more commonly are in a dynamic relation to each other. The second line goes beyond the first in poetic effect. For **Behold** see 1.12.

Eliphaz proposes to speak to Job by reminding him that once Job was the one who gave advice and confidence to discouraged people, as Job himself says in 29.21-25. **Instructed** translates a verb meaning "corrective teaching or disciplinary instruction," as found in Proverbs 19.18, "discipline your son." The object of **instructed** in RSV is **many**, which means "many people," as in TEV. NEB translates "those who faltered," to make it closer in meaning to the next line.

Strengthened the weak hands is a metaphor meaning that Job helped people who were helpless. The expression is used in Isaiah 35.3 and is found in Hebrews 12.12, where the parallel expression is "weak hands and feeble knees." Translators must deal with the two lines as a unit in which line b carries the thought of Job's helping other people, not only by teaching them but also by helping them in their weakened condition. In English the two lines may be rendered, for example, "Listen, Job, you have not only taught many people, you have also come to their rescue when they were helpless" or ". . . you have even made weak people strong again."

4.4   RSV   TEV

> Your words have upheld him who
>   was stumbling,
> and you have made firm the
>   feeble knees.

> When someone stumbled, weak
>   and tired,
> your words encouraged him to
>   stand.

This verse has a pair of parallel lines which pick up the thought of "weak hands" from 3b and intensify it through the figures of **stumbling** and **feeble knees**. **Stumbling** is used in Proverbs 4.12b to refer to falling from the path of wisdom. Both **stumbling** and **weak knees** are used metaphorically for failure in faithfulness to live in the right way. The words of instruction uphold the stumbler and firm up the feeble knees. TEV rearranges the poetic parallelism into two clauses related as background condition to consequence: "When someone . . . your words encouraged him to stand." Both metaphors are kept and put into line a. A further figure "stand" is introduced into line b. In some languages the figures will have to be replaced by nonfigures; for example, "By teaching people who needed help, you kept them living in the right way, and you were able to give them strength to go on."

4.5   RSV   TEV

> But now it has come to you, and
>   you are impatient;
> it touches you, and you are
>   dismayed.

> Now it's your turn to be in trou-
>   ble,
> and you are too stunned to
>   face it.

This verse has two parallel lines in which **comes to you** in line a is matched in line b by the more specific **touches you**. Eliphaz's opening words can be seen as both compassionate and critical. **But now** marks a turn in his speech. It emphasizes the contrast between Job's former role and his present desperate situation. **It comes** translates an impersonal form, "it comes or happens." In line b **it touches** is the same verbal form meaning "it strikes," and in Hebrew the matching in the two lines is more apparent than in RSV. **It** refers to the same discouragement Job has seen in those whom he helped in verses 3 and 4. Eliphaz generalizes because the writer has not allowed him to know what has happened in the first two chapters, namely, that Job is being put to a test. It may be necessary to make clear what **it** refers to; for example, "trouble comes to you," or "suffering happens to you," or "when you suffer." In some languages "trouble" and "suffering" will serve as agents of the action; for example, "trouble takes hold of you."

Impatient translates a Hebrew term which Dhorme renders "dejected." Other translations use "discouraged, falter, lose patience," and TEV "in trouble." The parallel verb in the second line is more forceful, as seen in both RSV **dismayed** and TEV "stunned." Mft. represents effectively the poetic movement: "But now that your own turn has come, you droop; it touches you close, and you collapse."

4.6   RSV   TEV

Is not your fear of God your
    confidence,
and the integrity of your ways
    your hope?

You worshiped God, and your life
    was blameless;
and so you should have confi-
    dence and hope.

This verse has two parallel lines which RSV takes to be rhetorical questions expressing emphatic denial. Eliphaz appears to admit that Job's faith in God and his personal integrity should give him confidence and hope that God will deal justly with him. **Fear of God** translates the Hebrew "your fear" and can mean here the same as religion or belief. "Fear of Yahweh" in Proverbs 1.7,29; 2.5; 9.10 is the religious source and substance of wisdom. Mft renders this line "Let your religion reassure you," and NEB "Is your religion no comfort to you?" **Confidence** and **hope** are the qualities which Job should have as the result of his religious life and integrity, as expressed in TEV. **Integrity** is the noun form of the Hebrew word translated "blameless" in 1.1. **Confidence** is often rendered idiomatically; for example, "resting the heart on someone" or "putting the innermost on someone." **Hope** refers here to possessing a hidden source of strength and purpose in the face of disaster. It is used with the same meaning in 5.16 "The poor have hope," and in 14.7 "There is hope for a tree, if it is cut down, that it will sprout again."

Although the two lines are parallel, there is little increase of poetic effect in the second line. Translators who are able to keep the poetic form of parallel lines will want to try to maintain the synonyms **confidence** and **hope**. Others may restructure the lines as two statements followed by a question, as in SPCL "You who are a faithful servant of God, a man of good conduct, how is it that you don't have full confidence?" TEV keeps all the elements of the parallelism but redistributes them so that "worshiped God" and "life was blameless" are the basis for the joint consequences of "confidence and hope."

The Hebrew noun for **hope** is an important word in the Book of Job. It usually carries the meaning of the verb "to hope," from which the noun is derived, and therefore it refers to the attitude of expecting or trusting that some good will occur. Sometimes it refers to that which is hoped for, or to the reason for hoping, as when Yahweh is called "the hope of Israel." In the Book of Job much emphasis is given to hope that is left unfulfilled. The noun happens to sound like the Hebrew word for "thread," and so in at least two places there seems to be a wordplay on these terms, as will be noted in the discussion.

3A-2. The righteous do not suffer from God's anger (4.7-11)
          RSV   TEV

7   "Think now, who that was innocent ever
        perished?
       Or where were the upright cut off?

8   As I have seen, those who plow iniquity
       and sow trouble reap the same.

9   . By the breath of God they perish,
       and by the blast of his anger they are
       consumed.

7   Think back now. Name a single case
       where a righteous man met with disas-
       ter.

8   I have seen people plow fields of evil
       and plant wickedness like seed;
       now they harvest wickedness and evil.

9   Like a storm, God destroys them in his
       anger.

10	The roar of the lion, the voice of the fierce lion, the teeth of the young lions, are broken.	10	The wicked roar and growl like lions, but God silences them and breaks their teeth.
11	The strong lion perishes for lack of prey, and the whelps of the lioness are scattered.	11	Like lions with nothing to kill and eat, they die, and all their children are scattered.

Subdivision Heading

Translators using the subdivision heading for verses 7-11 may have to adjust the wording to say, for example, "If you are good, Job, God will not make you suffer," "God does not punish good people," or "God destroys only wicked people." TOB has "Sowers of misery."

4.7   RSV   TEV

> "Think now, who that was innocent ever perished? Or where were the upright cut off?

> Think back now. Name a single case where a righteous man met with disaster.

Eliphaz now shifts away from Job's person to generalize, reminding him that, according to their shared store of wisdom, the suffering of the righteous is for discipline and not for destruction. This verse sums up the main argument of Job's three friends. The two lines are parallel, with a step-up of feeling brought about in line b, where the figurative **cut off** matches the more general **perish** in line a. Psalm 37 represents the view that the innocent do not perish, and 37.9 says "For the wicked shall be cut off; but those who wait for the LORD shall possess the land." The same thought is expressed in Proverbs 12.21, "No ill befalls the righteous, but the wicked are filled with trouble."

Think now is literally "recall or remember now." **Innocent** in line a and **upright** in line b refer to the same people, not to two different groups. The same combination is found in 2 Samuel 14.9 with the meaning of "blameless." Such persons are called **innocent** because they are innocent of doing evil and so are "righteous, good, just, upright." In other contexts **innocent** refers to people who are helpless in that they have no way to provide for themselves (see Psa 10.8). For the translation of **upright** see comments on 1.1.

If the translator is translating Job as prose, TEV offers a model in which **innocent** and **upright** are reduced to "a righteous man," and **perish** and **cut off** are condensed to "meet with disaster." On the other hand, if the parallel lines are to be kept, we may translate, for example, "Think about it, Job, did a just person ever meet his doom, or was a good person ever actually destroyed?" In languages in which active verbs will be required, we may say, for example, "Did God ever bring an innocent person to his death, or did God ever snatch away the life of a good person?" Mft attempts to represent the poetic movement: "What guiltless man has ever perished? When have the just ever been swept away?"

4.8-9   RSV   TEV

8   As I have seen, those who plow   8   I have seen people plow fields of
        iniquity   evil
     and sow trouble reap the   and plant wickedness like seed;
        same.   now they harvest wickedness
9   By the breath of God they perish,   and evil.
     and by the blast of his anger   9   Like a storm, God destroys them
        they are consumed.   in his anger.

Eliphaz now calls upon his personal experience regarding the teaching of retribution, or punishment. In the two-line parallelism, line a is the process and line b the consequence. Plowing and sowing are the process, and harvesting the consequence. These agricultural images provide the link between wickedness and destruction. For similar usage see also Proverbs 22.8; Hosea 8.7; 10.13; and Galatians 6.7-8.

In many languages the metaphor **plow iniquity** will have to be expressed as a simile; for example, "Like a farmer prepares the ground for planting, some people are busy sinning." **Sow trouble** may have to be restructured to say "and spread trouble like a farmer spreads seeds." The final clause may then be "The sin and trouble they make is like a harvest," "They get back sin and trouble like a harvest," or "For a harvest they gather sin and trouble." FRCL says "Plowing injustice or sowing misery leads to a harvest of injustice and misery." SPCL has reduced the figures to two and says "Experience has taught me that those who sow crime and evil reap what they sow."

In verse 9 Eliphaz qualifies his statement made in verse 8 by adding that it is God's anger that destroys the wicked. The two lines are parallel with dramatic heightening in line b, where the image of snorting anger matches the more prosaic **breath of God** in line a. The same image is seen in Exodus 15.8; 2 Samuel 22.16; Hosea 13.15. **Blast of his anger** translates "the wind of his anger," which is the same term for "wind" or "spirit" used in Genesis 1.2. **Perish** in line a is matched by the more dramatic **consumed** in line b. The picture may be that of the hot wind blowing from the desert, and TEV takes it in that sense: "Like a storm, God destroys them . . . ." The noun phrase **breath of God** may have to be expressed as a clause; for example, "God breathes on them and they die." In a poetic rendering which attempts to reflect the form of the Hebrew, we may translate, for example, "God breathes on them and they die; he blows on them and they disappear completely."

4.10-11   RSV   TEV

10   The roar of the lion, the voice of   10   The wicked roar and growl like
        the fierce lion,   lions,
     the teeth of the young lions,   but God silences them and
        are broken.   breaks their teeth.
11   The strong lion perishes for lack   11   Like lions with nothing to kill
        of prey,   and eat,

and the whelps of the lioness	they die, and all their children
are scattered.	are scattered.

Verses 10 and 11 may be taken together, since they employ the same image, and they are related by 10 being the reason and 11 the result. It is the picture of the fate of a family of lions, apparently understood as an illustration of what happens to the wicked. Some scholars regard these verses as later additions and question their relevance to the context. However, their style is that of the author of Job, and the lion is commonly used as an image of enemies and the wicked, as in Psalm 17.12; 22.13,21; Proverbs 28.15.

The lion was a real source of danger to shepherds in that part of the world. Job could easily understand from these words that he is the evil person in the guise of the lion, but Eliphaz does not assert this. The intent of the two verses is simply to say the lion is dead, and therefore the young have no food; so they are forced to scatter.

Verse 10 has only one verb, **broken**, and three subjects: **roar, voice,** and **teeth**. Literally the verb can apply only to teeth. But in poetry words are not always used in the regular manner. Here the verb **broken** applies to the roar and the growling, in the sense that the noise of them has "broken off, faded away, disappeared, become silent," and the young hunting lions can't kill their prey because their teeth have been broken. That is to say, they have lost their power.

In verse 11 the mature lion dies because there is no **prey**, and the small offspring are forced to scatter in search of something to eat. **Prey** refers to animals that lions capture, kill, and eat. Verse 10 provides the reason for the more straightforward consequence in verse 11. The poetic effect of placing the process (or cause) before the result in Hebrew poetry is always to give emphasis and focus to the latter.

TEV has made the implication clear in line a with "The wicked roar and growl like lions." A simile has been used in both verses, and "the wicked" and "their children" are associated with the lions and their offspring. In verse 10 TEV has introduced God as the one who "silences them and breaks their teeth." The metaphor of breaking the teeth now applies to the wicked. This may not be appropriate in some languages. It is not necessary to use several synonyms for lion or even various attributives, as seen in FRCL "God silences the growling of lions, and he breaks the teeth of these ferocious beasts. Without any prey, the wild animals perish, while their little ones are scattered far." In areas where people are not familiar with the lion, it may be necessary to use a different animal of prey. An illustration may be helpful; see *Fauna and Flora of the Bible*, pages 50-51.

3A-3. Eliphaz reports a vision: no one is righteous in God's eyes (4.12-21)

RSV	TEV

12	"Now a word was brought to me stealthily,	12	Once a message came quietly,
	my ear received the whisper of it.		so quietly I could hardly hear it.
		13	Like a nightmare it disturbed my sleep.
13	Amid thoughts from visions of the night,	14	I trembled and shuddered;
	when deep sleep falls on men,		my whole body shook with fear.
14	dread came upon me, and trembling,	15	A light breeze touched my face,

	which made all my bones shake.		and my skin crawled with fright.
15	A spirit glided past my face;	16	I could see something standing there;
	the hair of my flesh stood up.		I stared, but couldn't tell what it was.
16	It stood still,		Then I heard a voice out of the silence:
	but I could not discern its appearance.	17	"Can anyone be righteous in the sight of God
	A form was before my eyes;		or be pure before his Creator?
	there was silence, then I heard a voice:	18	God does not trust his heavenly servants;
17	'Can mortal man be righteous before God?		he finds fault even with his angels.
	Can a man be pure before his Maker?	19	Do you think he will trust a creature of clay,
18	Even in his servants he puts no trust,		a thing of dust that can be crushed like a moth?
	and his angels he charges with error;	20	A man may be alive in the morning,
19	how much more those who dwell in houses of clay,		but die unnoticed before evening comes.
	whose foundation is in the dust,	21	All that he has is taken away;
	who are crushed before the moth.		he dies, still lacking wisdom."
20	Between morning and evening they are destroyed;		
	they perish for ever without any regarding it.		
21	If their tent-cord is plucked up within them,		
	do they not die, and that without wisdom?'		

Subdivision Heading

Since verse 12 marks a clear shift of topic, it is advisable to place a subdivision heading at this point. If translators find the Handbook heading too long, they may adjust it to say, for example, "What Eliphaz saw and heard in a dream," "Eliphaz has a vision," or "A question is put to Eliphaz in the night." TOB has "Nocturnal vision," and Habel "A teaching revealed to Eliphaz."

4.12-13	RSV		TEV
12	"Now a word was brought to me stealthily, my ear received the whisper of it.	12	Once a message came quietly, so quietly I could hardly hear it.
13	Amid thoughts from visions of the night, when deep sleep falls on men,	13	Like a nightmare it disturbed my sleep.

Eliphaz prepares to deliver to Job the "word" mentioned in 4.2. He begins by describing the communication which came to him. His account is very different from the way traditional prophets of Israel spoke of their revelations. It is more akin to the experience of Abraham in Genesis 15.12, in which a "dread and great darkness fell on him." Verse 12 has two parallel lines which form the process, and verse 13 has another pair of related lines which form the circumstances of verse 12.

A word was brought to me stealthily: a word, although singular in Hebrew, refers to the whole message Eliphaz received and is correctly translated "message" by TEV, FRCL, SPCL, and others. **Brought to me stealthily** translates Hebrew "was stolen to me," a metaphor used also in 2 Samuel 19.3 to underline the quiet, furtive nature of this ghostly visit. Line b is chiastic in relation to line a, that is, it has the parallel elements in reverse order, since line a ends with "was stolen," and line b begins with "received" (for the definition of "chiasmus" see the Glossary). In line b the poet shifts to more concrete language, **ear** and **whisper**, to dramatize the emotion. TEV has preserved something of this with "so quietly . . . ." Some languages will prefer to keep the noun **ear** rather than shift to the verb "hear."

In some languages it will be necessary to shift to an active construction in line a and say, for example, "Someone quietly spoke a message to me" or "I heard a message someone quietly spoke to me." The two lines may be rendered, for example, "Someone stole in quietly and spoke a message to me; I could hardly hear what was said."

The parallel lines of verse 13 serve as the circumstances for verse 12 and for verse 14. The matching terms in verse 13 are **thoughts from visions** in line a and **deep sleep** in line b. **Thoughts** translates a Hebrew form of the same noun used in Psalm 94.19 ("cares"), where the idea is that of troubled or disturbed thoughts, and in the context of night sleep this would be a "bad dream" or, as in TEV, "nightmare." **Deep sleep** translates a Hebrew noun which in Genesis 2.21 God imposes on Adam in order to remove one of his ribs. In Isaiah 29.10 the LORD pours out on the leaders of Jerusalem a "spirit of deep sleep," which is here a stupor, and in Job 33.15-16 it is a terrifying dream. TEV in a very plain form reduces the two poetic lines to one. FRCL keeps both lines, saying ". . . during a dream at night, when the thoughts are confusing, when stupor pounces on human beings."

In some languages it will be necessary to shift from noun phrases to clauses and say, for example, "While I was having a nightmare (a confusing dream) one night, at that time when people fall into a deep sleep" or "One night I had a nightmare; it happened when I fell into sleep that was like fainting."

4.14	RSV	TEV
	dread came upon me, and trem- bling, which made all my bones shake.	I trembled and shuddered; my whole body shook with fear.

Dread came upon me and trembling: **dread** and **trembling** describe the mental and physical reaction of Eliphaz to his nightmarish revelation. The parallelism shows a change from the mental emotion of being terrorized to the picturable trembling of the entire body. **Dread** translates a Hebrew term used also in Genesis 15.12, when Abraham went into a deep sleep. It is the same term used in Job 3.25. Job there experienced it only as terror, "the thing that I fear." For Eliphaz it is associated with revelation. **Come upon me** in Hebrew means to confront or to meet up with. It is used in that sense in Numbers 23.3, where Balaam tells Balak "Perhaps the LORD will come to meet me."

Which made all my bones shake: the implication is that, as a result of the trembling, Eliphaz's entire body shook with fear. **Bones** is a typical poetic usage of a part of the body for the whole body. **Shake** translates a form of the Hebrew word translated **dread** in line a. The meaning of the full expression is "My whole body shook with fear," as in TEV. In some languages physical and emotional states act grammatically as agents, so that we can say, for example, "Terror and trembling took hold of me" or "Fear and trembling caught me by the throat."

4.15	RSV	TEV
	A spirit glided past my face; the hair of my flesh stood up.	A light breeze touched my face, and my skin crawled with fright.

Eliphaz continues his narrative use of parallel lines. Verse 15 presents in line a the cause and line b the effect.

A spirit glided past my face: **A spirit** translates Hebrew *ruach,* which does not likely refer to the spirit of God but to an eerie wind or breeze. In many languages the use of spirit without qualification will imply a bad spirit. If it were a disembodied spirit, it would be the only such usage in the Old Testament. However, in Eliphaz's speech there may be a play on words here. The Hebrew verb translated **glided past** is used in Isaiah 21.1 to describe the movement of whirlwinds in the desert. Although the source of the wind is not disclosed, its purpose was clearly not evil in intent. Therefore something like breeze or breath is to be preferred; for example, "A breath of air brushed against my face" or "I felt air blow against my face."

The hair of my flesh stood up is a natural reaction to a frightening experience. The word translated **hair** is the subject of various interpretations. As used here the term means a single hair, which, of course, in poetic discourse can be understood as a part standing for the whole. Some scholars suggest changing the Hebrew word for **hair** to get "horror" or "tempest." Habel believes the parallelism of the text favors a reading that gives "whirlwind" and so says "A whirlwind made my flesh shiver." However, it seems best to take line a as the cause of line b, and all other translations agree with RSV and TEV. In some languages the hair does not "stand up," but the "skin gets cold" or "bumps form on the skin."

4.16	RSV	TEV
	It stood still, but I could not discern its appearance. A form was before my eyes; there was silence, then I heard a voice:	I could see something standing there; I stared, but couldn't tell what it was. Then I heard a voice out of the silence:

Eliphaz describes the presence of the mysterious form as being silent and hidden. Verse 16 has two sets of two lines in which only the first lines of each pair are parallel in meaning.

It stood still translates Hebrew "It stood." The subject **It** is a prefix on the Hebrew verb that requires a masculine antecedent, which may eliminate "spirit" from the previous verse, since this noun is normally feminine. It is no doubt the intention of the author to leave the reader wondering, because a visible visit from God would, in Old Testament terms, result in the death of the viewer. For this reason Eliphaz is kept from recognizing the form it took. Translators will not always be able to use ambiguity to get around this point. TEV renders the indefinite subject as "something," "I could see something standing there," and does this by incorporating line a of the second pair of lines into line a of the first pair.

I could not discern its appearance: the word translated **appearance** and also the word **form** in the next line are used only of God's appearance to Moses in Numbers 12.8. **A form was before my eyes**: the poet is using repetition to create suspense before coming to the message that was spoken. The **form** is something visible, but it represents something other than itself. The Hebrew word is *tamuna,* and Israelites were forbidden to make *tamuna* of their deity in Exodus 20.4. Moses alone was allowed to see the *tamuna* of God. In some languages it may be necessary to reverse the two lines to say, for example, "I could see a shape but could not tell what it was" or "I could make out a form but could not see clearly to know what it was."

There was silence: the silence before the voice spoke is used in Psalm 107.29 as the silence before a storm breaks. The idea is that a hush precedes and at the same time prepares for the frightening words that will be spoken. In translation it may be necessary to say, for example, "everything became silent" or "there was no noise anywhere."

Then I heard a voice: Eliphaz's description of his vision began in verse 12 with something audible, **A word was brought to me**. Now the vision will close with the hearing of the actual words. So the poetic effect has been moved from the abstract "word" in verse 12 to the concrete **voice** in 16. The voice finally comes as the climax of a series of images: nightmare, terror, stupor, a breeze against the face, vague shapes, and then at last a speaking voice. Eliphaz makes no claim as to whose voice it is. Translators who are translating this Hebrew poetry as prose will do well to follow the model of TEV. Those who are translating it as poetry should try to avoid creating more ambiguity than the author did. A compromise solution may be something like this: "Something was standing there, but I could not tell what it was. I could see a shape; then, everything was hushed and I heard a voice ask: . . . ."

4.17	RSV	TEV

'Can mortal man be righteous
    before[d] God?
Can a man be pure before[d] his
    Maker?

"Can anyone be righteous in the
    sight of[g] God
or be pure before[h] his Cre-
    ator?

[d] Or *more than*

[g] righteous in the sight of; *or* more righteous than.
[h] be pure before; *or* be more pure than.

Verses 17-21 contain the essence of the traditional argument, which is to say that people are mortal and should accept their mortality. In a sense the message, coming after all the suspense, is less than might have been expected. It charges Job with no sin and yet offers him no relief. Since in Hebrew there are no quotation marks, it is not possible to be certain that the voice carries on through verse 21. Most translations assume it does.

Can mortal man be righteous before God? Mortal man renders the Hebrew *'enosh,* a possible play on words, since it means "weak" as well as "man." **Be righteous** translates the Hebrew *tsadaq,* and in the context of Eliphaz's speech, it is understood by many interpreters to take on the sense of being morally and spiritually right, just, sinless, or perfect. Job himself uses this term in a more legal sense, having the idea of "innocent" or "guiltless." The word translated "blameless" in 1.8 by RSV is a different Hebrew word. FRCL translates "Can a man claim to be blameless . . . ?" SPCL "Can a man be considered just before God?" NJB "Can a mortal seem upright to God?" The marginal alternative given in RSV and TEV is taken up by NEB, "Can mortal man be more righteous than God?" "More righteous than God" and **righteous before God** are alternative interpretations of the same Hebrew text, which arise from the ambiguity in the Hebrew preposition *min.* It is unusual for it to have the meaning "before" (RSV) or "in the sight of," but it is the word generally used when comparing, as in Genesis 38.26 "She is more righteous than I am," where the same Hebrew verb meaning "to be in the right" is used as here in Job. TEV "in the sight of God" translates the meaning intended by RSV. Both RSV and TEV provide the alternative rendering in a footnote. **Mortal man** may be rendered as TEV "anyone," "a person," or "an ordinary person." If the poetic intensification in line b is to be kept, then the step-up will be from "anyone" in line a to something like "greatest person" in line b.

Can a man be pure before his Maker? This line is parallel to the first. Here the word translated **a man** is *geber.* It focuses on male gender in contrast to female and carries the sense of power, force, strength. Job describes himself as a *geber* whose way has been blocked by God (3.23). Later God challenges Job to gird up his loins and act like a true *geber* (38.3; 40.7). In its poetic order line a is general, "Can an ordinary man," and line b is raised by being specific, "Can even a real man." The Hebrew word translated **pure** is often used of people, but only in Habakkuk 1.13 of God, "Thou who art of purer eyes than to behold evil." In Leviticus 15.13; 22.4 the word for **pure** refers to being ritually clean in worship of God. In the present context, however, it refers to moral perfection in relation to the creator. The rhetorical question may be shifted to an emphatic denial; for example, "No ordinary person can be more righteous than God, and not even the bravest person can be more pure than the creator."

4.18	RSV	TEV
	Even in his servants he puts no trust, and his angels he charges with error;	God does not trust his heavenly servants; he finds fault even with his angels.

Verse 18 makes the argument of verse 17 still stronger by not allowing even angels to be without error. The two lines are again parallel, the first being negative and the second positive. **Even** translates the Hebrew particle often rendered in RSV as "behold." In the present context the meaning is "if" or "even." **Servants** refers not to earthly servants but to those like the angels and perhaps the beings who serve God in heaven. TEV, SPCL, and some others have described the servants as "heavenly." **Angels** is the regular term used in the Old Testament for these heavenly creatures. In Psalm 34.7 "The angel of the LORD encamps around those who fear him." **Angels** are God's heavenly messengers known for caring for, protecting, and guarding his people in Exodus 23.20 and Joshua 5.13-15. As is common in parallel lines, **angels** in line b is a more specific term than **servants** used in line a. In **charges with error** the Hebrew word translated **error** is found only here in the Old Testament. Some scholars change the vowels of this word to get "folly," the thing Job refused to charge God with in 1.21 (see discussion there on "wrong"). Others suggest changes which give "deception" or even "praise." Most translations are similar to RSV, or TEV "find fault." RSV begins verse 18 as a concessive clause, **Even in his servants**, which signals a degree of surprise in what follows. TEV does the same but places "even" in line b. In some languages it may be necessary to make the two lines of verse 18 into two "if" clauses; for example, "If God does not trust . . ." and "if God finds fault . . . ."

4.19   RSV   TEV

how much more those who dwell   Do you think he will trust a crea-
   in houses of clay,   ture of clay,
whose foundation is in the   a thing of dust that can be
   dust,   crushed like a moth?
who are crushed before the
   moth.

This verse begins with a Hebrew particle which can have the sense of RSV's **how much more**, in which verse 18 is the base for the comparison. That is, God will trust human beings less and find even more fault in them than in angels. The verse has three lines which are all parallel. They all emphasize the frailty of human life.

Who dwell in houses of clay: human beings were formed from the dust of the earth in Genesis 2.7; 3.19; also Job 10.9; 33.6; 1 Corinthians 15.47. The figure of a house or tent representing the physical body is common in the Old Testament. **Whose foundation is the dust**: the solidity of a building depends upon the firmness of its foundation, and man's "house of clay," which is his body, rests on nothing more substantial than dust (Psalm 103.14).

If the figure **dwell in houses of clay** is likely to be understood as referring to people who live in mud-walled houses, it will be necessary to shift to a different figure or to say, for example, "a human being," or "an ordinary person," or "ordinary people whose bodies God created from clay." If the figure of the dwelling is not kept in line a, it will not be possible to keep **foundation of dust** in line b. In that case we may sometimes say, for example, "who are nothing more than dust" or "who are weak as dust."

The final line of this verse shifts the metaphor to another frail creature, the moth, which is used to emphasize the vulnerability of human beings. **Who are crushed before the moth**: this expression is to be taken to mean "who are crushed quicker than a person can crush a moth." It fits the context to understand this line to mean "They (human beings) are crushed like a moth," and this is the way most translators understand it. So man is crushed by God as easily as a person crushes a fragile moth. **Crushed before the moth** must often be restructured to say, for example, "who are as fragile as a moth" or "who die as easily as a person crushes a moth." For pictures and a description of moths, see *Fauna and Flora of the Bible,* pages 55 and 56.

4.20

RSV	TEV

Between morning and evening
   they are destroyed;
they perish for ever without
   any regarding it.
	A man may be alive in the morn-
	   ing,
	but die unnoticed before eve-
	   ning comes.

Between morning and evening: in Psalm 90.5-6 the passing of a person's life is compared to the fresh green grass of the morning, which fades and withers by evening. There is no attempt to give a precise time in the expression **between morning and evening**. The meaning is that an individual is alive and well in the morning and before the day is over he is dead. TEV is an accurate model in this verse.

They are destroyed: they refers not to the moth of verse 19c but to those who live in houses of clay and whose foundation is dust. **Destroyed** translates a Hebrew verb meaning to "pound or pulverize." It is used of the warriors beaten down in Jeremiah 46.5 and of images being smashed to pieces in Micah 1.7. **They perish forever** is the consequence of the previous line.

Without any regarding it: in order for this expression to mean "without anyone noticing it," it is necessary to add the Hebrew word for heart as a complement of the verb, which is "place, lay," thus "lay it in the heart." The idiom is used in that way in Isaiah 57.1, which RSV translates "No one lays it to heart." This solution has not been widely accepted, and other suggestions have been made to correct the Hebrew text. However, as recognized by Gordis, the force of the parallelism of thought between 20a and 21a, and between 20b and 21b, makes it possible to understand **without any regarding it** to refer to those who perish as being unaware of their dying. Thus, for example, "they die and know nothing of it" or "they die and do not know it."

4.21

RSV	TEV

If their tent-cord is plucked up
   within them,
do they not die, and that with-
   out wisdom?'
	All that he has is taken away;
	   he dies, still lacking wisdom."

If their tent-cord is plucked up: the Hebrew noun translated **tent-cord** by RSV is understood by Dhorme to mean "what remains," and it has that meaning in Exodus 23.11; Psalm 17.14; Isaiah 44.19. The noun therefore refers to excess wealth being taken away; but this does not fit the context. Consequently Dhorme transfers 21a to 5.5b (so also NEB and REB). This has the advantage of making 19c parallel to 20a, and verse 20b parallel to 21b. However, the Hebrew word translated **tent-cord** can mean "abundance," and TEV therefore translates "all that he has." **Plucked up within them** translates a verb used for pulling up a tent-peg, or striking camp. However, it is necessary to take the full expression as an idiom referring to the loss of a person's wealth to others in death. In languages which do not use a passive construction, it will be necessary to shift to an active verb; for example, "Others will take the wealth he owns."

And that without wisdom may be taken to mean that the one who died did so without having gained wisdom, or without understanding why he was dying. Most translations agree with the first alternative. **Wisdom** in Proverbs 4 is a guide and goal of life, and in Psalm 111.10 "The fear of the LORD is the beginning of wisdom." In wisdom literature wisdom is an attitude and a discipline, and to die without attaining it is a disaster. Wisdom should not be translated as knowledge or information or intelligence but, if necessary, as "knowing the way of the LORD" or "wisdom that comes from God." Accordingly we may suggest "they die without knowing God's way" or "when they finally die they still do not understand the way of God."

3A-4. Eliphaz says Job alone is to blame (5.1-7)

RSV	TEV
1 "Call now; is there any one who will answer you? To which of the holy ones will you turn?	1 Call out, Job. See if anyone answers. Is there any angel to whom you can turn?
2 Surely vexation kills the fool, and jealousy slays the simple.	2 To worry yourself to death with resentment would be a foolish, senseless thing to do.
3 I have seen the fool taking root, but suddenly I cursed his dwelling.	3 I have seen fools who looked secure, but I called down a sudden curse on their homes.
4 His sons are far from safety, they are crushed in the gate, and there is no one to deliver them.	4 Their sons can never find safety; no one stands up to defend them in court.
5 His harvest the hungry eat, and he takes it even out of thorns; and the thirsty pant after his wealth.	5 Hungry people will eat the fool's crops— even the grain growing among thorns— and thirsty people will envy his wealth.
6 For affliction does not come from the dust, nor does trouble sprout from the ground;	6 Evil does not grow in the soil, nor does trouble grow out of the ground.
7 but man is born to trouble as the sparks fly upward.	7 No indeed! Man brings trouble on himself, as surely as sparks fly up from a fire.

For an account of the content in chapter 5, see under **3A. Eliphaz's First Speech (4.1–5.27)**, page 89.

Subdivision Heading

Chapter 5 continues without repeating the formula of 4.1, "Then Eliphaz the Temanite answered." Accordingly some translations have no heading at this point. Some say "Eliphaz continues." TOB uses a subdivision heading for 5.1-7, "The origin of evil," and Habel has "A teaching verified by Eliphaz." Translators wishing to use the Handbook heading may find it necessary to say, for example, "Eliphaz says Job brings his troubles on himself" or "Eliphaz accuses Job of causing his own suffering."

5.1	RSV	TEV

"Call now; is there any one who will answer you? To which of the holy ones will you turn?	Call out, Job. See if anyone answers. Is there any angel to whom you can turn?

In Dhorme's view verse 1 does not seem to relate to what goes before or after. Therefore he shifts verse 1 to immediately before 5.8. Many translations, however, keep verse 1 in its traditional position. **Call now**: Job is challenged to make a futile appeal by shouting out. This may be understood as a rebuke for Job's calling upon the forces of destruction to remove his origins in 3.3-9. That it is a rebuke is not certain, however, because Eliphaz has until this point been sympathetic with Job. **Is there anyone who will answer you?** The very general term **anyone** is matched in line b by **holy ones**. **Call now** may sometimes be rendered "shout to someone," "call someone's name," or "make a shout." **Answer** is not to reply to a question but simply to respond to Job's call, that is, "help you" or "listen to you."

To which of the holy ones . . . ? In 33.23 angels are referred to as mediators, and Eliphaz seems to suppose that Job might think of appealing to them for help. **Holy ones** translates Hebrew *qedoshim,* the same beings that were referred to in 4.18 as "servants" and "angels." Eliphaz has argued there that these creatures are not fully trustworthy. In the present verse, translations are divided between those that follow RSV **holy ones** and those that follow TEV "angels." Translators should make certain that a translation of **holy ones** does not mean "religious teachers or leaders," as it does in some languages. For further discussion see 4.18. **Will you turn**: the meaning is look to, appeal to for help, guidance, deliverance. In some languages this expression may be rendered "which angel will you ask to come and help you?" or, as direct address, "to which angel will you say 'Help me!'?"

5.2	RSV	TEV

Surely vexation kills the fool, and jealousy slays the simple.	To worry yourself to death with resentment would be a foolish, senseless thing to do.

Surely vexation kills the fool: the two lines of verse 2 are parallel; however, there is little if any intensification in the second line. **Vexation** translates a Hebrew term used in Proverbs 12.16; 14.17 meaning passion, anger, resentment or "short temper." **Kills** in line <u>a</u> means to murder and is more specific than the general term translated **slays** in line <u>b</u>. This is an example of parallelism in which the more specific term occurs in the first line and the general term in the second, and so is an exception to the general pattern. **Fool** translates a noun used in Proverbs 12.15 of a person who is brash and impulsive: "the way of a fool is right in his own eyes." **Fool** is contrasted in line <u>b</u> of that proverb by "a wise man listens to advice." Normally in the Old Testament the **fool** is not a senseless person but rather one who stubbornly rejects the highest wisdom, the fear of God (Prov 1.7). However, in the present context the term refers to an impulsive, brash person who is wise in his own eyes (Prov 12.15), and means a senseless, foolish, silly person. Idiomatic expressions are used in some languages to describe such people; for example, "gourd-headed people," "hollow heads," or "mind-gone-away people." In some languages it will not be possible to employ anger or resentment as the agent of killing, and in those cases it will be necessary to say, for example, "When a foolish person gives himself to anger, it kills him" or "When a foolish person is filled with anger . . . ." In some languages it will also be necessary to say against whom the anger is directed. Mft and FRCL make God the object of the anger, so FRCL says "The fool is angry with God, and that is what kills him."

Jealousy slays the simple: **jealousy** translates a noun found also in Proverbs 14.29-30, where the meaning is that of jealous anger. NEB calls it "childish resentment," and FRCL says "the silly person loses his temper." **The simple**: the verb related to this noun is used in 31.9,27, where the meaning focuses on being enticed by a woman and by nature. The idea is that **the simple** are people who are easily led astray, deceived. So Eliphaz uses this proverbial saying to make the point that anger and indignation destroy people. They reveal their stupidity by allowing themselves to be led astray.

5.3   RSV   TEV

I have seen the fool taking root,	I have seen fools who looked
but suddenly I cursed his	secure,
dwelling.	but I called down a sudden
	curse on their homes.

Eliphaz now calls upon his own experience to substantiate the proverb he has just cited. **I have seen the fool taking root**: for **fool** see 2a above. The picture is that of a tree putting down roots to provide nourishment for itself, and is used here to mean prosperity, solidity, security, well-being. The same verb is used in Isaiah 27.6, where "Jacob will take root," and in Psalm 80.9, where the vine brought from Egypt "took root and filled the land." Some commentators change the form of the verb to get "uprooted," and this is followed by NEB with no marginal note. In languages in which the figure of taking root is not applied to a person, it will be necessary to recast the expression to say, for example, "I have seen how prosperous fools can become" or "I have seen how well some fools live."

But suddenly I cursed his dwelling: RSV follows the Hebrew text, but the Septuagint and the Syriac version have "a curse fell." Some interpreters suggest changing the verb to get "it rots." However, a building does not suddenly rot. Others would change the verb to read "passes away," "is empty," or the passive "is cursed." Most translations agree with RSV and TEV. Dhorme recommends accepting the Hebrew as it stands. **Cursed** is the same as in 3.8. In Eliphaz's view the prosperity or security of the fool deserves to be cursed, and that is what Eliphaz does. **Suddenly** is used to say that Eliphaz was quickly, immediately moved to bring the well-being of the fool to an end, and may sometimes be rendered, for example, "I wasted no time in cursing his house" or "immediately I cursed his home." **Dwelling** refers to the house, home, or place where the fool lives. For **curse** see 1.5; 2.9; 3.1.

5.4   RSV   TEV

> His sons are far from safety,   Their sons can never find safety;
>   they are crushed in the gate,   no one stands up to defend
>   and there is no one to deliver   them in court.
>   them.

Eliphaz does not refer directly to Job's tragedy, yet the poetic language permits Job to interpret Eliphaz's words as alluding to the loss of all he owned (1.13-19). In verse 4 lines a and b are parallel. Line a is general in **far from safety**, while line b is more specific, naming the place where the lack of safety will be felt. Some interpreters take verses 4-5 to be curse petitions; for example, NJV says "May his children be far from success, may they be oppressed in the gate."

His sons are far from safety: when the father is destroyed, the offspring are in danger. Line a may sometimes be rendered, for example, "Their sons are always in danger" or "Their sons are never safe." **They are crushed in the gate**: justice was to be guaranteed at the entrance to the town, where social, economic, and legal matters were handled (Deut 21.19-21; Ruth 4.1-11; Prov 22.22). Proverbs 22.22 says "Do not rob the poor because he is poor, or crush the afflicted at the gate," where the same verb "crush" is used as in verse 4. The meaning is to exploit, take advantage of, take away their rights. Line b **crushed in the gate** may be translated in a legal sense; for example, "they lose their case in court," or as FRCL says, "condemned without recourse before the court."

And there is no one to deliver them: this statement is used frequently as a set phrase to underline the finality of an act of punishment, destruction, or disaster. See Psalm 7.2; 50.22; Isaiah 5.29. TEV has condensed lines b and c into one. If this third line is not condensed into line b, it may sometimes be rendered, for example, "there is no one to save them" or "there is no one to defend them."

5.5   RSV   TEV

> His harvest the hungry eat,   Hungry people will eat the fool's
>   and he takes it even out of   crops—
>   thorns;[e]   even the grain growing among
> and the thirsty[f] pant after his[g]   thorns[i]—
>   wealth.   and thirsty people will envy his

e Heb obscure
f Aquila Symmachus Syr Vg: Heb *snare*
g Heb *their*

wealth.

i Probable text even . . . thorns; *Hebrew unclear.*

His harvest the hungry eat: in Hebrew this line begins with the pronoun "whose," which refers back to the fool in verse 3. TEV has "Hungry people will eat the fool's crops." The meaning is that the fool (and his sons in verse 4) is so helpless that the poor and hungry can help themselves to his crops. If verse 4 has been translated as a petition, verse 5 should be also, as NJV "May the hungry devour his harvest." **Harvest** must be expressed in some languages as, for example, "the food he grows" or "the plants he has hoed."

The next two lines are difficult to interpret, and numerous changes in the text have been suggested. **And he takes it even out of thorns**: the Hebrew says literally "and to from thorns he takes it." The word translated **thorns** is found only here and in Proverbs 22.5. Some interpreters simply delete the line, feeling it is too unclear to bother with, but such a decision should be avoided. Others have proposed changes in the text that permit "and their sheaf the poor take it," or "all their substance he takes," or "a strong man snatches it from baskets." The latter refers to baskets of grain being taken to the threshing floor, which is the rendering followed in part by NEB, "The stronger man seizes it from the panniers," meaning large baskets. Dhorme changes one consonant in the Hebrew word **thorns** and gets "and carry it away to hiding places." Still others change thorns to "teeth," with the meaning "from their mouths." NJB has "God snatches it from their mouths." In spite of the variety of interpretations, NIV, TOB, FRCL, GECL, and SPCL translate similarly to RSV and TEV. The thought is "The hungry gather and eat the crops grown by the fool, even that part that grows among thorns" or ". . . even that part that is protected by thorns."

And the thirsty pant after his wealth renders what is literally "and inhales the snare their wealth." The word "snare" is found only here and in 18.9. In RSV and TEV **thirsty** translates the ancient versions. (See RSV and TEV footnotes.) This same text is followed by many other modern translations, although HOTTP finds "snare" the more likely text. Most modern translations use some form of greed, envy, or thirst. NJV takes verse 5b to be a continuation of the curse petition and says "May the thirsty swallow their wealth," with a note saying the Hebrew is uncertain. Many languages express consuming, destruction, and spending with the verbs swallow or eat. Translators must make certain that the verb is used naturally with the subject. If the "thirsty" do not eat, it will be better to say, for example, "greedy people eat his wealth," or as a curse, "may greedy people eat, take away, use up his wealth."

5.6-7	RSV	TEV
6	For affliction does not come from the dust, nor does trouble sprout from the ground;	6 Evil does not grow in the soil, nor does trouble grow out of the ground.
7	but man is born to trouble as the sparks fly upward.	7 No indeed! Man brings trouble on himself, as surely as sparks fly up from

a fire.[j]

[j] sparks fly up from a fire; *or* birds fly up
to the sky.

Having cited his wise sayings, Eliphaz now formulates the principle he draws
from them. In his view misfortune does not just spring out of the ground. However,
as he continues into verse 7, he seems to contradict himself by implying that
misfortune is the result of having been born.

Affliction does not come from the dust: affliction translates Hebrew *'awen*.
In 4.8 this term and *'amal* meaning "trouble" are in parallel, where the former was
rendered by RSV as "iniquity": "plow iniquity and sow trouble." **Affliction** is better
rendered "evil," as in TEV and others. This negative thought prepares for the positive
one that follows in 5.7. The two words translated **dust** and **ground** are matched in
lines a and b. In Hebrew **dust** means not only the fine powder called "dust" in
English, but the ground in general. It is used in the most general sense of ground in
8.19b. In line b of this verse the word for **ground** is *'adamah,* as found in 14.8, which
represents a shift to a more literary-level word and a resultant step-up of poetic
effect. The heightening of poetic effect may be illustrated in English by rendering
these lines with something like "Evil is not something that comes from the ground,
and even less do troubles grow out of the soil." If the poetic expression of evil
growing in the ground is not possible, the translator should find another poetic way
to phrase this, or to say it in prose fashion; for example, "evil is not something that
just happens," or "people are not evil just because they happen to touch the
ground," or as a simile, "evil does not grow out of the ground like a plant."

Nor does trouble sprout from the ground: this line is parallel to the previous
line. In languages in which **trouble** must be associated with people, it may be
necessary to employ a simile; for example, "and the trouble people have does not
spring up like a weed from the ground."

But man is born to trouble: man translates the Hebrew *'adam,* which relates
to the word for ground, *'adamah,* in verse 6b. The word translated **is born** may be
read with different vowels to form the word for "begets," which would mean that
"man is the source of his own troubles," and so TEV "Man brings troubles on
himself." Modern translations are divided between those which follow TEV and those
similar to RSV. HOTTP prefers "man is born." In many languages **is born to trouble**
will have to be expressed by saying, for example, "people will always have troubles
from the time they are born," "trouble will always bother people from their birth,"
or "people are certain to have misery." If the translator follows TEV, he may say, for
example, "people are the cause of their own unhappiness," as does also SPCL.

As the sparks fly upward: there are two main interpretations of this line.
According to RSV and TEV the comparison is made to the sparks flying upward from
a fire. NEB, BJ, and some others speak of birds or eagles soaring. **Sparks** translates
Hebrew "sons of *reshef.*" *Reshef,* according to Dhorme, was the name of the
Phoenician god of lightning. The bird associated with lightning was the eagle, and
according to this interpretation, "sons of *reshef*" means "sons of lightning," which is
taken to be eagles. **Fly upward** translates a verb phrase which means literally "raise
their flight" and is taken by some interpreters to mean to "fly high" or "soar aloft,"
which is descriptive of eagles and other large birds, but not of sparks. Nevertheless

many modern translations prefer to follow the rendering of RSV and TEV. Some provide an alternative rendering. No matter which image the translator follows, the meaning is clear, that "people create their own troubles (or are bound to have trouble) just as surely as sparks fly upward from a fire" or ". . . just as surely as eagles soar in the sky."

3A-5. Eliphaz advises Job to take his case to God (5.8-16)

RSV	TEV
8 "As for me, I would seek God, and to God would I commit my cause;	8 If I were you, I would turn to God and present my case to him.
9 who does great things and unsearchable, marvelous things without number:	9 We cannot understand the great things he does, and to his miracles there is no end.
10 he gives rain upon the earth and sends waters upon the fields;	10 He sends rain on the land and he waters the fields.
11 he sets on high those who are lowly, and those who mourn are lifted to safety.	11 Yes, it is God who raises the humble and gives joy to all who mourn.
12 He frustrates the devices of the crafty, so that their hands achieve no success.	12-13 He upsets the plans of cunning men, and traps wise men in their own schemes, so that nothing they do succeeds;
13 He takes the wise in their own craftiness; and the schemes of the wily are brought to a quick end.	14 even at noon they grope in darkness.
14 They meet with darkness in the daytime, and grope at noonday as in the night.	15 But God saves the poor from death; he saves the needy from oppression.
15 But he saves the fatherless from their mouth, the needy from the hand of the mighty.	16 He gives hope to the poor and silences the wicked.
16 So the poor have hope, and injustice shuts her mouth.	

Subdivision Heading

In verses 8-16 Eliphaz offers Job a message of assurance. Translators wishing to place a heading before this subdivision may follow the model of the Handbook, or adapt it to say, for example, "Eliphaz gives Job advice," "Eliphaz tells Job what he should do," or "Eliphaz offers Job some hope." Habel has "Eliphaz's affirmation of hope," Rowley "Eliphaz counsels Job," and TOB "Call to God."

5.8 RSV	TEV
"As for me, I would seek God, and to God would I commit my cause;	If I were you, I would turn to God and present my case to him.

Eliphaz begins by saying what he would do if he were in Job's situation. **As for me, I would seek God**: in verse 1 Eliphaz warned Job against appealing to angels. Now he advises him to trust God. This verse opens with a word that introduces a contrast with what precedes. See also 1.11 and 2.5. **Seek** translates a word that means to address or make an appeal to. It is used in Genesis 25.22 of Rebekah inquiring of the LORD, and in 1 Samuel 9.9 with the same sense.

And to God I would commit my cause: **God** in this line is *'Elohim*. **Cause** renders a Hebrew word which here has the meaning of cause, complaint, or (legal) case. **Commit my cause** means to put a person's complaint before a legal hearing. In some languages this expression may be rendered, for example, "I would put my words in God's hands" or "I would tell my complaint to God."

5.9   RSV   TEV

who does great things and un-
   searchable,
marvelous things without num-
   ber:
	We cannot understand the great
	   things he does,
	and to his miracles there is no
	   end.

Who does great things and unsearchable: this line is part of a praise to God built on the pattern of Psalm 145.3, "Great is the LORD, and greatly to be praised, and his greatness is unsearchable." As is customary, the praise opens with a participle, "Doing great things." **Unsearchable** translates what is literally "no investigation" and means "beyond understanding," "unfathomable," "deep." The structure of RSV is plainly awkward. TEV has introduced "We," which would not conflict with Eliphaz's point of view here. This line may be rendered as a reason; for example, "because God does great things that people do not understand."

Marvelous things without number: this line is parallel to the previous line, with little attempt to heighten the poetic effect. The content of these marvels is developed in verses 10-16. Some translators may be translating into prose or into languages where close repetition will not be acceptable; in that case they may wish to incorporate 9b into 9a as a single statement; for example, "God does many great and marvelous things which we do not understand" or "the great and wonderful things God does are many, and we do not understand them."

5.10   RSV   TEV

he gives rain upon the earth
   and sends waters upon the
   fields;
	He sends rain on the land
	   and he waters the fields.

He gives rain upon the earth: this line is parallel to the line that follows. The praise begins as in verse 9 with a participle, "Giving rain . . . ." In Hebrew the rain is given to "the face of the earth." Unlike the fertility gods who make it rain routinely, God's gift of rain is always viewed as a miracle. See also Psalm 104.10-13; Jeremiah 10.12-13. In Jeremiah 14.22 it is neither the idols nor the heavens which "give the rain" but God alone. **Earth** should be understood in the widest sense and not limited to the land of Israel.

And sends water upon the fields: the matching expression is again in Hebrew "upon the face of the fields." In characteristic fashion the poet moves line b to the more specific "fields" or "countryside."

5.11   RSV   TEV

he sets on high those who are
    lowly,
and those who mourn are
    lifted to safety.

Yes, it is God who raises the
    humble
and gives joy to all who
    mourn.

He sets on high those who are lowly: following God's action in nature, there follows now his action on the human level. The sense of this verse can be compared to 1 Samuel 2.8, "He raises up the poor from the dust; he lifts the needy from the ash heap." **Those who are lowly** translates a plural noun derived from a verb meaning to be down, or to be low and therefore "humble." God sets these people "on high." In some languages **those who are lowly** is rendered, for example, "people who have no position," "people whose necks are bent down," or "people who are looked down on." The poet makes a clear contrast in his use of **high** and **lowly**. However, the contrast cannot be retained with the proper meanings in many languages, particularly where the humble are not associated with the position "low." We may, however, say, for example, "God gives strength to the humble" or "God enables the weak to stand up."

And those who mourn: the word translated **mourn** means "blackened ones" and depicts a person whose head and face have been dirtied with ashes in ritual mourning, as in Psalm 35.14; 38.6. The expression may have to be filled out to say, for example, "those who mourn for the dead." **Are lifted to safety** translates Hebrew "raise to safety" and is expressed in Psalm 12.5 as "I will place him in the safety for which he longs" (RSV). Interpreters understand the expression **lifted to safety** variously. NJV and NEB have "victory." Another group of translations including BJ, GECL have "prosperity, happiness," in line with TEV "gives joy." The translator has a considerable range of choice; for example, "God gives victory to those who mourn," "gives them happiness," "makes them joyful," or "makes them safe."

5.12-13   RSV   TEV

12 He frustrates the devices of the
        crafty,
    so that their hands achieve no
        success.
13 He takes the wise in their own
        craftiness;
    and the schemes of the wily
        are brought to a quick end.

12-13 He upsets the plans of cunning
        men,
    and traps wise men in their
        own schemes,
    so that nothing they do suc-
        ceeds;

Note that TEV has reduced verses 12 and 13 to a single three-line sentence.

He frustrates the devices of the crafty: the form of the Hebrew verb translated **frustrates** may be taken in the sense of "cause to break or crumble." When used with plans, thoughts, or designs, it means to cause them to fail, turn out badly, ruin them. TEV has "upsets the plans." **Devices** refers to mental activities such as plans, schemes, intentions. **Crafty** describes people who use cunning to reach their objectives, and is used in Genesis 3.1 of the serpent, who "was more subtle than any other wild creature" (RSV). Therefore "God ruins the plans thought up by cunning people" or "God causes the schemes of cunning people to fail."

So that their hands achieve no success: this line is the consequence of the previous line. **Hands** refers to the persons themselves. The Hebrew word translated **success** denotes foresight to plan ahead, and so the meaning is "They did not accomplish what they had planned." The reason is that God upset their plans.

Takes the wise in their own craftiness: see 1 Corinthians 3.19. **Takes** translates a Hebrew term which means to ensnare or catch in a trap. Other forms of the same verb are used in 36.8 as "caught in cords of affliction" (RSV). See also 38.30, "is frozen"; 41.17 (41.9 in Hebrew), "they clasp each other." The same picture is drawn in Psalm 7.16; Proverbs 26.27, where the wicked fall into their own pit. **The wise** refers not to people who have attained godly wisdom but rather to clever people who consider themselves wise. They are cunning, wily, crafty people. So "God catches crafty people in their own craftiness."

The schemes of the wily are brought to a quick end: here another word of similar meaning to plots, plans is used. **Wily** translates a word derived from the same root used in Proverbs 8.8, where the reference is to twisted or crooked words. It is used in Psalm 18.26 with reference to people who are crooked in their conduct. **Wily** may be rendered, for example, "people who deceive others," or idiomatically in some languages, "people with double tongues." In the expression **brought to a quick end**, God is the implied agent of the action, which is to cut short, stop, bring to an end the plots of such people. So "God cuts short the plots hatched up by crooked people."

5.14	RSV	TEV
	They meet with darkness in the daytime, and grope at noonday as in the night.	even at noon they grope in darkness.

They meet with darkness in the daytime: Eliphaz expands the picture to describe how those who seek advantage over others are brought down. Like the Syrians whom Elisha led to Samaria in broad daylight (2 Kings 6.18-23), they run into darkness. Line a in the Hebrew has the order "by day, by night," and line b reverses this order to "night, day." The two lines are parallel. Line a uses the common verb meaning to meet or encounter, while line b shifts to the more specific and striking **grope**, which means to feel about as if blind or in the dark. The same verb is used in Deuteronomy 28.29, "You shall grope at noonday, as the blind grope in the darkness." Job will return to this theme in 12.25. **Grope** in line b steps up the poetic intensity and gives greater coherence to the two-line parallelism. By reducing the two lines of verse 14 to one, TEV does not retain the poetic intensification and unity of the lines, which may be rendered in English "In daylight they run into darkness; in broad daylight they grope like blind men in the dark." This may also be translated, for example, "When it is light they are in the dark, and in broad daylight they stumble like blind persons in the dark."

5.15   RSV   TEV

> But he saves the fatherless from   But God saves the poor[k] from
>   their mouth,[h]   death;
> the needy from the hand of the   he saves the needy from op-
>   mighty.   pression.

[h] Cn: Heb uncertain   [k] *Probable text* poor; *Hebrew unclear.*

But he saves the fatherless from their mouth: the Hebrew reads "But he saves from the sword from their mouth" and lacks the words **the fatherless.** Many interpreters believe that an object of the verb **saves** is needed in line a to match **the needy** in line b. It may have been left implicit in the Hebrew in order to keep the number of words the same in the four poetic lines of verses 15-16. Therefore some modify the word "sword" to get **the fatherless.** Gordis understands the Hebrew to mean "from the sharp tongue," and that without any change. Numerous other suggestions have been made, but most of these differ as to deliverance being from the sword or from the mouth. HOTTP suggests "from a sword," "from their mouth," or "from their sharp mouth." This solution leaves unanswered the question who is delivered or saved in line a. Most modern translations name the object of the verb **save** (fatherless, poor, helpless, destitute, ruined), and NJB has "the bankrupt." Most have a note saying "Hebrew unclear." **From their mouth** is to be taken as referring to the tyrants who are pictured as wild animals devouring the poor, as in Proverbs 30.14, and this is matched in line b by **the mighty.** TEV has "saves the poor from death," where "death" means destruction at the hands of the powerful.

5.16   RSV   TEV

> So the poor have hope,   He gives hope to the poor and
>   and injustice shuts her mouth.   silences the wicked.

This verse summarizes Eliphaz's view of God's intervention on behalf of the poor, and in his view justice always wins in the end. **So the poor have hope: the poor** translates a word referring to the weak, similar in meaning to **the needy** in verse 15. See 4.6 for the word **hope,** also 14.7,19; 17.15; 19.10.

And injustice shuts her mouth: the same expression is found in Psalm 107.42. **Injustice** translates a noun which refers to evil or wicked conduct and is personified here as having a mouth, either to devour the poor or to boast. It is implied that God is the one who acts in both lines. In languages in which **injustice** cannot be personified, it may be necessary to express the thought as "and wicked people are stopped from doing evil things" or "God shuts the mouths of evil people."

3A-6. Eliphaz assures Job that God will restore him (5.17-27)

RSV	TEV

17 "Behold, happy is the man whom God reproves;
    therefore despise not the chastening of the Almighty.
	17 Happy is the person whom God corrects!
	    Do not resent it when he rebukes you.

18 For he wounds, but he binds up;
    he smites, but his hands heal.
	18 God bandages the wounds he makes;
	    his hand hurts you, and his hand heals.

19 He will deliver you from six troubles; in seven there shall no evil touch you.	19 Time after time he will save you from harm;

20 In famine he will redeem you from death,
    and in war from the power of the sword.
	20 when famine comes, he will keep you alive,
	    and in war protect you from death.

21 You shall be hid from the scourge of the tongue,
    and shall not fear destruction when it comes.
	21 God will rescue you from slander;
	    he will save you when destruction comes.

22 At destruction and famine you shall laugh, and shall not fear the beasts of the earth.	22 You will laugh at violence and hunger and not be afraid of wild animals.

23 For you shall be in league with the stones of the field,
    and the beasts of the field shall be at peace with you.
	23 The fields you plow will be free of rocks;
	    wild animals will never attack you.

24 You shall know that your tent is safe,
    and you shall inspect your fold and miss nothing.
	24 Then you will live at peace in your tent;
	    when you look at your sheep, you will find them safe.

25 You shall know also that your descendants shall be many, and your offspring as the grass of the earth.	25 You will have as many children as there are blades of grass in a pasture.
26 You shall come to your grave in ripe old age, as a shock of grain comes up to the threshing floor in its season.	26 Like wheat that ripens till harvest time, you will live to a ripe old age.
27 Lo, this we have searched out; it is true. Hear, and know it for your good."	27 Job, we have learned this by long study. It is true, so now accept it.

Starting with verse 17 Eliphaz opens a new topic, the assurance given to Job. Here he encourages Job to expect that God has a purpose and plan for his life. This purpose is interpreted by Eliphaz as being divine discipline which will eventually bring Job to full restoration of his former self.

Subdivision Heading

Translators may use the Handbook heading or adapt it by saying, for example, "Eliphaz tells Job that God will give him a new life," "A new life for Job," or "Job will live a happy and secure life." Habel has "Assurance of restitution," and TOB "Promise of renewal."

5.17   RSV   TEV

> "Behold, happy is the man whom   Happy is the person whom God
>   God reproves;   corrects!
>   therefore despise not the chas-   Do not resent it when he re-
>   tening of the Almighty.   bukes you.

Eliphaz's point of departure is that God is disciplining Job, although this could hardly be Job's view of the matter. **Behold, happy is the man: Behold** translates the same particle found in 4.3, but here it functions as a connective, according to Dhorme, linking verse 17 to verse 16. Its meaning as a linking word would be "and so, therefore, because of that"; however, most translations do not treat it as a linking word. In fact most do not translate it. **Happy** translates the same Hebrew expression found in Psalm 1.1; 94.12. It is the term used in the Old Testament to describe a fortunate person. Here it means that the person whom God reproves is to be considered fortunate, deserving congratulations. In translation the use of a term implying luck or chance should be avoided. The word for **man** is Hebrew *'enosh* and not *'ish* as in Psalm 1.1. However, in the present context the word is general and refers to "anyone," and so TEV "Happy is the person." **God reproves** translates "*'Eloah* corrects (or, disciplines)." The word is used as a legal term in 13.3, where it has the meaning of making a charge against someone, "argue my case." Here it means to correct someone for misconduct, to reprimand, rebuke.

The verb in line a of verse 17, **reproves**, is in the third person singular, but the verb **despise** shifts to the second person imperative in line b. Such a shift is not natural in some languages. Therefore it will sometimes be necessary to shift line a to the second person; for example, "You are a fortunate person to have God correct you," or idiomatically, ". . . when God makes you walk a straight path." Alternatively we can translate both lines as third person, so that line b would be, for example, "Therefore such a person should not resent it when God rebukes him."

Despise not the chastening of the Almighty: despise is not to be taken in the sense of "to hate" but rather "reject, refuse, repel, turn down." **Chastening** translates a Hebrew term for disciplined teaching in wisdom, as seen in Proverbs 1.3; 23.12. In Proverbs 3.11-12 "The LORD reproves him whom he loves." The word is close in meaning to **reproves** in line a.

The Almighty translates Hebrew *Shaddai*, which appears here for the first time in Job but occurs thirty-nine times throughout the book. *Shaddai* is a name for God used mainly in Genesis and Exodus. Some interpreters suggest that the poet uses this name to give his poem the atmosphere of the patriarchal setting. The meaning of *Shaddai* is obscure, and some translations retain it as a proper name (NJB, BJ, Dhorme). Others like TEV translate it here as "God," but elsewhere TEV uses "Almighty God," and once "The Almighty." (See the section entitled "The names of God" in the introduction, "Translating the Book of Job," page 21.) Based on the traditional usage of **the Almighty,** translators may wish to adapt this to say something like "God who is very powerful," "God the great and mighty one," "The mighty God," "The most powerful God," "God who can do all things," or "The most powerful One." The two lines are parallel, with little if any step-up of intensification in the second line. "God corrects" in line a is matched by "*Shaddai* disciplines" in line b. The noun phrase **chastening of the Almighty** must often be expressed as a clause; for example, "The teaching (guidance, discipline) which God gives you," or "When God instructs and corrects you."

5.18   RSV   TEV

> For he wounds, but he binds up;   God bandages the wounds he
>   he smites, but his hands heal.   makes;
>   his hand hurts you, and his
>   hand heals.

Verses 18-23 give the reasons which justify accepting the correction which comes from God. **He wounds, he binds up**: the statement opens with the Hebrew particle *ki,* which indicates that what follows is additional and not by way of conclusion or contrast. The two lines of this verse are parallel in meaning as well as in structure. Job's friends are painfully aware of Job's suffering, as seen in 2.13. Deuteronomy 32.39 says "I kill and I make alive; I wound and I heal." Since God is the one who, in Eliphaz's view, has wounded Job, God will also bandage his wounds.

He smites, but his hands heal: smites is to be understood as poetic strengthening of the term translated **wounds** in line a. It means here to hurt, harm, inflict injury. **His hands** is a poetic way of saying "he" or God, seen as the one who reaches out to bind up the wounds and bring healing. In some languages it will be necessary to express the object of God's wounding and bandaging; for example, "God wounds a person, but he also bandages up his wounds." It may also be necessary to do the same in line b; for example, "He injures a person, but he also heals him."

5.19   RSV   TEV

> He will deliver you from six trou-   Time after time he will save you
>   bles;   from harm;
>   in seven there shall no evil
>   touch you.

Deliver you from six troubles: this verse represents a common biblical pattern called "number parallelism." As is seen in nearly all poetic expansion, line b tends to follow a step-up pattern. Number parallelism is no exception. In 40.5 the step-up from line a to line b is from one to two: "I have spoken once . . . twice but I will proceed no further." In 33.29 the step-up is from two to three, in Amos 1.3 from three to four. In Proverbs 6.16 the movement upward is from six to seven, as in the present verse: "There are six things which the LORD hates, and seven which are an abomination to him." These numbers are not to be taken as each having a precise meaning in itself, but as conveying an emphasis of the idea from line a to line b. Therefore it is futile to expect exactly seven troubles in the verses following Proverbs 6.16. Generally translators must avoid using numbers to translate this kind of emphasis, unless the language itself calls for the use of numbers.

In seven there shall no evil touch you: TEV has reduced line a and line b to one and translated the number parallelism by "time after time." However, other

modern versions retain the two lines, some expressing the number parallelism as in
TEV. GECL says "As often as you run into misfortune, he will help you and protect
you from injury." **Evil** in this context may be translated harm, injury, misfortune,
misery.

5.20   RSV   TEV

In famine he will redeem you from death,	when famine comes, he will keep you alive,
and in war from the power of the sword.	and in war protect you from death.

In famine he will redeem you from death: Eliphaz now begins to list some
of the ways in which God intervenes on man's behalf. **Redeem** translates the word
used, for example, in Exodus 13.13-15, in which it has the sense of regaining
possession of something or someone by payment and is translated "buy back" by TEV.
In our context **redeem you from death** suggests that death personified has
possession of the person. This is a poetic context and so is acceptable. However, the
expression "buy back" may not be meaningful in the receptor language and may not
even have the possibility of becoming so. The thought here is that even in famine
God will not allow his own to die. In some languages it will be necessary to recast
line a to say, for example, "When people suffer from famine, God will not let you
die," or as in TEV ". . . he will keep you alive."

And in war from the power of the sword: the verb **redeem** from line a is
understood as the verb in line b. **Power of the sword** is literally "hands of the
sword," which occurs in parallel with **famine** also in Jeremiah 18.21. The expression
power of the sword (see also Psalm 63.10) is less common than the literal "mouth
of the sword," which is said to devour, as in Exodus 17.13; Numbers 21.24. Eliphaz
follows the set order in verses 20-21 of famine, war, pestilence. In line b it will often
be necessary to introduce a parallel verb; for example, "and when there is war, he
will keep you from being killed" or ". . . he will protect your life." When translating
Job as poetry, the translator should attempt to retain or substitute equivalent images.

5.21   RSV   TEV

You shall be hid from the scourge of the tongue,	God will rescue you from slander;
and shall not fear destruction when it comes.	he will save you when destruction comes.

Be hid from the scourge of the tongue: **be hid from** means to be saved,
spared, protected, sheltered. **Scourge of the tongue** means malicious gossip or
slander. In this metaphor the tongue is made to appear like a whip or scourge that
inflicts painful punishment. In a similar vein Psalm 31.20 says "Thou holdest them
safe under thy shelter from the strife of tongues" (RSV). TEV renders that verse "you
hide them from the insults of their enemies." RSV uses the passive **shall be hid,**

which must be shifted to an active verb in many languages; for example, "God will protect (shelter, defend, help, hide) you." If the figure of being protected from gossip or slander is not natural, the translator may be able to say, for example, "God will protect you from people who speak bad words about you" or ". . . from people who tell lies about you."

And shall not fear destruction when it comes: TEV has made "will save you" in line b more parallel to "will rescue you" in line a than the text justifies. As RSV shows, line b is a consequence of line a, and most translations use some form of **shall not fear. Destruction** translates a noun meaning violence, devastation, ruin, misfortune. Contrary to the normal arrangement of poetic parallel lines, **destruction** is the general term and occurs in the second line, where we would expect the specific or figurative phrase. Note, however, its position in verse 22. There is no indication of the exact nature of the destruction. It sums up all the misfortunes in verses 20-21. In some languages it is not possible to "fear destruction," and so the expression must be recast to say, for example, "You will not be afraid when violent things happen" or ". . . when disaster takes place," or better, ". . . when these bad things happen to people."

5.22	RSV	TEV
	At destruction and famine you shall laugh, and shall not fear the beasts of the earth.	You will laugh at violence and hunger and not be afraid of wild animals.

At destruction and famine you shall laugh: verse 22 forms a link between verses 21 and 23. The Hebrew word for **destruction** is repeated from verse 21, but the word for **famine** is Aramaic, a different word than is used in verse 20. There is no real change in meaning. Some interpreters would drop verse 22, believing it serves no purpose. However, Dhorme points out that verse 23 explains verse 22. Also 23a gives the reason for 22a, while 23b explains 22b. **Laugh** translates a verb which here suggests scorn, scoff, or deride. It is also used in 39.7, where it is translated "scorns" by RSV. In some languages, to laugh at something means only to show puzzlement or embarrassment. Since that is not the idea here, the expression must often be adjusted to say, for example, "You will scorn violence and famine," "You will scoff at . . . ," or sometimes idiomatically, "You will say that violence and famine are only small things."

Beasts of the earth: these animals are wild animals in contrast to domestic animals, and the same as referred to in verse 23b. Wild animals are sometimes called "bush animals," "animals that eat in the forest," or "animals that people hunt."

5.23	RSV	TEV
	For you shall be in league with the stones of the field,	The fields you plow will be free of rocks;

and the beasts of the field shall be at peace with you.	wild animals will never attack you.

In league with the stones of the field: this line has been the subject of much speculation. Only a few opinions need be mentioned. Some understand it to mean that the stones in the field will not become numerous and make cultivation difficult. Others take it to mean that property boundaries marked by stones will not be violated by enemies. Some make a change in the word **stones** to get "lords." This would then refer to spirits which inhabit a field. Still others change **stones of the field** to get "sons of the field," which would mean something like "beasts of the field," and so be parallel with the next line. All of these interpretations are represented in modern translations. RSV and some others leave the meaning unclear. TEV, SPCL, Mft, NEB, FRCL, GECL, and others, while not agreeing, do give some sense to the expression. Both **stones** and **beasts** are normally things that make a farmer's work difficult and dangerous; but in these lines Eliphaz speaks of a peaceful relation existing between them and Job. The translator is advised to follow the meaning suggested by TEV, or one of the other translations which avoid the literal rendering of RSV. FRCL says "You will be protected from damage to your fields, from rocks which are thrown there . . . ."

Beasts of the field shall be at peace with you: as in verse 22b the reference is not to domestic animals but to wild animals. The prophetic vision of Isaiah 11 is summarized here. In Ezekiel 14.21 four scourges are listed: "sword, famine, evil beasts, and pestilence." **Be at peace with you** translates a form of Hebrew *shalom* with the meaning of making peace with someone. Translators may find it is not appropriate in their language to give the impression that animals make some kind of peace treaty with people or vice versa. It will be better to use some expression as in TEV, or SPCL "and the wild animals will be your friends." GECL says "and every wild animal leaves you there in peace," implying as TEV states negatively, "will never attack you." NEB has replaced **beasts** with "weeds" and offers no explanation for this.

5.24	RSV	TEV

You shall know that your tent is safe, and you shall inspect your fold and miss nothing.	Then you will live at peace in your tent; when you look at your sheep, you will find them safe.

You shall know translates the opening word, which has a prefix to mark a transition between the list of disasters in verse 20-23 and the concluding part of the chapter. The whole expression is translated by TEV as "Then." Its fuller meaning is "You will have the satisfaction of knowing," or as Mft says, "You may be sure." **Tent is safe**: **tent** translates a noun which may be used in the general sense of a dwelling, or by extension a household, that is, those who live in the house. NEB renders it "household." The English word "tent" is more specific than the context suggests, although it is used by both RSV and TEV. **Safe** translates the Hebrew *shalom*, which refers to "good health, prosperity, blessing, peace, safety, and well being." RSV **tent**

is safe implies in English that the structure of the tent is sound, that it is not likely to collapse. This is not the idea. TEV "live in peace" is far better. SPCL says "You will have prosperity."

Inspect your fold: the word translated **fold** can refer to the place where domestic animals are kept or to the animals themselves. In the present context the phrase means "to look at your sheep," as in TEV. **Fold** may be understood as a parallel term for **tent** in line <u>a</u>, and FRCL takes it in this way: "You will experience peace in all your house; when you inspect it, nothing will be missing." NEB is similar, with "you will look around your home . . . ." In language areas where sheep are unknown, it is sometimes possible to use a generic term such as animals, provided they refer to domestic and not wild animals. We may also say, for example, "the animals you keep," or "the animals you own."

5.25　　　　RSV　　　　　　　　　　　　TEV

> You shall know also that your　　　　You will have as many children
> 　descendants shall be many,　　　　　as there are blades of grass in
> and your offspring as the grass　　　　a pasture.
> 　of the earth.

Your descendants shall be many: verse 25 begins by repeating the assurance given in verse 24, **You shall know**. Most translations do not repeat this mechanically. **Your descendants** translates "your seed" and is parallel to **your offspring** in the next line. In Genesis 3.15 "seed" refers to human offspring, and it has that meaning here.

Offspring as the grass of the earth: offspring translates a word used in Isaiah 34.1; 42.5 referring to the natural produce of the land. It is used in Job 31.8 in the same sense. Eliphaz may be foreseeing Job's future or may have forgotten that Job's children are all dead. **Grass of the earth:** this simile is used to give a picture of numerous offspring (see TEV "blades of grass"). The parallelism between **many** in line <u>a</u> and **grass** serves to step up the poetic intensity through this figurative expression. For those who are translating Job as poetry, the two lines may be rendered, for example, "You will also have many children; they will be like grass growing everywhere."

5.26　　　　RSV　　　　　　　　　　　　TEV

> You shall come to your grave in　　　Like wheat that ripens till har-
> 　ripe old age,　　　　　　　　　　vest time,
> as a shock of grain comes up　　　　you will live to a ripe old age.
> 　to the threshing floor in its
> 　season.

In this verse line <u>b</u> is a statement and line <u>b</u> a simile which illustrates it. The parallelism is in the time of the two events as well as in the events themselves. **Come to your grave** in line <u>a</u> means to approach death, be near death, ready to die. **Ripe**

old age translates a word whose meaning is uncertain. It occurs also in 30.2, where it is translated by RSV as "vigor." The idea is that Job will die when he is ready, just as a sheaf of grain can only be threshed when it has been made ready (ripe, mature) by the growing cycle. In line b **a shock of grain** refers to a stack of sheaves, probably wheat.

Comes up to the threshing floor: the word translated **comes up** suggests a picture of harvest time, when heaps or stacks of sheaves appear to rise up over the fields. Some translators take this to refer to the elevated threshing floor, where the wind would blow the chaff away (RSV, NEB). TEV compares the ripe grain to life rather than to death: "You will live to a ripe old age." NJV implies death by saying "as shocks of grain are taken away in their season . . . ," and Mft "like a sheaf borne home in harvest." TEV has placed the simile in line a, and in some languages the same will be necessary. In languages where threshing is unknown, it may be necessary to say, for instance, "in the place where the grain is cleaned" or "the place for separating the grain." If such an expression does not result in a clear picture, it may be better to follow TEV and others which speak of wheat, or "grain that ripens until harvest," or "until ready to be gathered up." If grains are largely unknown, a local plant which is gathered when it ripens may be able to be used.

5.27	RSV	TEV
	Lo, this we have searched out; it is true. Hear, and know it for your good."[i]	Job, we have learned this by long study. It is true, so now accept it.

[i] Heb *for yourself*

Speaking finally on behalf of the three friends, Eliphaz brings his speech to a close. He approached Job apologetically in 4.2, and now he ends, calling on Job to learn the truth as Eliphaz perceives it. **Lo** translates a phrase meaning literally "Look at this" and is rendered by TEV as "Job," addressed by his name.

We have searched out: Eliphaz refers to himself and his colleagues, and in the context this excludes Job. **Searched out** translates a verb used again in 28.3. It means "give careful thought to something, study, observe." **It is true** translates Hebrew "so it is," a self-assuring affirmation. The first half of line a is the reason, and the second half is the conclusion. In some languages it will be necessary to make clear what the referent of **it** is in the expression **it is true**. This may be rendered, for example, "What we have learned is true," "All the things we have discovered are true," or "Everything I have told you is true."

Hear, and know it for your good: in place of **hear** as a command, some interpreters prefer "we have heard" (NEB, Mft). Most, however, like RSV and TEV, have an imperative such as "listen, be informed, pay attention." **Good**, as the RSV footnote says, is literally "for yourself," and many translations keep it in that form; for example, SPCL says, "Listen to this and prove it to yourself." GECL says "You should take note of it for yourself, because it is so." Both of these are good translation models.

3B. JOB REPLIES (6.1–7.21)

In chapters 6 and 7 Job replies to Eliphaz. The topic of chapter 6 is Job's accusation that his three visitors are not true friends. Job leads up to this theme indirectly, as the reader by now would expect him to do. He begins in verses 2-3 with a cry of anguish, asking that his grief be put on a scale for his friends to see how great it is. It would weigh more than the sands of the sea. In verse 4 Job places the responsibility for his suffering on God, and then uses a series of similes based on foods to justify his complaint against his maker (verses 5-7). In verses 8-9 Job returns to his pleas to be "cut off." If this were possible, Job would be delighted. He would not be in anguish because he knows that God is holy and Job has not opposed him. In verses 11-13 Job acknowledges his human frailty, and finally, before he unleashes his accusation against his friends, he admits there is nowhere he can turn for help.

Verses 14-27 make up the main body of Job's charges against his friends. He begins indirectly by speaking in the third person. In verse 14 Job claims that lack of kindness or loyalty to a friend comes from losing respect for *Shaddai*. Just as Job used similes to state his complaint against God in 5-7, he prepares the next step of his charge against his friends, whom he sarcastically calls "my brethren," by comparing them to a treacherous dry stream bed that leads a caravan of travelers out into the desert and to their deaths (15-20). He concludes this comparison in verse 21, addressing them in the second person plural, applying it directly to them. He accuses them of being afraid, even though he has never asked material help from them (21b-23).

With verse 24 Job's tone changes, but only momentarily. If he has made a mistake, he is willing to be instructed, but he finds no truth in what he has heard. He accuses his friends of assuming that his own complaints are only idle talk, wind. In verse 27 Job hands his visitors one last stinging observation. He accuses them of being willing to throw dice to see who gets an orphan, the most helpless person in society, and to haggle like market vendors over the fate of a friend. All of this is to say that these visitors are more concerned with scoring points in debate than in practicing human compassion.

Job concludes with an appeal for them to be honest with him and stop their deceit (verses 28-30). He wants them to accept his true situation, which is that a righteous man is suffering, even if they have never believed such a thing could happen. He begs them to rethink their position because his vindication is at stake. Job's suffering gives him the insight which his friends lack.

As the translator reads chapter 6, it will become evident that certain patterns of theme and structure recur. In order to illustrate these patterns and to show where they occur, a display is given below.

Job's **complaint**	verse 2	against his troubles
The argument		
Illustration	3	like sand on scales
Reason	4	shot by God's arrows
Illustration	5-7	*rhetorical questions:* on animals, Job, and food

Job's **request**	8-9	that God crush him, cut him off
The argument		
Result	10a	would be happy
Reason	10b	never opposed God
	11-13	*rhetorical questions:* no strength or hope to go on
Job's **complaint**	14	against his friends
The argument		
Illustration	15-23	friends like dried up streams *rhetorical questions:* never asked for gifts, or asked for help
Job's **request**	24	teach me
The argument		
	25	friends are deceitful with words
Illustration	26	*rhetorical questions:* why do you argue with the wind?
Illustration	27	cast lots and bargain
Job's **request**	28-29	look at me, stop doing what you are doing
The argument		
	30	*rhetorical questions:* you think I am lying and ignorant

Division Heading

Many translations supply a division heading such as "Job replies," "Job replies to Eliphaz," or "Job's first reply." TEV has "Job," and RSV, which does not use headings, translates verse 1. FRCL has "Job's reply: He complains about his friends," GECL "Job: Despair expresses itself," NJB "Only the sufferer knows his own grief."

3B-1. Job is weighed down by grief (6.1-7)

RSV	TEV

	RSV		TEV
	1 Then Job answered:	*Job*	
2	"O that my vexation were weighed, and all my calamity laid in the balances!	1-2	If my troubles and griefs were weighed on scales,
3	For then it would be heavier than the sand of the sea; therefore my words have been rash.	3	they would weigh more than the sands of the sea, so my wild words should not surprise you.
4	For the arrows of the Almighty are in me; my spirit drinks their poison; the terrors of God are arrayed against	4	Almighty God has shot me with arrows, and their poison spreads through my body. God has lined up his terrors against me.

	me.	5	A donkey is content when eating grass,
5	Does the wild ass bray when he has grass,		and a cow is quiet when eating hay.
	or the ox low over his fodder?	6	But who can eat flat, unsalted food?
6	Can that which is tasteless be eaten with-		What taste is there in the white of an
	out salt,		egg?
	or is there any taste in the slime of the	7	I have no appetite for food like that,
	purslane?		and everything I eat makes me sick.
7	My appetite refuses to touch them;		
	they are as food that is loathsome to		
	me.		

Subdivision Heading

For the content of verses 1-7 Habel has "Explanation of current plight," and TOB says "Arrows from the Almighty." The Handbook heading may be adjusted to say, for example, "Job complains of his sufferings," "Job complains that God has made him suffer," or "Job accuses God."

6.1   RSV   TEV

Then Job answered: *Job*

Then Job answered: TEV and others place verses 1 and 2 together, since 6.1 is replaced by "Job" as the identification of the speaker. For comments see 4.1.

6.2-3   RSV   TEV

2	"O that my vexation were weighed,	2	If my troubles and griefs were weighed on scales,
	and all my calamity laid in the balances!	3	they would weigh more than the sands of the sea,
3	For then it would be heavier than the sand of the sea;		so my wild words should not surprise you.
	therefore my words have been rash.		

Verses 2-3 are closely linked, in that verse 2 is a condition which is beyond fulfillment, and verse 3 is the hypothetical result. The images used are poetic kinds of reality in which anger and misfortune are depicted as solid objects and therefore capable of being weighed like sand.

O that my vexation were weighed: Job complains that his circumstances have not been understood by Eliphaz. Job's bitter complaints in chapter 3, which his visitors heard, must be judged in the light of his agony. **Vexation,** which was used by Eliphaz in a proverbial saying in 5.2, is now picked up by Job, and means the same as in 5.2. It is matched in the next line by **calamity,** meaning resentment, anger, anguish. It appears that Job has taken Eliphaz's proverb and applied it to himself, and he rejects being labeled as a "fool." If his misfortune could be properly understood, Eliphaz would not have suggested that "vexation kills the fool." **Were weighed** is a poetic way of saying "could be understood, evaluated, appreciated." Job does not suggest that his anguish could be weighed, but rather "if only it were possible," since he says in verse 3 that it would have an impossible weight, more than the sand of the sea.

All of my calamity laid in the balances: this is line <u>b</u> of a pair of lines, and it is parallel to line <u>a</u>, with step-up of feeling through the use of the more specific **laid in the balances.** This expression matches the more general term **weighed** in line <u>a</u>. **Calamity** translates a word found in the margin of the Hebrew text. The fact that the two lines of this verse show some intensification in the second line can be expressed in English by "If it were possible to weigh my anger, or rather, if someone were able to lay all my misfortune on a scale . . . ." If the translator is forced to abandon figurative expressions, the verse can be translated as prose: "If it were possible for others to understand how angry I am and how much misfortune I've been through . . . ." TEV manages to retain the metaphor of weighing Job's feelings with "If my troubles and griefs were weighed on the scales."

Would be heavier than the sand of the sea: this line is the first result of verse 2, and the next line is the second result. The two lines are not parallel in this case. If Job's suffering could be placed on one scale pan and all the sand of the sea placed on another, the scale would tip down on the side of Job's suffering. **Sand** is most often used in Old Testament comparisons to indicate an uncountable number, usually offspring or soldiers (see Gen 22.17; 32.12). The Hebrew says literally "sands of the seas," implying all the sand from all seas, and so NJB, TOB, NIV, and others. In some language areas this imagery will not be meaningful, and it may be necessary to substitute "rivers" and "deserts," or even to change **sand** to a different figure which is more natural in this context.

Therefore my words have been rash: in this line Job explains or justifies the "wild words" which he used in chapter 3, which his friends sat through in silence. He wishes to establish that his outburst does not make him a "fool" (5.2). This line is the conclusion to be drawn from verses 2 and 3a combined. Verses 4-7 will expand the reason, which is the intolerable treatment Job has received at the hands of Almighty God. **Rash** translates a Hebrew verb which may rest on a root meaning to stammer or stutter, and is used in this sense by Dhorme; but the context does not seem to support this meaning. A better equivalent would be reckless, impetuous, unrestrained. FRCL says "This is why I spoke without rhyme or reason." GECL has "It is no wonder that I carry on muddled talk." NEB translates "What wonder if my words are wild?" In order to show clearly that 3b is a consequence of verses 2 and 3a, it may be necessary to say, for example, "That is the reason why I spoke so wildly."

6.4	RSV	TEV
	For the arrows of the Almighty are in me; my spirit drinks their poison; the terrors of God are arrayed against me.	Almighty God has shot me with arrows, and their poison spreads through my body. God has lined up his terrors against me.

The three lines of verse 4 are so arranged that lines a and c are parallel, with **arrows of the Almighty** in line a matched by **terrors of God** in line c. Line b has two functions: it depicts the effects of line a, and it adds something to **arrows**, saying they are poisoned. **The arrows of the Almighty are in me**: the image of God as an archer is common in the Old Testament (Deut 32.23; Ezek 5.16; Lam 3.12-13; Psa 7.13). In 4.8 Eliphaz asserted that disaster is the harvest of evil that a person has sown or, in 5.17, the result of discipline from Almighty God. Obviously Job does not accept these theories. From Job's perspective, God has chosen without purpose to shoot him down like a wild animal. **The arrows** represent Job's suffering. In 16.12 Job says, as TEV puts it, "God uses me for target practice." **The Almighty** translates the Hebrew *Shaddai*. See 5.17 for discussion of this name. This is the first time Job accuses God of attacking him.

The expression **arrows of the Almighty are in me** implies that the arrows were shot into Job by God, and for this reason it may be necessary to translate, for example, "God has shot his arrows into me (into my body)" or "God has shot me with his arrows." If the picture is not clear, it may be necessary to use a word explaining the metaphor of the arrows. For example, "God has shot me with arrows of suffering." Or we may shift to a simile; for example, "God has made me suffer, like a person shot by arrows." If none of this is possible, a less poetic effort can be made by saying, for example, "God has made me suffer." This last rendering requires a further adjustment for line b, such as "and I am dying from it" or "and it is killing me."

My spirit drinks their poison: the arrows are tipped with poison to bring death, and the author speaks of Job's **spirit** drinking that poison. Poisoned arrows are not mentioned anywhere else in the Old Testament. TEV and SPCL say "my body . . . ." The poetic meaning, however, is more than Job's physical body absorbing the poison. It is his innermost, his center of being. Many translations follow RSV. TOB has "My breath breathes the poison." BJ says "My mood drinks the poison." FRCL avoids saying that a part of the person takes in the poison: "I have absorbed the terrible poison."

Line b in verse 4 implies that the arrows from line a are poisoned. This information may have to be built into line a. In some languages, therefore, line a will have to say something like "God has shot me with poisoned arrows" before line b can go on to say, for example, "and my spirit (soul, innermost, I) is drinking (absorbing) it." Instead of the figure of something drinking the poison, it may be necessary to use a different figure or to use a nonfigure such as "it enters all of me," "goes in to me," or "soaks into me."

The terrors of God are arrayed against me: the verb "terrify" occurs frequently in Job, but the plural noun form is found only here and in Psalm 88.15, where TEV translates it "punishments." In the present context it is associated with fear, fright, awesomeness that goes with God when he overwhelms the enemy. The expression **terrors of God** means "the terror which God causes others to experience." It is the latter sense which must be understood here. **Arrayed against me** depicts a line of troops in battle formation ready for the attack. This is well expressed by TEV: "God has lined up his terrors against me." **The terrors of God** must often be restructured in translation to say, as in SPCL for example, "God has filled me with terror with his attacks." NEB has "God's onslaughts wear me away." Or we may say "God has prepared to attack me, and I am full of fear."

6.5-6 RSV	TEV

5   Does the wild ass bray when he has grass,
     or the ox low over his fodder?
6   Can that which is tasteless be eaten without salt,
     or is there any taste in the slime of the purslane?[j]
	5 A donkey is content when eating grass,
	     and a cow is quiet when eating hay.
	6 But who can eat flat, unsalted food?
	     What taste is there in the white of an egg?

[j] The meaning of the Hebrew word is uncertain

Job sets out now to match Eliphaz's proverbs (5.2-7) with two of his own. These are stated as rhetorical questions, meaning emphatic denials. The two lines are parallel but without increasing the emphasis. **Wild ass bray** and **grass** in line a̲ is matched in line b̲ by the domestic **ox low** and **fodder**. What do these rhetorical questions refer to? According to Habel, verse 5 is linked back to verses 2-3. Then the interpretation is that the **ass** and **ox**, which refer to Job, do not complain when there is fodder to eat, and so Job would not complain if God were not causing him all this trouble. On the other hand, the hungry animals may still refer to Job, but the fodder may be taken as the comfort that is not forthcoming from his friends. A somewhat parallel picture is found in Psalm 69.21-22. The point of the second view is that, if Job had received proper food (true words of comfort), he would not now be in such anguish.

Does the wild ass bray when he has grass: the **wild ass** is portrayed fully in 39.5-8. (See *Fauna and Flora of the Bible,* pages 5-7.) The despair of this wild creature when it lacks food is seen in Jeremiah 14.6. **Grass** translates the term for wild pasture grass used also in Genesis 1.11 for "vegetation" in general. **Ox low over his fodder**: the Hebrew term translated **ox** is defined by Holladay as "fully grown male bovine, whether castrated or not." The word is also used sometimes of cattle in general. TEV says "cow," SPCL "bull," and NEB, like RSV, "ox." This range of renderings covers all possibilities, and translators are free to take their choice. In contrast with **grass** which the wild animals find growing on the hillsides, **fodder** is more specifically food for domestic animals, and the word is found only here and in Isaiah 30.24.

In some languages other animals will have to be substituted for ass and ox, but the translator should attempt to maintain the contrast between the wild animal that eats grass in line a̲ and the domestic animal that eats food supplied by its owner in line b̲. If it is not possible to contrast actual species of animals, we may often shift to a generic usage; for example, "Does a wild animal cry when it can find something to eat, or a tame animal when its owner gives it something to eat?" Rhetorical questions must often be answered "Certainly not!" Or negative statements may be used instead of rhetorical questions. Those finding a positive statement more natural will find a good model in TEV. TEV does not attempt to make the distinction between wild and domestic animals.

In RSV and other translations, Job continues with still another rhetorical question. In order to vary the style, TEV, which avoided the question form in the previous verse, now translates with a question. **Can that which is tasteless be eaten without salt**: this figure may refer to the words of Eliphaz, which were arguments without consolation or comfort. Line a asks rhetorically if anything that is in itself tasteless can be eaten without adding salt to give it flavor. The answer is an emphatic "No."

Any taste in the slime of the purslane?: the first line of this pair is straightforward in its literal meaning. However, this line is more of a problem. **Slime** translates a word found only here and in 1 Samuel 21.13, where RSV renders it "spittle." **Purslane** is a pod-bearing plant that secretes a runny, sticky sap. (See *Fauna and Flora of the Bible,* pages 170-171.) The name of this plant has also been associated by some interpreters with the "mallow" (NEB) and the milkweed. A rabbinical interpretation, "slime of the yolk," preferred by many scholars, is the basis for "white of the egg" used by TEV and others. SPCL avoids identifying any form of substance and says "What pleasure is there in a flavorless thing?" Because of the uncertainty in this line, translators are advised to follow TEV, or if people do not eat eggs, SPCL offers an adequate model.

In line a **that which is tasteless** is matched in line b by the tastelessness of **slime of the purslane**. Line b follows the regular pattern in being more specific than line a. The way in which line b goes beyond line a can be rendered in English, for example, "Food without salt is tasteless, and there is even less taste in the white of an egg" or "Saltless food is tasteless, but not as tasteless as the white of an egg."

6.7	RSV	TEV

	My appetite refuses to touch them;
	    they are as food that is loath-
	      some to me.[k]
		I have no appetite for food like that,
		    and everything I eat makes me
		      sick.[l]

[k] Heb obscure

[l] *Probable text* sick; *Hebrew unclear.*

My appetite refuses to touch them: my appetite translates the Hebrew term which is literally "my soul" but which can also mean "my throat." More commonly it is translated "I," as in TEV, "I have no appetite for food like that," referring to the tasteless food in verse 5. **Touch them**: the Septuagint has "to rest," which means "my soul refuses to be quiet." Most translators, however, follow a form similar to RSV or TEV in this line.

The next line is more problematic, and the translations of it appear to have little in common. Literally the line says, "they like sickness of my bread." It is not clear what "they" refers to, and so some interpreters change "they" to another word which means loathes or hates. The second Hebrew word may be modified slightly to give "my palate," "my life," or "my heart." In this way the line is similar to 33.20a, "so that his life loathes bread." Using "palate" the expression reads "My palate loathes my food." Finally, by changing two consonants the Hebrew can yield the meaning "my bowels resound with suffering." Modern translations vary greatly in the way they relate bread or food to sickness. NJV says "They are like food when I am sick," which could mean either that the food is undesirable due to his sickness, or that sickness makes him desire the food. FRCL has "My suffering is a bread which I find nauseating." TOB translates "They are unclean foods," and NEB "My bowels rumble with an echoing sound." There is no note to clarify. Most modern translations offer a note giving the literal form, which is of little help, or say "Hebrew unclear."

In many languages there are special terms used to speak of different tastes; for example, sweet, sour, bitter, salty, saltless, and the like. Line a can sometimes be rendered "I do not eat saltless foods." For line b the translator is advised to follow the model of a major language known to many of the people, if there is one. Otherwise the models of RSV or TEV may be followed.

3B-2. Job is without hope and strength (6.8-13)

	RSV		TEV
8	"O that I might have my request, and that God would grant my desire;	8	Why won't God give me what I ask? Why won't he answer my prayer?
9	that it would please God to crush me, that he would let loose his hand and cut me off!	9	If only he would go ahead and kill me!
		10	If I knew he would, I would leap for joy, no matter how great my pain.
10	This would be my consolation; I would even exult in pain unsparing; for I have not denied the words of the Holy One.		I know that God is holy; I have never opposed what he commands.
11	What is my strength, that I should wait? And what is my end, that I should be patient?	11	What strength do I have to keep on living? Why go on living when I have no hope?
12	Is my strength the strength of stones, or is my flesh bronze?	12	Am I made of stone? Is my body bronze?
13	In truth I have no help in me, and any resource is driven from me.	13	I have no strength left to save myself; there is nowhere I can turn for help.

Subdivision Heading

Translators wishing to use a heading for the content of verses 8-13 may modify the Handbook heading to say, for example, "Job asks God to cut him off" or "Job wants God to destroy him." Habel has "Explanation of personal hope," and TOB "Empty consolations."

6.8-9	RSV		TEV
8	"O that I might have my request, and that God would grant my desire;	8	Why won't God give me what I ask? Why won't he answer my prayer?
9	that it would please God to crush me, that he would let loose his hand and cut me off!	9	If only he would go ahead and kill me!

It is best to consider verses 8 and 9 together, since verse 8 is only introductory to verse 9. With verse 8 Job returns to his plea to God to release him from life, as in chapter 3. Job hopes that his outburst will make God strike him down and finish him. The two lines of verse 8 are very similar, but there is little if any intensification in the second line.

That I might have my request: God is implicit in this line and expressed in the next. TEV has taken God from the next line and placed it here, and has structured this line as a question rather than as a petition.

That God would grant my desire: **desire** translates the Hebrew term for "hope," which was used in 4.6, where Eliphaz asked Job if his hope was not built on his fear of God and his integrity. Job's hope is that God will kill him, which he expresses in the words of the next line. NEB says "That God would grant what I hope for," and this is followed by FRCL, NIV, NJB, TOB, and others.

If the translator is able to maintain meaningful parallel lines, they may be translated, for example, "I beg God to do what I ask him, to give me what I want." If the parallel lines can not be kept, verse 8 may be rendered as a single line; for example, "Grant me, God, what I ask you to do."

Verse 9 gives the content of Job's prayer from verse 8, that God should destroy him.

That it would please God to crush me: Job pleads that God be willing to **crush** him. **Crush** translates the same verb Eliphaz used in 4.19, "crushed like a moth" (TEV). There it was used literally. In 5.4 and here it is used figuratively. **That he would let loose his hand and cut me off**: the form of the verb **let loose** is causative and means detach, release, free. The picture is that of God freeing his hand (from some engaging action) so that he can cut Job loose. **Cut me off**: in the light of the usage in Isaiah 38.12, the expression depicts God cutting Job out of the thread of the fabric being woven on the loom. For Job to be cut off, the act must be done by God, not by Job taking his own life.

The two lines of this verse are parallel, with the figure of thread being cut from the loom making the second line more visible in the image. The poetic strengthening can be expressed in English, for example, "If God would only crush the life out of me, if only he would take his hand and cut off my life as a thread is cut out of a cloth" or ". . . cut out when cloth is woven."

6.10 RSV	TEV
This would be my consolation; I would even exult[l] in pain unsparing; for I have not denied the words of the Holy One.	If I knew he would, I would leap for joy, no matter how great my pain. I know that God is holy; I have never opposed what he commands.

[l] The meaning of the Hebrew word is uncertain

This would be my consolation: **This** refers back to the previous verse, so that Job is saying "My death would be my consolation." TEV and others avoid beginning with **This** and relate the line clearly to verse 9, with a condition: "If I knew he would (kill me)." Pope suggests that Job thinks God owes him the favor of putting him out of his misery, because Job has always been faithful. TEV assumes that Job will accept the decree of death just as he accepted the earlier decrees of God. **Consolation** is comfort or being cheered up when in distress.

I would even exult in pain unsparing: exult translates a verb found only here. Some interpreters read "jump for joy" as in TEV. **In pain unsparing:** that is, without regard to the pain involved, in spite of the pain. **Pain unsparing** is pain that has no mercy on the one suffering.

For I have not denied the words of the Holy One: some scholars drop this line. NEB does not translate it but places it in the margin. However, HOTTP considers it an "A" rating, meaning that in all probability this is the correct text. God is called **the Holy One** in Isaiah 40.25; Habakkuk 3.3; Sirach 45.6-7. Only in the plural does this term have the meaning of "angels" (5.1; 15.15).

In the Hebrew text verse 10 has three lines. TEV, which reduced verse 8 to one line, has increased verse 10 to four lines by splitting line c into two: "I know that God is holy" and "I have never opposed what he commands." For the purpose of making the lines parallel, the poet matches **consolation** in line a with **exult** in line b. Line c is not parallel with either a or b, but rather is the reason underlying both a and b. If the reason clause is more natural at the beginning, we may translate, for example, "I have always obeyed what God has commanded me, and so if I could die, I would jump for joy and not even think of the pain of death."

6.11 RSV	TEV
What is my strength, that I should wait? And what is my end, that I should be patient?	What strength do I have to keep on living? Why go on living when I have no hope?

Feeling that he has endured all he can, Job's implies that his strength cannot hold out. Eliphaz's promise of a secure future and death at a ripe old age is more than Job can wait for. He is impatient to be finished with his miserable existence.

Lines a and b are parallel, with **wait** being matched by **patient**. **What is my strength, that I should wait:** Job's rhetorical question is a way of saying "I do not have the strength, stamina, courage to wait for a happy end." **And what is my end, that I should be patient: end** translates a word which in Psalm 39.4 is parallel with "the measure of my days," that is, the span of life that remains to be lived, and therefore "my future," "the remainder of my life." FRCL says "But I no longer have the strength to continue: why should I be patient, I no longer have a future." Alternatively we may say, for example, "I do not have the strength to go on living, so why should I be patient when I have no future?" or ". . . why should I wait patiently for the end of my life?" or ". . . for the time when I will die?"

6.12 RSV	TEV
Is my strength the strength of stones, or is my flesh bronze?	Am I made of stone? Is my body bronze?

Is my strength the strength of stones: strength translates the same word as in 11a, and it is used twice in 12a. Lines a and b are parallel, matching **bronze** with **stones,** both being figures of hardness and of insensitivity to pain. See 40.18 for comments on **bronze.** Job, by contrast, is a man of flesh and blood who cries out in his anguish. **Or is my flesh bronze:** in typical emphasis line a **strength** is matched in line b by the more specific **my flesh.** GECL is even more specific, with "my muscles." FRCL, like TEV, says "Am I a rock, I, to resist everything? Is my body bronze?" In some languages verse 12 may be rendered, for example, "Am I strong as a rock or am I made of bronze? Certainly not!" or "I am not as strong as a rock, and much less am I made of bronze." If **bronze** is unknown, the translation can be "metal."

6.13	RSV	TEV

	In truth I have no help in me,
	  and any resource is driven
	    from me.
		I have no strength left to save
		  myself;
		there is nowhere I can turn for
		  help.

In truth I have no help in me: in truth translates a word that occurs elsewhere only in Numbers 17.13. There it is translated as introducing a question. The remainder of the line is literally "not my help within me," which appears most likely to mean "I am unable to help myself." Many modern translations understand this line to be a question; for example, NEB has "Oh how shall I find help within myself?" and NJB "Can I support myself on nothing?" Syriac and Vulgate render it "behold there is no . . . ." Dahood combines the first two Hebrew words of the line to get "Should I increase a hundredfold." The basic meaning is that Job is at the end of his power to endure.

The two lines are parallel in sense. **And any resource is driven from me:** **resource** translates the same word rendered "success" by RSV in 5.12. In the present verse it means help, counsel, support. Some scholars suggest a modification to the text to get deliverance or salvation, which is reflected in TEV as "strength left to save myself." In many languages the passive **is driven from me** will have to be replaced by an active construction; for example, "I cannot depend on anyone to support me," "there is no one else to strengthen me," or "there is no one to rescue me."

3B-3. Job complains that his friends deceive him (6.14-23)

	RSV		TEV
14	"He who withholds kindness from a friend forsakes the fear of the Almighty.	14	In trouble like this I need loyal friends— whether I've forsaken God or not.

15	My brethren are treacherous as a torrent-
	  bed,
	as freshets that pass away,
		15	But you, my friends, you deceive me like
			  streams
			that go dry when no rain comes.

16	which are dark with ice, and where the snow hides itself.	16	The streams are choked with snow and ice,
17	In time of heat they disappear;	17	but in the heat they disappear, and the stream beds lie bare and dry.

when it is hot, they vanish from their place.

18   The caravans turn aside from their course;
      they go up into the waste, and perish.

19   The caravans of Tema look,
      the travelers of Sheba hope.

20   They are disappointed because they were confident;
      they come thither and are confounded.

21   Such you have now become to me;
      you see my calamity, and are afraid.

22   Have I said, 'Make me a gift'?
      Or, 'From your wealth offer a bribe for me'?

23   Or, 'Deliver me from the adversary's hand'?
      Or, 'Ransom me from the hand of oppressors'?

18   Caravans get lost looking for water;
      they wander and die in the desert.

19   Caravans from Sheba and Tema search,
20   but their hope dies beside dry streams.

21   You are like those streams to me,
      you see my fate and draw back in fear.

22   Have I asked you to give me a gift
      or to bribe someone on my behalf

23   or to save me from some enemy or tyrant?

Subdivision Heading

The Handbook heading for verses 14-23 may be adjusted to say, for example, "Job's friends are false," "Job's friends are not true friends," or "Job complains against his friends." Habel has "Portrayal of false friends," TOB "The emptiness of friendship," and Rowley (verses 14-30) "Job's disappointment in his friends."

6.14   RSV   TEV

"He who withholds[m] kindness from a friend
forsakes the fear of the Almighty.

In trouble[m] like this I need loyal friends—
whether I've forsaken God or not.

[m] Syr Vg Compare Tg: Heb obscure

[m] *Probable text* trouble; *Hebrew unclear.*

He who withholds kindness from a friend: the first line of this verse is difficult to interpret. Nearly every translation consulted is different. Since the next line is clear, it sometimes helps to start from there; and most interpreters look for something that will match **forsakes the fear of the Almighty**. Dhorme makes a change in the first word in line a to get "despise or scorn," and the subject of this action is **a friend**. By his account line a would be "His friend has scorned compassion" or "His friend has refused to be compassionate." **Forsakes** is thus matched by "scorn." HOTTP considers the word rendered "scorn" to mean "the one who collapsed" and rates the reading "B," which means that there is some doubt about the word translated **withholds** in RSV. **Kindness** and TEV "loyal" translate Hebrew *chesed,* meaning pity, mercy, compassion, which are the result of a relationship of loyalty. If line a is taken to mean "His friend has failed to show mercy," it matches extensively with the whole of line b.

In nearly all translations line a is in the third person singular. Only TEV shifts to "I," Job speaking of himself. NJB keeps it general but shifts to second person.

Translators are free to follow RSV, TEV, or another translation, but may need to provide a note saying the Hebrew is unclear in line a. Some other renderings which may be used are: FRCL "The downtrodden man has a right to a bit of goodness from a friend"; GECL "He who is down and out needs a true friend"; TOB "The man who has collapsed has the right to the mercy of his neighbor"; NJB "Refuse faithful love to your neighbor (and you forsake the fear of Shaddai)"; NIV "A despairing man should have the devotion of his friends." Many of these translations are followed in line b by a concessive clause such as "even though he forsakes the fear of God."

The difficulties in verse 14a are such that a clear translation decision is not possible. The Handbook, however, prefers to interpret Job as saying that failure to be compassionate to another person is the same as turning away from the fear of God; that is, it is the same as having no reverence for God. In this view it is the person who shows no love for a friend who also shows no respect for God. Translators may find that the use of the third person is unclear. (Note that in verse 21 Job switches to the second person.) In that case it is possible to speak here in the second person so that Job is addressing the friends: "When you (plural) fail to show kindness to me, you (plural) also show no respect for God." If the third person is used, we may say, for example, "People who do not show love for their friends likewise do not show reverence for God Almighty."

6.15	RSV	TEV
	My brethren are treacherous as a torrent-bed, as freshets that pass away,	But you, my friends, you deceive me like streams that go dry when no rain comes.

Verses 15-20 compare Job's friends to treacherous desert stream beds that give hope to traveling caravans but in the end lead them to their deaths. Line a of verse 15 is a simile in which **torrent-beds** matches **freshets** in line b. Line b is not the intensification of line a but rather serves as an extension of the simile in line a.

My brethren are treacherous as a torrent-bed: Job addresses his friends as **my brethren**. In 19.13 the same term includes all of Job's kinsmen, but here he uses this expression of close relationship to refer ironically to his visitors. TEV says "But you, my friends." Job is speaking sarcastically because he has no reason to look on them as being brotherly or friendly. **Treacherous** here means fickle, undependable, deceptive. In Jeremiah 15.18 the brook whose waters fail is called "deceitful." **Torrent-bed** translates Hebrew *nachal,* which refers to the stream beds in the Middle East that carry off rain and ground water, but in the hot season may be completely dried up. Because they may be running with water one month and completely dry the next, they are deceptive and even treacherous for travelers. **As freshets that pass away: freshets**, an archaic English word for streams, translates the Hebrew for "like river beds streams," where the plural of *nachal* from line a is used again. They refer to dry stream beds, or as TEV makes explicit in the text, those "that go dry when no rain comes." If such dry stream beds are unknown, an explanatory note may be required for the reader, or "when no rain comes," as TEV says, may be used in the text.

6.16   RSV   TEV

which are dark with ice, and where the snow hides itself.	**The streams are choked with snow and ice,**

Dark with ice: the author is more concerned to create suggestive poetic images than to describe physical realities. An ice-covered stream need not be dark; but poetically **dark** gives a hint as to the hidden nature of these friends whom Job sees as concealing their true intentions and failing to be honest and open with him. TEV has avoided **dark** but has used "choked with snow and ice," which may serve a similar poetic purpose in English.

Where the snow hides itself: **hides itself** translates a verb which is similar to one used in Exodus 15.8 translated "piled up." Some take this line to mean "the snow piles up on them," and NEB gives both meanings: "are hidden with piled up snow." NJV takes the verb hidden in an active sense, "snow obscures them," that is, snow hides the stream beds. The translator who is trying to follow the poetic language of the author will pay particular attention to the images, while at the same time keeping to the meaning of the text. There does not appear to be any good reason for departing from the meaning of the RSV here. In areas where snow and ice are unknown, it may be necessary to say, for example, "The water in these streams is cold and dark." If **snow** is unknown and the term cannot be borrowed from a major language, it may be necessary to shift to something like fog or clouds and say, for example, "and the fog hides them" or "the clouds cover them."

6.17   RSV   TEV

In time of heat they disappear; when it is hot, they vanish from their place.	**but in the heat they disappear, and the stream beds lie bare and dry.**

In time of heat they disappear: the two lines of this verse are parallel, with only a bit more imagery in the second line. **In time of heat** translates a verb form found only here. In Ezekiel 20.47 another form of the same verb means "scorched." Here the most probable meaning is "melt"; for example, "When the snow and ice melt, they (the streams) soon disappear." **Disappear** translates a word used poetically here, meaning "are made silent." **When it is hot they vanish from their place: they** refers to the stream beds with water, not to the beds themselves. **Vanish** means the water dries up.

Line b repeats the thought of line a and adds nothing new. TEV has kept both lines and has made line b the consequence of line a. TEV has also linked verse 17 to 16 as a contrast by beginning verse 17 with "but." In Hebrew it is not a consequence, but rather a step-up of the depiction of the change from warm melting to the heat of the hot season. We may relate verse 17 to 16 as a contrast; however, the more natural relation is that of time sequence. In languages which do not have terms for snow and ice, the translator may say, for example, "When the weather warms, the streams disappear."

6.18   RSV   TEV

> The caravans turn aside from   Caravans get lost looking for
>   their course;   water;
>   they go up into the waste, and   they wander and die in the
>   perish.   desert.

The caravans turn aside from their course: **caravans** refers to a line of camels with riders and merchandise, crossing the desert. They turn aside from their route in search of water, but find none and so die. **Turn aside** means to leave, abandon, stray from their path.

They go up into the waste and perish: the first part of this line is parallel to the previous line, and the final part is a consequence. **Waste** translates the Hebrew word *tohu,* used in Genesis 1.2 in combination with the similar sounding *bohu* and translated by RSV "without form and void." This same term is used in 26.7, where RSV says "he stretches out the north over the void," and which TEV renders "empty space." In Isaiah 45.18 TEV renders it "desolate waste." Here the meaning is trackless waste land. Its most conspicuous feature is its emptiness. **Perish** is a literary word in English, meaning to die, which was also used in 3.3. The image of the lost caravan in hopeless search of life-sustaining water is the poet's way of intensifying Job's feeling of deception in the advice Eliphaz has offered him.

Caravans may be translated by some such expression as "travelers," "camels and their riders," or "travelers on camels." The author and his readers knew why the caravans **turn aside**, but in some languages it will be necessary to say, as in TEV, "looking for water." If an empty desert area is unknown, it may be necessary to say, for example, "They wander far from where people live" or "They wander into the empty land where nothing lives, and they die there."

6.19   RSV   TEV

> The caravans of Tema look,   Caravans from Sheba and Tema
>   the travelers of Sheba hope.   search,

The caravans of Tema look: **Tema** is believed to be an oasis southeast of the head of the Gulf of Aqaba. (See also Isaiah 21.14; Jeremiah 25.23.) Eliphaz is said in 4.1 to be a Temanite. **The travelers of Sheba hope**: this line emphasizes the deception of failure to find water.

In translation it may be necessary to relate these caravans to the preceding verse by saying, for example, "Some of these caravans (travelers) come from the place called Tema, and they search in the desert for water. Others who come from the place called Sheba hope they will find water."

6.20   RSV   TEV

> They are disappointed because   but their hope dies beside dry
>   they were confident;   streams.

> they come thither and are
>   confounded.

They are disappointed because they were confident: the two lines are parallel, with little if any intensification. **They** most logically refers to all the caravans in verses 18 and 19. **Disappointed** translates a verb meaning "ashamed." They are deceived because they were sure the stream beds would have water, and so they feel ashamed. Using the same word, Psalm 22.5 says "In thee they trusted and were not disappointed." **Because they were confident:** they were certain, sure, convinced that they would find water.

They come thither: thither is an old English word meaning "to that place," and so we can translate "when they got there," "when they reached the place where they were going," or "when they arrived there." **Confounded** translates a word found also in Psalm 35.26 as "confusion." It is rendered somewhat poetically by NJV as "when they reach the place, they stand aghast," which is stronger than NIV, "They arrive there only to be disappointed."

Verse 20 may have to be restructured in some languages to give a clear translation. The following points should be considered: (1) It may be necessary to shift the reason clause from line a to the beginning of the line. (2) It may be necessary to combine the result clauses from both halves of the verse. (3) It may be necessary to make clear that the reason for being disappointed is the failure to find water, as implied in verses 15-18. As an example we may translate "Because they were sure they would find water, they went there, but they were disappointed and confused" or "The caravans were certain they would find water, but when they reached the place, they were confused and disappointed."

6.21   RSV   TEV

> Such you have now become to
>   me;[n]
> you see my calamity, and are
>   afraid.

> You are like[n] those streams to
>   me,[o]
> you see my fate and draw back
>   in fear.

[n] Cn Compare Gk Syr: Heb obscure

[n] *Probable text* like; *Hebrew* because.
[o] *Some ancient translations and one Hebrew manuscript* to me; *most Hebrew manuscripts have two different expressions:* nothing *in the text and* to him *in the margin.*

Such you have now become to me: the Hebrew text says, literally, "because you have become nothing." The marginal reading in the Hebrew Bible says "You have become it." RSV follows the Septuagint and Syriac, which have "You also have become to me." TEV and others change the first word from "because" to "like" and get "You are like those streams to me." NIV has "You too have proved to be of no help." Although the HOTTP committee rates both the Masoretic text and the marginal reading as "C," the recommended translation of the text "you are nothing" and of the margin "you have become it" seem to imply the sense rendered more clearly by TEV. Job is comparing his friends to the treacherous desert streams.

You see my calamity and are afraid: there is here a play on the words **see** (*tir'u*) and **are afraid** (*tira'u*). The word translated **calamity** occurs only here and so is different from that used in 6.2. Its meaning is seen in NEB "dismay," NJV "misfortune," NIV "something dreadful," SPCL "horrible situation." Just as the caravan travelers were dumbfounded at the dried-up streams, Job accuses his friends of reacting the same way to his misfortunes. In verse 14 Job equates failure to be compassionate to a friend with forsaking the fear of God. As a result the sight of his suffering produces not compassion but fear.

The two lines of this verse are not parallel. Line a is a conclusion by way of comparison to verses 15-20. For this reason it will often be clearer, as in TEV, to make the comparison to the treacherous streams; for example, "You are just like those dry stream beds to me" or "You have dealt with me like those dry stream beds which disappointed the travelers."

6.22-23 RSV	TEV
22 Have I said, 'Make me a gift'? Or, 'From your wealth offer a bribe for me'? 23 Or, 'Deliver me from the adversary's hand'? Or, 'Ransom me from the hand of oppressors'?	22 Have I asked you to give me a gift or to bribe someone on my behalf 23 or to save me from some enemy or tyrant?

Job now adds sarcasm to his observations. The two lines are parallel with increased emotion in the second line. **Have I said, 'Make me a gift'?** If Job had asked his visitors to use their wealth to help him, he could have understood their attitude; such is the effect of money on good human relations. The Hebrew says, literally, "Is it because I say give to me?" RSV and TEV understand the final Hebrew verb phrase as giving a gift.

'From your wealth offer a bribe for me'? In 1.3 Job's prestige rested on his great wealth, and after losing all of it, he has not attempted to regain anything by asking his visitors for gifts or to bribe someone to help him. The word for **bribe** is also used in Ezekiel 16.33, where Jerusalem is accused of playing the role of the prostitute who bribes her lovers to come to her. A **bribe** is money or a reward promised or given to someone to influence them to act on behalf of the one giving the money. The word suggests that the one accepting the money is being corrupted, that is, has lost the desire to be honest. In RSV and TEV verses 22-23 are translated as rhetorical questions. In some languages it will be necessary to reply to these questions with something like "Certainly not!" Other languages will prefer strong negative statements; for example, "I have never said to you 'Give me a gift,' and I certainly never asked you to bribe someone for me."

Job continues his rhetorical question, **'Deliver me from the adversary's hand'?** Again there are two parallel lines with some poetic reinforcing in the second line. These lines may be understood as the reasons Job might have asked for money in verse 22. As in 29.12, **deliver** translates a verb meaning free, rescue, save from one who has power or control. **Adversary's hand** is the poetic use of a part for the whole. Job does not name a specific enemy, and so it is best to say, as TEV, "from some enemy" or "from an enemy."

Ransom me from the hand of the oppressors is also used in 5.20 and 33.28 and implies payment to the captor or oppressor. **Oppressors** translates a plural noun derived from a verb root meaning to terrify or inspire fear. It is translated by RSV in 15.20 as "ruthless," and by TEV "tyrant." **Ransom** is more specific than **deliver**, and it is this movement toward the concrete idea in line _b_ that gives the step-up of poetic feeling. **Ransom** must sometimes be translated "pay money to the oppressors so they will free me" or "give a gift to buy me back from people who treat me badly."

3B-4. Job insists that he is innocent (6.24-30)

	RSV		TEV
24	"Teach me, and I will be silent; make me understand how I have erred.	24	All right, teach me; tell me my faults. I will be quiet and listen to you.
25	How forceful are honest words! But what does reproof from you reprove?	25	Honest words are convincing, but you are talking nonsense.
26	Do you think that you can reprove words, when the speech of a despairing man is wind?	26	You think I am talking nothing but wind; then why do you answer my words of despair?
27	You would even cast lots over the fatherless, and bargain over your friend.	27	You would even roll dice for orphan slaves and make yourselves rich off your closest friends!
28	"But now, be pleased to look at me; for I will not lie to your face.	28	Look me in the face. I won't lie.
29	Turn, I pray, let no wrong be done. Turn now, my vindication is at stake.	29	You have gone far enough. Stop being unjust. Don't condemn me. I'm in the right.
30	Is there any wrong on my tongue? Cannot my taste discern calamity?	30	But you think I am lying— you think I can't tell right from wrong.

Subdivision Heading

As suggested in the display at the beginning of chapter 6, verses 24-30 contain two requests. These are placed under a single heading in the Handbook. Job is requesting his friends to recognize his innocence, so suitable headings would be "Job asks his friends for help" or "Job asks his friends to stop condemning him." Habel has (for verses 22-27) "Interrogation of false friends" and (for verses 28-30) "Closing appeal to friends." TOB has "Words of a desperate man."

6.24	RSV	TEV
	"Teach me, and I will be silent; make me understand how I have erred.	All right, teach me; tell me my faults. I will be quiet and listen to you.

Eliphaz has generalized about Job's suffering and bases his arguments on the assumption that Job has sinned. Job is willing to listen in silence if they will show him how he is at fault. **Teach me, and I will be silent**: Job will be silent so that he can listen, or as TEV says, "and listen to you." **Teach me** is matched in the next line by **make me understand**, which translates the causative form of the Hebrew verb.

How I have erred: **erred** translates a verb used in Leviticus 4.13, "If . . . Israel commits a sin unwittingly . . ." (RSV); "sins . . . without intending to" (TEV). The note in NJB says "sinning inadvertently or through ignorance." So Job is asking his friends to show him how he has unintentionally sinned. In some languages it will be clearer to say, for example, "I will be quiet so you can teach me." If being silent does not infer clearly the act of listening, it will be better to say, for example, "I will be quiet and listen to you; go ahead and teach me." **How I have erred** may need to be recast, and may be rendered idiomatically in many languages; for example, "how I have strayed from the right path," "how I have failed to walk straight," or "the wrong path I have taken."

6.25	RSV	TEV

How forceful are honest words!
But what does reproof from
   you reprove?

Honest words are convincing,
   but you are talking nonsense.

How forceful are honest words: the Hebrew word translated **forceful** is problematic. The word is *nimretsu*. Some scholars replace *r* with *l* and get "pleasant," arguing that the substitution of *l* for *r* is a common dialect variation. RSV translates another form of the same root found in 1 Kings 2.8 as "grievous," and in TEV as "bitterly." Some take the meaning to be "painful," as this is the meaning of the cognate word in Akkadian. The Koehler-Baumgartner lexicon (K-B) gives "offending." If Job is referring to his own words, the meaning can well be "painful" because he speaks his words out of his anguish, and so NIV says "How painful are honest words." On the other hand it seems best to take the adjective in line a to be in contrast with the thought in line b, that is, honest words spoken by anyone are pleasant, but the arguments coming from Job's visitors are criticisms which correct nothing. Not surprisingly translations vary greatly. FRCL has "Honest arguments wound no one," and SPCL says "No one can refuse a correct argument." It seems best to understand this verse as a complaint about the critical attitude in Eliphaz's words, words which Job does not accept as honest arguments.

What does reproof from you reprove? Job is repeating his demand to know for which of his sins Eliphaz is correcting him. The final word in Hebrew is *mikkem,* "from you," which some scholars suggest should be *hakam,* "wise," and get "what does reproof of the wise prove?" NEB, which made a change in the first line to get "How harsh are the words of the upright man," accepts "wise" in the second line and gets a better parallel line: "What do the arguments of wise men prove?" (It gives a note on "wise men" saying "Hebrew unintelligible.") However, a clear rendering is possible without changing the Hebrew text, by saying as does NIV "But what do your arguments prove?" TEV "You are talking nonsense" expresses Job's thought, but little of the original form of it. If the translator has used a positive word such as "pleasant" or "convincing" in line a, it will be necessary to link line b to line a by a strong contrast; for example, "but your words are not pleasant, and they correct nothing" or "but your arguments are not like that, and they do not show me what is right."

6.26   RSV   TEV

> Do you think that you can re-   You think I am talking nothing
>   prove words,   but wind;
> when the speech of a despair-   then why do you answer my
>   ing man is wind?   words of despair?

That you can reprove words: Job is driven to the conclusion that his visitors are deceitful, because they devise arguments to correct him and disregard what he says in his despair. **Reprove words** should be taken to mean "make up words of reproof," "correct what I say," "set me right."

Speech of a despairing man is wind: as a dependent clause, line b in RSV implies that what Job says is really wind, a position which Job obviously does not accept. TEV avoids this by making line b a statement: "You think I am talking nothing but wind." To do this TEV has switched the order of the lines. It is not necessary, however, to switch the lines. NIV, for example, says "Do you mean to correct what I say, and treat the words of a despairing man as wind?" **Despairing man** translates a word also found in Isaiah 57.10 and Jeremiah 2.25, where RSV has "hopeless" in both places. NJV translates line b "but count a hopeless man's words as wind." **Wind** translates "for the wind," meaning without substance, not serious, foolish. In some languages this verse may be restructured to say, for example, "Do you think you can correct my ways when you look on me as hopeless and speaking foolish words?" or ". . . as a man who has lost hope and speaks foolishness?"

6.27   RSV   TEV

> You would even cast lots over the   You would even roll dice for
>   fatherless,   orphan slaves
> and bargain over your friend.   and make yourselves rich off
>   your closest friends!

Job's criticism of his visitors reaches a high point of insult now. **Cast lots over the fatherless**: **cast lots** translates the verb element "you cause something to fall," which is taken by RSV, TEV, and most others to mean "cast lots, throw dice." The same word is used in 1 Samuel 14.42, where Saul asks for guilt to be fixed by the use of Urim and Thummim. Some scholars, however, divide the following two words in the Hebrew text and get "Will you even fall on the blameless one?" This is the basis for NEB "Would you assail an orphan?" Some interpreters do not feel that this verse fits at this point and so place it after verse 23 (see Mft). It seems best, however, to accept the Hebrew text as it stands, with the verse in its traditional position.

In some languages casting lots or throwing dice is unknown. In such cases it may be necessary to shift to a different image; for example, "You would even play a game with someone to win an orphan" or "You would even have a contest to see who gets an orphan as the prize."

And bargain over your friend: bargain over translates a word which has the meaning of argue over the price, haggle, barter, as if a friend were merchandise. Several suggestions are made for changes in the text. NEB proposes different vowels for the verb to get "Would you hurl yourselves on a friend?" However, there does not appear to be any need to change. FRCL has "And you would go so far as to sell your own friend!" NJB translates "and selling your friend at a bargain price." TEV shifts the idea away from selling and says "make yourselves rich off your closest friends!" TEV implies that they cheat their friends to enrich themselves.

6.28   RSV   TEV

> "But now, be pleased to look at   Look me in the face. I won't lie.
>   me;
>   for I will not lie to your face.

Job now concludes his speech by asking them to face him honestly and stop trying to deceive him. He is a righteous sufferer and wants them to accept him as such.

But now be pleased to look at me: Job is not asking them to look at him and be pleased with what they see, but rather to "be so good as to look at me," "please look at me." NJV has "Be so good as to face me." In Hebrew the verb "face" in line a is matched by the noun "face" in line b. TEV "Look me in the face" is abrupt but gives the meaning. The two lines are not parallel apart from the matching of "face" in both. Line b is something of a consequence of line a. **I will not lie to your face**: RSV uses the word **face** in line b only, perhaps to avoid repetition. Job is appealing for an open and sincere communication in which they will look each other in the eye. Translators should not attempt to preserve "face" in both lines unless it is perfectly natural.

6.29   RSV   TEV

> Turn, I pray, let no wrong be   You have gone far enough. Stop
>   done.   being unjust.
>   Turn now, my vindication is at   Don't condemn me. I'm in the
>   stake.   right.

Turn translates a common Hebrew word *shub,* which literally means "return," in the sense of repeating an action or starting again; and in the present context it is a plea for his friends to make a new start in their attitude toward him. A literal translation of "return," as in KJV, gives the impression the three friends are walking away from Job and he is calling them back; RSV **turn** is little better. Here the word means "relent, think again, think it over." GECL goes to the point directly with "stop

143

judging!" which gives the reason behind TEV "You have gone far enough," that is, in your judgmental attitude. **I pray** can be rendered beg, ask, request; or it may not even be necessary to translate it at all. **Let no wrong be done: wrong** translates a word meaning injustice. It occurs in 11.14, where TEV translates "evil" and RSV "wickedness." The sense is that Job's friends should stop being unjust in their criticism of him, and it may be rendered "Stop being unjust to me" or "Stop being unfair to me."

The second line begins with the same verb **turn** as in the first, and so Job repeats his plea for them to "stop being unfair." **My vindication is at stake** is literally "my righteousness is in it." Some interpreters propose changing the text to say "My righteousness is still in me" or "My righteousness is still intact." Rowley argues for the translation in RSV, since the word righteousness here has a legal sense meaning to clear a person from charges. The phrase "in it" in Hebrew means here "in question," or as RSV says, **at stake**. The injustice Job feels is what has been done against him in Eliphaz's speech. It is far too serious to leave as is, and that is the reason for his appeal.

Line b̲ matches line a̲ by repeating and thus emphasizing the idea "stop doing what you are doing" or "think again about what you are saying." **My vindication is at stake** may be translated, for example, "admit that I am right," "recognize that I have done no wrong," or "acknowledge that right is on my side."

6.30 RSV	TEV
Is there any wrong on my tongue? Cannot my taste discern ca-lamity?	But you think I am lying— you think I can't tell right from wrong.

In these two parallel lines Job is saying that he understands (tastes) the flavor of his suffering, even if they cannot. **Is there any wrong on my tongue: wrong** is the same word as in 29a. **On my tongue** is matched in the next line by **taste**, or more literally, "palate." Job is not inquiring if what he has said might be wrong, but rather if his friends think he has lost the taste of injustice. He is emphatically denying that he has said anything untrue, and TEV, which avoids the images of **tongue** and **taste**, says "But you think I am lying." GECL implies lying by translating "I do not go too far with my words," and SPCL has "Do you think I am a liar?" In some languages there are figurative expressions which can be used to preserve something of the poetic impact of line a̲; for example, "Does my tongue speak false words?" or "Is my mouth a crooked path? Certainly not!"

Cannot my taste discern calamity? Just as his tongue is incapable of lying, so his palate is incapable of being mistaken about the nature of his misfortune. The mouth with its tongue and palate are used in different ways; in line a̲ the tongue is associated with speech, and in line b̲ the palate with taste. **Discern** means to understand, discriminate, or distinguish between things that are different. For **calamity** see 6.2. In some languages this verse can be rendered figuratively as "Do you think I cannot feel (taste, smell, see) misfortune?"

3B-5. Job complains to God about his oppressive existence (7.1-8)

RSV	TEV

1 "Has not man a hard service upon earth,
    and are not his days like the days of a
    hireling?
2 Like a slave who longs for the shadow,
    and like a hireling who looks for his
    wages,
3 so I am allotted months of emptiness,
    and nights of misery are apportioned
    to me.
4 When I lie down I say, 'When shall I
    arise?'
    But the night is long,
    and I am full of tossing till the dawn.
5 My flesh is clothed with worms and dirt;
    my skin hardens, then breaks out
    afresh.
6 My days are swifter than a weaver's shut-
    tle,
    and come to their end without hope.

7 "Remember that my life is a breath;
    my eye will never again see good.
8 The eye of him who sees me will behold
    me no more;
    while thy eyes are upon me, I shall be
    gone.

1 Human life is like forced army service,
    like a life of hard manual labor,
2 like a slave longing for cool shade;
    like a worker waiting for his pay.
3 Month after month I have nothing to live
    for;
    night after night brings me grief.
4 When I lie down to sleep, the hours drag;
    I toss all night and long for dawn.
5 My body is full of worms;
    it is covered with scabs;
    pus runs out of my sores.
6 My days pass by without hope,
    pass faster than a weaver's shuttle.

7 Remember, O God, my life is only a
    breath;
    my happiness has already ended.
8 You see me now, but never again.
    If you look for me, I'll be gone.

In chapter 6 Job accused his three visitors of being less than true friends. Now, however, he shifts his theme to general remarks about people and specific comments about his own suffering. The outline below is adapted from Habel, who points out that chapter 7 is carefully crafted by the author into three units which follow the same basic pattern in each unit.

Unit A

General observation	verses 1-2	Human beings are oppressed Their days are limited
Complaint	3-4 5-6	My nights are oppressive My body is diseased My life is short
Reproach	7-8a	My life is a breath The Eye will not see me
The end	8b	I will not be

Unit B

General observation	9-10	People vanish They go to Sheol
Complaint	11-12	I won't be restrained I will complain Why put a guard on me?
	13-14	God torments me
Reproach	15-16a	I prefer death I hate life Leave me alone
The end	16b	My days are a breath

Unit C

General observation	17-18	People are important They have God's attention
Plea	19	Look elsewhere Leave me alone
Reproach	20a	If I sin are you hurt, you watcher of men?
Complaint	20b	Why am I your target?
Reproach	21a	Why don't you pardon me?
The end	21b	You will look for me, but I'll be gone

Subdivision Heading

Translators wishing to introduce the content of chapter 7 with a subdivision heading may modify the Handbook heading by saying, for example, "Job complains to God," "Job tells God that life is hard labor," or "Job complains that everyone lives like a slave." Habel has "Human existence is servitude," TOB "Forced labor." TEV, which identified Job as the speaker at the opening of chapter 6, makes no additional identification in chapter 7. Some translations use one heading for the chapter; for example, FRCL has "Job complains against God," and GECL "Why doesn't God leave people in peace?" Translators should note that the white space used by both RSV and TEV to represent changes in the discourse (see "Headings" in the Introduction to the Handbook, and the display above) do not correspond to the three recurring units outlined above. Where there is a very clear structural arrangement of the content, it is advisable to reflect this in the use of subdivision headings.

7.1-2	RSV		TEV
1	"Has not man a hard service upon earth, and are not his days like the days of a hireling?	1	Human life is like forced army service, like a life of hard manual labor,
2	Like a slave who longs for the shadow, and like a hireling who looks for his wages,	2	like a slave longing for cool shade; like a worker waiting for his pay.

Verse 1 takes the form of a rhetorical question. Job speaks of man in a universal sense, which would include himself. **Has not man a hard service upon earth**: the term translated **man** is general and inclusive, referring to all people, everyone. **Hard service** translates a word meaning "army" and is extended to refer to the term of military service, as it does in Numbers 1.3, where all males were counted for military service. Life in a military camp suggested continuous hard labor. TEV's "forced army service" expresses the idea well. Instead of rhetorical questions TEV has used two statements employing similes, "Human life is like . . . ." In some languages **man** can be shifted to the more general idea of life, as in TEV, or as in FRCL "Life is hard . . . ." It may also be necessary to say "People have to work hard," or "Everyone is forced to do hard labor . . . ," or using a simile, "The life of people is like doing hard army duty . . . ." **Upon earth**, which is not translated as such by TEV, does not refer to the earth in contrast to another place, but serves to draw attention to man's physical existence in the sense of "as long as he is alive" or "in this life." **Upon earth** may be rendered, for example, "As long as people are alive," "During life," or "While they live." In some languages, if the rhetorical question form is used, a reply may be required; for example, "They certainly do!"

Are not his days like the days of a hireling? This line does not parallel the first in structure but in word association, in which **hireling** is associated with **hard service**. A **hireling** is a person who is hired to work for daily wages. The term is also used of a mercenary or soldier who serves for money, as in 2 Samuel 10.6, where the Ammonites hired Syrians and others to fight Joab. The **hireling** or day wage earner was to be paid daily (Deut 24.15; Matt 20.8), and his wages were not to be kept from him until the following morning (Lev 19.13). Every day consisted of hard labor, with the uncertainty of being paid at the end of the day. **Days of a hireling** may refer to the working days, or more generally, to the life or way of life of the worker. In situations where people are not familiar with the idea of day labor, it may be necessary to say, for example, "a person who works each day for someone else" or "a person who gets money by working for an employer." **His days** refers to the suffering struggle of the person in line a of the verse, and to make this clear it may be necessary to say "Isn't what he does like the things a day laborer does?" In some languages it will be best to shift **his days** to something like "Is not his suffering like the suffering of the day laborer?" or "Does he not endure the same

147

pain as the day laborer?" TEV shifts from **his days** in line b again to "like a life," which gives balance to the two lines.

Verse 2 continues the chain of similes begun in verse 1b. The two lines of this verse are parallel in structure; and there is a shift of images from military service and daily wage earner in verse 1 to **slave** in this verse.

Like a slave who longs for the shadow: shadow is taken in the sense of "cool shade," as in TEV. **Like a hireling who looks for his wages**: the word **hireling** is the same as in 1b and can refer to the mercenary soldier or to the day laborer. He **looks for his wages** in the sense that he anticipates, is anxious for, is expecting his daily pay. In the thought of the author, to exist is to be enslaved, and only the end of life brings freedom. It is important in continuing the simile that the subject **man** from verse 1 be clearly indicated; for example, "People's (or, Human) life is like a slave longing for the shade." Or "Our lives on earth are . . . ."

In languages in which the word **slave** is unknown, it may be necessary to use a descriptive phrase; for example, "a poor person who has been sold to someone" or "a person whom an owner has bought (or, captured)." The reason the slave longs for the shade is that his labor is in the hot sun. This may not be clear, and that information may need to be given, as in FRCL "A slave in the sun who would like some shade." It may be necessary to say, for example, "As a slave who works in the hot sun wants to rest in the cool shade."

RSV **look for his wages** does not mean that the worker has lost them and is searching for them, but rather as in TEV "waiting for his pay." In some languages it will be necessary to shift to a verb, "waiting for the boss to pay him" or ". . . to give him what he has earned."

7.3	RSV	TEV
	so I am allotted months of emptiness, and nights of misery are apportioned to me.	Month after month I have nothing to live for; night after night brings me grief.

Beginning with verse 3 in unit A, Job shifts from the general observation to concentrate on his personal complaints. Verse 3 has two lines, in which **months** in line a is paralleled by **nights** in line b.

So I am allotted months of emptiness: so translates a Hebrew connective which indicates that the following clause is a logical sequence to what has come before; that is, Job applies the misery of the soldier, worker, or slave to himself. **So I am allotted** is literally "Thus I am caused to inherit." Just as an heir receives property from his ancestors without having chosen them, so Job receives his misery without having any say in the matter. What Job has inherited is **months of emptiness. Emptiness** translates a word meaning "vanity" or "futility" which occurs also in Psalm 89.47, translated by RSV "for what vanity thou hast created all the sons of men." The reference is to the short span of a person's life and is rendered by TEV "you created all of us mortal!" The figure of **months of emptiness** refers back to the **days** of verse 1 and extends the picture of suffering from days to months over these verses.

The expression **I am allotted** may have to be shifted to an active voice, with God as the actor; for example, "God makes me spend months . . . ." It may be unnatural to receive something abstract such as months of futility, and so the translator must often shift to something like "month after month my life is useless." In some languages it is possible to assign this emptiness to Job's fate in the sense "It is my lot to spend month after month for nothing" or ". . . to live for months with no purpose."

Nights of misery are apportioned to me: this line is a generalized introductory statement followed in verse 4 by the picture of Job tossing on his bed, trying to go to sleep. **Misery** translates a term meaning "sorrow, grief, oppression, suffering." As in line a there is no attempt to say how many nights were involved. However, the time span is seen as a cycle of inescapable repetition, or as TEV says, "month after month" and "night after night." It is not stated who has caused Job's grief, but in verse 7 Job, without addressing God by name, calls upon God to remember how short Job's life is. So here, as in the previous line, it is God who has handed out to Job his months and nights of misery. Line b may parallel line a in a stylistically acceptable manner; for example, if it is possible to say "pass month after month of futility," line b may say "and night after night in suffering."

7.4	RSV	TEV
	When I lie down I say, 'When shall I arise?' But the night is long, and I am full of tossing till the dawn.	When I lie down to sleep, the hours drag; I toss all night and long for dawn.

There is considerable variation in the translations of this verse. Some render the opening clause as a condition, "If I lie down," while others prefer a continuous state, "Lying in bed," and others again as a dependent time clause, "When I lie down."

When I lie down refers to going to bed to sleep at night. **I say** is the literal Hebrew form, but the meaning in the context is something like "I ask myself" or "I wonder." **When shall I arise** is not a question concerning what time to get up in the morning, but rather an expression of the tiresome length of the night while waiting anxiously for dawn. **But the night is long** emphasizes the slow passage of the night and the wearisome delay of the dawn. **I am full of tossing till the dawn**: the expression **I am full** or "I am filled" is the preferred Hebrew text (an "A" decision, according to HOTTP) but may not be an appropriate translation in some languages. **Full of tossing** means turning over and over in bed while not being able to fall asleep, and may sometimes be rendered "I keep turning on my bed until dawn comes" or "I turn over again and again until I see the light of morning."

TEV has reduced the three Hebrew lines to two. NEB modifies the text, as do some of the ancient versions, and gets four lines. SPCL has shifted the order of clauses to say "I lie down and the night becomes endless for me. I grow tired from tossing till dawn and think to myself: 'When will I ever get up?'" Translators may feel that some adjustments of order will make the flow of ideas more coherent, such as placing the question **When shall I arise?** at the end, as in SPCL. TEV has avoided this problem by recasting the question into a statement which follows logically, "The hours drag." This expression means that the hours pass by slowly, and combines both the question and the following line **But the night is long.**

7.5   RSV   TEV

> My flesh is clothed with worms   My body is full of worms;
>   and dirt;   it is covered with scabs;
>   my skin hardens, then breaks   pus runs out of my sores.
>   out afresh.

Verse 5 consists of two vivid statements describing Job's body in terms of his **flesh** and **skin**. **My flesh is clothed with worms and dirt**: **my flesh** means "my body" and is the poetic use of a part of the body to represent the whole body. The figure of clothing is used to indicate that the entire body is covered with disease. The term translated **worms** is found only in Exodus 16.24, where it refers to worms that destroy food, and in Isaiah 14.11, where it is associated with the dead body. In 17.14 and 21.26 worms are also associated with the dead body, and so the term has the sense of "maggots." The word translated **worm** here is related to a verb meaning to grow rotten. In 25.6 the same word is used to symbolize human insignificance and is used in parallel with another word for worm. The choice of a term to translate **worm** should be appropriate to the context. For a discussion of **worm** see *Fauna and Flora of the Bible,* page 86. **Dirt** translates "clod of dust" and may suggest dirt caked on the skin. Dust as well as worms is a symbol of death, as seen in 17.16 "descend together into the dust." The particular expression used here may mean scabs, and TEV and some others take it in that sense.

In some languages translators must avoid speaking of **flesh** and **skin** and must thus perhaps modify the parallelism. However, it is often possible to substitute "body" for **flesh,** or even for both terms. It may not be possible in translation to keep the metaphor **clothed with worms and dirt,** but it may be possible to employ a different figure. "Full of worms" may give the wrong idea, and in such cases we can often say, for example, "Worms crawl all over my body," "Worms and dirt are everywhere on my body," or "I have worms and scabs from head to foot."

In line b Job extends the description of his body as having dried skin running with pus from open sores. **My skin hardens:** translators render this line in various ways. The Hebrew says "My skin is broken and it runs." The word "runs" is derived from a verb meaning to melt or flow, and HOTTP thinks it has that meaning here, and so Job's skin is covered with festering running sores. In translation it is best to keep this as a general description and not identify it as a particular disease, such as yaws.

7.6   RSV   TEV

My days are swifter than a weaver's shuttle,
and come to their end without
hope.

My days pass by without hope,
pass faster than a weaver's
shuttle.[p]

[p] WEAVER'S SHUTTLE: *A small device in
the loom which carries threads back and
forth rapidly in weaving cloth.*

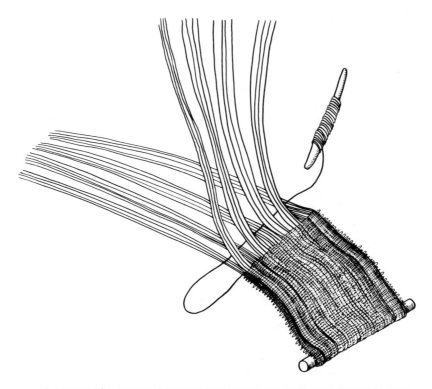

A WEAVER'S SHUTTLE PASSES THROUGH THREADS TO FORM CLOTH

In verse 6 Job seems to reverse the image seen in verse 4 of the slowness of
his life, and complains now, **My days are swifter than a weaver's shuttle**. The
shuttle is the small device used by the weaver to carry the "woof" (or "weft") thread
from one side of the loom to the other. The shuttle darts quickly across the loom,
between the "warp" threads, leaving the "woof" thread stretched behind. The "warp"
threads then close over and under the "woof" thread, holding it in place. In this way
another line of thread has been added to form the cloth. A skilled weaver causes this
to happen quite rapidly, with the shuttle moving back and forth constantly, until a
whole piece of cloth is formed. One day is here compared with one swift movement
of the shuttle.

And come to their end without hope: the Hebrew word for **hope** here can also mean thread. It is used in the sense of thread in Joshua 2.18, where the scarlet thread or cord was displayed to show where Rahab the harlot lived. NEB translates "and come to an end as the thread runs out." The meaning is that life speeds past faster than a weaver's shuttle, and consequently the shuttle is unable to keep supplying thread for the cloth (life). This may be rendered, for example, "My days come to an end for lack of thread," or ". . . when the thread runs out." Many translations, however, follow RSV and TEV, **without hope**. FRCL brings out the double meaning of thread and hope by saying "My life will have passed faster than a weaver's shuttle, it reaches its end when the thread of hope runs out."

Translators must take into account familiarity with the loom in deciding which expression to follow. Since **shuttle** is a technical term, it is best to identify it in a note, as in TEV. In languages where weaving and the loom are unknown, it may be necessary to avoid the expression **swifter than a weaver's shuttle** and use a local alternative. If none is available it is possible to translate without the image by saying simply "My days pass by quickly" or "My life is very short." **And come to their end without hope** may be restructured, particularly if the shuttle figure is avoided; for example, "my days pass by and I have nothing to look forward to" or "and my life ends without hope of being well again."

7.7

RSV	TEV
"Remember that my life is a breath; my eye will never again see good.	Remember, O God, my life is only a breath; my happiness has already ended.

In verse 7 Job's complaint now seems to take on a tone of irony, and so it has been labeled as a reproach against God in the outline. Job calls upon God to remember that his life is nothing more than wind. According to Genesis, it is the breath of God which, when breathed into a person, makes him a living soul. Job sees it differently. To him life is nothing but a breath; life is ebbing away from him.

Remember that my life is a breath: **remember** is a plea to God for him to become again the active Yahweh who showed his people mercy through the covenant. The same expression is used repeatedly by the psalmist in Psalms 20.3; 25.6; 79.8; 106.4. Here the call to God to remember is said in irony. **Breath** translates the Hebrew term *ruach*, which in Psalm 104.29-30 is the wind or spirit that creates life out of dust. By contrast Job uses the term as a symbol of the emptiness of life. **Remember** may sometimes have to be rendered negatively, "Do not forget," or idiomatically, "Do not remove it from your heart." TEV has added the word "only" in "my life is only a breath." This helps to emphasize the limited nature of **breath**. We may also say, for example, "My life is nothing more than a breath." In some languages it may be better to shift to a simile and say "My life is like a breath," as in SPCL.

My eye will never again see good: **my eye** is the poetic use of a part for the whole, and means that Job will not see, experience, witness joy or happiness in life. TEV has restructured this expression to make "happiness" the subject, where **good**

is the object in RSV. In some languages an idiomatic expression will be appropriate; for example, "My mouth will never again taste happiness" or "Happiness will never again hold my heart." FRCL says "My eyes will never again see happiness."

7.8	RSV	TEV

The eye of him who sees me will
    behold me no more;
    while thy eyes are upon me, I
    shall be gone.

You see me now, but never again.
If you look for me, I'll be gone.

This verse is omitted in the Septuagint, but there are no grounds for omitting it in translation. In verse 7 it was Job's eye that would never again see good; now he shifts to **the eye of him who sees me**. In verse 20 God is called "watcher of men," and it would seem that God is the one who sees in verse 8. TEV has made this clear by use of the second person, "You see me now." In some languages it may be necessary to make clear that "you" refers to God, and say accordingly "God, you see me now . . . ." **Will behold me no more**: in Hebrew this clause comes first. The word translated **behold**, meaning to gaze at or look at intently, occurs six times in the book of Job.

While thy eyes are upon me I shall be gone: according to Habel, Job reaches a state of defiance here. The idea is "You will look for me, but I won't be there." Job's absence will frustrate the scrutinizing eyes of God in his search for the Job that was. In some languages the expression "I won't be" or "I won't be there" would be unclear, and we must say, for example, "but I will no longer exist," "I will not be where you look," "I'll be dead and gone away," or "I'll be gone because I will be dead."

3B-6. Life is short and Job wishes God would leave him alone (7.9-16)

RSV	TEV

	RSV		TEV
9	As the cloud fades and vanishes, so he who goes down to Sheol does not come up;	9-10	Like a cloud that fades and is gone, a man dies and never returns; he is forgotten by all who knew him.
10	he returns no more to his house, nor does his place know him any more.	11	No! I can't be quiet! I am angry and bitter. I have to speak.
11	"Therefore I will not restrain my mouth; I will speak in the anguish of my spirit; I will complain in the bitterness of my soul.	12	Why do you keep me under guard? Do you think I am a sea monster?
12	Am I the sea, or a sea monster, that thou settest a guard over me?	13	I lie down and try to rest; I look for relief from my pain.
13	When I say, 'My bed will comfort me, my couch will ease my complaint,'	14	But you—you terrify me with dreams; you send me visions and nightmares
14	then thou dost scare me with dreams and terrify me with visions,	15	until I would rather be strangled than live in this miserable body.
15	so that I would choose strangling and death rather than my bones.	16	I give up; I am tired of living. Leave me alone. My life makes no sense.

16   I loathe my life; I would not live for ever.
         Let me alone, for my days are a
            breath.

Subdivision Heading

Verses 9-16 form the second unit of chapter 7. Translators may modify the Handbook heading to say, for example, "Job complains that God will give him no rest" or "Job is angry with God." Habel has "Human life is futility."

7.9-10 RSV	TEV

9   As the cloud fades and vanishes,
      so he who goes down to Sheol
      does not come up;
10 he returns no more to his house,
      nor does his place know him
      any more.
	9-10 Like a cloud that fades and is
	      gone,
	   a man dies and never returns;
	   he is forgotten by all who knew
	   him.

The second unit opens, as did the first, with a generalized observation. Verse 9 is a simile in which a person who dies and goes down into Sheol is compared to a vanishing cloud. **As the cloud fades and vanishes**: Hosea 13.3 uses similar images, with mist, dew, and smoke to represent how temporary those things are which fade away. **Fades** does not refer to the gradual loss of color but to the gradual dispersion of the drifting cloud. **Vanishes** refers to the final stage of fading so that the cloud is no longer visible.

So he who goes down to Sheol does not come up: Sheol was believed to be beneath the earth. In 1 Samuel 28.15 Samuel complained of Saul's disturbing him by "bringing him up." In 10.21 **Sheol** is a place from which the dead do not return, a land of gloom and darkness. It is the place where all living beings go after death. It may be more natural to place the comparison after the thing compared; for example, "A person dies and does not come back again; he is like a cloud that fades and disappears" or "After a person dies he does not live again; he is like a cloud that fades away and vanishes."

He returns no more to his house: this line simply repeats with a little more detail the end of verse 9b, **he . . . does not come up**, and is omitted by TEV. **Nor does his place know him any more: place** refers to the people where he lived. They do not know him, in the sense that the memory of him vanishes, and so TEV says "he is forgotten." We may sometimes translate "The people who knew him forget him," "He is forgotten by his relatives," or "Those where he lived soon forget him."

7.11-12 RSV	TEV

11 "Therefore I will not restrain my
      mouth;
    I will speak in the anguish of
      my spirit;
	11 No! I can't be quiet!
	    I am angry and bitter.
	    I have to speak.

I will complain in the bitterness of my soul.
12 Am I the sea, or a sea monster, that thou settest a guard over me?

12 Why do you keep me under guard?
Do you think I am a sea monster?[q]

[q] SEA MONSTER: *A reference to ancient stories in which sea monsters had to be guarded so that they would not escape and do damage.*

Verse 11 has three lines. Line a is stated negatively while lines b and c are positive. The parallelism is in the matching of **I will not restrain my mouth, I will speak,** and **I will complain.** There is steady intensification as Job becomes more specific in line c. Job shifts back to himself as he did in verse 3 and begins his second complaint. Verse 11 is introductory to what follows.

Therefore I will not restrain my mouth: Therefore introduces a conclusion, presumably from the generalized statements in verses 9-10. **Restrain my mouth** means to prevent myself from speaking. TEV gives this line considerable emotive impact with "No! I can't be quiet!" **I will speak** in line b matches the negative statement in line a. Job says he will speak out **in the anguish of my spirit,** which is to say in his pain or distress. In line c **complain in the bitterness of my soul** makes specific the nature of Job's speaking and calls attention to his deep negative feelings. **Bitterness of my soul** is another way of saying "I am deeply angry." **Anguish of my spirit** in line b matches **bitterness of my soul** in line c. These expressions are often rendered through other idiomatic expressions; for example, "My heart heat rises" or "The fingers of my stomach seize me."

In verse 12 Job addresses himself directly to God. The form of this verse is a rhetorical question which serves poetically to express a strong denial. **Am I the sea, or a sea monster?** In Hebrew there are two distinct words, rendered by RSV as **sea** and **sea monster.** TEV renders the two as one, "sea monster." The reference to the sea has generally been understood along the lines suggested by such passages as 38.10-11, where God claims to have marked a boundary for the sea. But it is more likely that there is a reference here to Canaanite legends in which Yam, the sea god, is defeated by Baal. The "sea monster" is mentioned in Genesis 1.21; Psalm 74.13; 148.7. In Isaiah 27.1 it is closely associated with Leviathan, and in Isaiah 51.9 with Rahab. In several of these passages there is an allusion to the Mesopotamian story of creation, with its description of the defeat of the forces of chaos by the creator. Translators will no doubt wish to provide a note to explain "sea monster" and can refer to the TEV footnote as a guide. **That thou settest a guard over me:** TEV restructures this dependent clause as a question and places it first. Job complains that he is not a threat to God, like the sea monster that had to be watched over to prevent its causing chaos. Dahood understands the word translated **guard** to mean "muzzle." Most modern translations take the meaning as given in RSV and TEV. In translation it may be clearer to say, for example, "I am not the sea or a great sea snake, dragon, monster, that you have to keep an eye on me" or ". . . that you have to watch what I am doing all the time."

7.13-14   RSV   TEV

	RSV		TEV
13	When I say, 'My bed will comfort me, my couch will ease my complaint,'	13	I lie down and try to rest; I look for relief from my pain.
14	then thou dost scare me with dreams and terrify me with visions,	14	But you—you terrify me with dreams; you send me visions and nightmares

In these verses Job continues his complaint against God. Verse 13 is dependent on verse 14 to complete its thought, and may be taken as in RSV or as a conditional sentence "If I say . . . ." **My bed will comfort me**: Job in his anguish hopes he will find comfort and relief when he goes to bed to sleep. **My couch** is parallel to **my bed** in the previous line but is without heightened poetic effect. **Will ease my complaint** matches **comfort me**. Job's complaint is not just for his physical illness but for the deeper anguish he is unable to escape. In some languages it will not be possible to find a pair of words with similar meaning such as **bed** and **couch**. It is possible in many cases to avoid one or even both nouns and employ verb phrases; for example, "When I lie down to sleep" and "When I go to bed."

Verse 14 completes the thought of verse 13. The two lines of this verse are parallel, saying something very similar. Their purpose is to emphasize Job's complaint against God, who will not even leave him alone in peace while he sleeps. **Then thou dost scare me with dreams**: **then** refers to the time when Job is in bed and sleeping. Eliphaz received his revelations in a vision of the night. For Job such visions are a further source of torment. **Terrify me with visions** is not intended to represent a different reaction nor a different experience. The two lines say very much the same thing. However, the verb translated **terrify** is in the Hebrew intensive form, which heightens the poetic feeling in line b. In some languages it may be necessary to say, for example, "You give me bad dreams that scare me" or "You make me have bad dreams and they scare me." There is no attempt to distinguish **visions** from **dreams** in the parallel lines. The focus is rather on Job's reaction to these nighttime experiences.

7.15   RSV   TEV

RSV	TEV
so that I would choose strangling and death rather than my bones.	until I would rather be strangled than live in this miserable body.

As in the first unit (verses 7-8), Job again seems to be taunting God by rejecting life and preferring death. **So that I would choose strangling** is literally "so chooses strangling my soul." **I** translates the Hebrew "my *nefesh*," which can mean "my soul, throat," or be used as a substitute for the personal pronoun. The one who chooses is the "soul," which here is Job. The word translated **choose** is used in Psalm 84.10 with an additional particle and means "prefer" (RSV "I would rather"); and it seems best to understand it here also as "I would prefer strangling" or "I would prefer to be strangled." In some languages it will be necessary to supply a subject of strangling; for example, "I would prefer to have someone strangle me." Line b has no verb, and the verb from line a must be used again, which makes line b read "I prefer death rather than my bones." Job would rather die than go on being like a bag of bones, which TEV renders "miserable body." Others change a single letter to get "sufferings." HOTTP regards "than my bones" as an "A" reading and suggests a meaning such as "being reduced to a skeleton." In some languages it is possible to say "And I would rather die than go on suffering" or, if **bones** is used, "I would rather die than be a pile of bones" or " . . . than turn into nothing but bones."

7.16   RSV   TEV

> I loathe my life; I would not live   I give up; I am tired of living.
>   for ever.   Leave me alone. My life makes
> Let me alone, for my days are   no sense.
>   a breath.

I loathe my life is literally "I despise" with no object stated. Therefore an object must be supplied from the context. "Death" may be supplied from verse 15, but "life" is more likely as in RSV, in accordance with 9.21, which says plainly "I loathe my life." Some take the meaning of the verb translated **loathe** to mean "give in, succumb," which does not require supplying an object, and so TEV has "I give up." Either RSV or TEV may be followed by translators. In languages in which **life** cannot be used as the object of "hate," we may say, for example, "I hate to go on living" or "I hate to be alive."

I would not live for ever: it hardly seems necessary for Job to make such an obvious remark. Habel thinks Job is making a mock rejection of God's offer of eternal life. He does this on the basis of a comparable situation in a Canaanite legend. However, it does not seem necessary to go outside the text. We can still understand Job's remark as irony, since he does not need to inform God that he is a mortal and will soon die. In the context of Job's life being a mere breath, it does not seem justified to take **for ever** to refer to living eternally, as in the New Testament concept of eternal life; rather, to live "always," to always remain alive.

Let me alone, for my days are a breath: in 10.20 Job says "are not the days of my life few?" Here he pleads that God will leave him alone, or leave him in peace because he has such a short life span. The same word translated **breath** is used in Psalm 144.4, "Man is like a breath, his days like a passing shadow." There does not seem to be any justification for TEV to shift from the image of the frailty of life to its meaninglessness: "My life makes no sense." **For my days are a breath** may be rendered "because I have only a short time to live" or "after only a few breaths I will be dead."

3B-7. Job asks God why he watches him so closely (7.17-21)

RSV   TEV

17 What is man, that thou dost make so   17 Why is man so important to you?
        much of him,   Why pay attention to what he does?
    and that thou dost set thy mind upon   18 You inspect him every morning
        him,   and test him every minute.
18 dost visit him every morning,   19 Won't you look away long enough
    and test him every moment?   for me to swallow my spit?
19 How long wilt thou not look away from   20 Are you harmed by my sin, you jailer?
        me,   Why use me for your target practice?
    nor let me alone till I swallow my   Am I so great a burden to you?
        spittle?   21 Can't you ever forgive my sin?
20 If I sin, what do I do to thee, thou watch-   Can't you pardon the wrong I do?
        er of men?   Soon I will be in my grave,
    Why hast thou made me thy mark?   and I'll be gone when you look for me.
    Why have I become a burden to thee?
21 Why dost thou not pardon my transgres-
        sion
    and take away my iniquity?
    For now I shall lie in the earth;
        thou wilt seek me, but I shall not be."

Subdivision Heading

A heading at this point will provide a sign that the third unit now begins. The Handbook heading may be modified to say, for example, "Job calls God 'You jailer!'" or "Job asks God, 'Won't you ever leave a person alone?'" Habel has "Human beings are humiliated," and TOB "Failure of God."

7.17-18   RSV   TEV

17 **What is man, that thou dost**   17 **Why is man so important to you?**
        make so much of him,   **Why pay attention to what he**
    and that thou dost set thy   **does?**
        mind upon him,   18 **You inspect him every morning**
18 **dost visit him every morning,**   **and test him every minute.**
    and test him every moment?

What is man, that thou dost make so much of him: in Psalm 8.5 the psalmist asks the same question in an attitude of praise and marvel at God's gracious care of his creatures. (See also Psalm 144.3 for a similar question.) Job's attitude is very different from that of the psalmist. Job sees man as being insignificant, and this should be reason enough for God to turn his attention elsewhere and mind his own business. (Translators should review the discussion of irony in the introduction, "Translating the Book of Job," page 19.) RSV **make so much of him** translates the causative form of a Hebrew verb which takes on the meaning of "extol, magnify." In the present context it means "appreciate, think highly of." The form of this question must often be restructured in translation; for example, "Why is a human being so important to you?" or "Why are people so important that you pay attention to them?" **Set thy mind upon him** is expressed in Hebrew as "place the heart on" and

158

refers to mental action such as "concentrate on, pay attention to." In 1 Samuel 4.20 the same expression is used of the mother of Ichabod, who did not pay attention to the women who told her she had given birth to a son. In English the literal expression "set the heart on something" means to desire to possess or accomplish it, which is not the sense in this passage.

Translators should keep in mind that these verses represent some of the most ironic remarks Job makes. In some cases it may be better to shift from the rhetorical questions to negative statements; for example, "I wish you would not think so highly of people, or pay so much attention to them."

In RSV verses 17-21a are translated as rhetorical and why-questions. In some languages these may need to be recast as statements or as statements combined with questions.

Verse 18 continues the generalized introduction. **Visit him every morning**: the Hebrew term for **visit** has a wide range of meaning according to the particular context. Here it means "observe, investigate, inspect, pay attention to." TEV "inspect him every morning" is more precise and satisfactory than RSV. In some languages the sense of **visit** used here is expressed idiomatically; for example, "You put your eyes on him every morning" or "You sniff at him each time the sun rises." **Test him every moment**: the word translated **test** is used of discovering the degree of purity of a metal, and is used metaphorically to mean to examine carefully. **Visit** and **test** are parallel in meaning, with the second being more specific. In the same manner **morning** in line a is paralleled by the smaller time unit **moment** in line b. Line b has the effect of heightening both the time and the event.

7.19   RSV   TEV

> How long wilt thou not look away   Won't you look away long enough
>   from me,   for me to swallow my spit?
> nor let me alone till I swallow
>   my spittle?

Although this verse is stated as a question, the force of Job's words is a plea for God to take his eyes off Job and leave him in peace. **How long wilt thou not look away from me?** This question is awkwardly constructed in English. NEB, which retains the liturgical language when addressing God, says "Wilt thou not look away from me for an instant?" **Nor let me alone until I swallow my spittle?** Job complains that God does not take his observant gaze off Job long enough for him to swallow his spittle. In 9.18 Job asks for time to take a breath. If the expression **swallow my spittle** is unfamiliar or has a different meaning than in Hebrew, it should be avoided or replaced by an equivalent expression. In Arabic the same expression is commonly used with the meaning "to take a break" or "to catch one's breath." The two lines of verse 19 need to be more closely related than they are in RSV. This is done well in TEV: "look away long enough for me . . . ."

7.20   RSV   TEV

If I sin, what do I do to thee, thou watcher of men? Why hast thou made me thy mark? Why have I become a burden to thee?	Are you harmed by my sin, you jailer? Why use me for your target practice? Am I so great a burden to you?

Job now begins to reproach God for treating him unjustly. The first sentence is long for Hebrew poetry and may be understood as a conditional clause, as in RSV **If I sin, what do I do to thee?** Job is not admitting (here or elsewhere) that his troubles have come on him because he has sinned; he is establishing the imaginary context or condition which is required to get relief from God, who is his tormentor. In the next verse he will make a plea for forgiveness for his supposed sin. The question, then, is how should that affect God? This question may sometimes be rendered "If I were to sin, how would it affect you?" or " . . . how are you hurt?" or " . . . what have I done to harm you?" **Thou watcher of men**: God is addressed in this expression of irony, which alludes to verse 12, "You have set a guard over me." Normally in the Scriptures, when God watches, it is for care and protection, but here it is to keep an eye on, that is, to confine or restrict. So TEV translates "you jailer." **Why hast thou made me thy mark?** In 6.4 Job complained of being shot by God's arrows. In 16.12 Job says "He set me up as his target." The word translated "target" means something aimed at. Here **mark** translates a different word, but clearly it has the meaning of target in the present context. In languages where shooting at targets is unknown, it may be necessary to restructure this question to say, for example, "Why have you beaten me" or "Why have you hit me again and again?" The third question **Why have I become a burden to thee?** presents a problem, in that Hebrew says not **to thee** but "to myself," and this is followed by some translations. According to Jewish tradition "to myself" in this passage is one of the eighteen scribal corrections where the original text was altered out of reverence to God. The rabbinical idea was that for Job to be a burden to God would be blasphemy, and this could not be read. RSV and TEV follow "to thee." HOTTP rates "to thee" as a "B" reading. **Why have I become a burden to you?** may have to be restructured to say, for example, "Why have I become something heavy for you to carry?" or "How is it that I am like a load that you have to carry?"

7.21   RSV   TEV

Why dost thou not pardon my transgression and take away my iniquity? For now I shall lie in the earth; thou wilt seek me, but I shall not be."	Can't you ever forgive my sin? Can't you pardon the wrong I do? Soon I will be in my grave, and I'll be gone when you look for me.

Having completed his complaint about being God's target, Job reproaches God with a set of parallel questions. **Why dost thou not pardon my transgression?** Here Job appears to make a mock plea. He makes no request for pardon with an affirmation of trust in God's mercy, nor does he confess guilt. The only reason God would pardon him is because Job will soon be dead and gone. Dhorme suggests that the verb translated **pardon,** which means to "raise, carry, lift, endure," takes on the meaning of tolerate when used with **transgression** or fault as its object, and so translates "And why dost thou not tolerate my transgression and overlook my fault?" **Take away my iniquity** is parallel in both meaning and structure to the previous line. FRCL says "Why do you refuse to put up with my sin, to forgive my wrongs?" GECL says "Can you not take away my mistakes, and simply overlook my sins?"

For now I shall lie in the earth: **For now** introduces the reason for Job's ironical request. Job will soon be dead and in the grave, and it will be too late to consider him further. **In the earth** translates Hebrew "in the dust." In 20.11 and 21.26 the expression "lie down in the dust" means to die. In 17.16 Job asks "Shall we descend together into the dust?" Dust is one of the characteristics of Sheol. TEV says "Soon I will be in my grave." Translators may keep the poetic effect by using an appropriate metaphor for death. SPCL says "Soon I will be stretched out in the dust." **Thou wilt seek me:** **seek** translates a word meaning to seek diligently, carefully. The word is used in Psalm 63.1 for worshipers who eagerly seek Yahweh in the temple. Job ironically reverses the picture and has God seeking Job, his victim. **But I shall not be:** although Psalm 139.8 claims it is impossible to escape God in Sheol, Job asserts that once he dies God will no longer be able to hound him or to pardon him. For Job the land of the dead is the only place of freedom, the only escape. **But I shall not be** may have to be expanded to complete the sense; for example, "But I will no longer exist" or "But I will have ceased to be a living person."

3C. BILDAD'S FIRST SPEECH (8.1-22)

Chapter 8 is the first speech of Bildad. Unlike chapter 7, it is not organized into recurring themes. Rather, it consists of three unique parts. Bildad begins by scolding Job for his long discourse in chapters 6 and 7. He considers Job's talk nothing more than hot air, which he calls "wind." In the first section (verses 2-7) Bildad discourses on God's justice. In the second section (verses 8-19) he appeals to the wisdom of the ancient fathers as the authority for his argument. In this section Bildad uses ancient sayings which refer to two plants, to illustrate his point. In the final section (verses 20-22) Bildad concludes his speech, arguing that God is on the side of the blameless person and will reward the good and punish the wicked.

Division Heading
Many versions use a division heading similar to that in the Handbook. TEV identifies the speaker as Bildad and does not formally translate verse 1, allowing "*Bildad*" to represent it. The translator may prefer something like "Bildad makes his first argument" or "The friend Bildad takes his turn to argue." GECL has "The second friend: be warned!" FRCL has "Bildad's speech: accounts must be settled

sooner or later," NJB "The unswerving course of God's justice," and Habel "Bildad's ancient parable of the two plants."

3C-1. Bildad advises Job to plead with God and have his fortunes restored (8.1-7)

	RSV		TEV
	1 Then Bildad the Shuhite answered:	*Bildad*	
2	"How long will you say these things, and the words of your mouth be a great wind?	1-2	Are you finally through with your windy speech?
3	Does God pervert justice? Or does the Almighty pervert the right?	3	God never twists justice; he never fails to do what is right.
4	If your children have sinned against him, he has delivered them into the power of their transgression.	4	Your children must have sinned against God, and so he punished them as they deserved.
5	If you will seek God and make supplication to the Almighty,	5	But turn now and plead with Almighty God;
6	if you are pure and upright, surely then he will rouse himself for you and reward you with a rightful habitation.	6	if you are so honest and pure, then God will come and help you and restore your household as your reward.
7	And though your beginning was small, your latter days will be very great.	7	All the wealth you lost will be nothing compared with what God will give you then.

Subdivision Heading

Translators wishing to provide a subdivision heading for verses 2-7 may modify the Handbook heading to say, for example, "Job should beg God to help him," "God always does what is right," or "If you ask God, he will restore you." Habel has "Counsel on El's justice," Rowley "Bildad's affirmation of the justice of God," and TOB "Justice of the Almighty."

8.1-2	RSV		TEV
	1 Then Bildad the Shuhite answered:	*Bildad*	
2	"How long will you say these things, and the words of your mouth be a great wind?	1-2	Are you finally through with your windy speech?

Then Bildad the Shuhite answered: see 2.11 for discussion of the names and origins of Job's three friends. For comments on verse 1 see also 4.1. Although in Hebrew each speaker is identified at the beginning of his speech, some languages prefer to place such an identification at the end; for example, "I am Bildad from Shuah and this is what I said to Job." It may be necessary in some languages to provide a transition from one discourse to the next by saying, for example, "After Job

finished speaking, then Bildad from Shuah began to speak." **Answered** does not
mean that Bildad is replying to a question posed by Job, but that he will now take
his turn to address Job, to give him his wise counsel. Having identified Bildad as the
speaker by means of the heading, TEV and others do not repeat the information in
a formal translation of verse 1.

How long will you say these things is the first part of a double rhetorical
question. **How long** is not used to ask a question about the time, but rather to ask
why Job does not stop talking, or to rebuke him for talking at such length. **These
things** refers to the content of Job's speech in chapters 6 and 7, "all these things you
have been saying." NJB says "How much longer are you going to talk like this?"

And the words of your mouth be a great wind: Bildad's question refers to
the opinions Job has expressed in chapter 7. The expression **of your mouth**
frequently occurs with **words**, but it adds nothing to the meaning and most often will
not be translated. **Great wind** is a derogatory way of referring to all that Job said.
TEV renders it "windy speech," and FRCL calls it "that whirlwind of words." In some
languages **great wind** could imply that Bildad is impressed with the powerful and
effective nature of Job's speech. This is not the sense of Bildad's words.

Translators may find it necessary to reduce the parallelism of verse 2 into one
coherent question as in TEV. If the question form must be avoided, it is possible to
say, for example, "You talk and talk, and what you say is like the wind" or "You talk
and never stop. It is like a wind storm."

8.3	RSV	TEV

	Does God pervert justice?
	  Or does the Almighty pervert
	    the right?
		God never twists justice;
		  he never fails to do what is
		    right.

With verse 3 Bildad shifts from scolding Job to instructing him, and begins his
discourse on God's justice with a pair of parallel rhetorical questions whose meanings
are about the same. **Does God pervert justice?** Bildad blames Job for accusing God
of not being just, because Job insists that he is innocent. Even if he has sinned, Job
demands that God leave him in peace, because his time to live is so short (7.20-21).
In Bildad's view God can only act fairly. The word translated **pervert** means "to bend
or distort" and is used of falsifying scales in Amos 8.5. TEV "twist" applies well in
English when used with "justice." **Justice** or judgment refers not only to the act of
judging but also to what is right. If the rhetorical question must be answered in
translation, the reply will be "No." It may be necessary to shift to a negative
statement, "God does not pervert justice!" **Pervert** in the sense used here may
sometimes be rendered, for example, "God does things in the right way," or "God
judges things straight," or sometimes idiomatically, "When God judges people he
does not do it with two mouths."

Or does the Almighty pervert the right? This line expresses the same
thought as the previous line. In line a **God** translates *'El*, and in line b **Almighty**
translates *Shaddai*. **Almighty** is discussed in 5.17. Instead of a word with similar
meaning being used to replace **pervert** in line b, the same Hebrew verb is repeated.
Right translates Hebrew *tsedeq* and in this context has the same meaning as **justice**.

Because the two parallel lines are so close in meaning, SPCL condenses the two into one by saying "God, the Almighty, never twists justice nor the right."

8.4   RSV   TEV

> If your children have sinned   Your children must have sinned
>   against him,   against God,
> he has delivered them into the   and so he punished them as
>   power of their transgression.   they deserved.

In this verse Bildad refers to the death of Job's children and assumes the cause of their death was their sinfulness. The destruction of Job's family proves for Bildad the validity of the doctrine of retribution, that is, if a person sins he will be punished. This is the evidence of God's justice. **If your children have sinned against him**: the form of this clause is conditional as in RSV. However, in the present context there is very little room for doubt, and consequently TEV and others make it a statement, "Your children must have sinned." SPCL is even more certain: "Certainly your children sinned against God." **Sinned against him** means to do what God has commanded people not to do, and is sometimes rendered "Your children have sinned by doing what God said not to do" or ". . . sinned by not obeying God."

He has delivered them into the power of their transgression: into the power of their transgression translates what is literally "He sent them away in the hand of their transgression." The idea is that they sinned, and God used their sins to punish them. It is clear that God is the one who took the initiative to punish them, and so TEV has "He punished them as they deserved." However, it may be preferable to keep the transgressions in focus as the secondary agent; for example, NEB "so he left them to be victims of their own iniquity"; NIV "He gave them over to the penalty of their sin." In some languages it is not possible for sins to serve as the primary agent in punishing people, and so we must often translate "God has punished them through the bad things they did" or "God used the evil they had done to punish them."

8.5-6   RSV   TEV

> 5   If you will seek God   5   But turn now and plead with
>   and make supplication to the   Almighty God;
>   Almighty,   6   if you are so honest and pure,
> 6   if you are pure and upright,   then God will come and help
>   surely then he will rouse him-   you
>   self for you   and restore your household as
>   and reward you with a rightful   your reward.
>   habitation.

Verses 5 and 6 take the form of a long conditional sentence in Hebrew. The "if" clause runs from 5a to 6a, with the consequence in 6b and 6c.

If you will seek God: Job spoke in 7.21 of God seeking him, but Bildad's advice is that Job should seek God. **Seek** does not mean to look for something that is lost or misplaced, but rather implies that Job should change his attitude toward God by going to him for help. **Seek God** may be rendered "Ask God for help," or "Look to God for help," or "Pray that God will hear you and help you." If the two parallel lines are repetitive in translation, and since there is little poetic heightening, it may be possible to adjust the lines; for example, "Seek God the Almighty, and ask him to have mercy on you."

Make supplication to the Almighty: as in verse 3, the first line has *'El* and the second *Shaddai*. The two lines are parallel, but they are varied poetically so that in Hebrew they form a chiasmus:

　　　　(a) seek . . . God　　　　　　(b) Almighty . . . supplication

Make supplication translates a verb meaning "implore, ask for mercy."

If you are pure and upright makes up the third clause. Dhorme regards this line as a scribal addition on the basis that it is alien to the main theme, and consequently omits it. In 1.1 Job is described as being "blameless and upright," where the same term occurring here is translated "upright." In 16.17 Job says his "prayer is pure." See 1.1 for translation suggestions about **upright**. For suggestions concerning **pure** see 4.17.

The consequence of these conditions is **he will rouse himself for you**. **Rouse** translates a verb meaning to wake someone from sleep or to wake up. In Hebrew no object is expressed, but it is implied that it is reflexive. In the present context the sense is not simply that of waking up, but rather of keeping awake and so keeping watch over. This is the suggestion of Dhorme, and NEB translates "Then indeed will he watch over you."

Reward you with a rightful habitation: the word translated **reward** is *shalam*, which means to restore something to its original wholeness, to repair, or to reestablish. **Rightful habitation** translates a phrase which may mean the dwelling which is rightfully his, as in Jeremiah 23.5, or the dwelling which characterizes his righteousness. In Jeremiah 31.23 it is applied to the "land of Judah" and in Jeremiah 50.7 to God himself. Here it may refer either to the dwelling where Job is to live as a righteous man, or to the dwelling which is rightfully his. It is best to take it as TEV has done, "restore your household as your reward." So Job will be given back his family and prosperity. This expression may sometimes be rendered "and give you as a gift the family you once had."

8.7	RSV	TEV
	And though your beginning was small, your latter days will be very great.	All the wealth you lost will be nothing compared with what God will give you then.

The two lines of this verse are in sharp contrast, with **small** in line a̲ and **great** in line b̲. Bildad's promise seems to overlook the fact that Job began, not with small things, but as "the greatest man in the east." However that may be, the words are probably taken from a wise saying that assures the upright of great prosperity. His future wealth will far exceed what he has known in the past, as is seen in 42.12.

Though your beginning was small refers to Job's past life, before his tragedy, not to the time of his birth. **Small** translates "trifle, little thing, something of little importance." In Genesis 19.20 the same term is used, where Lot pleads with the destroying angels at Sodom to allow him to flee to a neighboring city, which he calls a "little one." **Your latter days will be very great: your latter days** translates Hebrew "your end," and when applied to a person, according to Dhorme, it refers to a person's new condition in contrast to his former state. It does not mean "at the end of your life." **Be very great** translates "grow greatly." The term is used in Psalm 92.12, where it refers to physical growth and is parallel to "flourish": "The righteous flourish like the palm tree, and grow like a cedar in Lebanon." If the translator wishes to maintain the contrast of a small beginning with greatness in latter days, it may be necessary to restructure the first clause by saying, for example, "What you had before was small compared with all the wealth you will have later."

3C-2. The ancients know that the godless suffer (8.8-19)

RSV	TEV
8 "For inquire, I pray you, of bygone ages, and consider what the fathers have found;	8 Look for a moment at ancient wisdom; consider the truths our fathers learned.
9 for we are but of yesterday, and know nothing, for our days on earth are a shadow.	9 Our life is short, we know nothing at all; we pass like shadows across the earth.
10 Will they not teach you, and tell you, and utter words out of their understanding?	10 But let the ancient wise men teach you; listen to what they had to say:
11 "Can papyrus grow where there is no marsh? Can reeds flourish where there is no water?	11 "Reeds can't grow where there is no water; they are never found outside a swamp.
12 While yet in flower and not cut down, they wither before any other plant.	12 If the water dries up, they are the first to wither, while still too small to be cut and used.
13 Such are the paths of all who forget God; the hope of the godless man shall perish.	13 Godless men are like those reeds; their hope is gone, once God is forgotten.
14 His confidence breaks in sunder, and his trust is a spider's web.	14 They trust a thread—a spider's web. 15 If they lean on a web, will it hold them up?
15 He leans against his house, but it does not stand; he lays hold of it, but it does not endure.	If they grab for a thread, will it help them stand?"
16 He thrives before the sun, and his shoots spread over his garden.	16 Evil men sprout like weeds in the sun, like weeds that spread all through the garden.
17 His roots twine about the stoneheap; he lives among the rocks.	17 Their roots wrap around the stones and hold fast to every rock.
18 If he is destroyed from his place, then it will deny him, saying, 'I have never seen you.'	18 But then pull them up— no one will ever know they were there.
19 Behold, this is the joy of his way; and out of the earth others will spring.	19 Yes, that's all the joy evil men have; others now come and take their places.

Subdivision Heading

The Handbook heading may be modified to say, for example, "The ancestors knew that evil people suffer" or "It has always been known that sin brings suffering." TOB has two subheadings, "Testimony of the ancestors" (verses 8-12) and "Fate of the wicked" (verses 13-19). Habel (verses 8-20) has "Parable of the two plants," and Rowley "Bildad's appeal to the wisdom of the ancients."

8.8	RSV	TEV
	"For inquire, I pray you, of by- gone ages, and consider what the fathers have found;	Look for a moment at ancient wisdom; consider the truths our fathers learned.

Bildad now claims that his argument is supported by the wisdom of the fathers and wise men of past ages. **For inquire, I pray you, of bygone ages**: his opening phrase is a formula used to appeal to ancient traditions. It is used in Deuteronomy 4.32, where Moses reminds the people of the covenant and asks them to "search the past." See also Jeremiah 18.13. **Bygone ages** translates the Hebrew for "first generation." Interpreters vary greatly as to the meaning of this phrase. It can hardly refer to the patriarchal period, because that is the time setting of the Job story. Some take it to mean the generation immediately past, but others feel that one generation is too limited to accumulate wisdom. It seems best, in spite of the singular, to understand the plural, as in RSV. The command **inquire, I pray you, of bygone ages** must often be restructured to say, for example, "I beg you to ask the people who lived long ago." If such an expression is not possible, since these persons are no longer living, it may be necessary to say "I ask you to find out what the people taught who lived long ago." Line b specifies the content of line a, and in languages where this is required to make line a clear in any case, it may not be necessary to repeat line b.

Consider what the fathers have found: **consider** represents a verb meaning "establish, determine." Many editors change one consonant to get "consider." **What the fathers have found** is literally "the search of their fathers" and may most likely be taken to mean the "fruit of their search, the results of their investigations." **Fathers** refers to the ancestors.

8.9	RSV	TEV
	for we are but of yesterday, and know nothing, for our days on earth are a shadow.	Our life is short, we know noth- ing at all; we pass like shadows across the earth.

The two lines of verse 9 are parallel and stress the need to make use of the experience of the past because of the limited knowledge and life of the living generation. **For we are but of yesterday**: in 14.1-2 Job observes that a person's life "is of few days," which he compares to a flower that blooms and withers. By contrast the fathers, men like Enoch and Noah, lived long lives and gained vast experience. The sense of this expression is as in TEV, "Life is short." Translators should seek to use equivalent sayings that express the shortness of life. In some languages it is necessary to express life as a verb; for example, "We live only a short while," "We do not live long," or "We live very few years and then die." **And know nothing** is understood to be in contrast with the great knowledge accumulated in past ages. **Our days on earth are a shadow: shadow** is used in Old Testament poetry as a symbol of the briefness of life; for example, Psalm 144.4, "Man is like a breath, his days are like a passing shadow." The same thought is expressed in 1 Chronicles 29.15. In translation it may be necessary to shift to a simile and to complete the comparison; for example, "The time we live on earth passes the way a shadow passes" or ". . . goes away as a shadow disappears."

8.10

RSV	TEV
Will they not teach you, and tell you, and utter words out of their understanding?	But let the ancient wise men teach you; listen to what they had to say:

This verse is in the form of a question and has two verbs: **Will they not teach you, and tell you. They** refers to the fathers in verse 8. **Utter words out of their understanding: utter words** translates "bring forth words." This line parallels **teach . . . and tell** in the first line. The words which they bring forth are from "their heart" in Hebrew, which means from the depths of their understanding. The heart in Hebrew stands for the intelligence. The force of the negative question is to make a positive statement: "Indeed, they will teach you." In translation it may be better to reduce the three verbs to two as in TEV and others. In some languages it will be necessary to make explicit what they teach; for example, "They will teach you their wisdom" or ". . . what they have learned."

8.11

RSV	TEV
"Can papyrus grow where there is no marsh? Can reeds flourish where there is no water?	"Reeds can't grow where there is no water; they are never found outside a swamp.

In RSV this verse consists of two rhetorical questions which anticipate "No" as a reply. These questions are thought to be proverbial sayings which reflect the wisdom Bildad cherishes. Scholars emphasize that the terms for **papyrus** and **reeds** have an Egyptian connection. Note that TEV makes verses 11-14 the teachings of the ancestors.

Can papyrus grow where there is no marsh? Papyrus is an aquatic (water) plant of the sedge family that grew in the shallow waters of the Nile river. It was used for making an early form of paper, among other things (the word "paper" is derived from "papyrus"). **Marsh** translates a word which occurs only in 40.21 and in Ezekiel 47.11. **Marsh** is another name for swamp. **Reeds flourish where there is no water? Reeds** are like papyrus, tall grassy plants that grow near water. The same Hebrew term is found in Genesis 41.2,18. For a description of these plants, see *Fauna and Flora of the Bible,* pages 125 and 171-172. The point of the saying is that people need to have a dependable source of life, just as these plants require abundant water to sustain them.

PAPYRUS PLANTS

The questions of verse 11 are rhetorical and parallel. The translator must decide whether to keep them as questions and whether or not a "No" is required. In some languages it may be better to translate as SPCL does, "Reeds and papyrus only grow where water is plentiful." In some languages well-known swamp grasses will substitute. However, the names of these grasses should be familiar. If no such grasses are known, a single generic term may be used.

REEDS

8.12   RSV   TEV

While yet in flower and not cut down,	If the water dries up, they are the first to wither,
they wither before any other plant.	while still too small to be cut and used.

While yet in flower translates "while it is in its greenness" and refers most likely to the early or blossoming stage of the plant, a plant that is not yet ripe or mature for use. **They wither before any other plant**: this line is the main clause, and in some languages it must come before the line above. It is implied that these plants will wither more quickly than any other plant "if the water dries up," as TEV makes clear.

8.13   RSV   TEV

Such are the paths of all who forget God;	Godless men are like those reeds; their hope is gone, once God is forgotten.
the hope of the godless man shall perish.	

Bildad now draws his conclusion from the saying and its explanation. **Such are the paths of all who forget God: paths** translates a word meaning "destiny, fate, future." The Septuagint translates "latter end" by making a change in the text, and this is followed by some editors. Dhorme retains the Hebrew text and finds support in Proverbs 1.19, where the same term is said to mean "fate" and is rendered "this is what happens to anyone" by TEV. **Who forget God** does not mean to fail to remember God, but as in Deuteronomy 8.11-20, to refuse to acknowledge God's authority, or to disobey him. This line may be rendered, for example, "People who disobey God are like those plants" or "This is what happens to people who pay no attention to God."

The hope of the godless man shall perish: hope refers to the source of renewal which an individual needs to survive, and is the spiritual equivalent of the sustaining water for the plant. For comments on **hope** see 4.6. **Godless man** parallels **all who forget God** in the previous line. The word translated **godless** occurs repeatedly in Job and is based on a verb meaning "to be profane"; that is, the person has turned aside from God and has therefore cut himself off from worship and contact with God, almost as if ritually unclean—but by his own decision. The term is used especially in connection with murder and adultery, but here is closely parallel in meaning with **all who forget God**. In many languages it is not possible to say that "hope perishes or dies." However, it is often possible to express this line as "Godless people perish without hope."

8.14   RSV   TEV

His confidence breaks in sunder,   They trust a thread—a spider's
  and his trust is a spider's   web.
  web.°

° Heb *house*

His confidence breaks in sunder: **breaks in sunder** translates a word
(uncertain whether noun or verb) that occurs only here. Assuming that its meaning
matches **spider's web** in the next line, interpreters have deduced a wide range of
meanings. It is impossible with the evidence available to say with any degree of
certainty what the meaning is. The apparent reference is to something fragile, and
modern translators use "thread, feather," or "gossamer." NIV says "fragile," and the
use of such a general description may be better than the more specific objects that
symbolize it. Note also that the occurrence of "hope" in verse 13, which in Hebrew
sounds like "thread," may mean the author is using a wordplay here, to show that
hope is fragile as thread, or even as a spider's web. For **confidence** see 4.6. In some
languages this idea is expressed idiomatically; for example, "He places his heart on
something that is easily broken."

His trust is a spider's web: RSV has a note "Hebrew *house*." In Hebrew, as
in Arabic, a spider's web is literally "spider's house." The word translated **trust**
means "security" and occurs in 18.14, and also in 31.24, where the same parallelism
is found again. This series of images highlights the inevitable failure of the godless,
according to Bildad's understanding. From a general statement in the first line, the
thought moves to something much more specific with the use of **spider's web** here.
This line means that his security or safety is as fragile as a spider's web, and it may
be appropriate to translate with a simile making clear the fragile aspect: "His safety
is as fragile as a spider's web" or "He cannot be protected more than a spider's web
would protect him."

8.15   RSV   TEV

He leans against his house, but it   If they lean on a web, will it
  does not stand;   hold them up?
he lays hold of it, but it does   If they grab for a thread, will
  not endure.   it help them stand?"

Bildad continues the metaphor depicting the insecurity of the godless person.
He leans against his house, but it does not stand: the image of the fragile
spider's web is continued here in terms of the evil man's house. **His house** may refer
to his dwelling, but more probably it refers to his prosperity or wealth. If the godless
man relies on any of these, he will find them no more substantial than the web. **Lean**
can refer to placing physical weight on something or to finding support and security.
TEV and others take **house** to refer to the "web" of verse 14, while other translators
follow RSV **his house**. The line may be rendered, for example, "He relies on his
wealth to protect him, but it cannot."

He lays hold of it, but it does not endure: **lays hold of** translates the same word used in 2.3, where God reminds Satan that Job "still holds fast his integrity." Here it refers to grasping or clutching his dwelling or wealth to maintain his security, that is, "He holds on to what he owns, but it does not last."

8.16   RSV   TEV

He thrives before the sun,
  and his shoots spread over his
    garden.
	Evil men sprout like weeds in the
	    sun,
	  like weeds that spread all
	    through the garden.

The image of the two plants which was introduced in verses 11-12 is brought back, but now they are in a garden, not a marsh. Here evil people are like a well-watered plant that spreads throughout a garden but is soon destroyed. **He thrives before the sun**: **thrives** translates a word meaning "moist" or "sappy" and is found only here. The verb form is found in 24.8, where RSV renders it "They are wet." This line may be taken to mean "He is watered before the sun rises." The watering may be the work of the owner of the garden or may be the result of the early morning dew. In some languages it will be necessary to adjust the third person singular pronoun **he**, which goes back to the **godless man** in verse 13, and shift to a simile; for example, "They are like plants that are watered before the sun rises." If the passive voice must be avoided, we may translate, for example, "They are like plants which a gardener waters before the sun rises."

His shoots spread over the garden does not parallel the first line but is its consequence. **Shoots** are the new growth that spreads out from the parent plant. TEV has "weeds"; however, the reference is not to individual weeds, which would have separate roots from the main plant. **His garden** is changed by some editors who feel that, since the evil person is compared to the plant, the garden is not meant to refer to the same person. However, the meaning is not that he is the owner of the garden, but simply that the garden is the place where he grows. We can translate line b, for example, "and their shoots come up everywhere in the garden."

8.17   RSV   TEV

His roots twine about the stone-
    heap;
  he lives among the rocks.ᴾ
	Their roots wrap around the
	    stones
	  and hold fast toʳ every rock.

ᴾ Gk Vg: Heb uncertain   ʳ *Probable text* hold fast to; *Hebrew* see.

His roots twine about the stone-heap: the image and wording lend themselves to contrasting points of view. Although the plant will be torn out in verse 18, here it may mean that the roots are solidly entwined about the stones. This is the picture in TEV. It may also be taken to mean that, because the plant is on stony ground, it is weak, and so NEB "but its roots become entangled in a stony patch." It seems preferable to take it as in TEV, so that the wicked appear to be flourishing and secure, yet will be destroyed. **Twine** means to wind and twist about the stones, penetrating through the cracks. If **he** has been replaced by "evil people" or "they" in the translation of previous verses, it is important to maintain the same subject also in verses 17-19.

He lives among the rocks translates the Hebrew text, "He sees the house of stones." The Septuagint has "He lives in the midst of stones," which involves making two changes in the Hebrew and is the form of RSV. The RSV footnote says "Hebrew uncertain." TEV follows a widely-supported textual change giving the meaning "They grasp it," and so has "holds fast to every rock." Both TEV and RSV follow a change from Hebrew *beth* "house" to *ben* "among" in the expression "house of stones." HOTTP considers "he sees" to be a "B" reading but gives it the meaning "to investigate" or "to break through." It is possible to interpret the Hebrew text as presenting a picture of spreading roots from garden to rock pile in 16b and 17a and then to the house in 17b, in which the house of stones is ripped apart. In this way the poetic effect is built up in 17b. We may then render the Hebrew of verse 17 "His roots entangle themselves in the rock pile, and his stone house is ripped apart."

8.18

RSV	TEV
If he is destroyed from his place, then it will deny him, saying, 'I have never seen you.'	But then pull them up— no one will ever know they were there.

Once the plant is uprooted, it is forgotten, and such is the implied fate of the wicked. **If he is destroyed from his place** is literally "If one destroys him." **Destroy** translates Hebrew "swallow" and is used also in 7.19; 20.15,18 with the same meaning. **His place**, like **his garden** in verse 16, means the place where he is rooted. This line, which is an "if" clause, is rendered by TEV as a command. It is not clear to whom this command should be addressed. NEB has "Then someone uproots it from its place."

Then it will deny him: the subject of **deny** is **his place** in the first line. **Deny** has the sense of "disown" and is used also in 31.28 (RSV "been false to"). Psalm 103.16 says "and its place knows it no more." **I have never seen you**: in poetic terms the garden itself speaks these words, which is a way of saying that the plant disappears without a trace, and the wicked man will do the same. If the poetic image of the garden disowning the uprooted plant and speaking is not possible, the translator may have to follow something along the lines of TEV, "No one will ever know they were there" or "Everyone will say that there never was anything there."

8.19

RSV	TEV
Behold, this is the joy of his way; and out of the earth others will spring.	Yes, that's all the joy evil men have; others now come and take their places.

Behold, this is the joy of his way: this verse is problematic. Many scholars believe the Hebrew word translated **joy** makes no sense in the context. Consequently Dhorme drops one consonant and gets a word meaning "rotting" and translates "Behold him rotting on a path." NEB seems to follow this proposal as well and translates "That is how its life withers away." Others make far-reaching changes. Gordis suggests a change that means "depart" and translates "Behold, it goes on its way." Habel prefers to keep the Hebrew text as it is and accepts the tone of the speaker as ironic, with a meaning suggesting that the root "rejoices in the earth that swallows it." If the translator accepts the Hebrew text and the ironical force of the statement, the meaning is as in TEV, "that's all the joy evil men have," or "the joy of evil people does not last long," or "evil people are not joyful long."

Out of the earth others will spring: in Hebrew the subject is singular, but it must be understood as collective, since the verb is plural. **Earth** translates "dust" as in 5.6, but here with the meaning of soil. The godless person has been compared to a healthy plant that is pulled up and thrown out, and where it grew other plants will shoot up and take its place. **Out of the earth** refers to other plants sprouting to take the place of the one uprooted. However, as in TEV, it may be necessary to refer not to the plants but to the evil persons represented by the plants; for example, "Others now come and take their places" or "Other evil people come and take their places."

3C-3. God will help Job if he is faithful (8.20-22)

	RSV		TEV
20	"Behold, God will not reject a blameless man,	20	But God will never abandon the faithful or ever give help to evil men.
	nor take the hand of evildoers.	21	He will let you laugh and shout again,
21	He will yet fill your mouth with laughter, and your lips with shouting.	22	but he will bring disgrace on those who hate you,
22	Those who hate you will be clothed with shame,		and the homes of the wicked will vanish.
	and the tent of the wicked will be no more."		

Subdivision Heading

Translators may wish to show that Bildad has reached his conclusion. The Handbook heading may be worded, for example, "God will help Job" or "If you are faithful, Job, God will take care of you." Habel has "Closing assurance," Rowley "Summary," and TOB "Promises of happiness."

8.20	RSV	TEV
	"Behold, God will not reject a blameless man, nor take the hand of evildoers.	But God will never abandon the faithful or ever give help to evil men.

Bildad has reached the conclusion of his speech and now summarizes his advice to Job in terms of the divine justice in which God takes care of good people but refuses his protection to the wicked. **Behold, God will not reject a blameless man**:

Bildad's principle is first stated in negative terms; the positive expression of it is to come in the next two verses. **Blameless** is the quality which the poet used to describe Job in 1.1, and which God used of him in 1.8. **Not reject** may be expressed positively in some languages; for example, "God will accept a blameless person." **Nor take the hand of evildoers**: line b contrasts **evildoers** with **blameless man** in line a. **Take the hand** is used in Isaiah 42.6 meaning that God supported, protected, helped. This line is negative and may be translated "But God will not help evil people."

8.21   RSV   TEV

He will yet fill your mouth with laughter, and your lips with shouting.	He will let you laugh and shout again,

Verse 21 has two parallel lines, in which **mouth** and **laughter** in line a match **lips** and **shouting** in b. The verb **fill** does duty for both lines. **He will yet fill your mouth with laughter**: **yet** translates a Hebrew adverb which may, according to HOTTP, mean "until, again, or while," with "until" the most probable meaning. On the other hand, Dhorme takes it to mean "again" and translates as a passive, "Your mouth will again be filled with laughter." **And your lips with shouting**: **shouting** translates a word which means "shout of joy" but can also mean "war cry" and is used in this sense in 39.25. In the sense of repeating the action, SPCL says "He will cause you to laugh again." There is little intensification in the two parallel lines, and so some translators may find it best to reduce the two lines to one; for example, "He will cause you to laugh and shout with joy again."

8.22   RSV   TEV

Those who hate you will be clothed with shame, and the tent of the wicked will be no more."	but he will bring disgrace on those who hate you, and the homes of the wicked will vanish.

Those who hate you will be clothed with shame: **who hate you** is the common expression in the Psalms for the enemies of the righteous, and this is matched in the next line by **the wicked**. The metaphor **clothed with shame** is used in Psalm 35.26 as a plea: "Let them be . . . ." **Shame** is pictured as a garment that clothes the enemies of good people in Psalm 109.29; 132.18. In languages in which the passive cannot be used, it will be necessary to say, for example, "God will clothe with shame those who hate you," or if the metaphor must be replaced by a nonmetaphor, "God will bring shame on the people who hate you," or idiomatically, "God will cause those who hate you to have hot faces."

The tent of the wicked will be no more: **tent of the wicked** is a common image from the Psalms, where the "tents of wickedness" are contrasted with the "tents of the righteous"; for examples see Psalm 84.10; 118.15. The reference is to their dwelling or home. **Will be no more** means "vanish, disappear, be destroyed." This line may sometimes be rendered "and God will destroy the houses where wicked people live."

3D. JOB REPLIES (9.1–10.22)

Job's speech (chapters 9–10) consists of four themes, three of which are repeated, and the fourth, Job's plea to be left alone to die, serves as the conclusion. Job begins speaking of the impossibility of answering God (9.2-4). This is followed in 9.5-13 by a discourse on God's wisdom and power in nature. Then in 9.14-21 Job returns to his first theme. In 9.22-31 he opens a third theme, that God is unjust in his dealing with people. Again in 9.32-35 he returns to the first theme, the impossibility of answering God. In 10.1-7 he renews the theme of God's injustice. In 10.8-13 he discourses again on the greatness of God in creating and caring for him, although with a bad motive. In 10.14-17 Job again depicts God as being unjust. Finally in 10.18-22 Job regrets his birth and pleads with God to let him die in peace.

The following display illustrates how Job moves back and forth between these themes. Translators will note that the headings in the Handbook are not entirely in the same positions as the themes in the display. This is because the Handbook sometimes covers more than one theme under a single heading. See, for example, page 192, in which a single heading serves for verses 25-35, which involves two themes. Alternative suggestions for the placement of headings are suggested in the text.

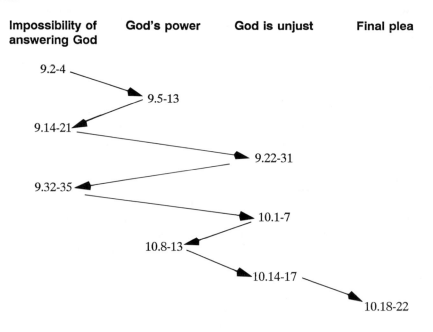

Impossibility of answering God	God's power	God is unjust	Final plea
9.2-4			
	9.5-13		
9.14-21			
		9.22-31	
9.32-35			
		10.1-7	
	10.8-13		
		10.14-17	
			10.18-22

Division Heading

For suggestions regarding the division heading, see comments on the same in 3-B (6.1–7.21). Other translations have, for example, FRCL "God is too strong for me"; Habel "Job on the futility of litigation"; NJB "God's justice is above all law"; Rowley "Job answers Bildad"; NAB "Job's second reply."

3D-1. Job sees no way to win his case with God (9.1-4)

	RSV		TEV
	1 Then Job answered:	*Job*	
2	"Truly I know that it is so:	1-2	Yes, I've heard all that before.
	But how can a man be just before		But how can a man win his case
	God?		against God?
3	If one wished to contend with him,	3	How can anyone argue with him?
	one could not answer him once in a		He can ask a thousand questions
	thousand times.		that no one could ever answer.
4	He is wise in heart, and mighty in	4	God is so wise and powerful;
	strength		no man can stand up against him.
	—who has hardened himself against him,		
	and succeeded?—		

Subdivision Heading

The Handbook heading includes only verses 2-4, which is the first expression of the impossibility of answering God. Translators wishing to place a heading before verse 2 may say, for example, "Job knows he cannot answer God" or "Job admits it is impossible to argue with God."

9.1-2	RSV		TEV
	1 Then Job answered:	*Job*	
2	"Truly I know that it is so:	1-2	Yes, I've heard all that before.
	But how can a man be just		But how can a man win his
	before God?		case against God?

Then Job answered: see comments on 4.1 and 8.1. **Truly I know that it is so: Truly** is a characteristic expression used in Job (12.2; 19.4; 34.12; 36.4) and may be rendered "certainly, indeed, yes." Job says in 13.2 "What you know I also know; I am not inferior to you" (RSV). Job may be dismissing most of what Bildad has said as being common knowledge, and therefore TEV has "I've heard all that before." However, Bildad has said that God does not pervert justice, whereas Job will argue the contrary. So we must understand a certain irony in Job's reply. He does not mean that he agrees and accepts all that Bildad has said. The relationship between the two lines in verse 2 may be understood in different ways. Some take line b to be the object of the verb **know** in line a. For example, NEB translates "Indeed this I know for the truth, that no man can win his case against God." Others make 2b a contrast with 2a, and so the thing which Job knows refers to the traditional wisdom expounded by Bildad in chapter 8. FRCL translates 2a "Certainly, I am well acquainted with this point of view," which is similar to TEV. In some languages this line may be rendered, for example, "Yes, I know well the path of your words" or "I certainly know the story your words tell."

But how can a man be just before God? Line b begins with a contrast in which Job picks up Eliphaz's question in 4.17, "Can mortal man be righteous before God?" The Hebrew verb *tsadaq* is here translated **be just** and means to be righteous or to be in the right. It is used in the legal sense in Exodus 23.7. In 4.17 Eliphaz used it in the moral and religious sense. The entire thrust of chapter 9 has to do with the hopelessness of obtaining justice from God, and *tsadaq* is therefore understood in the sense of being acquitted by winning a lawsuit against one's opponent, in this case God. This is the meaning as translated by TEV, Mft, NEB, and NJV. In languages in which legal cases are not heard formally by a judge, it may be necessary to say, for example, "How can a person prove to God that he is innocent?" "How can a person show God that he is not in the wrong?" or as a direct statement, "A person cannot say to God 'I am innocent.'"

9.3	RSV	TEV

<table>
<tr><td>

If one wished to contend with
   him,
   one could not answer him once
    in a thousand times.

</td><td>

How can anyone argue with him?
   He can ask a thousand ques-
    tions
    that no one could ever an-
     swer.[s]

</td></tr>
</table>

[s] He can ask . . . answer; *or* A man could ask him a thousand questions, and he would not answer.

If one wished to contend with him: in Hebrew there are only third-person singular pronouns in verse 3, and in translation it will often be necessary to replace these with nouns. TEV, like RSV, understands that it is man who may wish to **contend** (argue a case, go to a law court) with God. **One could not answer him once in a thousand times** translates what is literally "with him he cannot answer him once in a thousand times." This is best expressed in TEV as "He (God) can ask a thousand questions that no one could ever answer," and TEV offers an alternative in the margin, "A man could ask him (God) a thousand questions and he (God) would not answer." RSV, like TEV text, assumes that God asks the questions which **one could not answer.**

Once in a thousand times: the two main interpretations of this phrase are that God could pose a thousand questions which would be beyond man's ability to answer (as in RSV and others), or that God will not answer an accusation by man, not even once in a thousand times, which is to say "not ever" or "not at all." NEB follows the latter in the text and the former in the margin. Translators should follow the text of TEV. Chapters 38–41 illustrate God's asking Job numerous questions which he cannot answer, or at least he makes no attempt to answer. In languages in which **once in a thousand times** would be understood literally as a slight probability of answering successfully, it will be better to translate as in TEV, "no one could ever answer."

9.4

RSV	TEV
He is wise in heart, and mighty in strength —who has hardened himself against him, and succeeded?—	God is so wise and powerful; no man can stand up against him.

He is wise in heart: as usual in the Old Testament, **heart** here represents intelligence. The same expression is used in 37.24. The Hebrew does not specify the one who is **wise in heart**, but the following question makes clear that it refers to God and not to man. **Wise in heart** may have to be restructured in translation to say, for example, "God is wise," "God's heart is wise," or "there is wisdom in God's heart." **Mighty in strength**: verse 19 confirms that the qualities of intelligence and strength belong to God. **Mighty in strength**, if rendered literally, may be unnecessarily redundant. The whole line may be rendered "God is wise and powerful."

Who has hardened himself against him and succeeded? This line is a rhetorical question requiring in many languages the reply "No one." The form of the Hebrew for **hardened** has no object, the usual one being "nape of the neck," with the meaning of "oppose, resist." It is best to take it here with that meaning as in TEV, "No man can stand up against him." In some languages a suitable figure may be used; for example, "who has raised his hand against God?" "Who has pushed out his lip at God?" If no figurative expression exists, it may be necessary to ask "Who has said 'No' to God?" or "Who has said to God 'I will not obey you'?" **Succeeded** translates a form of the verb *shalam* meaning "to be safe, intact, whole." The meaning of the line may be rendered as a question, "Who can defy God and get away with it?" or "Can anyone challenge God and win his case? Certainly not."

3D-2. Job cannot confront a powerful God (9.5-13)

	RSV		TEV
5	he who removes mountains, and they know it not, when he overturns them in his anger;	5	Without warning he moves mountains and in anger he destroys them.
6	who shakes the earth out of its place, and its pillars tremble;	6	God sends earthquakes and shakes the ground; he rocks the pillars that support the earth.
7	who commands the sun, and it does not rise; who seals up the stars;	7	He can keep the sun from rising, and the stars from shining at night.
8	who alone stretched out the heavens, and trampled the waves of the sea;	8	No one helped God spread out the heavens or trample the sea monster's back.
9	who made the Bear and Orion, the Pleiades and the chambers of the south;	9	God hung the stars in the sky—the Dipper, Orion, the Pleiades, and the stars of the south.
10	who does great things beyond understanding, and marvelous things without number.	10	We cannot understand the great things he does, and to his miracles there is no end.
11	Lo, he passes by me, and I see him not; he moves on, but I do not perceive him.		

12	Behold, he snatches away; who can hinder him? Who will say to him, 'What doest thou'?	11	God passes by, but I cannot see him.
		12	He takes what he wants, and no one can stop him; no one dares ask him, "What are you doing?"
13	"God will not turn back his anger; beneath him bowed the helpers of Rahab.	13	God's anger is constant. He crushed his enemies who helped Rahab, the sea monster, oppose him.

Subdivision Heading

The Handbook heading recognizes verses 5-13 as Job's inability to confront the power of God. Translators may wish to modify this to say, for example, "Job acknowledges that God is great," "God is too great for our understanding," or "God is wise and powerful." Habel has "Characterization of the adversary."

9.5   RSV   TEV

> he who removes mountains, and they know it not,
> when he overturns them in his anger;

> Without warning he moves mountains
> and in anger he destroys them.

Verses 5-13, which form a doxology, or expression of praise to God, begin with a particle implying God as the subject, and in translation this should be made clear. In verses 1-12 God is actually named as the subject only in verse 2. In these verses of praise to God, Job shows that he knows as much theology as his friends. In RSV verses 4-10 make up one long sentence. Because verse 5 begins a new subdivision of the text, it is important to begin verse 5 with a new sentence.

He who removes mountains: the picture is that of an earthquake, with the shaking of the pillars upon which the earth rests. In Psalm 75.3 the earth is shaken when God judges. **Remove mountains** may have to be expressed differently in some languages to say, for example, "shake mountains," "cause mountains to fall down," "shakes down the mountains with an earthquake." **They know it not**: in RSV the literal rendering gives the meaning that the mountains do not know when they are moved or shaken by God. TEV understands the verb **know** in an impersonal sense, implying "nobody knew what would happen," and translates "Without warning." Dhorme understands the object of the verb to be the following line, that is, the mountains "know not the one who has overturned them in his anger." NEB takes the verb to mean "to be still or at rest" and translates "It is God who moves mountains, giving them no rest." Some scholars prefer to follow the Syriac, which has "and he does not know it," meaning that shaking mountains is such a common event that God could do so without even knowing it. Probably the best understanding is "suddenly," or "before they knew anything about it," and so the text is best expressed by TEV "Without warning." "Without warning" may be rendered "Without saying a word," "Without telling anyone."

When he overturns them in his anger: the verb translated **overturns** means to knock over, turn upside down. The word is used in connection with the destruction of Sodom in Genesis 19. The reference is to the violent action of turning the mountains over or causing them to collapse. TEV "destroy" is less descriptive and more general. **In his anger**: in 4.9 Eliphaz speaks of God cutting off the wicked, literally, "by his nostril." The same expression is used here and may suggest the picture of a hot blast of breath through the nostril. In some languages the expression **in his anger** must be expressed as a reason clause; for example, "when he overturns the mountains because he is angry" or "because of his anger he throws them down."

9.6	RSV	TEV
	who shakes the earth out of its place, and its pillars tremble;	God sends earthquakes and shakes the ground; he rocks the pillars that support the earth.

Who shakes the earth out of its place: Job continues to describe God as one who creates chaos in the universe, just as he has brought fear and chaos into Job's own life. In connection with God's judgment, **out of its place** refers to the foundation upon which the earth rests, and this is spelled out in the next line.

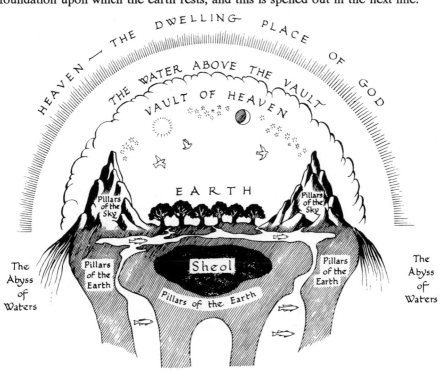

AN ANCIENT CONCEPT OF THE UNIVERSE

And its pillars tremble: the supports on which the earth is thought to rest are mentioned in Psalm 75.3, "when the earth totters, and all its inhabitants, it is I who keep steady its pillars" (RSV). In 26.11 the heavens are said to be supported on pillars. In this verse the shaking of the pillars causes the earthquake. In some translations it may be necessary to provide a note as well as cross references to explain the ancient biblical picture of the world resting on pillars over the water. In some languages it may be necessary to translate, for example, "God shakes the earth on its foundations, and makes the stones it rests on to tremble."

9.7 RSV	TEV
who commands the sun, and it does not rise; who seals up the stars;	He can keep the sun from rising, and the stars from shining at night.

Who commands the sun and it does not rise: the author shifts from speaking of the earth in verse 6 to speaking of the heavens. The agent of the verb continues to be God. The command not to rise is given to the sun, which is here not the usual term for sun, but rather a poetic term. In some languages it may be necessary to shift to direct address; for example, "God says to the sun, 'Do not rise,' and to the stars, 'Do not shine.' " **Who seals up the stars**: the action of sealing up the stars would be to cover them and not allow them to shine. So Job describes God as one who keeps the heavens in darkness, and this is similar to their condition in 3.4-9, when he called on God to "let that day (of his conception) be darkness."

9.8 RSV	TEV
who alone stretched out the heavens, and trampled the waves of the sea;[q]	No one helped God spread out the heavens or trample the sea monster's back.[t]
[q] Or *trampled the back of the sea dragon*	[t] TRAMPLE THE SEA MONSTER'S BACK: *A reference to ancient stories in which a sea monster was killed and then trampled (see also 26.13).*

Who alone stretched out the heavens: the Hebrew of this line differs from Isaiah 44.24 only by "I . . . alone." Both passages emphasize that God created the heavens by his own power, with nobody to help him. For similar references see Psalm 18.9-15; 144.5-7. In Isaiah 40.22 and Psalm 104.2 God stretches out the heavens like a tent or curtain. In many languages the sky is not thought of as something that can be stretched across space, and in such cases we must often say "God alone put the sky in its place" or "without anyone's help God put the sky above."

Trampled the waves of the sea: the RSV footnote reads "trampled the back of the sea dragon." This reading derives from the assumption that Hebrew *yam* "sea" is to be identified here with Ugaritic *yammu* "sea dragon," and the word **waves**, literally "heights," is to be taken as meaning "back." Another interpretation understands the expression to mean "the back of the sea." **Trample the waves** does not refer to merely walking on the waves, but rather to subduing the sea, or controlling it. The same notion applies where "the sea dragon" replaces "the sea." Translators may be able to use a figurative expression for this thought; for example, "he puts down his foot on the waves of the sea," "he stops the waves of the sea with his hand." If a figurative expression is not possible, we may sometimes translate "he subdues the waves of the sea," or if the animal is used, "he destroys the sea monster." For suggestions regarding "sea monster," see 7.12.

9.9 RSV	TEV
who made the Bear and Orion, the Pleiades and the chambers of the south;	God hung the stars in the sky— the Dipper, Orion, the Pleiades, and the stars of the south.

This verse introduces references to groups of stars in the sky. A fuller description is provided in the Appendix, page 781, so that translators may be able to identify them and mention them according to names already existing in the receptor language.

Who made the Bear and Orion, the Pleiades and the chambers of the south: in 38.31-32 the order of these constellations is reversed and the Hebrew term for the Bear is different. The Septuagint and Syriac reverse the order here also. Due to the inconsistent use of these names, there appears to have been no clear-cut identification for them, although Orion is more consistently identified by the name used here than the other two. Although the first three names in Hebrew do not identify with any certainty the three constellations suggested in RSV and others, translators are advised to use the names of these constellations in their own languages.

Bear may refer to either the Big Dipper or the Little Dipper, both being constellations in the region of the sky near the north celestial pole. **Orion** is a conspicuous constellation and can be located in the winter skies of the northern hemisphere by extending a line drawn from Polaris, the North Star, through the star Capella in the constellation Auriga. **Pleiades** is a small cluster of stars located in the shoulder of the bull in the constellation Taurus. If specific names for constellations are lacking or are too little known to be of any value to the reader, the translator may borrow these terms from a major language. If this would not be helpful, we may translate, for example, "He made the group of stars in the northern sky, the group of stars in the middle sky." The former would apply to the **Bear**, and the latter to **Orion** and **Pleiades**.

And the chambers of the south: this expression does not seem to identify any constellation. Pope suggests that, since "chamber" is the source of the tempest in 37.9, the reference may be to the place from which the south winds blow. TEV and others understand it to be a general term for southern stars. In many languages it will be best to translate **chambers of the south** as in TEV, "stars of the south," or "stars in the southern skies."

9.10   RSV   TEV

> who does great things beyond
>   understanding,
> and marvelous things without
>   number.

> We cannot understand the great
>   things he does,
> and to his miracles there is no
>   end.

Who does great things beyond understanding: this verse repeats the thought of Eliphaz's words in 5.9, perhaps with a touch of irony. **Marvelous things without number**: this line parallels the previous line in both meaning and structure. There is little rhetorical heightening, however. In translation it may be necessary to indicate the ones possessing understanding; for example, "beyond the understanding of people" or "far greater than people can understand." **Without number** may be rendered "More marvelous things than a person can count."

9.11   RSV   TEV

> Lo, he passes by me, and I see
>   him not;
> he moves on, but I do not
>   perceive him.

> God passes by, but I cannot see
>   him.

Lo, he passes by me, and I see him not: in these parallel lines Job speaks of the mystery of God's ways in relation to his own. God is not only the powerful creator who hangs the stars in the sky, but he is also elusive and invisible. In 4.15-16 Eliphaz experienced an eerie wind gliding over his face. Here Job cannot see him. For comments on **Lo** see 5.27; and see discussion on the synonymous term "behold" in 1.12,19. **Passes by me** means that God passes close to where Job is. The verb translated **see** carries also the connotation of "being acquainted with." **He moves on, but I do not perceive him**: **perceive** translates a word very close in meaning to **see** in line a, so that TEV reduces the two lines to one. **Perceive him** may need to be expressed "I do not know that he is there" or "I am not aware of him."

9.12   RSV   TEV

> Behold, he snatches away; who
>   can hinder him?
> Who will say to him, 'What
>   doest thou?'

> He takes what he wants, and no
>   one can stop him;
> no one dares ask him, "What
>   are you doing?"

Behold, he snatches away: the verb translated **snatches away** is found nowhere else in the Old Testament, although a noun form is found in Proverbs 23.28 with the meaning "robber" in RSV. The Hebrew particle translated **Behold** is not the same as that in 1.12,19; this one may also be rendered as "if," as in NEB and NIV, or be omitted as in TEV. Job's thought is that God is able to do exactly as he wishes, with no accountability to anyone. In Hebrew **snatches away** has no object, but in many languages an object must be supplied; for example, "He takes something away." FRCL translates "Who will make him let go what he has taken by force?" Another model may be "Who can prevent him from taking away what he wants?" **Who can hinder him? Hinder** translates the causative form of the verb "return" and here means "prevent," or as TEV says, "No one can stop him."

Who will say to him, 'What doest thou?' In this verse line b is more dramatic than line a and heightens the poetic effect. It serves to emphasize the point that God is responsible to himself only. The use of **who** in both lines introduces a rhetorical question meaning "No one can . . ."; it does not introduce a question asking for the name of the person who can stop him. These two "who" questions may be rendered "No one can stop him" and "No one can say to him . . . ."

9.13   RSV   TEV

"God will not turn back his an-   God's anger is constant. He
    ger;   crushed his enemies
beneath him bowed the helpers   who helped Rahab,ᵘ the sea
    of Rahab.   monster, oppose him.

                        ᵘ RAHAB: *A legendary sea monster which
                        represented the forces of chaos and evil.*

God will not turn back his anger: no one can stop God from taking what he wants, and he unleashes his anger on anyone he pleases. In verse 5 God overturns mountains in his anger. The expression **turn back his anger** reflects the literal Hebrew, which is the causative form of "return," translated as "hinder" in verse 12. Since God does not restrain his anger, it continues always to operate, and so TEV "God's anger is constant." **Turns back his anger** is idiomatic and may be restructured as a conditional sentence, as in SPCL "If God is angry he does not calm himself easily." It may be necessary to express this negative thought in positive terms; for example, "God will let his anger have its way" or "God will be angry when he acts."

Beneath him bowed the helpers of Rahab: this line is given as evidence of the constant nature of the divine anger. **Rahab** has been identified by some scholars with Leviathan in 3.8 and the sea monster in 7.12. It is a symbol of the sea and in particular the Red Sea, and so it stands for Egypt in Isaiah 30.7 and Psalm 87.4. In the Babylonian creation myth Rahab's helpers are the ones that help the monster Tiamat create chaos. **Beneath him** suggests submission, defeat. The thought may be expressed, for example, "He defeats the helpers of Rahab" or "He crushes the helpers of Rahab under his feet." TEV has identified these helpers of Rahab as "his enemies." It is recommended that translators identify Rahab in a note. An example is found in TEV. A cross reference to 26.12 should also be given.

3D-3. It is futile for Job to attempt to prove he is innocent (9.14-24)

RSV	TEV
14 How then can I answer him, choosing my words with him?	14 So how can I find words to answer God?

15 Though I am innocent, I cannot answer
      him;
      I must appeal for mercy to my accuser.
	15 Though I am innocent, all I can do
	      is beg for mercy from God my judge.

16 If I summoned him and he answered me,
      I would not believe that he was listen-
      ing to my voice.
	16 Yet even then, if he lets me speak,
	      I can't believe he would listen to me.

17 For he crushes me with a tempest,
      and multiplies my wounds without
      cause;
	17 He sends storms to batter and bruise me
	      without any reason at all.

18 he will not let me get my breath,
      but fills me with bitterness.
	18 He won't let me catch my breath;
	      he has filled my life with bitterness.

19 If it is a contest of strength, behold him!
      If it is a matter of justice, who can
      summon him?
	19 Should I try force? Try force on God?
	      Should I take him to court? Could anyone
	      make him go?

20 Though I am innocent, my own mouth
      would condemn me;
      though I am blameless, he would prove
      me perverse.
	20 I am innocent and faithful, but my words
	      sound guilty,
	      and everything I say seems to condemn
	      me.

21 I am blameless; I regard not myself;
      I loathe my life.
	21-22 I am innocent, but I no longer care.
	      I am sick of living. Nothing matters;
	      innocent or guilty, God will destroy us.

22 It is all one; therefore I say,
      he destroys both the blameless and the
      wicked.
	23 When an innocent man suddenly dies,
	      God laughs.

23 When disaster brings sudden death,
      he mocks at the calamity of the inno-
      cent.
	24 God gave the world to the wicked.
	      He made all the judges blind.
	      And if God didn't do it, who did?

24 The earth is given into the hand of the
      wicked;
      he covers the faces of its judges—
      if it is not he, who then is it?	

Subdivision Heading

Translators may wish to adapt the Handbook heading by saying, for example, "Job knows he cannot answer God," "I know God would not listen to me," or "God will not let me prove that I am innocent." Habel has "Considering the difficulty of litigation," and Rowley "The impossibility of facing God in court."

9.14   RSV   TEV

How then can I answer him,   So how can I find words to an-
   choosing my words with him?   swer God?

How then can I answer him: **How** may also be read as an exclamation meaning "How much more!" or, as in the present context, "How much less!" The monster is helpless against God, and so by comparison how much less powerful would Job be against him! In 9.3 Job admits the impossibility of entering into a legal dispute with God. The same thought is renewed here with **answer him**. The same

Hebrew verb will be repeated in verse 32, where "answer" means to defend oneself in a legal dispute. **Answer him** does not refer, therefore, to making a simple response to a question, but rather to rebutting the charges or accusations that God would bring against Job. NJB translates **answer** as "And here am I, proposing to defend myself."

The parallel line **choosing my words with him** is condensed into the first line by TEV. This is more logical, since a person selects the words to use before defending himself of the charges. RSV **with him** is ambiguous, since it may mean either "choosing my words in cooperation with him" or "choosing my words to use against him." Since the meaning is the latter, it would be better to say, for example, "choosing my words to speak to him," ". . . to defend myself," or ". . . to answer his charges." In translation it may be necessary to make an adjustment similar to that made in TEV; for example, "How can I choose the words to defend myself?" "How can I think of the arguments which I will use to answer the charges he brings against me?"

9.15	RSV	TEV
	Though I am innocent, I cannot answer him; I must appeal for mercy to my accuser.[r]	Though I am innocent, all I can do is beg for mercy from God my judge.

[r] Or *for my right*

Though I am innocent, I cannot answer him: **innocent** translates the Hebrew *tsadaq* "to be righteous," which also occurs in 4.17; 9.2,20; 10.15; 15.14; 22.3; 34.5; 35.7; here it means innocent of wrongdoing, and therefore to be in the right in a lawsuit. (See also the language of a lawsuit in 11.2; 13.18; 40.8.) **I cannot answer him** is rendered by some of the ancient versions as a passive, "I am not answered." In verse 3 it was said that God does not answer his opponents, and here the passive seems to fit this context. But in verse 16 there is the possibility of God replying. Job does not doubt his innocence of wrongdoing, and therefore RSV and TEV are to be preferred over NIV "Though I were innocent." **I cannot answer him: answer** in the sense of defending oneself against charges is used in verses 14, 15, and 16. Job's failure to answer his accuser is not because he has no defense, but rather because God will not listen to anything Job says.

I must appeal for mercy to my accuser: since Job has no possibility of answering or defending himself before God, he has no recourse but to throw himself on God's mercy. Translations differ in their rendering of the term translated **accuser** by RSV. TEV and others have "judge." It is evident that Job's opponent is also the one who judges him, and "judge" appears to render the term better in English than does "accuser," which carries no special legal connotation. **Appeal for mercy** must often be restructured to say, for example, "ask God to be kind to me" or "beg the one who judges me to have mercy on me."

9.16   RSV   TEV

> If I summoned him and he an-   Yet even then, if he lets me
>   swered me,   speak,
> I would not believe that he was   I can't believe he would listen
>   listening to my voice.   to me.

If I summoned him and he answered me: Job continues by imagining how it would be if he could call God to appear in a lawsuit. **Summoned** translates Hebrew "called" with the sense to notify to appear in court. In translation it may be necessary to fill out the legal context of **summoned** by saying, for example, "If I asked him to come to court and argue his case" or "If I said 'You must appear before a judge with me . . . .'" **Answered me** refers not to defending himself, but simply to accepting the summons or call to appear in court.

I would not believe that he was listening to my voice: because the possibility of this happening is out of the question for Job, he would not believe God was hearing the call to appear in court. This may sometimes be rendered "I would not believe God heard my voice" or "I would not believe God paid attention to what I said."

9.17   RSV   TEV

> For he crushes me with a tem-   He sends storms to batter and
>   pest,   bruise me
> and multiplies my wounds   without any reason at all.
>   without cause;

For he crushes me with a tempest: RSV **For** implies a consequence, although this is not necessarily implied in Hebrew. **Crushes me** translates the verb "bruise" used in Genesis 3.15, "he shall bruise your head, and you shall bruise his heel" (RSV). Translations differ in the rendering of the word translated **tempest** by RSV and "storms" by TEV. Syriac translators read the word as "hair," that is, "with or for a hair." This same sense is preferred by Dhorme, who understands it to mean "for a trifle," an expression which parallels **without cause** in the next line. HOTTP rates the reading "storm" only with a "C" evaluation but thinks that either "hair" or "storm" is possible. FRCL avoids both metaphors and translates "He crushes me for no significant reason," giving the alternatives of "storm" and "hair" in the margin. In translation **crushes** may imply total physical destruction, which is not correct in this context. Therefore it may be necessary to say, for example, "He pounds me, beats me, whips me"; and the full expression may be rendered "He blows against me with a storm which whips me" or "He makes a storm strike me down."

And multiplies my wounds without cause. This clause may need to be restructured to say, for example, "he bruises me all over with no reason at all" or "although I am innocent, he wounds me over and over."

9.18 RSV TEV

he will not let me get my breath, but fills me with bitterness.	He won't let me catch my breath; he has filled my life with bitterness.

He will not let me get my breath: in 7.19 Job complained that God gave him no time to swallow his saliva, and here he objects that God repeatedly attacks him without giving him time to catch his breath. **Fills me with bitterness**: line b extends the complaint in line a and carries it further in the sense that "not only will he not allow me to get my breath, but he even fills my life with bitterness." **Bitterness** is a taste which symbolizes suffering, and in languages where the taste of bitterness has no such meaning, it is better to say, for example, "he makes me suffer" or "he fills my life with suffering."

9.19 RSV TEV

If it is a contest of strength, behold him! If it is a matter of justice, who can summon him?[s]	Should I try force? Try force on God? Should I take him to court? Could anyone make him go?[v]

[s] Compare Gk: Heb *me*. The text of the verse is uncertain

[v] *Probable text* make him go; *Hebrew* make me go.

If it is a contest of strength, behold him! In the first line of this verse Job expresses the impossibility of matching his strength with that of God. By changing Hebrew *hinneh* "behold" to *hu* "he," some interpreters translate "If it is a question of strength, he (God) is the mighty one"; that is, "If it is a contest between my strength and God's, God is the stronger one." It is best to retain the Hebrew text and translate, for example, "If it is a contest of strength, God says, 'Here I am.'"

The second line of the verse, which also begins with an "if" clause, has in Hebrew the question "who will appoint me a time?" The sense here is probably "a time to appear in court." RSV and TEV follow the Septuagint and Syriac, which have "summon him" instead of "summon me," and so TEV has "make him (God) go (to court)." It is recommended that translators follow the Hebrew in the form of a question, "Who can cause me to meet (him) at the appointed time?" This may be rendered "Who would take charge of my trial?" or "Who would set a time for my case to be heard?"

9.20 RSV TEV

Though I am innocent, my own mouth would condemn me;	I am innocent and faithful, but my words sound guilty,

> though I am blameless, he
> would prove me perverse.

> and everything I say seems to
> condemn me.

Though I am innocent, my own mouth would condemn me: the Hebrew text has "my mouth"; however, some editors change this to "his mouth" on the assumption that it is God's mouth that condemns Job. HOTTP accepts "my mouth" as an "A" reading but suggests three ways to interpret the expression: (a) my mouth will condemn me; (b) with my mouth he will condemn me; and (c) if I am justified by my mouth, he will condemn me all the same. It seems best to understand Job's thought as representing his fear that he will be so confused by God's presence that he will even argue against himself. The words he uses in his own defense will condemn him. Line a may also be rendered, for example, "Although I am innocent (have done no wrong), God would still condemn me for what I say" or "Even though I am innocent, God would use my own words to show that I am guilty."

Though I am blameless closely parallels the previous line. For comments on **blameless** see the following paragraph. **He would prove me perverse**: **perverse** translates a root which means "twisted, bent." The thought is either that God would twist what Job says and turn his words against him, or God would prove that Job is in the wrong. NEB translates "he twists my words," and Mft "he would prove me wrong." Either of these is an adequate model for translating.

9.21-22   RSV   TEV

21   I am blameless; I regard not myself;
      I loathe my life.
22   It is all one; therefore I say,
      he destroys both the blameless and the wicked.

21-22 I am innocent, but I no longer care.
      I am sick of living. Nothing matters;
      innocent or guilty, God will destroy us.

The three short lines of verse 21 appear to be irregular in their rhythm and are considered by some scholars as a poetic device for expressing the intense emotion under which Job is now speaking. **I am blameless**: Job has asserted in verses 9, 15, and 20 that he is innocent. In order to preserve his innocence, he is willing to give up all else, including his very life. The word translated **blameless** is the same as that used in 1.1; 1.8; and 2.3. Bildad had assured Job in 8.20 that God does not spurn the "blameless." But Job's frustration comes from being blameless and unable to prove it. **I regard not myself** translates what is literally "I do not know my soul." The verb translated "know" here has the meaning of "concern" in such passages as Exodus 2.25, where God "saw the slavery of the Israelites and was concerned for them" (TEV). Job is therefore saying that he no longer is concerned for himself, or "I do not care what happens to me." He then goes further in the next line by saying **I loathe my life**. In 10.1 Job will say again the same thing. TEV translates this as "I am sick of living." **Loathe** translates a word meaning "despise or reject." Job is prepared to risk his life by taking up charges against God. In some languages it may be necessary to shift **life** to a verb and say, for example, "I hate living" or "I hate the way I have to live."

It is all one: these words are omitted by the Septuagint, and some editors invert the two lines to say "Therefore, I say: it is all one." Dhorme translates "That is why I have said: 'It is all one.'" TEV combines verses 21 and 22 and translates "Nothing matters." The literal translation is "One it is, therefore." Here "one" carries the sense of "It is all the same" or "It all amounts to the same thing." "Nothing matters" may be expressed as "Nothing is important to me," or idiomatically as in some languages, "Nothing touches my head" or "Nothing takes hold of my heart." The reason for this despairing remark is that **he destroys both the blameless and the wicked.** Since the good and the evil share the same fate, Job is saying that God is not a just judge but a heartless destroyer of life. **Destroys** is general and may have to be expressed more specifically in some languages; for example, "he kills both . . ." or "he takes away the life of . . . ."

9.23	RSV	TEV
	When disaster brings sudden death, he mocks at the calamity[t] of the innocent.	When an innocent man suddenly dies, God laughs.

[t] The meaning of the Hebrew word is uncertain

The thrust of verses 23-24 is to assert that God does not discriminate between the innocent and the guilty. **When disaster brings sudden death: When** may also be taken in the sense of "If." The intention is to say "Whenever a disaster occurs." **Disaster** translates Hebrew "whip" or "scourge," and some interpreters understand it to refer to a natural disaster such as a plague or flood, which carries off the good and evil together. TEV has shifted the focus from the disaster to the sudden death of the innocent. There is therefore no suggestion in TEV that the sudden death is due to a disaster. In 4.7 Eliphaz asked Job "who that was innocent ever perished?" Line 23a may have to be restructured in some languages to say, for example, "When a disaster causes people to die suddenly . . . ," or more specifically, "If a flood or storm suddenly kills people . . . ."

In 5.22 Eliphaz told Job that "At destruction and famine you shall laugh." But Job turns this around and asserts now that it is God who **mocks at the calamity of the innocent.** According to the marginal note in RSV, the meaning of the term translated **calamity** is uncertain. Some scholars modify the word to get the meaning "melt," implying that the heart melts, and the word is therefore a figure meaning "despair." This is followed by several modern translations. TEV says only "When an innocent man suddenly dies, God laughs." Line b is the consequence of line a, which FRCL translates "God has nothing but ridicule for all their distress." We may also render this line, for example, "God makes fun of the innocent in their troubles" or "God laughs at the innocent when they suffer."

9.24   RSV   TEV

> The earth is given into the hand   God gave the world to the wick-
>   of the wicked;   ed.
> he covers the faces of its judg-   He made all the judges blind.
>   es—   And if God didn't do it, who did?
> if it is not he, who then is it?

Verse 24 continues the same observation of God's indifference to the innocent. There are three lines in this verse, and only the first two are parallel. **The earth is given into the hand of the wicked:** the verb is passive, and the implied subject is God. Translations are divided between those which take **earth** to refer to an individual nation and those which understand it to refer to the world generally. It seems preferable to assume with RSV and TEV that the general meaning is intended. **Into the hand** means into the power or control of wicked people. In languages in which a passive verb cannot be used, it may be necessary to say, for example, "God gives the earth to wicked people" or "God lets evil people have power over the earth."

He covers the faces of its judges: in Exodus 23.8 bribery is condemned because it covers the eyes of officials so they can not see where justice lies. Translators are probably familiar with the image of justice represented as a feminine figure holding a scale in one hand and a sword in the other, and whose eyes are blindfolded. The blindfold is supposed to suggest that justice should be dispensed without prejudice. The picture in this verse is quite different. Here it is God who covers the eyes of the judge so he cannot see the truth and judge fairly. If the metaphor of covering the face or eyes gives the wrong meaning, translators may restructure this expression to say, for example, "He blinds the eyes of judges so they cannot judge fairly" or "He prevents justice being given, by blinding the eyes of judges."

If it is not he, who then is it? Job's friends have argued that a man's good fortune is the result of his merits, because God rewards the innocent. Job argues against that position from his own innocence. Since Job's friends cannot accept that God has brought on his suffering, Job puts this question to them: "If it is not God, then who is it?" NEB does not translate the question in its text, but HOTTP rates it an "A" reading, and translators should retain it. This question may have to be restructured to say, for example, "If it is not God who does these things, then who does them?"

3D-4. Job recognizes there is no one to mediate between him and God (9.25-35)

                     RSV   TEV

25   "My days are swifter than a runner;   25   My days race by, not one of them good.
         they flee away, they see no good.   26   My life passes like the swiftest boat,
26   They go by like skiffs of reed,   as fast as an eagle swooping down on a
         like an eagle swooping on the prey.   rabbit.
27   If I say, 'I will forget my complaint,   27-28 If I smile and try to forget my pain,
         I will put off my sad countenance, and   all my suffering comes back to haunt

	be of good cheer,'		me;
28	I become afraid of all my suffering,		I know that God does hold me guilty.
	for I know thou wilt not hold me inno-	29	Since I am held guilty, why should I both-
	cent.		er?
29	I shall be condemned;	30	No soap can wash away my sins.
	why then do I labor in vain?	31	God throws me into a pit with filth,
30	If I wash myself with snow,		and even my clothes are ashamed of
	and cleanse my hands with lye,		me.
31	yet thou wilt plunge me into a pit,	32	If God were human, I could answer him;
	and my own clothes will abhor me.		we could go to court to decide our
32	For he is not a man, as I am, that I might		quarrel.
	answer him,	33	But there is no one to step between us—
	that we should come to trial together.		no one to judge both God and me.
33	There is no umpire between us,	34	Stop punishing me, God!
	who might lay his hand upon us both.		Keep your terrors away!
34	Let him take his rod away from me,	35	I am not afraid. I am going to talk
	and let not dread of him terrify me.		because I know my own heart.
35	Then I would speak without fear of him,		
	for I am not so in myself.		

Subdivision Heading

The Handbook heading covers two of the themes shown in the display. Translators may supply one heading for verses 22-31 and another for verses 32-35. For example, as a heading for verses 22-31, "God is unjust," "God does not do things fairly," or "God is the cause of my suffering." A heading for verses 32-35 may be "There is no one to judge both God and Job," "Job needs someone to decide things between him and God," or "An umpire for Job and God." Rowley has "God flouts justice indiscriminately," and TOB "The inhumanity of God."

9.25-26   RSV   TEV

	RSV		TEV
25	"My days are swifter than a runner;	25	My days race by, not one of them good.
	they flee away, they see no good.	26	My life passes like the swiftest boat,
26	They go by like skiffs of reed, like an eagle swooping on the prey.		as fast as an eagle swooping down on a rabbit.

Job returns to the theme of the swiftness with which life passes away. In 7.6 he said "My days are swifter than a weaver's shuttle." He now uses the figure of a **runner**. **My days are swifter than a runner**: the word **runner** is found also in 2 Samuel 18.19-33, where the runner is a bearer of an urgent message for the king. TEV avoids the analogy of the runner and says "My days race by." This line may also be rendered "the days of my life pass swiftly" or "my days are all quickly gone." **They flee away** repeats the thought of the first line without using a parallel comparison. **They see no good** is an idiomatic way of saying the days are without happiness, or nothing good happens during the passage of the days. In many languages **days** cannot be described as being able to see, like people, and so we may have to restructure this expression to say, for example, "nothing good happens to me" or "my days pass by without anything good happening to me."

They go by like skiffs of reed: the comparison shifts from the runner on land to small, speedy boats made of reeds. The word for **reed** is used only here. The more common term is "papyrus" as in 8.11 and in Isaiah 18.2. **Skiffs of reed** or papyrus were Nile boats whose sides were made of papyrus reeds and which were known for their swift travel on the river. Line a may be rendered, for example, "My days go quickly like fast sailing boats." In areas where sailing boats are unknown, the comparison may be shifted to any swift water craft; for example, "My days flow swiftly like a fast dugout." Where boats are completely unknown it may be necessary to drop the image and say, for example, "My life is very soon over" or "The days of my life come quickly to an end."

Like an eagle swooping on the prey: the third analogy shifts again, from water to the air. This time the comparison is to the **eagle** or hawk pictured as swooping down out of the sky to snatch its prey. **Prey** translates Hebrew "food," and TEV attempts to be more specific still with "rabbit." Translators may find it necessary to substitute another bird of prey. The pictures of the runner, the skiff, and the eagle all emphasize the swiftness of the passing of time, and so whatever comparisons are used, they must be characterized by swiftness of movement.

9.27-28 RSV	TEV

27   If I say, 'I will forget my com-
      plaint,
     I will put off my sad counte-
      nance, and be of good
      cheer,'
28   I become afraid of all my suffer-
      ing,
     for I know thou wilt not hold
      me innocent.
	27-28 If I smile and try to forget my
	      pain,
	     all my suffering comes back to
	      haunt me;
	     I know that God does hold me
	      guilty.

Verse 27 offers two conditions, with the consequences appearing in verses 28 and 29. Job is here addressing his conditions to God. **If I say, 'I will forget my complaint . . .'**: it may be necessary to indicate who is addressed by **say**, such as "If I say to you, God," or "God, if I tell you . . . ." Job does not mean that he will forget that he has a complaint against God, but that he will stop voicing it, that is, "I will stop complaining to you." The second condition is **I will put off my sad countenance**, which translates the Hebrew "I will leave my face." This means that Job will give up the look he has been wearing; that is, "I will change the look on my face" or "I will smile." The word **sad** does not occur in Hebrew but is implied in the expression. **And be of good cheer** is literally "brighten (my face)." If Job does these things, the result nevertheless is **I become afraid of all my suffering**. When Job resolves to cheer up, he is afraid that some new pain will afflict him. The reason for his reaction is **for I know thou wilt not hold me innocent**; he knows that God does not treat him as an innocent man, does not clear him and acquit him of his crime, whatever crime he is supposed to be guilty of. The final line may be rendered, for example, "I know you will not say 'Job, you are innocent' " or ". . . 'Job, you are not guilty.' "

9.29 RSV TEV

I shall be condemned;
    why then do I labor in vain?
	Since I am held guilty, why
	    should I bother?

The final consequence of the conditions in verse 27 is **I shall be condemned**; most of the ancient versions treated this short clause as meaning "Since I am already condemned," or as in SPCL, "If I am condemned . . . ." Job is saying that, since it is so certain that God will find him guilty, there is no use arguing. In many languages this line must be expressed in the active; for example, "You will condemn me," "You will hold me guilty," or "You, God, will not say that I am innocent."

Why then do I labor in vain? The word translated **labor** means "tire oneself out, exhaust oneself." Job's labor is the futile effort of arguing his defense. In some languages this may be rendered "Why do I keep on trying to defend my case?" "Why do I continue to argue against you?" or "Why don't I give up?"

9.30 RSV TEV

If I wash myself with snow,
    and cleanse my hands with lye,
	No soap can wash away my
	    sins.

Verse 30 has two "if" clauses which are followed in 31 by two consequences. The two "if" clauses are parallel, both having to do with physical cleansing. **If I wash myself with snow**: there are two forms of the Hebrew text; the one has "with snow water" and the other "with snow." Washing with snow or with water from melted snow would not produce anything more than a symbolic cleansing. Pope understands the Hebrew word for snow here to refer to the soapwort plant, whose roots were used for making soap, and so TEV has "No soap can wash away my sins." HOTTP reports that its committee members were equally divided between "soap" and "snow," and so offers translators equal choice.

And cleanse my hands with lye: I in the first line shifts to **my hands** here, which represents a sharpening of focus in the second line. TEV has chosen to disregard this focusing and has condensed the two lines into one. The term translated **lye** refers to an alkaline substance made from the ashes of vegetable matter and used for cleansing. The poetic intensification in the movement from line a to line b is based on the shift from washing with **snow** or "snow water" (clean but not particularly cleansing) to **lye** in line b (a specific cleansing agent). Hence the heightening may be expressed "If I wash myself with snow or even cleanse my hands with lye . . . ." In languages where snow is unknown, water which is known to be particularly clear and clean may be used, such as spring water, or simply "very clean water." A natural soap known to get things especially clean may be used for **lye**. If neither image can be used, verse 30 may be rendered, for example, "If I wash myself with water and cleanse my hands completely . . . ."

9.31   RSV   TEV

yet thou wilt plunge me into a   God throws me into a pit with
    pit,   filth,
and my own clothes will abhor   and even my clothes are
    me.   ashamed of me.

The consequences of the "if" clauses in verse 30 are drawn out in verse 31. God is still being addressed by Job. **Yet thou wilt plunge me into a pit**: no matter how hard Job tries to cleanse himself, God's superior power will undo him and act against him. Scholars propose changing the word translated **pit** to get "cesspool" or "filth." Dhorme believes the line should be read "plunge me into filth," which contrasts sharply with the cleansing images of the previous verse. Pope argues that the Hebrew means "filth" and does not require any change. The context suggests the contrast of cleanliness in verse 30 with its opposite in this verse. TEV translates "a pit with filth." This line may be rendered, for example, "you will still push me down into the dirt" or "you will throw me into a dirty hole."

My own clothes will abhor me: in this expression the **clothes** act like a person. Job becomes repulsive to the clothes that cover his body. Some scholars suggest changing "my clothes" to "my friends," but clothes is more logical in the context. In languages in which **clothes** cannot be used as the subject of a verb of emotion, it may be necessary to expand this line to say, for example, "my own clothes will be ashamed of me like one person is ashamed of another" or "my own clothes will turn against me like a false friend."

9.32   RSV   TEV

For he is not a man, as I am,   If God were human, I could an-
    that I might answer him,   swer him;
that we should come to trial   we could go to court to decide
    together.   our quarrel.

Job now turns to his friends and explains why God would act in such a manner. Since Job is a man and God is not a man, there can be no possibility of dealing with God in a legal manner, as he has argued in verses 14, 15, and 16. **For he is not a man, as I am, that I might answer him**: TEV has restructured the first clause as "If God were human." **As I am** is not translated by TEV, it being clearly supposed of Job. **Answer** is the same word used in verse 14, where the sense is "defend himself" in a legal dispute. This is strengthened by the next line, **that we should come to trial together**. The RSV way of relating the clauses is awkward in English, and the relationship is more clearly expressed in TEV. RSV **together** translates a Hebrew expression used also in 2.11 and is expressed by TEV in the use of the first person plural pronouns in "we could" and "our quarrel," an action involving both Job and God. In translation we should not give the impression that God is implied to be somehow inferior to Job. It may therefore be necessary to restructure this line to say, for example, "I am only a man, but because God is much more than a man . . . ," "because I am only human and God is much greater than I am . . . ," or "If God were a mere human like me . . . ." The consequence of the first clause may sometimes be rendered "then we could argue our case in court" or "we could hear each other's case before a judge."

9.33   RSV   TEV

> There is no[u] umpire between us,   But there is no one to step be-
>   who might lay his hand upon   tween us—
>   us both.   no one to judge both God and
>   me.

[u] Another reading is *Would that there were*

There is no umpire between us: as the RSV footnote says, this expression can be read "Would that there were," meaning "I wish there were." This is the rendering of the Septuagint and the Syriac. Job seems to be seeking reconciliation at this point and wishes there were an **umpire**, arbiter, or mediator between him and God. TEV avoids these noun forms and uses "no one to step between us." Job cannot go to court with God because there is no judge to decide between him and God. **Umpire** may also be rendered, for example, "a person to decide who is right" or "someone to hear our arguments and decide who is right." **Who might lay his hand upon us both**: the idea is that the judge lays his hands on (takes hold of) both parties in a dispute, and so exercises his authority over both. The same expression of God acting with authority is found in Psalm 139.5, "Thou dost beset me behind and before, and layest thy hand upon me." The whole verse may be restructured to say, for example, "I wish there were someone to listen to both of us, someone who had authority over us."

9.34   RSV   TEV

> Let him take his rod away from   Stop punishing me, God!
>   me,   Keep your terrors away!
>   and let not dread of him terri-
>   fy me.

Let him take his rod away from me: in Psalm 23 the rod in the hand of the shepherd protects the sheep. Here the **rod** is a symbol of God's punishment and is mentioned again with the same sense in 21.9. In 13.21a Job cries out for God to remove his hand from Job. TEV has avoided the image of the punishing rod, with the direct command "Stop punishing me, God." Although the verbs in both lines in Hebrew are in the third person, TEV has shifted to the second person with direct address. The result is a more natural and vivid account. If the translator finds it best to stay closer to the form of the Hebrew, it may be possible to restructure line a as "I ask that God stop beating me with his stick," "I ask you, God, to stop beating me," or "God, stop beating me."

Let not dread of him terrify me: in 7.14 Job accuses God of terrifying him with dreams and visions in his sleep. Here he asks God to stop terrifying or frightening him. If direct address is continued in line b, this may be expressed, for example, "and stop frightening me." If verse 34 is taken as addressed to the imaginary judge in verse 33, the verse may be expressed as a request; for example, "Make God stop beating me and causing me to be afraid."

9.35

RSV	TEV
Then I would speak without fear of him,	I am not afraid. I am going to talk
for I am not so in myself.	because I know my own heart.

RSV makes the first line of this verse a consequence of verse 34 but leaves the second line obscure and ambiguous. **Then I would speak without fear of him**: RSV takes this line to mean that only if God's terrors were removed would Job be able to speak out fearlessly in his own defense. TEV, which provides another model, does not relate the line as a consequence of verse 34, but rather as a sudden shift in outlook: "I am not afraid."

There is furthermore the problem of the second line: **for I am not so in myself.** This line by itself is obscure and is translated literally by RSV. Some scholars understand the line to mean "in my own conscience I am not what God thinks"; and closely related to this is TEV "because I know my own heart." NJB similarly has "I do not see myself like that at all," and NRSV, NEB "for I know I am not what I am thought to be." Dhorme, on the other hand, shifts line b to the beginning of the verse and translates "Since it is not so (that is, because Job cannot deal with God as a human, verse 32), I with myself will commune and will not fear Him." In this sense Job will make his defense to himself. The context suggests that Job is contrasting himself in his normal state with that of being terrified by God. In his normal situation he would be himself and speak freely without intimidation. Translators may follow Dhorme's model by saying, for example, "Since I am not truly myself, I cannot defend myself freely," "Since I cannot do as I normally would . . . ," or "Since I am terrified by God, I am unable to argue my case as I should."

3D-5. Job accuses God of being unfair to his creatures (10.1-7)

	RSV		TEV
1	"I loathe my life; I will give free utterance to my complaint; I will speak in the bitterness of my soul.	1	I am tired of living. Listen to my bitter complaint.
2	I will say to God, Do not condemn me; let me know why thou dost contend against me.	2	Don't condemn me, God. Tell me! What is the charge against me?
3	Does it seem good to thee to oppress, to despise the work of thy hands and favor the designs of the wicked?	3	Is it right for you to be so cruel? To despise what you yourself have made? And then to smile on the schemes of wicked men?
		4	Do you see things as we do?

4	Hast thou eyes of flesh?	5	Is your life as short as ours?
	Dost thou see as man sees?	6	Then why do you track down all my sins
5	Are thy days as the days of man,		and hunt down every fault I have?
	or thy years as man's years,	7	You know that I am not guilty,
6	that thou dost seek out my iniquity		that no one can save me from you.
	and search for my sin,		
7	although thou knowest that I am not guilty,		
	and there is none to deliver out of thy hand?		

Subdivision Heading

Since chapter 10 is a continuation of Job's speech begun in chapter 9, no division heading is required. The Handbook heading reflects the theme of God's injustice, as shown in the introduction to chapters 9–10. Translators wishing to place a heading before 10.1 may say, for example, "God is unfair," "God does not do things justly," or "God does not treat people fairly." Habel has "Rehearsal of the case against God," and TOB "Contempt of the creature," meaning that God scorns his own creatures.

10.1
RSV
TEV

"I loathe my life;
  I will give free utterance to my complaint;
  I will speak in the bitterness of my soul.

I am tired of living.
  Listen to my bitter complaint.

I loathe my life: (see 9.21.) It is apparent from the following verses that Job imagines how it would be to take God to court. The verb translated **loathe** in 9.21 is different from the verb found here. In both verses the object is Job's *nefesh* "life, soul," but the verb here is better expressed "to be weary, tired, exhausted," and so TEV "I am tired of living." Mft says a bit more forcefully "I am sick of life, sick of it." Some translators understand this line as a reason clause to explain the next line, and so NJB "Since I have lost all taste for life, I shall . . ."; FRCL "So, since my life makes me sick . . ."; NIV "I loathe my very life; therefore, I will . . . ."

I will give free utterance to my complaint translates the Hebrew "I will let loose my complaint upon myself." This clause is open to various interpretations. Dhorme and others understand that Job will let loose his complaint "to myself." That is, he will inwardly vent his anger against God. Habel understands that Job is preparing to make a public rehearsal of his legal complaint. TEV has taken the verb of this line to mean the same as **speak** in the next line and has combined the two lines into one. "Let loose" is to say that Job can no longer keep his complaint to himself, and so FRCL "I will not keep to myself any longer my complaints"; SPCL "I will relieve myself of my complaints." GECL, which makes this a reason clause, says "Therefore I cannot hold back my complaint." Job's complaint is not to be understood as a traditional lament such as Psalm 55.17, "Evening and morning and at noon I utter my complaint and moan." The **complaint** of Job is a legal dispute or charge he would take up against God if he were able to take God to court. This line may be rendered, for example, "I cannot keep my complaint to myself," "I will openly bring charges against God," "I will not hide the things I have to complain against God," or "I will tell everyone the charges I have against God."

I will speak in the bitterness of my soul describes the manner and not the place where Job will let loose his accusations. **Bitterness of my soul** is a widely used metaphor in which bitterness of taste is extended to feelings of disappointment, anger, resentment. In this verse as a whole, line c is parallel to line b, and **bitterness of soul** also serves the poetic purpose of intensifying line a, going beyond it in rhetorical vividness. The term *nefesh* is rendered **soul** here by RSV but **life** in line a. In translation **bitterness** may be associated with various parts of the body. FRCL says "bitter heart," and GECL avoids the term bitter and translates "What has left me in despair . . . ." **Bitterness of my soul** may sometimes be rendered "the anger in my heart," "the sourness in my stomach," or "the heat in my liver." The full line may be translated, for example, "I will tell him how sour my stomach is" or "I will tell him from the heat in my innermost."

10.2

RSV	TEV
I will say to God, Do not condemn me; let me know why thou dost contend against me.	Don't condemn me, God. Tell me! What is the charge against me?

I will say to God, Do not condemn me: Job begins the rehearsal of his charges, the words he would say to God in a lawsuit. In 9.27-28 Job said that if he dropped his complaint against God, God would still not find him guiltless. Now he has moved to the point of telling God what his complaints are, knowing full well that it will do no good. At least his friends will hear it all. Job, as well as his friends, assumes that God holds him guilty. In 9.29 Job says "I shall be condemned." There is no umpire or judge to weigh his complaints against God, as he said in 9.33. Job, without any means of appeal, can only ask that he be heard before being judged as guilty, that is, before being condemned. This line may also be translated, for example, "I will say to God 'Do not judge me guilty,'" "'Do not find me in the wrong,'" or positively, "I will say to God 'Judge me innocent.'"

Let me know why thou dost contend against me: Job does not want to be condemned in advance, at least not until he knows the reason; and so he asks God to specify the charges God has against him. This line may also be expressed, for example, "Tell me what wrongs you accuse me of," "Let me hear what the charges against me are," or "Show me why you accuse me of wrong doing."

10.3

RSV	TEV
Does it seem good to thee to oppress, to despise the work of thy hands	Is it right for you to be so cruel? To despise what you yourself have made? And then to smile on the

and favor the designs of the	schemes of wicked men?
wicked?	

Job, of course, receives no reply, but the next step in his rehearsal will be to put a series of rhetorical questions to his oppressor. The purpose of these questions is to make God think again about his actions against Job.

In verses 3-7 and 9-10 RSV uses rhetorical questions. Translators should determine whether all, part, or none of these should be translated as rhetorical questions. See the comments on this device in "Translating the Book of Job," page 16.

Does it seem good to thee to oppress . . . : this expresses the irony of Job's mood. In Genesis 1.31 "God saw everything that he had made, and behold, it was very good." By contrast the manner in which Job has been dealt with by his creator suggests not only that God looks upon the creation of Job as bad, but that God looks upon it as actually something to be oppressed and despised. The word translated **oppress** is used again in 40.23 ("is turbulent"). The meaning here is "to be strong and violent" and is well rendered by TEV as "cruel." Job's question can be restated as "What benefit (pleasure) do you get by torturing me?" Other translation models: "What good does it do you to treat me badly?" or "What purpose is there in your hurting me?"

To despise the work of thy hands: despise means "spurn, reject, consider of no value." **The work of thy hands** refers to God's act of creating, or to the things he has made. Other renderings are "Why do you reject what you yourself have made?" "Why do you throw away as worthless what you have created?" or "Why do you discard the thing you have made with your own hands?"

And favor the designs of the wicked: favor translates a verb meaning to have a glowing face, to be radiant or to smile. Therefore Dhorme translates "to smile at the counsel of the wicked?" Similarly TEV "smile on the schemes of wicked men?" **Designs** translates the same expression used in Psalm 1.1, "the counsel of the wicked," and elsewhere is rendered "schemes, plans, projects, intrigues." This line may be expressed, for example, "and then look with satisfaction on the deceits of evil people" or "and be happy with the schemes of wicked people."

10.4	RSV	TEV

Hast thou eyes of flesh?	Do you see things as we do?
Dost thou see as man sees?	

Hast thou eyes of flesh? To have **eyes of flesh** means to see (understand) things in a human way, as Job does. TEV has "Do you see things as we do?" meaning "Do you understand things as we humans do?" **Dost thou see as man sees?** does not go beyond the first line in intensity or in emphasis. Neither does it serve to refine the focus of that line. Therefore TEV has reduced the two lines to one.

Job's question in the first line may be expressed "Do you see things the same way a person sees them?" "Do you understand things the way we do?" "Are your eyes like our eyes?" If the translator preserves the two lines, the first may be expressed, for example, "Do you see things the way a human being does," and the second, "and do you understand as a person does?"

10.5	RSV	TEV

> Are thy days as the days of man,
> or thy years as man's years,

Is your life as short as ours?

Are thy days as the days of man: that is, "Do you have as few days to live as a man does" or "... as a human being does?" "Is your life as short as a person's?" By asking this question Job widens the scope of his inquiry. This question asks if God is not afraid Job will die before he can fully complete his torture of him. In putting his question in this way, Job continues his sarcasm. Line b **or thy years as man's years** is in Hebrew "or your years like the days of a man?" **Man** in line a is the Hebrew term *'enosh,* which is translated "mortal" by NEB, NIV. **Man** in line b renders the Hebrew term *geber,* which denotes a human of male gender. There is little poetic movement between the lines, and so TEV has reduced them to one with "Is your life as short as ours?"

10.6	RSV	TEV

> that thou dost seek out my iniq-
> uity
> and search for my sin,

Then why do you track down all
my sins
and hunt down every fault I
have?

Verse 6 begins with the Hebrew connective translated "that," which links verse 6 to verse 5 in a general way. TEV uses "Then why" as a more natural way to make verse 6 a question following verse 5.

That thou dost seek out my iniquity: according to Rowley, it is Job's view that God has not found him guilty of wrongdoing but is torturing him to make him confess his evil, and thus God wishes to justify himself. The word translated **seek** is followed by a particle before its object, which denotes an intensive action. The words translated **iniquity** in line a and **sin** in line b are parallel. In 14.16-17 the same word pair occurs in essentially the same context. The verb translated **search** is parallel to **seek** in line a and has the sense of "investigate" or "inquire into." Line b **and search for my sin** in the Hebrew reverses the order of verb-subject found in line a and thus creates a chiasmus, "and for my sin search?"

The question in this verse is: are the **sins** and **iniquities** being searched, investigated sins which Job has committed and not confessed, or is God looking to see if he can find some hidden guilt in Job? TEV seems to understand the former, "why do you track down all my sins?" However, in the light of Job's constant claim of being innocent of wrongdoing, NEB and REB take the other view: "that thou lookest for guilt in me and dost seek in me for sin." In other words Job is protesting that God is keeping his eye on him, trying to find guilt in him. Translators may render verse 6 as a question or as a statement subordinated to verse 5, as in RSV. In question form verse 6 may be rendered, for example, "Why do you want to discover sin in me, and investigate me to find evil?"

10.7 RSV TEV

although thou knowest that I am not guilty, and there is none to deliver out of thy hand?	You know that I am not guilty, that no one can save me from you.

Although thou knowest that I am not guilty: verse 7 opens with a concessive clause, which translates the Hebrew "in spite of your knowledge." Job has insisted all along upon his innocence, and believes that God knows the truth of Job's innocence but is acting otherwise. TEV has avoided the use of the concessive clause and makes an equally valid independent statement, "You know that I am not guilty." This line may also be expressed "even though you know I am innocent . . ." or "even though you know I have done no wrong . . . ."

And there is none to deliver out of thy hand: some scholars see a break in sense between lines a and b and therefore propose changing either the first or the second to give the two halves a closer relationship. However, it is not necessary to establish a close parallelism between the lines. It is best to leave them as they stand in the Hebrew text. To be delivered **out of the hand** means to be "rescued, saved, spared" from whatever God may care to do to him: "There is nobody who can save me from you, God"; "No one can help me escape from you"; or "There is no one to rescue me."

3D-6. Job accuses God of watching over him to destroy him (10.8-17)

RSV TEV

#	RSV	#	TEV
8	Thy hands fashioned and made me; and now thou dost turn about and destroy me.	8	Your hands formed and shaped me, and now those same hands destroy me.
9	Remember that thou hast made me of clay; and wilt thou turn me to dust again?	9	Remember that you made me from clay; are you going to crush me back to dust?
10	Didst thou not pour me out like milk and curdle me like cheese?	10	You gave my father strength to beget me; you made me grow in my mother's womb.
11	Thou didst clothe me with skin and flesh, and knit me together with bones and sinews.	11	You formed my body with bones and sinews and covered the bones with muscles and skin.
12	Thou hast granted me life and steadfast love; and thy care has preserved my spirit.	12	You have given me life and constant love, and your care has kept me alive.
13	Yet these things thou didst hide in thy heart; I know that this was thy purpose.	13	But now I know that all that time you were secretly planning to harm me.
14	If I sin, thou dost mark me, and dost not acquit me of my iniquity.	14	You were watching to see if I would sin, so that you could refuse to forgive me.
15	If I am wicked, woe to me! If I am righteous, I cannot lift up my	15	As soon as I sin, I'm in trouble with you, but when I do right, I get no credit.

head,
for I am filled with disgrace
and look upon my affliction.
16 And if I lift myself up, thou dost hunt me
       like a lion,
    and again work wonders against me;
17 thou dost renew thy witnesses against me,
    and increase thy vexation toward me;
    thou dost bring fresh hosts against me.
	I am miserable and covered with shame.
	16 If I have any success at all,
	    you hunt me down like a lion;
	    to hurt me you even work miracles.
	17 You always have some witness against
	    me;
	    your anger toward me grows and
	    grows;
	    you always plan some new attack.

Subdivision Heading

The Handbook suggests a single heading for two themes, as seen in the introduction to this division. Translators may wish, however, to provide two, one for verses 8-12 and another for verses 13-17. In the first case we may say, for example, "You marvelously created me," or "Job says, 'I am your creature.'" In the second case, "Job says, 'God wants to destroy me,'" or "You are always watching for me to sin." Habel covers verses 8-17 with "The charges against God."

10.8 RSV	TEV

Thy hands fashioned and made
    me;
    and now thou dost turn about
    and destroy me.^{v}
	Your hands formed and shaped
	    me,
	    and now^w those same hands
	    destroy me.

^{v} Cn Compare Gk Syr: Heb *made me* *together round about and thou dost de-* *stroy me*	^{w} *Some ancient translations* and now; *Hebrew* together.

Thy hands fashioned and made me: in verse 3 Job acknowledges that he is the result of the work of the creator's hands. See also 14.15. **Fashioned and made** express two closely-related process words. The two together suggest movement from bringing something into a recognizable form to giving it a specific shape, as in TEV "Your hands formed and shaped me." **Made** translates a word meaning "cut out or hew" and depicts God as carving a statue, and consequently the verb is related to the noun "idol." **Thy hands** is a part standing for the whole and may be expressed "You formed me and shaped me." From a poetic point of view it is desirable to retain the figure of God's hands at work; for example, "Your own hands created me and formed this body of mine."

And now thou dost turn about and destroy me is literally "together round about and yet you destroy me." Instead of "together" the Septuagint and Syriac have "afterwards." HOTTP rates "altogether, round about" as "B" and concludes that these words belong to the preceding verb. Line a is then understood from the Hebrew to mean "you made every bit of me," and the second line "and now you destroy me." In this way a satisfactory rendering is made from the Hebrew and is little different from RSV. This line may also be restructured to say, for example, "After creating me, you waste it all and destroy me," or "You create me, then go on to destroy me."

10.9   RSV   TEV

Remember that thou hast made   Remember that you made me
   me of clay;[w]   from clay;[x]
and wilt thou turn me to dust   are you going to crush me
   again?   back to dust?

[w] Gk: Heb *like clay*   [x] *One ancient translation* from clay; *He-
                                            brew* like clay.

Remember that thou hast made me of clay: both RSV and TEV follow the
Septuagint. Job addresses God with an imperative. **Made me** is repeated as it is in
verse 8. The picture is that of the potter fashioning pots from clay, as in Isaiah 45.9
and Jeremiah 18.1-12. Job is here asking God to remember that he has made Job
with great care, and he asks how such a labor of love can be reduced to nothing. Job
recognized in 1.21 that he would return naked to his starting point, but here his
complaint is that God is arbitrary in the way he discards his work of creation. In
some languages the command to remember is more effectively expressed as "Don't
forget": "Don't forget, God, that you made me from a piece of clay." In languages
in which clay utensils are unknown, one may say, for example, "Don't forget that you
created me from a bit of mud."

Wilt thou turn me to dust again? Although this line may be read as a
statement or a question, it seems in the context to be understood best as a question.
Job does not question that he will eventually return to dust, but rather asks why God
is grinding him down to nothing. The Hebrew word translated **dust** is the same word
translated "soil" by TEV in Genesis 3.19: "You will have to work hard and sweat to
make the soil produce anything."

Turn me . . . again translates the Hebrew for "to turn," in the sense of
transforming, converting. However, the verb is in the causative mood, and TEV's
"crush" fits the context well. This line may sometimes be expressed "Are you going
to grind me into dust?" or "Are you going to smash me into dust?"

10.10   RSV   TEV

Didst thou not pour me out like   You gave my father strength to
   milk   beget me;
and curdle me like cheese?   you made me grow in my mot-
                                               her's womb.

Didst thou not pour me out like milk: related thoughts on the formation of
the embryo are expressed in such passages as Psalm 139.13, "For thou didst form my
inward parts, thou didst knit me together in my mother's womb." Some of the
ancient Greeks taught that the semen clotted to form the fetus. The Koran speaks
of the marvel of procreation through a drop of semen or a clot of blood. **Pour**
translates the causative form of the Hebrew verb, which means to make flow, and is
used in Ezekiel 22.20 in the sense of making metals molten, and in 2 Kings 22.9 of
melting down silver coins for other purposes. TEV has chosen to set aside the

metaphors in this verse with "You gave my father strength to beget me" in line <u>a</u>. In so doing TEV changes the nature of the poetic description of procreation. In verse 9 Job says God has made him of clay. Gordis sees the process referred to in this verse as the semen being poured like milk into the womb, where it solidifies like cheese. In verse 11 it will finally be knitted with bones and muscles and covered with skin.

This poetic description appears to be unaware of the active participation of the female ovum uniting with the male sperm to form the fetus. The adjustments made by TEV affect the intention of the author and distort the nature of his description of prenatal formation. It is likely that the significance of the images in verse 10 will be lost in many languages unless more of the implied information supporting the images of **milk** and **cheese** is provided. For example, FRCL translates verse 10 "One day you formed me in the body of my mother as one curdles milk in the bottom of a pot." It is also possible to render the line as a rhetorical question, "Did you not pour me like milk into my mother's womb?"

And curdled me like cheese: this line is parallel to the previous line, and a comparison is used again here. This time it is the curdling of cheese. The primary meaning of the verb translated **curdled** is "coagulate." Here it is used in its causative form, meaning to "stiffen or congeal," and so with cheese, **curdle**. The word translated **cheese**, which is cognate with Arabic, is found only here. The line may be rendered, for example, "and caused that milk to curdle like cheese." In areas in which the making of cheese is unknown, it will be better to avoid these images and say, for example, "Did you not pour me like water into my mother's womb and make my body start growing there?"

10.11   RSV   TEV

| Thou didst clothe me with skin and flesh, and knit me together with bones and sinews. | You formed my body with bones and sinews and covered the bones with muscles and skin. |

Thou didst clothe me with skin and flesh: Job continues to remind God how he has been intimately responsible for Job's prenatal development. Some translations take this verse to be a question, as in verse 10. God is the subject of the verb. **And knit me together with bones and sinews**: the verb translated **knit** implies in today's English the use of needles to intertwine two threads to form a fabric or cloth. The meaning of the Hebrew term is better conveyed by "weave, intertwine, form, or shape." TEV reverses the two lines to give a more logical sequence. That is, it prefers to have the body formed first with bones and sinews and then covered with muscles and skin, and this may be preferred in other languages. Reversing the sequence in this fashion, the whole verse may be expressed as "wove my body together with bones and muscles, and covered it with flesh and skin."

10.12   RSV   TEV

> Thou hast granted me life and   You have given me life and con-
>   steadfast love;   stant love,
> and thy care has preserved my   and your care has kept me
>   spirit.   alive.

Thou hast granted me life and steadfast love: as Pope says, these lines refer probably not to Job's prenatal days, but to God's providential care before tragedy struck him. **Thou hast granted** translates what is literally "You have made (done) with me." The verb here is often used in combination with the Hebrew term *chesed,* **steadfast love**. Apart from the word translated **life**, the remainder of the line means "show loyalty and kindness," as in 2 Samuel 9.3. This expression occurs almost always with a human subject, but in this verse God is the subject. Since **life** is not part of the usual expression, NIV uses two verbs, "You gave me life and showed me kindness." *Chesed* is better rendered in English as in TEV "constant love," but NIV is an adequate model for translation. Other models: "You have given me life and love," "You have caused me to live and have loved me," or "You have enabled me to exist and have been kind to me."

And thy care has preserved my spirit: not only has God given Job life and shown him constant love, he has also preserved his life. The word translated **care** means "visit, inspect, guard," and in the form used in this verse means "careful, watching, vigilant care." Thus Job emphasizes the extraordinary care God has taken of him before turning against him. **Preserved** translates the verb also used in the phrase in 2.6 "spare his life." **My spirit** translates Hebrew *ruach* or "my breath," which is the basis for physical life, and that which God breathed into man's nostrils (Gen 2.7). This line may also be rendered, for example, "you have also watched carefully over my life," "you have taken good care of me," or "you have guarded my life well."

10.13   RSV   TEV

> Yet these things thou didst hide   But now I know that all that
>   in thy heart;   time
> I know that this was thy pur-   you were secretly planning to
>   pose.   harm me.

Yet these things thou didst hide in thy heart: **these things** refers to the things which Job is about to mention in verses 14-17 and is paralleled by **this** in the next line. Job is about to tell openly the things which God has been keeping secret. **Hide in thy heart** means to keep them secret, not to let anyone know about them. The whole line may be rendered "What I will tell now you have kept secret," "You did not let me know what you were planning to do," or "You did not let anyone know the things you would do to me." **I know that this was thy purpose**: this line has a parallel in 27.11 "I will not conceal the purpose of the Almighty" (NEB). In Job's view God's kindness in his earlier happy life was part of God's cruel plan to ruin him. So he says now "I know that you were planning to do these things to me."

10.14   RSV   TEV

> If I sin, thou dost mark me,   You were watching to see if I
>   and dost not acquit me of my   would sin,
>   iniquity.   so that you could refuse to
>   forgive me.

With verse 14 Job begins to reveal those secrets which God has had in his mind. **If I sin, thou dost mark me**: RSV does not make clear the conditional nature of the "if" clause, which is brought out by TEV, "If I would sin," or NEB, "If I sinned, thou wouldst be watching me." **Mark** translates the same verb rendered "preserved" in verse 12. It means to guard or watch. In verse 12 it was used positively, but here its sense is "spy on," "keep a close watch on," "keep an eye on." The line may be rendered, for example, "You were spying on me to see if I would sin" or "You kept your eye on me, waiting for me to do something evil."

And dost not acquit me of my iniquity: line b takes the thought of line a further. In 7.21 Job inquires why God does not pardon his sin. The word translated **iniquity** is the same as used in 10.6 and means the same as "sin." **Acquit** translates the same verb as in 9.28 rendered by RSV "hold me innocent." Job looks upon God as the watcher of people, who is concerned with catching them in their sins.

TEV has restructured the verse as a statement in line a followed by a purpose in line b that he accuses God of having: "so that you could refuse to forgive me." If the translator follows the TEV logical sequence, line b may also be expressed "so that you could accuse me of doing evil" or "in order to hold me guilty for my sin."

10.15   RSV   TEV

> If I am wicked, woe to me!   As soon as I sin, I'm in trouble
>   If I am righteous, I cannot lift   with you,
>   up my head,   but when I do right, I get no
> for I am filled with disgrace   credit.
>   and look upon my affliction.   I am miserable and covered with
>   shame.^y

> ^y *Probable text* covered with shame;
> *Hebrew* see my shame.

If I am wicked, woe to me! In 9.22 Job says that whether he is guilty or innocent, it is all the same to God. He now repeats the same utterance of despair. Job believes it is God's intention to make him suffer, whether he is wicked or righteous. The exclamation translated **woe to me!** is found only here and in Micah 7.1, where it is rendered by RSV as "Woe is me!" This somewhat archaic exclamation is translated "I'm in trouble with you" in TEV. SPCL says "I am lost," FRCL "too bad for me," and GECL "it goes badly for me." If the translator keeps the "if" clause, line a may be expressed in some languages "If I am wicked, pain is mine," "If I am evil, suffering takes hold of me," or "If I am bad, trouble awaits me." Line b gives the contrast: **if I am righteous, I cannot lift up my head**. Being **righteous** is to act

rightly in regard to God and one's fellow beings, or, as TEV says, "When I do right
. . . ." **Lift up my head** is an expression meaning to have self respect, to be
unashamed, or to act with a clear conscience. In Judges 8.28 the Midianites were
subdued and therefore "lifted up their heads no more." In Psalm 83.2 the same
expression is taken as a sign of defiance. Some translations express the negative side
of shame as in FRCL: "Even if I am innocent (of wrongdoing), I must keep my head
bowed." SPCL translates "If I am innocent, there is little I can be happy about." Mft
says "I must hang my head!" which expresses the Hebrew idiomatically. TEV "get no
credit" is less forceful and far less picturable, and is typical of the frequent
demetaphorizing in TEV. In many languages it will be appropriate to use a different
figure to represent **lift up my head** to convey the notion of self-respect; for example,
"I cannot see with clear eyes" or "I cannot walk a straight path."

For I am filled with disgrace and look upon my affliction: it is necessary to
examine this pair of lines as a unit. **Filled with disgrace** means "covered with
shame," "dishonored," "humiliated." Some scholars delete this line as a gloss (in this
case, for example, supposing it was an explanatory remark someone added next to
the text). Others, including HOTTP, understand the word translated **look upon** to
mean "saturated, soaked, drunk," and therefore "I am filled with disgrace and drunk
with my affliction." The word translated **filled with** means having plenty of food, and
its parallel suggests having plenty of drink. There is clearly poetic intensification in
the movement from "filled" in the first half line to "drunk" in the second, with the
idea "I am not only filled with disgrace, I am even drunk from suffering." FRCL
translates this pair of lines "and I am tipsy with disgrace, drunk with my misery." The
whole expression may also be rendered, for example, "I am dishonored and suffer
greatly." If the receptor language permits, the translator may be able to reflect the
intensification in the second half; for example, "I am dizzy with dishonor and drunk
with suffering."

10.16   RSV   TEV

    And if I lift myself up,[x] thou dost   If I have any success at all,
      hunt me like a lion,   you hunt me down like a lion;
    and again work wonders   to hurt me you even work
      against me;   miracles.

[x] Syr: Heb *he lifts himself up*

And if I lift myself up, thou dost hunt me like a lion: the Hebrew text is
literally "And he lifts himself." Interpreters have tried different ways to identify the
subject of the first verb. RSV and TEV understand that the verb should be in the first
person and so follow the Syriac version. **Lift myself up** is understood by SPCL, GECL,
TEV to refer to Job's proud doings. NEB and BJ translate "Proud as a lion." Still other
translations (Mft, FRCL, NIV) understand the first half of the line to mean "If I lift
my head," without making clear what such a gesture may mean, other than
contrasting it with "when I lower my head" in the previous verse. It is not entirely
clear from the text whether Job compares himself to a hunted lion, or compares God
to a lion on the prowl. However, in view of 6.4, in which God's arrows are shot into

Job, it is probably best to assume that Job is here again the object of God's hunting, and so now God is depicted as a prowling lion. RSV's translation, as well as TEV, "You hunt me down like a lion," may mean either that God is a hunting lion, or that Job is the lion being hunted. It is best to avoid the ambiguity of RSV and TEV by translating as FRCL does: "As soon as I lift up my head, you are there taking up the hunt against me, like a lion" (similarly Mft and NIV). We may also translate, for example, "If I do anything to be proud of, you become like a lion and hunt me down to destroy me."

And again work wonders against me: this statement adds irony to Job's words and translates what is literally "and again you show yourself wonderful through me." The wonderful works of God's creation mentioned in verses 8-11 are now wonderful works of torment. TEV is quite right in expressing the purpose in the translation "to hurt me." This line may also be rendered, for example, "You even do amazing things just to harm me" or "You make miracles to cause me to suffer."

10.17 RSV	TEV
thou dost renew thy witnesses against me, and increase thy vexation toward me; thou dost bring fresh hosts against me.^y	You always have some witness against me; your anger toward me grows and grows; you always plan some new attack.

^y Cn Compare Gk: Heb *changes and a host are with me*

Thou dost renew thy witnesses against me: scholars differ regarding the meaning of the word translated **witnesses**. Some hold that these refer to Job's sufferings which testify (give evidence) to his guilt. Dhorme and others read the Hebrew word with different vowels and get "your hostility," which serves as a parallel for **thy vexation** in the following line. It does not seem necessary, however, to change the Hebrew just for the sake of parallelism. The line may sometimes be translated, for example, "You make new attacks on me," "You attack me again in order to make me suffer."

And increase thy vexation toward me: **vexation** translates a word meaning "to be angry, to be irritated." According to Eliphaz it is anger which causes the downfall of the fool in 5.2. Job says that God's anger toward him increases, or, as TEV translates, "grows and grows." The line may be rendered "and you become more and more angry with me" or "your anger against me gets greater all the time."

Thou dost bring fresh hosts against me translates the Hebrew "changes and hosts with me." See RSV footnote. The word translated **fresh** refers to military reliefs, troops who are sent in to relieve (take over from) combat-weary soldiers, and so are said to be rested or fresh. Job pictures himself pitted against an unending supply of fresh troops, a picture which is far more vivid than the abstraction of TEV, "You always plan some new attack." FRCL translates "and you throw troops who are always fresh against me." This line may also be translated, for example, "You send troubles on me like rested soldiers ready for battle."

3D-7. Job asks God to leave him alone as he is near death (10.18-22)

RSV	TEV
18 "Why didst thou bring me forth from the womb? Would that I had died before any eye had seen me,	18 Why, God, did you let me be born? I should have died before anyone saw me.
19 and were as though I had not been, carried from the womb to the grave.	19 To go from the womb straight to the grave would have been as good as never existing.
20 Are not the days of my life few? Let me alone, that I may find a little comfort	20 Isn't my life almost over? Leave me alone! Let me enjoy the time I have left.
21 before I go whence I shall not return, to the land of gloom and deep darkness,	21 I am going soon and will never come back— going to a land that is dark and gloomy,
22 the land of gloom and chaos, where light is as darkness."	22 a land of darkness, shadows, and confusion, where the light itself is darkness.

Subdivision Heading

The Handbook suggests that a heading be placed before verse 18 to show that this is the closure of Job's speech. Translators may wish to modify the Handbook heading to say something like "Leave me alone!" "I am about to die," or "Job's final plea to God." Habel has "Closing complaint and plea."

10.18-19   RSV   TEV

RSV	TEV
18 "Why didst thou bring me forth from the womb? Would that I had died before any eye had seen me,	18 Why, God, did you let me be born? I should have died before anyone saw me.
19 and were as though I had not been, carried from the womb to the grave.	19 To go from the womb straight to the grave would have been as good as never existing.

Job again picks up his death wish from 3.11-26. **Why didst thou bring me forth from the womb**: Job does not repeat the exact words of 3.11 which ask "Why did I not die at birth, come forth from the womb and expire?" In 3.11 Job did not ask why God allowed him to be born, but here in verse 18 he blames God directly for his tragic existence. The line may be rendered "Why did you allow me to be born?" "Why did you let me come out of my mother's womb?" or "I wish you had never let me come out of my mother's womb."

Would that I had died before any eye had seen me: in 3.16 Job envies babies that never lived to see the light of day, and here in a similar vein he wishes that nobody had ever seen him alive. The line may also be expressed "I wish I had died before anyone saw me" or "I wish I had died before I was born."

And were as though I had not been, carried from the womb to the grave: this verse continues the lament begun in verse 18. The RSV wording follows closely the structure of the Hebrew text and therefore is not particularly clear. Job is saying that he wishes he had never lived but had died at birth and been buried. TEV makes this clear with a noun clause as subject: "To go from the womb straight to the grave would have been . . . ." This line may also be translated, for example, "I wish I had died and they had buried me immediately. That would have been better than living."

10.20   RSV   TEV

Are not the days of my life few?[z]   Isn't my life almost over? Leave
Let me alone, that I may find   me alone!
a little comfort[a]   Let me enjoy the time I have
                                                         left.

[z] Cn Compare Gk Syr: Heb *Are not my days few? Let him cease*
[a] Heb *brightens up*

Job now begins to close his discourse and asks rhetorically **Are not the days of my life few?** The words **of my life** are not in the Hebrew text. The Septuagint and Syriac have "the days of my life," which is followed by RSV, TEV, and others. The Hebrew text adds a word which may be rendered "let him cease," as in the RSV note. Gordis understands this word to have contrasted meanings, both "cease" and "continue." He translates "but little will my days continue." KJV translates this verb as an imperative, "cease then," a request Job addresses to God. This verb may also be read as indicative, and that is a suggestion of HOTTP: "Will not the fewness of my days soon cease?" The line may also be rendered, for example, "Isn't my life almost finished?" or as a statement, "I have only a short time left to live."

Let me alone, that I may find a little comfort: Psalm 39.13 says "Look away from me, that I may know gladness" (RSV). In 7.19 Job asked God "How long wilt thou not look away from me?" In 14.6 Job, speaking about mankind in general, asks God to "look away from him . . . that he may enjoy . . . ." Many scholars propose changing the Hebrew text to get "look away from," as in the Septuagint. The Hebrew of the first clause says "put from me," and this may expect the reader to understand "thy hand" or "thy attention," according to Rowley. In any event Job is pleading with God to leave him in peace. **A little comfort** translates the same term used in 9.27, "be of good cheer." The line may be rendered, for example, "Stop your attacks; let me rest a little" or "Leave me alone to enjoy myself awhile."

10.21-22   RSV   TEV

21	before I go whence I shall not return,	21	I am going soon and will never come back—
	to the land of gloom and deep darkness,		going to a land that is dark and gloomy,
22	the land of gloom^b and chaos, where light is as darkness."	22	a land of darkness, shadows, and confusion, where the light itself is darkness.

^b Heb *gloom as darkness, deep darkness*

Before I go whence I shall not return: verses 21-22 are subordinate clauses dependent upon verse 20b in RSV. Job realizes that it is useless to regret that he was born, and the best he can hope for is that God will cease to take any notice of him. As in Psalm 39.13, the reference to Job's not returning is to Sheol, the world of the dead.

To the land of gloom and deep darkness: a description of Sheol. **Gloom** translates the same word used in 3.5, where Job asked that "gloom and deep darkness claim" the day he was born. The term for **deep darkness** is sometimes rendered by "shade" or "shadow of death." Translators may find it better to rearrange the lines of verse 21 as follows: "before I go to the land of gloom and darkness and will not return," "before I go to the place that is full of shadows and darkness and will not come back again."

The land of gloom and chaos: this extends the description of Sheol. In verses 21-22 there are four terms used in Hebrew to speak of the darkness of Sheol, and two of these are repeated, so that these two verses are overloaded with six references to the gloominess of Sheol. RSV, as the note indicates, reduces to **gloom and chaos** what is literally "as darkness, deep darkness." TEV uses "darkness, shadows." **Chaos** translates what is literally "without order" and conveys the idea of disorder or confusion.

Where light is as darkness: light and darkness are contrasting terms, and where there is no light, all is darkness. In the poetry of Job, it is so dark in Sheol that it is as though the shining of Sheol's light were darkness, or as TEV says, "the light itself is darkness." In some languages verse 22 will serve in apposition to verse 21 only by repeating the subject; for example, "That place is a land of darkness, shadows, and disorder," or "There in that place it is dark, and there are shadows and confusion." In some languages abstracts such as "disorder and confusion" must be expressed as descriptive statements; for example, "where everything is scattered about" or "where no two things are kept side by side." **Where light is as darkness** must be restructured in some languages; for example, "where even the light would be like darkness," "where the light that shines is not light but darkness," or "where there is no light and all is darkness."

3E. ZOPHAR'S FIRST SPEECH (11.1-20)

Chapter 11 contains the speech of Job's third and probably youngest friend, Zophar the Naamathite. Zophar's speech is again the counsel of a wise man or teacher who disputes Job's interpretation of God's wisdom. Zophar is plainly disgusted with Job's claims of innocence and says that God is not treating Job as severely as his guilt deserves. He offers Job advice on how he should conduct himself and thereby be restored to fellowship with God. Zophar implies that he has received secret wisdom not known to Job.

Zophar's speech is organized into three parts. In verses 2-6 he rebukes Job and wishes that God would speak out clearly against Job. In verses 7-12 Zophar praises the wisdom of God, and in verses 13-20 he turns again to Job and tells him that he should repent so that he can be made whole again.

Division Heading

Chapter 11 is the first speech of Zophar and should be headed as such. Some translations use a heading which attempts to do the duty of both division and subdivision headings. For example, FRCL has "Zophar's speech: return to God"; GECL "The third friend: You are guilty, God is in the right"; Habel "Zophar on God's inscrutable wisdom." Others are similar to the Handbook heading; for example, TOB "First poem of Zophar."

3E-1. Zophar says God has not punished Job to the extent his guilt demands (11.1-6)

RSV	TEV
1 Then Zophar the Naamathite answered:	*Zophar*
2 "Should a multitude of words go unanswered, and a man full of talk be vindicated?	1-2 Will no one answer all this nonsense? Does talking so much put a man in the right?
3 Should your babble silence men, and when you mock, shall no one shame you?	3 Job, do you think we can't answer you? That your mocking words will leave us speechless?
4 For you say, 'My doctrine is pure, and I am clean in God's eyes.'	4 You claim that what you say is true; you claim you are pure in the sight of God.
5 But oh, that God would speak, and open his lips to you,	5 How I wish God would answer you!
6 and that he would tell you the secrets of wisdom! For he is manifold in understanding. Know then that God exacts of you less than your guilt deserves.	6 He would tell you there are many sides to wisdom; there are things too deep for human knowledge. God is punishing you less than you deserve.

Subdivision Heading

Translators wishing to provide a subdivision heading may use the Handbook heading, or adapt it to say, for example, "Job, God ought to punish you more," "Much talk does not make you right," or "I wish God would answer you."

11.1   RSV   TEV

Then   Zophar   the   Naamathite   *Zophar*
answered:

Then Zophar the Naamathite answered: see 2.11 for suggestions regarding
the names **Zophar** and **Naamathite**. See comments on 4.1 for the prose formula
Then . . . answered. The marker that is used to translate **Then** should show that
the action has now shifted forward to the next scene and signals a change in speaker.
In some languages it may be necessary to say, for example, "After Job had finished
speaking," "When Job stopped talking," or "When Job became silent again." In
some languages it will be best to avoid using the word "answer" and say, for example,
"When Job stopped talking Zophar was the next one to speak to him."

11.2-3   RSV   TEV

2   "Should a multitude of words go   2   Will no one answer all this non-
          unanswered,   sense?
     and a man full of talk be vindi-   Does talking so much put a
          cated?   man in the right?
3   Should your babble silence men,   3   Job, do you think we can't an-
     and when you mock, shall no   swer you?
          one shame you?   That your mocking words will
                                                       leave us speechless?

   Should a multitude of words go unanswered: verses 2-3 are rhetorical
questions, as were the openings of Eliphaz's and Bildad's speeches in 4.2 and 8.2
respectively. Zophar's questions are directed against beliefs that Job has expressed.
Multitude of words is a literal translation of the Hebrew text. Most of the ancient
versions, however, have changed this to "he who is a great talker," which was no
doubt influenced by Proverbs 10.19. HOTTP believes the expression **multitude of
words** has the sense of "he who multiplies words," which means that it has the same
sense as the ancient versions without changing the text. Zophar asks if a big talker,
one who talks much, should be allowed to go on without being corrected. In 8.2
Bildad also accused Job of producing words like a "great wind." In some languages
it is not the words that may be said to go unanswered, but rather the speaker.
Accordingly we may translate, for example, "Should one who talks so much not be
answered?" "Should a person who uses so many words not have someone speak back
to him?" or as a statement, "Anyone who talks as much as you do, Job, should listen
to someone else."
   And a man full of talk be vindicated: the second line is parallel in meaning
to the first. **Man full of talk** translates Hebrew "man of lips," which is Zophar's way
of scolding Job. The occurrence of this figurative expression in the second line results
in heightening the poetic effect. **Man full of talk** or "man of lips" contrasts sharply
with the persons referred to in 8.10, who "utter words out of their understanding,"
which is literally "from the heart." **Vindicated** translates Hebrew *tsadaq,* meaning
"to be right, justified, acquitted of doing something wrong." See comments at 9.15.

Zophar does not say who will vindicate or put Job in the right. It is implied that Zophar himself will respond to what Job has been saying. TEV renders **multitude of words** as "nonsense" and in line b makes "talking" the subject of "put a man in the right." "Does talking so much put a man in the right?" The question implies a negative answer. If a rhetorical question is used, it may be expressed, for example, "And can so much talk prove you to be innocent?" or "Can your words show you are not guilty?" As a statement, "All of your talk will not prove you to be guiltless."

Should your babble silence men: babble translates a word rendered "boasts" by RSV and TEV in Isaiah 16.6. The same word has the meaning of "chatter," which is empty, meaningless talk and expresses well the idea in this verse. **Silence** used here as a verb does not mean to cause them to be totally silent but rather to be made speechless or unable to answer back; so TEV has "Do you think we can't answer you?" **Men** here and in verse 11 is the Hebrew word for "males" and is not the usual word for human beings. However, there does not seem to be any attempt to emphasize that they are males in contrast to females, and a general word such as "anyone" is more suitable in translation. TEV translates "we," referring to Zophar and his two companions. If the translator follows TEV, "we" must be expressed as excluding Job in those languages which make this kind of distinction. "Do you think all your chatter is going to keep us (the speaker and others) from talking?" Other question models are: "Will your wordy speeches leave people silent?" "Will all your talk cause others to remain silent?" The line may be stated negatively: "All of your talk will not keep others from speaking back to you."

And when you mock, shall no one shame you? In 9.23 Job says that God "mocks at the calamity of the innocent" (RSV). Rowley says that Job's mocking is not directed at his friends, but rather at their teaching that suffering is the result of sin. **Mock** means "deride, ridicule, make fun of." Many languages use idiomatic expressions for **mock**; for example, "to laugh at someone," "to make up funny words about," "to wag the head at," or "to smack the lips at." **Shame** translates a word with the same meaning as in English, but also with the sense of scolding someone, as in Ruth 2.15, where Boaz instructs the harvesters, "Let her glean . . . and do not reproach her." NIV has "Will no one rebuke you . . . ?" and Dhorme translates "without anyone rebuking you." The line may be rendered, for example, "When you make fun of others, do you think no one will scold you?" "When you wag your head at people, won't they correct you?" or "When you smack you lips at us, won't we shake our fingers at you?" In some languages these questions must be answered positively; for example, "Certainly we will." Some languages will prefer a conditional sentence, "If you mock us, we will reprimand you."

11.4 RSV	TEV
For you say, 'My doctrine is pure, and I am clean in God's eyes.'	You claim that what you say is true; you claim you are pure in the sight of God.

For you say, "My doctrine is pure": this verse begins with the Hebrew word meaning "you have said" followed by direct speech, so that the impression given is of a quotation from Job. However, Job did not actually say these words. He has only claimed that he is innocent, not that his doctrine is pure. The word translated **doctrine** is the usual term for teaching found in Wisdom literature (see Prov 1.5, "learning"; 4.2, "precepts"). Some scholars suggest a change in the Hebrew text, to get "conduct." This is probably unnecessary. Job has clearly rejected the traditional teaching or doctrine of his friends and has claimed to have as good knowledge as they have about such things. TEV has avoided both the words doctrine and teaching and has translated "what you say." NEB has "opinions" and NIV "beliefs," which are preferable to TEV. **Pure** translates a different word than the one used in 4.17, "Can a man be pure before his maker?" **Pure** as a description of something abstract such as doctrine refers to its being "authentic, original, not mixed with false teachings," and may sometimes be translated as being "all good" or "having nothing false in it." The term is also used in 16.17, where it describes prayer. Other possible renderings: "You say that your views are the right ones," "You claim that what you believe is the truth," "You, Job, say 'What I believe is the true teaching,'" or "You claim that your opinions are not mixed with false beliefs."

"I am clean in God's eyes": this line is parallel with the previous line and completes the quotation. Job's objection is that God considers him wicked and treats him as unclean. The word **clean** refers in Hebrew here to what shines. It is not applied to something physical but is used in the moral sense. The meaning is the same as "without reproach, guiltless, innocent." **In God's eyes** translates the Hebrew "in your eyes." Some scholars change this to "in my eyes," that is, "in Job's own opinion." However, Job has consistently argued that he is innocent in God's eyes, and that God knows this to be true. Pope changes the text to get "You are clean in your own eyes." It is best, however, to follow RSV and TEV. The line may also be expressed, for example, "I am innocent before God," "I have done no wrong in God's sight," "In God's eyes I have no guilt," "God sees me as an innocent man," or "God looks on me as having done no bad things."

11.5   RSV   TEV

> But oh, that God would speak,   How I wish God would answer
>   and open his lips to you,   you!

Zophar imagines a situation where God would confront Job directly, similar to Job's wish for God to appear in court with him. **But oh, that God would speak and open his lips to you**: Zophar's wish is that God would answer, reply, speak directly to Job, and correct him of his errors. The formula for expressing this kind of a wish in Hebrew is literally "Who will give (to me), that . . . ," and in English the same thought is generally expressed by "Would that . . ." or "How I wish that . . . ." (This formula appears again in 23.3 and 29.2.) In this verse line b **open his lips to you** is parallel to line a. The poetic force of the parallelism with the figurative expression in line b is that of giving greater emphasis. The meaning in line b is the same as in line a, and TEV has accordingly condensed the two lines into one. The translator who is translating Job as poetry should employ whatever device is natural in the poetry of the receptor language to preserve the heightening of poetic feeling. The whole line may be expressed, for example, "I wish that God would speak directly to you" or "I would love God to tell you exactly what he knows." The heightened parallelism may be expressed in a form such as "I wish God would speak, that he would say it directly to you."

11.6   RSV   TEV

> and that he would tell you the
>   secrets of wisdom!
> For he is manifold in under-
>   standing.[c]
> Know then that God exacts of
>   you less than your guilt
>   deserves.

> He would tell you there are many
>   sides to wisdom;
> there are things too deep for
>   human knowledge.
> God is punishing you less than
>   you deserve.

[c] Heb obscure

And that he would tell you the secrets of wisdom! Verse 6 is complex grammatically and textually. Translators will note that the order of lines in RSV and TEV are different. In Hebrew there are three lines. TEV also has three, but the content of lines a and b have been transposed. RSV and others take line a as a continuation of Zophar's wish in verse 5, thus expressing in verse 6a a third wish, **tell you the secrets of wisdom. Secrets,** which is plural here and in Psalm 44.21, refers to things which are hidden. In 28.11 it is used in the singular (RSV "the thing that is hid"). This line becomes line b in TEV, ". . . things too deep for human knowledge." **Wisdom** in Job refers to understanding the hidden principles of order guiding creation and the organization of the universe. Those who possess **wisdom** have gained understanding and appreciation of the mystery of God's ways. TEV has rendered this line "There are things too deep for human knowledge." Translators following RSV, in which verse 6a continues Zophar's wish from verse 5, may render line a, for example, "that he would tell you the mysteries of his ways" or ". . . the hidden thoughts of his mind."

For he is manifold in understanding: the RSV footnote says "Hebrew obscure." The Hebrew says literally "it is double for effectual wisdom." Some take "double" to mean "double what you think it is." Others make a change in the Hebrew term for "double" to read "wonders" so that the meaning would be "They (the secrets) are like wonders." Others object that God's secrets are not "like wonders" but are truly wonders. Another textual change gives "They are wonderful (full of mystery) to the understanding." Rowley takes the line to mean that the wisdom of God cannot be grasped by the human mind. TEV "There are many sides to wisdom" follows Pope, who says this means that God knows both sides of everything—the hidden as well as the known. TEV gives the translator a base from which to adapt. Following TEV it may be necessary to express "many sides to wisdom" differently, since in many languages wisdom cannot be handled as an object having sides; for example, "there are many ways to look at wisdom," "wisdom must be considered from many points of view," or "God's understanding is not on one path, but on many."

The third line, **know then that God exacts of you less than your guilt deserves**, is considered an addition by some scholars, who therefore drop it. HOTTP rates it "B" and recommends "God forgets for you (part) of your fault." TEV, however, gives a better model: "God is punishing you less than you deserve." This may be expressed in some languages, for example, as "You deserve much punishment, but God punishes you a little" or "God makes you suffer a little, but he should make you suffer more."

3E-2. God's wisdom is beyond Job's understanding (11.7-12)

RSV	TEV
7 "Can you find out the deep things of God? Can you find out the limit of the Almighty?	7 Can you discover the limits and bounds of the greatness and power of God?
8 It is higher than heaven—what can you do? Deeper than Sheol—what can you know?	8 The sky is no limit for God, but it lies beyond your reach. God knows the world of the dead, but you do not know it.
9 Its measure is longer than the earth, and broader than the sea.	9 God's greatness is broader than the earth, wider than the sea.
10 If he passes through, and imprisons, and calls to judgment, who can hinder him?	10 If God arrests you and brings you to trial, who is there to stop him?
11 For he knows worthless men; when he sees iniquity, will he not consider it?	11 God knows which men are worthless; he sees all their evil deeds.
12 But a stupid man will get understanding, when a wild ass's colt is born a man.	12 Stupid men will start being wise when wild donkeys are born tame.

Subdivision Heading

Verses 7-12 take up the theme of God's greatness. Translators wishing to place a heading here may follow the Handbook suggestion, or they may say something like "God is great," "God sees the evil deeds of people," or "You cannot know the limits of God's greatness." Rowley has "The unsearchable wisdom of God," and TOB "God's justice."

11.7   RSV   TEV

"Can you find out the deep   Can you discover the limits and
    things of God?   bounds
Can you find out the limit of   of the greatness and power of
    the Almighty?   God?

In verses 7-12 Zophar enlarges upon the theme of God's vast wisdom and man's inability to grasp it. The two lines of verse 7 are parallel, but there is little increase in poetic effect in the second line, and TEV combines them into a single sentence printed on two lines. The same verb translated **find out** occurs in both lines. **Find out** translates a verb meaning "explore, investigate, probe, discover the deep truth of a matter." Zophar's question is a way of saying that the mystery of God is beyond man's ability to understand. Both lines of this verse are rhetorical questions, as were the two parts of verse 2, and may be rendered as negative statements, that is, "You cannot find out the deep things of God," and "You cannot find out the limit of the Almighty." **Deep things of God** may be restructured to say, for example, "the things about God that are difficult for people to understand." The whole line may be rendered, for example, "Can you investigate and learn the things about God that are difficult for people to understand?" The answer to this question is "No!"

Can you find out the limit of the Almighty? Limit translates a word meaning "completeness, end, totality." It is used in 28.3 to refer to the extremities or depths a miner digs into the earth. In 26.10 it refers to the outer limit of the earth, where darkness and light meet. The **limit** of God is the mysterious depth, the unknowable truth of God's wisdom, and this is parallel to **the deep things of God** in the previous line. TEV has transposed the two lines so that "limits and bounds" express the unlimited nature of God's "greatness and power." **Almighty** translates Hebrew *Shaddai*; for a discussion of **Almighty** see 5.17. Line b̲ asks essentially the same question as line a̲. There is little heightening of movement in line b̲. This line may sometimes be expressed "Can you also discover the truth about God's wisdom which people cannot grasp?" or "Can you dig down and reach the truth of God that is beyond understanding? Of course not!" This may also be expressed as a negative statement, "You certainly cannot dig down and reach the truth . . . ."

11.8   RSV   TEV

> It is higher than heaven[d]—what
>   can you do?
> Deeper than Sheol—what can
>   you know?

> The sky is no limit for God,
>   but it lies beyond your reach.
> God knows the world of the dead,
>   but you do not know it.

[d] Heb *The heights of heaven*

It is higher than heaven—what can you do? RSV and others follow the Vulgate, because the Hebrew of the first clause appears to be only a fragment of a sentence. However, in the poetic expression it is forceful, concise, without conforming to a normal sentence structure. The poet uses this space image with only two words, "heights (of) heaven," to point visually to God's wisdom as being beyond human reach. Therefore in translation into a poetic form we often need an equivalent expression and not necessarily a complete sentence. We may suggest, for example, "High above," "Like the sky," "Beyond the heavens." The depths or limits of God in the preceding verse are here said to be beyond the reach of human thought. In languages in which degree of greatness is not expressed as a space relation, **higher than heaven**, it may be necessary to restructure this to say "The wisdom of God is greater than the heavens are high" or "The wisdom of God is so great, it is like the heavens." **What can you do?** This rhetorical question expects the reply "Nothing!" or as NEB says, "You can do nothing," meaning "You can do nothing to obtain God's limitless wisdom." TEV expresses this verse in idiomatic

English as "The sky is no limit for God, but it lies beyond your reach." It is, however, not the sky itself that is meant, but "the greatness of God's wisdom." This question may have to be restructured in translation to say, for example, "There is nothing you can do to understand it" or "You are not great enough to understand it."

Deeper than Sheol—what can you know? In line a of this verse the extremity or limit is in terms of the heavens, that is, upward. In line b the image is the reverse, the depths of the earth or **Sheol. Sheol** is the place of the dead. See 7.9 for discussion. The comparison is with the deep wisdom of God. Sirach 1.3 speaks of the vastness of God's wisdom as extending beyond all dimensions. To this the author of Job adds the dimension of Sheol. (See also Paul's allusion to four dimensions in Eph 3.18.) **What can you know?** has the same meaning as the question in line a, and some may want to translate it only once, unless they want to keep the total parallelism. TEV translates "God knows the world of the dead, but you do not know it." This rendering shifts the reference from the depth and limits of God's wisdom, which cannot be known, to knowledge about **Sheol.** TEV is the only translation which restructures in this way and should not be followed here. In some languages **deeper than Sheol** must follow the same pattern as in line a; for example, "It is greater than Sheol" or "Its greatness surpasses the greatness of Sheol." It may be necessary to combine the two lines by saying, for example, "The wisdom of God is greater than the heavens above or the place of the dead below."

11.9	RSV	TEV
	Its measure is longer than the earth, and broader than the sea.	God's greatness is broader than the earth, wider than the sea.

Its measure is longer than the earth: the dimension of length is now added and compared to the earth. The Babylonians divided the universe into four zones, each having its own lord: heaven, earth, sea, and underworld. The view in Job is similar, in which Sheol represents the underworld. In verse 9 the two dimensions are length and width. In languages in which the earth is thought of as a sphere, length does not apply well. Accordingly TEV has used "broader than the earth," which NEB uses for the sea, "broader than the sea." In translation it is important that what is referred to, the depths of God's wisdom in verse 7, be clear, since it has been substituted by pronouns in verses 8 and 9. Accordingly the translator may wish to reintroduce the subject from verse 7, as TEV has done, rather than using pronouns, as RSV has done.

And broader than the sea: in 37.10 breadth is used in connection with the wide expanse of "waters." In many languages the spatial comparison of wisdom must be restructured as in verse 8. Verse 9 may be expressed, for example, "God's wisdom is greater than the earth is large and greater than the sea is wide, and you cannot understand it."

11.10   RSV   TEV

If he passes through, and impris-   If God arrests you and brings
    ons,   you to trial,
  and calls to judgment, who can   who is there to stop him?
    hinder him?

If he passes through, and imprisons: in this verse Zophar shifts from the greatness of God's wisdom to his power and authority. There are two major variations in the translation of this verse. One group, Dhorme, NEB, and others, understands the word translated **imprisons** to mean "keep something secret," and in this case it would refer to keeping his passing by a secret. More commonly the meaning is taken as in RSV, TEV, and others to mean "arrest, capture, put in jail." TEV and some others consider **passes through** to express a casual appearance related to the main event, as in the English expression "he comes and [does so-and-so]." Therefore they do not translate it but begin with the "if" clause: "If God arrests you." If **passes through** is to be translated, it can be rendered "If God happens to arrest you" or "If God should decide to arrest you." RSV, unlike TEV, does not specify an object for the verb **imprison**. In TEV it is "you." In English this can refer to Job in the context of Zophar's talk, but it is also general and slightly more direct than saying "arrests somebody." The line may be expressed "If God should come along and arrest you" or "If God should put you in jail."

Verse 10 must be understood in part in the light of verse 11, as has been done in RSV and TEV. The verb translated **calls to judgment** means "summon an assembly, call people to a meeting," but in the context of verse 11 it refers more specifically to a court case or hearing, and therefore TEV "brings you to trial" is a good model; other possibilities are "and brings you before the judge" or "puts you in a law court." **Who can hinder him** translates the Hebrew for "who can turn him back." **Hinder** means to be an obstacle in someone's progress. TEV "stop" is more forceful. If a general object is used as the object of **imprisons** in line a, then this line may sometimes be rendered, for example, "and sends a person to trial, what can he do about it?" ". . . there is nothing he can do to prevent it," or ". . . that person will have to go ahead and suffer."

11.11   RSV   TEV

For he knows worthless men;   God knows which men are worth-
  when he sees iniquity, will he   less;
    not consider it?   he sees all their evil deeds.

For he knows worthless men: Zophar asserts that God does not have to investigate people to know their wickedness. **Worthless men** translates the Hebrew "men of emptiness," which is used also in Psalm 26.4, "I do not sit with false men" (RSV), where the expression is parallel in meaning with "dissemblers" and so suggests "deceitful people." **Worthless men** is translated "deceitful men" by NIV, "liars" by SPCL, and "false" by NEB. This line may also be expressed as "God knows a liar when he sees one," "God knows if you are worthless," or "God knows which people are deceitful."

When he sees iniquity: in 7.8,20; 10.14 Job sees God as a spy working against him. Now, however, Zophar tells Job that what God is seeing is **iniquity**, Job's sin. In Zophar's view God knows deceitful men and sees their sins. RSV, NIV, and NEB express the final part of this verse as a question, **will he not consider it? Will he not** implies a positive reply is expected: "Yes, he will." Some scholars suggest that the negative particle should be read with a different vowel as an object pronoun, giving "he does consider it." Rowley suggests it be read "without considering it." A good translation model is "When God sees iniquity (sees a person sin), he takes note of it, pays attention to it, does not let it pass unnoticed," or "When God sees people do bad things, he does not forget what they have done," or "God knows when people do bad things, and he keeps these in his heart."

11.12	RSV	TEV
	But a stupid man will get under-standing, when a wild ass's colt is born a man.	Stupid men will start being wise when wild donkeys are born tame.

But a stupid man will get understanding when a wild ass's colt is born a man: this verse has been understood in various ways:

(1) As two parallel lines: "And so an empty man gets understanding, and a wild ass's colt is born a man." That is, the stupid man becomes clever, and the ass becomes a man. The two parts are separate statements.

(2) As a sarcastic comparison: "The stupid man will have understanding only when an ass gives birth to a man." In this sense the stupid person will never understand.

(3) A suggestion made by Pope and followed by TEV is that the word translated **colt**, which is here the offspring of the donkey, really means "male domestic donkey" rather than offspring. The other Hebrew word means a wild donkey as in 6.5. The Hebrew word *'adam,* translated **man,** should be read *'adamah* "open country" and modifies wild donkey. This permits the translation to read "A stupid man will get understanding just as easily as a wild donkey of the open country will be born tame," or, as TEV translates, "Stupid men will start being wise when wild donkeys are born tame." This rendering is more natural as a proverbial saying than RSV and is recommended to translators.

This saying is made up of a comparison in which the unlikeliness or impossibility of the first clause is matched by the impossibility of the second. In some languages the comparison will not be evident; for example, where wild and domestic donkeys are unknown. In other languages the comparison may be too obscure to be understood. In the first case it may be possible to substitute other animals; for example, "Stupid men will become wise men when snakes are tame as dogs." Another solution is to substitute a general word such as "animal"; for example, ". . . when wild animals give birth to tame animals." In some cases it may be necessary to make the comparison within each clause more redundant; for example, "Stupid people will stop being stupid and act like wise men when wild donkeys stop giving birth to wild young and give birth to tame young" or "It is as impossible for stupid people to be wise as it is for wild animals to give birth to domestic animals." Some languages may have local expressions that convey these comparisons more clearly, and in such cases these may be used.

3E-3. Zophar assures Job that God will reward him if he will renounce his evil (11.13-20)

RSV	TEV
13 "If you set your heart aright, you will stretch out your hands toward him.	13 Put your heart right, Job. Reach out to God.
14 If iniquity is in your hand, put it far away, and let not wickedness dwell in your tents.	14 Put away evil and wrong from your home.
15 Surely then you will lift up your face without blemish; you will be secure, and will not fear.	15 Then face the world again, firm and courageous.
16 You will forget your misery; you will remember it as waters that have passed away.	16 Then all your troubles will fade from your memory, like floods that are past and remembered no more.
17 And your life will be brighter than the noonday; its darkness will be like the morning.	17 Your life will be brighter than sunshine at noon, and life's darkest hours will shine like the dawn.
18 And you will have confidence, because there is hope; you will be protected and take your rest in safety.	18 You will live secure and full of hope; God will protect you and give you rest.
19 You will lie down, and none will make you afraid; many will entreat your favor.	19 You won't be afraid of your enemies; many people will ask you for help.
20 But the eyes of the wicked will fail; all way of escape will be lost to them, and their hope is to breathe their last."	20 But the wicked will look around in despair and find that there is no way to escape. Their one hope is that death will come.

Subdivision Heading

In verses 13-20 Zophar tells Job what he must do to receive God's blessing and be restored. Translators may wish to modify the Handbook heading by saying, for example, "Do these things, Job, and God will protect you," "Repent, Job, and God will reward you," or "Here is how you can forget your troubles." Habel has "Conditional assurance," TOB "New life," and Rowley "Repentance is the way to restoration."

11.13-14

RSV	TEV
13 "If you set your heart aright, you will stretch out your hands toward him.	13 Put your heart right, Job. Reach out to God.
14 If iniquity is in your hand, put it	14 Put away evil and wrong from your home.

> far away,
> and let not wickedness dwell in
>   your tents.

In these two verses Zophar sets out four conditions required for Job to be accepted by God. **If you set your heart aright**: this advice is similar to that given by Bildad in 8.5-7. Zophar's advice is shallow, and the poetic language used to express it should be appropriate. **You** is emphatic and in contrast with the stupid person referred to in verse 12. This may require translators to say something like "As for you, Job" or "But if you, Job . . . ." **Set your heart aright** means "repent, change your heart, live in the right way." TEV has expressed the conditions as commands, which may be a good model for some languages to follow. Expressing it as an "if" clause, we may translate "If you, Job, change your heart . . ." or "Job, if you will repent . . . ."

You will stretch out your hands toward him: the same expression is used in Isaiah 1.15. It refers to the attitude and gesture of addressing prayer to God, as NEB makes clear, "and spread out your hands to pray to him!" TEV "Reach out to God" implies the gesture of extending the hands but leaves the purpose unclear. A better rendering would be "Reach out to God in prayer" or "Extend your hands to God in prayer."

If iniquity is in your hand: **in your hand** is the expression of a part for the whole person and means "if you have sinned." **Put it far away**: **it** refers to the sin or iniquity said in the first line to be in Job's hand. The sense of **put it far away** is "stop sinning!" RSV has rendered this line as a command, which has the effect of interrupting the conditions before reaching the consequences in verse 15. **Put it away** can also be understood as a condition in Hebrew, so that the meaning would be as in NIV, "If you put away the sin that is in your hand . . . ." A translator may use either a series of commands as in TEV or a series of "if" clauses. Both ways are preferable to RSV.

And let not wickedness dwell in your tents: this is the fourth condition set down by Zophar and the second to be stated in the negative. **Wickedness** is pictured as a person living in Job's tents or home. Bildad used the expression "tent of the wicked" in 8.22, where TEV translates "home" as here. Zophar is saying "You must stop sinning and not allow anyone in your house to sin."

Verse 14 uses figurative expressions, **iniquity in your hand** and **wickedness in your tents,** so that the poetic intensification does not build up from line a to line b. TEV considers line a as being contained in line b and does not translate it. However, the author is no doubt making a distinction between Job's personal sin and that of his family, and this distinction should be reflected in the translation. Verse 14 may be expressed, for example, "If you have done evil things, stop them, and let justice be done at home." FRCL translates "If your hands are soiled by evil, clean them, and do not give place to injustice in your house," which is a good model for those who can retain the image of the hands.

11.15   RSV   TEV

> Surely then you will lift up your   Then face the world again, firm
>   face without blemish;   and courageous.
>   you will be secure, and will not
>   fear.

Verses 15-19 contain a list of rewards that Job will enjoy if he follows Zophar's advice. Job, however, has no intention of following the advice of his friends.

Surely then you will lift up your face without blemish: this expression means "be free from shame, be self-confident, have hope for the future." TEV translates "face the world again," which is a sign of having hope and confidence. **Without blemish** means "without a stain on his conscience" or "with a clear conscience." Line 15a may also be rendered, for example, "Then you will certainly face the future without shame," "Then you will be strong and have a clear heart," or sometimes "You will walk a straight path and have a clean eye."

You will be secure, and will not fear: **secure** translates a Hebrew verb applied to casting molten metal to form a statue. The form of the verb used here has the sense of being "hard, firm, solid," not in a physical sense but socially, spiritually, emotionally. NEB translates "man of iron," that is, of iron-like character, a solid, sound personality. The text does not say what it is that Job will not fear. But in languages which must provide an object, it will be best to keep the object general and say, for example, "You will be afraid of nothing," or "Nothing or no one will cause you to be afraid."

11.16   RSV   TEV

> You will forget your misery;   Then all your troubles will fade
>   you will remember it as waters   from your memory,
>   that have passed away.   like floods that are past and
>   remembered no more.

You will forget your misery: **misery** translates a word used in 3.10 and 4.8, where it was rendered "trouble" by RSV. It refers to the pain and suffering Job has gone through. **You will remember it as waters that have passed away**: in 6.15 river beds were used as an image for treachery. Here a similar image is used to speak of forgetting. The comparison to **waters that have passed away** means the memory of something so indistinct it is forgotten, or remembered in the faintest way possible. The idea is expressed in English as "water under the bridge." Verse 16 may be rendered in some languages, for example, "You will forget your sufferings just like water that has flowed away in the river" or "You will forget your troubles like a person forgets the water that flowed down the river." Translators may have other traditional sayings that express this notion.

11.17 RSV TEV

And your life will be brighter
than the noonday;
its darkness will be like the
morning.

Your life will be brighter than
sunshine at noon,
and life's darkest hours will
shine like the dawn.

In 10.22 Job finished his speech by referring to Sheol as the place where "light is as darkness." Zophar assures Job now that instead of darkness **your life will be brighter than noonday**. The line is literally "(More) than noonday will be (or, stand) your life." The word translated **life** also means "world," so that Gordis translates "brighter than noonday will be your world." **Brighter**, although not expressed in Hebrew, is clearly implicit in the comparison with **noonday**. Translators in many languages will find it difficult to speak of Job's life or world being brighter than the noonday sun, since a person's life is not spoken of in those terms, and "world" is not used in this way, which may imply that Job owns the world. Therefore it may be necessary to say, for example, "The noonday sun will shine on you," or "The sun will shine brightly on all you own, as it shines at noonday."

Its darkness will be like the morning: the exact meaning of this line is uncertain. **Darkness** is obtained by a slight change in the vowels of the Hebrew and is preferred by many scholars. Zophar appears to reinforce his assertion of the previous line by saying that Job will find that even what he thinks of as darkness will be light. TEV shifts away from the comparison of darkness to morning light with "Your life will be brighter than sunshine at noon." In many languages it will be clearer to speak of a change from darkness to light rather than comparing them; for example, "The darkness in your life will change to sunlight" or "The troubles you suffer will change as darkness of night changes to morning sunlight."

11.18 RSV TEV

And you will have confidence,
because there is hope;
you will be protected[e] and take
your rest in safety.

You will live secure and full of
hope;
God will protect you and give
you rest.

[e] Or *you will look around*

And you will have confidence because there is hope: the verb translated **have confidence** occurs in 6.20, "they were confident" (RSV). The expression means "have a sense of security, live confidently, securely, without fear." In 7.6 Job complained that he was "without hope," but Zophar promises him a life full of hope in the future. For a discussion of **hope** see 4.6. Line 18a may also be expressed "You will gain new confidence and new hope," "You will look to the future without fear and with confidence," or " You will have no more fear and will be filled with hope."

You will be protected and take your rest in safety: **protected** translates a verb which normally has the sense of "dig or search for something," and RSV has "you will look around" in a footnote. However, these more common meanings do not fit the context. HOTTP gives three suggestions: (1) "and you will be ashamed," (2) "and you will dig," and (3) "you will protect." BDB (Brown, Driver, and Briggs Hebrew-English lexicon) explains the usage here as "search or look carefully about before going to rest." NIV follows this with "You will look about you and take your rest in safety." RSV, TEV, and others accept a change in the Hebrew text to get "protect," as in HOTTP's third suggestion. However, the implied subject of "protect" is God, as in TEV, "God will protect you." This seems the best solution and is the one followed by Dhorme and other interpreters. "God will guard you and you will rest without fear," or "God will keep anyone from harming you, and you will rest securely."

11.19	RSV	TEV
	You will lie down, and none will make you afraid; many will entreat your favor.	You won't be afraid of your enemies; many people will ask you for help.

You will lie down: this expression is nearly the same in meaning as the last clause of verse 18, "take your rest." It is found in the identical words in Isaiah 17.2; Zephaniah 3.13, apart from the pronominal differences. NEB considers it a later addition and puts it in a footnote. TEV does not translate it here in order to avoid the repetition with verse 18. **And none will make you afraid**: the same expression is used in Micah 4.4 to express confidence. TEV has made the object of the verb "enemies": "You won't be afraid of your enemies." Another possibility is "No one will cause you to fear."

Many will entreat your favor translates the Hebrew "many will soften your face." This figurative expression is sometimes used of begging favors from God. Applied to people it refers to saying sweet or flattering words in order to obtain something. When Job is prosperous again many people will again be asking him for favors. In some languages this expression takes on figurative forms, as in Hebrew; for example, "Many people will stroke your back," "Many people will hold out their hands to you," or "Many people will open their hands and smile at you."

11.20	RSV	TEV
	But the eyes of the wicked will fail; all way of escape will be lost to them, and their hope is to breathe their last."	But the wicked will look around in despair and find that there is no way to escape. Their one hope is that death will come.

Having completed his list of promised rewards for a new life, Zophar ends his speech with a warning to Job that if he does not change his ways, he will be lost. **But the eyes of the wicked will fail**: as in the case of Bildad's speech in 8.20-22, this saying expresses the miserable fate of the wicked. **Eyes** is used as the image that will "cease, fade, disappear, grow dim" in such passages as Psalm 119.82,123. The meaning here is not to be taken literally, since the physical eyes of the good and evil fail alike. The point here is that the wicked fail to see (understand, grasp) the significance of their true situation. It is their spiritual eyes which fail them, or as TEV says, "The wicked will look around in despair." That is, they will be in trouble and look around for a way out. Line 20a may need to be restructured in some languages to make clear the nature of the failing vision; for example, "The wicked will fail to see the truth," or without the figure, "Evil people will not understand what is happening to them."

All way of escape will be lost to them: Zophar emphasizes the frustration in store for the wicked because they cannot find a way to escape from their troubles. The inability of the wicked or the troubled to escape from a dreadful end is a common poetic picture in the Old Testament. For example, in Psalm 88.8 the psalmist cries out to God, "I am closed in and cannot escape . . ." (TEV). Psalm 142.4 expresses the same thought, "no refuge remains to me . . ." (RSV). On the other hand it is the righteous who escape from troubles (Prov 12.13). Because the vision of the wicked is impaired, they do not see their way out of their troubles; and this may be expressed, for example, "They are unable to find a way to escape," "They do not see how they can be freed," "They do not see a place where they can take refuge."

And their hope is to breathe their last translates the Hebrew "and their hope the breathing out of the soul." This refers to giving up the ghost, to die. The brightest hope of the wicked is to die. Job has already expressed this as his hope. Zophar aims his final blow at Job by saying that death is his final hope, unless of course he changes according to Zophar's advice. This line may be rendered, for example, "And these people can only hope for death," "People like these have only one last hope: death," or "There is no hope for such people; they die."

3F. JOB REPLIES (12.1–14.22)

This speech by Job closes the first cycle of speeches. Job opened this series in chapter 3, followed by Eliphaz (chapters 4–5), Bildad (chapter 8), and Zophar (chapter 11). Now Job will speak again in 12–14 before the three friends respond again in the same order as before.

In 12.2-6 Job claims that his knowledge is as great as that of his friends. He resents his three friends assuming that they are his superiors in matters of wisdom, and so his words are filled with sarcasm. In verses 7-12 Job appeals to nature as the witness to God's wisdom. Verses 13-25 consist of a hymn of praise of God's wisdom, but still in a somewhat satirical tone. Within this hymn there are three recurring themes: in verses 13-16 God can destroy and nothing can be done about it; in verses 17-21 God can discredit and destroy leaders; and in 22-25 he can confuse nations and their leaders. Chapter 13.1-5 is a part of the theme structure of chapter 12, since it closes the theme by returning to the subject of 12.3, "I am not inferior to you" (13.2), and closes with a final reference to wisdom with which chapter 12 began. In this way the theme of God's wisdom encloses the section of text from 12.2 to 13.5. The discussion of the content of 13.6–14.22 will be taken up at 13.6.

Division Heading

TEV and many others indicate with a heading that Job is again the speaker. Some provide more than speaker identification; for example, NAB has "Job's third reply," and TOB, which counts from Job's speech in chapter 3, says "Fourth poem of Job." Some combine the division with at least part of the subdivision headings; for example, FRCL has "Job's reply: God, an implacable tyrant"; GECL "Job: what God does is beyond understanding." NJB has "God's wisdom is best seen in the awesome works of his omnipotence," Habel "Job on knowledge and wisdom," and Rowley "Job answers Zophar."

3F-1. Job claims he is just as wise as the friends (12.1-6)

	RSV		TEV
	1 Then Job answered:	*Job*	
2	"No doubt you are the people, and wisdom will die with you.	1-2	Yes, you are the voice of the people. When you die, wisdom will die with you.
3	But I have understanding as well as you; I am not inferior to you. Who does not know such things as these?	3	But I have as much sense as you have; I am in no way inferior to you; everyone knows all that you have said.
4	I am a laughingstock to my friends; I, who called upon God and he answered me, a just and blameless man, am a laughingstock.	4	Even my friends laugh at me now; they laugh, although I am righteous and blameless; but there was a time when God answered my prayers.
5	In the thought of one who is at ease there is contempt for misfortune; it is ready for those whose feet slip.	5	You have no troubles, and yet you make fun of me; you hit a man who is about to fall.
6	The tents of robbers are at peace, and those who provoke God are secure, who bring their god in their hand.	6	But thieves and godless men live in peace, though their only god is their own strength.

Subdivision Heading

Translators who wish to provide a heading for verses 1-6 may follow the suggestion of the Handbook, or say, for example, "Job accuses his friends," "Job accuses his friends of taking advantage of his weakness," or "You think you know everything."

12.1	RSV		TEV
	Then Job answered:	*Job*	

Then Job answered: see comments on 4.1

12.2   RSV   TEV

"No doubt you are the people,   Yes, you are the voice of the
  and wisdom will die with you.   people.
                                       When you die, wisdom will die
                                         with you.

No doubt you are the people: **No doubt** translates a word meaning "truly,"
which, when followed as it is by the Hebrew conjunction *ki,* has the meaning "It is
true that, doubtless, certainly." The word translated **people** has no article in the
Hebrew, as it normally would have to give the RSV meaning. However, in poetry
articles are not always found as they are in prose, and so the RSV meaning can still
be obtained. Many different changes to the text have been proposed by scholars, but
none are convincing. Job is saying in a sarcastic way "You are the important people,
the ones who count, the people everyone listens to." TEV "the voice of the people"
means "You are the ones who speak for the people." In some languages this
expression is rendered, for example, "You are the mouths of the village," "Out of
your mouths the people speak," or "Your tongues speak for everyone."

And wisdom will die with you: this line is not parallel with the first line but
is a separate thought in the form of a relative clause describing **the people** in that
line. "you are the people with whom wisdom will die out" or "after you die there will
be no more wise people alive."

12.3   RSV   TEV

But I have understanding as well   But I have as much sense as you
  as you;   have;
I am not inferior to you.   I am in no way inferior to you;
Who does not know such   everyone knows all that you
  things as these?   have said.

But I have understanding as well as you: verse 3 has three lines as in RSV,
but as the second line is identical with the second line of 13.2, some interpreters
think it is out of place here and omit it. However, it makes good sense and appears
to be part of the design for the closure of the first unit of the poem, and so it should
not be omitted in translation. **Understanding** translates the Hebrew term "heart,"
which is rendered "sense" in TEV, NEB, and others. FRCL says "I know how to think
as well as you do." The line may also be expressed "But I understand things as well
as you do," "Your sense does not surpass mine," or "How you understand matters
is not greater than the way I understand them."

I am not inferior to you is a more general statement than lines a or c of the
verse. Accordingly GECL places it at the beginning. Translators may wish to do the
same. This line translates a Hebrew idiom "I do not fall from you," meaning "I do
not fall short of you" or "I am not less than you." NEB translates "In nothing do I
fall short of you." Job is assuring his friends that he is their equal. This line may also
be rendered, for example, "I am equal to you" or "What you are in thinking I am
also."

Who does not know such things as these? The verb **know** does not occur in Hebrew but is clearly implied. RSV translates Job's remark as a negative question which expects the reply "Everybody knows." TEV and others translate as a statement: "Everyone knows all that you have said." Job thus continues to ridicule his friends' wisdom, saying that all they have said is nothing new. This line may be rendered as a question by translating, for example, "Is there anyone who does not know these things you are saying?" "Doesn't everyone know these words you speak? Of course they do!" As a statement we can say "There is no one ignorant of what you have said" or "Everybody knows the things you have said."

12.4   RSV   TEV

RSV	TEV
I am a laughingstock to my friends;	Even my friends laugh at me now;
I, who called upon God and he answered me,	they laugh, although I am righteous and blameless;
a just and blameless man, am a laughingstock.	but there was a time when God answered my prayers.

Verse 4 is difficult to translate. Like verse 3 it has three lines, but their relation is not clear. There is an awkward shift from first to third person. **I am a laughingstock to my friends** translates the Hebrew "I am an object of laughter to his friends." There are two ways to interpret this verse. One is as RSV and TEV. Job is speaking of himself, and so Hebrew "his friends" is changed to "my friends." In line b then Hebrew "answers him" is changed to "answers me." TEV differs from RSV in that it transposes lines b and c. If the translator follows the line order of TEV (a, c, b), this verse may be rendered in some languages, for example, "My friends now laugh and make fun of me. They do this even though I am righteous and innocent; but before this happened, God used to answer me when I prayed to him." Another way to interpret the verse is to change the first line to third person; for example, "Anyone becomes a laughingstock to his friends" (NJB). Line b likewise may be kept in the third person, "If he cries to God and expects an answer." In this interpretation there is no reference to Job; it is a general reference to any righteous and blameless person as being the object of scorn and laughter. Both interpretations are possible.

I, who called upon God and he answered me translates the Hebrew "One calling unto God and he answered him." RSV and TEV (third line) change "him" to "me" so that it refers to Job, as in line a. **Call upon God** means "ask God for help."

A just and blameless man, am a laughingstock: the RSV wording keeps the reference to Job (not to a generalized subject) through the use of **am. Just** translates Hebrew *tsadiq* discussed in 4.17; 10.15. See also 1.1,8 for a discussion of **blameless. Laughingstock** refers to a person who is made fun of or laughed at.

12.5   RSV   TEV

RSV	TEV
In the thought of one who is at ease there is contempt for	You have no troubles, and yet you make fun of me;

> misfortune;
> it is ready for those whose feet
> slip.

> you hit a man who is about to
> fall.

In the thought of one who is at ease there is contempt for misfortune: the Hebrew of verse 5 is far from clear, and numerous changes have been proposed but little agreement reached. The first word in Hebrew is a prepositional prefix and noun translated **for misfortune** by RSV. The word also has the meaning "lamp, torch, flame," and the Vulgate and others translate "lamp." This usage does not, however, fit the context here. The word translated **thought** in RSV is found nowhere else in the Old Testament, and so its meaning is not certain. However, taken with the word that follows it, the sense seems to be "in the mind of those who have no troubles . . . ." Job sees that the beliefs of his friends enable the prosperous and comfortable to look down on the unfortunate. Moreover they withhold their sympathy, believing that such people as Job have brought on their own troubles. RSV makes a general statement, whereas TEV relates it to Job: "You have no troubles, and yet you make fun of me." Translators may do the same or follow RSV. If kept general, we may translate, for example, "People who have no troubles despise those who suffer misfortune" or "Those who are always at ease make fun of those who have troubles."

It is ready for those whose feet slip: RSV supplies **it is** and makes **it** refer back to **misfortune** in line a. In this interpretation **misfortune** is ready and waiting for **those whose feet slip**, meaning "for someone who is about to fall, to have troubles, to suffer." TEV again makes the line applicable to Job's friends, and not to someone in general. "Hit" in TEV translates the same word rendered **ready** by RSV; this is supported by Dhorme and many other commentators and is recommended to translators as making the best sense. **Those whose feet slip** means "people who are stumbling, falling, staggering." It is a figure of speech depicting people who are suffering, who are miserable. If the translator follows RSV, it may be best to make **misfortune** the subject of this line, "misfortune is ready . . . ." However, in some languages **misfortune** cannot serve as a subject in this kind of construction. Therefore the expression must often be restructured to say, for example, "Misfortune always happens to people who are already suffering" or "People who are already suffering always have still more misfortune." The better rendering, which is TEV, may have to be restructured in some languages to say, for example, "You cause troubles for a person who is falling," or "You make troubles for someone who is already suffering."

12.6	RSV	TEV

RSV	TEV
The tents of robbers are at peace, and those who provoke God are secure, who bring their god in their hand.[f]	But thieves and godless men live in peace, though their only god is their own strength.

f Hebrew uncertain

The tents of robbers are at peace: in this verse Job is saying that, while the prosperous or fortunate people are causing misery for the unfortunate and looking down on them as wicked, violent robbers and godless people are enjoying a good life. There are three lines, with a and b being closely alike in meaning. **Tents of robbers** refers to the homes of those lawless people who violently attack others. TEV "thieves" is less satisfactory, as the aspect of violence is largely lacking. **At peace** means that they live at home without trouble, threat, worry, or concern. This line reinforces the thought of verse 5. TEV contrasts line a with the last line of verse 5. We may also say, for example, "But robbers who attack people live at home in security," "But the tents of plunderers are left unharmed," or "But bandits live at home in peace."

And those who provoke God are secure: the shift in line b is from **robbers** who attack people to those who provoke God or make him angry. TEV calls them "godless men" and combines this line with line a. It is not suggested how people provoke, irritate, or anger God. **Are secure** is parallel in meaning with **in peace** in line a. Line b may be rendered, for example, "and people who make God angry are without threat," "and nobody threatens people who make God angry," "and no one threatens the peace of those who make God angry," or "and no one disturbs the safety of those who cause God to be angry."

Who bring their god in their hand: this line is literally "whom *'eloah* brings in his hand." Numerous attempts have been made to understand these words. Leaving aside all the proposed emendations or changes in the Hebrew vowels to make it clearer, there are two major approaches. The first is that of Gordis, who asserts that it is a Hebrew idiom which means to deceive; and he translates "all those who have deceived him (God)." However, Gordis gives no evidence of such an idiom used elsewhere in the Bible. The second interpretation is based on similar language used in Genesis 32.29; Deuteronomy 28.32; Micah 2.1. Each of these passages contains the term *'el,* which is taken by Dhorme to refer to God, and he translates these passages respectively "Their hand serves as their God," "My hand serves me as God," and "Your hand will not be able to serve as God."

As is seen in RSV and TEV, *'eloah* is here an object under the control or power of the thieves and godless people in line a and is appropriately translated "god." The best sense that can be made is that some people think they control or have power over God, but in reality they have only a god, idol, false god in their hand or power.

TEV translates as a concessive clause "though their only god is their own strength." We may also say, for example, "They are the ones who have power over their gods" or "Their strength is the god they trust." In languages in which it is difficult to express the idea of a "god," we may say, for example, "What they worship is their own power" or "Their own strength takes the place of God."

3F-2. God has given wisdom to the animals (12.7-12)

	RSV		TEV
7	"But ask the beasts, and they will teach you;	7	Even birds and animals have much they could teach you;
	the birds of the air, and they will tell	8	ask the creatures of earth and sea for

you;

8   or the plants of the earth, and they will
     teach you;
     and the fish of the sea will declare to
     you.
9   Who among all these does not know
     that the hand of the LORD has done
     this?
10   In his hand is the life of every living thing
     and the breath of all mankind.
11   Does not the ear try words
     as the palate tastes food?
12   Wisdom is with the aged,
     and understanding in length of days.

their wisdom.

9   All of them know that the LORD's hand
     made them.
10   It is God who directs the lives of his crea-
     tures;
     every man's life is in his power.
11   But just as your tongue enjoys tasting
     food,
     your ears enjoy hearing words.

12-13 Old men have wisdom,
     but God has wisdom and power.
     Old men have insight;
     God has insight and power to act.

Subdivision Heading

The major subject of verses 7-12 is Job's suggestion that his friend should learn about God from nature, and particularly from the animals. The Handbook heading may be reworded to say, for example, "Ask the animals to tell you about God," "The animals can tell you about God," or "The animals know about God even if you don't."

12.7   RSV   TEV

"But ask the beasts, and they   7   Even birds and animals have
   will teach you;   much they could teach you;
the birds of the air, and they
   will tell you;

But ask the beasts and they will teach you: Job addresses someone (probably Zophar) in the singular. **But** translates a connective used to call attention to the subject now taken up, and so TEV has "Even." **Beasts**, as well as **birds** in the next line, are followed in Hebrew by singular verbs but are to be taken as collectives, and therefore are translated in English as plurals in RSV, TEV. The word **beasts** is used in 18.3 in association with "stupid." The word emphasizes these creatures' inferiority to human beings. The feminine singular form of the Hebrew word translated **beasts** can mean "animal" or even "cattle" and often refers to living creatures generally, excluding humans, and particularly the larger animals. The term refers generally to domestic animals, but it can also refer to wild animals. The plural feminine form, as used in this verse, refers to the hippopotamus in Job 40.15. However, in the present context it refers to animals in the general sense. In languages which must distinguish between domestic and wild animals, it will be best to use a term designating domestic animals. TEV uses "animals," since **beasts** has a very wide range of meanings in modern English. The implication is that Job's friends should talk with the animals to learn about God, since their traditional knowledge has taught them nothing valuable. In translation it may be necessary to express **ask the beasts** as "ask the animals to tell you what they know about God," or "ask the animals to tell you about God," or ". . . to teach you about God."

The birds of the air, and they will tell you: in Hebrew **ask** is not repeated in this line. In 35.11 the author of Job asks "Who teaches us more than the beasts of the earth, and makes us wiser than the birds of the air?" In 11.7 Zophar asked "Can you find out the deep things of God?" and in 11.8 "it is higher than the heaven." Job now replies to Zophar that he should inquire from the **birds of the air**, literally "of heaven." TEV has condensed these two lines into one. In translation it will be necessary to repeat the verb "ask" in the second line, unless of course the two lines are joined to say "Ask the animals and birds to teach you about God." **Birds of the air**, if translated literally, may cause readers to ask if these are different from other kinds of birds. If a language makes a distinction based on birds that fly and birds such as chickens and other domestic fowl, the former should be used.

12.8	RSV	TEV
	or the plants of the earth,[g] and they will teach you; and the fish of the sea will declare to you.	ask the creatures of earth and sea for their wisdom.

[g] Or *speak to the earth*

Or the plants of the earth, and they will teach you: verse 8 is patterned on verse 7 and repeats the same idea. The word rendered **plants** occurs in 30.4,7, but the same word is more commonly read as a verb that means "meditate, think about," and in 7.11 it is translated "speak" by RSV. Some modern translators adopt a change from **plants of the earth** to get "creatures that crawl." This supports the usual order of beasts, birds, fishes, and creeping things, and RSV is alone among modern versions to use **plants**. This leaves two choices, both of which are recommended to translators: "Speak to the earth" as in FRCL, SPCL, GECL, NIV, and TOB, or "creatures of the earth" as in TEV and others. **Earth** is used here in the sense of "the ground or land," rather than the earth as a planet. In languages in which inanimate objects cannot be used with a verb like **teach**, it may be possible to say, for example, "and you will learn by watching them" or "you will become wise by watching what they do." **And they will teach you** is repeated from verse 7a in the Hebrew. TEV condenses the second part of both lines into one, "for their wisdom."

And the fish of the sea will declare to you: as with the previous two lines, the verb **ask** is implied in Hebrew. **Fish** is plural in Hebrew. The order of beasts, birds, reptiles, and fish is nearly the opposite of that in Genesis 1.26. In languages in which the sea is unknown, it may be necessary to translate, for example, "and the fish in the rivers will tell you."

12.9	RSV	TEV
	Who among all these does not know	All of them know that the LORD's hand made them.

that the hand of the LORD has
   done this?

Some translators do not believe that verses 9-10 fit at this point. Dhorme, for
example, places verses 9-10 after verses 11 and 12. NEB has the order 9, 11, 12, 10.
There does not seem to be sufficient reason to transpose these verses, and it is
recommended to translators that they keep them in their traditional order.

**Who among all these does not know that the hand of the LORD has done
this?** Verse 9 in Hebrew is a rhetorical question as in RSV. TEV has expressed it as
a statement. **Who does not know** may refer either to the creatures in verses 7-8, or
to the humans who can learn from the creatures. Both RSV and TEV understand it
to refer to the creatures, that is, "All of those creatures know." **Hand of the LORD**
translates "hand of Yahweh." This is a rare usage because nowhere else does the
name *Yahweh* occur as the name of God in the speeches between Job and his friends.
Some Hebrew manuscripts read "Eloah," which may be a correction made by
copyists. **This** at the end of the verse may refer to all that Zophar has said. It seems
best, however, to take it as referring to what God has done with his creatures, that
is, that he has given them life, which witnesses to his wisdom. This idea is expressed
by TEV, "The LORD's hand made them." FRCL translates "Among all these creatures,
which one still does not know that all that happens is the work of the Lord?" SPCL
says "Is there still anyone who does not know that God has done all this with his
hand?" Either of these, as well as TEV, are good models to follow.

12.10   RSV   TEV

In his hand is the life of every   It is God who directs the lives of
   living thing   his creatures;
and the breath of all mankind.   every man's life is in his pow-
                                            er.

Verse 10 expands on verse 9 and gives the reason why God's creatures are able
to know him. The two lines of verse 10 are closely parallel in meaning. **In his hand
is the life of every living thing: In his hand** means "in God's power, under God's
control, directed by God." **Life** translates *nefesh*, which is paralleled by *ruach* **breath**
in the next line. In 7.11 these same two terms are rendered "soul and spirit." There,
as well as here, the meanings are the same. When God takes away the *nefesh* "soul,"
death results, so here "soul" is the life principle or life force that sustains a creature.
TEV translates **soul** as "lives," since it refers to the collective, **every living thing.**
This expression includes all forms of life, including animal life. Line a then says "In
God's hands are the lives of everything that lives" or "God has power over the lives
of everything that lives."

And the breath of all mankind: In his hand in the first line applies also to
this line. **Breath** translates Hebrew *ruach*. Until God gives man **breath**, he is not a
living creature. **All mankind** translates "the flesh of man," which refers more
specifically to the life or spirit of people, in contrast to the term in the first line,
which is all-inclusive. This line may be expressed as "The breath which gives people
their life" or "The breath which causes people to live."

12.11   RSV   TEV

> Does not the ear try words
>   as the palate tastes food?

> But just as your tongue enjoys
>   tasting food,
>   your ears enjoy hearing words.

Does not the ear try words as the palate tastes food? The point of this proverb is that the ear judges between what is true and false, good and bad, just as the mouth distinguishes between what tastes good and what tastes bad. Job appears to claim for himself the right to discern what is good and true from the false teachings of his friends. The proverb serves as a sarcastic climax to verses 7-10. The ear and the palate, although only parts of the body, serve for the whole person in this saying. TEV has placed the emphasis upon enjoying rather than upon distinguishing. However, enjoying food and words is not what Job is saying here, therefore TEV should not be followed. The same saying will be used by Elihu in 34.3, where TEV gives a better translation. In languages where these respective parts cannot by themselves perform these functions, it may be necessary to adjust the proverb to say, for example, "When a person hears words spoken, does he not test them to decide which are true? Of course he does. It is the same as when he tastes food and finds some tastes good and some tastes bad."

12.12   RSV   TEV

> Wisdom is with the aged,
>   and understanding in length of
>   days.

> 12-13 Old men have wisdom,
>   but God has wisdom and pow-
>   er.
> Old men have insight;
>   God has insight and power to
>   act.

This verse is handled in a variety of ways by scholars. Some go so far as to delete verse 12 as an intrusion; but the verse has clear continuity with verse 11, although TEV combines 12-13 and places them in a new paragraph.

Wisdom is with the aged: most modern translators take this to be Job's own comment. GECL, Mft, and Habel make it refer to the belief of Job's friends; for example, "Wisdom, you argue, lies with aged men" (Mft). It seems preferable to translate it as Job's own statement. **Wisdom** is here understood as the ability to discriminate, know the difference, between what is true and what is not true. It is said to be **with the aged**, which means it is found among old people who have practiced it over many years. Bildad had expressed the same in 8.8-10: "Inquire . . . of bygone ages, and consider what the fathers have found." Eliphaz will do the same again in 15.10. In some languages a very old person is called "a person with one remaining hair" or "a person with a wrinkled face."

And understanding in length of days: this line is parallel in meaning with the previous line. The Hebrew says only "and length of days understanding." **Length of days** is a poetic equivalent of "old age," and **understanding** means the same as **wisdom** in line <u>a</u>. The two lines therefore say essentially the same thing. However, the occurrence of the figure **length of days** for "old men" in line a tends to heighten the poetic effect somewhat. In translation it may be possible to keep the parallelism as in RSV. Some translators may find a rendering such as SPCL a better model: "Old people have wisdom; age has given them understanding." In some languages **understanding** as a noun creates difficulties, since it may be necessary to know what it is that is understood. We may therefore suggest another model: "Old people know the difference between what is true and what is not true. When they become old they understand things."

Translators will notice that TEV restructures verses 12-13 so that the order is 12a, 13a, 12b, 13b. The effect of this change in order is to emphasize the superior "wisdom and power" of God in comparison to that of men. However, the contrast is also present in the usual line order; and such rearrangement is not required to obtain the contrast, although it may give more emphasis to it.

3F-3. God is the divine destroyer (12.13-25)

RSV	TEV
13 "With God are wisdom and might; he has counsel and understanding.	12-13 Old men have wisdom, but God has wisdom and power. Old men have insight; God has insight and power to act.
14 If he tears down, none can rebuild; if he shuts a man in, none can open.	14 When God tears down, who can rebuild, and who can free the man God imprisons?
15 If he withholds the waters, they dry up; if he sends them out, they overwhelm the land.	15 Drought comes when God withholds rain; floods come when he turns water loose.
16 With him are strength and wisdom; the deceived and the deceiver are his.	16 God is strong and always victorious; both deceived and deceiver are in his power.
17 He leads counselors away stripped, and judges he makes fools.	17 He takes away the wisdom of rulers and makes leaders act like fools.
18 He looses the bonds of kings, and binds a waistcloth on their loins.	18 He dethrones kings and makes them prisoners;
19 He leads priests away stripped, and overthrows the mighty.	19 he humbles priests and men of power.
20 He deprives of speech those who are trusted, and takes away the discernment of the elders.	20 He silences men who are trusted, and takes the wisdom of old men away.
21 He pours contempt on princes, and looses the belt of the strong.	21 He disgraces those in power and puts an end to the strength of rulers.
22 He uncovers the deeps out of darkness, and brings deep darkness to light.	22 He sends light to places dark as death.
23 He makes nations great, and he destroys them: he enlarges nations, and leads them away.	23 He makes nations strong and great, but then he defeats and destroys them.
24 He takes away understanding from the chiefs of the people of the earth, and makes them wander in a pathless waste.	24 He makes their leaders foolish and lets them wander confused and lost;
25 They grope in the dark without light; and he makes them stagger like a drunken man.	25 they grope in the dark and stagger like drunkards.

Subdivision Heading

As pointed out in the introduction to division 3F (12.1–14.22), verses 13-25 make up a hymn on God's wisdom and power, with three recurrences of a single theme. The Handbook suggests a single heading. Translators may wish to adjust the Handbook heading to say, for example, "God has the power to do as he pleases," "God destroys and people can do nothing about it," or "God is all powerful."

12.13 RSV	TEV
"With God[h] are wisdom and might; he has counsel and understanding. [h] Heb *him*	12-13 Old men have wisdom, but God has wisdom and power. Old men have insight; God has insight and power to act.

With God are wisdom and might: the Hebrew text has "with him," where "him" can refer only to God and not to the old men in verse 12. **Wisdom** translates the same noun used in verse 11. The contrast between verses 12 and 13 is that God has both **wisdom and might**, while people have only wisdom. **Might** translates a word meaning "power, strength, force." The same word occurs in 26.14, "the thunder of his power." It is God's **might** that enables him to carry out his will. In translation it may be necessary to mark the contrast between people and God by saying, for example, "On the other hand, God has both wisdom and power," "But God who has wisdom also has power," or "God is both wise and powerful."

He has counsel and understanding. Isaiah 28.29 expresses the same idea with "he is wonderful in counsel and excellent in wisdom." **Counsel** here does not mean giving advice but rather devising plans, thinking ahead, having insight. **Understanding** is the same word as used in 12b.

12.14 RSV	TEV
If he tears down, none can rebuild; if he shuts a man in, none can open.	When God tears down, who can rebuild, and who can free the man God imprisons?

If he tears down, none can rebuild: it is not clear whether **tears down** is to be taken literally or figuratively, and whether the object torn down is physical or emotional. God is clearly implied as the one who **tears down**, but he is not named. RSV translates with an "if" clause followed by a statement. TEV uses a "when" clause followed by a question which expects the reply "Nobody." In translation it will often be necessary to provide an object; for example, "If God tears something down, nobody can build it again" or "When God tears down a building, no one can rebuild that building." GECL translates "What he lays in ruins no one can build again." FRCL has "One does not rebuild what God demolishes."

If he shuts a man in, none can open: this line is more specific in that **man** is mentioned as the one whom God shuts in, probably suggesting to put in prison, make captive. FRCL translates "One does not free the person he (God) imprisons." TEV translates as a question and reverses the order of the two lines, and thus gives the entire verse a balanced chiastic structure. In translation it is best to avoid the literal **shuts a man in**, as this can be construed to have many different meanings. A rendering closer to TEV or FRCL is preferred. In cultures that do not have jails or prisons, it may be necessary to use a more general expression as in RSV, or say, for example, "If God takes people captive, who can free them?" or "Who can set people free if God has captured them?"

12.15   RSV   TEV

> If he withholds the waters, they   Drought comes when God with-
>   dry up;   holds rain;
> if he sends them out, they   floods come when he turns
>   overwhelm the land.   water loose.

If he withholds the waters, they dry up: Job asserts that God is free to do as he wishes, and that drought and floods are part of what he does. RSV follows the Hebrew order of placing the verb clause first in each line of verses 14 and 15. TEV shifts in verse 15 by placing the "when" clause at the end, and thus breaks up the monotony of the structure. God is pictured as restraining the waters which would burst loose. The reference is to the rains, and the drying up occurs where the rains do not reach. Accordingly it may be clearer in many languages to say, for example, "When God does not let it rain, everything dries up" or "If God does not let the rain fall, the ground dries up."

If he sends them out, they overwhelm the land: this line contrasts with the previous line. **Sends them out** refers to releasing the rain water, causing it to rain. **Overwhelms** translates a word meaning "overturn, upset, knock down." In 9.5 it was translated "remove mountains" (RSV). It is used in connection with the overthrow of Sodom and Gomorrah (Gen 19.25). TEV translates "floods came," since the result comes from causing great rains to fall. The line may also be rendered "If he sends a flood, it runs everywhere" or "If he lets the flood waters loose, they destroy everything."

12.16   RSV   TEV

> With him are strength and wis-   God is strong and always victori-
>   dom;   ous;
> the deceived and the deceiver   both deceived and deceiver are
>   are his.   in his power.

With him are strength and wisdom: the structure of verses 13 and 16 is the same; however, the words translated **strength and wisdom** in verse 16 are different from the words translated "wisdom and might" in verse 13. In 16 the word rendered

wisdom refers to the effects of wisdom in terms of success and is therefore more correctly translated "victorious" in TEV. NEB translates "Strength and success belong to him." FRCL has "strength and skill." This line may also be expressed, for example, "God is powerful and defeats his enemies" or "God is strong and able to do as he wishes."

The deceived and the deceiver are his: the two subjects in this line have similar sounds in Hebrew and are therefore an example of the poetic feature called alliteration. They are used to include both extremes, and another set with the same function is found in the Hebrew of "bond or free" in Deuteronomy 32.36. **Deceived** refers to one who goes astray, gets lost. **The deceiver** is the one who causes someone to go astray or become lost. This line begins a theme of aimless wandering which continues to verse 25. The intention is primarily upon humanity as a crowd drifting about without purpose. This may include the moral aspect of going astray. The thought is that nothing escapes the wisdom of God. **Are his** translates the Hebrew "to him," but **are his** is ambiguous, suggesting wrongly that he keeps them. They do not escape his power and wisdom, and so TEV "are in his power" is to be preferred. SPCL has "subject to him." This line may be rendered, for example, "If a person becomes lost or causes others to become lost, God is in control of them" or ". . . they have not escaped from God's power."

12.17   RSV   TEV

> He leads counselors away
> stripped,
> and judges he makes fools.

> He takes away the wisdom of
> rulers
> and makes leaders act like
> fools.

In verses 17-21 Job describes how God can discredit and bring down leaders of society. **He leads counselors away stripped**: **counselors** translates a term for officials in 3.14 who are ranked with kings. FRCL calls them "great men of state," and TEV "rulers." They may also be advisers to the king. **Stripped** translates a word used only here, in verse 19, and in Micah 1.8, where it means "barefooted." According to Dhorme, to go barefooted is the sign of extreme grief. HOTTP does not support any change in the text but considers the received Hebrew text an "A" reading and suggests the meaning "despoiled," which means to plunder or rob. TEV "takes away the wisdom of rulers" expresses the same idea in more general terms. FRCL agrees with Dhorme: "He makes great men of state go barefooted." Gordis suggests that the meaning "stripped of clothes" has an extended sense meaning "stripped of sense," and so "mad" or "crazy." Translators should render **stripped** in such a way that the symbolic meaning is clear. SPCL translates in its text "He causes the wise to lose their intelligence," and in the margin gives what it says represents the Hebrew: "He removes the wise from their positions." The line may also be expressed "He takes from the leaders their wisdom" or "He causes the rulers to be dumb."

And judges he makes fools: **judges** translates the same word used in 9.24 "He covers the faces of its judges" (RSV). **Judges** are a class of authorities or rulers and not just court judges. **Makes fools** translates a verb meaning "drive someone mad" in the sense of causing them to loose their mind or become crazy. This line may be expressed, for example, "He also causes those in authority to go crazy," "He also makes the chiefs of the people to lose their minds," or "He makes the chiefs to become like mad men."

12.18 RSV TEV

> He looses the bonds of kings, and binds a waistcloth on their loins.

> He dethrones kings and makes them prisoners;

He looses the bonds of kings: bonds translates the Hebrew "discipline, correction," which most scholars read with different vowels to get **bonds** or "chains." It is not certain if the meaning is that God removes the chains which kings put on others, or if God takes away some symbol of royal authority belonging to kings. HOTTP understands it in the latter sense, as do TEV and others: "He dethrones kings." SPCL has "He leaves kings without authority." NIV represents the former sense, "He takes off the shackles put on by kings," referring to the bonds kings put on people. Dhorme thinks **the bonds of kings** refers to chains which keep kings in bondage, so that the meaning is "He sets kings free from chains."

The understanding of the first line is partly dependent upon the second, **and binds a waistcloth on their loins.** In RSV the relation between the two lines is not clear. The Hebrew says "and he binds a girdle on their waist." Some take this to mean that he strengthens the kings by placing a girdle or wide band about their middle. However, it is more probable that the meaning is that God, having removed their symbol of authority, puts on the kings a waistcloth which is worn for doing hard physical labor, and so depicts a slave. TEV translates this entire line "and makes them prisoners." A literal rendering of line b̲ such as NIV, "and ties a loincloth around their waist," would require an explanatory note to show that he reduces the king to a slave. It is better to give the fuller cultural significance in the text by saying, for example, "and makes them slaves" or "and ties a loincloth on them and makes them slaves." Another translation model is "God takes away the authority of kings and makes them like slaves." If the translator wishes to keep the change of clothes image in each line, it may be possible to say, for example, "He takes away from kings their robes of authority and puts on them the loin cloth of a slave."

12.19 RSV TEV

> He leads priests away stripped, and overthrows the mighty.

> he humbles priests and men of power.

He leads priests away stripped: verses 17a and 19a are the same, except that **counselors** is replaced by **priests.** This is the only mention of **priests** in the book of Job. Most translators will have a term for **priests** from the translation of the New Testament. If a descriptive term must be used here, we may say, for example, "the one who makes sacrifices," "the one who leads the prayers," or "the one who prays to God for the people." For comments on **stripped** see verse 17.

And overthrows the mighty: God overthrows those whose positions seem permanent. **Overthrows** is used here as in Psalm 21.12, "For you will put them to flight." It refers to getting rid of, bringing down, taking power from the rulers. **Mighty** translates an adjective meaning "perpetual, unceasing." Here it refers to authorities whose power is continuous, not subject to change. These are rulers who have great power and continuity. The line may also be expressed "He brings to an end the established authorities" or "He takes away power from those who rule the people."

12.20   RSV   TEV

> He deprives of speech those who   He silences men who are trusted,
>   are trusted,   and takes the wisdom of old
> and takes away the discern-   men away.
>   ment of the elders.

He deprives of speech those who are trusted: **deprives of speech** translates the Hebrew idiom "removes the lip," and this is rendered by TEV "He silences . . . ." **Those who are trusted** translates a word which has the meaning of "truthful, sincere" as well as "steadfast, faithful, trusted." Dhorme translates "He deprives of speech the truthful," but this sense does not fit the context as well as RSV, TEV, and others. The line may be rendered, for example, "He closes the mouths of those whom the people trust," "He will not allow truthful people to speak," "He causes the faithful to be silent," or "He causes people whom others trust to be silent."

And takes away the discernment of the elders: **discernment** translates Hebrew "taste" and refers to the capacity to distinguish between right and wrong. It is rendered in English by such words as "judgment, insight, good sense." In 12.12 wisdom is a quality of "the aged," and TEV, which translated there "old men have wisdom," here says "wisdom of old men." This line may also be expressed, for example, "and he takes away from the old people their good judgment" or "and he removes from old people their ability to know right from wrong."

12.21   RSV   TEV

> He pours contempt on princes,   He disgraces those in power
>   and looses the belt of the   and puts an end to the
>   strong.   strength of rulers.

He pours contempt on princes: for the same expression see Psalm 107.40a. The scorn or **contempt** is literally "poured" in the Hebrew. This figure refers to expressing disgust, disdain, extreme displeasure, and is close in meaning to "mock, ridicule, deride, make fun of." **Princes** does not refer to sons of a king but translates a category of authorities known as "noblemen, persons of authority," and therefore TEV "rulers." The line may be rendered, for example, "He scorns those who are in positions of authority," "He ridicules the leaders," or "He mocks the rulers of the people."

He looses the belt of the strong renders the literal form of the Hebrew and is similar to verse 18a. **Belt** translates a word found only here but which is similar to a word used in Psalm 109.19, "like a belt with which he daily girds himself." Although many changes in the text have been suggested, it is best to read the text here as it stands. The sense is as in 12.18a, so that here again Job says God takes power and authority away from the rulers. In some contexts the word translated **the strong** refers to "river beds," but in this verse that meaning is inappropriate. FRCL translates, "He suddenly leaves the tyrants without any defense." This line may also be rendered, for example, "He leaves the powerful without any strength" or "He takes away from the mighty their strength."

12.22   RSV   TEV

He uncovers the deeps out of   He sends light to places dark as
   darkness,   death.
  and brings deep darkness to
   light.

He uncovers the deeps out of darkness: this verse has been handled variously by different scholars. Some find it does not fit the larger context and so delete it. NEB keeps it and shifts it to the end of the chapter. However, translators should not delete nor shift it to another position. As in 3.5 and 10.21, **darkness** and **deep darkness** are parallel terms in which the second term is more intensive. The meaning of this verse is not clear, and translating it literally, as RSV does, does not help the reader. According to Dhorme this verse alludes to the action of God in nature. **Uncovers** translates a verb meaning "unveil" or "strip," that is, take away something so that what is covered, hidden, can be seen. The **deeps** may be taken as referring to the depths of *Sheol,* which is the dark place of the dead in the depths of the earth. It is also possible that the **deeps** refers to the plans and schemes of men which God brings to light, or it can be God's own deep or hidden purposes, which are seen as God carries them out (Rowley's view).

The second line **and brings deep darkness to light** says almost the identical thing as the first line, and so TEV reduces both lines to one: "He sends light to places dark as death." The whole verse may be rendered, for example, "He unveils the darkness of Sheol," "He brings the darkness of Sheol to light," or "He makes the hidden Sheol to be seen." If the translator is able to retain the parallelism of the two lines, it may be possible to say, for example, "He takes away the darkness of the place of the dead, and makes the darkest of places light."

12.23   RSV   TEV

He makes nations great, and he   He makes nations strong and
   destroys them: great,

| he enlarges nations, and leads them away. | but then he defeats and destroys them. |

He makes nations great, and he destroys them: in Job's view God makes some nations great, but without any moral principle. Nations rise and fall because he has the power to cause them to do so. **Makes nations great** translates the causative form of the verb "grow." In 8.11 it is used to refer to the reeds that grow in the water. Each line has two contrasting verbs to depict how God causes a nation to be great and then causes it to become worthless. NJB says in the first line "builds up . . . ruins," GECL "grow . . . fade away." This line may also be expressed, for example, "He makes nations to grow large and he makes them grow small" or "He makes tribes of people become powerful and then he makes them become weak."

He enlarges nations, and leads them away: **enlarges** translates the Hebrew "spread out," which NEB understands to mean "flatten" and so translates "He lays them low." **Nations** refers to a group of people who have a common history and share a sense of belonging together. In many languages this kind of body is known as a tribe or ethnic group. In some languages it is possible to speak of "the people who follow one leader." **Nations** is the same Hebrew word in both lines. TEV makes both verbs in line a positive, "He makes nations strong and great," and then uses two negative verbs in line b, "defeats and destroys them." Aside from stylistic arrangement, TEV agrees with the meaning in RSV. Some take the first verb in line b to mean "scatter" (SPCL). FRCL translates "expand," a positive action paralleling "make great" in line a. The second verb in line b means "guide," which would be a positive action, and so many interpreters supply "into captivity" to get a negative sense. Some change the vowels of the verb to get "abandons," while others change one consonant and get "exterminates them." It seems best to recommend the meaning suggested by RSV and TEV. The stylistic arrangement will depend on the way the translator's own language handles two lines in which contrasting actions are expressed. In translation it is important that it be made clear that God does both events, the positive one and the negative one. In order to make this clear in some languages, it may be necessary to say, for example, "God makes some nations great, and he also destroys those nations. He builds up some nations, and he ruins those same nations."

12.24   RSV   TEV

| He takes away understanding from the chiefs of the people of the earth, and makes them wander in a pathless waste. | He makes their leaders foolish and lets them wander confused and lost; |

Job speaks of rulers in verses 17-21. In verse 23 he focuses upon nations. In verses 24-25 he speaks again of the leaders. **He takes away understanding from the chiefs of the people of the earth**: this translates the Hebrew "He takes away the heart of the heads of the people of the earth." Some interpreters believe the first line is too long due to the putting together of two readings, **of the people** and **of the earth**. The Septuagint omits **of the people**. In 3.14 the parallel expression "counselors of the earth" is used. "Take away the heart" is a Hebrew idiom meaning to cause someone to be stupid, ignorant, or as TEV says, "make their leaders foolish." **Chiefs of the people** is a general designation of rulers or persons in authority. TEV takes **of the earth** to be redundant, since all rulers are "of the earth." The line may also be rendered, for example, "He also takes away the intelligence of those who rule the people" or "He makes the rulers of the people stupid."

And makes them wander in a pathless waste is identical to Psalm 107.40b. **Makes them wander** translates a verb meaning "stagger, go astray." Here they drift about, wandering aimlessly. **Pathless waste** translates "a waste (where there is) no path." **Waste** is the word translated "without form" (RSV), "formless" (TEV), in Genesis 1.2. The reference here is to a trackless, empty desert, as used in 6.18, where TEV says "They wander and die in the desert." Here TEV understands the **waste** to be a confused state of mind rather than a physical place. However, Job's description is figurative in both places. Line 24a may be rendered, for example, "He makes the rulers wander about in the desert" or "He makes the rulers of the people drift about, not knowing where they are."

12.25   RSV   TEV

> They grope in the dark without
>   light;
> and he makes them stagger
> like a drunken man.

> they grope in the dark and
>   stagger like drunkards.

They grope in the dark without light: the verb translated **grope** is used also in 5.14. **Grope** means to feel with the hands in the dark so as not to fall. **In the dark without light** translates the Hebrew "darkness and not light" and refers to a complete and total darkness where there is no sign of light. The line may be rendered, for example, "These rulers feel about like blind men in the dark," "They put out their hands to feel their way in the darkness," or "They do not know where they are going in the darkness."

And makes them stagger like a drunken man: **stagger** is the same verb used to translate "makes them wander" in verse 24. It may be clearer in translation to rearrange and transpose the two lines of verse 25; for example, "Like drunkards they stumble and grope about in the darkness" or "They stagger about like drunk men as they feel their way through the darkness."

3F-4. Job's argument is with God (13.1-5)

RSV   TEV

1	"Lo, my eye has seen all this,
	    my ear has heard and understood it.
		1-2	Everything you say, I have heard before.
			    I understand it all; I know as much as

2	What you know, I also know;
	    I am not inferior to you.
			you do.
			    I'm not your inferior.

3	But I would speak to the Almighty,
	    and I desire to argue my case with
	        God.
		3	But my dispute is with God, not you;
			    I want to argue my case with him.

		4	You cover up your ignorance with lies;

4	As for you, you whitewash with lies; worthless physicians are you all.
5	Oh that you would keep silent, and it would be your wisdom!

	you are like doctors who can't heal anyone.
5	Say nothing, and someone may think you are wise!

In these five verses Job begins by assuring the friends that what they tell him he has heard before. His argument, however, is not with them but with God.

Subdivision Heading

Translators may wish to use the Handbook heading or modify it to say, for example, "Job wants to argue his case with God," "Job says, 'I want to take up my case with God,'" or "My case is against God." TOB has "Plaster-work of lies," meaning that the friends have covered over their ignorance with lies (see verse 4).

13.1-2   RSV   TEV

1	"Lo, my eye has seen all this, my ear has heard and under- stood it.	1-2	Everything you say, I have heard before.
2	What you know, I also know; I am not inferior to you.		I understand it all; I know as much as you do. I'm not your inferior.

Lo, my eye has seen all of this: Lo translates the common Hebrew particle *hen* translated as "Behold" in 8.19,20, and gives emphasis to the following word, which in Hebrew is **all this**. TEV provides this emphasis for English by beginning the sentence with "Everything you say"; NEB has "All this I have seen . . . ." **All this** may refer to the way God's wisdom is shown in nature and society in chapter 12 (so Habel and Dhorme) TEV takes **all this** to refer to what Job's friends have said, but it seems best to understand it as referring to what Job has just been saying, and many translations understand **all this** in this way. **My eye has seen**: in 12.25 Job spoke of leaders that "grope in the dark without light." In contrast to these Job claims that he has light and is able to see. In Hebrew usage the eye and ear are expressions for knowing and understanding. This is Job's claim to wisdom. He has seen and heard personally, and not depended on the traditions of others.

My ear has heard and understood it: in 12.11 Job asks "Does not the ear try words?" The parallelism of **my eye has seen** in line a and **my ear has heard** in line b has been restructured in TEV so that no mention is made of seeing in either line. This is because TEV assumes **all this** to mean the words spoken by Job's friends, and reinforces this interpretation by combining verses 1 and 2. If the translator interprets **all this** in line a to refer to what Job has been saying, then the translation will follow RSV, or say, for example, "All that I have said I have seen with my own eyes, and heard with my own ears, and understood it."

What you know, I also know: the images of eye and ear from verse 1 are here replaced by the verb **know**. Zophar asked Job in 11.7 "Can you find out the deep things of God?" To him God is beyond human knowing, but Job is not impressed with Zophar's argument. This line may also be expressed, for example, "I know everything you know" or "Whatever you know I know too." The next line, **I am not inferior to you**, is repeated exactly from 12.3b.

13.3   RSV   TEV

> But I would speak to the Al-   But my dispute is with God, not
>   mighty,   you;
> and I desire to argue my case   I want to argue my case with
>   with God.   him.

But I would speak to the Almighty: Job has just said in 12.14 that "if God shuts a man in, none can open." In spite of Job's fateful picture of the God who acts to suit himself, Job will still appeal to God to hear his case. Verse 3 opens with a conjunction marking strong contrast. The contrast is between appealing to his friends and appealing to God. TEV has brought this contrast out clearly by adding "not you": "but my dispute is with God, not you." **Almighty** translates the Hebrew *Shaddai*. See comments on **Almighty** in 5.17. **Speak** in line a is general, with the more specific kind of speaking in line b, **argue**, which produces poetic heightening.

And I desire to argue my case with God: aside from the poetic intensification in this line, the two lines say much the same thing. **Argue my case** translates a single Hebrew verb meaning "convince, correct, rebuke." It is used as a reflexive verb in Isaiah 1.18, "Come now, let us reason together, says the LORD" (RSV). **Argue my case** may be expressed "I want to talk to God and prove I am innocent" or "I want to speak to God and show him I am not guilty of wrong."

13.4   RSV   TEV

> As for you, you whitewash with   You cover up your ignorance
>   lies;   with lies;
> worthless physicians are you   you are like doctors who can't
>   all.   heal anyone.

As for you, you whitewash with lies: **As for you** translates the same contrastive conjunction used in verse 3. Here it serves to shift the focus from God in verse 3 to **you** (plural). **Whitewash with lies** translates "plasterers of lies" and is similar to Psalm 119.69 "The godless besmear me with lies" (RSV). **Whitewash** is lime mixed with water and is used for painting on walls to make them white and cover ugly rough surfaces. (See Matt 23.27; Acts 23.3, "whitewashed tombs.") Here the lies are the whitewash that conceals the truth. In English the expression "whitewash" is used to say that something ugly and distasteful has been covered up to improve its appearance. In this case Job pictures the friends as disturbed by the ugly truth, and thus they attempt to hide, or cover, it with lies, as one uses whitewash. Job's friends are depicted as "falsehood-plasterers," meaning they have covered over the truth with a coating of lies, and so TEV has "You cover up your ignorance (of the truth) with lies." This may also be rendered, for example, "You tell lies to hide the truth" or "You hide what you don't understand by telling lies."

Worthless physicians are you all: this line should be seen as parallel in meaning to the previous line. Job accuses his friends of covering the truth with lies in line a, and in line b of being healers with worthless medicines. Job's friends who came to give him comfort and healing are failures. This is the sense of TEV "like doctors who can't heal anyone." Another interpretation is that the word **physicians** is to be read "patchers," and so "worthless patchers" who try to cover up the tears in a garment. NEB "stitching a patchwork of lies" follows this sense, which makes the two lines similar in meaning. Although nearly all translations follow RSV and TEV, the understanding of NEB is likewise possible, but the first is more likely. This line may be translated, for example, "You are like doctors who treat the sick with bad medicines," "You are false doctors unable to cure the sick," or "You give out medicines that will cure no one."

13.5   RSV   TEV

Oh that you would keep silent,   Say nothing, and someone may
  and it would be your wisdom!   think you are wise!

Oh that you would keep silent: Job concludes this section on the contrast of his wisdom with that of his friends by suggesting that silence on their part would show them to be wise. It is the wisdom suggested in Proverbs 17.28: "Even a fool who keeps silent is considered wise."

And it would be your wisdom is literally "and that it may be wisdom to you." It refers to keeping silent in the previous line. TEV has restructured this verse so that **wisdom** is a verb which requires a subject, "someone may think you are wise," which expresses the idea clearly. Verse 5 may also be expressed, for example, "I wish you would keep silent and show you are wise," or by reversing the two lines, "I wish you would show that you are wise by not saying anything."

3F-5. Job questions the friends' worth as witnesses against him (13.6-12)

RSV   TEV

	RSV		TEV

6	Hear now my reasoning,
	  and listen to the pleadings of my lips.
		6
		7
			Listen while I state my case.
			  Why are you lying?
			  Do you think your lies will benefit God?

7	Will you speak falsely for God,
	  and speak deceitfully for him?
		8	Are you trying to defend him?
			  Are you going to argue his case in

8	Will you show partiality toward him, will you plead the case for God?		court?

9	Will it be well with you when he searches
	  you out?
	  Or can you deceive him, as one de-
	  ceives a man?
		9	If God looks at you closely, will he find
			  anything good?
			  Do you think you can fool God the
			  way you fool men?

10	He will surely rebuke you
	  if in secret you show partiality.
		10	Even though your prejudice is hidden,
			  he will reprimand you,

11	Will not his majesty terrify you, and the dread of him fall upon you?	11 12	and his power will fill you with terror. Your proverbs are as useless as ashes;
12	Your maxims are proverbs of ashes, your defenses are defenses of clay.		your arguments are as weak as clay.

In verses 6-12 Job accuses the friends of lying and pretending to defend God's cause.

Subdivision Heading

Translators may wish to adapt the Handbook heading by saying, for example, "Job says the friends are not fit to testify against him," "Job accuses the friends of lying," or "Job tells the friends that they cannot defend God."

13.6	RSV	TEV

Hear now my reasoning,
and listen to the pleadings of
my lips.

Listen while I state my case.

Hear now my reasoning: in two parallel lines Job opens this part of his speech, just as he will do again in verses 13 and 17. The two lines of verse 6 form a chiastic structure in Hebrew which has the form:

> Hear now my arguments
> And to the pleadings of my lips listen.

In Hebrew **my reasoning** is a noun derived from the verb translated "argue my case" in verse 3. It can also be translated "argument, defense," or "Listen while I present my case."

And listen to the pleadings of my lips: the root of the word translated **pleadings** means "contend, dispute, quarrel" and is used in 9.3; 10.2. **Pleadings of my lips** is figurative and heightens the poetic image of the more direct "arguments" or **reasoning** of the first line. TEV "Listen while I state my case" translates a summary of the meaning of the two lines but makes no attempt to handle the poetic intensification. Also TEV reduces the two lines to one. Verse 6 may be rendered, for example, "Listen to what I have to explain to you; just be quiet so you can hear my protests" or "Be quiet while I present my case, and listen to my arguments."

13.7	RSV	TEV

Will you speak falsely for God,
and speak deceitfully for him?

Why are you lying?
Do you think your lies will
benefit God?

Will you speak falsely for God: this line begins the first of four questions which Job asks his friends (verses 7, 8, 9, 11). He addresses them in the plural and so is not singling out Zophar, who was the last to address him in chapter 11. **Speak falsely** is literally "speak injustice." In 6.29 the same noun is translated "wrong." In 27.4 it is translated "falsehood" and is parallel with "deceit." **For God** in Hebrew stands at the beginning of the line and receives the emphasis. Therefore Job is asking "Is it for God that you speak falsely?" or "Do you think it is for God that you lie?"

And speak deceitfully for him: in Hebrew the line begins with **for him**, which repeats the emphasis of line a. Contrary to normal poetic style, **speak** is used in both lines rather than employing a different word of similar meaning in the second line. The two lines are therefore parallel without poetic intensification. TEV adjusts the two lines so that **for God** is translated only once, "for the benefit of God," in line b. This verse may be rendered as in SPCL, "Do you think you are defending God with your lies, and that you are rendering him a service through your deceitful words?" As a negative command this verse may be rendered, for example, "Don't think you are helping God and serving him by lies and deceit!" or as a negative statement, "You are not helping God or serving him by lying and deceiving people."

13.8   RSV   TEV

> Will you show partiality toward   Are you trying to defend him?
>   him,   Are you going to argue his
> will you plead the case for   case in court?
>   God?

Will you show partiality toward him: show partiality toward him translates "lift up his face." This is an idiom referring to the act of a superior to an inferior that allows the inferior person to face the superior after having been granted a special favor. In other words Job is asking if his friends will do God a special favor that will allow God to look up at them. The tone is very sarcastic. In some languages the first clause may be expressed figuratively; for example, "Will you hold out your right hand to God?" "Will you put your right hand on God's head?" or "Will you make God's face shine?"

Will you plead the case for God: in this line Job shifts his thought only slightly but maintains his sarcasm. **Plead the case** is used in Judges 6.31, where it is rendered "defending" by TEV and "defend his cause" by RSV. In other words Job is asking his friends if God has hired them to be his defense lawyer in court. In legal terms verse 8 can be rendered "Will you show favors to God, and will you defend him in court?" or alternatively, "Will you show God a special favor by being his lawyer?"

13.9   RSV   TEV

> Will it be well with you when he   If God looks at you closely, will
>   searches you out?   he find anything good?
> Or can you deceive him, as one   Do you think you can fool God
>   deceives a man?   the way you fool men?

Job continues his irony with a further question: **Will it be well with you when he searches you out?** Job's friends would come under the sharp examination of the judge (God) by pretending to represent him in court. The Hebrew for **searches** was used by Zophar in 5.27, where he claimed that the friends had searched out the truth. According to Job, Zophar and his friends will be "searched out" by God. The question can be rendered "Will you come out all right when God observes you closely?" or "Will you pass the test when God examines you?"

Or can you deceive him, as one deceives a man: deceive translates a verb which is used in Jeremiah 9.5, where TEV translates "mislead." In other words Job is warning his friends against treating God as though he were a human being whom someone could mislead or misguide without being punished. NJB says "Can he be duped as mortals are duped?" Dhorme has "seeing that, as one trifles with a man, you trifle with Him." TEV "fool God as you fool men" is a good model. "Men" may be better represented by "people."

13.10

RSV	TEV
He will surely rebuke you if in secret you show partiality.	Even though your prejudice is hidden, he will reprimand you,

After these three questions Job now makes a statement in verse 10a followed by a condition in verse 10b. **He will surely rebuke you: rebuke** translates the same verb rendered "argue my case" in verse 3. However, with God as subject the meaning here is "punish, correct, chastise." TEV has "reprimand."

If in secret you show partiality: In secret suggests a guilty action, one that must be kept hidden. **Show partiality** is the same expression used in verse 8a. In some languages it will be necessary to place the final clause at the beginning; for example, "If you show hidden favors to God, he will certainly punish you"; or in some languages "If you secretly lay your hand on God's head, he will certainly stop you." In the Hebrew order we may translate "God will surely correct your way of doing things, if you try to show him secret favors."

13.11

RSV	TEV
Will not his majesty terrify you, and the dread of him fall upon you?	and his power will fill you with terror.

For the fourth time Job addresses his friends with a question: **Will not his majesty terrify you?** Rowley suggests that in Hebrew the word translated **his majesty** is literally "lifting up," and "show partiality" in 10b is literally "lift up the face." Consequently **his majesty** forms a play on words, and so Job is saying that, if the friends lift up the face of God, his lifting up will cause them terror. On the other hand a person who enjoys high status or elevated rank is said in Hebrew to be "lifted up." A high standing authority evokes "respect, fear, awe." In this sense **majesty** is a good rendering. This line may also be expressed, for example, "Won't his greatness terrify you?" "Won't his being like a chief scare you?" or as a statement, "He will frighten you because he is so great and powerful."

And the dread of him fall upon you: dread, which means great fear, terrible fright, is said to "fall" on someone, and so this line means almost the same as the first line. Therefore TEV has reduced the two lines to one. In some languages "fear" is said to take hold of a person, so that line b may be rendered, for example, "Fear of him will take hold of you," "Fear of him will seize you," or more dramatically "You will be so badly frightened by him that your knees will shake."

13.12   RSV   TEV

> Your maxims are proverbs of
>   ashes,
>   your defenses are defenses of
>   clay.

> Your proverbs are as useless as
>   ashes;
>   your arguments are as weak as
>   clay.

Your maxims are proverbs of ashes: **maxims** translates a Hebrew term whose basic sense is "remember." Here it refers to what is remembered by old people—their sayings, proverbs, and traditional wisdom from past ages. Job considers his friends' proverbs to be **of ashes**. Like any burned material, they have been used up and reduced to a useless left-over state with no further value. They are lifeless like the remains of a burned out fire. TEV describes the proverbs as "useless as ashes." This line may be rendered, for example, "Your proverbs are like the ashes left over from a fire" or "What you say are old proverbs, like the old ashes from a burned out fire."

Your defenses are defenses of clay: **defenses** translates a Hebrew word referring to the rounded ornamental knob on a shield. By extension it may also refer to the shield itself and also to the function of a shield, that is, "defense." Here **your defenses** refers to the words of Job's friends, what they say to Job. And, as in the previous line, Job considers them to be as fragile as **clay**. A shield made of clay would break in pieces at the first blow. TEV translates **defenses** as "arguments" which crumble like "clay." The line may be rendered, for example, "The words you use to defend yourselves are as weak as clay" or "Your arguments are no better than a shield made of clay."

3F-6. Job will argue his case face to face with God (13.13-16)

RSV   TEV

13   "Let me have silence, and I will speak,   13   Be quiet and give me a chance to speak,
          and let come on me what may.   and let the results be what they will.
14   I will take my flesh in my teeth,
          and put my life in my hand.   14   I am ready to risk my life.
15   Behold, he will slay me; I have no hope;   15   I've lost all hope, so what if God kills me?
          yet I will defend my ways to his face.   I am going to state my case to him.
16   This will be my salvation,   16   It may even be that my boldness will save
          that a godless man shall not come   me,
              before him.   since no wicked man would dare to
                                                                   face God.

In verses 13-16 Job expresses his determination to confront God. For the second time he asks for silence and says that he will defend his innocence regardless of the consequences.

Subdivision Heading

The Handbook heading may be modified to say, for example, "Job will state his case to God," "I will argue with God no matter what happens to me," or "Job is ready to risk his life by facing God."

13.13 RSV	TEV
"Let me have silence, and I will speak, and let come on me what may.	Be quiet and give me a chance to speak, and let the results be what they will.

Let me have silence, and I will speak: the first clause is literally "Be silent from me." "From me" has been rendered variously by different translators. Dhorme says it means "Abstain from speaking to me." The Septuagint and some others omit "from me." TEV renders the line accurately with "Be quiet and give me a chance to speak."

And let come on me what may: this line in Hebrew ends with "what," but the meaning is to be taken as "come what may," "let be what will be." So Job is saying he is ready to pay the price for whatever may happen to him for speaking out. The line may be expressed "it is unimportant what happens to me," "let happen whatever will happen," or "I don't care what may happen to me."

13.14 RSV	TEV
I will take[i] my flesh in my teeth, and put my life in my hand.	I am[z] ready to risk my life.
[i] Gk: Heb *Why should I take?*	[z] *One ancient translation* I am; *Hebrew* Why am I.

I will take my flesh in my teeth: in Hebrew verse 14 begins with "Why" as if a question is being asked. However, "Why" spoils the sense, and most scholars understand it to be a copyist's repetition of the last word in verse 13. So they omit it and express the line as a statement, as in RSV, TEV. **Flesh** in this line can best be equated with **life** in the next line. This parallelism is the reverse of the more common occurrence of the figurative element in the second line. **My flesh** and **my life** refer to Job's life. Together the two lines say "I will risk my life." See Judges 12.3; 1 Samuel 19.5 for the same expression. Various explanations have been given for the saying in line a. However, many of these can be dismissed because line b makes clear that Job is ready to risk his life. Consequently line a must also mean that he is ready to risk his life, called **flesh**. If it is possible to retain the parallelism by using two expressions meaning "I am willing to risk my life," this is recommended. However, it is also possible to follow the model of TEV. Line a may also be rendered, for example, "I am willing to risk my life" or "I am ready to put my life on the line."

And put my life in my hand: since the meaning of this line is about the same in sense as the figure used in line a, TEV reduces the two lines to one. SPCL translates the verse "I will risk my life; I will bet everything for everything." FRCL says "Here I am ready for it all, even to risk my life."

13.15   RSV   TEV

> Behold, he will slay me; I have   I've lost all hope, so what if God
>   no hope;   kills me?
> yet I will defend my ways to   I am going to state my case to
>   his face.   him.

Behold, he will slay me; I have no hope: KJV translates "Though he slay me, yet will I trust in him" and so pictures Job as a man of unconquerable trust in God. However, this rendering is wrong. The context is that of challenging God to do his worst to Job. The word translated **Behold** can also carry the meaning "if, although," or as introducing a command or conjecture, and NEB translates "If he would slay me . . ."; Mft "He may kill me . . ."; NJB "Let him kill me if he will"; SPCL "Although he kills me . . . ." The usual meaning of the word translated **hope** is "wait," as in 6.11; 14.14; 30.26. The translation of line b is not in doubt, and it clearly shows that Job is determined to argue his case and prove himself innocent in an encounter with God. Therefore translators are encouraged to follow the Hebrew text in this line and express Job's lack of "hope, expectation." Accordingly NEB has "I should not hesitate"; FRCL "I no longer have anything to lose"; NJB "I have no other hope"; Mft "What else can I expect?" RSV's rendering is correct but does not provide an adequate model for translators. TEV reverses the two clauses of line a: "I've lost all hope, so what if God kills me?" The "so what" question is striking as a translation but does not reflect the Hebrew very well. The line may also be expressed, for example, "Let God kill me if he wishes, what more do I have to lose?" "If God wishes to kill me, that is the end of my hopes," or ". . . then I have nothing more to look forward to."

Yet I will defend my ways to his face: Job is certain about his cause and is prepared to defend himself. **Yet** introduces strong opposition to what has just been said, and may be rendered "nevertheless, in spite of that, regardless." The sense of this line in its context is "In spite of the fact that I've lost all hope (of being declared innocent by God), I will argue my case before him." **To his face** means "directly, before him, in his presence."

13.16   RSV   TEV

> This will be my salvation,   It may even be that my boldness
>   that a godless man shall not   will save me,
>   come before him.   since no wicked man would
>   dare to face God.

This will be my salvation: scholars have different understandings of what **This** refers to. In RSV **This** refers to the whole of the line that follows. TEV makes it refer to "my boldness" just expressed by Job in verse 15. **This** may point back to verse 15b or forward to verse 16b. In either case Job's **salvation** or success is attained by his being able to stand before God to argue his case. **Salvation** here is to be understood as the successful outcome of Job's argument, since being willing to come face to face with God is something no sinful man would ever consider. The line may also be expressed, for example, "And by doing this I will be saved," "By appearing before God I will come out safely," "Standing before God will show that I have succeeded," or "I will stand in God's presence and he will save me."

The second line states Job's conviction **that a godless man shall not come before him.** If Job were a godless man (a sinner, as suggested by his friends), he would not dare appear before God to argue his case. Job's willingness to challenge God is itself evidence that God must eventually acquit him of wrongdoing. **Godless man** means "sinner, wicked person, one who does not acknowledge God." TEV has related line b to line a as a subordinate clause, "since no wicked man would dare to face God." This line may also be translated, for example, "because a wicked person will not come before God" or "because evil people are not able to stand in God's presence."

3F-7. Job calls on God to appear in court with him (13.17-23)

RSV		TEV
17	Listen carefully to my words, and let my declaration be in your ears.	17 Now listen to my words of explanation. 18 I am ready to state my case, because I know I am in the right.
18	Behold, I have prepared my case; I know that I shall be vindicated.	
19	Who is there that will contend with me? For then I would be silent and die.	19 Are you coming to accuse me, God? If you do, I am ready to be silent and die.
20	Only grant two things to me, then I will not hide myself from thy face:	20 Let me ask for two things; agree to them, and I will not try to hide from you:
21	withdraw thy hand far from me, and let not dread of thee terrify me.	21 stop punishing me, and don't crush me with terror.
22	Then call, and I will answer; or let me speak, and do thou reply to me.	22 Speak first, O God, and I will answer. Or let me speak, and you answer me.
23	How many are my iniquities and my sins? Make me know my transgression and my sin.	23 What are my sins? What wrongs have I done? What crimes am I charged with?

In these verses Job calls on God to speak out and to declare the charges he is bringing against Job.

Subdivision Heading

Translators wishing to provide a subdivision heading may adjust the Handbook heading to say, for example, "Job asks God to declare the charges against him," "Tell me, God, what crime I am charged with," or "Job says to God, 'Tell me what wrongs I have done.'" TOB has "Petition to the hidden God" (verses 20-28).

13.17   RSV   TEV

> Listen carefully to my words,
>   and let my declaration be in
>   your ears.

> Now listen to my words of expla-
>   nation.

For the third time in this chapter, Job emphasizes his message by calling for attention. **Listen carefully to my words**: Job's call for a hearing is in the prophetic style of Isaiah 6.9, which is literally a double verb, "Hear and hear." The same formula will be repeated by Job again in 21.2 and by Elihu in 37.2.

And let my declaration be in your ears: in line b there is no verb; instead **in your ears** parallels the double verb translated **Listen carefully** in line a. (See also 15.21.) **Declaration** refers to the argument that Job will set forth. TEV "explanation" is to be preferred. The two lines of verse 17 are typical of parallelism in which line b heightens the poetic tone through the use of a figure of speech, **in your ears.** TEV does not handle the poetic intensification, and reduces the two lines to one. Verse 17 may be rendered, for example, "Listen carefully to what I have to say, and think about what I will explain to you" or "Listen to what I say, and pay attention to the words of my argument."

13.18   RSV   TEV

> Behold, I have prepared my case;
>   I know that I shall be vindicat-
>   ed.

> I am ready to state my case,
>   because I know I am in the
>   right.

Behold, I have prepared my case: **Behold** translates here two Hebrew forms in which the first acts as an imperative, and in which the combined sense is "look here, see now," or "attention please." **Prepared** translates an expression drawn from marshaling troops in battle formation. Applied to Job's words it refers to arranging the thoughts and words that Job will use to argue his case. **My case** refers to a case in law or a lawsuit: "Pay attention. I have lined up the arguments for my defense," "Listen carefully because I have put together all the arguments in my case."

I know that I shall be vindicated: **vindicated** translates the word used in 9.15 ("innocent"); 11.2 and means "to be right, innocent of wrong, not guilty." The line may also be expressed, for example, "I know that God will declare me innocent of wrongdoing" or "I know that God will say to me, 'Job, you are not guilty.'"

13.19   RSV   TEV

> Who is there that will contend
>   with me?
> For then I would be silent and
>   die.

> Are you coming to accuse me,
>   God?
> If you do, I am ready to be
>   silent and die.

Who is there that will contend with me? Job believes his case is so sure that no one would dare go against him. There are two problems in the translation of this verse. First, line a is a question that may imply the answer "God," as in TEV, or may refer to whoever might challenge Job, as in RSV. The Hebrew does not mention God, but Job's dispute is with God, and so TEV is probably correct: "Are you coming to accuse me, God?" **Contend** translates the same verb used in 9.3 meaning "dispute, argue, plead" in a lawsuit. If the translator takes God to be the one implied, it is also possible to render the line, for example, "God, are you going to argue against me?" or "Is it you, God, who will oppose me in court?" If the one contending with Job is taken as someone else, then the rendering may be, for example, "Is there someone who is going to oppose me?" "Who is going to argue against me?" or "Who is going to dispute my case with me?"

For then I would be silent and die: the second problem is the relation between the two lines. If Job is willing to take his flesh in his teeth, that is, to risk his life, it seems contradictory that he is now ready to be silent and die if God or someone else should challenge him. However, if God is willing to argue against Job, he would then know why God has caused him to suffer, and he would be willing to be silent and to die. To make this clear FRCL translates "Consequently, who will dare contest my legal right? I am ready, if I am in the wrong, to silence myself and die." Although not in the Hebrew, the phrase "if I am in the wrong" is understood as being the implied consequence in line b. FRCL offers a good translation model, and its approach may also be expressed, for example, "If I am in the wrong, I am ready to become silent and even to die" or "If God proves me to be guilty, I am ready to stop arguing and to die."

13.20　　　RSV　　　　　　　　　　　　　TEV

Only grant two things to me,　　　　　Let me ask for two things; agree
　　then I will not hide myself　　　　　　　to them,
　　　from thy face:　　　　　　　　　and I will not try to hide from
　　　　　　　　　　　　　　　　　　　　you:

Only grant two things to me is literally "Two things only do not do to me." Job addresses God in verse 20, and his two requests are spelled out in verse 21. These are conditions which Job requires to insure himself a fair hearing. If these requests are granted, Job says, **then I will not hide myself from thy face**, meaning that he will appear before God to hear God's accusations against him. **From thy face** means "from you" or "from God." In translation it may be necessary to rearrange verse 20 so that line b is stated first, as a condition, and then line a as an "if" clause; for example, "I will not hide myself from you, God, if you will give me two things," or stated positively, "I will appear before you, God, if you will grant me two requests." In some languages the "if" clause must precede the consequence; for example, "If you will grant me two requests, God, I will come into your presence."

13.21   RSV   TEV

> withdraw thy hand far from me,   stop punishing me, and don't
>   and let not dread of thee terri-   crush me with terror.
>   fy me.

     · The first request is **withdraw thy hand far from me**. In 9.34a Job expressed this plea with the words "Let him take his rod away from me," where the sense is "Let him stop punishing me." **Withdraw thy hand** refers to the hand that is causing Job to suffer. Line <u>b</u> **and let not dread of thee terrify me** repeats 9.34b with only a pronominal difference. Verse 21 contains Job's two requests and should be brief in translation; for example, "First stop punishing me, and second stop making me afraid" or "Stop hurting me and stop terrorizing me."

13.22   RSV   TEV

> Then call, and I will answer;   Speak first, O God, and I will
>   or let me speak, and do thou   answer.
>   reply to me.   Or let me speak, and you an-
>   swer me.

    Then call and I will answer: in line <u>a</u> Job shifts the responsibility for the initiative to God. Job is ready to accuse or defend. The choice he leaves to God. **Call** means "tell me, speak to me, let me know." **I will answer** means "I will respond, reply, be ready." If God does not want to start the argument, then Job is willing to do so, as he says in line <u>b</u>, **or let me speak, and do thou reply to me**. Under this alternative Job is willing to **speak**, "state his case," first, and God is then expected to reply. TEV provides a good model for translation: "Speak first, O God, and I will answer. Or let me speak, and you answer me." Alternatively, "God, you speak first and I will reply, or I will speak first then it is your turn."

13.23   RSV   TEV

> How many are my iniquities and   What are my sins? What wrongs
>   my sins?   have I done?
> Make me know my transgres-   What crimes am I charged
>   sion and my sin.   with?

    Job wants to be ready to defend his case and so asks **How many are my iniquities and my sins?** Three terms for sin are used in verse 23. In line <u>a</u> the word translated **iniquities** comes from the root meaning "to err," and **sins** from the root meaning "to miss the mark," while in line <u>b</u> **transgression** comes from a verb meaning "to rebel." However, these terms are used interchangeably, and it is unlikely that the author is attempting to draw out different shades of meaning between the three terms. The term **sin** is repeated in both lines; however, in line <u>b</u> it is singular, since Job is not asking for their number here but what they are as a collective. In line a Job seems to be asking for the quantity of his sins, and so many translations render line a in terms of number; for example, "How many sins . . . ." Others such as TEV take both lines to refer to the nature of the sins; for example, "What are my sins?" Both interpretations are accepted.

In many languages there are not three different words for **sin**. Consequently it is sometimes necessary to use two or to reduce them to one. Another solution is to use verbs; for example, "God, tell me how many times I have done wrong and how many times I have failed to walk on your path." Line b may sometimes be rendered "Show me how I have disobeyed you and done wrong."

3F-8. Job complains again against God (13.24-28)

	RSV		TEV
24	Why dost thou hide thy face, and count me as thy enemy?	24	Why do you avoid me? Why do you treat me like an enemy?
25	Wilt thou frighten a driven leaf and pursue dry chaff?	25	Are you trying to frighten me? I'm nothing but a leaf; you are attacking a piece of dry straw.
26	For thou writest bitter things against me, and makest me inherit the iniquities of my youth.	26	You bring bitter charges against me, even for what I did when I was young.
27	Thou puttest my feet in the stocks, and watchest all my paths; thou settest a bound to the soles of my feet.	27	You bind chains on my feet; you watch every step I take, and even examine my footprints.
28	Man wastes away like a rotten thing, like a garment that is moth-eaten.	28	As a result, I crumble like rotten wood, like a moth-eaten coat.

In these verses Job complains bitterly that God attacks him even though he is nothing more than dry straw. Job states that God even charges him for mistakes of his youth, and that he is constantly under God's distrustful eye.

Subdivision Heading

The Handbook heading may be modified to say, for example, "Job complains that God frightens and spies on him," "Job resents God's treating him like an enemy," or "Why do you watch every step I take?"

13.24   RSV   TEV

Why dost thou hide thy face,   **Why do you avoid me?**
   and count me as thy enemy?   **Why do you treat me like an**
                                                enemy?

Why dost thou hide thy face: in Psalm 27.9; Isaiah 54.8 **hide thy face** means to be angry, while in Psalm 30.7; 104.29 it has the sense of unfriendliness, as it does here. In other words Job is asking "Why do you refuse to be friendly with me?" or as TEV says, "Why do you avoid me?"

And count me as thy enemy: there are two matters to consider in regard to **enemy**. First, it may represent an increase of degree over the idea of being

261

"unfriendly" in line a, so that what is avoidance in line a becomes the role of the enemy in line b. Secondly, the author may be making a play on words. The Hebrew term used here for **enemy** is *'oyeb*. Job's name in Hebrew is *'eyob*. The idea in the author's mind may have been to say "Why do you consider me your *'oyeb*? I am *'eyob*." Line a may be rendered, for example, "God, why are you angry with me," or idiomatically in some languages, "God, why is your heart hot with me?" ". . . why do your insides boil when you think of me?" or "Why are you so unfriendly toward me?" In some languages the expression for "my enemy" is "one who hates me." Thus one may say "Why do you act as if I hate you?" The whole verse may be translated so that the intensification from "unfriendly" to "enemy" is brought out; for example, "Why are you unfriendly toward me and even consider me your enemy?"

13.25	RSV	TEV

Wilt thou frighten a driven leaf	Are you trying to frighten me?
and pursue dry chaff?	I'm nothing but a leaf;
	you are attacking a piece of
	dry straw.

Wilt thou frighten a driven leaf: Job looks on himself as a flimsy object blown about by God. He compares himself to a **driven leaf** in a and **dry chaff** in b. The picture is that of a dry leaf that is blown from its tree and whirled away by the wind. The poetic expression suggests that the wind-blown leaf feels frightened. TEV has created a model for languages in which inanimate objects do not have such sensations. Line a is made a question, which is followed by a statement in line b, so that it is Job who is "frightened" and then compared to the leaf. "Are you trying to frighten me? I am nothing but a leaf."

And pursue dry chaff: **pursue** translates a verb meaning "chase, hunt down, go after." When used with a human object it can mean "persecute." **Dry chaff** refers to the bits of straw separated from the grain in winnowing. Job is asserting that it is unworthy of someone with God's power to use it to chase a flimsy bit of straw, such as Job is. FRCL translates verse 25 "Whom are you pursuing?—A flying leaf! Whom do you ceaselessly chase?—A bit of dry straw!" This verse may also be rendered, for example, "Why do you frighten me and make me like a dry leaf blown from a tree, and chase me like straw blown by the wind?"

13.26	RSV	TEV

For thou writest bitter things	You bring bitter charges against
against me,	me,
and makest me inherit the	even for what I did when I was
iniquities of my youth.	young.

For thou writest bitter things against me: Job now develops a picture of God as the judge writing down the charges against him. (See also 31.35.) **Bitter things**

describes the charges against Job, as seen from Job's point of view. In 20.14 the same word means "poison," and in 20.25 it refers to the organ which secretes bile, the gall bladder. In some languages it will be necessary to express **bitter things against me** in a different way, since written words may not be called **bitter**; for example, "You write in a book and accuse me of doing bad things," "You bring charges against me and write them in a book," or "In the book of the judge you write words which tell the wrongs I have done."

And makest me inherit the iniquities of my youth: Job considers it would be unjust for him to be punished now for what he may have done when he was young. **inherit** here means "receive the consequences, be paid back for" his youthful sins. TEV avoids the word **inherit** by making "even for what I did when I was young" the second object of "bring bitter charges" in line <u>a</u>. This line may also be expressed, for example, "in this way you make me remember the sins I did as a youth," "and so you pay me back by recalling the wrong things I did as a child," or "so you make me suffer for the sins of my youth."

13.27   RSV   TEV

> Thou puttest my feet in the stocks,
> and watchest all my paths;
> thou settest a bound to the soles of my feet.

> You bind chains on my feet;
> you watch every step I take,
> and even examine my footprints.

Thou puttest my feet in the stocks: here Job pictures himself as God's prisoner, with his movements severely restricted. **Stocks** translates a word found only here and in 33.11. (See also Acts 16.24.) The term refers

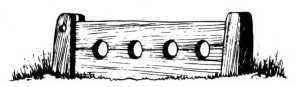

STOCKS

to a wooden block in which a prisoner's feet were locked, but according to line <u>b</u> there may have been some possibility of movement. TEV translates "You bind chains on my feet." This line may also be expressed, for example, "You tie my feet together" or "You tie my feet so I cannot walk."

And watchest all my paths: this line pictures God as Job's guard who will not let him get away. According to Dhorme the word translated **paths** refers more to the way one walks than to the place where one walks. The sense in his view, therefore, is "step," and so TEV "You watch every step I take." This may also be expressed, for example, "You keep guard on my every movement," "You keep your eye on me all the time," or "You never take your eyes off me." In 7.20 Job called God a "Watcher of men."

Thou settest a bound to the soles of my feet: this line is rendered in a variety of ways. The problem is the relation of **settest a bound** to **soles of my feet**. The word translated **soles** usually means "roots" and in the context refers to the part of the foot that "touches the ground." **Settest a bound** translates a verb meaning "engrave, carve out." Some understand the meaning then to be that God engraves a mark on the soles of the feet, perhaps to track down the prisoner who might escape. Others take it to mean that God marks a line around Job's feet, draws a circle, and does not allow him to move out of it. Still further, Dhorme understands the word to mean "examine," and this is followed by TEV and others, and is a recommended model for translators. The line may also be expressed, for example, "You examine the ground my feet have touched," "You inspect my footprints," or "You study the footprints I make in the dust."

13.28   RSV   TEV

Man[j] wastes away like a rotten   As a result, I crumble like rotten
    thing,   wood,
  like a garment that is moth-   like a moth-eaten coat.
    eaten.

[j] Heb *He*

In verse 28 there is a sudden switch to third person, and many translators do not believe 28 fits after 27. Accordingly they move it elsewhere: after 14.2a, 14.3, or 14.6; some put it after 13.24, while a few delete it. TEV and RSV keep it in its place, and translators should to do the same.

Man wastes away like a rotten thing: Hebrew begins with an emphatic "He" or "It." By translating **Man** RSV has attempted to represent the third person, but without some further adjustment it does not fit the context. Accordingly some modern translations shift to the first person and make a linkage with verse 27: TEV "As a result I crumble like rotten wood"; FRCL "But my life falls apart like rotten wood"; GECL "Therefore I am falling apart like rotten wood." On the whole it seems better for translators to make this kind of adaptation than to shift the verse to a new location. It may be advisable to provide a note in some translations to say "Hebrew says 'He.'"

Like a garment that is moth-eaten: a similar expression is used in Isaiah 50.9. This line may be rendered, for example, "like clothes that have been chewed by moths" or "like clothes that moths have been eating." The moth is used here as something that destroys silently, slowly, and surely. This image fits with the slow wasting away of man in line <u>a</u>. The female moth lays its eggs in woolen material, and it is the larvae that feed on the wool, not the adult moth. For details and picture see *Fauna and Flora of the Bible,* pages 55 and 56.

3F-9. Job describes the briefness of life (14.1-6)
                RSV   TEV

1   "Man that is born of a woman is of few   1   We are all born weak and helpless.
        days, and full of trouble.   All lead the same short, troubled life.
2   He comes forth like a flower, and withers;   2   We grow and wither as quickly as flowers;
        he flees like a shadow, and continues   we disappear like shadows.
            not.   3   Will you even look at me, God,

3   And dost thou open thy eyes upon such a
         one
     and bring him into judgment with
         thee?
4   Who can bring a clean thing out of an
         unclean?
     There is not one.
5   Since his days are determined,
         and the number of his months is with
         thee,
     and thou hast appointed his bounds
         that he cannot pass,
6   look away from him, and desist,
         that he may enjoy, like a hireling, his
         day.

         or put me on trial and judge me?
4   Nothing clean can ever come
         from anything as unclean as man.
5   The length of his life is decided before-
         hand—
     the number of months he will live.
     You have settled it, and it can't be
         changed.
6   Look away from him and leave him alone;
         let him enjoy his hard life—if he can.

In chapter 13 Job spoke of his personal struggle to confront God, but in chapter 14 he speaks of the experience of people generally. The general theme is a lament for the short span of human life coupled with the finality of death. This chapter consists of two major divisions. The first is verses 1-6, and the second is verses 7-22. Habel analyzes the chapter as a series of axioms, generally accepted truths, and analogies or comparisons taken mainly from nature. These elements recur in both sections of the chapter.

It is also possible to view chapter 14 as three discourses on despair alternating with two on hope. In verses 1-6 Job speaks of the inevitability of death for everyone. In verses 7-9 he looks to nature and sees hope for the tree stump that it may sprout again. In verses 10-12 his mood again switches to despair as he compares man's death to a dried-up lake. In verses 13-17 he again regains hope, thinking how God could hide him in Sheol until God's anger is past and God would call him. But in verses 18-22 he switches back to lament that God destroys a man's hope.

This scheme may be diagramed:

Despair   1-6   God has made men weak and short of life.

Hope   7-9   A tree stump can sprout again.

Despair   10-12   Man dies like a lake or river that has dried up.

Hope   13-17   God could preserve Job in Sheol until his anger is past.

Despair   18-22   God destroys man's hope to live.

Verse 1 opens with the general statement or axiom that a person's life is short and filled with trouble. This is then followed by comparing life to a flower and a shadow. Verses 3-4 interrupt the sequence to return to Job's unending question of going to court with God and being acquitted. Verse 5 picks up the axiom concerning the brevity of life in terms of time and space, and ends in verse 6 with a plea for God to leave people alone so they can enjoy their "day," their brief moment of existence.

Subdivision Heading

Translators wishing to use a subdivision heading here may follow the Handbook heading or say something like "Job complains that life is very short," "Job says that God has given people only a short time to live," or "Job complains that people are weak and life is short." Habel has "On the limits of mortal life." Translators who wish to provide a single heading for chapter 14 may find suggestions in some of the modern versions. For example, FRCL has "Job's reply: the sad human condition," GECL "God leaves human beings without hope," TOB "Death cannot be changed," and Rowley "Job's lament on the brevity of life and the finality of death."

Translators will note that the Handbook has not suggested a heading for each of the despair and hope sections displayed above, though translators may wish to include them. In that case the translator may wish to mark each alternation of subject by saying, for example, "Job despairs" and "Job hopes," or, more fully, "Job despairs of the shortness of life," "Job sees hope for a tree that is cut down," and similarly the remaining three subjects.

14.1   RSV   TEV

> "Man that is born of a woman is   We are all born weak and help-
>   of few days, and full of trou-   less.
>   ble.   All lead the same short, trou-
>   bled life.

Job begins by making a general assertion: **Man that is born of a woman is of few days, and full of trouble. Man** translates Hebrew *'adam* and refers to humankind, or everyone. TEV makes it inclusive with "We are all born . . . ." **Man** is followed in verse 1 by three attributive phrases. The first, **that is born of a woman**, focuses upon the frailty of a person's beginnings. In verse 4 (also 15.14 and 25.4) this thought is made more specific in terms of ritual impurity or uncleanliness associated with childbirth. **Born of a woman** is rendered "weak and helpless" by TEV, which makes clear the significance of the expression. The author is not making a distinction between people born of women and those born from some supernatural birth. He is emphasizing the frailty of human existence. FRCL keeps the Hebrew expression but makes its significance clear with "A man is nothing more than a child of a woman." GECL translates "From birth a human being is weak and helpless." This expression may be rendered, for example, "A human is born frail and helpless," "A person is born from a woman and has no strength," or "A woman gives birth to a child, and it is helpless." The second characteristic is **of few days**, which translates the Hebrew "short of days," meaning that human beings have a short life; they do not live long. Jacob complained in Genesis 47.9 that his long life was brief. Job complained of the shortness of life in 7.6-7; 9.25-26. The third quality of life is that it is **full of troubles**. In 3.17 Job said that in Sheol "the wicked cease from troubling," meaning they have ceased from doing evil. The last part of the verse may also be expressed "He lives for only a short time, and during his life he suffers," "People die soon and while they live they have troubles," or "Their lives have many troubles and they die quickly."

14.2   RSV   TEV

He comes forth like a flower, and   We grow and wither as quickly as
   withers;   flowers;
he flees like a shadow, and   we disappear like shadows.
   continues not.

This verse follows the general assertion, not by giving evidence for it, but rather by offering a comparison. The comparisons or analogies are drawn from nature, which everyone should be able to observe.

He comes forth like a flower, and withers: the fragile aspect of human life is compared with a flower. Psalm 90.6 speaks of the grass in the same way: "In the morning it flourishes and is renewed; in the evening it fades and withers." See also Psalm 103.15; 144.4; Isaiah 40.6-8. **Comes forth** translates "goes out" and is used here to depict the young plant springing up from the soil. Nothing is said about the duration of the flower. The focus is placed on the quick transition from young plant to withered, wilted flower. The line may be rendered, for example, "They begin their life like a growing flower, but then wither away" or "They grow like a flower, then dry up and fade away."

The second line is parallel to the first, **he flees like a shadow, and continues not**. The image is that of silent and sudden disappearance. In 9.25 Job said "My days are swifter than a runner; they flee away . . . ." The same verb translated **flee** is also used here. Psalm 144.4 says "Man is like a breath, his days are like a passing shadow." In this verse it is the person who is pictured as rushing past like a shadow. **And continues not** translates "and stays not," which serves to emphasize the passing, transient nature of a shadow. TEV "We disappear like shadows" conveys the idea well in English. This line may have to be restructured, since in some languages a shadow does not act independently of the object which casts the shadow; for example, "They disappear like a person's shadow" or "Like a person's shadow moves away, they are soon gone."

14.3   RSV   TEV

And dost thou open thy eyes   Will you even look at me, God,
   upon such a one   or put me on trial and judge
and bring him[k] into judgment   me?
   with thee?

[k] Gk Syr Vg: Heb *me*

In spite of Job's concentration on the shortness of life and its comparison to aspects of nature, he cannot forget his concern with God's unjust treatment of him. In this verse Job expresses surprise that God should examine anything as unimportant as a human being.

And dost thou open thy eyes upon such a one: **open thy eyes upon** means "pay attention to, take notice of, look at," the same as was used in 7.8. **Such a one** translates the Hebrew "this person," which TEV renders "me." The pronoun in the second line is "me" in the Hebrew text. Consequently if "me" is used in line b, it probably should also be used in line a. However, the Septuagint, Syriac, Vulgate, RSV, and others change to "him" in line b in order to match the previous verses. HOTTP recommends following the Hebrew "me" in line b. This line may also be expressed, for example, "Do you bother to notice me, God?" or "Do you even notice that I am here, God?"

And bring him into judgment with thee: bring to judgment means "take to court, bring a lawsuit against, take someone before the judge." **With thee** refers to God as the one who judges, so that the line says "And take me to court to be judged by you" or ". . . for you to judge me."

14.4

RSV	TEV
Who can bring a clean thing out of an unclean? There is not one.	Nothing clean can ever come from anything as unclean as man.

Some scholars believe that verse 4 does not fit the context, because it is not clear whether verse 4 refers back to the uncleanness implied in verse 1. It is omitted in one Hebrew manuscript. Some translators delete it, and NEB places it in a footnote. Most modern translations keep it, and users of this Handbook should do likewise.

Who can bring a clean thing out of an unclean? Who can bring is literally "Who can give," which is an idiom used a number of times in Job. It is used to express a strong wish such as "How I wish someone could . . . !" but this does not fit the context, and if the translator wishes to keep the question form, it is best to follow something like RSV. TEV uses a negative statement, "Nothing . . . ." **Clean** and **unclean** have been understood in three way. Some hold that **clean** refers to being morally good, and **unclean** to being evil. This thought is held to be Job's paraphrase of Eliphaz's question in 4.17, "Can mortal man be righteous before God? Can a man be pure before his maker?" In Gordis' view Job is now saying "You, God, should have no difficulty in telling the pure man apart from the impure, since you created men and know their nature and limitations."

A second interpretation is that **clean** refers to being innocent of guilt in a legal sense, and **unclean** refers to being guilty.

A third understanding is that **unclean** refers to ritual impurity resulting from childbirth. In this view Job may assume the traditional teaching that "if a woman conceives and bears a male child, then she shall be unclean seven days" (Lev 12.2b; see also Psa 51.5). This view is reinforced in 15.14 and 25.4b. In both of these references uncleanliness is associated with birth. This is the view preferred by the Handbook. However, in many languages the words used to translate **clean** and **unclean** will not necessarily be associated with ritual impurity. That is acceptable, since the translator may prefer to avoid associating **unclean** with ritual impurity as described in the third interpretation.

The concept of ritual purity is difficult to express in some languages. In some cases this notion can best be expressed in terms of defilement or taboo; for example, "Who can cause something that is defiled to be undefiled?" "Can a person who is taboo be made free of taboo?" or "Can a person who is ritually forbidden be made free of what is forbidden?" FRCL retains the rhetorical question, and answers it: "But who can bring out something pure from what is impure? Nobody on earth!" SPCL uses a statement to say "Nobody can get purity out of impurity." GECL has "You must know therefore that he is unclean, and that nothing clean comes out of him."

Translators will often find this line difficult to make clear, since **clean** and **unclean** do not seem to describe anything. Therefore it will often be necessary to translate something similar to TEV: "Nothing clean can ever come from anything as unclean as man" or "A human who is ritually unclean cannot give birth to one who is ritually clean."

There is not one: this short line is in no way balanced with line a, which is part of the reason some scholars delete the entire verse. However, short lines often serve the purpose of creating a striking imbalance in structure in order to call attention to themselves and their message. Line b is the reply given to the rhetorical question in line a; and it may also be expressed in that way in translation; that is, "Nobody!"

14.5 RSV	TEV
Since his days are determined, and the number of his months is with thee, and thou hast appointed his bounds that he cannot pass,	The length of his life is decided beforehand— the number of months he will live. You have settled it, and it can't be changed.

This verse follows on more suitably from verse 3 than from verse 4, and leads naturally to verse 6, which is the consequence of the dependent clauses of verse 5. Verses 5-6 are saying that, since a person's life is short and he cannot break out of the limits God has imposed, God should leave mankind in peace to enjoy his short life. Verse 5 has three lines in Hebrew, the first beginning with "If" (RSV **Since**) and the other two likewise being dependent clauses. Many translators, however, translate all three as statements.

Since his days are determined: his days means the number of days a person will live, his length of life. **Determined** translates the Hebrew for "cut," which is idiomatic for "decided." It is God who has decided how long a person's life will be (TEV "decided beforehand").

And the number of his months is with thee: this expression expands from **days** to **months** but is parallel in meaning to the first line. In some languages it may be best to reduce lines a and b to one by saying, for example, "Since you have decided to make a human's life short" or "Because you have decided not to give a person a long life."

And thou hast appointed his bounds that he cannot pass: appointed translates the Hebrew "made" and has the sense of "fix, place, set." **His bounds** refers to a fixed limit of time, not to a geographical place. Thus line c continues to speak of the limits of time a person will live. **That he cannot pass** means that humans are not able to go beyond or exceed the time limit, the length of life that

God has fixed for them. The line may also be expressed, for example, "you also fixed the length of life that he can live" or "you also set a limit to the length of time he could live."

There is a progression in the three lines going from **days** to **months** to a general designation of limits of time. TEV has retained the three lines. It is not clear in TEV until line c̲ that God is the one who has limited man's life span. It would be better to make this clear in line a̲; for example, "You decided beforehand how long he could live."

14.6　　　　RSV　　　　　　　　　　　　TEV

> look away from him, and desist,[1]
>   that he may enjoy, like a hire-
>   ling, his day.

[1] Cn: Heb *that he may desist*

> Look away from him and leave
>   him alone;[a]
>   let him enjoy his hard life—if
>   he can.[b]

[a] *One Hebrew manuscript* and leave him alone; *most Hebrew manuscripts* so that he may rest.
[b] let him . . . can; *or* until he finishes his day of hard work.

Look away from him and desist: the RSV footnote shows the wording of the Hebrew text, "that he may desist." The TEV footnote refers to one Hebrew manuscript which has "leave him alone," which is also the text of TEV. Most Hebrew manuscripts have the same verb, but with one additional letter, which TEV translates in a footnote "so that he may rest." In effect there is no great difference translation-ally between the meanings of the two forms of the Hebrew text, since if God leaves a person alone, the result would be that such a person would relax and be free from worry. If verse 5 has been translated as a series of conditions, then verse 6 should be rendered as their consequence; for example, "Therefore leave him alone," "Consequently don't bother him," or "So let him be."

That he may enjoy, like a hireling, his day: in 7.1 Job spoke of the hard days of work of the **hireling**, a workman who is paid at the end of his day's work. The **hireling** has only the short evening after his labor to enjoy himself. At that time he can take pleasure from what he has earned and from his rest. **Enjoy his day** is understood in various ways by interpreters. It is doubtful whether the Hebrew verb can mean "enjoy" in the RSV and TEV sense. If it is to be taken as in RSV and TEV, it will have to be understood as irony. TEV attempts to bring out this irony by adding "if he can." NEB represents another view, where the word translated **enjoy** means "count, pay off": "counting the hours day by day like a hired labourer." This interpretation may be the basis for NIV "till he has put in his time like a hired man." Dhorme takes **day** to refer to "his day's work," and so translates "Until, like a hireling, he finishes his day's work!" This sense seems better than imposing a tone of irony on the verse. FRCL translates "In order that he may finish his day's labor in peace," which provides translators with a good translation model. This line may also be rendered, for example, "so he can end the day and not worry" or "and in this way he can rest at the end of his day's work."

3F-10. Job complains that God destroys his hope to live (14.7-22)

	RSV		TEV
7	"For there is hope for a tree, if it be cut down, that it will sprout again, and that its shoots will not cease.	7	There is hope for a tree that has been cut down; it can come back to life and sprout.
8	Though its root grow old in the earth, and its stump die in the ground,	8	Even though its roots grow old, and its stump dies in the ground,
9	yet at the scent of water it will bud and put forth branches like a young plant.	9	with water it will sprout like a young plant.
10	But man dies, and is laid low; man breathes his last, and where is he?	10	But a man dies, and that is the end of him; he dies, and where is he then?
11	As waters fail from a lake, and a river wastes away and dries up,	11	Like rivers that stop running, and lakes that go dry,
12	so man lies down and rises not again; till the heavens are no more he will not awake, or be roused out of his sleep.	12	people die, never to rise. They will never wake up while the sky endures; they will never stir from their sleep.
13	Oh that thou wouldest hide me in Sheol, that thou wouldest conceal me until thy wrath be past, that thou wouldest appoint me a set time, and remember me!	13	I wish you would hide me in the world of the dead; let me be hidden until your anger is over, and then set a time to remember me.
14	If a man die, shall he live again? All the days of my service I would wait, till my release should come.	14	If a man dies, can he come back to life? But I will wait for better times, wait till this time of trouble is ended.
15	Thou wouldest call, and I would answer thee; thou wouldest long for the work of thy hands.	15	Then you will call, and I will answer, and you will be pleased with me, your creature.
16	For then thou wouldest number my steps, thou wouldest not keep watch over my sin;	16	Then you will watch every step I take, but you will not keep track of my sins.
17	my transgression would be sealed up in a bag, and thou wouldest cover over my iniquity.	17	You will forgive them and put them away; you will wipe out all the wrongs I have done.
18	"But the mountain falls and crumbles away, and the rock is removed from its place;	18	There comes a time when mountains fall and solid cliffs are moved away.
19	the waters wear away the stones; the torrents wash away the soil of the earth; so thou destroyest the hope of man.	19	Water will wear down rocks, and heavy rain will wash away the soil; so you destroy man's hope for life.
20	Thou prevailest for ever against him, and he passes; thou changest his countenance, and	20	You overpower a man and send him away forever; his face is twisted in death.
		21	His sons win honor, but he never knows it, nor is he told when they are disgraced.
		22	He feels only the pain of his own body and the grief of his own mind.

sendest him away.
21   His sons come to honor, and he does not
          know it;
          they are brought low, and he perceives
          it not.
22   He feels only the pain of his own body,
          and he mourns only for himself."

This section opens with a comparison rather than with an axiom. In verses 7-9 human life is contrasted with a tree that is cut down. The tree can sprout again where there is water, but man dies and that is his end, verse 10. In verse 11 the nature analogy applies to lack of water, in which the dried-up lake or river is compared in verse 12 to humans who die and never rise again. Verses 13-17 interrupt the sequence, as did verses 3-4 in the first section, to express a hope for release from endless death. In verse 13 Job wishes that a time could be set for God to remember him. In verses 14-15 he is willing to wait for God to call him, and in verses 16-17 he longs for the time when God would not watch over his sins, but would forgive him. The nature analogy then picks up again with verse 18, in which the falling mountains, the erosion made by streams, is compared to the ways in which man's hope is destroyed by God. The section, and the whole speech, concludes with man's suffering and death as a final statement of the human condition.

Subdivision Heading

The Handbook heading may be modified to say, for example, "Job will wait, but God will destroy him" or "Job in hope and despair." Habel has "On the hope of new life." Translators wishing to provide headings according to the alternating patterns of despair and hope should refer to the suggestions before 14.1.

14.7   RSV   TEV

"For there is hope for a tree,   There is hope for a tree that has
    if it be cut down, that it will   been cut down;
    sprout again,   it can come back to life and
and that its shoots will not   sprout.
    cease.

The verse opens with another comparison from nature. This time it is another plant, but a much larger one than the flower in verse 2.

For there is hope for a tree: For translates a Hebrew conjunction which refers back to verse 5 and the time limits imposed on human life by God. The world of vegetation is not restricted the way human beings are, because the tree can be cut down and then send out new shoots that will become another tree. By contrast human death is the final end. Job repeats Zophar's expression of **hope** from 11.18. In 5.16 Eliphaz said "So the poor have hope" (RSV). The hope expressed for the tree is that being cut down is not the end of its life. In translation it may be necessary to combine lines a and b to make clear that the tree is one that has been cut down; for example, "If someone cuts down a tree, there is hope for it to sprout again" or "We can hope that a tree that has been cut down will sprout again."

If it be cut down, that it will sprout again expresses both the condition and the consequences. The second consequence, which is parallel to the first, is **that its shoots will not cease.** TEV has reduced the two consequences to "come back to life and sprout," which expresses the meaning economically and adequately. In translation it will often be necessary to say who is hoping. For example, "If a person cuts down a tree, he can expect that tree to come back to life and sprout again" or "When someone cuts down a tree, he can hope to see that tree continue to live and send out shoots." If it appears in translation that it is the rootless trunk of the tree that continues to live, it will be better to say, for example, "He can expect to see the tree stump send out shoots and go on living."

14.8	RSV	TEV
	Though its root grow old in the earth, and its stump die in the ground,	Even though its roots grow old, and its stump dies in the ground,

Though its root grow old in the earth: the poet has in mind the stump of the tree dying and with no new shoots coming up because of lack of water, as becomes clear in verse 9. Verse 8 is related to verse 7 as something unexpected in the light of what was said in verse 7, and the relationship may be expressed in English by such logical connectors as "Even though" or "In spite of the fact." Verse 7 spoke of the tree and the new shoots above ground, and verse 9 speaks of the stump of the tree and the roots beneath the ground. **In the earth** in line <u>a</u> is parallel with **in the ground** or "dust" in line <u>b</u>. In typical fashion the poet shifts from the larger image **earth** to the smaller **ground.**

And its stump die in the ground: die in the ground in this context means to rot in the ground.

14.9	RSV	TEV
	yet at the scent of water it will bud and put forth branches like a young plant.	with water it will sprout like a young plant.

This verse states two consequences which can happen to the apparently dead tree stump.

Yet at the scent of water renders the vivid poetic imagery of the Hebrew, suggesting that at the slightest contact with water the tree stump will take on new life. TEV has not attempted to retain the metaphor nor to adapt it: "with water it will sprout." SPCL, on the other hand, says idiomatically "Upon smelling the freshness of water . . . ." GECL has "It has only to feel a tiny bit of water . . . ," and FRCL "A bit of water suffices for it to regain life."

It will bud and put forth branches like a young plant: **It** refers to the apparently dead tree stump. **Bud** and **put forth** describe the growth process from budding to growing a branch. **Young plant** suggests the tree that has been freshly planted or transplanted.

We may translate verses 8-9, for example, as follows:

> 8 Even if the roots grow old,
>   and the stump decays.
> 9 it will send out new sprouts,
>   when it gets a bit of water.

14.10   RSV   TEV

> But man dies, and is laid low;   But a man dies, and that is the
>   man breathes his last, and   end of him;
>   where is he?   he dies, and where is he then?

But man dies, and is laid low: **But** marks the sharp contrast between the living, growing tree in verse 9 and the person who dies like the rotting stump of verse 8. **Man** in line a renders Hebrew *geber,* which is associated in meaning with the root meaning "be strong, powerful." **Man** in line b is *'adam* as in 14.1. The strength of mankind is **laid low**, which translates a Hebrew root meaning "be weak" and is used in this sense in Joel 3.10. NEB uses "disappears" in the text and gives "is powerless" in a footnote. The expression **laid low** should not be interpreted to mean "laid in the grave." So the meaning is either that **man** who is "strong" becomes weak and powerless, or that even a strong man dies and becomes weak and powerless.

Man breathes his last translates the Hebrew "expires," which is parallel with **dies** in the previous line. **And where is he?** This is a rhetorical question whose intention is to say "and that is the end of him." It may be better in some languages to place this question before the first clause, so that the full line will read, for example, "and then where is he when he dies? or "and what happens to him when he dies?"

14.11   RSV   TEV

> As waters fail from a lake,   Like rivers that stop running,
>   and a river wastes away and   and lakes that go dry,
>   dries up,

This verse opens with another comparison taken from nature. This time man, when he dies, is compared to a body of water that dries up.

As waters fail from a lake: **As** is supplied by the RSV translators to mark the comparison; the Hebrew text does not have any such marker. **Lake** translates Hebrew *yam,* which usually means "sea," but covers the area of meaning of both seas and lakes. Since line b has **river**, it is better to use "lake" in line a. **And a river**

wastes away and dries up: wastes away is the gradual process that results in the final state of being dry, or in the final process of drying up.

It is usual in Hebrew parallelism to shift to the smaller item in the second line. TEV has reversed the two images, putting "river" in the first and "lake" in the second line. There does not appear to be any good reason for doing this. The nature of the comparison is between the verbs associated with the bodies of water and death. The whole verse may be expressed, for example, "Like a lake that dries up or a river that stops flowing." In languages in which the comparison can only come after the thing compared, it may be necessary to say, for example, "a person's life is like . . . ."

14.12   RSV   TEV

> so man lies down and rises not
> again;
> till the heavens are no more he
> will not awake,
> or be roused out of his sleep.

> people die, never to rise.
> They will never wake up while
> the sky endures;
> they will never stir from their
> sleep.

So man lies down and rises not again: so translates the common Hebrew connective *waw,* literally "and," used here to mark a conclusion. **Man** translates still another term different from the two in verse 10. There is, however, no attempt in line a to give a further nuance of meaning through the use of this different term. **Lies down** sounds as if the dead man reclined himself into a lying position. However, the verb suggests lying in bed or in a tomb as a state and not a process. **Rises not again** serves to emphasize the timelessness of death or lying down in death. TEV "They will never wake up" puts the emphasis on the permanence of death and omits **lies down** as redundant. The line may also be rendered, for example, "in the same way a human being dies and does not come back to life," or "so also a person who dies is laid down and does not stand up again."

Till the heavens are no more, he will not awake: the Hebrew construction of this line is unusual and has led to varying interpretations. Some omit one consonant and get "till the heavens wear out," which is similar to Psalm 102.26, where the heavens "will all wear out like a garment." Others understand the text to mean "so long as the heavens are not torn apart," and delete line c as a copyist's mistaken explanation of the verb after the meaning of the verb had become lost. HOTTP gives the expression only a "C" rating and translates it as in RSV. TEV "while the sky endures" is a positive form of RSV. The expression is used to refer to the endless state of death. It does not mean to suggest that, when the sky finally disappears, then the dead will rise. This expression may also be rendered, for example, "as long as the sky is above, he will never come back to life" or "the dead person will remain dead as long as the heavens exist."

Or be roused out of his sleep: this line is parallel with **will not wake up** in the previous line. It is not suggested that God is the one who would rouse them from sleep. In languages which do not use a passive voice in this construction, it may be necessary to say, for example, "or wake up from his sleep."

14.13   RSV   TEV

> Oh that thou wouldest hide me
>   in Sheol,
> that thou wouldest conceal me
>   until thy wrath be past,
> that thou wouldest appoint me
>   a set time, and remember
>   me!

> I wish you would hide me in the
>   world of the dead;
> let me be hidden until your
>   anger is over,
> and then set a time to remem-
>   ber me.

Oh that thou wouldest hide me in Sheol: in sharp contrast to verses 7-12, which hold out no hope of future life for people, Job now longs for future fellowship with God. The construction in this line is an idiom that suggests that Job realizes that his wish is unlikely to be granted. **Hide** means to place Job in a position of safety in Sheol where he will be free from his present sufferings. For **Sheol** see 7.9. It may be necessary to restructure the line to make clear that hiding Job in Sheol is for his safekeeping; for example, "I wish you would keep me safe in Sheol" or "If only you would hide and protect me in the place of the dead."

That thou wouldest conceal me until thy wrath be past: conceal has the same meaning as **hide** in the previous line. The thought moves forward to a time when **thy wrath be past,** or as TEV says, "until your anger is over," or we may also say "until you have stopped being angry at me."

That thou wouldest appoint me a set time, and remember me: a set time translates the same word rendered "bounds" in verse 5. It refers here to a certain time to be fixed. Job is asking God to fix a limit for his time to spend in Sheol. **And remember me!** God would remember, keep his word with Job, that the end for the time in Sheol would be as agreed. The second half of verse 13 may have to be recast to make clear what God is to remember. This may need to be expressed, for example, "I wish you would set the number of days for me to spend there (in Sheol) and not forget me" or ". . . remember that I am waiting for you there."

14.14   RSV   TEV

> If a man die, shall he live again?
>   All the days of my service I
>   would wait,
> till my release should come.

> If a man dies, can he come back
>   to life?
> But I will wait for better times,
>   wait till this time of trouble is
>   ended.

If a man die, shall he live again? Job's question at this point seems to interrupt what comes before and what follows. Accordingly some transfer this line to follow verse 19. However, most modern translations keep it at this point, and it is recommended that translators do the same. Rather than an interruption, Job's rhetorical question may be understood to be Job reflecting to himself on the arrangement he would like God to make with him in verse 13. Such a deal with God would mean that Job would live again. It is perhaps in this mood that we should understand his question. The Septuagint changes the question to an affirmative assertion that man will live again. Some treat the line as a wish: "If only a man might die and live again!" However, taken as a whole it seems best to follow RSV and TEV by translating the line as an "if" clause followed by a rhetorical question. In some languages this will require a negative reply; for example, "If a person dies, will he come back to life? No!" or "Can a man who has lived and then died live again? Certainly not!"

All the days of my service I would wait. For discussion of **service** see 7.1. **Wait** translates the same verb translated "have . . . hope" in 13.15 and so includes the idea of patient expectation which Job rejected earlier. **Till my release should come**: this expression is based on a military metaphor in which Job pictures himself standing at his post in Sheol, waiting to be relieved by another soldier. Mft translates "I could endure my weary post until relief arrives." However, the military picture need not be pushed here and TEV "wait for better times," while very general, expresses the idea. TEV has transposed lines b and c and has repeated the verb "wait" in each line. This part of the verse may also be expressed "I will wait as long as is necessary until someone comes to release me."

14.15	RSV	TEV
	Thou wouldest call, and I would answer thee; thou wouldest long for the work of thy hands.	Then you will call, and I will answer, and you will be pleased with me, your creature.

Thou wouldest call, and I would answer thee: Job hopes that God will wish to renew his broken fellowship with his servant. It may be necessary in some languages to express the object of **call**; for example, "I will answer when you call me" or "When you call my name I will reply." **Thou wouldest long for the work of thy hands: work of thy hands** is used in 10.3 and 34.19. The reference is to Job, which TEV translates "your creature." This may also be rendered "me whom you have created" or "me, Job, your creature." In some languages it may be best to transpose lines a and b so that the longing precedes the call. In this case we may translate, for example, "When you want to see me, your creature, you will call me and I will answer you."

14.16	RSV	TEV
	For then thou wouldest number my steps, thou wouldest not keep watch over my sin;	Then you will watch every step I take, but you will not keep track of my sins.

For then thou wouldest number my steps: scholars disagree about the application of this verse. Some take it to be a complaint such as Job had voiced against God in 13.27, when he said bitterly "you watch every step I take" (TEV). Those who understand this line as an unfriendly act make a contrast between it and verse 15. For example, NEB "But now thou dost count every step I take." RSV and TEV see the line as continuing verse 15, and describing the way God counts Job's steps as watching over him in a friendly way. Translators are advised to follow RSV and TEV, since their sense seems to fit the context and requires no modification of the text. **Then**, in this view, refers to the imagined future in which Job sees himself as being called by God in Sheol and given new life. **Number my steps** or "count my steps" is best taken here as "watching over, protecting, guiding." This line may be rendered, for example, "Then you would look after me," "Then you would guard over me," or ". . . take care of me."

Thou wouldest not keep watch over my sin: TEV begins this line with "but" to strengthen the contrast of God's care of Job in line a and his not keeping track of Job's sins in line b. **Watch over** translates the same verb used in 10.14, which TEV renders "You were watching to see if I would sin." There Job complained of God's spying on his sin. As he looks to the imagined future, God will no longer spy on him and his sins. This line may also be expressed, for example, "You would not keep your eye on my sins" or "You would not spy on me to see if I sinned."

14.17	RSV	TEV
	my transgression would be sealed up in a bag, and thou wouldest cover over my iniquity.	You will forgive them and put them away; you will wipe out all the wrongs I have done.

My transgression would be sealed up in a bag: according to Pope this may refer to an ancient system of keeping inventory on animals. Small stones were dropped into a container or removed from it as the number and kind of animals a person owned changed. The translation of verse 17 will depend on the way verse 16 has been understood. RSV, TEV, and others translate verse 17 as a continuation of the thought of verse 16, so that God would seal up Job's sins in a bag, that is, keep them out of sight. NEB and others take the other view that Job's sins are put in safe keeping where they can be brought out and used in evidence against him later. The view of RSV and TEV is recommended to translators. In verse 16 God would cease "to notice, pay attention, see" Job's sins. This line may also be translated, for example, "You will forgive and hide my sins," "You will take away the wrong I have done," or, keeping the figurative language, "You will hide my sins like a person hides things in a bag."

And thou wouldest cover over my iniquity: cover over translates the same verb used in 13.4 and translated "whitewash" (RSV). See comments on 13.4. **Iniquity** has the same meaning as **transgression** in the previous line. This line may also be expressed, for example, "You will cover up my sins the way a person paints whitewash on a wall" or "You will cover over and hide my sins."

14.18   RSV   TEV

"But the mountain falls and   There comes a time when moun-
   crumbles away,   tains fall
   and the rock is removed from   and solid cliffs are moved
     its place;   away.

This verse again picks up the comparison from nature. The **mountain** and **rock** are frequently used images of strength and security. The tone is again pessimistic and compares the wearing away of the **mountain** and **rock** to the destruction of "man's hope" in verse 19.

But the mountain falls and crumbles away: Job has apparently given up his vision of a temporary stay in Sheol. This line begins with a term marking strong contrast, which can be rendered in English "But on the other hand" or "in spite of all this." The word translated **crumbles away** has the sense of "fade" as applied to flowers and withering leaves. The word is not normally used of a mountain, but for the poet it contains an allusion to the opening comparison in verse 2. The poet's intention is to say that what is solid and permanent is no different than the fading flower. The line may also be expressed, for example, "But even mountains fall apart" or "But even the highest and strongest hills are shaken down."

And the rock is removed from its place: line b repeats the same message as line a. It shows typical parallelism in which the smaller image is placed in the second line. **Removed from its place** is better rendered "dislodged from its place" as in NEB. TEV and SPCL have shifted from **rock** to "cliffs" to relate the imagery of the two lines more closely. In languages in which the passive is not used, it may be necessary to express line b as an active construction; for example, "and the rocks tumble down" or "and the cliffs fall from their places."

14.19   RSV   TEV

the waters wear away the stones;   Water will wear down rocks,
   the torrents wash away the soil   and heavy rain will wash away
     of the earth;   the soil;
   so thou destroyest the hope of   so you destroy man's hope for
     man.   life.

The nature analogy continues with water, stones, and torrents. **The waters wear away the stones**: **wear away** translates the timeless action of erosion in which moving water "pounds, crushes, rubs" the stones in the stream bed. In some languages it may be necessary to say, for example, "The river's waters erode the stones in the stream bed" or "The water in the river flows against the stones in the stream bed and wears them down."

The torrents wash away the soil of the earth: **torrents** translates a word meaning "rain storms, torrential rains." TEV says "heavy rains." Their action is applied to the **soil of the earth**, which in English is better stated as "the soil," (TEV). This line may also be expressed, for example, "the big rains wash away the soil" or "the heavy winter rains take away the earth."

So thou destroyest the hope of man: this line provides the application of the nature analogy. **Destroyest** translates the Hebrew "cause to perish." God's action against man's hope is destructive, just as erosion is in nature. NEB succeeds nicely in the context of water eroding the soil: "So thou hast wiped out the hope of frail man." FRCL has "You too, you bring to ruin the hope of man." **Hope of man** refers to his hope to go on living instead of being destroyed by death, and to make this clear TEV says "you destroy man's hope for life." In some languages it may be necessary to place this line at the beginning of this verse and say, for example, "You destroy man's hope for life, the way the river waters erode . . . ."

14.20

RSV	TEV
Thou prevailest for ever against him, and he passes; thou changest his countenance, and sendest him away.	You overpower a man and send him away forever; his face is twisted in death.

Thou prevailest forever against him: **prevailest** translates a word whose root means "to be powerful," and which has the sense here of "attack." This meaning is well conveyed by TEV "You overpower a man." **For ever** is connected more naturally with **prevailest** as in RSV, and NIV "You overpower him once for all." **And he passes** translates the Hebrew "and he goes," which is an indirect manner of speaking about death, as in English "pass away." The line may also be expressed, for example, "You defeat him and he dies," "You overcome him and he gives up his life," or "You subdue him and he is finished."

Thou changest his countenance is in the Hebrew "changing his face" and refers to the distorted face of the dead person. RSV reflects the Hebrew form and does not say what kind of change takes place, but TEV does not leave it in doubt: "His face is twisted in death." RSV and others understand God to be the one who changes the face. Others, like TEV, take it that the face is changed as a result of death. It seems best to take it as in TEV, which is closer to the Hebrew idea. In languages in which a passive construction cannot be used, it may be necessary to say, for example, "You distort his face," "You cause his face to twist," or "You give him an ugly face in death." **And sendest him away** is parallel to **and he passes** in line a. TEV does not repeat the expression but uses "and send him away" for both expressions.

14.21

RSV	TEV
His sons come to honor, and he does not know it; they are brought low, and he perceives it not.	His sons win honor, but he never knows it, nor is he told when they are disgraced.

This verse emphasizes that those in the world of the dead know absolutely nothing regarding even those matters which most closely concern them, such as the welfare of their families.

His sons come to honor, and he does not know it: **come to honor** in this line is positive, and **brought low** in line b̲ is the opposite. **Come to honor** translates a verb meaning "to be honored, given recognition." The dead man's sons rise to positions of importance which in life would make the father proud. But the dead father knows nothing of it. It is the same if **they are brought low**. The same contrast is brought out in Jeremiah 30.19, "I will make them honored and they shall not be small" RSV. This line may also be expressed, for example, "People honor his sons, and he does not even know it" or "People speak well of his sons, but he never knows it."

Brought low translates a verb meaning "being small, weak, insignificant." By contrast the honored one is "a person of weight, a notable." **And he perceives it not**: TEV translates "Nor is he told when they are disgraced" and thus constructs a well balanced set of lines. This is a good translation model. Other models are: "People shame them and neither does he know this" or "Even when his sons are disgraced he knows nothing of it."

14.22   RSV   TEV

> He feels only the pain of his own   He feels only the pain of his own
>   body,   body
> and he mourns only for him-   and the grief of his own mind.
>   self."

He feels only the pain of his own body: RSV and TEV give the traditional sense that the dead body, for at least a time, continues to feel pain. And this no doubt is the meaning the poet intended. He is saying that the dead man is unaware of the important things taking place around him, such as the honor or disgrace of his sons. His only awareness is confined to his own death pains. The line may be rendered, for example, "He knows nothing but his own pain," or "He feels nothing but his own body's pains."

And he mourns only for himself translates the Hebrew "and his *nefesh* mourns for him." This line reinforces the thought in line a̲. He does not know what happens to his own sons, cannot feel pain for them, and cannot mourn for them. His mourning is only for himself. In many languages it will seem strange to speak of a dead person mourning for himself, and in some cases this will have to be expressed as a simile; for example, "And he will be like a person who can only mourn over his own death" or "He will be like one who can mourn for nobody but himself."

4. Second Round of Speeches

(15.1–21.34)

Section 4 contains the second of three rounds or series of speeches or arguments given by Job and his three friends. As in the first round (4.1–14.22) the order of speakers is Eliphaz, Bildad, Zophar, with Job responding to each of their speeches. Eliphaz speaks in chapter 15, with Job responding in chapters 16 and 17. Bildad presents his arguments in chapter 18, and Job replies in chapter 19. Zophar takes over in chapter 20, and the second round is closed with Job answering in chapter 21.

Section Heading

Translators wishing to follow the Handbook headings may need to modify this section heading to say, for example, "This is the second group of arguments," "Job and his friends argue a second time," or "The second arguments between Job and the friends." TEV has "The second dialogue," and NJB has "Second cycle of discourses."

4A. ELIPHAZ'S SECOND SPEECH (15.1-35)

Eliphaz is again the first to speak, as he was in chapters 4 and 5. There he concentrated on the moral perfection of God, which he drew from traditional teaching and personal experience. His aim was to convince Job that he could be restored to health by accepting Eliphaz's advice. This speech contains two major divisions: verses 2-16, and verses 17-35. In the first part Eliphaz scolds Job through the use of accusations and rhetorical questions. In the second section Eliphaz, who is a bit more diplomatic than the other friends, draws a picture of the wicked through the use of ironic allusions and indirect references, all of which are aimed at Job.

Division Heading

The Handbook heading shows this to be the second speech by Eliphaz. Translators may prefer to say, for example, "Eliphaz makes his second speech," "Eliphaz presents his second argument," or "Eliphaz argues again with Job." Some translators may prefer to combine the division and subdivision headings (see below). For example, FRCL has "Speech of Eliphaz: the evil person will not escape," GECL "The first friend: no man is guiltless."

4A-1. Eliphaz rebukes Job for his claims of innocence (15.1-16)

RSV   TEV

1 Then Eliphaz the Temanite answered:

Eliphaz

2 "Should a wise man answer with windy knowledge,
and fill himself with the east wind?

1-2 Empty words, Job! Empty words!

3 No wise man would talk the way you do
or defend himself with such meaningless words.

3 Should he argue in unprofitable talk,
or in words with which he can do no good?

4 If you had your way, no one would fear God;
no one would pray to him.

4 But you are doing away with the fear of God,
and hindering meditation before God.

5 Your wickedness is evident by what you say;
you are trying to hide behind clever words.

5 For your iniquity teaches your mouth,
and you choose the tongue of the crafty.

6 Your own mouth condemns you, and not I;
your own lips testify against you.

6 There is no need for me to condemn you;
you are condemned by every word you speak.

7 "Are you the first man that was born?
Or were you brought forth before the hills?

7 Do you think you were the first man born?
Were you there when God made the mountains?

8 Have you listened in the council of God?
And do you limit wisdom to yourself?

8 Did you overhear the plans God made?
Does human wisdom belong to you alone?

9 What do you know that we do not know?
What do you understand that is not clear to us?

9 There is nothing you know that we don't know.

10 Both the gray-haired and the aged are among us,
older than your father.

10 We learned our wisdom from gray-haired men—
men born before your father.

11 Are the consolations of God too small for you,
or the word that deals gently with you?

11 God offers you comfort; why still reject it?
We have spoken for him with calm, even words.

12 Why does your heart carry you away,
and why do your eyes flash,

12 But you are excited and glare at us in anger.

13 that you turn your spirit against God,
and let such words go out of your mouth?

13 You are angry with God and denounce him.

14 What is man, that he can be clean?
Or he that is born of a woman, that he can be righteous?

14 Can any man be really pure?
Can anyone be right with God?

15 Behold, God puts no trust in his holy ones,
and the heavens are not clean in his sight;

15 Why, God does not trust even his angels;
even they are not pure in his sight.

16 how much less one who is abominable and corrupt,
a man who drinks iniquity like water!

16 And man drinks evil as if it were water;
yes, man is corrupt; man is worthless.

In verses 2-16 Eliphaz intensifies his criticism of Job and accuses Job of attacking religion with his empty words. Through a series of rhetorical questions, Eliphaz accuses Job of ignorance and of being against God. By repeating Job's own words from 14.1, he reminds Job that he is a human creature and is entirely corrupt and without righteousness.

Subdivision Heading

Translators using subdivision headings may want to adjust the Handbook heading to say, for example, "Eliphaz scolds Job, who claims he is innocent," "Eliphaz accuses Job of being angry with God," or "Eliphaz asks Job, 'Do you think you know everything?' " TOB has "The impurity of man," Rowley "Rebuke of Job for rashness and irreverence," Habel "On the knowledge and language of Job."

15.1   RSV   TEV

> Then Eliphaz the Temanite an-   *Eliphaz*
> swered:

Then Eliphaz the Temanite answered: see 4.1 for discussion.

15.2   RSV   TEV

> "Should a wise man answer with   Empty words, Job! Empty words!
>   windy knowledge,
> and fill himself with the east
>   wind?

Verse 2, like the opening verse in each of Eliphaz's speeches, begins with a rhetorical question: **Should a wise man answer with windy knowledge . . . ?** This is the equivalent of a strong negative statement: "A wise man should not answer with . . . ." In 12.3 and 13.2 Job claimed that he was not inferior in wisdom to his friends. In 8.2 Bildad referred to Job's words as being "a great wind." Now Eliphaz picks up the same thought. It is clear from the next line that **wise man** refers to Job and not to Eliphaz. **Answer** refers to Job's reply to his friends and means anything that Job may say. **Windy knowledge** translates "knowledge (characterized by) wind." The sense of this expression is made clear only in the next line, **and fill himself with the east wind**. This line translates Hebrew "and fill his belly with the east." The reference to "the east" is to the scorching wind that blows from the east across the desert. In this sense Job is filling himself with "hot air," which in English describes his **knowledge** in the first line. In English **windy knowledge** can be expressed by Eliphaz calling Job a "bag of hot air," that is, someone whose talk has no substance.

TEV renders both lines of verse 2 "Empty words, Job! Empty words!" This rendering departs considerably from the form of the Hebrew, and although it does give an effective rendering of the sense, it is too direct to serve as a translation model in many languages. Most modern translations stay closer to the Hebrew form and translate **windy knowledge** as knowledge that has no true substance; for example, SPCL "He who is wise does not reply with empty words, nor does he swell himself up with reasons that are mere wind." FRCL has "Does a wise man like you feed himself on wind, does he also make replies that have no substance?" If the rhetorical question form is retained, it will often be necessary to add a negative reply. This line may also be expressed as a negative statement; for example, "A wise man should not talk with meaningless words" or "A wise man like you, Job, should not make speeches with words that are like hot air." Alternatively we can translate, for example, "Job, a wise man should not talk with words that have no meaning."

15.3   RSV   TEV

Should he argue in unprofitable   No wise man would talk the way
  talk,   you do
or in words with which he can   or defend himself with such
  do no good?   meaningless words.

Should he argue in unprofitable talk: in 13.3 Job said "I desire to argue my case with God." Eliphaz now picks up Job's thought and asks in a rhetorical question if such arguing would not be without profit, that is, without effect, accomplishing nothing. The word translated **unprofitable** is found only in Job. **Or in words with which he can do no good?** This line is almost identical in meaning to the first line, and some translators may find it best to combine the two into a single line.

The sense of verse 3 is essentially the same as verse 2. Translators may find it is best to continue the same kind of sentence construction in verse 3 as was used in verse 2; for example, if verse 2 was translated as a statement expressing obligation, then verse 3 may be best translated in a parallel form. For example, "You should not argue aimlessly," "You should not argue with words that do no good," or "Job, you should not argue, because your talk accomplishes nothing."

15.4   RSV   TEV

But you are doing away with the   If you had your way, no one
  fear of God,   would fear God;
and hindering meditation be-   no one would pray to him.
  fore God.

But you are doing away with the fear of God: in this verse Eliphaz drops the rhetorical question form to aim his rebuke directly at Job, and addresses him in the second person. **But** translates a Hebrew connective that intensifies the following clause in regard to the preceding one. It is equivalent to English "Indeed!" or "Why!" It may be translated "You even . . ." or "You go so far as to . . . ." Eliphaz accuses Job of **doing away with**, which translates a term meaning to "lower, diminish, decrease." TEV expresses this in a clause: "no one would fear God." GECL has "undermine," FRCL "ruin," NJB "suppress." **Fear [of God]** translates Hebrew "fear, reverence, worship," and is used also to mean "religion." Translations use such expressions as "faith," "belief," "religion," "reverence," or "piety," sometimes in association with God; for example, "reverence for God" or "belief in God." This line may also be expressed, for example, "You are even making reverence for God a thing of little importance," "Yes, you are reducing belief in God to nothing," or "Indeed, Job, you do away with religion."

And hindering meditation before God: **hindering** is parallel to **do away with** in the previous line. Its root meaning is "to pull down" and is again an accusation of destroying religion. **Meditation** translates a word which is used as a verb in Psalm 119.15 with the sense of "reflect, meditate." NJB, which translates "discussion before God," says in its note, "means the application of the mind to religious truths coupled with the idea of speech . . . ." Gordis supports this with "conversation, communion with God," and so TEV and others translate "pray to God." In many languages it will be difficult to express the destruction of an activity such as meditation or prayer, and so we must sometimes restructure this line to say, for instance, "you make it difficult for a person to pray to God," "you take away the practice of meditation before God," or "you take away the custom of speaking to God in prayer."

15.5-6	RSV		TEV

	RSV		TEV
5	For your iniquity teaches your mouth, and you choose the tongue of the crafty.	5	Your wickedness is evident by what you say; you are trying to hide behind clever words.
6	Your own mouth condemns you, and not I; your own lips testify against you.	6	There is no need for me to condemn you; you are condemned by every word you speak.

It is best to consider verses 5 and 6 together, since their subject matter is so closely linked, as well as their structures.

For your iniquity teaches your mouth: verse 5 begins with a Hebrew conjunction which here has the function of English "Since" or "Because," making both lines of verse 5 subordinate to verse 6. This first line is ambiguous because it is not certain from the Hebrew whether **your mouth** or **your iniquity** is the subject of **teaches**. Most translators take **iniquity** to be the subject, and so Eliphaz asserts that Job's wickedness teaches his mouth what to say. Some understand that it is the mouth (what Job says) that "reveals" his iniquity, and this seems to be the understanding of TEV, "Your wickedness is evident by what you say." These two meanings do not differ in substance. In many languages it is not possible to say that an abstract term such as wickedness teaches a body part such as the mouth. Therefore the construction must be changed to say, for example, "Because you are wicked, you talk the way you do" or "You are wicked, and that is what makes you say the things you say."

And you choose the tongue of the crafty: Eliphaz asserts that Job follows a form of speech used by people who deceive others. **Tongue of the crafty** is the "speech, language, manner of arguing" used by persons who are "cunning, clever, deceptive." This line may also be expressed, for example, "you talk like a deceiver," "you use deceptive words," or "you deceive people by using clever words." In many languages figurative expressions are commonly used to express this thought; for example, "you talk with a forked tongue" or "there are two hearts behind your words."

Your own mouth condemns you, and not I: verse 6 is the result of the two reasons given in verse 5; that is, "Because you are wicked and crafty, it is your mouth that condemns you." In 9.20 Job said "Though I am innocent, my own mouth would condemn me . . . ." Those words give Eliphaz the opening to agree with Job, but in a much wider context than Job meant in chapter 9. TEV has restructured line a by shifting **and not I** to the front, and combining **your own mouth** in line a and **your own lips** in line b. This line may also be rendered, for example, "I do not condemn you; your own mouth condemns you," "You do not need me to say you are guilty; your own mouth does that," or "I do not say 'Job, you are guilty.' Your own words say it."

Your own lips testify against you: the poet has moved from **mouth** to **tongue** to **lips** as images of Job's speech, none of which appear in TEV. **Lips testify against you** is a law court expression used similarly in Jeremiah 14.7; 2 Samuel 1.16. The meaning is "your words witness against you," "what you say accuses you," or "your talk shows that you are guilty."

15.7	RSV	TEV
	"Are you the first man that was born? Or were you brought forth before the hills?	Do you think you were the first man born? Were you there when God made the mountains?

Eliphaz now returns to the rhetorical question to remind Job of his human limitations: **Are you the first man that was born?** Zophar in 11.7-9 argued that knowledge of God reaches beyond the four dimensions of space and so cannot be reached by man. Dhorme believes this line is a clear allusion to Proverbs 8.22, which refers to wisdom when it says "The LORD created me at the beginning of his work, the first of his acts of old." It may also imply that the first man born would have the most ancient and therefore the most authentic knowledge. It may be necessary to express this question in such a way that **first** refers to the first in creation and not first among Job and his friends; for example, "Job, were you born before any other human was born?" or "Job, were there any other people alive when you were born?"

Or were you brought forth before the hills? Proverbs 8.25 makes wisdom the first of all the creatures of God: "Before the hills, I was brought forth." The only difference between this line and the equivalent line in Proverbs is the change from "I" to "you." In translation it may be necessary to say, for example, "Were you even born before the hills were created?" "Were you born before God created the hills?" or "Job, are you so old that you were born before God made the hills?"

15.8	RSV	TEV
	Have you listened in the council of God? And do you limit wisdom to yourself?	Did you overhear the plans God made? Does human wisdom belong to you alone?

287

Have you listened in the council of God: listened refers to listening to the talk that takes place in the council where God's plans are made. **Council of God** is the same assembly of heavenly beings described in 1.6; 2.1. See discussion there. This line may be rendered, for example, "When God held his council in the heavens, were you there listening?" "Did you hear God's plans discussed in his meeting in the heavens?" or "Were you there listening when God and his messengers held their meeting in the heavens?"

And do you limit wisdom to yourself? Limit translates the verb rendered "do away with" in verse 4, but here it has the meaning of attracting to oneself, of getting all there is. Dhorme therefore translates "Have you a monopoly on wisdom?" NEB has "usurp all wisdom for yourself alone?" TEV "belong to you alone" is clear and adequate. For discussion of **wisdom** see 11.6. This line may also be expressed, for example, "Are you the only human who has wisdom?" "Are you the only person who is wise?" or "Is there no one else in the world but you who is wise?"

15.9 RSV	TEV
What do you know that we do not know? What do you understand that is not clear to us?	There is nothing you know that we don't know.

What do you know that we do not know: the two lines of verse 9 are parallel without any effort at raising the intensity, and TEV reduces them to one. Line a echoes Job's claim in 12.3b and 13.2a, where he said "I am not inferior to you" and "what you know I also know." Neither Job nor his friends are winning this argument.

What do you understand that is not clear to us? Hebrew does not say **clear to us** but "with us," which some scholars take to mean that a person possesses a thing through knowledge of it. Translators must decide on the basis of style whether to translate verse 9 as questions or statements. As a statement verse 9 may be expressed, for example, "You know nothing that we don't also know, and all that you understand is also clear to us."

15.10 RSV	TEV
Both the gray-haired and the aged are among us, older than your father.	We learned our wisdom from gray-haired men— men born before your father.

Both the gray-haired and the aged are among us: in 12.12 Job said "Wisdom is with the aged." If Eliphaz is referring to himself, he is claiming wisdom by virtue of being older than Job. In that case he claims what he accused Job of claiming. There are several ways of understanding **gray-haired** and **aged**. Both are singular and may refer to a single class of people, that is, "old men." They may refer to Eliphaz and his companions, who then would be **older than Job's father**. Although this seems doubtful, it is the view taken by RSV, NEB, NIV, FRCL, and others. NJB translates "One of us is . . ."; TOB "Look, here among us is an old man, and the other older in years than your father." Another view is that Eliphaz refers to old men of wisdom in general, as Mft says, "Gray hairs and age are on our side," and as is shown in TEV. It is not possible to eliminate any of these, but it does seem best in the context to assume, as does TEV, that the wisdom of the **gray-haired and the aged** from times before Job's father is present in the learning of Eliphaz and his companions. FRCL renders verse 10 "There are among us people of great experience, richer in years even than your own father." In some languages the thought of TEV may be expressed "We learned our wisdom from men having only one hair; those men were born long before your father." In other languages this may be expressed "Old men with wrinkled faces taught us wisdom; they lived long before your own father."

15.11   RSV   TEV

> Are the consolations of God too   God offers you comfort; why still
>   small for you,   reject it?
>   or the word that deals gently   We have spoken for him with
>   with you?   calm, even words.

Are the consolations of God too small for you: Job's friends have tried to comfort him (2.11) by speaking to him about God and how God deals with sinners. These views are best seen in Eliphaz's speech in 5.17-27, Bildad's in 8.5-8, and Zophar's in 11.13-20. In 4.12-21 Eliphaz told of receiving a revelation. Job's friends hold their advice to be inspired by God, but Job calls them "miserable comforters" (16.2). **Consolations of God** is the comfort that God gives through the agency of the friends. TEV has expressed this noun phrase as a verb phrase: "God offers you comfort." SPCL says "Doesn't it suffice you that God himself comforts you?" This line may also be expressed, for example, "Is it not enough that God himself comforts you?" "Do you need still more than God's comfort?" or "God offers to make you feel better. Isn't that enough?"

Or the word that deals gently with you? The word is best taken as being in apposition with **consolations of God** and referring again to the words spoken by Eliphaz, or by all three of the friends (TEV "we"). **Deals gently with you** is the same expression found in 2 Samuel 18.5, when David ordered his military leaders to "deal gently for my sake with the young man Absalom." See also "gently" in Isaiah 8.6. Eliphaz is saying "We spoke gently with you" or "Our words to you were spoken calmly."

15.12   RSV   TEV

> Why does your heart carry you   But you are excited and glare at
>   away,   us in anger.
>   and why do your eyes flash,

Why does your heart carry you away translates the Hebrew "Why does your heart take you?" **Heart** here is the center of emotions, and Eliphaz is asking "Why do you allow yourself to be carried away by emotions?" TEV, which prefers a statement, has "But you are excited." The sense is that Job does not think calmly about what his friends say, but rather reacts emotionally. GECL says "Why do you let your feelings stir you up so badly?" FRCL "Why do you react with so much emotion?" This line may also be expressed figuratively in some languages; for example, "Why does your heart beat so fast?" "Why do you let your insides leap in you?" or "Why does your liver shake?"

And why do your eyes flash? Job's emotional outbursts are reflected in his eyes. **Flash** translates a word found only here. According to Rowley, Targum and Syriac equate it with an Aramaic verb found only in postbiblical Hebrew, but with the first and second consonants switched around, and meaning "wink." In many languages "wink" would carry a different meaning than what is intended here. The context makes clear that Job reacts with anger in his eyes, and so TEV "glare at us in anger" is a good rendering. This line may also be rendered idiomatically sometimes, "And why do your eyes turn red?" or "And why do your nostrils flare?"

15.13	RSV	TEV

RSV	TEV
that you turn your spirit against God,	You are angry with God and denounce him.
and let such words go out of your mouth?	

That you turn your spirit against God: *ki* is the opening connective in this verse, but interpreters disagree as to what things it connects. RSV **that** makes verse 13 a consequence of 12. SPCL makes verse 13 another "why" question parallel to verse 12. TEV does not use a connective but shows the connection through "anger" in verse 12b and "angry" in verse 13a. **Turn your spirit against God** translates the literal Hebrew form. Some scholars understand **spirit** here to mean "breath," but this destroys the parallelism. The Hebrew for **spirit** here means "anger," as it does in Judges 8.3; Proverbs 16.32. This line may also be rendered, for example, ". . . when you become angry with God" or "Why do you turn your anger against God?" In some languages this expression may best be expressed figuratively; for example, ". . . when your heart gets hot at God" or "Why does your innermost boil up at God?"

And let such words go out of your mouth: the word **such** is required in the RSV rendering, but is not in the Hebrew. Eliphaz is rebuking Job for being angry with God, and for this reason his words are harsh. TEV translates the whole line as "and denounce him." SPCL says "and give free rein to your protests." This line may also be rendered, for example, "and you say such bad words against God," "and you let such speeches against God fly from your mouth," or "and you pour out such speeches from your mouth."

15.14   RSV   TEV

What is man, that he can be   Can any man be really pure?
   clean?   Can anyone be right with God?
Or he that is born of a woman,
   that he can be righteous?

What is man, that he can be clean? In 4.17 Eliphaz asked a similar question in similar language, and Job asked the question in 9.2. Eliphaz's question refers to anyone generally, but indirectly to Job in this context. He is urging Job to see his iniquity in that light. For a discussion of **clean** in this context, see 14.4. Eliphaz's question implies the impossibility of being ritually clean. In translation it may be necessary to express this question in a form that brings this out; for example, "What is a human being that he should act as if he were ritually clean?" or "Can a person pretend to be ritually clean?" or as a negative statement, "No one can act as if he were undefiled."

Or he that is born of a woman that he can be righteous? Here the reference is clearly to "anyone," "everybody." The descriptive phrase is used to give added emphasis. **That he can be righteous** implies being righteous with regard to God, and TEV makes this clear with "can anyone be right with God?" TEV is the only translation consulted which makes this connection explicit. For discussion of **righteous** see 4.17. The line should be translated in a form that fits stylistically with the form of the previous line; for example, if a statement is used in line a, line b may also be rendered "and no one can be right in God's eyes."

15.15-16   RSV   TEV

15   Behold, God puts no trust in his   15   Why, God does not trust even his
      holy ones,   angels;
     and the heavens are not clean   even they are not pure in his
      in his sight;   sight.
16   how much less one who is abomi-   16   And man drinks evil as if it were
      nable and corrupt,   water;
     a man who drinks iniquity like   yes, man is corrupt; man is
      water!   worthless.

Verses 15-16 can best be treated as a unit. Verse 15 is made of two negative statements, and 16 goes beyond them in degree.

Behold, God has put no trust in his holy ones: line a is identical in Hebrew to 4.18a except that this verse has "his holy ones" and 4.18a has "his servants." Both refer to members of God's heavenly council. For **behold** see 1.12. 4.18b has "angels" in parallel with "servants," meaning the same heavenly beings. Accordingly TEV says "Why, God does not trust even his angels." This line may be translated, for example, "It is true that God does not trust even his angels," or "Indeed, God does not trust even his messengers," or ". . . the holy ones who serve him."

And the heavens are not clean in his sight: 25.5 says "The stars are not clean in his sight." Scholars disagree about the meaning of **heavens** in verse 15. TEV "even they are not pure" makes **heavens** refer to **the holy ones** or "angels" mentioned in the previous line. TEV has based its translation on the assumption of parallelism of meaning, but no other modern version agrees. In a number of passages in the Psalms, the heavens are addressed as a person, but nowhere do they appear to be identified with angels. In 25.5b, where the same expression occurs, TEV translates "stars," not "angels." It would be best, therefore, to render this line as "even the heavens are not pure in God's sight."

How much less one who is abominable and corrupt: Eliphaz begins the comparison with a Hebrew expression which can mean either "how much more" or "how much less." It is the latter in the present context. God, who was not named in verse 15, is likewise the implied actor in verse 16 who trusts even less. **Abominable** translates a word meaning "something which produces disgust, or which horrifies." It is often used of something that is physically revolting, repulsive to the senses. **Corrupt** translates a word found only here and in Psalm 14.3; 53.3, where it is used in the moral sense of corruption, "depraved" (RSV). SPCL, which translates the two lines of verse 15 as "if" clauses, renders verse 16 as a consequence of comparison: "If even the angels do not merit his confidence . . . how much less mankind, corrupt and disgusting!" NEB also translates verse 15 with an "if" clause and renders verse 16 "how much less so is man, who is loathsome and rotten." This line may also be expressed "God will trust even less a human who is worthless and does evil deeds."

A man who drinks iniquity like water: the point of this metaphor is that people do evil deeds with the ease with which they take a drink of water. Some commentators suggest that the mention of water rather than strong drink suggests that they do their evil in large doses, but this may be questioned. This line may be rendered, for example, "This is a person who does evil as easily as he drinks a cup of water," "a human being who likes to do evil as much as he likes to drink water," or "a person who fills himself with evil as easily as he fills his stomach with water."

4A-2. The fate of the wicked (15.17-35)

RSV	TEV
17 "I will show you, hear me; and what I have seen I will declare	17 Now listen, Job, to what I know.

18   (what wise men have told,
     and their fathers have not hidden,
	18 Wise men have taught me truths
	     which they learned from their fathers,
	     and they kept no secrets hidden.

19   to whom alone the land was given,
     and no stranger passed among them).
	19 Their land was free from foreigners;
	     there was no one to lead them away
	     from God.

20   The wicked man writhes in pain all his
     days,
     through all the years that are laid up
     for the ruthless.
	20 A wicked man who oppresses others
	     will be in torment as long as he lives.

21   Terrifying sounds are in his ears;
     in prosperity the destroyer will come
     upon him.
	21 Voices of terror will scream in his ears,
	     and robbers attack when he thinks he
	     is safe.

22   He does not believe that he will return
     out of darkness,
     and he is destined for the sword.
	22 He has no hope of escaping from dark-
	     ness,
	     for somewhere a sword is waiting to
	     kill him,

23   He wanders abroad for bread, saying,
     'Where is it?'
   He knows that a day of darkness is
     ready at his hand;
	23 and vultures are waiting to eat his
	     corpse.
	   He knows his future is dark;
	 24 disaster, like a powerful king,

24 distress and anguish terrify him;
    they prevail against him, like a king
      prepared for battle.
	is waiting to attack him.
	25 That is the fate of the man
	    who shakes his fist at God
	    and defies the Almighty.

25 Because he has stretched forth his hand
    against God,
    and bids defiance to the Almighty,
	26-27 That man is proud and rebellious;
	    he stubbornly holds up his shield

26 running stubbornly against him with a thick-bossed shield;	and rushes to fight against God. 28 That is the man who captured cities

27 because he has covered his face with his
    fat,
    and gathered fat upon his loins,
	and seized houses whose owners had
	      fled,
	    but war will destroy those cities and

28 and has lived in desolate cities,
    in houses which no man should inhabit,
    which were destined to become heaps
      of ruins;
	houses.
	29 He will not remain rich for long;
	    nothing he owns will last.

29 he will not be rich, and his wealth will not
    endure,
    nor will he strike root in the earth;
	Even his shadow will vanish,
	30 and he will not escape from darkness.
	He will be like a tree

30 he will not escape from darkness;
    the flame will dry up his shoots,
    and his blossom will be swept away by
      the wind.
	whose branches are burned by fire,
	    whose blossoms are blown away by the
	      wind.

31 Let him not trust in emptiness, deceiving
    himself;
    for emptiness will be his recompense.
	31 If he is foolish enough to trust in evil,
	    then evil will be his reward.

32 It will be paid in full before his time,
    and his branch will not be green.
	32 Before his time is up he will wither,
	    wither like a branch and never be
	      green again.

33 He will shake off his unripe grape, like
    the vine,
    and cast off his blossom, like the olive
    tree.
	33 He will be like a vine that loses its unripe
	    grapes;
	    like an olive tree that drops its blos-
	      soms.

34 For the company of the godless is barren,
    and fire consumes the tents of bribery.
	34 There will be no descendants for godless
	    men,
	    and fire will destroy the homes built by
	      bribery.

35 They conceive mischief and bring forth
    evil
    and their heart prepares deceit."
	35 These are the men who plan trouble and
	    do evil;
	    their hearts are always full of deceit.

In verses 17-35 Eliphaz appeals to both personal experience and tradition to describe for Job the miserable plight of the wicked.

Subdivision Heading

The Handbook heading may be modified to say, for example, "Eliphaz tells Job how the wicked suffer," "Eliphaz describes the suffering of wicked people," or "Eliphaz tells Job that there is no peace for the wicked."

15.17-19 RSV	TEV

17 "I will show you, hear me;
    and what I have seen I will
      declare
18 (what wise men have told,
    and their fathers have not hidden,
19 to whom alone the land was
	17 Now listen, Job, to what I know.
	18 Wise men have taught me truths
	    which they learned from their
	      fathers,
	    and they kept no secrets hid-
	      den.

given,   19   Their land was free from foreign-
and no stranger passed among   ers;
them).   there was no one to lead them
                                                  away from God.

Verses 17-19 are introductory to the second part of the chapter, in which
Eliphaz draws a picture of the fate of the wicked man. He does this by first asserting
that his knowledge and experience are in line with the true tradition of the fathers.

I will show you, hear me: this line introduces verses 18-19 and echoes Job's
repeated calls for silence in chapter 13. Eliphaz likes to argue on the basis of his
personal experience (4.8,12; 5.3). The Hebrew does not say **show** as in RSV, but says
literally "I will tell you, listen to me." This line is well rendered by FRCL, "Listen, I
have something to explain to you."

And what I have seen I will declare: in this line Eliphaz again appeals to the
mysterious vision that was revealed to him in chapter 4. TEV has reduced the two
lines to one: "Now listen, Job, to what I know." It is better, if the language permits,
to relate line b to what Eliphaz has seen; for example, "Listen and I will tell you; I
will explain to you what I have seen."

What wise men have told: as Dhorme says, "Wise men do not possess their
wisdom intrinsically; they hold it from their fathers and transmit it to their sons." The
line begins with a relative particle linking what Eliphaz has seen with the knowledge
that has been passed on by others. TEV makes Eliphaz the explicit recipient of the
teaching of the **wise men**. This is not stated in Hebrew, but TEV understands it to
be implicit. It will often be necessary in translation to express the objects of **told**, as
in TEV "Wise men have taught me truths," or "Wise men have told me what I
know."

And their fathers have not hidden: the Hebrew wording of this line suggests
that it be understood "and they did not hide it from their fathers." However, this
meaning does not suit the context. RSV makes **their fathers** the subject of **have not
hidden**. In Hebrew poetry a relative particle is frequently omitted where it would be
natural to expect it in prose. Consequently the Hebrew "from their fathers" should
be understood to mean "*which comes* from their fathers," that is, "the teaching given
by wise men and which comes from their fathers, their ancestors."

To whom alone the land was given: the forefathers who possessed the true
tradition or wisdom were the first to occupy the promised land, and pure teaching
could be maintained by not mixing with foreigners. The point of view is strictly
Israelite regardless of the origins of Eliphaz and Job. This line says, in effect, "The
land was given to their ancestors and to nobody else" or "God gave the land only to
these men, the wise fathers."

And no stranger passed among them: compare Joel 3.17 (4.17 in Hebrew)
"And Jerusalem shall be holy and strangers shall never again pass through it."
Stranger translates a noun meaning one who is not an Israelite. The second line in
TEV, "There was no one to lead them away from God," is an explanation of the
implication of the absence of non-Israelites in the land. Translators who use
footnotes may prefer in this case to stay closer to the text and give the TEV rendering
in a note. It is possible to retain the text and build in something of the implication.
For example, FRCL "They did not suffer from foreign influence," GECL "No
foreigners could lead them away from God." This line may also be expressed "and

foreigners did not cause them to turn away from God" or "and people from other tribes did not lead them away from God."

We may translate verses 17-19 as follows:

> 17 Listen, Job, while I tell you something;
>   I will explain to you what I have seen.
> 18 Wise men have taught me.
>   They learned their teachings from their ancestors.
> 19 God gave them the land,
>   and no foreigners turned their hearts away from him.

15.20

RSV	TEV
The wicked man writhes in pain all his days, through all the years that are laid up for the ruthless.	A wicked man who oppresses others will be in torment as long as he lives.

Verse 20 begins the detailed portrayal of the wicked. **The wicked man writhes in pain all his days**: the belief of Eliphaz is that the wicked person is punished on this earth. **Wicked** translates a noun which refers to one who causes others to suffer. It was used in 3.17 in the plural, "In the grave wicked men stop their evil" (TEV). Here TEV translates "A wicked man who oppresses others." **Writhe in pain** renders a verb form meaning "tormented, punished." This may be taken as physical, but more likely it refers to the conscience. NEB says "racked with anxiety." It can also be translated "tormented by worry." **All his days**: verse 20 begins in Hebrew with this phrase and is poetically related to its parallel expression in the following line. This line may be rendered, for example, "Evil people are made to suffer as long as they live," or "Wicked people are punished throughout their lives," or, as an active construction, "God punishes evil people during their lives."

Through all the years that are laid up for the ruthless: this expression of time which moved from **days** in line a to **years** in line b refers to the same thing, that is, the amount of time he is given to live. **That are laid up for** means "that are saved, reserved, stored up" for someone, just as in Psalm 31.19 "O how abundant is thy goodness which thou hast laid up for those who fear thee." TEV reduces the two time references to one and says "as long as he lives." FRCL keeps both time references with "every day" in line a, and in line b "the time of the tyrants is strictly counted." **Ruthless** translates the same term used in 6.23, translated "oppressors" (RSV) and "tyrant" (TEV). Due to the similarity of meaning in the two lines of this verse, some may prefer to reduce the two lines to one, or to translate line b, for example, "This goes on as long as these violent people live" or "These oppressors of people will suffer all their lives."

15.21   RSV   TEV

Terrifying sounds are in his ears;   Voices of terror will scream in
  in prosperity the destroyer will   his ears,
  come upon him.   and robbers attack when he
                                                  thinks he is safe.

Terrifying sounds are in his ears: here the inward violence which the wicked person suffers is pictured. **Terrifying sounds** translates Hebrew "voice of fears" and suggests the fright that the voice of his conscience arouses within him. TEV makes this intense, with "scream in his ears." It may be necessary in translation to express this line differently; for example, "He hears frightening sounds in his ears," "Frightening voices shout at him," or "He hears awful sounds that scare him."

In prosperity the destroyer will come upon him: **in prosperity** translates "in peace (*shalom*)" and suggests in this context "while all is peaceful, quite calm." TEV has "when he thinks he is safe." **The destroyer** translates the same noun rendered "robbers" in 12.6 by RSV, and that would be a better translation here. **Come upon him** means "assault, attack." This line may be rendered, for example, "while everything is quiet, robbers will attack him" or "when he thinks he is safest, bandits will leap on him."

15.22   RSV   TEV

He does not believe that he will   He has no hope of escaping from
  return out of darkness,   darkness,
  and he is destined for the   for somewhere a sword is wait-
  sword.   ing to kill him,

He does not believe that he will return out of darkness is literally "He does not believe a return from darkness." The subject is still the wicked man, but the meaning of **return out of darkness** is problematic. Some suggest that he fears the night, that he will not wake up. Others take **darkness** to mean "misfortune." That is, he will always remain unfortunate. Dhorme understands the verb form rendered **return out of** to mean "escape from," and translates "He does not expect to escape the dark," and this is followed by TEV and others. All of these express the torments which his conscience causes him. In this line **darkness** is thought of as a person, and in some languages it may be necessary to restructure **return out of darkness** by saying, for example, "He has no hope that he can avoid misfortune," "He knows he will have to suffer," or "There is no way he can avoid death."

And he is destined for the sword: the Hebrew verb translated **destined** is passive, "watched or waited for." However, this is the only place where this word is used in this way. TEV and others shift to the active: "for somewhere a sword is waiting for him." FRCL keeps the passive, "They feel themselves being spied on by a violent death." **Sword** is an image of violent death and refers to being killed. In some languages a **sword** does not operate without a person using it, and so this line must be expressed, for example, "and someone is waiting to kill him with a sword."

In languages in which the **sword** is unknown, it may be possible to substitute a local weapon or to say, for example, "somebody is waiting to murder him."

15.23 RSV	TEV
He wanders abroad for bread, saying, 'Where is it?' He knows that a day of darkness is ready at his hand;	and vultures[c] are waiting[d] to eat his corpse. He knows his future is dark;

[c] *One ancient translation* vultures; *Hebrew* where is he?
[d] *One ancient translation* are waiting; *Hebrew* he wanders.

He wanders abroad for bread, saying, 'Where is it?' RSV translates the Hebrew text, which suggests that the wicked person is troubled by poverty and lack of food. **Where is it?** is the question of the wicked person as he searches for food. However, the Septuagint translates "He has been appointed for food to vultures," that is, in verse 22 the wicked person fears being killed, and in verse 23 he fears that he will subsequently be eaten by vultures. The Hebrew word for "vulture" has the same consonants as the word meaning **Where is it?** Accordingly many translations prefer an expression similar to SPCL, "His corpse will be food for vultures," and this is recommended by HOTTP. Another model is "The vultures will eat his corpse for their food."

He knows that a day of darkness is ready at his hand: some interpreters follow the Septuagint and place **day of darkness** with verse 24a, but this is not necessary. **Day of darkness** is the appointed time for disaster or ruin. This line may also be expressed, for example, "He knows that he is about to be destroyed," "He knows he will soon be killed," or actively, "He knows somebody will kill him."

15.24 RSV	TEV
distress and anguish terrify him; they prevail against him, like a king prepared for battle.	disaster, like a powerful king, is waiting to attack him.

Distress and anguish terrify him: the Septuagint transfers "day of darkness" to this line and makes it the subject of **terrifies him**. NEB has "Suddenly a black day comes upon him." The advantage of following the Septuagint is that the remaining six Hebrew words are easily arranged into two more lines which NJB translates "Distress and anguish assail him as when a king is poised for the assault." In some languages **darkness** (shifted from verse 23) cannot serve as the subject of **terrify**. In such cases it may be necessary to say, for example, "He will find himself in darkness and filled with terror" or "Terror will fill him in the darkness." In the same way **distress and anguish** may have to become objects of a verb such as "suffer"; for example, "He will suffer from distress and anguish," that is, from worry and trouble. The entire verse is rendered by SPCL "Darkness will fill him with terror, and anxiety and disgrace will assault him, as when a king attacks in battle."

Like a king prepared for battle: the comparison is to a king about to lead his army in the attack. The word translated **battle** occurs only here in the Old Testament, but its meaning in this context has been widely accepted, even in the ancient versions. This line may be rendered, for example, "like a king who leads his army against enemies and makes them suffer." The comparison of distress and anguish with an attacking king is applied to the person who feels under siege from those difficulties.

15.25 RSV	TEV
Because he has stretched forth his hand against God, and bids defiance to the Almighty,	That is the fate of the man who shakes his fist at God and defies the Almighty.

Because he has stretched forth his hand against God: verses 25-28 give reasons for the suffering of the wicked which Eliphaz has described in verses 20-24. In order to make clear the relation of verse 25 to the preceding verses, it may be necessary to begin it with "All that is because . . ." or "The reason for all that is . . . ." TEV does this somewhat with "that is." **Stretched forth his hand** means for the purpose of striking, or as a symbol of challenging the one named, that is, God. Examples of this usage may be seen in Isaiah 5.25; 9.21. TEV "who shakes his fist at God" is a good translation for English. FRCL says "who raises his fist," SPCL "who raises his hand," and GECL "who clenches his fist." If the translator does not have a gesture, this line may also be expressed, for example, "This is because he has challenged God to fight him" or "The reason is that he has dared God to oppose him."

And bids defiance to the Almighty: the verb translated **bids defiance** is used in Isaiah 42.13, where RSV translates "He shows himself mighty against his foes." According to Dhorme the term means "behave like a champion" or "play the hero," that is, to act courageous and brave under danger. In the present context it can be taken to mean "defy, challenge." In 40.7-9, when God answers Job, he will challenge Job to gird up his loins like a "hero," based on the same Hebrew root. Two terms for God are used in this line, *'El* and *Shaddai*, but without any significant difference of meaning. Note that the figurative expression is placed in line a and not in line b. There is therefore little poetic movement between the lines. TEV serves as a good translation model.

15.26-27 RSV	TEV
26 running stubbornly against him with a thick-bossed shield; 27 because he has covered his face with his fat,	26-27That man is proud and rebellious; he stubbornly holds up his shield

298

and gathered fat upon his loins,	and rushes to fight against God.

Verse 26 continues the description of the wicked person's foolish defiance of God. It is his trust in his own strength that is described.

Running stubbornly against him translates the Hebrew "runs against him with neck." Numerous suggestions have been made by scholars to explain "with neck," which is rendered **stubbornly** by RSV. Tur-Sinai interprets the expression to refer to a piece of neck armor worn in battle. Some understand it to mean "with a stiff neck," and so "insolently, stubbornly." Others translate "headlong," meaning to charge straight ahead with the head lowered. While all these meanings are possible, the context seems to require something like RSV. TEV has transposed verses 26 and 27 so that verse 27 is the first line. TEV's second line is RSV verse 26a.

With a thick-bossed shield: see 13.12 for a discussion of this decorative part of the shield. Verse 26 may be rendered, for example, "The wicked person stubbornly attacks God, rushing at him with his shield in hand" or "Holding his shield up the evil person lowers his head and attacks God." In languages in which there is no word for shield, it may be possible to say, for example, "The wicked man tries to protect himself as he runs to attack God."

Because he has covered his face with his fat: here is another reason for the foolishness of the wicked person's attack on God. This may refer to the fat person who has lived luxuriously and is too excessively fat to attack anyone physically. Such a description of living in luxury and self-indulgence is found in Psalm 73.7, "Their eyes swell out with fatness." See also Jeremiah 5.28 and Deuteronomy 32.15. Most modern versions translate verse 27 as a nonmetaphor. A few, however, including TEV, take **fat** as a metaphor meaning "rebellion, pride, prosperity, power." Either is possible in translation. Some translators may find it convenient to follow the way in which TEV has condensed the two lines of verse 27 and placed them before verse 26. As a nonmetaphor we may sometimes say, for example, "He does this even though he is weighted down with fat" or ". . . even though he is swollen with fat." If **fat** is to be taken as a figure of speech, the translator may follow TEV or something similar to Mft, "so swollen in prosperity." Another model can be "He has become motionless from living like the rich" or "He has eaten so well he is useless."

And gathered fat upon his loins: if **fat** is taken literally in the first line, it should continue the same in this line. The word for **fat** in line b is found only here in the Old Testament but is cognate with an Arabic verb "to be fat." **Loins** here refers to the lower part of the back, but can be translated "waist, hips, middle." Mft translates the line "so bloated in his wealth." NEB avoids the figurative meaning, "and though his sides bulge with fat." This line may also be rendered, for example, "and his belly is enormously fat."

15.28   RSV   TEV

and has lived in desolate cities, in houses which no man should inhabit, which were destined to become	That is the man who captured cities and seized houses whose owners had fled,

> heaps of ruins;   but war will destroy those
>   cities and houses.

And has lived in desolate cities: it is hardly possible that Eliphaz is now thinking of Job. There are three main views taken by interpreters in regard to this verse. Some understand that the wicked person has destroyed these cities in order to occupy them. NJB says "Towns he had destroyed." Some understand all three lines of the verse to be a prediction of future events (NEB, NIV). According to Rowley the reference is to ruined cities believed to be under a curse, as in Joshua 6.26; Isaiah 13.20; 34.13-17. In this understanding the wicked man who trusts in his prosperity is willing to risk the curse to live in such places. TEV is closest to the first view with "That is the man who captured cities." This is not likely, since the cities seem already to be in ruins. The viewpoint taken by RSV seems to fit best with the overall context of challenging God by dependence upon a person's own power. **Desolate** translates a verb meaning "hidden or effaced" and refers to cities that are in ruins. This notion can be expressed in translation by saying, for instance, "He defied God by living in cities that were in ruins" or "He challenged God's might by living in these ruined cities." Although this interpretation seems to fit the context best, it may be necessary to add a note; for example, "Such places were believed to be under a curse. See Joshua 6.26; Isaiah 13.20."

In houses which no man should inhabit: this line refers to houses no longer occupied by their owners because they have fled, presumably out of fear for the wicked tyrant in their midst, or to the fact that these places were under a curse.

Which were destined to become heaps of ruins: **destined** translates the Hebrew "get ready, be ready," and refers to the advanced stage of collapsing, and can be rendered "which were about to fall down."

15.29   RSV   TEV

> he will not be rich, and his   He will not remain rich for long;
>   wealth will not endure,   nothing he owns will last.
> nor will he strike root in the   Even his shadow[e] will vanish,
>   earth;[m]
>   [e] *One ancient translation* shadow; *Hebrew*
> [m] Vg: Heb obscure   unclear.

He will not be rich: this line seems to contradict the context of the wealthy, wicked person, but the reference is to the future, and so it means, as TEV says, "He will not remain rich for long." **And his wealth will not endure** is the parallel of the previous clause, with no significant change in meaning and without heightening of poetic effect.

Nor will he strike root in the earth: in contrast with the clarity of the first two lines, the third is rendered in many different ways by translators. RSV and others have a note "Hebrew obscure" and base the translation on the Vulgate. TEV and others base their translation on the Septuagint, which says "He will not cast a shadow on the earth." K-B offers the meaning "possessions" for the word translated "shadow" by TEV, a word which is otherwise completely unknown. NIV follows this lead and says "nor will his possessions spread over the land." Translators may follow this suggestion (supported also by HOTTP), or follow TEV "Even his shadow will vanish." This line extends the thought of the previous line to say again that this person will disappear. We may translate, for example, "He will disappear; even his shadow will vanish" or "Both he and his shadow will disappear."

15.30	RSV	TEV
	he will not escape from darkness; the flame will dry up his shoots, and his blossom[n] will be swept away[o] by the wind.	and he will not escape from darkness. He will be like a tree whose branches are burned by fire, whose blossoms[f] are blown away by the wind.

[n] Gk: Heb *mouth*
[o] Cn: Heb *will depart*

[f] *One ancient translation* blossoms; *Hebrew* mouth.

He will not escape from darkness: some scholars omit this line as a misplaced variant of verse 22a. In 10.21 Job used the image of darkness to refer to death and Sheol, and this is the thought being expressed here. Therefore FRCL translates **darkness** as a metaphor for death: "He will not escape the night of death." If "darkness of death" or "night of death" are not suitable expressions in the receptor language, we may say, for example, "He will not escape death," or this may be translated positively as "He will certainly die."

The flame will dry up his shoots: **flame** translates a word used only in Ezekiel 20.47 (21.3 in Hebrew), where it refers to a forest fire. Eliphaz picks up the word **shoots** from Job's speech in 14.7. It is advisable in translation to use the same word as in 14.7, as this helps to relate the two speeches. It is the **shoots** of the tree, the young sprouts that will grow to be trees, that are dried up by the fire. Since the wicked person is here compared to a tree, TEV expresses part of this line as a simile, "He will be like a tree," and places this before "whose branches (shoots) are burned by fire." We may also express this as "He will be like a tree whose young shoots are burned by fire" or "He will be like a tree, and the fire will burn his branches."

The second aspect of failing to mature is **his blossoms will be swept away by the wind**. This translation and that of TEV are based on the Septuagint. The Hebrew text says "he shall depart by the breath of his mouth." This may be a reference to 4.9, in which Eliphaz claimed that the wicked, namely Job, perish "by the breath of God." Some interpreters object to "his mouth" referring to the mouth of God, since God has not been mentioned since verse 26. However, this does not seem to be adequate reason for departing from the Hebrew text.

According to the RSV footnote **swept away** represents a "correction" of the Hebrew "will depart." HOTTP, which gives "of his mouth" a "B" rating, recommends "by the breath of his (God's) mouth." "Will depart" in the Hebrew text may be understood in the sense of "carried off, taken away." We may then avoid both RSV and TEV by translating the Hebrew text of verse 30 as follows:

He will not escape from the darkness of death.
He will be like a tree whose young shoots are burned by fire,
  and the breath of God will blow him away.

15.31   RSV   TEV

Let him not trust in emptiness,   If he is foolish enough to trust in
  deceiving himself;   evil,
  for emptiness will be his rec-   then evil will be his reward.
  ompense.

This verse is best understood as a bit of proverbial wisdom.

Let him not trust in emptiness, deceiving himself: the Hebrew construction begins by expressing a negative imperative suitably translated by RSV. **Emptiness** translates a word used in 7.3, "I am allotted months of emptiness." Some suggest a change in the word to get "high rank" (NEB), "stature" (Dhorme). Other renderings are "lie, evil, deceit, worthlessness, vanity, fraud." In order to settle on a translation of **emptiness**, it is necessary to look at the next line.

For emptiness will be his recompense: the word translated **recompense** refers to exchange of goods in buying and selling, or to the profit made. TEV sums this thought up with "reward": "Then evil will be his reward." FRCL is better with "He makes a mistake by counting on fraud, because he will be paid back in the same coin." SPCL says "Let him not trust foolishly in deceit, because he will only be deceived." Translations which change the word translated **emptiness** to get "height or stature" are able to continue the analogy of the tree in verse 30. For example, NJB "Let him not trust in his great height, or delusion will be his."

Because the Hebrew is subject to so much variation of interpretation, it is not possible to insist on any one rendering as being superior. However, the proposed change to "height" or "stature" has the advantage of relating this verse with both verses 30 and 32. This verse may be rendered, for example, "Let him not trust in being great or he will be deceived," "He deceives himself if he relies on his high standing," or "He is bound to fall if he thinks of himself as great."

15.32   RSV   TEV

It will be paid in full before his   Before his time is up he will
  time,   wither,[g]
  and his branch will not be   wither like a branch and never
  green.   be green again.

[g] *Some ancient translations* wither; *He-brew* be filled.

It will be paid in full before his time: it is not clear what RSV **It** refers to. Hebrew says "Before his day it (he) shall be filled." This likewise is unclear. The Septuagint, Syriac, and Vulgate understand the Hebrew words meaning "It shall be filled" as "withered." Both words sound alike. This understanding is supported by the next line, which speaks of a tree. TEV refers to the man: "he will wither." NEB and others supply the subject "his palm tree" or "his vine" to get a line that is balanced with 32b. "Palm tree" is arrived at with a slight change to the Hebrew.

And his branch will not be green: branch translates a word which refers specifically to the palm branch and is found in Isaiah 9.14; 19.15. It is recommended that translators adapt some form of TEV; for example, "Very soon he will wither like a dry branch, and never be green again" or "He is like a branch that withers before its time and is never green again."

15.33	RSV	TEV
	He will shake off his unripe grape, like the vine, and cast off his blossom, like the olive tree.	He will be like a vine that loses its unripe grapes; like an olive tree that drops its blossoms.

He will shake off his unripe grape, like the vine: shake off translates a verb meaning "to use violence." TEV avoids the active verb and says "He will be like a vine that loses its unripe grapes." In both lines of the verse the thought is that the person is like a tree that will fail to bring its fruit to maturity. **Unripe grape** is used in Jeremiah 31.29; Ezekiel 18.2, where RSV translates "sour grapes." In languages in which grapes are unknown, it may be necessary to substitute another fruit, especially one that grows on a vine. The line may also be expressed "He will be like a vine whose fruit does not ripen, but drops to the ground while green" or "He will be like a vine whose fruit falls to the ground before it is ripe."

And cast off his blossom, like the olive tree. Rowley quotes Wetzstein (in Delitzsch): "In order to appreciate the point of comparison, it is needful to know that the Syrian olive tree bears fruit plentifully the first, third and fifth years, but rests during the second, fourth, and sixth. It blossoms in these years also, but the blossoms fall off almost entirely without any berries being formed." In languages in which the vine does not **cast off** its blossom, it may be necessary to change this expression to say, for example, "and like the blossom that falls from the olive tree" or "and like the olive tree whose blossom falls to the ground." In areas where the olive tree is unknown, another fruit tree may be substituted.

15.34	RSV	TEV
	For the company of the godless is barren, and fire consumes the tents of bribery.	There will be no descendants for godless men, and fire will destroy the homes built by bribery.

For the company of the godless is barren: company is a term used frequently in the Old Testament to refer to a "band, clique, faction, group" who adhere to a common leader. Mft says "For the godless are a barren tribe." These gangs of godless people are said to be **barren,** that is, will suffer the fate of being cut off without "descendants" (TEV). This line may be rendered, for example, "The bands of unbelievers will have no descendants," "The groups of people who do not trust God will come to an end," or "Gangs of people who do not put their trust in God will die without descendants."

And fire consumes the tents of bribery: fire suggests the kind of fire which came down and destroyed some of Job's wealth in 1.16. **Tents of bribery** is ambiguous since it may refer to those who give bribes or to those who receive them. Here the second meaning fits best the context of condemnation of the wicked. (For comments on "bribe" see 6.22.) TEV assumes it means "the homes built by bribery." This likewise is unclear as to who paid and who received the bribes. More suitable would be to make clear that **tents of bribery** refers to the homes of the gangs of the wicked who have received bribes for their oppressive acts and have built their homes from them. SPCL says "and their houses (of the godless company) enriched by bribes will burn in the fire." This line may also be expressed "the houses they have built from bribery money will be burned down" or "the houses they have built from the money they have gotten by taking bribes from the oppressed will burn down."

15.35   RSV   TEV

> They conceive mischief and bring   These are the men who plan
>   forth evil   trouble and do evil;
>   and their heart prepares de-   their hearts are always full of
>   ceit."   deceit.

They conceive mischief and bring forth evil. Chapter 15 begins with Eliphaz accusing Job of filling his belly with the east wind (15.2). He now ends his speech saying "their belly (RSV **heart**) prepares deceit." Psalm 7.14 expresses the same sentiment, "The wicked man conceives evil and is pregnant with mischief, and brings forth lies." In Job 4.8 the same thought is expressed as "Those who plow iniquity and sow trouble reap the same." See also Isaiah 59.4. TEV does not attempt to retain the productivity image but reproduces something of the progression: "These are the men who plan trouble and do evil."

And their heart prepares deceit: see above concerning **heart.** Translators who are striving to translate in poetry will want to retain the images in so far as they are suitable in their own languages, or else supply equivalent images. NEB keeps the images in a slightly modified form: "They conceive mischief, and give birth to trouble, and the child of their womb is deceit." If the reproduction images cannot be kept, it may be necessary to say something like "They are the people who think up trouble to cause others; they succeed in doing evil deeds, and their hearts are full of deceit."

4B. JOB REPLIES (16.1–17.16)

Chapters 16–17 form a single discourse unit and, like chapter 15, consist of a major theme alternating with a minor one, resulting in the same pattern as in the previous chapter: complaint, plea, complaint, plea, complaint.

In 16.2-5 Job bitterly complains of his miserable comforters. He too could string words together to relieve their pains. In 16.6-9 the target of Job's complaint is God. In 16.10 Job complains against people who have attacked him. In verses 11-14 Job complains again of God's attacks, and this time the treatment received by Job is more violent than in verses 6-9. In verses 15-17 Job's complaint continues as he tells how he has reacted to God's attacks, claiming that he is not violent and that his prayer is pure. In verses 18-21 Job shifts to a plea that earth should not hide the wrongs done to him, and he pleads for someone to mediate between God and him. In 16.22–17.2 Job again takes up his complaint against his coming death and his mockers. In 17.3-5 Job again makes a plea to God to accept what he is saying and not to allow his enemies to triumph over him. He concludes his plea with a proverbial saying. In 17.6-16 Job returns to his complaint, in which he describes his misery (verses 6-7) and attacks the friends in 8-10 for pretending to be honest, but who in his view are not even wise. Finally in 11-16 Job's complaint turns to despair as he nears death, and his only hope is to find comfort in the grave.

These two chapters may be displayed as follows:

16.2-17		Complaint	
	2-5		to the friends
	6-14		to God
	15-17		self defense
16.18-21		Plea	
16.22–17.2		Complaint	
17.3-5		Plea	
17.6-16		Complaint	
	6-7		against God and people
	8-10		against the friends
	11-16		against the friends (verse 12) to death and Sheol

Division Heading

The Handbook supplies a heading for Job's discourse in chapters 16–17. Translators may wish to do the same. Some versions combine division and subdivision headings in one. For example, FRCL "Job's reply: 'I have a witness in heaven,'" GECL "Job: God has dealt unjustly with me," BJ "From the injustice of men to the justice of God." See also TEV. Although the Handbook headings and the headings found in most versions do not entirely conform to the structure presented above, translators who care to may use a larger number of headings, provided those headings will be a help to readers.

4B-1. Job accuses Eliphaz of substituting words for comfort (16.1-5)

RSV	TEV
1 Then Job answered:	*Job*
2 "I have heard many such things;	1-2 I have heard words like that before;
miserable comforters are you all.	the comfort you give is only torment.
3 Shall windy words have an end?	3 Are you going to keep on talking forever?
Or what provokes you that you answer?	Do you always have to have the last word?
4 I also could speak as you do,	4 If you were in my place and I in yours,
if you were in my place;	I could say everything you are saying.
I could join words together against you,	I could shake my head wisely
and shake my head at you.	and drown you with a flood of words.
5 I could strengthen you with my mouth,	5 I could strengthen you with advice
and the solace of my lips would assuage your pain.	and keep talking to comfort you.

Subdivision Heading

The first subdivision heading used in the Handbook in this division may need to be modified in some languages to say, for example, "Job complains that the friends do not comfort him," "Job accuses his friends of making him feel worse," or "Job says to the friends, 'You are bad comforters.' " TOB uses "Wretched comforters," and Rowley has "Job's dismissal of the comfort of the friends."

16.1   RSV   TEV

Then Job answered: *Job*

Then Job answered: see 4.1; 6.1.

16.2   RSV   TEV

"I have heard many such things; miserable comforters are you all.   **I have heard words like that before; the comfort you give is only torment.**

I have heard many such things: the things Job refers to are the previous speeches of all three friends, not just the last speech of Eliphaz. In the next line he includes them all in his condemnation.

Miserable comforters are you all: **miserable comforters** is literally "comforters of trouble." Job picks up from Eliphaz's words in 15.35 "They conceive mischief," where "mischief" translates the same word rendered **miserable** here. These are comforters who increase trouble instead of removing it. The same term is used in 3.10; 4.8. Job's friends came expressly to comfort him, to relieve his suffering (2.11), but their ministry to Job is less than helpful. In some languages this line may be rendered, for example, "You (plural) do not relieve my sufferings; you (plural) make me miserable instead of helping me," "You (plural) do not help me; you make me suffer still more," or "Instead of making me feel better, you (plural) make me feel worse."

16.3	RSV	TEV
	Shall windy words have an end? Or what provokes you that you answer?	Are you going to keep on talking forever? Do you always have to have the last word?

Shall windy words have an end? Here Job throws back at them the words of Bildad in 8.2 and those of Eliphaz in 15.2. Job is asking if his friends will never come to an end with their speeches. TEV says it well: "Are you going to keep on talking forever?" This line may also be expressed, for example, "Will your windy speeches never finish?" "Will you go on making meaningless speeches forever?" or "Will you never cease talking nonsense to me?"

Or what provokes you that you answer? Job now switches to second person singular, prompting NEB to put verse 3 in quotation marks, thus making Job quote his friend's words. However, Job switches pronouns in 21.3 to address the last speaker, and it is not necessary to assume here that he is quoting them as in NEB. **Provokes** translates a word meaning "agitate" or "irritate." Job is scolding Eliphaz for being a person who itches to talk, as if he is possessed with an illness which makes him speak. **Answer** here refers to replying to Job's speech, and so TEV "have to have the last word." It may also be rendered "What bothers you so that you have to talk back to me?" or "What makes you want to make these speeches?"

16.4	RSV	TEV
	I also could speak as you do, if you were in my place; I could join words together against you, and shake my head at you.	If you were in my place and I in yours, I could say everything you are saying. I could shake my head wisely and drown you with a flood of words.

I also could speak as you do: this verse has four lines in Hebrew, as in RSV. Job is saying that if he and his friends changed places, he could be as unkind to them as they are to him. TEV transposes lines a and b in order to place the hypothetical condition at the opening.

If you were in my place is literally "If your soul (*nefesh*) were in the place of my soul." This idiomatic use of the word for "soul" means "you (plural)" and "I" respectively. In many languages it will be necessary to shift the "if" clause to the beginning and say, for example, "If you (plural) were me," "If we were in each other's place," or "If we changed places." Some languages may express this more idiomatically; for example, "If you were sitting on my stool" or "If you ate from my bowl."

I could join words together against you: the Hebrew word translated **join words together** has been subjected to much speculation and has been compared with similar words in Arabic and Ugaritic. There is little agreement, but the general sense seems clear: Job claims he could make brilliant speeches just as they do and get nowhere. This line may also be expressed, for example, "I could make great speeches criticizing you," or "I could say the same kinds of things about you."

And shake my head at you: this gesture is most often associated in the Bible with scorn, ridicule, and mockery; see Lamentations 2.15; Psalm 22.7; Matthew 27.39. However, in this context some interpreters see in the gesture a sign of sympathy or compassion, be it genuine or not. A number of English translations use "shake my head at you"; but this is ambiguous, because in English this expression means refusal or disagreement. TEV implies mockery with "shake my head wisely." FRCL says "I will shake my head as a sign of compassion." NEB, NJV, and NAB say "wag my head at (or, over) you," but this is not an English expression. SPCL says "I would mockingly shake my head at you." Translators should use the gesture which expresses ridicule in their own language. For examples see 11.3.

16.5   RSV   TEV

> I could strengthen you with my
>   mouth,
>   and the solace of my lips would
>   assuage your pain.

> I could strengthen you with ad-
>   vice
>   and keep talking to comfort
>   you.

I could strengthen you with my mouth: Job's tone is sarcastic. He could strengthen them by giving them nothing more than words. That is no real sympathy. **Mouth** is used here in place of words, since its parallel, **lips**, is used in the next line. TEV translates **mouth** as "advice." FRCL has "I would encourage you by sheer talk," meaning by doing nothing but talking. This line may also be expressed "I could help you by making long speeches," "I could strengthen you by using lots of words," or "I could give you lots of advice, and so make you strong."

And the solace of my lips would assuage your pain: **solace** translates a Hebrew word meaning "movement, agitation." It is the "movement of the lips" that is parallel to "my mouth" in line a. The movement of the **lips** is the figure representing talk or advice, and this is said to relieve the pain. In Hebrew the word translated **assuage** has no object, but **your pain** has been supplied by RSV. Some scholars interpret the word translated **assuage** to mean "restrain or withhold," and so Dhorme "The movement of my lips I would not restrain." In this view, if Job were in his friends' place, he would give them all the comfort they required. It seems best, however, to understand line b as Job's continuing sarcasm, and this may be expressed, for example, "and what I would say to you would make you feel good" or "the words I would say would be sufficient to relieve your pains."

4B-2. Job accuses God of treating him with violence (16.6-17)

	RSV		TEV
6	"If I speak, my pain is not assuaged, and if I forbear, how much of it leaves me?	6	But nothing I say helps, and being silent does not calm my pain.
7	Surely now God has worn me out; he has made desolate all my company.	7	You have worn me out, God; you have let my family be killed.
8	And he has shriveled me up, which is a witness against me; and my leanness has risen up against me, it testifies to my face.	8	You have seized me; you are my enemy. I am skin and bones, and people take that as proof of my guilt.
9	He has torn me in his wrath, and hated me; he has gnashed his teeth at me; my adversary sharpens his eyes against me.	9	In anger God tears me limb from limb; he glares at me with hate.
10	Men have gaped at me with their mouth, they have struck me insolently upon the cheek, they mass themselves together against me.	10	People sneer at me; they crowd around me and slap my face.
11	God gives me up to the ungodly, and casts me into the hands of the wicked.	11	God has handed me over to evil men.
12	I was at ease, and he broke me asunder; he seized me by the neck and dashed me to pieces; he set me up as his target,	12	I was living in peace, but God took me by the throat and battered me and crushed me. God uses me for target practice
13	his archers surround me. He slashes open my kidneys, and does not spare; he pours out my gall on the ground.	13	and shoots arrows at me from every side— arrows that pierce and wound me; and even then he shows no pity.
14	He breaks me with breach upon breach; he runs upon me like a warrior.	14	He wounds me again and again; he attacks like a soldier gone mad with hate.
15	I have sewed sackcloth upon my skin, and have laid my strength in the dust.	15	I mourn and wear clothes made of sackcloth, and I sit here in the dust defeated.
16	My face is red with weeping, and on my eyelids is deep darkness;	16	I have cried until my face is red, and my eyes are swollen and circled with shadows,
17	although there is no violence in my hands, and my prayer is pure.	17	but I am not guilty of any violence, and my prayer to God is sincere.

Subdivision Heading

Translators wishing to provide a subdivision heading at this point may use the Handbook heading or modify it to say, for example, "Job complains that God has torn him apart," "Job accuses God of violent attacks," or "Job says that God has broken him to pieces." TOB has "The target of God," Habel "Complaint against God as enemy," and Rowley "Job's abandonment by God and man."

16.6   RSV   TEV

> "If I speak, my pain is not as-
> suaged,
> and if I forbear, how much of
> it leaves me?

> But nothing I say helps,
> and being silent does not calm
> my pain.

Verse 6 begins the complaint against God, who treats Job as an enemy. God is seen at times acting like a wild animal, and like an enemy who turns people against him.

If I speak, my pain is not assuaged: in verse 5 "your pain" was supplied by RSV; here it is expressed in the Hebrew text. The same verb translated "assuaged" in verse 5 occurs here in the passive form. It means "to ease, lessen, relieve pain." TEV translates "help," that is, "Nothing I say helps." This line is in contrast to the preceding one and may need to be marked as such; for example, "But, on the other hand, however, nevertheless": "But when I speak, it does no good to relieve my suffering" or "However, if I make a speech, it does not make my pains go away."

And if I forbear, how much of it leaves me? The result clause is expressed in RSV as a rhetorical question. Neither by speaking nor by remaining silent can Job find any relief. **Forbear** translates a verb meaning "cease, stop, desist," and in the context refers to ceasing from speaking, saying nothing, as in TEV "being silent." **How much of it leaves me** translates the Hebrew "what am I eased?" Some interpreters understand the question word to be a negative and understand the clause to mean "it (the pain) does not depart," which is the basis for TEV "does not calm my pain." This line may also be expressed, for example, "even if I remain silent, I am still in pain," "keeping silent likewise does not remove my suffering," or "by not speaking I still do not get rid of my pains."

16.7-8   RSV   TEV

7   Surely now God has worn me
      out;
      he has[P] made desolate all my
      company.
8   And he has[P] shriveled me up,
      which is a witness against me;
      and my leanness has risen up
      against me,
      it testifies to my face.

7   You have worn me out, God;
      you have let my family be
      killed.
8   You have seized me; you are
      my enemy.
    I am skin and bones,
      and people take that as proof
      of my guilt.[h]

[h] *Verses 7-8 in Hebrew are unclear.*

[P] Heb *thou hast*

Verses 7 and 8 are closely related and need to be dealt with together. The TEV footnote says of these two verses: "Hebrew unclear."

Surely now God has worn me out: it will be noted that RSV has **God** in line a and **he** in line b, while TEV has "you" in both lines. Line a in the Hebrew text has neither "God" nor "you." Scholars have reconstructed both lines of this verse and get widely different results. Both TEV and RSV make God the subject of **has worn me out**, and this is the understanding of FRCL, SPCL, GECL, NJV, NIV, and Mft. On the other hand NJB and BJ understand "pain" from verse 6 to be the subject. If the translator follows RSV or TEV with God as the subject, this line may be rendered, for example, "Certainly God has taken away my strength" or "Yes, God has brought me to the end of my strength."

He has made desolate all my company: this line in Hebrew has "you (singular)." See RSV note. TEV introduces "you" into line a in order to be consistent with the Hebrew "you" in line b, while RSV, which supplied **God** in line a, translates **he** in line b. Translators may follow either model but should be consistent in the two lines. **Made desolate** translates a verb meaning "devastate, ruin, destroy," and so TEV "killed." **All my company** probably does not refer to all of Job's other friends but is more specifically his own closest kin, and so TEV "family." NIV has "You have devastated my entire household," which would include family and servants. Line b may also be rendered, for example, "You, God, have killed my entire family" or "God has destroyed my family." FRCL says "all those around me."

And he has shriveled me up: this line in Hebrew has "you (singular)," as in verse 7b. RSV keeps **he** in the interest of consistency with its change to "he" there. **Shriveled** translates an uncertain word found only here and in 22.16. It has the meaning of "seize, take hold of" in Syriac and postbiblical Hebrew, and this is followed by TEV "You have seized me." Translators express the line variously; for example, SPCL "He has put me in prison"; Dhorme "He has risen up against me"; NIV "You have bound me." Others follow RSV; for example, FRCL "The wrinkles he has given me are witnesses to it," GECL "He engraves my face with deep wrinkles." Because of the lack of certainty, translators are free to follow either RSV or TEV.

Which is a witness against me: according to Rowley, Job's being shriveled up is the evidence of his sin. **Which** in RSV refers back to the previous line and gives the meaning that Job's physical condition "shows, witnesses against him" that he is a sinner. Following RSV these lines may be rendered "He has inflicted my skin with deep wrinkles which are like witnesses against me" or "He has put wrinkles on my skin, and they are like witnesses who speak against me."

And my leanness has risen up against me: Job's physical condition, being bony like a skeleton, is again a testimony of his guilt. **Has risen up against me** is the personalization of **leanness**, which takes the stand, in court terminology, to testify against Job. TEV has translated this phrase "You are my enemy." Job's thought is more in terms of the contestants in a trial than "enemy" suggests.

It testifies to my face: this line is added to give emphasis to the metaphor in the previous line. In many languages **leanness** cannot be used as the subject of the verb "rise up or stand up." Therefore it will often be necessary to restructure these two lines and say, for example, "He has made me bony, and this too is like a witness who stands up to speak against me" or "He has reduced me to a skeleton, and this is like . . . ."

16.9	RSV	TEV
	He has torn me in his wrath, and hated me;	In anger God tears me limb from limb;

<table>
<tr><td>he has gnashed his teeth at
  me;
my adversary sharpens his
  eyes against me.</td><td>he glares at me with hate.</td></tr>
</table>

Job now speaks of God as if he were a wild animal tearing him apart. **He has torn me in his wrath and hated me**: the picture in RSV and TEV is that of a wild animal that has caught its prey and is tearing it to pieces, or as TEV says, "Tears me limb from limb." In translation it may be necessary to make this line a simile; for example, "As a wild animal tears the flesh of its prey, he has torn me apart." Translators may find it is better to shift **and hated me** to the beginning; for example, "He hated me and has torn me apart as a wild animal tears its victim." Otherwise the translator may follow the model of TEV. TEV has taken **and hated me** from line a and made it a description of line c, "He glares at me with hate."

He has gnashed his teeth at me means he shows his fury or anger. This line adds nothing to the meaning or intensity of line a, and TEV does not translate it.

My adversary sharpens his eyes against me: the wording of RSV is not idiomatic English. **Sharpens his eyes** is a figure meaning that the penetrating eyes of the animal (God) are fixed on Job as he tears Job's flesh apart. Unlike TEV, FRCL keeps all the lines and with some adjustments renders verse 9 "In his anger, God chooses me as his prey, he pursues me, he gnashes his teeth at me; he, my enemy, pierces me with his look." To gnash the teeth means to bare and strike the teeth together as a wild animal does when attacking its prey. SPCL translates lines b and c "He nails me with his eyes as if he were my enemy." Here **and hated me** is translated "as if he were my enemy." The whole verse may also be rendered, for example, "He has torn me like an angry animal; he has bared his teeth at me as though he hates me, and he fixes his angry eyes on me."

16.10   RSV   TEV

<table>
<tr><td>Men have gaped at me with their
  mouth,
they have struck me insolently
  upon the cheek,
they mass themselves together
  against me.</td><td>People sneer at me;
  they crowd around me and
  slap my face.</td></tr>
</table>

Men have gaped at me with their mouth: **men** translates an indefinite "they," which TEV renders "people." **Gaped at me** means they "stared at me with open mouths." It implies that the person whose mouth is open is in a state of wonder, dumbfounded by what he sees. This is not likely to be the sense here. TEV "sneer" is better. NIV has "Men open their mouths to jeer at me"; but it is hard to understand how a person can jeer without opening the mouth. It may be necessary in some languages to continue the animal simile in this line; for example, "Like wild animals they threaten me with their mouths." The next line continues the description of physical violence done to Job by his enemies.

They have struck me insolently upon the cheek: to slap a person's face is an extreme insult; for example, Psalm 3.7 "Arise, O LORD! Deliver me, O my God! For thou dost smite all my enemies on the cheek." See also Micah 5.1 (4.14 in Hebrew); Lamentations 3.30. **Insolently** means the act is done "to ridicule, scorn, mock." The Hebrew word translated **cheek** refers to the jaw and the cheeks. The line may be rendered, for example, "to ridicule me they have slapped my face" or "to make fun of me they have slapped me."

They mass themselves together against me: the form of the verb used here means "to pile up, press together" and applied to people is, as in TEV, "They crowd around me . . . ." The final line of verse 10 may be translated, for example, "they gang up to attack me" or "they crowd around me as they attack me." TEV has reduced lines b̲ and c̲ to one. The only verb in line c̲ is **mass against,** and the implication is that they do this to threaten, ridicule or attack.

16.11 RSV TEV

God gives me up to the ungodly, and casts me into the hands of the wicked.	God has handed me over to evil men.

God gives me up to the ungodly: the two lines of verse 11 are parallel, with the figurative expression occurring in line b̲, and this gives line b̲ an increase in poetic intensity. Job clearly blames God for causing him to suffer. The verb in line a̲ means "to hand over, deliver, give up." **Ungodly** translates a Hebrew noun meaning "child" and is used with that sense in 19.18; 21.11. However, "child" does not fit the context, and so most interpreters accept a change of vowels to give a similar sounding noun meaning "unrighteous," as in 27.7. The parallelism in line b̲ requires this change. Therefore RSV **ungodly** (TEV "evil men") is a common rendering. Although some translators follow the Hebrew text and translate "youth, child" (see FRCL, TOB), RSV and TEV are recommended. The line may be rendered, for example, "God hands me over to evil people," "God turns me over to people who do evil things," or "God gives me away to wicked people."

And casts me into the hands of the wicked: line b̲ is without a verb, and depends on the verb in line a̲. TEV, which does not often attempt to show poetic heightening in the second line, here also reduces the two lines to one. If poetic heightening is to be kept, the translator must express it in a poetic manner which is acceptable in his or her language. In English this may be said "God hands me over to evil people, right into their hands" or "God turns me over to the ungodly, turns me over to them right into their hands."

16.12-13 RSV TEV

12 I was at ease, and he broke me asunder; he seized me by the neck and dashed me to pieces;	12 I was living in peace, but God took me by the throat and battered me and crushed me.

	he set me up as his target,		God uses me for target practice
13	his archers surround me.	13	and shoots arrows at me from
	He slashes open my kidneys, and		every side—
	does not spare;		arrows that pierce and wound
	he pours out my gall on the		me;
	ground.		and even then he shows no
			pity.

The description of God attacking Job in verses 12 and 13 is best looked at as a single unit.

I was at ease, and he broke me asunder: in Hebrew the two clauses are reversed, but in English the state of being at ease is better placed before the abrupt action. The word translated **ease** is better expressed by TEV "living in peace." **Broke me asunder** means "smashed to pieces," in which the person thinks of himself as a breakable object like a clay pot. Another form of the same verb is used in Psalm 74.13 where God "breaks" the sea in order to make a way through it. In some languages it is not possible to speak of breaking a person as if he were a solid object, and so this line may have to be expressed, for example, "When I was happy God came and threw me about," ". . . shook me badly," or "I was living quietly when God suddenly crushed my body."

He seized me by the neck and dashed me to pieces: the first clause is literally "he seized my nape" and means "he grabbed me, took me by the nape of the neck." The nape of the neck refers to the back of the neck. **Dashed me to pieces** is a different verb than the one used in the previous line but means the same. "He grabbed me by the neck and threw me down."

The next line goes naturally with verse 13a and is parallel with it. **He sets me up as his target**: the picture is that of an archer, one who shoots arrows with a bow, placing a target for practice. The word translated **target** is not the same as used in 7.20, but it has the same meaning. It is also found in 1 Samuel 20.20; Lamentations 3.12. This line may require some adjustments in translation; for example, "he uses me as a thing to hit when he practices shooting arrows," "he practices on me by shooting arrows into me," or "he makes me like a target and shoots me with arrows." If bows and arrows are not known, another weapon may be used, provided that it can be used for target practice. However, a weapon such as a gun would be inappropriate.

His archers surround me: the word for **archers** is used in Jeremiah 50.29. It is unclear who these archers may be, other than Job's enemies or the wicked from verse 11. The ancient versions translate "arrows" instead of **archers**, and many translators follow them. See TEV "and shoots arrows at me . . . ." If the translator follows RSV, **archers** may be rendered, for example, "those who shoot arrows," "the shooters," or "the ones practicing." Otherwise the translator may use "arrows," as in TEV, "and shoots arrows at me from every side."

He slashes open my kidneys depicts the results of the arrow attack. RSV follows the Hebrew, but TEV shifts to "pierce and wound me." The verb translated **slashes open** is suitable for the action of a sword or knife, but not for an arrow, where "pierce" is more fitting. In some languages it may be better to make arrows the subject of "pierce"; for example, "His arrows go into my kidneys" or "He shoots me in the kidneys with his arrows." **And does not spare** is an awkward rendering of the Hebrew, which means "and he has no pity, mercy, compassion." He attacks without mercy. TEV "even then he shows no pity" expresses it well.

He pours out my gall on the ground: TEV takes this line to be the same as the previous line and therefore does not translate it. The word **gall** or "bile," the secretion in the liver, is found only here. A closely similar word translated "bitter things" occurs in 13.26 and is translated "gall" in 20.14,25. Verse 13 may be rendered, for example, "He shoots his arrows into my kidneys without any mercy and pours out the bile from my liver onto the ground."

16.14	RSV	TEV
	He breaks me with breach upon breach; he runs upon me like a warrior.	He wounds me again and again; he attacks like a soldier gone mad with hate.

The figure now shifts from the attack of God's arrows to the onslaught against a wall. **He breaks me with breach upon breach**: Hebrew has a verb which has a closely similar noun form used twice, and the result is poetic alliteration, which RSV manages to imitate to some extent with **breaks . . . breach . . . breach**. Job pictures himself here as a wall which God smashes through. TEV does not attempt to keep the image of storming a wall, but shifts to a nonfigurative expression: "He wounds me again and again."

He runs upon me like a warrior: **runs upon** refers to the attack or running over of an enemy by an attacking soldier. TEV has added to the expression of the simile **like a warrior** to give it the idea of anger: "like a soldier gone mad with hate." This seems unnecessary, since the figure of a warrior on the attack adequately conveys Job's thought. GECL translates "He wounds me again and again like a warrior breaking through a wall." In translation it may be better to shift the simile in line b to the opening; for example, "like a warrior he attacks me" or "he assaults me like a charging soldier." The whole verse may be rendered "He leaps on me like a warrior and wounds me again and again" or "Like a charging soldier he attacks me and leaves me with many wounds."

16.15	RSV	TEV
	I have sewed sackcloth upon my skin, and have laid my strength in the dust.	I mourn and wear clothes made of sackcloth, and I sit here in the dust defeated.

I have sewed sackcloth upon my skin: **sackcloth** refers to a coarse dark material made of goat or camel hair. It is a sign of mourning and was worn next to the skin (2 Kgs 6.30). Job's sackcloth is **sewed . . . upon my skin**, and this may suggest that he will wear it permanently, or that he wears it next to his skin. TEV "I wear clothes made of sackcloth" suggests neither the one nor the other. GECL, however, translates "The mourning clothes are my second skin," which implies that Job will wear them all the time. The line may be rendered, for example, "I have put mourning clothes on my body," "I have dressed myself in the clothes of those who mourn for the dead," or "I wear the rough cloth of those who are in mourning." In some languages it may be necessary to give a footnote explaining **sackcloth**; for instance, "Mourning clothes were coarse pieces of cloth sewed together from woven goat or camel hair."

And have laid my strength in the dust translates the Hebrew "I have thrust my horn in the dust." To raise a person's horn is an expression of pride, strength, or success. Here the meaning is the opposite: Job is totally "depressed, ruined, defeated." TEV "I sit here in the dust defeated" recalls the picture from 2.8, where Job sits in the ash heap scraping his sores. **Have laid** suggests a vigorless, passive act, whereas the word it translates refers to a determined, energetic gesture such as "thrust, jab shove." If the translator's language has an equivalent metaphor, it should be used. If not, we may also say, for example, "I am ruined," "I am totally defeated," or actively, "he (God) has crushed me," or "God has ground me down to dust."

16.16-17   RSV   TEV

| 16 | My face is red with weeping, and on my eyelids is deep darkness; | 16 | I have cried until my face is red, and my eyes are swollen and circled with shadows, |
| 17 | although there is no violence in my hands, and my prayer is pure. | 17 | but I am not guilty of any violence, and my prayer to God is sincere. |

Verse 16 gives two descriptions of Job's face, in the form of consequences he has suffered, and verse 17 states two concessive clauses, meaning that the results in verse 16 are true in spite of the condition in verse 17.

My face is red with weeping: the verb translated **is red** is found only here and seems to mean "is inflamed." It is obvious that the use of **red** to describe a person's face is not appropriate everywhere. It may be better to speak of the face as "swollen," "tear stained," or some similar description. In some languages people say, for example, "My cheeks are hot from crying" or "My face is washed by my tears." **With weeping** is the cause of Job's inflamed face.

And on my eyelids is deep darkness: **eyelids** stands here as a part for the whole and refers to Job's entire eyes. **Deep darkness** may perhaps be understood as "the shadow of death," which is used in 3.5, but the meaning in this verse is "darkened, very dark" or, as TEV graphically says, "circled with shadows." These are not shadows of objects cast on Job, but the darkening of the skin around the eyes. FRCL translates this line "My eyes are completely red and circled by shadows from much crying." SPCL has "My face has swollen from crying and my vision has become blurred." We may also say, for example, "I have cried until my eyes are red and I can hardly see" or "I have shed so many tears my eyes are red and swollen with dark circles."

Although there is no violence in my hands: here Job denies that he has been violent. Zophar advised Job in 11.14 to get rid of the iniquity in his hands. **Violence** is probably used here to symbolize evil. The line may be rendered, for example, "although I have done nothing wrong," "and in spite of this I am not guilty of wrong," or "but I have committed no crime." **My hands** is a part for the whole. Job claims that he is innocent, using an expression meaning that he has done no wrong act, has committed no crime, has been violent against no one.

And my prayer is pure: in Isaiah 1.15, when the hands are not clean, prayer is unacceptable to God. In 31.7 Job says his hands are clean. **Pure** in relation to prayer refers to respecting and honoring God. This line may also be expressed, for example, "and in my prayers I have shown honor to God" or "and my prayers to God have shown him reverence."

4B-3. Job hopes someone in heaven will witness for him (16.18–17.2)

	RSV		TEV
18	"O earth, cover not my blood, / and let my cry find no resting place.	18	O Earth, don't hide the wrongs done to me! / Don't let my call for justice be silenced!
19	Even now, behold, my witness is in heaven, / and he that vouches for me is on high.	19	There is someone in heaven / to stand up for me and take my side.
20	My friends scorn me; / my eye pours out tears to God,	20	My friends scorn me; / my eyes pour out tears to God.
21	that he would maintain the right of a man with God, / like that of a man with his neighbor.	21	I want someone to plead with God for me, / as a man pleads for his friend.
22	For when a few years have come / I shall go the way whence I shall not return.	22	My years are passing now, / and I walk the road of no return.
17.1	My spirit is broken, my days are extinct, / the grave is ready for me.	17.1	The end of my life is near. I can hardly breathe; / there is nothing left for me but the grave.
2	Surely there are mockers about me, / and my eye dwells on their provocation.	2	I watch how bitterly everyone mocks me.

Subdivision Heading

Translators may wish to use the Handbook heading or modify it to say, for example, "Job says he has a witness in heaven" or "Job says, 'A witness in heaven will speak for me.'" Habel has (16.18–17.1) "Cry of hope amid despair," TOB (16.22–17.5) "Witness of the crime," Rowley (16.18–17.9) "Job's appeal to his witness in heaven."

16.18

RSV	TEV
"O earth, cover not my blood, / and let my cry find no resting place.	O Earth, don't hide the wrongs done to me! / Don't let my call for justice be silenced!

Verse 18 is a transition to the final section of chapter 16, in which Job appeals to his witness in heaven.

O earth, cover not my blood: Job is convinced that death is about to cut him off, and he calls on the earth to allow his blood to cry out to God for vindication. A similar thought is in Genesis 4.10, "Your brother's blood is crying out to me from the ground . . ." (TEV). As long as the blood is not covered over and hidden, it can cry out (Ezek 24.7). This verse can be compared with Isaiah 26.21b, "And the earth will disclose the blood shed upon her and will no more cover her slain." The form of the verb translated **cover** is causative, meaning "hide, conceal." TEV "Don't hide the wrongs done to me" is less compelling than the thought demands. Job sees himself as a murder victim whose blood is on the ground. In many languages it will be necessary to restructure this line. SPCL provides a good model: "This crime against me cries out for justice." In many languages in which "crime" and "earth" cannot be personalized, we may say, for example, "My blood has been shed; do not keep this secret," or "I am like a murdered man; this must not be concealed," or "I am like a man who has been murdered; don't anyone try to hide this crime."

And let my cry find no resting place is literally "Do not let a place be for my cry." RSV has supplied **resting** to qualify **place**. There are two traditions in the understanding of **place**. One refers to the place where a person stops to rest temporarily, such as to spend the night, and the other is a place to hide. The parallelism favors the latter as a secret place where someone goes to hide from whatever may be pursuing. It is the cry for justice or vindication which should not go away and be hidden and silenced in a secret place, but remain where its voice can be heard. This line may also have to be expressed differently, since a **cry** may not be said to seek a hiding place; for example, "do not forbid me from crying out," "do not let my cry for justice be silenced," "let no one try to silence my demand for justice," or "let me cry out and say, 'God should act fairly with me.' "

16.19   RSV   TEV

Even now, behold, my witness is   There is someone in heaven
    in heaven,   to stand up for me and take
  and he that vouches for me is   my side.
    on high.

Even now, behold, my witness is in heaven: Job does not name his **witness** as God, but many interpreters take it in that sense. **Even now** translates an expression meaning "right now, at this very time," referring to the present time while Job is suffering, and so "Right now while all this is happening to me." **Behold** calls special attention to what follows, but is often best left untranslated in English. Pope does not think **my witness** can refer to God, who is already seen by Job as accuser, judge, and executioner. Gordis sees no problem in Job's oriental logic, in which God can be seen as both judge and witness at the same time. The idea is that, while God has caused Job's suffering, Job still retains trust in the God of righteousness and love. Habel takes the position that the **witness** is a third party, a counterpart to the Satan of 2.3, a lawyer who can act to defend Job in the heavenly council. The interpretation of this verse is linked to 19.25. Taken as a whole it seems best to follow RSV and TEV and not identify **my witness** explicitly with God. The clause may also be expressed "there is someone in heaven who will testify in my favor," "somebody in heaven will stand up for me," or "a witness is in heaven who will speak for me and defend me."

And he that vouches for me is on high: this line repeats the previous line but substitutes an Aramaic word for "witness." In this context line b may be used as a parallel line to confirm what was said in line a, but which does not really go beyond line a; for example, "Yes, it is true that up there is one who will say I am right."

16.20	RSV	TEV

My friends scorn me;	My friends scorn me;
my eye pours out tears to God,	my eyes pour out tears to God.

My friends scorn me is literally "My scorners are my friends." The word translated **friends** is used in reference to Eliphaz, Bildad, and Zophar in 2.11; 32.5; 42.10. The word translated **scorn** has the meaning "mediator" in 33.23; Isaiah 43.27, and "interpreter" in Genesis 42.23. However, the usual meaning of the word is "scorn, ridicule, deride, mock," and it occurs with that meaning in Proverbs 3.34; Hosea 7.5; Psalm 119.51.

My eye pours out tears to God: although the singular is used in Hebrew, the reference is to "the eyes," as in TEV. Here Job says that he cries constantly. This line may need to be expressed differently in some languages to say, for example, "I look to God with tears in my eyes," "my eyes fill with tears as I plead for God's help," or "I cry to God to help me."

16.21	RSV	TEV

that he would maintain the right	I want someone to plead with
of a man with God,	God for me,
like^q that of a man with his	as a man pleads for his friend.
neighbor.	

^q Syr Vg Tg: Heb *and*

That he would maintain the right of a man with God: in 9.33 Job complained "There is no umpire between us" (RSV). Job's desire is that his witness be an "arbiter, umpire, mediator" between man (himself) and God. RSV **that he** links verse 21 to verse 19 by referring apparently to "my witness in heaven." **Maintain the right** translates the verb from which the noun "umpire" comes in 9.33. It means "reprove, argue, or reason," as in Isaiah 1.18. If the translator does not interpret the line to mean "that God would argue a man's case with God," he must, like RSV, refer to someone already mentioned; for example, "my witness in heaven," or, as in TEV, repeat an indefinite "someone." NEB says "If only there were one to arbitrate between man and God." FRCL makes the reference back to verse 19: "Oh! That my witness would arbitrate between God and me!" If the translator follows RSV or FRCL, linking this verse to verse 19, this line may be rendered "I want my witness to speak to God for me" or "I wish my witness would take up my case with God." If the one to plead on Job's behalf is understood to be someone else, TEV provides a good model for translating.

Like that of a man with his neighbor: the Hebrew text has the connective *waw* "and," and not "like." However, the ancient versions understood the connective to serve here as a comparison, and it is best to take it as in RSV, TEV. **Man** in this line translates the Hebrew "son of man," but this expression simply means "a man." Some scholars change the Hebrew word for "son" to "between" and understand the meaning to be "as between a man and his neighbor." The verb in this line must be supplied from the previous line. **Neighbor** translates the word for "friend" used in verse 20. In some languages the simile may have to be placed at the beginning of the verse; for example, "As a person pleads for his friend, I want someone to speak to God for me."

16.22   RSV   TEV

> For when a few years have come   My years are passing now,
>   I shall go the way whence I   and I walk the road of no re-
>   shall not return.   turn.

As indicated in the outline of chapters 16 and 17 (page 305), verse 22 opens the second of Job's complaints. This will be followed by a second plea in 17.3-5. Although the Handbook has not used a subdivision heading before 16.22, translators may prefer to do so. For example, a heading may say "Job sees his life ending" or "Job complains that he will soon die."

For when a few years have come I shall go the way whence I shall not return: this verse is best understood as Job expressing the shortness of time left for him to live. Job has spoken before of his approaching death in 10.21-22. **A few years** translates "years of number," meaning that the years are so few that they can be counted easily. The similar idiom "men of number" is used in Genesis 34.30; Psalm 105.12; Ezekiel 12.16. Here this is equivalent to "After a few short years . . . ."

Line b emphasizes the fact that Job will not be able to return from the dead. In 7.9-10 Job said "So he who goes down to Sheol does not come up. He returns no more to his house." In 10.21 Job said "Before I go whence I shall not return, to the land of gloom and deep darkness." The main clause of this verse is expressed metaphorically in TEV as "and I walk the road of no return." The verse may have to be restructured in some languages to say, for example, "After a few short years I will die and will not live again," "My days are numbered and I will go where people do not return," or sometimes idiomatically, "I am about to depart, and when I follow the path of death, I will not walk this way again."

17.1   RSV   TEV

> My spirit is broken, my days are   The end of my life is near. I can
>   extinct,   hardly breathe;

the grave is ready for me.   there is nothing left for me but
                                                        the grave.

Chapter 17 is a continuation of chapter 16, and 17.1-2 belongs to the theme
structure of the subdivision beginning at 16.22.

My spirit is broken: in Hebrew this verse has three lines, each line consisting
of two words. There are two major interpretations of line a, depending on the way
the Hebrew term *ruach* (**spirit**) is understood. It can mean "breath" as in 9.18, or
"wind" as in 15.30. It may also refer to a person's spirit as "life force, human
vitality," something akin to "strength," as in 10.12; 12.10a. TEV and others prefer to
take it in the sense of "breath"; that is, Job appears to be approaching death in great
pain, and so he says "I can hardly breathe." NJB has "My breathing is growing
weaker." Translators who understand **spirit** to mean "life force" or "the principle
that sustains life" tend to translate like RSV, **My spirit is broken**. This expression
in English, however, means something different than the translators intend. In
current English it means to lose the will or desire to go on living. A better translation
is "My strength is gone" or "I have no strength left." This is expressed idiomatically
in some languages as "My spirit has vanished" or "My innermost has laid down."

My days are extinct: **my days** refers to the days of Job's life, the time he has
lived, his years of life. **Extinct** translates a verb found in an Aramaic form in 18.5-6,
where it refers to a lamp being "put out." It occurs in that form in a number of
manuscripts in 6.17, where it refers to desert stream beds that are drying up. So for
Job the days of his life are coming to their end, vanishing, disappearing, or as TEV
says, "The end of my life is near." This may also be expressed, for example, "I am
about to die" or "My life is almost over."

The grave is ready for me is literally "graves for me," which expresses in
poetically compressed form the idea that the graveyard or death lies ahead. **Grave**
is plural in Hebrew, to suggest the place of tombs or graves, that is, the graveyard
or cemetery. This line may also be expressed "They have prepared my grave for me,"
"People have dug my grave," or "My grave is ready and waiting for me."

17.2   RSV   TEV

Surely there are mockers about   I watch how bitterly everyone
    me,   mocks me.
and my eye dwells on their
    provocation.

Surely there are mockers about me: according to Rowley **Surely** translates
a Hebrew phrase used in 31.36 which expresses an oath: "I swear that . . ." However,
no translation uses that expression. Dhorme understands it to make both clauses into
questions. Most translators, however, render both lines as statements. **Mockers are
about me** is a noun phrase which TEV expresses as a clause, "everyone mocks me,"
and this is clearer in English.

And my eye dwells on their provocation: this line is obscure in Hebrew, and
the various changes proposed do not improve it, according to Pope. Consequently

translators vary greatly in the way they express it. **Provocations** is modified by some to get "bitterly," and so TEV has "how bitterly everyone . . . ." The verb translated **dwells** means "rest, stay, pass the night," and suggests "keeping an eye on" or "watching closely." TEV reduces the two lines to one with "I watch how bitterly everyone mocks me." This is as good a model as translators will find. Verse 2 may also be expressed, for example, "Everywhere there are people who laugh at me, and I watch as they cruelly attack me."

4B-4. Job asks God to be his guarantor (17.3-5)

	RSV		TEV
3	"Lay down a pledge for me with thyself; who is there that will give surety for me?	3	I am being honest, God. Accept my word. There is no one else to support what I say.
4	Since thou hast closed their minds to understanding, therefore thou wilt not let them triumph.	4	You have closed their minds to reason; don't let them triumph over me now.
5	He who informs against his friends to get a share of their property, the eyes of his children will fail.	5	In the old proverb a man betrays his friends for money, and his children suffer for it.

In verses 3-5 Job switches from complaint to plea and asks God to serve as his guarantor, which means that God would be legally responsible for Job's freedom.

Subdivision Heading

Translators who wish to follow the outline of the Handbook may place a heading before verse 3. Other suggestions are "Job pleads with God," "Job asks for God's help," or "Job needs God to be responsible for him."

17.3

RSV	TEV
"Lay down a pledge for me with thyself; who is there that will give surety for me?	**I am being honest, God. Accept my word. There is no one else to support what I say.**

Lay down a pledge for me with thyself translates the Hebrew "lay down, pledge me." The language is that of the law court. Job appears now to address God and ask him to act as his guarantor. A guarantor is a friend or relative who provides bail money to obtain a prisoner's release and guarantee his good conduct. TEV does not keep the legal images. FRCL says "O God, bring me your own guarantee." GECL translates "God, do you provide bail? Be my surety." Other translation models are: "God, pay the price to have me released," "God, provide the money to free me from prison," or "Pay the price to set me free."

Who is there that will give surety for me? translates an idiomatic expression, "who will strike hands with me?" TEV translates this same expression in Proverbs 6.1;

17.18; 22.26, as "responsible for someone else's debts." This line is a question whose expected answer is "No one!" TEV translates the line as a negative statement: "There is no one else to support what I say." FRCL keeps the question: "Aside from you, who else would want to involve himself for me?" GECL also asks a question and substitutes a different metaphor: "Who else puts his hand in the fire for me?" Job's only hope depends on whether God himself will be willing to commit himself on Job's behalf. This line may also be expressed, for example, "Is there anyone else who will do this for me?" or as a statement, "Nobody else will speak on my behalf."

17.4

RSV	TEV
Since thou hast closed their minds to understanding, therefore thou wilt not let them triumph.	You have closed their minds to reason; don't let them triumph over me now.

Since thou hast closed their minds to understanding: in this line Job seems to say that God has hidden the truth from the friends. **Their minds,** in Hebrew "their hearts," does not actually say that the minds are the minds of the friends. Nevertheless, in this context it is best to assume it. FRCL has "You have removed all reason from my friends." They are not qualified to serve as Job's guarantor. **Understanding** has its seat in the "heart," and in Isaiah 44.18 the Hebrew for "heart" is the organ of mental activity, usually rendered "mind" in English. This line may also be rendered, for example, "You have shut their minds so they cannot think," "You have made my friends so they cannot understand," or "You have deadened my friends' minds and they cannot think."

Therefore thou wilt not let them triumph: therefore expresses the consequence of the previous line and can be translated "that is why, for that reason, due to that." TEV expresses the line as a plea, but this seems unnecessary. In Hebrew the verb translated **let . . . triumph** has no object, and so one is supplied by most translators. **Triumph** here has the sense of "conquer, win, be successful." The thought is the same as that of the psalmist who pleads that his enemies should not "triumph over him," Psalm 13.3-5; 30.2; 38.19; 41.11. The line may be rendered, for example, "stop them from defeating me" or "keep them from conquering me."

17.5

RSV	TEV
He who informs against his friends to get a share of their property, the eyes of his children will fail.	In the old proverb a man betrays his friends for money, and his children suffer for it.[i]

[i] a man . . . suffer for it; *or* a man entertains his friends while his children go hungry.

In verse 4 Job said that God would not allow his friends to triumph over him, and here he asserts that their betrayal of him will have its effect on their offspring. TEV has introduced verse 5 with "In the old proverb," which gives verse 5 a more logical connection with the previous verse. FRCL and GECL also refer to a proverb.

He who informs against his friends to get a share of their property is in the form and style of a proverb, which is TEV's reason for introducing the verse with "In the old proverb." Interpreters have found this verse confusing and open to many variations of meaning. The first part is literally "for a share he tells his friends," and the remainder says "and the eyes of his children fail." Jewish commentators understood the phrase translated **share of their property** (a single word in Hebrew) to mean "flattery," and so KJV has "He that speaketh flattery to his friends." **Informs** translates a word that usually means "tell," but here it is best taken as in RSV or as "denounce, betray." TEV has "betrays his friends for money," which is equivalent to RSV.

The eyes of his children will fail: the thought in this line is that the children of the traitor in the previous line will suffer for the evil act of their parent. The wording here is similar to 11.20: "But the eyes of the wicked will fail." RSV, which rearranged the Hebrew form of line a to obtain a good rendering, reverts to a literal translation here in line b. TEV "and his children suffer for it" is a suitable translation model.

The TEV footnote offers another rendering of verse 5. FRCL follows this interpretation: "They are like the man of whom the proverb speaks: inviting his friends to share his bread, he leaves his children to wait in vain for their part." Mft is similar: "Like one who bids friends to a feast, and lets his children starve." We may also translate, for example, "As the saying goes, share your food with your friends and let your children starve." However, translators will do well to follow RSV or TEV in line a, and TEV in line b.

4B-5. Job complains that people think he is godless (17.6-10)

RSV	TEV
6 "He has made me a byword of the peoples, and I am one before whom men spit.	6 And now people use this proverb against me; they come and spit in my face.
7 My eye has grown dim from grief, and all my members are like a shadow.	7 My grief has almost made me blind; my arms and legs are as thin as shadows.
8 Upright men are appalled at this, and the innocent stirs himself up against the godless.	8 Those who claim to be honest are shocked, and they all condemn me as godless.
9 Yet the righteous holds to his way, and he that has clean hands grows stronger and stronger.	9 Those who claim to be respectable are more and more convinced they are right.
10 But you, come on again, all of you, and I shall not find a wise man among you.	10 But if all of them came and stood before me, I would not find even one of them wise.

Subdivision Heading

In verses 6-10 Job continues his lament or complaint against people who are against him—indirectly meaning the friends. Other headings that may be used for these verses are, for instance, "Job complains against the friends," "Job's friends think they are right," or "Job refuses to consider his friends wise."

17.6 RSV TEV

"He has made me a byword of
  the peoples,
 and I am one before whom
  men spit.

And now people use this proverb
  against me;
 they come and spit in my face.

He has made me a byword of the peoples: Hebrew uses an impersonal construction "one has made me," which can be expressed as singular or plural. RSV has supplied **he**, and TEV "people." The Septuagint refers to God as the one who has made Job a **byword**: "You have made me . . . ." Dhorme takes it as the equivalent of a passive in English: "I have been made . . . ." NIV is more specific than RSV: "God has made me . . . ." The preferred solution is to consider the construction as intending to be impersonal, and use something like "they," "one," or "people." **Byword** translates a word meaning "proverb, parable, wise saying." In Psalm 44.14 and elsewhere it has the meaning of "object of contempt" (TEV "a joke among the nations"), or "laughingstock." In this line the reference is to Job as someone to be ridiculed, laughed at. TEV "people use this proverb" refers to the proverb in verse 5, which is not explicitly called a proverb in the Hebrew of verse 5. In some languages a special name is given to shaming songs which are sung to ridicule someone. The name for these songs is appropriate here. "He has made the people sing ridicule songs to me" or "He has made the people sing songs that make fun of me."

And I am one before whom men spit is literally "I am a spitting in the faces." RSV, which follows the ancient versions here, intends to give the meaning of being an object of contempt. Spitting in the face is a most serious insult (Deut 25.9; Isa 50.6; Mt 26.67). Job expresses this thought again in 30.10b. However, spitting in the face has different meanings in different cultures. In some places and contexts this gesture is used to confer a blessing from a father to his son. It is important in translation that the gesture, if used, means "to insult, reject, despise." If the gesture does not, it is better to use a nonfigurative expression, "they insult me" or "they despise me." It may be possible to retain the gesture and say "they spit on the ground in front of me to show their hatred" or "they spit at me because they reject me."

17.7 RSV TEV

My eye has grown dim from
  grief,

My grief has almost made me
  blind;

| and all my members are like a shadow. | my arms and legs are as thin as shadows. |

My eye has grown dim from grief: the verb translated **has grown dim** is used of failing eyesight in Genesis 27.1; Deuteronomy 34.7. **Grief** or sorrow is said to be the cause of Job's failing eyes. The line may also be expressed, for example, "My eyes have gotten dim because of my sadness," "My vision grows dark because I grieve," or "I can hardly see any more because my grief is so great."

And all my members are like a shadow: **members** refers to Job's limbs; TEV has "my arms and legs." They are compared to a **shadow** not because of their darkness but because of their thinness. In languages in which thinness of a person's limbs cannot be compared to a shadow, it may be necessary to modify this line to say, for example, "my arms and legs are thin as sticks" or "my limbs are so thin they hardly cast a shadow."

17.8   RSV   TEV

| Upright men are appalled at this, and the innocent stirs himself up against the godless. | Those who claim to be honest are shocked, and they all condemn me as godless. |

Some commentators believe verses 8, 9, and 10 are out of place here, since they seem to interrupt the flow of thought, and that verse 11 should stand in their place. Dhorme defends keeping these verses where they are, and most modern translators do that.

Upright men are appalled at this: **Upright men** translates a word meaning "the honest, the straight, the good" and is used in parallel with "the innocent" in 4.7. There are differences of opinion regarding who these **upright men** are. The two equally valid views are that they are good people anywhere who would be shocked at Job's conditions, or that Job is speaking sarcastically about the friends. SPCL takes the first view: "On seeing this, good people are amazed." It is the second view which TEV adopts when it says "Those who claim to be honest . . . ." FRCL and others follow TEV. **Appalled** translates a verb found also in Isaiah 52.14, where RSV has "astonished." In the present context the word has the meaning of "amazed, shocked, astonished, upset." We may translate with the general meaning of "uprightness"; for example, "When good people see how much I've suffered, they are shocked," "Good people see my condition and they are amazed," or, referring to Job's friends, we may translate "People who think they are sincere (honest) are amazed."

And the innocent stirs himself up against the godless: the two understandings of **upright men** in line a apply equally to the parallel **the innocent** in line b. Because the subject in both lines is expressed in words of similar meaning, TEV replaces **the innocent** with "they." **Stirs himself up** translates a verb meaning "to arouse, excite." The result can be pleasurable excitement as in 31.29, but in verse 8 it is more likely to mean displeasure, which FRCL translates as "indignant." TEV "condemns" is stronger than the text suggests. SPCL has "get angry." **The godless** refers to the wicked, or to the unbelievers, and is used in 8.13 "The hope of the godless man shall perish." The line may be translated "The innocent person is troubled, disturbed, annoyed, distressed by the one who does not trust God." There is little doubt that Job refers to himself as seen from the point of view of the friends, and TEV makes this clear with "They all condemn me as godless." This line may also be expressed, for example, "They become angry and say, 'He does not trust God.'"

17.9   RSV   TEV

> Yet the righteous holds to his   Those who claim to be respect-
>   way,   able
> and he that has clean hands   are more and more convinced
>   grows stronger and stronger.   they are right.

Yet the righteous holds to his way: TEV follows the same wording as in verse 8a, making **the righteous** an ironical reference to Job's friends: "Those who claim to be respectable." FRCL agrees basically with TEV: "Let the faithful persevere, they say." NEB and others understand the reference to be to the righteous in general who do not deviate from their chosen way: "In spite of all, the righteous man maintains his course." NJB avoids referring either to Job or to the friends, with "Anyone upright grows stronger step by step." **The righteous** is represented by the person mentioned frequently in the Psalms as one who keeps the law. He is one who is faithful in his relationship to God and to what God requires. Translators who have made verse 8 refer to Job's friends should continue to do so in verse 9, as in TEV and others. If, however, the "upright" and the "innocent" in verse 8 were interpreted to be general, then verse 9 will be understood in the same way. Both understandings are acceptable. Accordingly we may translate as in TEV, or say, for example, "And in spite of everything the good person will not fail," "However, the person who trusts God will keep on trusting him," or "Nevertheless, the person who follows God will not stumble."

And he that has clean hands grows stronger and stronger: in 11.14 Zophar warned Job "If iniquity is in your hand, put it far away." The man of **clean hands** is parallel to **the righteous** in line a. The removal of iniquity from the hands results in **clean hands,** which is to say the person is "upright, honest, good, respectable." **Grows stronger and stronger** translates the Hebrew "adds strength," which is moral, spiritual strength. In languages in which **clean hands** will have the sense of being upright, honest, and good, this line may be rendered, for example, "and the person who has clean hands becomes stronger," ". . . grows stronger day by day," ". . . becomes stronger all the time," or ". . . becomes stronger in his spirit."

17.10   RSV   TEV

> But you, come on again, all of   But if all of them came and stood
>   you,   before me,
> and I shall not find a wise man   I would not find even one of
>   among you.   them wise.

Job is not overwhelmed or discouraged by the attacks of the friends, and so he invites them now to repeat what they have said.

But you, come on again, all of you: some hold that verse 10 has little connection with the context, and that line a is too long and some of it should be eliminated; but there is no agreement on what should be removed to improve it. The Hebrew has "all of them" in line a, but switches to "you (plural)" in line b. However, this is not uncommon, and most translations are in agreement with RSV, which changes from third plural in verse 9 to second plural in verse 10 (TEV is exceptional). **Come on again** is literally "go back and turn again!" "Turn again" is used as in Proverbs 1.23, where it is rendered by RSV "Give heed." It is the teacher's challenge to the learner to examine a matter again for its deeper meaning. TEV expresses this command as an "if" clause: "But if all of them came and stood before me . . . ." This rendering restructures the Hebrew considerably but succeeds well in expressing Job's intention. This line may also be rendered, for example, "Come again and repeat what you have been saying," "Come on then, all of you, attack me again," or "Speak up all of you; let's hear your words again."

And I shall not find a wise man among you: in Job's mind a **wise man** would not be one as in 17.4, whose mind has been closed, who is appalled at his situation (17.8). He would be wise by showing sympathetic understanding of Job's plea to God to hear the argument of his innocence. By contrast the friends offer pious advice and attempt to show that Job is not innocent of wickedness. The line may also be expressed, for example, "I know I won't find one of you to be a wise man" or "I have listened, but will not find that one of you is wise."

4B-6. Job's only hope is to die (17.11-16)

	RSV		TEV
11	My days are past, my plans are broken off, the desires of my heart.	11	My days have passed; my plans have failed; my hope is gone.
12	They make night into day; 'the light,' they say, 'is near to the darkness.'	12	But my friends say night is daylight; they say that light is near, but I know I remain in darkness.
13	If I look for Sheol as my house, if I spread my couch in darkness,	13	My only hope is the world of the dead, where I will lie down to sleep in the dark.
14	if I say to the pit, 'You are my father,' and to the worm, 'My mother,' or 'My sister,'	14	I will call the grave my father, and the worms that eat me I will call my mother and my sisters.
15	where then is my hope? Who will see my hope?	15	Where is there any hope for me? Who sees any?
16	Will it go down to the bars of Sheol? Shall we descend together into the dust?"	16	Hope will not go with me when I go down to the world of the dead.

In verses 11-16 Job continues his complaint, but now he finds there is no way left for him but to die.

Subdivision Heading

The Handbook heading may be modified to say, for example, "Job's hopes have gone," "Job says 'My only hope is in the grave,' " or "Job says he will be in the grave and without hope." Rowley has "Job's anticipation of death as the end of his troubles."

17.11 RSV	TEV
My days are past, my plans are broken off, the desires of my heart.	My days have passed; my plans have failed; my hope is gone.

This verse has been analyzed by many scholars in order to get a satisfactory understanding of it. It is not clear how the Hebrew is to be divided into lines, and the two lines of RSV are just one way of looking at its structure. For the purpose of discussion we will refer to the three parts of the verse as lines a, b, and c.

My days are past: this line (a) is equivalent to verse 1 "my days are extinct." **My plans are broken off** makes sense as line b in parallel to line a, but this then leaves line c **the desires of my heart** dangling on the end without any connection to the rest of the verse. Dhorme thinks line c is not be tied in with line b, but that it is a suspended thought, an idea that the author does not wish to complete: "The desires of my heart are . . . ." TEV translates lines b and c independently by supplying a verb for line c: "My plans have failed; my hope is gone." FRCL uses the verb of line b to apply to both **plans** and **desires**: "The plans I have made and my most cherished desires have been reduced to nothing." HOTTP refers to BJ, which divides the verse after **my plans** and attaches the verb **are broken** to line c, as in the Septuagint. Furthermore, BJ adopts a Hebrew variant which gives "the strings of my heart" in place of the Masoretic text, "desires of my heart," which HOTTP rates as a "B" reading. Therefore NJB translates "My days have gone, along with my plans, and the strings of my heart are broken." This gives a good translation with limited change to the Hebrew text and is recommended to translators. The whole verse may also be rendered, for example, "The days I have to live are finished; my plans, too, have ended, and my heart is broken." The final clause is rendered idiomatically in many languages; for example, "my innermost has laid down," "my liver has fallen," or "my stomach has become silent."

17.12 RSV	TEV
They make night into day; 'the light,' they say, 'is near to the darkness.'[r] [r] Heb obscure	But my friends say night is daylight; they say that light is near, but I know I remain in darkness.

They make night into day: translators differ greatly on who or what makes night into day. TEV assumes that Job refers here to his friends ("My friends say

. . ."), and this is probably best. The idea is that the friends who pretend night is day would deceive Job into thinking in their confused manner. FRCL translates it well: "If I believe my friends, my night will be day." This is better than RSV **They,** which can refer only to elements of verse 11. NEB prefers to use a passive with no subject indicated, "Day is turned into night." The line may also be expressed "My friends say that night is day" or "My friends do not know night from day."

The light, they say, is near to the darkness: they say is supplied by RSV, making it refer to the friends. There are variants of this verse, but HOTTP regards the Hebrew text as an "A" reading and suggests translating both lines "They claim that night is the day and that light is near although I am confronted with darkness." This requires supplying "they claim," as in RSV **they say,** and "although I am" in line b. HOTTP's recommendation is essentially TEV's rendering and is recommended to translators. Verse 12 may also be rendered, for example, "When it is night, my friends claim it is daylight; when it is growing dark, they claim it is getting light."

17.13	RSV	TEV

RSV	TEV
If I look for Sheol as my house, if I spread my couch in dark- ness,	My only hope is the world of the dead, where I will lie down to sleep in the dark.

If I look for Sheol as my house: RSV begins verses 13-14 with **If,** and verse 15 is taken as a consequence stated in question form. TEV, on the other hand, uses a disguised negative statement ("My only hope . . .") in verse 13 and future statements in verse 14. FRCL begins verse 13 with a question: "What am I still waiting for? A place for myself in the world of the dead." This variety points out the range of different ways in which the same Hebrew construction can be translated. **Look for** translates a word meaning "hope for, expect, wait for," and so TEV has "My only hope is . . . ," and NJB "All I want, in fact, is to dwell in Sheol." Job expects **Sheol,** the place of the dead, to become his **house** (see 7.9). In many languages it will be better to avoid the repetitive use of "if" clauses in RSV and translate verses 13 and 14 as statements. This line may also be rendered, for example, "The only thing I can look forward to is death," "My only hope is to die and be buried," or "I still wait to live in the world of the dead."

If I spread my couch in darkness is a metaphor meaning to go to the place of the dead. The language used here concerning going to sleep is found also in Psalm 63.6; 132.3; 139.8. The word translated **spread** means "prop up or support" and refers to arranging the cushions on which one will lie down. **Couch** is the object for sleeping on, usually translated "bed." In some languages the metaphor in line b must be adjusted to say, for example, "and I will sleep there in the dark," "I will lie there in the dark," or "I will always be there in the darkness."

17.14   RSV   TEV

if I say to the pit, 'You are my   I will call the grave my father,
    father,'   and the worms that eat me
and to the worm, 'My mother,'   I will call my mother and my
    or 'My sister,'   sisters.

If I say to the pit, 'You are my father': RSV begins again with an "if" clause,
as do NIV and NEB. The word translated **pit** is rendered "corruption" by KJV, NIV; but
most scholars agree that this noun is derived from the verb meaning "to sink down"
and not from the verb "to ruin," so **pit** is better. The same word is used for the grave
or tomb in 33.18,22,24,28,30. **Pit** refers to the grave, and **worms** to those that eat the
dead body in the tomb.

And to the worm, 'My mother' or 'My sister': **worm** is singular, to be in
parallel with **pit**; however, the thought is of a mass of worms that will eat Job's
remaining flesh in the grave, not the worms that are already eating him. He will be
so familiar with them that he can address them as members of his family. In some
languages it will be necessary to express the verse in the form of a simile and say, for
example, "I will speak to the grave as if it were my father, and I will talk to the
worms as if they were my mother and sister." Other models are: "I will be so close
to the grave and the worms that eat me that I can call them my father, my mother,
and my sister," "I will say to the grave 'You, grave, are like a father to me,' and to
the worms I will say 'You, worms, are like a mother or sister to me.' " In languages
which must distinguish between younger and older sister, the appropriate term would
probably be the one that implies endearment.

17.15   RSV   TEV

where then is my hope?   Where is there any hope for me?
Who will see my hope?   Who sees any?

Where then is my hope? In RSV verse 15 is treated as a consequence of the
two preceding verses, which is preferred. The clear implication of the question is that
there is no hope. In languages in which **hope** must be expressed as a verb phrase,
it may be necessary to express this question differently; for example, "What is there
for me to hope for?" or "What do I have to look forward to?"

Who will see my hope? It is uncommon for a word to be in parallel with itself
in two consecutive lines. Because of this the ancient versions use a different word in
line b. For example, the Septuagint has "my good." NJB follows one Hebrew variant,
"any happiness," and NEB another, "my piety." TEV avoids the repetition of **hope** in
line b by asking "who sees any?" This line must often be expressed differently from
the RSV form to say, for example, "Does anyone see a future for me?" or "Does
anyone know?"

17.16   RSV   TEV

> Will it go down to the bars of
>   Sheol?
> Shall we descend together into
>   the dust?"

> Hope will not go with me[j]
>   when I go down to the world of
>   the dead.

> [j] *One ancient translation* with me; *He-*
> *brew unclear.*

Will it go down to the bars of Sheol: it translates a Hebrew form that is in the feminine plural, which, according to Dhorme, suggests that originally there were two different words for "hope" in verse 15. TEV is also singular, "Hope will not . . . ." **Bars of Sheol** is an uncertain translation. Some scholars take the expression to be a substitute for "gates of Sheol" as in Isaiah 38.10. The Septuagint has "with me to Sheol," which is the source of TEV's "Hope will not go with me." HOTTP recommends a change in the Hebrew vowel, giving the meaning "with me" or "beside me." In languages in which "Hope" must be expressed as a verb, TEV's rendering will require some adjustments; for example, "Will what I look forward to come to an end with me in the world of the dead?" or "Will all that I hope for disappear with me in the world of the dead?"

Shall we descend together into the dust: this translation follows the Septuagint. HOTTP suggests "Shall we not together go down to the dust?" This is based on a Hebrew vowel change and is close to the Septuagint meaning. **Dust** is parallel with **Sheol** and refers to the world of the dead. This line adds nothing new to the thought of the previous line and does not heighten the poetic intensity. However, in poetic translation which keeps the parallelism, **Sheol** and **dust** may be retained. In languages in which "hope" is a verb in verse 15, the use of **we** in verse 16 may make no sense. In that case it may be necessary to say, for example, "and I and all I looked forward to (or all I hoped for) will go down into the dust."

4C. BILDAD'S SECOND SPEECH (18.1-21)

Chapter 18 is the second speech of Bildad the Shuhite. His speech has two parts: verses 2-4 serve as an introduction, in which Bildad accuses Job of playing word games, treating the friends like dumb animals, and expecting the order of nature to change in order to suit Job. In verses 5-21 Bildad portrays the fate of the wicked through the use of a series of images.

The underlying thought of each of the friends is that suffering is the evidence of sin, and the logic of this doctrine forces them to conclude that Job is guilty of wrongdoing, an accusation which Job battles against tirelessly.

Division Heading
Translators may wish to translate the Handbook heading or follow the form used for the heading in Bildad's first speech in chapter 8 (division 3C). TOB has "The second poem of Bildad," FRCL "Bildad's speech: a trap for the wicked," GECL "The

second friend: Evil men are appointed to an evil end," and NJB "The inevitable fate of the wicked."

4C-1. Bildad scolds Job for his talk (18.1-4)

RSV	TEV
1 Then Bildad the Shuhite answered:	*Bildad*
2 "How long will you hunt for words? Consider, and then we will speak.	1-2 Job, can't people like you ever be quiet? If you stopped to listen, we could talk to you.
3 Why are we counted as cattle? Why are we stupid in your sight?	3 What makes you think we are as stupid as cattle?
4 You who tear yourself in your anger, shall the earth be forsaken for you, or the rock be removed out of its place?	4 You are only hurting yourself with your anger. Will the earth be deserted because you are angry? Will God move mountains to satisfy you?

Subdivision Heading

Translators may care to translate the Handbook heading or adapt it to say, for example, "Bildad tells Job to be quiet" or "Job, do you think we are stupid?" TOB has "Threat to the earth," Habel "Bildad on the world of the wicked," and Rowley "Why is Job so contemptuous?"

18.1   RSV   TEV

Then Bildad the Shuhite answered: *Bildad*

For comments on the name of Bildad the Shuhite, see 2.11.

18.2   RSV   TEV

**"How long will you hunt for words?
Consider, and then we will speak.**

**Job, can't people like you ever be quiet?
If you stopped to listen, we could talk to you.**

In characteristic fashion Bildad opens his speech with a question. **How long will you hunt for words?** is literally "How long will you (plural) set a trap for words?" In Bildad's first speech in chapter 8 he asked Job "Are you finally through with your wordy speech?" That appears to be the thrust of his opening question here. Bildad seems to be addressing Job, but the Hebrew verbs of verse 2 are in the plural. The Septuagint has singular verbs. Modern translations handle the problem of the plural address in three ways: RSV and others assume that Bildad is speaking to Job only and change to the singular like the Septuagint. TEV and others take the position that

Bildad is speaking to Job, not as an individual, but as a representative of a group, so TEV identifies Job and says "people like you." Another group of translations (FRCL, BJ, NJB, TOB) assume that Bildad is addressing the other two friends; for example, NJB "What prevents you others from saying something?" These translations take the view that **We will speak** in the second line refers to Bildad and his two friends, and so NJB has "Think—for it is our turn to speak!" TEV assumes that Bildad uses the first person plural in line b to mean Bildad and Job. The advantage of interpreting line a as Bildad addressing the other two friends is that no change is required in the Hebrew text. While it is not possible to insist on one view at the expense of the others, in verse 4 Job is clearly addressed, and the remainder of the chapter is intended for Job's ears, not for the other friends; therefore RSV and TEV are to be preferred.

Hunt in **hunt for words** translates a word some scholars say is derived from the Akkadian word for "trap." The word occurs nowhere else in the Old Testament. Some medieval Jewish interpreters understood the word to mean "end," and so NJV has "Put an end to talk!" This is the recommendation of HOTTP. Pope relates the word rendered **hunt** to an Arabic root of the same meaning and translates "How long will you set word snares?" Habel takes the expression to be the equivalent of "playing word games." It is possible that readers will interpret **hunt for words** as implying that Job is not fluent in his language. This is hardly the meaning. Consequently in many languages it will be necessary to say, for example, "When will you put a stop to your speeches?" "Will you go on talking forever?" or "When are you going to be silent?"

Consider, and then we will speak: **Consider** does not make good sense here, and the Hebrew verb it translates would be better rendered "Be sensible!" Dhorme suggests a change in one letter, which gives "Listen!" and this seems to be the basis for TEV "If you stopped to listen." NJB, which assumes Bildad is speaking to the other two friends, says "Think—for it is our turn to speak!" One of the alternative renderings in a footnote of FRCL is a good model for translators: "Come to your senses, and then we will talk." This line may also be expressed, for example, "If you would be reasonable, we could talk," "Stop to think for a while, and then we can speak together," or idiomatically, "Let your tongue rest so that we can speak together."

18.3   RSV   TEV

> Why are we counted as cattle?   What makes you think we are as
>   Why are we stupid in your   stupid as cattle?
>   sight?

Why are we counted as cattle? The reason for Bildad's question probably arises from Job having said in 12.7 "Ask the beasts and they will teach you." There Job declared that even dumb animals know as much as his friends. The two lines of this verse are parallel rhetorical questions which TEV reduces to one. The thought of the verse is echoed in Psalm 73.22: "I was stupid and ignorant, I was like a beast toward thee" (RSV). **Counted** does not refer to numbering but rather translates a verb meaning "consider, look upon, think of as": "Why do you think of us as animals?" **Cattle** translates a collective noun meaning animals in general, including wild and domestic animals as well as cows, but in the present context the reference is to a dumb beast symbolizing stupidity. **Cattle** is perhaps more specific than the context requires, unless the translator's language uses "cattle" in that rhetorical manner. So the question of this line is "Why do you consider us like beasts?" or "What makes you think of us as dumb animals?"

Why are we stupid in your sight? The meaning of the Hebrew word translated **stupid** is uncertain, and some interpreters connect it with a root meaning "to be unclean." HOTTP says the word may have either meaning, and GECL gives both meanings by adding a line: "Are we dumb as cattle, as he (Job) asserts? Is he of the opinion that we are unclean?" It is better to select one meaning and to place the other in a footnote, as in NJB. **In your sight** translates the Hebrew "in your (plural) eyes." HOTTP suggests that **in your sight** refers to the other two friends, and so Bildad is asking "Are we (all three of us friends of Job) stupid like animals in your (you two others') eyes?" or, Bildad addressing the two friends, "Friends, do you think we are stupid as cattle, as Job has said?" RSV **in your sight** implies "in Job's sight" but does not make it specifically so. FRCL follows HOTTP "Do you (plural) have the impression that we (all three friends of Job) are stupid?" In languages in which "we" and "us" must be either inclusive or exclusive, translators should use the form of **we** that means the speaker and others, but excludes Job, the one addressed. In some languages this may have to be expressed differently; for example, "Job, why do you think of us, who are your friends, as dumb animals? Why do you consider us stupid?"

It is also possible that Bildad addresses Job in the plural as a respectful or honorific way of speaking to him. In this case there is probably a strong note of irony, that is, meaning to be less than respectful. In that case we may translate "Job, do you, sir, really think we are stupid as cattle?" or "Job, your honor, . . . ?"

18.4	RSV	TEV
	You who tear yourself in your anger, shall the earth be forsaken for you, or the rock be removed out of its place?	You are only hurting yourself with your anger. Will the earth be deserted because you are angry? Will God move mountains to satisfy you?

You who tear yourself in your anger: this line translates the Hebrew "O tearer of himself in his anger." In 16.9 Job said God "has torn me in his wrath." However, Bildad says Job tears himself in his own anger. This line is the opening address of the two parallel lines which will follow. Here Bildad addresses Job in the third person singular in the Hebrew, but RSV and others translate with the second singular **You who . . . your anger**. According to Bildad it is Job's passion that carries him away and causes him injury. Although the line is translated in many ways, it is probably best to treat it as an address for the remainder of the chapter; for example, "Job, you injure yourself in your anger" or "Job, you get angry, and it is your anger that wounds you."

Shall the earth be forsaken for you? According to Bildad, Job thinks the very course of nature should be altered to suit him. Bildad has in mind that Job's complaints to God are like asking that the world be remade just to fit Job. According to the three friends the moral principle on which the world rests is that sin results in suffering. **Earth . . . forsaken** implies an earth whose inhabitants have abandoned it, gone away, all for Job's sake. This would be extreme chaos. This line and the next may be treated as sarcastic rhetorical questions; for example, "Do you think everyone must abandon the earth to prove you are right?" or "Do you believe the earth must become like a desert to show you are in the right?"

Or the rock be removed out of its place? In 14.18b Job laments that a man dies and disappears under the grinding force of God: "The rock is removed from its place." Bildad now picks up from this line to tell Job that such a thing does not take place just to satisfy Job. This line may also be translated, for example, "Do you think God must push over mountains to satisfy you?" or "Do you believe God must knock down the hills to make you happy?"

4C-2. How God punishes the wicked (18.5-21)

RSV	TEV

5   "Yea, the light of the wicked is put out,
    and the flame of his fire does not
    shine.
	5 The wicked man's light will still be put
	    out;
	    its flame will never burn again.

6 The light is dark in his tent, and his lamp above him is put out.	6 The lamp in his tent will be darkened.

7   His strong steps are shortened
    and his own schemes throw him down.
	7 His steps were firm, but now he stumbles;
	    he falls—a victim of his own advice.

8   For he is cast into a net by his own feet,
    and he walks on a pitfall.
	8 He walks into a net, and his feet are
	    caught;

9 A trap seizes him by the heel, a snare lays hold of him.	9 a trap catches his heels and holds him.

10 A rope is hid for him in the ground,
    a trap for him in the path.
	10 On the ground a snare is hidden;
	    a trap has been set in his path.

11 Terrors frighten him on every side,
    and chase him at his heels.
	11 All around him terror is waiting;
	    it follows him at every step.

12 His strength is hunger-bitten,
    and calamity is ready for his stumbling.
	12 He used to be rich, but now he goes
	    hungry;
	    disaster stands and waits at his side.

13 By disease his skin is consumed,
    the first-born of death consumes his
    limbs.
	13 A deadly disease spreads over his body
	    and causes his arms and legs to rot.

14 He is torn from the tent in which he
    trusted,
    and is brought to the king of terrors.
	14 He is torn from the tent where he lived
	    secure,
	    and is dragged off to face King Death.

15 In his tent dwells that which is none of
    his;
    brimstone is scattered upon his habita-
    tion.
	15 Now anyone may live in his tent—
	    after sulfur is sprinkled to disinfect it!

16 His roots dry up beneath,
    and his branches wither above.
	16 His roots and branches are withered and
	    dry.

17 His memory perishes from the earth,
    and he has no name in the street.
	17 His fame is ended at home and abroad;
	    no one remembers him any more.

18 He is thrust from light into darkness,
    and driven out of the world.
	18 He will be driven out of the land of the
	    living,
	    driven from light into darkness.

	19 He has no descendants, no survivors.
	20 From east to west, all who hear of his fate

19 He has no offspring or descendant among his people, and no survivor where he used to live.	shudder and tremble with fear.
	21 That is the fate of evil men, the fate of those who care nothing for God.
20 They of the west are appalled at his day, and horror seizes them of the east.	
21 Surely such are the dwellings of the ungodly, such is the place of him who knows not God."	

Bildad now portrays the fate of the wicked through the use of a series of images. In verses 5-6 the wicked are those without light, in verse 7 the darkness shortens his steps, in verses 8-10 the wicked is caught in a net, in verses 11-12 he is chased by fear, in verse 13 he is destroyed by disease, and in verses 14-15 he is marched off from his tent to death. Verses 16-21 present a picture of conditions after death. The wicked person dries up and withers away like a tree, no one remembers him, he is cast into darkness, and he has no offspring. Everyone is shocked by the thought of him. All of this happens to the wicked, which, by inference, means Job himself.

Subdivision Heading

Subdivision heading 4C-2 may be modified to say, for example, "This is what God does to the wicked," "Here is what will happen to wicked people," or "This is the way the wicked end." Rowley has "The fate of the wicked," TOB "Death of the wicked," and Habel "Plight and place of the wicked."

18.5-6 RSV	TEV
5 "Yea, the light of the wicked is put out, and the flame of his fire does not shine.	5 The wicked man's light will still be put out; its flame will never burn again.
6 The light is dark in his tent, and his lamp above him is put out.	6 The lamp in his tent will be darkened.

With verse 5 Bildad shifts his attention to the theme of the misfortunes of the wicked, which aims to impress on Job his need to confess his sins. Verses 5-6 have two parallel lines each, the images being light and darkness.

Yea, the light of the wicked is put out: see Proverbs 13.9; 24.20 for the same thought. **Yea** translates an adverb whose function is to affirm what follows as being in opposition to something said earlier, in this case the speeches of Job. It may be translated "In spite of your words" or "This is how it really is." NEB renders it "No." **Light** is a symbol of life and happiness (11.17). **Light . . . is put out** is a metaphor (see comments on "extinct" in 17.1) and means that death or disaster results. This line may also be expressed as a continuation of verse 4; for example, "Of course not. The wicked person comes to a bad end," "In spite of what you claim, the evil person is bound to die," or "No matter what you may think, death awaits all evil people." If it is possible in the translator's language to retain the life images of light and flame

337

in a meaningful manner, the poetry will no doubt be enhanced. This may mean expressing the line a bit differently; for example, "No, the light which is life in the wicked will go out" or "Certainly not, Job, the life of the wicked will go out like a light."

And the flame of his fire does not shine: flame is parallel with **light** of the previous line. Dhorme says the reference is not to "the flame of his hearth" (although FRCL and TOB take it this way), but it should be rendered **the flame of his fire**, as in RSV, symbolizing life and happiness as in line a. TEV and others render the verbs as future tense, whereas RSV and others use the present tense as a habitual condition. In some languages it may be necessary to express the line differently; for example, "and he will grow cold like a fire that has died" or "and he will be like a fire that burns no more."

The light is dark in his tent: this implies a process suggesting that the light in his house or dwelling will also go out, leaving his place in darkness. This line may have to be expressed, for example, "He will be like a light that no longer shines in his house," "He will be like a house where the light no longer shines," or "He will be like a darkened tent whose light has gone out."

And his lamp above him is put out may mean the lamp hanging from the roof of his tent (so Rowley), but it may also mean "beside him," as in NIV "The lamp beside him goes out." Here the meaning is taken best as in RSV, in which the lamp is elevated, probably placed on a stand as in Matthew 5.15. This line may be rendered, for example, "and the lamp that shone above him has gone out" or "and the lamp above his head is now dark."

18.7	RSV	TEV
	His strong steps are shortened and his own schemes throw him down.	His steps were firm, but now he stumbles; he falls—a victim of his own advice.

His strong steps are shortened: the wicked man is portrayed as taking short steps compared to the long confident strides he took before. TEV shows this process: "His steps were firm, but now . . . ." **Strong steps** translates "steps of his vigor" and refers to his confident way of walking. FRCL says "His confident gait will become hesitant," which reflects the Hebrew better than TEV "stumbles." SPCL has "His firm step will lose its strength." This line may also be rendered, for example, "He no longer walks with confidence" or "He now takes short steps in order not to stumble."

And his own schemes throw him down: schemes translates a word meaning "counsel, advice" in the positive sense, and is different from the word Job used in 17.11: "My plans are broken off." **Throw him down** is rendered by the Septuagint as "cause him to stumble," which is preferred by many. TEV uses "stumbles" in the first line and "falls" as completing the process here. "Victim of his own advice" expresses the idea well. The line may also be rendered, for example, "the advice he gives to others causes him to fall," "the words he gives to others make him stumble," or "what he tells others to do makes him fail in his own plans."

18.8-10 RSV TEV

	RSV		TEV
8	For he is cast into a net by his own feet, and he walks on a pitfall.	8	He walks into a net, and his feet are caught;
9	A trap seizes him by the heel, a snare lays hold of him.	9	a trap catches his heels and holds him.
10	A rope is hid for him in the ground, a trap for him in the path.	10	On the ground a snare is hidden; a trap has been set in his path.

These three verses may be taken together, since they use similar images to express Bildad's belief that the wicked cannot escape the disaster that is about to fall on them. In verses 5-6 there was a four-fold parallelism relating to light; in verses 8-10 there is a six-fold repetition of a single theme using six different words for various kinds of traps. TEV expresses verses 8 and 9 in one line each and uses three words for trap: "net, trap, snare." RSV uses five terms, and NEB six.

For he is cast into a net by his own feet: the word translated **net** refers to a large net capable of catching a person. It is used in Psalm 9.16; 25.15: "The wicked are snared in the work of their hands," and ". . . he will pluck my feet out of the net." **By his own feet** means that "his walk, his manner of living" leads him to the net. In languages which have a variety of traps for catching animals and birds, terms for these may be used, provided they are not too technical to be known by most readers. In languages in which no traps are known, considerable adjustments will be required. This line may also be rendered, for example, "His own feet cause him to fall into a net" or "His own feet carry him to a trap which catches him." If no such net or trap is known, we may say, for example, "His way of living causes him to fall" or "The evil he does causes him to stumble."

And he walks on a pitfall: the word translated **pitfall** suggests a covering of interwoven materials. Branches are woven lightly together and placed over a deep hole into which the victim falls when he walks over it. TEV reduces the two lines of verse 8 to one, and translators may also find this line redundant. In languages in which **pitfalls** are known, it may be necessary to say, for example, "he steps on a pitfall and falls in" or "he is caught when he walks across a pitfall."

A trap seizes him by the heel: trap translates a word which designates a bird snare in Hosea 9.8, where RSV calls it "fowler's snare." The nature of this trap is not entirely clear, but it seems to have been operated by a spring mechanism that trapped the bird's foot.

A snare lays hold of him: here again the translated word refers to some kind of woven material or mesh, but the nature of the snare and its use are not known. A general term for trap can be used, if there is such in the translator's language. The poetic device used by the poet is the progressive use of the smaller trap, which has the effect of focusing on the details in verses 9 and 10. **Heel** is probably used as a part of the foot standing for the whole foot. Since it may not be clear how one is trapped by the **heel**, it may be better to reduce the two lines to one and say, for example, "A trap catches him by the foot" or "He steps on a trap and it takes hold of his foot."

A rope is hid for him in the ground: rope here most likely refers to a hidden noose that is attached at the other end to a bent bough or small tree which springs upright and tightens the noose around the victim when the trap is sprung. For similar thoughts see Psalm 140.5; 142.3b.

A trap for him in the path: this line states that the noose would be placed in the path where he would walk and step on it. The word translated **trap** occurs only here in the Old Testament. It is derived from the verb meaning "to trap or catch animals" and so is a general term. Verse 10 may be rendered, for example, "The noose of a rope is hidden in his path." If the picture is not clear, it will often be sufficient to say, for example, "In the path where he walks, a trap is set for him," or in languages which avoid the passive, "Someone has set a trap for him on the path where he walks."

18.11   RSV   TEV

> Terrors frighten him on every   All around him terror is waiting;
>   side,   it follows him at every step.
>   and chase him at his heels.

Terrors frighten him on every side: Bildad does not specify the nature of these **terrors**. Pope takes them to be demons, and Dhorme suggests they are the fears of the guilty soul. In 15.21 Eliphaz spoke of "terrifying sounds" being in the ears of the wicked. The line may also be expressed "Things that cause him terror are around him" or "Frightening things are about him."

And chase him at his heels: whatever the nature of the **terrors**, they are now portrayed as animate creatures in hot pursuit of the wicked. The wicked person is unable to escape the hounding of his fears. The verb translated **chase** usually means "scatter," but this is unsuitable when one person is the object. Some scholars suggest changing the line to say "and compel him to make water over his feet," which NEB translates more graphically "and make him piss over his feet." The Hebrew text is clear as it stands without making changes. The line may be rendered, for example, "and these things run after him to catch him," "these frightening things are close to his heels chasing him," or ". . . chase him biting at his heels."

18.12   RSV   TEV

> His strength is hunger-bitten,   He used to be rich, but now he
>   and calamity is ready for his   goes hungry;
>   stumbling.   disaster stands and waits at
>   his side.

His strength is hunger-bitten is literally "His strength is hungry," but this figure of speech makes little sense in English, and RSV **hunger-bitten** makes even less sense. The word translated **strength** can also mean "wealth," and so TEV "He used to be rich." It may also mean "calamity," as in NIV "Calamity is hungry for him." It is not possible from the Hebrew to tell which is the better meaning here.

The subject **calamity** in the parallel line **b** makes **strength** the logical subject in line a. HOTTP prefers to understand the text to be "His strength is famished," which can be translated "Hunger robs him of his strength" or "He is hungry and so has no strength."

And calamity is ready for his stumbling: translators are divided between those who derive the word translated **stumbling** from a root meaning "to limp" and those who relate it to a word for "rib." RSV belongs to the first, and "Disaster stands and waits at his side" in TEV belongs to the second. TEV is preferred because it relates verse 12 more closely to verse 11. In some languages it will not be possible to speak of **calamity** or "disaster" as if they are persons. In these cases this line must be restructured to say, for example, "He stumbles into dangerous places," "He can never avoid suffering," or "Suffering is like his closest friend."

18.13 RSV	TEV
By disease his skin is consumed,[s] the first-born of death con- sumes his limbs.	A deadly disease spreads over his body and causes his arms and legs to rot.

[s] Cn: Heb *it consumes the limbs of his skin*

By disease his skin is consumed: the RSV footnote gives the literal Hebrew, "it consumes the limbs of his skin." RSV modifies the Hebrew text by changing several vowels and one consonant. This modification is followed by NEB and NJB. The ancient versions are in total disagreement among themselves: the Septuagint has "Let the branches of his feet be eaten," Syriac "His cities will be swallowed up by force," Vulgate "Let it devour the beauty of his skin," Targum "It will devour the linen garments which cover his skin." HOTTP evaluates "it consumes" as a "B" reading and "the limbs of his skin" as a "C" reading, and proposes three interpretations: (1) "He (death's first-born son from line **b**) consumes his limbs"; (2) "It (calamity from verse 12) consumes the members of his body"; and (3) "It or he consumes the skin of his limbs" (meaning either calamity from verse 12 or death's first-born from line **b**). From all of this it can be seen how the Hebrew verb does not indicate which is the subject or the object. As a result interpreters are forced to try out the possibilities and select something that fits the context. Both RSV and TEV follow the second suggestion of HOTTP and take the subject of line a to be **disease**, based on "calamity" or "disaster" in verse 12. Here TEV translates the word for **skin** as "body," and this is more satisfactory than **skin**, which can be interpreted as a part representing the whole.

The first-born of death consumes his limbs: in the light of the discussion above, this line is fairly clear. Nevertheless, great differences of opinion center on the interpretation of **the first-born of death**. However, Bildad is speaking to a man whose body is racked with disease and pain, and in this context **first-born of death** is best understood as parallel with **disease** in line a, but going beyond disease to terrible death. TEV expresses the image of **first-born of death** as "deadly disease" and makes it serve as the subject of both lines; this provides an adequate model for translators. Verse 13 may also be rendered, for example, "A disease causes his body to decay, and a deadly illness eats his limbs," "He is destroyed by disease, and his arms and legs are eaten by death," or "Sickness gnaws like a rat at his skin, and a deadly disease eats away his arms and legs."

18.14-15   RSV   TEV

	RSV		TEV
14	He is torn from the tent in which he trusted, and is brought to the king of terrors.	14	He is torn from the tent where he lived secure, and is dragged off to face King Death.
15	In his tent dwells that which is none of his; brimstone is scattered upon his habitation.	15	Now anyone may live in his tent—[k] after sulfur is sprinkled to disinfect it![l]

[k] Now anyone may live in his tent; *Hebrew unclear.*
[l] TO DISINFECT IT: *Sulfur was used in the ancient world as a disinfectant and to clean rooms that had contained corpses.*

He is torn from the tent in which he trusted: KJV takes **trusted** to be the subject "His confidence shall be rooted out of his tabernacle," but in verse 15 it is the wicked person who no longer inhabits his tent. Accordingly the wicked man should also be the subject of 14a, and **trusted** refers to his attitude toward his tent, as in RSV and TEV. **Torn from** translates a verb used of pulling up tent pegs and cords. In languages in which an active construction is required, the logical actor in this context is death, which is again personified. This line may be rendered, for example, "Death takes him away from the security of his home" or "Death pulls him away from his house where he has been safe." If death cannot be the actor in the receptor language, it may be necessary to employ a simile; for example, "Death takes him away from the safe home as people carry a dead man to his grave" or, keeping more of the imagery, we may say "As one pulls up tent pegs, death takes his life."

And is brought to the king of terrors: the subject of the verb **brought** may be understood as second singular, "you (singular) will bring him," or third singular, "it (or, he) will bring him." RSV follows a slight change in the text which gives third plural and which may be read as a passive, **is brought**, or as TEV, "is dragged off." The verb itself has a causative meaning, "to lead someone, to march someone off." NIV says "marched off to the king of terrors." **King of terrors** is found nowhere else in the Bible. Pope takes this title to refer to the Ugaritic god of death, *Mot.* Psalm 49.14 says "Like sheep they are appointed for Sheol; Death shall be their shepherd"; and "shepherd" is a royal title. The preferred rendering of **king of terrors** would be "King Death" as in TEV. The line may also be rendered, for example, "They bring him to the one who rules over the dead" or "They make him march away to the chief of those who have died."

In his tent dwells that which is none of his: RSV gives a meaningless translation for a line which is not entirely clear in the Hebrew. Numerous suggestions have been made to change the text. Pope accepts that of Dahood, based on the similarity of the Hebrew word used here to the Akkadian and Ugaritic words for "fire." NIV follows Dahood and translates "Fire resides in his tent." SPCL has "His house is set on fire." TEV "Now anyone may live in his tent," also recommended by HOTTP, is based on the view that, since the tent no longer belongs to its previous owner, it is empty and anyone may occupy it. Therefore we may translate the Hebrew "They live in his tent which is no longer his." If the translator follows TEV, this line may also be expressed "Anyone who wishes may move into his house" or "Anyone can occupy the house he has left behind."

Brimstone is scattered upon his habitation: **brimstone** is a poetic word for "sulfur," a substance which burns to produce an acid gas. It is associated in Genesis 19.24 and Revelation 14.10 with divine judgment. As the TEV footnote explains, sulfur was used to disinfect rooms, particularly where corpses had laid. TEV has made explicit in the text "to disinfect it." There are other reasons for the use of sulfur, such as to rid a place of evil spirits or to make the ground sterile. GECL has a note on sulfur which says "By scattering sulfur the land is symbolically cleansed or a curse is expelled." In most translations this line will remain unclear unless further information is supplied, either in the text or in a note, and in some cases in both. In languages in which sulfur is unknown, one may translate, for example, "yellow stones called sulfur" or "yellow rocks that burn, called sulfur." It is recommended that translators follow TEV, which may also be expressed, for example, "they sprinkle sulfur on his house to remove the disease."

18.16	RSV	TEV

	His roots dry up beneath,
	    and his branches wither above.
		His roots and branches are with-
		    ered and dry.

His roots dry up beneath: for similar figures of roots and branches, see 8.16-19; 14.7-9. RSV translates all the redundancy of the Hebrew, but TEV does not state the obvious, that **roots** are **beneath** and that **branches** are **above**. TEV also reduces the two parallel lines to one. For similar use of set expressions, see Amos 2.9, "fruit above and roots beneath."

And his branches wither above. It is possible that the images here refer to ancestors and descendants, as in Isaiah 11.1,10. See also Judges 5.14 (RSV note "From Ephraim their root"); Isaiah 14.29. However, this thought comes out clearly in the progression leading up to verse 19. It is best therefore to translate the comparison of Job to the tree in verse 16; for example, "He becomes like a tree which is decaying from the roots in the ground to the branches up high."

18.17	RSV	TEV

	His memory perishes from the
	    earth,
		His fame is ended at home and
		    abroad;

and he has no name in the
    street.

no one remembers him any
    more.

His memory perishes from the earth refers to the memory people had of
him, or as TEV says, "his fame." **Earth** is here in parallel with the word translated
street in the next line. **Street** translates Hebrew word which refers to the area
outside or beyond; thus **street** is a satisfactory rendering when the word is used in
relation to a house. However, in this verse the word refers to the area that lies
outside or beyond a city or inhabited area. The two terms taken together are used
to give a picture of the totality of space. **Earth** refers here to the inhabited, cultivated
area, and the word translated **street** to the remaining areas, which are best described
in English as wilderness or uninhabited areas. The two are used in parallel to express
"the whole world, everywhere," or as TEV says, "at home and abroad." In 5.10 the
same words are translated "earth and fields." The line may also be expressed
"Nobody on earth remembers him" or "He is forgotten by everyone on earth."

And he has no name in the street: for the meaning of **street** see the
previous paragraph. Having **no name** is equivalent to not being remembered. It
serves to give some poetic heightening to this line. Verse 17 may be rendered, for
example, "Nobody anywhere remembers him, and he has been forgotten by all" or
"Everyone in the world has forgotten him; no one at all remembers who he was."

18.18   RSV   TEV

He is thrust from light into dark-
    ness,
    and driven out of the world.

He will be driven out of the land
    of the living,
    driven from light into dark-
    ness.

He is thrust from light into darkness translates the impersonal "they push
him . . . ." It is not said who **thrusts** him. Some interpreters suggest changing the
Hebrew to "He shall thrust him," in which the subject is God and the object is the
wicked person. Dhorme objects to making God the subject, on the basis that God has
not been mentioned in the chapter. However, this is hardly reason enough. The
subject is far more likely to be God than people, and in languages which do not use
an impersonal subject or a passive construction, it will be best to say "God thrusts
him out . . . ." **Light** and **darkness** are here contrasting images of life and death. In
17.13 darkness is the symbol of Sheol.

And driven out of the world: the world here does not mean the physical
earth, but the line speaks of being driven from the place where people live into
Sheol, the place of the dead; that is, from the place of the living or "land of the
living" (TEV, NEB). In languages which do not use a passive, it will be necessary to
adjust the line to say, for example, "God will drive him from life into the darkness
of death" or "God will push him out from the living people and make him go to the
dark land of the dead."

18.19   RSV   TEV

He has no offspring or descen-   He has no descendants, no survi-
   dant among his people,   vors.
and no survivor where he used
   to live.

He has no offspring or descendant among his people: verse 19 provides
the explanation of verses 16 and 17. The wicked person's roots dry up in verse 16,
and he is forgotten in verse 17, because he has no **offspring or descendant**.
Offspring or descendant translates a Hebrew fixed pair of terms, "son or
kinsman," which Gordis tries to parallel in English with "neither kith nor kin."

And no survivor where he used to live: that is, "in his dwelling." Some
interpreters take this to mean "in his home." However, his home has been destroyed.
Other suggestions do not throw significant light on the phrase, and TEV considers it
redundant and so does not translate it. FRCL sees it as placing emphasis upon the
lack of members of his family to live on after him, and translates "Of all his
household no one will survive." GECL translates verse 19 "No son or grandson to
carry on the family, and from his household not one survivor." Other translatable
models are: "He leaves behind no children or other offspring, and where he used to
live there are no survivors" or "He is without offspring, and no one has survived in
the house where he once lived."

18.20   RSV   TEV

They of the west are appalled at   From east to west, all who hear
   his day,   of his fate
and horror seizes them of the   shudder and tremble with fear.
   east.

They of the west are appalled at his day: some translators have understood
this line (and the next line) as referring to time, because the Hebrew says "Those
after him and those before him." KJV translates "They that come after . . . as they
that went before." Gordis suggests "later generations . . . earlier generations."
However, the author is speaking about the fate of the wicked person, and people
who lived before him in time could not know of his fate, nor could future generations
know, since the wicked man is cut off without any future. A better interpretation is
that Bildad is speaking about the wicked man's contemporaries. Bildad and Job's
space orientation would come from facing the rising sun. The east would then be
"before," and the west would be the direction which was "behind" or "after." He
therefore divides people into two directions, those in the east and those in the west.
TEV "from east to west" is more idiomatic for English than RSV. **Appalled** translates
a word meaning "stupefied." It is used in Jeremiah 4.9, where TEV translates it
"shocked." **His day** refers to the day of the ruin or death of the wicked person, his
fate, the time when he receives his just reward. For him it is a day of doom and
destruction.

And horror seizes them of the east: there is no intended difference in the reactions of the people in the east from those in the west. The two lines have essentially the same meaning, and together they cover all people everywhere. In some languages it is necessary to express verse 20 differently; for example, "Everyone who lives where the sun goes down and those who live where the sun rises will be shocked to learn what a bad end he suffered" or "All the people upriver and those downriver will be amazed at his ruin and death."

18.21 RSV	TEV
Surely such are the dwellings of the ungodly, such is the place of him who knows not God."	That is the fate of evil men, the fate of those who care nothing for God.

Surely such are the dwellings of the ungodly: in verse 21 Bildad intends to assure Job that the teaching which Bildad has delivered, that wickedness brings doom and destruction, is a reliable teaching. **Surely** translates a different expression than that used in 17.2. Here it serves to express certainty, as in "certainly, yes, no doubt about it, for sure." Bildad speaks of the **dwellings of the ungodly**, which will appear again in 21.28. **Dwellings** is parallel to **place** in the next line. Bildad is referring to the wicked person, not just to the place where he lives, and so TEV "This is the fate of evil men." NJV, FRCL, and TOB understand verse 21 to be a quotation, the opinion expressed by the appalled people from east and west in verse 20.

Such is the place of him who knows not God: in 8.13 Bildad spoke of these as people "who forget God." The expression does not refer to not being acquainted with God or not knowing about him, but rather, as TEV and NEB say, "who care nothing for God." The meaning is as in Amos 3.2, when God says to Israel, "You only have I known" (RSV), "you are the only one I have known and cared for" (TEV). Verse 21 may also be rendered, for example, "For certain, the wicked person is doomed in this way, and all those who have no reverence for God" or "Certainly evil people are punished like that, and the same happens to all who do not trust God."

Bildad ends his speech with no appeal to Job to repent. In Bildad's view God belongs to the realm of light, and by implication Job is destined for the realm of darkness, which is death.

4D. JOB REPLIES (19.1-29)

In chapter 19 Job replies to Bildad. His speech may be divided into four or five sections. Following a sharp rebuke handed to the friends (verses 2-6), Job opens a major complaint against God, who is portrayed as an attacking enemy army (verses 7-12). In verses 13-22 Job complains that his relatives, servants, and friends have all deserted him. In verses 23-27 Job's attitude suddenly changes from despair to hope. Picking up the theme of a witness in heaven from 16.19, Job believes that a defender will step forward and uphold his claim to innocence. Finally in verses 28-29 Job addresses the friends and warns them that they are in danger of being judged by God.

Division Heading

Chapter 19 is again the speech of Job. Translators may wish to show this clearly for their readers by using a heading like the Handbook, or adapt it to say, for instance, "Job's speech to Bildad" or "Job argues back." TOB has "Sixth poem of Job." Some versions combine a division and subdivision heading; for example, FRCL "Job's reply: In the end my defender will intervene," GECL "Job: God does me an injustice."

4D-1. Job accuses the friends of being arrogant (19.1-6)

RSV	TEV
1 Then Job answered:	*Job*
2 "How long will you torment me, and break me in pieces with words?	1-2 Why do you keep tormenting me with words?
3 These ten times you have cast reproach upon me; are you not ashamed to wrong me?	3 Time after time you insult me and show no shame for the way you abuse me.
4 And even if it be true that I have erred, my error remains with myself.	4 Even if I have done wrong, how does that hurt you?
5 If indeed you magnify yourselves against me, and make my humiliation an argument against me,	5 You think you are better than I am, and regard my troubles as proof of my guilt.
6 know then that God has put me in the wrong, and closed his net about me.	6 Can't you see it is God who has done this? He has set a trap to catch me.

Subdivision Heading

Translators may use the Handbook heading or adapt it by saying, for example, "Job says his friends insult him," "Job asks, 'Why do you insult me?' " or "You think my troubles show I am guilty." Rowley has "Job's impatience with his friends."

19.1   RSV   TEV

Then Job answered: *Job*

Then Job answered: see 4.1.

19.2   RSV   TEV

"How long will you torment me, and break me in pieces with words?   **Why do you keep tormenting me with words?**

How long will you torment me . . . ? How long is the question with which Bildad began both his speeches in 8.2 and 18.2. Since the verbs are in the plural, it is clear that Job is throwing Bildad's questions back at him and the friends. **Torment**

me translates "torment my soul (*nefesh*)," which Dhorme renders "distress my soul." Job is not attempting to separate his soul from his person, and it is better to translate **me** as in RSV and TEV.

And break me in pieces with words? The verb translated **break in pieces** is used in 4.19; 6.9 and translated "crushed" by RSV and TEV. Here Job is emotionally crushed by the words of his friends. Their crushing words do not lead him to have sorrow for his sin; on the contrary, they only increase his pain. God is responsible for Job's physical torments. The **torment** he speaks of is mental. Verse 2 may also be expressed, for example, "How long will you make me suffer anguish and crush me with your long speeches?" or "Will you never stop making me pained in my heart and wounding me with your sharp words?"

19.3   RSV   TEV

> These ten times you have cast   Time after time you insult me
>   reproach upon me;   and show no shame for the
>   are you not ashamed to wrong   way you abuse me.
>   me?

These ten times you have cast reproach upon me: ten times is not to be taken literally, but rather as a round number, as in Genesis 31.7; Numbers 14.22. NEB has "time and time again," GECL "already too many times," SPCL "over and over." **Cast reproach** translates a verb meaning "to shame, outrage, insult." This line may also be rendered, for example, "Over and over you insult me," "You repeat the same insults again and again," or idiomatically in some languages, "You pile up insults higher and higher on my head."

Are you not ashamed to wrong me? The word translated **ashamed** is not the same word used in line a but the word that was used in 6.20 and rendered "confounded" by RSV. The word translated **wrong** is found nowhere else in the Old Testament. Scholars have proposed numerous changes to get a more certain sense. In some Hebrew manuscripts the initial consonant is replaced by another consonant that looks similar, and Dhorme takes the variation in spelling to represent a variant pronunciation that does not affect the meaning. The NEB footnote implies that there are two different verbs, one as in RSV **wrong me** and the other meaning "others are astonished at me." NJB has "maltreating me," SPCL "Aren't you ashamed for treating me like this?" This provides a good model for translation. The line may also be expressed "Aren't you ashamed for making me suffer from your speeches?" or "You should be ashamed to make me suffer this way."

19.4   RSV   TEV

> And even if it be true that I have   Even if I have done wrong,
>   erred,   how does that hurt you?
>   my error remains with myself.

And even if it be true that I have erred: this line appears clear enough by itself, but it cannot be considered without regard to the second line, where scholars differ greatly in their interpretations. In this first line Job is not likely to be admitting that he has sinned, because elsewhere he has repeatedly defended his innocence (9.21; 10.7; 16.17). Some scholars understand that Job is using sarcasm and attacking his friends. If he had erred it was between him and God, not a matter for their eyes. His argument is with God. Dhorme and others also take the view that any error Job may have committed is strictly his own business. Rowley, on the other hand, thinks that Job is striking back at the friends, not because they pry into his affairs, but because of their hostility toward him.

My error remains with myself: in this line Job is saying "I have not injured you," or as TEV translates, "How does that hurt you?" Pope takes the view that if Job sinned, the fault lies with God. It is not possible to exclude these varying interpretations; however, all the modern translations consulted take the view of Dhorme that Job's error, if he ever had such, is his own business and does not concern the friends. Verse 4 may be rendered, for example, "Even if I sinned, that has nothing to do with you," "If it is true that I have done wrong, how does that affect you?" or "If I have sinned, that would hurt me, not you."

19.5-6	RSV		TEV
5	If indeed you magnify yourselves against me, and make my humiliation an argument against me,	5	You think you are better than I am, and regard my troubles as proof of my guilt.
6	know then that God has put me in the wrong, and closed his net about me.	6	Can't you see it is God who has done this? He has set a trap to catch me.

Translators vary greatly as to the form of the two lines in verse 5. Some translate them as questions, some as conditions, and some as statements. RSV and others translate verse 5 as two conditions and verse 6 as their consequence.

If indeed you magnify yourselves against me: **magnify yourselves** translates the Hebrew literally, but when the object is a person, the expression means "to appear superior, to look down on someone." For similar usages see Psalm 35.26; 38.16. NEB translates "You lord it over me," and TEV "You think you are better . . . ." The line may also be expressed in some languages, for example, "If you (plural) think you are great and I am small" or "If you think you are chiefs and I am a slave."

And make my humiliation an argument against me: the verb in this line, **make . . . an argument,** is the same as used in 5.17 with the sense of "reproach, rebuke." In 16.21 it has the meaning of "argue, reason, reprove." Job's friends use his humiliation as an argument to prove him guilty of sin, or as TEV says, "(You) regard my troubles as proof of my guilt." The word translated **humiliation** means "shame, disgrace" as in 16.10, "insolently." The same noun is used in 1 Samuel 25.39, "insult," and in 2 Samuel 13.13, where it refers to the shame accompanying a crime. Job's friends have always looked upon Job's misery as the effect of his sin, while in reality the cause is God, as Job argues. The line may continue as an "if" clause; for example, "If you (plural) use my suffering to show that I have sinned"; or it may be a statement, if a statement was used in the first line; for example, "You consider my sufferings as evidence that I have sinned" or "You think that because I suffer, that proves I have done wrong."

Know then that God has put me in the wrong: verse 6 makes clear that in verse 4 Job is not admitting that he has sinned, for here it is clear that it is God who gives rise to all his troubles. The expression translated **know then** is used here as in 2 Kings 10.10, to introduce a serious and important assertion: "Know then that there shall fall to the earth nothing of the word of the LORD . . . ." Here NEB translates "I tell you . . . ." In 8.3 Bildad asked if God perverts (TEV "twists") justice. Job uses the same verb here to say that is exactly what God has done to him. TEV "God . . . has done this" refers to "troubles" in verse 5b. FRCL is more precise, ". . . it is God who has wronged me," as is GECL, ". . . God has done me an injustice." The line may also be expressed, for example, "You should understand that God is the one who has made me suffer," "Know for sure that God has caused me these troubles," or "Look here, God is the one who has wronged me."

And closed his net around me: in 18.8-10 Bildad spoke at length of the traps, snares, and nets which catch the wicked. Job knows only the ones God has set for him. The term for **net** is derived from a verb meaning "to hunt and fish," which implies a general word for net. The use of the **net** is, however, restricted by the verb translated **closed**, which suggests "to turn around," and implies, therefore, a net which can encircle its victim. TEV "a trap to catch me" is general both in object and process. NJB has "and enveloped me in his net," NEB "He has drawn the net round me." In languages in which a term for a net large enough to encircle a person is available, this should be used. However, a casting net used in fishing may not always be appropriate in this context. It may be necessary to use a general term for "trap" or to shift to another image; for example, "He has caught me in his grip" or "He has snatched me up in his hand."

4D-2. Job accuses God of treating him violently (19.7-12)

	RSV		TEV
7	Behold, I cry out, 'Violence!' but I am not answered; I call aloud, but there is no justice.	7	I protest his violence, but no one is listening; no one hears my cry for justice.
8	He has walled up my way, so that I can-not pass, and he has set darkness upon my paths.	8	God has blocked the way, and I can't get through; he has hidden my path in darkness.
9	He has stripped from me my glory, and taken the crown from my head.	9	He has taken away all my wealth and destroyed my reputation.
10	He breaks me down on every side, and I am gone, and my hope has he pulled up like a tree.	10	He batters me from every side. He uproots my hope and leaves me to wither and die.
11	He has kindled his wrath against me, and counts me as his adversary.	11	God is angry and rages against me; he treats me like his worst enemy.
12	His troops come on together;	12	He sends his army to attack me; they dig trenches and lay siege to my tent.

they have cast up siegeworks against
me,
and encamp round about my tent.

Subdivision Heading

Translators may adapt the Handbook heading to say, for example, "Job says God is destroying him," "Job accuses God of treating him like his worst enemy," or "Job says God attacks him like an army." Habel (6-12) has "Complaint against God's siege tactics," and Rowley "God's abandonment and assault."

19.7

RSV	TEV
Behold, I cry out, 'Violence!' but I am not answered; I call aloud, but there is no justice.	I protest his violence, but no one is listening; no one hears my cry for justice.

Behold, I cry out, 'Violence!' For **Behold** see 4.18; 13.15. As RSV translates, Job cries out or shouts the word **Violence!** which is used also in 16.17. Here **Violence!** is used as in Jeremiah 20.8, "For whenever I speak, I cry out, I shout, 'Violence and destruction!' " In verse 7 Job's shout is equivalent to the cry "Help!" NEB translates "Murder!" SPCL "They are killing me!" TEV's statement "I protest his violence" is subdued and lacking in impact. The line may also be expressed, for example, " 'Look,' I shout, 'Save me!' " or as a condition: "If I cry out 'Stop!' " "Even if I cry out 'I'm being attacked!' " **But I am not answered** translates the passive, which must often be expressed as in TEV "No one is listening," or FRCL "Nobody answers me."

I call aloud, but there is no justice: TEV does not repeat the words **I call**. **Aloud** emphasizes the parallel **I cry** in line a, but it may be better rendered by being more specific, as NEB "If I appeal for help," or "If I shout for help." **No justice** is poetically compressed to say that there is no one to do justice, to do the right thing for Job. **There is no justice** may be rendered, for example, "nobody treats me fairly," "nobody does what is right for me, "there is no one to judge what is right," or "no one stands up to decide what is fair."

19.8

RSV	TEV
He has walled up my way, so that I cannot pass, and he has set darkness upon my paths.	God has blocked the way, and I can't get through; he has hidden my path in darkness.

He has walled up my way: this line is similar to Lamentations 3.7 "He has walled me about so that I cannot escape." Job has expressed similar thoughts in 3.23; 13.27; 14.5. In 1.10 Satan spoke of God having placed protective walls around Job. **Walled up** translates a verb meaning to enclose with a wall or fence. It can be translated "He has blocked my way so that I can't get through" or, as FRCL says,

"God bars my way, preventing me from getting through." This line may also be rendered, for example, "He has cut off my path," "He has thrown up a barrier on my path," or "He has put up a wall so I can't get by."

And he has set darkness upon my paths translates literally the Hebrew of line <u>b</u>. Some scholars change the word translated **darkness** to get "thorn hedge," and so NEB "He has hedged in the road before me." But no change is required, since the Hebrew as it stands can be rendered, for example, "he has left me in the dark to find my way."

19.9   RSV   TEV

He has stripped from me my glory, and taken the crown from my head.	He has taken away all my wealth and destroyed my reputation.

He has stripped from me my glory: The verb translated **stripped** is used for taking away a person's clothing, since **glory** as well as shame (see 8.22a) is often treated in this figurative way. God has taken away Job's good reputation, and the honor in which his friends regarded him. **Glory** translates the Hebrew term *kabod,* which means "glory, honor, wealth." Job has lost all of these. TEV prefers "all my wealth" in this line. GECL translates "well-being."

And taken the crown from my head: in Psalm 8.5 **glory** is spoken of as a **crown**. Just as a crown is removed from the head, so Job's glory, honor, and wealth have been removed. Verse 9 may be rendered, for example, "He has taken from me the honor people gave me, and removed my good reputation" or "He has snatched away my wealth and even taken my honor, which I wore like a crown."

19.10   RSV   TEV

He breaks me down on every side, and I am gone, and my hope has he pulled up like a tree.	He batters me from every side. He uproots my hope and leaves me to wither and die.

He breaks me down on every side: the verb translated **breaks me down** means "demolish" and implies that Job has now switched to the image of a building. In 16.14 Job speaks of himself as a wall that is "broken down breach upon breach." TEV "He batters me from every side" is a good rendering. The line may also be rendered, for example, "He smashes me like one demolishes the walls of a house," "He destroys me like someone destroying a building," or "He ruins me completely."

And I am gone translates the Hebrew "and I go," which emphasizes the extreme degree of being demolished or battered down. It does not mean that Job has departed from the scene or from life. In some languages it will be best to treat this expression as part of the first clause, as is done by means of the adverb "completely" in the example above.

And my hope has he pulled up like a tree: the image changes again, this time to a tree. TEV represents the image without mentioning the tree. "He uproots my hope." For discussion of **hope** see 4.6; 14.7,19; 17.15. This line may be rendered, for example, "What I looked forward to he has pulled up like a tree" or "What I wanted most has been cut down as one cuts down a tree."

19.11 RSV TEV

He has kindled his wrath against me, and counts me as his adversary.

God is angry and rages against me; he treats me like his worst enemy.

He has kindled his wrath against me: **kindled** implies fire or heat, and the Hebrew can also be translated "His anger glows at me." TEV avoids the suggestion of fire or heat and says "rages against me." FRCL has "unleashing the fire of his anger against me." The line may also be expressed, for example, "He burns me with the heat of his anger" or "He has lit his anger like a person lights a fire and turned it against me."

And counts me as his adversary: the Hebrew says "his adversaries," while the Septuagint and Syriac have the singular, which is followed by RSV, TEV, and most others. **Counts me as** means "treats me as, considers me as." TEV "worst" is not supported by the Hebrew. This line may also be expressed "he treats me as one of his enemies," "he acts as if I were his enemy," or "he fights me as if I were his enemy."

19.12 RSV TEV

His troops come on together; they have cast up siegeworks[t] against me, and encamp round about my tent.

He sends his army to attack me; they dig trenches and lay siege to my tent.

[t] Heb *their way*

With the introduction of "enemy" in verse 11, verse 12 develops the image of the military.

His troops come on together: **troops** translates a word meaning "companies," which are here God's companies of soldiers. For similar military images see 10.17; 16.14; 30.12. The same expression occurs in 25.3. **Come on together** means these troops are advancing in the attack or, as TEV says, "He sends his army to attack me." Because these **troops** have not been mentioned before, it will often help stylistically to keep God as the subject, as in TEV, "God sends his army to attack me," or "God attacks me with companies of soldiers."

They have cast up siegeworks against me translates the Hebrew "And they heap up against me in their way." This may refer to attacking forces digging under or piling up dirt against a wall in order to overrun it, which is the meaning of **siegeworks**. This line has been given many different interpretations, and many scholars consider RSV's rendering largely guesswork. Some interpreters take this line to be an explanation of 30.12b added by copyists, and so delete it. HOTTP rates this line in the Hebrew text as an "A" reading, and accordingly it should not be deleted. FRCL avoids the idea of **siegeworks** by translating "They lay down a road in order to reach me." Translators may follow this, or the models of RSV and TEV, since nothing better has been convincingly presented. Translators may adapt RSV's rendering to say, for example, "They are preparing to overrun me," "They tunnel through to reach me," or "They are getting ready to attack my position."

And encamp around my tent: the figure of **siegeworks** in line b is not appropriate for line c, since an attack on a tent would hardly use such methods. However, regardless of the military tactics in line b, in line c the enemy troops are camped around his tent. SPCL places this line at the beginning of line b and says "They camp around my house and prepare the attack." Translators may find this a suitable way to relate line c to line b.

4D-3. Job accuses God of turning his family and servants against him (19.13-22)

RSV	TEV
13 "He has put my brethren far from me, and my acquaintances are wholly estranged from me.	13 God has made my brothers forsake me; I am a stranger to those who knew me;
14 My kinsfolk and my close friends have failed me;	14 my relatives and friends are gone.
15 the guests in my house have forgotten me; my maidservants count me as a stranger; I have become an alien in their eyes.	15 Those who were guests in my house have forgotten me; my servant girls treat me like a stranger and a foreigner.
16 I call to my servant, but he gives me no answer; I must beseech him with my mouth.	16 When I call a servant, he doesn't answer— even when I beg him to help me.
17 I am repulsive to my wife, loathsome to the sons of my own mother.	17 My wife can't stand the smell of my breath, and my own brothers won't come near me.
18 Even young children despise me; when I rise they talk against me.	18 Children despise me and laugh when they see me.
19 All my intimate friends abhor me, and those whom I loved have turned against me.	19 My closest friends look at me with disgust; those I loved most have turned against me.
20 My bones cleave to my skin and to my flesh, and I have escaped by the skin of my teeth.	20 My skin hangs loose on my bones; I have barely escaped with my life.
21 Have pity on me, have pity on me, O you my friends, for the hand of God has touched me!	21 You are my friends! Take pity on me! The hand of God has struck me down.
22 Why do you, like God, pursue me?	22 Why must you persecute me the way God does? Haven't you tormented me enough?

Why are you not satisfied with my
flesh?

In these verses Job laments that those closest to him have deserted him.

Subdivision Heading

The Handbook heading may be adapted to say, for example, "Job says, 'Those I loved most have turned against me,' " "Job accuses God of turning his best friends away from him," or "God has made Job's loved ones desert him." Habel has "Complaint against friends for desertion," and Rowley "Job laments his forsaken state and appeals to his friends."

19.13 RSV	TEV
"He has put my brethren far from me, and my acquaintances are wholly estranged from me.	God has made my brothers forsake me; I am a stranger to those who knew me;

He has put my brethren far from me: Job begins by accusing God of making his brothers desert him. **My brethren** is an archaic term for "my brothers." The Septuagint has "My brothers have gone far." HOTTP, however, translates the Hebrew "He has put my brothers far from me." **Brethren** may be taken as a general term for kin (Mft translates "clansmen"), but there is no reason not to use "brothers," which would probably include the sons of Job's father's brothers. A satisfactory translation model is "God has taken my brothers and put them far from me" or "God has removed my brothers from me."

And my acquaintances are wholly estranged from me: acquaintances is literally "those who know me" and is parallel to **brethren** in the first line. In 42.11 "all his brothers and sisters and all who had known him before" come to Job and eat with him. **Estranged** or "alienated" is translated by TEV as "stranger." The line may also be rendered, for example, "all the people who knew me are now strangers," "all my former friends are like foreigners to me," or "none of my former friends know me any more."

19.14-15 RSV	TEV
14 My kinsfolk and my close friends have failed me; 15 the guests in my house have forgotten me; my maidservants count me as a stranger; I have become an alien in their eyes.	14 my relatives and friends are gone. 15 Those who were guests in my house have forgotten me; my servant girls treat me like a stranger and a foreigner.

Scholars generally agree that in the Hebrew text verses 14-15 are unnatural in form, verse 14 being too short and verse 15 too long. Therefore the first two words of verse 15, translated **the guests** and **in my house**, are joined with the last word of verse 14, translated **have forgotten me**: verses 14 and 15a are thus one line in the Hebrew, and 15b,c compose the next line. RSV demonstrates the result of this shift.

My kinsfolk and my close friends have failed me: **kinsfolk** refers to "relatives," as in TEV, without specifying the degree of closeness of kinship. **Close friends** is "those knowing me," similar to verse 13b. Job complains that these persons **have failed me**. The sense is that they have disappeared or "are gone" (TEV). This line may also be expressed, for example, "My relatives and friends have abandoned me" or "My kinsmen and friends have left me."

The guests in my house have forgotten me: these people have been visitors who have been guests in Job's house, ones he has entertained. They have no need of Job now, and so they have forgotten him. These are former guests. In some languages **guests** must be rendered, for example, "people who have eaten my food" or "people who have slept in my house."

My maidservants count me as a stranger: the Hebrew word translated **maidservants** also means "concubines." Job begins with **maidservants** here and continues with "manservant" in verse 16a, a good reason for not taking **maidservants** to mean "concubines" here. **Stranger** translates a general word for foreigner, one who is not from the in-group or tribe; that is, an alien. This line may also be expressed "my (feminine) servants treat me as they would treat a stranger," "my servants pay no more attention to me than they would pay to a stranger," or "the women who work in my house treat me like a stranger." If the treatment of strangers is ambiguous, it will be better to make it clear by saying, for example, "pay no attention to me" or "do not obey my orders."

I have become an alien in their eyes: **alien** translates a word referring to a person from a strange land, or native from a different tribe. The words for **stranger** and **alien** overlap greatly in their meanings. In English "stranger" and "foreigner" are approximate equivalents. This line may be expressed "I am nothing more than a stranger to them." According to chapters 1 and 2, Job's servants have been killed, but nothing is gained by pressing this matter in a poetic story such as Job.

19.16	RSV	TEV
	I call to my servant, but he gives me no answer; I must beseech him with my mouth.	When I call a servant, he doesn't answer— even when I beg him to help me.

I call to my servant, but he gives me no answer: Job's servants pay no attention even to his voice. As pointed out in the discussion of verse 15, Job now speaks of the "manservant" or "male servant." Psalm 123.2 says ". . . the eyes of servants look to the hand of their master." A servant is ready to obey his master and watches for his orders from the slightest gesture of the master's hand. By contrast Job cannot get obedience from servants even by calling aloud to them.

I must beseech him with my mouth: this line emphasizes the deserted role Job now plays. His servant does not respond to him in the expected ways, and Job is reduced to making pleas and begging his servant to help him. Verse 16 may be expressed, for example, "If I call my (male) servant, he does not answer, no matter how much I beg" or "I call my servant and even insist, but he pays no attention to me."

19.17   RSV   TEV

> I am repulsive to my wife,
>   loathsome to the sons of my
>   own mother.

> My wife can't stand the smell of
>   my breath,
> and my own brothers won't
>   come near me.

I am repulsive to my wife is literally "My *ruach* is repulsive to my wife." *Ruach* means "spirit, "wind," or "breath," and, like *nefesh* "soul," sometimes represents the living person, usually translated "I." Here "breath," meaning halitosis or a bad odor from the breath, best suits the context; so FRCL, TEV, NJB, BJ, GECL, TOB, NIV, and others. The line may be expressed, for example, "My bad breath is disgusting to my wife," "My breath is so foul my wife turns away from me," or "My bad breath offends my wife."

Loathsome to the sons of my own mother: loathsome translates a verb which is parallel with **repulsive** in line a and means "to have a foul smell." **Sons of my own mother** would refer to Job's true brothers, male children born to the same mother. The Hebrew expression is literally "sons of my belly," which would normally refer to Job's own offspring. However, these children have been killed. Interpreters have suggested that these **sons** are children of his concubines (who have never been mentioned), or his clansmen, or his grandchildren. Translators are divided between those like RSV and TEV, who understand these to be Job's brothers, and those who consider them to be his own children. In regard to the latter, Pope believes that the author does not bother himself with the details of the prose section of the story, and so has no problem calling them Job's own children. Both interpretations are possible. Therefore we may translate, for example, "my own brothers can't stand my odor" or "I am a terrible stench to my own children."

19.18   RSV   TEV

> Even young children despise me;
>   when I rise they talk against
>   me.

> Children despise me and laugh
>   when they see me.

Even young children despise me: Even translates an expression that calls attention to the extent in which everyone has abandoned Job. **Young children** translates a word found only here and in 21.11, and which is correctly translated as RSV has it. These **young children** are old enough to understand how to ridicule and to employ the words and gestures this may have involved. **Despise** translates a verb also meaning "to scorn, ridicule, make fun of." This line may also be rendered, for example, "Even young children make fun of me" or "Even the children laugh at me."

When Job struggles to his feet these children jeer or laugh at him. **When I rise they talk against me**: **when I rise** refers to Job's getting to his feet to stand and move about. **Talk against** is the literal Hebrew, but the preposition represented by **against** when following the word **talk** takes on the meaning of "scoff, ridicule." These children are not using conversation to discuss Job negatively; they are in all likelihood depicted as using words, sounds, and gestures to make fun of, deride, laugh at Job. The line may also be expressed "when I get up to go, they make fun of me" or "when I stand up . . . ."

19.19   RSV   TEV

> All my intimate friends abhor
>   me,
>   and those whom I loved have
>   turned against me.

> My closest friends look at me
>   with disgust;
>   those I loved most have turned
>   against me.

All my intimate friends abhor me: **intimate friends** is literally "all the men of my confidence." These are Job's most trusted friends or "closest friends" (TEV), as expressed in Psalm 55.13-14. They are said to **abhor** Job, which is to be disgusted by him, to be repulsed by his condition. This line may be rendered, for example, "The dearest friends I had detest me," "My closest friends hate me," or in some languages, "The friends I shared my food with now hate me."

And those whom I have loved have turned against me: these are the closest relatives and friends whom Job loved most of all. This verse is a summary of Job's feeling of despair and neglect. **Turned** is the same verb used in 9.5 of God overturning mountains. Here it is followed by a preposition which gives it the sense of "abandon, desert, be unfaithful to." In some languages line b may be rendered, for example, "the people I loved most turn their backs to me" or "the ones I loved most say 'We don't know him.'"

19.20   RSV   TEV

> My bones cleave to my skin and
>   to my flesh,
>   and I have escaped by the skin
>   of my teeth.

> My skin hangs loose on my
>   bones;
>   I have barely escaped with my
>   life.[m]

> [m] *Verse 20 in Hebrew is unclear.*

Verse 20 is a problem for interpreters and is the first in a series which makes the remainder of this chapter exceedingly difficult, if not impossible, to be certain about. Although numerous changes have been suggested, scholars are unable to find much agreement on verse 20. The first line is too long and the second is obscure. The repetition of **skin** in both lines leads to further problems. In spite of all this, it seems evident, according to Rowley, that Job is saying that he has been reduced to a shadow of his former self and has barely survived.

My bones cleave to my skin and to my flesh: **cleave** means to "cling, adhere, stick to." Lamentations 4.8c says "their skin has shriveled upon their bones," and Psalm 102.5b "my bones cleave to my flesh." Verse 20a seems to have brought both ideas into one line. Consequently many translations remove **flesh** from line a and get something similar to TEV "My skin hangs loose on my bones." FRCL has "I have nothing more than skin on my bones," SPCL "My skin sticks to my bones," NIV "I am nothing but skin and bones," and GECL "Only skin and bones can be seen on me." This line may also be expressed, for example, "My limbs are like sticks."

And I have escaped by the skin of my teeth: the Septuagint, which translates line a "In my skin the flesh is rotten," takes **my bones** in line a as part of line b and translates "My bones are held in my teeth," and **by the skin of** is omitted. NJB has adapted its translation to the Septuagint: "My flesh is rotting under my skin, my bones are sticking out like teeth." This rendering does not give the idea of bare survival suggested by TEV "I have barely escaped with my life." FRCL interprets the expression **by the skin of my teeth** to mean "I come through this disaster by having lost everything." HOTTP, which considers line b to be a "C" reading, recommends "I have escaped with the skin of my teeth" (that is, there is no soundness in me, or I have just bare life, with nothing more, safe). This agrees essentially with TEV and others. The expression **by the skin of my teeth** has become proverbial in English, meaning to accomplish something, but just barely. This line may also be expressed, for example, "I have almost died, but not quite," "Death has almost seized me," "I have barely escaped death," or "By only a tiny bit am I still alive."

19.21

RSV	TEV
Have pity on me, have pity on me, O you my friends, for the hand of God has touched me!	You are my friends! Take pity on me! The hand of God has struck me down.

Have pity on me, have pity on me, O you my friends: the double plea for mercy in this line is seen in Psalm 123.3a "Have mercy on us, O LORD, have mercy on us." TEV and others do not repeat the plea. Its purpose is to express the degree of Job's need for a show of compassion on the part of his friends. The word translated **friends** does not occur in the list of persons in verses 13-14, and is applied here to the three friends, Eliphaz, Bildad and Zophar. In some languages the line may be rendered idiomatically; for example, "You who are my friends, have a warm heart for me," "My friends, I beg you let your livers feel for me," or "You friends, warm your insides for me."

For the hand of God has touched me: the image is that of God's hand representing the action of God which is responsible for Job's suffering. **Touched** is an understatement. The sense is that God's hand has struck Job down—a violent, destructive blow. It is used in this sense in 1.11,19; 5.19. This line gives the reason why Job calls for mercy. In languages in which **touch** will not signify the violence done to Job, the thought must be expressed differently; for example, "because God has struck me down," "because the hand of God has knocked me to the ground," or "because God has violently attacked me."

19.22   RSV   TEV

> Why do you, like God, pursue
>   me?
> Why are you not satisfied with
>   my flesh?

> Why must you persecute me the
>   way God does?
> Haven't you tormented me
>   enough?

Why do you, like God, pursue me: in 13.25 Job asked God "Wilt thou frighten a driven leaf and pursue dry chaff?" The verb translated **pursue** is not meant in the sense of follow or chase, but "to afflict, persecute, punish, cause to suffer."

Why are you not satisfied with my flesh? Satisfied translates a word meaning "being satiated or filled up"; that is, eating so much that you become weary of it. So Job is accusing his friends of acting like human flesh eaters that cannot get enough. However, since they are not literally eating his flesh, the expression must be taken figuratively. Tur-Sinai says the expression "to be sated with another's flesh" derives from the practice of sexual abuse carried out on captives of war and other helpless victims. Psalm 27.2b, which literally says "eat up my flesh," is translated by RSV "uttering slanders against me." Translators are divided between those who keep the literal expression, as RSV, and those who translate the figurative meaning as "attack, torment, slander, malign." For clarity it is better to translate the figure. Verse 22 may be rendered, for example, "Why do you make me suffer as God does? Why do you keep on attacking me?" or "God has punished me; why do you do the same? Do you have to go on saying evil things about me?"

4D-4. Job is sure of having one in heaven who will defend him (19.23-29)

RSV   TEV

23   "Oh that my words were written!
         Oh that they were inscribed in a book!
24   Oh that with an iron pen and lead
         they were graven in the rock for ever!
25   For I know that my Redeemer lives,
         and at last he will stand upon the
         earth;
26   and after my skin has been thus de-
         stroyed,
         then from my flesh I shall see God,
27   whom I shall see on my side,
         and my eyes shall behold, and not
         another.
         My heart faints within me!
28   If you say, 'How we will pursue him!'
         and, 'The root of the matter is found

23   How I wish that someone would remem-
         ber my words
         and record them in a book!
24   Or with a chisel carve my words in stone
         and write them so that they would last
         forever.
25   But I know there is someone in heaven
         who will come at last to my defense.
26   Even after my skin is eaten by disease,
         while still in this body I will see God.
27   I will see him with my own eyes,
         and he will not be a stranger.

         My courage failed because you said,
28   "How can we torment him?"

	You looked for some excuse to attack
29 be afraid of the sword,	me.
for wrath brings the punishment of the	29 But now, be afraid of the sword—
sword,	the sword that brings God's wrath on
that you may know there is a judg-	sin,
ment."	so that you will know there is one who
	judges.

Job's thoughts in verses 23-29 are adjusted by some interpreters to make it a clear insight into the concept of resurrection. A GECL footnote says regarding these verses: "The traditional translation of verses 25-27 in which Job expresses his hope of resurrection are based upon the Latin Vulgate translation and have no basis in the Hebrew text." Rowley says "There is no thought of more than the moment of his consciousness of his vindication, and certainly not the thought that the bliss of the Afterlife will make amends for the suffering of this life. It is not bliss for which Job longs, but vindication."

Subdivision Heading

Translators may wish to place a heading before verse 23. If the Handbook heading is not suitable, other suggestions are: "Job is sure that someone in heaven will defend him" or "Job says he will see God." Habel has "Job's hope of a redeemer," TOB "The living redeemer," and Rowley "Job's assurance of vindication."

19.23 RSV	TEV
"Oh that my words were written! Oh that they were inscribed in a book!	How I wish that someone would remember my words and record them in a book!

Oh that my words were written! My words refers to Job's repeated protests of his innocence. Job's concern is that his words be written for future generations to know. FRCL translates **my words** as "my protest," which expresses the thought more accurately than "words." GECL says "I wish someone would write it all down." TEV introduces "remember" into this line, which explains the purpose for the writing of Job's protests. This line may also be rendered, for example, "I wish someone would write down my complaints" or "If only somebody would write down my arguments against God."

Oh that they were inscribed in a book: line b shows the rise of emotion as the thought of line a repeats but becomes more specific, **inscribed in a book**. **Inscribed** translates a verb meaning carve or engrave. The word translated **book** normally refers to a scroll, but when used with "engrave," scroll is inappropriate. Pope suggests that the word translated **book** can mean a record or document but may be related to an Akkadian word for "copper." Such an engraved copper treasure scroll was found at Qumran. Translators should use a term that the reader will recognize as referring to something appropriate for writing on, which most often will be something like **book**. This line may show the intended heightening of intensity by saying, for example, "If they would only put them permanently into a record," "Even better—have my case put into a book," or "Better still, record my words on something that will last."

19.24   RSV   TEV

Oh that with an iron pen and   Or with a chisel carve my words
      lead   in stone
   they were graven in the rock   and write them so that they
      for ever!   would last forever.[n]

                                    [n] last forever; *or* be on record.

Oh that with an iron pen and lead they were graven in the rock forever: the first part is literally "with an engraver of iron and lead." This can refer to the instrument for engraving on rock, or perhaps to the material on which engraving took place. It is difficult to understand how an instrument of lead could be used for engraving, due to its softness; and so HOTTP "suggests tablets of iron and lead" or "with lead," meaning melted lead placed into the spaces of the inscription. This is the thought of NEB: "cut with an iron tool and filled with lead." FRCL has "engraved with an iron point which one blackens with lead." That refers to filling the engraved lettering with molten lead, giving it a dark color. RSV **iron pen** is misleading for present day readers. Job wants future generations to have access to his argument so that they will know the truth, and so these rock inscriptions should last **for ever**. Verse 24 may need to be expressed differently in some languages to say, for example, "Let someone even scratch them into a rock with an iron tool so they will last," "Let my words even be dug into the face of a rock with an iron tool so they will not disappear," or "Let someone engrave my words on a rock and fill the letters with melted lead so they will last."

19.25   RSV   TEV

For I know that my Redeemer[u]   But I know there is someone in
      lives,   heaven
   and at last he will stand upon   who will come at last to my
      the earth;[v]   defense.

[u] Or *Vindicator*
[v] Or *dust*

For I know that my Redeemer lives: the word translated **Redeemer** is the Hebrew *go'el*, and it is found only here in the book of Job. An RSV footnote has "Vindicator" as an alternative translation. In other parts of the Old Testament the word has a variety of meanings. In such passages as 2 Samuel 14.11 it means "avenger of blood," who is a kinsmen who avenges his dead relative. In Ruth 4.4-6 it is the relative who buys back the property of the dead man. In Numbers 5.8 he is the one to whom restitution is made (payment made in case of guilt). The term is applied to God as the one who delivers Israel from slavery in Egypt (Exodus 6.6) and from exile (Jer 50.34). In Psalm 103.4 God is the one who "redeems your life from the pit." In the context of this verse in Job, **Redeemer** means generally "defender, protector, helper" and more specifically "the one who wins my case" or "the one who stands up for me in court." Job is saying again that the one who will defend him in his argument or lawsuit with God "lives." As Rowley says, Job is not asking God to rescue him from Sheol. That would be the task of a "deliverer." Job wants his name and honor vindicated. He wants everyone, now and in the future, to know that he was innocent of wrongdoing. His vindicator, defender, is the one who will do this for him.

A much debated question is the identity of Job's *go'el*. For every argument that concludes that it is God, there is an equally good argument that it is not. Habel suggests that the obvious resolution of the identity of the **Redeemer** lies in relating verse 25 to 16.19, and so TEV "I know there is someone in heaven . . . to my defense." TEV makes use of the same wording as in 16.19. However, TEV does not thereby resolve the question (nor need it do so) whether "someone in heaven" means God or a third party. Many modern translations which assume it is God do this by spelling with an initial capital, and so "Defender, Vindicator, Redeemer." Translators who assume Job has a third party in mind will usually spell with a lower-case initial letter.

This Handbook recommends the use of "defender, vindicator, helper." However, if the translator prefers to indicate that this refers to God, there is a strong body of translations to support that. Translators should bear in mind that people hearing the Scriptures read do not know if a word is capitalized or not. In writing systems which do not use capitals letters, the problem is irrelevant. GECL makes the identification with God explicit: "I know that God, my advocate, lives." Vindicator may be rendered, for example, "The one who proves I am innocent" or "The person who defends my right." In any case "defender" and **Redeemer** are used in almost the same way in this context. In some languages it may be better to say, as FRCL does, "I know, myself, that I have a living defender."

And at last he will stand upon the earth: just as with the first line, interpreters come to totally different meanings for this line. RSV and others make **at last** an expression of time, meaning "finally, in the end." Not so, argues Dhorme, who sees "The First and the Last" as titles for God, as used in Isaiah 44.6; 48.12; and so he translates "And then, as the Last, he will arise on the earth." Translators differ most concerning **at last** and **will stand upon the earth**. BJ follows Dhorme "he, the last, will stand . . . ." Mft shifts **at last** to line a, "I know One to champion me at last." However, many modern translations understand **at last** to be used adverbially, as in RSV and TEV. **Earth** translates the Hebrew "dust," and so some take it to refer to the grave, as in the NIV footnote, "Or, *upon my grave.*" Most scholars, however, agree that **stand upon the earth** is a courtroom expression used to mean "to take the stand as a witness" in 31.14; Deuteronomy 19.16; Psalm 12.5; Isaiah 19.21. It is in this sense that TEV renders "come to my defense." NEB translates this line "and that he will rise last to speak in court." The thought is that he will have the final word; thus FRCL translates "and that he will have the final word on this earth." Translators may follow either interpretation; for example, "I know that he will have the final word," meaning that his decision will be final, authoritative, and with no further recourse. Or one may say, for example, "he will be my lawyer in this final court" or "he will take the stand finally for me on this earth."

19.26 RSV TEV

RSV	TEV
and after my skin has been thus destroyed, **then from[w] my flesh I shall see God,[x]**	**Even after my skin is eaten by disease,** **while still in this body[o] I will see God.[p]**
[w] Or *without* [x] The meaning of this verse is uncertain	[o] while still in this body; *or* although not in this body. [p] *Verse 26 in Hebrew is unclear.*

And after my skin has been thus destroyed: verse 26 offers even more scope for textual changes, conjectures, and outright guesses. While the individual words are fairly clear, the clause as a whole is far from clear. The list of proposals given by interpreters is too long and doubtful to make even a partial list. HOTTP recognizes that the Hebrew text is probably damaged in line a and gives it only a "C" rating, meaning that there is considerable doubt about it. Modern translations seem to fall into three groups regarding the meaning of this line: (1) those like NEB, which put "Hebrew unintelligible" in the footnote and then embark on changes which give renderings that bear no relation to the Hebrew; (2) those which try to keep the Hebrew text, but adjust the translation with some conjecture, such as TEV "Even after my skin is eaten by disease," FRCL "When they have finished tearing off my skin"; (3) those like Mft, which switch from "skin" to "body": "This body may break up . . . ." Translators can follow the Hebrew in cases (2) and (3) by following some model such as TEV or FRCL. TEV's translation may need to be expressed as an active construction; for example, "When disease has eaten away my skin."

Then from my flesh I shall see God: **from my flesh** can also be understood as "without my flesh," as in the RSV footnote, or the TEV footnote "although not in this body." The question most argued is the manner of Job's seeing God. Job's overwhelming desire so often repeated is to come to court face to face with God (13.15,20,24). He wants to confront God as a living human being, not as a spirit, and in verse 27 he hopes to see God with his eyes. As KJV says, "In my flesh shall I see God," or as TEV translates, "while still in this body I will see God." In some languages it may be necessary to transpose the two lines of verse 26 to say, for example, "While I still have my physical body, I shall see God even though disease has eaten away my skin."

19.27 RSV TEV

RSV	TEV
whom I shall see on my side,[y] **and my eyes shall behold, and not another.** **My heart faints within me!**	**I will see him with my own eyes,** **and he will not be a stranger.**

^y Or *for myself*   My courage failed because you
                                                    said,

Whom I shall see on my side: on my side translates the Hebrew "for myself," as in the RSV footnote. RSV and others interpret Job to mean that he will see God taking his part, being on his side in the argument, or as NJB translates, "He whom I shall see will take my part." This rendering implies that God is Job's defender and not his enemy. FRCL translates this line more naturally with "I will see him myself, with my own eyes," and this is essentially the meaning of TEV. The renderings of TEV and FRCL are preferred and may be followed by translators.

And my eyes shall behold, and not another: RSV, like the Hebrew, has no object for **behold**. The object must be understood from the previous line. The word translated **another** has the meaning of "stranger" in Proverbs 27.2 and is taken in that sense here by TEV: "and he will not be a stranger." FRCL also translates "stranger" but with a different meaning: "I am the one who will see him, and not a stranger." NJB is like TEV: "My eyes will be gazing on no stranger." The thought of the line probably is that Job's struggle with God as his enemy will be over, that God will no longer be an enemy or stranger to him; and so TEV serves as a good model. This line may also be expressed "and God will not be a stranger to me," or "and he will not be a foreigner." This line may also be rendered positively, "and I will see him as a friend" or "I will see him as one whom I know."

My heart faints within me is literally "My kidneys grow faint in my breast." The kidneys are considered the center of emotions in Hebrew thought. This line is taken by most translators to go with the two preceding lines of verse 27, as though the thought Job has just expressed has overwhelmed him emotionally. TEV, on the other hand, relates this line to what follows, and adjusts this line with "because you said . . . ," placing verse 28a in quotation marks. FRCL and others keep this line as part of verse 27 by saying "My heart is exhausted waiting for that moment," that is, the moment when Job will see God. Translators may follow this. A better possibility is to relate the line to what follows, as in TEV and others.

19.28-29 RSV	TEV
28 If you say, 'How we will pursue him!' and, 'The root of the matter is found in him'; 29 be afraid of the sword, for wrath brings the punishment of the sword, that you may know there is a judgment."	28 "How can we torment him?" You looked for some excuse to attack me. 29 But now, be afraid of the sword— the sword that brings God's wrath on sin, so that you will know there is one who judges.^q

^q one who judges; *or* a judgment.

Since verses 28 and 29 form a separate subject, translators may wish to consider placing a subdivision heading before them, although the Handbook has not done so.

Some suggestions are: "Job warns the friends," "God will judge you," or "You should be afraid of God's anger."

Verses 28 and 29 go together and are translated by RSV so that the conditions expressed in 28 are followed by the consequences in 29.

If you say, 'How we will pursue him!' RSV and others express this line as an exclamation, TEV as a question. The Hebrew seems to favor the question form. **Say** is not natural before a question, and FRCL translates "You ask yourselves." **Pursue** translates the same verb used in verse 22; see comments there. If the translator follows TEV, as suggested above, verse 28, or at least verse 28a, is understood as Job quoting the friends. The line may also be expressed "How can we make him suffer most?" or "What is the best way to injure him?"

And the root of the matter is found in him: RSV now switches to a statement and makes this line a second quotation from the friends. RSV translates the Hebrew literally, except **in him**, which in Hebrew is "in me." The Hebrew has switched in this line to indirect speech. Most interpreters and translators, including the ancient versions, change the Hebrew "in me" to "in him." **Root of the matter** or Hebrew "root of the word" means "ground, basis, reason," or "excuse" (TEV). They look for an excuse to accuse Job. FRCL, which continues the question form as in the first line, translates "What pretext can we find in order to charge him?" There is considerable manuscript support for keeping verse 28b as part of the quotation. This line may be rendered, for example, "The root of the trouble lies in himself," "The basis for his suffering is in him," "The cause of his troubles is himself," or "No one is to blame for his suffering but Job himself."

Job now sounds a stern warning to the friends. **Be afraid of the sword: the sword** is the instrument of God's vengeance in Deuteronomy 32.41; Isaiah 34.5-8, and of his anger in Zechariah 13.7. In Romans 13.4 it is the symbol of authority. In some languages this line will have to be adjusted to say, for example, "You should fear the sword," or more fully, "When God uses the sword, you should be afraid for your lives." In many languages the identification of **sword** with God's anger will not be made without further adjustments. Accordingly we may translate "You should fear God's judgment," "God will judge people, so you should fear him," or "You should fear the anger of God, who judges people."

For wrath brings the punishment of the sword: from this point onward verse 29 becomes obscure and is regarded by some interpreters as untranslatable. Nevertheless modern translations do show general agreement as to the essential thought expressed in RSV and TEV. Some editors take **wrath** to mean "these things," referring to the thoughts expressed in verse 28. TEV and others understand **wrath** to be "God's wrath." Dhorme suggests a slight change in the Hebrew to get "wrath is kindled as against iniquities," and this is followed by NJB "since the wrath bursts into flame at wicked deeds." (A note on "bursts into flame" says "Hebrew unintelligible.") GECL translates "Because such crime merits the death sentence," SPCL "The sword with which God punishes evil," and NIV "Wrath will bring punishment by the sword." HOTTP supports RSV with "wrath deserves or brings punishments of the sword," or, similar to GECL, "crimes liable to the sword." If sword has not been mentioned in the previous line, this clause may be rendered, for example, "God's anger will cause him to punish sin" or "God will be angry and punish sinners."

That you may know there is a judgment: most arguments on this line center on the word translated **judgment**. Some interpreters believe this word is a misspelling of the name for God, *Shaddai*, which is used frequently in Job, but the spelling never varies. Gordis points out that knowing God is always used in a favorable sense and refers to worshiping God and obeying the law. Job's thought is a warning to the friends, and therefore it is better to understand this line as in RSV. TEV expresses the noun **judgment** as "one who judges." In many languages the verb "to judge" requires an object; for example, "So that you will know there is one who judges the affairs of people" or "one who judges sinners." In some cases this may be rendered idiomatically, "So you will know that God cuts the affairs among people who do evil."

4E. ZOPHAR'S SECOND SPEECH (20.1-29)

Zophar, who last spoke in chapter 11, responds now to Job. His words seem to burst forth from his anger as he attacks Job. His speech falls into four parts. He opens with a short introduction (verses 2-3). In verses 4-11 he describes the short-lived happiness of the wicked. In verses 12-22 he employs the images of eating and wealth to show how the wicked are doomed. Finally in verses 23-29 he describes how God strikes the wicked down in his anger.

Division Heading

Translators should indicate that chapter 20 is Zophar's second speech, and should refer to the wording used in chapter 11. Translators may wish to follow some modern versions which do not use subdivision headings but select one heading for the chapter. Some examples are: GECL "The third friend: The deserved punishments that befall the criminal," FRCL "Zophar's discourse: The misfortunes of the wicked," NJB "The course of justice admits of no exception."

4E-1. Zophar is anxious to speak to Job (20.1-3)

RSV	TEV
1 Then Zophar the Naamathite answered:	*Zophar*
2 "Therefore my thoughts answer me, because of my haste within me.	1-2 Job, you upset me. Now I'm impatient to answer.
3 I hear censure which insults me, and out of my understanding a spirit answers me.	3 What you have said is an insult, but I know how to reply to you.

Subdivision Heading

In verses 2 and 3 Zophar expresses his desire to speak to Job. Translators wishing to place a subdivision heading here may follow the Handbook or say, for example, "Zophar knows what to tell Job" or "Zophar is upset with Job's talk."

20.1   RSV   TEV

> **Then Zophar the Naamathite an-**   *Zophar*
> **swered:**

For suggestions on the name of **Zophar the Naamathite**, see 2.11. For **answered** see 4.1.

20.2   RSV   TEV

> "Therefore my thoughts answer   Job, you upset me. Now I'm im-
>   me,   patient to answer.
>   because of my haste within me.

Therefore my thoughts answer me: Therefore translates an expression at the opening of a speech, one which has the meaning "That is why . . . ." It is equivalent to "In response to what you have said" or "What you have said is the reason why . . . ." Dhorme translates "This is why . . . ," and Mft "Now this does . . . ." **Answer me** does not suit the context. Accordingly some suggest a textual change to get "My thoughts disturb me." Dhorme keeps the Hebrew with the meaning "My thoughts bring me back," which is to say "cause me to speak to you again." The form of **answer** is causative, and so NEB translates "forces me to reply," which is better than RSV. FRCL has "My reflections urge (literally push) me to reply." TEV has transposed lines a and b: "Now I'm impatient to answer." This line may also be rendered, for example, "What you have said makes me speak up," "I have heard you and so I have to reply to you," or "Because of this I want to say something to you."

Because of my haste within me: the word translated **haste** is disputed by interpreters. Some take it to mean "feeling or emotion," and so Dhorme "because of the sensation I feel." TEV, which places this line before line a, translates "Job, you upset me." Others like NEB keep **haste**, as in RSV, "And this is why I hasten to speak." In some languages it is obligatory to place line b before line a, while in others considerations of style may make it preferred. This second line may be expressed, for example, "You have upset me so," or idiomatically, "You have made my heart run wild" or "You have made my stomach twist." The whole verse may be rendered, for example, "Because of the way I feel inside me, I have to reply to what you have said" or "My heart stirs within me, and because of what you have said I have to speak up now."

20.3   RSV   TEV

> I hear censure which insults me,   What you have said is an in-
>   and out of my understanding a   sult,
>   spirit answers me.   but I know how to reply to
>   you.

I hear censure which insults me: this line consists of three words which are literally "I hear the rebuke of my chastisement." **Censure** here means "reproof or correction." In other words Zophar is saying "I hear you scolding, and it insults me." TEV says it well: "What you have said is an insult." In this way Zophar complains that he is humiliated by Job's speech. This may refer to all of chapter 19, but in particular to the final verses. This may also be expressed "I hear your words which insult me," "When you speak you insult me," or "Your talk is an insult."

And out of my understanding a spirit answers me: literally "the *ruach* ('spirit, wind, breath') from my understanding makes me reply." This statement is not clear, and interpreters differ greatly in their understanding of it. Pope, following Dahood, changes **understanding** to get "frame," "The spirit of my frame answers me." Habel rejects that and translates "My discerning spirit," so that Zophar is speaking with the authority of his inner wisdom. In 32.8 Elihu uses the same word with reference to God's spirit, which gives men wisdom. NEB suggests a meaning similar to "inspiration," with "a spirit beyond my understanding." TEV takes *ruach* to refer to the person speaking: "I know how to reply to you." FRCL expresses *ruach* as a verb: "My reason inspires in me the reply to give." It is evident that translators are divided between those who consider "spirit" as a reference to the person of Zophar, and those who see in it something akin to inspiration. It is not possible to be certain which is best, and translators may choose either. Understanding *ruach* to refer to Zophar's person, we may translate, for example, "but I know how to answer you" or "but I am capable of replying to you." Likewise, using the definition of inspiration, we may translate "my understanding gives me the right answer for you" or "because I understand things I can give you a reply."

4E-2. Zophar describes the fate of the wicked (20.4-11)

RSV	TEV

4   Do you not know this from of old,
    since man was placed upon earth,
	4 Surely you know that from ancient times,
	    when man was first placed on earth,

5   that the exulting of the wicked is short,
    and the joy of the godless but for a
    moment?
	5 no wicked man has been happy for
	    long.

6   Though his height mount up to the heav-
    ens,
    and his head reach to the clouds,
	6 He may grow great, towering to the sky,
	    so great that his head reaches the
	    clouds,

7   he will perish for ever like his own dung;
    those who have seen him will say,
    'Where is he?'
	7 but he will be blown away like dust.
	Those who used to know him
	    will wonder where he has gone.

8   He will fly away like a dream, and not be
    found;
    he will be chased away like a vision of
    the night.
	8 He will vanish like a dream, like a vision
	    at night,
	    and never be seen again.

9   The eye which saw him will see him no
    more,
    nor will his place any more behold
    him.
	9 He will disappear from the place where
	    he used to live;

10   His children will seek the favor of the
    poor,
    and his hands will give back his wealth.
	10 and his sons will make good what he
	    stole from the poor.

	11 His body used to be young and vigorous, but soon it will turn to dust.

11   His bones are full of youthful vigor,
            but it will lie down with him in the
                dust.

Zophar now takes up the theme presented by Bildad in his first speech (8.11-19) and Eliphaz in his second speech (15.29-35). Zophar deals in generalities in describing how the wicked person comes to his end before his time.

Subdivision Heading
The Handbook heading for verses 4-11 may be adapted to say, for example, "Zophar tells Job what happens to the wicked," "Zophar tells how wicked people come to a bad end," or "There is no future for evil people." Habel has "The rapid fall of the wicked," Rowley "The brevity of the triumph of the wicked," and TOB "The extinction of the wicked."

20.4-5	RSV	TEV

	RSV	TEV
4	Do you not know this from of old, since man was placed upon earth,	4	Surely you know that from ancient times, when man was first placed on earth,
5	that the exulting of the wicked is short, and the joy of the godless but for a moment?	5	no wicked man has been happy for long.

Do you not know this from of old: in the Hebrew the question is not negative: "Do you know this?" TEV expresses the question as a statement: "Surely you know." **From of old** refers to times past and extending into the present, and so TEV "from ancient times." This line may also be rendered, for example, "Have you not always known?" or "Have you not always been aware?"

Since man was placed upon the earth: this expression refers, as in Deuteronomy 4.32, to the time of creation; that is, "ever since God created people and put them on the earth." RSV and TEV use the passive but imply that God is the one who created; compare FRCL "Since God placed man on the earth." This line may also be rendered "ever since God created mankind" or "ever since people have been on the earth."

Verse 5 completes the thought of verse 4. **That the exulting of the wicked is short**: **exulting** translates a word meaning "joy, happiness, gladness," usually expressed with a sound or a shout. In other words, "The joy of the wicked does not last long." **Wicked** here is plural in Hebrew, but Zophar will switch to the singular in the verses which follow. This may imply that he is applying this traditional teaching to Job in particular. The wicked (plural) come under attack by Bildad (8.11-19), Eliphaz (15.29-35), and Bildad again (18.5-21). The same teaching finds expression also in Psalm 37. **Short** translates "very near," which means that the end of the time the wicked have left to rejoice is near; that is, their time will soon be finished. This line may also be expressed "that the wicked do not enjoy long life," "that the joy of the wicked is only for a short while," or "that the happiness of evil people lasts only for a moment."

And the joy of the godless but for a moment: line b says essentially the same as line a with little poetic intensification, and so TEV has reduced the two lines to one: "No wicked man has been happy for long." For **godless** see 8.13. Line b may be translated as emphasizing line a; for example, "Yes, it is true that people who do not trust God are not happy for long" or "Yes, people who do not remember God (who forget God) are happy only for a moment."

20.6-7	RSV		TEV
6	Though his height mount up to the heavens, and his head reach to the clouds,	6	He may grow great, towering to the sky, so great that his head reaches the clouds,
7	he will perish for ever like his own dung; those who have seen him will say, 'Where is he?'	7	but he will be blown away like dust. Those who used to know him will wonder where he has gone.

Verse 6 states two imagined conditions which are concluded in verse 7, and so the two verses should be considered together.

Though his height mount up to the heavens: some interpreters see verse 6 as alluding to a tree, but this is largely imagination. It seems better to take it as referring to the man's physical height or stature, and it can be expressed "He may be so tall he reaches the sky" or "Even if he is so tall he reaches the heavens."

And his head reach to the clouds: the significance of the wicked being so high is only made clear in verse 7, where he is brought down to the level of his excrement. This line may be rendered, for example, "and he is so tall his head touches the clouds" or "and he is as tall as the clouds are high in the sky."

He will perish for ever like his own dung: interpreters find numerous ways to avoid **like his own dung,** which is considered crude. Syriac has "like a whirlwind," and Dhorme associates the Hebrew word **dung** with Assyrian and Greek and gets "like a ghost he vanishes for ever." NJB follows this, "but he vanishes like a phantom, once for all." Some scholars understand **dung** to refer to piles of animal manure stored and dried for use in making fire. NAB accepts this: "yet he perishes for ever like the fuel of his fire." The most likely idea is that he is compared to **dung** which returns to the soil and so disappears. FRCL "He will end up like his own excrement." Translators must be sensitive to public reading and should avoid an expression which will provoke amusement or disgust in handling this line. If the reference to **his own dung** is inappropriate or subject to conflicting interpretations, it will be better to follow one of the suggested interpretations. The point is that he will vanish, disappear forever; and therefore many other similes will convey this, or we may follow TEV "be blown away like dust." For languages which do not use the passive, it may be necessary to say, for example, "he will disappear like dust" or "the wind will blow him away like dust."

He will so completely disappear that **those who have seen him will say,**

371

'**Where is he**'? RSV makes the question direct and places it in quotation marks. TEV makes it indirect. The question "Where is he?" is asked the first time in Job's speech in 14.10. Verse 7 is similarly expressed in Psalm 37.35-36.

20.8   RSV   TEV

> He will fly away like a dream,   He will vanish like a dream, like
>   and not be found;   a vision at night,
> he will be chased away like a   and never be seen again.
>   vision of the night.

He will fly away like a dream: the fleeting **dream** is used in Psalm 73.20 to illustrate the temporariness of the wicked. TEV translates "vanish like a dream," which is more suitable for English. In some languages it may be necessary to replace the pronoun **He** with "the wicked person." The Hebrew appears to be in the passive, "He is driven away like a dream." Again the thought is focused not on how the dream goes away, but on the fact that a dream is impermanent. Therefore "disappear, vanish, go away" may express the thought better as an active construction; for example, "He will disappear like the dream a person had during his sleep."

He will be chased away like a vision of the night: this line recalls Job's complaint in 7.14 that God terrified him with night visions. TEV has removed the passive sense of **be chased away** by employing "He will vanish" and using it for both the dream in line a and the **vision of the night** in line b. As in 7.14 there is no attempt here to distinguish between **dream** and **vision**. The poet uses **vision of the night** to extend the sense of **dream** and to go beyond it poetically, but not to speak of two different experiences. Therefore the translator should not make an artificial distinction in the meanings. In languages in which there is only one word for **dream**, it may be possible to use a descriptive phrase in the second; for example, "he will disappear like images seen during sleep" or "like thoughts that pass through the mind while asleep."

20.9   RSV   TEV

> The eye which saw him will see   He will disappear from the place
>   him no more,   where he used to live;
> nor will his place any more
>   behold him.

The eye which saw him will see him no more: some understand this to refer to the eye of God, as in 7.8, where Job said "The eye of him who sees me will behold me no more." In 7.19-20 Job complains about God spying on him and calls God "Thou watcher of men." It is not recommended that the allusion be made explicit by saying "The eye of God . . . ." It is more probable that the reference is to people generally who were accustomed to seeing Job go about each day, and this fits better with the next line. TEV has transposed verse 9a to before verse 8b and made it a passive, "and never be seen again." Modern translations tend to use:

(1) the literal form "the eye accustomed to see him" (NJB); (2) an impersonal subject "one used to see him," (FRCL); or (3) the subject supplied from the next line, "those who lived with him and saw him" (SPCL).

Nor will his place any more behold him: in this line **his place,** meaning "the place where he lived," is parallel to **the eye** in the first line. It is necessary in many languages to express this line differently in translation, since **his place** is not an animate object that sees. Accordingly SPCL has "Those who lived with him." NJB translates "His home [meaning the people of his home] will never set eye on him again." TEV has translated the implication of no one seeing him: "He will disappear from the place where he used to live." This line may also be expressed "nor will his family members see him again" or "nor will those of his household see him again."

20.10	RSV	TEV
	His children will seek the favor of the poor, and his hands will give back his wealth.	and his sons will make good what he stole from the poor.

His children will seek the favor of the poor: some interpreters believe verse 11, which speaks of the father, should come before verse 10, and so NEB and Mft transpose them. This is not necessary. Scholars disagree on the origin of the verb root translated **seek the favor of.** Dhorme gives the verb the sense as in TEV "His sons will compensate the poor." Dhorme also transfers verse 10 to follow verse 19. The Septuagint and others derive the meaning from the root of the verb "crush" found in verse 19 and translate "The poor shall oppress his children." Tur-Sinai suggests "will indemnify," and Pope "must redress." The thought of Zophar is that the sons will be forced to return the ill-gotten wealth the wicked father has taken from the poor, and so something similar to TEV is recommended. This line may also be expressed, for example, "and his children will give back the wealth he stole from the poor" or "The sons of the wicked father will have to return to the poor what their father took from them."

And his hands will give back his wealth: his hands translates the Hebrew. NEB, NJB, and others make a change to get "his children." **His hands** would refer to the father, who has disappeared from the scene in the previous line. Gordis argues that **his hands** has the extended meaning of "offspring" and should be translated "his children" without any change. Since line b of the verse is parallel to line a, TEV does not repeat the subject in line b, and thus makes "his sons" the subject of the main clause covering the whole verse. The recommended translation is "his sons" or "his children." If line a is understood as recommended, line b is almost a repetition, and so some translators will prefer to reduce the two lines to one, as does TEV. **His hands** is the poetic use of a figure in the second line which gives a degree of intensification over line a.

20.11   RSV   TEV

His bones are full of youthful   His body used to be young and
　　vigor,   　　vigorous,
　　but it will lie down with him in   　　but soon it will turn to dust.
　　the dust.

His bones are full of youthful vigor: verse 11 says that the wicked person will
die prematurely, before he is very old. RSV translates **are full of** in the present tense,
but TEV "used to be" is past tense. It is not certain from the Hebrew which the
author had in mind, but either is appropriate. **Bones** is used as a part representing
the whole, referring to his body. **Youthful vigor** means that his body is still strong
and young, not having grown old and weak. This line may also be expressed, for
example, "Although he is still young in his body," "Although his body is still young
and strong," or "While he still has the strength of his youth."

But it will lie down with him in the dust: in the poetic expression it is his
youthful vigor that will **lie down**, be buried with him. Since these are physical
qualities that do not of themselves **lie down**, some translators will have to express
the thought differently; for example, SPCL says "In full vigor and youth he will go
down to the grave." If the translator has used a dependent clause in the first line, this
line will complete the thought; for example, "he will be buried," "they will put him
in his grave," or "he will die and be buried."

4E-3. Zophar compares evil to food eaten by the wicked (20.12-22)

　　　　　　　　RSV   TEV

12　"Though wickedness is sweet in his   12-13　Evil tastes so good to him
　　　　mouth,   that he keeps some in his mouth to
　　　though he hides it under his tongue,   enjoy its flavor.
13　though he is loath to let it go,   14　But in his stomach the food turns bitter,
　　and holds it in his mouth,   as bitter as any poison could be.
14　yet his food is turned in his stomach;   15　The wicked man vomits up the wealth he
　　it is the gall of asps within him.   stole;
15　He swallows down riches and vomits them   God takes it back, even out of his
　　up again;   stomach.
　　God casts them out of his belly.   16　What the evil man swallows is like poison;
16　He will suck the poison of asps;   it kills him like the bite of a deadly
　　the tongue of a viper will kill him.   snake.
17　He will not look upon the rivers,   17　He will not live to see rivers of olive oil
　　the streams flowing with honey and   or streams that flow with milk and
　　curds.   honey.
18　He will give back the fruit of his toil,   18　He will have to give up all he has worked
　　and will not swallow it down;   for;
　　from the profit of his trading   he will have no chance to enjoy his
　　he will get no enjoyment.   wealth,
19　For he has crushed and abandoned the   19　because he oppressed and neglected
　　poor,   the poor
　　he has seized a house which he did not   and seized houses someone else had
　　build.   built.
　　　　　　　　　　　　　　　　　　　　　　　20　His greed is never satisfied.

20	"Because his greed knew no rest, he will not save anything in which he delights.	21	When he eats, there is nothing left over, but now his prosperity comes to an end.
21	There was nothing left after he had eaten; therefore his prosperity will not endure.	22	At the height of his success all the weight of misery will crush him.
22	In the fulness of his sufficiency he will be in straits; all the force of misery will come upon him.		

Subdivision Heading

The Handbook heading may be adapted to say, for example, "Zophar says that evil tastes good to the wicked," "For the wicked, doing bad things is like eating good food," "The evil a person does will turn sour," or "Evil tastes good, but goes bad." Habel has "The poisonous food of the wicked."

20.12-14   RSV   TEV

12 "Though wickedness is sweet in his mouth, though he hides it under his tongue, 13 though he is loath to let it go, and holds it in his mouth, 14 yet his food is turned in his stomach; it is the gall of asps within him.	12-13 Evil tastes so good to him that he keeps some in his mouth to enjoy its flavor. 14 But in his stomach the food turns bitter, as bitter as any poison could be.

Verse 12 begins Zophar's portrayal of the ways in which the wicked is paid back for his sins. Verses 12 and 13 describe a condition whose consequences are seen in verse 14. These three verses form one long sentence in Hebrew.

Though wickedness is sweet in his mouth: here the poet depicts the wicked man making the enjoyment of sin last as long as possible and getting out of it everything he can. The imagery is that of a sweet taste in the mouth. In languages in which an abstract quality like **wickedness** cannot be said to be **sweet**, it will often be necessary to express the thought in the form of a simile; for example, "Although doing evil things may be like sugar in a person's mouth . . ." or "Even though doing evil is like having sugar in his mouth." In some languages it will not be advisable to have a string of concessive clauses as in verses 12 and 13. These may be expressed as statements.

Though he hides it under his tongue: the purpose of putting the sweet object under the tongue is to make it last and so keep the taste of sweetness lingering in the mouth. This line may be rendered, for example, "even if he keeps the sweetness hidden under his tongue" or "even if he prolongs the sweetness by putting it under his tongue."

Though he is loath to let it go: verse 13 expresses the purpose of verse 12b, and TEV accordingly reduces these two lines to one, "that he keeps . . . flavor," and joins verse 13 with verse 12.

And holds it in his mouth: FRCL has not condensed these lines like TEV, and for translators who are able to preserve them meaningfully, this translation offers a good model:

> 12 In his mouth evil is sweet like candy,
>   and he slips it beneath his tongue.
> 13 He holds it there for a long time, he does not let it go,
>   prolonging the pleasure of its flavor.

Yet his food is turned in his stomach: the conclusion of this pleasurable savoring of sweetness is that it turns bitter and even poisonous. **Turned** was used in 19.19, where it referred to "turning against Job." Here it is used of food that goes bad, becomes sour and indigestible, or, as TEV, "But in his stomach the food turns bitter." It may be necessary to adjust verse 14a to show how it is linked with verses 12 and 13; for example, "Yet when the sweetness reaches his stomach" or "However, when he swallows the sweetness."

It is the gall of asps within him: the ancient view was that the gall bladder of snakes secreted poison, and consequently **gall of asps** means "snake poison." The word translated **asps** refers to a poisonous snake, but not exclusively to the **asp**. **Within him** is literally "in his intestines." TEV "as bitter as any poison could be" is somewhat misleading. This line is an excellent example of raising poetic intensity of a general word in line a through the use of a more specific term in line b. In this way **his food** in line a is bitter in his stomach, but in line b it is more than bitter; it is poison in him. The conclusion of verse 14 may be expressed, for example, "it becomes like snake poison inside him" or "it is as deadly as snake venom in his intestines."

20.15   RSV   TEV

> He swallows down riches and   The wicked man vomits up the
>   vomits them up again;   wealth he stole;
> God casts them out of his   God takes it back, even out of
>   belly.   his stomach.

He swallows down riches and vomits them up again: in verses 12-14 it was wickedness that lay behind the image of sweetness in the mouth. In verse 15 it is **riches**, which may be taken as the ill-gotten gain in verse 10. **Swallows down riches** is a figure for getting wealth through dishonesty, corrupt dealings or, as TEV says, "The wealth he stole." He is forced to **vomit** it; that is, he cannot keep it and enjoy it, but it is forced abruptly from him. In many languages the figure of swallowing riches and vomiting them conveys clearly the poetic intention. In other languages some adjustments may be required; for example, "He is dishonest and steals people's wealth, but he has to give it up" or "Being corrupt he steals money from people, but he cannot hold on to it."

God casts them out of his belly: here it is God himself who is said to be the cause for him to vomit up his riches. This recalls Jeremiah 51.44 "And I will punish Bel in Babylon, and take out of his mouth what he has swallowed." TEV makes more definite the way in which God acts in this line: "God takes it (the riches) back, even out of his stomach." This may also be rendered, for example, "it is God who makes him vomit them up" or "God is the one who takes riches away from him."

20.16	RSV	TEV

He will suck the poison of asps; the tongue of a viper will kill him.	What the evil man swallows is like poison; it kills him like the bite of a deadly snake.

He will suck the poison of asps: in verse 12 the wicked hid his wickedness under his tongue in order to taste it and prolong its sweetness. In 16, instead of sweetness he finds himself sucking out the flavor of snake poison, or more poetically "serpent venom." Because verse 16 seems more closely related to verse 14, some editors have suggested it was originally a marginal comment on that verse. Consequently Mft places verse 16 immediately after verse 14 and places 16b before 16a. Such textual revisions are not necessary, as the sense is clear as it stands in the Hebrew. This line may be rendered, for example, "He has been sucking the poison of snakes" or "What he has been sucking is snake poison."

The tongue of a viper will kill him: it is not the tongue as such that causes death. **Tongue of a viper** is parallel to **poison of asps** in the previous line. Therefore it is the **poison** symbolized by the **tongue** that kills. In translation it may be difficult to make this point clear without some adjustment such as TEV "it (the poison) kills him like the bite of a deadly snake." GECL translates verse 16 "What he has swallowed (his riches) works on him like poison; it is as deadly as the bite of a viper." **Viper** occurs elsewhere only in Isaiah 30.6; 59.5, where TEV translates "poisonous snake." The exact meaning of the Hebrew word translated **viper** is uncertain, and a generic term for "deadly snake" such as in TEV may be adequate. Translators may use a term for **viper** that is the most deadly among known poisonous snakes. The line may be rendered, for example, "the bite of the viper will kill him" or "it is the snake poison that will kill him."

20.17	RSV	TEV

He will not look upon the rivers, the streams flowing with honey and curds.	He will not live to see rivers of olive oil[r] or streams that flow with milk and honey.

[r] *Probable text* He will . . . oil; *Hebrew unclear.*

He will not look upon the rivers, the streams . . . : this verse is difficult to understand. **He will not look upon** is generally agreed to mean "He will not live to see." However, the preposition which follows the word translated **look** gives the sense of seeing with pleasure or satisfaction, so SPCL has "He will not be able to enjoy," which can also be translated "He will not live to enjoy." The word translated **rivers** is a rare word in Hebrew and is followed by the more familiar word for river translated **streams** in RSV. Some scholars believe that the common word was inserted later to explain the meaning of the less common word. Consequently some suggest a change in **streams** to get "oil," which TEV translates as "olive oil." TEV appears to have used **streams** twice, once as "olive oil" and once as "streams," in order to get a better set of parallel lines. The figure "rivers of olive oil" would refer to great wealth and blessings. NEB, following the Septuagint, translates "rivers of cream." The wicked will not be able to share in this blessing, and the first line may also be rendered, for example, "He will not have a part in rivers that flow with oil" or, if this is unclear, "He will not share in the blessings of prosperity" or "He will not receive the wealth and blessings God gives his people."

Streams flowing with honey and curds: in Isaiah 7.15 the order is "curds and honey." **Curds** refers to the coagulated or thickened milk for making cheese. It was much valued as a refreshment, as in Judges 5.25. "Milk," "butter," "cream," and "curds" are all used to translate the Hebrew word. In Exodus 3.8 God spoke to Moses and told him that he had come to deliver the Hebrews out of Egypt to a land "flowing with milk and honey." There again the order is the reverse of that in our verse. This phrase is another figure of prosperity and well-being. In some languages it may be necessary to adjust this line to say, for example, "and the vast amounts of honey and milk that God gives his people." If these figures must be set aside, the translator may say, for example, "He will not see prosperity flowing like a river" or "He will not see the blessings from God that are as plentiful as a river full of water."

20.18-19   RSV   TEV

18   He will give back the fruit of his toil,
     and will not swallow it down;
     from the profit of his trading
     he will get no enjoyment.
	18 He will have to give up all he has worked for;
	     he will have no chance to enjoy his wealth,

19   For he has crushed and abandoned the poor,
     he has seized a house which he did not build.
	19 because he oppressed and neglected the poor
	     and seized houses someone else had built.

Verse 18 describes the misfortune of the wicked person, and verse 19 gives the reason for his disaster. These two verses are linked in Hebrew by the connective meaning "because." In some languages it may be necessary to transpose verses 18 and 19 so that the reason clauses of verse 19 come before the consequences of verse 18.

He will give back the fruit of his toil: verse 18 is similar in meaning to verse 15, whose thought is giving back his wrongly acquired wealth to the poor. The noun translated **fruit of his toil** is not found elsewhere, but the verb form meaning "to toil or labor" gives another noun form in 10.3 rendered "the work of thy hands." The parallelism in the second line **profit of his trading** gives **fruit of his toil** the more specific meaning of "gains, profits, acquisitions," which is more specific than TEV "all he has worked for." This first line may be translated "He has to give back all he has gained" or "He has to return all the money he has acquired."

    And will not swallow it down: swallow translates the same verb used in verse 15. Here **swallow** is again used figuratively. TEV considers **not swallow** to repeat **give back** and does not translate it separately: "He will have to give up all he has worked for." NEB and others keep **swallow**, but do not give it a clear sense, "He must give back his gains without swallowing them." FRCL is clearer: "He will give back his gains before being able to use them." This gives a good model for translation.

    From the profit of his trading he will get no enjoyment: from the profit is based on a change in the Hebrew text. Otherwise the text would mean "according to the profit," which does not seem to make sense. **Trading** or "exchange" presupposes that the wicked person has been engaged in business, but even here he will not be able to enjoy the wealth he acquired from it. These lines may also be expressed, for example, "he will have no happiness from the wealth he has earned" or "the money he has earned from his business will give him no joy."

    For he has crushed and abandoned the poor: although interpreters have suggested various changes in this first line of verse 19, the Hebrew is not obscure. The wicked man has done two things to the poor: "oppressed" and "neglected" them, as in TEV, and this is the reason why he has to do the things required in verse 18. In some languages it may be necessary to adjust the reason clause of verse 19 by saying, for example, "The reason is that he has done nothing to help the poor and has treated them badly" or "Because he has treated the poor badly and paid no attention to their needs."

    He has seized a house which he did not build: the sense here is "he has taken over houses instead of building them." Hebrew speaks in the singular, as in RSV. FRCL refers to the house of the poor in the previous line: "He has seized their house instead of building them one." However, this appears to be the wicked person's regular practice and not an individual case. TEV and others therefore shift to the plural: "and seized houses someone else (not necessarily the poor) had built." This line may also be expressed, for example, "he has also taken people's houses away from them" or "he has also put people out of their own houses."

    It was suggested above that it may be more natural in some languages to switch verses 18 and 19 so that the reason the wicked person will have to give up his wealth is stated first. We may translate, for example, "[18] Because he has done nothing to help the poor, has treated them badly, and has thrown people out of their homes, [19] he will have to give back all the money he has obtained before he ever has a chance to benefit from it."

20.20-21	RSV		TEV
20	"Because his greed knew no rest,	20	His greed is never satisfied.
	he will not save anything in	21	When he eats, there is nothing

which he delights.	left over,
21 There was nothing left after he	but now his prosperity comes
had eaten;	to an end.
therefore his prosperity will	
not endure.	

These two verses are treated together, since they use the same imagery and express the same thought. However, translators relate them in various ways.

Because his greed knew no rest is literally "He knew no quietness in his belly." In RSV line a is the cause and line b the consequence. NEB, on the other hand, takes the whole of verse 20 as the cause, with the result or effect set out in verse 21. From the Hebrew it is not clear whether the greed of the man is the cause of his inability to save what he enjoys, as in RSV, or whether the relationship between the lines is to be taken as in NEB. TEV seems to agree with NEB. However, TEV has condensed the two lines of verse 20 into one. This line is idiomatic; "to know no quietness in the belly" is the equivalent of saying "his insides are never at ease," that is, "he is always gluttonous, greedy, piggish." This line may be rendered, for example, "His appetite is never satisfied," "He can never get enough," or "He always wants more than he gets."

He will not save anything in which he delights is literally "He will not cause his valued things to escape." This line has been given many interpretations. The most probable is that, due to his greed in the previous line, he goes too far and in the end has nothing left. RSV's meaning is appropriate. The whole of verse 20 may be rendered "Because of his greed he is unable to save any of his treasured belongings" or "He is so greedy he cannot save any of the things he likes."

Verse 21 repeats in different words the thought expressed in verse 20. **There was nothing left after he had eaten** is literally "There is no survivor from his eating." **Nothing left** translates the same Hebrew word which RSV renders "survivor" in 18.19. It is not food that he devours, but the poor. TEV keeps only the image of food with "When he eats there is nothing left over," which depicts a gluttonous person at his food. NIV improves on this: "Nothing is left for him to devour." SPCL improves on that again: "Nothing escapes his voracity" (gluttonous appetite). FRCL is still better: "No one escapes his voracity." This line may also be rendered, for example, "He is so greedy that nobody can escape him" or "He wants everything, and so he catches everybody." In some languages we may say idiomatically, "He is greedy and eats everybody," or "He is so greedy he doesn't stop until he has eaten up everybody."

Therefore his prosperity will not endure: this line expresses the final condition of the prosperity of the wicked. The word translated **prosperity** is taken by some translators in the sense of "well-being, happiness." In 21.16, where RSV translates the same word as "prosperity," TEV shifts to the verb form, "succeed." This line may also be expressed "his happiness will not last," "he is not happy long," or "his well-being soon comes to an end."

20.22
RSV   TEV

> In the fulness of his sufficiency
>   he will be in straits;
> all the force of misery will
>   come upon him.

> At the height of his success
>   all the weight of misery will
>   crush him.

In the fulness of his sufficiency he will be in straits: the wicked man is now said to be in trouble "at the height of his success, wealth." He cannot find satisfaction no matter how much he succeeds nor how much wealth he obtains. It is not the absence of satisfaction that strikes him, but more actively, "anguish takes hold of, seizes him." This line may be rendered, for example, "When he has acquired everything he is full of trouble," "No matter how much wealth he has, he is never happy," or "Even though he succeeds in all he does, anguish gets him down."

All the force of misery will come upon him is literally "Every hand of the unfortunate will come on him." The Septuagint and Vulgate make a change in the text to get the rendering of RSV. **Force of misery** translates the Hebrew "hand of the unfortunate," which implies striking a blow. In figurative terms "misery strikes him down," or "all the weight of misery will crush him" (TEV). In some languages the line may have to be restructured to say "misery will grab him like a person grabs something with his hand," or without the figure, "he will suffer greatly."

4E-4. Zophar describes disasters that happen to the wicked (20.23-29)

RSV   TEV

23 To fill his belly to the full
    God will send his fierce anger into
      him,
    and rain it upon him as his food.
24 He will flee from an iron weapon;
    a bronze arrow will strike him through.
25 It is drawn forth and comes out of his
      body,
    the glittering point comes out of his
      gall;
    terrors come upon him.
26 Utter darkness is laid up for his treasures;
    a fire not blown upon will devour him;
    what is left in his tent will be con-
      sumed.
27 The heavens will reveal his iniquity,
    and the earth will rise up against him.
28 The possessions of his house will be car-
      ried away,
    dragged off in the day of God's wrath.
29 This is the wicked man's portion from
      God,
    the heritage decreed for him by God."

23 Let him eat all he wants!
    God will punish him in fury and anger.
24 When he tries to escape from an iron
      sword,
    a bronze bow will shoot him down.
25 An arrow sticks through his body;
    its shiny point drips with his blood,
    and terror grips his heart.
26 Everything he has saved is destroyed;
    a fire not lit by human hands
    burns him and all his family.
27 Heaven reveals this man's sin,
    and the earth gives testimony against
      him.
28 All his wealth will be destroyed
    in the flood of God's anger.
29 This is the fate of wicked men,
    the fate that God assigns to them.

Subdivision Heading

The Handbook heading may be modified to say, for example, "Zophar tells how God punishes the wicked," "God's anger will destroy the evil person," or "The wicked person and his family will be destroyed." Rowley has "The swift stroke of God upon the wicked," and Habel "The disasters prepared for the wicked."

20.23   RSV   TEV

To fill his belly to the full
   God[z] will send his fierce anger
     into him,
   and rain it upon him as his
     food.[a]
	Let him eat all he wants!
	   God will punish him in fury
	     and anger.

[z] Heb *he*
[a] Cn: Heb *in his flesh*

Verse 23 has three lines, but TEV has merged the second and third lines. The figure of eating continues in this verse.

To fill his belly to the full: this line is omitted by the Septuagint and also by NJB and NEB. The meaning of the line is not very clear. Dhorme understands it to carry the same thought as the preceding verses; that is, in the moment when the wicked man is filling his belly (taking from the poor), God will strike him down. So Dhorme translates "When he is occupied in filling his belly." TEV "Let him eat all he wants" interprets **belly** to refer to literal eating, and this is what most translators understand here.

The second line, **God will send his fierce anger into him**, is literally "He will send . . . ." Nearly all interpreters agree that "he" refers to God, and so TEV "God will punish him in fury and anger" is a good rendering. This line may also be rendered "God will be angry and make him suffer" or "God will angrily punish him."

The third line, **and rain it upon him as his food**, is more problematical. The RSV footnote says "in his flesh," which is the Hebrew text. The expression "in his flesh" as used here is found elsewhere only in Zephaniah 1.17, where RSV translates "flesh" and TEV "dead bodies." RSV **food** is obtained by reading a closely similar Hebrew word meaning "bread." Although many changes have been proposed, that of RSV involves the slightest change in the Hebrew and gives a satisfactory sense in the context. TEV considers line c as saying the same thing as line b and so does not translate it again. This line may also be expressed "and God will cause his anger to come down on him as the food he eats," or "God's anger will pour down on him and be his food," or "he will have God's anger for his food."

20.24   RSV   TEV

He will flee from an iron weapon;
   a bronze arrow will strike him
     through.
	When he tries to escape from an
	   iron sword,

> **a bronze bow will shoot him
> down.**

He will flee from an iron weapon: translators differ in the way they relate the two lines of this verse to each other. TEV and others make line <u>a</u> a dependent clause, "When he tries to escape . . . ," "If he flees . . ." (Dhorme). RSV and others form two parallel clauses. Both approaches are possible. TEV follows the pattern found for the same idea expressed in Amos 5.19. **Iron weapon** is a weapon made of iron. Dhorme takes the word translated **weapon** to mean "armor of iron," but "weapon" suits the context better. This line may also be rendered, for example, "He will run away to escape being wounded by an iron weapon," "If he runs away to escape being struck down by an iron weapon," or "He will run away to avoid being wounded by a soldier using an iron weapon."

A bronze arrow will strike him through: the Hebrew has "bow of bronze," but bows are not made of bronze, and a bronze bow would not shoot an arrow. (See 40.18 for a comment on **bronze**.) **Bow of bronze** is also used in Psalm 18.34. The poet attributes to the **bow** the effect which is produced by the arrow. RSV has shifted to **bronze arrow**, but TEV has kept "bronze bow." FRCL translates "a bronze point," that is, "a bronze arrowhead." This line may need to be adjusted as in the case of **iron weapon** to say, for example, "an arrow with a bronze point will hit him" or "an enemy will shoot an arrow with a bronze point into him." If **bronze** is unknown, the translator may say "iron" or "metal."

20.25	RSV	TEV

It is drawn forth and comes out	An arrow sticks through his
of his body,	body;
the glittering point comes out	its shiny point drips with his
of his gall;	blood,
terrors come upon him.	and terror grips his heart.

It is drawn forth and comes out of his body is literally "One draws it comes out of his back." Many interpreters suggest changing the word translated **drawn forth** to get "arrow shaft" and translate "And a shaft (of an arrow) comes out of his back." The picture is the arrow penetrating completely through his body. This is followed by TEV "An arrow sticks through his body" and is preferred.

The glittering point comes out of his gall: glittering point translates the Hebrew for "lightning," and in Deuteronomy 32.41 it is translated by TEV as "flashing sword," and in Habakkuk 3.11 "shining spear." The word here is in parallel with "arrow shaft" in the previous line. In Assyrian the cognate term designated the bolts of lightning with which the storm god was armed. TEV "shining point" refers to the bronze point of the arrow shaft. **Comes out of his gall** is the poet's way of fixing the position where the arrow point sticks out of his body. FRCL makes it a bit more general with "liver." Mft is more general still with "entrails." TEV and GECL are less specific but more graphic, with "drips with his blood." This line may be rendered, for example, "the shining arrow point sticks out of his gall bladder." If this picture is not clear, the translator may adjust it to say, for example, "the arrow point that pierced his body passes through his liver."

Terrors come upon him: the result of seeing the bloodied arrow piercing his body brings **terror** as he begins to faint and die. This line may also be expressed, for example, "he is in terror," "he is afraid," or idiomatically in some languages, "fear has taken hold of him," or "everywhere he smells fear."

20.26	RSV	TEV

RSV	TEV

Utter darkness is laid up for his treasures;
   a fire not blown upon will devour him;
 what is left in his tent will be consumed.
	Everything he has saved is destroyed;
	   a fire not lit by human hands burns him and all his family.

Utter darkness is laid up for his treasures is literally "All darkness is hidden for his laid up things." Dhorme takes "hidden" to mean "reserved, destined for," and translates "Thick darkness is reserved for him." FRCL follows this with "It is the night that is kept for his fate," as does Mft, "Deep darkness is his doom." HOTTP suggests "All darkness is hidden as a thing reserved for him." NEB follows the Septuagint, "Darkness unrelieved awaits him." TEV follows RSV but attempts to give it a clearer meaning: "Everything he has saved is destroyed." From the wider context it would appear that **darkness** here refers to death, but when applied to his possessions it is their destruction. This line may also be expressed, for example, "His possessions are destroyed" or "They take his wealth from him and destroy it."

A fire not blown upon will devour him: this is a fire which has not been kindled by a person blowing on it to get it started. It is a negative way of saying "a divine fire" or "a fire sent by God," as in Numbers 16.35; 26.10. FRCL calls it "a supernatural fire." A footnote in FRCL clarifies that this is "a fire not lit by human hands," and this is also the translation given by TEV. The translator may keep the indirect association with God's action by translating, for example, "A fire that was not started by a human being will burn him up" or "A fire that does not need to be kindled by someone will eat him." An NJB note has "thunderbolt."

What is left in his tent will be consumed: what is left translates the word used in 18.19; 20.21, with the meaning "survivor," and it is used in a similar sense here. Obviously they are not "survivors" after they have been consumed by the fire. They were the ones who "lived in his tent, his home," the ones TEV calls "all his family."

20.27	RSV	TEV

RSV	TEV

The heavens will reveal his iniquity,
   and the earth will rise up against him.
	Heaven reveals this man's sin,
	   and the earth gives testimony against him.

The heavens will reveal his iniquity: Dhorme considers verses 27 and 29 to form the conclusion of Zophar's speech and so transposes verses 28 and 27. Through the use of **heavens** in line a and **earth** in line b, the poet asserts that the whole universe condemns the wicked man. In 16.18-19 Job called upon the witnesses of heaven and earth. For a similar idea of the participation of heaven and earth in legal dispute, compare Deuteronomy 32.1; Isaiah 1.2; Micah 6.1-2. In some languages it is not possible to say that **the heavens** can **reveal** something. In such cases it may be possible to express verse 27a as a simile; for example, "The heavens will be like a witness and shout that he is guilty" or "The heavens will be like a witness against him and shout 'You are wicked!'"

And the earth will rise up against him is probably to be taken in the legal sense of taking the witness stand to testify against someone, and so TEV "earth gives testimony against him," and NEB "And earth will rise up to condemn him." The line may be expressed "Even the earth will be like a witness who stands up to testify against him," or "The earth will be like a witness in court and will say 'You are guilty!'"

20.28	RSV	TEV
	The possessions of his house will be carried away, dragged off in the day of God's[b] wrath.	All his wealth will be destroyed in the flood of God's anger.

[b] Heb *his*

The possessions of his house will be carried away: **possessions** translates a noun which elsewhere always means "produce of the earth" or "fruit of the soil." In Hebrew "the fruits of his house" may refer to "his wealth," as in TEV, or to his possessions generally, as in RSV. Another interpretation is arrived at by changing **possessions** to "flood." This is based on equating the word translated **possessions** here with a similar word in Isaiah 30.25 translated "brooks running with water" (RSV) and "streams of water" (TEV). "Flood" gives a sense that is more suitable in the context, so that the line will say "A flood will carry away his house." **Carried away** translates a verb meaning "go into exile." Some interpreters change the vowels of this verb to get the word "roll," and so NEB and others "A flood will sweep away his house." If the translator follows the change to "flood," this line may be rendered, for example, "A flood will carry off his goods" or "A flood will wash away his house."

Dragged off in the day of God's wrath: some scholars derive this verb from a root meaning "drag away," but others base it on a root meaning "pour out." Therefore Dhorme translates "waters which flow," and Pope "torrents." **God's wrath** is "his wrath" in the Hebrew, but, as in verse 23b, nearly all agree that God is the agent of the action. The expression **God's wrath** refers to divine retribution, that is, God punishing someone. Therefore **wrath**, meaning anger, fury, portrays God as furiously punishing someone as he judges them. **Day of God's wrath** refers to the time when God judges, and so the line may be rendered "when God in his anger judges sinners." We may also translate verse 28 "A flood will wash away his house on the day when God angrily judges sinners."

20.29   RSV   TEV

> This is the wicked man's portion   This is the fate of wicked men,
>   from God,   the fate that God assigns to
>   the heritage decreed for him   them.
>   by God."

Verse 29 is a summary conclusion of Zophar's speech, in which the things said about the wicked man are the things he can expect to receive from God. In a similar vein Eliphaz summarized his conclusions in 5.27, and Bildad also, in 18.21.

This is the wicked man's portion: this line refers to all that Zophar has said to depict the fate of the wicked. **Portion** translates the same word found in 27.13; 31.2, and refers to the "fate, doom, lot" of the wicked. It is what will happen to them because of their wickedness, their inevitable end. **Portion** often refers to family property, land, that is passed on to the next generation as an inheritance. Thus the image of fate or doom is expressed in terms of inheritance, but that figure is limited because it does not assume that God dies to make it become effective. SPCL says "This is what God has destined for the wicked person," Mft "This is what God bestows upon a sinner," NEB "Such is God's reward for the wicked man." **Wicked man** is singular in Hebrew, but the reference is collective, and so TEV "wicked men." This line may also be rendered, for example, "This is how wicked people come to their end" or "This is the way God judges sinners."

The heritage decreed for him by God: heritage is parallel to **portion** in the previous line and also refers to a kind of inheritance, whether land or other possessions. **Decreed for him by God** means that God gives to the wicked this fate or doom. If the lines are to be kept parallel, some form of "wicked person" must be supplied in the second line: TEV "them" and RSV **him.** Line b expands line a only slightly, and it may be expressed, for example, "it is the fate that God has decided for him" or "this is the doom (bad ending) that God has arranged for them" (sinners).

4F. JOB REPLIES (21.1-34)

Chapter 21 marks the closure of the second cycle of speeches. This means that each speaker has now spoken twice. In this chapter Job replies to the friends about the fate of the wicked, which has been a major topic discussed by all three friends: Eliphaz (15.20-30); Bildad (18.5-21); and Zophar (20.5-29). In their speeches they have used words which they have heard Job use, and have implied that Job is one of the wicked, the people who are doomed. In Job's previous speeches (chapters 16, 17, and 19) he concentrated his attention on his argument with God and his determination to get a fair hearing that would show him to be innocent of wrong-doing. However, in chapter 21 Job shifts the focus of his attention to the assertions of the friends and argues against their teaching. He does this by appealing to the evidence around him, and claims that wicked individuals, instead of suffering the doom the friends claim they must suffer, live happily and die in peace and prosperity.

Job's presentation consists of an introduction (verses 2-6) and three major sections. In the first part (verses 7-16) Job depicts the general happiness of the wicked as secure, surrounded by happy, playing children, and as prosperous, and still they have no use for God. In the second section (verses 17-26) Job draws attention to the lack of suffering among the wicked. He refutes the idea that the sons of the wicked father are caused to suffer, and instead insists that wicked people must suffer for their own sins. The rich dies in his riches and the poor in his poverty, and that is their common end. In the final section (verses 27-34) Job's observations are said to be confirmed by practical experience, by people who travel widely. Without suffering or being punished, the wicked is carried off to his burial, where he is buried in pomp and glory. Job concludes, therefore, that the friends offer him no comfort at all with their hollow and meaningless answers to his problem.

Division Heading

Translators may use the Handbook heading or adapt it by saying, for example, "Job speaks back to Zophar," "Job argues with Zophar," or "Job tells Zophar what he thinks." Some translations that have only a division heading are: GECL "Job: Indeed God lets the wicked go unpunished!" and FRCL "Job's response: the happiness of the wicked is a fact."

4F-1. Job asks his friends to listen to him (21.1-6)

RSV		TEV	
	1 Then Job answered:	*Job*	
2	"Listen carefully to my words, and let this be your consolation.	1-2	Listen to what I am saying; that is all the comfort I ask from you.
3	Bear with me, and I will speak, and after I have spoken, mock on.	3	Give me a chance to speak and then, when I am through, sneer if you like.
4	As for me, is my complaint against man? Why should I not be impatient?	4	My quarrel is not with mortal men; I have good reason to be impatient.
5	Look at me, and be appalled, and lay your hand upon your mouth.	5	Look at me. Isn't that enough to make you stare in shocked silence?
6	When I think of it I am dismayed, and shuddering seizes my flesh.	6	When I think of what has happened to me, I am stunned, and I tremble and shake.

Subdivision Heading

The Handbook heading may be modified to say, for example, "Job asks Zophar to listen," "Job demands attention," or "Listen to what I have to say." Rowley has "Job appeals for a hearing," and TOB "The courage of truth."

21.1   RSV   TEV

Then Job answered: *Job*

Then Job answered: see 4.1 for a discussion of **answered**.

21.2	RSV	TEV

RSV	TEV
"Listen carefully to my words, and let this be your consolation.	Listen to what I am saying; that is all the comfort I ask from you.

Job appeals for the close attention of the friends. **Listen carefully to my words:** see the comments on 13.17, where Job used the same words.

And let this be your consolation: RSV is misleading in its wording, which sounds as if Job is giving consolation to the friends. **Your consolation** means "the consolation or comfort which you give me." In 15.11 Eliphaz claimed to offer Job "the consolations of God." Job has received no comfort from the friends, but if they will only listen to him, by doing so they will be able to comfort him. This verse may be rendered "Please listen carefully to what I have to say; this is the only comfort I expect from you," or idiomatically sometimes, "Open your ears for me; then you will be able to help me."

21.3	RSV	TEV

RSV	TEV
Bear with me, and I will speak, and after I have spoken, mock on.	Give me a chance to speak and then, when I am through, sneer if you like.

Bear with me, and I will speak: **Bear with me** translates a verb meaning "tolerate, endure, have patience." In 7.21 it was used to translate "pardon." Mft translates it "pray let me . . . ," NJB "Permit me." The element of politeness is somewhat lowered in TEV, "Give me a chance." In Hebrew Job addresses the friends in the plural. This line may also be expressed, for example, "Have patience and I will tell you something," or idiomatically sometimes, "Let your hearts rest cool and I will talk to you."

And after I have spoken, mock on: **mock** is the same root used in 9.23; 11.3; 22.19. Here Job switches to the singular as if addressing Zophar, who was the last to speak. However, many scholars understand him to be speaking to all three, as in the previous line, and so translate in the plural. English does not make an obligatory distinction between singular and plural in the pronoun and verb. **Mock on** or "go ahead and mock me," ". . . and make fun of me," ". . . and laugh at me," or ". . . and ridicule me."

21.4	RSV	TEV

RSV	TEV
As for me, is my complaint against man?	My quarrel is not with mortal men;

Why should I not be impatient?	I have good reason to be impatient.

As for me, is my complaint against man? This question implies that Job's complaint is not with men but with God, and so assumes a negative reply. The Hebrew favors a question, as in FRCL "Is it against a man that I myself complain? No!" TEV translates this line as a negative statement: "My quarrel is not with mortal men." **Complaint** is used in 10.1, where TEV translates "complaint" and not "quarrel," as it does here. This line may be rendered, for example, "I have no complaint against people," "My quarrel is not with people," or "Do I complain against people? Of course not."

Why should I not be impatient? is literally "And why should not my *ruach* ('spirit, breath') be short?" The word which introduces the question has the meaning "and if that is so" or "and in that case." SPCL translates "because of this," and FRCL "why therefore." Shortness of *ruach* is a Hebrew idiom which means to be impatient. Translators may find it better to shift this line to a positive statement: "I have a right to be impatient." In some languages **impatient** is expressed figuratively; for example, "I have good reason to have boiling insides" or "I am right to have hot kidneys."

21.5 RSV TEV

Look at me, and be appalled, and lay your hand upon your mouth.	Look at me. Isn't that enough to make you stare in shocked silence?

Look at me and be appalled: in this verse Job gives three commands translated **Look, be appalled,** and **lay.** RSV fails to relate these verbs in a stylistically appropriate manner for English. TEV "Isn't that enough to make you . . ." improves the style considerably. Job is not asking the friends to **be appalled** by looking at his physical appearance. Rather he is asking them to get ready to hear something that will appall, amaze, astound, surprise, them, and will cause them to become silent. Instead of drawing attention to his diseased body, he is asking them to look at his particular story, his situation, or as FRCL says, "Be sensitive to my case; you'll be amazed." NJB has "Give your attention to me; you will be dumbfounded." This line may also be rendered, for example, "Think about what has happened to me, and you'll be amazed," "Consider my situation and let it grasp you," or idiomatically, "Let what has happened to me stop your hearts."

And lay your hand upon your mouth: Job's experience so completely contradicts the pious teaching of the friends that, if they will hear him out, they will, as TEV says, "stare in shocked silence." Laying the hand over the mouth is a gesture of silent amazement which has been found depicted in archaeological objects from Mesopotamia; see Pope. Verse 5 may be rendered, for example, "look at what has happened to me and let it stop your talking, let it make you put your hands over your mouths" or "Think how God has treated me; then you will be silently amazed and cover you mouths with your hands." In some languages putting the hand over the mouth means to speak with respect to a superior, and so the expression must be adjusted to say, for example, "be quiet," "don't speak any more." If the expression "put your hand over your mouth" implies speaking to someone secretly, it may be necessary to avoid the literal expression and translate something like "stop talking."

21.6	RSV	TEV

RSV	TEV

When I think of it I am dismayed,
    and shuddering seizes my
    flesh.
	When I think of what has happened to me,
	I am stunned, and I tremble
	    and shake.

When I think of it I am dismayed: the first word in this line in Hebrew usually means "if," but it can also mean **When** in the sense of "Whenever" or "Every time." **Think** translates the Hebrew for "remember, recall." In Hebrew there is no object equivalent to **it**; therefore it is not clear exactly what it is that Job remembers. It may refer, as in TEV, to what he has already suffered, or to the thoughts that will appear in the rest of the chapter. NEB and others avoid any reference to the past or present, with "when I stop to think . . . ." FRCL and GECL, like TEV, refer to Job's past sufferings. In 4.5 Eliphaz used the passive form of the verb translated **dismayed** to depict the attitude of Job in the face of misfortune. Here it means "to be terrified, frightened," or as in NEB, "to be filled with horror." In some languages it will be necessary to make clear what Job is thinking of, and TEV's rendering may serve as a guide; for example, "When I think how much I have suffered, it terrifies me" or "When I think about my troubles I am frightened."

And shuddering seizes my flesh: RSV gives a literal translation which expresses the correct thought. It means that the **flesh**, the "body," is caused to tremble. NJB has "my flesh creeps," which is a diminished kind of trembling. NEB "My whole body is convulsed" is a more accurate statement. This line may also be expressed "I tremble all over" or "my whole body shakes with fear."

4F-2. Job claims the wicked are happy (21.7-16)

	RSV		TEV

7	Why do the wicked live,
	    reach old age, and grow mighty in
	        power?
		7	Why does God let evil men live,
			    let them grow old and prosper?

8	Their children are established in their
	        presence,
	    and their offspring before their eyes.
		8	They have children and grandchildren,
			    and live to watch them all grow up.

9	Their houses are safe from fear,
	    and no rod of God is upon them.
		9	God does not bring disaster on their
			        homes;
			    they never have to live in terror.

10	Their bull breeds without fail;
	    their cow calves, and does not cast her
	        calf.
		10	Yes, all their cattle breed
			    and give birth without trouble.

11	They send forth their little ones like a
	        flock,
	    and their children dance.
		11	Their children run and play like lambs

12	They sing to the tambourine and the lyre,
	    and rejoice to the sound of the pipe.
		12	and dance to the music of harps and
			        flutes.

		13	They live out their lives in peace and quietly die without suffering.
		14	The wicked tell God to leave them alone;

13	They spend their days in prosperity, and in peace they go down to Sheol.
14	They say to God, 'Depart from us! We do not desire the knowledge of thy ways.
15	What is the Almighty, that we should serve him? And what profit do we get if we pray to him?'
16	Behold, is not their prosperity in their hand? The counsel of the wicked is far from me.

they don't want to know his will for their lives.
15 They think there is no need to serve God nor any advantage in praying to him.
16 They claim they succeed by their own strength, but their way of thinking I can't accept.

Job has completed his introductory words of appeal for attention and now shifts into the first major part of his speech on how the wicked prosper. This is the opposite of the assertion of the friends. The prosperity of the wicked is a problem which recurs many times in the Old Testament. See Jeremiah 12.1-2; Malachi 3.5; Psalm 73; Habakkuk 1.13.

Subdivision Heading

Translators using a heading at this point may wish to adjust the Handbook heading to say, for example, "God does not punish the wicked," "God lets the wicked live happy lives," or "Job argues that God takes care of the wicked." TOB (7-18) has "Success of the scoundrels," and Rowley "The wicked who renounce God prosper."

21.7	RSV	TEV

RSV	TEV
Why do the wicked live, reach old age, and grow mighty in power?	Why does God let evil men live, let them grow old and prosper?

Why do the wicked live: Job's question is in reply to Zophar's claim that the wicked die prematurely (20.11). Job sees that the wicked are still living on, not dying off, as the friends would have him believe. The first part of the question has the sense of "Why do the wicked go on living, keep on living (and not die out)?" In the light of the next line, NEB refers to living a long time: "Why do the wicked enjoy long life?" TEV and GECL introduce God into the question, although other modern translations do not. However, God is an actor in verses 9b, 14a, 15a, and 15b, and even more frequently in the second section. Consequently it is evident that God is implied in Job's speech, beginning with this verse: "Why does God let evil men live?" (TEV).

Reach old age, and grow mighty in power: not only do the wicked go on living instead of dying prematurely, but they **reach old age**; that is, they live to become old people, advanced in years. **Mighty in power** is taken by some to mean that they prosper in wealth, as suggested by TEV ". . . and prosper." Some take it to mean physical strength, which seems less likely. Others refer to a more abstract kind of power; for example, NJB "their power increasing with their age." Translators may take **mighty** in any of these senses; for example, "Why does God let evil people go on living, get old and powerful?" or "Why does God allow wicked people to get old and become rich?"

21.8   RSV   TEV

> Their children are established in   They have children and grand-
>   their presence,   children,
> and their offspring before their   and live to watch them all
>   eyes.   grow up.

Job again contradicts the claims made by the friends in 15.33; 18.19; 20.21. **Their children are established in their presence**: **children** translates the Hebrew for "seed," which usually means descendants in the general sense. The two terms translated **children** in line a and **offspring** in line b occur in parallel both here and in 5.25. They therefore refer to the same descendants. The general term is used in line a and the more specific one in line b. Various translations reproduce this kind of parallelism: NJB "posterity" and "offspring," FRCL "descendants" in line a and "grandchildren" in line b. **Established in their presence** translates an awkward Hebrew wording, literally "before their face with them." HOTTP, which gives the Hebrew text only a "D" rating, suggests "before their face" means "while they (the wicked) are still alive," and "with them" means "not separated from them." Dhorme takes "with them" to be an unnecessary repetition which adds no further meaning. RSV takes the double expression as alternative expressions which say the same thing, and so it has omitted "with them." **Established** translates the idea of being settled and secure. NEB translates "They live to see their children settled." TEV has reordered the components of verse 8, putting "children and grandchildren" together in the first line.

And their offspring before their eyes: they live to watch their children become settled. TEV has kept this line and incorporated **offspring** as "grandchildren" into line a. **Before their eyes** is parallel to **in their presence** in line a but is idiomatic in order to heighten the intensity of the first line. The thought may be expressed "They even live to see their grandchildren." TEV shifts **established in their presence** from line a to line b and translates "and live to watch them all grow up." If the translator wishes to retain the force of the parallelism, verse 8 may be rendered, for example, "They see their children settle down near them, and even live to watch their grandchildren grow up."

21.9   RSV   TEV

> Their houses are safe from fear,   God does not bring disaster on
>   and no rod of God is upon   their homes;
>   them.   they never have to live in ter-
>   ror.

Their houses are safe from fear: this line reflects the assurance Eliphaz gave to Job in 5.24, which depended on Job's acceptance of his misfortunes as divine punishment, "You will live in peace in your tent." Now, however, Job says the same thing of wicked people, without any conditions attached. These people live in their homes securely and without being afraid. In verse 8 the focus was on their children; in 9 it is on their homes; and in 10 it will be on their livestock. TEV has shifted God from line b into line a and translates the line negatively: "God does not bring disaster on their homes." However, line a in Hebrew emphasizes the positive aspect of dwelling securely. SPCL and others reflect the Hebrew better with "nothing threatens the peace of their homes." This line may also be rendered, for example, "They do not need to be afraid that someone will destroy their houses" or "They live in peace in their houses and are not afraid."

And no rod of God is upon them: in 9.34 Job complained that there was no one to remove the "rod of God" from him. **Rod of God** refers, as earlier, to divine punishment, and so "God does not punish them." NEB calls it "the rod of God's justice." Because the sense of the metaphor is apparent, FRCL translates "The rod of God never strikes them." The line may be translated, for example, "God does not use his rod to punish them," "God does not punish them," or "God's switch (cane, stick) is never used to punish them."

21.10   RSV   TEV

> Their bull breeds without fail;   Yes, all their cattle breed
>   their cow calves, and does not   and give birth without trouble.
>   cast her calf.

Fertility among livestock was considered a sign of God's blessing (Deut 28.11; Psa 144.13). **Their bull breeds without fail:** the Hebrew has "his bull," referring to any bull owned by the wicked person. The bull of the wicked man succeeds in fertilizing the cow at every attempt, and so the owner prospers. Although both **bull** and **cow** are singular, the sense is collective and some translators shift to the plural. The first half of each line in this verse is positive and the second half negative, giving a poetic balance to the verse. TEV reduces **bull** in line a and **cow** in line b to "their cattle," which has the effect of blurring the male and female contributions to the act of procreation. The language is starkly simple, but NEB has made it pompous: "Their bull mounts and fails not in its purpose." **Breeds** translates a verb meaning to mount a female animal in mating. In Hebrew no object is expressed since the cow is mentioned in line b. The negative verb translated **does not fail** refers to successful mating each time. The line may be rendered "Every time the bull mates with a cow, she gets pregnant," or "Each time the bull is put with the cows, all the cows conceive," or "The bull and the cow mate successfully every time."

Their cow calves, and does not cast her calf is also expressed "the cows of the wicked have their calves without miscarriage" or "their cows give birth and never miscarry."

21.11-12   RSV   TEV

11	They send forth their little ones like a flock, and their children dance.	11	Their children run and play like lambs
12	They sing to the tambourine and the lyre, and rejoice to the sound of the pipe.	12	and dance to the music of harps and flutes.

They send forth their little ones like a flock: each pair of lines in verses 11 and 12 is closely parallel in meaning; for this reason TEV reduces each verse to one line. Job depicts the children of the wicked running and playing like lambs in a pasture. A similar picture is found in Zechariah 8.5. **Send forth** is used to portray the children going out from their homes like sheep leaving the enclosure and going to the pasture. **Their little ones** means young children old enough to run and play. Lambs are known for their playful behavior. This line may be rendered, for example, "Their children run like lambs as they play" or "Their children play like lambs in a flock." In languages in which sheep are not known, it may be possible to substitute another domestic animal or, more often, "Their children run about in happy play."

And their children dance: children is parallel with **little ones** in line a and refers to the same children. BJ and NJB translate "Their children dance like deer." This addition is inspired by Psalm 114.4-6 but not recommended by HOTTP. TEV has transferred **dance** to verse 12, "and dance to the music," which makes a smoother translation.

They sing to the tambourine and the lyre: in Hebrew there are three musical instruments named in verse 12. The first is a percussion instrument translated **tambourine**, the second a stringed instrument most often translated "harp" but sometimes **lyre**, and the third, which is in line b, is a wind instrument translated **pipe** or more commonly "flute." For more detailed descriptions and use of these instruments, translators should consult a Bible dictionary. TEV translates only "harps and flutes." The sense is that the children sing to the accompaniment of these instruments, that is, while the instruments are playing. TEV has shifted **dance** from verse 11 to verse 12 and omits **sing**, but the text portrays the children doing both. For the stringed instrument which accompanied the tambourine, FRCL has "guitar" and BJ has "zither," which seems to be the instrument used in 1 Samuel 10.5. This line may also be expressed "The children sing as people play the tambourine and the lyre." In some languages these instruments will be a local drum and a stringed instrument; the latter may be a guitar.

And rejoice to the sound of the pipe: translators differ somewhat as to the activity of the children in this line. The general sense is "to make merry," which does not specify any particular kind of action, but for children it implies jumping, skipping, or dancing about. They do this in response to the sounds made by the **pipe** or "flute," the wind instrument. If there is no wind instrument available to translate **pipe**, a different kind of instrument may be used. If no musical instrument is available, it may be necessary to borrow a word and say, for example, "a musical instrument called the flute." If this is not possible, the translator may have to express verse 12 differently; for example, "The children dance and sing and make joyful sounds."

21.13

RSV	TEV
They spend their days in prosperity, and in peace they go down to Sheol.	They live out their lives in peace and quietly die without suffering.

Job now shifts from the children to the adults. **They spend their days in prosperity**: the reference is not to passing their time but to "living out their days, bringing their lives to an end, completing their lives." They grow old and end their days in prosperity. Instead of dying prematurely and having everything taken from them, as Zophar claimed in 20.11, Job sees the wicked coming to the end of their lives as prosperous and wealthy people. Translators must be careful that **They** does not refer any longer to the children. Therefore it may be better to say "Those wicked parents live all their lives having wealth" or "Those wicked parents have wealth all their lives."

And in peace they go down to Sheol: **in peace** is literally "in a moment." The sense is that they die quickly without lingering in illness and suffering. So TEV "and quietly die without suffering." **Go down to Sheol** is not a punishment but the expected departure from life as portrayed throughout the Old Testament. **Sheol** is the place of the dead. It is not thought of as a place of punishment and should not be translated by a word equivalent to "hell." This line may be rendered, for example, "and when they die they go peacefully to the place of the dead," or "and they go to the grave in peace," or "they die in peace and are buried."

21.14

RSV	TEV
They say to God, 'Depart from us! We do not desire the knowledge of thy ways.	The wicked tell God to leave them alone; they don't want to know his will for their lives.

They say to God, 'Depart from us!' RSV begins verses 8-14 with "they" or "their," which refers in each instance to the wicked, and in translation may require being replaced by "the wicked" or "wicked people." In 22.17 Eliphaz quotes this line almost word for word. TEV's rendering through indirect speech is less emotive than RSV: "The wicked tell God to leave them alone." Better would be "They say to God 'Leave us in peace!' "

We do not desire the knowledge of thy ways: the wicked do not want to know the ways of God. God's **ways** are the way of life, conduct, that he requires of those who worship and follow him. This line may also be expressed, for example, "We do not want to know what you want," "We do not care to learn what you require of people," or "We do not want to know your laws."

21.15   RSV   TEV

> What is the Almighty, that we   They think there is no need to
>   should serve him?   serve God
> And what profit do we get if we   nor any advantage in praying
>   pray to him?'   to him.

What is the Almighty that we should serve him? This continues the quoted speech of the wicked, who now ask a question which can be rendered "Who does the Almighty God think he is that we should be his slaves?" TEV remains less emotive with "They think there is no need to serve God." **Almighty** translates the Hebrew *Shaddai*. See 5.17 for a discussion on "Almighty." Both questions in verse 15 are rhetorical and expect a negative reply. The Septuagint translators omitted this verse, possibly because they regarded it as blasphemous, that is, speaking badly against God. The word translated **serve** is rendered "worship" by NEB, a meaning the word often carries, and fits better with the following line.

And what profit do we get if we pray to him may also be expressed "What use is it for us to pray to him?" or "What good does it do for us . . . ?" This question is asked in Malachi 3.14, where TEV translates "What is the use of doing what he says . . . ?" TEV, which does not use direct speech, translates this line "nor any advantage in praying to him." If translated as a rhetorical question, the verse may be rendered, for example, "Who is the Almighty God to expect us to serve him? He is no one at all! What advantage is there for us if we pray to him? There is none!"

21.16   RSV   TEV

> Behold, is not their prosperity in   They claim they succeed by their
>   their hand?   own strength,
> The counsel of the wicked is   but their way of thinking I
>   far from me.   can't accept.

Interpreters point out that verse 16 is difficult to relate to the wider context. Pope suggests it may be regarded as the protest of someone who was shocked at the idea that the attitude of the wicked was acceptable, and so Pope and others put the verse in brackets. However, the Handbook recommends that translators do as in RSV and TEV.

Behold, is not their prosperity in their hand? Dhorme takes the word translated **Behold** (also in 13.15; 19.7) to transform a statement into a question and translates "Does not their happiness lie in their hands?" FRCL has "Aren't those people masters of their own happiness?" TEV adds the words "they claim" in order to make a statement rather than a question. GECL renders verse 16 "They believe every man is maker of his own fortune, but their way of thinking is far from mine."

The counsel of the wicked is far from me: Eliphaz repeats this line in 22.18b. **Counsel of the wicked** is mentioned in Psalm 1.1. RSV shifts in this line to a statement. Many scholars follow the Septuagint in this line in changing "from me" to "from him"; that is, "far from God." However, as Rowley points out, **is far from me** means that Job refuses the prosperity of the wicked and desires the fellowship with God which he has been denied, and so TEV translates "Their way of thinking I can't accept." Verse 16 may also be rendered "These wicked people think they make their own prosperity, but I don't accept what they say" or "These people believe they decide their own happiness, but that way of thinking is not what I believe."

4F-3. Job claims the wicked go unpunished (21.17-26)

RSV	TEV
17 "How often is it that the lamp of the wicked is put out? That their calamity comes upon them? That God distributes pains in his anger? 18 That they are like straw before the wind, and like chaff that the storm carries away?	17 Was a wicked man's light ever put out? Did one of them ever meet with disaster? Did God ever punish the wicked in anger 18 and blow them away like straw in the wind, or like dust carried away in a storm?
19 You say, 'God stores up their iniquity for their sons.' Let him recompense it to themselves, that they may know it. 20 Let their own eyes see their destruction, and let them drink of the wrath of the Almighty.	19 You claim God punishes a child for the sins of his father. No! Let God punish the sinners themselves; let him show that he does it because of *their* sins. 20 Let sinners bear their own punishment; let them feel the wrath of Almighty God.
21 For what do they care for their houses after them, when the number of their months is cut off? 22 Will any teach God knowledge, seeing that he judges those that are on high?	21 When a man's life is over, does he really care whether his children are happy? 22 Can a man teach God, who judges even those in high places?
23 One dies in full prosperity, being wholly at ease and secure, 24 his body full of fat and the marrow of his bones moist. 25 Another dies in bitterness of soul, never having tasted of good. 26 They lie down alike in the dust, and the worms cover them.	23-24 Some men stay healthy till the day they die; they die happy and at ease, their bodies well-nourished. 25 Others have no happiness at all; they live and die with bitter hearts. 26 But all alike die and are buried; they all are covered with worms.

Subdivision Heading

The Handbook heading may be modified to say, for example, "Job asks if God ever punished the wicked," "Job claims that God does not punish wicked people," or "The good and the bad all die alike." Rowley has (17-22) "How often do the godless suffer?" Habel "No calamity for the wicked," and TOB (19-34) "Impunity of the criminals."

	RSV		TEV
17	"How often is it that the lamp of the wicked is put out? That their calamity comes upon them? That God^c distributes pains in his anger?	17	Was a wicked man's light ever put out? Did one of them ever meet with disaster? Did God ever punish the wicked in anger
18	That they are like straw before the wind, and like chaff that the storm carries away?	18	and blow them away like straw in the wind, or like dust carried away in a storm?

^{c} Heb *he*

The questions of verses 17-18 assume the answer "Never!" or "No!" In 18.5 Bildad said that the light of the wicked is put out. Job now asks **How often is it that the lamp of the wicked is put out?** Job is not asking to know how many times this has happened, but is denying that it happens at all. **Lamp of the wicked** refers to their physical life. To have their **lamp** put out is to die prematurely or unexpectedly. Translators may be able to use a similar metaphor for unexpected death; for example, "Is it often that the fire in them grows cold?" If there is no figurative expression, we may express this line, for example, "Does it ever happen that they just fall dead? or "Did you ever see such people die unexpectedly?" As a statement, "They don't often die prematurely" or "They don't often die before they are old."

That their calamity comes upon them: it is necessary to understand **How often . . . ?** as applying to this line and the next. **Calamity** translates the same word used by Bildad in 18.12, meaning "misfortune, suffering." He asks "Do you ever see misfortune strike them? No!"

That God distributes pains in his anger? The RSV footnote shows that the Hebrew has "he"; but God is clearly implied, as in RSV and TEV. RSV follows the Septuagint with **distribute pains**. However, the word translated **pains** would refer to childbirth pains from the same root meaning "give birth to." This is hardly applicable. The same word means "ropes" and refers to the inheritance that is given after a field has been measured and divided. NIV follows this sense "The fate God allots in his anger," and NAB "The portion he allots . . . ." Dhorme relates the noun to an identical root with a different meaning, "to destroy, ruin, to act badly," and translates "How often does he destroy evildoers in his wrath?" and this is close to TEV "Did God ever punish the wicked in his anger?" This gives a much better translation model than RSV. This line may also be rendered, for example, "Does God ever get angry at them and make them suffer? No!" or "God never shows his anger at them and causes them to suffer."

Job continues the questions in verse 18, but without any imagery drawn from the earlier speeches of the friends. **That they are like straw before the wind**: this expression finds an echo in Psalm 1.4, "but are like chaff which the wind drives away." In verse 18 Job questions what Psalm 1 affirms. The questions in verse 18 still depend on **How often?** from verse 17. TEV avoids this and connects verse 18a closely to verse 17c so that God in verse 17 is the one who "blows them away." This hardly seems necessary, since it is the *ruach* "wind" which carries away the straw. This may also be expressed "Does the wind ever blow them away like straw? Not at all!" "They are not like straw that the wind blows away."

And like chaff that the storm carries away: the word translated **chaff** is the same as used in Psalm 1.4 and is rendered "dust" by TEV. This word is never used in the Old Testament except in similes of something light that is blown away by the wind. Parallel to **wind** in line a is the **storm** here in line b. **Storm** translates "whirlwind," which gives a more picturable event. In Hebrew the whirlwind "steals" the chaff away. It is the silent movement of the wind that slips in like a thief and is gone with the chaff. This line may also be rendered, for example, "and does a whirlwind pick them up and carry them off? Never!" or "no whirlwind ever slips in and carries them off." In areas where storms are cyclones or typhoons, and whirlwinds are less known, it will probably be best to say "wind."

21.19 RSV	TEV
You say, 'God stores up their iniquity for their sons.' Let him recompense it to themselves, that they may know it.	You claim God punishes a child for the sins of his father. No! Let God punish the sinners themselves; let him show that he does it because of *their* sins.

You say 'God stores up their iniquity for their sons': the words **You say** are not in Hebrew; they are supplied on the basis that Job is replying to an objection the friends may raise. The principle of children suffering for the sins of their parents is found in Exodus 20.5 and Deuteronomy 5.9. In 5.4 and 20.10 the friends spoke of the inheritance of suffering the wicked parent leaves for his children. Jeremiah (31.29 ff.) and Ezekiel (18.2 ff.) both reject the view that the sins of the parents cause their children to suffer. Compare also Matthew 27.25. **Store up** translates the Hebrew literally, a word meaning "to keep something in reserve, to save up." **Iniquity** means sin or wrongdoing. The Hebrew speaks of the wicked in the singular, "his (iniquity)" and "his (sons)," which RSV has generalized correctly in English as "their (iniquity)" and "their (sons)." This line may be rendered "You say that God holds on to their sins and makes their children suffer because of them," or "You believe that God punishes the children of these wicked people," or "You believe that God is saving his punishment for these people's children."

Let him recompense it to themselves, that they may know it: the wording of RSV is awkward and the meaning unclear. The Hebrew has only three words which translate literally "He repays him and he knows (it)." This line anticipates the friends' objection and is explained further by verse 20. The form of the verb translated **recompense** means "punish, carry out reprisals," and so means "Let him (God) punish him (the wicked person) himself." **Know it** is to be understood in the sense of "learn from it, profit from it." The final clause can be "so that they learn from it." TEV opens this line with "No!" as a strong objection to the teaching in the first line. TEV then repeats "God punish" from line a and supplies the object "sinners." A third line, which TEV has created, is to make very certain that the punishment is for "their sins," and "their" is placed in italics to emphasize that it is the sins of the wicked parent and not the sins of the children. TEV has gone further than is necessary, and the two lines can be clearly translated "You claim God punishes a child for the sins of his father; instead let God punish the father so that he will benefit from it."

21.20   RSV   TEV

> Let their own eyes see their de-   Let sinners bear their own pun-
>   struction,   ishment;
> and let them drink of the   let them feel the wrath of Al-
>   wrath of the Almighty.   mighty God.

In verse 20 Job continues to expand the view presented in verse 19. **Let their own eyes see their destruction:** in 19.27 a very similar construction is used: "my eyes shall behold." Here again the idea is that they (the wicked) should "witness" or "experience" their own **destruction. Destruction** translates a word found only here in the Old Testament, and so its meaning is largely arrived at from the context. Scholars differ greatly, however, in their interpretations of its meaning. Most employ terms which focus on a common area of meaning; for example, "punishment," "damnation," "misfortune," or "calamity"; and it is also translated "ruin" in the ancient versions. Dahood, Pope, and others see here the word "jar, pitcher, or cup." The allusion, they say, is to the cup of fate and divine wrath, as used in Psalm 16.5; 75.8; Isaiah 51.17; Jeremiah 25.15; Revelation 16.19. This interpretation has the advantage of paralleling the following line. Although none of the modern versions translates this as a figure, a reasonably good rendering is "Let him see the cup which he must drink" or ". . . the cup of punishment . . . ." However, since "cup" is a figurative expression for "punishment," many translators will prefer to avoid the figure, as in RSV. The first line may be rendered, for example, "They should see their own misfortune," "They should receive their own punishment," or "These wicked people themselves should be punished."

And let them drink of the wrath of the Almighty: if "cup" is used in the first line, this line may be translated as an apposition, that is, another expression referring to the same object: "the cup that is filled with the anger of Almighty God." On the other hand, if something like **destruction** or "punishment" is used in line a, then TEV's rendering will be appropriate: "Let them feel the wrath of Almighty God." Other suggestions are: "Let the anger of Almighty God fill them up," "Let them taste the anger of God the Almighty," or, if such idioms are inappropriate, "Let God Almighty punish them thoroughly."

21.21   RSV   TEV

> For what do they care for their   When a man's life is over,
>   houses after them,   does he really care whether his
> when the number of their   children are happy?
>   months is cut off?

For what do they care for their houses after them? Here Job is asking "What interest, concern, does a dead man take in the affairs of his family?" Whether his children are happy or punished makes little difference because his life is over. In 14.21 Job said "His sons come to honor and he does not know it," because he is dead. **Houses** is singular in Hebrew, "his house," but stands for "his family," or more specifically, "his children." **After them** means "after they (the wicked) have died." TEV transposes lines a and b in order to give a more natural English style. This line may also be expressed, for example, "After they die can they care what happens to their children? Certainly not!" "Can a dead man think about the well-being of his family? Not at all!" or, as a statement, "A dead man does not think about what happens to his family."

When the number of their months is cut off: their months is literally "his months." The same expression is found in 14.5. Elsewhere "the number of his days" is the equivalent, both terms meaning "his life span, the length of his life." The sense is not of the wicked man's time to live being fixed in advance, but rather "when his life is over" (TEV). Translators may need to transpose the two lines, as in TEV. This line may be rendered "once he is dead," "when his life is finished," or "after he has died."

21.22   RSV   TEV

Will any teach God knowledge,   Can a man teach God,
  seeing that he judges those   who judges even those in high
    that are on high?   places?

Will any teach God knowledge: some interpreters consider this verse to be a comment added later by someone objecting to the criticism of God's actions in verse 19. Tur-Sinai believes that Job is here expressing an objection of the friends. Dhorme, on the other hand, argues that Job is scolding the friends for imposing on God their own traditional teachings. According to the friends any lack of morality results automatically in physical suffering and death. But from verse 23 Job asserts that death happens to all alike, and so men should not try to teach God. **Teach God knowledge** is the literal form. God who has all knowledge cannot be given more by humans. NJB translates "But who can teach wisdom to God?" Use of the term "wisdom" or **knowledge** is redundant in English, and so TEV and others say "Can a man teach God?" This line may be rendered as a negative statement, "Men cannot teach God" or "People cannot give their knowledge to God."

Seeing that he judges those that are on high: this line explains why people cannot teach God. **Those that are on high** translates a single word in Hebrew, sometimes rendered "the exalted." Translators differ as to who these are. TEV "those in high places" refers to powerful people, rulers. NEB has "those in heaven above," and FRCL "angels." NJB "those on high" seems to be purposefully ambiguous. NJV takes **on high** to refer to the place of God, thus translating "he who judges from such heights." The reference is most probably to the heavenly council and echoes 16.19, Job's "heavenly witness." Since God controls the heavenly beings, he is no doubt capable of governing earth without being instructed by human beings. In some languages it may be more natural to transpose the two lines of this verse. This line may also be rendered "since God is the one who decides the affairs of even angels in heaven" or "because God even rules over those who serve him in heaven."

21.23-24   RSV   TEV

23   One dies in full prosperity,   23-24 Some men stay healthy till the
         being wholly at ease and se-   day they die;
         cure,   they die happy and at ease,
24   his body^d full of fat   their bodies well-nourished.
         and the marrow of his bones
         moist.

^d The meaning of the Hebrew word is
uncertain

These two verses may be taken together as a description of two contrasting groups, and representing all human beings. Death treats them without discrimination.

One dies in full prosperity: verses 23 and 25 begin with the same expression in Hebrew, "this one," but since they are in sequence and contrasted, it is better to reflect the contrast as RSV does. **In full prosperity** translates an idiomatic expression, "in the bone of his perfection"; that is, "the essence of health," which TEV renders "Some men stay healthy till the day they die." NJV says ". . . in robust health." In some languages it will be necessary to adjust the contrast contained in **One dies** in verse 23a and "another dies" in verse 25a by prefacing 23a with "There may be two people" or "If there are two people." Then verse 23a may go on with "the first person dies"; that is, "the first person dies while he is in perfect health."

Being wholly at ease and secure describes the first example as mentally and physically in the best of condition. This person has nothing to worry about, nothing to fear, and the line may be rendered, for example, "He is at peace and afraid of nothing."

His body full of fat: RSV notes that the word translated **body** is uncertain. It is found nowhere else in the Old Testament. Some scholars take it to mean "his pails" (buckets). NJV translates "His pails are full of milk." Syriac has "his sides," a word which some relate to an Aramaic root meaning "flank." This is the basis for RSV **body**. FRCL implies **body** in its translation, "well nourished . . . ." **Fat** translates the Hebrew for "milk," but if **body** is used as the subject, **fat** suits better and is obtained by a change of vowels only. The parallelism in line b makes **body** the preferred reading. This line may also be rendered "he has eaten plentifully," "he has had the best of food to eat," or "his body is fat from eating well."

And the marrow of his bones moist: the word translated **marrow** occurs only here in the Old Testament, but its connection with **bones** makes its meaning clear. The **marrow** in the bones is said to be **moist**, meaning "fresh, not dried up by old age." In Proverbs 3.8 the bones are said to be refreshed. TEV incorporates the meaning of this line with the previous line and joins verses 23 and 24 together. The sense of having moist marrow in his bones is translated by FRCL as "full of freshness, of youth." Translators may be able to replace the moist marrow figure by one that is more appropriate; for example, "and his skin is smooth like in his youth" or "his limbs are straight as those of a youth."

21.25   RSV   TEV

> Another dies in bitterness of   Others have no happiness at all;
>   soul,   they live and die with bitter
>   never having tasted of good.   hearts.

Another dies in bitterness of soul: Another translates "this one" as in verse 23a, but it refers to a different person or group of people and so must be contrasted with the person represented in 23a. If the translator has indicated something like "the first person" in 23a, verse 25 may begin "The second person" or "The other person." **Bitterness of soul** is "bitterness of *nefesh*." See 3.20; 7.11; 10.1 for discussion. TEV, which translates "with bitter hearts," transposes lines a and b. A person with **bitterness of soul** is "miserable, wretched, unhappy." This line may be rendered, for example, "The other person dies after a bitter life," "The second person lives an unhappy life and dies," or "Other people live miserable lives and die."

Never having tasted of good means "without ever having been happy." In contrast to the first person, who died healthy, well fed, and content, this wretched person has always been miserable and dies unhappily. Many translations, like TEV, will incorporate the sense of this line into the first line and need not repeat it.

21.26   RSV   TEV

> They lie down alike in the dust,   But all alike die and are buried;
>   and the worms cover them.   they all are covered with
>   worms.

They lie down alike in the dust: death treats all men alike. In 3.19 Job said that all kinds of people, the small and the great, the slave and the free, are all alike in death. TEV translates the expression **lie down . . . in the dust** as "die and are buried." In some languages it will be inappropriate to speak of the dead lying down, and so this must be expressed as in TEV, "They die and are buried" or "They die and people bury them."

And the worms cover them: in 17.14-16 Job called the worms in death "my mother and my sister." The portrayal of the worms as a covering in death is found in Isaiah 14.11: "Maggots are the bed beneath you, and worms are your covering." The **worms** referred to in this verse are the same as in 17.14 and refer to maggots that eat rotting flesh. This line may be rendered as "they all are eaten by worms" or "worms eat their bodies."

4F-4. Job claims that the wicked live well and are buried with honor (21.27-34)

RSV	TEV

27 "Behold, I know your thoughts,
    and your schemes to wrong me.
28 For you say, 'Where is the house of the
    prince?
    Where is the tent in which the wicked
    dwelt?'
29 Have you not asked those who travel the
    roads,
    and do you not accept their testimony
30 that the wicked man is spared in the day
    of calamity,
    that he is rescued in the day of wrath?
31 Who declares his way to his face,
    and who requites him for what he has
    done?
32 When he is borne to the grave,
    watch is kept over his tomb.
33 The clods of the valley are sweet to him;
    all men follow after him,
    and those who go before him are innu-
    merable.
34 How then will you comfort me with emp-
    ty nothings?
    There is nothing left of your answers
    but falsehood."
	27 I know what spiteful thoughts you have.
	28 You ask, "Where is the house of the
	    great man now,
	    the man who practiced evil?"
	29 Haven't you talked with people who trav-
	    el?
	    Don't you know the reports they bring
	    back?
	30 On the day God is angry and punishes,
	    it is the wicked man who is always
	    spared.
	31 There is no one to accuse a wicked man
	    or pay him back for all he has done.
	32 When he is carried to the graveyard,
	    to his well-guarded tomb,
	33 thousands join the funeral procession,
	    and even the earth lies gently on his
	    body.
	34 And you! You try to comfort me with
	    nonsense!
	    Every answer you give is a lie!

Subdivision Heading

The Handbook heading for the conclusion of chapter 21 may be modified to say, for example, "The wicked live happily and are buried with honor," "When God is angry he does not strike down the wicked," or "The wicked even enjoy their funerals." Habel has "On the glory of the Tyrant," and Rowley "The arguments of the friends are contradicted by universal experience."

21.27   RSV   TEV

"Behold, I know your thoughts,   I know what spiteful thoughts
    and your schemes to wrong   you have.
    me.

Verse 27 begins the final section of Job's speech in which his observations are said to be confirmed by those who travel.

Behold I know your thoughts: the Hebrew has two lines, the second of which develops the word **thoughts** in the first line. Job means here that he knows the friends refer to him when they talk about the doom awaiting the wicked. **Behold** here does not just emphasize something to follow, according to Dhorme, but rather affirms his statement as introducing a new theme. **Thoughts** in this context are hostile thoughts directed against Job, and so TEV says "I know what spiteful thoughts

404

you have." FRCL translates "Pay attention: I know what you have in the back of your minds." This refers to the ulterior motives of the friends.

And your schemes to wrong me: schemes is almost the same in meaning as **thoughts** in the previous line, and TEV therefore reduces the two lines to one. Verse 27 may be rendered, for example, "I know you have had thoughts and plan to do me wrong" or "I know what evil thoughts you think and how you plan to harm me."

21.28

RSV	TEV
For you say, 'Where is the house of the prince? Where is the tent in which the wicked dwelt?'	You ask, "Where is the house of the great man now, the man who practiced evil?"

For you say, 'Where is the house of the prince?' Here Job is anticipating a question which the friends might well ask. See the questions in 14.10; 20.7. In 8.14-15; 15.34; 18.14-21; 20.26,28, Job's friends claim that the houses of the wicked fall into ruin and vanish. **Prince** translates a word which Gordis renders "nobleman" and NJB "great lord." The parallel in line b is **the wicked**, and so **prince** in line a refers to an evil ruler; FRCL has "tyrants," and SPCL "evil tyrant." TEV "great man" lacks any sense of evil, but this is supplied in line b.

Where is the tent in which the wicked dwelt? House in line a and **tent** in line b provide the subject for the repetition of the thought. There is no attempt by the poet to heighten the intensity in the second line. Verse 28 may need to be expressed as a single line in some languages; for example, "You ask 'Where is the house of that wicked ruler?'"

21.29-30

	RSV		TEV
29	Have you not asked those who travel the roads, and do you not accept their testimony	29	Haven't you talked with people who travel? Don't you know the reports they bring back?
30	that the wicked man is spared in the day of calamity, that he is rescued in the day of wrath?	30	On the day God is angry and punishes, it is the wicked man who is always spared.

Job answers the question which he assumed the friends have asked, by asking another question which he then goes on to answer himself. He advised them to note what experienced travelers have said as evidence of what he himself believes to be true to experience. In 15.17-19 Eliphaz would show Job the truth that was fixed before any foreigner entered. Job, by contrast, appeals to them to widen their knowledge from the perspective of people such as travelers who have seen foreign places.

Have you not asked those who travel the roads: this thought is expressed in Psalm 80.12; 89.41; Lamentations 1.12; 2.15; Proverbs 9.15. This line may also be expressed "Have you never asked people who travel" or "You can learn from travelers."

And do you not accept their testimony: testimony translates a word meaning "sign or mark." Dhorme suggests that these travelers were laborers and tramps who moved from town to town and wrote down their names and occasional thoughts on small signs which they left at cross roads, and so Job is thought to be asking if the friends have not seen these "signs." Although interesting, this picture is not very likely because the **testimonies** or "signs" Job refers to are detailed abstract thoughts concerning the fate of the wicked. Therefore it seems more likely that Job has in mind people such as merchants, astrologers, and others who would travel widely and speak about the strange things they witnessed in far away places. This is in line with TEV "The reports they bring back." Verse 29 may also be rendered "Have you never talked with people who travel to other places, and do you not believe what they tell?" or "You should talk with people who travel and come back with their reports."

That the wicked man is spared in the day of calamity: verse 30 is the testimony that can be obtained from travelers who support Job's claim "that when misfortune strikes, the wicked person escapes unhurt." So Job contradicts the friends' teaching of retribution, being punished for evil. The verb translated **spare** can mean "to restrain or check" as in 7.11; 16.5-6, and so KJV says "reserved to the day." However, this is not the sense in verse 30, which has the same meaning as in 38.23 and may be translated **spared** as in RSV and TEV. **Day of calamity** refers to a time when many people, or a whole community, experience disaster or misfortune. God is not mentioned in this line but is clearly implied, and so TEV has "on the day God is angry and punishes." FRCL avoids "the day" and translates "The anger of God leaves him safe and sound." It is important that verse 30 be translated as the content of the travelers' reports from verse 29; for example, "Those travelers show that nothing happens to the wicked person when God is angry and punishes other people" or ". . . that wicked people escape God's angry punishment."

That he is rescued in the day of wrath: rescued is literally "led forth." Although various changes in the Hebrew text have been proposed, RSV **rescued** is a good rendering of the basic meaning and appropriate for the context. Line b means essentially the same as line a and is without poetic heightening, intensity, or focusing.

21.31   RSV   TEV

Who declares his way to his face,   There is no one to accuse a wick-
  and who requites him for what   ed man
  he has done?   or pay him back for all he has
                                               done.

Who declares his way to his face . . . ? Unfortunately RSV is unclear here. In this line Job returns to his own comments. The question expects the reply "Nobody!" and so TEV restructures the question as a negative statement: "There is no one to accuse a wicked man." God spares the wicked and, for fear of consequences, "No one accuses the wicked." **Declares** translates a word with the force of "denounce, expose," and **his way** refers to "his conduct, behavior." A better translation is "No one dares denounce the wicked man for the way he acts."

And who requites him for what he has done? Requites translates the Hebrew for "pay back, get even," and so TEV "Pay him back for all he has done." Verse 31 may also be rendered "No one dares denounce (accuse, condemn, expose, tell the truth about) the wicked person's bad ways, and no one dares to give him what he deserves" or ". . . and no one dares to punish him for what he has done."

21.32-33	RSV	TEV

	RSV	TEV
32	When he is borne to the grave, watch is kept over his tomb.	32 When he is carried to the grave-yard, to his well-guarded tomb,
33	The clods of the valley are sweet to him; all men follow after him, and those who go before him are innumerable.	33 thousands join the funeral procession, and even the earth lies gently on his body.

Verses 32 and 33 refer to the same event, the wicked man's burial. In Hebrew verse 32 has two lines and verse 33 has three. RSV keeps them in their Hebrew order. TEV, on the other hand, rearranges verse 33 so that lines b and c are combined and placed before line a. Other translations have different arrangements.

When he is borne to the grave: grave in Hebrew is plural here but singular in 17.1. The reference here is to the place of many graves, so TEV has "graveyard."

Watch is kept over his tomb: the lack of an expressed subject in this line has led to two kinds of adjustments: NEB transfers the last two words from verse 33, making them the subject of the verb: "and thousands (literally 'without number') keep watch at his tomb." On the other hand, TEV expresses this line as an expansion and specification of "graveyard" in the previous line: "to his well-guarded tomb." TEV is preferred because it does not disturb the order. Translators may combine the lines of verses 32 and 33 in various ways; for example, SPCL translates in the order 32a, 33b,c, 32b, 33a. The passive verbs in verse 32 must often be shifted to active constructions; for example, "When they carry him to his grave" or "When they bury him." This line may be expressed as "they guard his tomb" or "they watch over where they have buried him."

The clods of the valley are sweet to him: clods of the valley is parallel to **tomb** in verse 32b and refers to the dirt which covers his dead body or, as NEB translates, "the dust of the earth." **Sweet to him** is idiomatic, as in 20.12, where "wickedness is sweet in his mouth." The meaning is that the dirt that covers him is "pleasant, agreeable, comfortable." The dead man is depicted as consciously experiencing the mound of clods piled above him as being comfortable, pleasant. TEV and others translate "gentle or light." This is in contrast to "heavy" and "burdensome." TEV "even the earth lies gently on his body" is transferred to the end of verse 33. SPCL, which also places this line at the end, says, "Even the dirt is soft for him." **Valley** probably refers to the pit of the grave rather than the valley where the grave may be located.

All men follow after him: TEV transfers this line to verse 33a, so that the funeral events are told before telling the reaction of the dead man to his funeral, and this is recommended for translation. Everyone is present to follow the funeral procession taking the dead man to the grave.

And those who go before him are innumerable: this line and the one above are combined in TEV. NEB translates the two lines "all the world escorts him, before and behind." Translators may follow the order of TEV or that of SPCL, "And when they finally carry him to be buried all the procession accompanies him, some in front and some behind; they guard his tomb, and even the dirt is pleasant to him."

21.34   RSV   TEV

> How then will you comfort me   And you! You try to comfort me
>   with empty nothings?   with nonsense!
> There is nothing left of your   Every answer you give is a lie!
>   answers but falsehood."

Verse 34 marks the conclusion of the second round of arguments, in which Job shifts his attention back to the friends. He sums up all of their efforts to prove that he is guilty of wrong, stating that they are nothing more than **empty nothings**. Their mission to comfort Job has proven to be a miserable failure. The friends and their arguments are untrustworthy. Verse 34 marks not only a conclusion to the second round of speeches, but also a transition to the final round. Accordingly translators will want to watch for ways in which the concluding and transitional features may need to be marked.

Finally Job asks **How then will you comfort me with empty nothings?** In view of his observations and experience, the words of his comforters are lies. In 21.2 Job suggested that the consolation the friends wanted to give him would be accomplished by listening to his words. The word Job uses to describe their consolations is the Hebrew *hebel* "breath," that is, "whatever is vain, worthless." TEV translates this line with two exclamations: "And you! You try to comfort me with nonsense!" This line may also be rendered, for example, "How can you hope to comfort me with your foolish words?" or "It is foolish of you to think you can help me with your nonsense."

There is nothing left of your answers but falsehood: falsehood translates a word meaning "treachery" or "faithlessness" in regard to a person's relation to God or to his neighbor. Here the friends are unfaithful, disloyal to the truth, which FRCL translates "Your arguments are nothing more than a pretense of a reply." NEB has "How false your answers ring." This line can also be expressed "All you have said is a lie" or "There is no truth in anything you have said to me."

5. Third Round of Speeches

(22.1–27.23)

Section 5 contains the third and final round of arguments between Job and the friends. Unlike the first two rounds, in which each speaker is named at the beginning of the chapter, chapter 24 seems to combine speeches by Job and Zophar without naming Zophar. Job is named as the speaker of chapter 26; however, 26.5-14 is usually assigned to Bildad. There are other problems regarding the identification of the speaker in these chapters, and these will be discussed in the appropriate places.

Section Heading

Translators wishing to follow the Handbook headings may need to modify this section heading to say, for example, "This is the third group of arguments," "Job and the friends argue a third time," or "The final arguments between Job and the friends." Translators should word the section heading so as to conform to the usage in the first and second rounds. (See opening of chapters 4 and 15.) TEV has "The third dialogue," NJB "Third cycle of discourses."

5A. ELIPHAZ'S THIRD SPEECH (22.1-30)

This is the third speech of Eliphaz, the other two being chapters 4–5 and 15. The remarks of Eliphaz may be divided into three parts. In the first section (verses 2-11) he accuses Job of being one of the wicked. He makes no attempt to conceal his accusations through generalities and indirect address. He accuses Job directly. In the second part (verses 12-20) Eliphaz describes the wicked as thinking of God as being far removed and therefore having no control over them. In the third section (verses 21-30) he counsels Job to humble himself and receive instruction from God, and so be delivered from his misfortune.

Division Heading

Translators wishing to provide a division heading should use wording similar to that used in chapters 4 and 15, in which Eliphaz is the speaker.

5A-1. Eliphaz accuses Job of committing crimes against the poor (22.1-11)

RSV	TEV

	RSV		TEV
	1 Then Eliphaz the Temanite answered:	*Eliphaz*	
2	"Can a man be profitable to God?	1-2	Is there any man, even the wisest,
	Surely he who is wise is profitable to himself.		who could ever be of use to God?
3	Is it any pleasure to the Almighty if you are righteous,	3	Does your doing right benefit God, or does your being good help him at all?
	or is it gain to him if you make your ways blameless?	4	It is not because you stand in awe of God that he reprimands you and brings you to trial.
4	Is it for your fear of him that he reproves you, and enters into judgment with you?	5	No, it's because you have sinned so much; it's because of all the evil you do.
5	Is not your wickedness great? There is no end to your iniquities.	6	To make a brother repay you the money he owed, you took away his clothes and left him nothing to wear.
6	For you have exacted pledges of your brothers for nothing, and stripped the naked of their clothing.	7	You refused water to those who were tired, and refused to feed those who were hungry.
7	You have given no water to the weary to drink, and you have withheld bread from the hungry.	8	You used your power and your position to take over the whole land.
8	The man with power possessed the land, and the favored man dwelt in it.	9	You not only refused to help widows, but you also robbed and mistreated orphans.
9	You have sent widows away empty, and the arms of the fatherless were crushed.	10	So now there are pitfalls all around you, and suddenly you are full of fear.
10	Therefore snares are round about you, and sudden terror overwhelms you;	11	It has grown so dark that you cannot see, and a flood overwhelms you.
11	your light is darkened, so that you cannot see, and a flood of water covers you.		

Subdivision Heading

The Handbook heading may be modified to say, for example, "Eliphaz accuses Job of many wrongs," "Job, you are a great sinner," or "Job, you have cheated the poor." TOB (5-11) has "Crimes of Job," Rowley (6-11) "Job's sin, as deduced by Eliphaz," and Habel "Charge of gross sins."

22.1	RSV	TEV
	Then Eliphaz the Temanite answered:	*Eliphaz*

Then Eliphaz the Temanite answered: for comments see 2.11; 4.1.

22.2-3   RSV   TEV

2   "Can a man be profitable to   2   Is there any man, even the wis-
          God?   est,
     Surely he who is wise is profit-   who could ever be of use to
          able to himself.   God?
3   Is it any pleasure to the Almighty   3   Does your doing right benefit
          if you are righteous,   God,
     or is it gain to him if you make   or does your being good help
          your ways blameless?   him at all?

These two verses appear to support the claim Job made in 7.20 that God is indifferent to what takes place on earth, and is neither harmed by people's sin nor helped by their goodness. Eliphaz does not seem at all concerned to reply to Job's observations on the prosperity of the wicked in chapter 21. To Eliphaz and the other friends, prosperity is of no consequence. They are interested in piety and sin. If a person is pious and does his religious duties, he will be rewarded, and if he is wicked he will be punished. Their conclusion for Job is clear.

Can a man be profitable to God? As usual the friends begin their discourses with a rhetorical question. There is essential agreement between RSV and TEV in this line, in which Eliphaz asks "Is a man useful to God?" The negative of **profitable** was used in 15.3, "Should he (a wise man) argue in unprofitable talk?" There "unprofit-able" was paralleled by "can do no good." In a similar manner **profitable** here means "be of value, use, benefit, advantage." That is, "Can a person do God any good?" or as in NEB, "Can a man be any benefit to God?" This line may also be rendered, for example, "What can a person do that is valuable to God?" or "How can a man help God?"

Surely he who is wise is profitable to himself: in this line RSV and TEV differ in interpretation. RSV has **profitable to himself**, and TEV, which equates **he who is wise** in line b with **a man** in line a, asks if such a person "could ever be of use to God." In agreement with RSV are GECL, FRCL, NJB, BJ, TOB, NAB, Dhorme. **To himself** is similar to Proverbs 9.12 "If you are wise, you are wise for yourself." However, **to himself** can also be understood as "to him," in which case it would refer to God; so TEV, SPCL, NEB, NJV, NIV, and Mft. Translators may follow either. **Profitable** translates the same word as in line a. If the translator follows the model of RSV, the line may also be expressed, for example, "If the person is wise, he can certainly help himself" or "He can be of value to himself if he has wisdom." Verse 2 may also be translated, for example, "Job, do you think even a very wise person could be useful to God?"

Is it any pleasure to the Almighty if you are righteous ... ? Pleasure translates a word whose meaning is "concern, interest, advantage," and in the present context "benefit." TEV translates "benefit," which provides a good parallel to the second line. **Almighty** translates *Shaddai*. **Are righteous** is the Hebrew *tsadaq* (see Eliphaz's use of this word in 4.17; 15.14), which refers to being "pious, righteous, good." This line may also be rendered, for example, "If you are a good person, does that benefit God Almighty?" "How does your being good become an advantage to God?" or "Does God Almighty benefit from your being a good person?"

411

Or is it gain to him if you make your ways blameless? "Would God gain anything by your living in a good way?" **Gain** is here "profit, what can be obtained." It is the same word Judah used in Genesis 37.26, when he asked his brothers "What profit is it if we slay our brother and conceal his blood?" There was more to be gained by selling Joseph to the merchants. **To him** represents the Hebrew text and refers to God. **Make your ways blameless** translates "perfect your ways" and means "live without fault, be perfect, be without blemish." TEV "being good" appears to represent less of a quality of conduct than the text requires. This line may also be expressed, for example, "What does God get out of it if you live a perfect life?" or "What interest does God have in your living without fault?"

22.4-5	RSV	TEV
4	Is it for your fear of him that he reproves you, and enters into judgment with you?	4 It is not because you stand in awe of God that he reprimands you and brings you to trial.
5	Is not your wickedness great? There is no end to your iniquities.	5 No, it's because you have sinned so much; it's because of all the evil you do.

Is it for your fear of him that he reproves you . . . ? Eliphaz uses the word **fear** to express the idea of religion or piety, which refers to faithful devotion to a person's religious duties in 4.6; 15.4. The question in verse 4 assumes the reply "No." God would have no interest in correcting the religious person. If he corrects or punishes them, it is because they do not fear him. The question in this line is well translated by Mft "Why should he punish you for your religion . . . ?"

And enters into judgment with you: this line expands somewhat on "reproves" or "punishes" in the previous line. God not only punishes Job for his lack of "reverence, piety," but he even brings him to trial, takes him to court. Verse 4 may also be rendered as a statement with negative reasons; for example, "God punishes you and takes you to court because you show him no respect" or "God makes you suffer and tests you because you do not serve him faithfully." In languages in which the rhetorical question is preferred, we may translate, for example, "Do you think God judges you and punishes you because you are his faithful servant? Not at all!"

Is not your wickedness great? TEV answers "No" to the question in verse 4 as an introduction to the full reply in verse 5. (See also NEB.) For English style TEV's arrangement is better than repeating the question form in verse 5a as RSV does. If the translator prefers the question form in verse 5a, it may be necessary to mark the contrast; for example, "Is it not instead because you are very wicked?" In some languages it may be clearer to show the contrast between the questions in verses 2-4 and verse 5 by an introductory clause; for example, "The reason he punishes you is because you are such a sinner" or "He punishes you for your many sins."

There is no end to your iniquities: this line is a summary statement: "Your sins have no limit" or, as NEB forcefully says, "Your depravity passes all bounds." In Eliphaz's view there is no limit to the sins Job is capable of committing. This line may be expressed so that it continues to give, as in the previous line, the reasons why God punishes Job; for example, "and because you keep on sinning," "and because of the great extent of your sins," or "because the things you do are so very bad."

22.6

RSV	TEV
For you have exacted pledges of your brothers for nothing, and stripped the naked of their clothing.	To make a brother repay you the money he owed, you took away his clothes and left him nothing to wear.

In verses 6-9 Eliphaz specifies the sins Job has committed. They are all sins in which a man of power could oppress people and cause them to suffer.

For you have exacted pledges of your brothers for nothing: verse 6 begins with the link word *ki* "Because," "For the following reason," which leads up to the conclusion marked by "therefore" in verse 10. The tenses of the verbs imply habitual action. Eliphaz accuses Job of having **exacted pledges,** which means here that the lender of money takes an object belonging to the borrower and holds it until the debt is repaid. For the conditions required when accepting clothing as a pledge, see the next line. **Your brothers** can refer to Job's own brothers, close relatives, or more generally his kinsmen. **For nothing** translates the same expression used in 1.9, when Satan tells God that Job does not fear God "for nothing." In verse 6 it means "wrongly, unjustifiably." That is, Job, without any reason, unjustifiably, wrongfully, took pledges from his brothers.

The second half of this verse explains the first half. It was against the law to keep for more than one day a garment taken as a pledge (Exo 22.25-26). It was required by law to return it before night so that the poor debtor could have it to cover his body at night. **And stripped the naked of their clothing**: as prose this line would be considered inappropriate, since the naked are already stripped. The thought is, however, that these people become naked by being stripped of their clothing. TEV readjusts the elements of this expression: "to make your brother repay . . . you took away . . . and left him nothing to wear." Verse 6 may be rendered, for example, "You have done wrong by lending your brothers money, and took their things when they could not repay you; you even took their clothes and left them naked."

22.7

RSV	TEV
You have given no water to the weary to drink, and you have withheld bread from the hungry.	You refused water to those who were tired, and refused to feed those who were hungry.

The sins Eliphaz now mentions are contrary to the teaching of the prophets in such passages as Isaiah 58.7,10; Ezekiel 18.7.

You have given no water to the weary to drink: the weary or "tired" describes the condition associated with thirst in Isaiah 29.8; Jeremiah 31.25; Proverbs 25.25. The same is often said of the ground that is not watered.

And you have withheld bread from the hungry: verse 7 may be rendered, for example, "You never gave a drink of water to the thirsty nor a bite of food to the hungry" or "When you saw a thirsty person you never gave him a drink, and when you met a hungry person you never gave him something to eat."

22.8   RSV   TEV

| The man with power possessed the land, and the favored man dwelt in it. | You used your power and your position to take over the whole land. |

The man with power possessed the land: in this verse Eliphaz drops the second person singular pronoun and speaks in the third person. Translators deal with this sudden change in a variety of ways. RSV retains the third person, but this has the effect of breaking with the preceding verses. NEB treats the verse as a question which has arisen in the mind of Eliphaz as he reflects on the previous verses. "Is the earth then the preserve of the strong and a domain for the favored few?" TEV shifts to the second person singular. NJB uses still another technique. In verse 6 NJB has "You have exacted unearned pledges," then begins the following clause and each successive clause with the verb: "stripped people . . . failed to give . . . refused bread . . . handed the land over . . . sent widows . . . ." In this way NJB makes it clear that each of these acts was done by Job, but without directly saying "you." **Man with power** is literally "man of arm," the arm being a symbol of strength, as in Psalm 10.15, "Break thou the arm of the wicked . . . ."

And the favored man dwelt in it: favored man is literally "the lifted-up face." This probably refers to the one who has the right to raise his eyes and look directly at the master. Pope says "apparently an oblique reference to Job as an arrogant land-grabber who dispossessed his weaker neighbors." In the light of the prose introduction as well as the other comments on Job's life, Eliphaz's accusation here does not fit Job. TEV assumes **the man with power** in line a and **the favored man** in line b are the same person. There is no agreement concerning to whom this refers. TEV and GECL assume it is Job. NJB translates "You (in verse 6) handed the land over to a strong man, for some favored person to move in." Here the two persons may be the same or different. In FRCL Job is accused of letting someone else do it: "You allow the strong to take over the country and the most arrogant to occupy it." FRCL has an alternative rendering in its footnote: "You who are strong seize the country and you've had the nerve to make it your own." This agrees essentially with TEV, which is one model to be followed. The translator may also interpret **man with power** in line a and **favored man** in line b as different persons and translate, for example, "You help powerful people to take away other peoples' property, and then people with influence occupy it" or "You enable the strong to take the land of the weak, and your friends use it for themselves."

22.9   RSV   TEV

You have sent widows away emp-   You not only refused to help
    ty,   widows,
  and the arms of the fatherless   but you also robbed and mis-
    were crushed.   treated orphans.

The oppression of widows and orphans is condemned in the Old Testament (Exo 22.22; Deut 27.19; Jer 7.6; 22.3; Zech 7.10). Eliphaz returns to the use of the second person singular in the first line of this verse. The verb in the second line is in the passive, but many translators translate that line also with "you (singular)," referring to Job as the subject.

You have sent widows away empty: **sent** means "you dismiss, make them go away." The **widows** that come to the strong are asking for help but are sent away **empty**, which means "empty-handed, without receiving anything, without getting help." In some languages it will be necessary to express the line differently to make the context clear; for example, "When widows ask you for help, you give them nothing" or "If a widow comes to you for help, you send her away with empty hands."

And the arms of the fatherless were crushed: TEV translates this verse so that the poetic intensification in terms of increased violence is brought out: "You not only refused . . . but you also robbed . . . ." The heightening of poetic intensity in line b can also be expressed in English as "you even . . ." or "you even went so far as to . . . ." **Fatherless** refers to the orphaned children; **arms . . . crushed** means "destroyed, oppressed": "You have even oppressed children who have no fathers (to defend them)."

22.10-11   RSV   TEV

10 Therefore snares are round   10 So now there are pitfalls all
     about you,   around you,
    and sudden terror overwhelms   and suddenly you are full of
    you;   fear.
11 your light is darkened, so that   11 It has grown so dark that you
    you^e cannot see,   cannot see,
    and a flood of water covers   and a flood overwhelms you.
    you.

^{e} Cn Compare Gk: Heb *or darkness*

Therefore snares are round about you: in verse 10 Eliphaz's list of oppressive acts has built up to a conclusion marked by **therefore**, meaning "it is for that reason." **Snares are round about you** recalls the figurative language used by

Bildad in chapter 18. In 18.11 Bildad said "terrors frighten him on every side." The word translated **snares** is the same word translated "trap" in 18.9a (RSV). See 18.8-10 for discussion. TEV and NEB translate "pitfalls" and so have chosen a different kind of trap than that suggested by the Hebrew. In some languages where **snares** are not known, it may be necessary to say, for example, "And because of all this you are in danger" or "And now you are in trouble."

And sudden terror overwhelms you: **sudden** is often used with fear, panic, terror, or death in the Old Testament (Lev 26.16; Job 9.23; Prov 3.25; Zeph 1.18), and once with "destruction" in the New Testament (1 Thes 5.3). The **terror** or "fear" comes unexpectedly, when a person is least prepared for it. The word translated **overwhelms** was seen in 4.5 and 21.6. TEV renders it "suddenly you are full of fear," and NJB has "and sudden terrors make you afraid." This line may also be expressed, for example, "and without knowing it terror takes hold of you" or "suddenly you are badly frightened."

Your light is darkened so that you cannot see: this line in Hebrew is literally "Or darkness that you cannot see." RSV and others follow the Septuagint in adjusting verse 11a by changing the word translated "or" to **your light**, and "darkness" to **is darkened**, and supplying **so that** before **you cannot see**. These changes, which are considerable, followed by many interpreters. HOTTP admits that the Hebrew "or darkness" is very doubtful, giving it a "C" rating, but supplies "there is" to get "Or (there is) darkness." TEV has preferred to keep the Hebrew and thus avoid referring directly to **light**, by saying "It has grown so dark that you cannot see." FRCL has likewise avoided the Septuagint change by referring to the night: "The night darkens on you and you see nothing there." TEV and FRCL are preferred. However, if **light** is retained, it may be necessary to say in some languages, for example, "your light goes out and you cannot see in the dark," "everything becomes dark and you cannot see," or "you cannot see because the night is without any light."

And a flood of water covers you: the wording of verse 11b is the same as 38.34b, but in a different context. The thought of this line is expressed in greater detail in Psalm 69.1-2. Darkness and floods are common images for the threats of death. The line may also be expressed, for example, "and you are drowned by a flood" or "and you sink into the flood waters and drown."

5A-2. Eliphaz accuses Job of thinking God does not see his sinful deeds (22.12-14)

RSV	TEV
12 "Is not God high in the heavens? See the highest stars, how lofty they are!	12 Doesn't God live in the highest heavens and look down on the stars, even though they are high?
13 Therefore you say, 'What does God know? Can he judge through the deep darkness?	13 And yet you ask, "What does God know? He is hidden by clouds—how can he judge us?"
14 Thick clouds enwrap him, so that he does not see, and he walks on the vault of heaven.'	14 You think the thick clouds keep him from seeing, as he walks on the dome of the sky.

Subdivision Heading

The Handbook heading for verses 12-14 attempts to call attention to the alleged indifference of Job to God, who is far off. Translators wishing to place a heading before these verses may also say, for example, "You think that God does not judge people," "You think God is very far away," or "God is not as far away as you think, Job."

22.12   RSV   TEV

> "Is not God high in the heavens?   Doesn't God live in the highest
>   See the highest stars, how lofty   heavens
>   they are!   and look down on the stars,
>   even though they are high?

"Is not God high in the heavens? In Hebrew, as in RSV, this is a question. In Psalm 14.2 the psalmist describes God as "The LORD looks down from heaven upon the children of men to see if there are any that act wisely, that seek after God."

See the highest stars, how lofty they are! See translates the imperative "Look!" and can be understood as Eliphaz telling Job to "look at the highest stars." However, TEV, following the Septuagint, understands God as the one who looks down on the stars. The change from the imperative **See** to "sees" involves a very minor change of the Hebrew vowel markings. NEB also follows the change made in the Septuagint but understands the word translated **the highest** to mean the totality of stars, "God . . . looks down on all the stars . . . ." If the translator follows the thought of TEV, verse 12 may be rendered, for example, "God lives in the highest heaven and looks down on the stars" or "Doesn't God live high in the heaven, where he looks down on the highest stars? Certainly he does!" Verse 12 may also be translated as RSV; for example, "God is high in the heavens. Look up at the stars, how high they are." In order to relate verse 12 to verse 13, it may be necessary to translate verse 12 as the reason for verse 13; for example, "Because God is high in the heaven and you see how high the stars are, you ask . . . ."

22.13   RSV   TEV

> Therefore you say, 'What does   And yet you ask, "What does God
>   God know?   know?
>   Can he judge through the deep   He is hidden by clouds—how
>   darkness?   can he judge us?"

Therefore you say, 'What does God know?' The quotation in RSV closes after verse 14b. Job has not said this, but in 7.19 he recognized that God sees him and so begged God to look away from him. Eliphaz is putting words into Job's mouth, based on the inference drawn from God being high in the heavens and far away. In this way Eliphaz places Job with the godless, as expressed in Psalm 73.11, "And they say, 'How can God know? Is there knowledge in the Most High?'" See also Psalm 94.7. This line may continue verse 12b by saying, for example, "and so you conclude 'What can God know?' " or "and therefore you say, 'God can't know what is happening.' "

Can he judge through the deep darkness? Deep darkness translates the word rendered "dark cloud" by TEV in Exodus 20.21, in which God was present when he spoke to Moses after the people stood back (see also Deut 4.11). This line may also be expressed "How can he judge people when he is hidden by dark clouds?" or "He can't judge anyone because he is cut off by dark clouds."

22.14   RSV   TEV

> Thick clouds enwrap him, so that   You think the thick clouds keep
>   he does not see,   him from seeing,
> and he walks on the vault of   as he walks on the dome of the
>   heaven.'   sky.

Thick clouds enwrap him, so that he does not see: this is the description of the hidden God. RSV and others include the whole of verse 14 in the quotation which began in verse 13a. TEV closes the quoted question at the end of 13b and begins verse 14 with "You think . . . ." It also makes statements in both lines. This arrangement makes a clearer translation than RSV and is recommended to translators. **Thick clouds** translates "clouds that veil," suggesting a face veil, a cloth used to cover the face. (See 24.15c.) These are **thick clouds** in RSV and TEV. NEB has "His eyes cannot pierce the curtain of the clouds," and NJB "The clouds, to him, are an impenetrable veil," that is, a veil that cannot be seen through. FRCL translates "Their (the clouds from verse 13b) veil is too thick; God distinguishes nothing." This line may also be rendered, for example, "He can see nothing through such dark clouds" or "The dark clouds that hide him prevent him from seeing anything."

And he walks on the vault of heaven: this line describes an event happening at the same time as the main clause, which is in verse 14a. **Vault of heaven** is not an expression that is currently used in English. **Vault** is sometimes used to refer to an arched ceiling or roof, and as applied to heaven it suggests the dome-like appearance of the sky rising above the horizons. The term translated **vault** is used only here and in Proverbs 8.27; Isaiah 40.22. In the Proverbs reference TEV translates "horizon." The TEV footnote in the British edition has "Boundary between earth and sky: the horizon was regarded as a great circle where the earth met the sky and where God inspected the earth by walking around it." Modern translations use a variety of terms which have no clarifying note and often remain obscure; for example, NJB "rim of the heavens," NJV "circuit of heaven," and Dhorme "circle of the heavens." TEV has attempted to give an accurate rendering which conveys the idea, and translators will be helped by following it. This line may have to be rendered, for example, "He walks around the earth where the sky meets the ground" or "He walks where the sky and earth meet." It may also be necessary to provide readers with a footnote modeled on the TEV edition cited above.

5A-3. Eliphaz accuses Job of following the ways of evil men (22.15-20)

RSV	TEV
15 Will you keep to the old way / which wicked men have trod?	15 Are you determined to walk in the paths / that evil men have always followed?
16 They were snatched away before their / time; / their foundation was washed away.	16 Even before their time had come, / they were washed away by a flood.
17 They said to God, 'Depart from us,' / and 'What can the Almighty do to / us?'	17 These are the men who rejected God / and believed that he could do nothing / to them.
18 Yet he filled their houses with good / things— / but the counsel of the wicked is far / from me.	18 And yet it was God who made them / prosperous— / I can't understand the thoughts of the / wicked.
19 The righteous see it and are glad; / the innocent laugh them to scorn,	19 Good men are glad and innocent men / laugh / when they see the wicked punished.
20 saying, 'Surely our adversaries are cut off, / and what they left the fire has con- / sumed.'	20 All that the wicked own is destroyed, / and fire burns up anything that is left.

Subdivision Heading

The Handbook heading may be adjusted to say, for example, "Job wants to live like the wicked," "You want to follow those who reject God," or "Eliphaz warns Job that the wicked will be punished." TOB (12-20) has "Skepticism of Job," Habel (12-20) "A charge of siding with the wicked," and Rowley (12-20) "Job's assumption of divine indifference, as envisaged by Eliphaz."

22.15

RSV	TEV
Will you keep to the old way / which wicked men have trod?	**Are you determined to walk in / the paths / that evil men have always / followed?**

Eliphaz now challenges Job to say whether or not he intends to continue in the evil way of earlier generations. **Will you keep to the old way . . . ?** "Will you go on living like your ancestors?" **Way** translates the Hebrew for "road," used figuratively here to mean "conduct, behavior, way of life."

Which wicked men have trod? The verb **trod**, "walk," derived from the root meaning "road," is used to preserve the figure begun in the previous line. TEV would be closer to the Hebrew if it translated "Are you determined to go on walking in the old paths, the paths on which evil men have walked?" This verse may also be expressed "Have you decided to act the way evil people act?" or "Have you made up your mind to live as evil people live?"

22.16   RSV   TEV

> They were snatched away before
>   their time;
>   their foundation was washed
>   away.

> Even before their time had come,
>   they were washed away by a
>   flood.

They were snatched away before their time: due to **washed away** in line <u>b</u>, some think this verse refers to the flood in Genesis 7, but others take it to refer to a general drowning in a flood. The verb translated **snatched away** occurs only here and in 16.8, where TEV translated "seized." **Before their time** refers to a premature death, "died before they should have died" or "died before it was their time to die."

Their foundation was washed away: in Hebrew this line is not clear; it is literally "a river was poured out their foundation." The verb is passive in form, but there is no preposition corresponding to TEV's "by." RSV does not mention "river" or "flood," and TEV does not mention **foundation**. NIV translates "Their foundations washed away by a flood." Another possible meaning is "Their foundation is poured out like a river." The sense in this case would be that the house collapses as the foundation gives way, as though the foundation were liquid. However, the poet is thinking of the destruction of evil men themselves rather than their homes, and so a better translation of this line is "They were swept away like a building in a flood"; or the whole verse may be translated, for example, "As a building is washed away by a flood, so they died before their time to die had come."

22.17   RSV   TEV

> They said to God, 'Depart from
>   us,'
>   and 'What can the Almighty
>   do to us?'[f]

> These are the men who rejected
>   God
>   and believed that he could do
>   nothing to them.

[f] Gk Syr: Heb *them*

They said to God 'Depart from us': the similarity of the wording in this line to 21.14a suggests that Eliphaz is here referring back to those words spoken by Job. The only difference in the Hebrew is in the form of the verb at the beginning of the verse. In 21.14, as here, the Hebrew takes the form of direct speech. RSV maintains this, but TEV shifts to indirect. The line can be rendered "These are the men who said to God, 'Leave us alone.'"

And 'What can the Almighty do to us?' Most translations change the Hebrew from "them" to **us**, following the Septuagint. Both the sense and the parallelism require this change. The words of the unbelievers in this line are expressed in direct speech. Since the implied answer to this question is in the negative, TEV expresses it as negative statement: "and believed that he could do nothing to them." Verse 17 may be rendered, for example, "Those people said to God 'Leave us alone'; they believed Almighty God could not harm them" or " 'Let us be,' these evil people said to God; 'although he is the Almighty God, he can do nothing to us.' "

22.18

RSV	TEV
Yet he filled their houses with good things— but the counsel of the wicked is far from me.	And yet it was God who made them prosperous— I can't understand the thoughts of the wicked.

Yet he filled their houses with good things: this verse seems to be a thought which occurs to Eliphaz rather than something addressed directly to Job. RSV translates this line close to the Hebrew and clearly. TEV generalizes the expression **filled their houses with good things** to a more abstract level "made them prosperous." SPCL attempts to show that Eliphaz is addressing verse 18 to himself and so places it in parentheses. This may be helpful in some languages. Many English translations begin the line with **Yet**, as in RSV, meaning "in spite of that, nevertheless, still." The line may also be expressed "and in spite of all that, God made them rich" or "nevertheless God gave them all kinds of good things."

But the counsel of the wicked is far from me: this line is the same as Job said in 21.16. **Counsel of the wicked** was used by Job in 10.3 (translated there "designs of the wicked"). See the discussion there. The Septuagint has "far from him," but the Hebrew **far from me** is more effective. **Far from me** expresses Eliphaz's rejection of the schemes and plots of the wicked. He wants to have nothing to do with them. This is not reflected as clearly in TEV "I can't understand the thoughts of the wicked." RSV and TEV mark this line as a break in structure with the previous line by the use of a dash. The line may also be rendered, for example, "but the way the wicked make their plans is beyond me," "but I do not understand the way evil people scheme," or "I cannot grasp the way the mind of evil people works."

22.19-20

RSV	TEV
19 The righteous see it and are glad; the innocent laugh them to scorn, 20 saying, 'Surely our adversaries are cut off, and what they left the fire has consumed.'	19 Good men are glad and innocent men laugh when they see the wicked punished. 20 All that the wicked own is destroyed, and fire burns up anything that is left.

These two verses may be taken together as a description of the way in which the righteous react when they see the wicked experiencing disasters such as those referred to in verse 16. In Psalm 52.6-7 and 69.32 the psalmist speaks of the righteous rejoicing over the misfortunes of the wicked. The first line is the same as Psalm 107.42a.

The righteous see it and are glad: **the righteous** refers to those who are "faithful, upright, good." In the Hebrew "they see and are glad." What they see is the misfortune of the wicked in verse 16. TEV has made **it** explicit, "when they see the wicked punished," and transfers this to the second line. In translation it will often be necessary to state the object of seeing; for example, "Good people are happy to see the troubles of the wicked," "Good people rejoice when they see evil people have misfortune," or "The upright are glad when God punishes wicked people."

The innocent laugh them to scorn: **the innocent** does not refer to people who have been acquitted of a crime, but is in parallel with **the righteous** in the previous line and has the same meaning. **Laugh them to scorn** translates the same Hebrew expression used in Psalm 2.4, which means to laugh at someone with the purpose of "deriding, ridiculing, making fun of." TEV has joined "good men" and "innocent men" in line a as subjects of "glad" and "laugh," and has made line b a subordinate clause, "when they see the wicked punished." The purpose of this is to avoid the monotony of parallel lines in English. Translators may find it best to follow TEV as a model or to make a parallel line; for example, "they laugh and make fun of evil people" or "they laugh as they ridicule the wicked."

Saying, 'Surely our adversaries are cut off . . .': the word translated **adversaries** occurs only here in the Old Testament, and therefore its meaning is uncertain. Many guesses have been made. BDB suggests two possible changes. The first keeps the first person plural, as in RSV **our adversaries**. The use of the first person implies that this verse is a quotation of the words of **the innocent** in verse 19, and so RSV inserts the word **saying** between verses 19 and 20. The other change suggested substitutes a third-person plural suffix for the first plural, which is then attached to a word meaning "wealth." This avoids the need for introducing the word **saying**, since the third person now refers not to the enemies of the good men, but to the possessions of the evil men described in verses 15-17. Therefore NEB translates the line "for their riches are swept away." This change is used by most of the ancient versions and is the one followed by TEV. It has the additional advantage of providing a parallel to the third person in the next line, which is attached to a word meaning **what they left** or "their wealth" (NEB). The verb translated **cut off** is a passive form and has the sense of "are destroyed," "are ruined." This line may also be expressed either in terms of enemies or wealth; for example, "Indeed our enemies are destroyed" or "Certainly their wealth is destroyed." Stated as an active construction these alternatives may be "Certainly God destroys our enemies" or "Indeed God destroys their wealth." As indicated above, the recommended translation follows the change to wealth; for example, "Yes, God takes away their possessions."

And what they left the fire has consumed: SPCL translates verse 20 as the event witnessed by the upright in verse 19: "upon seeing the riches of the wicked being devoured by fire." This line seems to refer to "anything left over," which is then destroyed by fire. The picture is that of the total destruction of their possessions. In some languages the line is expressed "and fire eats the rest" or "what they leave behind, fire eats up."

5A-4. Eliphaz urges Job to give up evil, return to God, and be rewarded (22.21-30)

RSV	TEV

21 "Agree with God, and be at peace;
    thereby good will come to you.
	21 Now, Job, make peace with God
	    and stop treating him like an enemy;
	    if you do, then he will bless you.

22 Receive instruction from his mouth,
    and lay up his words in your heart.
	22 Accept the teaching he gives;
	    keep his words in your heart.

23 If you return to the Almighty and humble
    yourself,
    if you remove unrighteousness far from
    your tents,
	23 Yes, you must humbly return to God
	    and put an end to all the evil
	    that is done in your house.

24 if you lay gold in the dust,
    and gold of Ophir among the stones of
    the torrent bed,
	24 Throw away your gold;
	    dump your finest gold in the dry
	    stream bed.

25 and if the Almighty is your gold,
    and your precious silver;
	25 Let Almighty God be your gold,
	    and let him be silver, piled high for
	    you.

26 then you will delight yourself in the Al-
    mighty,
    and lift up your face to God.
	26 Then you will always trust in God
	    and find that he is the source of your
	    joy.

27 You will make your prayer to him, and he
    will hear you;
    and you will pay your vows.
	27 When you pray, he will answer you,
	    and you will keep the vows you made.

28 You will decide on a matter, and it will
    be established for you,
    and light will shine on your ways.
	28 You will succeed in all you do,
	    and light will shine on your path.

29 For God abases the proud,
    but he saves the lowly.
	29 God brings down the proud
	    and saves the humble.

30 He delivers the innocent man;
    you will be delivered through the
    cleanness of your hands."
	30 He will rescue you if you are innocent,
	    if what you do is right.

In verses 21-30 Eliphaz counsels Job to humble himself and receive instruction from God, and so be delivered from his suffering.

Subdivision Heading

The Handbook heading may also be stated as "Eliphaz asks Job to make peace with God," "Job, you must humbly return to God," or "Give up everything and surrender to God." Habel has "Counsel to accept the terms of Shaddai," Rowley "Eliphaz's appeal and promise to Job," and TOB "Fruits of reconciliation."

22.21 RSV	TEV

"Agree with God, and be at
    peace;
  thereby good will come to you.
	Now, Job, make peace with God
	    and stop treating him like an
	    enemy;
	  **if you do, then he will bless
	    you.**

Agree with God and be at peace: Agree translates a verb which is used in various forms with different meanings. Here it has the meaning "to become familiar with, to be reconciled with," and therefore TEV "stop treating him like an enemy." NJB translates "be reconciled." The Hebrew has "with him," but God is clearly meant, as in RSV and TEV. Some translations shift **be at peace** to the beginning of the line, to be followed by **agree with**, and so NJB has "Make peace with him, be reconciled." This line may also be rendered, for example, "Make peace and be friends with God," "Make friends and be at peace with God," or idiomatically, "Eat from one bowl with God and let your heart rest with his."

Thereby good will come to you: the Hebrew is difficult. TEV has taken it in the sense of blessing: "if you do, then he will bless you." The Hebrew has "by them," probably referring to the two commands in the previous line, "be at peace" and "be reconciled." Dhorme changes some vowels in the word rendered **will come to you** and gets "gain, profit, yield (of the land)"; he translates "By this means your yield will be good!" This makes a mockery of Job's true problem and shows Eliphaz to be a merciless materialist, which may well be true. Translators interpret the word translated **good** by RSV as "happiness, good fortune, wealth," which TEV shifts to the verb "bless." In many languages it will be preferable to use a verb phrase in an active construction; for example, "and so God will give you happiness (wealth, good fortune)."

22.22	RSV	TEV
	Receive instruction from his mouth, and lay up his words in your heart.	Accept the teaching he gives; keep his words in your heart.

Receive instruction from his mouth: Eliphaz thinks of himself as the spokesman for God. In 15.11 he referred to his advice as "consolations from God." He has already established that he possesses a revelation (4.12-21). The word translated **instruction** (Hebrew *torah*) often refers to the law, but in this context it means **instruction** or "teaching." **From his mouth** may be translated "which he himself gives." This line may be rendered, for example, "Let God instruct you," "Listen to what God teaches you," or "Learn the lessons God gives you."

And lay up his words in your heart: compare Psalm 119.11 "I have laid up thy word in my heart." The heart is the place of meditation and memory. FRCL translates "Take his words to heart." **Lay up** translates a verb meaning "to keep, store." This line may be rendered, for example, "store up God's words in your heart," "put God's words in your heart and keep them there," or "engrave his words on your mind."

22.23	RSV	TEV
	If you return to the Almighty and humble yourself,[g] if you remove unrighteousness far from your tents,	Yes, you must humbly[s] return to God and put an end to all the evil that is done in your house.

^g Gk: Heb *you will be built up*   ^s *One ancient translation* humbly; *Hebrew* be built up

In Hebrew verse 23 begins with "If," and verses 24 and 25 begin with "and," expressing implied conditions, each of which RSV translates with "if."

If you return to the Almighty and humble yourself: return to the Almighty means "to be converted from your ways, to change your ways," and most modern translations use "return to" or "turn to." The thought is that Job has strayed from the ways of God and must "come back to God." **Humble yourself** follows the Septuagint, which is preferred by many interpreters. The Hebrew has "you will be built up." (See RSV and TEV footnotes.) TEV and others express **humble yourself** as a qualifier of return: "You must humbly return to God." HOTTP rates the Hebrew as "B" and translates "You will be restored." In this case the Hebrew text makes good sense and should be followed.

In some languages it will not be natural to have so many "if" clauses (verses 23-25) before the consequence (verse 26). In such cases it may be necessary to shift to a different type of construction in 23-25; for example, "Return to the Almighty," "Remove unrighteousness." If the translator follows **humble yourself**, this is sometimes expressed idiomatically; for example, "make yourself a bowed person," "hold your hands upon your breast," "be a head-lowered person." This line may be rendered, for example, "If you change your ways, look down with the eyes and follow the Almighty God." Following the Hebrew text one may translate, for example, "If you will trust the Almighty, he will restore you" or "If . . . , he will make you what you used to be."

If you remove unrighteousness far from your tents: see comments on 11.14.

22.24-25	RSV	TEV
24	if you lay gold in the dust, and gold of Ophir among the stones of the torrent bed,	24 Throw away your gold; dump your finest gold in the dry stream bed.
25	and if the Almighty is your gold, and your precious silver;	25 Let Almighty God be your gold, and let him be silver, piled high for you.

Verses 24-25 are clearly linked in grammar and sense. **If you lay gold in the dust:** the Hebrew text of this verse has had two major interpretations. The first is "You will gather gold in the dust," in which Eliphaz is promising Job that he will be rich again. In 5.17-27 Eliphaz told Job that he would be restored to greatness. The other major understanding of the verse is that Eliphaz is urging Job to renounce wealth, and the consequence in verse 25 is that *Shaddai*, "Almighty God" (TEV), will take the place of his wealth. As Rowley points out it would be strange for Eliphaz to urge Job to get rid of gold when everything but his life has been taken from him. However, it is unfair to impose too much logic and too many demands for consistency on the ancient poet. In addition to these two interpretations, the ancient Syriac modified the Hebrew to get "You will count gold as dust," which makes a simile and means that Job will value gold no more than dust, or as Dhorme translates, "Then you will esteem gold as though it were dust." Among all the translations of this passage, only KJV views Eliphaz's words as a promise for the future, "Then shalt thou lay up gold as dust." In other words, to Job gold will be as common as dust. Most modern translations understand verse 24 to mean that Job is told to get rid of his gold. TEV and others have "Throw away your gold."

The advantage of understanding verse 24a to mean the renouncing of wealth is that it seems to make the best sense in the context and leads in smoothly to verse 25. NEB follows Syriac's simile and translates "If you treat your precious metal as dust . . . ." Verse 24 has poetic alliteration, that is, similar sounds that recur. For example, the word *'aphar* "dust" in line a is echoed by *'Ophir* in line b. *Betzer*, a rare word for "gold" in line a, is matched in line b by *betzur* "rocks."

And gold of Ophir among the stones of the torrent bed: **gold of Ophir** translates the Hebrew proper noun **Ophir**, which is an unknown place famed for its gold. (See Psa 45.9; Is 13.12.) Only here and in 28.16 is gold described by giving it this place name. TEV translates "finest gold." The verb in this line is to be understood from line a or supplied as a word of similar meaning, so TEV "dump." For **torrent bed** see 6.15. Verse 24 may be rendered, for example, "Get rid of your gold; throw your best gold among the rocks in the dry bed of the river," or somewhat differently and as an "if" clause, "If you will consider the most precious gold as if it were dust and nothing more than the stones of a river bed . . . ."

And if the Almighty is your gold: in RSV verse 25 contains two more "if" clauses, which TEV renders as "let" commands. **Gold** translates the same rare word used in verse 24a. This line may also be expressed, for example, "If you will accept Almighty God as your gold," "If you will let Almighty God be like gold to you," or "Let Almighty God be like gold to you."

And your precious silver: the meaning of the word translated **precious** is uncertain. It occurs elsewhere only in Numbers 23.22; 24.8 ("horns"), and in Psalm 95.4, where it is translated "heights" in contrast with "depths of the earth." In the present context the sense suggested by Dhorme is "heaped up piles" of silver, which is nearly equivalent to TEV "silver piled high." This line is an example of parallelism in which line b goes beyond, or carries the thought of line a, to a more intense level. In translation it will be necessary in some languages to shift to a simile and say, for example, "and let him be like piles of silver" or "let God be like silver that is heaped up."

22.26   RSV   TEV

then you will delight yourself in   Then you will always trust in
        the Almighty,   God
and lift up your face to God.   and find that he is the source
                                                            of your joy.

Verse 26 in RSV and TEV is the consequence of verses 23-25. **Then you will delight yourself in the Almighty**: **delight yourself** translates the reflexive form of a Hebrew verb meaning "to find joy, to take pleasure, to be happy." It is used in regard to Yahweh in Isaiah 58.14; Psalm 37.4. TEV has reversed lines a and b but has not gained any particular advantage by doing so.

And lift up your face to God: this Hebrew expression was also used in verse 8b, where RSV translates "favored man." For comments on this expression see 11.15. TEV "Then you will always trust in God" is a loose rendering and would be better rendered "Then you will face God with a clear conscience" or "Then you will not be ashamed before God." SPCL says "and you can look at him with confidence." Verse 26 may also be expressed, for example, "As a result the Almighty God will give you great joy, and you can look at him with a clear conscience" or "Then the Almighty God will fill you with joy, and you will look at him with a clean heart."

22.27-28   RSV   TEV

27 You will make your prayer to   27 When you pray, he will answer
      him, and he will hear you;   you,
    and you will pay your vows.   and you will keep the vows you
28 You will decide on a matter, and   made.
      it will be established for you,   28 You will succeed in all you do,
    and light will shine on your   and light will shine on your
      ways.   path.

These two verses add two more consequences which Eliphaz holds out to Job if he will repent and return to God.

You will make your prayer to him: Job has complained bitterly that God does not hear him. In 8.5-7 Bildad said that if Job was pure and upright he could pray to Almighty God, and that God would rouse himself for Job. Now Eliphaz has set new conditions that will enable God to hear Job and answer him.

And you will pay your vows: prayer may be accompanied by a vow, which is a promise to do something in payment to God for answering a request. See Psalm 22.25; 61.5,8; 65.1. Here Eliphaz assumes Job's prayer request will be granted, and that Job will back up his prayer with a vow to do something for God. Verse 27 may also be rendered, for example, "You will also pray to God, and you will keep the promises you make to him" or "God will hear your prayers, and you will do what you promised God you would do."

You will decide on a matter, and it will be established for you: "Anything you decide to do will be successful." This translates what is literally "And cut a word it stands for you," where "cut a word" means "decide something." **Established** translates a verb form meaning "arise, stand"; that which is "stood up, raised" is accomplished and so it succeeds. Some interpreters take the literal expression "cut a word" to mean "make a decree," so KJV "Thou shalt also decree a thing." The recommended sense is as in NJB: "Whatever you undertake will go well." This line may also be expressed "Whatever you decide to do will turn out well," "The things you want to do you will do them successfully," or "You will have success in everything you undertake."

And light will shine on your ways: instead of the darkness in which Job walks (19.8; 22.11), there will be light shining on his paths. This line may also be rendered "and your path will be lighted," "wherever you go you will walk in the light," or "the path you walk on will not be in darkness."

22.29   RSV   TEV

For God abases the proud,[h]   God brings down the proud[t]
  but he saves the lowly.   and saves the humble.

[h] Cn: Heb *when they abased you said,*   [t] *Probable text* proud; *Hebrew unclear.*
Proud

Eliphaz now summarizes his thoughts. **For God abases the proud**: as the TEV footnote says, the Hebrew of this line is unclear. Fortunately the next line is clear enough: **but he saves the lowly**. The person in line b is described in Hebrew as having "downcast eyes" and is in contrast to **the proud** person in line a. Line a is literally "When they have humbled you, you say 'Pride!'" The words "humbled" and "pride" have been the subject of numerous proposals for change, but few agreements. However, "you said" is generally felt to be out of place. Both RSV and TEV supply God as the subject of the active verb **abases** and translate line a as "God humbles the proud," which is clearly in contrast to **but he saves the lowly**. HOTTP gives the Hebrew text a "B" rating and attempts to keep it by offering two renderings: (a) "When they are brought low, you will say: 'restoration' and he (God) will save (the man with) lowered eyes"; and (b) "When they are brought low, you will say: '(it is because of) pride,' but (the man with) lowered eyes he (that is, God) saves." The second alternative can be translated into English as "When a person is humbled you say it is because he was proud, but God saves the humble person." Verse 29 may also be rendered, for example, "When God humbles people you say he did it because they were proud, but it is God's way of saving them."

22.30   RSV   TEV

He delivers the innocent man;[i]   He will rescue you if you are
  you will be delivered through   innocent,[u]
    the cleanness of your   if what you do is right.[v]
    hands."

                                                [u] *Some ancient translations* innocent;
[i] Gk Syr Vg: Heb *him that is not inno-*   *Hebrew* not innocent.
cent   [v] *Verse 30 in Hebrew is unclear.*

He delivers the innocent man: both RSV and TEV call attention to the difficulty of the Hebrew text of this verse. The problem centers on **the innocent man**, which most likely means "not innocent" as it stands. In this sense the meaning would be that God rescues, delivers the "man who is not innocent"; that is, Job, who is guilty. God delivers him because his hands are clean. Even though Job is not innocent, God would save him because he does what is right. Many scholars change the Hebrew word translated "not" by the addition of a consonant to get "man," and so RSV **innocent man**. This is one of the possibilities recommended by HOTTP. This sense seems to agree with the trend of Eliphaz's thought. When Job has clean hands, that is, when he does what is right, he is no longer sinning and God will rescue him.

TEV makes the reference to Job clear with "He will rescue you if you are innocent." It is necessary to make clear the relation of 30a to 30b, and this may be done in some languages by making line a a dependent clause; for example, "Since God rescues the innocent person" or "Because God rescues the innocent person from evil."

You will be delivered through the cleanness of your hands: cleanness of your hands is parallel with **innocent** in the previous line and has the meaning of being innocent of doing wrong, not guilty of living in a bad way, and so "doing the right thing." (See 2 Sam 22.21; Psa 18.20, 24.) The main clause of verse 30 may be translated, for example, "He will rescue you if you are not guilty." Verse 30 may be expressed, for example, "Because God saves the person who is innocent of wrong doing, he will save you if you are not guilty." The verse may also be expressed "If you are not guilty, God will rescue you from evil, because God saves people who are not guilty of doing wrong."

5B. JOB REPLIES (23.1–24.25)

Chapters 23 and 24 contain Job's seventh speech, in which he does not reply to Eliphaz's speech in chapter 22 but rather takes up his own agenda. The major theme of chapter 23 is Job's complaint that he cannot find God and therefore is unable to present his case to him.

Job's moods in this chapter are arranged in an alternating series of negative and positive outlooks. In verses 2-5 Job complains against God and his inability to find God. In verses 6-7 Job's attitude changes, and he feels that God would listen to his case and declare him innocent. However, with verses 8-9 Job is again hopelessly looking about for God. In verses 10-12 the positive attitude again comes to the surface as Job expresses confidence in God and himself. But finally Job's feeling in verses 13-17 is very low as he admits that God terrifies him.

Division Heading

In previous speeches made by Job, it was appropriate to say, for example, "Job replies to Eliphaz." Since chapter 23 is not a response to anything Eliphaz said in chapter 22, it is better to say, for example, "Job speaks again," "Job's turn again," or "Job." Some translations use only a single heading; for example, FRCL has "Job's discourse: God refuses to dialogue with me," and Habel "Job's quest to face God." Other suggestions are: "Job looks for God," "Job is unable to find God," or "Job seeks God, but cannot find him."

5B-1. God would listen to Job if Job knew where to find him (23.1-7)

RSV	TEV
1 Then Job answered:	*Job*
2 "Today also my complaint is bitter, his hand is heavy in spite of my groaning.	1-2 I still rebel and complain against God; I cannot keep from groaning.
3 Oh, that I knew where I might find him,	3 How I wish I knew where to find him, and knew how to go where he is.

that I might come even to his seat!	4 I would state my case before him
4 I would lay my case before him	and present all the arguments in my
and fill my mouth with arguments.	favor.
5 I would learn what he would answer me,	5 I want to know what he would say
and understand what he would say to	and how he would answer me.
me.	6 Would God use all his strength against
6 Would he contend with me in the great-	me?
ness of his power?	No, he would listen as I spoke.
No; he would give heed to me.	7 I am honest; I could reason with God;
7 There an upright man could reason with	he would declare me innocent once
him,	and for all.
and I should be acquitted for ever by	
my judge.	

Job cannot keep silent (verse 2) and is anxious to bring his case before God (verses 3-7), just as he has argued from chapter 6 onward.

Subdivision Heading

The heading for verses 1-7 may be modified to say, for example, "Job says, 'I wish I knew where to find God'" or "I would state my case if I could find him." Rowley has "Job's longing to meet God," TOB (2-9) "Absence of God."

23.1   RSV   TEV

Then Job answered: *Job*

Then Job answered: see 4.1 for a discussion of **answered**.

23.2   RSV   TEV

"Today also my complaint is   I still rebel and complain against
   bitter,[j]   God;
   his[k] hand is heavy in spite of   I cannot keep from groaning.
   my groaning.

[j] Syr Vg Tg: Heb *rebellious*
[k] Gk Syr: Heb *my*

Today also my complaint is bitter: **Today** is the only apparent reference in Job to the time of an action, and it has been interpreted by some as indicating that the poet is calling attention to the passing of days during which the speeches took place, or that chapter 23 takes place a day or more following chapter 22. It seems more probable that **Today also** signals that Job is renewing his old complaint even after having heard all his friends have to say. Therefore it may be better to translate "In spite of what has been said" or "Just the same." TEV "I still . . ." gives the expression this sense. For **complaint** see 7.13; the term is also used in 9.27; 10.1; 21.4. As the RSV footnote indicates, **bitter** follows a textual change made by the ancient versions. The Hebrew has "rebellious," so NJB translates "My lament is still

430

rebellious." Job's complaint is against God, and TEV makes this clear with two clauses: "I still rebel and complain against God." God is not mentioned by name in verses 1-15 but is represented by pronouns. In translation it will often be necessary to replace some pronouns by the noun "God." This line may also be expressed "In spite of what you have said, my complaint is as strong as before," "I'll tell you again, my complaints are bitter," or "Once more I object and complain against God."

His hand is heavy in spite of my groaning is literally "My hand is heavy on my groaning." RSV and others follow the change made by the Septuagint, **his hand**, which NJB renders more clearly than RSV as "despite my groans his hand is just as heavy"; that is, God goes on causing Job to suffer in spite of Job's groans. Dhorme and others keep the Hebrew "my hand," with the sense that Job tries to suppress his groans by laying his hand over his mouth. FRCL translates "I have really wanted to suppress my groans," and it transposes lines a and b so that a follows b with the sense "In spite of wanting to suppress my groans, still my complaint is stronger than ever." TEV translates "I cannot keep from groaning," which follows the Hebrew text rather than the Septuagint. TEV's rendering would be more accurate by including an expression to cover the sense of "my hand": "in spite of trying to suppress them, I can't hold back my groans." HOTTP retains the Hebrew and recommends a literal translation, which it explains as "My silence is an enforced one." RSV translates the Hebrew preposition in line b as "in spite of." In other words, God pays no attention to Job's groans but goes on punishing him. Taken as a whole it seems best to recommend the change followed by RSV, **his hand**. Line b is taken as the reason for the complaint or rebellion in line a. RSV can be expressed differently to say, for example, "because God keeps on punishing me in spite of my groaning" or ". . . in spite of my painful cries."

23.3	RSV	TEV
	Oh, that I knew where I might find him, that I might come even to his seat!	How I wish I knew where to find him, and knew how to go where he is.

Oh, that I knew where I might find him: Job despairs at not being able to lay his case before God. (See 9.34; 13.15.) He now laments the fact that he does not know where to find God. The form used here to express a wish is found also in 11.5, where TEV translates "How I wish God would answer you!" This line may also be expressed, for example, "If only I knew where to find him" or "I wish I could find God."

That I might come even to his seat: if Job knew where to find God, he would go to the place where he is. **Seat** translates a Hebrew noun whose meaning is uncertain. In Ezekiel 43.11 it means "arrangement, structure." In Nahum 2.9 it alludes to a "collection of treasure." As a verb it may mean "prepare, set, arrange"; in Psalm 9.7; 103.19 the verb means "established (his throne)," and in Exodus 15.17 Yahweh's hands have "established" his sanctuary. TEV translates very generally: "and knew how to go where he is." NJB has "dwelling," NEB "court," and Mft "throne." RSV **seat** refers to the place from which God judges, and so has the sense of "court."

In translation it will be best to be more specific than TEV and use a place where legal matters are held, or to shift to a verb; for example, "the place where God judges matters" or "the place where God listens to complaints."

23.4   RSV   TEV

> I would lay my case before him
> and fill my mouth with argu-
>   ments.

> I would state my case before him
> and present all the arguments
>   in my favor.

I would lay my case before him: this line recalls Job's comment in 13.18, which TEV renders "I am ready to state my case." The verbs in verses 4 and 5 have the sense of conditionals: "I would state my case if I could speak with him." See a similar conditional in 16.4. **Lay . . . before** translates a verb meaning "arrange, draw up a lawsuit"; that is, Job would state the details of his complaint, or "I would state my case before him" (TEV). This line may also be expressed, for example, "I would argue my case with him," "I would explain why I am innocent," or "I would prove to him that I have done no wrong."

And fill my mouth with arguments: "I would present him every detail." **Fill my mouth** is a poetic way of expressing the thoroughness and extent of Job's arguments in favor of his innocence. NEB has "and set out my arguments in full," TEV "and present all the arguments in my favor." This line may be expressed idiomatically in some languages; for example, "I would give him every breath of my argument," "I would leave no track unobserved," or "I would show him every pebble in the river bed."

23.5   RSV   TEV

> I would learn what he would
>   answer me,
> and understand what he would
>   say to me.

> I want to know what he would
>   say
> and how he would answer me.

I would learn what he would answer me: if Job could get his case before his judge, he **would learn**, meaning "know, find out." TEV has not repeated **I would** in this line but has shifted to "I want to know . . . ." TEV has also transposed the two lines of verse 5, which places the more specific **answer** in the second line and provides a better style for English. **What he would answer me** refers to God's defense of himself in the trial. NJB translates "I could learn his defence." If court room terms are not to be used in translation, we may say, for example, "I would find out what he has to say" or ". . . how he speaks for himself."

And understand what he would say to me: the two lines of verse 5 are closely parallel in meaning, since **learn** in line <u>a</u> is matched by **understand** in line <u>b</u>, and **he would answer me** in line <u>a</u> by **what he would say to me** in line <u>b</u>. In 15.9 the same Hebrew words translated here as **learn** and **understand** are used in parallel. There is no attempt to make a distinction in meaning nor to effect poetic heightening. In some languages it may be necessary to shorten and combine the two lines of verse 5; for example, "I would find out what he would say when he answered me." Others may prefer to keep the two parallel lines.

23.6 RSV	TEV
Would he contend with me in the greatness of his power? No; he would give heed to me.	Would God use all his strength against me? No, he would listen as I spoke.

Would he contend with me in the greatness of his power? In 9.29 Job was convinced that God would condemn him. In 13.21 Job asked God to withdraw his hand "and let not dread of thee terrify me." Now, however, he does not believe that God would overwhelm him with his might. Perhaps verse 6 can be taken as God having granted Job's request in 13.21. In the Hebrew line a is a question which Job answers negatively in line b. **Contend** translates the same word used in 9.3 and 13.19, meaning "dispute, argue, plead." **In the greatness of his power** is a phrase that is best taken in an instrumental sense, that is, **the greatness of his power** is the instrument or weapon which God uses in the contest against Job. "Will he use his great power to argue with me?" or "Would God use all his strength against me?" (TEV). However, TEV leaves unclear in what respect God uses his strength. FRCL is more specific with "Does it take a very great effort for him to confront me?" This line may also be expressed "Does it take great strength for him to dispute with me?" or "Would he crush me with his might in an argument?"

No; he would give heed to me is literally "No, surely he would place (attention) on me." Job answers his own question with confidence. The verb translated **give heed** usually means "place, put," but there is no object expressed in Hebrew, and so one must be supplied. NEB understands the object to be a charge: "No; God himself would never bring a charge against me." Dhorme proposes changing the word translated **give heed** by adding one consonant to get "He would only have to listen to me," which is the basis for TEV "He would listen as I spoke." This line may also be rendered "No, he would give me a fair hearing," "No, he would pay attention to what I say," or "He would not do that; he would listen to what I say."

23.7 RSV	TEV
There an upright man could reason with him, and I should be acquitted for ever by my judge.	I am honest; I could reason with God; he would declare me innocent[w] once and for all.

[w] he would declare me innocent; *or* then my rights would be safe.

Job is confident that God would find him innocent of all charges. **There an upright man could reason with him: There** translates the Hebrew word which normally has that meaning. It can refer back to the seat where God judges in verse 3, although verse 3 is four verses back. Some scholars give it the meaning "Then" as a reference to the time of Job's future court case with God. Dhorme suggests a change to get "he would observe . . . ." While NEB, NIV, NJV, and RSV keep **There**, TEV and others do not translate it. NJB follows Dhorme but joins verse 7a to verse 6b. The meaning may also be taken as "when he hears my case." Although verse 7 is separated from verse 3, there does not seem to be any valid reason for omitting the word. **Upright man** translates the same word used to describe Job in 1.1. It is also used in 5.17; 6.25, and has the meaning of "good, honest, respectable." See also 1.8; 2.3; 8.6. **Reason** translates a verb used in Isaiah 1.18 and means "discuss, argue, dispute." RSV follows the Hebrew quite literally and translates this line without direct reference to Job. However, the next line makes it clear that Job speaks of himself. Therefore TEV breaks the line into two sentences: "I am honest; I could reason with God." This line may also be rendered, for example, "When that time comes I will reason with him because I am honest," "When we meet he will listen to my argument because I am honest," or "At that time he will listen to a good argument from an honest man like me."

And I should be acquitted forever by my judge: this line is the consequence of the previous line. **Acquitted** translates a verb used reflexively with the sense "to deliver one's self." **By my judge** is in the Hebrew "from my judge." As it stands the text seems to give the sense "And I would be forever delivered from my judge" (Dhorme). This also seems to be the understanding of HOTTP. However, there are other ways to understand and translate this line. The Septuagint and the Vulgate have "from my judgment," that is, from the judgment God has taken in regard to Job, and so NJB translates "judgment" as "case": "So I should win my case forever." TEV shifts to the active and, instead of **by my judge**, has "he (God) would declare me innocent once and for all." The line may also be rendered, for example, "and he will declare me innocent and free forever," "and God, who is my judge, will say 'Not guilty, freed forever,'" or "and my judge who is God will set me free forever and declare me to be innocent."

5B-2. Job has searched everywhere for God (23.8-12)

	RSV		TEV
8	"Behold, I go forward, but he is not there; and backward, but I cannot perceive him;	8	I have searched in the East, but God is not there; I have not found him when I searched in the West.
9	on the left hand I seek him, but I cannot behold him; I turn to the right hand, but I cannot see him.	9	God has been at work in the North and the South, but still I have not seen him.
10	But he knows the way that I take; when he has tried me, I shall come forth as gold.	10	Yet God knows every step I take; if he tests me, he will find me pure.
11	My foot has held fast to his steps;	11	I follow faithfully the road he chooses, and never wander to either side.
		12	I always do what God commands;

| | I have kept his way and have not turned aside. | I follow his will, not my own desires. |
| 12 | I have not departed from the command-ment of his lips; I have treasured in my bosom the words of his mouth. | |

In verses 8 and 9 Job again picks up the problem of locating God. Although he cannot find God to present his case, he has confidence that God will judge him innocent when finally God tries him (verse 10). In verses 11-12 Job expresses the reasons for his confidence in God, namely, that he has not departed from God's commandments.

Subdivision Heading

The Handbook heading may be modified to say, for example, "I have looked in all directions for God," "I always do what God wants me to do," or "I follow faithfully on God's road."

23.8-9 RSV	TEV
8 "Behold, I go forward, but he is not there; and backward, but I cannot perceive him;	8 I have searched in the East, but God is not there; I have not found him when I searched in the West.
9 on the left hand I seek him,¹ but I cannot behold him; Iᵐ turn to the right hand, but I cannot see him.	9 God has been at work in the North and the South, but still I have not seen him.

ˡ Compare Syr: Heb *on the left hand when he works*
ᵐ Syr Vg: Heb *he*

These two verses need to be discussed together. In verse 3 Job said that he could not find God. Now he tells how he has searched for him in all directions. **Behold, I go forward, but he is not there**. For **Behold** see 4.18; 12.14; 13.15. **Forward** in line a and **backward** in line b describe a person facing the east. Here we have an example of the standard Hebrew way of telling directions, or what modern people call the four points of the compass. Before him is the direction "east," and in back of him is "west." To his left is "north" and to his right is "south." TEV is correct, therefore, in translating "I have searched in the east." The sense of going **forward** or to the "east" is "searching in the east" or "If I look for him in the east." The negative consequence is "I do not find him in that direction." In some languages the directions in this line may be rendered, for example, "But if I look for God where the sun rises" or ". . . at the headwaters of the river."

And backward, but I cannot perceive him: "even looking for him in the west I have not seen him." The verb must be supplied from line a. Languages that designate "east" as "where the sun rises" often designate "west" as "where the sun dies, sets, sinks, or falls off."

On the left hand I seek him, but I cannot behold him: the RSV footnote shows that the Hebrew says "on the left hand when he works," which TEV translates "God has been at work in the north . . . ." RSV follows Syriac in changing the verb "work" to mean "I seek him," the subject now being Job, not God. There does not seem to be any compelling reason to depart from the Hebrew text, and so TEV, which has joined the two lines of verse 9, is recommended.

I turn to the right hand, but I cannot see him: the RSV footnote shows that the Hebrew has "he turns . . . ." RSV follows the Syriac and Vulgate in changing this to **I turn**. Another verb which has the same consonants means "cover," as used in Psalm 104.2 "who coverest thyself with light as with a garment." Gordis accepts this sense, "He is hidden in the south," and FRCL does likewise, translating with a question. HOTTP accepts the two meanings "turn" and "hide." TEV combines "he turns to the south" with the previous line as "at work in the north and the south." A fuller rendering is "When he turns to the south, I cannot see him." Some translators may find that verses 8 and 9 are better expressed by joining them into a single sentence. This may be done by placing the verse numbers 8 and 9 before verse 8 and translating in summary fashion; for example, "I have searched for God in every direction, and still I have not found him." If translators employ the directions for "east" and "west" in verse 8, they should continue with the expressions for "north" and "south" in verse 9.

23.10	RSV	TEV
	But he knows the way that I take; when he has tried me, I shall come forth as gold.	Yet God knows every step I take; if he tests me, he will find me pure.

In contrast to his inability to find God, Job is confident that God knows where to find him. **But he knows the way that I take**: **But** may be understood as introducing a contrast between verse 10 and the two previous verses, or it may have the sense of "Although." **The way that I take** is well rendered by TEV "every step I take." Syriac has "my way and my standing," which Dhorme accepts and translates "my going and my staying." RSV and TEV are preferred, or we may also translate, for example, "But he knows the path I follow" or "But he knows where he can find me."

When he has tried me, I shall come forth as gold: **tried** translates the same verb used in 7.18 "and test him every moment," where it refers to God testing Job's faithfulness. See 7.18 for discussion. TEV has dropped the simile **as gold** and gives instead the sense of the simile, with ". . . find me pure." For this kind of testing compare Zechariah 13.9 "I will . . . test them as gold is tested." By appealing to Arabic and Ugaritic evidence, Dahood understands the verb translated **come forth** to mean "shine," referring to the shining surface of the gold in the heated crucible when the impurities have been removed. FRCL translates "but I will come out of it (the testing) pure, as the gold in a crucible." In languages in which this metaphor is not current, perhaps because smelting of precious metals is also unknown, it will be best to follow TEV. In other languages people do not speak of a person as being "pure." In such cases it may be possible to express this line as a simile; for example, "If he examines my ways, he will find me clean as pure water."

23.11   RSV   TEV

> My foot has held fast to his   I follow faithfully the road he
>   steps;   chooses,
> I have kept his way and have   and never wander to either
>   not turned aside.   side.

My foot has held fast to his steps translates the Hebrew literally. The two lines of verse 11 are closely alike in meaning. It is an example of the reverse of the usual practice of parallelism, in which the figurative term occurs in line b̲ with the more general one in line a̲. In a similar manner Psalm 17.5 says "My steps have held fast to thy path." **My foot** is the specific part of the body representing the person's action, "walk, go"; **hold fast** means "loyally, faithfully"; and **his steps** is a poetic metaphor for "the way he goes," "wherever he goes," or "the way he takes." NJB translates "My footsteps have followed close in his." This line may sometimes be rendered, for example "I take each step by walking in his footprints" or "I follow him by walking on his footprints."

I have kept his way and have not turned aside: **his way** means "the way God has shown" or "the way God has marked out" In some languages this can be expressed as "the trail God himself has cut out." **Not turned aside** means being "loyal, faithful, devoted, unswerving." This line may be expressed, for example, "I have gone the way he has shown me and been faithful to him" or "I have followed faithfully the path he has shown me."

23.12   RSV   TEV

> I have not departed from the   I always do what God commands;
>   commandment of his lips;   I follow his will, not my own
> I have treasured in[n] my bosom   desires.
>   the words of his mouth.

[n] Gk Vg: Heb *from*

I have not departed from the commandment of his lips: said positively this means "I have done everything he has commanded me to do"; expressed negatively, "I have not neglected, (failed) to keep his commands." **Commandment of his lips** means the law God has spoken and which he requires people to obey. SPCL has "I have always followed his laws and commandments." TEV shifts to "what God commands."

I have treasured in my bosom the words of his mouth: this line in Hebrew is unclear. RSV follows the Septuagint and Vulgate. See RSV footnote. TEV follows the Hebrew text without any change and does not call attention to the textual difficulty. **I have treasured** translates a verb meaning "I have kept, stored up, hidden away." **In my bosom** follows the Septuagint. The Hebrew has a preposition and a possessed noun which HOTTP interprets as "from the statute (law) concerning me" or "more than my portion." The HOTTP committee was divided, with half of the members accepting the Hebrew text with a "C" rating, and the other half favoring the Septuagint as representing the oldest and best text, also with a "C" rating. Translators should consult the full recommendation of HOTTP. In brief they recommend two alternatives: (1) follow the Hebrew with two possible phrase divisions, as in TEV, or (2) follow the Septuagint, as in RSV, with the possibility of putting an alternative translation in a note. FRCL, which follows the Septuagint, offers a good translation model: "I have kept in my heart everything he commanded me." This model may also be rendered, for example, "I have guarded in my heart all he told me to do" or "I have been faithful to do all he has required of me."

5B-3. Job believes God has a plan for him (23.13-17)

	RSV		TEV
13	But he is unchangeable and who can turn him?	13	He never changes. No one can oppose him
	What he desires, that he does.		or stop him from doing what he wants to do.
14	For he will complete what he appoints for me;	14	He will fulfill what he has planned for me;
	and many such things are in his mind.		that plan is just one of the many he has;
15	Therefore I am terrified at his presence;		
	when I consider, I am in dread of him.	15	I tremble with fear before him.
16	God has made my heart faint;	16-17	Almighty God has destroyed my courage.
	the Almighty has terrified me;		It is God, not the dark, that makes me afraid—
17	for I am hemmed in by darkness,		even though the darkness has made me blind.
	and thick darkness covers my face.		

Job now acknowledges that God does as he pleases (verses 13-15), and this thought terrifies him, because he feels enclosed in darkness (verses 16-17).

Subdivision Heading

The Handbook heading may be changed to say, for example, "I am afraid of God" or "God will do what he wants." Rowley (8-17) has "The inaccessibility and power of God," and TOB (10-17) "Presence of God."

23.13	RSV	TEV
	But he is unchangeable and who can turn him? What he desires, that he does.	**He never changes. No one can oppose him or stop him from doing what he wants to do.**

But he is unchangeable and who can turn him? Unchangeable translates the Hebrew "in one." Some interpreters supply "mind" to complete the sense, "he is of one mind"; that is, he is not divided but knows exactly what he wants. Pope and Dhorme make a textual change to get "he chooses," which is followed by NJB and NEB. HOTTP rates the Hebrew as an "A" reading and recommends two meanings: "and he is unique" or "and he alone." RSV, and TEV "He never changes," follow the Hebrew text but understand it differently than HOTTP. The sense of the question **who can turn him?** is well expressed by NEB, "who can turn him from his purpose?" The point is that God freely chooses what he will do, and no one can change the course he has chosen. TEV expresses the first part of verse 13 as two statements.

What he desires, that he does is literally "And his *nefesh* does what he desires." *Nefesh,* often translated "soul, breath, throat, neck," is also the center of emotions and particularly expresses desire, even selfish desires, in such passages as Hosea 4.8, where RSV translates it "greedy." This line is well translated by NEB, "He does what his own heart desires," or it may be expressed in some languages as "What his liver (stomach, throat) desires, he will do." In some languages translators may find that RSV's statement-plus-question in line a followed by a further statement in line b would be better changed to two statements; for example, "When he decides to do something, he does it; nothing can change his mind" or "What God decides to do he does, and he does whatever his heart desires."

23.14	RSV	TEV
	For he will complete what he appoints for me; and many such things are in his mind.	He will fulfill what he has planned for me; that plan is just one of the many he has;

For he will complete what he appoints for me: **complete** translates a verb meaning "accomplish, achieve, carry out his purpose, fulfill." **What he appoints for me** translates the same term TEV translated as "my own desires" in verse 12. The word here means "my decree"; that is, "what God decrees for me," not "what I decree." TEV uses "plan": "He will fulfill what he has planned for me." The line may also be rendered, for example, "He will do what he has planned for me" or "Whatever he has decided to do, he will carry it out for me."

And many such things are in his mind: things here is to be taken as referring to "plans" in the previous line. This line may be rendered "and he has many plans for me."

23.15	RSV	TEV
	Therefore I am terrified at his presence; when I consider, I am in dread of him.	I tremble with fear before him.

As in 21.6, the thought Job has just expressed causes him to be afraid. **Therefore I am terrified at his presence**: in 22.10 Eliphaz introduced the argument that Job's misery is the result of his criminal acts of oppressing the poor: "Therefore snares are round about you, and sudden terror overwhelms you." According to Job in 13.14, God has put it in his mind to do these things to Job, and nothing else accounts for them. It is the mystery of God's ways which frightens Job. **His presence** is literally "his face." The thought of meeting God face to face strikes terror into Job. The line may be rendered "It is because of this that I am afraid of him."

When I consider, I am in dread of him: this line adds little to the previous line. **Consider** translates a word meaning "ponder, reflect, think about," and so NEB "When I think about him, I am afraid." TEV does not translate this phrase, but it combines the entire line with line a. However, the two lines are not identical in meaning, and so TEV's translation is somewhat lacking. This line may be rendered "When I think about him, it fills me with fear" or "The thought of meeting him terrorizes me."

23.16-17   RSV   TEV

16	God has made my heart faint;	16-17	Almighty God has destroyed my
	the Almighty has terrified me;		courage.
17	for I am° hemmed in by dark-		It is God, not the dark, that
	ness,			makes me afraid—
	and thick darkness covers my		even though the darkness has
	face.ᴾ			made me blind.

° With one Ms: Heb *am not*
ᴾ Vg: Heb *from my face*

God has made my heart faint: verse 16 has two closely parallel lines. **My heart faint** is idiomatic in Hebrew and refers to a person who is "timid, fearful." Since God has done this to Job, TEV translates "Almighty God has destroyed my courage," that is, "made me timid." **The Almighty has terrified me**: line b adds little to line a except the substitution of *Shaddai* for *'El* "God." TEV has reduced the two lines to one, incorporating **Almighty** into line a. Many languages use figurative expressions to speak of a timid, fearful person; for example, "God has given me a quivering liver," "God has made my stomach shake," or "God has given me a cold innermost."

For I am hemmed in by darkness: verse 17 is difficult to understand in Hebrew. It says literally "Because I am not cut off by reason of darkness and from my face which thick darkness covers." RSV, like many other translations, has omitted the negative and translates **I am hemmed in**. HOTTP favors keeping the negative and translates "for I was not annihilated (before darkness came)." The verb translated **hemmed in** is rendered "be silent" by Syriac, and so Dhorme retains the negative and translates "I have not been silent because of darkness." NEB has "Yet I am not reduced to silence by the darkness," FRCL "However, in spite of the night, I have not kept silent." TEV has sought to make clear that "It is God, not the dark, that makes me afraid," and it does this by joining verse 16b to verse 17a in one line. Translators

440

may express TEV differently; for example, "I am not afraid of the darkness, but I am afraid of God" or "Darkness does not frighten me, but God does."

And thick darkness covers my face: RSV follows the change made by the Vulgate. The Hebrew has "from my face." See the RSV footnote. Job expresses despair in this line. He suffers from being blinded by the darkness that prevents him from seeing the God he seeks. TEV "Even though darkness has made me blind" translates the same idea as that of RSV. FRCL understands that God is the one who has caused Job to be placed in the darkness, and translates verse 17 "However, in spite of the night, I have not kept silent; in spite of the darkness that he makes fall upon me." Translators may find this a suitable model to follow or may adapt it to say, for example, "In spite of the darkness I have not stopped crying out, even though I can't see in this dark night."

Note on the text of chapter 24

Scholars generally agree that chapter 24 is the most difficult part of the entire book. The problems are ones of form as well as content, and even the relevance of the material to the rest of the poem. As to its form, it has more three-line verses than any other chapter. The text itself is obscure at more points, and HOTTP has comments on 12 verses.

As to its content, verses 1-17 appear to form a unit. However, many interpreters have found it necessary to shift verses about, to obtain a satisfactory flow of discourse. For example, NEB has reordered verses 1-9 in the following manner: 1, 2, 6, 3, 9, 4, 5, 7, 8. Unlike NEB, NJB has kept verses 1-5 in the traditional order but modified the arrangement of verses 6-12 as 6, 10, 11, 7, 8, 9, 12.

Translations which reorder verses frequently do so because the translators have not taken sufficiently into consideration the discourse structure of the poem, or if they have, they fail to recognize that poetic structures are often not neatly symmetrical. Since the Handbook will follow the Hebrew text verse order, as do also RSV and TEV, a display of the structure of chapter 24 shows that the verses have a pattern of alternating themes characteristic of the entire poem. The Handbook deals with the entire chapter as Job's speech.

A (1) God does not act justly

B (2-4) The wicked oppress the poor

C (5-8) The oppressed struggle and suffer

B' (9) The wicked oppress the orphan and poor

C' (10-11) The oppressed go naked, hungry, and thirsty

A' (12) God pays no attention to them

B" (13-17) The wicked hide, oppress the poor, do evil in darkness

D (18-20) Retribution for the wicked

B‴ (21) The wicked oppress women

A″ (22-23) God finally acts to destroy the wicked (RSV God favors the wicked. See comments on text.)

D′ (24) Retribution for the wicked

(25) Concluding challenge as to truth asserted

5B-4. Job complains that evil men exploit the poor (24.1-12)

RSV	TEV
1 "Why are not times of judgment kept by the Almighty, and why do those who know him never see his days?	1 Why doesn't God set a time for judging, a day of justice for those who serve him?
2 Men remove landmarks; they seize flocks and pasture them.	2 Men move property lines to get more land; they steal sheep and put them with their own flocks.
3 They drive away the ass of the fatherless; they take the widow's ox for a pledge.	3 They take donkeys that belong to orphans, and keep a widow's ox till she pays her debts.
4 They thrust the poor off the road; the poor of the earth all hide themselves.	4 They prevent the poor from getting their rights and force the needy to run and hide.
5 Behold, like wild asses in the desert they go forth to their toil, seeking prey in the wilderness as food for their children.	5 So the poor, like wild donkeys, search for food in the dry wilderness; nowhere else can they find food for their children.
6 They gather their fodder in the field and they glean the vineyard of the wicked man.	6 They have to harvest fields they don't own, and gather grapes in wicked men's vineyards.
7 They lie all night naked, without clothing, and have no covering in the cold.	7 At night they sleep with nothing to cover them, nothing to keep them from the cold.
8 They are wet with the rain of the mountains, and cling to the rock for want of shelter.	8 They are drenched by the rain that falls on the mountains, and they huddle beside the rocks for shelter.
9 (There are those who snatch the fatherless child from the breast, and take in pledge the infant of the poor.)	9 Evil men make slaves of fatherless infants and take the poor man's children in payment for debts.
10 They go about naked, without clothing; hungry, they carry the sheaves;	10 But the poor must go out with no clothes to protect them; they must go hungry while harvesting wheat.
11 among the olive rows of the wicked they make oil; they tread the wine presses, but suffer thirst.	11 They press olives for oil, and grapes for
12 From out of the city the dying groan, and the soul of the wounded cries for help; yet God pays no attention to their prayer.	

wine,
but they themselves are thirsty.

12   In the cities the wounded and dying cry
out,
but God ignores their prayers.

Subdivision Heading

Translators wishing to provide readers with headings may wish to follow the structural display given above. For example, before verse 1 the heading may say "God does not act justly," "Job argues that God does not act fairly," "Job says that God is unfair," or "God does not do the right thing." Habel has "The question in dispute." Those who wish to combine larger parts of the discourse within a single heading, as does the Handbook, may say, for example, "God does nothing when the wicked exploit the poor," or "Job asks, 'Why doesn't God act when the wicked harm the poor?' " For 2-12 Habel has "The exploitation of the poor," Rowley (1-17) "The inactivity of God in the face of human oppression and injustice," and TOB "The injustice of society."

24.1	RSV	TEV

"Why are not times of judgment
    kept by the Almighty,
and why do those who know
    him never see his days?
	Why doesn't God set a time for
	    judging,
	a day of justice for those who
	    serve him?

Why are not times of judgment kept by the Almighty . . . ? is literally "Why have times not been hidden from *Shaddai*? The Hebrew word for **times** is translated by RSV as **times of judgment** and by TEV as "time for judgment," which give the complete sense in the context. The Hebrew verb for "hidden" may also be translated "store up, reserve," as in 15.10; 21.19, and therefore RSV has **kept**. The meaning is therefore "Why doesn't God fix a time to judge evil people?" God's judgment should be applied to the list of exploiters Job will go on to enumerate in verses 3-17. Dhorme follows the Septuagint in this line: "Why are times hidden from the Almighty?" However, this sense is incomplete, and it is better to follow RSV or TEV. This line may also be rendered as a negative statement; for example, "God Almighty does not fix a time to judge wicked people" or "God Almighty does not say when he will judge the wicked." The line may also be translated as an obligation placed on God: "God Almighty should fix a time to judge the wicked."

And why do those who know him never see his days? In Psalm 36.10 "those who know thee" is paralleled in the following line by "the upright of heart." The same sense applies here, so that **those who know him** are his "followers, the faithful, the upright," or "those who serve him" (TEV). RSV retains the negative in both lines. **Never see his days** means they never see God acting against lawless or evil people. **His days**, parallel with **times** in line <u>a</u>, refers to God's act of judging. God's faithful ones do not see him pronouncing judgment on evildoers, because God fails to interfere in these matters and allows the wicked to have their way. TEV does not have a parallel clause in line <u>b</u> but makes the whole line an explanation of "time for judging" in line <u>a</u>. This line may be rendered, for example, "and why don't God's followers see him judging sinners?" or "why don't his faithful ones see him carry out justice?" The line may also be rendered as a negative statement: "and those who serve him do not see him judge the wicked."

24.2	RSV	TEV

RSV	TEV
Men remove landmarks; they seize flocks and pasture them.	Men move property lines to get more land; they steal sheep and put them with their own flocks.

Having set forth the general question in verse 1, Job now goes on to illustrate examples of evil acts which God fails to judge.

Men remove landmarks is in the Hebrew "they remove landmarks," and the Septuagint has added "the wicked." **Landmarks** are boundary stones placed at the edges of property to show where one man's field ends and another's begins. By moving these a person could increase his holdings at the expense of his neighbor. TEV has made the purpose of moving the landmarks clear: "to get more land." This practice is condemned in Deuteronomy 19.14; 27.17. See also Proverbs 22.28; 23.10; Hosea 5.10. "They" refers in these verses to the powerful, the rich, in contrast to the poor. Where such landmarks used to signify land ownership are unknown, this line will require some adjustments; for example, "Men take land that is not theirs," "People farm without permission on other people's land," "People farm other people's land and the owners don't know it," "People grow their crops on other people's land," or "People steal their neighbor's farm lands."

They seize flocks and pasture them: flocks refers to groups of animals which are not specified here. To pasture animals is to let them graze (feed) in a pasture, or where there is grass. By changing the vowels of **pasture**, the Septuagint gets "and their shepherd," which is preferred by Dhorme and others. HOTTP rates the Hebrew text as a "B" reading and recommends the rendering as in RSV, which TEV expands to make more specific: "and put them with their own flocks." So the powerful take the herds of animals and the pastures from their weaker neighbors. They feed these stolen animals as if they were their own. As in the first line, this line may also require adjustments in some languages; for example, "these same people steal animals and feed them as if they were their own," or "the rich steal animals and feed them among their own flocks," or "these people pasture herds of animals they have stolen."

24.3	RSV	TEV

RSV	TEV
They drive away the ass of the fatherless; they take the widow's ox for a pledge.	They take donkeys that belong to orphans, and keep a widow's ox till she pays her debts.

They drive away the ass of the fatherless: **drive away** can be misleading in English. The verb refers to taking away a flock or herd after it has been stolen. These animals are not just driven away to get rid of them, but rather taken away as stolen property, so TEV "They take donkeys that belong to orphans." The word **ass**, which has some unfavorable meanings in modern English, is replaced in TEV and others by the more common word "donkey." In Hebrew the word is singular, probably to emphasize the general poverty of the orphans. TEV has made it plural since "orphans" is plural. This line may also be expressed, for example, "They steal the donkeys that belong to orphans" or "They take away the donkeys of the orphans."

They take the widow's ox for a pledge: **ox**, also singular, refers to a bull or a cow used for plowing or other farm work. See *Fauna and Flora of the Bible,* pages 62-63. For a discussion of **pledge** see comments on 22.6. The law forbade taking a widow's garment as a pledge, that is, as security for a loan (Deut 24.17). To take away a widow's **ox** was to leave her with no means for doing heavy work. In languages in which cattle are not known, or where cows are not used for labor, it may be possible to substitute another domestic animal. Where no animals are used in cultivation, it may be necessary to borrow a term from a major language and say, for example, "they lend money to a widow and keep her animal called ox until she repays them" or, if this is unsatisfactory, "they lend . . . and take her best animal . . . ."

24.4	RSV	TEV

RSV	TEV
They thrust the poor off the road; the poor of the earth all hide themselves.	They prevent the poor from getting their rights and force the needy to run and hide.

They thrust the poor off the road: RSV understands the verb here to be transitive, with **the poor** as the object. NJB makes **the poor** the subject and translates "The needy have to keep out of the way." RSV is preferred. Some take this line to mean that the poor have no rights on the public road, while others understand it to mean "The poor have no rights (anywhere.)" TEV's rendering, "They keep the poor from getting their rights," represents the second view and is clearly parallel to Amos 5.12, "prevent the poor from getting justice in the courts" (TEV). Whether or not the translator retains the literal figure of pushing someone off the road will depend on how the figure is interpreted. Most modern translations follow RSV. We may also translate, for example, "They keep the poor from using the road" or "They push the poor out of their way." Using the model of TEV we may also render the line, for example, "They do not allow the poor any rights," "They keep the poor from being protected," or "They will not let the poor do what they have a right to do."

The poor of the earth all hide themselves: in this line **poor of the earth** is the subject. **Of the earth** is taken by some as "the poor of the land," but this has no real difference in meaning. The expression means "all the poor." **Hide themselves** translates the Hebrew "are hidden together," an expression which here has a reflexive sense, so RSV **hide themselves**. The thought expressed is that the poor have no rights, and to survive they are forced to conceal themselves, or to hide from their oppressors.

24.5   RSV   TEV

> Behold, like wild asses in the
>   desert
>   they go forth to their toil,
>   seeking prey in the wilderness
>   as food^q for their children.

> So the poor, like wild donkeys,
>   search for food in the dry
>   wilderness;
>   nowhere else can they find
>   food for their children.

^q Heb *food to him*

In the following verses the oppressed poor are compared to wild asses (donkeys) exposed to merciless conditions. **Behold, like wild asses in the desert they go forth to their toil**: for **Behold** see 4.18; 12.14; 13.15. For **wild asses** see comments on 11.12. **Desert** translates the Hebrew *midbar*, the most common term for desert in the Old Testament. At least in biblical times such areas, although uninhabited and not used for farming, had enough rain and grass to support certain wild animals, including the **wild ass**. **To their toil** translates the Hebrew "in their work" or "when they work." Dhorme places this expression after **seeking prey** in the next line. He also changes **in the desert** to get "in the evening." TEV has taken **to their toil**, with **seeking prey** of the next line, to mean "search for food," so "The poor, like wild asses, search for food in the dry wilderness." Because of the parallelism translators may find it best to follow TEV. This may also be expressed "Like wild donkeys these poor people look for food in the desert" or "These poor people live in the desert and are forced to search for something to eat, as wild donkeys do."

Seeking prey in the wilderness: **seeking prey** is not suitable for this kind of animal, and means "looking for food," which is parallel with **go forth to their toil**. **As food for their children** is literally "food to him for young." RSV changes "food to him" to read **as food**. HOTTP recommends taking "to him" in a distributive sense: "for each one of them" or "for him (the poor person) the wilderness is bread (food) for the young." Translators will notice a bewildering variety of translations of this textually confused verse. However, TEV has translated it in a clear way that reflects the idea, and with a minimum of textual adjustments. The poet is saying that the poor are no better off in their search for food than are the wild donkeys. This line may also be rendered, for example, "this is the only way they get food for their children" or "this is the way they feed their children."

24.6   RSV   TEV

> They gather their^r fodder in the
>   field
>   and they glean the vineyard of
>   the wicked man.

> They have to harvest fields they
>   don't own,^x
>   and gather grapes in wicked
>   men's vineyards.

^r Heb *his*

^x FIELDS THEY DON'T OWN: *Having been cheated out of their own land, the poor are forced to work for others for very small pay.*

They gather their fodder in the field: this line continues to describe the struggle of the poor as they try to find food to maintain their meager existence. **Their fodder** is in the Hebrew "his fodder." See the RSV footnote. However, the meaning of this word is far from certain. There are at least three other ways to interpret it: (a) NJB says "field of some scoundrel," where the word is taken to be the same as used in 1 Samuel 25.25, translated as "good-for-nothing" by TEV; (b) by changing the vowels only, some get the meaning "at night," and so Dhorme "In the fields during the night they reap"; (c) TEV and NEB divide the Hebrew word into two parts, one part being a negative, and so meaning "they don't own" or "what is not theirs." This is one of the recommendations of HOTTP. See the explanation in the TEV footnote. **Fodder** is not human food, and so RSV is not a satisfactory rendering. TEV and NEB are preferred. This line may also be rendered, for example, "They have to pick up what they can in other people's fields" or "They are forced to gather up something to eat from other people's fields."

And they glean the vineyard of the wicked man: **glean**, meaning to gather what is left in the fields after the harvest, translates a word found only here, and its meaning is not certain. TEV does not say **glean**, which was the legitimate work of the poor. It seems that the poor are taking the grapes without asking. TEV remains somewhat neutral with "gather grapes," whereas NEB says "filch the late grapes." "Filch" means to steal. NJB "pilfering in the vineyards" has the same meaning. **Wicked man** is sometimes translated "rich man" or "the rich." The wicked oppressed the poor and took their lands, and consequently became rich. In this context **wicked** has the sense of "rich, wealthy." A **vineyard** is a field of cultivated grape vines on which the grapes grow. In languages in which **vineyards** are unknown, it may be best to shift to "fields" or "gardens"; for example, "and they steal their food from the rich people's gardens."

24.7	RSV	TEV
	They lie all night naked, without clothing, and have no covering in the cold.	At night they sleep with nothing to cover them, nothing to keep them from the cold.

They lie all night naked, without clothing: this verse describes the poor people as being inadequately dressed and suffering from the cold. **Lie all night** translates a verb meaning "spend the night," which may be with or without sleep. TEV has "sleep," which is used generally for spending the night, and in English does not imply necessarily that the person actually sleeps. RSV **naked, without clothing** is repetitive. The idea is that "Being without clothes they spend the night naked," or "Because they have no clothing they pass the night naked," or "They spend the night naked because they lack clothing."

And have no covering in the cold: the first line does not necessarily depict miserable conditions in the heat of summer, but this line draws attention to times that are cold. **Covering** may refer to a blanket, or to the outer garment a person normally would have to use as a covering at night. In some languages it may be necessary to reduce the two lines of verse 7 to one and say "They spend the cold night naked because they have nothing to cover themselves."

24.8	RSV	TEV
	They are wet with the rain of the mountains, and cling to the rock for want of shelter.	They are drenched by the rain that falls on the mountains, and they huddle beside the rocks for shelter.

They are wet with the rain of the mountains: **rain** translates a word which refers to the heavy winter storms. These rains drench the miserable people who have no clothes to protect themselves. **Rain of the mountains** does not refer to rain produced by the mountains but, as TEV says, "rain that falls on the mountains." The coldness of such rain may not be recognized in tropical areas, and so it may be better to say "The cold rain in the mountains soaks their bodies" or "The cold mountain rains pour down on them."

And cling to the rock for want of shelter: **cling** is literally "embrace" and is used in Genesis 29.13 of Laban embracing Jacob and kissing him. The poet draws a picture of wet, miserable creatures hugging the rocks in search of warmth: "they huddle beside the rocks for shelter" (TEV). The line may also be expressed, for example, "they hug the rocks to warm themselves because they have no houses" or "because they have no shelter, they embrace the rocks to get warm."

24.9	RSV	TEV
	(There are those who snatch the fatherless child from the breast, and take in pledge the infant of the poor.)	Evil men make slaves of fatherless infants and take the poor man's children in payment for debts.

RSV encloses this verse in parentheses to indicate that it is out of place. Dhorme, NEB, and Mft put it between verses 3 and 4. NJB places it after verse 8 but follows it with verse 12. Pope puts it after verse 3 and follows it with verse 21. TEV and many other modern translations leave white space between verses 8 and 9 to indicate a shift in thought. Certainly there is a shift in the subject: from verse 5 to verse 8 it has been the poor, but in verse 9 it is the wicked, although in verse 10 the subject is again the poor.

There are those who snatch the fatherless child from the breast: in Hebrew verse 9 has "they" as subject, which RSV translates **There are those**. If verse 9 began with "They," as in verses 6, 7, and 8, the reader would wrongly assume

"They" to mean the poor, and the sense would be contradictory. Unfortunately KJV does just that. TEV replaces "They" in Hebrew with "Evil men." NIV avoids supplying a different subject, by translating the verse with passive verbs: "The fatherless child is snatched from the breast; the infant of the poor is seized for a debt." This is just as much a modification as supplying a new subject. **Snatch** translates the same verb used in verse 3, where it was translated "seize" (RSV) and "steal" (TEV). **Fatherless child** translates a noun often rendered in English as "orphan" (see NEB), but the reference is specifically to a male child who has become fatherless. **Breast** is a figure in which a part stands for the whole; it means the mother of the child. The child is snatched from its widowed mother, as the next line goes on to say, in payment for a loan. Therefore TEV is correct in translating "make slaves of fatherless infants." The line may also be rendered, for example, "The wicked steal an orphan boy from his mother's breast" or "Evil people will take a child who is nursing away from its mother."

And take in pledge the infant of the poor: for **take in pledge** see comments on 22.6. The Hebrew is literally "take as pledge upon the poor." Some interpreters change the vowels of the preposition "upon" to get "suckling," a nursing infant, which gives a good parallel with line a and appears to be the basis for RSV. Line b is parallel in meaning to line a and does not refer to a different child, but rather makes clear the reason for line a. FRCL and SPCL follow a suggestion which gives "mantle" or "coat." However, the poor described here have no such clothes to give as a pledge, and so this is inappropriate. It may be best to transpose the lines of verse 9 so that the reason clause comes first; for example, "They lend money to the poor, and when the poor cannot repay, they take away their children; they even snatch a fatherless baby from its mother's breast."

24.10 RSV	TEV
They go about naked, without clothing; hungry, they carry the sheaves;	But the poor must go out with no clothes to protect them; they must go hungry while harvesting wheat.

They go about naked, without clothing: the subject is again the poor, and so TEV makes this clear "But the poor . . . ." This line closely resembles verse 7a, differing only in the verb **go about**. TEV "go out" seems to imply leaving a dwelling, which they do not have. The sense is as in RSV, which suggests "wander here and there." **Without clothing** may be taken as an explanation for why they are naked. "They wander about naked because they have no clothes to wear."

Hungry, they carry the sheaves: this line emphasizes their misery as they carry **sheaves** (bundles of grain in the stalks), probably to the threshing floor where they will beat out the grain. The paradox is that the people who harvest the grain do so for the owners' benefit while the workers go hungry. TEV generalizes the picture with "while harvesting wheat." The line may also be expressed "they go hungry while they thresh out the grain," "while their backs are loaded with grain their stomachs pain from hunger," or "they carry another's grain on their backs and emptiness in their stomachs."

24.11   RSV   TEV

> among the olive rows of the wick-
> ed[s] they make oil;
> they tread the wine presses,
> but suffer thirst.

> They press olives for oil, and
> grapes for wine,
> but they themselves are
> thirsty.

[s] Heb *their olive rows*

Among the olive rows of the wicked they make oil: as RSV notes, the Hebrew is literally "between their rows they press out oil." The Hebrew can also be understood as "between their walls," which would refer to some kind of structure or enclosure where the olives are pressed. RSV **among the olive rows** suggests "between the rows of olive trees," but this is a very unlikely place to put equipment for pressing olives. Dhorme makes a slight change to get "between two millstones." Another proposed change gets "between their songs." The verb translated **they make oil** is found only here, but it is derived from the common term for "oil" and most likely has the meaning as in RSV. On the other hand, **they make oil** can be derived from the word for "noonday," used in Syriac and Vulgate. The idea here would be that they are forced to work through the heat of the day. TEV incorporates "and grapes for wine" from line b into line a and has "They press olives for oil and grapes for wine," which provides a good rendering to follow. However, TEV has not translated the location where this work is said to take place. In languages in which olives and grapes are unknown, it may be possible to substitute local fruits if a process of extracting oil and juice is used; for example, palm oil in many areas. Another possibility is to substitute some kind of generic expression; for example, "Near the trees belonging to the wicked, they squeeze out oil from the fruit."

A WINE PRESS

They tread the wine presses, but suffer thirst: here the picture is that of thirsty workers tramping their feet up and down on the grapes inside a vat to press out the juice, but they are not allowed to drink it. **Tread** translates the same verb rendered "trampled" in 9.8 and "trod" in 22.15. The word translated **wine presses** is found in Isaiah 16.10 "no treader treads out wine in the presses." **Wine press** refers to a large wooden or stone vat or container which was connected to a lower container by a pipe or channel. As the grapes were mashed in the upper vat, the juice ran into the lower one. It may be necessary to make clear that these oppressed people are surrounded by juice and, although thirsty, they are not allowed to drink. In some languages the line may have to be expressed as, for example, "While they suffer from thirst, they mash the fruit into juice, but cannot drink."

24.12   RSV   TEV

From out of the city the dying
    groan,
and the soul of the wounded
    cries for help;
yet God pays no attention to
    their prayer.

In the cities the wounded and
    dying cry out,
but God ignores their prayers.

Verse 12, as shown in the display at the beginning of this chapter, repeats the opening theme of God's indifference to the suffering of the oppressed. In this way the poet has enclosed the arguments from verses 2-11 between the common theme of verses 1 and 12.

From verse 12 to verse 25 there are a number of three-line verses in Hebrew. Until now Job has been speaking of the suffering of the poor in the countryside; now he shifts his attention to the city.

From out of the city the dying groan: RSV is not clearly translated. TEV makes this thought clear with "In the cities the . . . dying cry out." **Dying** translates the Hebrew for "men." This is a change of one vowel and follows the Syriac. **Dying** provides a better parallel with **wounded** in line b and is accepted by TEV and many others. TEV has incorporated **the wounded** from line b and for stylistic reasons placed it before **the dying**, and translates only the verb of line b. RSV keeps the two parallel lines. **Groans** translates the word used in Ezekiel 30.24, "and he will groan before him like a man mortally wounded." These are the cries of wounded, dying people. In some languages it may be necessary to say "the wounded and dying cry out to God" or "people who are wounded and dying cry to God for help."

And the soul of the wounded cries for help: it is the *nefesh* that cries for help. This same word can also mean "throat" or "neck," and so NJB translates "and the gasp of the wounded crying for help." This line does not suggest that the disembodied souls of the wounded cry for help; **soul of the wounded** is a poetic way of speaking of the wounded. **Cries for help** carries forward the thought of **groan** in line a by intensifying it. Translators who retain the parallel lines may wish to render this line, for example, "and the wounded ones cry out to God for help" or ". . . cry out 'God, help us!' "

Yet God pays no attention to their prayer is literally "but God does not charge madness," in which the final word is the same as in 1.22, which RSV translates "Job did not sin or charge God with wrong." NIV and others therefore translate "But God charges no one with wrongdoing." The Syriac translation and some Hebrew manuscripts change the vowels of the final word to get **prayer**, and this is followed by RSV, TEV, and many others. The verb in this clause is the same as used in 23.6, where RSV translates "give heed." The line is correctly translated by both RSV and TEV. HOTTP rates the Hebrew text as "B" and understands that "madness" refers to the unjust treatment of the poor in the previous verses. In this view the line can be rendered "But God pays no attention to the wrongdoing of the rich" or "yet God pays no attention to the evil things the rich do to the poor." In this way we can follow the Hebrew text and get a satisfactory translation.

5B-5. Job describes the crimes of evil men carried out under cover of darkness (24.13-17)

RSV	TEV
13 "There are those who rebel against the light, who are not acquainted with its ways, and do not stay in its paths.	13 There are men who reject the light; they don't understand it or go where it leads.
14 The murderer rises in the dark, that he may kill the poor and needy; and in the night he is as a thief.	14 At dawn the murderer gets up and goes out to kill the poor, and at night he steals.
15 The eye of the adulterer also waits for the twilight, saying, 'No eye will see me';	15 The adulterer waits for twilight to come; he covers his face so that no one can see him.
	16 At night thieves break into houses,

and he disguises his face.	but by day they hide and avoid the
16 In the dark they dig through houses;	light.
by day they shut themselves up;	17 They fear the light of day,
they do not know the light.	but darkness holds no terror for them.
17 For deep darkness is morning to all of	
them;	
for they are friends with the terrors of	
deep darkness.	

In verses 13-17 the thought shifts to particular kinds of evil persons: murderers, adulterers, and burglars. All of these persons carry out their evil under the cover of darkness. They are people who rebel against the light, go out in the dark, at night, at twilight. Every verse in this section has a reference to avoidance of light.

Subdivision Heading

The Handbook heading may be modified to say, for example, "Crimes committed in the dark," "Evil people love the darkness," or "At night is the time for wrongdoing." Habel has "The flagrant lawbreakers."

24.13 RSV	TEV
"There are those who rebel against the light, who are not acquainted with its ways, and do not stay in its paths.	There are men who reject the light; they don't understand it or go where it leads.

There are those who rebel against the light: this verse serves as an introduction and title to verses 14-17. **There are those** does not translate the same expression as in verse 9a, where RSV uses the same wording. Dhorme says the pronominal form used here refers back, not forward. It is clearer to avoid a pronoun and say "These are people who," "These are the kind of people who," or "Evil people are among those who . . . ." **Rebel against the light** is a literal translation of the Hebrew. It means they "hate, reject, avoid" the light. In view of the contrast between **light** and darkness, **light** must be understood, not as a spiritual or moral symbol, but as the opposite of night. The line may be rendered "Evil people are among those who hate the daylight," or "Wicked people hate to see daylight come," or ". . . to see the day dawn."

Who are not acquainted with its ways: lines b and c of this verse are closely parallel in meaning and are reduced to one by TEV. RSV **ways** gives the impression that the light is animate and operates like a person. **Ways** translates "roads," which is parallel with **paths** in the next line. These people are "unfamiliar with," "do not recognize" the roads that are clearly seen in the daytime, because they only use them in the dark of night. FRCL translates "They do not frequent lighted roads"; or the line may be rendered "they do not travel on lighted roads" or "they refuse to walk the roads in the daylight."

And do not stay in its paths: it is not always necessary to repeat **paths** just to get another parallelism. The thought is that these people "wander off, stray away" by not keeping on the visible and well marked paths.

24.14	RSV	TEV

RSV	TEV
The murderer rises in the dark,[t] that he may kill the poor and needy; and in the night he is as a thief.	At dawn the murderer gets up and goes out to kill the poor, and at night he steals.

[t] Cn: Heb *at the light*

The crimes mentioned in verses 14-16 are those listed in Exodus 20.13-15; Hosea 4.2; Jeremiah 7.9; only the order differs.

The murderer rises in the dark: Hebrew has "at the light." See RSV footnote. "At the light" appears to contradict the evil person's efforts to avoid the light. For translators such as Dhorme, who have shifted this verse to follow verse 12, the contradiction does not arise. However, most translators will keep the Hebrew order of verses, and some adjustment is required. Some take "at the light" to mean before daylight (NEB). HOTTP suggests "at day break." Pope has "at twilight," and NJB "when all is dark." TEV says "At dawn." **Murderer** is sometimes rendered "killer of men" or "one who kills people." The line may also be expressed "While it is still dark the murderer gets up" or "The murderer gets up before dawn."

That he may kill the poor and needy: some have made a change in **the poor and needy** to get "his enemy and his adversary," since there would be little to gain in murdering the poor. Such a change is uncalled for. In Psalm 10.8,9; 37.14, the wicked are accused of killing the poor and needy. TEV has reduced the **poor and needy** to "the poor." The line may be rendered, for example, "in order to go out and kill the poor man who has nothing."

And in the night he is as a thief: the simile in this line may mean that the murderer who gets up at dawn to kill is like the thief who works at night. However, TEV and others understand the line to mean that when night comes he also goes out and acts as a thief by stealing, so he is both murderer and thief. Some interpreters change **he is as a thief** to get "the thief prowls," and transfer it to precede verse 16, which describes the burglar. This line may also be expressed "when it is night the murderer goes out to steal" or "when the night comes this killer becomes a thief."

24.15	RSV	TEV

RSV	TEV
The eye of the adulterer also waits for the twilight, saying, 'No eye will see me'; and he disguises his face.	The adulterer waits for twilight to come; he covers his face so that no one can see him.

The eye of the adulterer also waits for twilight: this line may be compared to Proverbs 7.9, which depicts a young man going secretly at twilight to his prostitute. **The eye** draws attention to the watching and waiting of the adulterer, and so TEV "The adulterer waits . . . ." **Adulterer** translates a word which refers to a man who has sex with someone other than his marriage partner. FRCL translates "the unfaithful husband." In the Old Testament adultery took place between any man and a married or engaged woman. The result was an offense against the woman's husband, never against the male adulterer's wife. In some languages **adulterer** must be expressed as, for example, "The man who sleeps with other women" or "The man who takes another man's wife." The Hebrew for **twilight** is used in 7.4, where it refers to the "dawn." As in English the Hebrew word for this time refers to the scant light between sunset and full night, and it is this time that most probably is to be understood in RSV and TEV; it may also refer to the time between full night and sunrise, but not in this context. This line may be rendered "the adulterer watches and waits until it is almost dark."

Saying, 'No eye will see me': RSV translates the Hebrew literally. It is not **the eye of the adulterer** who speaks or thinks this line to himself, but the **adulterer**. "He says to himself 'No one will notice me.' " The line may also be expressed "He says to himself 'Nobody will see me' " or ". . .'Nobody will recognize who I am.' "

And he disguises his face: this expression is used in 13.24a, where Job asks God "Why dost thou hide thy face?" See there for comment. The expression refers to putting on a face veil; that is, "veil the face." TEV shifts line c of the verse so that it precedes line b and thus provides a reason before the result: "He covers his face so that no one can see him." The adjustment made by TEV will recommend itself to many translators. The translator should not give the impression that the adulterer wears a mask, which may be associated with local religious rites. In some languages it will be necessary to say, for example, "he keeps his face covered" or "he hides his face."

24.16	RSV	TEV
	In the dark they dig through houses;	At night thieves break into houses,
	by day they shut themselves up;	but by day they hide and avoid the light.
	they do not know the light.	

In the dark they dig through houses: this line does not continue the description of the adulterer but passes on to tell what the thief does. **They dig** is in the Hebrew "he digs." The verb in the next line has "they" as subject, and so RSV and others change to **they** in this line. TEV shifts to a more general kind of entry with "Thieves break into houses." The Hebrew expression is equivalent to Matthew 6.19. Compare also John 10.1. **Dig through houses** means to "dig, pierce, bore" a hole in the walls of houses. This practice is referred to in Ezekiel 8.8; 12.5,7,12. It is a common practice in some areas for thieves to gain entrance to a building by making a hole through the back wall, where they will not be seen. RSV does not say directly that this is the work of thieves, but translators should make it clear, as in TEV

"At night thieves break into houses." If the expression "dig through the walls of houses" is apt to be misunderstood, it is better to follow TEV. We may also say, for example, "thieves make holes in the walls of houses" or "thieves get into houses by making a hole in the wall."

By day they shut themselves up: since Hebrew has a singular subject in the first line and a plural here, some interpreters have understood this line to refer to all three groups of evildoers. Others, such as TEV, take verse 16 to refer to the thieves only. Both views are possible. The Hebrew verb in this line usually means "to seal something shut," as in sealing a document. NEB agrees with KJV in interpreting the verb as referring to the thief going about in the daylight, marking the doors of suitable houses for robbing: "and in the darkness breaks into houses which he has marked down in the day." This involves altering the verb to the singular to refer to the thief. But the verb nowhere else has the meaning given to it here in NEB, and no thief would be likely to attach his personal seal to a house or door in this way so that he could later be identified. So most translators interpret the verb to mean **shut themselves** in the dark. This line may also be expressed "they stay indoors during the day" or "in the daytime they keep themselves hidden."

They do not know the light: because they keep themselves shut up in the dark during the day, and only go out to do evil in the night, "they are unfamiliar with the light," "they do not know what is in the daylight," or "they have no idea what the daylight is like."

24.17	RSV	TEV
	For deep darkness is morning to all of them; for they are friends with the terrors of deep darkness.	They fear the light of day, but darkness holds no terror for them.

For deep darkness is morning to all of them: the order of the Hebrew words of this line does not indicate clearly whether the emphasis is as in NJB, "morning is a time of shadow dark as death," or as in RSV. According to NJB's interpretation, which is the same as TEV, the criminals dread the morning as that which brings to an end their favorite nighttime occupations. On the other hand, NEB agrees with RSV and translates "but dark night is morning to them." In this sense darkness is the favorite time for criminals. NIV gives two alternatives: "For all of them, deep darkness is their morning," and in a footnote, "For all of them, their morning is like the shadow of death." **Morning** translates a word referring to "dawn," and so TEV "light of day." TEV's rendering follows suitably after verse 16 and is preferred over RSV. This line may also be expressed "They are afraid when morning light comes" or "They are afraid when daylight comes."

For they are friends with the terrors of deep darkness: the Hebrew is "he knows the terrors of deep darkness." Hebrew "knows" is the same verb found in verse 13b and usually means "recognize, be familiar with." RSV has translated this verb as **they are friends with**. This rendering is possible, but preferred is "they are familiar with the terrors of the night" or "they are accustomed to the fear of the dark."

Note on the text of verses 18-25

Scholars have taken various positions regarding verses 18-25. Dhorme and Pope hold that these verses belong to Zophar and place them after 27.12. TEV does not shift them from their traditional position but attributes them to Zophar. Others assign verses 18-25 to Bildad. Another view suggested by Gordis is that in these verses Job is quoting the friends, and this is the position reflected in RSV with respect to verses 18-20. Still others claim these verses to be an independent poem inserted into the book. However, on the basis of the discourse structure, the Handbook prefers to treat verses 18-25 as an integral part of Job's argument. Accordingly the Handbook treatment is different from both RSV and TEV.

5B-6. The fate of the wicked and God's judgment described (24.18-25)

RSV	TEV
	[Zophar]
18 "You say, 'They are swiftly carried away upon the face of the waters; their portion is cursed in the land; no treader turns toward their vineyards.	18 The wicked man is swept away by floods, and the land he owns is under God's curse; he no longer goes to work in his vineyards.
19 Drought and heat snatch away the snow waters; so does Sheol those who have sinned.	19 As snow vanishes in heat and drought, so a sinner vanishes from the land of the living.
20 The squares of the town forget them; their name is no longer remembered; so wickedness is broken like a tree.'	20 Not even his mother remembers him now; he is eaten by worms and destroyed like a fallen tree.
21 "They feed on the barren childless woman, and do no good to the widow.	21 That happens because he mistreated widows and showed no kindness to childless women.
22 Yet God prolongs the life of the mighty by his power; they rise up when they despair of life.	22 God, in his strength, destroys the mighty; God acts—and the wicked man dies.
23 He gives them security, and they are supported; and his eyes are upon their ways.	23 God may let him live secure, but keeps an eye on him all the time.
24 They are exalted a little while, and then are gone; they wither and fade like the mallow; they are cut off like the heads of grain.	24 For a while the wicked man prospers, but then he withers like a weed, like a stalk of grain that has been cut down.
25 If it is not so, who will prove me a liar, and show that there is nothing in what I say?"	25 Can anyone deny that this is so? Can anyone prove that my words are not true?

This passage deals with the fate of evil people. Verse 25 closes with a challenge to anyone who wishes to dispute the truth of the matter.

The preceding verses have plural subjects, but beginning with verse 18 the subject is singular. Therefore translators attempt to provide a transition to this section. RSV puts verses 18-20 in quotation marks on the assumption that these verses are the words of one (or more) of the friends, and adds at the beginning **You**

say as Job's introduction of words of the friends which he is about to quote. NEB keeps verses 18-25 with the rest of chapter 24 and connects to the previous verses by adding "such men are . . . ." In these verses the Hebrew text shifts several times between singular and plural. For consistency RSV has kept these references all in the plural and TEV all in the singular.

Subdivision Heading

Translators may wish to provide more than one heading for verses 18-25. As the display at the beginning of chapter 24 shows, verses 18-20 deal with the retribution of the wicked, verse 21 speaks of the oppression of women, and then verses 22-23 depict God as finally acting against the wicked. The Handbook suggests a single heading, but translators may wish to use one heading before verse 18 and another before verse 22. For example, Habel has (18-21) "Destiny of the wicked" and (22-25) "Resolution of the question." The Handbook heading may be reworded to say, for example, "God will judge the wicked" or "God will cause the wicked to come to a bad end."

24.18	RSV	TEV
	"You say, 'They are swiftly carried away upon the face of the waters; their portion is cursed in the land; no treader turns toward their vineyards.	*[Zophar]*^y 18 The wicked man is swept away by floods, and the land he owns is under God's curse; he no longer goes to work in his vineyards.

^y Zophar *is not named in the text, but this speech is usually assigned to him.*

You say, 'They are swiftly carried away upon the face of the waters . . .': this is literally "He is swift on the face of the waters." The word translated **They are swiftly** may be translated as a verb meaning "to be swift" or as an adjective meaning "light, insignificant." In the latter sense **They** would refer to the wicked as being something light floating on the waters. TEV keeps the singular "the wicked man" and translates "is swept away by the floods." Hosea 10.7 has as parallel form "like a chip on the face of the waters," which is a figurative expression similar to NEB "Such men are scum on the surface of the water." NIV calls them "foam," and NJB says "He is no more than a straw floating on water." Translators may decide to provide a transition to this section, such as in RSV, or to attribute verses 18-25 to Zophar, as in TEV.

Their portion is cursed in the land refers to the portion of the land or earth they own, occupy, and labor on. **Is cursed** is a rare passive construction which TEV expresses as an active: "the land he owns is under God's curse." Such land is unproductive, useless, and lying in ruins. This line may also be rendered, for example, "God curses the land he owns" or "the place where he lives is cursed by God."

No treader turns toward their vineyards is more or less literally "he does not face in the direction of the vineyards," which makes little sense in the context. At least two changes are required to get RSV's translation. "In the direction of" becomes by a change of vowels **no treader,** meaning "no wine presser" or "no one to tread on the grapes to make wine." The Septuagint adjusts **vineyards** to get **their vineyards,** which RSV follows. It is not clear what changes TEV may have followed to get its translation, but it appears to be a more general sense of the changes accepted by RSV and is clear in meaning. Other models that may be followed are SPCL "and no one works again in his vineyard," NIV "so that no one goes to the vineyards" (because of the curse in line b), and NEB "and no laborer will go near their vineyards."

24.19	RSV	TEV
	Drought and heat snatch away the snow waters; so does Sheol those who have sinned.	As snow vanishes in heat and drought, so a sinner vanishes from the land of the living.

Drought and heat snatch away the snow waters: some interpreters think verse 19 is a proverbial saying. Whether that is true or not, it represents a sudden change of subject. Other examples of sayings in Job are found in 5.7 and 14.11-12. The two lines are not balanced, the second line being very short. TEV fills out the comparison with "As snow vanishes in heat and drought, so a sinner vanishes . . . ." RSV translates the line quite literally. The verb **snatch** has to do service for both lines. However, in English **snatch** does not describe the action of heat on snow, which involves gradual disappearance as in melting. SPCL translates "in the heat of the drought, the snow melts." TEV attempts to build the parallel around a common verb "vanish" in both lines and does it well. FRCL does not attempt to have a single verb in both lines but allows the implication of disappearance in the simile: "Like snow in the sun, so they [that is, all who are guilty, as mentioned in the next line] disappear into the world of the dead." All of these are adequate translation models. In languages in which **snow** is unknown and a borrowed word is not sufficiently understood by readers and listeners, it may be possible to substitute frost, hail, or dew. In such cases the simile will need to be shifted to say, for example, "Just as frost (hail, dew) disappears in the heat and drought . . . ."

So does Sheol those who have sinned: this line has two words in the Hebrew, "Sheol (those) sinning." The parallel event is pictured as Sheol snatching away the sinner (the verb being supplied from line a). This requires treating Sheol as a living being. Most modern translations adjust this line as noted above. According to the expression suggested for the first line, this line may be rendered, for example, "in the same way those who have sinned disappear into Sheol."

24.20   RSV   TEV

The squares of the town[u] forget   Not even his mother remembers
   them;   him now;
their name[v] is no longer re-   he is eaten by worms and de-
   membered;   stroyed like a fallen tree.
so wickedness is broken like a
   tree.'

[u] Cn: Heb obscure
[v] Cn: Heb *a worm*

The pattern of this verse is unusual. Instead of the usual two lines of equal length, which are normal in Job, the first half of the Hebrew text has three sentences of two words each. The second half consists of a line of the normal length. The clue to the pattern of parallelism in the first half of the verse consists of the balancing of **forget** and **no longer remembered**. But this leaves the middle section of the first part disconnected from the other two. So in order to make two lines of average length in the first half of the verse, in place of the three short lines, RSV distributes the three lines into two.

The squares of the town forget them: the RSV footnote indicates that the Hebrew is obscure. The Hebrew has "the womb forgets him," and RSV has changed the word for "womb" and the following word to get **The squares of the town**, meaning "the centers of the towns." This change does not seem necessary. Dhorme keeps the Hebrew and translates "The womb which has formed him forgets him," which TEV translates more naturally as "Not even his mother remembers him now." HOTTP supports this. In some languages it will be more meaningful to express "mother" as "the one who gave birth to him."

Their name is no longer remembered is literally "the worm sucks on him and he is not remembered." Aside from Exodus 16.24 and Job 25.6, the word rendered "worm" in Hebrew is always used with dead or decaying bodies, so TEV has "he is eaten by worms . . . ," the reason being that he is dead. RSV **their name** is a change based on the word for "worm" and is preferred by Dhorme. RSV has made one line of what can also be read as two lines in the Hebrew. TEV does not repeat **no longer remembered**. This line may be translated without any change, as suggested by TEV and others; for example, "worms eat his corpse" or "his dead body is eaten by worms (maggots)."

So wickedness is broken like a tree: this line is a summary statement of the preceding thoughts. RSV makes no textual changes. TEV takes **wickedness** to be the same subject as in the two preceding lines. **Broken like a tree** is at best a vague simile; only certain kinds of trees can be described as broken. Therefore TEV translates more meaningfully "destroyed like a fallen tree." This line may also be expressed "he is destroyed like a tree that is cut down," or "like a tree he is cut down," or "they destroy him in the same way as they cut down a tree and destroy it."

In RSV verse 20 concludes Job's quoting the friends. Verses 21-25 in RSV are Job's own words.

24.21   RSV   TEV

"They feed on the barren child-   That happens because he mis-
    less woman,   treated widows
  and do no good to the widow.   and showed no kindness to
                                             childless women.

They feed on the barren childless woman: verses 18-20 describe the unhappy fate of the wicked person. Verse 21, however, speaks of the evil things such a person does. To make a connection with the previous verse, TEV supplies "That happens because . . . ," which is not in the text but helps relate 21 to the previous context. **Feed** translates a verb form derived from a root meaning "to graze," or to another verb meaning "to associate with." Both verbs are written alike, and so only the context can determine which verb is meant. The Septuagint has "mistreat," and this is followed by TEV and others. The reference seems to be again to the wicked man who oppresses the weak and unfortunate. Line a has **barren childless woman**, and line b **widow**. TEV shifts the more specific term to line a for style and clarity. There is a difference between being a childless woman and a **barren childless woman**. The latter is to be pitied even more than the former, because in the Old Testament view God withholds children from her. The line may also be rendered, for example, "He also made the widow who could have no children to suffer" or "He oppressed the barren, childless widow."

And do no good to the widow: the sense of the verb translated **do no good** is "treat unkindly, ungraciously, fail to behave well toward." The widow has a right to special care, as she has no husband to protect her. This line may also be expressed "and was unkind to her" or "and behaved badly to her."

24.22   RSV   TEV

Yet God^w prolongs the life of the   God, in his strength, destroys the
    mighty by his power;   mighty;
  they rise up when they despair   God acts—and the wicked man
    of life.   dies.

^w Heb *he*

Yet God prolongs the life of the mighty by his power: this verse can be interpreted in various ways. RSV depicts God as being gracious to the mighty but destroying them in verse 24. Another view is that the person who seizes the mighty rises up in his place. The Hebrew has "he draws the mighty one." Although the subject appears to be the same as in the preceding verses, most interpreters take the subject here to be God. **The mighty**, which is plural, cannot be the grammatical subject, because the verbs are singular. RSV understands the first verb to mean **prolong**, and supplies **the life of** as the object. The verb used here normally has an unfavorable connotation, so NEB "Yet God in his strength carries off even the mighty." TEV "God destroys the mighty" is correct but less specific. FRCL translates

"But God has the strength to expel the tyrants." These renderings are to be preferred over RSV.

They rise up when they despair of life: Hebrew has "he rises up." RSV has now changed to the plural and assumes the subject is the men, not God. But it is more likely that the subject is still God, as in NJB, TEV, and others. **When they despair of life** translates the Hebrew "and he does not establish them in life." The same idiomatic phrase is found in Deuteronomy 28.66, translated by RSV "and have no assurance of life." This is taken to be the consequence of God rising up against a person, or as TEV says, "God acts . . . ." FRCL translates "God rises up and these (the mighty) are no longer sure of living." NJB says "to take away a life that seemed secure." TEV identifies the subject as "the wicked man" and says more directly than NJB "and the wicked man dies." The line may also be rendered, for example, "God lifts his hand and the wicked person dies," "God takes action and so the evil person dies," or "when God decides the matter, the evil person's life is finished."

24.23   RSV   TEV

> He gives them security, and they   God may let him live secure,
>   are supported;   but keeps an eye on him all
> and his eyes are upon their   the time.
>   ways.

He gives them security and they are supported: the subject of this line is again **He**, which most probably refers to God, as God is the logical subject in the next line. The sense in this verse is that God allows the wicked person to have a feeling of security, to feel safe and confident, but all the while God is watching what he is doing in preparation for his destruction. Implied is a contrast between the security the wicked is allowed to feel and the impending disaster that will follow. **And they are supported** translates "and he leans." This phrase adds little information to the preceding clause. NJB says "He lets him build his hopes on false security," and FRCL "He sometimes lets them think they are secure, but . . . ." TEV expresses the tentativeness of the security as "God may let him live securely, but . . . ." All of these are good translation models.

And his eyes are upon their ways: RSV begins this line with **and**, which fails to mark the contrast with the first line. The view of RSV can only be that God is watching the wicked to take care of them. This interpretation does not fit with the fate of the wicked in verse 24 and so is not recommended to translators. **His eyes** means "God watches, observes." TEV "keeps an eye on him" means "watch carefully, spy on every move he makes." NJB says it well: "but kept his eyes on every step he took."

24.24   RSV   TEV

> They are exalted a little while,   For a while the wicked man pros-
>   and then are gone;   pers,
> they wither and fade like the   but then he withers like a

mallow;[x]	weed,
they are cut off like the heads	like a stalk of grain that has
of grain.	been cut down.

[x] Gk: Heb *all*

This verse has three lines, with the parallelism being between lines b and c. The thought of this verse is that the wicked are fortunate for a while and then are cut off. Although the sense seems to be clear, numerous changes have been proposed; but these need not be considered.

They are exalted a little while, and then are gone: exalted is literally "be lifted up." It is sometimes rendered "They became great," "They had great glory," or "They were made to be powerful people." NEB says "They rise to the heights," that is, of fame and glory. Their greatness lasts only for **a little while. And then are gone** translates the Hebrew "and is not," which represents the typical shifting between singular and plural in this section. TEV understands this phrase to be adequately expressed in the simile in the following line. FRCL keeps it as "These people hold their heads high for a bit, and then nothing more." This line may also be expressed, for example, "The wicked become great people for a little while, but then they are nothing" or ". . . but afterwards they are great no more."

They wither and fade like the mallow: wither translates a verb meaning "to lower, bend, collapse," and describes the drying of the flower that withers and droops. **Fade** translates a verb whose basic meaning is "close," and may suggest the closing up of the petals of the flower. **Mallow,** as the RSV footnote shows, is from the Septuagint, which Pope says is "saltwort" transcribed from Hebrew to Greek. However, the Hebrew has a word which can mean "like all," and so KJV "They are taken out of the way as all other," and NIV "They are brought low and gathered up like all others." According to HOTTP the same word can mean "like the umbel," which refers to a botanical structure more than to a particular flower. In translation the point is sometimes lost by using a technical term or a term that is too specific. It is better to translate generally as "flower." However, TEV has sought to give the bad sense, which is missing in "flower," and accordingly says "like a weed." FRCL says "They bend down their heads like a dying flower." This may also be rendered "they droop and fade like a dried-up flower."

They are cut off like the heads of grain: cut off translates a verb used in 14.2; 18.16, where it is translated "withers" by RSV and TEV, but this verb does not suit for stalks of grain. Therefore RSV, TEV, and others translate **cut off.** FRCL does both: "They dry up like an ear of grain that has been cut." **Heads of grain** refers to the top of the stalks where the grains form. In languages in which an active construction is required, we may say, for example, "they are like an ear of grain someone has cut from the stem" or "they are like the heads of grain the farmer cuts off."

24.25   RSV   TEV

If it is not so, who will prove me	Can anyone deny that this is so?
a liar,	Can anyone prove that my words

>   and show that there is nothing   are not true?
>   in what I say?"

If it is not so, who will prove me a liar . . . ? Dhorme and NJB connect this verse with Job's speech that ended with verse 17. TEV keeps it as the final verse of Zophar's speech. FRCL closes the quotation at the end of verse 24, so that verse 25 is again the words of Job. In other translations (including RSV), which do not set off verses 18-25 from the rest of chapter 24, verse 25 will be taken as the words of Job. All of these solutions have their merits, since the challenge in verse 25 suits Job just as well as the friends or Zophar in particular. RSV translates the line with **if . . . who**. TEV expresses both lines as questions. **It** refers to all that has been said in verses 18-24. If the translator follows RSV, this line may be rendered, for example, "If what I have said is not true, is there someone who will show me I am wrong?" "If all that I said is not true, please prove me a liar," or "If I have said things that are wrong, show me that I am a liar."

And show that there is nothing in what I say is literally "and make into nothing my speech." This may be rendered "show that I am mistaken," or as TEV, "prove that my words are not true."

5C. BILDAD'S THIRD SPEECH (25.1-6)

Chapter 25 contains only six verses and repeats things said earlier by Eliphaz. Following the identification of Bildad as the speaker, the opening verse is not a question, the form normally used by the friends to begin their speeches. Many scholars agree that verses 5-14 of chapter 26 are a continuation of chapter 25, and so these later verses are also attributed to Bildad. Therefore the complete speech of Bildad is 25.1-6; 26.5-14, with a short speech from Job (26.1-4) inserted at the beginning of chapter 26. TEV marks verses 5-14 of chapter 26 as the speech of Bildad. Although scholars have proposed numerous rearrangements of the verses in chapters 25, 26, and 27, there has been little agreement and even less general acceptance. Therefore the Handbook will discuss these verses in the order they occur in the text as it stands.

Division Heading

For the wording of this heading, translators should refer to the heading used before 8.1 and 18.1.

5C-1. Mankind's lowly place in God's great design (25.1-6)

RSV	TEV
1 Then Bildad the Shuhite answered:	*Bildad*
2 "Dominion and fear are with God; he makes peace in his high heaven.	1-2 God is powerful; all must stand in awe of him; he keeps his heavenly kingdom in peace.
3 Is there any number to his armies? Upon whom does his light not arise?	
4 How then can man be righteous before	3 Can anyone count the angels who serve

	God?		him?
	How can he who is born of woman be clean?		Is there any place where God's light does not shine?
5	Behold, even the moon is not bright and the stars are not clean in his sight;	4	Can anyone be righteous or pure in God's sight?
6	how much less man, who is a maggot, and the son of man, who is a worm!"	5	In his eyes even the moon is not bright, or the stars pure.
		6	Then what about man, that worm, that insect? What is man worth in God's eyes?

The theme of this speech is the power of God in contrast to the weakness of man.

Subdivision Heading

The Handbook heading may be modified to say, for example, "What is man compared to the greatness of God?" "Compared with God people are nothing," or "God's greatness in the universe." Habel has "Mortals and the moon before El," Rowley "God's might and purity," TOB "The sovereignty of God," FRCL "Bildad's speech: The universal power of God," GECL "The second friend: No man can stand before God," and NJB "A hymn to God's omnipotence."

25.1   RSV   TEV

Then Bildad the Shuhite answered: *Bildad*

Then Bildad the Shuhite answered: see suggestions on 2.11; 4.1.

25.2   RSV   TEV

"Dominion and fear are with God;^y he makes peace in his high heaven.	God is powerful; all must stand in awe of him; he keeps his heavenly kingdom in peace.

^y Heb *him*

Dominion and fear are with God: as the RSV footnote indicates, the Hebrew has "with him," but RSV correctly translates **with God**. In 12.13,16 Job said "With God are wisdom and might" and "With him are strength and wisdom." This line is built on the same pattern. These are characteristics of God. **Dominion** translates a word meaning "the capacity to rule." The word is used as a noun but has the form of the causative of an infinitive verb, and so it means "that which gives power or domination." Some translate it "sovereignty," which means supreme authority, the highest ruling power. **Fear** is used as in 13.11. See comments there. **Fear** is caused by, or inspired by, God's power. RSV fails to show the relation between **dominion** and **fear**. God has **dominion**, sovereign power over everything, and this causes people to **fear**, which means "be awed, have reverence for him." In order to show the relation between what appears to be two nouns, TEV has expressed the line as two clauses: "God is powerful; all must stand in awe of him." NJB translates verse 2 as an exclamation: "What sovereignty, what awe is his . . . !" FRCL says "God has a sovereign power which is frightening." The line may also be rendered, for example, "God rules with frightening force," "God is powerful, and people should have reverence for him," or "God's power causes people to be awed."

He makes peace in his high heaven is literally "making peace in his heights." According to Dhorme the Hebrew verb **make** with **peace** as the object means "to establish peace," that is, to impose peace where there is strife. The reference may be to conflicts between angels, as in Daniel 10.13,20-21; destruction of the monster Rahab in Job 9.13; 26.12; Isaiah 51.9; or destruction of the hosts in heaven in Isaiah 24.21. TEV renders **high heaven** as "heavenly kingdom": "He keeps his heavenly kingdom in peace." This translation is less exact than that of FRCL, "He imposes peace up to the highest heaven." GECL translates both lines "God rules with frightening power, with a strong hand he establishes peace in heaven." This line may also be expressed "he causes there to be peace in heaven," "he brings about peace in heaven," or "he establishes peace where he rules in heaven."

25.3

RSV	TEV
Is there any number to his armies? Upon whom does his light not arise?	Can anyone count the angels who serve him? Is there any place where God's light does not shine?

Is there any number to his armies? This rhetorical question expresses the thought that God's troops, armies, are limitless in number. In 19.12 Job said God's "troops . . . cast up siege works against me." There the same word for "troops" is used as here. In 2 Kings 13.20-21 these troops are "marauding bands." TEV "angels" is questionable. There is no evidence that angels or stars are meant here and so "troops," "armies," or "bands" are preferred. Translated as a negative statement this line may be rendered, for example, "There is no end to the number of his troops," "His armies cannot be numbered," "No one can count how many armies he has," or "He has so many armies that no one can count them." The translator will note that the two lines of this verse are not parallel in meaning in the RSV form. This is discussed in the next paragraph.

Upon whom does his light not arise? RSV translates the Hebrew word **light**. By a change of one letter the Septuagint gets "his ambushes," and this is followed by Dhorme and NEB. The HOTTP committee was divided, half favoring the Hebrew and half the Septuagint (and both with a "C" rating), and so it recommends either. The use of "his ambushes" provides a parallel for line a; for example, "His squadrons are without number, at whom will they not spring from ambush?" (NEB). Following the Hebrew, TEV translates "Is there any place where God's light does not shine?" Following the Septuagint we may also render the line as a statement, particularly if the previous line was translated as a statement. In some languages this line will have to be expressed as a positive statement; for example, "They will attack anyone from ambush" or "They wait in hiding to attack anyone." RSV's rendering may also be expressed as a positive statement, "His light shines everywhere," or as a double negative statement, "There is no place where his light does not shine."

25.4	RSV		TEV
	How then can man be righteous before God? How can he who is born of woman be clean?		Can anyone be righteous or pure in God's sight?

How then can man be righteous before God? Bildad now uses the argument of Eliphaz in 4.17-19. The wording of this question is identical with Job's own question in 9.2b. See 9.2 for exegesis and translation comments. TEV translates 9.2b "But how can a man win his case against God?" but it renders the identical question here "Can anyone be righteous . . . ?" It would be better to keep the sense of this question the same in both places. Therefore translators should refer to the way they have translated 9.2b. In 14.1 **man** is described as being "born of a woman," and that expression is repeated in line b and in 15.14 as a sign of human frailty or weakness. The word translated **man** is not man in contrast to woman, but humanity in contrast to God, and in some languages it will be better translated "human being," as FRCL says, "And how can a human being pretend to be pure?"

How can he who is born of woman be clean? For **clean** see comments on 15.14. To be **clean** is to be free from ritual contamination. Since giving birth caused a woman and her child to be unclean, impure, they had to be ritually cleansed. TEV has shortened and combined both lines of verse 4: "Can anyone be righteous or pure in God's sight?" "In God's sight" has been shifted from line a.

25.5-6	RSV		TEV
5	Behold, even the moon is not bright and the stars are not clean in his sight;	5	In his eyes even the moon is not bright, or the stars pure.
6	how much less man, who is a maggot, and the son of man, who is a worm!"	6	Then what about man, that worm, that insect? What is man worth in God's eyes?

These two verses can be taken together, since they are linked by the Hebrew words meaning either "how much more" or "how much less," depending on the context. A similar pattern is found in the speeches of Eliphaz in 4.18-19 and 15.15-16.

Behold, even the moon is not bright: in 15.15b Eliphaz argued that "the heavens are not clean in his sight." In line b of this verse the **stars** will be substituted for the "heavens." TEV has shifted **in his sight** from line b to the beginning of the verse to reinforce the parallel statement made in verse 4, and so it will apply to both lines of verse 5. In RSV **in his sight** mistakenly applies only to line

b. It is better to translate **Behold** as "If," which enables the connection between verses 5 and 6 to be understood, and so "If in God's eyes even the moon is without brightness . . . ." (HOTTP prefers ". . . does not shine.")

And the stars are not clean in his sight: this line reproduces 15.15b, with **stars** replacing "heavens." In many languages it will be awkward or impossible to speak of stars being pure or clean. The thought here is that both the moon and the stars fail to shine as they should, and so they are dim. Therefore it will sometimes be possible to translate "and if the stars are dim," "if the stars give little light," or, as in FRCL, "and if the stars appear to him (God) as tarnished."

Verse 6 expresses a negative comparison. **How much less man who is a maggot**: the two lines of this verse are closely parallel in meaning and serve to emphasize the insignificance of human beings. To Bildad man is morally worth little because of his humble origins. **Man** translates the same Hebrew term used in verse 4a and may be rendered "person" or "human being." The parallel form in line b is **son of man**, and this means the same as the "human person" in line a. Humankind is likened to a **maggot**. The same word is used to describe Israel in Isaiah 41.14. The word here translated **maggot** is used in 7.5; 17.14; 21.26, and in those passages RSV translates it "worm." See the comments on "worm" in 7.5. In those and other passages **maggot** is associated with a dead body. Only here and in Psalm 22.6 is the term used to express man's insignificance. According to Dhorme the term is properly **maggot**, as in RSV, and **worm** (from the verb meaning "to gnaw") in line b refers to the "earthworm."

And the son of man who is a worm: **son of man** is parallel in meaning to **man** in line a. This expression represents the poet's way of intensifying the thought. The heightening of emphasis is not in the pair of terms **maggot . . . worm**, but in **man . . . son of man**. Since it is the poet's purpose to depict the insignificance of mankind, translators must find the most effective way to do this. For example, TEV has used the pair "worm" and "insect." FRCL says "What will become of these miserable humans as insignificant as an ordinary earthworm?" and SPCL "How much less mankind, this miserable worm." TEV's rendering of the line, "What is man worth in God's eyes?" does not translate the content of this line but seems to summarize verses 4-6. It is better to stay closer to the text. Due to the complex set of grammatical relations involved in verses 5 and 6, translators may find it necessary to state some aspects of the meaning more directly than the translations cited have done; for example, "If God does not consider the moon and stars to shine brightly, he considers human beings to be even less. To him they are maggots and worms"; "When God looks at the moon and the stars he considers them to be dim lights. When he looks at human beings they are nothing more to him than maggots and worms."

5D. JOB INTERRUPTS (26.1-4)

Only the first four verses of chapter 26 are considered to be the words of Job. Verses 5-14, the remainder of the chapter, continue the theme of chapter 25 and so are held by most to be the continuation of Bildad's speech. These verses are identified in TEV as belonging to Bildad.

It was said in the introduction to chapter 25 that scholars reorder parts of chapters 25, 26, and 27 in order to obtain a more coherent flow of thought from each speaker. Many different arrangements of the text have been proposed, but translators have as a rule not followed these, since they tend to be the opinions and preferences of individual interpreters. Nevertheless translators should know what some of the proposals for rearranging the verses in these chapters are, and why they have been suggested. What follows is a list of the major reordering by Habel, Dhorme and Pope. "+" means "followed by."

Habel: 25.1-6 + 26.5-14; 26.1-4 + 27.1-12; 27.13-23.

Dhorme: 25.1-6 + 26.5-14; 26.1-4 + 27.2-12; 27.13 + 24.18-24 + 27.14-23.

Pope: 24.1-17; 25.1-6 + 26.5-14; 27.1 + 26.1-4 + 27.2-23 + 24.18-25.

In addition to the block arrangements above, Dhorme and Pope shift a few individual verses. It will be noted that all three (and many others) agree that 26.5-14 belong with 25.1-6; they all attribute these verses to Bildad. Rather than explain the reasons for these rearrangements here, this Handbook will call attention to the explanations in the appropriate sections of the text.

5D-1. Job ridicules Bildad's speech (26.1-4)

RSV	TEV
1 Then Job answered:	*Job*
2 "How you have helped him who has no power!	1-2 What a big help you are to me— poor, weak man that I am!
How you have saved the arm that has no strength!	3 You give such good advice and share your knowledge with a fool like me!
3 How you have counseled him who has no wisdom, and plentifully declared sound knowledge!	4 Who do you think will hear all your words? Who inspired you to speak like this?
4 With whose help have you uttered words, and whose spirit has come forth from you?	

Verses 2-4 of chapter 26 appear to be only the introductory remarks of Job addressed to the friends, or to Bildad in particular. Job's exclamations and questions are bitterly satirical and express stinging criticism of the worthless counsel of the friends.

Subdivision Heading

Translators wishing to provide a heading for the content of these verses may follow the suggestion of the Handbook or say, for example, "Bildad, you are of no help to me," "Your advice, Bildad, is not worth hearing," or "Job rejects Bildad's advice." TOB has "Reply to Bildad," Rowley "Job answers Bildad," FRCL "What sad help you offer me," and NJB "Bildad's rhetoric is beside the point."

26.1   RSV   TEV

Then Job answered: *Job*

Then Job answered: see comments on 4.1.

26.2   RSV   TEV

"How you have helped him who   What a big help you are to me—
    has no power!   poor, weak man that I am!
How you have saved the arm
    that has no strength!

How you have helped him who has no power! Here and in the following two verses Job uses **you** (singular). This is in contrast to his use of "you" (plural) when addressing the friends, and the singular here suggests that he is replying to Bildad's last speech. **Him who has no power** refers to Job and means "someone who is weak or oppressed." TEV renders the expression "poor, weak man that I am." Job is sarcastically asking "Do you think you have been a help to this weak person?" The expected reply is "No!" This line may also be translated as a negative statement, "You certainly have been no help to me, poor and weak as I am." TEV brings out the irony better with an exclamation: "What a big help you are . . . !" Translators must be alerted to irony and reminded to use the appropriate devices in their own languages which will signal to the reader that Job is saying one thing and meaning another. Literal translations of irony may result in distortion of the author's purpose. In some languages there are special particles that convey the sense of irony. In others this is done by restructuring. In some languages irony is expressed by adding an expression like "Someone might think . . ." or "You must imagine . . . ." Special sound repetitions called ideophones are sometimes used in African languages to signal this kind of irony.

How you have saved the arm that has no strength: this line introduces a figure to heighten the sarcasm. The word **saved** also means "help." Since **helped** in line a and **saved** in line b have essentially the same meaning, TEV does not repeat "help" in line b. RSV **saved** is less satisfactory in this context than another word meaning help such as "assist" or "aid." **Strength** is symbolized by **arm** and was used in 22.8, translated "the man with power . . . ." **The arm that has no strength** is a literal rendering of the Hebrew and means "a powerless person" or "a man without power." NJB expresses the satire of the verse well: "To one so weak, what a help you are, for the arm that is powerless, what a rescuer!" NEB translates this line "What deliverance you have brought to the powerless!" Verse 2 may be rendered in some languages, for example, "You must imagine how you (singular) have helped me in my weakness, and imagine also how you came to the rescue of such a weakling!"

26.3   RSV   TEV

How you have counseled him who has no wisdom, and plentifully declared sound knowledge!	You give such good advice and share your knowledge with a fool like me!

How you have counseled him who has no wisdom: counseled is the same term used in 12.13b, in which God "has counsel and understanding." As a verb it means "advise, give advice." **Him who has no wisdom** is literally "the one not wise" and therefore "ignorant, uninformed." TEV says "fool," and NJB "the unlearned." The line may be translated "You have done so well giving advice to this simple-minded person" or "Just look how well you have informed this ignorant man."

And plentifully declared sound knowledge is a literal translation of the Hebrew. Job is being doubly sarcastic in saying that Bildad's very brief remarks in 25.1-6 were **plentifully declared**. The word translated **declared** means "show, make known, demonstrate." **Sound knowledge** is a single word in Hebrew. It is used in 5.12 in the sense of planning ahead ("success"), and so "having foresight in making plans." It is often used in the wisdom literature of the Old Testament for the wisdom possessed by both people and God. NEB translates it "sound advice." If the translator is retaining the parallelism, this line may be translated, for example, "and shown me great amounts of wisdom!" "and helped me greatly to plan ahead well!" or "and you have shown me so much clear understanding!"

26.4   RSV   TEV

With whose help have you uttered words, and whose spirit has come forth from you?	Who do you think will hear all your words? Who inspired you to speak like this?

In this verse Job continues his sarcasm as he inquires about the source of Bildad's great knowledge. **With whose help have you uttered words . . . ?** Translators will note a difference in the meaning in this line in RSV and TEV. The Hebrew can be understood to mean "To whom have you uttered words," which TEV expresses as "Who do you think will hear all your words?" Another way of taking the Hebrew is "With whom" in the sense of **With whose help** or "By means of whom." This second sense, which is that of RSV, provides a parallel for line <u>b</u>. It seems more fitting in the context of Job's sarcasm to take it as in RSV. NIV has "Who has helped you utter these words?" and NEB says "Who has prompted you to say such things?" This line may also be expressed "Who helped you think up all these words?" or "Who helped you speak so well?"

And whose spirit has come forth from you? Spirit is literally "breath." It can refer to the breath or spirit of God or of a human. This line asks the same question as line <u>a</u>, but it moves to a more specific level. The question **whose spirit** implies that Job does not accept Bildad's words as originating within himself, but hears them flowing out of his mouth like the breath or inspiration of someone else.

Thus TEV has "Who inspired you to speak like this?" In some languages "inspire" is rendered "caused, made, gave you the thoughts"; for example, "Who caused your mouth to speak this way?" or "Who gave you the thoughts to speak as you do?"

5E. BILDAD CONTINUES HIS SPEECH (26.5-14)

Verses 5-14 are understood here to be the continuation of 25.1-6, the speech of Bildad. TEV and others identify Bildad as the speaker. Habel, Dhorme, and Pope place 26.5-14 immediately after 25.1-6 in order to continue Bildad's speech and its common theme without interruption.

Division Heading

Translators may wish to retain the order of verses as in the Hebrew Bible, the Handbook, TEV, and RSV. In that case they may want to show that verses 5-14 are assigned to Bildad and so are a continuation of Bildad's speech in 25.1-6. The Handbook heading may be modified to say, for example, "Bildad continues to address Job" or "More of Bildad's speech."

5E-1. The greatness of God (26.5-14)

RSV	TEV
	[Bildad]
5 The shades below tremble,	5 The spirits of the dead tremble
the waters and their inhabitants.	in the waters under the earth.
6 Sheol is naked before God,	6 The world of the dead lies open to God;
and Abaddon has no covering.	no covering shields it from his sight.
7 He stretches out the north over the void,	7 God stretched out the northern sky
and hangs the earth upon nothing.	and hung the earth in empty space.
8 He binds up the waters in his thick clouds,	8 It is God who fills the clouds with water and keeps them from bursting with the weight.
and the cloud is not rent under them.	
9 He covers the face of the moon,	9 He hides the full moon behind a cloud.
and spreads over it his cloud.	10 He divided light from darkness
10 He has described a circle upon the face of the waters	by a circle drawn on the face of the sea.
at the boundary between light and darkness.	11 When he threatens the pillars that hold up the sky,
11 The pillars of heaven tremble,	they shake and tremble with fear.
and are astounded at his rebuke.	12 It is his strength that conquered the sea;
12 By his power he stilled the sea;	by his skill he destroyed the monster Rahab.
by his understanding he smote Rahab.	13 It is his breath that made the sky clear,
13 By his wind the heavens were made fair;	and his hand that killed the escaping monster.
his hand pierced the fleeing serpent.	
14 Lo, these are but the outskirts of his ways;	14 But these are only hints of his power,
and how small a whisper do we hear of him!	only the whispers that we have heard.
But the thunder of his power who can understand?"	Who can know how truly great God is?

Verses 5-14 describe the awe and mystery of God's power.

Subdivision Heading

The Handbook heading may be reworded to say, for example, "God's power causes people to fear," "God is great in all the universe," or "Who can know how truly great God is?" Habel has (5-9) "The awesome mysteries of God" and (10-14) "The establishment of cosmic order." Rowley has "God's all embracing rule," TOB "The transcendence of God," and FRCL "The universal power of God."

26.5	RSV	TEV
	The shades below tremble, the waters and their inhabitants.	*[Bildad]*[z] The spirits of the dead tremble in the waters under the earth.

[z] Bildad *is not named in the text, but this speech is usually assigned to him.*

The shades below tremble: shades, meaning the spirits of the departed dead, translates the Hebrew *repha'im*. The last references in 25.5-6 were to the moon and stars in the heavens and to people on earth. The thought continues its downward direction and now speaks of the lower regions and Sheol. Although the *repha'im* are also giants in Genesis 14.5; 15.20; Deuteronomy 2.11, 20, their association in verse 6 with Sheol gives the sense of the "spirits of the dead." This term is found in Psalm 88.10, "Do the shades rise up to praise thee?" and Isaiah 14.9, "The ghosts of those who were powerful on earth are stirring about" (TEV). In Hebrew the word translated **below** belongs to line b, and so some translate "beneath the waters." RSV and others transfer **below** to the first line. NEB and NJB make the same shift (or divide the verse) as does RSV, but supply a verb for line b where there is none in Hebrew. TEV does not place **below** with line a: "The spirits of the dead tremble." **Below** is to be understood as "below the earth."

For many languages there are basic differences from the Hebrew thought of the departed spirits of the dead being in a deep place below the earth. In many societies the spirits of the ancestors inhabit local springs, caves, groves, or rocks. Since readers must understand the Hebrew view in order to comprehend the poem as a whole, translators may find it best to say "The spirits of the dead (ancestors) tremble in Sheol" or "The spirits of the ancestors tremble in the place of the dead." In some languages it may be necessary to make clear the reason for the trembling of these departed dead. The reason goes back to 25.1-6. It is the awe which God's power and presence inspires that causes the trembling. Accordingly it may be necessary to render the line "The spirits of the dead ancestors tremble with fear at God's power" or "God's greatness makes the spirits of the dead in Sheol tremble with fear."

The waters and their inhabitants: it is unlikely that in the context of Sheol the author is speaking here of sea life, as RSV seems to imply. He is most likely thinking of the same spirits as in line a, who are thought to occupy a vast pit beneath the waters of the underworld. **Tremble** in line a is to be understood as the verb also in line b. Dhorme believes that, in the process of copying, the similarity between the Hebrew for **below** and "terrify" caused the verb to drop out, and so he restores it to give "the waters and their inhabitants became terrified." NEB follows this: "The waters and all that live in them are struck with terror." It seems more likely that line b is the location of the place of the **shades** in line a, as in TEV. In some languages it will be more natural to place line b before line a and translate, for example, "In Sheol, in the water under the earth, the spirits of the dead tremble with fear." For an artists view of the ancient concept of the universe, see the illustration on page 181.

26.6	RSV	TEV

Sheol is naked before God,
    and Abaddon has no covering.
	The world of the dead lies open
	    to God;
	    no covering shields it from his
	    sight.

Sheol is naked before God: the thought here, as in Psalm 139.8, is that God's presence is everywhere. Job expressed the wish to be hidden in Sheol (14.13), but such a thought is contrary to the idea of the God who is everywhere, and thus even the darkness of Sheol is not hidden from him. TEV, which has combined **Abaddon** from line b with **Sheol**, translates "The world of the dead lies open to God." This line will sometimes have to be expressed differently in translation; for example, "God sees the place of the dead called Sheol," "God knows all about the place of the dead called Sheol," or "God sees all of Sheol as he sees all of a naked person." ·

And Abaddon has no covering: **Abaddon** is used for Sheol in 28.22; 31.12; Proverbs 15.11; 27.20; and Psalm 88.11. In Revelation 9.11 this name is written in Greek. **Abaddon** is a noun formed from the verb meaning "to perish." In Psalm 88.11 TEV translates it "the place of destruction." **Has no covering** has the literal meaning of "unveiled." The parallelism means "Abaddon is uncovered, unveiled, exposed (to the eyes of God)." FRCL translates "No veil hides the abyss from his eyes." Since **Sheol** and **Abaddon** have the same meaning here, translators may wish to follow TEV and not mention **Abaddon** as a noun in line b. The line may be rendered, for example, "and it is exposed to his eyes" or "and he sees all of it."

26.7	RSV	TEV

He stretches out the north over
    the void,
    and hangs the earth upon
    nothing.
	God stretched out the northern
	    sky
	    and hung the earth in empty
	    space.

He stretches out the north over the void: the verbs in this verse are participles and so contain no marked subjects, but God is clearly the implied subject. The verb translated **stretches out** is used in 9.8, in which Job said God "alone stretched out the heavens." **Stretches out** is also the common verb used with "tent" as its object. **The north** translates the Hebrew *tsafon*, which some interpreters equate with the mythological mountain from where the god Baal ruled (Isa 14.13). However, "stretching out the heavens" is a common expression in the Old Testament (Psa

474

104.2; Isa 40.22; 44.24; 45.12; Jer 10.12; 51.15), and the verb is not used with the earth or mountains. Since line b parallels line a with **earth**, the reference in line a is to the heavens, and in this case "the northern sky" (TEV). **Void** is the same term used in Genesis 1.2, which represents the chaos before creation. In 6.18 and 12.24 it refers to the desert ("waste"). The same term is used in Jeremiah 4.23, where TEV translates it "barren waste." In this verse TEV translates **void** as "empty space" and transfers it to line b. Line a will require some adjustments in some languages; for example, "God places the northern sky in its place" or "God puts the northern sky where there was nothing."

And hangs the earth upon nothing: in 1 Samuel 2.8 and Psalm 75.3, the earth is pictured as supported on pillars. An earth hanging in empty space appears to depict an earth as people have come to know it in modern times, but in verse 11 there is the picture of the heavens supported on pillars. Nothing is said as to what supports the pillars. In some languages it will be awkward if not impossible to speak of "hanging the earth," and especially when it is hung on **nothing**. However, this line may be restructured to say, for example, "and he puts the earth where there is nothing to hold it," or "He sets the earth where there is nothing." (For an artist's view of this ancient concept of the universe, see the illustration, page 181.)

26.8	RSV	TEV
	He binds up the waters in his thick clouds, and the cloud is not rent under them.	It is God who fills the clouds with water and keeps them from bursting with the weight.

He binds up the waters in his thick clouds: binds up translates a verb meaning to "close in, put in a container, wrap up." The picture is of God wrapping up water in the clouds in such a way that the clouds do not split under the weight of the water. Proverbs 30.4 says "Who has ever . . . wrapped up water in a piece of cloth?" (TEV). Psalm 33.7 has a similar thought: "He gathered the waters of the sea as in a bottle." **Waters** refers to "rain water" more than to water generally. This line may be rendered, for example, "He wraps up the rain in his clouds," "He uses the clouds to bag up the rain," or "He fills the clouds with rain water."

And the cloud is not rent under them: in Hebrew **cloud** is singular in this line but expresses the same plural image as in the first line. **Rent** translates the verb used in Genesis 7.11, in which the rain came in the Noah story: "all the fountains of the great deep burst forth . . . ." In 38.37 the clouds are called the "waterskins of the heavens," comparing them with sacks made of animal skins, for containing water. The poet pictures them as being so firm they are not "burst, broken, split, torn" by the weight of the rain water in them. In languages in which an active construction must be used, we may translate, for example, "and the rain does not burst the cloud" or "the rain water does not tear the cloud."

26.9 RSV	TEV
He covers the face of the moon,[z] and spreads over it his cloud.	He hides the full moon behind a cloud.

[z] Or *his throne*

He covers the face of the moon: as the RSV footnote indicates, **moon** is "throne" in the Hebrew text. **Moon** or **full moon** is obtained by a change of vowels in the word for "throne." HOTTP gives the Hebrew an "A" rating and translates "the front of the throne," which is accepted by TOB and GECL. Poetic passages such as Psalm 11.4 and 103.19 speak of God's throne being in the heavens. God's throne is likewise associated with the flood in Psalm 29.10, where "flood" may refer to the waters above the firmament of heaven in the diagram on page 181. It is quite natural, therefore, that the sense here can be that God veils his throne with the clouds to conceal himself. Translators can follow HOTTP and use, for example, GECL as a model: "In thick clouds he covers his throne."

And spreads over it his cloud: his cloud is not meant to imply that he has only one cloud, as it would in some languages. The sense is "a cloud" or "clouds." Verse 9 may also be expressed "He hides his throne by covering it with a cloud" or "He darkens his throne with a cloud." In languages in which "throne" is unknown, we may say, for example, "He covers the place where he rules, by spreading a cloud over it."

26.10 RSV	TEV
He has described a circle upon the face of the waters at the boundary between light and darkness.	He divided light from darkness by a circle drawn on the face of the sea.

He has described a circle upon the face of the waters: this translation is based on a change of vowels in the verb translated **described** and the word translated **circle**. In Hebrew the sense is "he has prescribed a limit." Proverbs 8.27, speaking of creation, has "he drew a circle on the face of the deep." Many interpreters believe this is also the intended meaning here, which Syriac has, and it is followed by RSV and TEV. TEV transposes the lines. **Upon the face of the waters** means "on the surface of the oceans, seas." The idea is that the earth stood between seas, and upon these the dome of the sky came down to the surface, like an inverted cup. Within this dome, light alternated with darkness as the sun passed overhead. (See Psa 19.4-6.)

At the boundary between light and darkness: this line has no verb. TEV has supplied "divided," so that it is God who "divided light from darkness." **Boundary** refers to the horizon, which is said to be **between light and darkness**. This line becomes the first line in TEV, and the other line becomes the means. FRCL says it well and keeps the Hebrew order: "He drew a circle around the ocean, out there where light gives way to darkness." NIV translates "He marks out the horizon on the face of the waters for a boundary between light and darkness." It is unlikely that many readers will understand how drawing a circle on the sea can divide day from night. The flat earth was thought of as surrounded by water, and the horizon (the circle on the face of the waters) was the place where night would end and daylight would begin, and vice versa. Accordingly we may translate, for example, "He has placed the horizon on the seas like a circle around the earth, and at the horizon daylight changes to night."

26.11   RSV   TEV

> The pillars of heaven tremble,   When he threatens the pillars
>   and are astounded at his re-   that hold up the sky,
>   buke.   they shake and tremble with
>   fear.

The pillars of heaven tremble: in 9.6 Job speaks of the "pillars that support the earth." **Pillars of heaven** refers to the distant mountains that support the dome of the heavens. In Greek mythology the Atlas Mountains served this function. (See the illustration on page 181.) **Pillars** are solid columns or supports for holding up a heavy object, such as the roof of a building. **Tremble** translates a word found only here, but from related languages and the context it is clear that these supports "tremble" or "shake." TEV has transposed a part of this line so that it becomes the consequence of the action in line b of RSV.

And are astounded at his rebuke: the **pillars** of the first line are personified in that they **are astounded**, which translates a verb meaning to be "stupefied, stunned, shocked." **His rebuke** translates a noun derived from a verb which means "threaten" when the object is the enemy or the physical elements, as it is here. By rearranging the lines as in TEV, we may translate "When God threatens the mountains that hold up the sky, they are stunned and tremble with fear." Since the cause for the shaking of the pillars is stated in line b, it will be more natural in some languages to transpose the two lines. Also in some cases the translator must state the object of God's threat to the pillars; for example, "When God threatens to destroy the pillars that hold up the heavens" or "If God threatens to knock down the mountains that support the sky, they shake with fear." If pillars and mountains may not be said to tremble with fear, it may be possible to shift to a simile and say, for example, "they tremble with fear like a frightened person."

26.12   RSV   TEV

> By his power he stilled the sea;   It is his strength that conquered
>   by his understanding he smote   the sea;[a]
>   Rahab.   by his skill he destroyed the
>   monster Rahab.[b]

[a] CONQUERED THE SEA: *A reference to*
an ancient story in which the sea fought

against God.
b RAHAB: *See 9.13.*

By his power he stilled the sea: as suggested by the note in TEV, the background of verse 12 is the ancient Mesopotamian and Ugaritic stories of the conflict between the creator and the sea. Both lines allude to the way in which God created by conquering his enemies. The word translated **stilled** is disputed by scholars. In Isaiah 51.15 and Jeremiah 31.35, the same Hebrew verb is used in the sense of "stir up." But a separate root with the same spelling is translated by RSV and others as **stilled**. This is the sense most appropriate here, and since God uses his power to still the sea, TEV correctly translates "conquered the sea." This line may be translated, for example, "The power (or, strength) of God conquered (or, defeated) the ocean (or, sea)" or "God who is powerful conquered the sea."

By his understanding he smote Rahab: according to Jeremiah 10.12 "The LORD made the earth by his power; by his wisdom he created the world and stretched out the heavens" (TEV). The same Hebrew word meaning "wisdom" is used here and translated **understanding**. According to Pope **understanding** would no doubt be taken as "cunning" in terms of the Mesopotamian story, but Job belongs to the Hebrew wisdom literature, and this term is probably best translated "wisdom, intelligence, understanding." **Smote** translates a verb meaning "to strike," but in the context it refers to striking for the purpose of conquering or destroying, and so TEV is correct in saying "destroyed." For **Rahab** see comments on 7.12 and 9.13. This line may also be rendered, "because he is intelligent he destroyed the sea animal called Rahab" or "he is wise, and because of this he was able to kill the sea monster Rahab."

26.13 RSV	TEV
By his wind the heavens were made fair; his hand pierced the fleeing serpent.	It is his breath that made the sky clear, and his hand that killed the escaping monster.*c*

c ESCAPING MONSTER: *See 9.8.*

By his wind the heavens were made fair: **his wind** translates the Hebrew *ruach* "spirit, wind, breath." Since this word is paralleled by **hand** in line b, it is best to take the meaning to be "breath." However, in the context "wind" and "breath" are very similar. **Were made fair** translates a root meaning "sparkling, bright, pretty." Dhorme takes this word to mean "sweep" and translates "His breath has swept the heavens." This is followed by FRCL and TOB. NJB says "His breath has made the heavens luminous" (meaning "bright"), and TEV ". . . made the sky clear." This line may also be rendered, for example, "God blew and made the sky clear," "God's breath blew away the clouds from the sky," or "God made the sky bright by blowing away the clouds with his breath."

His hand pierced the fleeing serpent: this is no doubt a reference to the same event described in Isaiah 27.1: "In that day the LORD with his hard and great and strong sword will punish Leviathan the fleeing serpent, Leviathan the twisting serpent, and will slay the dragon that is in the sea." This monster is mentioned in 3.8 (see there for comments) and again in 41.1. See also Psalm 74.14 and 104.26. **Hand** may be taken as part for the whole, representing God, or as a substitute for "sword." **Pierce** depicts the action resulting from the use of the sword in God's hand, and may more generally be rendered "killed or destroyed." **Fleeing** in **fleeing serpent** is uncertain. It may have been a conventional adjective used by poets in speaking of this sea monster. TEV prefers "escaping," but "gliding," "slippery," or "wriggling" express its movements. The line may be expressed, for example, "with his hands he killed the slippery snake" or "with the sword in his hand he destroyed the wriggling snake."

26.14	RSV	TEV
	Lo, these are but the outskirts of his ways; and how small a whisper do we hear of him! But the thunder of his power who can understand?"	But these are only hints of his power, only the whispers that we have heard. Who can know how truly great God is?

Lo, these are but the outskirts of his ways: **Lo** translates a Hebrew particle which most probably introduces a condition, and Dhorme and others translate "If such are . . . ." Many others, however, translate this line as a statement. **These** refers to the descriptions of God's power in the preceding verses. **Outskirts** translates a space term which in this context refers not to a distant area such as **outskirts** suggests (as when referring to the distant outskirts of a city), but rather to something only partially disclosed or revealed; the term can be translated as "outline, glimpse, a small part of," which NJB renders "only a fraction of," and TEV "only hints of." **His ways** is translated "his power" by Pope, based on Dahood. FRCL has "his actions," and NJB "what he has done." Dhorme supports these with "his works." All of these are better translations than **his ways**. The line may also be rendered, for example, "All that I have been saying is only a small part of what he has done" or "These things are only a hint of his great acts."

And how small a whisper do we hear of him! **Whisper** translates a word found only here and in 4.12. The Hebrew interrogative particle is used in this line as an exclamation marker; an English equivalent may be "How small is the whisper we hear of him!" This line can follow the "if" clause which may be used in line a, or it can be translated as a separate comment on line a. NJB translates "and all we catch of it is the feeblest echo." TEV translates line b as being in apposition with line a, so that "only the whispers" refers back to the content of line a. Line b may also be rendered "what we have heard is hardly a whisper," or "and we only catch a slight whisper of all that he does," or "we know almost nothing of the things he does."

But the thunder of his power who can understand? The thought now takes shape for the entire verse: if we hear only the tiny whispers (the faintest noises) of God's great acts, how can we grasp the true greatness of his power? Psalm 104.6-7 says that God rebuked the waters above the mountains and they fled: "at the sound of thy thunder they took to flight." The threatenings of God in verse 11 are thus expressed in his thunder. In poetic terms **thunder** in this line stands in sharp contrast to **whisper** in line b. However, **thunder of his power** intends to convey far more than "powerful thunder." Zophar made the point in 11.6-9 that God's ways belong to the secrets or "mysteries of his wisdom." They are hidden. The question now asked is who can "grasp, comprehend," not just the loudness of his power displayed in thunder, but his true greatness? As GECL translates, "How truly great and powerful God must be!" or TEV "Who can know how truly great God is?"

Note on the text of chapter 27

It was pointed out in the introduction to division 5D that 26.1-4 appears to be the introductory section of an address by Job, which is then followed at 26.5 by Bildad, and remains Bildad's speech until the end of chapter 26. Habel, Dhorme, and Pope place 26.5-14 immediately following 25.1-6. Also, with some slight variations, all three place Job's speech 26.1-4 immediately before 27.1-12. Habel and Dhorme consider 26.1-4; 27.1-12 to be Job's address, and 27.13-23 to be that of Zophar. TEV identifies 27.13-23 as belonging to Zophar because, according to its footnote, "this speech is usually assigned to him."

An examination of the discourse structure of 27.1-23 makes it necessary to consider the possibility that chapter 27 is entirely the speech of Job, and not of Job and Zophar. The following display shows the typical pattern of alternating themes:

A (2-6) Job defends his integrity before his opponents

B (7-10) The wicked will fail

A' (11-12) Job would instruct his opponents

B' (13-23) The wicked will fail

In the light of the above unifying pattern, it does not seem necessary to assign, as do TEV and others, verses 13-23 to Zophar, or to any other speaker. For further advice see the note on verses 13-23, page 489.

5F. JOB REPLIES (27.1-23)

Division Heading

This heading may be reworded to say, for example, "Job replies to the friends" or "Job speaks again." TOB has "Job's tenth poem."

5F-1. Job affirms that his conscience is clear (27.1-6)

RSV	TEV
1 And Job again took up his discourse, and said:	*Job*
2 "As God lives, who has taken away my	1-2 I swear by the living Almighty God, who refuses me justice and makes my

	right,		life bitter—
	and the Almighty, who has made my	3	as long as God gives me breath,
	soul bitter;	4	my lips will never say anything evil,
3	as long as my breath is in me,		my tongue will never tell a lie.
	and the spirit of God is in my nostrils;	5	I will never say that you men are right;
4	my lips will not speak falsehood,		I will insist on my innocence to my
	and my tongue will not utter deceit.		dying day.
5	Far be it from me to say that you are	6	I will never give up my claim to be right;
	right;		my conscience is clear.
	till I die I will not put away my integri-		
	ty from me.		
6	I hold fast my righteousness, and will not		
	let it go;		
	my heart does not reproach me for		
	any of my days.		

In chapter 27 Job begins his final speech. His arguments cease at the end of chapter 31. Using a series of questions in 26.2-4, Job bitterly denounced the friends for their failure to offer him wise and helpful counsel. In 27.1-6 Job swears to his own integrity. He does this through the use of legal terms, as if he were testifying in court in his own defense. These six verses are particularly significant in the overall structure of the book, in that they are the beginning of the final speech by Job in his defense. Also Yahweh refers to this statement when he speaks later.

Subdivision Heading

The Handbook heading may be adjusted to say, for example, "Job defends himself," "Job swears to God that he is innocent," or "Job swears that he is telling the truth." Habel has "Job's oath of integrity," TOB (1-10) "Oath of innocence," FRCL "Would a guilty person appeal to God?" GECL "My conscience is clear."

27.1	RSV	TEV

And Job again took up his dis-   *Job*
course, and said:

And Job again took up his discourse, and said: in Hebrew Job is identified as the speaker beginning with chapter 26, and normally nothing is said to remind the reader who is speaking until a new speaker starts. Therefore the prose formula in this verse is unusual and suspicious. In 29.1 the same formula is appropriately used following chapter 28. However, in 27.1 it seems out of place. Dhorme explains it as the result of separating 27.2 and the following from 26.4. Therefore, he argues, the natural sequence is 25.1-6 + 26.5-14; 26.1-4 + 27.2-12. The speech of Job continues in 27.2, and 27.1, which is borrowed from 29.1, is no longer necessary. TEV follows this by identifying "Job" as the speaker and by indicating verses 1-2 as the opening verse. **Took up** is literally "raised," and **discourse** translates the Hebrew *mashal,* which has the meaning of "proverb, parable, saying," but in Isaiah 14.4 it refers to a larger composition, as here. In the context of Job it may be rendered "speech, address, discourse, argument, presentation." Verse 1 may be rendered, for example, "Job began to argue again," "Job picked up his argument again," or "Job began to speak again."

27.2　　　　RSV　　　　　　　　　　　　　　　TEV

> "As God lives, who has taken　　　　　I swear by the living Almighty
> away my right,　　　　　　　　　　　　God,
> and the Almighty, who has　　　　　who refuses me justice and
> made my soul bitter;　　　　　　　　makes my life bitter—

Verse 2 is introductory and requires verses 3 and 4 to complete the thought.

As God lives, who has taken away my right begins literally "As *'El* lives" or "'*El* is alive" and is the formula used in swearing an oath that what the speaker says is true. Note that the use of the name *Yahweh* is avoided in the oath. The thought expressed is "What I say is just as true as the truth that God is alive." In English the equivalent is "I swear by God." **Taken away** translates a verb meaning "remove," but with the object **my right**, it has the sense of denying Job access to justice, and so NJB "denies me justice," or TEV and others "refuse me justice." **Right** translates the term which often means "judgment" and refers here to what is "right and just." The same noun is used in 8.3, where RSV translates it "justice." TEV has transposed *Shaddai* from <u>b</u> to line <u>a</u> and rendered the oath formula as "I swear by the living Almighty God." Because of the nature of the grammatical relations and the links in meaning in verses 2, 3, and 4, it may be necessary to adjust the order of some of the elements. For example, **As God lives** is followed in the rest of verse 2 by actions that God has taken against Job. Verse 3 has two conditions which accompany the oath and the content of the oath comes in verse 4. Therefore in some languages it may be clearer to shift the opening words **As God lives** in verse 2a to verse 4. In this case verse 2 can begin, for example, "God has not allowed me to have justice," "God has prevented me from getting fair treatment," or "God has not treated me fairly."

And the Almighty, who made my soul bitter: **Almighty** translates *Shaddai* which is parallel with *'El* in line <u>a</u>. Job has spoken of the bitterness of his *nefesh* "soul" in 7.11 and 10.1. This bitterness or resentment is caused by God's refusal to hear his case. TEV has transferred "who refuses me justice" from line <u>a</u> and joined it with "and makes my life bitter" so that the two actions are made coordinate verb phrases. If the translator wishes to keep the two lines closer to the Hebrew form, he may translate, for example, "I swear by God who denies me justice, and who makes me feel bitter" or ". . . fills me with resentment." TEV ends verse 2 with a dash, "—," showing that something is to follow. This line may also be rendered "Because of what the Almighty has done to me, I resent it," or idiomatically sometimes, "The Almighty has made me bitter in my innermost" or "The Almighty has made my liver sour."

27.3　　　　RSV　　　　　　　　　　　　　　　TEV

> as long as my breath is in me,　　　as long as God gives me
> and the spirit of God is in my　　　breath,
> nostrils;

As long as my breath is in me: verse 3 may be taken as the conditions which will keep Job faithful to his oath. "I swear . . . that as long as my breath is . . . and the spirit of God . . . ." Job is frail and probably near death but still has the **breath** which comes from God's act of creation in Genesis 2.7. To have **breath** is to have life, and FRCL translates "As long as I have a little bit of life left in me." TEV reduces verse 3 to one line: "as long as God gives me breath."

And the spirit of God is in my nostrils: **spirit of God** translates *ruach Eloah*, in which the first word can mean "spirit, wind, breath," but in association with **nostrils** "breath" is the sense to be understood. Although the two lines of verse 3 are the same in meaning, line a is general and line b specific, which is the stylistic technique often used to raise the poetic intensity in the second line. So Job is saying that he swears "that as long as I have a spark of life and a breath from God in me . . . ." In languages in which the parallelism is to be retained, verse 3 may be rendered, for example, "As long as I have a bit of life, and as long as God enables me to breathe." Some may find that the meaning of the two lines is too similar to retain the double lines.

27.4	RSV	TEV
	my lips will not speak falsehood, and my tongue will not utter deceit.	my lips will never say anything evil, my tongue will never tell a lie.

In this verse Job finally states what it is he will swear to refrain from doing: **my lips will not speak falsehood. My lips** is a part of Job representing his whole being. **Falsehood** translates the same Hebrew word used in 13.7, where TEV translated "lying." In the negative this line may be rendered "I will never tell lies," or positively, "I will always speak the truth." The Hebrew word may refer to wickedness or evil, but in the context of speaking and lips, it is to be taken as falsehood or lying.

And my tongue will not utter deceit: **tongue** is parallel to **lips** in line a. **Utter** translates a word that is parallel with "speak" in Psalm 37.30 and has here the same meaning as in line a. The word translated **deceit** is used in parallel with **falsehood** in 13.7 ("falsely . . . deceitfully"). Aside from the changes in images, these two lines say the same thing. TEV, which often reduces synonymous lines to one to avoid monotony of style in English, keeps both lines, including **lips** and **tongue**. Translators who find it best to shift **as God lives** to verse 4 should express the oath in a fully idiomatic manner, provided it is acceptable in the mouth of Job; for example, "I tell this truth and God hears my words; I will not lie," "I say this before God who lives; I will not lie," "May God who hears me strike me dead if I tell lies." Translators may find the thought of line b is adequately expressed by line a, or may incorporate it into line a; for example, "I will not lie and will deceive no one."

27.5   RSV   TEV

Far be it from me to say that you are right; till I die I will not put away my integrity from me.	I will never say that you men are right; I will insist on my innocence to my dying day.

Far be it from me to say that you are right: Job appears to address the friends directly, and insists again on his innocence. The opening phrase is an emphatic denial. Job cannot accept the thought of the friends that he is guilty of wrongdoing. **Far be it from me** is translated by NEB as "God forbid . . . ," and by Mft as "When I maintain (by God!) that you . . . ." This phrase may require an idiomatic translation to express the equivalent idea. TEV translates the idea but lacks the force of the original: "I will never say that . . . ," and NIV "I will never admit . . . ." **To say that you are right** translates the Hebrew "that I should justify you," where "justify" represents the causative form of the verb *tsadaq* "to be right." It is used in 9.15; 11.2; 13.18. The meaning is "admit that you (plural) are right." RSV and TEV make **till I die** part of line b, and this is correct. To place that phrase in line a, as some translators do, is to destroy the balance of the two lines. This line may also be expressed, for example, "I will never admit that you (plural) are right" or "As God sees me, you are certainly in the wrong!"

Till I die I will not put away my integrity from me: **till I die** is not intended to suggest that Job will be willing to renounce his integrity after he dies, but rather that he will never renounce it, or as FRCL says, "Never, even till my death." **Put away** translates a verb whose meaning is "set aside, remove" but in this context means "renounce, deny." **Integrity** is the term God used to refer to the character of Job in 2.3 when speaking to Satan, "He still holds fast his integrity." Job is not claiming perfection or blamelessness, but innocence of wrongdoing, and so TEV and others translate positively, "I will insist on my innocence." Negatively this may be rendered "I will not say that I am guilty of wrongdoing."

27.6   RSV   TEV

I hold fast my righteousness, and will not let it go; my heart does not reproach me for any of my days.	I will never give up my claim to be right; my conscience is clear.

I hold fast my righteousness and will not let it go: verse 6 develops further the notion of verse 5b. Just as in 2.3,9, where Job is said to "hold fast his integrity," so here too he "clings to, maintains" his being in the right. NEB translates "I will maintain the rightness of my cause . . . ." **Righteousness** refers to Job's right behavior, conduct unspoiled by wrongdoing. SPCL says "I will not cease to insist on my honor." It is also used in the sense of "innocence" from wrong and is translated in Psalm 7.8 "Judge in my favor O LORD; you know that I am innocent" (TEV). **And will not let it go**: this statement reinforces the first part **I hold fast**. TEV represents it by "never" in "I will never give up . . . ." In this line **righteousness** or "being in the right" is treated as a physical object which can be held. In some languages this thought must be expressed differently; for example, "I insist I am innocent and will not change my mind" or "I know I am in the right and will never surrender."

My heart does not reproach me for any of my days: a literal translation of this line gives poor sense, as RSV shows. This is due to the uncertainty of the meaning of the Hebrew verb and its relation to the other words in the sentence. The word translated **heart** here evidently has the meaning of "conscience," as in TEV. In a similar way, in 1 Samuel 24.5 David's heart smites him. The Hebrew verb is usually translated as "reproach," but there is no object in the Hebrew. Most translators supply **me** as the object, but TEV expresses the meaning effectively with "my conscience is clear." **For any of my days**, which is not represented in TEV, means "as long as I live" and is translated by NEB as "so long as I live." "My conscience is clear" is sometimes expressed idiomatically; for example, "my heart does not speak behind me" or "my shadow does not tell me things." In some languages this line may be rendered "my heart does not scold me as long as I live."

5F-2. Job asks God to punish those who have opposed him (27.7-10)

RSV	TEV
7 "Let my enemy be as the wicked, and let him that rises up against me be as the unrighteous.	7 May all who oppose me and fight against me be punished like wicked, unrighteous men.
8 For what is the hope of the godless when God cuts him off, when God takes away his life?	8 What hope is there for godless men in the hour when God demands their life?
9 Will God hear his cry, when trouble comes upon him?	9 When trouble comes, will God hear their cries?
10 Will he take delight in the Almighty? Will he call upon God at all times?	10 They should have desired the joy he gives; they should have constantly prayed to him.

Some scholars find that 27.7-23 is inappropriate for Job. In verses 7-12 the speaker observes that God pays no attention to the cry of the wicked. Job's complaint is different in that God gives no heed to Job's cry, even though he is innocent. Although some think verses 7-23 are the words of Bildad, many others would assign them to Zophar. Some, like TEV, start Zophar's speech at verse 13. The Handbook, however, like RSV, considers all of chapter 27 to be the speech of Job.

Subdivision Heading

The Handbook, which follows the display at the beginning of this chapter, suggests a heading for verses 7-10. This may be reworded to say, for example, "Job says the wicked have no hope," "Let the wicked be punished," or "God will punish those who oppose me." Habel has (7-12) "Imprecation against Job's adversary," Rowley (7-12) "Desolate state of the godless."

27.7   RSV   TEV

> "Let my enemy be as the wicked,
>   and let him that rises up
>   against me be as the un-
>   righteous.

> May all who oppose me and fight
>   against me
>   be punished like wicked, un-
>   righteous men.

Let my enemy be as the wicked: the same words translated **wicked** and **unrighteous** in the following line are found in parallel in Job's speech in 16.11. Dhorme believes this fact connects verse 7 to verse 6, and so this is still the speech of Job. This line says that **my enemies** should suffer, that is, they ought to have the same fate as **the wicked**. TEV uses the passive in line b "be punished," which will often have to be shifted to the active with God as the actor: "May God punish my enemies (cause them to suffer) the way he punishes the wicked."

And let him that rises up against me be as the unrighteous: **him that rises up** translates a Hebrew participle which may be rendered "my opponents" or "those who . . . fight against me," as in TEV. **Be as the unrighteous** is parallel in meaning to the expression **be as the wicked** in line a. They are to suffer the same fate. TEV has brought the two parallel expressions together in line b as "be punished like wicked, unrighteous men."

27.8   RSV   TEV

> For what is the hope of the god-
>   less when God cuts him off,
>   when God takes away his life?

> What hope is there for godless
>   men
>   in the hour when God de-
>   mands their life?

For what is the hope of the godless when God cuts him off: most translations understand this verse the same as RSV and TEV, namely, that there is no hope for the godless when they come to the end of life. **Cuts off** translates a verb which has the meaning "to make illicit profit" and which is used in this way in some of the ancient versions and in TOB. However, most modern translations use it as RSV and TEV in the sense of "God requires a person's life," that is, "brings his life to an end." Dhorme, however, changes **cuts him off** to "he prays," which is followed by BJ and NJB. Preferred is the meaning understood by RSV and TEV, "What hope does a godless person have when God takes away his life?" TEV translates **the godless** as plural and maintains the plural through verse 10. **When God takes away his life** is almost the same in meaning to the previous line, and in those translations which cannot keep the parallelism, these two lines are sometimes reduced to one.

27.9   RSV   TEV

> Will God hear his cry,
>   when trouble comes upon him?

> When trouble comes, will God
>   hear their cries?

Will God hear his cry when trouble comes upon him? This rhetorical question anticipates a negative reply and may also be translated as a negative statement, "God will certainly not hear." **His cry** means "his cry for help" or "when he cries for help." **Trouble** translates the same word used in 5.19. See there for comments. For stylistic reasons TEV reverses the two clauses. **Him** refers to the godless person in verse 8a. Verse 9 may also be rendered, for example, "When times of distress come, will God hear his cry for help? Certainly not!"

27.10   RSV   TEV

> Will he take delight in the Al-   They should have desired the joy
>   mighty?   he gives;
> Will he call upon God at all   they should have constantly
>   times?   prayed to him.

Will he take delight in the Almighty? As in verse 9, this is a question that expects a negative reply, and the next line is usually translated as a question also, in order to make the connection between the two lines clear. In 22.26a Eliphaz says to Job "Then you will delight yourself in the Almighty." Dhorme interprets verse 10a as Job repeating Eliphaz in order to challenge the friends, and accordingly Job is still the speaker in verse 10. For **take delight** see 22.26a. TEV "They should have . . ." implies in fact that the godless did not do that. Using negative statements we may translate, for example, "He is not a person (or, They are not people) who finds joy (or, happiness) in worshiping the Almighty God."

Will he call upon God at all times? This echoes Psalm 86.3b, "for to thee do I call all the day." **Call upon** means "to call for help, to pray." **At all times** means "all the time, at any time." This may be understood to mean that Job (assuming he is the speaker) does not admit that the godless can call upon God. The friends, who refuse to recognize Job's innocence, urge him to do just that. But Job constantly calls on God to hear his case. Therefore the friends and Job are at a total impasse. The only way it can be resolved is for the friends to recognize Job's innocence, and they cannot do this because of the evidence before their eyes: Job's misfortune.

5F-3. Job wishes he could instruct his opponents (27.11-12)

	RSV		TEV
11	I will teach you concerning the hand of God; what is with the Almighty I will not conceal.	11	Let me teach you how great is God's power, and explain what Almighty God has planned.
12	Behold, all of you have seen it yourselves; why then have you become altogether vain?	12	But no, after all, you have seen for yourselves; so why do you talk such nonsense?

Subdivision Heading

Translators who wish to follow the Handbook may supply a heading for verses 11-12. The heading may also be worded "It is useless to teach you anything" or "No one can teach you; you know everything."

27.11   RSV   TEV

> I will teach you concerning the
>   hand of God;
>   what is with the Almighty I
>   will not conceal.

> Let me teach you how great is
>   God's power,
>   and explain what Almighty
>   God has planned.

I will teach you concerning the hand of God: you is plural, which gives evidence for those who hold that Job is speaking. **Hand** is used many times in Job, and particularly as an image of God's power or action in 10.7; 12.9,10; 19.21. NJB translates "But I am showing you the way that God works," FRCL "I myself will show you what the action of God is," and SPCL "I will show you the great power of God." All of these are good translation models.

What is with the Almighty I will not conceal: what is with the Almighty means "that which is in the mind or thoughts of the Almighty." This refers to God's "plans, purposes, what he has kept hidden in his mind." **Not conceal** or "not hide" may be rendered positively as "explain, reveal, show." TEV has "and explain what Almighty God has planned." As Rowley says, "The assumption of superior insight marked all the parties to the debate." This line may also be rendered "and I will show you what Almighty God has in his thoughts" or "I will explain to you the purpose God has in mind."

27.12   RSV   TEV

> Behold, all of you have seen it
>   yourselves;
>   why then have you become
>   altogether vain?

> But no, after all, you have seen
>   for yourselves;
>   so why do you talk such non-
>   sense?

Behold, all of you have seen it yourselves: here **Behold** is better translated "If" or else left untranslated: "If you all have observed this." TEV translates "But no, after all . . . ." **All of you . . . yourselves** translates a pair of pronouns "you (plural), all of you." In 13.4 these are used in parallel, and here they are put side by side, but the meaning is as in RSV and TEV. In Hebrew **seen** has no object but appears to refer to verse 11b, which speaks about what is in God's mind.

Why then have you become altogether vain? This is best handled as a question, as in RSV and TEV. The Hebrew construction translated **become altogether vain** is the noun "vain thing" followed by a verb of the same root, and so "become vain with a vain thing." It may represent an intensification of the worthlessness Job attributes to the friends. TEV renders the line well: "So why do you talk such nonsense?" Verse 12 may also be expressed, for example, "All of you have

488

seen these things, so why do you talk in such a foolish way?" or "You have all seen these things for yourselves; why then do you talk such nonsense?"

Note on verses 13-23

As indicated at the beginning of this chapter, TEV and others accept Zophar as the speaker of verses 13-23. If translators wish to follow the Handbook and consider Job as the speaker of the entire chapter, they may do so. However, in some languages it may be advisable to follow the lead of a major language Bible read in the area, or to state in a footnote, for example, "Some translations assign verses 13-23 to Zophar."

5F-4. How God punishes the wicked (27.13-23)

RSV	TEV
	[Zophar]
13 "This is the portion of a wicked man with God, and the heritage which oppressors receive from the Almighty:	13 This is how Almighty God punishes wicked, violent men.
14 If his children are multiplied, it is for the sword; and his offspring have not enough to eat.	14 They may have many sons, but all will be killed in war; their children never have enough to eat.
15 Those who survive him the pestilence buries, and their widows make no lamentation.	15 Those who survive will die from disease, and even their widows will not mourn their death.
16 Though he heap up silver like dust, and pile up clothing like clay;	16 The wicked may have too much silver to count and more clothes than anyone needs;
17 he may pile it up, but the just will wear it, and the innocent will divide the silver.	17 but some good man will wear the clothes, and some honest man will get the silver.
18 The house which he builds is like a spider's web, like a booth which a watchman makes.	18 The wicked build houses like a spider's web or like the hut of a slave guarding the fields.
19 He goes to bed rich, but will do so no more; he opens his eyes, and his wealth is gone.	19 One last time they will lie down rich, and when they wake up, they will find their wealth gone.
20 Terrors overtake him like a flood; in the night a whirlwind carries him off.	20 Terror will strike like a sudden flood; a wind in the night will blow them away;
21 The east wind lifts him up and he is gone; it sweeps him out of his place.	21 the east wind will sweep them from their homes;
22 It hurls at him without pity; he flees from its power in headlong flight.	22 it will blow down on them without pity while they try their best to escape.
23 It claps its hands at him, and hisses at him from its place.	23 The wind howls at them as they run, frightening them with destructive power.

This part of chapter 27 repeats the theme of verses 7-10. The subject is the fate of the wicked, and verse 13 serves as a title. The speaker then proceeds step by step through the loss and destruction the wicked suffer: children and wives (verses 14 and

15); silver and clothing (verses 16 and 17); house and wealth (verses 18 and 19); and natural disasters (verses 20-23).

Subdivision Heading

The Handbook heading may be modified to say, for example, "God will not allow the wicked to succeed," "The wicked have no secure future," or "The wicked are bound to fail." Habel has "Zophar on the destiny of the wicked," Rowley "The fate of the godless," and FRCL "A fleeting success."

27.13   RSV   TEV

> "This is the portion of a wicked
>   man with God,
>   and the heritage which oppres-
>   sors receive from the Al-
>   mighty:

> *[Zophar]*[d]
> 13   This is how Almighty God
>   punishes wicked, violent men.
>
> [d] Zophar *is not named in the text, but this speech is usually assigned to him.*

This is the portion of a wicked man: these words point forward to the verses that follow. In 20.29 "this" pointed back to what had already been said. For comments on **portion** and **heritage**, see 20.29. These terms normally refer to good things or to wealth received, and so their use here represents a form of irony. Hebrew has "with God"; but in 20.29 it has "from God," and the same should be read here. TEV expresses this verse in an active mode: "This is how Almighty God punishes . . . men." RSV keeps the singular in reference to the wicked in this section, but TEV translates in the plural—a more normal way in English for referring to a class of people. In some languages the appropriate form used will point forward. In others it may be necessary to make it clear by saying, for example, "I will tell you now how God punishes wicked people" or "Here is how God punishes the wicked."

And the heritage which oppressors receive from the Almighty: **heritage** is parallel in meaning to **portion** in the previous line, and **oppressors** (plural) to **a wicked man** (singular). These occurred in parallel in 15.20, where the same Hebrew word is translated "the ruthless" by RSV and "who oppresses others" by TEV. For **oppressor** see comments on 6.23. TEV reduces the parallelism to a single thought by joining "violent men" with "wicked," and **Almighty** with "God." Verse 13 is translated by SPCL as "This is the punishment that God, the Almighty, will give to cruel and evil men." Translators wishing to avoid the parallel line arrangement may follow this model. To make clear that **This** points forward to the remaining verses, translators may have to adjust the above model to say, for example, "God Almighty will punish cruel and evil people in the following way" or ". . . in the way I will tell you now."

27.14   RSV   TEV

> If his children are multiplied, it
>   is for the sword;

> They may have many sons,
>   but all will be killed in war;

and his offspring have not	their children never have
enough to eat.	enough to eat.

If his children are multiplied, it is for the sword: the Hebrew has "sons" in this line and "shoots" of a plant used figuratively to mean **offspring** or "children" in the next line. **Are multiplied** means "are increased in number." **It is for the sword** means "they will be killed by the sword," that is, "they will die in war." The line may be rendered "If he has many sons, they will be killed in war."

And his offspring have not enough to eat: **offspring** generalizes "sons" from line a but does not suggest a different group of people. They suffer death and starvation. The Hebrew is literally "they will not be satiated by bread," that is, "they will not have bread to satisfy them," "they will not have enough to eat," or "they will starve."

27.15   RSV   TEV

Those who survive him the pesti- lence buries, and their widows make no lamentation.	Those who survive will die from disease, and even their widows will not mourn their death.

Those who survive him the pestilence buries: **those** refers to the **children** in verse 14. **Him** refers to their father, the wicked man in verse 13. Any children not killed by war and famine "will die from disease" (TEV). The Hebrew says "those who survive him are buried by death." Here "death" is personified as in Jeremiah 15.2; 18.21; 43.11; and so it is taken as the plague, that is, RSV **pestilence**. The implication is that they will have no other burial—a tragic end. TEV avoids the term **pestilence** in favor of the more common word "disease." This line may also be rendered, for example, "The children of the wicked who survive will be killed by disease" or "The offspring of the wicked will die from disease."

And their widows make no lamentation: the Hebrew has "his widows," namely, the widows of the wicked man. The Septuagint has "their widows," which refers to the widows of the surviving family members. Since the subject in line a is plural, it is best to take **widows** as belonging to those who survive. Translators must make certain that **their widows** is appropriate in combination with the term used for "offspring" or "survivors" in the previous line. **Make no lamentation** means, as in TEV, "will not mourn their death." This line is identical in wording with Psalm 78.64b.

27.16-17   RSV   TEV

| 16 | Though he heap up silver like
dust,
and pile up clothing like clay; | 16 | The wicked may have too much
silver to count
and more clothes than anyone
needs; |
| 17 | he may pile it up, but the just
will wear it, | 17 | but some good man will wear the |

491

and the innocent will divide   clothes,
the silver.   and some honest man will get
                                                 the silver.

In the next two verses the speaker shifts from the family of the wicked to his wealth. These two verses form a chiastic structure in which the first line is balanced by the fourth and the second by the third. Verse 16 is conditional and verse 17 the consequence. Accordingly the two are handled here as a unit.

Though he heap up silver like dust: heap up is used in Genesis 41.49; Psalm 39.6. In Zechariah 9.3 it is used as here, referring to silver, and with the same simile "like dust." TEV has dropped the similes of **heap . . . like dust** and **pile up . . . like clay** and expressed abundance in a nonfigurative way: "too much to count" and "more than anyone needs." The translator must decide if heaping or piling up silver is a natural way to speak of having it in great quantities, and furthermore, if comparing great quantities to **dust** gives the sense of it being common and plentiful. If these images give another sense, or no sense at all, adjustments must be made. For example, it may be more natural to say "Although the wicked pile up silver like dirt" or "like sand."

And pile up clothing like clay: the verb here is different than the one in the previous line, but it is used commonly with the sense of "prepare, arrange, put in a pile." When **pile up** is used with **clay**, it refers to heaping the clay in a mound in preparation for shaping it into a vessel. A verb that is parallel to the one in line a, but which can be used with clothing, is desirable. **Clothing** is a general term and refers to any kind of clothing that is worn on the body. **Clothing** was a symbol of wealth and so is used in parallel with **silver**. **Clay** and **dust** are used in parallel in 4.19; 10.9; 30.19. **Clay** and **dust** may not be appropriate as images for quantity in some languages. FRCL says "and piles of clothing like mud," and SPCL avoids the image, "and may have clothes in large quantities."

He may pile it up, but the just will wear it: this refers to the clothing in verse 16b. **Pile it up** repeats the same verb used of **clothing** there. NJB, which translates **pile up** in verse 16b as "gather," translates it here as "let him gather!" TEV does not repeat the verb. **Just** refers to a person who is the opposite of the wicked, often translated "righteous," as in NJV and NIV. The sense is "a good, honorable, upright person," and so TEV, NJB, and others have "some good man." **Wear it** translates the Hebrew verb from which the noun **clothing** is derived. **It** refers to the **clothing** and will often be translated by a plural pronoun. This line may also be rendered, for example, "The wicked person may have great amounts of clothing, but the good person will wear those clothes." In some languages the failure of the rich to keep his own possessions may not be clear without further information. In such cases it may be necessary to say, for example, "The wicked person may have lots of clothes, but he will not live to wear them; some good person will wear them instead."

And the innocent will divide the silver: in 17.8 the "upright" and "the innocent" are used in parallel. See also 22.19. For comments on **innocent** see 4.7. **Divide the silver** may be understood as sharing it as one would an inheritance, and so NEB "His silver will be shared among the innocent," or as in TEV, "some honest man will get the silver."

27.18 RSV TEV

The house which he builds is like
   a spider's web,[a]
like a booth which a watchman
   makes.

The wicked build houses like a
   spider's web[e]
or like the hut of a slave
   guarding the fields.

[a] Cn compare Gk Syr: Heb *He builds his house like the moth*

[e] *Some ancient translations* spider's web; *Hebrew* moth *or* bird's nest.

The house which he builds is like a spider's web: as RSV's note indicates, the Hebrew is "he builds his house like a moth"; but moths do not build houses, unless the poet has the cocoon in mind. The Septuagint has "as moths, as a spider," and Syriac "as a spider," which many translators follow, including RSV and TEV. (See TEV note.) Dhorme opposes the Septuagint and has "nest," which NEB follows. TOB has kept "moth," adding a note: "He believes he is building, but in fact is destroying." HOTTP supports the Hebrew text but gives no reason or explanation of how it is to be understood. **Spider's web** occurs in 8.14 in a similar context, where frailty is emphasized through this image. If "moth" is not suitable in making clear sense, the translator is forced to choose between what are two kinds of guesses. **Spider's web** is a change based on a guess and confirmed by an ancient version, which probably made the same guess, whereas "nest" is a translation guess. In both cases the sense of "weakness, frailty" is involved. If "moth" is used, we may translate as does NIV, "like a moth's cocoon." FRCL has still another solution which avoids both spider and moth: "The house these people have built is fragile," with a note added, "Like a moth's or like a bird's nest." This is a happy compromise. SPCL says "fragile as a nest," NJB "All he has built himself is a spider's web." Whether the translator uses "moth," "spider's web," or "nest," it should be made clear that the image is used to show how impermanent and frail his efforts are.

Like a booth which a watchman makes: **booth** refers to a hut put together by using fragile materials, where a person stays to protect the harvest from birds and other intruders. (See Isa 1.8.) A literal translation such as RSV may require some expansion to give adequate information. In the context, as in the previous line, this hut or shelter is temporary and fragile. FRCL adds the adjective "shaky, rickety" to suggest its lack of firmness. In language areas in which such temporary shelters are not put up or are even unknown, we may sometimes translate "as a shack put in a garden to guard the crop" or "as a hut where a person stays to guard the field."

27.19 RSV TEV

He goes to bed rich, but will do
   so no more;[b]
he opens his eyes, and his
   wealth is gone.

One last time[f] they will lie down
   rich,
and when they wake up, they
   will find their wealth gone.

[b] Gk compare Syr: Heb *shall not be gathered*

[f] *Some ancient translations* One last time; *Hebrew* They will not be gathered.

He goes to bed rich, but will do so no more: this translation rests on the Septuagint and Syriac. In place of **will do so no more**, the Hebrew has "he will not be gathered." Similar expressions using the same Hebrew verb, but in different forms, are found in 20.9; 34.32; 40.5. TEV translates the same as RSV but in different words, "one last time." HOTTP suggests two ways to understand the line based on the Hebrew: "As a rich man he lies down (to sleep) while his house has not yet been taken away"; or "He lies down (dies) as a rich man without (however) being buried (that is, being reunited in the family tomb)". In the latter sense the Hebrew "they will not be gathered" is understood as the typical euphemism for death: "he was gathered to his ancestors." There is, however, no reference to ancestors in this verse. The line may also be rendered, for example, "For the last time he goes to bed as a rich man" or "Only once more he goes to bed still having his wealth."

He opens his eyes, and his wealth is gone: for **his wealth is gone** the Hebrew has "it is not" or "he is not." RSV, TEV, and others understand "it is not" to mean **his wealth is gone**. HOTTP's first interpretation continues in this line, "he opens his eyes (he awakens) and it (the house in verse 18) is no more"; the second alternative continues "he opens his eyes (in death?) and is no more (that is, he dies in an instant)." It is not possible to say for certain if the man has lost his house, his wealth, or his life. However, other modern translations understand this line in the same way as RSV and TEV, namely, "he wakes up to find his wealth gone," or "when he awakens he has no more wealth," or "he awakens as a poor man."

27.20	RSV	TEV

RSV	TEV

Terrors overtake him like a flood;
    in the night a whirlwind carries him off.
	Terror will strike like a sudden flood;
	    a wind in the night will blow them away;

Terrors overtake him like a flood: in 18.11 Bildad says "terror frightens the wicked man." **Terrors** expresses either the "fear, dread, fright" that is within the heart of the wicked, or things which cause him to be terrified, frightened. **Overtake** translates a verb whose usual meaning is "strike." The Hebrew "like the waters" is translated **like a flood**. TEV has "strike like a sudden flood," since it is the action of the flooding waters that strike him. HOTTP rates "like the waters" as an "A" reading, meaning there is no doubt about its being original. Their remark is "The waters are those of a *wadi* (stream bed) which unexpectedly take the traveler by surprise." Others propose changing the Hebrew for "like the waters" to get "daylight," which is a contrasting parallel with **in the night** in line b. Dhorme translates "terrors strike him in broad daylight." This is followed by NJB and others. It is best here to stay with the Hebrew, as in RSV and TEV. This line may also be expressed "Terror surprises him like a sudden flood," or "He is caught by terror as a sudden flood that washes things away," or "As a sudden flood comes and carries things away, fright does the same to him."

In the night a whirlwind carries him off: the words translated **whirlwind carries him off** are a repetition of the words spoken by Job in 21.18. **Whirlwind**

translates a word meaning a destructive or violent wind. This may or may not be a **whirlwind.** TEV has "a wind." Its force is implied by "blow them away."

27.21-23   RSV   TEV

21 The east wind lifts him up and   21   the east wind will sweep them
    he is gone;   from their homes;
    it sweeps him out of his place.   22   it will blow down on them
22 It^c hurls at him without pity;   without pity
    he flees from its^d power in   while they try their best to
    headlong flight.   escape.
23 It^c claps its^d hands at him, 23 The wind howls at them as they
    and hisses at him from its^d run,
    place.   frightening them with destruc-
                  tive power.

^{c} Or *he* (that is God)
^{d} Or *his*

These three verses will be handled together, since each describes the effect of the wind.

The east wind lifts him up and he is gone: the east wind blows from the desert towards the Mediterranean Sea, bringing scorching heat. Here it is violent, like a tornado or whirlwind, in that it picks the man up and carries him away. In 15.2 Eliphaz asked if a wise man should fill himself with the **east wind,** using the same Hebrew term. See there for comments. **Lifts him up** implies for the purpose of taking him away, and so "picks him up and carries him off." TEV reduces the two lines to one.

It sweeps him out of his place: sweeps describes the action of the violent wind and is used in Psalm 58.9b. **Out of his place** is best taken here as meaning "out of his house" or "out of the place where he lives." **Sweeps** may require adjusting in some languages to a nonfigure like "It blows him out of his house," or to a different figure.

It hurls at him without pity: It refers to the east wind. RSV notes that the Hebrew has "he," which RSV thinks refers to God, although God has not been mentioned since verse 13. TEV also makes the east wind the subject. **Hurls** translates a verb meaning "to throw at." There is no direct object expressed in this line nor in Numbers 35.20, where the same verb is used, but according to Dhorme, no object is required. Accordingly FRCL, which makes God the subject, translates "Without having pity on them, God uses them as targets." NJB says "Piteously he is turned into a target." If the east wind is the subject, then the verb "blows" is more appropriate than **hurls:** "It will blow down on them" (TEV, which keeps the plural for the wicked). **Without pity** is literally "not sparing," that is, "without holding anything back." This line may be expressed "This wind blows at them with full force" or ". . . with all its might."

He flees from its power in headlong flight: here the wicked man **flees from** what is literally "his (or, its) hand," which RSV translates **its power,** meaning "the force of the wind." **In headlong flight** is used translationally by RSV to bring out the force of the Hebrew construction, which serves to intensify the main verb. In a similar way TEV "they try their best to escape" emphasizes the urgency of the wicked person's flight. This line may also be rendered, for example, "he does all he can to run from its power" or "he tries hard to run away from this powerful wind."

It claps its hands at him: RSV and TEV continue with "the wind" as the implied subject. The Hebrew has only the third person singular pronoun prefixed to the singular verb **clap**. An RSV note indicates "he (that is God)." Mft understands it in this sense and translates "God openly derides him." BJ and TOB translate with an impersonal subject, as does FRCL: "One applauds on seeing them in this state." NJB has "His downfall is greeted with applause." It seems most consistent with the context to keep "the wind" as the subject, even though the noun is not present in the Hebrew. **Claps** translates what is literally "beats his palms." In Numbers 24.10 this gesture symbolizes anger: "And Balak's anger was kindled against Balaam, and he struck his hands together . . . ." In Lamentations 2.15 it is used to show "scorn, ridicule, derision." The sense of scorn is to be taken here as it parallels the similar use of **hiss** in the next line. Neither RSV nor TEV gives the meaning of these two gestures. TEV transposes the two lines, but "howls at them" is not made clear, and "frightening them" does not suggest scorn or ridicule. NIV is to be preferred here, with "It claps its hands in derision." In English "The wind howls scornfully at them" would be better. If the image of the wind clapping its hands in ridicule is not clear, it may be necessary to shift to a simile; for example, "The wind howls at them (him), like a person scorning them" or "The wind is like a person shouting ridicule at him."

And hisses at him from its place: **hisses** is used in Jeremiah 49.17 and Zephaniah 2.15 to express ridicule, and so is parallel with **claps** in the previous line. In Lamentations 2.15 the people who pass by "clap their hands at you; they hiss and wag their heads at the daughter of Jerusalem." **From its place** is understood variously by different interpreters. It may mean the place from which the wind **hisses**, as RSV, or the place wherever the wicked person may be, so NEB "wherever he may be." TEV "as they run" seems to follow somewhat the second interpretation. In English verse 23 may be rendered "The wind howls scornfully at them, and laughs at them wherever they go." In some languages it will be possible to make a parallel line in verse 23b by saying "and whistles at him wherever he goes" or "and whistles at him to scorn him wherever he may be." In some languages to whistle at a person has a connotation which may be undesirable in this context. SPCL translates verse 23 as "The wind pursues him with loud noises and whistles." Translators may be able to adapt from this model.

6. A Poem about Wisdom

(28.1-28)

Chapter 28 differs significantly from the other chapters of Job. There are no accusations, complaints, or responses to previous comments by earlier speakers. Many scholars consider it an intrusion, a chapter which does not seem to fit the overall design of the book. As it stands Job may be implied as the speaker, and some see in it Job giving up his case in despair. Others views are: that it was inserted later to express a judgment on the previous speeches; that it is a bridge between the speeches in chapters 4–27 and the closing speech of Job in chapters 29–31; that it resolves Job's problem and therefore makes Yahweh's speeches unnecessary; that it summarizes Job's case and forms the introduction to Yahweh's speeches.

There is no doubt that chapter 28 continues the imagery of earlier speeches. For example, in verse 9 "overturn mountains" recalls 9.5; "the thing that is hid he brings forth to light" in verse 11 echoes 11.6 and 12.22; the overall theme of chapter 28 is similar to that in chapter 11, namely, that divine wisdom cannot be attained by human beings unless God reveals it.

The Handbook views chapter 28 as an interlude or bridge between chapters 4–27 and chapters 29–42.6. Before chapter 28 Job is engaged in a dispute with three friends. After chapter 28 Job is confronted by Elihu and God. The overview of the structure of chapter 28 is given below, and the details are handled in the discussion of the verses. This outline agrees generally with "Patterns of Inclusion in Job: Their form and functional significance," an unpublished paper by Ernst R. Wendland. For a somewhat different approach to the outline of chapter 28, see Habel.

A (1-6) Men mine the earth for precious metals and stones

B (7-8) The way to the mines is not known

A′ (9-11) How men mine for precious stones

B′ (12-14) The source of wisdom is not known

A″ (15-19) Wisdom is more valuable than precious stones

B″ (20-22) The source of wisdom is not known

C (23-28) God alone knows the way to wisdom

Section Heading

The section heading used in the Handbook covers only chapter 28, and a division heading, if used, will cover the same material; therefore a division heading is unnecessary. Other titles for chapter 28, for example, are "In search of wisdom" or "Only God knows where wisdom is found." GECL has "From where does wisdom come," FRCL "The mystery of wisdom," NJB "Wisdom is beyond human reach," and TEV "In praise of wisdom."

6-1. The places where precious metals are mined (28.1-6)

	RSV		TEV
1	"Surely there is a mine for silver, and a place for gold which they refine.	1	There are mines where silver is dug; There are places where gold is refined.
2	Iron is taken out of the earth, and copper is smelted from the ore.	2	Men dig iron out of the ground And melt copper out of the stones.
3	Men put an end to darkness, and search out to the farthest bound the ore in gloom and deep darkness.	3	Men explore the deepest darkness. They search the depths of the earth And dig for rocks in the darkness.
4	They open shafts in a valley away from where men live; they are forgotten by travelers, they hang afar from men, they swing to and fro.	4	Far from where anyone lives Or human feet ever travel, Men dig the shafts of mines. There they work in loneliness, Clinging to ropes in the pits.
5	As for the earth, out of it comes bread; but underneath it is turned up as by fire.	5	Food grows out of the earth, But underneath the same earth All is torn up and crushed.
6	Its stones are the place of sapphires, and it has dust of gold.	6	The stones of the earth contain sapphires, And its dust contains gold.

Habel sees the basic structure of chapter 28, based as it is on the search for what is rare and precious, consisting of three recurring elements: the place or source of the precious item, the way or means of getting that item, and the process of discovering. Logically it may seem better for the last two to be interchanged, but the logic of the poem is determined by the flow of the poet's ordering of the items. Verses 1-2 list the places: "mine," "place," "earth," and the metals "silver," "gold," "copper." Verses 3-4 depict the difficult means for obtaining these. Verses 5-6 begin again with the place: "earth," "underneath it," and the precious objects "sapphire" and "gold."

Subdivision Heading

The Handbook supplies headings according to the outline presented at the beginning of this chapter; however, translators may prefer to give only a single heading for verses 1-11. For example, Rowley has "There is no known road to wisdom." If translators wish to follow the Handbook, they may say, for example, "Men dig in the earth for ore," "People search the earth for precious stones," or "Miners explore inside the earth to find ore."

28.1   RSV   TEV

"Surely there is a mine for silver,   There are mines where silver is
    and a place for gold which they   dug;
    refine.   There are places where gold is
                                                  refined.

Surely there is a mine for silver: **Surely** translates the Hebrew word
commonly translated "for" or "because." It may seem strange to open a discourse
with **Surely**; however, the Hebrew for **Surely** is frequently used to introduce an
emphatic assertion. Translators may use whatever structure is available in the
receptor language to supply this emphasis. In some languages this opening assertion
may be something equivalent to "It is certain that," "It is true," or "Indeed it is so."

Mine translates a word meaning "source" or "outlet" and normally refers to a
place in the ground from which water flows. In the context of verse 1 it refers to the
place of origin, and for the origin of a precious metal, **mine** is appropriate. In
English the plural is more natural, as in TEV. In Jeremiah 10.9 and Ezekiel 27.12,
silver is said to be imported from Tarshish, possibly Tartessus in Spain. **A mine for
silver** means a mine or mines where silver is obtained or, as TEV says, "where silver
is dug." This line may also be rendered "There are mines where men dig silver." In
languages in which there is no word for **silver** or **gold**, the translator may do one of
the following: (a) use a loan word from a major language; (b) use a loan word with
a classifier; for example, "a valuable metal called silver"; or (c) use a substitute metal
if one is known and is highly valuable; this may be the least desirable alternative.

It may be suggested that some adaptation be made in verse 1 that will prepare
for the contrast of obtaining wisdom in verses 12-28. For example, Mft places verse
12 before verse 1 and renders verse 1a "For silver there are mines," and then repeats
verse 12 after verse 11. However, Mft did not use headings, which can accomplish
this task even better.

And a place for gold which they refine: **a place** is parallel to **mine** in the
previous line and means the same thing. TEV again pluralizes **a place** so as to make
it general, like "mines" in line a. RSV reflects the Hebrew form, **gold which they
refine**. The plural form of the verb has the meaning of a passive, "where gold is
refined," or of an impersonal actor, "where one refines gold." **Refine** refers to the
process of heating gold to a liquid and then removing the impurities that float to the
surface. In languages which must employ active constructions, this line may be
rendered, for example, "and places where men dig gold and refine it." **Refine** may
sometimes be translated as "purify, clean." A translation should not attempt to
explain in the text the process of refining, as this would place more emphasis on it
than is given in the flow of the poem's discourse. A note may be used in some cases.

28.2   RSV   TEV

Iron is taken out of the earth,   Men dig iron out of the ground
    and copper is smelted from the   And melt copper out of the
    ore.   stones.

Iron is taken out of the earth: in verse 2 **iron** and **copper** continue the list of valuable metals. In Deuteronomy 8.9 the promised land is described as "a land . . . in which you will lack nothing, a land whose stones are iron, and out of whose hills you can dig copper." The verb translated **is taken** is in the passive. However, the parallel verb in line b is active. RSV shifts both verbs to the passive, and TEV has both as active. In translation either is possible and should follow the regular rules of style of the translator's language. **Earth** translates the Hebrew for "dust," but the meaning in this context is as in RSV and TEV. In languages which lack words for **iron** and **copper**, the same procedure suggested in verse 1a should be followed.

And copper is smelted from the ore: **copper** is said to have been plentiful in the Middle East, and it was mined and smelted in Cyprus, Edom, and the Sinai Peninsula. **Smelted** translates a verb meaning "to melt." Dhorme, however, takes it as an adjective meaning "hard" and translates "and a hard stone becomes copper." It seems best, however, to follow RSV. **Ore** translates Hebrew "stones." TEV "melt copper out of the stones" may give the wrong impression that the copper remains in liquid form. **Smelted** refers to the process of heating the ore in order to extract the copper from it. The copper hardens as it cools. In these verses "refine" (verse 1) and **smelt** have similar meanings.

28.3   RSV   TEV

Men put an end to darkness,   Men explore the deepest dark-
   and search out to the farthest   ness.
     bound   They search the depths of the
  the ore in gloom and deep   earth
    darkness.   And dig for rocks in the dark-
                                ness.

Men put an end to darkness: this verse, like the following one, has three lines in Hebrew. It describes the miner working under the ground. **Men put** translates the Hebrew for "one puts." **Put an end to darkness** probably means that the miners work in the dark mine by using lamps, or as FRCL translates, "Below the ground, miners carry light." This is clearer than TEV "explore the deepest darkness," which does not show how they overcome the darkness inside the earth. The line may also be rendered "Miners take lamps (lights, torches, fire) into the dark mines" or "They carry their lights into the dark places."

And search out to the farthest bound: **farthest bound** translates the term used in 26.10 referring to the boundary between light and darkness. Here it refers to the limit or extent to which the miner can explore underground. This may be rendered "They dig to the very limit" or ". . . as far as they can possibly go."

The ore in gloom and deep darkness: according to the Hebrew punctuation the main division in this verse comes at the end of the second line, but this leaves line c unconnected with the rest of the verse. Accordingly NEB and NAB omit it. However, better sense is made by making the chief division after the first line, as in RSV and TEV. **Ore** translates the Hebrew for "stone," as in verse 2b. In RSV **search** in line b serves also as the verb for line c. TEV, which makes lines b and c separate clauses, supplies "dig" as the verb in line c. Either solution is possible, but RSV is closer to the Hebrew form. **Gloom and deep darkness** translates the same expression used in 10.21. There the expression referred to Sheol. Here it refers to the darkness inside the mine. It may be translated "and dig out the ore in the deep darkness" or "search for the rocks in the darkness."

28.4	RSV	TEV

	They open shafts in a valley away
	    from where men live;
	  they are forgotten by travelers,
	  they hang afar from men, they
	    swing to and fro.
		Far from where anyone lives
		Or human feet ever travel,
		Men dig the shafts of mines.
		There they work in loneliness,
		Clinging to ropes in the pits.

They open shafts in a valley away from where men live: verse 4, like verse 3, has three lines. However, verse 4 is unclear. The translator need only compare KJV's rendering with TEV to see how two translations based on the Hebrew text as it stands can differ. KJV has "The flood breaketh out from the inhabitant; (even the waters) forgotten of the foot: they are dried up, they are gone away from men." Some scholars have found this verse to be almost meaningless, and NAB omits it. The literal Hebrew of line <u>a</u> is approximately "One opens a valley from with a sojourner." The Hebrew for "valley" probably refers here to a mine shaft, tunnel, or, as HOTTP suggests, "gorge." RSV seems to translate this word as both **shaft** and **valley**. Dhorme and others change the expression translated **away from where men live** to get "a foreign people," which is then used as the subject: "A foreign people has pierced shafts." TEV does not make any change in the text, but expresses **away from where men live** as an adverbial clause placed at the beginning: "Far from where anyone lives . . . ." It is possible to keep the Hebrew as it stands and translate "They dig mine tunnels far away from where people live," or "Miners dig mine shafts in remote places," or "In isolated places people dig for precious metals."

They are forgotten by travelers is literally "they are forgotten by the foot." This line is usually taken to mean that the people who pass by above these mine tunnels or shafts are unaware of what lies beneath their path, but it may also mean "people never pass by there" due to the extreme isolation. It is in this sense that TEV translates its second line, "Or human feet ever travel"; this may also be expressed as "No one ever travels that way" or "Travelers don't even know what is there."

They hang afar from men, they swing to and fro: this line is commonly interpreted as referring to clinging to a rope while being lowered into the mine. TEV has placed part of line <u>a</u> at this point, making it the first verb phrase, "Men dig the shafts of mines," and has made two lines of line <u>c</u> so that it ends up with five lines. **Afar from men** repeats the thought **away from where men live** in line <u>a</u>. RSV **they hang . . . they swing . . .** may be misunderstood if deep shaft mining is unknown to the reader. One restructuring which may be useful is shown in FRCL, "They open tunnels beyond the inhabited places. Far from humans, in inaccessible places, the miners swing back and forth, suspended by ropes." Another sense suggested by HOTTP is that the word translated "valley" refers to a "gorge," and the two verbs in line <u>c</u> depict a miner suspended by a rope, high above the bottom of the gorge, against one of the rocky walls in which the galleries are cut. TEV has made this clearer with "clinging to ropes in the pits." Without doubt verse 4 will require some restructuring in many languages. Translators may follow the model of TEV or, if FRCL is followed, they must be careful not to give the impression that the miners have been executed by hanging from a rope. Accordingly it should be made clear that these miners are either lowered by ropes into the mine or are suspended by ropes while they dig into the walls of the mine shaft. For example, "They dig out the ore while suspended by ropes that swing back and forth."

28.5   RSV   TEV

> As for the earth, out of it comes   Food grows out of the earth,
>   bread;   But underneath the same earth
>   but underneath it is turned up   All is torn up and crushed.
>   as by fire.

As for the earth, out of it comes bread: here the contrast seems to be between what happens on the surface of the ground and what takes place underneath. **As for** has no verbal equivalent in the Hebrew, which is literally "Earth out of it comes bread." The thought is that the surface is orderly and produces what the farmer expects of it, namely, **bread**. **Bread** here symbolizes "food" generally, or "crops": "Food grows on the surface of the earth." In order to make the contrast between the two lines of the verse clear, it may be necessary to say, for example, "On top of the ground they harvest crops, but under the ground . . . ."

But underneath it is turned up as by fire: the meaning of this line is not certain. It may refer to the process of heating rocks in a fire and cooling them to split them open. Another suggestion is that the poet thinks of igneous rocks being formed in fire. TEV does not mention the fire, which it takes as a metaphor on the view that the poet was describing the layers of rock under the ground in terms of the havoc left in a town after a severe fire. This line should show a strong contrast with the previous line: "but under the ground it is as if fire had turned everything upside down" or "but below the surface it looks like fire has stirred everything up."

28.6   RSV   TEV

> Its stones are the place of sap-   The stones of the earth contain
>   phires,[e]   sapphires,
>   and it has dust of gold.   And its dust contains gold.

[e] Or *lapis lazuli*

Its stones are the place of sapphires: **Its** refers to "the earth" in verse 5a, and so TEV "the stones of the earth." In English "rock" is more commonly used when speaking of ore bearing minerals or precious stones. Rowley says that **sapphires** were probably unknown before Roman imperial times, and that the stone discussed were probably *lapis lazuli,* as in the RSV footnote. **Sapphires** are bluish transparent gems. *Lapis lazuli* is deep blue and is not transparent. This line may be rendered, for example, "Men find sapphires in the rocks of the earth" or "Men find (blue) gems in the rocks in the earth."

And it has dust of gold: *lapis lazuli* is speckled with yellow iron pyrites, which give the impression of being gold dust. NEB, which translates the word for **sapphires** as *lapis lazuli*, renders this line "dusted with flecks of gold." Some believe that this is the preferred meaning, since the metal "gold" was mentioned earlier, in verse 1. Most modern translations, however, follow RSV and TEV. If *lapis lazuli* is known in the language, NEB may serve as a good translation model. Otherwise it is better to follow TEV or to say, for example, "and they find gold in the dirt."

6-2. Birds and wild animals do not know the way (28.7-8)

	RSV		TEV
7	"That path no bird of prey knows, and the falcon's eye has not seen it.	7	No hawk sees the roads to the mines, And no vulture ever flies over them.
8	The proud beasts have not trodden it; the lion has not passed over it.	8	No lion or other fierce beast Ever travels those lonely roads.

Verses 7-8 show the way in which the poet uses generic vocabulary followed by more specific terms to emphasize how not even birds or animals know the way to the mines. Verse 7 has "bird of prey" followed by "falcon," while in verse 8 "proud beasts" is followed by "lion."

Subdivision Heading

The Handbook heading may be modified to say, for example, "Not even falcons and lions know where the mines are" or "The mines are hidden from the birds and animals."

28.7	RSV	TEV
	"That path no bird of prey knows, and the falcon's eye has not seen it.	No hawk sees the roads to the mines, And no vulture ever flies over them.

That path no bird of prey knows: here the poet may be using an exaggerated image to emphasize the remoteness of the mines. **That path**, however, may refer either to the path leading to the remote mine, or to wisdom. It is unlikely that the **path** leads here to wisdom, since the verses which follow speak of the work of the miners. TEV says "the roads to the mines." **Bird of prey** translates a generic term which TEV prefers to render as "hawk," since **bird of prey** is not common English. **No bird . . . knows**: strictly speaking, a bird does not need to know the road to find something. TEV shifts to "does not see," which is little different. This line may also be translated "No bird of prey knows the path to the mine." There are many birds of prey such as the hawk, eagle, falcon, or vulture, and the translator may use the one best known to his readers. If no such birds are known, the translator may say, for example, "No bird that soars in the sky knows the path to the mine" or "Not even a soaring bird knows."

And the falcon's eye has not seen it: the word translated **falcon** is included in the list of birds not to be eaten (see Lev 11.13-19; Deut 14.11-20). TEV and others translate "vulture," as does the Septuagint. The exact identification of this bird is uncertain. TEV "no vulture ever flies over them" does not represent the Hebrew text too well, although it is implied that the bird is in flight. In this verse line b is specific while line a is general, and it thus follows the Hebrew device for intensifying the second line. So the sense is "Not even the falcon's eye has seen that path." If the language has neither **falcon** nor other birds of prey, it may be possible to say, for example, "and not even the best-sighted bird has ever seen that path" or "and not even the bird with the best eyes (vision) has ever seen it."

28.8   RSV   TEV

The proud beasts have not trod-   No lion or other fierce beast
    den it;   Ever travels those lonely roads.
  the lion has not passed over it.

The proud beasts have not trodden it: verse 8, like verse 7, has the generic animal in line a and the specific one in line b, which is one of the poetic techniques in parallelism for heightening the poetic effect. **Proud beasts** translates the Hebrew "sons of pride" and is found in 41.34, which describes Leviathan or the crocodile. **Proud beast** is a wild or fierce beast or animal. **Beast** is a more poetic term in English than "animal" and in this context suggests an untamed animal. This line may be rendered "Wild animals do not go along these roads."

The lion has not passed over it: **lion** translates the same word used in 4.10 and 10.16. Pope, following Mowinckel, argues for "serpent" here, and NEB translates "And no serpent comes that way." Although Dhorme translates "leopard," most translations keep **lion**. Because verse 8 moves from a general animal in line a to the specific one in line b, this line may be rendered "Not even the lion has passed over it." In some languages **lion** must be replaced by another wild animal that prowls.

6-3. How men mine in the earth (28.9-11)

	RSV		TEV
9	"Man puts his hand to the flinty rock, and overturns mountains by the roots.	9	Men dig the hardest rocks, Dig mountains away at their base.
10	He cuts out channels in the rocks, and his eye sees every precious thing.	10	As they tunnel through the rocks, They discover precious stones.
11	He binds up the streams so that they do not trickle, and the thing that is hid he brings forth to light.	11	They dig to the sources of rivers And bring to light what is hidden.

Verses 9-11 consider the manner in which miners dig into the earth to extract the ore. These verses are an example of the way in which the poet makes specific the material contained in verses 1-6, and accordingly the display on page 497 shows them to be A'.

Subdivision Heading

The Handbook heading may be replaced by another to say, for example, "Here is how men dig out the ore" or "This is the way miners get out the ore."

28.9	RSV	TEV

"Man puts his hand to the flinty rock,
  and overturns mountains by the roots.

Men dig the hardest rocks,
Dig mountains away at their base.

Having concentrated on the remoteness of the mines, the poet now speaks of the work of miners whose great feats enable them to extract precious stones. **Man puts his hand to the flinty rock**: this line is patterned after verse 3a. The subject **man** is impersonal. **Puts his hand** is used as in Genesis 37.22, in which Reuben advises his brothers not to harm Joseph. The expression carries the thought of "attack." What someone attacks here is **the flinty rock**, which some render as "the granite rock." The term meaning "flint stone" is used to indicate a hard rock that resists the efforts of the miners. TEV emphasizes the hardness of the rock rather than its mineral nature, with "men dig the hardest rocks." This line may also be rendered "Miners attack the hardest rocks to remove their ore" or "They dig into solid granite."

And overturns mountains by the roots: **overturns** translates the same verb root used in verse 5, where it is rendered "turned up." It is used of the destruction of Sodom and Gomorrah in Genesis 19.21-29. The word translated **roots** is the same as for the "roots" of trees and is used to express the extent of the excavation of the mountain. TEV calls it "their base." SPCL says "and pulls up the roots of the mountains." The picture given is somewhat exaggerated, but if the receptor language permits this kind of figurative expression, the translator should use it; for example, "they turn mountains upside down," "they pull up mountains by their roots (feet),"or more subdued, "they dig into the very bottoms of the mountains."

28.10	RSV	TEV

He cuts out channels in the rocks,
  and his eye sees every precious thing.

As they tunnel through the rocks,
They discover precious stones.

He cuts out channels in the rocks: the word translated **channels** is commonly used in the singular to refer to the Nile. Here it is used as in Isaiah 33.21, as a poetic parallel with the singular term for river translated "streams" in the next verse. The word may refer to the canals along the Nile. Accordingly NJB translates

"He cuts canals through the rock." Another possibility is that the **channels** are either drainage gutters or sluices connected with the mining operation. **Cuts** translates the same word used in Psalm 74.15, where RSV translates "Thou didst cleave open springs and brooks." TEV uses "tunnel through the rocks," which is expressive and very likely says what the poet meant.

And his eye sees every precious thing: **his eye sees** is a poetic manner of saying "he sees," but it has also an element of close attention, as if he is carefully watching for something as he works. The expression is used in 7.7; 13.1a; 29.11. It is more than seeing and passing on, and so TEV translates "discover." NJB says "on the watch for." **Every precious thing** is general, but in the context it naturally refers to precious stones or ores: "he watches carefully to find every precious stone" or "he watches every rock to find anything that is valuable."

28.11   RSV   TEV

> He binds up the streams so that   They dig to the sources of[h] rivers
>   they do not trickle,   And bring to light what is hid-
> and the thing that is hid he   den.
>   brings forth to light.

> [h] *Some ancient translations* dig to the
> source of; *Hebrew* bind from trickling.

He binds up the streams so they do not trickle: the word translated **binds up** is uncertain, since it is only used elsewhere in the sense of binding up wounds. Some of the ancient versions substituted another Hebrew verb which differs only in the middle consonant, and they get the meaning "search." Accordingly NJB translates "explores." HOTTP, however, prefers to keep the Hebrew and translates "he dams up." RSV and TEV differ significantly at this point. RSV follows the traditional rendering of the Hebrew, which has "from weeping," and takes this to mean "he dams up rivers so they do not leak into the mines." If this is followed, "weep" is understood figuratively. HOTTP rejects the traditional vowel pointing of the word translated "weep" and substitutes other vowels to give the meaning "sources," that is, the spring waters where a river begins. This is followed by TEV and many others and is recommended to translators. "They discover the sources of rivers" gives a better parallel for the following line than "He dams up the sources of rivers." The line may also be rendered, for example, "They find out where rivers begin" or "They find where water comes out of the ground to form rivers."

And the thing that is hid he brings forth to light: this line is parallel in sense to verse 10b. **The thing that is hid** is general and may refer to things in the earth as well as to the sources of rivers, and so means "whatever is hidden." **Brings forth to light** means "makes them known" or "makes them visible," and so "brings things that are not seen out to the light where people can see them."

6-4. The source of wisdom is not known (28.12-14)

RSV		TEV	
12	"But where shall wisdom be found? And where is the place of understanding?	12	But where can wisdom be found? Where can we learn to understand?
13	Man does not know the way to it, and it is not found in the land of the living.	13	Wisdom is not to be found among men; No one knows its true value.
14	The deep says, 'It is not in me,' and the sea says, 'It is not with me.'	14	The depths of the oceans and seas Say that wisdom is not found there.

Verses 12-14 reflect the thought of verses 7-8, in that the latter showed that birds and animals do not know the way to the mine, so also neither people nor the depths of the sea know the source of wisdom.

Subdivision Heading

This heading may be expressed differently; for example, "No one knows the way to wisdom," "Not even the deep sea knows where wisdom is."

28.12

RSV	TEV
"But where shall wisdom be found? And where is the place of understanding?	But where can wisdom be found? Where can we learn to understand?

Mankind's great industry in penetrating the earth for precious stones is now compared to his inability to get to the source of wisdom. Verse 12 is the key to the understanding of the whole chapter. The contrast between the success of the miners in the previous verse and the search for wisdom is marked by **But** in RSV and TEV. People know where to find silver, gold, and precious stones, but they do not know where to find wisdom. Between verse 12 and the next refrain in verse 20 there is a series of negative answers to the question asked here.

But where shall wisdom be found? This verse is repeated as a question with a few small changes in verse 20 and as a response in verse 28. The answer to the question comes in the final verse of the chapter, where **wisdom** is defined as "the fear of the Lord" and **understanding** as "to depart from evil."

The introduction of **wisdom** as new information may require in some languages an introductory statement; for example, "But let us talk also of wisdom," "But what about finding wisdom?" or "But how does a person become wise?"

And where is the place of understanding? Here **understanding** is used in parallel with **wisdom,** just as in Proverbs 1.2; 4.5; 7.9; 9.10; 16.16. Dhorme says **wisdom** expresses what is handed down by tradition, while **understanding** is acquired by discernment, insight, and judgment. However, in these verses the two are to be taken as two ways of referring to a single virtue.

28.13   RSV   TEV

Man does not know the way to   Wisdom is not to be found
 it,^f   among men;
 and it is not found in the land   No one knows its true value.
 of the living.

^f Gk: Heb *its price*

Man does not know the way to it: as the RSV note shows, **the way to it** is based on the Septuagint; Hebrew has "its price." HOTTP recommends the Hebrew, although only with a "C" rating, and TEV, which has transposed the two lines of verse 13, follows this with "No one knows its true value." The value of wisdom occurs again in verses 15-19. Translators are encouraged to follow TEV. The TEV form may also be expressed "No one knows how great its value is" or "No one knows how valuable it is."

And it is not found in the land of the living: in TEV this is the first line of the verse, and it fits better there in English, for stylistic reasons. **Land of the living** renders the Hebrew literally. The expression is found in Psalm 52.5; Isaiah 38.11; 53.8, and is the opposite of Sheol, which is the land of the dead. NJB says "She is not to be found on earth where they live," in which "they" refers to "no human being" used in line a̲. SPCL has "and does not find it in this world." The line may also be expressed "it (wisdom) cannot be found on this earth" or "no one will find it in this world."

28.14   RSV   TEV

The deep says, 'It is not in me,'   The depths of the oceans and
 and the sea says, 'It is not   seas
 with me.'   Say that wisdom is not found
                                              there.

The two lines of this verse are closely parallel in meaning and have been rearranged by TEV so that the first line contains both subjects. Nature is here personified as speaking.

The deep says, 'It is not in me': **the deep** refers to the water beneath the earth from which the sea is fed, and which is the source of floods in Genesis 7.11. The parallelism of **the deep** and **the sea** in line b̲ occurs again in 38.16. TEV "depths of the oceans" expresses the idea adequately. RSV reflects the Hebrew structure, in which **the deep** speaks directly.

And the sea says, 'It is not with me': the slight difference in the quoted words is not significant. Translators may find the parallelism so close in meaning that the two lines may be handled as a single thought. In many languages **the sea** cannot be personified as speaking directly or indirectly. In such cases we may translate, for example, "Wisdom is not found in the deepest parts of the oceans," or actively, "You will not find wisdom at the bottom of the sea." For comments on the translation of **sea** in areas where seas are unknown, see 6.3; 12.8.

6-5. Wisdom is more valuable than precious stones (28.15-19)

RSV	TEV

15 It cannot be gotten for gold,
   and silver cannot be weighed as its
      price.
16 It cannot be valued in the gold of Ophir,
   in precious onyx or sapphire.
17 Gold and glass cannot equal it,
   nor can it be exchanged for jewels of
      fine gold.
18 No mention shall be made of coral or of
      crystal;
   the price of wisdom is above pearls.
19 The topaz of Ethiopia cannot compare
      with it,
   nor can it be valued in pure gold.

15 It cannot be bought with silver or gold.
16 The finest gold and jewels
   Cannot equal its value.
17 It is worth more than gold,
   Than a gold vase or finest glass.
18 The value of wisdom is more
   Than coral or crystal or rubies.
19 The finest topaz and the purest gold
   Cannot compare with the value of wis-
      dom.

In verses 15-19 wisdom is depicted as something of surpassing value, and nothing can be given in exchange for it.

Subdivision Heading

The Handbook heading may be modified to say, for example, "Silver and gold are not valuable enough to buy wisdom," "No amount of wealth will purchase wisdom," or "The value of wisdom surpasses all other valuable things."

28.15   RSV   TEV

**It cannot be gotten for gold,
and silver cannot be weighed
      as its price.**

**It cannot be bought with silver or
      gold.**

It cannot be gotten for gold: in this verse TEV reduces lines a and b to one. Wisdom cannot be found, but if it could, gold and silver would be inadequate to buy it. **Gold** translates a different Hebrew word here than in verses 1 and 6. The word is found only here, and Dhorme takes it to refer to "solid gold," which would probably apply to a "bar of gold" in contrast to nuggets or gold dust. In any event an adequate translation will depend on the knowledge and experience of the readers. In some cases "gold" without further description may be adequate. This line may also be expressed, for example, "Even the best gold is not enough to buy it" or "You cannot buy it with gold."

And silver cannot be weighed as its price: this line extends the thought of the previous line by suggesting a transaction in the market, where **silver** is weighed on a scale by the merchant. The thought is parallel to line a, namely, "neither can one purchase it with silver." If the translator has to combine the two lines into one, verse 15 may be rendered "Neither gold nor silver will buy it," "You cannot buy it even if you have gold and silver for money," or "No amount of wealth will buy it, not even gold and silver."

28.16   RSV   TEV

> It cannot be valued in the gold of   The finest gold and jewels
>   Ophir,   Cannot equal its value.
>   in precious onyx or sapphire.[g]

[g] Or *lapis lazuli*

It cannot be valued in the gold of Ophir: the verb translated **valued** occurs only here and in verse 19, and in another form in Lamentations 4.2 ("worth their weight"). It has to do with weighing to determine value and is adequately translated in English by RSV or by saying "You cannot measure its worth . . . ." In the expression **Gold of Ophir**, the word for **gold** is again different, but coupled with **Ophir** it clearly refers to a fine quality of gold. **Ophir** was used in 22.24 as the name of a place known for its gold. See there for comments. SPCL says "One cannot pay for it with the most precious gold."

In precious onyx and sapphire: the word translated **onyx** is paired with "fine gold" in Genesis 2.12. The identification of the precious stones named in this verse is not possible. The one translated **onyx** has been rendered by many other names of gems, such as sardonyx, beryl, carnelian, and malachite. It was found on the breast plate of the high priest's robe (Exo 28.20), and on the ephod (Exo 25.7). **Sapphire** is the same gem as in verse 6. TEV avoids reference to any specific gems by saying "The finest gold and jewels cannot equal its value." Since the exact nature of these gems is uncertain, a translation using generic terms such as TEV is quite adequate.

28.17   RSV   TEV

> Gold and glass cannot equal it,   It is worth more than gold,
>   nor can it be exchanged for   Than a gold vase or finest glass.
>   jewels of fine gold.

Gold and glass cannot equal it: **Gold** translates the same term used in verse 1. **Glass** translates a word found only here, but the meaning is quite certain from related languages. In the ancient world **glass** was rare and therefore highly prized. TEV says "fine glass" to give a higher value than the common value that glass has today. NEB and others accomplish the same thing with "crystal." The phrasing in Hebrew is negative, as reflected in RSV. It may be necessary in translation to shift this to the positive by saying, for example, "It is worth more than gold and fine glass," as TEV does. In some languages the word **glass** is unknown except as applied to drinking glasses, which today are often made of plastic. In some cases **glass** is known by such descriptive phrases as "see-through stone." Where the term cannot be modified appropriately with "fine, pure, costly," it may be better to substitute a word such as "beads," which often are of considerable value for their color and rarity.

Nor can it be exchanged for jewels of fine gold: the Hebrew has "a vessel of fine gold." This is the only occurrence in Job of the word translated **fine gold**, although it is found in Psalm 19.10; Proverbs 8.19; Song of Solomon 5.11. TEV and others understand "vessel" to refer to a "gold vase," which is probably more accurate than **jewels**. In some languages a "vessel of gold" may be rendered "a pot made of fine gold."

28.18 RSV	TEV
No mention shall be made of coral or of crystal; the price of wisdom is above pearls.	The value of wisdom is more Than coral or crystal or rubies.

No mention shall be made of coral or of crystal: the intention of the poet is to say once again that wisdom is worth more than any precious stones rather than to identify the exact stones. There is little agreement among interpreters as to which stones these may be. **Coral** is a black, white, or pinkish limestone formed by sea plants and animals, and was and is still valued for making ornaments. The term translated **crystal** is not the same as the one rendered "glass" in verse 17. The word is found only here, and a related word found in Ezekiel 13.11,13; 38.22 means "hailstones." Both RSV and TEV as well as many others translate these two items as **coral** and **crystal**, and it is recommended that translators do likewise if possible. Many peoples living near the ocean in tropical areas are acquainted with coral in the form of coral reefs or atolls. Coral may be used for building roads, but in many communities it is not cut, polished, and carved into ornaments. To speak of coral as a gem or something precious may seem strange and inappropriate. In such cases it is better to substitute another known gem. If coral is not known, we may translate by borrowing a foreign word, using a borrowed word with a classifier such as "valuable stone called coral," or substituting a known stone that is valuable. **Crystal** refers generally to quartz that is transparent or partially so. Translators should follow the same suggestion given for **coral**. The negative wording of this line may have to be expressed differently to make its meaning clear; for example, "It is the same for coral and crystal" or "Nor will coral or crystal be valuable enough to buy it."

The price of wisdom is above pearls: the Hebrew word translated **pearls**, and somewhat doubtfully by TEV as "rubies," appears to refer to something red or pink in color, judging by Lamentations 4.7, where it is mentioned as a standard for comparing redness. The word translated by RSV as **price** sounds very much like another word which means "to draw, to drag," possibly with reference to the process of fishing for pearls. In agreement with this interpretation NJB translates this line as "better go fishing for Wisdom than for pearls!" This gives a parallel in thought to the first line, which may be rendered "Coral and crystal are not worth mentioning." Against this suggestion it should be noted that **pearls** are not known to have been discovered at so early a period as the writing of Job. Consequently it is probably safer to translate "red coral," in view of the scarcity of any early references to rubies. Translators should not make decisions by voting with the majority of versions, because there are usually a number of factors to consider when deciding which item to use. In the case of **pearls** in this line, the following modern translations use **pearls**: RSV, GECL, FRCL, SPCL, BJ, NJB, TOB; these use "rubies": TEV, NJV, NIV, Mft,

LB. NEB has "red coral." Translators will find themselves in good company with any of these.

28.19   RSV   TEV

> The topaz of Ethiopia cannot   The finest topaz and the purest
>   compare with it,   gold
>   nor can it be valued in pure   Cannot compare with the value
>   gold.   of wisdom.

The topaz of Ethiopia cannot compare with it: Ethiopia is known in Hebrew as "Cush." Here the place name probably designates the quality of the gem and not its place of origin. The word translated **topaz** also occurs in Exodus 28.17 and Ezekiel 28.13. It is a yellow stone found on the shores of the Red Sea.

Nor can it be valued in pure gold: **gold** is the same word used in verse 16. This line is about the same as verse 16a. **Topaz** may be handled in the same way as suggested for "coral" in verse 17.

6-6. The source of wisdom is not known (28.20-22)

	RSV		TEV
20	"Whence then comes wisdom? And where is the place of understanding?	20	Where, then, is the source of wisdom? Where can we learn to understand?
21	It is hid from the eyes of all living, and concealed from the birds of the air.	21	No living creature can see it, Not even a bird in flight.
22	Abaddon and Death say, 'We have heard a rumor of it with our ears.'	22	Even death and destruction Admit they have heard only rumors.

Just as in verses 7-8 the way to the mines is not known, in verses 20-22 the way that leads to wisdom is not known. This heading may also be worded, for example, "No one knows the way to wisdom," "No one knows how (or, where) to find wisdom," or "Wisdom cannot be found."

28.20   RSV   TEV

> "Whence then comes wisdom?   Where, then, is the source of
>   And where is the place of un-   wisdom?
>   derstanding?   Where can we learn to under-
>   stand?

Whence then comes wisdom? This line repeats the refrain in verse 12 with the exception that **comes** replaces "shall be found." The answer to the question is in two parts: verses 21 and 22, which continue the theme that wisdom is hidden; and verses 23-27, which claim that God alone has the answer.

And where is the place of understanding? See verse 12b for comments.

28.21　　　RSV　　　　　　　　　　　　　　TEV

It is hid from the eyes of all
　　living,
and concealed from the birds
　　of the air.

No living creature can see it,
Not even a bird in flight.

It is hid from the eyes of all living: the poetic movement between the two lines of this verse is from the general to the specific. In line a wisdom is hidden from **all living,** which means "all living creatures." This includes mankind and animals.

And concealed from the birds of the air: here, as in verse 7, wisdom is hidden even from a bird whose sight is keen at great distances. The heightening of poetic effect gives the meaning "Wisdom is hidden from all living creatures; even the birds soaring in the sky cannot see it."

28.22　　　RSV　　　　　　　　　　　　　　TEV

Abaddon and Death say,
　'We have heard a rumor of it
　　with our ears.'

Even death and destruction
Admit they have heard only ru-
　mors.

This verse has no two-line parallelism: only the two subjects are parallel in meaning. **Abaddon,** meaning "destruction," was used in 26.6. See there for comments. **Death** also is personified. The allusion is to the place of the dead, as in 30.23; 38.17.

We have heard a rumor of it with our ears: **rumor** translates a noun form of the verb "hear" and means "what one hears," "what is talked about." **With our ears**: this expression is also found in Psalm 44.1. FRCL translates "Yes, indeed, we have heard it spoken of." In languages in which **Abaddon and Death** cannot be said to speak, translators will have to express the verse differently; for example, "In the place of the dead, only a rumor of it has been heard" or "Those in the world of the dead have only heard it spoken of."

6-7. God alone knows the way to wisdom (28.23-28)

RSV　　　　　　　　　　　　　　　　　　TEV

23 "God understands the way to it,
　　and he knows its place.
24 For he looks to the ends of the earth,
　　and sees everything under the heavens.
25 When he gave to the wind its weight,

23 God alone knows the way,
　　Knows the place where wisdom is found,
24 Because he sees the ends of the earth,
　　Sees everything under the sky.
25 When God gave the wind its power

and meted out the waters by measure;	And determined the size of the sea;

26 when he made a decree for the rain,
     and a way for the lightning of the
     thunder;
	26 When God decided where the rain would
	     fall,
	     And the path that the thunderclouds
	     travel;

27 then he saw it and declared it;
     he established it, and searched it out.
	27 It was then he saw wisdom and tested its
	     worth—
	     He gave it his approval.

28 And he said to man,
     'Behold, the fear of the Lord, that is
     wisdom;
     and to depart from evil is understand-
     ing.'"
	28 God said to men,
	     "To be wise, you must have reverence for
	     the Lord.
	     To understand, you must turn from evil."

In verses 23-28 chapter 28 comes to a climax in the form of a confession which declares that no one but God has access to wisdom. Therefore in verse 28 God reveals to humankind that to know the "fear of the Lord" is wisdom.

Subdivision Heading

The Handbook heading may also be worded, for example, "To worship the Lord is wisdom," "Here is the way to wisdom," or "The answer to the question of wisdom." Rowley has "God alone has wisdom, and only by revelation can man possess it."

28.23-24   RSV   TEV

23 "God understands the way to it,
     and he knows its place.
	23 God alone knows the way,
	     Knows the place where wisdom is
	     found,

24 For he looks to the ends of the
     earth,
     and sees everything under the
     heavens.
	24 Because he sees the ends of the
	     earth,
	     Sees everything under the sky.

These two verses are related in that verse 24 provides the reason for verse 23. The answers to the questions in verse 20 were first given negatively, but from verse 23 to the end of the chapter the answers to verse 20 are all positive.

God understands the way to it: **God** is emphatic in this line, and so TEV translates "God alone." The Hebrew says literally "God understands its way." This means that God knows the "way, path, road" that leads to wisdom.

And he knows its place: this line is essentially the same in meaning as the previous line, which is well expressed by TEV as "God . . . knows the place where wisdom is found." Verse 23 may also be rendered, for example, "God is the one who knows the way to the place of wisdom" or "But God knows the path to wisdom, only he knows how to find it."

For he looks to the ends of the earth: although the Hebrew has different verbs for **look** and **see** in these two lines, the meaning is the same, as in TEV. Since God sees and knows all things, he knows where wisdom is found. **Ends of the earth** is used in Isaiah 40.28; 41.5,9 and is a use of spatial terms to indicate the vast extent of God's wisdom. SPCL says "to the last corner of the earth," and NJB "to the remotest parts of the earth."

And sees everything under the heavens: nothing escapes the eyes of God. He sees everything on earth. Verse 24 may also be expressed "He can see to the end of the earth, and sees everything under the sun" or "God can see as far as the end of the earth and see everything on it."

28.25 RSV	TEV
When he gave to the wind its weight, and meted out the waters by measure;	When God gave the wind its power And determined the size of the sea;

When he gave to the wind its weight: RSV, TEV, and others construct verses 25 and 26 as subordinate clauses of time, and verse 27 as the main clause, which gives the result of the action. Other translations relate these verses differently. Pope does essentially the same as RSV but begins verse 24 with the "when" clause. Dhorme also begins the subordination with verse 24, discontinues it in verse 25, and starts it again in verse 26. Since the verbs in verse 24 imply continuous present action, as in TEV, rather than a past event, it is better to follow RSV and TEV. Most interpreters understand the thoughts of verses 25 and 26 as referring to God's activity in creation. The Hebrew of verse 25 has no explicit subject and says literally "making for the wind a weight." The subject is God, from verse 23. The idea is that the wind, which is not normally thought of as a solid object, is here poetically given weight, and in these terms we may translate "When God set the weight of the wind," or "When God fixed the weight of the wind," or "When God decided how much the wind should weigh." If the association of weight with wind is poetically meaningless, it may be possible to translate as in TEV or to say, for example, "When God decided how strong the wind should be."

And meted out the waters by measure: RSV uses **meted out** and **by measure** to represent the two words used in the Hebrew of this line. The literal meaning is "to measure with a measuring instrument," that is, "to measure with a gauge." The expression depicts a carefully conducted process. **The waters** probably refers to the waters carried by the wind in the previous line, which then becomes specifically rain water in the next verse. TEV is the only translation consulted that has "seas." Better than "seas" is "the water in the clouds." The line may be rendered "and when he measured the amount of water in the clouds."

28.26 RSV	TEV
when he made a decree for the rain, and a way for the lightning of the thunder;	When God decided where the rain would fall, And the path that the thunder-clouds travel;

When he made a decree for the rain: translators differ in the interpretation of the word rendered **decree**. The basic meaning of the word seems to be "law," as implied by RSV. Dhorme interprets it as "limit," "he imposed on the rain a limit." Pope agrees with Dhorme but appeals to the basic meaning of the verb root, which is "to engrave" and, as applied to the rain, suggests "groove." In 38.25 a word translated "channel" is used in a similar context. The idea is then that God makes a channel for the rain to flow down to the earth. TEV perhaps follows this lead with "When God decided where the rain would fall." A word suggesting the path that the rain follows fits best in the next line. Nevertheless, most modern translators prefer some form such as "law," "rule," or "limit." Translators are advised to follow the form that best suits their own language style. This line may also be expressed, for example, "When God made a rule to guide the rain" or "When God fixed a law the rain has to follow."

And a way for the lightning of the thunder: **way** translates the Hebrew for "road, path." The RSV expression **lightning of the thunder** translates what is literally "voices of lightning." In 38.25 RSV translates the same expression "thunderbolt." Translations differ greatly in the rendering of this expression, but it is clear that the reference is to a storm accompanied by thunder. Dhorme translates "the rumble of thunder," and Rowley prefers "thunderstorm." TEV has supplied a verb to accompany **way**, "and the path that the thunder clouds travel," while NEB has "and a path for the thunderstorm," which is a good translation model. This expression may have to be expanded to say, for example, "and a path for the thunderstorm to follow" or "and a path to guide the thunderstorm."

28.27	RSV	TEV
	then he saw it and declared it; he established it, and searched it out.	It was then he saw wisdom and tested its worth— He gave it his approval.

Then he saw it and declared it: this verse describes what happened when the events of verses 25 and 26 had taken place, and is introduced by a word meaning **then**, marking a concluding event. In the four verbs which follow, God is the subject and wisdom the object. RSV follows the order of the Hebrew verbs: **saw, declared, established**, and **searched**. Translators will no doubt feel that the sequence of events here is not entirely chronological, since the search or testing should happen before declaring or establishing. (The Hebrew text may be following some form of chiastic ordering.) See below for a discussion of these terms. Note that TEV has arranged these events in the order "saw, tested, gave approval." We may also place them in the order **searched, saw, declared, established**. It should be noted that the poet, when placing **searched** at the end, has also added to it a Hebrew form often translated "even" or "also." This may give it the sense of "having already searched." RSV **he . . . declared it** (wisdom) is unclear. Dhorme interprets the expression to mean "appraise," "evaluate," which NJB follows with "then he saw and evaluated her (wisdom)." NEB is similar, with ". . . he saw wisdom and took stock of it." HOTTP recommends "he explained it." The line may also be rendered, for example, "Then he saw wisdom and saw its worth" or "Then he saw how valuable wisdom was," or following HOTTP, ". . . and explained how it is."

He established it: some Hebrew manuscripts have "discerned it," which NJB follows with "looked her through and through," a translation that may cause English speaking readers some confusion. FRCL, which follows the same thought, translates "He observed it." SPCL has "examined it," and GECL "acknowledged its worth."
Searched it out translates the same verb rendered "search out" in verse 3. In this line the verb is used as in 5.27, "This we have searched out; it is true." As there, the meaning here is "to study, examine." TEV translates this verb as "tested its worth." Translators should decide if any meaningful advantage is gained by reordering the verbs, and if so, may follow the order of TEV. The line may be expressed "he examined it and gave it his approval" or "he looked at it carefully and said that wisdom was good." Following the suggestion above, that **searched** may be taken as what was done first, we may translate verse 27 "After searching out the matter he saw how wisdom was and gave it his approval."

28.28	RSV	TEV
	And he said to man,	God said to men,
	'Behold, the fear of the Lord,	"To be wise, you must have rev-
	that is wisdom;	erence for the Lord.
	and to depart from evil is un-	To understand, you must turn
	derstanding.' "	from evil."

Some scholars omit verse 28 on the basis that only here is the Hebrew *'adonai* "Lord" to be found in Job, or that this verse is inconsistent with the rest of the chapter. Neither of these reasons is convincing. The book of Job contains many words that are used only once. From chapter 1 Job is described as a man who "fears God and turns away from evil." Therefore verse 28 is consistent with God's view of Job from the beginning of the poem.

And he said to man: this line is in prose. **Man** translates the Hebrew *'adam,* which refers to mankind and is translated as a plural in TEV. It is the equivalent of "God said to human beings, or to humanity, to all people, to mankind."

Behold, the fear of the Lord, that is wisdom: for comments on **Behold** see 4.18; 13.15. **Fear of the Lord** and **depart from evil** are parallel expressions found in a similar form in 1.1,8; 2.3; Proverbs 3.7; 14.16; 16.16. **Fear of the Lord**, which means "honor, respect, worship of the Lord," is the same as being wise or having wisdom. In other words "respect for the Lord is wisdom" or "a person who worships the Lord is wise."

RSV and TEV follow the English tradition in which the name of God, *Yahweh,* is translated and written "LORD," using all capital letters, and the Hebrew title *'adonai* is written "Lord." It is *'adonai* that occurs in this verse. Normally the reader will be accustomed to the term which translates **Lord** in the New Testament, or in other parts of the Old Testament such as the Psalms. For a discussion of the translation of **Lord**, see "Translating the Book of Job," page 21. Because the term *'adonai* occurs only once in Job, and because the reference is clearly to God, the translator may prefer to translate it as "God."

   And to depart from evil is understanding: depart from evil means "turn away from all that is bad," "avoid doing evil things." Most translators will want to keep a degree of parallelism between the two lines, so that if in line a "To be wise is" is used, then in line b it will be appropriate to say "to be intelligent is . . . ." For further comments see 1.1 and 1.8. This line may also be expressed, for example, "and separating yourself from evil ways is acting intelligently," "and avoiding bad conduct is the same as being intelligent," "intelligence is the same as staying away from evil ways," or "intelligence is avoiding doing evil things."

7. Job's Final Statement of His Case

(29.1–31.40)

Chapters 29, 30, and 31 form a unit in the book of Job. In these chapters there is no reply made by Job to the friends. Job's final speech is presented here in three stages: the opening, continuation, and conclusion. In chapter 29 Job looks back and remembers his life as a great man, recalling the good that he has done. In chapter 30 he looks at his present sufferings in relation to his past glories and accuses God of denying him justice. In chapter 31 he defends his integrity and challenges his adversary, God, to answer him. After chapter 31 Job says nothing further. In these three chapters Job speaks as if he were addressing a general audience. Before the first friend, Eliphaz, spoke in chapter 4, Job delivered a similar address. Now he concludes his remarks so that the poetic dialogues between Job and the friends are enclosed at both ends by the two speeches of Job.

Section Heading

Translators may wish to follow the Handbook by giving a section heading for chapters 29–31. This heading may be reworded to say, for example, "Job's final arguments," "Job completes his arguments," or "Job rests his case." Rowley has "Job's concluding soliloquy," and TOB "Job's eleventh poem."

7A. THE OPENING OF JOB'S FINAL SPEECH (29.1-25)

The structure of chapter 29, like much of the Book of Job, is one of repeated themes separated by other themes. Verses 2-6 speak of God's blessing in Job's past life. Verses 7-10 deal with Job's former social status in his community. In verses 11-17 Job tells how he treated people justly. In verses 18-20 he again picks up the theme of his earlier blessed condition, and the chapter ends with verses 21-25, in which Job again returns to the theme of his social status in the community. Chapter 29 may be displayed as follows:

A (2-6) God's blessing in former days

  B (7-10) Job's former status

    C (11-17) Job's just social acts

A' (18-20) Job's expectations from God's blessings

B' (21-25) Job's former social status

Division Heading

The Handbook division heading may be modified to say, for example, "Job begins his final argument" or "This is the start of Job's final speech." Habel calls it "Job's speech of remembrance." FRCL has "Job's final reply: Oh for the good old days of by-gone times," and GECL "If it were only as it used to be."

7A-1. Job recalls his prosperous and honored life (29.1-10)

RSV	TEV
1 And Job again took up his discourse, and said:	1 Job began speaking again.
2 "Oh, that I were as in the months of old, as in the days when God watched over me;	Job 2 If only my life could once again be as it was when God watched over me.
3 when his lamp shone upon my head, and by his light I walked through darkness;	3 God was always with me then and gave me light as I walked through the darkness.
4 as I was in my autumn days, when the friendship of God was upon my tent;	4 Those were the days when I was prosperous, and the friendship of God protected my home.
5 when the Almighty was yet with me, when my children were about me;	5 Almighty God was with me then, and I was surrounded by all my children.
6 when my steps were washed with milk, and the rock poured out for me streams of oil!	6 My cows and goats gave plenty of milk, and my olive trees grew in the rockiest soil.
7 When I went out to the gate of the city, when I prepared my seat in the square,	7 Whenever the city elders met and I took my place among them,
8 the young men saw me and withdrew, and the aged rose and stood;	8 young men stepped aside as soon as they saw me, and old men stood up to show me respect.
9 the princes refrained from talking, and laid their hand on their mouth;	9 The leaders of the people would stop talking;
10 the voice of the nobles was hushed, and their tongue cleaved to the roof of their mouth.	10 even the most important men kept silent.

Subdivision Heading

Although the display indicates five subdivisions in chapter 29, the Handbook uses only three headings. This is because there is a close relation in meaning between some of the adjoining parts of the chapter. Translators are, of course, free to provide as many as five if they think their readers will benefit from them. This heading may be reworded to say, for example, "Job remembers how he became rich and was honored" or "Job recalls how God blessed him and men honored him."

Rowley has "Job's former happiness," Habel "Remembrance of blessings and honor," and TOB "The happiness of former days."

29.1   RSV   TEV

| And Job again took up his discourse, and said: | Job began speaking again. |

And Job again took up his discourse, and said: see comments on 27.1. TEV says "Job began speaking again," which it did not say in 27.1 because 27.1 was the continuation of Job's speech begun in chapter 26. The word translated **again** seems to reinforce the idea that another speech or poem (chapter 28) has interrupted the speech of Job begun in chapter 26.

29.2   RSV   TEV

| "Oh, that I were as in the months of old, as in the days when God watched over me; | If only my life could once again be as it was when God watched over me. |

Oh, that I were as in the months of old: this verse uses the same formula for wishing that is seen in 11.5; 23.3. Job wishes that he could relive his past times of happiness. The formula means "How I wish I could relive . . ." or, as TEV says, "If only my life could . . . ." Line a has **months of old**, which is paralleled in line b by **days**. Chapter 7.3 follows the same pattern, with "months" in a and "nights" in b. **As in the months of old** translates the Hebrew literally. The expression refers to the past, or times gone by. Job wants to recapture the past: "Oh, if only I could relive the past," "I wish I could return to my former days," "I wish I were as I used to be," or "If I could only be again as I used to be!"

As in the days when God watched over me: the second line expresses the shorter time, as is typical of time units in parallelism. **Watched over me** refers to God's guarding, caring for Job. The same verb is used of God spying on Job in 10.14; 13.27; 14.16, but here the sense is as in Psalm 91.11, "For he will give his angels charge of you to guard you in all your ways." SPCL says "God protected me," and NJB "When God was my guardian," that is, "When God took good care of me."

29.3   RSV   TEV

| when his lamp shone upon my head, and by his light I walked through darkness; | God was always with me then and gave me light as I walked through the darkness. |

When his lamp shone upon my head: RSV begins verses 2b, 3a, 4b, 5a, 6a, and 7a with **when**, which translates the Hebrew form. However, this repetition creates a monotonous style in English. Therefore TEV varies these constructions. Translators should consider the stylistic effect of a repeated structure and vary it if necessary. God's **lamp** in line a and **light** in line b are images which represent God's blessing and guidance. The same pair is used in 2 Samuel 22.29, "Yea, thou art my lamp, O LORD, and my God lightens my darkness." See also Psalm 18.28; 36.9. **Lamp** refers to a stone or pottery bowl with olive oil for fuel, and with a wick which absorbs and burns the oil. **Upon my head** gives the impression of the light being focused on Job's head. Most take it to mean "over my head, above my head, above me." TEV avoids the parallelism of **lamp** and **light** and expresses this line as "God was always with me then," which gives the thought in prose terms and without the poetic imagery. If translators are translating as poetry and the images of **lamp** and **light** will not be clear, they may make the meaning clear in the text, substitute other images, or follow TEV. The first approach may be, for example, "When God blessed me by shining his lamp on my way." The second solution may be "When God cleared the branches from my path."

And by his light I walked through darkness: **by his light** is to be taken as "by means of his light," "in his light," or "in the light he provides"; so the line can be expressed as "He guided me through the dark with his light."

29.4	RSV	TEV
	as I was in my autumn days, when the friendship of God was upon my tent;	Those were the days when I was prosperous, and the friendship of God protected my home.

As I was in my autumn days: **autumn days** most likely refers to the time of harvest, when crops have reached their full maturity. NJB translates "Shall I ever see my days of harvest again . . . ?" FRCL has "at the time of maturity." The thought expressed is not that of advanced age and decline, but of fruitfulness, which TEV translates "when I was prosperous," and NEB "days of my prime." K-B lists the word as meaning "youth," but the sense is more equivalent to "maturity of life" in the light of Job's children being with him in the next verse. In English **autumn days** or "autumn of life" is misleading, since it suggests the physical and mental decline of advancing age. Translators should use a term or expression that suggests the full vigor of life. This may be later in life in some cultures than in others. "At that time I was in the prime of life," or "When I was a strong man," or "When I had all my powers."

When the friendship of God was upon my tent: **friendship of God** is uncertain. The Hebrew expression occurs in 15.8, where it is translated by RSV as "counsel of God." NJB and NEB translate "protected," and BJ has a note indicating that this follows the Septuagint and Syriac. The ancient versions substituted a Hebrew final k for a final d in order to get "protected." However, HOTTP keeps the Hebrew text and says that the expression may be rendered in three ways: (1) "with the friendship of God"; (2) "with the counsel of God"; or (3) "with the protection of God." TEV translators felt that "friendship of God" puts in focus the idea of protection and so used both (1) and (3): "the friendship of God protected . . . ." **My tent** is often rendered by TEV and others as "my home." The line may be rendered, for example, "When God protected my home" or "When God befriended me and took care of my home."

29.5   RSV   TEV

when the Almighty was yet with me,	Almighty God was with me then, and I was surrounded by all
when my children were about me;	my children.

When the Almighty was yet with me: Almighty translates *Shaddai,* regularly translated "Almighty God" by TEV. TEV avoids the repetition of "when" clauses in reference to past time by using an independent clause: "Almighty God was with me then." The idea is that God, who is no longer with Job, was still near him at that earlier time.

When my children were about me: children translates a word used in 1.19, where it is translated "young people" (RSV). It may also have the meaning of "my servants," which NEB prefers. However, most translations consulted take it to refer to Job's own children. Languages differ greatly in the way they express the idea of having one's children close by in the home. For example, "when my children sat about my fire," "in the times when my children ate from my bowl," or "when my children cultivated and planted with me."

29.6   RSV   TEV

when my steps were washed with milk,	My cows and goats gave plenty of milk,
and the rock poured out for me streams of oil!	and my olive trees grew in the rockiest soil.

Job's wealth and the fertility of his herds are expressed here in figurative terms. **When my steps were washed with milk: milk** translates the same word rendered "curds" in 20.17. Some translate "cream," or "butter." TEV has expressed this line differently: "My cows and goats gave plenty of milk." This may imply wealth but has reduced the poetic force to nearly nothing. NIV keeps the poetic figures: "when my path was drenched with cream." It makes little sense in English to say "when my feet were bathed in milk" (NJB) or "my path flowed with milk" (NEB). If "milk, cream, curds, butter" are not elements of a recognized expression of wealth, it is better to substitute a different figure or to translate without a metaphor; for example, "my path was paved with gold" or "I was a wealthy man."

And the rock poured out for me streams of oil: the rock most likely refers to the oil press, which is a hollowed-out rock where the crushed olives are pressed for their oil. Deuteronomy 32.13 has a similar reference to getting oil from the rock.

TEV "and my olive trees grew in the rockiest soil" may suggest that these trees do not normally grow well in rocky soil, but this is contrary to fact. It is more accurate to speak of the quantity of oil that was obtained from the oil press; for example, "And oil flowed richly from my olive presses." For translation comments on "olive press," see 24.11.

29.7-8	RSV	TEV

7   When I went out to the gate of the city,
    when I prepared my seat in the square,
8   the young men saw me and withdrew,
    and the aged rose and stood;

7   Whenever the city elders met and I took my place among them,
8   young men stepped aside as soon as they saw me, and old men stood up to show me respect.

TEV translates verse 7 as two dependent conditional clauses and verse 8 as the main clause. Verses 9 and 10 are extensions of the main clause in verse 8. Only verses 7 and 8 will be dealt with here as a unit.

When I went out to the gate of the city: Job's point of view is from within the city. **Gate of the city** refers to the large doors in the wall surrounding the city. These gates were open during the day, but closed at night or during attacks on the city. TEV avoids any reference to the traditional location of the meeting place in **the gate** and **in the square**, but identifies both of these places in terms of their function in the context. In languages in which **gate of the city** will refer only to a place but not to its social function, it will be better to translate as in TEV or, for example, "Whenever I attended the meeting of the town elders" or "Whenever the town's leaders met to discuss business."

When I prepared my seat in the square: **prepared my seat** means "when I sat down" or "when I took my seat." **Square** refers to the open area inside the city wall, near the city gates, where town administration meetings (Deut 21.19), legal transactions (Ruth 4.1, 11), or markets (2 Kgs 7.1,18) were held.

The young men saw me and withdrew: in this line it is the **young men** who move out of Job's way. **Withdrew** translates a verb meaning "hid," but these young men did not literally "hide"; they made themselves inconspicuous. They did not want to intrude, but they withdrew from the presence of older men, especially at the approach of a dignitary such as Job. TEV says they "stepped aside." Or we may translate "Young men saw me coming and so moved back" or "Young men gave me room as I approached."

And the aged rose and stood: in this line, which is line b of verse 8, **the aged**, the old men who have higher status in the town meetings, did not withdraw like the young men, but "stood to their feet." They would remain standing until Job invited them to be seated. In this way they would show respect for their leader. The sense of the verbs used here is past habitual action, which may be translated in English "would step aside" and "would stand up." TEV indicates the purpose of standing up: "to show me respect"; that is, "the old men stood up to honor me" or "the old men arose to show I was their superior."

29.9   RSV   TEV

> the princes refrained from talk-
>   ing,
> and laid their hand on their
>   mouth;

> The leaders of the people would
>   stop talking;

The princes refrained from talking: princes translates the same word as in 3.15, which TEV there renders "princes." In the context of a town gathering these men are city officials and other leaders, and not literally the sons of the king. The Hebrew term often translated "princes" never refers to sons of kings unless they happen to have this position of leadership. **Refrained from talking** means "they stopped talking" or "they would stop talking." Out of respect for Job even the highest officials ceased talking when Job appeared. TEV reduces the two lines of verse 9 to a single line.

And laid their hand on their mouth: in 21.5 Job told the friends "Look at me, and be appalled, and lay your hand upon your mouth." This gesture is used here to show the superior that they are keeping silent in his presence so that he may speak to them. The same gesture is used in some parts of the world to indicate that the one covering his mouth is addressing his superior. If the gesture has a different meaning, the translator should substitute an appropriate equivalent that means "to refrain from speaking," or say, for example, "and they kept their silence" or "they hushed their speaking."

29.10   RSV   TEV

> the voice of the nobles was
>   hushed,
> and their tongue cleaved to the
>   roof of their mouth.

> even the most important men
>   kept silent.

The voice of the nobles was hushed: nobles translates a word used in 31.37, where RSV translates "prince." The term suggests a leader who is below the rank of the "leaders" mentioned in verse 9, and in English, **nobles** is adequate. However, the context is most likely a town meeting, and TEV distinguishes between the two bodies of officials as "leaders" in verse 9a and "the most important men" here. Although the verb here is the same as the verb in verse 8a, where it is translated as "withdrew," it cannot have that meaning here; but **hushed** translates it well. This line may also be expressed as "the important men of the town became silent" or "the big men of the village stopped talking."

And their tongue cleaved to the roof of their mouth: in Psalm 137.6 the psalmist prays "Let my tongue cleave to the roof of my mouth, if I do not remember you." This entire line is reduced to "kept silent" by TEV and attached to the first line of the verse. NJB says "their tongues stayed still in their mouths." In translation it is important to use a figurative expression which means "to keep silence." In some areas a literal translation of this expression will appear so severe as to seem to be the result of a curse which Job's presence placed on these men. Accordingly it will often be better to use a more appropriate expression, or to avoid the figure and follow TEV.

7A-2. Job recalls his fair treatment of the oppressed (29.11-17)

RSV	TEV
11 When the ear heard, it called me blessed, and when the eye saw, it approved;	11 Everyone who saw me or heard of me had good things to say about what I had done.
12 because I delivered the poor who cried, and the fatherless who had none to help him.	12 When the poor cried out, I helped them; I gave help to orphans who had nowhere to turn.
13 The blessing of him who was about to perish came upon me, and I caused the widow's heart to sing for joy.	13 Men who were in deepest misery praised me, and I helped widows find security.
14 I put on righteousness, and it clothed me; my justice was like a robe and a turban.	14 I have always acted justly and fairly.
15 I was eyes to the blind, and feet to the lame.	15 I was eyes for the blind, and feet for the lame.
16 I was a father to the poor, and I searched out the cause of him whom I did not know.	16 I was like a father to the poor and took the side of strangers in trouble.
17 I broke the fangs of the unrighteous, and made him drop his prey from his teeth.	17 I destroyed the power of cruel men and rescued their victims.

Verse 11 is the start of a new line of thought, namely, the good Job had done for the oppressed. NJB, NEB, Dhorme, and others insert verses 21-25 between verses 10 and 11, since those verses continue the theme of respect given to Job by the people. The Handbook follows the order of the Hebrew text.

Subdivision Heading

Translators may wish to adapt the Handbook heading to say, for example, "Job remembers how well he treated the poor," "Job remembers that he treated the oppressed fairly," or "Job tells how he was always kind to those who suffered." Rowley has "The benevolence of Job," Habel (verses 11-24) "Remembrance of administering justice."

29.11 RSV	TEV
When the ear heard, it called me blessed, and when the eye saw, it approved;	Everyone who saw me or heard of me had good things to say about what I had done.

When the ear heard, it called me blessed: a similar statement is used in 13.1 in reference to Job having seen and heard what the friends were asserting. In the Hebrew of this line, **the ear** is a part of the body which stands for the whole, meaning "people," or as TEV says, "Everyone who . . . ." **Called me blessed** is literally "pronounced me happy." The verb used here is also found in Genesis 30.13; Proverbs 31.28. Here the word has the sense of "declare happy" or "congratulate," and FRCL translates it well: "I was congratulated by those who heard me"; other possibilities are "Everyone who heard me speak congratulated me," or "All those who heard me spoke highly of me," or ". . . said good words about me."

And when the eye saw, it approved: the eye represents the same subject as in the preceding line. Therefore TEV is correct in combining the two actions, with "Everyone who saw me or heard of me." **It approved** translates a verb meaning "to be a witness" or "to witness something regarding someone." The witness given may be favorable or unfavorable, but in the present context it clearly means "to speak in favor of someone." NEB keeps both lines parallel, with "whoever heard of me spoke in my favour, and those who saw me bore witness to my merit." FRCL translates this line "upon seeing me, all assured me of their esteem." The line may also be rendered "and everyone who saw me said good things about me." Some translators may prefer to rearrange the verse slightly to say, for example, "When the people heard and saw me, they congratulated me and said many good things about me."

29.12 RSV	TEV
because I delivered the poor who cried, and the fatherless who had none to help him.	When the poor cried out, I helped them; I gave help to orphans who had nowhere to turn.

Verse 12 supplies the reason for the praise in verse 11. **Because I delivered the poor who cried**: in 22.6-9 Eliphaz alleged that Job oppressed the poor. But Job is saying that he did not oppress them. "I rescued, saved the poor when they cried for help." It is probably implied that **the poor** cried to Job for help. This line echoes Psalm 72.12, in which the ideal king behaves in the same manner in regard to the poor. TEV and others do not make verse 12 the reason for the actions in verse 11, but make both verses independent statements of Job's conduct. Translators may find this fits the style of their language better and may wish to do the same. **Who cried** must often be expressed as "who cried to me for help," "who begged me to help them," or "who came crying to me for help."

And the fatherless who had none to help him: fatherless is parallel with **the poor** in the previous line. See 5.15; 6.27. The same pairing was used in 24.9; see there for comments. The line has no verb in Hebrew, and so a verb of similar meaning to that used in the first line must often be supplied. This line may also be expressed "and I rescued the orphan who had no one to help him" or "I helped orphans who are without fathers to help them."

29.13 RSV	TEV
The blessing of him who was about to perish came upon	Men who were in deepest misery praised me,

me,   and I helped widows find secu-
and I caused the widow's heart   rity.
to sing for joy.

The blessing of him who was about to perish came upon me: verse 13 is
closely parallel in meaning to verse 12. This line is literally "The blessing of the
perishing came upon me." This sounds as if someone's death was a blessing to Job.
The meaning can be expressed better as implying that Job rescued them: "Those who
were about to die (and would have died if Job had not saved them) gave me their
blessing." **Him who was about to perish** translates the present participle of the
verb "to perish, to die." **Perish** suggests dying with suffering and misery. TEV
expresses the aspect of suffering as "Men who were in deepest misery . . . ." In the
context of the poor, orphans, and widows, **him . . . about to perish** has the sense
of one who is in great suffering. It may also be possible to translate, for example,
"People who were suffering near death said good things about me" or "People in
great misery gave me their blessing."

And I caused the widow's heart to sing for joy: this statement may be taken
in reply to Eliphaz's claim in 22.9, "You have sent widows away empty." The verb
translated **caused to sing** is general in sense and means "to raise a loud cry," which
may be either of grief or joy; in this context it is a shout of joy. Most translations
leave the content indefinite; for example, "I put back some joy in the hearts of
widows" (FRCL), but TEV has tried to be more specific with "I helped widows find
security." This line may also be rendered, for example, "the help I gave even made
widows happy," "what I did for widows made their hearts rejoice," or "widows were
full of joy for the help I gave them."

29.14   RSV   TEV

I put on righteousness, and it   I have always acted justly and
clothed me;   fairly.
my justice was like a robe and
a turban.

I put on righteousness, and it clothed me: in Psalm 132.9; Isaiah 59.17,
righteousness is spoken of as a garment. It is paired here with **justice**, as in
Jeremiah 22.15; 23.5; 33.15, and means the same. The metaphor of putting on
righteousness as if it were clothing may mean that Job dressed himself in the clothing
(robes) worn by a leader of the community when he took his seat in the square
(verse 7). In this sense the garment was the symbol of his position. Just as a person
may be clothed with righteousness, he may also be clothed with shame (Psalm
132.18). For Job **righteousness** and **justice** are like a garment which, in his case,
adorns him and shows that he acted rightly and justly when he made decisions in
regard to the oppressed. All of this is in contrast to the unjust treatment he claims
to receive from God. Verse 14 is constructed as a chiasmus in Hebrew, with
righteousness coming at the beginning of line a and **justice** at the end of line b.
Put on means to dress oneself with clothing, but in English "put on" can give the
idea of pretense, and so TEV has modified this expression to say, "I have always acted

justly and fairly." This removes all traces of the imagery, which is not necessary to do; for example, in Isaiah 59.17 TEV translates clearly, "He will wear justice like a coat of armor, and saving power like a helmet . . . . He will clothe himself with the strong desire to set things right." FRCL is more poetic in its rendering of 14a: "A sense of justice was my garment . . . ." GECL says "Righteousness was always my clothing." We may wish to express the line as, for example, "I did what was right, and it was like the clothes I wore" or "Doing the right thing to people was as important to me as being clothed."

My justice was like a robe and a turban: line b with **robe** and **turban** makes more precise what was expressed in line a. **Justice** is the noun form of the verb "to act justly" or "to do the right, fair thing." **My justice** refers to the just, fair, good acts which Job did for others. **Robe** translates the same noun as in 1.20, where "Job arose, and rent his robe." **Robe** here refers to the outer garment, the one which is visible to the public. **Turban** translates the noun form of the verb meaning "to wind or wrap around" and applies here to the headdress that is wound about the head, and no doubt worn on the occasions mentioned above. In this line again the symbols of Job's office are appealed to as representing his fairness in making decisions or judgments. We may translate, for example, "When I judged matters fairly it was as clear as the robe and turban I wore." in areas where robes and turbans are unknown, it may be necessary to retain the general comparison in both lines a and b; for example, "I did things that were right, and it was like putting on my clothes; I judged matters fairly, and that was a common as getting dressed."

29.15	RSV	TEV
	I was eyes to the blind, and feet to the lame.	I was eyes for the blind, and feet for the lame.

I was eyes to the blind: Job claims to supply what was lacking to those in the community who were in need of help, acting as their guide and support. In Numbers 10.31 Moses said to Hobab ". . . you will serve as eyes for us." This meant that Hobab was to guide the Hebrews through the desert. The words **blind** and **lame** are a fixed pair which recur in such passages as Leviticus 21.18; Deuteronomy 15.21; 2 Samuel 5.6, 8; Jeremiah 31.8. **And feet for the lame**: in some languages it may be better to shift this to a simile; for example, "I was like eyes for the blind and feet for the lame." These similes may require some adjustments in translation; for example, "I guided the blind and supported the lame" or "I led the blind and helped the lame."

29.16	RSV	TEV
	I was a father to the poor, and I searched out the cause of him whom I did not know.	I was like a father to the poor and took the side of strangers in trouble.

I was a father to the poor: TEV improves this line by saying "I was like a father to the poor." This line may also be rendered "I protected the poor" or "I cared for the poor like a father."

And I searched out the cause of him whom I did not know: "I investigated the case of those I did not know." It was particularly in legal cases that the poor were without protection, and so Job undertook to help them. Job claims he sought the truth in legal suits and did not favor those he knew, his own community, at the expense of strangers. **Searched out** translates the same verb used in 28.3. This line may also be expressed "I defended strangers in court" or "I defended the rights of foreigners in legal cases."

29.17	RSV	TEV
	I broke the fangs of the unright- eous, and made him drop his prey from his teeth.	I destroyed the power of cruel men and rescued their victims.

I broke the fangs of the unrighteous: the wicked person is here compared to a wild animal. **Fangs** translates a noun derived from the verb "to gnaw." It is used in parallel with teeth in Joel 1.6 and Proverbs 30.14. **Unrighteous** translates the same word used in 16.11, which RSV renders "ungodly." To break the fangs of an animal is to disable it so that it is largely defenseless and unable to capture its victim. Therefore Job is saying that he not only rescued the oppressed, but he also disabled the oppressor so he could not continue his crimes. If the breaking of the teeth does not convey the thought of "taking away power," it will be better to follow a nonfigurative translation such as TEV: "I destroyed the power of cruel men." In some languages another figure may be more appropriate; for example, SPCL says "I broke the jaw of evil doers." In some languages it may be better to translate "I broke the hands of evil men."

And made him drop his prey from his teeth: an animal whose **fangs** are broken will lose hold of its **prey**, that is, its victim. **Teeth** parallels **fangs** in the previous line. It may be clearer to say "drop his prey from his mouth." TEV "and rescued their victims" is a good model for translators who are avoiding the poetic images in this line. This line should be translated in such a way as to be consistent with the figure or nonfigure used in line a. For example, if "broke the hands" is used in line a, then line b may be rendered "and took his victim from him" or "and rescued his victim."

7A-3. Job recalls how people respected him (29.18-25)

	RSV		TEV
18	Then I thought, 'I shall die in my nest, and I shall multiply my days as the sand,	18	I always expected to live a long life and to die at home in comfort.
19	my roots spread out to the waters,	19	I was like a tree whose roots always have water

	RSV		TEV
	with the dew all night on my branches,		and whose branches are wet with dew.
20	my glory fresh with me,	20	Everyone was always praising me,
	and my bow ever new in my hand.'		and my strength never failed me.
21	"Men listened to me, and waited,	21	When I gave advice, people were silent
	and kept silence for my counsel.		and listened carefully to what I said;
22	After I spoke they did not speak again,	22	they had nothing to add when I had
	and my word dropped upon them.		finished.
23	They waited for me as for the rain;		My words sank in like drops of rain;
	and they opened their mouths as for the spring rain.	23	everyone welcomed them just as farmers welcome rain in spring.
24	I smiled on them when they had no confidence;	24	I smiled on them when they had lost confidence;
	and the light of my countenance they did not cast down.	25	my cheerful face encouraged them. I took charge and made the decisions;
25	I chose their way, and sat as chief, and I dwelt like a king among his troops, like one who comforts mourners.		I led them as a king leads his troops, and gave them comfort in their despair.

Beginning with verse 18 and ending with verse 20, Job will speak of his former confidence in his future, a future that has been radically changed by events. In verses 21-25 he recalls again his honored status.

Subdivision Heading

Translators who wish to provide a heading for verses 18-20 may say, for example, "Job's former confidence" or "This is what Job expected." The Handbook gives one heading for the two final subdivisions and may be reworded to say, for example, "Job remembers how people honored him," "Job recalls that he led the people," or "The people respected Job as he led them." Rowley has (verses 18-20) "Job's former serene confidence," and (verses 21-25) "The esteem in which Job was formerly held."

29.18   RSV   TEV

Then I thought, 'I shall die in my
nest,
and I shall multiply my days as
the sand,

I always expected to live a long
life
and to die at home in comfort.

Then I thought 'I shall die in my nest': in my nest translates the Hebrew phrase "with my nest." In Isaiah 16.2 the word rendered **nest** here has the meaning of the contents of the nest and is translated "nestlings," that is, "baby birds." Mft translates "I shall grow old among my brood." That is to say, Job expected to grow old, with his children at home with him. HOTTP translates "in my nest," which probably means "I shall die at home." **Nest** is a figure of the comfort and security of home. The Septuagint has "my age will grow old," which Dhorme adjusts to "I shall die in a ripe old age." TEV has reversed the two lines of verse 18 to put the two thoughts into a more logical order, and says in its second line "(I always expected) to die at home in comfort." "In comfort" is added to give the connotation of being "in the nest." FRCL has "then I said to myself 'I will die in my nest.'" There appears

531

to be no good reason why the Hebrew text cannot be translated as it stands. If "die in the nest" cannot be used as a suitable figure of dying at home where a person is comfortable, then another figure may be used, or we may translate as in TEV.

And I shall multiply my days as the sand: translations differ greatly in the interpretation of this line. RSV and TEV understand **as the sand** to mean that Job will live a long life. **Sand** is used in Genesis 22.17 as a way of expressing numerous descendants, but there is no place in the Old Testament in which **sand** is used to signify long life. Nevertheless **sand** as "grains of sand" expresses in figurative terms a great number. The Septuagint makes a change from **sand** to get "like the palm tree." The Greek word for "palm tree" is *phoinix*, a word which means, among other things, the "Phoenix bird," a mythical bird which burned itself in its nest, and renewed itself from the ashes, and so was a symbol of immortality. GECL, FRCL, TOB, NAB, Gordis, NJV, and Habel follow the Greek. On the other hand Dhorme, Pope, NJB, BJ, SPCL, NIV, and, by implication, TEV prefer **sand**. The interpretation of the former group of translations gives a good parallel between the two lines. For example, GECL says "I had hoped to grow old like the phoenix, and to die like it in the nest." However, there is no certainty that the legend of the phoenix was known in Palestine at the time Job was written. Taken on the whole it seems preferable to recommend that translators follow RSV or, if the image of **sand** is not used, to follow TEV. In many languages the inverted order of the lines will produce better logic and clearness of thought. Verse 18 may also be rendered, for example, "I said to myself, 'I will live a long life and die at home'" or "I said, 'I will live to be a very old man and then die peacefully with my own people.'"

29.19	RSV	TEV
	my roots spread out to the wa- ters, with the dew all night on my branches,	I was like a tree whose roots always have water and whose branches are wet with dew.

My roots spread out to the waters: Job compares himself in this verse to a tree whose roots have plenty of water to nourish them. The thought is similar to Psalm 1.3, "He is like a tree planted by streams of water." Similar comparisons were made in 8.16-17; 14.7-9; 18.16. **With the dew all night on my branches**: at night the warm air cools, and dew forms on the leaves of the branches, appearing as small drops of water. TEV makes the comparison with the tree clearer: "I was like a tree . . . ." Verse 19 may also be rendered "I was like a tree planted close to water and with branches wet at night from the dew."

29.20	RSV	TEV
	my glory fresh with me, and my bow ever new in my hand.'	Everyone was always praising me, and my strength never failed me.

My glory fresh with me: in verse 20 there is no parallelism between the two lines, although some scholars suggest a change from **glory** to get "spear" in order to create a parallelism with **bow** in line b̲. However, there is no need to create parallel lines where they do not exist. **Glory** here refers to Job's position of honor, his reputation as a man of respect, as seen in verses 7-10. **Fresh** translates an adjective meaning "new," and **glory** is **fresh** in that it is constantly being "renewed within me." In other words Job was constantly being reminded by the people of his honor and prestige, and Mft translates the line as "Fresh honors fall to me," and TEV "Everyone was always praising me." The line may be rendered, for example, "The people were always telling me how much they respected me" or "People never ceased showing me great respect."

And my bow ever new in my hand: the idea is not that Job was ready to fight, but that he had constant and unfailing strength. FRCL keeps the metaphor: "and my strength to act like a well-strung bow." **Ever new** translates the causative form of a verb meaning "renew." The same verb is used in 14.7, which TEV translates "come back to life." TEV "My strength never failed me" expresses the sense correctly, avoiding the figure of the **bow**. This line may also be expressed "I was always receiving new strength," "new strength was always filling me," "I was constantly being strengthened," or "I never lacked for strength."

29.21 RSV	TEV
"Men listened to me, and waited, and kept silence for my counsel.	When I gave advice, people were silent and listened carefully to what I said;

Verses 21-25 are shifted by some translators to follow verse 10 because their content follows the same theme as in verses 1-10. In the Hebrew of verses 21-25 there is no expressed subject, and all the verbs are plural. This fact supports those who insert these verses between 10 and 11. RSV and TEV keep the order of the Hebrew text. The theme of these verses is the honor Job is given by his community.

Men listened to me and waited: **men** is supplied as the subject to accompany the plural form of the verb in Hebrew. TEV supplies "people." If this verse follows verse 10, then the subject is "princes and nobles" from verses 9 and 10. The order of the verbs in this verse may need to be rearranged to give a better sequence of actions. For example, "People waited for me and listened to what I said." NJB has "They waited anxiously to hear me." TEV transposes the two lines to give a more logical flow of thought.

And kept silence for my counsel: **kept silence** is parallel with **listened to me** in the previous line. **My counsel** may need to be expressed, as in TEV, as a verb phrase; for example, "I gave them advice" or "I advised them."

29.22   RSV   TEV

> After I spoke they did not speak   they had nothing to add when I
>   again,   had finished.
> and my word dropped upon   My words sank in like drops of
>   them.   rain;

After I spoke they did not speak again: Job always had the last word. What he said was final, and people did not argue with him.

And my word dropped upon them: **dropped**, as used in RSV, suggests a single act. The Hebrew verb, however, suggests the dripping of a liquid, drop after drop, and so TEV "My words sank in like drops of rain" conveys the idea accurately and in a pleasing manner. This line may be rendered, for example, "my words were pleasant to them like drops of rain" or "my words fell on them like rain drops on dry ground."

29.23   RSV   TEV

> They waited for me as for the   everyone welcomed them
>   rain;   just as farmers welcome rain
> and they opened their mouths   in spring.
>   as for the spring rain.

They waited for me as for the rain: in line <u>a</u> the word translated **rain** is a general term, and in line <u>b</u> **spring rain** translates a specific term for the rain that falls in March and April and is essential for the young plants which will face dry periods during the summer growing season. Accordingly these rains are sometimes translated "the latter rains." Since there is poetic heightening in the movement between the two lines, line <u>a</u> may be rendered in a general manner; for example, "They waited for me as people wait for rain."

And they opened their mouths as for the spring rain: **opened their mouths** is a poetic way of expressing anticipation and anxiety for the rain. In the poetic heightening of this verse, line <u>b</u> carries line <u>a</u> forward and to a more intense level through the use of a metaphor and a specific parallel, **spring rains**. The entire verse may be translated in such a way as to reflect this poetic movement; for example, "The people waited for me just as they wait for the rain, in fact, they were like anxious farmers looking for their last spring rain."

29.24   RSV   TEV

> I smiled on them when they had   I smiled on them when they had
>   no confidence;   lost confidence;
> and the light of my counte-   my cheerful face encouraged
>   nance they did not cast   them.
>   down.

I smiled on them when they had no confidence: most interpreters agree that Job's gesture is to be understood as favorable. KJV has "If I laughed on them . . . ," which mistakenly gives the idea of ridicule. RSV and TEV agree in the translation **when they had no confidence**. The Hebrew of this clause is a negative followed by the verb "believe." Dhorme argues that the Hebrew verb is regularly used with the negative in 4.18; 9.16; 15.15, 22,31; 24.22 ("despair"); 39.24 ("cannot stand still"), and that the meaning here is "they would not believe it"; that is, "If I smiled on them, they could not believe it." This is the thought expressed by Pope, Habel, BJ, NJB, NJV, TOB, FRCL, SPCL, NIV. Following this line of interpretation, we may have to make some adjustment that will make clear that the smile was an unexpected reward. Accordingly we may sometimes translate "If I smiled at them, they could hardly believe it because they did not expect it."

And the light of my countenance they did not cast down: RSV gives a literal rendering of the Hebrew. **Light of my countenance** expresses a happy, cheerful, smiling face, as in Psalm 4.6 "Lift up the light of thy countenance upon us, O LORD." See also Proverbs 16.15. **They did not cast down** translates the causative form of the Hebrew verb "to fall." RSV takes **light of my countenance** to be the object of the verb, but parallelism between the two lines suggests a meaning closer to TEV, in which "the light of my face" ("my cheerful face") is the subject and **did not cast down** is taken in the positive sense, meaning "encouraged them." The line may then be rendered positively as in TEV, "my cheerful face encouraged them," or "I gave them strength with my cheerful face," or negatively, "my cheerful face did not discourage them."

29.25 RSV	TEV
I chose their way, and sat as chief, and I dwelt like a king among his troops, like one who comforts mourners.	I took charge and made the decisions; I led them as a king leads his troops, and gave them comfort in their despair.

I chose their way, and sat as chief: verse 25 has three lines. **I chose their way** expresses the thought of Job making the decisions affecting the lives of his people as he guided and directed them. **And sat as chief**: this phrase, which states Job's position of authority, may best be placed at the beginning of the line, before what he does as chief; for example, "I was their leader and showed them the way" or "I was the one who led them and made their decisions."

And I dwelt like a king among his troops: the second line extends the idea of **sat as chief** to being **king** of an army. The reference to **troops** is not to be taken as implying that Job was a military leader. Job depicts himself in the role of the highest leadership, and the people as faithful and obedient followers. "I was their leader as a king is over his troops" or "I lived among them like a king among his soldiers."

Like one who comforts mourners is less certain than the previous lines. Dhorme claims the meaning of RSV has no connection with the context, and so he makes a change to get "Where I led them, they were willing to go," which NJB follows with "and I led them wherever I chose." Although Dhorme's suggestion seems to fit the context, the Hebrew is perfectly clear and serves as a good conclusion to this part of the speech. HOTTP supports RSV and TEV and is recommended to translators. The line may also be rendered "and I comforted them like one who consoles those who mourn" or "when they were sad I consoled them."

7B. JOB CONTINUES HIS FINAL SPEECH (30.1-31)

As Job continues his final speech, there is no break with the preceding part, but only a contrast drawn between those who formerly honored him and those who mock him now. In verses 1-8 Job ridicules the fathers of those who now make fun of him. He then picks up again the theme of mistreatment in verses 9-15. In verses 16-26 God mistreats Job regardless of Job's pleas. In verses 27-31 in spite of Job's good deeds, pain and the public assembly add their abuse, and he can only cry out like an animal and weep.

Division Heading

Translators who wish to use a division heading may modify the Handbook heading to say, for example, "Job continues," "Job's final speech continues," or "Job goes on speaking." Habel has "Job's final complaint," and TOB "Today's misery."

7B-1. Job considers the fathers of those who ridicule him as worthless (30.1-8)

RSV	TEV

1 "But now they make sport of me,
    men who are younger than I,
    whose fathers I would have disdained
    to set with the dogs of my flock.
	1 But men younger than I am make fun of
	    me now!
	    Their fathers have always been so
	    worthless
	    that I wouldn't let them help my dogs
	    guard sheep.

2 What could I gain from the strength of
    their hands,
    men whose vigor is gone?
	2 They were a bunch of worn-out men,
	    too weak to do any work for me.

3 Through want and hard hunger
    they gnaw the dry and desolate
    ground;
	3 They were so poor and hungry
	    that they would gnaw dry roots—
	    at night, in wild, desolate places.

4 they pick mallow and the leaves of bush-
    es,
    and to warm themselves the roots of
    the broom.
	4 They pulled up the plants of the desert
	    and ate them,
	    even the tasteless roots of the broom
	    tree!

5 They are driven out from among men;
    they shout after them as after a thief.
	5 Everyone drove them away with shouts,
	    as if they were shouting at thieves.

6 In the gullies of the torrents they must
    dwell,
    in holes of the earth and of the rocks.
	6 They had to live in caves,
	    in holes dug in the sides of cliffs.

7 Among the bushes they bray;
    under the nettles they huddle together.
	7 Out in the wilds they howled like animals
	    and huddled together under the bush-
	    es.

8 A senseless, a disreputable brood,	

they have been whipped out of the land.	8 A worthless bunch of nameless nobodies! They were driven out of the land.

Job begins by complaining of the mistreatment he now receives at the hands of young men or children whose fathers were worthless people. Job attacks the fathers and ridicules them as worthless people in these verses. These fathers have produced sons who have not been taught, and so they disregarded the law as expressed in Exodus 13.8; Deuteronomy 4.9; 6.7,20-25; Proverbs 3.12; 4.1. They are no doubt the very people who received just judgments when Job was their ruler (29.21-25). Job's scorn of the fathers is insulting to both the sons and their fathers.

Subdivision Heading

Translators wishing to provide a heading here may adapt the Handbook heading by saying, for example, "Your fathers were worth nothing," "Job ridicules the fathers of young men," or "Your worthless fathers!" Rowley has "The nobodies who now despise Job," and Habel (verses 1-11) "Abasement before outcasts."

30.1 RSV	TEV
"But now they make sport of me, men who are younger than I, whose fathers I would have disdained to set with the dogs of my flock.	But men younger than I am make fun of me now! Their fathers have always been so worthless that I wouldn't let them help my dogs guard sheep.

But now they make sport of me: verse 1 should be clearly marked as a contrast of past time in chapter 29 with present time in chapter 30. In Hebrew this verse has four lines, the first two being combined in TEV. RSV, which keeps the Hebrew form, does not name the subject until the second line. **Make sport of** translates the same verb which is rendered as "smiled" in 29.24. There Job "smiled" in kindness, but here Job is the object of someone's mockery. TEV has "make fun of me," and NEB "laughed to scorn." In translation we may use the same expressions for **make sport of** as were used for "scorn" in 16.20 and 22.19.

Men who are younger than I translates the Hebrew phrase "those smaller than I in days," which many translate as **younger**. The question is how much younger? Respect for a person's elders was expected as proper behavior. In 29.8 young men withdrew out of respect for Job. Dhorme suggests that the reference is to the mocking shouts of children, as in the case of Elisha in 2 Kings 2.23-24, and this is followed by FRCL, which says "But now I am ridiculed by urchins who don't respect my age." TEV "men younger than I" can imply that Job was making only a small distinction in age, whereas a significant age difference is intended, as is seen in the next line. GECL says "who are much younger than I," and Mft has "my juniors."

Whose fathers I would have disdained to set with the dogs of my flock: Job is concerned not only that they are children, or at least much younger than he, but that their status is inferior. Job **disdained** their fathers, which in Hebrew is "whom I would have refused . . ."; that is, "I would not have considered letting them

537

work with my sheepdogs." TEV and others translate this line as a fact; RSV and many others prefer a hypothetical statement with the implied meaning "Even if someone had requested me, I would not have allowed . . . ." Although sheepdogs were valued by shepherds (see Isa 56.9-11), they were also despised as being unclean animals that scavenged for their food (1 Kgs 14.11; 21.19,23; Psa 68.23). To call a person a "dog" was a serious insult (1 Sam 17.43; 2 Sam 3.8; 16.9), and this is still true in Arabic today. The meaning is not that Job would have disdained to turn his dogs on these people, but that he would not have hired them do the work of a sheepdog or, as Mft says, "I would have scorned to trust with a sheep-dog's task!" In languages in which sheep herding and the use of sheepdogs to keep the flock together are unknown, this line will require some adjustments. TEV "I would not let them help my dogs guard sheep" may be one such adjustment. Another may be "I would not let them do the dog's work of guarding the sheep" or "Dogs help guard the sheep, but I would not let their fathers help the dogs." In some languages a note may be required; for example, "Dogs are trained to look after sheep and to prevent them from straying."

30.2

RSV	TEV
What could I gain from the strength of their hands, men whose vigor is gone?	They were a bunch of worn-out men, too weak to do any work for me.

What could I gain from the strength of their hands: Job implies that these men, presumably the fathers, were physically weak and unfit for work. TEV shifts this to the second line. Even if they were strong enough to work, what good would it have done Job? TEV says "too weak to do any work for me."

Men whose vigor is gone: the meaning of this line is less clear. The word translated **vigor** is taken by some to mean "maturity." A number of changes have been proposed. For example, Dhorme modifies the preposition to get "men whose vigor had wholly perished." However, the sense of RSV and TEV does not require any change in the text. TEV "A bunch of worn out men" is more general and so is placed in the first line for reasons of English style. This verse may also be rendered, for example, "What good would I get out of people like that, all being worn out?" or "What use were they to me, since they were such weak men?"

30.3

RSV	TEV
Through want and hard hunger they gnaw the dry and desolate ground;[h]	They were so poor and hungry that they would gnaw dry roots— at night, in wild, desolate places.

[h] Heb *ground yesterday waste*

Through want and hard hunger: the Hebrew of this verse has three lines, but RSV reduces them to two. The word translated **hard** is rendered "barren" in 3.7.

There the basic meaning is "stony," and, as stony ground is unproductive, the meaning is extended to include "barren." The same allusion to stony ground here probably suggests "skinny, gaunt." It is here a description of the men in verse 2, which TEV renders "poor and hungry." NJB says "worn out by want and hunger."

They gnaw the dry and desolate ground is literally "those who gnaw the dry." TEV and others supply the word "roots," which Dhorme thinks fell out of the text in copying; but this expression may be a figure of speech, **dry** ground representing the roots that grow in it. RSV includes the words **and desolate ground** in the second line, and notes in a footnote that the Hebrew has "ground yesterday waste." RSV omits the words "yesterday" and "waste." NEB takes **dry** to mean "in the desert." HOTTP suggests either "those who gnaw the desert" or "those who flee to the desert." The words "ground yesterday waste" are much disputed. The word translated "yesterday" occurs in Genesis 19.34; 31.29,42, and is translated by TEV as "last night." Pope says the alliteration in this phrase is too striking for it to be removed, and translates "by night in desolate waste." HOTTP suggests "darkness/groping, waste and desolation." And the sense of this may be "They gnawed (something, perhaps roots) in the desert, where they groped in the waste and desolation of the darkness." Although no solution to the problems of this obscure verse can be at all certain, TEV is recommended as a meaningful attempt. The verse may also be rendered, for example, "These people were so poor and starved at night out in the deserts, that they would chew on dry roots in the ground."

30.4   RSV   TEV

> they pick mallow and the leaves   They pulled up the plants of the
>   of bushes,   desert and ate them,
> and to warm themselves the   even the tasteless roots of the
>   roots of the broom.   broom tree!

This verse continues the description of the miserable existence of these crude and inferior persons. Here attention is given to what they eat.

They pick mallow and the leaves of bushes: TEV has rendered **mallow** and **leaves of bushes** as "plants of the desert." It is difficult to be more specific about the identity of the one called **mallow**, since this is the only mention of it. It may also occur in 24.24, where RSV has also translated **mallow**. Most translations which mention a specific plant here identify it, as in NAB and NEB, with "saltwort," a plant with thick, sour leaves. Pope says of this plant that its foliage "is edible but has a sour taste and would be eaten only in dire extremity." RSV translates **and the leaves of** by adding one letter to the Hebrew of this line. A generic term translated **bushes** is found also in verse 7, and in Genesis 2.5, where TEV translates "plants," and in Genesis 21.15, where TEV has "bush." It is best not to attempt to be more specific than TEV in identifying these plants.

And to warm themselves the roots of the broom: RSV understands that they kept warm by burning the roots of the broom tree. TEV, NEB, Dhorme, Habel, and many others understand that they ate these roots. The Hebrew has "the root of the broom tree is their food." RSV and Pope interpret the words "their food" to mean "to warm oneself." The word is used in this way in Isaiah 47.14. Pope says the broom roots make good charcoal, and this is attested in Psalm 120.4, "A warrior's sharp arrows, with glowing coals of the broom tree." This small tree has long slender branches, small leaves, and produces a yellow flower. For illustration and technical name of the broom tree, see *Fauna and Flora of the Bible*, pages 100-101. Translators will often be required to substitute a local bush or small tree whose roots can be eaten if someone is starving. If the roots of the broom are not edible, as Pope says, this may be even more reason for Job to say that these miserable people are reduced to eating them. It is not likely that Job is congratulating them for keeping warm through the cold desert night. It seems preferable, therefore, to translate as TEV and others.

30.5   RSV   TEV

> They are driven out from among   Everyone drove them away with
> men;   shouts,
> they shout after them as after   as if they were shouting at
> a thief.   thieves.

They are driven out from among men: this construction is passive. These wanderers are driven out from "the midst," meaning from where people are settled, living. Wherever there are people living they drive these miserable persons away. TEV describes the action in this section as events that have already taken place: "drove them away." RSV describes it as present continuous action. This line will often have to be shifted to an active construction; for example, "People will not let them settle among them," "Villagers drive them away," or "Other people make them stay away from their settlements."

They shout after them as after a thief: TEV places "with shouts" in line a and "shouting" in line b. Not only are these people driven out from where others live, but at the same time people shout at them as when they shout to alert others that a thief has appeared. **As after a thief** is literally "like a thief."

30.6   RSV   TEV

> In the gullies of the torrents they   They had to live in caves,
> must dwell,   in holes dug in the sides of
> in holes of the earth and of the   cliffs.
> rocks.

In the gullies of the torrents they must dwell: the word translated **gullies** occurs only here in the Old Testament, and RSV and others base the translation on a similar word in Arabic. The sense seems to be the steep slopes of mountains along the edge of rivers, **torrents**, and this is translated as the final phrase of the second line in TEV, "in the sides of cliffs." NJB translates "in the sides of ravines." It is in these difficult places that they make their homes. The line may be translated, for example, "They look for a place to live on the steep mountain sides," "They have to find shelter in the gullies and ravines," or "They live on the sides of gullies near the stream beds."

In holes of the earth and of the rocks: it is difficult to tell from the Hebrew if **holes** is linked with **the earth** only, or also with **the rocks**. NEB says "they lived in gullies and ravines, holes in the earth and rocky clefts," which is better than RSV. This line may also be expressed "in holes in the ground and caves in the rocks."

30.7 RSV	TEV
Among the bushes they bray; under the nettles they huddle together.	Out in the wilds they howled like animals and huddled together under the bushes.

Among the bushes they bray: **bushes** translates the same word used in verse 4. **Bray** translates the same verb used in 6.5, "Does the wild ass bray when he has grass?" **Bray** represents the noise made by a donkey. **Bray** suggests these miserable people live like animals, specifically donkeys. Both Dhorme and Pope think their cries are from hunger. TEV has "howled like animals." FRCL shifts this line to second position and translates "One could hear their cries from the thickets." If necessary we may avoid naming the noise made by a specific animal by saying, for instance, "They make their cries among the bushes" or "They made noises like wild animals out in the far places."

Under the nettles they huddle together: **nettles** translates a word for the kind of vegetation that grows up in deserted ruins, as expressed in Zephaniah 2.9. In Proverbs 24.31 it is said to grow on the field of the idle farmer. It may be translated specifically as "thistles" or "thorns," or more generally as "undergrowth" or "bushes." **Huddle together** depicts them pressed together, perhaps to keep warm, or from fear. "They crowd together under the bushes" or "they cling to each other under the bushes to keep warm."

30.8 RSV	TEV
A senseless, a disreputable brood, they have been whipped out of the land.	A worthless bunch of nameless nobodies! They were driven out of the land.

A senseless, a disreputable brood is literally "sons of a senseless person, sons of a nameless person." "Sons of" is an expression which indicates the nature of these people. It does not refer to their being someone's male offspring. They have neither good morals nor respectability, and TEV calls them "A worthless bunch of nameless nobodies!" The word translated **senseless** is the word Job used of his wife in 2.10. The term refers to persons who lack moral judgment. See 2.10 for comments. And so they are "a foolish gang of nameless people," "A bunch of senseless people nobody knows," or "A worthless bunch of people and nobody knows their names."

They have been whipped out of the land: the word translated **whipped** is used as a transitive verb in 1 Samuel 2.14 with the meaning "to drive or thrust," and may be translated here without any change in the text, as in TEV, "They were driven out of the land." This line may have to be shifted to an active construction; for example, "People have beaten them and forced them from the country" or "People have used clubs to drive them from the land."

7B-2. Job describes the attacks of those who mock him (30.9-15)

RSV	TEV

9   "And now I have become their song,
    I am a byword to them.
	9 Now they come and laugh at me;
	    I am nothing but a joke to them.

10   They abhor me, they keep aloof from me;
    they do not hesitate to spit at the sight
    of me.
	10 They treat me with disgust;
	    they think they are too good for me,
	    and even come and spit in my face.

11   Because God has loosed my cord and
    humbled me,
    they have cast off restraint in my pres-
    ence.
	11 Because God has made me weak and
	    helpless,
	    they turn against me with all their fury.

12   On my right hand the rabble rise,
    they drive me forth,
    they cast up against me their ways of
    destruction.
	12 This mob attacks me head-on;
	    they send me running; they prepare
	    their final assault.

13   They break up my path,
    they promote my calamity;
    no one restrains them.
	13 They cut off my escape and try to destroy
	    me;
	    and there is no one to stop them.

14   As through a wide breach they come;
    amid the crash they roll on.
	14 They pour through the holes in my de-
	    fenses
	    and come crashing down on top of me;

15   Terrors are turned upon me;
    my honor is pursued as by the wind,
    and my prosperity has passed away like
    a cloud.
	15 I am overcome with terror;
	    my dignity is gone like a puff of wind,
	    and my prosperity like a cloud.

Subdivision Heading

The Handbook heading may be adjusted to say, for example, "Those who mistreat Job want to destroy him," "Job is under attack," or "No escape for Job." Rowley has "The indignities Job suffers."

30.9

RSV	TEV

"And now I have become their
    song,
I am a byword to them.
	Now they come and laugh at me;
	I am nothing but a joke to
	    them.

And now I have become their song: this verse repeats the thought of verse 1. The ones who do this to Job are not the miserable fathers Job depicted in verses 2-8, but their children from verse 1. FRCL makes this clear with "Now their children make up songs about me." The word translated **song** here refers to the music of stringed instruments and is used in many psalm titles. In Psalm 69.12 it is used of drinking songs: "I am the talk of those who sit in the gate, and the drunkards make songs about me." See also Lamentations 3.14, where it indicates mocking songs. In languages which do not use songs to ridicule someone, it may be necessary to say, for example, "But now their children make fun of me," "They tell stories about me," or "They makes jokes of me."

I am a byword to them: byword translates a form of "word" used frequently in Job. Only here does the context give it the sense of "ridicule." TEV expresses the thought effectively with "I am nothing but a joke to them."

30.10

RSV	TEV
They abhor me, they keep aloof from me; they do not hesitate to spit at the sight of me.	They treat me with disgust; they think they are too good for me, and even come and spit in my face.

They abhor me, they keep aloof from me: in Hebrew there are three verbs in the two lines of this verse, and TEV represents them with three lines. **Abhor me** translates a verb used in 19.19. The thought is not that of hatred, but disgust at Job's repulsive physical conditions. NJB says "Filled with disgust, they keep their distance." FRCL translates "They turn their back to me to show their disgust." **They keep aloof** is translated by TEV, more in terms of attitude than physical avoidance, as "they think they are too good for me." However, it is the reaction to Job's physical condition that is intended here, as in FRCL and NJB.

They do not hesitate to spit at the sight of me is literally "and from my face they do not spare spit." These persons are ready at any time to spit with disdain at the face of Job. The thought is that they spit into his face, and not that they spit on the ground **at the sight** of him, or when they see him. TEV has "They . . . even come and spit in my face." Spitting in the face has different meanings in different cultures. In languages in which this is a gesture of blessing, it may be necessary to say "they insult me by spitting on me" or "they spit on me to show they despise me."

30.11

RSV	TEV
Because God has loosed my cord and humbled me, they have cast off restraint in my presence.	Because God has made me weak and helpless, they turn against me with all their fury.

Because God has loosed my cord and humbled me: the written Hebrew text has "his cord," and the margin has a notation that it is to be read "my cord," which both RSV and TEV accept. The Hebrew of the verbs translated **loosed** and **humbled** are in the singular, and **cast off** in the next line is plural. RSV and TEV supply **God** as the subject of the verbs in this line. **My cord** is understood by some to mean "my bowstring," as in Judges 16.7-9 "God has loosed my bowstring," which means that God has left Job defenseless or, as TEV says, "Because God has made me weak and helpless." The HOTTP committee was divided between choosing "my cord" or "his cord" as the better text. The expression is obviously figurative and must be interpreted in order to be translated with meaning. Therefore TEV provides a good model for translation. In languages in which the cause is better stated following the consequence, it will be necessary to transpose the lines of verse 11. If the figure of loosening the bow string does not mean to weaken a person, the translator may be able to supply a different figure or may shift to a general term; for example, "God has broken my weapon." It may be possible in some languages to retain the image of the bow string and say "God has cut my bow string and now I am helpless."

They have cast off restraint in my presence: **restraint** translates the Hebrew for "bridle" and is used in Isaiah 30.28 and Psalm 32.9. A "bridle" is a harness placed on the head of a horse to control its movements, and it is used here as a symbol of restraint. The thought expressed in this line is that, when people saw that Job was helpless, they turned on him violently, as an unbridled horse that is no longer under control. NEB has "At sight of me they throw off all restraint." GECL says "Therefore they let every restraint go." NJB has "They too throw off the bridle in my presence," but this does not convey the idea in English of abandoning restraints. Other models are "when they saw me they did to me whatever they wished" or "so they let themselves do whatever they wished."

30.12	RSV	TEV
	On my right hand the rabble rise, they drive me[i] forth, they cast up against me their ways of destruction.	This mob attacks me head-on; they send me running; they prepare their final assault.

[i] Heb *my feet*

On my right hand the rabble rise: this verse has three lines in Hebrew. TEV marks the three independent clauses with semi-colons instead of commas, but it combines the second and third lines into one. The meaning of **right hand** is uncertain. In Hebrew thought the right hand implied strength as well as honor and prestige. The context may imply an attack against Job, and if this is correct, Job is saying that the mob rises up even where he is strongest, on his right hand. NEB is similar to this with "On my right flank they attack in a mob." TEV probably has a military assault in mind, with "This mob attacks me head on." **The rabble** translates a word which occurs only here in the Hebrew Bible. The context favors something like "mob" or a word suggesting "violent youth." This line may also be expressed as "Gangs of them attack me" or "The mobs gang up on me."

They drive me forth: there is so much uncertainty about this line that it is omitted by many translators, including NEB. As the RSV footnote indicates, the Hebrew has "my feet" in place of **me**. The verb is the same as in verse 11, so the Hebrew is literally "they have cast off my feet." This may suggest that the verb for **cast off** was mistakenly copied from verse 11. HOTTP suggests "My feet they have cast forth," meaning "They make me give ground," which is as good a guess as that of TEV. TEV translates "They send me running," which is another guess but which can serve as part of the description of the result of the attack on Job.

They cast up against me their ways of destruction: in Hebrew this line is similar to the second line of 19.12. See there for discussion. Job 19.12b, which has "their way" in the Hebrew, was interpreted in its context as placing "siege works" against Job. This line differs only by substituting another word, "path," rendered **ways** by RSV, followed by a word meaning "ruin, disaster" or **destruction**. Pope suggests the expression translated **their ways of destruction** refers to "siege works" as in 19.12, and NIV translates "They build their siege ramps against me." FRCL states it more generally and makes **destruction** a verb phrase involving Job: "They assault me in order to destroy me." Either NIV or FRCL may serve as a translation model for this line. We may also translate the line "they attack me and try to kill me."

30.13	RSV	TEV

<table>
<tr><td>

They break up my path,
   they promote my calamity;
   no one restrains[j] them.

j Cn: Heb *helps*

</td><td>

They cut off my escape and try to
   destroy me;
   and there is no one to stop[i]
   them.

i Probable text stop; *Hebrew* help.

</td></tr>
</table>

The division of this verse is abnormal, and so translators divide it in various ways. Most translators reduce the three Hebrew lines to two. Verses 13 and 14 continue the military figure of verse 12. Job is depicted as being cut off and unable to escape, and without anyone to come to his rescue.

They break up my path: the verb in this line is used only here, but may be an irregular spelling or another form of a similar verb used in 19.10, which RSV translates "he breaks me down." Job's enemies **break up** his path in order to prevent him from escaping; as NJB says, "They cut off all means of escape." TEV combines this line with the following as "They cut off my escape and try to destroy me." In translation a literal rendering will leave the reader wondering how breaking up the ground on the path can prevent someone from escaping. Accordingly it is better to give the meaning as in NJB or TEV, or to say, for example, "They have cut off my path so I cannot escape," "They cut me off so that I can't escape," or "They guard the road and I can't get away from them."

They promote my calamity is literally "from my ruin they profit"; NIV translates this as "They succeed in destroying me," which is preferable to TEV "try to destroy me." HOTTP translates "they contribute usefully to [meaning, 'promote'] my calamity." We may also render this line as "they bring about my downfall" or "they cause me to fail." It appears best to join this with the previous line, as in TEV.

No one restrains them: footnotes in both RSV and TEV indicate that the Hebrew verb translated **restrains** has been changed from the Hebrew for "help." The Hebrew verbs meaning "restrain" and "help" differ by only one letter. Dhorme and Pope suggest a change from "help" to get "prevent." NEB has "unhindered." The Hebrew term "no helper" can mean, as TOB says, "without needing any help," which is one of the recommendations of HOTTP, and since good sense can be made without changing the text, translators are encouraged to follow this; for example, "and no one needs to help them" or "they can do this without any help."

30.14

RSV	TEV
As through[k] a wide breach they come; amid the crash they roll on.	They pour through the holes in my defenses and come crashing down on top of me;

[k] Cn: Heb *like*

As through a wide breach they come: the figure of an assault on a besieged city continues. The enemy is depicted as making a hole in the city wall and pouring in, wave upon wave. The RSV footnote implies that there has been a textual change, but this is a translational matter. **Through a wide breach** translates the same expression found in Amos 4.3. **They come** refers to soldiers or enemies entering the city. The action is seen from Job's point of view inside the besieged city, or as TEV says, "in my defenses." This line may be more clearly translated as a simile; for example, "They attack me like soldiers breaking through a wall" or "They break through the wall that defends me."

Amid the crash they roll on: the subject is the same as in the first line, an indefinite **they**. The Hebrew has "under the crash," probably giving the picture that the invaders rush in while the stones of the wall are still falling. NEB expresses this as "at the moment of the crash." The word translated **roll on** has the same root as in Amos 5.24, "Let justice roll down like waters." The noun form of this verb means "wave," and the succession of troops pouring through the gap in the wall is described as being like a series of ocean waves. On the whole, RSV is a clear rendering of this verse, closer to the Hebrew form, and to be recommended to translators rather than TEV.

30.15

RSV	TEV
Terrors are turned upon me; my honor is pursued as by the wind, and my prosperity has passed away like a cloud.	I am overcome with terror; my dignity is gone like a puff of wind, and my prosperity like a cloud.

Terrors are turned upon me: the Hebrew of this verse has three lines, the second and third being parallel in meaning. **Terrors** is the same noun used by Bildad and Zophar in 18.11,14; 27.20. The meaning here is "fear, fright." **Are turned upon me** means "overwhelms me," or as in TEV, "I am overcome with terror."

My honor is pursued as by the wind: **honor** translates a word found only here and in Isaiah 32.8 ("noble"). It may be expressed as "dignity" or "confidence." It is related to the word for "noble" or "prince" found in 12.21; 21.28. It is Job's "princely dignity," which may refer mainly to his status in the community. **Pursued as by the wind**: we may render this as "it is as if my dignity were driven away by the wind." FRCL has "sweeping away my dignity like a gust of wind." TEV is expressive, with "my dignity is gone like a puff of wind." In some languages **my honor** may have to be expressed differently; for example, "the honor the people gave me" or "the respect I received from the people."

And my prosperity has passed away like a cloud: the word translated **prosperity** is related to the verb meaning "to save," so it has traditionally been rendered "salvation" and is so rendered by Dhorme. It can also be understood as "well-being, welfare," and many modern translations take it in one of these senses. The word occurs in Job in only one other place, namely, in 13.16, where RSV translates "salvation" but NEB has "success." The causative form of the verb can mean "is victorious" as in Zechariah 9.9, and "victorious" in the context in which God rescues or saves his people. Accordingly NEB translates "And my hope of victory vanishes like a cloud." This rendering fits the context better than **prosperity** or "welfare" and should be considered by translators as a translation model.

7B-3. Job accuses God of attacking him (30.16-26)

RSV	TEV
16 "And now my soul is poured out within me; days of affliction have taken hold of me.	16 Now I am about to die; there is no relief for my suffering.
17 The night racks my bones, and the pain that gnaws me takes no rest.	17 At night my bones all ache; the pain that gnaws me never stops.
18 With violence it seizes my garment; it binds me about like the collar of my tunic.	18 God seizes me by my collar and twists my clothes out of shape.
19 God has cast me into the mire, and I have become like dust and ashes.	19 He throws me down in the mud; I am no better than dirt.
20 I cry to thee and thou dost not answer me; I stand, and thou dost not heed me.	20 I call to you, O God, but you never answer; and when I pray, you pay no attention.
21 Thou hast turned cruel to me; with the might of thy hand thou dost persecute me.	21 You are treating me cruelly; you persecute me with all your power.
22 Thou liftest me up on the wind, thou makest me ride on it, and thou tossest me about in the roar of the storm.	22 You let the wind blow me away; you toss me about in a raging storm.
23 Yea, I know that thou wilt bring me to death, and to the house appointed for all living.	23 I know you are taking me off to my death, to the fate in store for everyone.
	24 Why do you attack a ruined man, one who can do nothing but beg for pity?
24 "Yet does not one in a heap of ruins stretch out his hand, and in his disaster cry for help?	25 Didn't I weep with people in trouble and feel sorry for those in need?
25 Did not I weep for him whose day was	26 I hoped for happiness and light, but trouble and darkness came instead.

> hard?
>   Was not my soul grieved for the poor?
> 26 But when I looked for good, evil came;
>   and when I waited for light, darkness
>   came.

In verses 16-26 Job shifts his attention to another source of his misery, namely, God.

Subdivision Heading

The Handbook heading may be adjusted to say, for example, "God also mistreats me," "God treats me cruelly," or "God does not listen to my cries."

30.16   RSV   TEV

"And now my soul is poured out   Now I am about to die;
    within me;   there is no relief for my suffer-
days of affliction have taken   ing.
    hold of me.

And now my soul is poured out within me: And now, as in verses 1 and 9, contrasts the past with the present (the Hebrew uses the identical expression in all three verses). In these verses Job compares the former times, when he enjoyed God's favor, with the present, when God is his enemy. RSV renders the Hebrew line literally, but **my soul** (*nefesh*) **is poured out within me** makes little sense. The same Hebrew expression is found in Psalm 42.4, where the context is a sad person recalling the past and longing for God's presence. In a similar way Job is downcast and in despair. The meaning here is that Job's suffering has reduced his existence to nothing, and so the Hebrew concept must have been that the *nefesh* was like a liquid that could be poured out in death. NJB translates "And now the life in me trickles away," and TEV "Now I am about to die." SPCL has "I have no more desire to live." All of these are adequate translation models.

Days of affliction have taken hold of me: this is again a literal rendering of the Hebrew. A similar expression occurs in verse 27 and in Lamentations 1.7. **Days of affliction** expresses the continuous nature of Job's suffering and misery, or as NEB says, "Misery has me daily in its grip." **Days** in this line is matched by "nights" in verse 17a. TEV has kept the meaning but dispensed with the poetic images of **days** and the depiction of being aggressively seized by suffering: "There is no relief for my suffering."

30.17   RSV   TEV

The night racks my bones,   At night my bones all ache;
    and the pain that gnaws me   the pain that gnaws me never
    takes no rest.   stops.

The night racks my bones is literally "the night pierces my bones from upon me." In RSV **The night** is taken as the subject and personified as "boring into, piercing" Job's bones. Another interpretation is that "he," namely God, does this to Job at night. Dhorme and others render the verb as a passive: "At night my bones are pierced." As noted above, the Hebrew adds "from upon me," which the Septuagint does not translate, and neither does RSV. HOTTP, which nearly always attempts to preserve a form of the Hebrew text, suggests "At night it pierces my bones, they drop from off me," which may mean "Suffering pierces my bones at night, and they fall off." GECL improves on this with "At night pain bores into all my bones, as though they were falling from my body." No doubt the poet was expressing severe pain in Job's body through these figures, but it may be necessary to avoid the figures and express the idea in a general way, as does TEV, "At night my bones all ache."

And the pain that gnaws me takes no rest: **that gnaws me** is literally "my gnawers." Some take this to mean the worms in Job's sores, as in 7.5. A word with similar sounds in Arabic means "veins," and Dhorme and NEB follow this. The Septuagint translates "my nerves." There is little certainty about the exact meaning of this Hebrew expression. **Takes no rest** translates a verb meaning "to lie down" for the purpose of sleeping; that is, "to go to bed" or "to sleep." Here the expression is used figuratively, and TEV translates without a figure of speech: "The pain that gnaws me never stops." Although "nerves" or "veins" may make a better parallel with **bones**, that is not sufficient reason to depart from the Hebrew text. In some languages **pain that gnaws** may have to be expressed differently; for example, "the pain that burns in me does not stop" or "the pain that makes me suffer goes on all night."

30.18	RSV	TEV

With violence it seizes my gar- ment;[1] it binds me about like the collar of my tunic.	God seizes me by my collar and twists my clothes out of shape.

[1] Gk: Heb *my garment is disfigured*

With violence it seizes my garment: as the RSV footnote shows, the Hebrew has "my garment is disfigured." RSV takes the subject to be "pain" from the previous verse. Dhorme and others understand God to be the subject, and so God is depicted as grabbing Job by his clothes and throwing him down. RSV follows the Septuagint in changing "is disfigured" to **seizes**. This involves the dropping of one letter in Hebrew. The line may be rendered, for example, "God has brutally grabbed, seized, taken hold of my clothes." TEV has reversed the order of the two lines in this verse to give a more logical order for English but does not change the text, and so "twists my clothes out of shape" translates the Hebrew "my garment is disfigured." The HOTTP committee was divided, one half giving the Hebrew text as we have it a "C" rating, and the other half giving the Septuagint a "C" rating as well. Consequently they suggest either text for translation. HOTTP understands the Hebrew text to mean "my skin is disfigured," and the Septuagint to mean "he seizes my garment." The Hebrew for **my garment** may be a metaphor referring to the skin.

It binds me about like the collar of my tunic: in RSV **it** refers again to "the pain" from verse 17 and from the first line of this verse. This line is not clear in its reference to the binding like the collar of the tunic, or outer garment. **The collar** (literally "mouth") is depicted as being tight, but Middle Eastern garments were not tight. It may be better to take this as a generalized simile and translate as in FRCL, "He grabs me by the neck, like a collar that fits too tightly." Without the simile the whole verse may be rendered, for example, "God grabs my clothes violently, he takes hold of me by the collar of my coat." We may also attempt to remain closer to the Hebrew form by saying, for example, "and seizes me and wrinkles my skin. It clings to me like the collar of my tunic."

30.19   RSV   TEV

God has cast me into the mire,   He throws me down in the mud;
and I have become like dust   I am no better than dirt.
and ashes.

God has cast me into the mire: in this verse, as in verse 18, God is not mentioned in the Hebrew. RSV, which had **pain** as the subject in verse 18, now introduces God as the subject. The sense of this line is not in doubt: "God throws me down in the mud." In verse 18b, if God has grabbed Job by the coat collar, then this is the follow-up event.

And I have become like dust and ashes: here Job echoes the language of Abraham in Genesis 18.27, "I am but dust and ashes." There, as here, **dust and ashes** expresses a person's lowly state or humiliation. TEV has done this in English with "I am no better than dirt." In 42.6 Job concludes his final answer to God by repenting "in dust and ashes." In some languages it may not be clear that **like dust and ashes** means "humble." In some language areas ashes are associated with mourning rituals. Accordingly we may have to translate, for example, "God has humbled me like dust and ashes," "God has made me low like dust and ashes," or, avoiding the simile, "God has humbled me," or idiomatically, for example, "God has made me a person with bowed head."

30.20   RSV   TEV

I cry to thee and thou dost not   I call to you, O God, but you
answer me;   never answer;
I stand, and thou dost not[m]   and when I pray, you pay no
heed me.   attention.

[m] One Heb Ms and Vg: Heb lacks *not*

I cry to thee and thou dost not answer me: TEV says, "I call to you, O God, but you never answer." God is not mentioned in the Hebrew, but there is no one else Job cries out to.

I stand, and thou dost not heed me: the Hebrew has "I stood and you looked at me." **Stand** is used here, as in Jeremiah 15.1, with the sense of "to pray," and so TEV "when I pray." **Thou dost not heed me** lacks a negative in Hebrew, as RSV indicates. RSV follows the Vulgate and one Hebrew manuscript which has the negative. See the RSV footnote. Some translate the line without adding the negative; for example, NEB "I stand up to plead, but thou sittest aloof." NIV is better: "I stand up, but you merely look at me." HOTTP has "I stood up and you fixed (your gaze) on me," with a second suggestion, "I halted (that is, 'I became silent') and you gazed at me." This agrees in part with Gordis' rendering, "If I remain silent, you pay me no heed." Gordis argues that the negative in line a applies equally to line b. On the same basis TEV translates "You pay no attention." The line may also be expressed "I came before you, but you do not listen to me," "I call to you for help, God, but you do not hear me," or "I pray to you, God, but you pay no attention to me."

30.21	RSV	TEV

Thou hast turned cruel to me;		You are treating me cruelly;
with the might of thy hand		you persecute me with all your
thou dost persecute me.		power.

Thou has turned cruel to me: Job is unable to account for the change of God's attitude toward him. Here Job renews his longstanding complaint against God expressed in 13.24; 16.9; 19.11. **Turned** in the sense of "became" is used also in Isaiah 63.10. **Cruel** is used the same way in Lamentations 4.3. The phrase suggests that God has become cruel, whereas in former times he was not. NJB renders it "You have grown cruel to me," and SPCL "You have become cruel to me." NEB says "Thou hast turned cruelly against me." All of these appear to be better than TEV, "You are treating me cruelly."

With the might of thy hand thou dost persecute me: **might of . . . hand** occurs also in Deuteronomy 8.17 and expresses, as in TEV, "with all your power." And so Job says "You use all your power to make me suffer."

30.22	RSV	TEV

Thou liftest me up on the wind,		You let the wind blow me away;
thou makest me ride on it,		you toss me about in a raging
and thou tossest me about in		storm.
the roar of the storm.		

In verse 19 God throws Job to the ground. Now he is picked up by the wind and helplessly tossed about.

Thou liftest me up on the wind: the poet depicts more variety of movement than is suggested by TEV "You let the wind blow me away." RSV expresses these movements through the translation of the Hebrew verbs translated **liftest me up** and

makest me ride. This may be translated, for example, "You cause the wind to pick me up and make me ride away on it."

And thou tossest me about in the roar of the storm: the verb translated **tossest** can mean "melt" and is translated "soften" in Psalm 65.10. That sense does not seem to be appropriate in the context of this verse. In Amos 9.5 TEV renders it as "the whole world rises and falls like the Nile river." A similar word in Arabic is used of the surging of the ocean, and this is the sense of RSV **tossest**, meaning to throw up and down. TEV has "You toss me about." **The roar of the storm**: there are two alternatives for the word translated **storm** in the Hebrew. The one means "success" as found in 5.12; see there for comments. The other form is a variant of the word meaning "crash" and is used in Isaiah 22.2 as "shoutings." Pope interprets the word as "noise," and in this context it refers to that which makes the noise, namely, **the storm**. There are numerous other suggestions, but RSV and TEV, which are supported by many other modern translations, are as good if not better than most and so are recommended to translators. This line may also be expressed "and you cause the storm to pitch me up and down" or "you cause the storm to throw me here and there."

30.23   RSV   TEV

> Yea, I know that thou wilt bring
>   me to death,
> and to the house appointed for
>   all living.

> I know you are taking me off to
>   my death,
> to the fate in store for every-
>   one.

Yea, I know that thou wilt bring me to death: Job acknowledges a number of times that death comes to everybody. **Yea** translates the Hebrew *ki*, whose function is not to join verses 22 and 23 but to introduce the clause beginning **I know**. Since it often marks an emphatic statement, it should be taken here as emphasizing Job's certainty that he must die some day. **Bring me** translates the Hebrew "bring me back, return me," which is probably used as a reflection of 1.21, in that death meant a return to the place from which a person started, namely, the earth. **Death** is personified here as in 28.22 and is the same as Sheol. GECL translates "I know you bring me toward the world of the dead." This line may also be rendered, for example, "I know you are taking me to my death" or "I know you are carrying me away to the land of the dead."

And to the house appointed for all living: the verb in line <u>a</u> serves also for line <u>b</u>. The movement from line <u>a</u> to line <u>b</u> is from the nonfigurative to the figurative. **House appointed** is "house of meeting" or "meeting place." It expresses the place where the dead are brought together, and it means the same as Sheol. This place is **for all living**, that is, "for everyone." **All living** seems to carry a bit of irony, reminding those now living that some day they will no longer be living. TEV avoids the figure "house of meeting" and translates "the fate in store for everyone." In this line FRCL emphasizes the parallelism in terms of a place: "that meeting place set for all the living." Other possible translations are "the place where all living people will meet when they die" or "the meeting place set aside for all who live and die."

30.24   RSV   TEV

"Yet does not one in a heap of   Why do you attack a ruined man,
    ruins stretch out his hand,   one who can do nothing but
  and in his disaster cry for   beg for pity?[j]
    help?[n]

                             [j] *Verse 24 in Hebrew is unclear.*

[n] Cn: Heb obscure

Job continues to cry out but gets no response. This verse is exceedingly difficult, and translators and commentators interpret it in various ways. Both RSV and TEV margins indicate that the Hebrew is unclear. Pope says it is one of the most difficult in the entire poem.

Yet does not one in a heap of ruins stretch out his hand: the first problem is the subject of **stretch out his hand**. In TEV the subject is "you," referring to God. In RSV it is Job himself. Both RSV and TEV understand **one in a heap of ruins** to be Job describing his own condition, which TEV renders "a ruined man." **Stretched out his hand** is a phrase used in Genesis 37.22, in which Reuben warns his brothers to "lay no hand upon" Joseph to do him harm. TEV, Dhorme, Pope, and many others interpret this expression as meaning "to do harm," and so TEV "Why do you attack?" On the other hand RSV and some others understand it to mean "to obtain help." Furthermore the word translated **heap of ruins** is interpreted by many, including Dhorme, to mean "poor man," and so Dhorme translates "I (Job) did not strike the poor man with my hand," and NJB "Yet have I ever laid a hand on the poor?"

And in his disaster cry for help: this line seems to state the conditions for the question or statement made in the previous line. Most modern translators make a change in the words translated **cry for help**. TEV is close to RSV in "beg for pity." In both RSV and TEV Job speaks of himself indirectly, as in FRCL "In distress, doesn't one cry out for help?" FRCL has a note saying "Verse obscure, meaning uncertain." Dhorme changes the text to say "If in his distress he cried out for my help," referring to the same person as in the first line. Translators appear to be divided into two groups: (1) those who depict Job as defending himself for not harming the unfortunate person who called out for help; and (2) those like RSV who depict Job justifying his pleas for help in the midst of his suffering. In the light of the following verse, it is preferable to follow the first group and translate, for example, "I never did anything to harm a person who was suffering, and who called out to me in his troubles."

30.25   RSV   TEV

Did not I weep for him whose   Didn't I weep with people in
    day was hard?   trouble
  Was not my soul grieved for   and feel sorry for those in
    the poor?   need?

Did not I weep for him whose day was hard? This verse is clearly linked with verse 24 and continues the theme of Job's defense of his past conduct. Not only did Job not harm the unfortunate person, but he was compassionate toward him. The question in this verse expects a "Yes" reply. The negative here continues into line b, as in 28.17. **Weep** means to cry with grief at the sight of the sufferer, showing that Job is affected emotionally. **Whose day was hard** translates the Hebrew "harsh of day," referring to a person whose daily life is spent under difficult, harsh circumstances. The expression calls attention to their poverty and is parallel with **the poor** in the following line. This line may also be translated "I have often cried for the one who suffered" or "Didn't I cry for those who were unfortunate? Of course I did!"

Was not my soul grieved for the poor? Job's **soul** (*nefesh*) is saddened by the poor. **Grieved** translates a word found only here. A similar verb meaning "to be sad" is found in Isaiah 19.10, and so TEV "and feel sorry for those in need?" Another rendering: "Wasn't I sad because of the people who had nothing? I certainly was sad!"

30.26 RSV	TEV
But when I looked for good, evil came; and when I waited for light, darkness came.	I hoped for happiness and light, but trouble and darkness came instead.

But when I looked for good, evil came: looked for is to be taken in the sense of "expected, looked forward to, hoped for." **Good** is "good fortune" or "happiness," as in TEV, and is symbolized by **light** in the next line. TEV shifts **light** from the next line to say "I hoped for happiness and light."

And when I waited for light, darkness came: waited translates a different verb in this line, but it has the same meaning as **looked for** in line a. **Darkness** symbolizes **evil**, which may best be taken in this context as "misfortune" or "misery" in contrast to "happiness." TEV takes **evil** from line a and associates it with **darkness** in line b: "but trouble and darkness came instead." Job's upright life gave him reason to expect happiness, while the friends, on their side, argued that turning away from his sin would return happiness or good fortune to him. The line may be expressed, for example, "I expected to have happiness, but got misery instead," "I hoped for good fortune, but got nothing but unhappiness," or "I hoped I would be happy, but I was always in trouble."

7B-4. Job cries for help, but none comes (30.27-31)

	RSV		TEV
	RSV		TEV
27	My heart is in turmoil, and is never still; days of affliction come to meet me.	27	I am torn apart by worry and pain; I have had day after day of suffering.
28	I go about blackened, but not by the sun; I stand up in the assembly, and cry for help.	28	I go about in gloom, without any sunshine; I stand up in public and plead for help.
29	I am a brother of jackals, and a companion of ostriches.	29	My voice is as sad and lonely as the cries of a jackal or an ostrich.

30	My skin turns black and falls from me, and my bones burn with heat.	30	My skin has turned dark; I am burning with fever.
31	My lyre is turned to mourning, and my pipe to the voice of those who weep.	31	Where once I heard joyful music, now I hear only mourning and weeping.

In the final verses Job appeals for help to the assembly where once he was the leader. But now his appeals go unheard.

Subdivision Heading

The Handbook heading may be reworded to say, for example, "No one listens to Job's cries," "No help for Job," or "No one will help Job." Rowley has "The contrast between then and now," Habel (verses 20-31) "Denial of justice."

30.27   RSV   TEV

My heart is in turmoil, and is
     never still;
days of affliction come to meet
     me.

I am torn apart by worry and
     pain;
I have had day after day of
     suffering.

My heart is in turmoil, and is never still: the first clause is literally "My bowels boil," and NEB offers the odd rendering "My bowels are in ferment." In Hebrew "bowels" represent the center of powerful emotions, as is seen also in Isaiah 16.11; Lamentations 1.20; 2.11 (RSV uses "my soul" in all three examples). The expression is well translated by both RSV, **My heart is in turmoil**, and TEV, "I am torn apart," which makes no reference to an organ of the body. **And is never still** translates "and they have not remained calm." The reference is to the "bowels." This phrase emphasizes the permanence of Job's painful emotional stress, which NJB translates "My stomach seethes, is never still." Languages differ greatly in the way they express psychological states, and the translator should use an idiomatic phrase that expresses it clearly and acceptably; for example, "My innermost is churning within me," "My liver will not sit still," "My stomach rolls over in me."

Days of affliction come to meet me: this line gives the reason for the physical and emotional distress in the previous line. **Days of affliction** calls attention to the prolonged aspect of Job's suffering. FRCL relates this line to the previous one by translating "ever since I confronted this life of misery." TEV has an independent sentence: "I have had day after day of suffering." **Come to meet me** is a literal rendering. In English it may be more natural to say, for example, "I face endless days of suffering." NJB keeps **days of suffering** as the subject, with "Days of suffering have struck me."

30.28   RSV   TEV

I go about blackened, but not by
     the sun;

I go about in gloom, without any
     sunshine;

I stand up in the assembly, and cry for help.	I stand up in public and plead for help.

I go about blackened, but not by the sun: **blackened** translates a word whose primary meaning is as in RSV. Dhorme takes it to mean "tanned," but when this is followed by **but not by the sun**, "tanned" is inappropriate in English. The most likely sense seems to be "darkened by disease," and by extension "sad, depressed, downcast," or as TEV says, "I go about in gloom." **But not by the sun** is literally "and not in heat," where "heat" is used as in Psalm 19.6. It is most likely that Job is saying here that he is dejected, in despair, and there is no sunshine or warmth to make him feel better. NJB has made a change to get "Yet no one comforts me." FRCL and others take **blackened** to mean "mourn," and translate "I am in mourning; there is no sun for me!" This line may also be rendered, for example, "I live a sad life and without the sun to cheer me up" or "I am discouraged and the sun does not shine to encourage me."

I stand up in the assembly, and cry for help: **stand up** translates the same verb used in verse 20. The purpose of Job's standing is to **cry for help**. **Assembly** refers to a public gathering of the leaders of the community, a town council meeting. This line may be expressed differently; for example, "I even call out in public and ask for help," "I stand up in the town meeting and beg the people to help me," or "I plead in the public meetings 'Someone please help me!' "

30.29   RSV   TEV

I am a brother of jackals, and a companion of ostriches.	My voice is as sad and lonely as the cries of a jackal or an ostrich.

I am a brother of jackals: **jackals** and **ostriches** inhabit the deserts and are known for their mournful cries. The **jackal** resembles the fox in appearance, but, unlike the fox, **jackals** go about in bands. See *Fauna and Flora of the Bible*, pages 31-32.

And a companion of ostriches: 39.13-18 contains a detailed description of the **ostrich**. For further information see *Fauna and Flora of the Bible*, pages 60-61. Job associates himself with these animals as **brother** and **companion**. It is unlikely that he means he lives with them in the desert. Instead he compares his pleas, his crying out to God and to the public, with their mournful wails in the desert, where no one replies. TEV translates "My voice is as sad and lonely as the cries of a jackal or an ostrich." FRCL has "By my sad cries, I have become a companion of jackals and a brother to the ostrich," which seems to fit French style better. In languages which must indicate older or younger brother, it will be best to use the term for "younger brother" to emphasize Job's dependence and inferior feelings. In many languages **jackal** may be translated by the word for "fox." If, however, the fox is unknown, it may be possible to substitute another animal known to make mournful cries. If these solutions are unsatisfactory, it may be possible to use a borrowed word and a classifier; for example, "a wild animal called . . . ." A term for **ostrich** is more difficult because it is found in fewer areas. Because of the peculiarities of the ostrich, it is harder to find an equivalent bird. Furthermore, the ostrich is described in some detail in chapter 39. Consequently, if the ostrich is unknown, it will often be best to use a borrowed word; for example, "big bird called . . . ." If this solution is unsatisfactory, it may be possible to say "big bird." In any case, it will be helpful to have an illustration of the ostrich in chapter 39.

30.30   RSV   TEV

> **My skin turns black and falls**   **My skin has turned dark; I am**
> **from me,**   **burning with fever.**
> **and my bones burn with heat.**

My skin turns black and falls from me: black does not translate the same word used in verse 28, but a verb related to the adjective translated "very dark" in Song of Solomon 1.5. **And falls from me** is a wrong translation of a preposition, which means "on me." It is unlikely that Job's skin could darken anywhere else than "on him," so TEV does not reproduce the phrase "on me." The implication is that, regardless of what color Job's skin was before his suffering, it has now become darker than before. The line may be rendered "My skin has turned dark and peels off."

And my bones burn with heat is literally "burn from heat," which is a metaphor used also in Psalm 102.3, meaning "My body is burning with fever" or, as TEV has it here, "I am burning with fever."

30.31   RSV   TEV

> **My lyre is turned to mourning,**   **Where once I heard joyful music,**
> **and my pipe to the voice of**   **now I hear only mourning and**
> **those who weep.**   **weeping.**

My lyre is turned to mourning: in 21.11-12 Job described the happiness of the children of sinners dancing to the music of harps and flutes or, as RSV says, "lyre" and "pipe." Here the same two instruments are mentioned. For comments on these see 21.11-12. **My lyre is turned to mourning** means that now, in contrast to former times, the instrument plays only the sounds of mourning or mournful music, and so FRCL has "My guitar plays only tunes for mourning." TEV does not mention any specific instrument but captures the contrast well: "Where once I heard joyful music, now I hear only mourning and weeping." Following FRCL's model, we may also translate "On my instrument I can now only play the sad music of those who mourn for the dead." The two lines may be combined to say "I can play on my instruments nothing but the sad music of those who weep and mourn for the dead."

And my pipe to the voice of those who weep: that is, "Now my flute plays only the tunes of those who weep." By keeping the instruments (whatever they may be) and representing Job as the musician, the reader gets a picture of Job as a person whose spirit is capable of making music, even if it has to reflect the sorrow of his mood.

7C. JOB CONCLUDES HIS FINAL SPEECH (31.1-40)

Chapter 31 brings Job's arguments to a close. His final statement is a series of oaths of innocence in which he declares that he is not guilty of having committed certain sins, and he invokes curses upon himself to defend his integrity. These sins or crimes are often viewed as a random list, but Habel discerns a design which gives a more coherent structure to the chapter. He calls the design of this chapter a "double frame," in which there is an outer frame and an inner frame.

The outer frame consists of verses 1-4 and verses 38-40, which contain the covenant and curse themes. For example, verse 1 mentions "a covenant with my eyes." The word "covenant" does not occur in verses 38-40; however, in these verses we are reminded how the earth served as a witness to covenant treaties in Deuteronomy 30.19. In Genesis 4.10, when innocent blood was shed, the ground cried out for justice. In the same manner Job asks the ground to cry out against him if he is guilty.

The inner frame in this view consists of verses 5-6 and 35-37 and contains challenges. In verse 6, for example, Job cries out "Let me be weighed in a just balance," and in verse 35 he says "Let the Almighty answer me."

Between the verses of the inner frames are most of the crimes Job denies having committed (verses 7-34). Aside from sexual impurity and falsehood in verses 1 and 5, these are: impurity of heart and hand (7), adultery (9), indifference to servants (13), hardheartedness toward the poor and oppressed (16-17), indifference to the poor (18), indifference to the unclothed (19), injustice to orphans (21), trust in riches (24-25), worship of sun and moon (26-27), rejoicing over the misfortune of others, cursing enemies (29-30), refusing hospitality (32), and hypocrisy (33).

Within the body of the oaths of innocence (verses 7-34) and including the end of the outer frame (verses 38-40), there are in Hebrew sixteen 'im or "if" clauses accompanied by interpretive comments. Of these sixteen clauses only verses 7, 9, 21, and 38 contain the introductions to formal oaths whose completion in the form of "Let such and such happen to me" is given in the following verse, that is, in verses 8, 10, 22, and 39.

Most of the "if" clauses are not followed by the completion of the oath in an explicit form but rather by comments Job makes in regard to the crime he has denied committing. For example, in 11-12 he exclaims how horrible such as crime would be. In verses 14-15 and 23 his comments reflect his relationship with God. In 18, 20, and 31 he comments on the close relationship he had to the persons he denies having sinned against.

Translators who are interested may care to compare Job's oaths of guiltlessness with similar negative confessions of ancient Egyptians in *The Book of the Dead*.

The structure of chapter 31 may be displayed as follows:

A	Covenant and curse	1-4
B	Challenge to God	5-6
C	List of crimes denied	7-34
B'	Challenge to God	35-37
A'	Covenant and curse	38-40

This view of chapter 31 helps us retain the integrity of the entire chapter and thus avoid shifting verses about because they do not seem to fit the context. It does not follow, however, that we require a subdivision heading for each part of the frame. For example, in the outline of section 7, division C, the initial outer and inner frames are contained under one heading, and the same is true of the final inner and outer frames in verses 35-40.

Division Heading

The Handbook heading may be modified to say, for example, "Job completes his argument" or "These are Job's final words." FRCL has "Job's final reply: I present myself to God with my head held high"; GECL has "I swear that . . . ," TOB "Affirmation of innocence."

7C-1. Job has sworn an oath and challenges God (31.1-6)

	RSV		TEV
1	"I have made a covenant with my eyes; how then could I look upon a virgin?	1	I have made a solemn promise never to look with lust at a girl.
2	What would be my portion from God above, and my heritage from the Almighty on high?	2	What does Almighty God do to us? How does he repay human deeds?
3	Does not calamity befall the unrighteous, and disaster the workers of iniquity?	3	He sends disaster and ruin to those who do wrong.
4	Does not he see my ways, and number all my steps?	4	God knows everything I do; he sees every step I take.
		5	I swear I have never acted wickedly and never tried to deceive others.
5	"If I have walked with falsehood, and my foot has hastened to deceit;	6	Let God weigh me on honest scales, and he will see how innocent I am.
6	(Let me be weighed in a just balance, and let God know my integrity!)		

Subdivision Heading

The Handbook heading combines the two initial frames of the Habel outline and may be reworded to say, for example, "Job has sworn to live a clean life," "Job has promised himself not to be false but also challenges God," or "God sees all I do so I will live right." Habel has "Covenant oath and opening challenge."

31.1   RSV   TEV

**"I have made a covenant with my eyes;
how then could I look upon a virgin?**

I have made a solemn promise never to look with lust at a girl.

This verse seems to open the chapter in an abrupt manner. Consequently some transfer it to another position. See discussion below.

I have made a covenant with my eyes: RSV and TEV differ significantly in the way they relate the two lines of this verse. TEV interprets line <u>b</u> as the content of the covenant in line <u>a</u>, whereas RSV makes line <u>b</u> a rhetorical question that assumes a negative answer. **Made a covenant** translates a Hebrew phrase which is literally "cut a covenant," as demonstrated in Genesis 15.7-21. There Abraham cut animals into two parts, and the covenantor (the LORD) passed between the halves of the animals. The probable implication was "May I be cut in half like these animals if I fail to keep my promise." See also Jeremiah 34.18. **Covenant** is a formal "agreement, treaty, pact" between two parties, in which each assumes some obligation. In the Old Testament **covenants** were made between God and Abraham, Laban and Jacob, David and Jonathan, as well as between husband and wife, and between nations. In verse 1 Job says he has made such a treaty or agreement **with my eyes**. Since the usage is metaphorical, we need not ask what obligation his eyes undertook. Accordingly TEV "I have made a solemn promise" expresses the thought appropriately. FRCL says "I have solemnly forbidden myself . . . ." GECL retains the metaphor: "I have concluded a treaty with my eyes." In many languages this line must be expressed differently; for example, "I have promised that I . . . ," "I have agreed never to . . . ," or "I have agreed to prevent my eyes from . . . ."

How then could I look upon a virgin? RSV interprets a Hebrew word here as a question marker, but it may also be taken as a negative indicator, which then translates literally as "I could not look intently at a virgin." The negative use of a rhetorical question, as in 16.6 "how much," is followed by most modern translations. **Look upon** translates a verb meaning "pay close attention to," and TEV qualifies it as "to look with lust," which is clearly implied in this context. Mft says "to look with longing," and FRCL "every look of desire." Such a qualification is usually required. **Virgin** in English refers to a young woman who has not had sexual relations; the Hebrew term, however, refers more often than not to an unmarried woman. The English term tends to emphasize the absence of sexual contact, but the covenant Job has made with his eyes is against having sexual desire for the kind of person **virgin** represents, and so it is more generally "young girl," FRCL *jeune fille,* SPCL *soltera,* and GECL *Mädchen.* Some scholars think **virgin** is out of place in verse 1, since sexual matters are taken up later. Consequently NEB places verse 1 after 5, while others place it after verse 12. Pope thinks that transferring verse 1 leaves verses 2-4 without connection, and so proposes keeping verse 1 in its traditional place but suggests a change in the term **virgin** to get "folly." However, there is no need to change nor to transfer verse 1. Job is citing sexual desire as an example which would be recognized immediately. Translations of this line will depend on the construction used in the previous line; for example, "I have promised never to stare lustfully at a young woman," "I have taken it upon myself to avoid looking with desire at a young woman," or "I have sworn not to look with sexual desire at young women."

31.2   RSV   TEV

What would be my portion from   What does Almighty God do to
    God above,   us?
  and my heritage from the Al-   How does he repay human
    mighty on high?   deeds?

What would be my portion from God above . . . ? This verse consists of two
rhetorical questions written as two lines that are parallel in meaning. Job is thinking
here of his former days when he was prosperous and fortunate. At that time he
expected his upright life to be rewarded with blessings. In his present state of
suffering he knows that he was mistaken. In 21.7-16 Job argued that it is the wicked
who prosper, and the innocent like himself are made to suffer. The words translated
portion and **heritage** are the same as in 20.29 and 27.13. See there for discussion.
God above is used also in 3.4. If the line is translated as a question, it may be
rendered "What then would God do to me?" "What would my reward from God
be?" or "How would God treat me?"

And my heritage from the Almighty on high? Almighty on high translates
"*Shaddai* from the heights," which Dhorme says means the "heights of heaven." In
any event it has the same meaning as its parallel expression, **God above**. SPCL puts
the question this way: "What is the reward the Almighty gives to every man from the
heights of heaven?" This serves as a usable translation model for these two lines.
·Verse 2 may also be expressed "What would the Almighty in the highest heaven
reward me?" "How would the Almighty in the highest heavens treat me?" Since it
is understood that God's reward would be punishment, in some languages it may be
better to translate this as a negative statement: "The Almighty in the highest heaven
would give me no good reward."

31.3	RSV	TEV
	Does not calamity befall the un- righteous, and disaster the workers of iniquity?	He sends disaster and ruin to those who do wrong.

Does not calamity befall the unrighteous . . . ? This verse follows the same
pattern as verse 2, and it supplies the answer to verse 2. The answer is in the thought
of the friends and is the one which Job had always depended upon before his
misfortune. He therefore seems to be agreeing with the traditional view of the
friends. However, he may be representing their teaching without agreeing that it is
true. See FRCL's rendering discussed in the following paragraph, "You say . . . ."
Calamity means misfortune, as used in 18.12. In 21.17,30 Job argued that the wicked
are spared **calamity**. **Unrighteous** translates the same Hebrew noun used in 16.11,
"ungodly," referring to wicked or evil people.

And disaster the workers of iniquity? Disaster means the same as **calamity**
in the previous line, just as **workers of iniquity** means the same as **the unrighteous**. For **workers of iniquity** see also Psalm 6.8; 28.3; Proverbs 10.29; 21.15. There
is little or no poetic intensification in these two lines, and TEV, while making two
lines, reduces the parallelism to a single sentence: "He sends disaster and ruin to
those who do wrong." FRCL says clearly that Job is attributing these thoughts to the
friends but does not hold to them himself: "You say the criminal receives misfortune,
and the people who do evil get harsh troubles." Translators must decide what form
verse 3 should take in relation to the longer discourse. Use of the question form as
a statement of what happens to the unrighteous may be inappropriate, and in such

cases verse 3 may be expressed as a strong statement; for example, "Certainly God makes evildoers suffer disaster and ruin."

31.4   RSV   TEV

> **Does not he see my ways,**   **God knows everything I do;**
> **and number all my steps?**   **he sees every step I take.**

Does not he see my ways . . . ? Like the previous verse the two lines of verse 4 are questions which expect an affirmative answer. Job may be thinking back to earlier times, but as Rowley suggests, it is more probable that he asks how it can be possible that God would make him suffer. If God truly saw him as he is, God could not bring misfortune on him. RSV translates the verse in a way that accurately shows the Hebrew form. **He** is replaced by "God" in TEV and others. **My ways**, which is found also in 4.6; 13.15; 22.3, refers to Job's life, actions, conduct, or as TEV translates, "everything I do." NJB has "But surely he sees how I behave." TEV translates "knows" in line a and "sees" in line b; but this variation does not appear necessary. This line may also be expressed, for example, "Doesn't God see how I live? Of course he does!" or "God sees all that I do."

And number all my steps? In 14.16 Job said the same thing of God as he does here. There the sense is that God watches over, protects, and guides Job. Here it is more probable, as in the previous line, that God is aware of every move Job makes. God not only sees everything he does but even counts his footsteps. Line b is more specific than line a and heightens the intensity, so that the meaning is "God not only sees everything I do, he even counts every step I take."

31.5   RSV   TEV

> **"If I have walked with falsehood,**   **I swear I have never acted wick-**
> **and my foot has hastened to**   **edly**
> **deceit;**   **and never tried to deceive**
>   **others.**

If I have walked with falsehood: RSV interprets verse 5 in the form of an "if" clause which is continued in verse 7. Verse 6 is treated as a parenthetical statement breaking the connection between verses 5 and 7. Whether or not verses 5 and 7 are translated as "if" clauses depends on the interpretation of the Hebrew *'im*, the first word in these verses. Dhorme and others take this word to be a question marker and translate "Have I walked with falsehood?" The use of the question form has the advantage of establishing a connection between verses 5 and 6, instead of making verse 6 a kind of parenthetical remark as in RSV. TEV, GECL, NEB, and SPCL, on the other hand, understand this structure to be an oath in the form of a strong denial; that is, "I swear I have never acted wickedly." Translating as in TEV also makes a better connection with verse 6. Translators may find either that the denial statement is more natural, or that the question form is more natural in their languages, and should be guided accordingly. Still others may find that the "if" clause is more appropriate in this kind of context. It is important that the translator decide how this structure is to be translated, because it occurs so frequently throughout the chapter. The word **walked** in the phrase **walked with falsehood** gives coherence and poetic continuity with "ways" in verse 4. The expression means "to walk with falsehood as a companion," and since this is figurative language, it may be translated, for example, "guided by what is false," "directed by lies," "led by wrong," or nonfiguratively as TEV, "acted wickedly," or Mft "lived a false life."

And my foot has hastened to deceit: foot gives continuity to **steps** in verse 4. **Foot has hastened** is a vivid way of expressing eagerness to carry out an act; that is, "made an attempt," "exerted an effort," or as in TEV, "tried to." **Deceit** is parallel with **falsehood** in the previous line and has been expressed as a verb phrase in TEV, "tried to deceive others." In some languages **hastened to deceit** is best expressed idiomatically; for example, "and I have acted with two hearts," "and I have worn two faces," or "and I have lived with a double tongue."

31.6 RSV	TEV
(Let me be weighed in a just balance, and let God know my integrity!)	Let God weigh me on honest scales, and he will see how innocent I am.

Let me be weighed in a just balance: for comments on the parentheses in RSV, see verse 5. With these words Job challenges God to act fairly with him. Only in the next line is God mentioned. TEV has shifted "God" to line a and followed with "he" in line b. This is more natural for English style. The image of weighing is found also in Daniel 5.27. **A just balance** translates a phrase which is literally "scales of justice" and is used in Leviticus 19.36 and Ezekiel 45.10. It refers to scales that weigh fairly, and so TEV "honest scales," that is, scales that give correct weights. If translators find that the image of being weighed on a just scale is inappropriate, it may be possible to express the sense without the image; for example, "Let God judge me fairly" or "Let God decide honestly about me."

And let God know my integrity: this is best understood as a consequence of the previous line, "so that God will know . . . ." If God will only measure Job's life with respect to his guilt or innocence, that will prove that Job is innocent. This was Job's claim in 29.14, where he says he has always acted justly. **Integrity** translates the same word used in 2.3,9; and in 27.5, "till I die I will not put away my integrity from me." See 2.3 for discussion. This line may be translated as either consequence or purpose; for example, "so that he will know how innocent I am" or "and then God will know I am not guilty of any wrong."

7C-2. Job swears he has avoided adultery (31.7-12)

	RSV		TEV
7	if my step has turned aside from the way, and my heart has gone after my eyes, and if any spot has cleaved to my hands;	7	If I have turned from the right path or let myself be attracted to evil, if my hands are stained with sin,
8	then let me sow, and another eat; and let what grows for me be rooted out.	8	then let my crops be destroyed, or let others eat the food I grow.
9	"If my heart has been enticed to a woman, and I have lain in wait at my neighbor's door;	9	If I have been attracted to my neighbor's wife, and waited, hidden, outside her door,
10	then let my wife grind for another, and let others bow down upon her.	10	then let my wife cook another man's food and sleep in another man's bed.
11	For that would be a heinous crime; that would be an iniquity to be punished by the judges;	11	Such wickedness should be punished by death.
12	for that would be a fire which consumes unto Abaddon, and it would burn to the root all my increase.	12	It would be like a destructive, hellish fire, consuming everything I have.

Subdivision Heading

The Handbook heading may be modified to say, for example, "Job takes an oath to show he has not been unfaithful to his wife," "Job swears that he has not gone after another woman," "Job swears that he has been faithful to his wife," or "Job swears he has not slept with another man's wife." Habel has "Oaths on impurity and adultery."

31.7-8

	RSV		TEV
7	if my step has turned aside from the way, and my heart has gone after my eyes, and if any spot has cleaved to my hands;	7	If I have turned from the right path or let myself be attracted to evil, if my hands are stained with sin,
8	then let me sow, and another eat; and let what grows for me be rooted out.	8	then let my crops be destroyed, or let others eat the food I grow.

These two verses may be taken together, since verse 8 is the consequence of the "if" clause in verse 7. In the Hebrew verse 7 has three lines.

If my step has turned aside from the way: the thought here draws upon the thought of 23.11: "My foot has held fast to his steps. I have kept his way and have not turned aside." **The way** refers to the path or way God has shown his followers as being right (Deut 9.12, 16). So TEV translates "If I have turned from the right path." We may also say, for example, "If my steps have wandered away from the path he has marked out."

And my heart has gone after my eyes: as in verse 1 the thought is that the eyes are the means through which temptation comes. This is well rendered by FRCL: "if my heart has followed the desires of my eyes." TEV is less poetic and more abstract with "let myself be attracted to evil." In some languages the line may be rendered "and I have desired the things I look at," "and my eyes have caused my heart to be led astray," or "and my eyes have seen things that I have desired."

And if any spot has cleaved to my hands: in 11.14; 16.17; and in Isaiah 1.15, the **hands** are depicted as being stained by sin. By contrast clean **hands** symbolize righteousness, as in 22.30 and Psalm 24.4. So the sense is "if my hands are dirtied by evil acts," "if I have been soiled by doing evil things," or "if I have become unclean by doing wrong." There are also alternatives to the Hebrew text in this line. TEV follows one which means "to stick," together with a word whose meaning is probably "stain." Alternatively the word translated "stain" may be a term meaning "anything," an understanding probably influenced by Deuteronomy 13.17. SPCL seems to prefer the second alternative: "If anything foreign is found in my possession." This rendering seems to fit well with the following verse, but most modern translators follow the understanding of the text taken in TEV. If the translator follows TEV, this line may be rendered, for example, "if my hands are dirtied by doing bad things" or, if **hands** is taken to represent the whole person, "if I have become stained by sin" or "if doing bad things has left a stain on me."

In verse 8 Job calls down upon himself the punishment he would deserve if he had committed the sins in verse 7. **Then let me sow, and another eat**: for his punishment Job asks that the crops he plants should be eaten by someone who did not plant them. TEV has reversed the two lines of verse 8. **Then let me** is not an appeal to someone but a dire consequence of his wrong. In some languages "let" or "may" statements must be reinforced; for example, "God take from me the food I raise and give it to others" or "God take my crops from me and let someone else eat them."

And let what grows for me be rooted out: **what grows for me** translates a single Hebrew word meaning "my shoots" as in 5.25; 21.8; 27.14. It may refer to "offspring," and Pope understands it this way: "and my offspring be uprooted." However, given the context it seems best to take the meaning as in RSV and TEV. This line may also be expressed, for example, "and take away from me the plants I cultivate" or "and destroy all my crops."

31.9-10	RSV	TEV
9	"If my heart has been enticed to a woman, and I have lain in wait at my neighbor's door;	9 If I have been attracted to my neighbor's wife, and waited, hidden, outside her door,
10	then let my wife grind for another,	10 then let my wife cook another man's food

and let others bow down upon   and sleep in another man's
   her.   bed.

These two verses, like 7 and 8, consist of conditions in verse 9 followed by consequences in verse 10. These verses move directly into the specific sins.

If my heart has been enticed to a woman: enticed translates the Hebrew for "seduced," which recurs in verse 27. It is the **heart** that is seduced. In verse 7 the **heart** follows after the eyes. The eye is the means by which the temptation reaches the center of desire and turns it into action. **Woman** here refers to a married woman, in contrast to the unmarried girl in verse 1. TEV says "neighbor's wife," which it takes from the next line. GECL is similar, with "If I become passionate for my neighbor's wife."

And I have lain in wait at my neighbor's door: the thought here is of the male adulterer who watches for the opportunity to sin with his neighbor's wife. **Lain in wait** is the same expression used in Proverbs 7.12, where, however, it is the woman waiting for the man. This is a military expression and is used in reference to setting up an ambush; that is, hiding to take someone by surprise. In 24.15 "the eye of the adulterer also waits for the twilight." Here too the man lurking outside is probably thought of as being in the dark or, as TEV says, "hidden." **Neighbor** translates the same word used in Exodus 20.17, "You shall not covet your neighbor's wife." **Neighbor's door** does not mean that the adulterer is to be pictured as lying close to the door, but at a distance where he can keep his eye on the door to see when the woman's husband leaves the house. By placing "neighbor's wife" in line a, TEV has changed the poetic intensification between the two lines. However, translators may also find that this provides a clearer translation, since **woman** in line a may not be associated with **neighbor's door** in line b. In some languages it may be necessary to make clear the implication of **lain in wait at my neighbor's door** by saying, for example, "and I have waited for my neighbor to leave his house," or the two lines may need to be transposed to say, for example, "If I have waited for my neighbor to leave his wife alone, because my heart has become passionate for her."

Then let my wife grind for another: in Exodus 11.5; Isaiah 47.2, grinding is the work of the slave. According to Gordis the thought expressed here through the use of **grind** is sexual. This is a rabbinical interpretation followed by the Targums and the Vulgate. The following line makes this clear. If **grind** is not to be taken as having sexual relations, the sense is that his wife should become the servant and concubine of another man, and so sexual relations are implied. On one level **grind** is to be understood as being humiliated or placed in the relation of servant to another man. On another level the thought is that of being used sexually.

Translators must decide whether to use an expression which focuses upon grinding for another as a servant or as suggesting sexual relations. In some languages to cook for another has clear implications of having sexual relations. Because line a is more indirect than line b, it is better to reserve the direct expression of sexual relations for line b.

TEV and GECL have substituted "cook," which is more general. FRCL says "work for another" in its text and gives the literal translation in a note. Mft gives a stronger sense to **grind** with "may my own wife be a slave to strangers," and NEB is similar but has a note in some editions: "*lit.* grind corn for another." This line may also be

 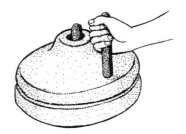

MILLSTONES, FOR GRINDING GRAIN INTO FLOUR

expressed, for example, "Then let my wife become another man's servant," ". . . my wife obey another man's orders," or ". . . my wife do what another man wants."

And let others bow down upon her: in the view of the Old Testament, adultery was an offense against the husband of the adulteress. Adultery always involved a married woman; the marital status of the man was not considered. The punishment which Job calls down on himself really falls on his wife. However, according to Leviticus 20.10, both the adulterer and the adulteress were to be killed. (See TEV verse 11.) **Bow down** translates a verb meaning "to bend or crouch down." It is used in 39.3 of mountain goats squatting down to deliver their young. Here the term is used as a way of saying "let others have sexual relations with her." TEV "sleep in another man's bed" is likewise the use of a mild figure which avoids a bolder expression such as "have sex with." In many languages it will be necessary to avoid an expression that cannot be read in public. This may require the use of an indirect expression such as "sleep with," "lie down with," "go to bed with."

31.11	RSV	TEV
	For that would be a heinous crime; that would be an iniquity to be punished by the judges;	Such wickedness should be punished by death.

For that would be a heinous crime: Dhorme omits this verse, assuming that it is a comment added by later copyists. NEB prints both verse 11 and verse 12 between brackets for the same reason. **That** refers back to the content of verse 9, not to verse 10. The word translated **heinous crime** is used especially in connection with sexual crimes in Leviticus 18.17; 20.14; Judges 20.6. NJB translates it as "a sin of lust."

That would be an iniquity to be punished by the judges: this expression is almost identical to that in verse 28b. **Punished by the judges** probably refers to a crime that must be submitted to the judges for decision. The word translated **judges** is the same as used in Exodus 21.22; Deuteronomy 32.31. TEV, which reduces this verse to a single line, translates "should be punished by death." The basis for this rendering is that in Old Testament thought the penalty was to be death, as in

Leviticus 20.10. Most translations stay closer to the Hebrew and translate something like "Doing that would be a crime; it would be an offense to be punished by the law."

31.12   RSV   TEV

> for that would be a fire which   It would be like a destructive,
>   consumes unto Abaddon,   hellish fire,
>   and it would burn to the root   consuming everything I have.
>   all my increase.

For that would be a fire which consumes unto Abaddon: Job expresses here his horror of the sin of adultery. The thought is evidently based on Deuteronomy 32.22, "For a fire is kindled by my anger, and it burns to the depths of Sheol, devours the earth and its increase, and sets on fire the foundations of the mountains" (RSV). Adultery is compared with fire in Proverbs 6.27-29. For comments on **Abaddon** see 26.6. **Abaddon** is here equated with Sheol. TEV expresses the line as a simile, "like a destructive, hellish fire," in which "hellish" corresponds to **Abaddon**. It may be clearer in translation to avoid a pronoun like **that** and say "adultery" or "committing adultery." In many languages the thought needs to be expressed as a simile: "adultery would be like a fire." The whole line may be rendered "Adultery would be like a fire that would burn and destroy me."

And it would burn to the root all my increase: **burn to the root** translates the Hebrew verb "uproot." However, rooting out something is not what fire does, and so many scholars agree to change one letter to get "burn"; RSV translates **burn to the root**, which TEV renders "consuming." **My increase** translates "my income or revenue." In this context, if one assumes that "roots" are somehow involved, the income is in terms of the produce of the land. NEB translates specifically, "crops," but FRCL remains general like TEV, with "all that I have acquired." Both are appropriate. The line may also be rendered, for example, "it would destroy everything I own" or "and burn away everything I have."

7C-3. Job swears that he never wronged the unfortunate (31.13-23)

	RSV		TEV
13	"If I have rejected the cause of my man-servant or my maidservant, when they brought a complaint against me;	13	When one of my servants complained against me, I would listen and treat him fairly.
14	what then shall I do when God rises up? When he makes inquiry, what shall I answer him?	14	If I did not, how could I then face God? What could I say when God came to judge me?
15	Did not he who made me in the womb make him? And did not one fashion us in the womb?	15	The same God who created me created my servants also.
		16	I have never refused to help the poor; never have I let widows live in despair
		17	or let orphans go hungry while I ate.

16 "If I have withheld anything that the poor
  desired,
  or have caused the eyes of the widow
  to fail,
17 or have eaten my morsel alone,
  and the fatherless has not eaten of it
18 (for from his youth I reared him as a
  father,
  and from his mother's womb I guided
  him);
19 if I have seen any one perish for lack of
  clothing,
  or a poor man without covering;
20 if his loins have not blessed me,
  and if he was not warmed with the
  fleece of my sheep;
21 if I have raised my hand against the fatherless,
  because I saw help in the gate;
22 then let my shoulder blade fall from my
  shoulder,
  and let my arm be broken from its
  socket.
23 For I was in terror of calamity from God,
  and I could not have faced his majesty.

18 All my life I have taken care of them.
19 When I found someone in need,
  too poor to buy clothes,
20 I would give him clothing made of
  wool
  that had come from my own flock of
  sheep.
  Then he would praise me with all his
  heart.
21 If I have ever cheated an orphan,
  knowing I could win in court,
22 then may my arms be broken;
  may they be torn from my shoulders.
23 Because I fear God's punishment,
  I could never do such a thing.

In verses 13-23 Job denies that he has abused his power over those less
fortunate than himself.

Subdivision Heading

The Handbook heading may be adjusted to say, for example, "Job swears that
he has never failed to do the right thing for the oppressed" or "Job swears that he
has acted fairly to the unfortunate." Habel has "Denial of inhumanity to the
unfortunate," and Rowley "Denial of abuse of power."

31.13-14   RSV   TEV

13 "If I have rejected the cause of
  my manservant or my maidservant,
  when they brought a complaint
  against me;
14 what then shall I do when God
  rises up?
  When he makes inquiry, what
  shall I answer him?

13 When one of my servants complained against me,
  I would listen and treat him
  fairly.
14 If I did not, how could I then
  face God?
  What could I say when God
  came to judge me?

RSV translates the Hebrew of line 13a as an "if" clause, and that of verse 14 as
two questions which are asked in consequence of verse 13. The RSV rendering of
verse 14 appears to leave in doubt whether or not Job would concern himself with
the claims for justice coming from his servants. TEV overcomes this problem by

restructuring these two verses. The translator should remember that verse 13 follows the "if" style of oath; however, in place of the curse placed upon himself if he has acted wrongly, Job asks the two rhetorical questions seen in verse 14. For every language, it will be necessary to determine whether the translation can maintain the same pattern for expressing all the "if" oaths in this chapter. In 19.15-16 Job relates how his servants have turned against him. Here he defends his dealings with them before his misfortune.

If I have rejected the cause of my manservant or my maidservant: **rejected the cause** translates a phrase which can mean "refused to listen to the claim" or "failed to recognize the rights." In a positive way the oath can also be translated, for example, "I always did what was right . . . ." **My manservant or my maidservant**: The Hebrew language requires that these two separate terms must be used. The meaning is "my male slave and my female slave." NEB translates them "my slave and my slave-girl." Some translations keep the separate male and female categories, and others, like TEV, reduce them to one, "one of my servants." The rights of slaves, though not many, are set forth in Exodus 21.1-11. In verse 15 Job sees both himself and the slave as creatures of God.

When they brought a complaint against me: the slave or servant is seen here as claiming one of his rights, or complaining to Job of some injustice. Job is the object of the complaint. TEV has made this line the first line, "When one of my servants complained against me," and line a becomes line b in TEV, so that circumstance or setting is followed by consequence, "I would . . . treat him fairly," which is a positive rendering of line a. "One of my servants," which translates **manservant** and **maidservant**, is kept as the subject of line a. FRCL also rearranges the structure in a similar manner: "Whenever my male or female servant had a complaint to present to me, I always respected their rights." Verse 13 may also be expressed "Whenever a man or woman who worked for me complained, I always listened to their case" or "If a man or woman servant wished to complain against the way I treated them, I respected their right to speak."

What then shall I do when God rises up? RSV translates the Hebrew literally. The expression **when God rises up** is found in Psalm 76.9, "When God arose to establish judgment . . . ." TEV renders this "when God came to judge me."

When he makes inquiry, what shall I answer him? When he makes inquiry translates the Hebrew for "When he visits." "Visits" is used in the sense of "inquiring" in 7.18, as "inspect" in 5.24, and as "punish" in 35.15. TEV relates verse 14 to verse 13 by the connecting expression "If I did not," that is, "If I did not treat my servants fairly." The question which follows in TEV, "how could I then face God?" is the rendering of **what shall I answer him?** TEV joins **rises up** and **makes inquiry** into "when God came to judge me." Translators should consider TEV's rendering as a model for clear meaning. However, translators may wish to keep more of the parallelism in the two lines of verse 14. The verse may also be rendered "If I did not treat them fairly, what would I answer God when he comes to judge me?" or "If I failed to act justly, I would not be able to answer God when he examines me."

31.15   RSV   TEV

> Did not he who made me in the   The same God who created me
>   womb make him?   created my servants also.
> And did not one fashion us in
>   the womb?

Job spoke in 10.8-12 of God's wondrous act of creating him in the womb. Here he acknowledges that the same is true for the slave. By saying this Job gives the reason why he respected the rights of his servants. The two questions in this verse ask nearly the same thing, and both assume a positive answer. TEV reduces them to one and recasts them as a single statement.

Did not he who made me in the womb make him: translators vary considerably in the way they express the translation of this verse. **Womb** translates the Hebrew for "belly" and is used in 3.10; 10.19; 15.35 ("heart"). The two different words translated **womb** are used as a set pair in parallelism, with the more general word in the first line followed by the more specific term in the second line. It may be necessary to express the line, for example, as "Did not God make me in my mother's womb the same as he made my servant in his mother's womb?" In some languages this line will be better translated as a statement.

And did not one fashion us in the womb: womb translates the more specific female organ used in Genesis 49.25; Proverbs 30.16. In the Hebrew the line ends with the word **one**, which can then be understood as **did not one fashion us** or as "did he not fashion us in one womb." However, **one** is parallel with the maker in line a, and so the first interpretation is the better one, and the singular **womb** can then be understood as the respective womb from which each came. RSV remains slightly ambiguous, in that it can imply that both Job and the slave were fashioned in the same womb. The ambiguity can be removed by leaving the womb implicit; for example, "Was it not the same God who made us both?" In translation it may be best to say in line a, for example, "Did not God . . . ," and in line b "and did not the same one (or, the same God) . . . ?" Dhorme prefers "was it not He alone . . . ?"

31.16-17   RSV   TEV

16 "If I have withheld anything that   16 I have never refused to help the
        the poor desired,   poor;
    or have caused the eyes of the   never have I let widows live in
        widow to fail,   despair
17 or have eaten my morsel alone,   17 or let orphans go hungry while
    and the fatherless has not   I ate.
        eaten of it

Verses 16 and 17 (and also verses 19, 20, and 21) are translated in RSV as a string of "if" clauses, which are followed by the consequence of punishment in verse 22. Verse 23 then provides the reason why Job avoided doing the wrong things he mentioned. In these verses Job speaks of the poor, widows, and orphans—people who

571

were dependent upon Job's goodness. These denials are a reply to Eliphaz, who accused Job of refusing to feed the hungry.

If I have withheld anything that the poor desired: that is, "If I have refused to give to the poor what they wanted." TEV and others express this oath as a strong denial, "I have never refused to help the poor"; and others use a rhetorical question; for example, NJB "Have I been insensitive to the needs of the poor?" which implies an oath as the answer, "Never!"

Or have caused the eyes of the widow to fail: RSV can be understood as causing widows to have poor eyesight. The expression is used in 11.20, where it means "to cause despair." (See 11.20 for comments.) Psalm 69.3 refers to the eyes growing dim through crying. TEV "never have I let widows live in despair" gives the right thought here. The line may also be expressed "I have never caused widows to be without hope," or stated positively, "I always gave widows reason to hope."

Or have eaten my morsel alone: **morsel** translates a word meaning "piece," which may or may not be accompanied by the word "bread." However, even here "morsel of bread" is understood. Eating alone would be a selfish act, and the **morsel** here refers to food in general, or to a small meal. TEV avoids **morsel**, "food," or "meal" by saying "while I ate." As a rhetorical question this can be expressed "Have I ever eaten by myself?" "Have I ever eaten a piece of my bread alone?" In many languages "to eat alone" means selfishly refusing to share food with others. However, in other languages this attitude will not be clear without further information; for example, "Am I guilty of not sharing my food with others?" or "Am I guilty of eating my food without sharing it with other people?"

And the fatherless has not eaten of it? The **fatherless** means "orphan" and refers to orphans generally, and so TEV and others translate "orphans." To avoid repetition TEV has "or let orphans go hungry . . . ." It may be best to combine the two lines of verse 17 to say, for example, "am I guilty of not sharing my food, and letting orphans go hungry?"

31.18	RSV	TEV
	(for from his youth I reared him as a father, and from his mother's womb I guided him°);	All my life I have taken care of them.ᵏ

ᵏ All my life . . . them; *Hebrew unclear.*

° Cn: Heb *for from my youth he grew up to me as a father, and from my mother's womb I guided her*

Verse 18, like verse 6, breaks the continuity of the "if" clauses leading up to verse 22, and so RSV places it between parentheses.

For from his youth I reared him as a father: as the footnote in RSV shows, this verse in Hebrew may be understood as "for from my youth he grew up to me as a father, and from my mother's womb I guided her." The expression "he grew up to me as a father" is unclear. The verb translated "grew up" is always intransitive, but in Hebrew the verb contains the suffix meaning "me," which translates as "to

me." HOTTP suggests "he grew up with me." Supposedly HOTTP can be expressed as
"I reared him as his father," and this is essentially the meaning of TEV. The
expression "from my youth" is translated by TEV as "all my life," which is more
general. TEV "taken care of them" refers to the poor, widows, and orphans in verses
16-17. RSV, on the other hand, has made a change in "from my youth" to get "from
his youth," referring to the orphan. Translators may follow either RSV or TEV; for
example,"I have been like a father to him nearly all his life," "I brought him up like
his own father," or "I have been like a father to them all my life."

And from his mother's womb I guided him: RSV has made a change from
"my mother's womb" to refer to the womb of the mother of the orphan, meaning
"from the birth of the orphan." RSV has also changed "guided her" to **guided him**,
the orphan. It no doubt seems exaggerated to say, as the Hebrew does, that Job took
care of widows from the time he was born; but it is not unlikely that he was taught
to do this in his earliest training. It is then possible to keep the Hebrew text without
change and say, for example, "and I have always taken care of widows." Translators
who follow the Hebrew as it stands produce quite different renderings of this verse.
For those who have to reduce parallelism, TEV provides an adequate translation
model. For others TEV will appear too abbreviated. A better model may be SPCL,
which keeps the parallel lines: "I have always treated the orphan as if I were his
father; I have always been a defender of widows."

31.19	RSV	TEV
	if I have seen any one perish for lack of clothing, or a poor man without covering;	When I found someone in need, too poor to buy clothes,

If I have seen anyone perish for lack of clothing: in RSV verse 19 is an "if"
clause, which is followed by a second "if" clause of a negative kind in verse 20. Like
previous verses of this kind, translators may also render these "if" clauses as
statements, as in TEV, "When I found someone in need," or as a question, as in NJB,
"Have I ever seen a wretch in need of clothing?" The two lines of verse 19 are
parallel. **Perish for lack of clothing** suggests that people actually died because of
no clothing.

Or a poor man without covering: **covering**, which is parallel with **clothing**
in line a, occurs in 24.7, also paired with **clothing**. Dhorme translates **covering** as
"coat," but a parallel expression such as NJB "with nothing to wear" is probably
better. It is recommended to translators that they follow some such restructuring as
in TEV, so that verse 19 is the condition and verse 20 the consequence. Verse 19, as
an introduction to the oath of verse 20, may be handled as an "if" clause, a "when"
clause, or any of the other types of introductory clauses that express verse 19 as the
circumstances under which verse 20 occurs; for example, "Every time I saw a poor
person dying from lack of clothing . . ." or "Whenever I found needy people who did
not have clothes to keep them warm . . . ."

31.20   RSV   TEV

if his loins have not blessed me, and if he was not warmed with the fleece of my sheep;	I would give him clothing made of wool that had come from my own flock of sheep. Then he would praise me with all his heart.

This verse has two lines in Hebrew, which are restructured in TEV so that the first line is placed at the end of the verse as an independent sentence, and the second line in Hebrew is made into two lines which express the consequence of the situation described in verse 19.

If his loins have not blessed me: his loins is a part of the body representing the whole body, or at least the lower part of the body suffering from the cold. In poetic terms the **loins** are pictured as a person expressing gratefulness to Job. NJB and others render this expression "bless me from his heart." FRCL, which translates verse 19 as a question, has "Have I ever seen a poor person . . . , someone in misery . . ." and follows in verse 20a with "without their thanking me . . . ?" This line may be shifted to the end of verse 20, as in TEV, or kept before verse 20b by relating it properly to verse 19b. For example, "Whenever I found . . . he would thank me because . . . ."

And if he was not warmed with the fleece of my sheep: in languages which do not use the passive, this question may be translated, for example, "is there anyone who has not warmed himself by wearing clothes made from the wool of my sheep?"

The two lines of verse 20 may be transposed, as in TEV, or kept in their Hebrew order, provided they are related in a clear way. For example, verses 19 and 20 may be expressed "If I ever saw a person dying from lack of clothing, I would give him clothes made from the wool of my own sheep, and he would be full of thanks" or "I never saw a person suffering from lack of clothing without giving him clothes made from the wool of my own sheep, and he always gave me thanks for them."

31.21   RSV   TEV

if I have raised my hand against the fatherless, because I saw help in the gate;	If I have ever cheated an orphan, knowing I could win in court,

Verse 21, in RSV as in Hebrew, is the final "if" clause in the string which began with verse 13. Verse 22 contains the punishment Job calls down on himself if he is guilty of committing the crimes mentioned in 13-21. TEV makes verse 22 the punishment only for the offense mentioned in verse 21, as do some other modern translations. This is done usually by putting a blank space between verses 20 and 21, and making verses 21-23 a unit.

If I have raised my hand against the fatherless: raised my hand translates a phrase meaning to shake the hand at someone in a threatening gesture. Job is claiming that he never used his power to oppress people or his influence to deprive them of justice. **The fatherless** translates the usual word for "orphan." Some scholars feel that the word for "orphan" is inappropriate here, having already been mentioned in verse 17. Accordingly they divide the Hebrew words meaning **against the fatherless** to get "the innocent." However, HOTTP classes the Hebrew phrase "against the orphan" as an "A" reading and translates it that way. The idea is that Job could easily threaten to have the orphan punished by raising his hand in a threatening gesture. TEV translates "If I have ever cheated . . . ." The context justifies this rendering, but the poetic language calls for an expression of a threatening nature; for example, TOB says "brandishing my fist at an orphan." If a threatening gesture is not available in the language, we may translate, for example, "I have never threatened an orphan" or "Have I ever threatened to harm an orphan?"

Because I saw help in the gate: line <u>b</u> gives the imagined reason why Job could have done harm to an orphan, something which he says he did not do. **Help in the gate** refers to having the support and backing of the other officials in the town. If Job had wanted to mistreat anyone, he could have counted on those men who sat in the town council to defend him. TEV "knowing I could win in court" means that Job has the support of the local court system (that met in the gate of the city) to defend his case. We may also say, for example, "I have never threatened to harm an orphan, even though I knew the officials would be on my side if I did."

31.22	RSV	TEV
	then let my shoulder blade fall from my shoulder, and let my arm be broken from its socket.	then may my arms be broken; may they be torn from my shoulders.

In verse 22 Job calls for a suitable punishment which is expressed in terms of damage to his shoulder and arm, presumably so he could no longer use threatening gestures. Translators differ greatly in the wording of this verse. **Then let my shoulder blade fall from my shoulder**: in this line of the Hebrew, there are two words meaning **shoulder**. The first refers to the **shoulder blade** and the other to the back of the neck. Dhorme tries to represent these with an awkward rendering, "then let my shoulder fall from its nape of neck." This makes little or no sense. It is clearer to say, for example, "Let my shoulder and shoulder blade be torn out." Since, however, the arm is attached to the shoulder, when the shoulder is torn away, the arm also will go.

The second line deals with the arm separately. **And let my arm be broken from its socket** is literally "and let my arm from the socket be broken." The word translated **socket** normally refers to a "reed" or "stalk," which has a hollow center and may give rise to the idea of **socket**. Dhorme takes this word to refer to the humerus, the upper arm bone, and Pope agrees but takes the other word for **arm** to mean the lower arm. Accordingly he translates "let my arm be wrenched off above the elbow." FRCL follows this with "and my arm be broken at the elbow." TEV, which refers only to the arm, understands the second line to be the lesser of the two punishments, and so transposes the two lines to give an increasing punishment at the climax: "may my arms be broken; may they be torn from my shoulders." Among the many conflicting translations of this verse, TEV offers a clear model to follow. Verse 22 may have to be expressed as an active construction; for example, "let someone break my arms and tear them from my shoulders."

31.23   RSV   TEV

> For I was in terror of calamity   Because I fear God's punish-
>   from God,   ment,
>   and I could not have faced his   I could never do such a thing.
>   majesty.

In verse 23 Job says that he feared God would send misfortune on him if he committed the wrongs he denies having done. Many scholars have proposed changes in this verse to get other meanings, but the Hebrew text can be translated satisfactorily without changes.

For I was in terror of calamity from God is literally "for a terror for me the calamity of God." The form is, as HOTTP translates, "For the calamity of God was a terror for me," which may be rendered "I was afraid that God would bring some disaster upon me."

And I could not have faced his majesty is literally "because of his majesty I could not do." **Majesty** here is not some royal aspect of God but is in parallel with **terror** in the previous line. The Hebrew requires completion of its thought, which NEB does with "could do none of these things." Other possibilities are "I could never do such a thing" (TEV) or "I could never do such a thing because I was afraid of him."

7C-4. Job denies avarice and idolatry (31.24-28)

               RSV   TEV

24	"If I have made gold my trust,		24	I have never trusted in riches
	or called fine gold my confidence;		25	or taken pride in my wealth.
25	if I have rejoiced because my wealth was great,		26	I have never worshiped the sun in its brightness
	or because my hand had gotten much;			or the moon in all its beauty.
26	if I have looked at the sun when it shone,		27	I have not been led astray to honor them
	or the moon moving in splendor,			by kissing my hand in reverence to them.
27	and my heart has been secretly enticed,			
	and my mouth has kissed my hand;		28	Such a sin should be punished by death;
28	this also would be an iniquity to be punished by the judges,			it denies Almighty God.
	for I should have been false to God above.			

Subdivision Heading

The Handbook heading may be modified to say, for example, "Job denies that he loves wealth or worships the heavens," or "Job swears that he does not love money, nor worship the sun and moon." Habel has "Denial of avarice and idolatry," and Rowley (verses 24-34) "Job's declaration of purity of heart."

31.24-25 RSV	TEV

24 "If I have made gold my trust,
    or called fine gold my confidence;
25 if I have rejoiced because my
    wealth was great,
    or because my hand had gotten much;
	24 I have never trusted in riches
	25 or taken pride in my wealth.

In verses 24 and 25 Job swears that he has not trusted in wealth. The expected consequence of these two verses, and the following two, does not come until verse 28. Job is here denying the charges made against him by Eliphaz in 22.24 and following.

If I have made gold my trust: the two lines in this verse are parallel, with only a slight degree of poetic intensification in line b, in which a more specific form of **gold** is used. (See 28.16.) The pair translated **trust** and **confidence** are used in the opposite order in 8.14. For translators who find it best to reduce a pair of parallel lines to one, TEV may be a good model: "I have never trusted in riches." Translators will often have to shift verses 24-27 to emphatic statements or rhetorical questions, or combinations of these, in order to avoid the series of "if" clauses.

Or called fine gold my confidence: the poet varies the style in this line by switching to what in the Hebrew is direct address, as in 17.14. Dhorme translates "And have I said to pure gold: 'My security!'" FRCL, which uses the question form, provides a model for those who attempt to retain the parallelism "Have I put my confidence in gold? Where have I ever said of it 'This is my security'?" In some languages this translation model may be rendered more idiomatically; for example, "Have I put my heart on gold? Never!" "Have I ever said, 'Gold, you are the one who takes care of me'? Never!"

If I have rejoiced because my wealth was great: the two lines of verse 25 say about the same thing, with the second line carrying the figure of the **hand** obtaining wealth. As in verse 24, TEV reduces this verse to a single line. In 22.25-26 Eliphaz advised Job "if the Almighty is your gold . . . then you will delight yourself in the Almighty." **Rejoiced** is the usual translation of the word used here, the idea being that Job denies that his great wealth was the source of his "joy, satisfaction, delight." Pope and NJB translate "Have I ever gloated . . . ," and TEV "taken pride," while GECL says "My wealth has never made me proud." These translations give the sense of misplaced delight, which is apparently the idea intended by the poet. The line may also be rendered, for example, "I never let my great wealth be my joy" or "my satisfaction never depended on the large amounts of wealth I had." Some translators will find it best to combine the two lines into one; for example, "I have not rejoiced just because I had great wealth," "I had lots of wealth, but this was not the source of my satisfaction" or ". . . was not what filled me with happiness."

Or because my hand had gotten much: my hand is a part for the whole and so refers to Job himself: "or because I had obtained great amounts of wealth" or "or because I made lots of money."

31.26-27 RSV	TEV
26 if I have looked at the sun[p] when it shone, or the moon moving in splendor, 27 and my heart has been secretly enticed, and my mouth has kissed my hand;	26 I have never worshiped the sun in its brightness or the moon in all its beauty. 27 I have not been led astray to honor them by kissing my hand in reverence to them.

[p] Heb *the light*

These two verses refer to the worship of nature. **If I have looked at the sun when it shone**: as RSV indicates, **sun** translates the Hebrew for "light." The accompanying verb, and **moon** in the following line, justify translating as **sun**. **Looked** does not by itself suggest to look on with awe or reverence, but means "when I looked at the shining sun" or "when I saw the sun shining in the sky."

Or the moon moving in splendor: in splendor is literally "as a precious thing" and is used of precious stones. This qualification accompanies the Hebrew verb "walk," and so depicts the **moon** as walking majestically across the heavens. NEB translates "or the moon moving in her glory," and GECL has "and watched the moon along its course in full splendor." In some languages the line may be expressed, for example, "or if I have watched the beautiful moon in the sky" or "or if I have gazed up at the beauty of the moon."

And my heart has been secretly enticed: Job denies that the **sun** and the **moon** have tempted him to worship them. The worship of heavenly bodies is condemned in Deuteronomy 4.19; 17.2-7; 2 Kings 23.5; and Jeremiah 8.1-3. **Enticed** is in the sense of "tempted, allured," or as TEV says, "led astray." **Secretly,** as in 13.10, probably refers to the secret manner of some cult worshipers in Job's time. "I have not been led astray secretly," or more fully, "I have not been tempted to worship them secretly."

And my mouth has kissed my hand translates the Hebrew clause "and my hand has kissed my mouth." The reference is to the worshiper kissing his hand and holding it out for the sun or moon to receive. The idea is clear enough but is rendered in various ways in different translations. For example, NJB has "so that I blew them a kiss," NIV "and my hand offered them a kiss of homage," NAB "to waft them a kiss with my hand," TEV "by kissing my hand in reverence to them." FRCL avoids **kissed my hand** by translating "Have I taken them for gods and have I worshiped them?" In languages in which kissing is unfamiliar, it may be necessary to provide another gesture; for example, "and I have not folded my hands to honor them" or "I have not bowed down to show them reverence." It may also be possible to retain the kiss gesture by adding the purpose, as in TEV.

31.28 RSV TEV

this also would be an iniquity to be punished by the judges, for I should have been false to God above.	Such a sin should be punished by death; it denies Almighty God.

This also would be an iniquity to be punished by the judges: the thought is repeated from verse 11b. According to Deuteronomy 17.2-7 the worship of heavenly bodies was punishable by death. **Punished by the judges** is rendered correctly by TEV as "punished by death." The idolater was to be stoned to death.

For I should have been false to God above: the sense is that Job would have been disloyal or unfaithful to God if he had been an idolater. **False to God** translates a verb meaning "to deny, to reject as true." TEV says "it denies . . . ," where "it" refers to "sin" in the previous line. However, Job is saying that if he sinned in this way, he himself would be "denying God on high." FRCL says "because I would have been a traitor to God on high." Translators may find that the two lines of this verse should be transposed; for example, "Doing that would have been unfaithfulness to God, . . ." or "That would have made me disloyal to God, and the judges would have condemned me to die for that sin."

7C-5. Job denies revenge, inhospitality, and hypocrisy (31.29-34)

RSV TEV

29	"If I have rejoiced at the ruin of him that hated me, or exulted when evil overtook him	29	I have never been glad when my enemies suffered, or pleased when they met with disaster;
30	(I have not let my mouth sin by asking for his life with a curse);	30	I never sinned by praying for their death.
31	if the men of my tent have not said, 'Who is there that has not been filled with his meat?'	31	All the men who work for me know that I have always welcomed strangers.
32	(the sojourner has not lodged in the street; I have opened my doors to the wayfarer);	32	I invited travelers into my home and never let them sleep in the streets.
33	if I have concealed my transgressions from men, by hiding my iniquity in my bosom,	33	Other men try to hide their sins, but I have never concealed mine.
34	because I stood in great fear of the multitude, and the contempt of families terrified me, so that I kept silence, and did not go out of doors—	34	I have never feared what people would say; I have never kept quiet or stayed indoors because I feared their scorn.

Subdivision Heading

The Handbook heading may be modified to say, for example, "Job denies that he wanted his enemies to die, or that he closed his doors to strangers or deceived people" or "Job says he never wanted to get revenge, he was hospitable, and he did not deceive." Habel has "Denial of vindictiveness and hypocrisy."

31.29   RSV   TEV

> "**If I have rejoiced at the ruin of**   I have never been glad when my
>   **him that hated me,**   enemies suffered,
>   **or exulted when evil overtook**   or pleased when they met with
>   **him**   disaster;

In RSV verse 29 begins with another "if" clause as a form of oath denying a particular sin. Verse 30 interrupts the "if" clause by making a statement of denial. The same procedure is repeated in verses 31 and 32, to be followed in verse 33 by still another "if" clause. Instead of Job calling down a punishment at verse 34, there is a suggested cause why Job may have been tempted to be hypocritical in verse 33. With verse 34 the build-up of denials breaks off without the self-cursing the reader has been led to expect. Accordingly many scholars transfer verses 38-40 to other locations throughout the chapter. Translations such as TEV, which do not use the "if" clause structure in verses 29-34, are able to present the sequence of denials in these verses without the sense of incompleteness in RSV.

If I have rejoiced at the ruin of him that hated me: rejoiced translates the same word used in verse 25a, but here the sense is "to take satisfaction, to be pleased." **The ruin** translates a word found only here and in Proverbs 24.22, and means "misfortune, disaster." **Him that hated me** translates a form of the verb "hate" which may best be rendered as "enemy," as in TEV and others. This line may also be expressed "I have never been glad to see my enemies in trouble" or "I have never been pleased when people who hate me have misfortune."

Or exulted when evil overtook him: exulted occurs also in Isaiah 51.17. Here it is used in the reflexive form and means to be glad, but in this context, at another person's expense—a cruel joy that comes from seeing someone else suffer. **Evil** is parallel with **ruin** in the previous line and refers to "misfortune, trouble." TEV translates both these parallel lines rather than shortening and combining them into one.

31.30   RSV   TEV

> (**I have not let my mouth sin**   I never sinned by praying for
>   **by asking for his life with a**   their death.
>   **curse);**

I have not let my mouth sin: Job's denial in this verse refers to his enemy in verse 29. For the use of parentheses see verses 5 and 18. **Mouth** is literally "palate." Job is saying in his denial that he did not even let his palate (the roof of the mouth) sin. As one of the speech organs, it is a more specific form of **my mouth**. Rowley thinks that "palate" suggests taste, and so Job never even had a taste of cursing his enemy. TEV combines the two lines of this verse, dispenses with the image, and says, "I never sinned . . . ." FRCL has "I never even allowed myself the wrong . . . ." NJB substitutes "tongue" for "palate": "I, who would not allow my tongue to sin . . . ." These examples give models that are both poetic and nonpoetic. In some languages a part of the body cannot be said to sin; accordingly we may say, as in TEV, "I never sinned."

By asking for his life with a curse: life in the Hebrew is *nefesh*, which may mean "soul" or **life**. In 1 Kings 3.11 Solomon is rewarded for not demanding the *nefesh* of his enemies. A curse may be put on someone in order to kill him, and thus NJB translates "or to lay his life under a curse," NIV "by invoking a curse against his life." Other translators assume that God must be named as the one who operates the curse; for example, FRCL "of cursing him by asking God for his death." TEV "I have never sinned by praying for their death" seems to dismiss the curse completely. Verse 30 may also be expressed "I never sinned by cursing his life" or "I never put a curse on his life and so did not sin."

31.31-32 RSV TEV

	RSV		TEV
31	if the men of my tent have not said, 'Who is there that has not been filled with his meat?'	31	All the men who work for me know that I have always welcomed strangers.
32	(the sojourner has not lodged in the street; I have opened my doors to the wayfarer);	32	I invited travelers into my home and never let them sleep in the streets.

See the paragraph introducing verse 29 for comments on the relationship of these verses to those before and after it.

If the men of my tent have not said: RSV continues to translate with an "if" clause, while Dhorme continues to use the question form, and here TEV uses a strong positive statement. The "if" clause is the least satisfactory for English, since there is no consequence to follow, either immediately or later in the chapter. The question form assumes a positive answer, which makes the positive statement a more direct and satisfactory form to use, at least for English. **The men of my tent** is understood by TEV as "all the men who work for me." However, the reference is more to Job's own "household." The Hebrew word for **tent** is nearly the same as the Arabic word for "family." **Tent** may be taken in a wide sense to include one's relatives, and so NJV translates "my clan." The idea of the kin group expressed as "household" is followed by NEB, NIV, Mft, Pope, Habel. SPCL has "those who lived with me." GECL has "guests," and FRCL "those whom I lodged."

Who is there that has not been filled with his meat? This line, which is a quotation in RSV, has three principal interpretations. The least likely, proposed by Tur-Sinai and supported by Pope, takes **filled with his meat** to mean "to abuse him sexually," which Pope renders "If males of my household ever said, 'O that we might sate ourselves with his flesh,'" that is, "have homosexual relations with him," as in the case of the men of Sodom in Genesis 19. Another view is related to the expression "eat my flesh," which occurs in Psalm 27.2 and which RSV renders "uttering slanders against me"; NEB takes this view and translates here "speak ill of."

The weakness of appealing to Psalm 27.2 is that the idiom used there refers to death and destruction of the psalmist, and not just to slander. Certainly the most widely accepted meaning is that no one would say that Job has not satisfied their appetites and filled their stomachs with his food. NJB translates "Will anyone name a person whom he has not filled with meat?" TEV avoids misunderstandings that can arise from being too specific in this verse, by saying "I have always welcomed strangers." GECL is similar but more detailed with "Whoever was my guest will testify for me that everyone was richly and well entertained."

Translators are faced with several ways to formulate the relation of the lines of verse 31. As a question we may translate "Have not the men who live in my house asked, 'Who is there who has not eaten well at Job's table?'" As a statement we may translate, for example, "Everyone in my family knows that anyone who came to me was well satisfied with the food he got."

The sojourner has not lodged in the street: for the use of parentheses in RSV, see verses 5 and 18. **Sojourner** translates the word used in 19.14-15, where it is rendered "alien." It refers to the outsider who comes seeking refuge and help. In English the usual terms are "stranger, foreigner, alien." NEB and TEV attempt to show that the person has come from elsewhere and is staying temporarily, and so they have "travelers." **Lodge** translates a verb meaning "to spend the night." **In the street**, which may mean "outside, without shelter," would leave the stranger exposed, not only to the weather, but more seriously to abuse.

I have opened my doors to the wayfarer: the Hebrew has "to the way," which is changed by nearly all to get **wayfarer**. The change is supported by the parallel **sojourner** in line a. **Wayfarer** refers to a person who is "traveling, passing through." Because the two terms mean about the same, TEV says "I invited travelers into my home and never let them sleep in the streets." If the two-line parallelism is being maintained, we can translate "I never let the stranger spend the night outdoors, and my doors were always open to receive travelers."

31.33	RSV	TEV
	if I have concealed my transgres- sions from men,[q] by hiding my iniquity in my bosom,	Other men try to hide their sins, but I have never concealed mine.

[q] Cn: Heb *like men* or *like Adam*

RSV has one last "if" clause before verse 38. Job is here denying that he has been a hypocrite, a double-minded person. Dhorme places verses 38-40 in the place of verse 33, and places verses 33-37 at the end of the chapter. However, note the structure Habel recognizes for these verses in their present position, as explained in the introduction to this chapter, page 558.

If I have concealed my transgressions from men: **conceal** translates "to cover" and carries the sense of pretending or deceiving. **Transgressions** and **iniquity** in the next line are commonly-paired terms. See comments on 10.6. **From men**, as the RSV footnote shows, may also be taken as "like Adam." Most modern translations understand this as in the RSV text. It is a common characteristic of people to hide their sins from others. TEV expresses the denial of line a as "Other men try to hide their sins . . . ." RSV's rendering is based on a change to **from men**, but TEV translates the Hebrew "like men," so that an alternative rendering can be "I have not hid my sins as others do."

By hiding my iniquity in my bosom: the word translated **bosom** is found only here in the Old Testament, but its meaning is clear from Aramaic usage. The clothing which Job wore was without pockets. However, with a belt tied around the waist, the inside upper part of the garment served as a spacious inner shirt pocket, and this was the "bosom." The picture here is of Job stuffing his sins inside his garment, where they could be carried but not visible to others. TEV translates "but I have never concealed mine." The verse may also be rendered, for example, "I have not done like other people who hide their sins, like people who put things away in their pockets."

31.34   RSV   TEV

because I stood in great fear of the multitude, and the contempt of families terrified me, so that I kept silence, and did not go out of doors—	I have never feared what people would say; I have never kept quiet or stayed indoors because I feared their scorn.

Verse 34 has three lines in Hebrew, but it is not clear how they relate to verse 33, or even to the previous verses. RSV and others translate the opening of 34 with **because** and thus make it an explanation for Job's refusal to be a hypocrite in verse 33. TEV, on the other hand, renders lines a and c as denials, and makes line b the explanation for line c, which is placed ahead of line b.

Because I stood in great fear of the multitude: in Hebrew the word translated **great** accompanies **multitude**. However, **great** is here in the feminine form in Hebrew and therefore cannot modify **multitude**, which is masculine. RSV therefore translates **great fear**. Dhorme and others make a change in a single vowel to get "the noise of the city," which is supposed to refer to the idle talk that takes place there, and which may be the basis for TEV ". . . what people would say." NJB translates "Have I ever stood in fear of common gossip?" "Stand in fear" in English does not mean to rise to the feet but attempts to reflect the Hebrew imperfect form of the verb, "to be (always) afraid." It is clear that **fear of the multitude** is fear of what the people generally will "say, talk about, gossip."

And the contempt of families terrified me: in this line the movement is from the generalized **multitude** or crowd to the more specific **families**, which refers to the same people. Line b explains line a, in that it is the "ridicule" or "scorn" that these people would express for such a hypocrite, which TEV translates as line c, "because I feared their scorn."

So that I kept silence, and did not go out of doors: RSV gives the impression that, because of what is referred to in the earlier part of the verse, Job kept silence and did not go outside. However, it is because he did not fear what people said that he was not afraid to go outside and face them; he had nothing to hide. If this verse is treated as a question, as many translations prefer, we may translate, for example, "Have I ever been so afraid of people's gossip or terrified by their ridicule that it caused me to stay at home and keep silent?"

7C-6. Job's final challenge and final oath (31.35-40)

RSV	TEV
35 Oh, that I had one to hear me! (Here is my signature! let the Almighty answer me!) Oh, that I had the indictment written by my adversary! 36 Surely I would carry it on my shoulder; I would bind it on me as a crown; 37 I would give him an account of all my steps; like a prince I would approach him. 38 "If my land has cried out against me, and its furrows have wept together; 39 if I have eaten its yield without payment, and caused the death of its owners; 40 let thorns grow instead of wheat, and foul weeds instead of barley." The words of Job are ended.	35 Will no one listen to what I am saying? I swear that every word is true. Let Almighty God answer me. If the charges my opponent brings against me were written down so that I could see them, 36 I would wear them proudly on my shoulder and place them on my head like a crown. 37 I would tell God everything I have done, and hold my head high in his presence. 38 If I have stolen the land I farm and taken it from its rightful owners— 39 if I have eaten the food that grew there but let the farmers that grew it starve— 40 then instead of wheat and barley, may weeds and thistles grow. The words of Job are ended.

In his last desperate effort Job, who has nothing to hide, challenges God to show him openly the charges he brings against Job. For the combining of verses 35-40 as the two frames at the end of the chapter, see the introduction to chapter 31, page 558 and following page.

Subdivision Heading

Translators may wish to modify the Handbook heading to say, for example, "Show me what you have against me, God," "I have nothing to fear from an open hearing," "Let me see the crimes I am charged with," or "This is Job's final challenge to God and his final oath of innocence."

31.35   RSV   TEV

Oh, that I had one to hear me!   **Will no one listen to what I am**
(Here is my signature! let the   **saying?**

Almighty answer me!)
Oh, that I had the indictment
written by my adversary!

I swear that every word is true.
Let Almighty God answer me.

If the charges my opponent
brings against me
were written down so that I
could see them,

Oh, that I had one to hear me! the Hebrew says literally "Who would give me a listener?" Job has made his appeal to God for a hearing many times, and so he is again appealing to God but does not use **the Almighty** until the following line. The line may be translated, for example, "Oh, how much I want to be listened to!" or "Oh, if only someone would listen to me!"

Here is my signature! let the Almighty answer me! My signature translates "my *Taw*," the final letter in the Hebrew alphabet. In ancient Hebrew writing this letter was written in the form of a cross. It is Job's signature or mark which makes any document of his authentic. Although Job does not mention a document, the expression calls up the image of authenticating a legal paper. Without referring to a signature TEV says "I swear that every word is true." FRCL translates "I can sign what I have said," meaning that signing it makes Job responsible for its truthfulness. Some take the word translated **signature** to mean "desire" and translate "This is my desire," which is completed with "that the Almighty would answer me." This is similar to NEB "Let the Almighty state his case against me!" or, in other words, "My desire is that the Almighty state his case against me." It is more probable, however, that Job is speaking of his signature and using the expression to claim that all he has said is true. This line may also be expressed, for example, "Oh, how much I wish Almighty God would speak out. I would sign my name to show that all I have said is true."

Oh, that I had the indictment written by my adversary! The words **Oh, that I had** are not in the Hebrew but are supplied by RSV to give balance between this line and the first. TEV translates the remainder of verse 35 as an "if" clause in order to link it with verse 36 as the consequence. Because this line opens up a new thought which has consequences in the next verse, such a restructuring, as in TEV, is recommended. Job has presented his case, but he has never seen the charges against him. **Indictment** translates a term meaning "letter, document, or book." In this context it refers to "the charges" brought against Job. **My adversary** is literally the "man of my case," that is, "the one I am involved with in a legal case," or as TEV rightly says, "my opponent." This line may be related to verse 36 by leaving blank space between it and the preceding line and by saying, for example, "As for the charges of my accuser, I wish I had them in writing" or "If I had the written charges made by the one who accuses me . . . ."

31.36   RSV   TEV

Surely I would carry it on my
shoulder;

I would wear them proudly on
my shoulder

I would bind it on me as a crown;	and place them on my head like a crown.

Surely I would carry it on my shoulder: in Isaiah 22.22 the key of the house of David is placed by God on the shoulder of his servant Eliakim. Carrying the indictment on the shoulder made it possible for everyone to see it. TEV says "I would wear them proudly on my shoulder." RSV's **carry it** refers to the singular "the indictment" of verse 35, while TEV's "wear them" refers to the plural "the charges." This line is taken as the consequence of the desire expressed in the previous line. In some languages it may be necessary to state the reason why Job would carry them on his shoulder; for example "Then I would carry them high on my shoulders where everyone could see them."

I would bind it on me as a crown: Job would go even further; if they would be visible on his shoulder, they would be even more visible on his head. And so Job is saying "I would not only carry them proudly on my shoulder, but would even wear them for a crown on my head." In some languages **as a crown** may have to be expressed as "I will even carry them on top of my head."

31.37   RSV   TEV

I would give him an account of all my steps; like a prince I would approach him.	I would tell God everything I have done, and hold my head high in his presence.

This verse appears to some as a natural conclusion and climax of Job's final speech (chapters 29-31). Verses 38-40 that now form the conclusion appear to be out of place, but translators are not agreed where else they should be inserted. NJB puts them after verse 15; NEB after verse 28; Pope and NAB after verse 8; Dhorme after verse 32; GECL between verses 34 and 35; and Mft between verses 22 and 24. However, the position taken by the Handbook, following Habel's outline, is that verse 37 is the end of the inner frame, and verses 38-40 make up the end of the outer frame. Therefore there is no need to change the position of any verse. See the introduction to chapter 31, page 558.

I would give him an account of all my steps: in 14.16 and 31.4 Job accepts that God counts his steps as expressing the totality of Job's actions. As TEV says, "I would tell God everything I have done." In some languages one may be able to stay closer to the Hebrew form than TEV does by saying, for example, "I would report to him every step I have taken" or "I would explain to him every thing I have done."

Like a prince I would approach him: **prince** translates a word meaning "chief, leader, or ruler," one who is in control. Nowhere else in the Old Testament is anyone said to approach God **like a prince**. The simile refers to the attitude of someone who has no reason to feel guilty or debased by his wrong, and is symbolized in TEV as "hold my head high in his presence." SPCL has "with dignity," GECL "and approach him like a prince without fear." Also possible are "I would present myself to him like a chief who is not afraid" or "I would stand before him like a proud leader."

31.38-39   RSV   TEV

38   "If my land has cried out against   38   If I have stolen the land I farm
       me,   and taken it from its rightful
     and its furrows have wept   owners—
       together;   39   if I have eaten the food that
39   if I have eaten its yield without   grew there
       payment,   but let the farmers that grew it
     and caused the death of its   starve—
       owners;

Verses 38-39 are translated as "if" clauses followed by the consequence in the form of a curse called down on Job in verse 40. It was pointed out in the opening of this chapter that verses 38-40 balance Job's opening statement in verses 1-4. Both relate to the covenant theme. In this end frame we encounter the earth or land crying out like a person, a reminder of the earth crying out for justice when Cain killed his brother in Genesis 4.10. In Deuteronomy 30.19 the earth was a witness in God's covenant with Israel.

If my land has cried out against me: verse 38 does not give the reason why Job's land would **cry out** against him. It is only in verse 39 that the reason comes to light. There the land could have been wrongfully acquired, and so TEV drops the figurative language in verse 38 to say "If I have stolen the land I farm." Some modern translations attempt to keep the image of the crying of the land; for example, FRCL says "Have I driven the fields to complain about me?" NJB "If my land cries for vengeance against me." If the land cannot be pictured as a person in this way, the translator may have to use an expression similar to TEV.

And its furrows have wept together: here TEV creates a parallel line based on its first line, "and taken it from its rightful owners," which means the same as "stolen the land" in the first line. In the parallelism of the Hebrew, the movement is from the general term for **land** in line a to a specific kind of land, **furrows**, in line b. If the poetic device of regarding the land as a person is unnatural in the language, the translator may follow TEV. **Furrows** are rows that have been plowed in preparation for planting. **Furrows** are side by side, and if they wept, it would be "in concert" or together. Verse 38 may be expressed as a question; for example, "Have I caused the owners of lands to cry, or made them cry together as furrows for planting are together?"

If I have eaten its yield without payment: yield translates a term meaning "strength." As in Genesis 4.12 it is the "strength" of the earth that produces crops, so that this line is "If I have eaten the crops, its produce, without paying for it" or ". . . profited freely from the harvests." Verse 39, like verse 38, may be translated as an "if" clause, a statement, or a question. Whatever form the translator prefers to follow, the structure must be adapted to that used in verse 38 and to the consequence in verse 40.

And caused the death of its owners: in this line some interpreters focus on "causing death," while others think it is speaking of "causing suffering by acting unjustly." RSV takes the former view, while TEV takes it to refer to oppressing the farmers. The latter seems to be preferred. FRCL says "without respecting the rights of their owners." TEV "farmers that grew it" seems to agree more with the meaning

587

required by the context. These would not be independent land owners such as Job, but rather "workers" or "farm hands." Verse 39 may also be expressed "If I have robbed anyone of his crops, or if I have exploited the farm workers." This may also be expressed as a statement of denial; for example, "I have never robbed anyone of his crops, nor have I made peasants starve."

31.40	RSV	TEV
	let thorns grow instead of wheat, and foul weeds instead of barley."	then instead of wheat and barley, may weeds and thistles grow.
	The words of Job are ended.	The words of Job are ended.

Verse 40 is the imprecation, or curse, that Job places upon himself if he is guilty of the crimes in verses 38 and 39. It is appropriate that the curse apply to the land, which has been the subject in the final three verses.

Let thorns grow instead of wheat: in Genesis 3.18 God told Adam that the ground is cursed and that thorns and thistles would come from it; however, the words are different from the ones used here. The word translated **thorns** is rendered in 2 Kings 14.9 as "thorn bush" (TEV) and in Isaiah 34.13 "thistles." **Wheat and barley** were the most prized grain crops and occur together in Deuteronomy 8.8 and Joel 1.11.

And foul weeds instead of barley: the word translated **foul weeds** occurs only here in the Old Testament, but it is derived from the verb meaning "to have a bad odor." There is little point in trying to be too specific in the translation of this term, unless there is a weed that commonly grows in uncultivated soil and has a bad odor. In languages in which **wheat** and **barley** are unknown, translators should follow the procedure suggested in 28.18.

The words of Job are ended: these words are in prose form. The reference is to all that Job has said in chapters 29–31. Job will speak again briefly in chapters 40 and 42. We may translate "Job has finished speaking" or "Job will not make any more speeches."

8. Elihu's Speeches

(32.1–37.24)

Chapter 32 marks the beginning of a series of speeches by Elihu, a discourse that continues through chapter 37. Elihu is presented to the reader, as were the other friends, in a brief prose introduction. Elihu has not previously been mentioned, and when his speech is completed he will not be mentioned again. Job does not reply to his long speech, and Elihu's words add little of substance to the book. He is introduced as a man younger than the friends, and one who is angry with the friends because they could not give Job a reply, and angry with Job because he justifies himself before God.

In chapter 32 Elihu, who has only listened to the debates between Job and the friends, decides that he must now, in spite of his youth, set the record straight. He addresses Job directly in chapter 33 and opposes Job's view of himself as innocent of wrongdoing. He challenges Job's insistence that God does not answer him, by pointing out the many ways God speaks to people, including through pain and suffering. Confession of sin, according to Elihu, is required before a person like Job can recover. Chapter 33 may be described as an unbalanced chiasmus, which will be discussed further in the introductory comments on that chapter. In chapter 34 Elihu continues to argue that God is all-powerful and punishes sinners, and so Job's only recourse is to stop his evil ways and cease to rebel against God. In chapter 35 Elihu, speaking directly to Job again, accuses him of being proud, suggesting that God does not answer him because of that. Elihu goes so far as to present himself as God's spokesman in chapter 36, and he claims to be a truly wise man. He describes God as great and righteous. God teaches men through suffering. Elihu's speech mounts rhetorically (36.27) as he depicts God as the force behind the thunder and lightning, and the whole of chapter 37 is a description of the God of nature. Elihu concludes that God ignores those (like Job) who claim to be wise.

Elihu's speech may best be viewed as consisting of four divisions: chapters 32–33, chapter 34, chapter 35, and chapters 36–37.

Section Heading

Most translators will want to give a special heading to Elihu's speeches, which are not interrupted in the manner of the earlier arguments. The Handbook heading may be modified to say, for example, "This is Elihu's series of speeches" or "A young man named Elihu now speaks."

8A. PROSE INTRODUCTION (32.1-6A)

RSV   TEV

1 So these three men ceased to answer Job, because he was righteous in his own eyes. 2 Then Elihu the son of Barachel the Buzite, of the family of Ram, became angry. He was angry at Job because he justified himself rather than God; 3 he was angry also at Job's three friends because they had found no answer, although they had declared Job to be in the wrong. 4 Now Elihu had waited to speak to Job because they were older than he. 5 And when Elihu saw that there was no answer in the mouth of these three men, he became angry.

6a And Elihu the son of Barachel the Buzite answered:

1 Because Job was convinced of his own innocence, the three men gave up trying to answer him. 2 But a bystander named Elihu could not control his anger any longer, because Job was justifying himself and blaming God. (Elihu was the son of Barakel, a descendant of Buz, and belonged to the clan of Ram.) 3 He was also angry with Job's three friends. They could not find any way to answer Job, and this made it appear that God was in the wrong. 4 Because Elihu was the youngest one there, he had waited until everyone finished speaking. 5 When he saw that the three men could not answer Job, he was angry 6a and began to speak.

Job's final words have been spoken. He has reached the climax of his argument and defense of his innocence by calling on God to defend himself in his suit against Job. Instead of God appearing, Elihu, who has never been mentioned, steps forth to argue that Job's desire to take God to court is wrong. Verses 1-6a are in prose.

Division Heading

Since the first five verses are in prose style and represent the words of the author, the Handbook has given these verses a title of their own. Translators may wish to do the same by saying, for example, "An angry young man speaks," "Elihu is angry and wants to speak," or "Introduction to Elihu."

32.1   RSV   TEV

So these three men ceased to answer Job, because he was righteous in his own eyes.

Because Job was convinced of his own innocence, the three men gave up trying to answer him.

So these three men: So translates the Hebrew connective *waw,* which here marks a consequence or result. TEV has shifted the reason clause beginning with **because** to the opening of the verse, and this makes verse 1 a reason followed by a result. Translators should follow the clause order that is most natural in the receptor language. **These three men** refers to Eliphaz, Bildad, and Zophar. The use of **men** here rather than "friends" has been taken by some scholars as an indication of a change of author. However, "friends" reappears in verse 3 and **men** again in verse 5. FRCL translates by using the names of the three friends. **Ceased** means "stopped, quit, gave up." **To answer** is the same term used at the opening of each speech by the friends and by Job. **Answer** does not mean reply to a question, but rather to pick up the argument, to carry the argument forward, or to respond to another's speech. See 4.1.

Because he was righteous in his own eyes: righteous translates the
Hebrew *tsadiq*. In the context it refers to being right in a legal suit, or being innocent
of charges made against one. So the author is saying that Job's insistence on being
right or being innocent has caused the friends to give up arguing with him. **In his
own eyes** means "in his own mind, opinion, heart," or as TEV says, "convinced." In
some languages the reason clause may have to come first, as in TEV: "Because Job
was so sure that he was not guilty of wrong . . . ."

32.2 RSV	TEV
Then Elihu the son of Barachel the Buzite, of the family of Ram, became angry. He was angry at Job because he justified himself rather than God;	But a bystander named Elihu could not control his anger any longer, because Job was justifying himself and blaming God. (Elihu was the son of Barakel, a descendant of Buz, and belonged to the clan of Ram.)

Elihu means "he is my God." The same name is found in 1 Samuel 1.1;
1 Chronicles 27.18. **Barachel**, which means "God has blessed," is not recorded
elsewhere in the Old Testament. The names of the father of Job and the fathers of
the three friends are never mentioned. **The Buzite** means a member of the clan
called Buz, who was the brother of Uz (Genesis 22.21). In 1.1 Job is said to be from
the land of Uz. In some languages it is necessary to translate the appositive
construction **Elihu the son of Barachel the Buzite, of the family of Ram** as one
or more complete sentences. For a model see TEV. We may also say "Elihu's father's
name was Barachel, who belonged to the clan called Buz, and who was a member of
the family called Ram." **Ram**, which means "lofty" or "exalted," is the family name.
In Ruth 4.19 it occurs as the name of one of David's ancestors. **Became angry**
translates the Hebrew clause "the anger burned." The same idiom is repeated later
in this verse and in verse 3.

Justified himself translates the verb form of the same word rendered
"righteous" in verse 1; that is, "he claimed he was right" or "he said he was
innocent." **Rather than God** refers to Job's failure to admit that God and not Job
was in the right, so that TEV says "Job was justifying himself and blaming God." TEV
rearranges verse 2 so as to leave the identification of Elihu's kinship at the end of
the verse, where it is enclosed in parentheses. This arrangement is particularly
helpful at the opening of this discourse in order to prevent the reader's attention
become focused on a detail which is secondary to the main line of Elihu's argument.
TEV also identifies Elihu as a "bystander," since Elihu has not been mentioned in the
prologue of 2.11, where the friends are introduced. FRCL does something similar by
saying "a certain Elihu," and SPCL "A man named Elihu." Translators should refer
to the suggestions for the translation and placing of the names of the three friends
in 2.11. **Justify himself rather than God** may also be rendered, for example, "he
was claiming to be innocent of wrong and accusing God of wrong" or "he said, 'I am
innocent, but, God, you are in the wrong.'"

32.3 RSV TEV

he was angry also at Job's three friends because they had found no answer, although they had declared Job to be in the wrong.	He was also angry with Job's three friends. They could not find any way to answer Job, and this made it appear that God was in the wrong.

In verse 3 Elihu "burns with anger" **at Job's three friends**. The reason is **because they had found no answer**. That is, the friends did not know how to respond to Job (for lack of wisdom). TEV has restructured the clause as a new sentence. Verse 3b in RSV says **although they had declared Job to be in the wrong**. On the other hand TEV says "this made it appear that God was in the wrong." Modern translations are divided between those that translate **Job** and those that translate "God." According to Jewish tradition **Job** in this passage is another of the eighteen scribal corrections where the original text of the Hebrew Bible was altered out of reverence to God. To write a clause saying that "God was in the wrong" would seem to be blasphemy, and they could not read it aloud; therefore the text was changed to read "Job." (The only other such scribal correction in the Book of Job occurs at 7.20.) The text that reads "God" implies that, by giving up the argument, the three friends were declaring Job right and God wrong.

Although many scholars prefer to take the text to be as in TEV, "God was in the wrong," others argue that giving up the argument does not imply putting God in the wrong, and so the present Hebrew text should be kept. Rowley would keep RSV but translate "and so (that is, by finding an answer) shown Job to be in the wrong." Tur-Sinai translates "because they had found no answer, and yet had condemned Job." HOTTP, which classifies the Hebrew text here as a "B" reading, suggests a rendering which may be reworded to say "Although the friends found no answer to give Job, they still found him unfaithful to God." Since it is not possible to rule out either possibility, translators are free to follow either TEV or one of the adaptations of RSV. Therefore we may translate, for example, "Elihu was also angry at the three friends because they could not show Job that he was wrong and so had let God appear to be wrong" or ". . . they could not refute Job, but still they condemned him." Some translations provide a footnote to say "The Hebrew reads 'thus leaving Job in the wrong.'"

32.4 RSV TEV

Now Elihu had waited to speak to Job because they were older than he.	Because Elihu was the youngest one there, he had waited until everyone finished speaking.

The Hebrew of this verse is literally "And Elihu had waited for Job with words, because they were older than he in days." The Hebrew does not make it clear whether Elihu had been waiting to speak to Job, or whether he was waiting while the friends were speaking. Some suggest changing the Hebrew "with words" to "while they were speaking." TEV does not make any change but takes "with words" to refer to the speaking done by the friends, and so "until everyone finished speaking." The friends **were older than he**; that is, older than Elihu, and therefore had more right to speak than Elihu. In translation it may be better to say, as does TEV, "because he was younger than they were," as this keeps the focus primarily on Elihu.

32.5   RSV   TEV

And when Elihu saw that there was no   When he saw that the three men could
answer in the mouth of these three   not answer Job, he was angry
men, he became angry.

Elihu is replaced by "he" in TEV. Rather than repeat a noun (**Elihu**), modern English style calls for a pronoun ("he") as a more natural expression. **No answer in the mouth** translates the Hebrew literally and means "had nothing to say in reply," "had no answer to give," or "could not answer." **Men** refers, as in verse 1, to the three friends. This is the fourth time Elihu is said to be angry.

32.6a   RSV   TEV

  And Elihu the son of Barachel the   and began to speak.
Buzite answered:

The first part of verse 6 is still in prose. The identification of Elihu is repeated as in verse 1, except his belonging to the "family of Ram." TEV does not repeat his kinship identification but shows that the following words are those of Elihu by placing *"Elihu"* in italics at the beginning of the speech. For **answered** see comments on 4.1.

8B. ELIHU'S FIRST SPEECH (32.6b–33.33)

The poetic section of Elihu's first speech (verses 6b-22) consists of three major units: In verses 6-10 Elihu argues that he has the right to reply to Job in spite of his youth, because it is not age that makes a man wise, but rather the spirit of the Almighty. In verses 11-16 Elihu argues that the friends have failed to disprove Job's arguments, and they have nothing more to say. In verses 17-22 Elihu presents himself as someone who must relieve himself of his words because he is like a wineskin ready to burst. Having been introduced as one who is angry at the friends and angry at Job, he foolishly claims (verse 21) that he will show partiality to no one, and claims that he does not know how to flatter a person. In this way Elihu is set up to make a fool of himself.

Division Heading
The Handbook division heading may be modified to say, for example, "Elihu now begins his speech," "This is what Elihu said," or "Elihu presents his arguments against Job."

8B-1. Elihu maintains his right to speak (32.6b-10)

	RSV		TEV
6b	"I am young in years, and you are aged; therefore I was timid and afraid to declare my opinion to you.	6b *Elihu* I am young, and you are old, so I was afraid to tell you what I think.
7	I said, 'Let days speak, and many years teach wisdom.'	7	I told myself that you ought to speak, that you older men should share your wisdom.
8	But it is the spirit in a man, the breath of the Almighty, that makes him understand.	8	But it is the spirit of Almighty God that comes to men and gives them wisdom.
9	It is not the old that are wise, nor the aged that understand what is right.	9	It is not growing old that makes men wise or helps them to know what is right.
10	Therefore I say, 'Listen to me; let me also declare my opinion.'	10	So now I want you to listen to me; let me tell you what I think.

Subdivision Heading

Translators wishing to provide a heading here may adapt the Handbook heading to say, for example, "It is God that makes a man wise," "You don't become wise just by growing old," "I am young, but I am also wise," or "Elihu's right to answer Job."

32.6b	RSV	TEV
	"I am young in years, and you are aged; therefore I was timid and afraid to declare my opinion to you.	*Elihu* **I am young, and you are old, so I was afraid to tell you what I think.**

Elihu is speaking to the three friends and does not address Job directly, not until 33.1. In many languages the plural form of **you** should be used.

I am younger in years translates the Hebrew for "I am younger in days," similar to 30.1, where the expression is "I am smaller in days" and has the same meaning as the expression here. In translation **in years** will often be unnecessary. **And you are aged**: that is, "You (plural) are old men." In 12.12 Job said "wisdom is with the aged." Elihu, however, does not consider age as a proof of wisdom.

The reason Elihu has not expressed his thoughts is that **I was timid and afraid**. **Timid** translates a verb found only here in the Old Testament. The two terms **timid** and **afraid** have the same meaning, and so many translators, like TEV, render them as a single expression such as "I was afraid" or "I was shy." **Declare my opinion** is not a good rendering, nor is TEV's "tell you what I think." Elihu is not speaking so modestly as to refer to his **opinion**, but rather to his "knowledge," and so the meaning of the Hebrew is really "in order to expose my knowledge to you," "so as to tell you what I know."

32.7   RSV   TEV

    I said, 'Let days speak,   I told myself that you ought to
      and many years teach wisdom.'   speak,
                                     that you older men should
                                     share your wisdom.

     I said, 'Let days speak . . .': this represents what Elihu thought to himself, not what he spoke; therefore TEV has "I told myself that you ought to speak"; or it can be expressed "I said to myself 'The old men should speak.' " **Days** is used figuratively to refer to the old friends, who have experienced many more days of life than Elihu, and so are more qualified to speak. Translators should retain a figurative expression if such is natural in the language.

     And many years teach wisdom completes the parallelism and what Elihu thought to himself. **Many years**, like **days**, refers to the friends as being older than Elihu. The meaning of this line is therefore "it is for the elderly to teach wisdom" or "the old men are the ones who should teach wisdom to others."

32.8   RSV   TEV

    But it is the spirit in a man,   But it is the spirit of Almighty
      the breath of the Almighty,   God
        that makes him understand.   that comes to men and gives
                                     them wisdom.

     But it is the spirit in a man: Elihu is saying in this verse that years alone, or having lived many years, does not give a person wisdom; it is rather the **spirit** which gives it. Elihu will conclude in verse 10 that he has such wisdom.

     The problem in this verse is the unclear relation between **spirit** in line a and **breath of the Almighty** in line b. There is, of course, some connection with the story of man's creation, Genesis 2.7, but that does not clarify this verse completely. One way to resolve the problem here is to make **spirit** refer to "the spirit of God," as in NEB, "But the spirit of God himself is in man and the breath of the Almighty gives him understanding," so that the two lines are then fully parallel. TEV accepts the parallelism but for clarity brings the two terms together: "It is the spirit of the Almighty God." However, some feel that parallelism should not be imposed here, and take **spirit in a man** to refer to his "intelligence" which he receives from God's spirit. In that case we may translate, for example, "It is true that everyone has intelligence, because the Almighty God has breathed it into him," or as FRCL says, "It is true that what makes a person intelligent is the Spirit, the inspiration of God Almighty." If **spirit** is taken as in FRCL, some translations will prefer to write "Spirit" with a capital "S." TEV has translated **man** as "men." Elihu is speaking generally here, and **man** is to be understood as "a person," or even more generally, as "people."

     Although the interpretation in FRCL seems preferable, it is not possible to rule out the implied parallelism of NEB. Translators are free to choose. However, it may be advisable to place the alternative rendering in a footnote.

32.9   RSV   TEV

> It is not the old[r] that are wise,
>   nor the aged that understand
>   what is right.

> It is not growing old that makes
>   men wise
> or helps them to know what is
>   right.

[r] Gk Syr Vg: Heb *many*

It is not the old that are wise: the RSV footnote indicates that the Hebrew has "many" instead of **old**. RSV follows the ancient versions, which makes for a better parallelism with the next line. However, as Dhorme points out, in Genesis 25.23 the singular of the Hebrew term means "elder," and so no change is required in the text to get **old**. RSV makes a general statement that the old are not wise. Elihu has just said that it is not age but God that gives wisdom. Therefore the meaning here needs to be made clear by qualifying the statement, which TEV has done well with "It is not growing old that makes men wise." In other words "Men do not become wise just by getting old."

Nor the aged that understand what is right: **what is right** translates the word commonly rendered "judgment," and refers here to what is just or right. FRCL restructures verse 9 in a way that may be helpful to translators: "To be wise, to recognize what is just, depends neither on age nor experience." SPCL says "Many years do not make a person wise, nor do beards bring with them proper understanding." This same thought may be expressed in some languages as "Being an old person with one hair does not make you wise, nor does having a wrinkled face give you understanding."

32.10   RSV   TEV

> Therefore I say, 'Listen to me;
>   let me also declare my opin-
>   ion.'

> So now I want you to listen to
>   me;
> let me tell you what I think.

Therefore I say, 'Listen to me . . .': Elihu now sums up: "This is the reason," "This is why," "In view of this." **Listen** is singular, which would imply that Elihu is addressing Job. The ancient versions and two Hebrew manuscripts have the plural, and it is more probable from the context that Elihu is speaking to both Job and the friends. Translators will note that RSV has translated as direct speech where TEV has used indirect speech. Whether to use direct or indirect in translation will depend on considerations of style and context.

Let me also declare my opinion: this line is similar to verse 6b. What Elihu wishes to say is more than **opinion**; it is his "knowledge"; that is, "Let me tell you what I know."

8B-2. Elihu accuses the friends of failing to answer Job (32.11-14)

RSV	TEV

11 "Behold, I waited for your words,
    I listened for your wise sayings,
    while you searched out what to say.
	11 I listened patiently while you were speaking
	    and waited while you searched for wise phrases.

12 I gave you my attention,
    and, behold, there was none that confuted Job,
    or that answered his words, among you.
	12 I paid close attention and heard you fail;
	    you have not disproved what Job has said.

13 Beware lest you say, 'We have found wisdom;
    God may vanquish him, not man.'
	13 How can you claim you have discovered wisdom?
	    God must answer Job, for you have failed.

14 He has not directed his words against me,
    and I will not answer him with your speeches.
	14 Job was speaking to you, not to me,
	    but I would never answer the way you did.

Subdivision Heading

The Handbook heading may be modified to say, for example, "Elihu says the friends did not speak the truth," "The friends did not answer Job correctly," or "The friends did not say what they should have said." Rowley (verses 6-14) has "Elihu's youth is wiser than the friends' age."

32.11 RSV	TEV

"Behold, I waited for your words,
    I listened for your wise sayings,
    while you searched out what to say.
	I listened patiently while you were speaking
	    and waited while you searched for wise phrases.

Verses 11 and 12 each have three lines in Hebrew. The three lines of verse 11 in RSV reflect their order in Hebrew. TEV has rearranged the verb order as "listen, waited, searched." There does not appear to be any advantage in doing this.

Behold, I waited for your words: **Behold** translates a Hebrew introductory word that has the effect of picking up again the subject of a previous verse, in this case verse 6. There Elihu said he was afraid to speak out. The sense of **Behold** is "As I was saying . . . ," but this may be expressed adequately in English as "Well" or "Well then." In some languages it need not be translated. **For your words** means "to hear what you (plural) were going to say" or "to hear the advice you (plural) would give Job."

I listened for your wise sayings: Elihu is saying that he listened intently to catch their "understanding, insight, or reasoning." The implication is that there was none, as he will make clear in verse 12. This line may be rendered, for example, "I listened carefully to see how you would argue."

While you searched out what to say is literally "while you searched words." The word translated **searched** is used throughout Job with various meanings:

"study" (29.16), "explore or investigate" (28.3), "scrutinize" (5.27; 13.9). **Words** in this context means "good words," "wise words," or "a good reply." GECL translates "I waited intently for your (plural) words; I hoped for a wise discourse while you (plural) struggled to find the right answer." We may also recast **words** and **sayings** as events and translate, for example, "Well, I waited to hear what you (plural) were going to say to Job. I listened to catch the way you (plural) understood things while you looked for ways to say it."

32.12

RSV	TEV
I gave you my attention, and, behold, there was none that confuted Job, or that answered his words, among you.	I paid close attention and heard you fail; you have not disproved what Job has said.

Elihu says he found no refutation, no argument put forth by the friends to show Job that he was wrong. Job would no doubt agree with Elihu here, but since he never replies to Elihu, it is impossible to know what he thinks of Elihu's speeches. None of the friends ever calls Job by his name. In contrast Elihu does so nine times during his long speeches.

I gave you my attention: Elihu is careful to emphasize that he paid close attention to the speeches of the friends. What he found was **there was none that confuted Job**: that is, "no one showed Job that he was wrong" or "and none of you has answered his arguments."

32.13

RSV	TEV
Beware lest you say, 'We have found wisdom; God may vanquish him, not man.'	How can you claim you have discovered wisdom? God must answer Job, for you have failed.

Elihu now warns the friends not to be confident that they have all the wisdom they need. **Beware lest you say** may also be expressed "Be careful, do not say . . . ." **We have found wisdom . . .** : in Proverbs 3.13 we have the thought "Happy is the man who finds wisdom." In Job, however, wisdom remains hidden to all except God (28.23). This line may be rendered, for example, "Don't say to yourselves, 'We have found wisdom'" or "Don't say to yourselves, 'We are the wise ones.'" In RSV the quotation which begins in line a continues through line b. However, Hebrew punctuation is not adequate to be certain where the quotation ends, and so some translate the next line as a separate statement made by Elihu. TEV expresses line a as a rhetorical question: "How can you claim you have discovered wisdom?" See the remark on direct and indirect speech in verse 11.

God may vanquish him, not man: if the quotation is taken as in RSV, it is unclear why the friends would need to ask God to deal with Job. The second line in

TEV suits the context better, since it means that Elihu himself is claiming that only God, and not the friends, can deal with Job. **Vanquish** translates a verb which HOTTP translates as "repulse." NEB has "rebut." TEV seems to accept the same sense as NEB in "God must answer Job," but completes it with a reason clause, "for you have failed." FRCL, which takes this line to be part of the quotation from line a, says "It is not we, but God who will refute him." In some languages this kind of construction is best handled as a negative followed by a positive statement; for example, "A man will not answer him; God will answer him."

32.14   RSV   TEV

| He has not directed his words against me, and I will not answer him with your speeches. | Job was speaking to you, not to me, but I would never answer the way you did. |

He has not directed his words against me: **He** refers to Job, who has not **directed** . . . , an expression meaning "to marshal" or "to line up in rows." HOTTP suggests "And he has not lined up (his arguments) against me." TEV "Job was speaking to you, not to me" gives the sense but loses the feeling of the original. We can translate "Job was not aiming his arguments at me" or "I was not the target of Job's words."

And I will not answer him with your speeches: Elihu is saying that he will not reply to Job with the poor arguments of the friends, or as TEV says, "but I would never answer the way you did."

8B-3. Elihu says he must speak or he will burst (32.15-22)

RSV   TEV

15	"They are discomfited, they answer no more; they have not a word to say.	15	Words have failed them, Job; they have no answer for you.
16	And shall I wait, because they do not speak, because they stand there, and answer no more?	16	Shall I go on waiting when they are silent? They stand there with nothing more to say.
17	I also will give my answer; I also will declare my opinion.	17	No, I will give my own answer now and tell you what I think.
18	For I am full of words, the spirit within me constrains me.	18	I can hardly wait to speak. I can't hold back the words.
19	Behold, my heart is like wine that has no vent; like new wineskins, it is ready to burst.	19	If I don't get a chance to speak, I will burst like a wineskin full of new wine.
20	I must speak, that I may find relief; I must open my lips and answer.	20	I can't stand it; I have to speak.
21	I will not show partiality to any person or use flattery toward any man.	21	I will not take sides in this debate; I am not going to flatter anyone.
22	For I do not know how to flatter,	22	I don't know how to flatter, and God would quickly punish me if I did.

else would my Maker soon put an end
   to me.

With verse 15 Elihu seems to direct his speech to Job; at least he no longer speaks to the friends, but about them. Nevertheless FRCL continues to the end of the chapter with Elihu addressing the friends rather than Job. Elihu's self-importance and wordiness grow with each new utterance.

Subdivision Heading

The Handbook heading may also be expressed, for example, "Elihu says if he doesn't speak he will burst open," "I have to speak," or "I can't wait any longer to speak." Rowley has "The collapse of the friends moves Elihu to speak."

32.15   RSV   TEV

"They are discomfited, they an-   Words have failed them, Job;
     swer no more;   they have no answer for you.
   they have not a word to say.

They are discomfited: They refers to the three friends. **Discomfited** translates a word meaning "dismayed, dumbfounded, speechless." **They have not a word to say** repeats the thought of the first line. TEV, which addresses these words to Job, reverses the lines for stylistic reasons. SPCL provides a good model: "Job, those three are confounded (speechless) and they do not know how to reply to you." This verse may also be expressed "Job, your three friends have no more words for you; they are unable to say anything more to you."

32.16   RSV   TEV

And shall I wait, because they do   Shall I go on waiting when they
     not speak,   are silent?
   because they stand there, and   They stand there with nothing
     answer no more?   more to say.

And shall I wait, because they do not speak . . . ? The rhetorical question in this verse expects the answer "No," which is given in verse 17. Elihu is emphasizing how patient he has been. If it is necessary in the receptor language to reduce the two lines, we may say, for example, "Because they stand there in silence, should I wait to speak to you?" or ". . . wait before I speak to you?" Another approach is to translate as a negative statement: "Just because they have nothing more to say to you, and stand there silently, I am not going to wait to speak to you."

32.17   RSV   TEV

>   I also will give my answer;   No, I will give my own answer
>   I also will declare my opinion.   now
>   and tell you what I think.

The two lines of this verse say the same thing. Both lines continue to pile up words as if a climax will be reached and Elihu will pronounce some momentous truth. Of course he never does. The Hebrew of line b is identical with that in verse 10b. Line a is literally "I will also answer my share." The word translated "share" normally means either a share of land or a share in a person's destiny. Neither of these meanings suits the idea here. NEB takes the expression to be an agricultural metaphor and translates "I, too, have a furrow to plough." A closer translation is "I will accept my share of the task of answering Job." TEV and most other modern translations make no attempt to focus on the word "share."

32.18   RSV   TEV

>   For I am full of words,   I can hardly wait to speak.
>   the spirit within me constrains   I can't hold back the words.
>   me.

For I am full of words is without question an honest remark. In some languages to be **full of words** implies that words have been eaten or drunk. Accordingly we must sometimes translate "I have many words to say," or "The words I have to say are endless," or "Words come from my mouth like air."

The spirit within me constrains me is literally "the *ruach* presses in my belly," where *ruach* can mean "wind," "breath," or "spirit." It is most likely that Elihu is being satirized by the poet, and so the *ruach* pressing in his belly is the equivalent of calling himself a "windbag," someone who talks endlessly and says nothing important. TEV keeps the focus on "words" from line a with "I can't hold back the words." This line may also be expressed as "I am bursting with words," "I am stuffed with words," or "I can't hold back the words that are in me."

32.19   RSV   TEV

>   Behold, my heart is like wine   If I don't get a chance to speak,
>   that has no vent;   I will burst like a wineskin full
>   like new wineskins, it is ready   of new wine.
>   to burst.

Behold my heart is like wine that has no vent: **heart** translates the Hebrew for "belly," as in the previous verse. The **wine** here is said to have no **vent**. Wine that is fermenting releases gas. If there is no escape for the gas, the pressure will build up and burst the container. Elihu is suggesting that his insides are like this, not from wine but from unexpressed words.

In the second line Elihu uses the simile **like new wineskins**. If the Hebrew word used here means **wineskins**, this is the only place in the Old Testament where it has that meaning. The sense of **wineskins** is based mainly on the word for **wine** in the first line. NEB follows the Septuagint in changing the word translated **new** in this line to read "blacksmith's bellows," and HOTTP supports this with a "C" rating, a rare decision on the part of HOTTP. However, all modern translations consulted are close to RSV, which is the form recommended here. The comparison is between Elihu's urge to speak and the pressure of the bursting wineskin, and TEV brings this out clearly by saying "If I don't get a chance to speak, I will burst like a wineskin full of new wine." TEV suggests that the wine is fermenting, by the expression "new wine." In languages in which **wineskins** are unknown, translators may be able to use a substitute expression. If **wineskins** is expressed through a loan word and a descriptive phrase, it may still be advisable to provide a note. In cases where the use of **wineskins** is totally unfamiliar, we may translate, for example, "See how I am bursting to speak. I am like a bag that will hold no more."

32.20   RSV   TEV

> I must speak, that I may find   I can't stand it; I have to speak.
>   relief;
> I must open my lips and an-
>   swer.

I must speak, that I may find relief: Elihu seems more concerned to take care of his own problem than to help Job. Verse 20 continues the depiction of Elihu under pressure and needing to ease his pain. To **find relief** is "to be comforted, to be freed from pain."

Open my lips and answer translates the Hebrew literally. This is a poetic way of saying "I must speak." It is implied that it is to Job that Elihu must speak. In some languages in which the parallel lines will be understood as describing events in sequence, it will appear odd that someone would speak and then open the lips, as if speaking in line a could be done without parting the lips. In such cases it may be best to omit the second line as redundant, or better, to say, for example, "yes, I must speak out."

32.21   RSV   TEV

> I will not show partiality to any   I will not take sides in this de-
>   person   bate;
> or use flattery toward any   I am not going to flatter any-
>   man.   one.

I will not show partiality is literally "I will not lift up the face." The expression is used in Leviticus 19.15, where the judges are told to treat the great and the poor alike. So Elihu is claiming that he will not show favors to anyone but will be impartial. TEV makes the matter of impartiality more specific with "I will not take sides in this debate." We may also translate, for example, "I will not side with any one person" or "I will be fair and treat everyone equally." RSV **man** means the same as **person** in line a and will be better translated as in TEV or as in the model translations given.

Use flattery translates a term meaning "give honorific titles." It is used in Isaiah 44.5 and 45.4. Elihu is thus saying that he will not treat anyone with special honor. The line may be expressed in some languages, for example, as "I will not warm people with words," "I will not speak big words about people," or "I will not make people great with my mouth."

32.22

RSV	TEV

For I do not know how to flatter,
    else would my Maker soon put
      an end to me.
	I don't know how to flatter,
	    and God would quickly punish
	      me if I did.

Elihu says **I do not know how to flatter**, in which **flatter** translates the same verb as in verse 21b.

Else would my Maker soon put an end to me is the reason Elihu gives for not using flattery. Elihu is afraid that God would take vengeance on him by getting rid of him: "If I did so my Creator would soon take me away" or ". . . destroy me."

8B-4. Elihu challenges Job to argue with him (33.1-7)

	RSV		TEV

1	"But now, hear my speech, O Job,
	  and listen to all my words.
		1	And now, Job, listen carefully
			  to all that I have to say.

2	Behold, I open my mouth; the tongue in my mouth speaks.	2	I am ready to say what's on my mind.

3	My words declare the uprightness of my
	      heart,
	  and what my lips know they speak
	      sincerely.
		3	All my words are sincere,
			  and I am speaking the truth.

4	The spirit of God has made me,
	  and the breath of the Almighty gives
	      me life.
		4	God's spirit made me and gave me life.

5	Answer me, if you can;
	  set your words in order before me;
	  take your stand.
		5	Answer me if you can. Prepare your arguments.

6	Behold, I am toward God as you are;
	  I too was formed from a piece of clay.
		6	You and I are the same in God's sight,
			  both of us were formed from clay.

7	Behold, no fear of me need terrify you;
	  my pressure will not be heavy upon
	      you.
		7	So you have no reason to fear me;
			  I will not overpower you.

In chapter 32 Elihu directed part of his remarks to Job's friends. Now in chapter 33 he turns his attention entirely to Job. The friends avoided playing the role of God's defense lawyer, but Elihu sees his task as doing just that. Consequently

Elihu confronts Job with legal language and arguments aimed to defend God against
Job's accusations.

At the beginning of this division, the structure of chapter 33 was described as
an unbalanced chiasmus. That structure is now spelled out in terms of the detailed
content. Elihu begins (verses 1-7) with a challenge to Job to listen to him and to
answer if he can. At the end of this speech, Elihu returns to the same theme,
challenging Job to listen and to answer if he can (verses 31-33). In verses 8-11 Elihu
restates Job's charges against God taken largely from Job's speech in chapter 13. The
imbalance in the structure appears in the lack of anything equivalent to verses 8-11
in the second half of the chapter. The third step in Elihu's speech (verses 12-14) is
his refutation or objection to Job's claims. In the second half of the chapter (verses
29-30), Elihu again overturns Job's arguments by claiming God acts to prevent a man
from going down to the grave. In the middle section of the speech (verses 15-28),
Elihu sets forth his strongest arguments in defense of God. This is essentially a
response to Job's charge that God does not answer. Elihu argues to the contrary
(15-18), insisting that God speaks in dreams, opens men's ears, terrifies them with
warnings to keep their soul from the grave. Further evidence that God answers men
is through physical suffering (19-22). The final way is through healing and restoration
(23-28). In all of this Elihu is implying that Job should confess and be restored, and
so there is really nothing new in Elihu's wisdom.

Subdivision Heading

Translators may wish to follow the Handbook heading or to modify it to say,
for example, "Now listen to me Job," "Job, I am ready to speak to you," or "Here
is what I have to say to you, Job." Habel has "Summons to testify in court," and
Rowley "Elihu invites the attention of Job."

33.1 RSV	TEV
"But now, hear my speech, O Job, and listen to all my words.	And now, Job, listen carefully to all that I have to say.

But now hear my speech, O Job: Elihu is now prepared to speak directly to
Job. **But** suggests a contrast with the close of the preceding chapter, but it is rather
a shift in topic and listener. "And now" expresses the linkage well in English. NJB has
"So, Job . . . ." The fact that Elihu addresses Job by name does not mean that Elihu
is a familiar friend or social equal of Job. It serves the purpose of keeping the focus
of Elihu's long speeches fixed on the principal character, who has now grown silent
but must not fade in the reader's mind. **My speech** refers to the arguments Elihu
will put forward. **O** in **O Job** is an English vocative form sometimes use when calling
to or addressing someone directly. The equivalent in many languages is the "you"
pronoun or no special form at all.

And listen to all my words forms a chiasmus in Hebrew with line a; that is,
the two lines are parallel in meaning, with the parallel elements coming in reverse
order in line b. TEV makes two lines but does not repeat the verbs: "And now, Job,
listen carefully to all that I have to say."

33.2　　　　RSV　　　　　　　　　　　TEV

> Behold, I open my mouth;　　　　I am ready to say what's on my
> 　　the tongue in my mouth　　　　　mind.
> 　　　speaks.

Behold, I open my mouth: Elihu's gift is in multiplying words. **Behold** translates a double expression, and the same as that used in 13.18. Here Elihu is calling attention to himself and his readiness to say something. Again the two lines have the same meaning, and no doubt the author is satirizing Elihu's self-importance. This line means "I am ready to speak" or "I am all set to present my arguments." NEB has "the words are on the tip of my tongue," which is a good idiomatic expression in English.

The tongue in my mouth speaks is literally "my tongue in my palate has spoken." Elihu wastes his words with empty phrases and says almost nothing of substance. It is also possible to understand these verbose lines as Elihu playing the role of God's attorney preparing to call Job to appear in court, as he finally does in verse 5. TEV reduces the two lines to one, "I am ready to say what is on my mind." TEV, however, loses some of the banality or emptiness in Elihu's talk by translating more economically and logically than the way Elihu speaks. If it is desirable to keep both lines, we may translate, for example, "I am all set to speak, and my tongue is forming words in my mouth."

33.3　　　　RSV　　　　　　　　　　　TEV

> My words declare the upright-　　All my words are sincere,
> 　　ness of my heart,　　　　　　　and I am speaking the truth.
> and what my lips know they
> 　　speak sincerely.

My words declare the uprightness of my heart is literally "Uprightness of heart are my words." **Declare** is supplied by RSV, since there is no verb in this line in Hebrew. According to RSV Elihu is trying to establish his honesty by what he says. Scholars differ considerably in their handling of this verse. This is mainly because the two lines are not balanced. Therefore it is necessary to look at the second line: **and what my lips know they speak sincerely**. Some feel that **lips know** is not a suitable combination, since lips **speak** but do not **know**. (But we can understand that this figure is a part [lips] representing the whole person [Elihu], and he is again attempting to state that he has knowledge.) By transferring the word **know,** which is the first word in line b in the Hebrew text, to line a, and changing the noun meaning **uprightness** to a similar verb meaning "confirm," NEB translates "My heart assures me that I speak with knowledge." This then allows NEB to render the second line "and that my lips speak with sincerity." Habel, on the other hand, keeps the two lines parallel, and without making any change in the text he translates "With uprightness my heart states my case; with knowledge my lips argue clearly." In this case the verb in line a is supplied from line b. This is preferable to TEV, which has not shifted **knowledge** to line <u>a</u> nor translated it in line <u>b</u>. The verse may also be expressed, for example, "I argue my case with a good heart and say it clearly."

33.4   RSV   TEV

> The spirit of God has made me,   God's spirit made me and gave
> and the breath of the Almighty   me life.
> gives me life.

The spirit of God has made me, and the breath of the Almighty gives me life: NJB, BJ, Mft, and Dhorme transfer this verse to follow verse 6. In 9.32 Job complained that God "is not a man, as I am, . . . that we should come to trial together." So Elihu assures Job that he is now to be confronted by one of God's creatures like himself. **Spirit of God** in line <u>a</u> is parallel in meaning to **breath of the Almighty** in line <u>b</u>. God in line <u>a</u> is *'El* and in line <u>b</u> *Shaddai*. **Made me** in line <u>a</u> is likewise parallel in meaning to **gives me life** in line <u>b</u>. TEV reduces these two lines to one. However, TEV could have kept the close parallelism by translating "God's spirit made me; the Almighty gave me life." FRCL prefers to keep both lines: "I was created by the Spirit of God, and was made to live by his almighty breath." SPCL has "God the Almighty made me and breathed his breath into me." Any of these are satisfactory translation models.

33.5   RSV   TEV

> Answer me, if you can;   Answer me if you can. Prepare
> set your words in order before   your arguments.
> me; take your stand.

Answer me, if you can is rendered alike by RSV and TEV, aside from punctuation. **Answer me** does not mean to reply to the question I will ask you, but rather "refute, argue against, disprove, defend yourself." FRCL and GECL have "contradict."

Set your words in order before me: **words** is not in the Hebrew. **Set in order** translates the same verb used in 32.14 meaning "to marshal or line up," and the implied object is Job's defense or his arguments, and so TEV has "Prepare your arguments." Since the term is from military usage, Dhorme takes it more literally as "prepare yourself." RSV understands **before me** to apply to the setting in order of the words. Others understand **before me** to go with the final verb translated **take your stand**; that is, "stand in front of me," which is more natural than RSV. This clause does not appear in TEV but should be translated, since the expression is appropriate in the context of the trial in which Elihu is acting as God's spokesman.

33.6 RSV TEV

Behold, I am toward God as you are;	You and I are the same in God's sight,
I too was formed from a piece of clay.	both of us were formed from clay.

Behold, I am toward God as you are: for **Behold** see comments on verse 2. **Toward God as you are** makes poor sense in English. A more natural translation is "I am the same as you are in God's sight" or "In God's eyes I am a man just like you." **As you are** is literally "like your mouth," in which a part is used for the whole, and so the expression means "like you."

I too was formed from a piece of clay: by saying **I too** Elihu includes them both. The rest of the line alludes to the creation in Genesis 2.7, although there the word "dust" is used for the material the LORD God used to form man, not **clay**. **Formed** translates a verb meaning "pinched off or broken off," as a potter breaks off a piece of clay from the mass to produce his object. TEV's rendering of both lines is clear and appropriate. This verse may also be expressed "Look, I am a man the same as you in God's eyes; I also was formed from a piece of clay" or ". . . and God made me too from a piece of clay."

33.7 RSV TEV

Behold, no fear of me need terrify you;	So you have no reason to fear me;
my pressure will not be heavy upon you.	I will not overpower you.

Behold, no fear of me need terrify you: This is the third time in seven verses that Elihu opens his sentence with **Behold**, calling attention to what he is saying, since the content itself is apparently insufficient to do this. In 9.34 Job asked God to "keep your terrors away," and 13.21 "don't crush me with terror" (TEV). Although Elihu calls on Job to stand before him, Job need not think he is standing before God, who causes him such terror. Elihu promises not to overwhelm him with his authority. "You need not fear me," he assures Job. But at the same time he does not invite Job to relax too much. Verse 7 is a consequence of verse 6 and so may be translated, for example, "And so (Consequently, Therefore) you don't have to be afraid of me."

My pressure will not be heavy upon you: **pressure** translates a noun found only here in the Old Testament, but the verb form occurs in Proverbs 16.26. The Septuagint either makes a change in the text to "my hand" or translates the Hebrew word in that way as a dynamic equivalent. NJB says "my hand will not lie heavy over you." FRCL translates "You have no reason to tremble before me or to think that I want to crush you." Verse 7 may also be rendered, for example, "So, you don't have to be afraid of me or think I will oppress you."

8B-5. Elihu restates Job's argument of his innocence (33.8-11)

	RSV		TEV
8	"Surely, you have spoken in my hearing, and I have heard the sound of your words.	8	Now this is what I heard you say:
9	You say, 'I am clean, without transgression; I am pure, and there is no iniquity in me.	9	"I am not guilty; I have done nothing wrong. I am innocent and free from sin.
10	Behold, he finds occasions against me, he counts me as his enemy;	10	But God finds excuses for attacking me and treats me like an enemy.
11	he puts my feet in the stocks, and watches all my paths.'	11	He binds chains on my feet; he watches every move I make."

Verse 8 introduces the content of verses 9-11, and so 8 and 9 will be treated together. Elihu will finally now get around to taking up Job's claims of innocence. Elihu does not accept that God would persecute anyone who was truly innocent. However, Elihu still needs one more piece of preamble (verse 8) before getting to the subject.

Subdivision Heading

The Handbook heading may be reworded to say, for example, "Elihu repeats Job's argument," "Elihu reviews what Job has said about his innocence," or "Elihu rewords Job's claims to be innocent." Habel has "Restatement of Job's case," Rowley (verses 8-13) "Job's affirmation of innocence and unjust treatment is false."

33.8-9	RSV		TEV
8	"Surely, you have spoken in my hearing, and I have heard the sound of your words.	8	Now this is what I heard you say:
9	You say, 'I am clean, without transgression; I am pure, and there is no iniquity in me.	9	"I am not guilty; I have done nothing wrong. I am innocent and free from sin.

Surely you have spoken in my hearing: Elihu is saying that he has heard all of Job's arguments, but the way in which he says it, according to Dhorme, is "You have done nothing but talk in my ears." TEV understands the two parallel lines as equivalent to a single line introducing the quotation that follows in verse 9. NJB, which translates this line as a question, makes it refer to Job's claim in verse 9: "How could you say in my hearing . . . ?" Others use various syntactic and stylistic means to relate verse 8 to verse 9. For example, FRCL says in line a, "I still have the sound of your voice in my ears"; this is followed by "since you did nothing but repeat this: . . . ," and the claims of Job's purity follow.

And I have heard the sound of your words is translated by RSV as nothing more than a parallel line, which does not attempt to tie it with verse 9. RSV supplies **You say** at the beginning of verse 9. It is better, however, to follow TEV if reducing the two lines to one, or FRCL if retaining both lines.

You say, 'I am clean, without transgression . . .': Elihu now begins to pick up words from Job's speech in 9.21, where he said "I am blameless." In 10.6-7 Job said "thou dost seek out my iniquity and search for my sin, although thou knowest that I am not guilty." In 16.17 Job said "There is no violence in my hands and my prayer is pure." There are further claims of this kind made by Job in 23.7,10; 27.4-6; chapter 31. None of these passages is actually quoted by Elihu. In fact the words which Elihu quotes in verse 9 are closer to the words of Eliphaz in 11.4, in which Eliphaz is paraphrasing Job. Job acknowledges his faults in 7.21 and 13.26, and has not claimed to be sinless, but Elihu has chosen to pay no attention to this. For discussion of **clean** see 11.4; on **transgressions** see 7.21.

I am pure, and there is no iniquity in me is parallel in meaning to the previous line. For **pure** see 11.4, and for **iniquity** see 7.21. In some languages it will be necessary to shift from nouns to verbs and say, for example, "You say, 'I have clean hands and have done nothing wrong; I live a pure life and have done no evil deeds'" or "You say, 'I have broken no taboo and have done no wrong; I live right and commit no crimes.'"

33.10	RSV	TEV
	Behold, he finds occasions against me, he counts me as his enemy;	But God finds excuses for attacking me and treats me like an enemy.

Behold, he finds occasions against me continues what Elihu considers a quotation from Job. This line reflects the kind of complaint Job makes against God in 10.13-17, but there is no passage which it closely resembles. **Behold** is used now by Elihu even when quoting Job. It may serve the purpose here of connecting verse 10 to verse 9 with an element of surprise, which in English, if it is translated at all, can be "Look here" or "Listen to this." **He** should often be rendered "God," since God has not been mentioned since verse 9. The word translated **occasions** is found elsewhere only in Numbers 14.34, where RSV translates "displeasure." Dhorme, Habel, and Pope propose a change to get "pretext." However, both ideas may be contained within the meaning range of the Hebrew word, and so that change is unnecessary. **Finds occasions against me** is incomplete and needs an explicit purpose; for example, as TEV says, "God finds excuses for attacking me" or "God looks for opportunities to make me suffer."

He counts me as his enemy nearly repeats 19.11, "and counts me as his adversary." **Counts** means "considers, regards, looks upon." TEV has "treats me like an enemy?"

33.11   RSV   TEV

he puts my feet in the stocks,
   and watches all my paths.'

He binds chains on my feet;
   he watches every move I
      make."

He puts my feet in the stocks repeats 13.27. For discussion of the terms see there. The only difference is that Job uses second person singular when he speaks to God, while Elihu uses third person singular. **And watches all my paths** closes the quotation which opened in verse 9a. **Paths** is used to represent the places where Job goes, or the steps he takes, which more generally means "everything I do."

8B-6. Elihu refutes Job's claim (33.12-14)

RSV   TEV

12   "Behold, in this you are not right. I will answer you.
    God is greater than man.
13   Why do you contend against him, saying, 'He will answer none of my words'?
14   For God speaks in one way, and in two, though man does not perceive it.

12   But I tell you, Job, you are wrong.
    God is greater than any man.
13   Why do you accuse God of never answering a man's complaints?
14   Although God speaks again and again, no one pays attention to what he says.

In verses 12-14 Elihu refutes Job's claims in verses 9-11.

Subdivision Heading

The Handbook heading may be modified to say, for example, "Elihu says Job's claim to be innocent is false," "Elihu tells Job that he is not speaking the truth," or "Job, you are wrong!" Habel has "Refutation of Job's claim."

33.12   RSV   TEV

"Behold, in this you are not right. I will answer you.
   God is greater than man.

But I tell you, Job, you are wrong.
   God is greater than any man.

Behold, in this you are not right: for **Behold** see verses 7 and 10. **This** refers to all that Job is quoted as saying in verses 9-11. **You are not right** is Elihu's legal pronouncement "you are not in the right," "the right is not on your side," or "you are in the wrong."

I will answer you refers to Elihu's reacting to what Job said, by telling Job that he is wrong; it does not mean that Elihu is answering a question. Therefore TEV rightly shifts this expression to the beginning and translates it "But I tell you, Job." Job is addressed in TEV, not in the Hebrew, in order to make clear that a transition from quoting Job to speaking to Job has been made. FRCL says clearly "You are wrong on this point, Job, and I must tell you so." This line may also be rendered, for example, "Job, you are wrong to say all that, and that is why I am telling you" or "I am telling you, Job, that you are wrong to say those things."

God is greater than man may mean that God is too great to be held accountable before people, as Job wants him to be, or it may mean that God is above the faults Job has attributed to him. FRCL takes it in the former sense, with "God is too great to discuss matters with a man." This is better than RSV and TEV, which translate this line literally. **Man** here does not refer exclusively to a male person but to anyone, male or female.

33.13   RSV   TEV

> Why do you contend against him,   Why do you accuse God
>   saying, 'He will answer none of   of never answering a man's
>   my^s words'?   complaints?

^s Compare Gk: Heb *his*

Why do you contend against him: in 9.2-3 Job recognizes that "if one wished to contend with him, one could not answer him once in a thousand times." **Contend** means "to argue a legal case, accuse, complain." Elihu's question is based on his observation in verse 12b, which Job himself has repeated, that if God is greater than a man, why should Job argue with him?

Saying, 'He will answer none of my words'? The RSV footnote shows that the Hebrew has "his words," which probably refer to "man" in verse 12, and so TEV "a man's complaints." FRCL offers two translations of this verse, one in the text and one in the footnote: "Why do you blame him for not answering questions put to him?" or "Why do you enter a lawsuit with him? He does not have to answer anyone's questions." HOTTP suggests three renderings, which are reworded here for clarity: (1) "God does not give answers to all of a man's questions"; (2) "God does not give account for all of his actions"; (3) "A reply cannot be given for all that God says." The second is similar to the translation in the NIV footnote: "That he does not answer for any of his actions"; and the third is similar to NEB, "For no one can answer his arguments." Job's concern throughout the book has been that God does not answer him; he is not concerned with a general or abstract problem. Therefore a translation should focus, not on the general, but on the specific application to Job, and so can be rendered "Why do you complain against God for not answering your questions?" or "Why do you object that God does not argue his case with you?" or "Why do you accuse God for not defending himself?"

33.14   RSV   TEV

> For God speaks in one way,   Although God speaks again and
>   and in two, though man does   again,
>   not perceive it.   no one pays attention to what
>   he says.

For God speaks in one way, and in two is understood variously by different translators. NJB seems to understand it as RSV may imply, "God speaks first in one way, and then in another." FRCL focuses on the manner of speaking, with "When God speaks he chooses one means of expression or another . . . ." NEB understands it to mean that God speaks but once: "Indeed, once God has spoken he does not speak a second time . . . ." This follows Dhorme, "The fact is that God speaks once, and He does not repeat His word."

What we have here is an example of number parallelism, which was presented in the introduction, "Translating the Book of Job," page 12, and discussed again in 5.19. Translators should review the comments there. Elihu is here using a common poetic device in which the second of two numbers is always greater than the first. The device is used in order to express the thought of doing something over and over, "again and again," as TEV says. We may also translate, for example, "God says something, then he says it over and over."

Though man does not perceive it is taken by some to mean "though one does not see him." Vulgate and Syriac change this line to mean "and he does not repeat it," which is the basis for Dhorme and NEB above. A better rendering is based on the Hebrew without any change, as in TEV, "No one pays attention to what he says."

8B-7. Elihu says God warns men in their dreams to stop sinning (33.15-18)

	RSV		TEV
15	In a dream, in a vision of the night, when deep sleep falls upon men, while they slumber on their beds,	15	At night when men are asleep, God speaks in dreams and visions.
16	then he opens the ears of men, and terrifies them with warnings,	16	He makes them listen to what he says, and they are frightened at his warnings.
17	that he may turn man aside from his deed, and cut off pride from man;	17	God speaks to make them stop their sinning and to save them from becoming proud.
18	he keeps back his soul from the Pit, his life from perishing by the sword.	18	He will not let them be destroyed; he saves them from death itself.

Subdivision Heading

The Handbook heading may be restructured to say, for example, "God warns people while they sleep," "God gives people dreams to warn them," or "God tells people to stop sinning." Habel has "Evidence from dreams," and Rowley (verses 14-28) "Job's complaint that God does not answer is belied by experience."

33.15-16	RSV		TEV
15	In a dream, in a vision of the night, when deep sleep falls upon men,	15	At night when men are asleep, God speaks in dreams and visions.
		16	He makes them listen to what he

<table>
<tr><td>

while they slumber on their
    beds,
16   then he opens the ears of men,
    and terrifies them with warn-
      ings,

</td><td>

says,
and they are frightened at his
    warnings.

</td></tr>
</table>

Since verse 15 is mainly setting, or background, with the main event in verse 16, the two will be discussed together. Verse 15 recalls Eliphaz's dream in 4.12 and nearly repeats it.

In a dream, in a vision of the night: "dreams" and "visions" are mentioned by Job in 7.14 as the means by which God terrifies him. There is no attempt here to distinguish between a **dream** and a **vision**, as there was none in 7.14, where they are in parallel position. Here **vision** is best placed in apposition to **dream**; that is, "in a dream, which is a vision in the night." **When deep sleep falls upon men** is the setting, and in English style it is best placed at the beginning, and so TEV has transposed these two lines.

While they slumber on their beds adds no new information and may be considered parallel in meaning with the previous line. TEV reduces lines b and c to one. Verse 15 may also be expressed "When a person goes to sleep at night and dreams and sees visions," or "When people lie on their beds and sleep at night, they have dreams," or ". . . God gives them dreams."

Then he opens the ears of men is literally "uncovers the ear" and means "to announce, inform, give news to." It is used in the sense of "inform" in Ruth 4.4; 1 Samuel 20.2,12,13. When God is the subject the verb means "to reveal," as in 36.10,15; 1 Samuel 9.15. FRCL translates "He brings to them a revelation."

And terrifies them with warnings is literally "and seals their bond." Most feel that the Hebrew text makes little sense, and so seek a way to change it. RSV's rendering is obtained by changing the vowels of the word meaning "seals," and in this way substituting the verb meaning "terrify," which is used in 7.14 in connection with **dreams** and **visions**. Consequently, by being spoken to through terrifying dreams, people learn their errors. However, HOTTP keeps the Hebrew "seals" and suggests "and he places under seal (his) warning (which concerns them)" or "he ratifies with a seal the warning (concerning) them." In this context Elihu is making the point that God does speak clearly to people over and over, and the Hebrew expresses the image of placing the seal on someone as meaning he stamps his warning on them. Thus the warning is clearly seen. We may then retain the Hebrew and translate, for example, "Then he tells people what he wants and makes his warnings as clear as a seal" or "He causes people to listen to what he says, and he leaves his mark to warn them."

33.17   RSV   TEV

<table>
<tr><td>

that he may turn man aside from
    his deed,
and cut off[t] pride from man;

</td><td>

God speaks to make them stop
    their sinning
and to save them from becom-
    ing proud.

</td></tr>
</table>

[t] Cn: Heb *hide*

That he may turn man aside from his deed is connected in RSV to verse 16 as the purpose of 16. TEV, on the other hand, translates this verse as an independent sentence. This first line is literally "to remove man's deed," which does not suggest a coherent meaning. Consequently the word translated **deed** is changed to read "evil," and then the entire phrase is translated "to prevent men from doing evil." Pope has "to deter men from evil." TEV takes the position that **deed** in the context refers automatically to "evil deeds," and so translates "God speaks to make them stop their sinning," which expresses the thought well. It is probably best to express verse 17 as the purpose for the events in verse 16, and so we may translate "He does this to make people stop doing evil deeds" or "This is to make them stop sinning."

And cut off pride from man: **cut off** translates the Hebrew term "hide," according to the RSV footnote. This line is literally "pride from man he covers." **Cut off** is a very slight change from the Hebrew "he covers" and is widely accepted. **Cut off pride from man** suggests "prevent people from being proud." TEV seems to accept the change but translates more clearly than RSV: "and to save them from becoming proud." In some languages this line may be rendered, for example, "and to keep them from having swollen hearts" or "and to stop them from acting with big heads."

33.18   RSV   TEV

> he keeps back his soul from the   He will not let them be de-
>   Pit,   stroyed;
> his life from perishing by the   he saves them from death
>   sword.   itself.

God's actions are taken to save man from a fate such as described in this verse. **He keeps back his soul from the Pit: keeps back** renders the terms used in 7.11; 16.5,6, with the sense of "restrain" or "check." Here it means "to spare, to save someone." NJB translates "preserves his soul." **Soul** translates the Hebrew *nefesh,* referring to a person's physical life. **Pit,** as in 17.14, refers generally to the world of the dead or more specifically to "the grave." TEV has avoided **pit** in this line, which it translates negatively, "He will not let them be destroyed." GECL is closer to the original with "So he rescues their life from the grave," which gives a good translation model. In some languages this expression may have to be restructured, for example, "When they are about to die and be buried, he saves them."

His life from perishing by the sword suggests a violent death, but there is nothing in the context to support this rendering. The verb translated **perishing** can mean "pass through, cross over," and although the word translated **sword** sometimes means "weapon," neither that meaning nor **sword** are suitable as a parallel to **pit** in line a. Accordingly some scholars identify the Hebrew word translated **sword** with a "canal" or "river," as in Nehemiah 3.15 and Isaiah 8.6, and associated in ancient mythology with the underground river on which the soul travels to its destination. Others, like TEV, understand **sword** not as the instrument of violent death, but of death generally, and so TEV "He saves them from death itself," which gives the same thought without the appeal to the mythological image of crossing the river to death. Some translators may feel that this line repeats line a so fully that to translate it will be repetitious. Parallelism may best be retained in the translation by following the thought of crossing the river, and translating similarly to NEB, "and stops him from crossing the river of death." In this case "river of death" may also be expressed as "the river that leads to death" or "the river that carries away the dead."

8B-8. Elihu says God sends sickness as a warning (33.19-22)

RSV	TEV
19 "Man is also chastened with pain upon his bed, and with continual strife in his bones;	19 God corrects a man by sending sickness and filling his body with pain.
20 so that his life loathes bread, and his appetite dainty food.	20 The sick man loses his appetite, and even the finest food looks revolting.
21 His flesh is so wasted away that it cannot be seen; and his bones which were not seen stick out.	21 His body wastes away to nothing; you can see all his bones;
22 His soul draws near the Pit, and his life to those who bring death.	22 he is about to go to the world of the dead.

Elihu now takes up the second way in which God warns men, which is suffering. This is particularly relevant to Job's case.

Subdivision Heading

The Handbook heading may be adjusted to say, for example, "God warns people by letting them become ill," "Suffering comes from God as a warning," or "The reason why people suffer." Habel has "Evidence from suffering."

33.19　　　　RSV　　　　　　　　　　　　　TEV

"Man is also chastened with pain upon his bed, and with continual strife in his bones;

God corrects a man by sending sickness and filling his body with pain.

Man is also chastened with pain upon his bed: is chastened is a passive construction which TEV expresses as active: "God corrects a man." **With pain** is the way God corrects, and may require a verb to relate it to the first clause; for example, as in TEV, "by sending pain," or "by means of sickness," or "by allowing him to become sick." TEV considers **upon his bed** as implied in "sending sickness." FRCL expresses this phrase as "sickness which sends him to bed."

And with continual strife in his bones: this line has an alternative reading in the Hebrew. RSV translates the form in the written text. KJV follows the other alternative: "and the multitude of his bones with strong pain." Most modern translations follow the same text as RSV. **Strife** is not a word that is used in English in connection with the bones. The reference is to suffering in the bones, which TEV translates as "pain." Dhorme prefers "a continual shaking of his bones, which may

615

imply fever," and FRCL says "Fever makes his limbs constantly tremble." TEV is an adequate rendering for the general picture; FRCL is better for capturing the poetic image.

33.20 RSV	TEV
so that his life loathes bread, and his appetite dainty food.	The sick man loses his appetite, and even the finest food looks revolting.

The result of sickness is his loss of appetite. **So that his life loathes bread**: **his life** refers to the sick man, and so TEV translates "The sick man" as the subject of line a. What the sick person **loathes**, "dislikes, has no desire for," is **bread**, which stands here for "food" in the general sense.

And his appetite dainty food: **appetite** is used here as the subject which **loathes . . . dainty food. Appetite** translates "his *nefesh*," which is commonly used in Hebrew in connection with desires and is suitably translated **appetite** in this context. **Dainty food** is literally "food of desire" and refers to the special foods a person likes, often referred to in English as "special or favorite dishes." Many languages have special terms to designate particular foods that appeal to the appetite. The line may be rendered "and he cannot stand his favorite dishes" or "and even his favorite dishes are repulsive to him."

33.21 RSV	TEV
His flesh is so wasted away that it cannot be seen; and his bones which were not seen stick out.	His body wastes away to nothing; you can see all his bones;

In a verse like this one, it is possible to forget for the moment that this is poetry and insist that the flesh does not disappear from view. Here **flesh** seems to refer to the muscles, which are not literally **seen** because skin covers them. Hunger and sickness can shrink the muscles so that they are no longer noticeable, and the skin then reveals the shape of the bones. However, the translator is not expected to be scientific but to reflect the author's poetic images in a suitable manner.

His flesh is so wasted away that it cannot be seen: there is a contrast between the visible flesh that has disappeared, and the invisible bones that now appear. **Flesh** can be the visible body in contrast to the bones, and so TEV translates more generally as "his body." It is also possible to refer to the person rather than to his **flesh** or "body"; for example, "He is so thin . . . ," or "He has lost so much weight . . . ," or "He has become like a skeleton." **That it cannot be seen** translates the Hebrew "from view" and is clearly implied in a rendering such as "he has become like a skeleton."

And his bones which were not seen stick out is translated by TEV "You can see all his bones." A more idiomatic rendering in English may perhaps be "and he is nothing but skin and bones."

33.22	RSV	TEV

<table>
<tr><td></td><td>His soul draws near the Pit,
  and his life to those who bring
    death.</td><td>he is about to go to the world
  of the dead.</td></tr>
</table>

His soul draws near the Pit translates the Hebrew "his *nefesh* approaches the pit." **Pit** translates the same word used in verse 18a and refers to the "grave" in the narrow sense, or to "the world of the dead" in the wider sense.

And his life to those who bring death: the verb in the first line serves also for this line, but the translation may require a verb to be used here. **His life** is parallel to **his soul** in line a. However, **those who bring death** is unclear. This expression is found nowhere else in the Old Testament. It appears to be a causative participle of the verb "to die" and so can be rendered "destroyers" or "killers," possibly referring to spiritual or even mythological beings that cause death. However, the expression is rendered variously by scholars. Dhorme follows the Septuagint to get "abode of the dead" as a parallel with **Pit**. TEV translates "world of the dead" to include both **pit** and **those who bring death,** and therefore reduces the two lines to one. It is possible to keep both lines and translate, for example, "He is about to go to his grave, and those who destroy life await him." It may be desirable to transpose the lines to give a more natural sequence; for example, "He is near death and approaches the grave" or "He is about to die and be buried."

8B-9. Elihu says God sends an angel to save men (33.23-30)

RSV	TEV

RSV	TEV

23   If there be for him an angel,
  a mediator, one of the thousand,
  to declare to man what is right for
   him;
	23 Perhaps an angel may come to his aid—
	  one of God's thousands of angels,
	  who remind men of their duty.

24   and he is gracious to him, and says,
  'Deliver him from going down into the
   Pit,
  I have found a ransom;
	24 In mercy the angel will say, "Release him!
	  He is not to go down to the world of
	   the dead.
	  Here is the ransom to set him free."

25   let his flesh become fresh with youth;
  let him return to the days of his youth-
   ful vigor';
	25 His body will grow young and strong
	   again;

26   then man prays to God, and he accepts
   him,
  he comes into his presence with joy.
  He recounts to men his salvation,
	26 when he prays, God will answer him;
	  he will worship God with joy;
	  God will set things right for him again.

27   and he sings before men, and says:
  'I sinned, and perverted what was right,
  and it was not requited to me.
	27 He will say in public, "I have sinned.
	  I have not done right, but God spared
	   me.

	28 He kept me from going to the world of
	   the dead,
	  and I am still alive."

28   He has redeemed my soul from going
        down into the Pit,
        and my life shall see the light.'
	29 God does all this again and again;
	30 he saves a person's life,
	        and gives him the joy of living.

29   "Behold, God does all these things,
        twice, three times, with a man,
30   to bring back his soul from the Pit,
        that he may see the light of life.

Subdivision Heading

The Handbook heading may be modified to say, for example, "God sends an angel to keep people from death" or "An angel can come and rescue you, Job."

33.23   RSV   TEV

If there be for him an angel,
   a mediator, one of the thou-
      sand,
   to declare to man what is right
      for him;
	Perhaps an angel may come to
	   his aid—
	   one of God's thousands of
	      angels,
	   who remind men of their duty.

If there be for him an angel, a mediator, one of the thousand: RSV translates verse 23 as an "if" clause, with the consequence of verses 23 and 24 coming in verse 26. TEV, which has shorter sentences, uses quite different sentence relations. The wording of RSV is rather literal and may be expressed "If an angel comes to him." In 5.1 a different word for **angel** was used, where TEV translated "Is there any angel to whom you can turn?" In both cases the reference is to someone who comes to help in a difficult situation. In apposition with **angel** is a second term, **mediator**, which translates a Hebrew word referring to one who interprets or comes between opposing parties to resolve their differences. TEV avoids **mediator** as a technical term and says "comes to his aid." **One of the thousand** makes it appear that there are exactly one thousand such beings. TEV is clearer with "One of God's thousands of angels." Daniel 7.10 refers to the vast numbers of heavenly servants as "a thousand thousands, and ten thousand times ten thousand."

To declare to man what is right for him is literally "to declare for man his uprightness." The purpose of the angel is to recall to the person what he should do, and so TEV "remind men of their duty." FRCL may serve as a translation model for verse 23: "But an angel, one of the thousands of God's mediators close to this man, is enough to make him know the right way." This may also be expressed "But one of the thousands of God's messengers (or, persons) who come to help someone is enough to show him what is right."

33.24   RSV   TEV

and he is gracious to him, and
   says,
   'Deliver him from going down
      into the Pit,
	In mercy the angel will say, "Re-
	   lease him!
	   He is not to go down to the
	      world of the dead.

| I have found a ransom; | Here is the ransom to set him free." |

And he is gracious to him: this verse has three short lines in Hebrew, divided as in RSV. No subject is used in line <u>a</u>. Some supply God as the subject, but it is more probably the angel, as TEV makes clear. **Gracious** translates a verb meaning "to have mercy, to take pity, to be compassionate." **Him** refers to the sick person mentioned in verses 19-23.

Deliver him from going down into the Pit are the words the angel speaks to God, and so FRCL says in line <u>b</u> "and he requests God 'Do not let him go down into the grave.'"

I have found a ransom is the continuation of the quotation of the angel. **Ransom** is usually a payment made to someone holding a person, in order to set that person free. TEV translates "Here is the ransom to set him free." In this way the angel buys the sick person some additional life. Verse 24 may also be expressed "The angel has pity on the sick person and says to God, 'Don't let him go to the world of the dead; I have found a way to free him.'"

33.25   RSV   TEV

| let his flesh become fresh with youth;
let him return to the days of his youthful vigor'; | His body will grow young and strong again; |

Let his flesh become fresh with youth: in RSV the quotation continues with verse 25. TEV, however, takes both 24 and 25 as a description of what happens as a result of the angel's request being granted. Both lines of verse 25 have about the same meaning, and they are reduced to one in TEV. **Becomes fresh** renders a Hebrew verb found only here in the Old Testament and having an unusual form. Pope and others change one letter to get "become plump," and Pope translates "His flesh becomes plump as a boy's." The same Hebrew root is found in 8.16 ("thrives") and 24.8 with the sense of "moist" or "sappy," and so Dhorme, like RSV, translates "His flesh becomes fresh with youth."

Let him return to the days of his youthful vigor may be rendered "he is again as he was when young" or "he finds his youthful strength all over again."

33.26   RSV   TEV

| then man prays to God, and he accepts him,
he comes into his presence with joy.
He recounts[u] to men his salvation, | when he prays, God will answer him;
he will worship God with joy;
God will set things right for him again. |

^{u} Cn: Heb *returns*

Then man prays to God, and he accepts him: **man** most likely refers to the sick person who has been restored through the mediation of the angel. The sense is as in 22.27, where Eliphaz says to Job, "You will make your prayer to him, and he will hear you." TEV makes this line clearer than RSV with "when he prays, God will answer him."

He comes into his presence with joy is literally "that he may see his face with joy." This is an idiom meaning to come before God as a servant, and in this context means more specifically "to come before God in worship," or as TEV says, "he will worship God with joy."

He recounts to men his salvation is literally "He will return to man his righteousness." The verb "return" is seen in the RSV footnote. According to the Hebrew it is implied that God restores righteousness to the person who was ill. However, RSV changes the text to **recounts**, meaning "announces, tells." Pope and NJB follow RSV. "Righteousness" can mean here "victory" or **salvation**. The idea here is that the restored man announces to others the mercy shown to him in his recovery, being saved from death. Some translators transfer this line to the end of verse 23, on the basis that it is out of place here but fits well after verse 23. Most, however, keep it in its traditional place and translate by following RSV's proposal, or as TEV, "God will set things right for him again." Verse 26 may be rendered, for example, "When the sick person prays to God, God listens to him. He will worship God joyfully because God has given him victory over death" or ". . . because God has not allowed him to die."

33.27   RSV   TEV

and he sings before men, and   He will say in public, "I have
   says: sinned.
   'I sinned, and perverted what   I have not done right, but God
     was right,   spared me.
  and it was not requited to me.

The restored person sings for joy as he tell others of his recovery. **And he sings before men and says**: **sings** translates a verb regarded as having an unusual form. It may also be rendered "tell, declare, make known," so "He begins to sing and tell everyone." **And says** serves in Hebrew as a kind of verbal opening quotation mark, and so many translations will leave it implicit.

I sinned and perverted what was right, together with the following line and verse 28, are the words of his song or hymn. **Perverted** translates a verb in the causative form meaning "to cause to deviate" and is well translated by TEV: "I did not do what was right." NJB says "I . . . left the path of right," which is clearer if rendered as "and wandered away from the right path."

And it was not requited to me: **requited** translates a verb not found elsewhere with that meaning. It does carry the meaning "to be equal," but "it was not equal to me" does not make clear sense. However, the expression may be taken in the sense that "the sin did not receive a penalty corresponding to the wrong," and this appears to be the meaning which RSV intends. TEV focuses on the result, "but God spared me," which is an active construction with God as the subject. FRCL is better: "But God spared me the pain I deserved." This line may be rendered negatively; for example, "but God did not punish me as I deserved" or "but God did not make me suffer as I should have."

33.28   RSV   TEV

He has redeemed my soul from   He kept me from going to the
    going down into the Pit,   world of the dead,
    and my life shall see the light.'   and I am still alive."

He has redeemed my soul from going down into the Pit: redeemed translates the same verb rendered "deliver" (RSV), "release" (TEV), in verse 24. NEB translates "saves," FRCL "He enables me to escape . . . ." **My soul** has an alternative reading for the Hebrew text, "his soul." RSV, TEV, and most others prefer **my soul**, but the meaning is as in TEV, "me." **Going down** translates the verb which can also mean "pass through" or "cross," and so the reference can again be to crossing the river of death, as in verse 18. **Pit** is as in verse 18. This line may also be expressed "He has not let me die" or "He has kept me safe from death."

And my life shall see the light uses an idiom that expresses satisfaction with something, "shall look upon." It has the meaning of "gloat over" when the object is one's enemies (Psa 22.17). In English "to see the light" is an idiom meaning "to see finally what one was doing wrongly." Therefore NEB, Pope, RSV, and others give a literal rendering which is wrong for English. It is better to avoid that idiom and say, as in TEV, "I am still alive." Or, to capture better the sense of the Hebrew idiom, "I shall continue to enjoy life (or, the light)."

33.29-30   RSV   TEV

29 "Behold, God does all these   29   God does all this again and
      things,   again;
    twice, three times, with a man,   30   he saves a person's life,
30 to bring back his soul from the   and gives him the joy of living.
      Pit,
    that he may see the light of
      life.ᵛ

ᵛ Syr: Heb *to be lighted with the light of life*

Behold, God does all these things, twice, three times means "repeatedly, over and over, again and again." For discussion see 5.19; 33.14.

To bring back his soul from the Pit: this is the fifth time Elihu has said this, with small variations.

That he may see the light of life is literally "that he may be enlightened with the light of life." RSV makes a change following Syriac. But it is not necessary to change the Hebrew; TEV "and gives him the joy of living" expresses the meaning suitably. This line may also be expressed "and make him happy to be alive."

8B-10. Elihu asks Job to be silent and learn (33.31-33)

RSV

31   Give heed, O Job, listen to me;
        be silent, and I will speak.
32   If you have anything to say, answer me;
        speak, for I desire to justify you.
33   If not, listen to me;
        be silent, and I will teach you wisdom."

TEV

31   Now, Job, listen to what I am saying;
        be quiet and let me speak.
32   But if you have something to say, let me
        hear it;
     I would gladly admit you are in the
        right.
33   But if not, be quiet and listen to me,
        and I will teach you how to be wise.

Subdivision Heading

The Handbook heading may be restated as, for example, "Be quiet, Job, and learn," "I will teach you to be wise," or "Listen to me, or speak if you can." Rowley has "Elihu's final appeal to Job."

33.31   RSV   TEV

Give heed, O Job, listen to me;   Now, Job, listen to what I am
   be silent, and I will speak.   saying;
                                                   be quiet and let me speak.

Give heed, O Job, listen to me: Elihu likes to demand Job's attention, which is no doubt lagging considerably by now!

Be silent, and I will speak shows how self-important Elihu considers himself, since Job has not uttered a sound since Elihu began in chapter 32.

33.32   RSV   TEV

If you have anything to say, an-   But if you have something to say,
   swer me;   let me hear it;
speak, for I desire to justify   I would gladly admit you are in
   you.   the right.

Elihu has just told Job to be silent. Now he tells him **If you have anything to say, answer me**. TEV's command is more natural, "let me hear it," or another expression can be "speak up."

For I desire to justify you may be rendered "I am anxious to find you innocent," "I want to prove you are in the right," ". . . that you are not in the wrong," or ". . . that you are not guilty."

33.33 RSV TEV

If not, listen to me; be silent, and I will teach you wisdom."	But if not, be quiet and listen to me, and I will teach you how to be wise.

If not, listen to me; be silent, and I will teach you wisdom: in 32.10,17 Elihu said he would tell his "opinion" or "knowledge," and now he calls it **wisdom**. **Wisdom** is far more than knowledge or information. **Wisdom** is an attitude and a discipline that comes from God. For discussions see 4.21; 11.6. Here Elihu refers more exactly to the wisdom he will teach Job in 34.16-30. In those verses he will speak about the way in which God rules the world and deals with wickedness. Also in 36.22–37.13 he will remind Job of God's mysterious ways and his powers in creating and sustaining nature. Verse 33 may be rendered, for example, "If you have nothing to say, be quiet and listen to me, and I will teach you to be wise." This remark is particularly ironic, since it has been made clear that fear of the Lord is wisdom (28.28).

8C. ELIHU'S SECOND SPEECH (34.1-37)

In chapter 34 Elihu defends God against charges brought by Job. In verses 2-9 he calls for a hearing of Job's case and lays out the charges against Job. In verses 10-15 he gives evidence of the character of God. Then in verses 16-30 he defends the manner in which God rules the world. Finally in verses 31-37 Elihu appeals to Job to confess his sins and cease his arguments.

Elihu arranges for Job to be tried in a human court because it is not proper for God to be hailed into court (verse 23). Job, who argues entirely from his own personal experience, concludes that God is unjust. By contrast Elihu argues the opposite, not from personal suffering but from his abstract theology. Consequently Elihu can no doubt convince the friends, who must still be listening, that Job's arguments are ignorant and uninformed.

Division Heading

The Handbook heading for this chapter is **Elihu's Second Speech**, which translators may wish to modify by saying, for example, "Elihu speaks again" or "Elihu continues to speak." Habel has "Elihu's defence of El's justice."

8C-1. Elihu criticizes the friends (34.1-4)

RSV TEV

1	Then Elihu said:	1-2	You men are so wise, so clever; listen now to what I am saying.
2	"Hear my words, you wise men, and give ear to me, you who know;	3	You know good food when you taste it, but not wise words when you hear them.
3	for the ear tests words as the palate tastes food.		

4	Let us choose what is right;
	    let us determine among ourselves what
	        is good.

4	It is up to us to decide the case.

Subdivision Heading

The Handbook heading may be adjusted to say, for example, "Elihu says the friends do not know wise words when they hear them," "Elihu accuses the friends of being dumb," or "You men are so clever!"

34.1-2   RSV   TEV

1	Then Elihu said:

2	"Hear my words, you wise men,
	    and give ear to me, you who
	        know;

1-2 You men are so wise, so clever;
        listen now to what I am saying.

Then Elihu said is the usual prose indication of the continuation of Elihu's argument.

Hear my words, you wise men closely resembles Elihu's appeal to Job in 33.1. Here Elihu addresses the three friends. The form of this verse is balanced, with "Hear, wise men" in line a and "Knowers, listen" in line b. There is typical poetic heightening in the movement between the lines, which has the common word for "listen" in line a, while line b is the more literary "give ear to." **You wise men** is "you (plural) who are wise," and **you who know** is "you (plural) who know things." Such words in Elihu's mouth are sarcasm. In 15.2,18 Eliphaz clearly identified himself with the **wise men**, but in 32.9 Elihu said that it is not the aged that are wise. So if Elihu is addressing the three friends, he is speaking ironically, and this is the best way to understand this verse. Elihu considers himself to be the teacher. TEV brings out the irony: "You men are so wise, so clever."

And give ear to me, you who know repeats the thought of line a with the poetic movement suggested above. **You who know** is a pluralized noun form of the verb "to know," and so "knowers," "people who know things." Habel translates this as "judges," but the sense is more that of "learned men," "those who have great experience."

Translators should express the sarcasm or irony of Elihu. Irony is the use of words whose intended meaning is the opposite of the literal sense of the words. In other words Elihu does not consider the friends to be wise, but calls them wise to ridicule them. In some languages special elements in the sentence are used to show that the reader or listener is to understand the meaning to be the opposite of what appears. In other languages it may be necessary to say, for example, "you men who people say are wise" or "you men who call yourselves wise." **You who know** may sometimes be rendered, for example, "you men who think you know things."

34.3   RSV   TEV

for the ear tests words
    as the palate tastes food.

You know good food when you
    taste it,

> but not wise words when you
> hear them.

For the ear tests words as the palate tastes food is almost an exact quotation of the words of Job in 12.11. There these words were in the form of a question. Here they are a statement. In both passages the point is that the tongue distinguishes between good and bad tastes, and the ear does the same in distinguishing between what is wise and what is not wise. TEV has translated this verse more accurately than it translated 12.11. The continuity from verse 2 to verse 3 is clear, since verse 2 ends with "give ear to" and verse 3 begins with **for the ear**. For discussion of this verse and for a translation model, see comments on 12.11.

34.4	RSV	TEV
	Let us choose what is right; let us determine among our- selves what is good.	It is up to us to decide the case.

Let us choose what is right: by **choose** Elihu refers to a process in which a person chooses after examination, and the focus of the meaning is on the analysis or examination. So "let us examine, take a close look at, discern." Many modern translations do not relate verse 4 directly to Job's case but translate as NIV, "Let us discern for ourselves what is right." However, Elihu is not calling for a general moral decision but for an examination of Job's claims. Therefore GECL says "Let us investigate together the case," and TEV "It is up to us to decide the case." The line may be rendered, for example, "Let us examine the case you have with God" or "We should look carefully at the argument you have with God."

Let us determine among ourselves what is good is parallel with the first line, and TEV does not repeat it, but GECL translates "We must recognize what is right and good." NIV, like many others, has "Let us learn together what is good." Habel translates the line "Let us decide between us what is defensible." **Good** is not to be taken as an abstract notion but as an evaluation of Job's charges against God. The line may also be expressed "let us see for ourselves what seems best" or "we should make up our minds what would be best."

8C-2. Elihu criticizes Job's claim to be innocent (34.5-9)

	RSV		TEV
5	For Job has said, 'I am innocent, and God has taken away my right;	5	Job claims that he is innocent, that God refuses to give him justice.
6	in spite of my right I am counted a liar; my wound is incurable, though I am without transgression.'	6	He asks, "How could I lie and say I am wrong? I am fatally wounded, but I am sin- less."
7	What man is like Job, who drinks up scoffing like water,		
8	who goes in company with evildoers and walks with wicked men?	7	Have you ever seen anyone like this man Job?

9   For he has said, 'It profits a man nothing   He never shows respect for God.
        that he should take delight in God.'   8   He likes the company of evil men
                                                             and goes around with sinners.
                                                    9   He says that it never does any good
                                                             to try to follow God's will.

Subdivision Heading

The Handbook heading may be modified to say, for example, "Elihu criticizes Job," "Job thinks he has done no wrong," or "Job is fatally wounded and still thinks he is sinless." Habel has "Charges against Job," and Rowley "Elihu declares Job to be essentially irreligious."

34.5   RSV   TEV

For Job has said, 'I am innocent,   Job claims that he is innocent,
    and God has taken away my   that God refuses to give him
    right;   justice.

For Job has said, 'I am innocent . . .': **For** links verse 5 to verse 4 as the reason why they must look into Job's case: he claims to be innocent of wrongdoing. In RSV and others the quoted words of Job begin at verse 5 and end with verse 6b. TEV makes only verse 6 a quotation. Contrary to his custom, Elihu quotes Job precisely here. In 9.15,20 Job claims his innocence by saying "though I am innocent . . . ."

And God has taken away my right is exactly what Job said in 27.2. See there for discussion.

34.6   RSV   TEV

in spite of my right I am counted   He asks, "How could I lie and
    a liar;   say I am wrong?
my wound is incurable, though   I am fatally wounded, but I am
    I am without transgression.'   sinless."

In spite of my right I am counted a liar: a comparison of RSV and TEV will show how differently this verse can be translated. A literal translation of line a in the Hebrew can be "Upon (or, With regard to, In spite of) my right I lie." The problem in line a is **I am counted a liar**, which translates the Hebrew "I lie," occurring in the intensive form of the verb. The Septuagint has "he lies." Scholars suggest that the Hebrew "I lie" is a scribal change to avoid calling God a liar. Dhorme therefore changes it to "he speaks falsely," and this is followed by NEB, "he has falsified my case," to which HOTTP agrees.

It should be remembered that Elihu is here quoting Job, and that in the previous line God is the subject. It is logical and fits the context to assume that God is the subject of this line also. Accordingly the preferred rendering of this line is something like "He (God) does not speak the truth about my case," "What God says about my case is not correct," "God lies about my right to be heard." FRCL says in its text "He (God) does not judge me according to the truth," and in its footnote "He lies concerning my case."

However, many modern translations keep "I lie" in the sense of RSV **I am counted** (by God) **a liar**. Some translations take "I lie" in a hypothetical sense; for example, SPCL says "It would be a lie to admit that I am guilty." TEV keeps "I lie" and makes it into a rhetorical question. Translators are advised to translate as in the previous paragraph.

My wound is incurable, though I am without transgression: my wound translates "my arrow," which is generally understood to be the poetic use of the instrument for wounding in place of the result. In 6.4 Job says "The arrows of the Almighty are in me." His wound is **incurable** and so leads to death. Accordingly TEV translates "I am fatally wounded." **Without transgression** means "I am innocent." So the whole line says "In spite of being innocent, I am dying from my wound." In some languages the cause of the wound may have to be stated, expressing this line as, for example, "although I am innocent, I am dying from the wounds God has given me" or "I have done no wrong, yet God has wounded me and I am dying." This line ends the quotation, as understood in RSV and others, and should be marked as such.

34.7	RSV	TEV

	What man is like Job,
	    who drinks up scoffing like
	        water,
		Have you ever seen anyone like
		        this man Job?
		He never shows respect for
		        God.

In asking **What man is like Job**, Elihu uses Job's name for the second time. Elihu's question is equivalent to "Is there anyone like Job?" or "What kind of a man is Job?"

Who drinks up scoffing like water? quotes 15.16b almost to the word. There Eliphaz said it of mankind in general, but here Elihu applies it strictly to Job. There it was "iniquity," but here it is **scoffing**. Job's "mockery, ridicule, scorn" are directed at religious and moral truths, as these are held by Elihu and the friends. In English the figure **drinks up scoffing** suggests that such a person can absorb or withstand a great deal of ridicule without being affected. But the figure as used here refers to a person who ridicules someone a great deal. The object of Job's scoffing is God, or perhaps religion as viewed by the friends. TEV, which translates the drinking figure as "never shows respect," has God as the object. FRCL has attempted to retain the figure through the use of a simile: "He deals in ridicule as easily as he drinks a glass of water." In some languages we may say "he pours out scorn as easily as he pours water out of a cup" or "he spits out ridicule as easily as he drinks water."

34.8	RSV	TEV

	who goes in company with evildo-
	        ers
	    and walks with wicked men?
		He likes the company of evil men
		    and goes around with sinners.

Who goes in company with evildoers: goes is literally "takes the path." The sense is as in RSV or, better expressed, "He goes about in the company of evildoers." His going about with such people may be taken in the literal sense of accompanying them as they go about or, more abstractly, as forming friendships with them, or having a common purpose with them.

And walks with wicked men: walks is parallel with **goes** in line a and is the same as in Psalm 1.1, "walks not in the counsel of the wicked," where "walk" refers to conduct. Here it may be translated, for example, "and acts like wicked people act," "does the things wicked people do," or "lives like wicked people live."

34.9	RSV	TEV

	For he has said, 'It profits a man nothing
	    that he should take delight in God.'
		He says that it never does any good
		    to try to follow God's will.

For he has said, 'It profits a man nothing that he should take delight in God' does not quote Job but may represent Job's opinion. In 9.22-24 Job said that calamity falls on the good and the bad without distinction. In 21.7-13 he argued that the wicked prosper. The thought is expressed in Malachi 3.14 that it is useless to serve God. Elihu attributes the same attitude to Job. **Profits a man nothing** means "it does a person no good," "there is nothing to be gained," or "there is no advantage in." The word translated **delight** is found in the same construction in Psalm 50.18, meaning "to be a friend of." The emphasis is upon a person's inability to be on good terms with God or, as Mft translates, "He says it is no use for man to be the friend of God." FRCL has "to seek good relations with God." GECL translates verse 9 "He says to himself that a person gets nothing out of it when he goes to the trouble to be always in friendship with God." This line may also be expressed, for example, "He asks, 'What good does it do to be on good terms with God?'" or "What advantage is there in being God's friend?" TEV's rendering is perhaps more specific than can be justified, "follow God's will."

8C-3. Elihu testifies to God's justice (34.10-15)

	RSV		TEV
10	"Therefore, hear me, you men of under-standing, far be it from God that he should do wickedness, and from the Almighty that he should do wrong.	10	Listen to me, you men who understand! Will Almighty God do what is wrong?
11	For according to the work of a man he will requite him, and according to his ways he will make it befall him.	11	He rewards people for what they do and treats them as they deserve.
12	Of a truth, God will not do wickedly,	12	Almighty God does not do evil; he is never unjust to anyone.
		13	Did God get his power from someone else? Did someone put him in charge of the world?
		14	If God took back the breath of life,

<table>
<tr><td></td><td>and the Almighty will not pervert justice.</td><td>15</td><td>then everyone living would die and turn into dust again.</td></tr>
</table>

13	Who gave him charge over the earth and who laid on him the whole world?
14	If he should take back his spirit to himself, and gather to himself his breath,
15	all flesh would perish together, and man would return to dust.

Subdivision Heading

The Handbook heading may be reworded to say, for instance, "God treats people as they deserve," "Can God do wrong?" or "God does not do evil." Rowley has "Elihu replies to Job's charge that God is unjust."

34.10   RSV   TEV

"Therefore, hear me, you men of
  understanding,
  far be it from God that he
    should do wickedness,
  and from the Almighty that he
    should do wrong.

Listen to me, you men who understand!
Will Almighty God do what is
  wrong?

Therefore, hear me, you men of understanding: **Therefore** translates a Hebrew connective which normally introduces a logical result, but in this context it introduces Elihu's opinion that stands in contrast with verse 9. NJB translates with "then." "But" in NEB is more appropriate in English to show the contrast. This verse has three lines. **Men of understanding** is literally "men of heart" and will be repeated in verse 34. The "heart" is the seat of intelligence in Hebrew thought. In verse 1 Elihu appealed to the "wise" and the "learned," and now he invites the "intelligent men," or as TEV says, "men who understand." Elihu is no doubt continuing to speak with sarcasm in addressing the friends, and translators should reflect this, as in verse 1.

Far be it from God that he should do wickedness is an emphatic negative statement in Hebrew, which TEV has expressed as a question expecting a negative answer, incorporating line c into line b. Lines b and c are parallel in meaning, with the usual word pair *'El* and *Shaddai* used in that order. **Far be it from** is found also in Genesis 18.25. We may translate this phrase "God would never consider doing evil" or "Evil is the last thing God would think of doing."

And from the Almighty that he should do wrong says almost the same thing as the previous line, but with *Shaddai* as the subject. The word pair translated **wickedness** in line b and **wrong** in line c is the same pair found in 27.7, rendered by RSV as "wicked" and "unrighteous," and translated by these same words in TEV. There is no essential difference intended in their meanings, and they may be translated by similar words for evil or wickedness. In such close parallelism translators may wish to reduce the two lines to one.

34.11   RSV   TEV

> For according to the work of a   He rewards people for what they
>   man he will requite him,   do
>   and according to his ways he   and treats them as they de-
>   will make it befall him.   serve.

For according to the work of a man he will requite him: this verse sets out Elihu's principle of justice, according to which God acts justly and pays a person according to what he has done. This thought is expressed similarly in Romans 2.6 and Matthew 16.27. The same thesis is argued by Bildad in chapter 8. Job asks in 21.31 "who requites him (the wicked) for what he has done?" **The work of a man** refers to "all that a person does." **He** refers to God, as in the preceding two lines. **Requite** means "to pay, compensate, give back," or as TEV says, "He rewards people for what they do." In some languages "rewards" refers only to positive acts or good gifts. Here the sense of **requite** refers to receiving what a person deserves. Accordingly we may also translate "God will pay him for the things he does" or "God will give him what he deserves, according to the good or bad things he has done."

And according to his ways he will make it befall him is an obscure translation of the Hebrew, which is literally "and according to the path of a man he makes him find it." The word translated **ways** is to be taken as "conduct, manner of living, things one does." The sense of conduct here is the same as used in 17.9; 21.31. The main verb in verse 11b can mean "to meet with," and RSV **befall** represents this meaning. Another sense is "he makes him find it"; that is, "God causes the person to find (thus, repays him) according to his conduct." The two parallel lines are well rendered by NEB: "For he pays a man according to his work, and sees that he gets what his conduct deserves." NEB offers a satisfactory translation model for verse 11. In saying this Elihu represents the same traditional wisdom as the three friends.

34.12   RSV   TEV

> Of a truth, God will not do wick-   Almighty God does not do evil;
>   edly,   he is never unjust to anyone.
>   and the Almighty will not per-
>   vert justice.

Of a truth, God will not do wickedly repeats the same thought Elihu voiced in verse 10. **Of a truth** translates the same Hebrew expression used at the opening of 19.4, rendered "even if it be true" by RSV. Here the expression may have the sense as in NEB, "the truth is," or else "it certainly is true." *'El* occurs in line <u>a</u> and *Shaddai* in line <u>b</u>, as in lines <u>b</u> and <u>c</u> of verse 10.

And the Almighty will not pervert justice is almost a quotation from 8.3a. See there for discussion. Verse 12 may be rendered, for example, "Certainly God will not do wrong, and God Almighty will not be unjust" or "It is true that God never does evil, and he will always judge things in the right way."

34.13   RSV   TEV

Who gave him charge over the earth and who laid on him[w] the whole world?	Did God get his power from someone else? Did someone put him in charge of the world?

[w] Heb lacks *on him*

Who gave him charge over the earth . . . ? is a rhetorical question which assumes the answer "Nobody," and in some languages the answer must be stated. God is supreme and answerable to no one, as Job says in 9.12. Job went on to conclude, therefore, that God is responsible for all injustices (9.24). **Gave him charge over the earth** means "put him in command of the earth," or "entrusted the earth to him." TEV attempts to make the rhetorical aspect of the question stronger in line a, focusing on who could possibly give God authority, by translating "Did God get his power from someone else?" Here the answer is emphatically "No!" His authority or power derives from himself. The question may be expressed as a strong negative statement: "God never got his power to rule the earth from anyone," or "No one had power to give God so he could govern the earth," or "God did not ask anyone for power to rule the earth."

And who laid on him the whole world? translates the Hebrew more or less literally, and supplies **on him,** as the RSV footnote indicates. The addition of **on him** is not a textual change but merely makes **him** in the first line do service in the second line also. **Laid on him** is parallel to **gave him charge** in line a. The question in line b assumes the answer "No one," the same as in line a; that is, "No one ever made him responsible" or "No one put him in control." The terms **earth** and **whole world** have the same meaning, referring to the world and all that is in it. In Hebrew this word pair most often occurs as it does here, but the second word has a more particular meaning and thus represents a poetic focusing of the concept from line a.

34.14-15   RSV   TEV

14	If he should take back his spirit[x] to himself, and gather to himself his breath,	14	If God took back the breath of life,
15	all flesh would perish together, and man would return to dust.	15	then everyone living would die and turn into dust again.

[x] Heb *his heart his spirit*

These two verses form two parts of a conditional sentence. Verse 14 has been rendered variously by different translators. **If he should take back his spirit to himself** is the first half of the condition and is literally "If he set his heart upon him." There are two problems here. First, the verb phrase translated "set his heart" can mean "pay attention, notice." Second, **upon him** may be taken to refer to God or to man. HOTTP offers two translations: "If he (God) should turn his attention only to himself" or ". . . to man." RSV follows the change made in the Septuagint and supported by Dhorme, that translates the verb as **takes back**. RSV omits "heart" as a scribal addition inserted in the text at an earlier stage when the verb in this line was misunderstood. However, the line can be adequately translated without change, as by Pope, "if he took it in his mind," or by Habel, "if he places in his heart . . . ," and by NIV, "if it were his intention . . . ."

And gather to himself his breath follows the tradition of dividing the text into lines in such a way that **spirit** is the object of the verb in line a̲. However, following the suggestion of Pope and others, "heart" is part of the idiom of "planning, deciding, taking in mind," and both **spirit** and **breath** may be taken as the objects of the verb **gather** (matching **take back**) in line b̲. Since the whole of verse 14 is the conditional clause, TEV has omitted the verb of line a̲, saying only "If God took back the breath of life." It would be more complete to say "If God should decide to take back the spirit and breath of life." This thought corresponds closely to that of Psalm 104.29; Ecclesiastes 12.7. "Breath of life" may also be rendered "his breath that gives people life" or "his breath that causes people to live." For a discussion of the distinction between *nefesh* **spirit** and *ruach* **breath**, see 12.10.

The consequence of the conditions in verse 14 is **all flesh would perish together**. **Flesh** refers to "all living things," as was used in 12.10; 28.21. **Perish together** means "die at the same time, at once, immediately."

The second condition is **and man would return to dust**. **Man** does not single out "human beings" as distinct from **all flesh** in line a̲, but allows poetic focusing on the more specific form of flesh. **Return to dust** is as TEV, "turn into dust again," as in Genesis 3.19. **Dust** has the sense of earth, soil, as in 10.9. Verse 15 may also be rendered, for example, "then every living thing would die at once, and mankind would return to dust" or "as a result all living creatures would die together, and mankind would become earth again."

8C-4. Elihu defends God's rule (34.16-30)

RSV	TEV
16 "If you have understanding, hear this; listen to what I say.	16 Now listen to me, if you are wise.
17 Shall one who hates justice govern? Will you condemn him who is righteous and mighty,	17 Are you condemning the righteous God? Do you think that *he* hates justice?
18 who says to a king, 'Worthless one,' and to nobles, 'Wicked man';	18 God condemns kings and rulers when they are worthless or wicked.
19 who shows no partiality to princes, nor regards the rich more than the poor, for they are all the work of his hands?	19 He does not take the side of rulers nor favor the rich over the poor, for he created everyone.
20 In a moment they die; at midnight the people are shaken and pass away, and the mighty are taken away by no human hand.	20 A man may suddenly die at night. God strikes men down and they perish; he kills the mighty with no effort at all.
	21 He watches every step men take.
	22 There is no darkness dark enough to hide a sinner from God.
	23 God does not need to set a time for men to go and be judged by him.
	24 He does not need an investigation

21 "For his eyes are upon the ways of a
    man,
    and he sees all his steps.
22 There is no gloom or deep darkness
    where evildoers may hide themselves.
23 For he has not appointed a time for any
    man
    to go before God in judgment.
24 He shatters the mighty without investiga-
    tion,
    and sets others in their place.
25 Thus, knowing their works,
    he overturns them in the night, and
    they are crushed.
26 He strikes them for their wickedness
    in the sight of men,
27 because they turned aside from following
    him,
    and had no regard for any of his ways,
28 so that they caused the cry of the poor to
    come to him,
    and he heard the cry of the afflicted—
29 When he is quiet, who can condemn?
    When he hides his face, who can be-
    hold him,
    whether it be a nation or a man?—
30 that a godless man should not reign,
    that he should not ensnare the people.

    to remove leaders and replace them
    with others.
25 Because he knows what they do;
    he overthrows them and crushes them
    by night.
26 He punishes sinners where all can see it,
27 because they have stopped following
    him
    and ignored all his commands.
28 They forced the poor to cry out to God,
    and he heard their calls for help.

29 If God decided to do nothing at all,
    no one could criticize him.
    If he hid his face, men would be helpless.
30 There would be nothing that nations
    could do
    to keep godless oppressors from ruling
    them.

Subdivision Heading

The Handbook heading may be reworded to say, for example, "Elihu says that God's rule is just," "Elihu argues that God knows how to rule the world," or "God is one who is just." Habel has "Defence of El's governance," and Rowley "Elihu defends the impartiality and omniscience of God."

34.16   RSV   TEV

"If you have understanding, hear   Now listen to me, if you are wise.
    this;
listen to what I say.

If you have understanding, hear this is literally "If understanding hear this." **If you have** is clearly implied. Elihu uses the singular in **hear this**, so he is no doubt speaking directly to Job. This line may need to be expressed differently; for example, "If you (singular) understand things" or "If you (singular) understand what I am saying to you."

Hear this in line a and **listen to what I say** in line b are the same in meaning. The two Hebrew verbs are the same as those used in verse 2. See there for comments.

34.17   RSV   TEV

> Shall one who hates justice gov-   Are you condemning the right-
>   ern?   eous God?
> Will you condemn him who is   Do you think that *he* hates
>   righteous and mighty,   justice?

Shall one who hates justice govern? begins with an interrogative that has
the sense of "Is it really so?" or "Is it really the case?" Dhorme translates "Do you
really think . . . ?" The expression introduces a proposition or thought that is not
acceptable to the speaker, and so assumes a negative answer. The verb **hate** is
associated with other abstract nouns, as in "hate knowledge" (Prov 1.22) and "hate
the good" (Micah 3.2). **Justice** is used in the same sense as in verse 5b (TEV).
Govern is literally "bind up" and is used in Hosea 6.1; Isaiah 1.6, where it refers to
bandaging wounds. However, it appears that the word has the sense of "rule or
control" only here. Dhorme argues in favor of **govern**, based on the use of the same
Hebrew word in Isaiah 3.7 ("a healer"), where he says the meaning is "bind on a
yoke," a figure for subduing and controlling. God, who governs all things, can not be
thought of as one who **hates justice**. TEV transposes the two lines of this verse.
TEV's rendering is questionable and should not be followed. It also destroys the
balance between the parallel lines. Verse 17 may also be rendered "Could God really
govern the world if he hates doing things fairly? Of course not!" Another translation
model is SPCL: "If God hated justice, he could not govern." This may also be
expressed as "If God really did not like judging matters fairly, how could he govern
the world?"

Will you condemn him who is righteous and mighty? is the second half of
Elihu's question to Job. In 40.8b God will put a similar question to Job. **Him who is
righteous and mighty** is literally "a righteous mighty one." **Righteous** means "fair,
just." **Mighty**, which TEV renders as "God," is used as a Hebrew adjective applied
to God only in 36.5. It never stands alone in the Old Testament as a name for God,
although the reference here is clearly to God and not to any human being. NEB says
"a sovereign whose rule is so fair," and NIV "the just and mighty One." The line may
also be expressed, for example, "Would you condemn God, who is great and does
things justly?" "Do you dare speak badly of the great God who rules the world
fairly?" or "Surely you wouldn't condemn God, who is great . . . ."

34.18-19   RSV   TEV

18 who says to a king, 'Worthless   18 God condemns kings and rulers
        one,'   when they are worthless or
    and to nobles, 'Wicked man';   wicked.
19 who shows no partiality to princ-   19 He does not take the side of
        es,   rulers
    nor regards the rich more   nor favor the rich over the
        than the poor,   poor,
    for they are all the work of his   for he created everyone.
        hands?

These two verses describe God in his dealings with human rulers and the poor.

Who says to a king, 'Worthless one': **who says** is literally "one says," and most adjust the vowels, as in the ancient versions, to make God the subject of **says**. Even HOTTP prefers the change as followed by RSV, which has no footnote. RSV makes verses 18 and 19 questions which begin with the relative **who** in the first line of each verse. The result is an awkward construction in English. Many translators prefer to translate these two verses as statements, and this is recommended. **Worthless one** translates a term of abuse found, for example, in 1 Samuel 25.25; 1 Kings 21.10. For a subject to address a king in this way was punishable by death (see 2 Sam 16.7,9; 1 Kgs 2.8). The Hebrew term is a compound word which means "having no value" or "good-for-nothing."

And to nobles, 'Wicked man': the thought in this line moves from the greater authority of kings to the lesser authority of **nobles**. These persons were referred to in 21.28 as "princes." The equivalent in many languages is "chief" and "elders," or "headman" and "old men." **Wicked man** or "evil person" is singular in Hebrew because it matches **worthless one** in the preceding line. In translation it will most often have to agree with **nobles**, which is plural. Many translations treat these abuse words as quotations, as in RSV. TEV treats them as part of a subordinate clause, "when they are worthless and wicked," and thereby loses much of the emotive impact in English.

Verse 19 is a second relative clause describing God's impartiality. **Who shows no partiality to princes** translates "does not lift up the face of princes." See 13.18 for discussion of this expression. The word translated **princes** is used in 3.15 and 29.9. These are high-ranking officials, not necessarily sons of a king. **Show partiality** means "to take the side of," "be unfairly in favor of," or "to like one more than the other."

Nor regards the rich more than the poor: the form of the parallelism is the reverse of the typical kind of poetic heightening, in that the metaphor occurs in line a and the common term in line b. **Regard the rich**, as in line a, means "favor the rich," "give the rich better treatment." The word translated **rich** is rare, but it occurs in parallel with "nobles" in Isaiah 32.5, and here with **princes**, and in contrast with **the poor**.

For they are all the work of his hands is the reason why God treats them all alike. In RSV this line is taken as part of the question which began in verse 17. TEV avoids the awkwardness of such a long question by making statements in verses 18 and 19. Verse 19 may also be rendered idiomatically in some languages; for example, "God does not share the seat of chiefs, and he does not treat the rich better than the poor, because he is the one who made them all" or "God does not sit down among the leaders, and he treats the rich and the poor alike, because he is their creator."

34.20 RSV	TEV

In a moment they die;
    at midnight the people are
    shaken and pass away,
    and the mighty are taken away
    by no human hand.
	A man may suddenly die at night.
	God strikes men down and
	    they perish;
	he kills the mighty with no
	    effort at all.

This verse has been modified in many ways to give a clearer sense. Its meaning appears to be that God's impartiality is shown in the way he destroys everyone alike.

In a moment they die: they seems to refer to the rich and the poor in the previous verse. The verb translated **die** is plural and so is best expressed with the pronoun **they**, as in RSV; TEV has adjusted it to the singular, "A man may . . . die," which in English refers to a general truth, not a specific instance, and therefore may be understood of either the rich or the poor. However, the form of RSV may be clearer for most languages. Many scholars take **at midnight**, the first words of line b in RSV, to be included in line a, as in TEV, "at night." This gives a better balance of lines in the Hebrew.

At midnight the people are shaken and pass away: RSV keeps **at midnight** with the second longer line. Dhorme evens up the line lengths by shifting **and pass away** to line a. **People** as the subject of **are shaken** is uncertain, since the Hebrew verb always refers to violent physical shaking of the earth, as in 2 Samuel 22.8, and it is not used figuratively. Some suggest that two letters of the verb have fallen out, and that its last two letters should have been joined to the following subject, which then reads "the rich," as in verse 19b; thus the verb and its subject would be "perish the rich." NJB follows this with "they perish—these great ones—and disappear." **Are shaken** is often changed to get "expire," or divided differently so as to mean "he strikes the rich." TEV seems to accept this change in word division, but keeps **the people** in the form of "men": "God strikes men down . . . ." **And pass away** has the sense of "disappear, perish, die."

And the mighty are taken away by no human hand: the mighty, as in 24.22, is singular and refers to a ruler, a powerful person. **Taken away** is plural, like the verbs in the preceding lines, and means "remove, depose, set aside, do away with." The thought is related to deposing a tyrant, or perhaps killing him, as in TEV. **By no human hand** is literally "not with a hand," an idiom meaning "effortlessly, easily, with the flick of a finger." Verse 20 may also be rendered, for example, "Suddenly death comes in the middle of the night, and God strikes people down and destroys them. He gets rid of the ruler with hardly any effort."

34.21	RSV	TEV
	"For his eyes are upon the ways of a man, and he sees all his steps.	He watches every step men take.

For his eyes are upon the ways of a man is a repetition of 24.23b. See there for comments.

And he sees all his steps would cause Job no surprise, since he himself asked in 31.4 "Does he not see my ways and number all my steps?" Elihu applies his words to people in general, but the inference concerns Job's case. This line may also be rendered "and God sees him everywhere he goes."

34.22   RSV   TEV

> There is no gloom or deep dark-   There is no darkness dark
> ness   enough
> where evildoers may hide   to hide a sinner from God.
> themselves.

There is no gloom or deep darkness where evildoers may hide themselves means that God's eyes can penetrate the deepest darkness so that no one is hidden from him. The thought is inspired by Psalm 139.11-12 and Jeremiah 23.24. For a discussion of **gloom and deep darkness**, see 3.5. **Evildoers** translates the same Hebrew term as "workers of iniquity" in 31.3. Verse 22 may also be expressed "For God there is no darkness dark enough to keep him from seeing people who do evil" or "The blackest darkness is not sufficient for the evildoer to hide from God."

34.23   RSV   TEV

> For he has not appointed a time[y]   God does not need to set a time[l]
> for any man   for men to go and be judged by
> to go before God in judgment.   him.

[y] Cn: Heb *yet*   [l] *Probable text* a time; *Hebrew* yet.

For he has not appointed a time for any man: in 9.32 and 14.13 Job complained of the lack of opportunity to face God in court, and in 24.1 he asked "Why doesn't God set a time for judging?" Elihu now answers Job's question. As the RSV note shows, the Hebrew text has "yet" where RSV translates **time**. Many scholars interpret the Hebrew word rendered "yet" as the result of its first letter having fallen out, due to the preceding word ending in the same letter, and the scribe copying only one letter where there should have been two. By restoring the dropped letter the word means "a set time, an appointment." RSV and TEV, which accept this change, have a note. Many other translations follow the change without a note. HOTTP understands the Hebrew word for "yet" to mean "in addition" and translates "for God need not make a further or special judgment." This seems to be followed by NIV, "God has no need to examine men further." FRCL translates "God has no need to summon a man," and in the footnote, "God has no need to examine a man in a special way . . . ." FRCL provides two satisfactory translation models.

In line b **to go before God in judgment** means "to appear before God to be judged" or "to go before God's court and be judged by him."

34.24   RSV   TEV

He shatters the mighty without   He does not need an investiga-
   investigation,   tion
  and sets others in their place.   to remove leaders and replace
                                           them with others.

He shatters the mighty without investigation: shatters translates a verb
meaning "to break to pieces." It is used in Isaiah 24.19 ("utterly broken") and Psalm
2.9 ("break"). When applied to persons it refers to causing their downfall, so that
TEV has "remove" in its second line. **The mighty** refers to the powerful rulers, as
used in verses 17 and 20. **Without investigation** translates the same Hebrew term
used in 5.9; 9.10 with the sense of "unsearchable," "not to be found out." Here the
sense is that God does not need to investigate because he already knows, or as TEV
says, "He does not need an investigation."

    And sets others in their place explains what God does after he has broken
the mighty in line a. **Sets others** means he "installs, appoints, gives their positions"
to other people.

34.25   RSV   TEV

Thus, knowing their works,   Because he knows what they do;
  he overturns them in the   he overthrows them and crush-
   night, and they are crushed.   es them by night.

    Thus, knowing their works, he overturns them in the night describes what
God does because he knows how they act. The word translated **Thus** commonly
means "therefore," but as the verse stands, that meaning is not appropriate. Dhorme
associates it with a similar connective in Arabic and translates "But." **Thus** is
achieved by dropping the prefix to the word. The best sense is probably "indeed,"
"certainly," "truly," giving a translation such as "There is no doubt; he knows their
deeds," "He certainly knows the things they do." **Overturns** means to take their
power and authority from them. "He overthrows them, puts them out of office,
removes them by force." **In the night** refers to the time of their overthrow and
emphasizes that it happens in the darkness of night, when they least expect it.
Crushed is the final consequence of being overthrown. **Crushed** is parallel with
shatters in verse 24a and shows the parallelism reaching from verse 24a through to
verse 25b.

34.26-27   RSV   TEV

26 He strikes them for their wicked-   26 He punishes sinners where all
    ness   can see it,
    in the sight of men,   27 because they have stopped
27 because they turned aside from   following him
    following him,   and ignored all his commands.

and had no regard for any of
his ways,

In RSV verse 26 is a statement whose reason is given in verse 27. **He strikes them for their wickedness** is literally "Under evil deeds he strikes them." There are numerous changes and rearrangements proposed for verse 26. However, it seems best to follow the suggestion of Pope, that the Hebrew word for "under" has both the sense of "Among" and " In the place of," as in 40.12 ("where they stand"). The word translated **their wickedness** is the plural of "evil," meaning "evildoers, criminals." The meaning of this line will then be "He strikes them down in the place for criminals," that is, "in the place where criminals are dealt with." The sense of this becomes clear only with line b.

In the sight of men is literally "in the place of onlookers," which means in the place where spectators gather, or the public square. TEV is similar, if less specific, with "He punishes sinners where all can see it." FRCL combines the lines: "He strikes them in public, like criminals." Pope, TEV, and FRCL are to be preferred to RSV.

Because they turned aside from following him explains the reason for verse 26: "because they no longer followed him," "because they were disloyal, unfaithful to him."

And had no regard for any of his ways: had no regard for translates a verb which can be rendered "paid no attention to, ignored." **His ways** refers to "his laws or teachings," or as TEV says, "commands." Verse 27 may also be rendered, for example, "because they became unfaithful to him and paid no attention to what he told them to do" or "because they no longer believed in him and would not obey his laws."

34.28   RSV   TEV

so that they caused the cry of the   They forced the poor to cry out
   poor to come to him,   to God,
and he heard the cry of the   and he heard their calls for
   afflicted—   help.

According to Pope verses 28-33 are full of difficulty: "The Septuagint originally omitted them entirely. Modern critics have suggested changes freely, with imagination and originality."

So that they caused the cry of the poor to come to him shows one of the ways in which sinners were disloyal to God. In their mistreatment of the poor, they cause the poor to cry out. "They treat the poor badly and so force them to cry out to God for help."

And he heard the cry of the afflicted: afflicted is the same as **the poor** in line a. God is not mentioned in either line in the Hebrew but is clearly implied.

29   When he is quiet, who can con-
     demn?
  When he hides his face, who
     can behold him,
  whether it be a nation or a
     man?—
30   that a godless man should not
     reign,
  that he should not ensnare the
     people.
	29 If God decided to do nothing at
	     all,
	  no one could criticize him.
	  If he hid his face, men would be
	     helpless.
	30 There would be nothing that
	     nations could do
	  to keep godless oppressors
	     from ruling them.

RSV places verse 29 between dashes to show that verse 30 connects in sense with verse 28 and that 29 is parenthetical. NEB encloses verses 29 and 30 in brackets to show these verses are secondary additions. NJB connects them closely in thought to 27 and 28. TEV and others link these two verses closely together grammatically—a solution that seems best to follow.

The first two lines of verse 29 present few difficulties. They are both parallel rhetorical questions expecting the answer "Nobody." **When he is quiet, who can condemn? He** refers to God. **Is quiet** translates a verb meaning "to be calm, taking no action," as used in 3.26. In Isaiah 57.20 and Jeremiah 49.23 it means "to rest" and has the sense of "ceasing to be active" or "doing nothing at all" (TEV). Dhorme and others transpose two letters in the verb translated **condemn** to get the meaning "stir up," and this is followed by NJB. This gives the sense "If God decides to rest, who can stir him up?" It seems best, however, to follow TEV and RSV. **Condemn** here may also be rendered "to accuse of doing wrong," and so TEV has "criticize," which is perhaps better than **condemn**, particularly when God is the object of man's accusations. TEV expresses the rhetorical question as a negative assertion.

When he hides his face, who can behold him is similar to Job's question in 13.24, "Why dost thou hide thy face?" Here the poetic heightening takes place with the figurative expression placed in the second line. **Behold** means "see, perceive," but the Hebrew has also been changed in many different ways by interpreters. TEV "men would be helpless" is an attempt to give a more specific meaning to the Hebrew, but there is no textual justification for it. It is best to accept the verb as meaning "see," as Job says in 23.9, "On the left hand I seek him, but I cannot behold him." We may translate, for example, "If he hid his face, none would be able to see him."

Whether it be a nation or a man? is literally "upon a nation or upon a man together." RSV keeps this oddly worded line within the section marked by dashes. Many translations, however, link it to verse 30. The word in Hebrew translated "together" has been changed in countless ways to obtain a more satisfactory rendering. None of these have met with general acceptance. TEV has translated lines b and c of the verse in its third line. That is, it has kept **When he hides his face** from line b and then joined the second half of line b with line c. Therefore **who can behold him** is translated "helpless," and **a man** is rendered as "men," and **nations** is shifted to verse 30a. This may require more adjustments than most translators will wish to follow. Dhorme links line c to verse 30 but adjusts the text to get "now he watches nations and persons." Since most modern translations connect line c to verse 30, it is necessary to look first at verse 30 before completing recommendations regarding verse 29c.

That a godless man should not reign translates the Hebrew closely. The second line, **that he should not ensnare the people,** is literally "from the snare of the people." HOTTP sets out the problems of verse 29c and verse 30 in four stages: (1) verse 29c should be linked to verse 30; (2) the word translated **man** in verse 29c probably means "humanity" as a collective noun; (3) "from the snares of the people" designates those who ensnare the people and so should be as in RSV; (4) and so the translation of verses 29c and 30 can be "And over a nation and over humanity alike, he makes king a godless man from among the seducers (those who ensnare) of the people." As a translation model this can be improved by saying, for example, "God chooses a man from among the deceivers of the people and makes him rule over their nations" or "God chooses godless men who lead the people astray, and he makes them rulers over nations."

8C-5. Elihu calls on Job to repent (34.31-37)

RSV	TEV
31 "For has any one said to God, 'I have borne chastisement; I will not offend any more;	31 Job, have you confessed your sins to God and promised not to sin again?
32 teach me what I do not see; if I have done iniquity, I will do it no more'?	32 Have you asked God to show you your faults, and have you agreed to stop doing evil?
33 Will he then make requital to suit you, because you reject it? For you must choose, and not I; therefore declare what you know.	33 Since you object to what God does, can you expect him to do what you want? The decision is yours, not mine; tell us now what you think.
34 Men of understanding will say to me, and the wise man who hears me will say:	34 Any sensible person will surely agree; any wise man who hears me will say
35 'Job speaks without knowledge, his words are without insight.'	35 that Job is speaking from ignorance and that nothing he says makes sense.
36 Would that Job were tried to the end, because he answers like wicked men.	36 Think through everything that Job says; you will see that he talks like an evil man.
37 For he adds rebellion to his sin; he claps his hands among us, and multiplies his words against God."	37 To his sins he adds rebellion; in front of us all he mocks God.

Subdivision Heading

Translators may wish to use the Handbook heading by adjusting it to say, for example, "Job, you must repent," "Job, stop doing evil," or "Job, you are the one who makes fun of God." Habel has "Appeal and verdict."

34.31-32   RSV   TEV

31   "For has any one said to God,   31   Job, have you confessed your
       'I have borne chastisement; I   sins to God
       will not offend any more;   and promised not to sin again?
32   teach me what I do not see;   32   Have you asked God to show you
       if I have done iniquity, I will   your faults,
       do it no more'?   and have you agreed to stop
                                                   doing evil?

Rowley says about verses 31-37 "These verses are among the most obscure and difficult in the book." Verses 31 and 32 appear to consist of a confession of sin followed by a promise not to repeat the sin.

For has anyone said to God has an indefinite subject. FRCL translates this line "Let us suppose someone said this to God." RSV and NEB assume Elihu is thinking in terms of Job specifically and so introduce direct speech. NJB understands the subject to be the godless ruler from the preceding verse. It is recommended that translators follow either RSV or TEV.

I have borne chastisement: chastisement does not occur in the Hebrew, but it is necessary for RSV to supply it in order to complete the Hebrew verb phrase "I have borne." Because there is no object for the verb in this line, many changes in the Hebrew text have been suggested. By a change of vowel markings, Dhorme and others get "I have been led astray." HOTTP suggests three ways in which the Hebrew may be understood: (1) "I raise my hand," as in swearing to the truth; (2) "I bear my sin"; (3) "I bear with what God sends me." The first two may be understood as admission of sin, and so the next line follows naturally, **I will not offend any more.** **Offend** translates a verb used in 21.17 meaning "to act wrongly," and so "to sin." The Hebrew does not have **any more**, but this is added on the basis that the consonants of this word, which appear again in the first word of the next verse, have fallen out. Verse 31 may also be expressed "Has anyone ever said to God, 'I am a sinner, but I will stop sinning?'" or more directly, "Job, have you ever admitted to God that you are a sinner and said you would confess your sins?"

Teach me what I do not see: teach has the sense here of "show, point out, make me aware of." **What I do not see** is literally "apart from I see." RSV's rendering is probably accurate. These words are still the words of the indefinite person Elihu is quoting, and so they are part of a confession and a request for help. **What I do not see** is taken to be the faults, sins, wrongs, of the confessing person. And so the line can be rendered "show me my sins that I have not recognized" or "show me how I have sinned without knowing it."

If I have done iniquity, I will do it no more: the confessor does not admit to having sinned but leaves this possibility open. He offers to sin no more. The consequence in this line is parallel in meaning to that in verse 31b. If Job has been addressed in verse 31, he should continue to be addressed in verse 32.

34.33 RSV TEV

Will he then make requital to
suit you,
because you reject it?
For you must choose, and not I;
therefore declare what you
know.[z]

Since you object to what God
does,
can you expect him to do what
you want?
The decision is yours, not mine;
tell us now what you think.

[z] The Hebrew of verses 29-33 is obscure

Will he then make requital to suit you . . . ? Elihu has completed his quotation of this imaginary question and now addresses Job directly, wanting to know what Job thinks of it. **Make requital** translates a verb meaning "to repay, get even, recompense." The repayment in this context would be punishment, and so Elihu asks "Will God punish him?" **To suit you** is literally "from with you" and probably means "according to you, in your opinion," and so Dhorme has "Is it your opinion that he will requite the wrong?"

Because you reject it: it is supplied in RSV, but in Hebrew there is no object. The sense may be "since you reject, oppose, dislike what God does." Dhorme thinks the missing object is "my doctrine or my teaching." These two lines may be translated, for example, "Since you don't accept the things God does, do you think God should punish such a person?"

For you must choose, and not I: in other words, "You are the one who has to decide, not me."

Therefore declare what you know: "Let's hear what you have to say." Since Job has expressed his disagreement with the way God handles justice (at least in Job's case), perhaps Job can tell Elihu how God should govern the world.

34.34-35 RSV TEV

34 Men of understanding will say to
me,
and the wise man who hears
me will say:
35 'Job speaks without knowledge,
his words are without insight.'

34 Any sensible person will surely
agree;
any wise man who hears me
will say
35 that Job is speaking from ignorance
and that nothing he says
makes sense.

Men of understanding will say to me: this verse in the Hebrew has two parallel lines with the verb in the first line serving for both lines. **Men of understanding** is the same as the expression used in verse 10. See there for comments. **The wise man** in line b matches "men of heart" or **men of understanding** in line a. Translators may prefer to bring the two lines of verse 34 together; for example, "People with good sense, who are intelligent and listen to me, say to me," or "Wise and intelligent people who hear me will say to me."

What the wise people in verse 34 will say is: **Job speaks without knowledge.**
In 33.3 Elihu boasts that he himself speaks words that are sincere and truthful.
Without knowledge means "with ignorance, without knowing what he is talking
about." In 15.2 Eliphaz accused Job of having only "windy knowledge." Job's words
are **without insight**, which TOB translates "without rhyme or reason." Job's speech
is senseless, or as TEV says, "makes no sense."

34.36   RSV   TEV

> Would that Job were tried to the   Think through everything that
>   end,   Job says;
>   because he answers like wicked   you will see that he talks like
>   men.   an evil man.

Would that Job were tried to the end begins with a word that can be read
as "my father" and is translated this way by the Vulgate. However, "my father"
makes no sense here. RSV **Would that**, expressing Elihu's desire, can be rendered
as in KJV, "My desire is that . . . ." In other words, "Job ought to be taken to court
to be tried . . . ." It is not entirely clear whether Job should be tried by men or by
God. If it is by God, Job would be fully in agreement, because that is what he has
asked for many times. Therefore it seems more likely that Elihu has men in mind,
and himself in particular. **To the end** means that Job should be tried "until the last
detail has been covered," "until there is not a word left to say." TEV "Think through"
does not render properly the idea of being tried in court.

The reason Job must be submitted to such a trial is **because he answers like
wicked men. Answers** refers to Job's speech in regard to God, and to his reply to
what the friends spoke. Here "Job speaks, talks," is better than **answers**. Verse 36
may be rendered, for example, "Job, you ought to be tried in great detail because you
talk like a criminal" or "Job should be brought to trial until every charge has been
covered, because he argues with God like an evil man."

34.37   RSV   TEV

> For he adds rebellion to his sin;   To his sins he adds rebellion;
>   he claps his hands among us,   in front of us all he mocks
>   and multiplies his words   God.
>   against God."

For he adds rebellion to his sin: Elihu has tried to obtain a confession from
Job, and this appears now to have failed. Job's refusal to confess his sin is therefore
the rebellion which he adds to his sin of accusing God of acting unjustly. Dhorme
and Pope transfer **rebellion** (translated "transgression") to line b in order to get a
better balance of lines. **Rebellion** or "revolt" means "to turn against, become unloyal
to." Some possible ways of expressing the line are: "He not only sins, he also revolts
against God," "He is a sinner and a rebel against God," "He is not only a sinner but
is also disloyal to God," or "He is a sinner and says 'No!' to God."

He claps his hands among us: his hands is not in the Hebrew text and has to be supplied in English. Dhorme and Pope propose changing the Hebrew verb translated **claps** to get "to doubt," and so Dhorme has "In our midst he casts doubt upon his transgressions," the last word having been brought over from the preceding line. FRCL is similar, with "He ends up by casting doubt among us." TEV understands it as ridicule and translates "in front of us all he mocks God." HOTTP says the verb translated **claps** means "to suffice" or "to strike" and offers two suggestions: "amongst us he fights (with words)," which means "he disputes with us." HOTTP's other suggestion confirms TEV's translation, and this is to be preferred.

And multiplies his words is Elihu's final observation in this chapter. Not only does Job mock God, he is also accused of "making long speeches, arguing at great length against God." TEV does not appear to have translated this line, or to have incorporated it into the previous line either; the translators may have thought it was sufficiently implicit in "he adds rebellion," but for most languages this will not be adequate. We may translate verse 37, for example, "He sins and says 'No' to God; he makes fun of God and never stops his talking." In some languages a gesture may be used for mocking or scorning God; for example, "he shakes sticks at God" or "he blows through his lips at God."

8D. ELIHU'S THIRD SPEECH (35.1-16)

In chapter 35 Elihu defends God in his silence toward Job. He begins in verse 2 by challenging Job's right to a hearing with God. Job has claimed that human conduct has no influence on the way God responds, and in verse 3 Elihu reminds Job of this remark. In verses 5-8 Elihu replies to Job that what humans do does not affect God, but only other people. In verses 9-13 Elihu shifts to the silence of God and argues that God does not respond to men because they are proud and evil. In the final three verses Elihu scorns Job for expecting to see God, and warns Job that he will be punished for his sin if he goes on speaking ignorantly of God.

Division Heading

The Handbook heading for this chapter is "Elihu's Third Speech," which translators may wish to modify by saying, for example, "Elihu speaks again" or "Elihu continues to speak."

8D-1. Elihu challenges Job's claim to innocence (35.1-4)

	RSV		TEV
1	And Elihu said:	1-2	It is not right, Job, for you to say
2	"Do you think this to be just?		that you are innocent in God's sight,
	Do you say, 'It is my right before God,'	3	or to ask God, "How does my sin affect you?
3	that you ask, 'What advantage have I? How am I better off than if I had sinned?'		What have I gained by not sinning?"
4	I will answer you and your friends with you.	4	I am going to answer you and your friends too.

645

In 34.36 Elihu expressed the wish that Job be tried to the end, and now he proceeds to question Job as he acts as God's defense lawyer.

Subdivision Heading
Translators may refer to the subdivision heading at 8C-2. Rowley has "Job's claim that virtue avails nothing refuted," Habel "Challenge to Job's claim."

35.1-3	RSV	TEV

	RSV	TEV
	1 And Elihu said:	1-2 It is not right, Job, for you to say
2	"Do you think this to be just?	that you are innocent in God's
	Do you say, 'It is my right	sight,
	before God,'	3 or to ask God, "How does my sin
3	that you ask, 'What advantage	affect you?
	have I?	What have I gained by not
	How am I better off than if I	sinning?"
	had sinned?'	

After being identified as the speaker, as at 34.1 and 36.1, Elihu questions Job about the claims he has made. **And Elihu said** is the author's way of telling the reader that Elihu's speech is continuing. **And** is seldom satisfactory as a marker to show the action is continuing. Better is "Then," or perhaps no linking word at all.

In 34.9 Elihu paraphrased Job's words: "It profits a man nothing that he should take delight in God." Job's assertion has been that being innocent of wrong has no effect on God. Elihu now examines this idea and sets forth two of Job's claims against each other. On the one side is Job's claim to have a just case to defend against God. On the other is Job's claim that it makes no difference to God whether a man sins or does not sin; God will always act entirely independently of what man does.

Do you think this to be just? Think translates the verb used in 13.24; 19.15; 33.10, and translated "to count" or "to consider." It may be rendered, for example, "Is it your opinion?" or "Does it appear to you?" **This** points forward to the questions in verse 3. **Just** translates the same word used in 32.9 and 34.4 meaning "right, justice." Elihu is asking if Job considers it right to claim what he says in the next line.

Do you say, 'It is my right before God' . . . ? My right translates the Hebrew *tsedeq*, the word used commonly throughout Job to refer to his claim to be "right, innocent, not guilty of wrongdoing." **Before God** is translated in various ways. Some understand it to mean "more than God," but Job has argued repeatedly that he is innocent in God's sight, and so the meaning is "I am right in my case against God," or as Habel translates verse 2, "Do you consider it just to claim 'I am right against El'?" In some languages this quoted question will have to be expressed, for example, as "Do you think it is fair for you to say to God, 'I am innocent, God'?" or indirectly, ". . . to say that you are innocent in God's eyes?"

That you ask, 'What advantage have I? You refers to Job. The Hebrew text shows that Job's quoted question is "What advantage (benefit) is there for you?" In 7.20 Job asked God "If I sin, what do I do to thee, thou watcher of men?" RSV and others change the Hebrew "you" to I in line a. However, Job has not asked how he benefits from sinning. Therefore we should retain the Hebrew "you" as referring to God. TEV has made clear that "you" refers to God, by saying "or to ask God, 'How does . . . you?' " Some translators may find it better to express the quoted questions in verses 2 and 3 as negative statements; for example, "or to say to God, 'My sin makes no difference to you.' "

How am I better off than if I had sinned?' is literally "what do I gain from my sin?" This line is at best ambiguous, since the final Hebrew word may be understood to mean "rather than my sin," which would mean "more than if I had sinned." The line may also be taken to mean "what do I profit without sin?" Dhorme and others follow the Septuagint, "What do I do if I sin?" Job has not admitted his sin as the cause of his suffering. However, since Job claims that a person's sins have no effect on God, "What have I gained by not sinning?" is a more likely meaning of this line. This line may be expressed as a positive question; for example, "What have I gained by being innocent?" or "What good has it done for me to be innocent?"

35.4	RSV	TEV

	I will answer you
	  and your friends with you.
		I am going to answer you and
		  your friends too.

I will answer you marks Elihu's decision to show Job Elihu's own wisdom.

And your friends with you: it is not certain whether **your friends** refers to just the other three, or to people who may share Job's ideas. In translation if **your friends** must be marked as present or absent, it is probably best to assume they are present listening to Elihu's speech. If verses 2 and 3 have been translated as questions, then verse 4 should be expressed as "I will answer." If statements have been used earlier, then verse 4 may require something like "tell, explain, teach."

8D-2. Elihu claims that it is not God but Job's fellow men who are affected by his sin (35.5-13)

	RSV		TEV
	RSV		TEV

5	Look at the heavens, and see;
	  and behold the clouds, which are high-
	  er than you.
		5	Look at the sky! See how high the clouds
			  are!

6	If you have sinned, what do you accom-
	  plish against him?
	  And if your transgressions are multi-
	  plied, what do you do to him?
		6	If you sin, that does no harm to God.
			  If you do wrong many times, does that
			  affect him?

7	If you are righteous, what do you give to
	  him;
	  or what does he receive from your
	  hand?
		7	Do you help God by being so righteous?
			  There is nothing God needs from you.

8	Your wickedness concerns a man like
	  yourself,
	  and your righteousness a son of man.
		8	It is your fellow-man who suffers from
			  your sins,
			  and the good you do helps him.

		9	When men are oppressed, they groan; they cry for someone to save them.
		10	But they don't turn to God, their Cre- ator,

9   "Because of the multitude of oppressions
        people cry out;
       they call for help because of the arm
        of the mighty.
10   But none says, 'Where is God my Maker,
        who gives songs in the night,
11   who teaches us more than the beasts of
        the earth,
       and makes us wiser than the birds of
        the air?'
12   There they cry out, but he does not an-
        swer,
       because of the pride of evil men.
13   Surely God does not hear an empty cry,
        nor does the Almighty regard it.

        who gives them hope in their darkest
          hours.
11   They don't turn to God, who makes us
        wise,
       wiser than any animal or bird.
12   They cry for help, but God doesn't an-
        swer,
       for they are proud and evil men.
13   It is useless for them to cry out;
        Almighty God does not see or hear
          them.

Subdivision Heading

The Handbook heading may be adjusted to say, for example, "God does not answer because people are proud," "Your sins harm your fellow beings," or "People want help, but their pride prevents God from helping them." Rowley has (verses 9-16) "When the cry of the afflicted goes unanswered, they have not learned their lesson."

35.5   RSV   TEV

Look at the heavens, and see;   Look at the sky! See how high
   and behold the clouds, which   the clouds are!
   are higher than you.

Look at the heavens, and see; and behold the clouds, which are higher than you: Zophar in 11.7,8 and Eliphaz in 22.12 have both responded to Job by comparing God's wisdom to the heavens. Even Job has done the same in 9.8-9. The poetic movement in this line is from the more remote **heavens** in the first line down to the closer and more specific **clouds** in the second line, which is one of the devices in parallelism for fine tuning or focusing. The suggestion is that God, symbolized as **heavens** and **clouds**, is above and beyond the reach of human beings. This verse serves only to introduce verse 6. Line a has two verbs for **see**, which reflect Elihu's emphatic kind of command. There is little point in attempting to translate with two different verbs for seeing; the meaning is "Look up at the sky!" **Behold** translates a verb meaning "to perceive, consider, view carefully," and so NJB translates "observe how high the clouds are above you."

35.6   RSV   TEV

If you have sinned, what do you   If you sin, that does no harm to
   accomplish against him?   God.
And if your transgressions are   If you do wrong many times,
   multiplied, what do you do   does that affect him?
   to him?

If you have sinned, what do you accomplish against him? Elihu again picks up the thought Job expressed as a rhetorical question in 7.20: "If I sin, what do I do to thee . . . ?" **What do you accomplish against him** translates "what do you do against him," which is equivalent to asking "how does that affect God?" or as a statement, "that does not affect God" or "that is nothing to God." The line may also be rendered, for example, "If you sin, that is nothing to God," or "If you sin, how does that do anything to God?" or ". . . what difference does it make to God?"

And if your transgressions are multiplied: transgressions means the same in noun form as **sinned** in line a. **Multiplied** means "over and over, again and again, repeatedly." The question part of the sentence has the same meaning as in line a. In Hebrew, as in RSV, both lines consist of an "if" clause followed by a question. TEV makes line a an "if" clause followed by a negative statement, but uses the question form in line b for variety of style.

35.7	RSV	TEV
	If you are righteous, what do you give to him; or what does he receive from your hand?	Do you help God by being so righteous? There is nothing God needs from you.

In 22.3 Eliphaz asked "Is it any pleasure to the Almighty if you are righteous?" It is the wisdom of Elihu to repeat what he has heard others say. **If you are righteous, what do you give to him: are righteous** here means "do what is right, live rightly, be upright." **Give to him** translates the Hebrew literally, and it contrasts with its parallel **receive** in the following line. TEV, which understands Elihu's question as irony, translates "Do you help God by being so righteous?" There is no indication in verse 6 that Elihu is using sarcasm, and it is probably not intended in verse 7 either. Elihu is attempting to make his point by using the words of Job and the friends. As in the preceding verse, the first half of the verse may be rendered as a question (RSV) or a statement (TEV). The line may be rendered, for example, "If you do what is right, what good are you doing for him?" or "If you do what is right, you are giving him nothing" or ". . . you are doing nothing for God."

Or what does he receive from your hand? This line is parallel in meaning to the question in line a. **Your hand** is a part referring to the whole and means "from you." The two lines may be shortened and combined; for example, "By doing what is right, how does that help God?" or "If you are innocent, what does God get from that?" In this view, it matters very little that Job has a claim against God based on Job's innocence, since Job's doing right would have no effect on God anyway. The logical implication is that Job should forget his complaint against God.

35.8	RSV	TEV
	Your wickedness concerns a man like yourself,	It is your fellow-man who suffers from your sins,

and your righteousness a son of man.	and the good you do helps him.

The statement **your wickedness concerns a man like yourself** has no verb in Hebrew, so RSV supplies **concerns**. The nouns in the two lines of this verse contrast, and so the verbs that are supplied must reflect the contrast. **Concerns** in line a in RSV leaves the reader to supply **concerns** in line b, but this fails to make clear the contrast. See the discussion in the next paragraph. In 22.2 Eliphaz said that a man's righteousness only profits himself. Elihu seems to see clearly that a man's sin and righteousness affect the lives of others. But even this is Job's argument, not Elihu's. In 24.2-17 Job spoke at length on how human suffering is caused by oppression, and that God pays no attention to the prayers of the oppressed. TEV has rendered this line very well: "It is your fellow-man who suffers from your sins." This may also be rendered, for example, "Your wickedness makes other people suffer," or "You do bad things and others suffer for it," or "Because of the evil you do, others have to suffer."

And your righteousness a son of man: **righteousness** is well translated in TEV by a phrase employing a verb, "the good you do." TEV supplies the appropriate verb "helps" in this line, which contrasts with "suffers" in line a. **Son of man** is the literal form of the Hebrew and matches **a man like yourself** in line a. TEV translates this expression as "him," referring to "fellow-man" in line a.

35.9   RSV   TEV

"Because of the multitude of oppressions people cry out; they call for help because of the arm of the mighty.	When men are oppressed, they groan; they cry for someone to save them.

Because of the multitude of oppressions people cry out probably refers again to Job's observations in 24.12, in which the oppressed cry out, but God does not hear them. Elihu will offer an explanation why God does not answer. **Multitude of oppressions** renders what in Hebrew probably means "excess of oppressions," which can be better translated as "being greatly oppressed." TEV translates this expression as a subordinate clause, "When men are oppressed . . . ." The reason **people cry out** is that they are severely oppressed.

They call for help because of the arm of the mighty: **arm of the mighty** refers to someone who is powerful, and is similar to the use of "arm of the man" in the Hebrew of 22.8. **For help** is not in the Hebrew, but RSV makes it explicit, as does TEV with "for someone to save them." **Because . . . mighty** may be omitted in translation if it results in bad style or is confusing; otherwise it should be retained as in the model examples. This line may also be expressed, for example, "and they call for someone to save them from the powerful" or "they call out for someone to defend them against those in power."

35.10   RSV   TEV

> But none says, 'Where is God my Maker,
> who gives songs in the night,

> But they don't turn to God, their Creator,
> who gives them hope in their darkest hours.

Elihu says the oppressed only call for relief from their oppressors. The point he wishes to make in verses 10 and 11 is that the cries of the oppressed are not heard because they do not call out to God. Verses 10 and 11 contain long rhetorical questions which may need to be recast as statements, as in TEV.

But none says, 'Where is God my Maker . . . ? God my Maker is translated by TEV as "God, their Creator" and by FRCL as "God, who made me." RSV and others begin the quotation here and continue it through verse 11. RSV follows the Hebrew form closely. TEV translates the singular **none** as "they," which is more natural in English. If the translator follows the pattern of RSV, this line may be rendered, for example, "But no one asks, 'Where is my creator?' " or "But no one calls on God his creator to save him."

Who gives songs in the night is generally understood in the sense that God enables people to sing even when they are surrounded by darkness. Nevertheless the word translated **songs** has been adjusted or interpreted in many different ways. Dhorme thinks it refers to "thunder," as in Psalm 29.3. Others take it to mean "lights," "star constellations," and Pope says the Hebrew root should be associated with a similar Arabic root meaning "violent, courageous, mighty," and so should be translated "strength or protection." Rowley observes wisely "It is a pity to rob Elihu of a poetic line when he creates one." However, similar lines are seen in Psalm 42.8; 77.6. TEV has "hope in their darkest hours." If **songs in the night** is not sufficiently meaningful, "songs that bring hope in their darkest hours" may be better. Or we may translate, for example, "who enables people to sing in times of great trouble."

35.11   RSV   TEV

> who teaches us more than the beasts of the earth,
> and makes us wiser than the birds of the air?'

> They don't turn to God, who makes us wise,
> wiser than any animal or bird.

Who teaches us more than the beasts of the earth: in 12.7 Job said that the beasts and birds could teach the friends. Dhorme thinks it is too commonplace to say that God has given man more understanding than the beasts and the birds, and so translates "He instructs us by the beasts of the earth," which the Hebrew construction also allows. FRCL follows the latter interpretation and translates "who uses the wild animals to teach us," and places the alternative rendering (as in RSV) in a footnote. Either rendering would be accurate and characteristic of Elihu. Following the Dhorme model we may need to adjust this slightly to say, for example, "God uses the lives of wild animals to teach us" or "God teaches us more than he taught the wild animals." The expressions **of the earth** and **of the air** will often be unnecessary in translation.

And makes us wiser than the birds of the air: RSV translates this line so as to follow on from the previous line. It states the obvious and is one of the two ways this line can be translated. The other way is to say "and makes us wise by means of the birds" or "he uses the birds to makes us wise." It is not clear what the animals and birds are supposed to teach, but the thought is probably that even the animals and birds in need cry out to God for help (see Psa 104.21; 147.9; Joel 1.20), and that people should follow their example. TEV can be understood in the same way: "Even though God makes people wiser than animals and birds, people still fail to turn to him for help."

35.12   RSV   TEV

> There they cry out, but he does   They cry for help, but God does-
>   not answer,   n't answer,
> because of the pride of evil   for they are proud and evil
>   men.   men.

There they cry out, but he does not answer: **There** seems to connect this line back to verse 9 by referring to the situation described in that verse. The word translated **There** normally has this meaning, but not as a connective. Dhorme suggests "Consequently," and Gordis "Then." TEV omits it with no loss of meaning. **He** refers to God.

Because of the pride of evil men is not entirely clear, because in Job's speech in chapter 24 it is the wicked ones who cause the oppressed to suffer. However, it appears to be Elihu's choice to call the oppressed **evil men**, because he is giving a theological reason for their failure to call on God's help. Therefore TEV "for they are proud and evil men" refers to the oppressed people in verse 9a. Verse 12 should be translated so that **they** refers to the people crying out in verse 9, and not to the animals or birds in verse 11. RSV **the pride of evil men** refers to those people who finally cry out to God for help, and may be expressed, for example, "because they are proud and evil people" or "because of their pride and evil."

35.13   RSV   TEV

> Surely God does not hear an   It is useless for them to cry out;
>   empty cry,   Almighty God does not see or
> nor does the Almighty regard   hear them.
>   it.

Surely God does not hear an empty cry is literally "Surely vanity God will not hear," which gives rise to different interpretations. Dhorme understands the two words translated "Surely vanity" to mean "a pure waste of time." NEB translates these words "All to no purpose." The cries of the people in verse 12 are addressed to nobody, and so their cries are useless, or as TEV says, "It is useless for them to cry out." In line a it is *'El* who does not hear their cries. In line b it is *Shaddai*. FRCL says "They cry out, but it is useless because God the Almighty does not hear it." This line may also be rendered, for example, "It is useless; God does not listen to them" or "There is no point in crying out; God does not listen." **Nor does the Almighty regard it** parallels the first line in meaning, with a shift from hearing to seeing, and from *'El* to *Shaddai*. The line may also be expressed "the Almighty does not even look their way" or "the Almighty does not even give them a glance."

8D-3. Elihu ridicules Job for being ignorant (35.14-16)

RSV	TEV
14 How much less when you say that you do not see him, that the case is before him, and you are waiting for him!	14 Job, you say you can't see God; but wait patiently—your case is before him.
15 And now, because his anger does not punish, and he does not greatly heed transgression,	15 You think that God does not punish, that he pays little attention to sin.
16 Job opens his mouth in empty talk, he multiplies words without knowledge."	16 It is useless for you to go on talking; it is clear you don't know what you are saying.

The preceding verses have dealt with the oppressed people, beginning with verse 9. Now Elihu speaks to and about Job's particular case, a transition TEV makes clear in verse 14a. Verse 14 is the logical follow-up to verse 13.

Subdivision Heading

The Handbook heading may be modified to say, for example, "Job, you are an ignorant man" or "Wait, Job, and you will see."

35.14

RSV	TEV
How much less when you say that you do not see him, that the case is before him, and you are waiting for him!	Job, you say you can't see God; but wait patiently—your case is before him.

How much less when you say that you do not see him suggests that if God does not hear the cries of the oppressed, because they are proud and evil, it is even less likely that he will listen to Job. RSV interprets the opening words of this line as in 15.16 and 25.6. These words are intended to relate verse 14 to verse 13, and this is followed by FRCL, BJ, NJB, NIV, and Dhorme. On the other hand TEV and others recognize a clear break between 13 and 14. A close connection in thought is to be preferred. RSV **How much less** implies more than it says and may be filled out by saying, for example, "How much less will God hear you, Job, who say you do not see him?" This line may also be expressed "If that is the case, Job, how will God ever hear you when you say you can't see him?"

The second line of verse 14 most probably refers to Job's statements in 13.18, "I have prepared my case; I know that I shall be vindicated," and in 31.35 (TEV), "Will no one listen to what I am saying? I swear that every word is true. Let Almighty God answer me."

That the case is before him: the verb **say** in the previous line serves also here. That is, "You also say that you have presented your case to him." The word translated **case** is not the usual one found in Job's speeches, but in some of its verb forms it means "to plead one's case." The final clause **and you are waiting for him** is understood to mean that Job is waiting for God to act on Job's case, that is, to make a legal decision for or against him. It is not in Elihu's manner to give Job gentle advice such as TEV suggests: "wait patiently—your case is before him." It is more realistic and accurate to retain in English the Hebrew clause order, as in RSV. Job's final words in 31.35 included "Let the Almighty answer me," and since then he has not spoken. So it is natural for Elihu to conclude that Job is waiting for God's decision regarding his case.

35.15-16	RSV	TEV
15	And now, because his anger does not punish, and he does not greatly heed transgression,[a]	15 You think that God does not punish, that he pays little attention to sin.
16	Job opens his mouth in empty talk, he multiplies words without knowledge."	16 It is useless for you to go on talking; it is clear you don't know what you are saying.

[a] Theodotion Symmachus Compare Vg: The meaning of the Hebrew word is uncertain

These two verses are handled as a unit by RSV but not by TEV. Verse 15 is obscure, and there are many different translations of it. Elihu may be referring to 21.14-26, in which Job asserted that God does not punish the wicked.

And now, because his anger does not punish seems to introduce still another complaint. **And now** suggests that something further is being added. It may be expressed as "What's more" or "In addition." TEV does not seem to represent it. The rest of this line is literally "surely (or, because) nothing his anger visited," where the verb means "visit, inspect, punish." "Nothing" is to be taken as the generalized object of the verb, and so "his anger does not punish anything," which is better rendered in this context as "anyone." TEV "You think" is supplied on the basis of "you say" in verse 14a and may also be rendered "You also say." **Anger** in Hebrew is used as the subject of **punish**. This must be recast in many languages to say, for example, "God in his anger does not punish . . . ."

Does not greatly heed is literally "does not greatly know," which seems strange, since we would expect something like "does not know at all." However, the word for "know" can mean **heed** as here, or "show concern for" as in Exodus 2.25, where TEV translates "was concerned for them." The same meaning is found in 9.21, where Job says "I no longer care" (TEV). RSV gives a satisfactory translation, but TEV is to be preferred: "that he pays little attention to sin." The word **transgression**, as noted in the RSV footnote, follows the ancient versions in which an obscure Hebrew word is changed to a similar sounding word meaning "sin," as in TEV.

Job opens his mouth in empty talk: Elihu again uses Job's name but is apparently addressing whoever may be listening, perhaps the friends and bystanders. TEV, which addressed Job directly and by name in verse 14a, continues to address Job with "you" in verses 15 and 16. Translators should follow the form of address that is most natural and is the least ambiguous. **Opens his mouth** means "he talks, makes speeches, gives discourses." **Empty talk** translates the word commonly rendered "vanity" by KJV and RSV in Ecclesiastes. The word is used in 21.34, where TEV translates it as "nonsense," and FRCL as "wind." In English this line can be rendered, for example, "Job talks like a windbag"; that is, he talks much and says little that is significant.

Elihu closes this chapter of his speech saying about Job that **he multiplies words without knowledge**, which is similar to what he said in 34.37. See there for comments. **Without knowledge** means "without knowing what he is saying" or "out of his ignorance." This line may be rendered, for example, "Job goes on talking about things when he knows nothing about them."

8E. ELIHU'S FINAL SPEECH (36.1–37.24)

Chapters 36 and 37 make up the fourth and final speech of Elihu. The theme of this final speech is a continuation of Elihu's defense of God. In 36.2-4 Elihu claims to speak on God's behalf. In verses 5-15 he testifies to God's character and explains to Job the purpose of suffering. In 16-21, a series of textually uncertain verses, Elihu accuses Job of allowing his prosperity to corrupt him and causing him to suffer. In 22-25 Elihu again reminds Job of the ways of God. Elihu then describes God's work in nature in 36.26–37.13. Finally, in verses 14-22 of chapter 37, Elihu asks Job to answer impossible questions about God in nature. Elihu concludes his speech in 37.23-24 with a testimony to God's power and justice.

Division Heading

Translators may wish to call this division something like "Elihu's fourth speech," "Elihu concludes his discourse," or "Elihu will say no more." Habel has "Elihu's second defence of El's justice."

8E-1. Elihu speaks the truth for God (36.1-4)

RSV	TEV
1 And Elihu continued, and said:	1-2 Be patient and listen a little longer
2 "Bear with me a little, and I will show	to what I am saying on God's behalf.

<table>
<tr><td>

you,
  for I have yet something to say on
    God's behalf.
3 I will fetch my knowledge from afar,
    and ascribe righteousness to my Mak-
      er.
4 For truly my words are not false;
    one who is perfect in knowledge is with
      you.

</td><td>

3 My knowledge is wide; I will use what I
    know
    to show that God, my Creator, is just.
4 Nothing I say to you is false;
    you see before you a truly wise man.

</td></tr>
</table>

Subdivision Heading

The Handbook heading may be reworded to say, for example, "I speak on behalf of God," "Elihu is God's spokesman," or "Elihu represents God."

36.1   RSV   TEV

  And Elihu continued, and said: *[See discussion below.]*

And Elihu continued, and said: Elihu, who began speaking in chapter 32, continues without interruption until the end of chapter 37. Verse 1 is the same conventional opening used for each of the friends of Job, except "answered" is here replaced by **continued**. This line may also be translated, for example, "Elihu continued speaking" or "Elihu went ahead with his speech."

Translators will notice that TEV leaves implicit the information that Elihu is continuing his speech. For those translations that consider this to be a fourth speech, or a fourth segment of the speech, it may be necessary to retain some kind of marker to indicate this kind of a break.

36.2   RSV   TEV

<table>
<tr><td>

"Bear with me a little, and I will
    show you,
  for I have yet something to say
    on God's behalf.

</td><td>

Be patient and listen a little
    longer
  to what I am saying on God's
    behalf.

</td></tr>
</table>

Bear with me a little, and I will show you: **Bear** translates a word which normally means "surround" as in RSV footnote to Judges 20.43; Psalm 22.12; Habakkuk 1.4. Here the sense is understood as used in the Aramaic and Syriac versions, "to wait or to be patient." **A little** refers to length of time, or as TEV says, "a little longer." **Show** refers here to presenting evidence that will convince Job. Therefore a more appropriate term is "teach, convince, enlighten, explain."

For I have yet something to say on God's behalf is literally "for there are still words for God." This line gives the reason why Job should be patient with Elihu. The "words" which Elihu refers to are his own, which he wishes to speak **on God's behalf**, as God's spokesman. In line a TEV has supplied "listen" and made line b the object of "listen." To speak **on God's behalf** means "in the place of God," "for God's cause," or "as the one who speaks for God." Verse 2 may also be expressed

"Wait a little longer and I will help you to understand, because I still have things to say as God's spokesman" or ". . . and I will tell you what God wants you to hear."

36.3   RSV   TEV

> I will fetch my knowledge from
>   afar,
>   and ascribe righteousness to
>   my Maker.

> My knowledge is wide; I will use
>   what I know
>   to show that God, my Creator,
>   is just.

I will fetch my knowledge from afar: fetch translates "carry" and means carry to where the speaker is; that is, "I will bring my knowledge." **Fetch . . . from afar** has the sense of "gather from widely different sources" or "bring in great variety," which Elihu does in the second part of his speech, when he deals with the variety of ways in which God is active in nature. NJB translates "I shall range far afield for my arguments." This may also be rendered "I will use great knowledge" or "I will show you how vast my knowledge is."

And ascribe righteousness to my Maker is a phrase which has the same meaning as "to justify" or "to show someone to be just or fair." **My Maker** renders the Hebrew literally and adequately. It is commonly translated "my Creator" by TEV and others. The word translated **my Maker** is not the usual verbal noun used in this sense, but its meaning as "my Creator" is not in doubt. This line may be translated, for example, "I will prove that my Creator is in the right," or "I will show you that my Maker is fair."

36.4   RSV   TEV

> For truly my words are not false;
>   one who is perfect in knowl-
>   edge is with you.

> Nothing I say to you is false;
>   you see before you a truly wise
>   man.

For truly my words are not false serves to certify that Elihu's words are to be accepted as true. Elihu is no stranger to immodest assurances about himself. FRCL translates the line as a positive statement: "What I have to say is the pure truth." It is because Elihu's **words are not false** that he is qualified to speak for God, or to represent God in Job's legal dispute with God. In some languages the line may be rendered idiomatically; for example, "I assure you my mouth speaks with one tongue" or "It is so that my words are all straight."

One who is perfect in knowledge is with you refers to Elihu himself, the same as in the previous line. **Perfect in knowledge** is used in 37.16, where it refers to God. **Perfect** translates a word meaning "complete" and is used in 1.1, and also in 1.8 and 2.3, where God uses the word to characterize Job. There it is translated "blameless" (RSV) and "faithful" (TEV). Used in relation to **knowledge** the meaning has to do with the degree of knowledge Elihu claims. TEV says "a truly wise man," FRCL "a man certain in his subject," Habel "perfect in reasoning," NEB "one whose conclusions are sound." We may also translate, for example, "a man whose knowledge is the highest" or "who has the best knowledge."

8E-2. God is just, and so people suffer (36.5-15)

RSV

5 "Behold, God is mighty, and does not despise any;
   he is mighty in strength of understanding.
6 He does not keep the wicked alive,
   but gives the afflicted their right.
7 He does not withdraw his eyes from the righteous,
   but with kings upon the throne he sets them for ever, and they are exalted.
8 And if they are bound in fetters
   and caught in the cords of affliction,
9 then he declares to them their work
   and their transgressions, that they are behaving arrogantly.
10 He opens their ears to instruction,
   and commands that they return from iniquity.
11 If they hearken and serve him,
   they complete their days in prosperity,
   and their years in pleasantness.
12 But if they do not hearken, they perish by the sword,
   and die without knowledge.

13 "The godless in heart cherish anger;
   they do not cry for help when he binds them.
14 They die in youth,
   and their life ends in shame.
15 He delivers the afflicted by their affliction,
   and opens their ear by adversity.

TEV

5 How strong God is! He despises no one;
   there is nothing he doesn't understand.
6 He does not let sinners live on,
   and he always treats the poor with justice.
7 He protects those who are righteous;
   he allows them to rule like kings
   and lets them be honored forever.
8 But if people are bound in chains,
   suffering for what they have done,
9 God shows them their sins and their pride.
10 He makes them listen to his warning
   to turn away from evil.
11 If they obey God and serve him,
   they live out their lives in peace and prosperity.
12 But if not, they will die in ignorance
   and cross the stream into the world of the dead.

13 Those who are godless keep on being angry,
   and even when punished, they don't pray for help.
14 They die while they are still young,
   worn out by a life of disgrace.
15 But God teaches men through suffering
   and uses distress to open their eyes.

In verses 5-15 Elihu defends the justice of God and attempts to show Job the purpose of his suffering.

Subdivision Heading

The heading of this unit may be worded, for example, "Suffering is to make you learn, Job," "Elihu tells Job that God allows him to suffer to teach him," or "Suffering is to make people turn away from their sins." Rowley has "The meaning and purpose of suffering," TOB "The divine education," and Habel "Interpreting affliction from El."

36.5   RSV   TEV

"Behold, God is mighty, and does   How strong God is! He despises
   not despise any;   no one;
he is mighty in strength of   there is nothing he doesn't
   understanding.   understand.

Behold, God is mighty, and does not despise any: the Hebrew has no
object for **despise**, and so RSV supplies **any**, meaning "anybody," and TEV does the
same with "no one." As the verse stands, line a reads "Yes, God is great and he does
not despise." Line b is literally "great by force of heart." Dhorme, supported by Pope
and others, transposes the word translated "force" in line b to qualify **mighty** in line
a and translates "Yes, God is great in might." He also makes a change in the Hebrew
word translated "great" to get "pure," and line b then becomes "and he does not
despise the pure in heart." HOTTP, which says the verb translated **despise** means "to
reject, not to care," gives a translation which can be reworded for clarity as "Behold,
God is mighty and he cares; he is a mighty judge by the strength of his decision."
However, no modern version supports HOTTP's rendering. Aside from supplying an
object for **despise**, RSV translates the Hebrew text and makes good sense. **Strength
of understanding** translates "strength of heart." In Hebrew "heart" symbolizes the
intelligence. TEV supports RSV, improves the style, and is recommended to
translators.

36.6   RSV   TEV

He does not keep the wicked   He does not let sinners live on,
   alive,   and he always treats the poor
but gives the afflicted their   with justice.
   right.

He does not keep the wicked alive is a reply to Job's question in 21.7, "Why
do the wicked live?" According to Elihu they do not remain alive. RSV's wording of
this line sounds as if God refuses to actively keep them alive by means of his divine
power. TEV is more satisfactory, as it reflects God in a more passive role of not
allowing them to live; or we may translate, for example, "He does not allow wicked
people to go on living."
   But gives the afflicted their right: but does not contrast the wicked with the
poor or what God does with each. Line a is negative and line b is positive.
Translators should employ the linking word that is suitable for this context. **The
afflicted** refers to people who suffer at the hands of the wicked, as in chapter 21.
There the ones who are suffering are the poor, and so line b is correctly rendered
by TEV as "and he always treats the poor with justice," which means "treats the poor
fairly."

36.7   RSV   TEV

> He does not withdraw his eyes
>   from the righteous,
> but with kings upon the throne
> he sets them for ever, and they
>   are exalted.

> He protects those who are right-
>   eous;
> he allows them to rule like
>   kings
> and lets them be honored for-
>   ever.

He does not withdraw his eyes from the righteous means that God "keeps his eyes on, watches with care, protects" the **righteous**. Dhorme makes a slight change in the Hebrew to get "He does not take away the right of the righteous." NEB and NJB connect this line to verse 6. RSV and TEV follow Pope by taking verse 7 as a unit. It is probably to be understood as an exaltation of the poor, as in Psalm 113.7-8. **The righteous** refers to "those who are faithful to God," "those who trust in God." The line may also be expressed "He watches over the righteous to take care of them," "He takes care of those who put their trust in him," or "God protects those who obey him."

But with kings upon the throne: the word translated **with** can also be taken as the sign of the direct object in Hebrew, and so NJB has "when he raises kings to thrones." NEB has "Look at kings on their thrones," and then goes on to treat verses 8-12 as a description of what happens to kings. However, it seems more likely, as in TEV, that these verses deal with two types of people: the righteous, exalted in verse 7, and those who fall into the sin of pride in verses 8-12. The latter view has the advantage of avoiding a break in the middle of verse 7, in which Elihu would have to change the subject.

But with kings is best understood as a comparison, in which **he sets them** in the next line describes what God does to the poor or "afflicted" of verse 6. That is, "He sets them on thrones like kings," or as TEV says, "He allows them to rule like kings." **For ever** modifies the verb **sets**, as in RSV.

And they are exalted is supported by Pope, and by TEV "honored." HOTTP gives a detailed discussion of the two possible senses of the Hebrew, "they are exalted," and "they become proud." This discussion does not allow for verses 8-12 to refer to the kings. On the whole TEV and RSV are to be recommended. The two final lines of the verse may need to be transposed in translation; for example "he honors them and treats them forever like kings on their thrones" or "he shows them honor by making them rule like kings forever."

36.8-9   RSV   TEV

> 8   And if they are bound in fetters
>   and caught in the cords of
>   affliction,
> 9   then he declares to them their
>   work
>   and their transgressions, that

> 8   But if people are bound in
>   chains,
>   suffering for what they have
>   done,
> 9   God shows them their sins and
>   their pride.

they are behaving arrogantly.

These two verses will be handled as a unit, since verse 8 contains the conditions
whose consequences are given in verse 9.

And if they are bound in fetters: in RSV **they** refers to the "righteous" in
verse 7. TEV makes the subject of this line "people." **Bound in fetters** is similar to
the thought expressed in 13.27 and 33.11. The feet of prisoners were chained to a
solid object to prevent them from escaping.

Caught in the cords of affliction introduces a metaphor meaning "made to
suffer" or, as FRCL says more poetically, "captives of a miserable situation." The
thought in verse 8 is that when the righteous suffer, before God rescues them, it is
because God is disciplining them. Verse 8 may also be expressed "If they are
imprisoned and are made to suffer" or "If they are made prisoners and suffer."

The purpose for which they are allowed to suffer is to make them aware of
their sins and to help them recognize that being raised to important positions has
made them proud. **Then he declares to them their work** is the consequence of the
"if" clause in verse 8. **He** should be changed to "God" in translation, if the pronoun
reference is not clear. **Declares** translates a verb meaning "reveals, shows, makes
clear." **Their work** is literally "what they have done" and is defined by the next
phrase **their transgressions**. These are not two separate events but rather a general
description followed by a more specific one. This line then says "God shows them
how they have committed sins" or ". . . how they have sinned."

That they are behaving arrogantly: the verb form in Hebrew is reflexive and
may be rendered, for example, "and allowed themselves to become proud." TEV has
reduced the two lines of verse 9 to one. The evil conduct of these people is brought
on by their becoming proud. Verse 9, the consequence of verse 8, may be rendered
"then God shows them how they have sinned and become proud."

36.10   RSV   TEV

He opens their ears to instruc-   He makes them listen to his
   tion,   warning
and commands that they re-   to turn away from evil.
   turn from iniquity.

He opens their ears to instruction describes how God continues to deal with
them. This verse repeats some of Elihu's talk in 33.16. **Opens their ears** means "to
cause to pay attention," or as TEV says, "He makes them listen." The phrase
translated **to instruction** means "to his warning." That is, "He makes them pay
attention to his warning."

And commands that they return from iniquity: **commands** here renders the
verb "says," which when followed by the content of the indirect address usually
means "to order or to command." **Return from iniquity** is an idiom meaning "to
return from evil to God" or "turn away from evil," as in TEV. The sense is "to stop
doing evil, renounce evil, give up wickedness, repent." Verse 10 may also be

rendered "He makes them listen carefully and orders them to stop their evil ways" or "He sharpens their hearing and tells them to repent of their sins."

36.11-12   RSV   TEV

11   If they hearken and serve him,   11   If they obey God and serve him,
        they complete their days in   they live out their lives in
        prosperity,   peace and prosperity.
     and their years in pleasant-   12   But if not, they will die in igno-
        ness.   rance
12   But if they do not hearken, they   and cross the stream into the
        perish by the sword,   world of the dead.
     and die without knowledge.

These two verses may be taken together as offering two alternatives. A similar contrast between obedience and disobedience is found in Isaiah 1.19-20. The first alternative is **If they hearken and serve him**, in which **hearken** is an archaic English verb meaning either "listen" or "obey." In the Hebrew no object is expressed with **serve**, but the implied object is clearly God, as in TEV. The consequences are described in the next two lines.

They complete their days . . . means that they will live their lives counted in line b as **days**, and in line c as **years**. In terms of parallelism line c goes beyond line b by shifting from the smaller time unit to the larger one. Line b expresses the same thought as in 21.13. **Prosperity** translates a Hebrew word which can have that meaning or "happiness, success, well-being." **Pleasantness** in line c is almost the same in meaning. TEV and others reduce lines b and c to one and use two nouns to describe the final state of their lives. TEV has "peace and prosperity," SPCL "happiness and felicity," GECL "happiness and peace," and FRCL "the greatest happiness." Translators should use expressions for **prosperity** and **pleasantness** that are fully natural in the receptor language.

But if they do not hearken presents the opposite condition of that in verse 11a, and the result is given in the last half of the line as **they perish by the sword**, which is the same expression used in 33.18. Many translations understand this expression to have the sense of crossing the river to death, as is possible also in 33.18. It is also possible to understand this as referring to their destruction, as in RSV, NJV, and NIV. FRCL, which uses the metaphorical expression in the text, has the nonfigurative rendering in a footnote. While both renderings are possible, it is recommended to translate verse 12 in the same way as in 33.18, and not change here as TEV does.

And die without knowledge gives the reason for their dying, not merely the circumstances. TEV has shifted this line to come before line a, which gives a more logical progression of thought. This line may be rendered, for example, "they die because they are ignorant" or "because they lack understanding they die."

36.13   RSV   TEV

"The godless in heart cherish
    anger;
  they do not cry for help when
    he binds them.

Those who are godless keep on
    being angry,
  and even when punished, they
    don't pray for help.

The godless in heart cherish anger: godless translates a word used in 8.13, which refers to people who do not trust God, and so "those who do not trust God" or "people who do not believe in God." Here **in heart** is added to make the expression more vivid. In some languages it is translated as "unbelievers in heart." Dhorme thinks it means "hypocritical," NJB calls them "stubborn," and FRCL "people of bad faith," that is, people who lack faith. **Cherish anger** is literally "put anger." Dhorme makes a change to get "keep their anger," and this seems to be followed by both RSV and TEV. The **anger** they have is their own, not God's.

These people **do not cry for help**; that is, "they do not ask God to help them." **When he binds them** describes the extent of the conditions God imposes on them, and still they do not ask for his help. Pope changes the Hebrew verb translated **binds** to get "chastises," but the general sense of putting them in bonds is for punishment, and so TEV "even when punished" is adequate without the need for any change. Verse 13 may be rendered, for example, "They are people who do not trust God and who stay angry. Even when God punishes them, they do not ask him to help them."

36.14   RSV   TEV

They die in youth,
    and their life ends in shame.[b]

They die while they are still
    young,
  worn out by a life of disgrace.

[b] Heb *among the cult prostitutes*

They die in youth implies that these people have no future. In line b **in shame** is literally "among the male prostitutes," as noted in the RSV footnote. Translations differ greatly in the rendering of this line. Some translations avoid the literal meaning and give a euphemism or substitute expression that parallels the idea of premature death in line a. Others seek to represent in some way the idea of the pagan temple male prostitute. The term occurs in both masculine and feminine forms in Deuteronomy 23.17; 1 Kings 14.24; 15.12; 22.46; 2 Kings 23.7. The practice of religious prostitution, which was frequently condemned in the book of Kings, was part of the fertility rituals of the Canaanites. Some have sought a parallel between dying **in youth** in line a and the supposed short lives of temple prostitutes, but according to Pope there is no evidence to support this view. RSV **their life ends in shame** avoids the literal rendering and gives a meaning which the literal expression suggests. The same is true of TEV. Dhorme thinks the reference to male prostitutes focuses upon their youthfulness and so translates "and their life ends in adolescence." This creates a good parallelism but does not seem to be justified. Elihu, like the friends, is sure that the wicked are headed for an untimely death and so must repent. On the whole the translations of RSV and TEV are recommended.

36.15   RSV   TEV

He delivers the afflicted by their   But God teaches men through
    affliction,   suffering
and opens their ear by adversi-   and uses distress to open their
    ty.   eyes.

He delivers the afflicted by their affliction describes Elihu's view of the meaning of discipline. God uses the suffering of the one who suffers to rescue him. This verse leads up to the application of Elihu's wisdom to Job's own case. **Delivers** means "saves, rescues, spares." TEV focuses on the sense of being disciplined, with "God teaches men through suffering," that is, "God teaches people by allowing them to suffer." Dhorme translates **afflicted** as "poor," and this is followed by FRCL. NEB says "those who suffer, he rescues through suffering."

Opens their ear is the same expression used in verse 10 and in 33.16, where the sense is "makes them listen," and it has that sense here also. **Adversity** translates a word meaning also "oppression or suffering" and is close in meaning to **affliction** in the previous line. TEV shifts from the ear to the eye with "he uses distress to open their eyes," that is, to make them see the error of their ways. The shift to "eyes" should only be used if it is natural in the receptor language and has the meaning as in TEV. Verse 15 may also be rendered "God uses suffering to save people who suffer; he uses pain to make them understand" or "God teaches people by allowing them to suffer, and he makes them listen to him by letting them have troubles."

8E-3. Elihu warns Job that he is being punished as he deserves (36.16-21)

RSV   TEV

16   He also allured you out of distress   16   God brought you out of trouble,
         into a broad place where there was no   and let you enjoy security;
             cramping,   your table was piled high with food.
         and what was set on your table was full 17   But now you are being punished as you
             of fatness.   deserve.
                                                     18   Be careful not to let bribes deceive you,
17   "But you are full of the judgment on the   or riches lead you astray.
             wicked;   19   It will do you no good to cry out for help;
         judgment and justice seize you.   all your strength can't help you now.
18   Beware lest wrath entice you into scoff-   20   Don't wish for night to come,
             ing;   the time when nations will perish.
         and let not the greatness of the ran-   21   Be careful not to turn to evil;
             som turn you aside.   your suffering was sent to keep you
19   Will your cry avail to keep you from   from it.
             distress,
         or all the force of your strength?
20   Do not long for the night,

when peoples are cut off in their place.
21 Take heed, do not turn to iniquity,
for this you have chosen rather than
affliction.

Verses 16-21 are extremely difficult to interpret and, as Rowley says, "scarcely any two interpreters are agreed as to their meaning." In verses 16-25 Elihu applies to Job's situation the principle expressed in verse 15, that God uses suffering to teach the sufferer.

Subdivision Heading

The Handbook heading may be modified to say, for example, "Job, God is punishing you as you deserve," "Job, God is trying to keep you from evil," or "Job, the wicked deserve to be punished." Habel has "Admonition to Job," Rowley (verses 16-25) "Elihu applies the principle to Job."

36.16 RSV	TEV
He also allured you out of distress into a broad place where there was no cramping, and what was set on your table was full of fatness.	God brought you out of trouble, and let you enjoy security; your table was piled high with food.

There are three lines in verse 16 instead of the usual two, and the division between the first two is uncertain.

He also allured you out of distress has no specific subject, but TEV and RSV are no doubt correct in making God the subject. **Allured** translates a verb whose tense does not make clear whether Elihu is describing Job's past experience, as in RSV, or some future possibility, as in NIV, "He is wooing you from the jaws of distress." **Allured** translates the same verb used in 2.3, where God says that Satan "moved me" (RSV), "persuaded me" (TEV). In Deuteronomy 13.6 the same verb is translated by RSV as "entices." Some interpreters consider it unlikely that God is the subject if this verb is used in its usual sense of "entice." Some take the subject to be **a broad place** in line b. Accordingly Mft translates "your wide freedom has beguiled you." **Out of distress** is literally "from the mouth of distress." Some change this to get "wealth," and so "wealth has enticed you" or "riches have seduced you." Dhorme understands the verb rendered **allured** to mean "remove," and regards it as a movement to a more specific term than the general verb **deliver** in verse 15a. He translates "and similarly he will remove you from the jaws of trouble." This is similar to TEV "God brought you out of trouble" and is recommended.

Into a broad place translates a single Hebrew word which has been rendered "expanse, freedom, abundance, amplitude" and is followed by **where there was no cramping,** which is literally simply "no cramping" and has the apparent sense of "unconfined, without restriction." Then the Hebrew adds "instead of it" or "beneath it." Dhorme transfers "instead of it" to the beginning of line b and makes line b contrast with **distress**: "instead of it (trouble), you will enjoy unrestricted abundance." TEV understands **a broad place** to refer to security and translates "and let you enjoy security." This is as good a guess as any, and far better than referring to unlimited space, as in RSV and others. This line may also be rendered "and takes good care of you" or "and provides for your needs."

And what was set on your table was full of fatness: set is uncertain. The word is used in Isaiah 30.15, where it means "quietness or resting." Dhorme gives it the meaning of "filled," "And your table will be filled . . . ." TEV has "Your table was piled high . . . ." **Fatness** in this context refers to rich food, as in Isaiah 55.2, where TEV translates "the best food of all." Although TEV is recommended as a suitable model for translating verse 16, Rowley offers a different one in which wealth is the subject in line a: "Wealth hath enticed thee, unlimited abundance behind thee, thy table loaded with rich food." Another possibility is "God took away your misfortune; in its place he gave you all you could want, and even your table was loaded with the richest foods."

36.17   RSV   TEV

"But you are full of the judgment   But now you are being punished
    on the wicked;   as you deserve.
judgment and justice seize you.

RSV suggests that Elihu is accusing Job of judging the wicked. But Job has done the contrary; he has argued that there is no one judging the wicked, and so they not only escape punishment, they thrive. Therefore it seems more probable that Elihu is condemning Job because he did not act justly when he had the power to do so, and therefore Job has brought his suffering on himself.

But you are full of judgment on the wicked is literally "but the wicked's judgment (condemnation, punishment, sentence) you have filled up." TEV reduces the two lines of this verse to one and understands them to be a statement by Elihu that punishment has caught up with Job. HOTTP relates verse 16c to verse 17a, so that the table that is full of food parallels Job's being full of the judgment that is for the wicked. The sense here is probably not to be taken that Job is judging, condemning the wicked, but that the punishment, judgment, condemnation due the wicked has come fully to Job. The context of verses 15-21 is about powerful people like Job who have been reduced to weakness, and who may be tempted to trust in their past glory. NIV attempts to keep the sense of being **full of judgment** by translating "But now you are laden with the judgment due the wicked." We may also say, for example, "But now you are getting the full punishment that other wicked people get."

Judgment and justice seize you: seize has no object, and most translations supply **you**, as in RSV. FRCL, which gives the sense of TEV but also retains both lines, says "However, you have been condemned, and the sentence which is handed to you is without appeal." The model of FRCL may have to be expressed differently in some languages; for example, "God has condemned you to suffer, and you cannot escape the punishment he gives you."

36.18 RSV TEV

Beware lest wrath entice you into scoffing; and let not the greatness of the ransom turn you aside.	Be careful not to let bribes deceive you, or riches lead you astray.

This verse is probably best understood as a warning against corruption and injustice. **Beware lest wrath entice you into scoffing: wrath** translates a word which normally has that meaning in the Old Testament. KJV understands it to refer to God's wrath, but RSV takes it to be Job's anger. However, there is no indication here as to what may call forth Job's anger. The noun translated **wrath** is feminine, but the verb form of **entice** is masculine. Moreover, as they stand, there is no apparent relation between the lines. Therefore the interpretation of the first line must depend upon the understanding of the second line, which is much clearer, referring as it does to corruption from bribes. Some interpreters recognize the word translated **wrath** in line a as a form of the verb "to see," and so translate as TEV "Be careful." RSV, which retains **wrath**, supplies **Beware** translationally. **Scoffing** translates a word which may mean either "sufficiency" as in 20.22, or "clap" as in 27.23. It is the second sense which gives RSV **scoffing**. Most translations take the first meaning and translate "riches, wealth, money," as in TEV. So Elihu's warning to Job is "Be careful not to let money deceive you."

And let not the greatness of the ransom turn you aside gives the impression that someone is being held for payment of ransom. **Ransom** here means "bribe." It translates a word meaning "to cover." It is used in Genesis 32.21, in which Jacob "covers Esau's face" with gifts to appease him. It is used in 1 Samuel 12.3, in which Samuel asks "from whose hand have I taken a bribe to blind my eyes with it?" See also Proverbs 6.35; Amos 5.12. **Turn you aside** means "corrupt you." TEV has shifted "bribes" to the first line for stylistic purposes. This line may be rendered, for example, "and don't let bribery corrupt you" or "and don't be corrupted by people paying you bribe money."

36.19 RSV TEV

Will your cry avail to keep you from distress, or all the force of your strength?	It will do you no good to cry out for help; all your strength can't help you now.

Dhorme rejects verses 19 and 20 as the comments of copyists. The interpretations of these verses and the changes proposed to give them sense are probably as numerous as there are translations. The Hebrew form is a rhetorical question assuming a negative answer. TEV has expressed this as a negative statement.

Will your cry avail to keep you from distress: your cry translates a word which elsewhere has the meaning "riches," and KJV translates "Will he esteem thy riches?" The word translated **avail** means "set in order, or compare," as used in Isaiah 40.18, and so "be equal to," and this is the sense of TEV "help you now."

From distress in the Hebrew is literally "not in (or, from) distress." Pope keeps **from distress**, but makes a small change from the Hebrew for "not" to get "to him" and translates "Will your opulence (wealth) avail with him in trouble?" This can be expressed in another way, "Will your wealth have any influence on God when you are in trouble?" As can be seen, translations differ as to **your cry** or "wealth" as the subject of this line. The word rendered **from distress** can be assigned other vowels in Hebrew to give "gold," as used in 22.24. FRCL reflects the latter change with "Neither your goods nor your gold will be sufficient . . . ." HOTTP accepts either "cry" or "fortune," and either "in distress" or "gold," as possible choices on which to base a translation. And so the thought is that Job's plea or his wealth will be no help to escape his troubles, which have been brought on by his own sin.

Or all the force of your strength merely strengthens the first line as another thing which cannot help Job, and is well translated by TEV. TEV's translation of verse 19 can be adapted to the notion of wealth in line a by saying, for example, "Your wealth will do you no good; all your strength can't help you now." This gives a suitable translation model for this verse.

36.20   RSV   TEV

> Do not long for the night,   Don't wish for night to come,
>   when peoples are cut off in   the time when nations will
>   their place.   perish.

Do not long for the night: Elihu appears to be telling Job that it will do him no good to curse the night in which he was conceived (3.3-8). It is also possible that **night** is used by Elihu to refer to death. Job asked in 3.16 why he was not hidden (died at birth) as an infant that never sees the light. Most translators agree with RSV and TEV. In Hebrew there is no structural link between the two lines, but **when** has been supplied by RSV, and "the time when" by TEV.

Peoples are cut off translates "peoples go up," which has a close parallel in Psalm 102.24, which TEV translates "take me away." **In their place** may also be rendered "on the spot" or in this context "suddenly." HOTTP's rendering can be adjusted to say, "Do not long for the night (death) to come, the time when the nations will suddenly disappear."

36.21   RSV   TEV

> Take heed, do not turn to iniq-   Be careful not to turn to evil;
>   uity,   your suffering was sent to keep
>   for this you have chosen rath-   you from it.
>   er than affliction.

Take heed, do not turn to iniquity echoes verse 18 as another warning. The first line is clear enough. **Turn to iniquity** means "to do evil deeds, become evil." Stated positively the sense is "avoid sin, get rid of evil ways, turn your back on wrongdoing."

In the second line **this** refers back to **iniquity** in the first line. The verb **chosen** can also have the meaning of "test or prove," particularly in the Aramaic sense. Dhorme translates "It is because of that that you have been tried by affliction." In order to keep Job from evil, he is being tested by suffering. TEV expresses this notion clearly as "Your suffering was sent to keep you from it," that is, to keep Job from doing evil.

8E-4. Elihu asks Job to remember how great God is (36.22-25)

	RSV		TEV
22	Behold, God is exalted in his power; who is a teacher like him?	22	Remember how great is God's power; he is the greatest teacher of all.
23	Who has prescribed for him his way, or who can say, 'Thou hast done wrong'?	23	No one can tell God what to do or accuse him of doing evil.
24	"Remember to extol his work, of which men have sung.	24	He has always been praised for what he does; you also must praise him.
25	All men have looked on it; man beholds it from afar.	25	Everyone has seen what he has done; but we can only watch from a distance.

In verses 22-25 Elihu now reminds Job of the purpose of suffering which his sin has brought on him, and how God is teaching him through it.

Subdivision Heading

The Handbook heading may be reworded to say, for example, "Job, you should praise God," "Remember how great and good God is," or "Elihu reminds Job how great God is."

36.22	RSV	TEV
	Behold, God is exalted in his power; who is a teacher like him?	**Remember how great is God's power; he is the greatest teacher of all.**

Behold, God is exalted in his power: **Behold** is Elihu's attention-getter for important messages to follow. "Look," "Listen," "See how" are some equivalents in English. TEV has "Remember." **Exalted** translates a verb form meaning "to be very high" in terms of honor. Dhorme translates "sublime," TEV "great," and NEB renders the line "God towers in majesty above us." FRCL has "Yes, God is sovereign, he has such power."

Who is a teacher like him? This rhetorical question can be expressed "what teacher can compare with him?" This question is expressed as a statement by TEV. NJB uses a verb phrase: "Who can teach lessons as he does?"

36.23   RSV   TEV

Who has prescribed for him his   No one can tell God what to do
   way,   or accuse him of doing evil.
or who can say, 'Thou hast
   done wrong'?

Who has prescribed for him his way . . . ? is the first of two rhetorical
questions in this verse, both of which TEV expresses as statements. The first question
follows the form of the question Elihu asked in 34.13, except for the final word.
However, here the sense of the verb is "assigned, given," or, using the words of TEV
as a rhetorical question, "Who can tell God what to do?" The answer expected is
"No one." And so TEV has "No one can tell God what to do."

Since no one has the right to tell God how he should act, the implication of the
second line is that God cannot be accused of failing to act in the right way. This line
in Hebrew is to be taken as direct address: **who can say, 'Thou hast done wrong'?**
Whether it is rendered as direct or indirect address will depend upon the best style
in the receptor language. The implication for Job is that he should not criticize God
for causing him to suffer, but instead he should try to understand what God is
seeking to teach him. Verse 23 may also be expressed, for example, "Who can tell
God what to do? No one! Or who can say to God 'You have done wrong'? No one!"

36.24   RSV   TEV

"Remember to extol his work,   He has always been praised for
   of which men have sung.   what he does;
                                            you also must praise him.

Following Elihu's advice, **Remember to extol his work**, would be wiser than
criticizing God for being unjust. **Extol** translates a verb meaning "to magnify, make
great, increase." The sense is "to praise, speak greatly of." **His work** is literally "his
doings" and relates to the same verb used in verse 23b. FRCL translates "Don't forget
to celebrate what he has done."

Of which men have sung refers to such people as the psalmist and poets who
have sung God's praises, taking as their theme the wondrous works of God. TEV
transposes the two lines for a more logical order and translates "praise" in both
lines. Another rendering, for example, is "Remember to praise God for what he has
done for us, things for which people sing his praises"; or, if the lines are transposed,
"People have always sung his praises. You too should remember to praise him for
what he has done."

36.25   RSV   TEV

All men have looked on it;   Everyone has seen what he has
   man beholds it from afar.   done;

> **but we can only watch from a distance.**^m

^m but we can only watch from a distance; *or* no one understands it at all.

All men have looked on it: it refers to the work of God in 24a. The subject in both lines of verse 25 is "mankind," and the verb in each line means "see." Line <u>a</u> may be rendered "Everyone sees God's work." The second line **man beholds it from afar** is better expressed in the TEV text than in the margin, "but we can only watch from a distance." If "everyone" is used in line <u>a</u>, "they" may be appropriate in line <u>b</u>. The idea is that human beings see God's works, but only imperfectly. Verse 25 may also be expressed "Everyone has seen the things God has made, but they have only seen them from a great distance."

8E-5. Elihu describes God's activity in the storm (36.26–37.13)

RSV	TEV
26 Behold, God is great, and we know him not; the number of his years is unsearchable.	26 We cannot fully know his greatness or count the number of his years.
27 For he draws up the drops of water, he distils his mist in rain	27 It is God who takes water from the earth and turns it into drops of rain.
28 which the skies pour down, and drop upon man abundantly.	28 He lets the rain pour from the clouds in showers for all mankind.
29 Can any one understand the spreading of the clouds, the thunderings of his pavilion?	29 No one knows how the clouds move or how the thunder roars through the sky, where God dwells.
30 Behold, he scatters his lightning about him, and covers the roots of the sea.	30 He sends lightning through all the sky, but the depths of the sea remain dark.
31 For by these he judges peoples; he gives food in abundance.	31 This is how he feeds the people and provides an abundance of food.
32 He covers his hands with the lightning, and commands it to strike the mark.	32 He seizes the lightning with his hands and commands it to hit the mark.
33 Its crashing declares concerning him, who is jealous with anger against iniquity.	33 Thunder announces the approaching storm, and the cattle know it is coming.
Chapter 37	*Chapter 37*
1 "At this also my heart trembles, and leaps out of its place.	1 The storm makes my heart beat wildly.
2 Hearken to the thunder of his voice and the rumbling that comes from his mouth.	2 Listen, all of you, to the voice of God, to the thunder that comes from his mouth.
3 Under the whole heaven he lets it go, and his lightning to the corners of the earth.	3 He sends the lightning across the sky, from one end of the earth to the other.
4 After it his voice roars; he thunders with his majestic voice and he does not restrain the lightnings	4 Then the roar of his voice is heard, the majestic sound of thunder, and all the while the lightning flashes.
	5 At God's command amazing things happen, wonderful things that we can't understand.

	when his voice is heard.	6	He commands snow to fall on the earth,
5	God thunders wondrously with his voice;		and sends torrents of drenching rain.
	he does great things which we cannot	7	He brings the work of men to a stop;
	comprehend.		he shows them what he can do.
6	For to the snow he says, 'Fall on the	8	The wild animals go to their dens.
	earth';	9	The storm winds come from the south,
	and to the shower and the rain, 'Be		and the biting cold from the north.
	strong.'	10	The breath of God freezes the waters,
7	He seals up the hand of every man,		and turns them to solid ice.
	that all men may know his work.	11	Lightning flashes from the clouds,
8	Then the beasts go into their lairs,	12	as they move at God's will.
	and remain in their dens.		They do all that God commands,
9	From its chamber comes the whirlwind,		everywhere throughout the world.
	and cold from the scattering winds.	13	God sends rain to water the earth;
10	By the breath of God ice is given,		he may send it to punish men,
	and the broad waters are frozen fast.		or to show them his favor.
11	He loads the thick cloud with moisture;		
	the clouds scatter his lightning.		
12	They turn round and round by his guidance,		
	to accomplish all that he commands them		
	on the face of the habitable world.		
13	Whether for correction, or for his land,		
	or for love, he causes it to happen.		

Beginning in verse 26 and continuing through chapter 37 verse 13 Elihu describes to Job the greatness of God as seen in nature, and verse 26 is the introduction to this section.

Subdivision Heading

The Handbook heading for this part may be modified to say, for example, "God sends storms upon the earth," "God sends down thunder and lightning," or "God commands the storms." Habel has "Interpreting storms from El (part 1)," and Rowley "God's work in nature."

36.26   RSV   TEV

Behold, God is great, and we   **We cannot fully know his great-**
   know him not;   **ness**
the number of his years is   **or count the number of his**
   unsearchable.   **years.**

Behold, God is great, and we know him not seems strange, since it denies that God is known at all. Dhorme says that the Hebrew, literally "we do not know," implies that the object is that which has just been stated. In other words, "God is great, and (or, but) we do not know how great." FRCL follows this suggestion: "Yes, God is great, so great that one has no idea." TEV is less explicit, with "We cannot fully know his greatness." Another model is "God is so great that we cannot know him completely."

The number of his years is unsearchable emphasizes how it is impossible to count God's age in human years, which is comparable to Psalm 102.27b, "and thy years have no end." This line may be rendered, for example, "We cannot count his years," "We cannot figure how many years God has lived," or "We cannot tell how old God is."

36.27-28 RSV	TEV
27 For he draws up the drops of water, he^c distils his mist in rain	27 It is God who takes water from the earth and turns it into drops of rain.
28 which the skies pour down, and drop upon man abundantly.	28 He lets the rain pour from the clouds in showers for all mankind.

^c Cn: Heb *they distil*

These two verses describe, first how rain is formed, and then how it comes down. Verse 27 is uncertain, and translations differ greatly in the way they handle it.

For he draws up the drops of water describes how God takes drops of water and causes them to go up to where he is thought to be. Some scholars make a change in the word **water** to get "from the sea." This, however, is unnecessary. TEV's translation "takes water from the earth" is not a change in the text but an attempt to say from where God takes the drops of water. The implication may be that God gets the water from the earth according to the description in Genesis 2.6, "a mist went up from the earth." It is sufficient to say "He (God) draws up to himself, lifts up, drops of water," or as GECL says, "He draws drops of water up to heaven."

He distils his mist in rain is literally "they distil," as the RSV footnote says. **He** refers to God, but the Hebrew "they" refers to the **drops of water** in the previous line. Thus "He draws the waterdrops that distil rain from the flood," and in verse 28a "that trickle from the clouds." **Distils** translates a transitive verb meaning "to filter, refine," and is used in 28.1 referring to refining gold. Many translations, including RSV and TEV, change to the singular subject, referring to God. Pope argues that **his mist** refers to the reservoir of underground water in Genesis 2.6, and translates "flood." Since it is God who is being praised for his ways in nature, it is probably best to make God the subject, as in RSV and TEV, and translate "and God turns the drops of water into rain."

Which the skies pour down begins with a relative particle referring to the drops of rain in verse 27b. **Skies** translates "clouds." **Pour** is plural in Hebrew and has "clouds" as its subject. The sense is "The clouds pour down the rain." TEV supplies God as the agent, "He lets the rain pour from the clouds," which most likely expresses the poet's thought.

And drop upon man abundantly: abundantly translates a word which most interpreters take to be an adjective rather than an adverb; they then translate, for example, "upon many men." However, Pope argues that the expression is an alternative form of the word translated "showers" in Deuteronomy 32.2; and since the Hebrew *'adam* "man" is a variant form of the word *'adamah* meaning "earth," he therefore translates "pour on the ground in showers." This suits the context better than TEV "in showers for all mankind." However, it is not possible to eliminate the interpretation of RSV or TEV, and so a wide range of choice is given for translation. In some cases translators may have to follow the interpretation of a major language Bible, provided that translation contains one of the suitable choices. Verse 28 may also be rendered "He makes the clouds send down rain that showers the earth" or "He makes the clouds send down rain upon people everywhere."

36.29 RSV	TEV
Can any one understand the spreading of the clouds, the thunderings of his pavilion?	No one knows how the clouds move or how the thunder roars through the sky, where God dwells.

Dhorme, NAB, NEB, NJB, BJ, Pope, Mft place verse 31 after verse 28, where it fits much better. This Handbook recommends that translators move verse 31 to this position, so that the order of verses will be: 28, 31, 29, 30, 32. It may be advisable to number this group of verses "28-32." If the traditional order of verses is retained, an alternative suggestion is given in the discussion of verse 31. The Hebrew text of verse 29a begins with "also," since Elihu is posing an additional rhetorical question.

Can anyone understand the spread of the clouds assumes a negative answer. **Spread** translates a verb meaning "stretch out" and is used in 26.9, where God is said to spread clouds over the face of the moon. In this context it refers to the drifting motion of the clouds. TEV expresses this line as a negative statement: "No one knows how the clouds move." Verse 29 may be rendered as a question: "Can anyone understand how God makes the clouds move across the sky, or how the thunder roars across the heavens where God lives? No one!"

The thunderings of his pavilion translates the Hebrew literally, but most readers will get little of its significance. **Thunderings** here refers to the noise made by lightning in a storm. The word for **pavilion** is used in 27.18, where it refers to the hut of a watchman. Here the reference is to God's abode in heaven, as in Psalm 18.11, "his canopy thick clouds dark with water." In order to make this line clear, TEV has used two lines to translate what in Hebrew is two words. TEV has expressed **thunderings** as a verb phrase, and **pavilion** as "the sky, where God dwells."

36.30 RSV	TEV
Behold, he scatters his lightning about him, and covers the roots of the sea.	He sends lightning through all the sky, but the depths of the sea remain dark.

Behold, he scatters his lightning about him: scatters is the same verb translated **spreading** in verse 29. The word translated **lightning** usually means "light." Dhorme adjusts it to get "mist," but in the context **lightning** is more appropriate. **About him** probably implies "the place where he dwells," and so TEV has "through all the sky." The line may also be translated "He makes the lightning strike all around him" or "He sends bolts of lightning flashing across the skies."

And covers the roots of the sea is a line that is translated in countless ways. The expression **roots of the sea** is found nowhere else in the Old Testament. Roots are associated with mountains in 28.9. Since the expression makes little sense, particularly in relation to the first line, many changes have been proposed. For example, NJB follows one change that gives "covers the tops of the mountains." Dhorme, who shows contrast between the two lines, adequately translates the Hebrew text without change, "and has veiled the depths of the sea," with which TEV agrees: "but the depths of the sea remain dark." This line may be rendered, for example, "he covers the sea with darkness" or "he covers the sea and leaves it dark."

36.31 RSV	TEV
For by these he judges peoples; he gives food in abundance.	This is how he feeds[n] the people and provides an abundance of food.

> [n] *Probable text* feeds; *Hebrew* judges.

See suggestion at beginning of verse 29.

For by these he judges people: as it stands in the traditional order, **these** seems to refer back to **roots of the sea** in verse 30b, and this is obviously not correct. Therefore, if the translator is keeping the numerical verse order, some adjustment should be made; for example, "It is by sending rain that . . . ." **Judges**, as in RSV, translates the usual meaning of the Hebrew word, but this gives a poor parallel with the second line. Therefore many translators change this word to one meaning "he feeds or nourishes," as the TEV footnote shows.

He gives food in abundance is parallel to the first line in its adjusted form. Verse 31 may be rendered, for example, "It is by means of the rains that he nourishes people and gives them plenty to eat."

36.32 RSV	TEV
He covers his hands with the lightning, and commands it to strike the mark.	He seizes the lightning with his hands and commands it to hit the mark.

Verses 32-33 are uncertain in meaning, as can be seen by comparing translations.

He covers his hands with the lightning is literally "upon hands he covers light." The word **covers** leaves the picture unclear as to what God actually does. Line b seems to require his hurling the light from his hands, and so TEV has expressed the idea clearly with "seizes." **Lightning** is again "light," just as in verse 30a. FRCL attempts to retain the thought of **covers**, with "He conceals the lightning in his two hands."

And commands it to strike the mark describes how God, as if he were a storm king, orders the lightning to strike where he wants. **Mark** or "target" is the same word used in 7.20. It is recommended that translators follow TEV, which may also be expressed "He grabs the lighting in his hands and makes it strike where he commands it."

36.33   RSV   TEV

> Its crashing declares concerning   Thunder announces the ap-
>   him,   proaching storm,
>   who is jealous with anger   and the cattle know it is com-
>   against iniquity.   ing.

Its crashing declares concerning him is literally "Its noise declares concerning him." In the light of the literal rendering, it is not surprising that a very great number of changes have been proposed. RSV sees the storm as the instrument of God's anger. Rather than deal with the many kinds of proposals for change and translations this verse has produced, in the interest of brevity and clarity it will be better to eliminate nearly all of these and follow the recommendations of HOTTP, which are basically in agreement with TEV. HOTTP defends the Hebrew text as it stands, saying that the consonantal text is certain because all the ancient versions are based on that form of the text. The vowel marking that has been added implies a different understanding of the consonantal text from that of the early versions. The suggested rendering of HOTTP can be adapted as follows: "The noise of the thunder warns that a storm is coming." This agrees basically with TEV's "Thunder announces the approaching storm." Either of these may serve as a translation model. In some languages it may be necessary to say "When people hear the noise of thunder they know a storm is coming."

Who is jealous with anger against iniquity represents a form that is changed from the literal text "cattle also concerning what rises." RSV follows a change from "cattle" to get "one who incites passion," and another change from "concerning what rises" to a word meaning "evil." In this way RSV accepts two changes proposed by Pope. Here again HOTTP suggests the Hebrew text can yield an appropriate sense: "the cattle too (announce) the rising (storm). In other words "and the cattle also show that a storm is coming" or "and the cattle too know a storm is blowing up." This agrees with TEV "and the cattle know it is coming."

37.1   RSV   TEV

> "At this also my heart trembles,   The storm makes my heart beat
>   and leaps out of its place.   wildly.

At this also my heart trembles continues without interruption from 36.33. **This** refers to the thunderstorm in the previous verse, which TEV makes clear by saying "The storm." **Also** establishes the connection structurally. The Septuagint has "your heart," but the Hebrew "my heart," referring to Elihu's heart, is to be followed. The word translated **trembles** is used in the causative form in 11.19, where it is translated "make you afraid" (RSV). The sense here is "quiver, shake" and, in relation to the heart, suggests the spasms of the heart at moments of fear and excitement.

And leaps out of its place refers to the action of the heart, which now goes beyond what it did in line a. The heart is described as "leaping, jumping," and **out of its place** means "out of the chest." The use of the metaphor in the second line intensifies the image of the trembling heart in line a. The intensification in the second line along with the figurative expression may be expressed in English, for example, as "My heart trembles, in fact it beats wildly." TEV, as is frequently the case, disregards intensification in parallelism, reduces the two lines to one, and uses a single verb, "makes my heart beat wildly." In translation it will normally be necessary to make clear that it is the storm in the previous verse that causes the heart to tremble. In some languages other figures express the idea of fear; for example, "The storm makes my liver move" or ". . . my innermost to rebel." Translators must follow the devices of their own language to show intensification when it is appropriate.

37.2   RSV   TEV

Hearken to the thunder of his
    voice
  and the rumbling that comes
    from his mouth.

Listen, all of you, to the voice of
    God,
  to the thunder that comes
    from his mouth.

Hearken to the thunder of his voice: Elihu invites all his hearers, since the verb translated **Hearken**, that is, "Listen," is in the plural, and so TEV has "Listen, all of you." **Thunder** translates a word meaning "trouble, agitation, anger." It is used in 3.17,26; 14.1, where it is translated "trouble." In 28.26 "thunder" is the voice of God. The second line makes clear that this word as used in line a means **thunder**. In line b the noun translated **rumbling** is found elsewhere only in Ezekiel 2.10, where RSV translates "mourning." In Isaiah 31.4 the verb is used of the growling of a lion. The two lines of this verse are parallel in meaning, with little intensification in the second line. TEV keeps both lines but reduces **thunder** and **rumblings** to "thunder" and places it in the second line. In Psalm 29 the voice of the LORD is associated with thunder, lightning, and storms. **Thunder of his voice** may be rendered "the thunder which is God's voice," "His voice which is like thunder," or "the thunder in which God speaks." The second line may also be rendered "Listen how he roars with his mouth," "Hear him roar," or "He roars like a lion when he speaks."

37.3   RSV   TEV

> Under the whole heaven he lets it
>   go,
>   and his lightning to the cor-
>   ners of the earth.

> He sends the lightning across the
>   sky,
>   from one end of the earth to
>   the other.

Under the whole heaven he lets it go describes how God makes it thunder and lightning everywhere. **Under the whole heaven** depicts the extent of the lightning flashes as seen from a human viewpoint on the ground. **It** in line a most likely refers to the lightning in line b, based on the way pronouns function in Hebrew discourse, and so TEV has "He sends the lightning . . . ." NEB and others, however, take **It** to refer to the thunder of verse 2. **Lets go** translates a verb meaning "looses, releases," and so "sends" in TEV. A verb such as "throws, hurls, casts" is also appropriate.

In English **lightning** in line b fits best when shifted to line a to replace the pronoun, and if necessary the pronoun may be used in line b. **Lightning** is literally "light," as in 36.32. **Corners** translates a word which means "fringes or borders," as in the borders of a carpet. The earth is thought of as flat, like a carpet that has four edges, borders, and corners. The expression may be rendered "the ends of the earth," "from one end of the earth to the other," or "all across the earth."

37.4   RSV   TEV

> After it his voice roars;
>   he thunders with his majestic
>   voice
>   and he does not restrain the
>   lightnings[d] when his voice is
>   heard.

> Then the roar of his voice is
>   heard,
>   the majestic sound of thunder,
>   and all the while the lightning
>   flashes.

[d] Heb *them*

After it his voice roars: After it refers to the time following the lightning flash in verse 3; this is better rendered "Then" by TEV. The poet recognizes the cause and effect relation of lightning and thunder. **Roar** translates a word rendered "groanings" in 3.24 and "roar" in 4.10. The voice is that of God, and so "Then God's voice roars." In line b **he thunders with** describes the kind of voice that creates the roar. The voice is said to be **majestic**, which in Hebrew often means "exalted, excellent," and is often used in parallel with "powerful." Due to the repetitions of thunder and voice, it may be possible to combine lines a and b; for example, "Then God's voice thunders powerfully."

In the third line **he does not restrain the lightnings** describes how God does not hold the lightning back, but rather releases it, sends it out. The RSV footnote indicates that the Hebrew has "them" where RSV has **lightnings**. This represents an interpretation of the plural object suffix on the Hebrew verb **restrain**. RSV here follows Dhorme, who considers this a change, but it is more properly a translational matter, making **the lightnings** explicit. **When his voice is heard** is considered by TEV to be a variation of a repeated thought that is becoming stylistically heavy. Accordingly TEV substitutes "all the while" before "the lightning flashes." **When his voice is heard** may be taken as referring to the simultaneous action of thunder and lightning, and so we may translate the second part of the verse, for example, "and at the same time he sends out flashes of lightning."

37.5	RSV	TEV
	God thunders wondrously with his voice; he does great things which we cannot comprehend.	At God's command amazing things happen, wonderful things that we can't understand.

God thunders wondrously with his voice is changed by some scholars on the basis that **thunders** has been repeated too often, but it may be best to allow Elihu to use his own repetitious style. **Wondrously** describes the reaction of the ones who hear it. Therefore it may be best to translate, for example, "God makes thunder with his voice, and it is amazing to hear it" or "When God speaks, it sounds like thunder, and it is an awesome noise to hear."

He does great things which we cannot comprehend: this line is a general statement, whereas the previous line is specific. This is the reverse of typical parallelism. Hebrew poetic style prefers the general statement to be given first. In actual fact TEV's rendering of these lines thoroughly mixes the segments of the two lines rather than transposing the lines. There is no reference to **thunder** nor to **voice**, and so on the whole TEV's translation is not recommended. It is probably best to understand line b, not as a parallel to line a, but rather as a transition to the following verses, which go on to speak of God's ways of working in nature other than through thunder and lightning. RSV can serve as a model for translating this line.

37.6	RSV	TEV
	For to the snow he says, 'Fall on the earth'; and to the shower and the rain,[e] 'Be strong.'	He commands snow to fall on the earth, and sends torrents of drenching rain.

[e] Cn Compare Syr: Heb *shower of rain and shower of rains*

For to the snow he says, 'Fall on the earth' depicts God as commanding the snow to fall. RSV and others use direct address, although TEV prefers the indirect form. Translators should use the form that is most natural in the receptor language. **Fall** translates a verb which has the meaning "to be" but is used here in its Aramaic form, and it is used similarly in Arabic. This line may be expressed "God says to the snow, 'Fall down to earth,'" or "God orders the snow, 'Snow on the earth.'"

Translated indirectly it can be "God orders the snow to fall on the ground." Since the snow can only fall earthward, it is sufficient to say, for example, "God orders the snow to fall" or "God orders it to snow." In languages where **snow** is unknown, it may be necessary to use a borrowed word or to substitute something like frost, hail, or mist.

And to the shower and the rain, 'Be strong' is literally "shower or rain and shower of rains of his strength." RSV gives the literal form in its footnote and adjusts the translation as shown. Syriac omits the second of these expressions, "shower of rains," and three Hebrew manuscripts omit the first expression but keep the second one. Dhorme takes these expressions to be redundant and translates "torrential rains." TEV follows this with "torrents of drenching rain." **Be strong** is obtained by changing the Hebrew vowels for "of his strength." This gives a parallel to the command in line a. GECL translates the parallel lines "To the snow he commands: 'Fall downward to the ground!' To the rain clouds he says: 'Let it pour!'" This provides a translation model that can be adapted.

37.7

RSV	TEV
He seals up the hand of every man, that all men may know his work.^f	He brings the work of men to a stop; he shows them what he can do.^o

^f Vg Compare Syr Tg: Heb *that all men whom he has made may know it*

^o *One ancient translation* them what he can do; *Hebrew* this to those whom he has made.

He seals up the hand of every man: verse 7 is interpreted and translated in various ways. RSV gives a literal translation whose probable meaning is that God prevents people from working, by causing it to rain and snow. Agricultural work in the fields is interrupted by the weather. TEV makes this clear by avoiding the figurative language. NEB has "He shuts every man fast indoors." This involves making a change in the Hebrew word for **hand**, and taking the word translated **seals up** to mean "close up," as it is used in Jeremiah 32.11 and Daniel 12.4.

That all men may know his work is literally "that all men of his work may know." The traditional Hebrew text uses a form that means "men of his work," that is, men whom he has made. Some scholars believe the last letter of the Hebrew for "men" was lost when the text was copied because it is the same as the first letter of the next word. In that case the text would say "that all men may know of his work." The RSV footnote gives the first meaning as representing the Hebrew text. The RSV text follows the opinion of the scholars so as to represent the second meaning, to which TEV agrees. The wording **all men** (TEV "them") has an added advantage in that it permits the parallelism of **every man** in line a and **all men** in line b. NEB follows an interpretation of the verb translated **know** to mean "rest," as in 20.20 "his greed knew no rest." And so NEB translates "and all men whom he has made must stand idle." Another possibility is "that every person may rest from his work." This suggestion provides an excellent parallel with line a, provided that line a is understood to mean "He brings the work of people to a stop" because of the rain and snow in verse 6. The TEV translation may be followed; however, the preferred rendering is "He brings all the work people do to a stop so that all may rest from their work."

37.8 RSV TEV

Then the beasts go into their
lairs,
and remain in their dens.

The wild animals go to their
dens.

Then the beasts go into their lairs explains that resting from work applies also to the wild animals. **Beasts** refers to wild animals in general, as in 5.23; 39.15; 40.20. **Lairs** is a noun based on a verb meaning "to ambush." It implies a hidden place where the animal stays concealed from view.

And remain in their dens depicts the animals as staying for a period of time inside and protected from the stormy weather. **Den** translates the plural of a word meaning "abode," a more general term than the one used in line <u>a</u>. TEV reduces these two lines to one with no significant loss of meaning or poetic effect. Verse 8 may also be rendered, for example, "The wild animals go into their dens and stay there through the storm."

37.9 RSV TEV

From its chamber comes the
whirlwind,
and cold from the scattering
winds.

The storm winds come from the
south,
and the biting cold from the
north.

From its chamber comes the whirlwind is the poet's way of speaking of the area, region, zone out of which winds blow. In 9.9 the expression used is "chamber of the south," in which the word for south occurs. Some interpreters understand **the chamber** here to refer to the same place as the more specific "chamber of the south" in 9.9. This is followed by Dhorme, TEV, FRCL, SPCL, NJB, BJ, and Mft. RSV and others use only **chamber**. TEV does not refer to a place which **chamber** represents, but refers to the direction only, which is the natural manner of speaking of winds in English. FRCL translates similarly, with "From the south comes the hurricane." **Whirlwind**, which may refer more generally to "hurricane, tempest, storm winds," is used in 21.18; 27.20. It is recommended that translators follow TEV, since RSV makes the thought somewhat vague. We may also say more poetically than TEV "Out of the south where they live come the storm winds." This thought will be expressed in some languages according to local geography; for example, "From down river where the winds come, they begin to blow."

And cold from the scattering winds translates two words in Hebrew, literally "from the scatterers cold." "The scatterers" may be handled as in RSV. However, Dhorme cites the Koran as using the same term to refer to the north winds that scatter the rain. While the words "south" and "north" do not occur in either line of verse 9, in some languages directions are the only recognized manner of speaking of winds. In such cases FRCL may be followed, which translates the whole of verse 9 "From the south comes the hurricane, from the north the cold." It is possible to stick closer to the Hebrew form, but this should not be done at the expense of clarity.

37.10   RSV   TEV

> By the breath of God ice is given,   The breath of God freezes the
>   and the broad waters are froz-   waters,
>   en fast.   and turns them to solid ice.

By the breath of God ice is given depicts ice as being formed by God's breath. In this case the cold north wind of verse 9b is pictured as **the breath of God. And the broad waters are frozen fast** translates "and the expanse of waters with narrowness." The word rendered **are frozen fast** may come from either of two Hebrew verbs. The one is "narrows," as suggested by the literal rendering. The other is used of a molten metal becoming a solid mass. It is the latter sense which applies here, as in TEV, "turns to solid ice." TEV has shifted "waters" to line a. However, we may translate as in FRCL, "God breathes, and the ice takes form; the surface of the water hardens like metal." In some languages **ice** is unknown and is expressed, if at all, with a borrowed word. In some cases it will be preferable to speak of the degree of cold; for example, "The breath of God blows so cold that the water becomes hard as metal."

37.11-12   RSV   TEV

> 11 He loads the thick cloud with   11 Lightning flashes from the
>   moisture;   clouds,P
>   the clouds scatter his light-   12 as they move at God's will.
>   ning.   They do all that God commands,
> 12 They turn round and round by   everywhere throughout the
>   his guidance,   world.
>   to accomplish all that he com-
>   mands them   P Verse 11 in Hebrew is unclear.
>   on the face of the habitable
>   world.

Verses 11 and 12 refer to the action of the clouds and so may be treated together. TEV notes that in Hebrew verse 11 is unclear. TEV assumes the sense of the two lines is the same and so combines them.

He loads the thick cloud with moisture: He loads occurs only here in the Hebrew Bible, and its meaning is uncertain, but in Isaiah 1.14 there is a corresponding noun form meaning "burden," and so **He loads** is likely the sense. **Moisture** translates a Hebrew word which occurs only here and whose meaning is uncertain.

The word seems to be clearly parallel to "his light" in line b, but other suggestions for its meaning are "hail" and "lightning."

The clouds scatter his lightning: as in 36.32; 37.3, the Hebrew for "light" is generally understood here to mean **lightning**. TEV's single-line translation is adequate to represent line a, but for line b something like RSV should be followed. It is apparent from the uncertainties in the Hebrew text that the translation of these two verses will remain doubtful. However, here are two models which may be suggested for verse 11: "God fills the clouds with rain and sends them out full of lightning" or "God fills the clouds with lightning and sends them flashing everywhere."

They turn round and round by his guidance describes how these natural forces obey God's commands. TEV links verse 12 to verse 11, making the **clouds** in verse 11 the subject of the verb "move" in verse 12a. According to Rowley the sense of verse 12a is "The cloud goes round in circles, wheeling about according to his plans." The word translated **turn round** is the same as that used to describe the turning round of the flaming sword in Genesis 3.24. **By his guidance** means "according to his plans or purposes."

To accomplish all that he commands them: that is, "they do all that God commands them to do." **On the face of the habitable world** is literally "on the face of the world the earth." The phrase translated **the habitable world** occurs elsewhere only in Proverbs 8.31. However, the sense of the full expression is as in TEV, "throughout the world," or as FRCL says more broadly, "in the universe." Verse 12 may also be rendered, for example, "The clouds whirl about as God directs them; they obey God's commands throughout the whole world" or "God sends the clouds whirling around; they obey him everywhere they go."

37.13	RSV	TEV
	Whether for correction, or for his land, or for love, he causes it to happen.	God sends rain to water the earth; he may send it to punish men, or to show them his favor.

Whether for correction, or for his land, or for love is translated in numerous ways. This verse does not consist of two parallel lines, but is a single statement in which the main clause comes at the end, as in RSV. **Correction** and **love** are easily paired as far as meaning is concerned, but **land** does not seem to fit. **Correction** translates the Hebrew "whip," a symbol of punishment. **Love** translates the Hebrew *chesed,* meaning "constant love, loyalty," and TEV renders it here as "favor." HOTTP makes three recommendations for translating this line. The first is the same as RSV. The second is "whether for correction, if it concerns his land, whether for a favor, he will bring it about." The third is "whether for a tribe, or for his land, or for a favor, he will make it happen." Pope suggests changing **for his land** to get "grace," but this makes "favor" redundant. Dhorme says that a verb is required in the first half of the verse. Accordingly he redivides the two words translated **or for his land,** and with a slight change in the Hebrew gets "God accomplished his will." This provides a parallelism, "Whether it be for punishment that he accomplishes his will, whether it be for mercy that he brings it to pass."

TEV's translation depends on the understanding of the main clause in RSV, **he causes it to happen.** TEV follows an observation made by Dhorme that the Targum translations saw here three different kinds of rain, and so TEV has taken this phrase to mean "God sends rain," and the poorly fitting **for his land** is taken as the general statement of purpose to be followed by the two specific purposes. TEV then translates "God sends rain to water the earth; he may send it to punish men, or to show them his favor." FRCL interprets **he causes it to happen** to mean the same as Dhorme's suggested change, and translates "God carries out his will on earth, either to punish or to show his goodness," and adds a note, "Probable meaning of an uncertain text." GECL translates "He sends rain to moisten the earth. Sometimes he sends it to punish people and sometimes as a sign of his goodness." It is not possible to make a reasonably clear translation of this verse without some textual or other adjustments, and TEV, FRCL, or GECL are suitable models to follow.

8E-6. Elihu challenges Job to reflect on God's greatness in nature (37.14-22)

RSV	TEV
14 "Hear this, O Job; stop and consider the wondrous works of God.	14 Pause a moment, Job, and listen; consider the wonderful things God does.
15 Do you know how God lays his command upon them, and causes the lightning of his cloud to shine?	15 Do you know how God gives the command and makes lightning flash from the clouds?
16 Do you know the balancings of the clouds, the wondrous works of him who is perfect in knowledge,	16 Do you know how clouds float in the sky, the work of God's amazing skill?
17 you whose garments are hot when the earth is still because of the south wind?	17 No, you can only suffer in the heat when the south wind oppresses the land.
18 Can you, like him, spread out the skies, hard as a molten mirror?	18 Can you help God stretch out the sky and make it as hard as polished metal?
19 Teach us what we shall say to him; we cannot draw up our case because of darkness.	19 Teach us what to say to God; our minds are blank; we have nothing to say.
20 Shall it be told him that I would speak? Did a man ever wish that he would be swallowed up?	20 I won't ask to speak with God; why should I give him a chance to destroy me?
21 "And now men cannot look on the light when it is bright in the skies, when the wind has passed and cleared them.	21 And now the light in the sky is dazzling, too bright for us to look at it; and the sky has been swept clean by the wind.
22 Out of the north comes golden splendor; God is clothed with terrible majesty.	22 A golden glow is seen in the north, and the glory of God fills us with awe.

After having addressed any who were listening from verse 2, Elihu now speaks directly to Job, as he did in 33.1.

Subdivision Heading

The Handbook heading may be reworded to say, for example, "Elihu's final challenge to Job," "Can you hang the sky in its place?" or "Job, think of the wonderful things God does." Rowley has "The majesty and unsearchableness of God," and Habel "Closing challenge to Job."

37.14   RSV   TEV

"Hear this, O Job;   Pause a moment, Job, and listen;
   stop and consider the won-   consider the wonderful things
      drous works of God.   God does.

Hear this, O Job: this refers to the great and wonderful things about God which Elihu will speak of in the following verses. Elihu's remarks are intended to produce humility in Job and to lead him to repent.

Stop and consider the wondrous works of God: stop is literally "stand" but here means "remain quiet" or "pause a moment," as TEV says. Elihu has not given Job opportunity to do anything else since he began speaking in 32.6 **Consider** translates the reflexive form of a verb meaning "observe, notice, pay attention." **The wondrous works of God** were introduced in verse 5. The verse may be translated "Give me your attention, Job, while you think about the wonderful things God does" or ". . . take time to think about the great things God does."

37.15   RSV   TEV

Do you know how God lays his   Do you know how God gives the
   command upon them,   command
and causes the lightning of his   and makes lightning flash from
      cloud to shine?   the clouds?

This subdivision contains a number of rhetorical questions that translators may need to recast in some other form according to the style of the receptor language.

Do you know how God lays his command upon them anticipates the kind of questions which God will put to Job in the following chapters. The Hebrew text has "Do you know how God placed on them?" Both RSV and TEV supply **command** translationally. **Them** refers back to the clouds in verse 11. NIV makes this line clear with "Do you know how God controls the clouds?" This line may also be expressed, for example, "Do you know how God orders the clouds to move?" or "Do you know how God makes the clouds obey him?

And causes the lightning of his cloud to shine: lightning translates the Hebrew for "light," as in 36.32; 37.3. **Shine** suggests a continuous glow which is not suitable when speaking of **lightning**. "Makes lightning flash from the clouds" (TEV) is far better.

37.16   RSV   TEV

> Do you know the balancings of   Do you know how clouds float in
>   the clouds,   the sky,
> the wondrous works of him   the work of God's amazing
>   who is perfect in knowledge,   skill?

Do you know the balancings of the clouds: **balancings** translates a word that occurs nowhere else in the Old Testament. A verb root with the same consonants meaning "equalize, balance" suggests the rendering of RSV. However, **balancings of the clouds** does not give a clear picture of cloud activity, and so TEV "float in the sky" is probably the intended idea. **Wondrous works** differs from the same wording used in verse 14 by only one letter and is best taken as a variation without trying to change it to something else. The expression is sometimes rendered "miracle" and refers to the activity in line a, as TEV makes clear: "the work of God's amazing skill." **Perfect in knowledge** is the way Elihu modestly describes himself in 36.4. Here the expression applies to God.

37.17   RSV   TEV

> you whose garments are hot   No, you can only suffer in the
>   when the earth is still because   heat
>   of the south wind?   when the south wind oppresses
>   the land.

You whose garments are hot translates a line beginning with the relative particle "whose" followed by "your (singular) hot garments." RSV takes "your garments" to tie in with "you" (singular) in verse 16, and so Elihu is speaking to Job. TEV expresses this line as a negative reply to the question in verse 16: "No, you can only suffer in the heat." TEV does not mention **your garments** but replaces this phrase with "you." NEB and others retain it, "sweating there in your stifling clothes." SPCL has "You are suffocating in your clothes from the heat."

When the earth is still because of the south wind describes the absence of moving air to bring coolness and relief from the heat. TEV makes "south wind" the subject of "oppresses the land." Many translations refer to the earth but fail to express the stillness of the heated air. It may be necessary to say, for example, "when the air is hot and heavy" or "when the air is too hot to breathe." **South wind** translates the Hebrew "from the south," which refers to the hot winds that blow across the desert from the south. It is this searing hot wind from the south that makes the air of the land hot. In some languages it will be more natural to transpose the two lines of verse 17 and say, for example, "When the burning winds blow from the south, you are suffocated in your clothes" or "When the hot winds blow, your clothes will make you suffer in the heat."

37.18   RSV   TEV

> Can you, like him, spread out the   Can you help God stretch out the
> skies,   sky
> hard as a molten mirror?   and make it as hard as pol-
>   ished metal?

Can you, like him, spread out the skies . . . ? is the final question Elihu asks
to remind Job of his frail human condition. **Like him,** which may also be understood
as "with him," is taken by TEV to mean working with God, alongside God, and so
TEV translates "Can you help God . . . ?" **Spread out** translates a verb meaning "to
hammer, beat out, flatten," and is used in Exodus 39.3; Numbers 16.39, referring to
the beating of metal into thin sheets. The related noun is used in Genesis 1.6, where
it refers to the "firmament" or "dome" (TEV) of the sky. **Spread out** or "stretch
out" gives a better picture of the process. NEB "beat out the vault of the skies, as he
does" is less clear than **spread out. Skies** is the same word translated "clouds" in
35.5. In languages in which **spread** or "stretch" cannot be used naturally with the
skies as object, it may be necessary to shift to an expression like "make" or "create."
For example, "Can you help God create the sky?"

Hard as a molten mirror: mirror translates a word found only here and in
Sirach 12.11. A related word occurs in Exodus 38.8. In ancient times mirrors were
made of polished bronze, not glass. The word translated **molten** is used to indicate
the formation of a solid mass in verse 10, and rendered as "fast" by RSV. NEB
translates "hard as a mirror of cast metal." "Cast metal" is metal that has been
heated to a liquid, poured into a particular shape, and then hardened while cooling.
In RSV this line gives a further description of the content of line a, but it may require
a verb to make it a separate clause, as in TEV. In some languages **molten mirror** will
have to be expressed differently; for example, "and make it like a mirror? or "and
make it shine like glass?"

37.19   RSV   TEV

> Teach us what we shall say to   Teach us what to say to God;
> him;   our minds are blank; we have
> we cannot draw up our case   nothing to say.
> because of darkness.

Teach us what we shall say to him is to be taken as Elihu's sarcasm. **Teach
us** translates the Hebrew "make us know." **Us** refers to Elihu and others, probably
the friends, but excludes Job, the person spoken to. **Him** refers to God. Dhorme
changes this to "Tell me what we shall say to Him."

In **we cannot draw up our case**, the verb has no object. The verb means
"arrange, set in order," as used in 33.5, where TEV translates "prepare your
arguments." RSV supplies **our case**, which suits the context well. **Darkness** in
because of darkness may refer to the darkness of the minds of Elihu and the
friends, or the darkness which conceals God from them. TEV takes it in the former
sense, "our minds are blank," and places it before **we cannot draw up our case,**

which is rendered as "we have nothing to say." GECL translates "Inform us! What should we say to him? We are in the dark and have nothing to report." This offers a clear translation model. In translation "we are in the dark" may have to be expressed as "we know nothing," or "we are ignorant."

37.20   RSV   TEV

> Shall it be told him that I would   I won't ask to speak with God;
>   speak?   why should I give him a
> Did a man ever wish that he   chance to destroy me?
>   would be swallowed up?

Shall it be told him that I would speak? reveals that Elihu is afraid to speak directly with God. Such an act could result in his death. RSV translates the Hebrew literally, and the result is not as clear as TEV. Elihu's question is rhetorical and is expressed clearly by TEV's negative statement, "I won't ask to speak with God."

Did a man ever wish that he would be swallowed up? represents a second rhetorical question whose assumed answer is "No." This line may be kept as a question or expressed again as a negative statement, "No one ever wanted to be swallowed up." TEV shifts to a "why" question to vary the style. **Swallowed up** translates the Hebrew passive. The word is used in its literal sense in 7.19, but it is used here figuratively, meaning "to be destroyed or killed." Dhorme, however, derives this verb from a root meaning "inform." FRCL follows this and translates "Or is someone going to inform him that somebody has spoken?" The sense of **swallow** used figuratively is clear and suits the context well, and so there is no need to change it. This line may also be expressed, for example, "Would anyone be foolish enough to risk being destroyed by God?" or "Would anyone be so foolish as to want God to kill him?"

37.21   RSV   TEV

> "And now men cannot look on   And now the light in the sky is
>   the light   dazzling,
> when it is bright in the skies,   too bright for us to look at it;
> when the wind has passed and   and the sky has been swept
>   cleared them.   clean by the wind.

Verse 21 appears to have little relevance to the rest of the context. However, Elihu has just rejected the idea of confronting God. The conclusion is that, if men cannot look at the bright glare of the sun, how much less can they look on the brightness of God.

And now men cannot look on the light: look is plural, but there is no subject for the verb. Therefore RSV has supplied **men**. It may be translated as a passive; for example, "The light cannot be looked upon." The word translated **light** is not to be taken as "lightning," as in 36.32; 37.3.

When it is bright in the skies: **bright** translates a word found nowhere else in the Old Testament, though a related word occurs in Leviticus 13, which means "white," as applied to a spot on the skin. However, the same word in Syriac means "to be dark or obscure," and Rowley translates "And now men saw not the light, it was obscure in the skies." This is followed by a number of other translations.

When the wind has passed and cleared them describes how the light becomes bright and impossible to look at. This line is translated by RSV as a subordinate time clause, which in translation may have to be shifted forward; for example, "When the wind has blown away the clouds, a person cannot look at the dazzling light in the sky."

37.22

RSV	TEV
Out of the north comes golden splendor; God is clothed with terrible majesty.	A golden glow is seen in the north, and the glory of God fills us with awe.

Out of the north comes golden splendor is literally "Out of the north comes gold." To speak of the precious metal gold is irrelevant to the context. Therefore RSV is no doubt correct in understanding "gold" as a description of a quality of God, and so translates **golden splendor**. Dhorme defends this and translates "rays of gold." TEV is similar with "golden glow." NIV is more explicit in reference to God: "Out of the north he comes in golden splendor."

God is clothed with terrible majesty is literally "upon God awesome majesty." RSV has translated using a metaphor where there is no figure in the Hebrew; however, a figure may be implied. The sense may also be expressed as in Habel, "around *'Eloah* the splendor is awesome." TEV makes the awe the experience of the imagined on-lookers and translates "And the glory of God fills us with awe," which is a satisfactory model for translating. Verse 22 may be expressed, for example, "From the north God comes bright as gold, and his glory (brightness) causes us to fear him" or "God comes from the north shining like gold, and his brilliance frightens all who see him."

8E-7. Elihu reminds Job that God ignores those who think they are wise (37.23-24)

RSV	TEV
23 The Almighty—we cannot find him; he is great in power and justice, and abundant righteousness he will not violate.	23 God's power is so great that we cannot come near him; he is righteous and just in his dealings with men.
24 Therefore men fear him; he does not regard any who are wise in their own conceit."	24 No wonder, then, that everyone is awed by him, and that he ignores those who claim to be wise.

Subdivision Heading

The Handbook heading may be adapted in translation sometimes by saying, for example, "God pays no attention to people who think they are wise" or "Everyone is amazed at God's greatness, except those who think they know everything."

37.23   RSV   TEV

The Almighty—we cannot find	God's power is so great that we
him;	cannot come near him;
he is great in power and jus-	he is righteous and just in his
tice,	dealings with men.
and abundant righteousness he	
will not violate.	

Elihu brings his speeches to a close by assuring Job that God does not pay attention to people like Job who claim to be wise. Ironically it is Elihu who has claimed to have knowledge, and so he is speaking against himself. Chapter 38 will open with God addressing Job from the whirlwind in contrast to what Elihu has said God would do.

In Hebrew verse 23 has two long lines which RSV divides into three shorter ones. Elihu asserts that God is unsearchable, cannot be fully known, remains a mystery. He cannot accept Job's view that God violates justice. TEV has retained the two long lines of the Hebrew and has produced a good rendering whose adjustments are explained below.

The Almighty—we cannot find him: Almighty translates *Shaddai*. The word translated **find** is used in 23.3, where Job desires to find God. **Find** does not imply that God is lost, but rather "beyond reach," or as Dhorme says, "we cannot attain to him," and TEV "we cannot come near him." RSV follows the Hebrew of line a, which has a topic followed by a comment, and which RSV separates with a dash. TEV takes **power** from line b and makes it part of the subject, to represent *Shaddai,* **the Almighty:** "God's power is so great . . . ." In terms of the three lines of RSV, the second line states that it is both God's power and justice that are qualified as **great.** **Abundant righteousness,** which is literally "greatness of righteousness," in RSV is made the object of **violate,** which is not likely to be the poet's intention. Many scholars make a slight change in "greatness of righteousness" to get "great in righteousness."

He will not violate is rendered by Dhorme and Pope as "he will not oppress." NIV has a rendering which is fairly close to the Hebrew and can serve as a basis for making translation adjustments: "The Almighty is beyond our reach and exalted in power; in his justice and great righteousness, he does not oppress." This verse may be expressed, for example, "God Almighty has great power, and we cannot come near him; he is righteous and just, and so does not oppress people" or "God the all-powerful one is too powerful for us to get close to him; he is good and treats everyone fairly."

37.24   RSV   TEV

> Therefore men fear him;
>   he does not regard any who
>   are wise in their own con-
>   ceit."

> No wonder, then, that everyone
>   is awed by him,
>   and that he ignores those who
>   claim to be wise.

Therefore men fear him means that people "revere, respect, have reverence for" God.

He does not regard: **regard** translates the Hebrew verb "see." The sense is that God does not need to take into account these wise persons, because he is sufficient in himself. "He does not pay attention to them," "God does not even notice them."

Wise in their own conceit translates "who are wise of heart." There are two interpretations of this expression: those like RSV and TEV, which assume it means they are not wise but think they are, and those that understand the expression to refer to wise people who really are wise. "Wise in heart" is used in 9.4 and has no bad sense intended. NEB translates "all who are wise look to him." Translations are divided between these two interpretations. NIV has in its text "does he not have regard for all the wise in heart?" and in the footnote "for he does not have regard for any who think they are wise." This may be the solution, at least for those who give alternative renderings in the notes. **Wise in their own conceit** may be rendered for example, "people who think they are wise, but are not," "people who say they are wise," or "people who act like wise people."

9. The LORD Addresses Job

(38.1–41.34)

In this section the LORD suddenly appears and addresses Job. The LORD's speech is divided into two major divisions. In the first (38.1–40.2) the LORD challenges Job to answer him, then goes on to give an overview of the mysteries of the sky and the earth, and follows with a survey of the mysteries of animal and bird life. After Job's confession of ignorance (40.3-5) the LORD again challenges Job to govern the universe, and then describes the monsters Behemoth and Leviathan (40.6–41.34).

Section Heading

Translators may wish to follow the Handbook heading or say something like "The LORD now appears to Job," "God comes to speak with Job," or "God confronts Job at last." Habel has "Yahweh's defence of his cosmic design," Rowley "The first divine speech." FRCL has "The LORD intervenes," and GECL "God answers Job with questions."

9A. THE LORD'S SPEECH: FIRST PART (38.1–40.2)

Chapters 38 and 39, and including 40.1-2, like chapters 36 and 37, form a unit within a larger unit of speeches, in which at last God appears on the scene and confronts Job with a mass of challenges. These challenges are in the form of questions which invite Job to reveal his wisdom, or lack of it. The intent of God's questions to Job is not to answer the problem of why the innocent suffer generally, nor even why Job has suffered, but rather to lead Job to an understanding of his case in the light of the great design for the universe which the Creator has made.

In verses 1-3 of chapter 38 God appears. He is called Yahweh. Except for 12.9 he has not been referred to by this name since the opening prose section of the book. Job is ordered to prepare to be questioned. All the questions put to Job by Yahweh concern creation and nature. In verses 4-11 the subject is the earth and the sea. Verses 12-21 relate to light and darkness. Verses 22-38 deal with aspects of the heavens. In 38.39–39.12 the subject is the wild life in nature. 39.13-30 take up the ostrich, the horse, and the eagle. Finally in 40.1-2 Job is asked by Yahweh to answer. And in 40.3-5 Job claps his hand over his mouth in amazement, saying he cannot answer.

Division Heading

The Handbook heading may be modified to say, for example, "God's first speech," "The LORD begins to challenge Job," or "The first challenge to Job."

9A-1. God challenges Job to answer his questions (38.1-3)

RSV	TEV

1 Then the LORD answered Job out of the whirlwind:
2   "Who is this that darkens counsel by
    words without knowledge?
3   Gird up your loins like a man,
    I will question you, and you shall de-
    clare to me.
	1 Then out of the storm the LORD spoke to Job.
	The LORD
	2 Who are you to question my wisdom
	    with your ignorant, empty words?
	3 Stand up now like a man
	    and answer the questions I ask you.

Subdivision Heading

The Handbook heading may be reworded to say, for example, "Answer me if you can, Job," "Who do you think you are, Job?" or "Job, can you answer these questions?" Rowley has "The LORD's opening challenge."

Because of the large number of topics touched on in this chapter, some translations separate these by blank space and with or without some symbol to call attention to the topical units. Each switch in topic is pointed out in the discussion in the Handbook, so that the translator may decide if a subheading at that point will be helpful.

38.1	RSV	TEV

Then the LORD answered Job out of the whirlwind:	**Then out of the storm the LORD spoke to Job.**

Verse 1 is in prose; it is phrased in the same manner as the introductions to the speeches of the friends, except that Job is named as the one being addressed. There is no reference to Elihu, who was the previous speaker, nor to anything Elihu has said.

Then the LORD answered Job out of the whirlwind: **Then** translates the Hebrew connective *waw*, which is used here to mark a transition which shifts the scene forward to a new setting. It is usually translated as **Then** in English, but can be "after that, when that was finished, later on." **LORD** translates the Hebrew name for God, *Yahweh*. For full discussion see "Translating the Book of Job," page 21, and comments on 1.6. **Answered** is not to be taken in the sense of answering a question, but more generally as "spoke to, said to, addressed." The first thing God says to Job is in the form of a question in verse 2. For comments on **answered** see 4.1. **Whirlwind** does not translate the same words for storm used by Elihu in chapters 36 and 37. This may be a way of avoiding any reference to Elihu's talk. The Hebrew term refers to a fierce, raging storm. **Whirlwind** is a rather more specific type of wind than the context suggests, and a more general term for a severe storm is better.

Storms were associated with appearances of God in Exodus 19.19-20; Judges 5.4-5; Habakkuk 3.5-6; Psalm 18.8-16. NEB and others use "tempest," and TEV "storm." In translation it may be necessary to restructure **out of the whirlwind**, which refers to the place from which the LORD speaks to Job. In some languages this is expressed "from inside the storm," "from the heart of the storm," or as a simile, "The LORD spoke to Job like a great wind storm."

38.2   RSV   TEV

    "Who is this that darkens coun-   *The LORD*
        sel by words without knowl-   Who are you to question my
        edge?   wisdom
                             with your ignorant, empty
                             words?

Who is this that darkens counsel . . . ? is a question directed to Job, and not to Elihu as some have argued. The question is rhetorical. It should be recalled that each of the three friends begins his speech in chapters 4, 8, and 11 with rhetorical questions. It is clearer to address a person in the second person, and so TEV and others change to "Who are you . . . ." **Darkens counsel** is literally "obscuring plans." **Counsel** translates a word meaning "plan, purpose, design." By accusing God of being unjust, Job is said to be "obscuring, doubting, clouding" the "purposes, wisdom" of God. TEV renders this phrase as "question my wisdom." This line may also be rendered, for example, as "Who do you think you are to doubt my plans?" or "What right have you to question what I have decided to do?"

By words without knowledge? describes the way in which Job "doubts, questions, obscures" God's wisdom or design for creation. In 35.16 Elihu accused Job in a similar manner. It is by the use of ignorant talk that Job does this: "You do this by speaking ignorantly" or "You talk but don't know what you are saying." Verse 2 may be expressed "Who are you to doubt my plans with your ignorant talk?" This verse may require shifting line <u>b</u> to line <u>a</u> and translating "Who are you who talks ignorantly and rejects what I plan to do?" If the rhetorical question form cannot be used in the sense of "What right have you," it may be necessary to say, for example, "Who gave you the authority?" or "Did someone give you the power?"

38.3   RSV   TEV

    Gird up your loins like a man,   Stand up now like a man
        I will question you, and you   and answer the questions I ask
        shall declare to me.   you.

Gird up your loins like a man is used again in 40.7. In Jeremiah 1.17 this expression refers to preparing for a hard task, in Isaiah 5.27 preparing for battle, and in 1 Kings 18.46 for running. See also Luke 12.35. When undertaking tasks that required freedom of the legs, it was necessary to pull the long shirt tail or lower part of the robe up between the legs and fasten it around the waist and hips with a cord or belt. The expression is used figuratively here in the sense of "get ready for action." **Like a man** translates a word for **man** that emphasizes "maleness" but is not the term meaning "strong man" or "warrior." TEV "stand up now like a man" expresses the thought well. We may also say, for example, "Be prepared like a man," "get yourself ready . . . ." In some languages this expression may be rendered idiomatically, for example, as "pull up your clothing," "tighten your belt," "tie up your waist band." In many languages, however, a nonfigurative expression such as "get ready" will be used. It is possible in some languages to combine the figurative and nonfigurative expressions.

Declare to me translates "make me know" and has been used by Job when addressing God in 10.2; 13.23, and by Elihu in 37.19 when speaking to Job. In this line God states clearly his course of action: "I am going to ask you questions and you are going to answer me."

9A-2. The earth and the sea (38.4-11)

	RSV			TEV
4	"Where were you when I laid the foundation of the earth?		4	Were you there when I made the world? If you know so much, tell me about it.
	Tell me, if you have understanding.		5	Who decided how large it would be?
5	Who determined its measurements— surely you know!			Who stretched the measuring line over it?
	Or who stretched the line upon it?			Do you know all the answers?
6	On what were its bases sunk, or who laid its cornerstone,		6	What holds up the pillars that support the earth?
7	when the morning stars sang together, and all the sons of God shouted for joy?			Who laid the cornerstone of the world?
			7	In the dawn of that day the stars sang together,
8	"Or who shut in the sea with doors, when it burst forth from the womb;			and the heavenly beings shouted for joy.
9	when I made clouds its garment, and thick darkness its swaddling band,		8	Who closed the gates to hold back the sea when it burst from the womb of the earth?
10	and prescribed bounds for it, and set bars and doors,		9	It was I who covered the sea with clouds and wrapped it in darkness.
11	and said, 'Thus far shall you come, and no farther,		10	I marked a boundary for the sea and kept it behind bolted gates.
	and here shall your proud waves be stayed'?		11	I told it, "So far and no farther! Here your powerful waves must stop."

With verse 4 God begins the questions which relate mainly to the earth, sea, and creation. The image is that of God as a master builder who has set up the earth on foundations, pillars, and with a cornerstone.

Subdivision Heading

Translators may wish to insert a heading before verse 4. Some suggestions are: "God is like a master builder," "God asks Job about the earth, the sea, and creation" or "God questions Job about creation."

38.4   RSV   TEV

> "Where were you when I laid the   Were you there when I made the
>   foundation of the earth?   world?
> Tell me, if you have under-   If you know so much, tell me
>   standing.   about it.

Where were you when I laid the foundation of the earth is similar to a sarcastic question Eliphaz put to Job in 15.7, "Are you the first man that was born?" God does not ask in order to know where Job was at the time of creation, but this is an ironic way of saying "you were not there." Both God and Job know that Job was not present at the creation. The implication is that to know the design of the universe would require having participated in the act of creation.

The foundation is the lower part of a structure upon which the structure rests. The usage of building terms is figurative, and TEV shifts to "made the world," which is more general but is also more appropriate when speaking of the earth. In language areas in which buildings lack a foundation, it may be necessary to say, for example, "Where were you when I set the earth on its resting place?" or ". . . when I set the earth down?"

Tell me, if you have understanding is literally "Tell if you know understanding." **Understanding** translates a Hebrew word meaning "discernment, insight" and is sometimes paired with "wisdom." According to Dhorme "to know discernment" is to know the inner truth of a matter, as in Proverbs 4.1, and seems to have the same meaning as "gaining wisdom" in Proverbs 4.5. According to Habel God appears to ask Job if he has acquired the wisdom to enable him to discern the mysteries of the design of the earth. FRCL transposes the two lines of verse 4 and translates "Explain to me, if you know the truth: where were you when I founded the earth?" This line is not parallel with line a but is a command that is added to line a. In some languages it will be more natural to place line b first; for example, "Tell me if you know so much, where were you when I set the earth on its resting place?"

38.5   RSV   TEV

> Who determined its measure-   Who decided how large it would
>   ments—surely you know!   be?
> Or who stretched the line   Who stretched the measuring
>   upon it?   line over it?
>   Do you know all the answers?

Who determined its measurements is a question concerning the work of the designer or architect. The question in the next line concerns the surveyor and in verse 6 the engineer. This line asks "Who decided what its dimensions would be?" or, as TEV says, "Who decided how large it would be?" **Surely you know!** would follow naturally as a conclusion if Job had been present at creation, but since he obviously was not, RSV makes this comment particularly ironical. As sarcasm it has the meaning "You don't know at all." NEB translates "surely you should know." Some translations play down the irony; for example, NJB says ". . . do you know?"

RSV is to be preferred. TEV's translation is a good model to follow. We may also say, for example, "Who decided what its measurements would be?" TEV rightly transfers **surely you know** to the end of verse 5 so that it applies to both lines, and this is recommended to translators.

Or who stretched the line upon it gives a picture of calculated measurements being made to assure the exactness of the construction. For the use of the measuring line see also Jeremiah 31.39; Zechariah 1.16. **Stretched** is the same verb used in 9.8, where Job says of God, "who alone stretched out the heavens." Stretching a line or cord between fixed points is the preliminary task in construction, equivalent to surveying to get the angles square and the sides straight. **Upon it** refers to the earth in verse 4. In many language areas no careful measurements are made when preparing to build a house. No angles are square nor are lines straight. However, it is often possible to say, for example, "Who walked across it to fix its direction?" or "Who laid a bamboo pole down to get it straight?"

38.6-7	RSV		TEV
6	On what were its bases sunk, or who laid its cornerstone,	6	What holds up the pillars[x] that support the earth? Who laid the cornerstone of the world?
7	when the morning stars sang together, and all the sons of God shouted for joy?	7	In the dawn of that day the stars sang together, and the heavenly beings[q] shouted for joy.

[x] PILLARS: *See 9.6.*
[q] HEAVENLY BEINGS: *See 1.6.*

These two verses are closely related in subject and structure and will be considered together. **On what were its bases sunk** translates the Hebrew literally. The earth was thought of as a building set on foundations, as in verse 4a, and also in Psalm 24.2; 89.11; 102.25; 104.5; Proverbs 3.19; Isaiah 48.13; 51.13, 16; Zechariah 12.1. In 9.6 Job reflects the traditional wisdom that the earth rests on pillars. These pillars in turn rest on **bases**. The reference in this line is not to the pillars, as in TEV, but to the **bases** or "footings" upon which the pillars rest. NEB translates it clearly as "On what do its supporting pillars rest?" This view of the earth is different from that expressed by Bildad in 26.7, who said that God "hung the earth in empty space," which sounds more like the view of the earth as confirmed by modern science. In Psalm 24.2 the earth rests upon the seas. This line may require more information to make it clear. For example, "On what do the bases rest that hold up the pillars of the earth?" or "What is beneath the footings that support the pillars holding up the earth?" It is likely that a detailed note will be required at 9.6, and a cross reference to that note may be placed here.

Or who laid its cornerstone: cornerstone translates a word which may refer either to the stone placed at the main corner in the foundation, or at the top as the final stone laid. The latter is referred to in English as the "capstone." Most modern translations have **cornerstone**, which refers to the final stage of laying the foundation, not to the completion of the construction. In languages in which cornerstones are unknown, it may be possible to say, for example, "or who finished the work of setting it in place?" or "who completed the place where it would rest?"

When the morning stars sang together makes the whole of verse 7 subordinate to something which may not be clear. The thought could go back to verse 4a, "Where were you," but this separates it very far. More likely it is to be understood in relation to verse 6, so that the singing of the morning stars takes place at the time of, or upon completion of, the laying of the **cornerstone**. From Ezra 3.10-11 it is known, for example, that the laying of the foundation of the Second Temple was accompanied by celebrations and music. The same is referred to in Zechariah 4.7 on the occasion of the laying of the capstone. So here the laying of the foundation of the earth is accompanied by singing. TEV translates "In the dawn of that day," but the reference of "that day" in TEV's own context is somewhat ambiguous. NJB relates verse 7a to verse 6b by translating "to the joyful concert of the morning stars." TOB has "while the morning stars sang in chorus," and NIV ends verse 6b with a dash: ". . . cornerstone—while the morning stars sang together." Translators should not rely on punctuation alone to show that verse 7a occurs simultaneously with or follows verse 6. For example, "Who laid the cornerstone as the morning stars began to sing?" Before the creation of man it is the stars which witness the creation of the earth, and are said to sing together, that is, in chorus. In 3.9 Job mentions the "stars of dawn." See the discussion there. The reference here is the same. **Sang together** implies singing as a chorus, uniting their voices.

Sons of God, which matches **morning stars**, refers to the angels, or more generally "heavenly beings" as in TEV. The expression **sons of God** occurs in 1.6 and refers to God's heavenly court. See comments on 1.6 and the TEV note there. In some languages "the singing of stars" may be meaningless. However, it may be possible to express this phrase as a simile and say, for example, "Who laid the cornerstone while the morning stars sang like people singing together?"

38.8	RSV	TEV

"Or who shut in the sea with doors,
  when it burst forth from the womb;

Who closed the gates to hold back the sea[r]
  when it burst from the womb of the earth?

[r] TO HOLD BACK THE SEA: *See 26.12.*

From verse 8 to verse 11 the topic is the sea. These four verses form one long sentence in the Hebrew and in RSV. By shifting to **who** RSV and others continue the question form as was done in verse 6b. **Or who shut in the sea with doors: who shut** is literally "and he shut," which the Septuagint changes to "I shut." **Shut** translates the word rendered as "hedge" in 1.10 and 3.23. **Doors** translates a word referring to the two leaves of a door; that is, a door made of a pair of boards. **Doors** is used figuratively and refers to the seashore or any natural barrier that keeps the sea from flooding the land. Similar thoughts are expressed in Psalm 104.9; Proverbs

8.29; Jeremiah 5.22. If this poetic image cannot be used, the translator is advised to seek another. If we must translate as prose, the thought may be expressed, for example, "Who stopped the sea from overflowing the land?" or "Who prevented the sea from running over the land?"

When it burst forth from the womb compares the rushing sea to a new-born baby coming out of the womb. The Hebrew does not suggest where the womb is, but TEV assigns it to the earth, "womb of the earth." FRCL omits the womb image and says "from the depths." The picture given may suggest the bursting of the waters in child birth, waters in the womb which protect the fetus, or unborn baby. Due to the problem of speaking of the sea as coming from the womb, it may be necessary in many languages to express this line differently; for example, "when the ocean poured out over the earth" or "when the waters of the rivers ran over the earth."

38.9	RSV	TEV
	when I made clouds its garment, and thick darkness its swaddling band,	It was I who covered the sea with clouds and wrapped it in darkness.

When I made clouds its garment continues the metaphor of birth, and this line depicts the clouds as being the clothing for the sea, which is the infant. TEV answers the question in verse 8 with "It was I" here in verse 9a. Translators may wish to do the same. This is far better than RSV **when I made** and permits the formation of a new sentence in verse 9a. TEV has departed from the image of making clothing for the newborn sea by switching to "covered the sea with clouds," which retains something of the purpose of these cloud garments.

And thick darkness its swaddling band is an even stranger metaphor, in which God is depicted as wrapping cloths around the infant sea. **Thick darkness** translates the same word used in 22.13b and translated as "deep darkness." The verb in line a must serve also in line b. The **thick darkness** is used as a **swaddling band**. The noun translated as **swaddling band** is found only here in the Old Testament. However, the verb is used in Ezekiel 16.4. The allusion is to wrapping a new born infant with strips of cloth to keep its limbs straight. The same was applied to the baby Jesus in Luke 2.7. As in the first line TEV has replaced the noun here with a verb, "wrapped it in darkness." NEB preserves the imagery of verse 9 with "When I wrapped it in a blanket of cloud and cradled it in fog." In some languages it will be necessary to avoid the images of **garments** and **swaddling bands** and say, for example, "I am the one who covered the sea with clouds and made it dark."

38.10	RSV	TEV
	and prescribed bounds for it, and set bars and doors,	I marked a boundary for the sea and kept it behind bolted gates.

And prescribed bounds for it: prescribed translates a word whose usual meaning is "break." However, the literal rendering of this line, "and I broke on it my boundary," leaves the sense uncertain. **Prescribed** follows the Septuagint and Vulgate. Most translations follow the Septuagint here with a verb meaning "set, place" without explaining how they have arrived at this meaning. SPCL, however, has "I set a limit," and in the footnote it has " 'set' is according to an ancient version." NJV has "When I made breakers My limit for it." "Breakers" probably refers to the breaking of the sea waves on the shore. FRCL has "I have broken its onrush, marked its limit," and TOB is the same in the first clause. These translations supply an object for the verb "break" and refer to the bursting forth of the sea, which seems to fit well with the next line. If this is not followed, something like TEV may be used.

And set bars and doors refers most probably to the natural barriers along the sea coast, such as cliffs, which prevent the ocean from flooding the land, as was expressed in verse 8a, where the word "doors" was used for the same purpose. **Bars** refers to the iron bars laid across the inside of a pair of double doors to prevent them from being pushed open, or as TEV says, "bolted gates." This line may be expressed, for example, "and shut it behind closed doors" or "and closed the doors to shut it in." If this kind of imagery is not suitable, we may also say, for example, "and would not let it flood the land" or "and stopped it from running over the land."

38.11	RSV	TEV
	and said, 'Thus far shall you come, and no farther, and here shall your proud waves be stayed'?	I told it, "So far and no farther! Here your powerful waves must stop."

Thus far shall you come, and no farther is God's command to the sea. "You can come up to here, but you can go no farther." God is represented here as quoting his own words addressed to the sea.

And here shall your proud waves be stayed translates the Hebrew "here he will put on the pride of your waves." This line makes sense only by supplying "a limit" as the object of the verb "put." The Septuagint has "shall be broken," expressing God's control over the movement of the sea. HOTTP takes two positions, each equally favored. One is to translate as in RSV. The other is to follow the Septuagint "and here will the pride of your waves be broken." Among modern translations which follow the Septuagint are NJB, BJ, and Habel. Those preferring the Hebrew text are Pope, NJV, TOB, FRCL, NIV, and others. Translators may follow either alternative. TEV has replaced **proud waves** with "powerful waves" as a more common expression. Verse 11 may also be rendered, for example, as "You, ocean, can come only this far and no farther. Here on the shore your mighty waves must break." In languages in which only rivers are known, "rivers" may substitute for "sea" or "ocean."

9A-3. Dawn, darkness and Sheol (38.12-21)

RSV

TEV

12   "Have you commanded the morning since
your days began,
and caused the dawn to know its place,
13   that it might take hold of the skirts of the
earth,
and the wicked be shaken out of it?
14   It is changed like clay under the seal,
and it is dyed like a garment.
15   From the wicked their light is withheld,
and their uplifted arm is broken.

16   "Have you entered into the springs of the
sea,
or walked in the recesses of the deep?
17   Have the gates of death been revealed to
you,
or have you seen the gates of deep
darkness?
18   Have you comprehended the expanse of
the earth?
Declare, if you know all this.

19   "Where is the way to the dwelling of
light,
and where is the place of darkness,
20   that you may take it to its territory
and that you may discern the paths to
its home?
21   You know, for you were born then,
and the number of your days is great!

12   Job, have you ever in all your life
commanded a day to dawn?
13   Have you ordered the dawn to seize the
earth
and shake the wicked from their hiding
places?
14   Daylight makes the hills and valleys stand
out
like the folds of a garment,
clear as the imprint of a seal on clay.
15   The light of day is too bright for the
wicked
and restrains them from doing violence.

16   Have you been to the springs in the
depths of the sea?
Have you walked on the floor of the
ocean?
17   Has anyone ever shown you the gates
that guard the dark world of the dead?
18   Have you any idea how big the world is?
Answer me if you know.

19   Do you know where the light comes from
or what the source of darkness is?
20   Can you show them how far to go,
or send them back again?
21   I am sure you can, because you're so old
and were there when the world was
made!

The earth and sea give way now as the divine speaker takes up the subject of
dawn, darkness, and the place of the dead.

Subdivision Heading

The Handbook heading may be modified to say, for example, "Do you know
about the dawn, darkness, and the world of the dead?" or "Can you control the
dawn?" Habel has "Dawn, darkness, and netherworld."

38.12   RSV

TEV

**"Have you commanded the morn-
ing since your days began,
and caused the dawn to know
its place,**

**Job, have you ever in all your life
commanded a day to dawn?**

Have you commanded the morning: day and night must be carefully regulated for natural life to succeed. In this line **morning** is regarded as a person receiving orders so that it will appear on time as it should. **Morning** in line a has the same meaning as **dawn** in line b. **Command** means "give the morning its orders," "tell the morning what it should do." **Since your days began**, which is the opening phrase in the Hebrew of verse 12, means "since you were born," "during your life time."

Caused the dawn reminds Job that in 3.7-9 he wanted to impose a curse on the dawn to prevent it from seeing the light of day. **To know its place** is to know where its position is in the order of creation. If Job knew its established place, he would know the design that regulates its appearance. TEV takes the two lines of verse 12 to mean the same and so reduces them to one. However, for those translators who seek to retain the focusing effect of the movement from one line to the next, **dawn** in line b is more specific than **morning** in line a. Verse 12 may be rendered, for example, as "During your lifetime have you told the morning what it should do or made the dawn start a new day?" In some languages it may be clearer to place **dawn** before the more general **morning**. For example, SPCL translates "Have you ever in your life given orders that dawn should come and day should break (begin)?" This may serve as a translation model for some languages.

38.13   RSV   TEV

    that it might take hold of the   Have you ordered the dawn to
       skirts of the earth,   seize the earth
    and the wicked be shaken out   and shake the wicked from
       of it?   their hiding places?

That it might take hold of the skirts of the earth expresses the purpose of verse 12. It refers to "the dawn." **Take hold** translates the usual word for "grasp, seize," and **skirts of the earth** is the same expression translated as "corners of the earth" in 37.3. See there for discussion. The poetic picture is the dawn reaching out to the edges of the earth, as though it were a blanket or garment, and shaking the wicked out. In many languages the figures in this verse will appear extreme and therefore may have to be expressed differently. TEV repeats "Have you ordered" from verse 12 in order to make the relation of verse 13 to verse 12 clear. The picture of the dawn taking hold of the **skirts of the earth** may easily be misunderstood. TEV "dawn to seize the earth" may have to be restructured to say, for example, "Have you ever made the light of dawn shine across the edges of the earth?" or "Have you ever sent the rays of morning light shining across the earth?"

And the wicked be shaken out of it: **the wicked** translates the word commonly having that meaning. Interpretations differ as to the meaning of **shaken out of it**. It seems best to take this expression to mean that the dawning light of morning causes the wicked to escape from the light (see 11.13-17; 24.13-17) and flee into the darkness. Accordingly this line may be rendered, for example, as "which makes the wicked flee" or "which causes evil people to run and hide." NEB translates "the Dog-stars" both here and in verse 15, which refers to the stars named Sirius and Procyon, visible in the late winter skies in the northern hemisphere. This rendering is based on the assumption that **the wicked** is out of place in a context describing God's activities in the created heavens. However, the poet deals separately with the stars in verses 31 and 32, and so **the wicked** is to be kept here.

38.14 RSV	TEV

It is changed like clay under the seal,
  and it is dyed[g] like a garment.
 	
[g] Cn: Heb *they stand forth*
	Daylight makes the hills and valleys stand out
	  like the folds of a garment,
	  clear as the imprint of a seal
	  on clay.

It is changed like clay under the seal describes by analogy how the darkened earth of verse 13 changes as dawn progresses into day. It is the appearance of the earth that changes. The analogy may be to a smooth piece of clay that takes on a definite shape when impressed with a seal, or signet ring. The expression translated as **clay under the seal** is literally "like clay a seal." Dhorme takes it to refer to a red-colored clay used in ancient medicine, and which is used here to suggest the pink color of the earth at sunrise. FRCL follows Dhorme in this but translates the first line in two ways: "The earth takes on a rose-colored hue," which is qualified with the more literal rendering "like clay on which seals are impressed"; and in the footnote it gives "like the clay under the imprint of the seal." TEV shifts the clay impression figure to the end of verse 14 and expresses **It is changed** as "Daylight makes the hills and valleys stand out."

And it is dyed like a garment is literally "and they stand forth like a garment," as the RSV note shows. TEV and others supply "folds" to get a more adequate parallel with line a and to complete the image in line b. FRCL renders this line "and all nature appears clothed in it." RSV follows a change also taken up by Dhorme, Pope, NJB, and BJ. Taken as a whole TEV is preferred. In many languages the expression **clay under the seal** in line a will have to be modified to give a better picture of the effect of the light of dawn on the earth's surface. SPCL has dropped the clay impression figure and translated "Then the relief of the earth appears, dyed in colors like a garment." This is also a good model, which may also be rendered as "Then the land stands out clearly like the folds in a rose-colored garment."

38.15 RSV	TEV

From the wicked their light is withheld,
  and their uplifted arm is broken.
	The light of day is too bright for the wicked
	  and restrains them from doing violence.

From the wicked their light is withheld: in 24.17 **the wicked** love to carry out their evil in the night, and so "deep darkness is morning to all of them." **Their light is withheld** therefore refers to the coming of dawn, which takes away the darkness referred to as **their light**. The use of **their light** meaning "darkness" is irony: "The wicked have their light taken away" or "What the wicked call their light is taken away from them."

And their uplifted arm is broken states that the wicked are unable to carry out their violent acts because the daylight has come. The **uplifted arm** is an image of violence. TEV says "and restrains them from deeds of violence." Because **their light** is irony and refers to the opposite of light, it may be necessary to translate this satire as "darkness" and restructure the sentence in line a to say, for example, "Daylight takes away darkness from the wicked," "When daylight comes the wicked lose their darkness," or "When it is daytime the wicked have no more darkness." Line b may then be expressed, for example, "and they can no longer hurt people" or "they lose the strength to injure people."

38.16   RSV   TEV

"Have you entered into the   Have you been to the springs in
    springs of the sea,   the depths of the sea?
    or walked in the recesses of   Have you walked on the floor
    the deep?   of the ocean?

Have you entered into the springs of the sea inquires of Job his knowledge regarding things that are not apparent to human vision. **Springs of the sea** refers to the underground sources of water thought to supply the oceans. The word translated as **springs** occurs only here, but another form of the word is found in 28.11 and is translated as "streams." This may be compared with "roots of the sea" used in 36.30.

Or walked in the recesses of the deep: recesses translates a word used in 11.7, "deep things," and has the sense of "something to be explored, researched, discovered, investigated," and so it implies here "to find out what is hidden." It is in this sense that RSV uses **recesses of the deep**; the meaning, in other words, is the hidden or mysterious depths of the ocean. NEB says "the unfathomable deep." A term suggesting the hidden or unknown is better than the "bottom of the ocean" or TEV "floor of the ocean." Verse 16 may also be rendered, for example, as "Have you been to the springs that give the water to the ocean, or investigated the dark depths of the sea?" In languages in which oceans are unknown, translators may have to refer to large lakes or rivers. "Have you gone to the place where the springs form the rivers, or studied the mysteries of the deep rivers?"

38.17   RSV   TEV

Have the gates of death been   Has anyone ever shown you the
    revealed to you,   gates
    or have you seen the gates of   that guard the dark world of
    deep darkness?   the dead?

Have the gates of death been revealed to you asks if Job has been shown the entrance to the world of the dead, or Sheol. **Gates of death** is found in Psalm

704

9.13; 107.18, and "gates of Sheol" in Isaiah 38.10. **Gates of death** are not gates that belong to death, but rather gates that mark the entrance to such a place.

The two lines of this verse are parallel in meaning. In line b **gates** in **gates of deep darkness** is the same word as in line a. **Deep darkness** is used in 3.5 and refers to the darkness of Sheol. That the world of the dead is thought of as a dark place is emphasized by Job in 10.21,22. TEV has not repeated **gates** but reduces the two lines to one: "gates that guard the dark world of the dead." In languages which do not use passive constructions, the first line must be reformed, as in TEV. For example, "Has anyone ever shown you the entrance to the world of the dead?" Some translators may prefer to reduce these two lines to one and say, for example, "Has anyone ever shown you the dark entrance (doors, gates) of Sheol, the world of the dead?"

38.18

RSV	TEV
Have you comprehended the expanse of the earth? Declare, if you know all this.	Have you any idea how big the world is? Answer me if you know.

Have you comprehended the expanse of the earth shifts the ironical questions away from Sheol to the earth. Here God asks Job if he understands how large the earth is. The word translated as **expanse** can mean "width" or more generally "the dimensions." TEV is clear with "how big the earth is." The rhetorical question is not intended to ask for a reply but to emphasize Job's ignorance of the size of the earth.

Declare, if you know all this: line b serves to group the previous questions into a small subdivision of the longer series of challenging questions.

38.19-20

RSV	TEV
19 "Where is the way to the dwelling of light, and where is the place of darkness, 20 that you may take it to its territory and that you may discern the paths to its home?	19 Do you know where the light comes from or what the source of darkness is? 20 Can you show them how far to go, or send them back again?

These two verses are closely related in meaning, with verse 20 expressing the purpose of knowing the locations mentioned in verse 19. In verse 19 **light** and **darkness** are regarded as persons who have dwellings. Each comes out from its dwelling and later returns to it. The light leaves its home in the morning and returns to it at night, then darkness comes from its dwelling to return at dawn. **Where is the way to the dwelling of light . . . ?** can be translated easily if it is possible to retain the personification. For example, FRCL says "Do you know where the light lives?"

TEV avoids the figurative expression: "Do you know where the light comes from?" **The light** refers to the kind of light made by the sun and is the same word used in Genesis 1.3.

And where is the place of darkness: place corresponds to **dwelling** in the previous line. This line recalls Job's question in 28.12b "where is the place of understanding?" FRCL pushes the irony of the personification further than the text may imply: "at what address can one find darkness?" TEV "or what the source of darkness is?" is a suitable rendering. GECL has "from what place does darkness come?" In some languages it may be possible to render verse 19 as "Do you know where to go to find the light or where to find darkness?" or "Do you know where the light goes or from where darkness comes?"

That you may take it to its territory: it in both lines is singular in Hebrew, but refers to the light and the darkness in verse 19. Therefore it is best to use the plural, as in TEV "them." The notion is that Job would have to know where light and darkness live in order to lead them out to **their territory**, that is, to the place where they do their work, ". . . so that you could show them the way to their place of work."

And that you may discern the paths to its home: only by knowing the path to their dwellings could the light and darkness know where to go when they stop working. It is possible to express verses 19 and 20 as condition and consequence. For example, "If you know the path to the dwelling of the light and the place where darkness lives, then you may lead them out to their work and back to their homes." In languages in which the figures of dwellings for light and darkness will be unclear, it may be possible to render verse 20 as "If you know, you should be able to show them where they are to go and where they are to return."

38.21	RSV	TEV
	You know, for you were born then, and the number of your days is great!	I am sure you can, because you're so old and were there when the world was made!

You know, for you were born then continues the divine speaker's sarcasm of Job's wisdom and is much like that of Eliphaz in 15.7. **You know** suggests "You know the answers to all these questions." **Born then** means that Job was alive then, that he existed that long ago. TEV has adapted verse 21a to refer to verse 20 by saying "I am sure you can." The sarcastic reason Job supposedly can **know** is that he was already born at the time of creation.

And the number of your days is great translates the Hebrew literally. Logically this line is a consequence of the previous line. That is, since line a is true, line b is also true. "Because you were already born at the time of creation, you must be a very old man" or "You know all this because you were born when I created the world, and so you are very old." These renderings may have to be restructured in some languages to bring out the irony; for example, "You think you know the answers as if you had been born when I created the world. You must certainly be a very old man."

9A-4. The heavens (38.22-38)

RSV		TEV

	RSV		TEV
22	"Have you entered the storehouses of the snow, or have you seen the storehouses of the hail,	22	Have you ever visited the storerooms, where I keep the snow and the hail?
23	which I have reserved for the time of trouble, for the day of battle and war?	23	I keep them ready for times of trouble, for days of battle and war.
24	What is the way to the place where the light is distributed, or where the east wind is scattered upon the earth?	24	Have you been to the place where the sun comes up, or the place from which the east wind blows?
25	"Who has cleft a channel for the torrents of rain, and a way for the thunderbolt,	25	Who dug a channel for the pouring rain and cleared the way for the thunder-storm?
26	to bring rain on a land where no man is, on the desert in which there is no man;	26	Who makes rain fall where no one lives?
27	to satisfy the waste and desolate land, and to make the ground put forth grass?	27	Who waters the dry and thirsty land, so that grass springs up?
28	"Has the rain a father, or who has begotten the drops of dew?	28	Does either the rain or the dew have a father?
29	From whose womb did the ice come forth, and who has given birth to the hoar-frost of heaven?	29	Who is the mother of the ice and the frost,
30	The waters become hard like stone, and the face of the deep is frozen.	30	which turn the waters to stone and freeze the face of the sea?
31	"Can you bind the chains of the Pleiades, or loose the cords of Orion?	31	Can you tie the Pleiades together or loosen the bonds that hold Orion?
32	Can you lead forth the Mazzaroth in their season, or can you guide the Bear with its children?	32	Can you guide the stars season by season and direct the Big and the Little Dip-per?
33	Do you know the ordinances of the heav-ens? Can you establish their rule on the earth?	33	Do you know the laws that govern the skies, and can you make them apply to the earth?
34	"Can you lift up your voice to the clouds, that a flood of waters may cover you?	34	Can you shout orders to the clouds and make them drench you with rain?
35	Can you send forth lightnings, that they may go and say to you, 'Here we are'?	35	And if you command the lightning to flash, will it come to you and say, "At your service"?
36	Who has put wisdom in the clouds, or given understanding to the mists?	36	Who tells the ibis when the Nile will flood, or who tells the rooster that rain will fall?
37	Who can number the clouds by wisdom? Or who can tilt the waterskins of the heavens,	37	Who is wise enough to count the clouds and tilt them over to pour out the rain,
38	when the dust runs into a mass and the clods cleave fast together?	38	rain that hardens the dust into lumps?

Subdivision Heading

The Handbook heading may be modified to say, for example, "What do you know about the rain clouds?" or "Who sends the rain down on the earth?" Habel has "Phenomena of the heavens"; FRCL has (verses 4-38) "God, master of the inanimate world."

38.22

RSV	TEV
"Have you entered the store-houses of the snow, or have you seen the store-houses of the hail,	Have you ever visited the store-rooms, where I keep the snow and the hail?

Have you entered the storehouses of the snow begins another question in the Hebrew with the verb **entered**, just as in verse 16. **Snow** and **hail** are depicted as kept by God in warehouses, stored up for the proper season or occasion. **Hail** particularly is used by God as a weapon in Joshua 10.11; Exodus 9.22; Isaiah 28.17; Ezekiel 13.13. **Storehouses** or "storerooms" may also be rendered more generally as "places where the snow is kept."

The second line matches the first in meaning. **Hail** refers to small balls of ice that fall to the earth from the cold sky, usually associated with thunderstorms. TEV reduces the two lines of verse 22 to ". . . storerooms, where I keep the snow and hail." In translation it may be best to reduce the repetition of **storehouses** in the two lines to say, for example, "Have you gone to the place where I store up the snow and hail?" In tropical areas **hail** is often better known than **snow**. In some languages it may be preferable to say "cold and hail" or "dew and hail."

38.23

RSV	TEV
which I have reserved for the time of trouble, for the day of battle and war?	I keep them ready for times of trouble, for days of battle and war.

Which I have reserved for the time of trouble: this line begins with a relative particle translated as **which**, connecting verse 23 to verse 22. God has kept snow and hail **for the time of trouble**.

The day of battle and war makes specific what is meant by the parallel **time of trouble** in line a. God threw hailstones down on the Amorites in Joshua 10.11 as they fled from Israel. **Battle and war** appear to be a fixed pair of expressions. No attempt is made to distinguish these as different kinds of events. In some languages it may be necessary to adjust verse 23 to say, for example, "I have kept them stored up in case of troubles when there is a war" or "I keep them stored for the times when people fight and have wars."

38.24　　　RSV　　　　　　　　　　　　　　TEV

What is the way to the place
　　where the light is distribut-
　　ed,
　　or where the east wind is scat-
　　tered upon the earth?

Have you been to the place where
　　the sun comes up,
　　or the place from which the
　　east wind blows?

What is the way to the place where the light is distributed . . . ? This line has the same wording in Hebrew as in verse 19a, except for the verb **is distributed.** The sense of the line is unclear in RSV. **What is the way** inquires how to find, and it is better rendered in English as "Where is?" "How does one get to?" "How does one find?" The Hebrew word translated as **light** has been changed in many different ways to produce a line that is more clearly parallel with the next line. Dhorme and others change **light** to get "mist." TEV understands **light** to refer to the sun, and then translates **is distributed** as "comes up." This may be the intention of the poet, but the Hebrew does not suggest it. NIV may be closer by taking **light** to refer to "lightning," as was the case in 36.30 and 32, "What is the way to the place where the lightning is dispersed," that is, "sent out." The line may also be rendered as "Do you know how to find the place where I send out the lightning?" or "Do you know how to go to where I cause the lightning to flash?"

Or where the east wind is scattered upon the earth? has given rise to numerous proposals for change to make this line more parallel with line a, but no such changes are necessary. **East wind** translates the same word as in 15.2 and 27.21. The reference is to the scorching winds that blow across the desert from the east. **Scatter** translates the Hebrew, but in English the action of the wind normally scatters objects in its path, and the action itself is expressed as "to blow." Therefore TEV has "or the place from which the east wind blows?" **East wind** should be translated to show the direction from which the wind blows; that is, "Or where the wind blows from the east," or "blows out of the east," or "blows from east to west."

38.25-27　　　RSV　　　　　　　　　　　　　TEV

25　"Who has cleft a channel for the
　　　torrents of rain,
　　　and a way for the thunderbolt,
26　to bring rain on a land where no
　　　man is,
　　　on the desert in which there is
　　　no man;
27　to satisfy the waste and desolate
　　　land,
　　　and to make the ground put
　　　forth grass?

25　Who dug a channel for the pour-
　　　ing rain
　　　and cleared the way for the
　　　thunderstorm?
26　Who makes rain fall where no
　　　one lives?
27　Who waters the dry and thirsty
　　　land,
　　　so that grass springs up?

In Hebrew, as in RSV, these three verses form a single sentence and so will be handled together. TEV expresses each verse as a separate "who" question. Verse 25 poses the question and verses 26 and 27 extend the question in terms of purposes. All three verses refer to God's activity in sending rain. The implied answer to God's question is "I did."

Who has cleft a channel for the torrents of rain depicts the rain as coming to the earth directed along grooves or trenches in the sky. The word rendered as **channel** is the same as the "trench" built around the altar in 1 Kings 18.32. In 28.26 the rain is said to follow a "decree" or "rule," which emphasizes the order of events in nature. These **channels** which guide the raindrops as they descend are in the sky, but TEV "dug a channel" is likely to give the impression that they are on the earth. The word translated as **cleft** means "to cut up or to divide" and pictures God cutting grooves in the sky to direct the raindrops. **Torrents of rain** translates a noun based on a verb meaning "to flood." These are rains which are so heavy that they cause flooding, and so "downpours, pouring rains, torrential rains." It may be clearer in some languages to speak generally and say, "Who made a way for the pouring rains to fall?" or "Who made the path down which the torrential rains flow?"

Verse 25b is identical to 28.26b in the Hebrew. **And a way for the thunderbolt** is parallel in meaning to line a. The verb in the first line serves in the second line also. **Way** translates "path, road," which is parallel to **channels** in line a. **Thunderbolt** translates "claps of thunder, rumble of thunder, noise of thunder." Even the sound of thunder is depicted as being under God's control. In some languages it may be preferable to join both lines of verse 25 into one and say, for example, "Who made a way for the pouring rain and the noise of thunder?" In some cases it will be better to shift "rains" to the end of verse 25 in order to relate it more closely to the subject "rain" in verse 26a.

To bring rain on a land where no man is states at least one of the purposes for which God controls the rain, and that is to make it rain where no human beings are found. The two lines are reduced to one by TEV. In line a the purpose is to bring rain on the uninhabited **land**. The verb phrase **to bring rain** is not repeated in line b but is understood as applying there also.

On the desert suggests intensification in line b. God not only makes it rain on uninhabited land, but even on the desert. The word translated as **man** in line a is different from the word translated as **man** in line b. However, this difference is not crucial for the poetic movement nor for the sense. Verse 26 may be rendered, for example, as "Who makes it rain in places where no one lives, and even in empty deserts?"

Verse 27 gives the reason or purpose of verse 26. **To satisfy the waste and desolate land: satisfy** translates the word used in 9.18, where it was rendered as "fills me." The sense is "to satisfy with water," and this may be more clearly expressed as "to water," as in TEV "who waters the . . . ." **Waste and desolate land** is a description of the desert. It translates the same Hebrew phrase used in 30.3, where TEV translates "wild, desolate places." A desolate place is one where human life cannot be sustained. Here TEV translates "dry and thirsty land," which appears to be a textual change, but no note is given. Job observes in 12.15 that if God "withholds the waters, they dry up." Here God replies by pointing out that he sends rain even in the places where no humans live, in order to give life to the grass.

And to make the ground put forth grass is literally "and cause to sprout the source of grass," which is not entirely clear. Dhorme makes a change to get "from the steppe." HOTTP gives "And make a yield of grass shoot up," which is expressed adequately by TEV "so that grass springs up." "Springs up" means "grows up quickly" due to the rains. Translators may follow TEV and others with another "who" question, or better RSV, which has a clause of purpose. The latter may be rendered, for example, as "This is done to water the dry desert so that grass grows."

38.28	RSV	TEV

	"Has the rain a father,
	    or who has begotten the drops
	        of dew?
		Does either the rain or the dew
		    have a father?

Has the rain a father asks a question as to the origin of the rain based on the human analogy. For Job the question has a clear answer: "No." **Who has begotten** in the Hebrew may suggest either the mother's or the father's role in giving birth. However, the mother's role will come up in the next verse, and so it is best to consider the second line as still referring to the father. **Drops** in **drops of dew** translates a word that occurs only here in the Old Testament, but in the context there is little uncertainty about the meaning. TEV has reduced the two lines to one with "Does either the rain or the dew have a father?" However, this loses some of the poetic effect. In languages in which the suggestion of the rain having a father or being conceived must be restructured for clarity, we may be able to say, for example, "Is the rain a person that must have a father? No!" "Has a human father made the rain?" "Does the rain come from a human father? Of course not!" The second line may be translated "Were the dew drops conceived like children? No."

38.29	RSV	TEV

	From whose womb did the ice
	    come forth,
	and who has given birth to the
	    hoarfrost of heaven?
		Who is the mother of the ice and
		    the frost,

From whose womb did the ice come forth shifts the imagery to the mother, and TEV asks "Who is the mother of the ice?" **Comes forth** is the same term that was used in 1.21; 3.11. The word translated as **womb** is literally "belly." **Ice** translates a word which is sometimes rendered appropriately as "hail," but due to verse 30 it is best understood here as **ice**, as in 6.16; 37.10.

In the second line the word translated as **given birth** has the same root as the verb in the causative form in verse 28b, which is rendered as **begotten** and applied to the father. Here it refers to the mother's act of giving birth. **Hoarfrost** refers to dew on the ground which freezes hard on cold, clear nights. Like the snow, the **hoarfrost** is sent from heaven by God, as in Psalm 147.16, "he scatters the hoarfrost like ashes." By reducing the two lines in verse 28 and the two lines in verse 29, TEV has created a parallelism between these two verses. However, unless there are linguistic reasons for avoiding the parallel lines in these two verses, they should be kept. Verse 29 may require adjustments in translation similar to those in verse 28. For example, "Did a mother give birth to the ice? No." "Does the ice have a mother as a child does? Of course not."

38.30   RSV   TEV

> The waters become hard like   which turn the waters to stone
>   stone,   and freeze the face of the sea?
> and the face of the deep is
>   frozen.

RSV translates verse 30 as an independent statement, but it is better as a consequence of verse 29, as in TEV.

The waters become hard like stone translates the Hebrew "the waters hide themselves." The word translated as "hide" has a variant form which means "harden," and so **become hard**, and this suits the context better than "hide." Habel analyzes the problem as a poetic case where the verb in the first line provides the sense for the verb in the second line, and the second for the first also. Normally the "deep is hidden" and water "freezes over," but here the verbs are reversed so as to apply to the subject in the other line. Even if this is the case, it is normally necessary to adjust the wording in order to make the meaning clear. Therefore it is best to translate line a, for example, as "which make the water hard like stone." In line b **face of the deep** refers to the surface of the ocean. The verb translated as **is frozen** means "to become set, to solidify or form a solid mass," and so TEV has "and freeze the face of the sea." In languages unacquainted with freezing it may be possible to say "and the surface of the sea becomes hard" or "becomes cold and hard."

38.31   RSV   TEV

> "Can you bind the chains of the   Can you tie the Pleiades together
>   Pleiades,   or loosen the bonds that hold
> or loose the cords of Orion?   Orion?

The questions now shift to the constellations of the stars. **Can you bind the chains of the Pleiades: bind** renders a verb meaning "to tie, knot together," and so the question refers to tying up the seven stars of the cluster called the Pleiades to keep them together in a group. **Chains** translates a word found elsewhere only in 1 Samuel 15.32, which RSV translates there as "cheerfully." That meaning is obviously not appropriate here. Scholars point out that most probably the word used here is related to the verb "to tie," but in this form two of the consonants have been switched. The combination **bind the chains** therefore means "to chain or tie together." The words for **the Pleiades** and **Orion** were used in 9.9. See there for comments, and note the descriptions and the star maps in the Appendix, page 781.

Or loose the cords of Orion puts the question in the reverse sense in regard to **Orion**. The word translated as **cords** occurs nowhere else in the Old Testament, but it is related to the verb meaning "to pull," and so the uncertainty is largely eliminated. It is not clear what the **cords of Orion** may be, other than a parallel for the similar expression in line a. NEB thinks **cords** may refer to the three aligned stars that make up Orion's belt. **The Pleiades** and **Orion** are found in the same general area of the night sky, **the Pleiades** being relatively small and indistinct, while **Orion** is vast and easily seen. This line may be rendered as in NEB, "or loose Orion's belt?" If readers are unfamiliar with these northern constellations, a note may be required. Otherwise we may translate more generally; for example, "or loose the cords that hold together the group of stars called Orion."

38.32	RSV	TEV
	Can you lead forth the Mazzaroth in their season, or can you guide the Bear with its children?	Can you guide the stars season by season and direct the Big and the Little Dipper?

Can you lead forth the Mazzaroth continues the questions regarding Job's control over the heavenly bodies. **Mazzaroth** is the transliteration of a Hebrew word which is much disputed. The word is similar to a word used in 2 Kings 23.5 translated as "constellations" (RSV) and "planets" (TEV), but in the form used here it is found nowhere else. Dhorme translates it as "Corona," by which he means *Corona Borealis*, the Latin name of the constellation "Northern Crown." Others take it to be the signs of the Zodiac, or the circle of the Zodiac. TEV avoids any reference to a specific constellation and translates "stars." FRCL translates in the text "signs of the Zodiac," and in a footnote says "Other possible translations of a unique Hebrew word of uncertain meaning: the planets, or Venus, or the constellation Corona Borealis." **In their season** refers to the right time for the stars to appear in their positions in the sky; that is, "to appear on time" or "to appear at the proper time." Translators are advised that it is better to err by being too general, due to the uncertainty involved if one attempts to be specific. Therefore TEV supplies a good model to follow. This line may also be rendered, for example, as "Can you tell the stars when they should appear?" or "Can you guide the stars so they will appear at the right time?"

Or can you guide the Bear with its children: the Bear, according to Dhorme, refers to the same constellation called by that name in 9.9, although there is a slight difference in the vowels. **The Bear** translates what is most probably the "Great Bear," known also by its Latin name *Ursa Major*, or in English "The Big Dipper." **Its children** are then the group of stars known as *Ursa Minor*, "Little Bear," also called "The Little Dipper," which contains Polaris, the North Star. Both of these are northern hemisphere constellations. (Note the description and the star map in the Appendix, page 781.) TEV is no doubt correct calling them "the Big and the Little Dipper." Translators in the northern hemisphere should be able to identify these stars easily, as they are visible throughout the year, weather conditions permitting. Translators in the southern hemisphere who are unacquainted with these constellations may find it best to speak of "stars in the northern skies" or, more specifically, "stars in the north called Big Bear and Little Bear."

38.33   RSV   TEV

> Do you know the ordinances of   Do you know the laws that gov-
>   the heavens?   ern the skies,
> Can you establish their rule on   and can you make them apply
>   the earth?   to the earth?

Do you know the ordinances of the heavens inquires if Job knows the laws that control the movements of the heavenly bodies, or as TEV says, "laws that govern the skies." This may also be expressed in some languages as "Do you know what roads the lights in the sky follow?" or "Do you know the way in which the lights in the sky are controlled?"

Can you establish their rule on the earth: **rule** translates a word found nowhere else in the Old Testament. It may be related to a root having to do with "writing, or what is written." In view of this Dhorme translates "Do you fulfill on earth what is written there?" The thought may be that the stars influence events on earth, and this is implied in RSV's rendering, which means "Can you make the laws in the heavens apply to the earth?" That is also the thought of TEV. Verse 33 may be rendered as "Do you know what rules the lights in the sky obey? Can you make the same rules apply on the earth? or "Can the same rules be followed on the earth?"

38.34   RSV   TEV

> "Can you lift up your voice to the   Can you shout orders to the
>   clouds,   clouds
> that a flood of waters may   and make them drench you
>   cover you?   with rain?

Can you lift up your voice to the clouds questions Job's ability to direct the clouds in a way similar to the question asked in verse 33b. The clouds are not ordered about by men. In 36.29 Elihu asks Job "Can anyone understand the spreading of the clouds?" **Lift your voice** means "shout out orders, call out commands."

That a flood of waters may cover you is identical to 22.11b, but the context is different. In the Septuagint **cover you** is translated as "answer you." The HOTTP committee was divided between those preferring the Septuagint and those wanting the Hebrew text, which RSV follows. Most modern translations follow the Hebrew. The line may be translated, for example, as "so that the rain will submerge you," "so that rain will flood over you," or "and cause the rain to drown you like a flood."

38.35   RSV   TEV

Can you send forth lightnings,   And if you command the light-
    that they may go   ning to flash,
    and say to you, 'Here we are'?   will it come to you and say,
                                             "At your service"?

Can you send forth lightnings asks if Job can make lightning like God does
in 36.32, where he commands the lightning to strike. The form of the verb translated
as **send forth** means "release, unleash," as in 12.15; 20.23. In 36.32; 37.11-13, the
lightnings are God's servants, and they do as he wishes. **That they may go** means
go to the place where Job is, or "come to where you are," as if these personal
servants are returning for further orders.

The lightnings then say **Here we are**, which is the plural form of the response
formula said by Moses to the LORD in Exodus 3.4, and by Samuel to Eli in 1 Samuel
3.4-6. TEV "At your service" suggests a servant ready to do what his master tells him.
TEV supplies a good translation model for verse 35. It may also be rendered, for
example, as "Can you send the lightning flashing so it will return to you and ask
'Where next, Master?' "

38.36   RSV   TEV

Who has put wisdom in the   Who tells the ibis[s] when the Nile
    clouds,[h]   will flood,
    or given understanding to the   or who tells the rooster that
    mists?[h]   rain will fall?[t]

[h] The meaning of the Hebrew word is   [s] IBIS: *A bird in ancient Egypt that was*
uncertain   *believed to announce the flooding of the*
                                             Nile River.

                                             [t] *Verse 36 in Hebrew is unclear.*

Who has put wisdom in the clouds is clear except for the words translated
as **clouds** in line a and **mists** in line b. The RSV note says the meaning of both
words is uncertain. The suggestions put forth by interpreters are numerous and
confusing, but there are four major lines of interpretation: (1) psychological terms
such as NJV "hidden parts" and "mind," or NEB "darkness" and "secrecy";
(2) meteorological (weather) terms such as RSV "clouds" and "mist"; (3) mythological terms: Pope has "Thoth," the Egyptian God, and "Sekwi," the Coptic name for
Mercury; (4) zoological terms (names of creatures) such as Dhorme "ibis" and
"cock." TEV has followed the lead of Dhorme and made the wisdom of the "ibis" and
"cock" specific by ". . . ibis when the Nile will flood or . . . rooster that rain will fall."
TEV also gives a note on the "ibis" and a note on the Hebrew text of this verse.
HOTTP admits the possibility of the meanings "ibis" and "cock," but denies the
possibility of psychological meanings such as "inward parts" and "heart." Rowley,
who summarizes many views, concludes "while there can be no certainty of the

meaning, RSV gives the most probable sense." The meteorological line of interpretation seems to fit the context of verses 34-38 best. However, TEV cannot be ruled out and is secondarily based on weather conditions. If the translator follows RSV, the expression **put wisdom in the clouds** may have to be restructured to say, for example, "Who has enabled the clouds to rain?" or "Who has made the clouds so that they know how to rain?" The second line may be rendered as "And who has shown the mist how to rise?" If these solutions are not satisfactory, translators may be able to follow a widely-used version of the language area.

38.37-38   RSV   TEV

37 Who can number the clouds by wisdom? Or who can tilt the waterskins of the heavens,	37 Who is wise enough to count the clouds and tilt them over to pour out the rain,
38 when the dust runs into a mass and the clods cleave fast together?	38 rain that hardens the dust into lumps?

These two verses are linked by **when**, referring to the time of the action in verse 37.

Who can number the clouds by wisdom asks if anyone has the wisdom to get an accurate count of the vast number of clouds in the sky. This may refer to the fact that their number changes constantly, and so before anyone could reach a total, the counting would have to begin again, and again. **Wisdom** here has more to do with skill than knowledge, and so FRCL "Who is sufficiently skilled to count the clouds?"

Tilt the waterskins of the heavens depicts the clouds as water containers, as in 26.8a. **Tilt** translates the causative form of a verb meaning "to lay something down," that is, "to turn on its side," or more specifically of a water-filled container, "to pour out." This line may be rendered, for example, as "and to pour out the rain from the water jars in the sky" or "turn over the clouds and pour out the rain."

When the dust runs into a mass depicts a situation that exists at the time of the pouring out of the rain in verse 37. It is the action of the rain that hardens the dust. A literal rendering can be "when the dust hardens into a mass."

The clods cleave fast together says something similar to the statement in line a, but **clods**, lumps of soil, replaces **dust**. As in line a, the action of the rain is to cause **clods** of earth to stick together and thus make larger **clods**. TEV reduces the two lines to one and places verse 38 in apposition to **rain** in verse 37. However, the rain is performing two distinct actions on the ground, one on the **dust** and the other on the **clods**. NEB expresses both lines well: ". . . when the dusty soil sets hard as iron, and the clods of earth cling together?" This may also be expressed, for example, ". . . when the dusty ground forms hard clumps, and the clods of earth stick together?"

9A-5. Wild life (38.39–39.12)

RSV	TEV

RSV

39   "Can you hunt the prey for the lion,
    or satisfy the appetite of the young
      lions,
40   when they crouch in their dens,
    or lie in wait in their covert?
41   Who provides for the raven its prey,
    when its young ones cry to God,
    and wander about for lack of food?

Chapter 39
1   "Do you know when the mountain goats
    bring forth?
    Do you observe the calving of the
      hinds?
2   Can you number the months that they
    fulfil,
    and do you know the time when they
    bring forth,
3   when they crouch, bring forth their off-
    spring,
    and are delivered of their young?
4   Their young ones become strong, they
    grow up in the open;
    they go forth, and do not return to
    them.

5   "Who has let the wild ass go free?
    Who has loosed the bonds of the swift
    ass,
6   to whom I have given the steppe for his
    home,
    and the salt land for his dwelling
    place?
7   He scorns the tumult of the city;
    he hears not the shouts of the driver.
8   He ranges the mountains as his pasture,
    and he searches after every green
    thing.

9   "Is the wild ox willing to serve you?
    Will he spend the night at your crib?
10   Can you bind him in the furrow with
    ropes,
    or will he harrow the valleys after you?
11   Will you depend on him because his
    strength is great,
    and will you leave to him your labor?
12   Do you have faith in him that he will
    return,
    and bring your grain to your threshing
    floor?

TEV

39   Do you find food for lions to eat,
    and satisfy hungry young lions
40   when they hide in their caves,
    or lie in wait in their dens?
41   Who is it that feeds the ravens
    when they wander about hungry,
    when their young cry to me for food?

Chapter 39
1   Do you know when mountain goats are
    born?
    Have you watched wild deer give
    birth?
2   Do you know how long they carry their
    young?
    Do you know the time for their birth?
3   Do you know when they will crouch down
    and bring their young into the world?
4   In the wilds their young grow strong;
    they go away and don't come back.

5   Who gave the wild donkeys their free-
    dom?
    Who turned them loose and let them
    roam?
6   I gave them the desert to be their home,
    and let them live on the salt plains.
7   They keep far away from the noisy cities,
    and no one can tame them and make
    them work.
8   The mountains are the pastures where
    they feed,
    where they search for anything green
    to eat.

9   Will a wild ox work for you?
    Is he willing to spend the night in your
    stable?
10   Can you hold one with a rope and make
    him plow?
    Or make him pull a harrow in your
    fields?
11   Can you rely on his great strength
    and expect him to do your heavy
    work?
12   Do you expect him to bring in your har-
    vest
    and gather the grain from your thresh-
    ing place?

The focus now shifts to wild life, and this will continue through 39.12.

Subdivision Heading

The Handbook heading may be modified to say, for example, "The LORD asks Job about the animals," "What do you know about the animals?" or "Do you provide for the animals?" Habel has "The kingdom of the wild," Rowley "A survey of the mysteries of animal and bird life surpassed Job's understanding," and TOB "Sovereign of the animals."

38.39-40   RSV   TEV

39 "Can you hunt the prey for the   39   Do you find food for lions to eat,
       lion,   and satisfy hungry young lions
     or satisfy the appetite of the   40   when they hide in their caves,
       young lions,   or lie in wait in their dens?
40 when they crouch in their dens,
     or lie in wait in their covert?

Can you hunt the prey for the lion . . . ? shows that God, in contrast to human beings, provides the lion with victims for food. **Hunt** translates the same verb used in 10.16. It means to search for the purpose of killing, not just to find. Lions stalk their victims, as all cats do, by quietly creeping toward them and then springing on them. Obviously Job is not capable of doing this. **Lion** translates one of the terms for "lion" or "lioness" used by Eliphaz in 4.11, and **young lions** is used in 4.10. See there for comments. The same term is used in Psalm 104.21, where God supplies their food. See also 4.11 for comments on **prey**.

Satisfy the appetite of means "give them all they can eat," "fill their stomachs."

When they crouch in their dens depicts the lions hidden from sight while they lie in their dens. The word rendered as **crouch** is used in 9.13 ("bowed") and 22.29 ("lowered [eyes]" for "lowly"), but in very different contexts. Here the sense is parallel to **lie in wait** in the next line. The word translated as **dens** was used in 37.8.

Lie in wait is what the lions are doing. **Covert** translates a word meaning "booth" or "hut," as used in 27.18, and is here qualified further with "of their ambush." So the whole phrase refers to a place such as a thicket where a lion can conceal itself and spring on its unsuspecting victim.

38.41   RSV   TEV

Who provides for the raven its   Who is it that feeds the ravens
     prey,   when they wander about hun-
  when its young ones cry to   gry,
     God,   when their young cry to me for
  and wander about for lack of   food?
     food?

Who provides for the raven its prey shifts from the king of beasts to another meat-eating creature, the bird called the **raven**. The **raven**, unlike the lion, feeds on dead flesh. It is a black bird similar to the crow. For details see *Fauna and Flora of the Bible,* pages 67-69. Psalm 147.9 says that "he gives . . . to the young ravens which cry." RSV follows the Hebrew order, which gives the impression in line c̲ that the baby ravens are wandering about outside the nest. In order to avoid this impression, TEV transposes lines b̲ and c̲, which makes "wander about hungry" apply to the ravens in line a̲ and not to their young. This improves the logic of the verse. The word translated as **prey** in line a̲ is not the same as the word used for the lion's **prey** in verse 39a. TEV has restructured the line to say ". . . feeds the ravens." The line may also be rendered, for example, as "Who provides food for the ravens."

When its young ones cry to God describes the baby ravens in the nest calling out to God for food. **Wander about** translates a verb which can also mean "stagger about." That is, a creature that is starving staggers when it moves. It is possible to understand this line as referring to their weakness from lack of food. In this case it is not necessary to transpose lines b̲ and c̲. For example, FRCL keeps the Hebrew line order and translates "Who provides food for the raven, when its little ones call out to God for help, and who are weakened by lack of something to eat." This provides a good translation model to follow.

39.1	RSV	TEV

<table>
<tr><td>"Do you know when the mountain goats bring forth? Do you observe the calving of the hinds?</td><td>Do you know when mountain goats are born? Have you watched wild deer give birth?</td></tr>
</table>

39.1-4 forms a unit describing the birth and growth of mountain goats.

Do you know when the mountain goats bring forth? The word translated as **when** is deleted by Dhorme and others in order to improve the meter of this line. The word is said to be an unintended repetition of the last two consonants of the phrase translated as **Do you know.** With its deletion the sense is "Do you know the bringing forth (giving birth) of mountain goats?" RSV and TEV retain the word so that the reference is to the time when they give birth. The reference may be to the season of the year and is so handled by FRCL; NJV says "Do you know the season when the mountain goats give birth?"

Mountain goats is literally "goats of the rock." NJB, NEB, NAB, RSV, and TEV have "mountain goats," Mft "wild goats," Dhorme "antelopes of the rock," and Pope translates "ibex." For a detailed description of the **mountain goat,** see *Fauna and Flora of the Bible,* pages 46-47. **Bring forth** means "to give birth." This refers to the female goat giving birth to her young. TEV shifts the focus to the young by asking ". . . when mountain goats are born?"

In language areas where wild mountain goats are unknown, it may be possible to substitute another animal of a similar nature. If domestic goats are known, it is usually possible to use the same term and qualify them as "wild" or, for example, "goats that run loose in the hills." This line may be rendered "Do you know the time of the year when wild goats have their young?" or ". . . give birth to their young?"

Do you observe the calving of the hinds? asks if Job spends his time in the isolated mountains where these wild animals are seldom seen, especially at the time when they give birth to their young. **Calving** means "to give birth to a calf," the young of certain kinds of animals such as cows and deer. The word **hinds** in Hebrew refers to the adult female deer. The matching units of lines a and b are "know . . . observe," "female wild goats . . . female wild deer," "giving birth . . . calving." In translation it may be necessary to substitute another wild animal for the deer if one is known. Line b shifts the thought to a more concrete act. As TEV says, "Have you watched wild deer give birth?" In both lines of verse 1, it is possible to speak of "small wild animals" and "big wild animals" if no substitute animals are available.

39.2	RSV	TEV
	Can you number the months that they fulfil, and do you know the time when they bring forth,	Do you know how long they carry their young? Do you know the time for their birth?

Can you number the months that they fulfil asks if Job can tell how many months these animals carry their young; that is, how long they are pregnant before giving birth. The question in verse 2b repeats the question of verse 1a and most probably refers to goats and deer. Verse 2 may also be expressed, for example, "Do you know how many months they carry their offspring?" or ". . . they are pregnant?" Line b may be joined to line a; for example, "Do you know how many months these animals carry their young (inside them) and the time when they give birth?"

39.3	RSV	TEV
	when they crouch, bring forth their offspring, and are delivered of their young?	Do you know when they will crouch down and bring their young into the world?

When they crouch repeats the thought of verse 2b by making the question somewhat more vivid. **Crouch** translates a verb used of women in childbirth in 1 Samuel 4.19, where it is translated as "bowed." In regard to the deer it depicts the animal bending the hind legs to lower the body to the ground so that the young one is close to the ground as it comes out. **Bring forth** translates a different verb than the one used in verses 1a and 2b. Here the word means "to cleave, divide in two," but with offspring as the subject that meaning is inappropriate. Therefore many scholars make a slight change in the Hebrew to get "drop." However, Driver defends the usage as idiomatic, and so NEB translates "to open their wombs." The sense is "to give birth" and is probably best left as a general statement, as in RSV.

And are delivered of their young renders what is literally "they send out their labor pains." However, in the context the reference is not to labor pains but to what causes the pains, namely, the offspring. FRCL gives a clear translation of verse 3:

"The females crouch down in order to put their young on the ground." This verse may also be rendered "The females lower themselves so their young do not fall to the ground in birth."

39.4	RSV	TEV
	Their young ones become strong, they grow up in the open; they go forth, and do not return to them.	In the wilds their young grow strong; they go away and don't come back.

Verse 4 is not related to the birth process of verses 1-3 but is a comment that emphasizes the early maturity of these wild animals. **Their young ones become strong** means that these newborn animals become healthy and vigorous. **In the open** translates an Aramaic word found only here and refers to the open countryside, free from restrictions put on domestic animals that are taken into enclosures to protect them. In the second line **they go forth** means "they leave"; that is, "they leave their mothers and do not return to them."

39.5	RSV	TEV
	"Who has let the wild ass go free? Who has loosed the bonds of the swift ass,	Who gave the wild donkeys their freedom? Who turned them loose and let them roam?

In verses 5-8 the writer thinks of the wild donkey as a domestic donkey that has been granted its freedom, released from its bondage to the city. Translators may consider leaving blank space before verse 5 to show that a new subject is beginning.

Who has let the wild ass go free? implies that it is God who has liberated these animals. **Wild ass** is the same animal named in 6.5. See there for comments. **Wild ass** is singular, but translators may find it more natural to use the plural and also the plural pronouns throughout these nature passages. Compare also 11.12 and 24.5. **Go free** means "to be free to go where it wishes."

Loosed the bonds is equivalent to "untied the ropes" or "taken off the rope that held the animal." This usage is figurative and means "given them their freedom" or "let them roam free." **Swift ass** translates an Aramaic word found nowhere else in the Old Testament. However, there is no reason to assume that the animal in line b is any other than the one in line a. Distinguishing between these two animals is not the point of the verse, and TEV and others use only one term. The meaning of the two lines is nearly identical and without poetic focusing or intensification. If the "who" questions are used here, it may be necessary in translation to insert the reply "I did." In some languages it will be clearer to translate "I let the wild donkey go free" or "I am the one who let the wild donkey roam." The line may be rendered, for example, "I am the one who gave them their freedom" or ". . . who let them go free."

39.6   RSV   TEV

> to whom I have given the steppe
>   for his home,
> and the salt land for his dwell-
>   ing place?

> I gave them the desert to be their
>   home,
> and let them live on the salt
>   plains.

The steppe for his home names the place God has given the wild donkey to live. In 24.5 the wild donkey is associated with the desert and the wilderness. Both terms emphasize the uninhabited and uncultivated nature of such a place. The term rendered **steppe** here is the same as the one translated as "wilderness" in 24.5. In the second line **salt land**, which matches **steppe** in the first line, refers to ground that is infertile, an area that will not produce grass or food. In Judges 9.45 the land was sown with salt to make it infertile. The "salt plains" near the Dead Sea were known to lack vegetation. See also Jeremiah 17.6; Psalm 107.34. TEV translates "salt plains." In some languages the word translated as **steppe** will be translated as "desert" or "place where no one lives or cultivates," and **salt land** as "a place where no grass grows." Verse 6 may then be translated as "I gave them a place to live where people do not live or farm, and a place where the grass does not grow."

39.7   RSV   TEV

> He scorns the tumult of the city;
>   he hears not the shouts of the
>   driver.

> They keep far away from the
>   noisy cities,
> and no one can tame them and
>   make them work.

He scorns the tumult of the city depicts the wild donkey **scorning** (literally "laughing at") the noisy city. The wild donkey sees no reward in living under the stress and din of civilization. In the open deserts he is free to roam, and, unlike his domesticated cousin, **he hears not the shouts of the driver. Shouts** translates the same word rendered "thunderings" in 36.29. In 3.18 the word here rendered **driver** was translated as "taskmaster," meaning the one who oversees slaves doing forced labor. See Isaiah 9.4. **Driver** refers here to the man who drives the animals, making them work, a task that is carried out by whipping the animals and shouting commands at them. The fortunate wild donkey hears none of this abuse. TEV's rendering is too general and should not be followed.

In languages in which **scorns** or "laughs at" cannot be said of a donkey or other animal, translators must often express this differently; for example, "He avoids the noise of the city," or as in TEV, "keep far away from the noisy cities." The second line may also be expressed "they never hear donkey-drivers shouting at them" or "they never hear men shouting at them to make them work."

39.8   RSV   TEV

He ranges the mountains as his
      pasture,
and he searches after every
      green thing.

The mountains are the pastures
      where they feed,
where they search for anything
      green to eat.

He ranges the mountains as his pasture depicts the wild donkey searching over great distances for his food, which is scarce in the deserts. **Ranges** translates a word meaning "to scour, search intensely, look everywhere for." Where the donkey searches is in the desert mountains. RSV **as his pasture** translates the words for "his pasture," which is in apposition with **mountains**.

He searches after every green thing represents a focusing of the animal's search for food. In line a he searches the mountains which are his pasture, barren as they are. In line b he tracks down every green thing that grows. Verse 8 may be rendered, for example, "He (they) looks everywhere in the mountains for his food, and searches out every green blade of grass to eat."

39.9   RSV   TEV

"Is the wild ox willing to serve
      you?
Will he spend the night at your
      crib?

Will a wild ox work for you?
Is he willing to spend the night
      in your stable?

Having dealt with the contrast between the domestic and wild donkey, the divine speaker now takes up the same contrasts between the domestic and wild ox.

Is the wild ox willing to serve you: **wild ox** translates a term used in Deuteronomy 33.17 which speaks of Joseph having horns like those of a wild ox, to "push peoples . . . to the ends of the earth." The parallelism in Psalm 29.6 and in Isaiah 34.7 implies that the term refers to some kind of ox. (KJV translates it as "unicorn.") Although **ox** in English refers mainly to a male bovine animal that has been castrated and is used for labor, the animal here was a powerful wild animal with dangerous horns, and in fact it was hunted by the ancient Assyrians. Its characteristics make it appear similar to the African "bush cow" or buffalo. Its strength and fierceness are mentioned in Numbers 23.22; Deuteronomy 33.17; Psalm 92.10. For a discussion of **ox** and "cow," see *Fauna and Flora of the Bible,* pages 62-63. Dhorme translates "buffalo," but in English this term requires a modifier such as "wild." **Serve you** refers to doing heavy labor such as pulling a cart or plow, as in TEV "work for you." In languages in which the **ox** is unknown, we may say "wild cow" or substitute another animal if appropriate. The evident answer to the question in line a is "No!"

Will he spend the night at your crib implies being closed up in a pen in order to eat. At night the domestic ox is brought from the fields to spend the night in a pen or stable. The word for **crib** occurs also in Isaiah 1.3; Proverbs 14.4 (RSV footnote). It refers to the feed box or "trough" where the owner places food for the animals. TEV "stable" is the building where the feed box is located. This line may also be expressed "Will the wild ox come to your feed box and spend the night?" or "Will the wild ox stay all night at the place where you feed your animals?"

39.10 RSV   TEV

Can you bind him in the furrow   Can you hold one with a rope
   with ropes,   and make him plow?
or will he harrow the valleys   Or make him pull a harrow in
   after you?   your fields?

Verse 10 is difficult as it stands. HOTTP gives three suggestions. However, the recommendations each contain the expression "bind or tie to the furrow," and the idea of an ox tied to a furrow is far from clear. **Can you bind him in the furrow with ropes**: in place of **him** the Hebrew text has "wild ox." A **furrow** is a trench in the ground made by a plow. Dhorme makes a change to get "If you tie a rope around his neck." Pope translates the Hebrew but substitutes **him**, as in RSV, "Can you hold him in the furrow with rope?" Kissane, quoted by Rowley, makes a slight change to get "Wilt thou bind him with a halter or cord?" NEB, which translates the word for **valleys** in line <u>b</u> to mean "strength," transposes "strength" and **furrow** to read "Can you harness its strength with ropes?" This gives a clear picture, but TEV translates it more clearly as "Can you hold one with a rope and make him plow?"

Before deciding finally on how to render the first line, it is necessary to look at the second line. **Or will he harrow the valleys after you? Valleys** most likely refers to the **furrows** in line <u>a</u>. **Harrow** as a verb means to drag a heavy instrument with spikes across a plowed field, to break up the clods of soil and make the ground smooth for planting. So the question in line <u>b</u> is "Will the wild ox pull a harrow across the fields for you?" or ". . . across the furrows?" Since the second line concerns the breaking up of the clods, one can assume that the first line concerns plowing and so may be translated as in TEV, or as saying, for example, "Can you hold him with a rope when you plow furrows?" In languages in which plowing and harrowing are unknown, the question in verse 10 may have to be recast to say, for example, "Can you put a rope on him and make him pull a load, or make him drag a log to smooth your ground?"

39.11 RSV   TEV

Will you depend on him because   Can you rely on his great
   his strength is great,   strength
and will you leave to him your   and expect him to do your
   labor?   heavy work?

The wild ox is powerful but cannot be trusted, and so God asks **Will you depend on him . . . ?** which means "Can you trust him?" "Can you rely on him?" or "Can you count on his great strength?" **Will you leave to him your labor** may be rendered "will you hand over to him your heavy jobs to do?" Again the clear answer is "No," because a wild ox will not work for a human being.

724

39.12   RSV   TEV

> Do you have faith in him that he
>   will return,
> and bring your grain to your
>   threshing floor?[i]

> Do you expect him to bring in
>   your harvest
> and gather the grain from
>   your threshing place?

[i] Heb *your grain and your threshing floor.*

In verse 12 there are two forms of the Hebrew text, one having the intransitive form of the verb *shub,* meaning "return" in the sense of "come back," and the other the transitive form, which means "to bring something back." RSV follows the first, while TEV follows the second, which requires an object such as "harvest." RSV has changed the text very slightly but gives clear sense and is recommended as a translation model.

Threshing floor is the level ground or platform on which the grain is removed from the cut plants by beating or dragging a heavy object over them. The grain and seed coverings are then tossed into the air so that the light straw (chaff) is blown away from the grain. Verse 12 may be rendered, for example, "Can you count on him to come back and bring your harvest (grain) to your threshing floor?"

9A-6. The ostrich, horse and eagle (39.13-30)

	RSV		TEV
13	"The wings of the ostrich wave proudly; but are they the pinions and plumage of love?	13	How fast the wings of an ostrich beat! But no ostrich can fly like a stork.
14	For she leaves her eggs to the earth, and lets them be warmed on the ground,	14	The ostrich leaves her eggs on the ground for the heat in the soil to warm them.
15	forgetting that a foot may crush them, and that the wild beast may trample them.	15	She is unaware that a foot may crush them or a wild animal break them.
16	She deals cruelly with her young, as if they were not hers; though her labor be in vain, yet she has no fear;	16	She acts as if the eggs were not hers, and is unconcerned that her efforts were wasted.
17	because God has made her forget wisdom, and given her no share in understanding.	17	It was I who made her foolish and did not give her wisdom.
18	When she rouses herself to flee, she laughs at the horse and his rider.	18	But when she begins to run, she can laugh at any horse and rider.
19	"Do you give the horse his might? Do you clothe his neck with strength?	19	Was it you, Job, who made horses so strong and gave them their flowing manes?
20	Do you make him leap like the locust? His majestic snorting is terrible.	20	Did you make them leap like locusts and frighten men with their snorting?
21	He paws in the valley, and exults in his strength; he goes out to meet the weapons.	21	They eagerly paw the ground in the valley; they rush into battle with all their strength.
		22	They do not know the meaning of fear, and no sword can turn them back.
		23	The weapons which their riders carry

22	He laughs at fear, and is not dismayed;		rattle and flash in the sun.
	he does not turn back from the sword.	24	Trembling with excitement, the horses
23	Upon him rattle the quiver,		race ahead;
	the flashing spear and the javelin.		when the trumpet blows, they can't
24	With fierceness and rage he swallows the		stand still.
	ground;	25	At each blast of the trumpet they snort;
	he cannot stand still at the sound of		they can smell a battle before they get
	the trumpet.		near,
25	When the trumpet sounds, he says 'Aha!'		and they hear the officers shouting
	He smells the battle from afar,		commands.
	the thunder of the captains, and the		
	shouting.	26	Does a hawk learn from you how to fly
			when it spreads its wings toward the
26	"Is it by your wisdom that the hawk soars,		south?
	and spreads his wings toward the	27	Does an eagle wait for your command
	south?		to build its nest high in the mountains?
27	Is it at your command that the eagle	28	It makes its home on the highest rocks
	mounts up		and makes the sharp peaks its fortress.
	and makes his nest on high?	29	From there it watches near and far
28	On the rock he dwells and makes his		for something to kill and eat.
	home	30	Around dead bodies the eagles gather,
	in the fastness of the rocky crag.		and the young eagles drink the blood.
29	Thence he spies out the prey;		
	his eyes behold it afar off.		
30	His young ones suck up blood;		
	and where the slain are, there is he."		

Verses 13-30 deal with the ostrich, the horse, and the eagle. The section on the ostrich was omitted by the Septuagint, and many interpreters omit verses 13-18. The reason for omitting these verses is the absence of any rhetorical questions, and the fact that in verse 17 God is referred to in the third person. Consequently some scholars have felt these verses to be the work of later copyists.

Subdivision Heading

Translators may wish to follow the Handbook heading or modify it to say, for example, "Think about these three animals," "Birds and animals you should think about," or "Have you considered the ostrich, horse, and eagle?"

39.13 RSV	TEV

"The wings of the ostrich wave
    proudly;
but are they the pinions and
    plumage of love?^{j}
	How fast the wings of an ostrich
	    beat!
	But no ostrich can fly like a
	    stork.^{u}

^{j} Heb obscure	^{u} *Verse 13 in Hebrew is unclear.*

In the Hebrew text of verse 13a, there is nothing that is fully certain. **The wings of the ostrich wave proudly: ostrich** translates a word that can mean "shrill cries." The word occurs nowhere else in the Old Testament. However, from the descriptions in the following verses, the ostrich is clearly the subject of these verses.

Waves proudly has been translated in countless ways. Pope has "flap wildly," NAB "beat idly," NJV "beats joyously," Dhorme "is gay," NEB "are stunted," NIV "flap joyfully," HOTTP "waves gaily." The Hebrew verb means "exult or rejoice," and "flap joyfully" is probably as near as any. In languages in which the **ostrich** is unknown, translators may use a descriptive term; for example, "big bird" or "big bird called ostrich." Otherwise it may be possible to substitute a different large bird which has some similar traits.

But are they the pinions and plumage of love? is even more uncertain than the first line, and the vast array of translations results from conjectures and changes too numerous to mention. RSV's footnote says "Heb obscure." In line b the words translated as **pinions** and **plumage** are in some sense parallel to **the wings** in line a. In Ezekiel 17.3 all three of these words are found: "great wings and long pinions, rich in plumage." The word translated as **wings** in line a is general, while those in line b are more specific. **Pinions** refers to the wing feathers that spread out to enable a bird to fly. **Plumage** refers to the outer feathers covering the body and wings. Most interpreters accept the meanings as in RSV.

The word translated as **love** is *chasid*, which appears to be the feminine form of the adjective *chesed*, which is usually rendered "constant love" and provides the basis for RSV's translation. RSV's rendering draws in part from the following verses, which describe the ostrich as abandoning her eggs in an unkind way. The cruelty of the ostrich was proverbial, judging from Lamentations 4.3. ". . . but the daughters of my people have become cruel, like the ostriches in the wilderness." HOTTP supports RSV with "but is it a pious plumage and down?" However, "pious" is not an appropriate qualification of feathers in English. HOTTP suggests there is a play on words between "pious" and "stork," since the same word can also mean "stork." The stork, in contrast to the ostrich, is known for the care it gives to its young. Furthermore TEV interprets the Hebrew word at the beginning of the line, not as a question but as a negative marker. TEV follows the interpretation "stork" and produces a translation that suits the context, is meaningful, and has some support in the early versions: "but no ostrich can fly like a stork." NIV retains the Hebrew more closely with "The wings of the ostrich flap joyfully, but they cannot compare with the pinions and feathers of the stork." Both of these are good translation models to follow. In language areas in which the stork is unknown, it may be possible to substitute another large bird that is known for its flight and care of its young.

39.14	RSV	TEV
	For she leaves her eggs to the earth, and lets them be warmed on the ground,	The ostrich leaves her eggs on the ground for the heat in the soil to warm them.

For she leaves her eggs to the earth: leaves in the sense of "abandon" is argued against by some scholars who understand the verb to mean "lays," and this implies that the ostrich cares for its eggs. From the content of verses 15-18 it is clear that the poet takes the proverbial view of the careless ostrich. Therefore TEV translates "The ostrich leaves her eggs on the ground."

And lets them be warmed on the ground implies that the ostrich does not cover the eggs with her body but wanders off and lets the heat from the sun and the earth keep them warm. Verse 15 makes clear that in this line the ostrich is not warming her eggs in the sand while she sits on them, but that they are warmed by other means after she has walked away, or, as NEB says, "she abandons . . . letting them be kept warm by the sand," which may also be rendered "letting the sand keep them warm."

39.15   RSV   TEV

> forgetting that a foot may crush   She is unaware that a foot may
>   them,   crush them
> and that the wild beast may   or a wild animal break them.
>   trample them.

Forgetting that a foot may crush them depicts the ostrich failing to think of the danger to her eggs when she is not sitting on them. **Forgetting** implies that the ostrich once knew but no longer does. TEV is better, with "She is unaware." **A foot** may be that of a human or animal, more likely the latter in the desert, as line b shows. In line b it is a **wild beast,** meaning a "wild animal." **Trample** is not a deliberate act. The animal may step on the eggs and crush them as it passes by. Verse 15 may also be translated as "She does not realize that something may crush them or that an animal may step on them."

39.16   RSV   TEV

> She deals cruelly with her young,   She acts as if the eggs were not
>   as if they were not hers;   hers,
> though her labor be in vain,   and is unconcerned that her
>   yet she has no fear;   efforts were wasted.

She deals cruelly with her young echoes the thought of Lamentations 4.3 cited in the discussion of verse 13. **Deals cruelly** translates a verb found in Isaiah 63.17, where it is used to describe "hardening of the heart." "She is cruel," "she acts harshly," "she is hard-hearted," all express the thought in English. **Her young** is literally "her children," and this Hebrew word may refer to either eggs or chicks of a bird, or both, in Deuteronomy 22.6,7. RSV assumes the eggs have hatched, which is not stated in the Hebrew. NEB has "chicks." TEV "She acts as if . . ." does not focus on the harsh treatment but on her indifference. FRCL says "She is a very hard (-hearted) mother to her little ones." **As if they were not hers** describes further the indifference or cruel attitude of the mother ostrich. In translation this clause may often have to be stated as a separate sentence, very much as TEV's first line, or, for example, "She acts as if they belonged to someone else."

Labor alludes to laying the eggs. **In vain** means "wasted, useless." **Yet she has no fear** is better expressed as "she has no concern" or "she is indifferent." NEB translates the line "not caring if her labour is wasted," and this is essentially the meaning of TEV. So the ostrich's young may hatch out or may not. The mother ostrich is not concerned about the effort of it all. Verse 16 may also be translated, for example, as "She is a hard-hearted mother to her little ones; she treats them as if they belonged to someone else, and it does not matter to her that laying her eggs was wasted effort."

39.17   RSV   TEV

> because God has made her forget   It was I who made her foolish
>   wisdom,   and did not give her wisdom.
>   and given her no share in
>   understanding.

Because God has made her forget wisdom makes it appear that the poet has forgotten that God is supposed to be speaking. In order to retain the first person for God, TEV shifts to "I." **Made her forget** translates the causative form of the verb **forget**. The sense is "to deprive, to prevent from having," and so "I have not allowed her to have wisdom" or ". . . her to be wise." FRCL says "It is because I have not granted wisdom to her."

Given her no share in understanding translates the Hebrew literally. "She did not get her share of intelligence." Gordis suggests that God is the subject in both lines, and translates "God forgot her when he allocated (distributed, gave out) wisdom, and he gave her no share in understanding." This rendering is particularly good for its parallelism. Another possibility is "It was I who kept her from being wise, and it was I who withheld intelligence from her."

39.18   RSV   TEV

> When she rouses herself to flee,[k]   But when she begins to run,[v]
>   she laughs at the horse and   she can laugh at any horse
>   his rider.   and rider.

[k] Heb obscure   [v] *Probable text* run; *Hebrew unclear.*

Comments on the failings of the ostrich end on a positive note: she can run faster than a horse. **When she rouses herself to flee** is literally "when on high she lifts up." The RSV footnote indicates that the word translated as **flee** is obscure. This verb occurs nowhere else, and so there have been numerous guesses as to its meaning. Since the second line is not in doubt, the first line should make a statement about the running of the ostrich, and not just "rearing up," as many translations have. For example, TOB says "But when she gets up and springs forward," SPCL "But when she gets up and starts to run," GECL "If she gets frightened and runs." All of these are good translation models.

She laughs at the horse and his rider describes the ostrich as ridiculing the horse and rider for not being able to run like her, or, as FRCL says, "For her it is a game to leave horse and rider behind." GECL translates "She laughs mockingly at horse and rider." For a discussion of an animal laughing to express scorn, see comments on verse 7.

39.19   RSV   TEV

> "Do you give the horse his
>   might?
> Do you clothe his neck with
>   strength?[l]

> Was it you, Job, who made hors-
>   es so strong
> and gave them their flowing
>   manes?

[l] Tg: The meaning of the Hebrew word is obscure

Verses 19-25 contain a description of the horse. Again the question is addressed to Job.

Do you give the horse his might? Might translates a word usually meaning physical as well as moral strength. It is used in 12.13, "with God are wisdom and might." See also 26.14. Here the reference is to physical strength. TEV makes it clear that Job is being addressed: "Was it you, Job, who made horses so strong?" The answer is obviously "No." RSV follows the Hebrew singular of **horse** in verses 19-25, but TEV makes the statements and questions more general for English by using the plural. This line may also be translated, for example, as "Are you the one who gave the horse his strength? Certainly not!" or "Do horses have great power because of what you did for them? Not at all!"

The figurative expression **clothe . . . with strength** is used in the sense of "make, give, cause to have." As the RSV footnote shows, RSV follows the Jewish Targum and translates a word found only here as **strength**. The Hebrew word is usually connected with the verb meaning "to thunder," but that sense is inappropriate here. HOTTP understands it to mean "trembling or quivering." As Pope says, "what clothes a horse's neck is the mane." Dhorme, NEB, and TEV translate "mane." TEV's rendering "and gave them their flowing manes" is a most satisfactory translation and may be followed by translators.

39.20   RSV   TEV

> Do you make him leap like the
>   locust?
> His majestic snorting is terri-
>   ble.

> Did you make them leap like
>   locusts
> and frighten men with their
>   snorting?

Do you make him leap like the locust? Leap translates a verb meaning "to quiver or shake," but that sense is inappropriate. In Joel 2.4 the locusts are compared to the running of the horse. See also Revelation 9.7. Here, however, the comparison is reversed, and so **leap** fits this context. **Locust** refers to the grasshopper-like insects that swarm in the air and make a whirring noise. They settle on crops and totally destroy them. See *Fauna and Flora of the Bible,* pages 53-54.

His majestic snorting is terrible: **majestic** translates a word meaning "glorious or proud," which characterizes the noise made through the horse's nostrils as he blows air. The sound the horse makes is awesome or terrifying. TEV has arranged this line so that **is terrible** is the effect experienced by people: "and frighten men with their snorting." This rendering can be improved by saying, for example, "and terrifying people with their fierce snorting."

39.21	RSV	TEV

	He paws^m in the valley, and
	    exults in his strength;
	    he goes out to meet the weap-
	      ons.
		They eagerly paw the ground in
		    the valley;
		    they rush into battle with all
		    their strength.

^m Gk Syr Vg: Heb *they dig*

He paws in the valley: **He paws** is singular and represents the ancient versions, as the RSV note shows. The Hebrew has "they dig." The first clause depicts the impatient and nervous war horse pawing the ground with its front hooves as it waits to attack the enemy line. **In the valley** translates a word which in Ugaritic can mean "force" or "valley," and some scholars prefer the former sense, as it provides a parallel for **strength** in the next clause. The first clause is then sometimes rendered "He paws vigorously." NEB has "He shows his mettle as he paws and prances." The expression "shows his mettle" means "he shows that he is a spirited horse, one full of energy." NIV is similar with "He paws fiercely." Armies were placed in battle formation in valleys in Genesis 14.8; Judges 7.1, and it is safe to retain the same expression here. **In his strength** is taken by some scholars as the beginning of line b. TEV follows this interpretation and places the two verbs together in line a, translating **exults** as "eagerly." NIV divides the verse into three clauses: "He paws fiercely, rejoicing in his strength, and charges into the fray." The first line may also be expressed "They dig up the ground with their hooves and show their strength."

He goes out to meet the weapons describes the war horse (and rider) racing forward to charge the enemy battle line. **Weapons** refers to both weapons and armor. TEV understands it as a figurative reference for the entire "battle." The translator may wish to make both explicit, as in "He charges into battle against the enemies' weapons."

39.22	RSV	TEV

	He laughs at fear, and is not
	    dismayed;
	    he does not turn back from the
	    sword.
		They do not know the meaning of
		    fear,
		    and no sword can turn them
		    back.

He laughs at fear depicts the war horse scorning the thought of fear just as the fast moving ostrich laughs at the horse and rider in verse 18, and the donkey at the noise of the city in verse 7. **Laughs at** means "to make fun, ridicule, scorn." Not only does the horse not show signs of fear, but he laughs at fear. **He is not dismayed** means "he is not afraid, is not frightened."

Turn back from the sword means he does not run away from where the sword is being used, or, more generally, "he does not run away from the heat of the battle." Verse 22 may also be expressed "He (they) has no thought of fear, and he does not run away from where the fighting is" or "Where others fear, he (they) snorts; he does not turn and run from the battle."

39.23   RSV   TEV

> Upon him rattle the quiver,   The weapons which their riders
>   the flashing spear and the   carry
>   javelin.   rattle and flash in the sun.

Upon him rattle . . . : rattle translates a verb found only here, but it appears to be associated with the verb "to sing," and so "to resound." The reference is to the noise of arrows rattling inside the **quiver**, which is the leather container holding the arrows, and is strapped to the rider's back. **Quiver** may have to be translated, for example, as "the container holding the arrows" or "the arrow box." No mention is made of the rider who carries the **quiver** and the other weapons. The focus is entirely on the action of the horse. TEV, however, places a rider on the horse, and this give a more adequate picture, since these weapons are useless to the horse alone.

The word translated as **flashing** (reflecting the sun) applies to the other two weapons commonly rendered as **spear** and **javelin**. The **spear** is a pointed blade fixed on a long wooden shaft. **Javelin** is a light spear suited for throwing at the enemy while riding on a swiftly moving horse. **Javelin** may be translated as "the throwing spear" or "the light spear."

39.24   RSV   TEV

> With fierceness and rage he swal-   Trembling with excitement, the
>   lows the ground;   horses race ahead;
> he cannot stand still at the   when the trumpet blows, they
>   sound of the trumpet.   can't stand still.

With fierceness and rage he swallows the ground describes the excitement of the horse. In Isaiah 14.16 the verbs which give rise to **fierceness** and **rage** mean "shake" and "tremble." TEV expresses the idea well with "tremble with excitement," and NEB "Trembling with eagerness." **Swallows the ground** is an idiom meaning "to run at full speed."

The phrase **he cannot stand still** translates the verb "to believe," whose root meaning is "to be firm," which many interpreters take to mean **stand still**. The blowing of a horn was the signal for the charge. **Trumpet** translates the Hebrew *shofar*, which is a ram's horn. Translators may find it best to transpose the two lines of verse 24 and say, for example, "He cannot stand still, and when the trumpet sounds 'Charge!' he trembles with excitement and charges forward at full speed."

39.25 RSV	TEV
When the trumpet sounds, he says 'Aha!' He smells the battle from afar, the thunder of the captains, and the shouting.	At each blast of the trumpet they snort; they can smell a battle before they get near, and they hear the officers shouting commands.

Verse 25 has three lines, as in RSV. **When the trumpet sounds, he says** depicts the horse as a human speaker. **When** translates a phrase meaning "As often as" or "Whenever." **Trumpet** is the same word used in verse 24. In RSV the horse says, **Aha**, which in Hebrew resembles the sound a person makes when discovering something joyful, *he-ach*. **Aha** may come close to the Hebrew expression if the horse is to speak English, but TEV is more realistic, with "at each blast of the trumpet they snort." NJB translates "he neighs exultantly." Neighing refers to the sounds a horse makes. SPCL says "At the sound of the trumpet he answers by neighing."

He smells the battle from afar means he picks up the scent of, or detects, the enemy troops and their horses from a great distance. **The thunder of the captains . . .** may also be the object of **smells** in the previous line. **Smells** may be used poetically in a wider meaning such as "recognizes, is aware of." FRCL translates "discerns" in line b and applies it by implication to line c. TEV supplies the verb "hear" in line c, and this is probably the best thing to do in translation. In line c **thunder** translates the same word used in 26.14, and refers to the commands and instructions being shouted to the soldiers by their leaders. **The shouting** is most probably an extension of the noise made by the officers, and so TEV has combined **thunder** and **shouting** into "officers shouting commands." Translators may wish to rearrange the order of lines in verse 25 to begin with line b: "He smells the battle in the air while still a long way off. He senses the leaders shouting out commands to the soldiers, and when the trumpet calls he snorts."

39.26 RSV	TEV
"Is it by your wisdom that the hawk soars, and spreads his wings toward the south?	Does a hawk learn from you how to fly when it spreads its wings toward the south?

In this final section, dealing with the hawk and the eagle, verses 26 and 27 are questions put to Job, and verses 28-30 are comments on the eagle.

Is it by your wisdom that the hawk soars . . . ? Wisdom translates the same noun rendered "understanding" in verse 17. **By your wisdom** can also be expressed "because you have taught it." **Hawk** translates a term used elsewhere in Leviticus 11.16 and Deuteronomy 14.15. At least eighteen species of hawks are reported to exist in Palestine, and it is not certain which one is referred to here. Both the **hawk** and the eagle are large meat-eating birds. See *Fauna and Flora of the Bible,* pages 40-41, 82-85. **Soars** translates a verb found only here, but the word is related to the term translated as "pinions" in verse 13. Dhorme thinks it means "grows feathers," but most take it to mean "use the wings," hence "to fly." **Soar** means to fly at a great height in the sky.

And spreads his wings toward the south depicts the hawk migrating to the south. **Spreads his wings** matches **soars** in line <u>a</u>; it also means "flies," but is stated with a more graphic verb. In nonpoetic terms the meaning is "and flies away to the south." If **spreads its wings** is retained, it may be necessary to indicate for the purpose of flying; for example, "and spreads its wings and flies to the south."

39.27   RSV   TEV

> Is it at your command that the   Does an eagle wait for your com-
> eagle mounts up   mand
> and makes his nest on high?   to build its nest high in the
>   mountains?

Is it at your command that the eagle mounts up . . . ? is the second question put to Job about a bird of prey; this time the bird is the **eagle** or vulture. The term translated as **eagle** is the same as that in 9.26. The Septuagint translated "vulture," and this is followed by FRCL, BJ, and NEB. Pope says the word *nesher* designates both eagles and vultures, including the golden eagle and the carrion vulture. For descriptions of these birds see *Fauna and Flora of the Bible,* pages 82-85. In modern times eight species of eagles and four of vultures are found in Palestine. Although most modern translations have **eagle**, the context of verses 28-30 describes the vulture better than the eagle. **Mounts up** refers to the soaring or high flying habits of these birds. Line <u>a</u> may be rendered "Do you give the eagle (vulture) the command that makes it fly high into the sky?" or "Do you order the vulture (eagle) to soar in the sky?"

The second question asks if Job commands this bird to make **his nest on high.** **On high** refers to a high mountainous area, which TEV translates "high in the mountains." In languages in which there are few hills and no mountains, the description in verse 27 will require saying something like "Does the eagle wait for you to tell it to build its nest on the highest rocks?" or ". . . on the highest place it can find?"

39.28   RSV   TEV

> On the rock he dwells and makes   It makes its home on the highest
> his home   rocks

in the fastness of the rocky crag.	and makes the sharp peaks its fortress.

Verse 28 carries verse 27 forward by making more graphic the eagle's habit of building its nest among the highest rocks in the mountains.

On the rock he dwells and makes his home: this line is exceptional, since it has two verbs of the same meaning translated as **dwells** and **makes his home**, while the next line has no verb but picks up the word translated as **rock** and elaborates it. **Rock** in line <u>a</u> refers to the rocks in the highest mountains, as line <u>b</u> shows. TEV has reduced the redundancy of the two verbs in this line to "makes its home."

In the fastness of the rocky crag: fastness or TEV "fortress" translates a term rendered "stronghold" in 1 Samuel 22.4; 24.22, referring to a place of safety in the remote mountains, where a person is secure from enemies. **Rocky crag** is literally "tooth of the rock" and is used also in 1 Samuel 14.4. The word refers to jagged rock formations that stand at the top of steep cliffs. TEV has supplied a verb for this line which gives a better parallel arrangement of the lines. In the language areas referred to in verse 27, verse 28 may again require some adjustments; for example, "It builds its nest on the highest rocks, and there it has a place where it is safe."

39.29   RSV   TEV

Thence he spies out the prey; his eyes behold it afar off.	From there it watches near and far for something to kill and eat.

From this secure fortress high in the rocks **he spies out the prey**. These birds are known to be able to detect even small warm-bodied rodents from great distances in the air. **Spies** translates a word meaning "to search." Since he searches from a great distance and without his prey knowing, **spies** expresses the action well. **Prey** translates the same word for food used in 38.41 in connection with the raven. TEV says "for something to kill and eat." TEV "kill" is not necessarily implied, particularly if the bird is the vulture. The vulture, like the raven, usually eats the flesh of animals that are already dead. See 38.41 for discussion.

His eyes behold it afar off depicts the distant eagle or vulture as having fixed its gaze on its victim.

39.30   RSV   TEV

His young ones suck up blood; and where the slain are, there is he."	Around dead bodies the eagles gather, and the young eagles drink the blood.

His young ones suck up blood describes the young birds eating the flesh referred to in the next line. Line a is abrupt, since the **blood** is not identified until line b; therefore TEV transposes the two lines. The word translated as **suck up** is found nowhere else in the Old Testament. By adding one letter to the Hebrew word it can be changed to "lick up," which is the Aramaic equivalent used in 1 Kings 21.19. However, sucking and licking do not express in English the way a bird takes up liquids, and so TEV has "drink."

And where the slain are, there is he is loosely quoted in Matthew 24.28 and Luke 17.37 as a proverbial saying. This saying may have already been in circulation before Job was written. In Hebrew the line is literally "and where the dead, there he." **The slain** refers to corpses of dead persons who have been fatally wounded, as in 24.12. By extension the word came to denote dead people, especially those killed violently, and to corpses which lay unburied on the battlefield, to be eaten by vultures. The line may be expressed "Where the dead bodies are, the vultures gather," "The vultures come where there are dead bodies," or "Where there are dead bodies the vultures gather to eat them."

9A-7. God challenges Job to answer (40.1-2)

	RSV		TEV
	1 And the LORD said to Job:	1-2	Job, you challenged Almighty God;
2	"Shall a faultfinder contend with the Almighty?		will you give up now, or will you answer?
	He who argues with God, let him answer it."		

The first two verses of chapter 40 consist of God's challenge to Job.

Subdivision Heading

Although the heading here involves only two verses, it is important to separate God's challenge to Job from Job's response in verses 3-5. Translators may follow the Handbook heading or say, for example, "Now will you answer me, Job?" "Let me hear what you have to say, Job," or "Job, it is time for you to answer me."

40.1-2   RSV   TEV

	1 And the LORD said to Job:	1-2	Job, you challenged Almighty God;
2	"Shall a faultfinder contend with the Almighty?		will you give up now, or will you answer?
	He who argues with God, let him answer it."		

The first verse is a prose introduction to God's question to Job in verse 2. The wording is the same as in 38.1, except the phrase "out of the storm" is lacking. Since 40.1 continues without interruption from 39.30, it is clear that God is still the speaker. 40.1 was omitted in the Septuagint. TEV reduces verse 1 to "Job" as a form of address and numbers the verses as 1-2.

Shall a faultfinder contend with the Almighty? This question asks if Job is prepared to argue against God. **Faultfinder** translates a word found only here, but it is based on a root meaning "to correct or reprove." Dhorme argues for a very slight change in this word to make it mean "yield, give up," which is followed by TEV. Dhorme also takes the word translated as **contend** to be a participle, "contender, one who argues," and translates "Will he who argues with Shaddai yield?" **Almighty**, as always in RSV, translates *Shaddai*. Translators may follow RSV or TEV. In some languages adjustments must be made in translating **contend with the Almighty** when God is speaking of himself. For example, the RSV form may be adjusted to say "You have criticized me, the Almighty God," or the TEV model "Will you now give up to me, God Almighty?" or "Will you now stop arguing with me, God Almighty?"

He who argues with God, let him answer it: argues may be taken to mean "criticize"; that is, the person who criticizes God should answer the questions that God has been asking Job. **God** in this line translates *'Eloah*. TEV has brought both terms for God together into line a as "Almighty God" and presents the alternative choices of action in the second line. This requires shifting "will you give up now" from line a to line b. This restructuring gives an adequate and clear translation. However, translators may prefer to retain the parallelism by translating, for example, "Job, will you now give up arguing against the Almighty? If you will criticize God, then you must answer the questions," or in some languages, "If you will criticize me, then . . . ."

9B. JOB WILL ANSWER NO MORE (40.3-5)

RSV	TEV
3 Then Job answered the LORD:	*Job*
4 "Behold, I am of small account; what shall I answer thee? I lay my hand on my mouth.	3-4 I spoke foolishly, LORD. What can I answer? I will not try to say anything else.
5 I have spoken once, and I will not answer; twice, but I will proceed no further."	5 I have already said more than I should.

Division Heading

The Handbook heading for Job's response to the LORD may be modified to say, for example, "I said foolish things," "Job admits his ignorance," or "How can I answer you?" Rowley (verses 1-5) has "Job's answer to the divine challenge," Habel (also verses 1-5) "Closing challenge and Job's reply," GECL "Job acknowledges God's wisdom," FRCL "It is up to Job to reply."

40.3	RSV	TEV
	Then Job answered the LORD:	*Job*

Then Job answered the LORD says in prose that Job replied to God. TEV places verses 3 and 4 together but does not translate the words of verse 3, since they are implied in the previous line, where the name of the speaker is given in italics. TEV and others show in the margin that verses 3-5 are the words of Job.

40.4	RSV	TEV

RSV	TEV

"Behold, I am of small account;
    what shall I answer thee?
I lay my hand on my mouth.
	I spoke foolishly, LORD. What
	    can I answer?
	I will not try to say anything
	    else.

Behold, I am of small account: **Behold** emphasizes the importance of Job's conclusion, in which he values himself as worthless. Many versions do not represent it in translation. **I am of small account** translates a verb meaning "to be swift, light, insignificant." The verb is found in 7.6 and 9.25 ("are swifter"); 1 Samuel 2.30 ("be lightly esteemed"); Nahum 1.14 ("are vile"). Job is admitting that he is of little importance in God's vast scheme of things. FRCL says "I am nothing at all," NIV "I am unworthy"; NEB translates "I who carry no weight," but in English this expression means "I have little influence on those above me." Since Job's quarrel with God has resulted in Job's speaking against God's justice, TEV says "I spoke foolishly, LORD." Translators should note that it may not be wise to add the name "LORD" here as TEV does, since Job uses it only once in all the discourses.

What shall I answer thee? is Job's way of saying "There is nothing I can say to you." In some languages, when one speaks to a superior, as Job does here, it is necessary to avoid the use of the pronoun alone. In these cases Job may say "How can I answer you, God?" In verse 2 Job was given the choice of giving up or answering. His choice will have to be to give up, surrender, submit. **I lay my hand on my mouth** expresses the gesture of placing the fingers or hand over the mouth as a sign of silence. In translation it may be necessary to state the purpose of the gesture; for example, "I place my fingers on my lips and remain silent."

40.5	RSV	TEV

RSV	TEV

I have spoken once, and I will
    not answer;
twice, but I will proceed no
    further."
	I have already said more than I
	    should.

I have spoken once shows how Hebrew parallelism almost always has a smaller number in the first line than in the second. For a similar example with the numbers six and seven, see 5.19. In line b the increase is plus one, and so **twice.** This does not mean that Job has spoken two or three times, but "again and again," "over and over," or perhaps in this context "I have already said too much." If the parallel lines are being retained, it is not necessary to keep the numerical device if that is not a natural figure in the translator's language. For example, "I have spoken out, and

so I will not say any more" or "I have said it too often, and now will say no more."
If the translator is not retaining the parallel lines, TEV may be followed.

9C. THE LORD'S SPEECH: SECOND PART (40.6–41.34)

Beginning with verse 6 God appears out of the storm, as in 38.1, and begins his
second discourse. In verses 7-14 God, who has been considered unjust by Job,
challenges Job to govern the world, to show that he has the integrity and power to
control the universe. If Job can do this, God will honor him. Beginning with verse
15 the theme shifts abruptly to God's control of Behemoth and continues to the end
of the chapter. In the Hebrew Bible chapter 40 has 39 verses. RSV and TEV follow
the tradition of ending chapter 40 with verse 24 and including verses 25-39 in chapter
41. The Handbook will mark the alternative numbering system, so that those who
follow the Hebrew system will not be confused. Translators whose readers do not use
any other language scripture will have no difficulty following the numbering system
used in RSV and TEV. However, where a major language Bible is read by enough
readers, it is often advisable to follow the numbering of that Bible, if the numbering
differs from RSV and TEV.

Some scholars have suggested that the verses dealing with Behemoth and
Leviathan (40.15–41.34) should be joined with the animal discourse in 38.39–39.30,
and that verses 40.7-14 should be joined to the first divine speech. According to this
view Job's words of submission in 40.3-5 should be joined to 42.2-6 to make a single
confession. The reason for these transpositions is that, as the text stands, Job has
submitted to God in 40.3-5, but in verses 7-14 God again challenges him to assume
control of the universe and show how it really should be operated. The sections on
Behemoth and Leviathan have nothing to do with this theme.

Division Heading

Translators providing a division heading here should adapt it to the wording
used in 9A (38.1–40.2).

9C-1. God challenges Job to punish the wicked (40.6-14)

RSV	TEV
6 Then the LORD answered Job out of the whirlwind:	6 Then out of the storm the LORD spoke to Job once again.

7 "Gird up your loins like a man;
    I will question you, and you declare to
        me.
	The LORD
	7 Stand up now like a man,
	        and answer my questions.

8 Will you even put me in the wrong?
    Will you condemn me that you may be
        justified?
	8 Are you trying to prove that I am un-
	        just—
	        to put me in the wrong and yourself in
	            the right?

9 Have you an arm like God,
    and can you thunder with a voice like
        his?
	9 Are you as strong as I am?
	        Can your voice thunder as loud as
	            mine?

10 "Deck yourself with majesty and dignity; clothe yourself with glory and splendor.	10 If so, stand up in your honor and pride;

739

11   Pour forth the overflowings of your anger,
      and look on every one that is proud,
      and abase him.
	clothe yourself with majesty and glory.
	11 Look at those who are proud;
	      pour out your anger and humble them.

12   Look on every one that is proud, and
      bring him low;
      and tread down the wicked where they
      stand.
	12 Yes, look at them and bring them down;
	      crush the wicked where they stand.
	13 Bury them all in the ground;
	      bind them in the world of the dead.

13   Hide them all in the dust together;
      bind their faces in the world below.
	14 Then I will be the first to praise you
	      and admit that you won the victory
	      yourself.

14   Then will I also acknowledge to you,
      that your own right hand can give you
      victory.	

Subdivision Heading

The Handbook heading may be adjusted to say, for example, "God invites Job to govern the universe," "Are you as strong as I am, Job?" or "Job, can you govern the world?" Rowley has "Job is invited to assume the throne of the universe," Habel "Challenge to govern like El," FRCL "Does Job take himself to be God?" and TOB "The condemnation of God."

40.6-7   RSV   TEV

> 6 Then the LORD answered Job out of the whirlwind:
> 7   "Gird up your loins like a man;
>   I will question you, and you
>   declare to me.

> 6 Then out of the storm the LORD spoke to Job once again.
>
> *The LORD*
> 7   Stand up now like a man,
>   and answer my questions.

These two verses are almost identical to 38.1-3. See there for comments. These verses introduce the second divine speech, which continues without interruption to 41.34, to which Job makes a final response (42.1-6).

40.8   RSV   TEV

> Will you even put me in the
>   wrong?
> Will you condemn me that you
>   may be justified?

> Are you trying to prove that I am
>   unjust—
>   to put me in the wrong and
>   yourself in the right?

Will you even put me in the wrong sums up the whole point at issue between God and Job. The question God put to Job in the first line is developed in the second line. The dispute between the two of them centers around the question of justice. By asking this question, which expects the answer "Yes," God is accusing Job of denying that God is just. In 9.22-24 Job has done just that. This question opens with the same word used in 34.17, meaning "truly?" "really?" and translated as **even**. **Put me in the wrong** is literally "break my judgment," which is equivalent to "make my judgment have no effect." As Rowley points out, if Job had only defended his

own integrity, he would have been in the right, but he has accused God of being
unjust and challenged God's moral right to rule the world.

In the second line **condemn** translates the same term used in 9.20; 15.6; 32.3.
Condemn me is parallel to **put me in the wrong. That you may be justified** is the
opposite of being in the wrong; that is, "so that you may be in the right," or as SPCL
translates, "so that you may appear innocent."

40.9   RSV   TEV

Have you an arm like God,   Are you as strong as I am?
   and can you thunder with a   Can your voice thunder as
    voice like his?   loud as mine?

Verses 9-14 are filled with satire. The questions and commands addressed to
Job carry a deep sense of ridicule which translators must take into account.
Translators should refer to the discussion of this subject under "Irony" in "Translat-
ing the Book of Job," page 19.

Arm refers to "power," so that **arm like God** means "strength or power such
as God has." Compare 22.8; Exodus 15.16; Psalm 77.15; 89.13. The implication is
that, since Job lacks God's power, he has no right to question his justice. The
question in both lines assumes the answer "No." TEV has changed the Hebrew for
like God to "as I" because God is the speaker, and it is more natural in English for
the speaker to speak of himself in the first person.

Can you thunder with a voice like his? expresses the thought of 37.4. God's
voice thunders. "Can your voice thunder like mine?"

40.10   RSV   TEV

"Deck yourself with majesty and   If so, stand up in your honor and
   dignity;   pride;
   clothe yourself with glory and   clothe yourself with majesty
    splendor.   and glory.

Deck yourself with majesty and dignity: this is a command to Job to adorn
himself with the symbols of power. The invitation to Job, if he can accept, gives him
the royal qualities of the divine ruler. The divine speaker seems almost harsh in his
sarcastic challenges to a ragged and sickly Job still sitting in a pile of ashes. **Majesty**
and **dignity** translate two words both beginning with the same letter in Hebrew and
each suggesting high, elevated, superior status. Translations differ considerably in the
way they render these: Pope "grandeur and majesty," NEB "pride and dignity," NJV
"grandeur and eminence," NIV "glory and splendor," TEV "honor and pride." TEV
drops the figure in this line, but keeps it in the next on the assumption that the
retention of one, rather than both, gains in clarity. This line may be expressed, for
example, "Show that you have honor and pride," "Show that you are a noble person
and have pride," or in some languages, "Let me see you act like a proud chief." An

exclamation mark can serve to signal a sarcastic remark, if the exclamation mark has that sense in the receptor language.

Clothe yourself with glory and splendor expresses the same idea as in the previous line. As in line a the two words translated as **glory** and **splendor** both begin with the same Hebrew letter. These two words are the ones used in Psalm 21.5; 96.6; 111.3. In Psalm 104.1 the psalmist says of God, "You are clothed with glory and honor," which uses the same words. In some languages the expression **clothe yourself** must be adjusted to say, for example, "become a great and powerful man," or "be great and glorious," or "show that you are great and that people honor you."

40.11   RSV   TEV

> Pour forth the overflowings of   Look at those who are proud;
>   your anger,   pour out your anger and hum-
> and look on every one that is   ble them.
>   proud, and abase him.

Pour forth the overflowings of your anger invites Job to exercise his power. Since Job supposes that the moral governing of the world calls for swift punishment of the wicked, he is now given a chance to do it. **Pour forth** translates the word used in 37.11 referring to the scattering of lightning. **Overflowings** translates a noun form of a verb which means "to exceed" and refers to his excess of anger, which TEV renders "pour out your anger." NJB has "Let the fury of your anger burst forth." TEV has transposed the two lines so that the object of Job's anger is identified in the first line, which gives a more logical order than the Hebrew poetic style followed by RSV. Verse 11 may also be expressed idiomatically sometimes; for example, "Let them know that you are angry, and lower the heads of everyone who has a swollen heart."

Although God alone has the right to humble the exalted and to raise the lowly (5.11; 1 Samuel 2.7; Isaiah 13.11; 25.11), Job is invited to perform that function. **Everyone that is proud** identifies the ones Job is to humble. **Abase** means "to humble, to cause someone to be made low."

40.12   RSV   TEV

> Look on every one that is proud,   Yes, look at them and bring them
>   and bring him low;   down;
> and tread down the wicked   crush the wicked where they
>   where they stand.   stand.

Except for "abase" verse 12a is identical to verse 11b, and the verb translated as **bring him low** means the same as the one translated as "abase." Some scholars delete this line as a copyist's error, but it is probably best understood as emphasis. TEV recognizes the repetition by prefixing "Yes" before this line.

And tread down is accurately and vividly expressed by "crush." **Where they stand** is literally "beneath them," but it also means "in their place" in 34.24; 36.20, and has the sense here of "on the spot." So Job is invited to crush the proud immediately before they can react. Verse 12 may also be rendered "Even more, make those who think they are important to become like nothing, and smash evil people right now" or "Make people with swollen hearts to be as if they were nothing, and crush the wicked quickly."

40.13   RSV   TEV

Hide them all in the dust together;
  bind their faces in the world
  below.[n]

Bury them all in the ground;
  bind them in the world of the
  dead.

[n] Heb *hidden place*

Hide them all in the dust together: **hide** here is a poetic term for "bury." **Them** refers to the proud ones in the previous verse. **Dust** refers to the grave, and so the line means "Bury them all in the ground" or ". . . in the grave."

Bind translates a verb meaning "to imprison." **Their faces** is the use of a part for the whole, meaning "them." **In the world below** translates a noun based on the verb "hide," and means "a hidden place," as the RSV footnote shows. The reference is to the dark places of Sheol, or TEV "world of the dead." The verse may be expressed "Put them in the ground in the prison which is Sheol, the place of the dead" or "Bury them and lock them up in the dark world of the dead."

40.14   RSV   TEV

Then will I also acknowledge to
  you,
  that your own right hand can
  give you victory.

Then I will be the first to praise
  you
  and admit that you won the
  victory yourself.

If Job can do all that God challenges him to do in verses 9-13, then he can take over God's management of the universe.

Then will I also acknowledge: **acknowledge** translates a verb meaning "praise." FRCL says "You will receive my congratulations," GECL "Then I will not hesitate to praise you."

That your own right hand can give you victory: **right hand** is used here as in Psalm 98.1 and means "your own strength" or "you yourself." **Give you victory** translates the Hebrew "save you." Pope says "If Job could do what he charges God of neglecting to do, then he could save himself." The thought is best expressed in terms of winning the struggle Job has set for himself with God, and therefore the whole verse may be rendered, for example, "Then I myself will praise you (recognize that you are great), and accept that your strength has given you the victory."

9C-2. God invites Job to think about the monster Behemoth (40.15-24)

RSV	TEV

15 "Behold, Behemoth,
    which I made as I made you;
    he eats grass like an ox.
	15 Look at the monster Behemoth;
	    I created him and I created you.
	    He eats grass like a cow,

16 Behold, his strength in his loins,
    and his power in the muscles of his
      belly.
	16 but what strength there is in his body,
	    and what power there is in his muscles!

17 He makes his tail stiff like a cedar;
    the sinews of his thighs are knit togeth-
      er.
	17 His tail stands up like a cedar,
	    and the muscles in his legs are strong.

18 His bones are tubes of bronze,
    his limbs like bars of iron.
	18 His bones are as strong as bronze,
	    and his legs are like iron bars.

19 "He is the first of the works of God;
    let him who made him bring near his
      sword!
	19 The most amazing of all my creatures!
	    Only his Creator can defeat him.

20 For the mountains yield food for him
    where all the wild beasts play.
	20 Grass to feed him grows
	    on the hills where wild beasts play.

21 Under the lotus plants he lies,
    in the covert of the reeds and in the
      marsh.
	21 He lies down under the thorn bushes,
	    and hides among the reeds in the
	      swamp.

22 For his shade the lotus trees cover him;
    the willows of the brook surround him.
	22 The thorn bushes and the willows by the
	      stream
	    give him shelter in their shade.

23 Behold, if the river is turbulent he is not
      frightened;
    he is confident though Jordan rushes
      against his mouth.
	23 He is not afraid of a rushing river;
	    he is calm when the Jordan dashes in
	      his face.

24 Can one take him with hooks,
    or pierce his nose with a snare?
	24 Who can blind his eyes and capture him?
	    Or who can catch his snout in a trap?

The theme now shifts abruptly to a description of **Behemoth**. (See *Fauna and Flora of the Bible*, pages 11-12.)

Subdivision Heading

Translators may use the Handbook heading or adapt it to say, for example, "Think about Behemoth," "Here is an animal for you to consider," or "Behemoth is a wonderful creature." Rowley has "The description of Behemoth," Habel "El's subjection of Behemoth," and FRCL "The hippopotamus."

40.15   RSV   TEV

"Behold, Behemoth,[o]
 which I made as I made you;
 he eats grass like an ox.

[o] Or *the hippopotamus*

Look at the monster Behemoth;[w]
 I created him and I created
 you.
 He eats grass like a cow,

[w] BEHEMOTH: *Some identify this with the hippopotamus, others with a legendary creature.*

744

Behold, Behemoth: Behold calls Job's attention, "Look at, consider, think about." **Behemoth** is the transliteration, or English spelling, of the Hebrew word. It is the plural of a common word meaning "animal" or "beast." In the singular it is sometimes used to refer to cattle or domestic animals. The plural form is rare, and in this verse and Psalm 73.22 the plural is used, but with a singular verb. According to Dhorme the pluralization adds a dimension of greatness to this creature. Some interpreters identify this animal with the Egyptian hippopotamus, as in the RSV footnote. Pope argues against **Behemoth** being a Nile hippopotamus and connects both **Behemoth** here and **Leviathan** in chapter 41 with ancient legends. There are two solutions taken by most modern translations in rendering **Behemoth**: many transliterate the word, while others use "hippopotamus." Some, like TEV, provide a note. Translators for languages in which the hippopotamus is as unknown as **Behemoth** may say: (a) "big animal called behemoth," or (b)"big animal that lives near the water." In most cases it is not sufficient to use a loan word with some defining words, and, because of the uniqueness of this beast, it is normally not advisable to suggest substituting some local animal. Many translators may wish to provide a note similar to TEV.

Which I made as I made you begins with a relative particle and emphasizes that **Behemoth** is a real creature, a part of God's creation just as Job is.

He eats grass like an ox: grass translates the same word rendered "plants" in 8.12. **Ox** translates a noun which may refer to cattle collectively, to a cow, or to a work animal, the ox. For a discussion of **ox** see 39.9. The hippopotamus eats water plants growing in and along the banks of rivers as well as grass and green plants growing some distance from rivers.

40.16   RSV   TEV

Behold, his strength in his loins,   but what strength there is in
    and his power in the muscles   his body,
    of his belly.   and what power there is in his
                                                    muscles!

His strength in his loins: loins refers to the thighs or the upper part of the legs. Some argue that the reference is to his sexual powers, but this is not confirmed by the second line. The **loins** are the proverbial seat of physical strength in Nahum 2.1; Psalm 69.23; Deuteronomy 33.11. TEV has generalized to "his body" so that "body" and "muscles" of the following line make a complete picture.

The **muscles of his belly**, according to Rowley, are known to be particularly thick on the hippopotamus. The reference is to the band of muscle that lies on the lower side of his body. It must be remembered, however, that this statement comes from a poet who is praising the strength of this beast. TEV has made the poet's bland statement more emphatic than the original.

40.17 RSV	TEV

He makes his tail stiff like a
    cedar;
    the sinews of his thighs are
    knit together.
	His tail stands up like a cedar,
	    and the muscles in his legs are
	    strong.

He makes his tail stiff like a cedar: **stiff** translates a word found only here, and so the meaning is uncertain. Another verb root that gives the same form as used here means to make stiff, and this is followed by RSV. This has sometimes been taken to mean "make erect," and so TEV "stands up like a cedar." BDB and K-B suggest "bend down." This may refer to the long branches of the cedar tree extending out and downward, in which case the beast may be thought of as having a long, sloping tail. **Cedar** refers to a type of evergreen tree known from Lebanon as a majestic tree with durable wood. For illustration and discussion see *Fauna and Flora of the Bible,* pages 107-108. Any large tree whose wood is used for construction may be used.

Sinews are tendons that join the muscles to the bone, but these are not visible as are the muscles. Therefore it is better to follow TEV and to translate "muscles." If the translator has chosen to translate "Behemoth" as "hippopotamus," the translation of verse 17a should be suitable for that animal. If "Behemoth" is rendered by a descriptive phrase or by transliteration, it will not matter greatly which of the comparisons with the cedar tree are chosen. In the first case one may say, for example, "His tail is stiff as . . ." or "His tail is hard as . . . ."

40.18 RSV	TEV

His bones are tubes of bronze,
    his limbs like bars of iron.
	His bones are as strong as
	    bronze,
	    and his legs are like iron bars.

His bones are described by another analogy. **Tubes** translates a word which first meant stream bed, and canal, and then pipes for carrying water. **Tubes** calls attention to their size and roundness. **Bronze,** which is a mixture of copper and tin, was typically used as an image to designate strength or hardness, as in 6.12; 20.24; 41.27.

Limbs like bars of iron continues the description of the animal's strength. **Limbs** translates another word for bones, but is better translated in this line as "legs." **Bars of iron** refers to rods of solid iron.

40.19 RSV	TEV

"He is the first of the works[P] of
    God;
    let him who made him bring
    near his sword!
	The most amazing of all my crea-
	    tures!
	    Only his Creator can defeat
	    him.

^p Heb *ways*

This verse and verse 20 seem to interrupt the description of Behemoth's body and his surroundings in verses 15-24. They do not connect with the preceding verses or with those that follow, so the context is not a clear guide to their meaning. The first line uses the same sort of language about Behemoth as is used of wisdom in Proverbs 8.22.

He is the first may mean first in time or first in importance or greatness. TEV understands the word in the second of these senses, as does NEB, "He is the chief of God's works." Since the LORD is speaking, TEV adjusts the expression meaning "God's creatures" (literally "God's ways") to "my creatures," as in verse 9. It is also possible that the writer may be speaking about the order in time at which God created various creatures. In Genesis 1.24 the Hebrew word *behemah*, the singular of *behemoth*, occurs as the first in the list of creatures made by God just before he made human beings. It is most likely that the reference here is to the animal being "the greatest."

Let him who made him bring near his sword! renders the Hebrew literally but with little clarity of meaning. This line has been interpreted in numerous ways, and many changes have been proposed to clarify the sense. **Sword** has often been interpreted to refer to the teeth or tusks of the hippopotamus, but a **sword** does not serve for cutting grass. Dhorme and others adjust the words translated as **bring near his sword** to get "a tyrant to his companions." The "companions" are then the other animals mentioned in verse 20. NEB follows Dhorme and translates "Made to be a tyrant over his peers," that is, "over his equals." TEV understands **sword** as a means of "defeat" and says "Only his creator can defeat him," a translation which the confusing Hebrew text supports in part. However, one of HOTTP's recommendations agrees essentially with TEV: "Only the one who made him (his creator) is able to kill him." HOTTP's other suggestion may be rendered "His creator holds him back with his sword," that is, so that the animal will not attack. Although Dhorme's proposal seems to fit the line to the following verse, the change in text is extensive, and so TEV or HOTTP is recommended.

40.20	RSV	TEV
	For the mountains yield food for him where all the wild beasts play.	Grass to feed him grows on the hills where wild beasts play.^x

^x *Verse 20 in Hebrew is unclear.*

For the mountains yield food for him begins with the connective *ki*, which does not seem to connect with the preceding verse. HOTTP interprets this connective in three ways: "Therefore," "But," or as an emphatic marker, "Yes indeed." This line, like verse 19b, has given rise to many interpretations. Some point out that **mountains** are not the habitat of the hippopotamus, are not near the Nile, and are totally bare of vegetation. Others point out that **mountains** can refer here to the low hills which do grow vegetation in the upper valley of the Nile, and that these places

are accessible to the hippopotamus. The word translated as **food** occurs only in
Isaiah 44.19, where it means "block of wood," but it is generally accepted as meaning
"produce, crop." RSV renders the line clearly without changing the text, and is
supported by HOTTP. TEV makes "produce" more specific as "grass," but gives a
rendering essentially agreeing with RSV.

Wild beasts is literally "beasts of the field." The thought is perhaps that the
wild animals have nothing to fear from Behemoth, who eats nothing but grass. Verse
20 may also be rendered "He eats his food in the hills while many other wild animals
are at play."

40.21	RSV	TEV
	Under the lotus plants he lies, in the covert of the reeds and in the marsh.	He lies down under the thorn bushes, and hides among the reeds in the swamp.

Under the lotus seems to depict the animal submerged in the water, but this
is most likely inaccurate. The word translated as **lotus plants** (also used in verse
22a) refers, not to the Egyptian water lily, but to a thorny tree found along the
eastern Mediterranean and in North Africa. It flourishes in damp hot areas and is
abundant around the Sea of Galilee. **In the covert** means "in a hidden place." TEV
says "hides." **Reeds** translates a common term for tall grass with thick stems which
grow in marshy ground. See *Fauna and Flora of the Bible,* pages 171-174. **Marsh** is
also found in 8.11 and refers to a low-lying area covered by shallow water and
grasses. The verse may be expressed, for example, "He goes off to lie under the
thorn bush or hides himself among the tall grass in the swamp waters."

40.22	RSV	TEV
	For his shade the lotus trees cover him; the willows of the brook surround him.	The thorn bushes and the willows by the stream give him shelter in their shade.

Lotus trees translates the same word rendered "lotus plants" in 21a. There is
no reason to make a distinction as RSV does. The animal is depicted as being shaded
by the thorn bush.

Willows of the brook suggests that the poet is thinking of his own country
rather than Egypt in this line. **Willows** are identified in *Fauna and Flora of the Bible,*
page 170, as poplar trees that grow along the banks of streams and stream beds in
the eastern Mediterranean. **Brook** is a small stream often referred to in biblical
literature by the Arabic word *wadi*. These stream beds are often dry except in the
rainy season. TEV has combined the two kinds of trees as the topic in line a, and
places the comment about them in line b. This give a good model for translators to
follow.

40.23   RSV   TEV

RSV	TEV

Behold, if the river is turbulent
  he is not frightened;
he is confident though Jordan
  rushes against his mouth.
	He is not afraid of a rushing
	  river;
	he is calm when the Jordan
	  dashes in his face.

If the river is turbulent, he is not frightened depicts the bravery of the animal. The word translated as **turbulent** commonly means "oppress," but that meaning does not suit the context here. Many changes have been suggested to give "overflows," "sinks," "gushes." The context suggests something such as TEV "rushing." RSV and others translate the Hebrew clause as a conditional sentence. NJB translates "If the river overflows . . . ," and FRCL "If the current is strong . . . ." TEV makes a statement.

The second line is exceptionally long, and consequently many interpreters switch some of it to the first line, but this is not necessary. Parallel with **he is not frightened** in line a is **he is confident** in line b, which means "he remains calm," "does not get upset." **Jordan** has no article in the Hebrew, which makes it likely that the word refers, not to the Jordan river, but to any river like the Jordan. FRCL translates it as "torrent," GECL "the river," SPCL "water." Nevertheless many translators keep **Jordan**. **Against his mouth** pictures the water rushing over the submerged head of the animal. When a hippopotamus comes to the surface of the river to breathe, its head is beneath the water, with only the eyes and nostrils protruding. If the water rushes over him, he merely closes his nostrils, and so "he is calm when the Jordan dashes in his face" (TEV). Another good translation model of verse 23 is SPCL: "If the river rises, he is not frightened; even when the water reaches his snout, he remains calm."

40.24   RSV   TEV

RSV	TEV

Can one take him with hooks,[q]
  or pierce his nose with a
  snare?
	Who can blind his eyes and cap-
	  ture him?
	Or who can catch his snout in
	  a trap?

[q] Cn: Heb *in his eyes*

Can one take him with hooks is literally "shall take him with (or, in) his eyes." **One** is supplied as the subject by RSV. **With hooks** follows a proposed change in the Hebrew. Other changes suggested are "by his teeth," "in his lair," and "by blinding his eyes," which is the choice of NEB and is also followed by TEV.

Pierce his nose with a snare: pierce does not describe the action of a snare or trap. Therefore Dhorme changes **snare** to get "thorns." If **snare** is to be retained, it is necessary to make some suitable adjustment in translation, which TEV does with "catch his snout in a trap," and NEB "or pierce his nose with the teeth of a trap." In some languages it may be best to translate verse 24 as a statement; for example, "Nobody can catch him with a hook nor pierce his snout with the teeth of a trap." This verse may also be rendered in the second person; for example, "Can you capture him and blind his eyes? Can you trap him and pierce his snout?"

Note on chapter and verse numbering, chapters 40 & 41

In the Hebrew Bible chapter 40 continues to verse 32, including the verses numbered 1-8 of chapter 41 in RSV and TEV, and chapter 41 in the Hebrew begins with what in RSV and TEV is verse 9 of the chapter. Some modern translations (NJB, BJ, FRCL, NJV, TOB, GECL, NAB) follow the Hebrew numbering. If the translator is preparing a Bible in a community where a major language used by readers follows the Hebrew numbering, it is advisable to do the same, or to place the second set of numbers in the margin with a brief note; for example, "Numbers to the right of the line follow the Hebrew Bible." The Handbook will use the same numbering system as RSV and TEV but will include the Hebrew numbering system within square brackets.

9C-3. God challenges Job to capture Leviathan (41.1-11 [40.25–41.3])

RSV	TEV
1 "Can you draw out Leviathan with a fishhook, or press down his tongue with a cord?	1 Can you catch Leviathan with a fishhook or tie his tongue down with a rope?
2 Can you put a rope in his nose, or pierce his jaw with a hook?	2 Can you put a rope through his snout or put a hook through his jaws?
3 Will he make many supplications to you? Will he speak to you soft words?	3 Will he beg you to let him go? Will he plead with you for mercy?
4 Will he make a covenant with you to take him for your servant for ever?	4 Will he make an agreement with you and promise to serve you forever?
5 Will you play with him as with a bird, or will you put him on leash for your maidens?	5 Will you tie him like a pet bird, like something to amuse your servant girls?
6 Will traders bargain over him? Will they divide him up among the merchants?	6 Will fishermen bargain over him? Will merchants cut him up to sell?
7 Can you fill his skin with harpoons, or his head with fishing spears?	7 Can you fill his hide with fishing spears or pierce his head with a harpoon?
8 Lay hands on him; think of the battle; you will not do it again!	8 Touch him once and you'll never try it again; you'll never forget the fight!
9 Behold, the hope of a man is disappointed; he is laid low even at the sight of him.	9 Anyone who sees Leviathan loses courage and falls to the ground.
10 No one is so fierce that he dares to stir him up. Who then is he that can stand before me?	10 When he is aroused, he is fierce; no one would dare to stand before him.
11 Who has given to me, that I should repay him? Whatever is under the whole heaven is mine.	11 Who can attack him and still be safe? No one in all the world can do it.

Chapter 41 is entirely taken up by descriptions of **Leviathan**, and the LORD again asks Job questions and makes comments. (See *Fauna and Flora of the Bible*, pages 73-74.)

Leviathan, like Behemoth, is the transliteration, or English spelling, of the Hebrew word. The TEV footnote at 3.8 defines **Leviathan** as "a crocodile or legendary monster." See the discussion of **Leviathan** in 3.8. Other Old Testament references to this animal are found in Psalm 74.14; 104.26; Isaiah 27.1. As in the case of Behemoth, most translations use either the word **Leviathan** adapted to the sound system of the language, or use the word "crocodile." In languages where the crocodile is unknown, and there is no equivalent animal, it may be necessary to use **Leviathan** with a qualifier such as "water animal called Leviathan," or "Leviathan" accompanied by a note explaining what a crocodile is. If the translator has used a transliteration of "Behemoth" in 40.15, it is advisable to do the same for **Leviathan**.

Subdivision Heading

Translators may follow the Handbook heading or adapt it by saying, for example, "Job, can you catch Leviathan?" or "Can you capture this animal?" Rowley has (verses 1-34) "The description of Leviathan."

41.1^r RSV	TEV
[40.25]	
"Can you draw out Leviathan^s with a fishhook, or press down his tongue with a cord?	Can you catch Leviathan^y with a fishhook or tie his tongue down with a rope?
^{r} Ch 40.25 in Heb	^{y} LEVIATHAN: *See 3.8.*
^{s} Or *the crocodile*	

Can you draw out Leviathan with a fishhook asks Job if he can catch this animal the way someone catches a fish. **Draw out** translates a verb meaning "to extract," in this case extract from the water, and the action is expressed in English as "catch." In some languages this is commonly expressed as "Can you fish the crocodile with a fishhook?"

The question **Can you . . . press down his tongue with a cord** sounds strange. **Press down** translates the causative form of a verb meaning "to sink," but the word is used in Leviticus 8.13 in the sense of "bind," and Dhorme takes that meaning to apply here. In order to prevent a crocodile from using its jaws, it is necessary to tie its jaws shut. If line <u>b</u> is to be taken as an action following line <u>a</u>, the captured animal would need to have its mouth tied shut. In this case **tongue** may be taken as representing the mouth, and the meaning can be "Can you tie his mouth shut with a rope?" The answer to both questions is then "No!" The questions in verses 1-7 as well as later in the chapter may require shifting to negative statements in some languages. In other languages it may be necessary to answer the question with a strong negative.

41.2
[40.26]

RSV	TEV
Can you put a rope in his nose, or pierce his jaw with a hook?	Can you put a rope through his snout or put a hook through his jaws?

Can you put a rope in his nose: rope translates a word for "reed" used also in Isaiah 9.14; 19.15; 58.5 ("rush"). Such reeds were made into ropes. The purpose of putting a rope through the nose of Leviathan would be to control its movements. It would be necessary to pierce the flesh between the nostrils, and pass the rope in one nostril and out the other. Translators should take care not to give the impression that the rope is stuffed up the animal's nose. It may be necessary to say, for example, "Can you thread a rope through his nostrils?" or "Can you put a ring and rope through his snout?"

Or pierce his jaw with a hook? Hook translates a word whose basic meaning is "thorn," as used in 31.40. It is used in the sense of **hook** in 2 Chronicles 33.11. This **hook** would be much larger than the fishhook in the previous verse. Verses 3-4 treat Leviathan as if he were a human prisoner, and Dhorme cites the treatment of Assyrian prisoners, in which a prisoner's jaw was pierced and rope put through it. The meaning may be expressed as "Can you pass a hook through his jaw?"

41.3
[40.27]

RSV	TEV
Will he make many supplications to you? Will he speak to you soft words?	Will he beg you to let him go? Will he plead with you for mercy?

After Leviathan is captured and made a prisoner, the questions become ironic. **Make supplications** translates "multiply the prayers." The reason he begs his captor is that he wants to be freed, and so TEV translates more specifically "Will he beg you to let him go?"

In the second line the irony heightens. **Speak to you in soft words** asks if Leviathan will use sweet talk, or honeyed words, which is flattery, to obtain his release. Dhorme translates "tender words," FRCL "fond words," NIV "gentle words."

Verse 3 may also be expressed, for example, "Will he beg you for mercy or flatter you with sweet words?" or "Will he beg you for his life or warm your heart with tender words?"

41.4
[40.28]

RSV	TEV
Will he make a covenant with you to take him for your servant for ever?	Will he make an agreement with you and promise to serve you for-ever?

Make a covenant with you is literally "cut a covenant with you," as in 31.1. See there for comments on this idiom as well as on the term **covenant**. **Servant for ever**, as in Deuteronomy 15.17; 1 Samuel 27.12, requires that Leviathan give up his freedom for all time to serve his captor. The idea is well expressed by TEV as "and promise to serve you forever?" We may also say, for example, "Will he promise always to be your faithful servant?" or "Will he agree with you to serve you forever? Certainly not!"

41.5
[40.29]

RSV	TEV
Will you play with him as with a bird, or will you put him on leash for your maidens?	Will you tie him like a pet bird, like something to amuse your servant girls?

The irony continues as the LORD asks Job if he will make a plaything out of this fierce beast. In Psalm 104.26 Leviathan is described as playing in the sea.

Play with him as with a bird probably refers to the practice in some areas of children catching small birds and tying a string to the bird's leg and letting it fly to the end of the string.

In the second line the question asks if Job will tie the beast with a rope to lead him and amuse his servant girls. **For your maidens** may require making the purpose clear; for example, "For your servant girls to watch." The verse may be expressed "Will you tie him as you tie a bird to play with, or will you lead him around with a rope so your servant girls can watch?"

41.6
[40.30]

RSV	TEV
Will traders bargain over him? Will they divide him up among the merchants?	Will fishermen bargain over him? Will merchants cut him up to sell?

Just as in the previous verse Leviathan is too huge to be a plaything for anyone but God, so here he is no ordinary fish to be dealt with in the usual way in the fish market.

The Hebrew word translated as **traders** refers to a group of fishermen owning a boat between them, and then getting together to bargain over what they have caught, deciding how much each should be paid before the fish are handed over to the **merchants**. They will divide Leviathan up to sell him as food. He is too big to be sold in one piece, so he has to be cut up. For **bargain over** see 6.27. The meaning of this verse may be expressed as "Will fishermen argue over how much he will sell for? Will merchants cut him up and sell him?"

41.7   RSV   TEV
[40.31]

> Can you fill his skin with har-   Can you fill his hide with fishing
>   poons,   spears
>   or his head with fishing   or pierce his head with a har-
>   spears?   poon?

The questions return to the subject of capturing Leviathan. NEB places this verse after 40.24.

Can you fill his skin with harpoons translates the Hebrew literally and is ambiguous. **Fill his skin** means "pierce his skin with many harpoons." **Harpoons** in this line and **fishing spears** in the next line occur only here in the Old Testament. The word for **harpoons** is connected with a word for "thorn" used in Numbers 33.55. It is not certain just how this instrument was made, but from its association with "thorn" it was probably a barbed spear, and the **fishing spears** must have been very similar, and also thrown by hand. One of these, or even both, may have been attached by a rope to a boat or held in the hand to prevent the weapon from being taken away by the wounded animal. The point of the question is that no amount of spearing the hide or the head of Leviathan would injure or kill it. **Harpoons** and **fishing spears** may have to be translated by a single term in some languages, or through the use of a descriptive phrase such as "spears used for killing fish."

41.8   RSV   TEV
[40.32]

> Lay hands on him;   Touch him once and you'll never
>   think of the battle; you will not   try it again;
>   do it again!   you'll never forget the fight!

Lay hands on him translates an imaginary command which is better expressed as an "if" clause. "If you lay your hands on him . . . ." This expression means "to take hold of him with the hands." TEV says "Touch him once." **Think** is also an imperative. **Think of the battle** means "imagine the struggle you would have" or "think of the fight that would cause." If the first clause begins with "if," we may translate, for example, as "If you lay a hand on him, you will never forget the struggle." **You will not do it again** or "You will never do it a second time" gives the result of the condition.

41.9^t RSV   TEV
[41.1]

> Behold, the hope of a man is   Anyone who sees Leviathan
>   disappointed;   loses courage and falls to the
>   he is laid low even at the sight   ground.
>   of him.

^{t} Ch 41.1 in Heb

In Hebrew verse 9 is numbered 41.1, as the RSV footnote indicates.

The hope of a man is literally "his hope." There is no noun for "his" to refer back to, and so RSV supplies **of a man**. In order to get around this problem, Dhorme transposes verses 9 and 10 so that the antecedent is found in verse 10b, which is placed before verse 9. HOTTP makes two suggestions: the first agrees with RSV, and the second "the hope in it," which they say means "the hope of attaining it." TEV restructures verse 9 and clearly states who the participants are. "Anyone" is supplied as the subject of the phrase in line b **at the sight of**, and so we get "Anyone who sees." **Him**, referring to Leviathan, is made the object of "sees." **Hope . . . is disappointed** becomes the main verb phrase translated as "loses courage," and **he is laid low** becomes "and falls to the ground," a coordinate clause with "loses courage." Although considerably rearranged, this rendering agrees with the thought expressed in RSV and is recommended to translators.

41.10	RSV	TEV
[41.2]		

RSV	TEV
No one is so fierce that he dares to stir him up. Who then is he that can stand before me?	When he is aroused, he is fierce; no one would dare to stand before him.

No one is so fierce that he dares to stir him up: **fierce** translates a word that usually means "cruel," but most take it here to refer to Leviathan, where **fierce** is more suitable. RSV makes it apply to Leviathan's opponent, which is less likely. The Hebrew of this line implies a negative question, "Is he not fierce . . . ?" TEV has switched to a statement: "When he is aroused . . . ." NEB expresses the line as an exclamation: "How fierce he is when he is roused!" **Stir him up** translates the same verb used in 3.8, where there is another reference to stirring up Leviathan.

The question **Who . . . can stand before me** is taken by some to mean "before God" and by others to mean "before Leviathan." Most Hebrew manuscripts have "before me," as in RSV, but a number of manuscripts have "before him," as in TEV. HOTTP favors the reading followed by RSV. In general it may be said that translations which agree with RSV's rendering interpret the adjective in the first line as referring to Leviathan's opponents, the meaning of the whole verse being "No one is daring enough to challenge Leviathan, so how can anyone dare to challenge God?" On the other hand, those who read the same Hebrew text as does TEV understand the adjective in the first line as referring to Leviathan: "He is so fierce when he is aroused that nobody would dare to face up to him." Since there is good manuscript evidence for both RSV and TEV, either may be recommended. Some translators may prefer to follow a widely-used translation in the language area.

41.11	RSV	TEV
[41.3]		

RSV	TEV
Who has given to me,[u] that I should repay him? Whatever is under the whole heaven is mine.	Who can attack him and still be safe? No one in all the world can do it.[z]

u The meaning of the Hebrew is uncer-   *z Verse 11 in Hebrew is unclear.*
tain

As the notes of RSV and TEV indicate, verse 11 is unclear in Hebrew. The basic problem is whether the verse is speaking about God or about Leviathan.

According to HOTTP the verb translated as **has given** means "to advance," that is, "to come before with gifts" or else "to challenge." In the first sense the committee suggests "Who has preceded me (with his gifts)," and in the second sense "Who has challenged me." It is the first of these which supports RSV's rendering. TEV on the other hand follows changes proposed by Dhorme and others which change the Hebrew for **me** to "him" in the first line and change **Whatever** to "No one" in the second. So the sense of "challenge" or "confront" in line a is translated in TEV as "attack," and the object of "attack" is "him," Leviathan. Furthermore, TEV follows the Septuagint, which changes the word translated as **repay him** to get "remain safe."

The second line in Hebrew is literally "under the whole heavens it is mine," which HOTTP understands as "everything under the heavens is mine" and so supports RSV. NEB, whose first line refers to an attack on Leviathan, as in TEV, changes to "not a man under the wide heaven." This is a reply to the question in line a. TEV is similar, with "no one in all the world can do it." The translation of verse 11 is determined in part by the choice in verse 10b, either to follow the Hebrew text as is or to accept a change. RSV does the former and TEV the latter. Both are possible. The advantage of RSV is that it changes the text less and still gives a clear translation. The advantage of TEV is that, aside from verses 10b and 11, all the other verses in chapter 41 speak only of Leviathan and never of God. Therefore, in the interest of the whole context, TEV has an even greater advantage.

9C-4. God describes the terror of Leviathan (41.12-34 [41.4-26])

	RSV		TEV
12	"I will not keep silence concerning his limbs, or his mighty strength, or his goodly frame.	12	Let me tell you about Leviathan's legs and describe how great and strong he is.
13	Who can strip off his outer garment? Who can penetrate his double coat of mail?	13	No one can tear off his outer coat or pierce the armor he wears.
14	Who can open the doors of his face? Round about his teeth is terror.	14	Who can make him open his jaws, ringed with those terrifying teeth?
15	His back is made of rows of shields, shut up closely as with a seal.	15	His back is made of rows of shields, fastened together and hard as stone.
16	One is so near to another that no air can come between them.	16	Each one is joined so tight to the next, not even a breath can come between.
17	They are joined one to another; they clasp each other and cannot be separated.	17	They all are fastened so firmly together that nothing can ever pull them apart.
18	His sneezings flash forth light, and his eyes are like the eyelids of the dawn.	18	Light flashes when he sneezes, and his eyes glow like the rising sun.
19	Out of his mouth go flaming torches;	19	Flames blaze from his mouth, and streams of sparks fly out.
		20	Smoke comes pouring out of his nose, like smoke from weeds burning under a pot.

sparks of fire leap forth.

21   His breath starts fires burning;
        flames leap out of his mouth.

20   Out of his nostrils comes forth smoke,
        as from a boiling pot and burning
        rushes.

22   His neck is so powerful
        that all who meet him are terrified.

21   His breath kindles coals,
        and a flame comes forth from his
        mouth.

23   There is not a weak spot in his skin;
        it is as hard and unyielding as iron.

22   In his neck abides strength,
        and terror dances before him.

24   His stony heart is without fear,
        as unyielding and hard as a millstone.

23   The folds of his flesh cleave together,
        firmly cast upon him and immovable.

25   When he rises up, even the strongest are
        frightened;
        they are helpless with fear.

24   His heart is hard as a stone,
        hard as the nether millstone.

26   There is no sword that can wound him;
        no spear or arrow or lance that can
        harm him.

25   When he raises himself up the mighty are
        afraid;
        at the crashing they are beside them-
        selves.

27   For him iron is as flimsy as straw,
        and bronze as soft as rotten wood.

28   There is no arrow that can make him run;
        rocks thrown at him are like bits of
        straw.

26   Though the sword reaches him, it does
        not avail;
        nor the spear, the dart, or the javelin.

29   To him a club is a piece of straw,
        and he laughs when men throw spears.

27   He counts iron as straw,
        and bronze as rotten wood.

30   The scales on his belly are like jagged
        pieces of pottery;
        they tear up the muddy ground like a
        threshing sledge.

28   The arrow cannot make him flee;
        for him slingstones are turned to stub-
        ble.

29   Clubs are counted as stubble;
        he laughs at the rattle of javelins.

31   He churns up the sea like boiling water
        and makes it bubble like a pot of oil.

30   His underparts are like sharp potsherds;
        he spreads himself like a threshing
        sledge on the mire.

32   He leaves a shining path behind him
        and turns the sea to white foam.

33   There is nothing on earth to compare
        with him;
        he is a creature that has no fear.

31   He makes the deep boil like a pot;
        he makes the sea like a pot of oint-
        ment.

34   He looks down on even the proudest
        animals;
        he is king of all wild beasts.

32   Behind him he leaves a shining wake;
        one would think the deep to be hoary.

33   Upon earth there is not his like,
        a creature without fear.

34   He beholds everything that is high;
        he is king over all the sons of pride."

Subdivision Heading

The Handbook heading may be reworded to say, for example, "God tells Job how awful Leviathan is" or "Leviathan is a terrible creature!" Habel has (verses 5-21) "The terror and invincibility of Leviathan."

41.12   RSV   TEV
[41.4]

"I will not keep silence concern-   Let me tell you about Leviathan's
    ing his limbs,   legs
or his mighty strength, or his   and describe how great and
    goodly frame.   strong he is.

I will not keep silence concerning his limbs begins a detailed description of Leviathan. **Will not keep silence** may be rendered positively; for example, "I will tell you about" or "I will describe to you." **Limbs** is the same word used in 18.13 and is best translated as "legs," as in TEV and others. However, Pope connects the word for **limbs** with "boasting," as in 11.3 ("mocking"), but this removes the line as an introduction to the physical description of Leviathan.

Or his mighty strength, or his goodly frame is literally "and the word of might and the grace of arrangement." The first of these two phrases may be rendered, according to HOTTP, as "the details of his exploits," which we may translate as "the great deeds he has done" or "the brave things he has done." The second description seems to apply to the frame or form of the animal. The word translated as **goodly** occurs nowhere else in the Old Testament, but it is generally thought to be connected to a similar word meaning "grace." Dhorme changes the expression to get "his incomparable might," and NJB follows this with "his matchless strength." Interpreters have questioned the idea that a crocodile could be considered graceful (if Leviathan is a crocodile). However, the important thing is what the poet thought, whether he had ever seen a crocodile or not. TEV combines the two statements into line b as "how great and strong he is." NIV may be closer to the poet's intention, with "his strength and his graceful form." Verse 12 may also be expressed, for example, "I will tell you about Leviathan's legs, and about the great things he has done, and how graceful he is."

41.13	RSV	TEV
[41.5]		

<table>
<tr><td>Who can strip off his outer garment?
Who can penetrate his double coat of mail?^v</td><td>No one can tear off his outer coat
or pierce the armor^a he wears.</td></tr>
</table>

^v Gk: Heb *bridle*

^a *One ancient translation* armor; *Hebrew* bridle.

Verses 13 and line 14a are the final questions regarding Leviathan. The remainder of the chapter is given over to descriptive statements.

Who can strip off his outer garment? assumes the answer "Nobody." TEV expresses the question as a negative statement. **Strip off** translates a verb used in 12.22 and 20.27 meaning "uncover." The expression is metaphorical in this line. The Hebrew says literally "the face of his garment," which is taken by Dhorme to mean the front of a garment as opposed to the back. Some take this to refer to the scales of the crocodile, and so the belly side of the animal. FRCL takes the expression to mean "who has removed his garment from the front," that is, from the mouth end of the animal. TEV and RSV, as well as many others, understand the reference to be to the **outer garment** in contrast to the double layer beneath, and this is satisfactory if the figure is to be retained in translation. In languages in which the figure may not be used, it may be necessary to express this question differently; for example, "Who can remove his hide or cut through to his armor?" or "Who can take away his skin or the iron-like covering that protects him?"

Penetrate his double coat of mail is literally "Who can enter into his double bridle?" In place of "bridle" the Septuagint has "coat of armor." This involves a change in the order of the consonants. Some retain "bridle"; for example, NIV has

"Who would approach him with a bridle?" HOTTP supports the change which underlies RSV and TEV. This gives a better parallel between the two lines. **Coat of mail** or "armor" refers to metal body coverings worn by soldiers in battle to protect them from their enemies' weapons. The fact that it is **double** means that it is twice as thick, and therefore twice as effective.

41.14	RSV	TEV
[41.6]		
	Who can open the doors of his face?	Who can make him open his jaws,
	Round about his teeth is terror.	ringed with those terrifying teeth?

Who can open the doors of his face continues the use of the figure. **The doors of his face** is figurative language referring to "his jaws." The sense is "Who has the strength to open his jaws?" or "Who has the strength to make him open his mouth?" The answer is "No one," and so the thought may also be expressed as "Nobody can make him open his jaws."

Round about his teeth is terror makes a separate statement in RSV. TEV links this line more closely to line a with "ringed with . . ." modifying "jaws." It is the teeth that cause terror, not something around them. "Seeing his teeth causes a person terror" or "His teeth frighten people."

41.15	RSV	TEV
[41.7]		
	His back[w] is made of rows of shields,	His back[b] is made of rows of shields,
	shut up closely as with a seal.	fastened together and hard as stone.

[w] Cn Compare Gk Vg: Heb *pride*

[b] *Some ancient translations* back; *Hebrew* pride.

His back is made of rows of shields follows the ancient versions, as the RSV and TEV notes indicate. The Hebrew text has "pride" instead of **back**. **Rows of shields** translates the literal Hebrew and refers to the hard scales or plates that cover the animal's back. The line may also be rendered, for example, "His back is covered with rows of thick scales" or ". . . rows of heavy scales that protect him."

The **shields** are said to be **shut up closely as with a seal**. In the second line RSV follows the Hebrew text, which may mean that the series of shields or scales are identical and tightly arranged, so they are like a row of impressions made by a single seal or stamp. On the other hand the sense may be that each scale is closed tightly as if sealed shut. TEV follows the Septuagint, which changed the vowel of the Hebrew word rendered **closely** to get "stone." In this understanding the scales are compared to the rock-hardness of the seal, and so TEV has "fastened together and hard as stone." Both RSV and TEV are recommended.

41.16   RSV   TEV
[41.8]
> One is so near to another   Each one is joined so tight to the
>   that no air can come between   next,
>   them.   not even a breath can come
>   between.

Verse 16 carries the compactness of the animal's hide a step further. **One is so near to another** means "each shield is so close to the next." The word translated as **air** is *ruach,* which is commonly translated as "breath, air, or spirit," but the last meaning is inappropriate here. The poet uses the image of **air** to depict the lightest and perhaps smallest thing to fit between the compact shields. RSV and TEV are very similar in their renderings; we may also translate "Each scale is so close to the next that not even a breath of air could enter between them."

41.17   RSV   TEV
[41.9]
> They are joined one to another;   They all are fastened so firmly
>   they clasp each other and   together
>   cannot be separated.   that nothing can ever pull
>   them apart.

Verse 17a repeats the thought of verse 16a but uses different wording. The reference is still to the armor-like hide of Leviathan. **Joined** translates the passive form of the same verb used in 38.38, where it is rendered "cleave fast together."

Clasp translates the reflexive form of the verb used in 38.30, and **separated** represents the reflexive form of the verb used in 4.11. FRCL may be translated as "Each scale is bound to the next, and nothing can undo such a connection" or "Each scale is so close to the next, they cannot be separated."

41.18   RSV   TEV
[41.10]
> His sneezings flash forth light,   Light flashes when he sneezes,
>   and his eyes are like the eye-   and his eyes glow like the ris-
>   lids of the dawn.   ing sun.

His sneezings flash forth light describes the effect of Leviathan's sneezing. Ancient writers observed that when the crocodile sneezed, tiny drops of water that sprayed the air caused the light to sparkle. **His sneezings** translates a word found nowhere else in the Old Testament, but is clearly related to the Aramaic and Arabic verbs with the same meaning. The Hebrew word *'atisha* resembles the sound made by a sneeze.

Eyes are like the eyelids of the dawn follows the same comparison used of the rising sun in 3.9, and so Leviathan's eyes are "like the rising sun," as in TEV. The whole verse may be rendered "When he sneezes the light sparkles, and his eyes are red as the rising sun."

41.19
[41.11]

RSV

TEV

Out of his mouth go flaming
torches;
sparks of fire leap forth.

Flames blaze from his mouth,
and streams of sparks fly out.

In the next three verses the imagery builds up so that the description goes well beyond that of a natural animal. It is more like that of a legendary dragon.

Flaming torches translates a word used in Genesis 15.17; Zechariah 12.6; Daniel 10.6. Here the focus is on the flame, not on the torch that contains the flame, and so TEV "flames blaze from his mouth." In the second line **sparks** in the phrase **sparks of fire** is found only here, but is clear as translated in RSV from its usage in Arabic. The expression suggests not only that flames come out of his mouth, but that the flames give rise to sparks that fly out from the flames, or as TEV says, "streams of sparks fly out." Verse 19 may also be expressed as "Fire flashes out of his mouth and sparks shoot outward."

41.20
[41.12]

RSV

TEV

Out of his nostrils comes forth
smoke,
as from a boiling pot and
burning rushes.

Smoke comes pouring out of his
nose,
like smoke from weeds burning
under a pot.

Out of his nostrils comes forth smoke: nostrils translates a word that occurs only here but is based on the root rendered "snorting" in 39.20. Where fire and sparks come from his mouth, now smoke is said to come from his nostrils: "Smoke pours out of his snout."

The second line is more complex. RSV, NIV, and TEV all translate the Hebrew text but reach somewhat different results, since a literal translation would give "like a blown pot of rushes." In Jeremiah 1.13 "a boiling pot" is literally "a blown pot," suggesting that it means a pot under which the flame is blown so that its contents boil from the increased heat. RSV interprets the rushes as **burning rushes**, while TEV describes the smoke pouring out of Leviathan's nose as being "like smoke from weeds," in which "weeds" represents a shift to a more general term. In TEV these weeds are said to be "burning under the pot." This is not a very close translation of the Hebrew. NIV apparently likens the smoke from Leviathan's nostrils to the vapor "from a boiling pot over a fire of reeds." This represents the Hebrew more closely than either RSV or TEV, but it is doubtful whether the reeds are really part of the picture in the writer's mind. A more satisfactory translation is "Smoke pours forth from his snout as from a boiling cooking pot."

NEB and NJB change the Hebrew word translated as **rushes** to a word not found elsewhere, which they understand to mean "hot, boiling," on the basis of a similar Arabic word. This is evidently how the Hebrew was understood by the translators of the Vulgate. So NJB has "like a cauldron boiling on the fire," with a literal translation in a footnote: "like a heated and boiling cauldron." NEB has "like a cauldron on a fire blown to full heat." In view of the support from the Vulgate and the clear sense given by this change, it is best to follow NJB in translating verse 20b.

41.21
[41.13]

RSV	TEV
His breath kindles coals, and a flame comes forth from his mouth.	His breath starts fires burning; flames leap out of his mouth.

Kindles means "to light, set on fire, to cause something to start burning." **Coals** refers to charcoal made from wood. "His breath ignites coals." This line is an example of what his flaming mouth does in verse 19a. Verse 21b repeats the thought of verse 19a.

41.22
[41.14]

RSV	TEV
In his neck abides strength, and terror dances before him.	His neck is so powerful that all who meet him are terrified.

The **neck** is thought of as the place of strength in Psalm 75.5. "He has a powerful neck."

Terror dances before him suggests a picture of an abstract quality performing a human action. The words translated **terror** and **dances** occur nowhere else in the Hebrew Bible. Therefore there is a degree of uncertainty in their meanings. The word for **terror** is related to a verb meaning to languish, that is, to lose strength, to wither. The withering away of one's strength is said to dance, jump, leap before this powerful monster. The picture created by this figurative language is probably that the awesome power of Leviathan as described in verses 18-21 produces such panic in the beholder or its victim that all sense of strength is transformed (dances) into weakness.

TEV "all who meet him are terrified" is a statement of the result of encountering this monster. It may be possible to keep some of the imagery by saying, for example, "and he causes everything to collapse with fear," or "and he makes his victims wither with fright," or "all who face him are terror-stricken."

41.23
[41.15]

RSV	TEV
The folds of his flesh cleave together, firmly cast upon him and immovable.	There is not a weak spot in his skin; it is as hard and unyielding as iron.

Folds in **folds of his flesh** translates a noun related to the verb "to fall," and so is literally "what falls down." NEB understands this to mean "underbelly." **Folds of his flesh** gives the picture of a fat animal with rolls of flesh. But the poet says that even these parts, which in another animal may be flabby and soft, are compact, or form a solid mass. The verb is the same as in 19.20 and 31.7. TEV "skin" is not a suitable model to follow.

The second line emphasizes again the hardness of Leviathan's flesh. **Cast** translates the verb used for casting or molding hot metal, and so the thought is that his flesh has been molded on him, like pouring hot liquid metal into a mold. This is a figure used to express hardness, and TEV expresses the figure as a simile which is clear: "it is as hard and unyielding as iron." Verse 23 may also be expressed, for example, "Even the meaty parts of his body are as hard as cast metal" or "Even the softest parts of his body are like iron."

41.24   RSV   TEV
[41.16]

RSV	TEV
His heart is hard as a stone, hard as the nether millstone.	His stony heart is without fear, as unyielding and hard as a millstone.

Hard translates the same word as that rendered "firmly cast" in verse 23b. Here the reference is to the fearlessness of Leviathan. TEV retains **stone** as an adjective, "his stony heart is without fear."

The poetic movement in line <u>b</u> is to a more specific kind of stone, **the nether millstone**, which refers to the lower of two circular stones in which the upper one is turned so that grain between the stones is ground to flour. The lower millstone was larger and harder than the upper stone which ground against it. For illustrations and descriptions see page 566.

41.25   RSV   TEV
[41.17]

RSV	TEV
When he raises himself up the mighty[x] are afraid; at the crashing they are beside themselves.	When he rises up, even the strongest[c] are frightened; they are helpless with fear.

[c] strongest; *or* gods.

[x] Or *gods*

When he raises himself up the mighty are afraid: mighty, as both RSV and TEV notes indicate, may be rendered "gods," which translates the plural of *'El*. According to Pope the cowering of the gods is a common mythological theme and is evidence that Leviathan is a mythological monster and not a Nile crocodile. This verse is difficult to interpret and has caused much discussion. The basic decision that must be made to translate this verse is whether the translator is to follow the Hebrew text or one of the many changes in the Hebrew recommended by scholars. Both RSV and TEV follow the Hebrew but interpret the Hebrew *'elim* to mean **the mighty** and "the strongest." The Hebrew word is translated "a mighty one" in Ezekiel 31.11 and "the mighty chiefs" in Ezekiel 32.21. Most of the ancient versions translate as in RSV except the Vulgate, which says "angels." Both RSV and TEV refer to mighty human beings. HOTTP, on the other hand, takes *'elim* to be "gods," some kind of supernatural beings, and so is closer to the Vulgate rendering "angels." The use of "gods" within the context of the increasing awesomeness of this creature is fully natural. Therefore the Hebrew may be interpreted to mean "gods," and this is followed by

SPCL and TOB. NJV has "divine beings." We may translate the first line as "When he (Leviathan) rises up, even the gods are frightened."

Crashing translates "breakings," which may also be rendered as "sea breakers," that is, ocean waves that break near the coastline. However, the Hebrew word rendered **crashing** has other meanings. In Isaiah 65.14 the word is translated "anguish (of spirit)." In Proverbs 15.4 the verb form is translated "it breaks (the spirit)." **They are beside themselves** translates a form of the verb that gives the sense of withdraw, fall back, retire. The reason the gods withdraw is that the fear of Leviathan is too great for them to withstand. Accepting the recommendation of HOTTP we may then translate verse 25 as "When Leviathan rises up, even the gods are frightened; they draw back through fear" or "When he rises up . . . they are filled with fear and flee."

41.26   RSV   TEV
[41.18]

> Though the sword reaches him, it   There is no sword that can
>   does not avail;   wound him;
>   nor the spear, the dart, or the   no spear or arrow or lance
>   javelin.   that can harm him.

In verse 26 and the following three verses the poet tells how useless it is to try to kill Leviathan.

Though the sword reaches him: reaches is literally "touches," but the sense is "is used to attack him." What is said of **sword** in the first line is true of the other three weapons mentioned. NEB combines them all in line a as "Sword, or spear, dagger or javelin, if they touch him, they have no effect." These weapons do not penetrate his hide. Instead they bounce off. The words translated as **dart** and **javelin** are found only here. Each of the weapons mentioned appears to be a hand-held weapon but may also be used by throwing. The exact nature of the weapons mentioned here is not the point. What is important is that, no matter how many weapons are used against him, they have no effect. In some languages there may not be terms for each of these different instruments. In such cases it may be necessary to say, for example, "Even if they attack him with a spear, or arrows, or any other weapon, none of these will wound him."

41.27   RSV   TEV
[41.19]

> He counts iron as straw,   For him iron is as flimsy as
>   and bronze as rotten wood.   straw,
>   and bronze as soft as rotten
>   wood.

He counts is as used in 13.24; 19.15; 33.10; and 35.2 ("think"), where the meaning is "he regards, considers," or as TEV says, "for him . . . ." The weapons of verse 26b are made of **iron** and **bronze**. **Bronze** is an alloy of copper and tin (see comment at 40.18). In line a "to him an iron weapon is no stronger than one made of straw," and in line b "a weapon made of bronze is as weak as rotten wood." In languages in which **bronze** is unknown, it may be necessary to translate, for example, "Iron is nothing more than straw to him, and any other metal is to him like rotten wood."

41.28
[41.20]

RSV

The arrow cannot make him flee;
for him slingstones are turned
to stubble.

TEV

There is no arrow that can make
him run;
rocks thrown at him are like
bits of straw.

In verse 26 the weapons are held or thrown. In verse 28 the weapons are shot by strings. **Arrow** in the first line is literally "son of bow," a different expression than that used in verse 26b. "Shooting an arrow at him does not make him run away." In the second line **slingstones** refers to stones that are thrown from a sling. A sling consists of two cords attached to a pouch where the stone is placed. The cords are held so that, as the sling revolves over the head of the thrower, one cord is released, the pouch opens, and the stone flies out. David used a sling to kill Goliath in 1 Samuel 17.49,50. For a further description see a Bible dictionary. **Turned to stubble** means they have no more effect than if they were made of straw. **Stubble** translates a word meaning "chaff," which is the lightest part of the straw blown from the grain in winnowing. See 5.26 for a description. TEV is correct, with "like bits of straw." In languages in which the slingshot is not known, the translator may follow something like TEV, "rocks thrown at him."

STONE IN SLING

41.29
[41.21]

RSV

Clubs are counted as stubble;
he laughs at the rattle of javelins.

TEV

To him a club is a piece of straw,
and he laughs when men
throw spears.

Clubs translates a word found only here. A similar word in Arabic has the same meaning. It refers to a wooden weapon used for beating or striking. It is usually tapered toward the hand-held end. Dhorme takes the word to refer to the shaft of an arrow. **Are counted as** translates the same expression used at the beginning of verse 27. **Stubble** is again as in verse 28b.

Just as the ostrich was said to "laugh at any horse and rider" (39.18, TEV), so Leviathan **laughs at the rattle of javelins. Rattle** seems to refer to the whir or noise made by the javelin or spear as it sails through the air toward its target. **Javelin** translates a different word than the one used in verse 26b but is the word found in 39.23. TEV makes it general: "He laughs when men throw spears." His laughing is to show how futile are their attempts to kill him. In some languages this line may have to be adjusted to say, for example, "He pays no attention when people throw spears at him" or "He doesn't even notice when spears are thrown at him."

41.30	RSV	TEV
[41.22]		

His underparts are like sharp
   potsherds;
he spreads himself like a
   threshing sledge on the
   mire.

The scales on his belly are like
   jagged pieces of pottery;
they tear up the muddy ground
   like a threshing sledge.[d]

> [d] THRESHING SLEDGES: *These had sharp pieces of iron or stone fastened beneath them.*

A THRESHING SLEDGE

His underparts are like sharp potsherds is literally "under him points of potsherds." The reference is to the belly of the crocodile, which is covered with scales. **Potsherds** is the same word used in 2.8, where Job scrapes his skin with these. See there for comments. As Leviathan crawls through the mud, the scales on his belly leave their marks on the ground. This action is compared to that of a **threshing sledge**, which consists of parallel boards with sharp stones and is dragged over the threshing floor to remove the grain from the seed coverings. For further details see a Bible dictionary. **Mire** refers to the muddy ground where the animal leaves and enters the water. "Beneath him his belly is like sharp pieces of broken pottery." **Threshing sledge** must often be adapted to some local piece of similar equipment, or a descriptive phrase may be used; for example, "When he drags himself through the mud, he leaves marks as if made by a board with spikes driven through it."

41.31	RSV	TEV
[41.23]		

He makes the deep boil like a
   pot;

He churns up the sea like boiling
   water

> he makes the sea like a pot of
> ointment.

> and makes it bubble like a pot
> of oil.

Verses 31 and 32 describe Leviathan in the water. **The deep** translates a word used in Psalm 69.2,15; 107.24, and refers to the water at the bottom of the sea, or to the depths of the sea. **Boil** translates the same word found in 30.27, where the heart is said never to be still. The thought is that he churns up the water so that it appears to boil, not that he makes it hot. **Pot** refers to a cooking pot.

In line b **sea** matches **deep** in line a. **Like a pot of ointment** has given rise to many different renderings. The Hebrew word for **pot of ointment** denotes perfume itself, as in Ezekiel 24.10 (RSV footnote), as well as a pot for making ointments or salves to be rubbed on the skin. In this sense the pot contains material for making medicine and so gives off a medicinal odor. TEV makes this general with "bubble like a pot of oil." NEB, which speaks of "lake" instead of **sea**, says "He whips up the lake like ointment in a mixing-bowl." The whole verse may be rendered "When he gets in the water he stirs up the sea like a pot of boiling water, like a pot of steaming medicine."

41.32   RSV   TEV
[41.24]

> Behind him he leaves a shining
>   wake;
> one would think the deep to be
>   hoary.

> He leaves a shining path behind
>   him
> and turns the sea to white
>   foam.

Behind him he leaves a shining wake is literally "Behind him he lights a path." The foam he leaves behind him as he swims through the water looks like a path. **Wake** refers to the wave, or momentary track, left on the water's surface by a boat or other surface object moving through the water. **Shining wake** refers to the whiteness of the foam.

One would think the deep to be hoary: the deep is the same word used in 28.14; 38.16,30. The reference is to the deep sea. **Hoary** translates "gray head," that is, a head covered with white or gray hair. Here it refers to the foam on the water, which is expressed by the metaphor of the white head of hair. TEV drops the figure and says "turns the sea to white foam." FRCL retains the image, with "silver hair floating on the surface of the deep water." The verse may be rendered "When he swims he leaves behind him a shining path of foam" or "When he goes through the water, he leaves behind a white and shining path of foam."

41.33-34   RSV   TEV
[41.25-26]

33 Upon earth there is not his like,   33 There is nothing on earth to
        a creature without fear.   compare with him;
34 He beholds everything that is   he is a creature that has no
        high;   fear.

> he is king over all the sons of   34   He looks down on even the
>   pride."   proudest animals;
>   he is king of all wild beasts.

The final two verses of the chapter sum up the description of Leviathan as superior to all other animals. In verse 33 line a may be rendered "There is nothing like him on earth." Line b is a second statement: **a creature without fear**. **Creature** translates "one made" and may be rendered "one made to be fearless" or "a fearless creature."

He beholds everything that is high is often adjusted and combined with verse 33b to give "everything that is high fears him." However, the Hebrew seems to make adequate sense without change. **Everything that is high** refers to proud or haughty animals, and so "He gazes at every proud animal" or, as Dhorme says, "every haughty creature." TEV has extended the meaning of **beholds** to "look down on," which fits well with the context of the next line. Line b is rendered literally by RSV as **sons of pride**. This expression is used in 28.8, "proud beasts," where it refers generally to "wild animals." See comments on 28.8. And so the description of Leviathan ends: "He is the king over all the wild animals" or "He considers every other animal to be less than he is. He is the ruler over all the wild animals."

10. The LORD Restores Job

(42.1-17)

Chapter 42 opens with Job's final speech, which consists of only five verses.

In addition to Job's second and final reply (42.2-6), verses 7-17, which are entirely in prose, are divided into two parts. Verses 7-9 deal with the final restoration of the three friends, who are reproached by God and told to offer a sacrifice. In verses 10-17 Job's fortunes are doubled and given back to him, and he dies a happy old man.

Section Heading

The Handbook heading may be reworded to say, for example, "God makes Job well again," "God gives Job back all he took from him," or "Job begins a new life." Rowley has "Epilogue," and Habel "The restoration of Job."

10A. JOB'S FINAL RESPONSE IS REPENTANCE (42.1-6)

RSV	TEV
1 Then Job answered the LORD:	1 Then Job answered the LORD.
2 "I know that thou canst do all things, and that no purpose of thine can be thwarted.	*Job* 2 I know, LORD, that you are all-powerful; that you can do everything you want.
3 'Who is this that hides counsel without knowledge?' Therefore I have uttered what I did not understand, things too wonderful for me, which I did not know.	3 You ask how I dare question your wisdom when I am so very ignorant. I talked about things I did not understand, about marvels too great for me to know.
4 'Hear, and I will speak; I will question you, and you declare to me.'	4 You told me to listen while you spoke and to try to answer your questions.
5 I had heard of thee by the hearing of the ear, but now my eye sees thee;	5 In the past I knew only what others had told me, but now I have seen you with my own eyes.
6 therefore I despise myself, and repent in dust and ashes."	6 So I am ashamed of all I have said and repent in dust and ashes.

Many views have been held regarding the meaning of Job's final statement. Habel summarizes four positions that are taken by interpreters: (a) That it represents a complete surrender of Job's will to the will of God. God's self-disclosure causes Job

769

to repent. (b) That Job perceives God in a new way, recognizes his control over the universe, and so is reconciled to God and reaffirms his faith. (c) That Job's final confession is part of the irony of the book. Job's insights have exposed God as "a blind force and a blustering orator." In spite of his innocence Job confesses, and his confession further exposes the duplicity of God. (d) That Job's final speech is his closing act of defiance. Job now sees God as he really is, unjust, unfeeling, and cruel. And he rejects a deity that confronts his cries for justice with proud boastings and irrelevant questions.

Habel takes the position that the conflict between Job and God is resolved in such a way as to preserve the integrity of each. In his first speech (chapter 38) God challenges Job to demonstrate his superior wisdom. This results in Job's first confession (40.3-5), which vindicates God's rule over the universe. In his second reply Job, who has been insistent that God appear in court with him, concludes that God's appearance is sufficient, and a declaration of Job's innocence is no longer required. In this way Job's integrity is also vindicated, and so he can repent in dust and ashes.

Division Heading

The Handbook heading may be modified to say, for example, "Job repents," "I repent of all I have said," or "I repent because I was ignorant." Rowley has "Job's answer to the divine challenge continued," Habel "Job's final response," GECL "Job submits to God," and FRCL "Job confesses his incompetence."

42.1   RSV   TEV

Then Job answered the LORD: **Then Job answered the LORD.**

Then Job answered the LORD is another of the many prose introductions to speeches in the book. It is identical to 40.3. In spite of this identification, TEV puts "*Job*" before verse 2.

42.2   RSV   TEV

"I know that thou canst do all   *Job*
things,   I know, LORD, that you are all-
and that no purpose of thine   powerful;
can be thwarted.   that you can do everything you
                                      want.

Job now makes two statements addressed to God. **I know that thou canst do all things: things** is implied but not expressed in Hebrew. The sense of this line is "I know you have the power to do anything" or TEV ". . . that you are all-powerful." Many translators will prefer to address God as LORD, as in TEV.

Job also knows **that no purpose of thine can be thwarted. Purpose** translates a word meaning "plan or idea"—anything that God plans to do will be done. TEV renders the thought positively: "you can do everything you want." This may also be rendered, for example, "you can do whatever you decide to do" or "no one can stop you from doing what you want."

42.3-4	RSV		TEV
3	'Who is this that hides counsel without knowledge?' Therefore I have uttered what I did not understand, things too wonderful for me, which I did not know.	3	You ask how I dare question your wisdom when I am so very ignorant. I talked about things I did not understand, about marvels too great for me to know.
4	'Hear, and I will speak; I will question you, and you declare to me.'	4	You told me to listen while you spoke and to try to answer your questions.

These two verses are handled together, since they share the same problems of interpretation and translation adjustments. Verse 3a is a variant of 38.2, in which God asks Job "Who is this that darkens counsel by words without knowledge?" In other words, "Job, who are you to question my wisdom . . ." (TEV). Aside from some small differences in the verbs used in 38.2 and here, it seems out of place for Job to be asking **'Who is this that hides counsel without knowledge?'**

In order to deal with this verse, various approaches have been made. Some scholars delete verses 3 and 4 as marginal notes that have been incorporated later into the text. See NEB. Others take these two verses to be original. RSV puts verses 3a and 4 in quotation marks to show that Job is quoting God. But quotation marks are of little help to people hearing a text read. NJB makes a more complex adjustment by giving the implied answer to the question the LORD had asked Job in 38.2: "I was the man who misrepresented your intentions with my ignorant words." NJB explains this adjustment in a footnote. FRCL places "You said" at the beginning of verse 3: "You said: I dared to make your plans obscure by speaking about things I was ignorant of." The same is done at the beginning of verse 4. TEV is similar to FRCL: "You ask how I dare question . . ." and "You told me to listen . . . ." TEV uses indirect speech to make the passage smoother and more natural in English.

In fairness to the text a note should call attention to 38.2-3 and the translation adjustment required. For example, "In verses 3 and 4 Job is using some of God's words from 38.2 and 3 to reply to him." Verse 3a may also be expressed, for example, "You asked me how I could doubt your wisdom" or "You asked me, 'What right have you to question my wise way of doing things?'"

The second line of verse 3 is Job's own statement, which is a reason clause beginning with **Therefore** or "because of that, accordingly, on that account." **Uttered** means "talked about, said." In effect Job says "Because of that I talked about things I knew nothing of." The subject of the final line of verse 3 is in apposition with line b. **Things too wonderful** translates "great things" and TEV "marvels too great." Job confesses that these "great things" are beyond his ability to know.

Verse 4 repeats with slight variations 33.31a; 38.3b; 40.7b. See these for comments.

42.5   RSV   TEV

I had heard of thee by the hear-   In the past I knew only what
   ing of the ear,   others had told me,
but now my eye sees thee;   but now I have seen you with
                                my own eyes.

According to Rowley Job's intellectual problem is unsolved, but he has gone beyond it. He has not learned the cause of suffering nor the explanation of injustice, but he has discovered that in his suffering he need not be cut off from fellowship with God. The two lines of verse 5 are in sharp contrast. Line <u>a</u> is Job's knowledge of God from others, and line <u>b</u> expresses his knowledge as an eye witness.

I had heard of thee means "I had heard about you" or "I heard people speak about you." **By the hearing of the ear** is literally "by report of ear" and means "by hearsay," that is, "by what someone else had said," usually taken as a rumor. NJB translates "Before, I knew you only by hearsay," FRCL "I only knew of you by what someone else said."

But now contrasts the former time with the present. **My eye sees thee**: eye is singular to match **ear**, which is also singular in line <u>a</u>. The line may be expressed "Now, however, I have seen you with my own eyes."

42.6   RSV   TEV

therefore I despise myself,   So I am ashamed of all I have
   and repent in dust and ashes."   said
                              and repent in dust and ashes.

Therefore opens Job's final statement. It introduces verse 6 as a consequence of verse 5: "that is why," "because I have seen you." **Despise** is the same word used in 7.5,16 with the meaning "melt away, sink down," according to Dhorme. Pope, on the other hand, argues that the object of **despise** is what Job has said about God, and so he translates "I recant and repent." "Recant" means to withdraw what has previously been claimed to be true. This translation is followed by NJV. NAB has "I disown what I have said," Habel "I retract," and FRCL "I withdraw that which I affirmed." TEV expresses more adequately the attitude of repentance, with "I am ashamed of all I have said." **Myself** is not in the Hebrew but is supplied by RSV, which follows the Septuagint.

Job's second act is to **repent in dust and ashes**. In 2.8 Job is depicted as sitting among the ashes. In 2.12 Job's friends see his condition, and to express their grief they sprinkle dust on their heads. In 30.19 Job compares his misery to dust and ashes. Sitting in dust and ashes and putting them on the head were rituals of mourning and repentance. See 2 Samuel 13.19; Isaiah 58.5; Jeremiah 6.26.

10B. THE LORD INSTRUCTS THE FRIENDS TO MAKE A SACRIFICE, AND JOB PRAYS FOR THEM (42.7-9)

RSV

TEV

Conclusion

7 After the LORD had spoken these words to Job, the LORD said to Eliphaz the Temanite: "My wrath is kindled against you and against your two friends; for you have not spoken of me what is right, as my servant Job has. 8 Now therefore take seven bulls and seven rams, and go to my servant Job, and offer up for yourselves a burnt offering; and my servant Job shall pray for you, for I will accept his prayer not to deal with you according to your folly; for you have not spoken of me what is right, as my servant Job has." 9 So Eliphaz the Temanite and Bildad the Shuhite and Zophar the Naamathite went and did what the LORD had told them; and the LORD accepted Job's prayer.

7 After the LORD had finished speaking to Job, he said to Eliphaz, "I am angry with you and your two friends, because you did not speak the truth about me, the way my servant Job did. 8 Now take seven bulls and seven rams to Job and offer them as a sacrifice for yourselves. Job will pray for you, and I will answer his prayer and not disgrace you the way you deserve. You did not speak the truth about me as he did."

9 Eliphaz, Bildad, and Zophar did what the LORD had told them to do, and the LORD answered Job's prayer.

The poem is concluded, but not the story. Verses 7-17 are often referred to as the "epilogue," which means something added to a story to bring out a particular point. These verses are in prose. Interpreters have expressed many different opinions about the significance of the conclusion of the book. Some feel that the conclusion proves that Satan was right about Job's serving God for material gain. Others point out that it proves the argument of the friends, namely, that if Job would confess his sin he could find happiness again.

It is clear that Job has come through successfully in the test devised by Satan in chapter 2: he has never cursed God. Therefore God must act to conclude the test and declare Job innocent. The trial has brought great suffering to Job. Now with the trial concluded, the suffering must cease, and it follows from the nature of the story that the innocent Job must be restored. His judge acts fairly by restoring him and rewarding him for his integrity.

Division Heading

The Handbook heading may be modified to say, for example, "God defends Job and criticizes the friends," "Job is the only one who spoke the truth about me," or "Job will pray for the friends." Rowley has "The LORD's censure of the friends and vindication of Job," Habel "Yahweh's verdict," GECL "God declares Job to be in the right," and TOB "Judgment of the friends."

42.7 RSV TEV

After the LORD had spoken these words to Job, the LORD said to Eliphaz the Temanite: "My wrath is kindled against you and against your two

After the LORD had finished speaking to Job, he said to Eliphaz, "I am angry with you and your two friends, because you did not speak the friends; for you have not spoken of me what is right, as my servant Job has. truth about me, the way my servant Job did.

The LORD translates the name of Israel's God *Yahweh,* which was used in chapters 1 and 2. See discussion of the name in "Translating the Book of Job," page 21, and in 1.7. **These words** creates confusion, since the last words were spoken not by the LORD but by Job. TEV avoids this problem by saying "After the LORD had finished speaking to Job." **Eliphaz** is the only one addressed, since he is probably the oldest of the friends. For the translation of **Eliphaz the Temanite**, see suggestions on 2.11.

My wrath is kindled means "I am angry with you." The reason for God's anger is **you have not spoken of me what is right. What is right** means what is correct and consistent with the facts. It is used in the Hebrew of Deuteronomy 17.4; 1 Samuel 23.23. TEV renders it here as "the truth." In some languages **against you and against your two friends** may create confusion. In such cases it may be better to translate "against you, Bildad, and Zophar."

Job's friends have insisted that Job's calamities were God's punishment for his sins. Job maintained that he had not brought this punishment on himself through sin. So the friends are saying things about God that are not true. Job is correct in what he is saying about God, but he draws conclusions from it that make God out to be unjust. It is for these wrong conclusions that Job has just repented. In some languages the contrast between Job's speaking the truth and what the friends said may have to be expressed in the following way: "Because you (plural) have lied in what you have said about me. Only my servant Job has told the truth" or "Because my servant Job has told the truth about me, but you (plural) have not told the truth." **My servant Job** is the same expression used by God in 1.8; 2.3. See there for translation suggestions.

42.8   RSV

Now therefore take seven bulls and seven rams, and go to my servant Job, and offer up for yourselves a burnt offering; and my servant Job shall pray for you, for I will accept his prayer not to deal with you according to your folly; for you have not spoken of me what is right, as my servant Job has."

TEV

Now take seven bulls and seven rams to Job and offer them as a sacrifice for yourselves. Job will pray for you, and I will answer his prayer and not disgrace you the way you deserve. You did not speak the truth about me as he did."

God now takes the initiative to reconcile the friends to himself and to Job. In 1.5 Job offered burnt offerings to God on behalf of his children. Job is now asked to make a similar sacrifice, which confirms the fact that God accepts Job.

Seven bulls and seven rams is a large sacrifice. Job is to play the role of the mediator, like Abraham in Genesis 20.7, Moses in Numbers 21.7, and Samuel in 1 Samuel 7.5; 12.19,23. However, it is the friends who supply the animals for the sacrifice. There is no evidence in the text that this sacrifice is made by priests on behalf of the friends. Therefore we must assume that the three friends take the animals to the place where Job is and perform the ritual of burned sacrifice themselves. Job's only function is to speak with God on behalf of the friends. The presence of Job is necessary, just as Samuel's presence was required at the sacrifice wrongly offered by Saul alone in 1 Samuel 13.8-13.

My servant is used three times in verse 8. This usage is rhetorical, that is, it functions as a device to associate Job with the LORD and to set Job apart from the three friends in the eyes of the LORD. Note that TEV has made no provision for this important detail in its translation of this verse. If translators find the expression **my servant** is redundant, they should explore ways of varying the expression so as to retain and emphasize the association of Job with the LORD, whom he serves.

Job shall pray for you means "Job will speak to me on your behalf." Intercessory prayer is mentioned in the Old Testament in Genesis 18.23-32; 20.7; Exodus 8.30; 32.11-13; Numbers 14.13-19; 21.7; Deuteronomy 9.20; 1 Samuel 7.5,8; 12.19,23; Isaiah 53.12; Jeremiah 37.3; Amos 7.2, 5. **Bulls** are male cattle. **Rams** are adult male sheep. For a discussion of **burnt offering**, see 1.5.

I will accept his prayer is literally "I will accept his face." It means "I will answer his prayer." The expression **deal with you according to your folly** is uncertain as to its meaning, since this is the only place where it occurs with God as the subject of the verb. Elsewhere folly always refers to someone committing some disgraceful act, as in Judges 19.23,24. NJB has "I . . . shall not inflict my displeasure on you." TEV "not disgrace you as you deserve" is most likely a correct rendering. In some languages this expression may be translated idiomatically as "I will not show your face even though I should," "I will keep your head covered even though you have done wrong," or "I will hide your bad liver even though it should be seen." **What is right** translates the same noun used in verse 7 meaning "the truth." For a second time God upholds Job as having spoken the truth.

42.9	RSV	TEV

So Eliphaz the Temanite and Bildad the Shuhite and Zophar the Naamathite went and did what the LORD had told them; and the LORD accepted Job's prayer.	Eliphaz, Bildad, and Zophar did what the LORD had told them to do, and the LORD answered Job's prayer.

No mention is made of Elihu. The listing of the names of the three friends is in the same order as when they were introduced in 2.11. TEV does not give the tribal or ethnic identifications of the three friends. These should be included in the translation, unless they are unacceptably redundant in the receptor language. In verse 8 God said that Job would pray for the friends, and in verse 9 Job has done this. Job's prayer was that God would not disgrace the friends as they deserve. In this way the friends also come out with their integrity intact.

As in verse 8, **the LORD accepted Job's prayer** is literally "the LORD accepted the face of Job," which is to be taken as "the LORD answered Job's prayer." NEB avoids the repetition by bringing forward from verse 10 "when he had prayed for his friends," and not repeating that clause again in verse 10. This is a recommended step, which gives a more logical order than either RSV or TEV. Therefore verse 9 may be translated, for example, as "Then Eliphaz the Temanite . . . did what the LORD told them to do, and God answered Job's prayer when he prayed for his three friends."

10C. THE LORD GIVES JOB TWICE AS MUCH AS WAS TAKEN FROM HIM (42.10-15)

RSV	TEV
10 And the LORD restored the fortunes of Job, when he had prayed for his friends; and the LORD gave Job twice as much as he had before. 11 Then came to him all his brothers and sisters and all who had known him before, and ate bread with him in his house; and they showed him sympathy and comforted him for all the evil that the LORD had brought upon him; and each of them gave him a piece of money and a ring of gold. 12 And the LORD blessed the latter days of Job more than his beginning; and he had fourteen thousand sheep, six thousand camels, a thousand yoke of oxen, and a thousand she-asses. 13 He had also seven sons and three daughters. 14 And he called the name of the first Jemimah; and the name of the second Keziah; and the name of the third Keren-happuch. 15 And in all the land there were no women so fair as Job's daughters; and their father gave them inheritance among their brothers.	10 Then, after Job had prayed for his three friends, the LORD made him prosperous again and gave him twice as much as he had had before. 11 All Job's brothers and sisters and former friends came to visit him and feasted with him in his house. They expressed their sympathy and comforted him for all the troubles the LORD had brought on him. Each of them gave him some money and a gold ring. 12 The LORD blessed the last part of Job's life even more than he had blessed the first. Job owned fourteen thousand sheep, six thousand camels, two thousand head of cattle, and one thousand donkeys. 13 He was the father of seven sons and three daughters. 14 He called the oldest daughter Jemimah, the second Keziah, and the youngest Keren Happuch. 15 There were no other women in the whole world as beautiful as Job's daughters. Their father gave them a share of the inheritance along with their brothers.

Division Heading

The Handbook heading may be adjusted to say, for example, "God gives Job back double the amount he took from him" or "God restores to Job his family and wealth." Rowley has "Job's fortunes restored," GECL "God gives Job new fortunes," and FRCL "The LORD restores Job."

42.10   RSV   TEV

And the LORD restored the fortunes of Job, when he had prayed for his friends; and the LORD gave Job twice as much as he had before.	Then, after Job had prayed for his three friends, the LORD made him prosperous again and gave him twice as much as he had had before.

And the LORD: And is not a suitable rendering of the Hebrew *waw* here. The conjunction serves to introduce a course of action following an earlier one. "Then," "After that," or "Later" are more appropriate in English. If the repetition of **LORD** results in bad style in the receptor language, the pronoun "he" may be used.

If the translator has not moved **when he had prayed . . .** to verse 9, it may be best to make this a time clause, as in TEV, "after Job had prayed . . . ," and shift this clause to the beginning for better sequence. **Restored the fortunes** is literally "turned the captivity." The expression has nothing to do with "captivity" or "exile" in the context of Job's restoration. The expression is normally applied to a nation and not to an individual. Here it has to do with the restoration of Job's prosperity. Job not only got back all he had before, he got back twice as much. If the translator follows the suggestion at the end of the preceding paragraph, verse 10 may be expressed as "The LORD gave back to Job his wealth and doubled everything he had before" or "The LORD again made Job a wealthy man and gave him twice as much as he had before." If the suggestion for shifting **when he had prayed . . .** to verse 9 is not followed, TEV may serve as a translation model for verse 10.

42.11	RSV	TEV

Then came to him all his brothers and sisters and all who had known him before, and ate bread with him in his house; and they showed him sympathy and comforted him for all the evil that the LORD had brought upon him; and each of them gave him a piece of money^y and a ring of gold.	**All Job's brothers and sisters and former friends came to visit him and feasted with him in his house. They expressed their sympathy and comforted him for all the troubles the LORD had brought on him. Each of them gave him some money and a gold ring.**

^{y} Heb *qesitah*

Job's restoration to God and the friends has been established. The circle now widens as he is restored to society in the form of his **brothers and sisters.** These probably include all those who had at least the same father but not necessarily the same mother. The larger circle is made up of **all who had known him before**; these are his "former friends." There is no suggestion that these people had come to help Job in his calamity. Job's wife is not mentioned but is present by implication when he has more children in verse 13. **Ate bread** is too limited to express in English the idea of feasting, and so TEV has "feasted with him." All of this celebration takes place in Job's house, and so it is a feast prepared by Job.

These friends and relatives **show him sympathy and comfort him,** which was the intention of the three friends in 2.11, but they never managed to do it. Their actions are in response to the **evil** inflicted on Job by God. In 2.10 Job asks "Shall we receive good at the hand of God, and shall we not receive evil?" In 30.26 Job says "when I looked for good, evil came." This is said in Job's complaint of the harsh treatment he receives from God. In translation a literal rendering of **evil** may be far more specific than the suffering and ill treatment Job has received. Job does not refer to such things as the evil eye, witchcraft, secret murders, and the kinds of things associated with **evil** as used in some languages. Accordingly it may be necessary to translate as misfortune, suffering, or trouble.

Each of them gave Job **a piece of money,** an expression which translates a Hebrew word used only in Genesis 33.19 and Joshua 24.32. This was an uncoined piece of silver used in buying and selling before coins were made. **A ring of gold** was an ornament worn by women in the nose (Gen 24.47; Isa 3.21), and by men and women in the ears (Gen 35.4; Exo 32.2-3; Judges 8.24).

42.12-13   RSV   TEV

12 And the LORD blessed the latter days   12 The LORD blessed the last part
of Job more than his beginning; and he   of Job's life even more than he had
had fourteen thousand sheep, six thou-   blessed the first. Job owned fourteen
sand camels, a thousand yoke of oxen,   thousand sheep, six thousand camels,
and a thousand she-asses. 13 He had   two thousand head of cattle, and one
also seven sons and three daughters.   thousand donkeys. 13 He was the father
                                                 of seven sons and three daughters.

The latter days is better expressed by TEV as "the last part" in contrast to "the
first part." It is not that the LORD blesses the days, but that he blesses Job during
that time. The number of animals is exactly double the number given in chapter 1.
In chapter 1 the sons and daughters are mentioned before the animals. In verse 13
the sons and daughters are mentioned after the animals, and unlike the animals they
are not doubled, unless the peculiar form of the word **seven** is to be understood as
a dual, as Dhorme suggests, and so would mean fourteen. This does not explain why
the number of daughters is not doubled. There is no mention of the servants.
Translators should refer to comments on **yoke** and each of the types of animals in
1.2-3.

42.14   RSV   TEV

And he called the name of the first   He called the oldest daughter Jemimah,
Jemimah; and the name of the second   the second Keziah, and the youngest
Keziah; and the name of the third   Keren Happuch.[e]
Keren-happuch.

                                                 [e] *In Hebrew the names of Job's daughters*
                                                 suggest beauty both by their sound and by
                                                 their meaning. JEMIMAH *means "dove";*
                                                 KEZIAH *means "cassia," a variety of*
                                                 cinnamon used as a perfume; and KEREN
                                                 HAPPUCH *means a small box used for eye*
                                                 make-up.

Note the meanings of the names of Job's three new daughters as explained in
the TEV footnote. In some languages it will be quite natural to use the translated
names rather than the transliterated ones. For example, NJB says "His first daughter
he called Turtledove, and the second Cassia, and the third Mascara." TOB translates
"The first he named Turtledove, the second had the name Cinnamon Bloom, and the
third Eyeshadow." Translators may wish to place the Hebrew names in a footnote.

42.15   RSV   TEV

And in all the land there were no wom-   There were no other women in the
en so fair as Job's daughters; and their   whole world as beautiful as Job's daugh-

father gave them inheritance among their brothers.

ters. Their father gave them a share of the inheritance along with their brothers.

In all the land may refer to the country where Job lived or more generally "in all the world"; "Job's daughters were the most beautiful women in the world."

Gave them inheritance: this way of passing on family property was a departure from Israelite laws of inheritance, which entitled a daughter to inherit only when there was no male heir (Num 27.1-11). Attention is no doubt called to it here by the author because of Job's desire to see justice done to all his children.

10D. JOB DIES (42.16-17)

RSV

TEV

16 And after this Job lived a hundred and forty years, and saw his sons, and his sons' sons, four generations. 17 And Job died, an old man, and full of days.

16 Job lived a hundred and forty years after this, long enough to see his grandchildren and great-grandchildren. 17 And then he died at a very great age.

Division Heading

The final heading brings the story to a close. The Handbook heading may be followed, or the translator may say, for example, "Job lived a long time and died," "This is the way Job ended," or "And now Job is old and so he dies."

42.16   RSV   TEV

And after this Job lived a hundred and forty years, and saw his sons, and his sons' sons, four generations.

Job lived a hundred and forty years after this, long enough to see his grandchildren and great-grandchildren.

As the text stands, **And after this** refers to Job arranging for his daughters to inherit along with the brothers. However, **after this** may also refer to the end of Job's troubles, and that Job lived 140 years after his restoration. The Septuagint has "Job lived after the affliction 170 years, and all the years he lived were 240 years." This makes Job 70 years old at the time of his misfortune, the end of one normal life span according to Psalm 90.10. **A hundred and forty years** may represent another example of doubling, so that Job lived 70 years before and 2 x 70 years after. The concluding paragraph gives Job's life an ending similar to that of the patriarchs in Genesis.

It is not known how the author counts generations when he says **four generations**. Job lived to see his sons and his son's sons, which would be his grandsons. If Job saw four generations of his descendants, as the Hebrew says, he probably would have seen his great grandsons. By contrast Joseph, who lived 110 years, saw his grandchildren to the third generation (Gen 50.23). According to Psalm 128.6, to see your children's children is a supreme blessing and the crown of old age (Prov 17.6). TEV is no doubt correct with "to see his grandchildren and his great-grandchildren." In some languages verse 16 may be translated as "After these matters were tied up, Job lived a hundred and forty years more. So he lived long enough to see his sons and the children of his sons and all others that were born, up to the fourth generation from Job." Or "After all this had taken place, Job lived another hundred and forty years. Thus he lived long enough to see four generations of descendants."

42.17   RSV   TEV

And Job died, an old man, and full of   **And then he died at a very great age.**
days.

The close of Job's life is described by the traditional formula used of Abraham in Genesis 25.8, of Isaac in Genesis 35.29, and of David in 1 Chronicles 29.28. In this way Job dies as **an old man full of days**, meaning "as a very old man." He takes his place with the patriarchs, the heroes of Israel's faith.

Ancient Star Patterns

From ancient times people have observed the stars and have seen how they seem to form certain patterns. These observers often associated the patterns with various figures they were acquainted with, and these were frequently figures from stories and myths. They therefore named the star patterns, or constellations, after the names of the figures they knew from mythology. Even today these names are used by astronomers to refer to certain star constellations.

In the Book of Job several constellations are mentioned, and it will be necessary for translators to determine how to identify and name them in the receptor language. Normally this is done by naming them according to the system used in schools for teaching students about the stars. In some cases there may be local names for groups of stars, and translators should be prepared to investigate this possibility and translate accordingly.

The constellations mentioned in the Book of Job include the Big and Little Bear, Orion, and the Pleiades. The Pleiades is a small cluster of six stars which can be hidden by your thumb even if you hold your thumb at arm's length. The ancient story was that there were seven sisters, and these were pursued by the hunter, Orion. The gods rescued them by carrying them off into the sky, where they became stars. Only six can be seen; the seventh was hidden completely from Orion!

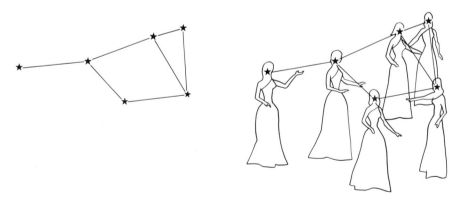

THE PLEIADES

Orion, the hunter, is depicted carrying a club in one hand and the skin of a lion in the other hand. Stars form his belt as well as a sword that hangs from it. Orion can be seen directly above the equator. He looks toward the northwest, where he can see but can never reach the Pleiades.

ORION

The tail of the Little Bear ends with the North Star, which is positioned almost directly over the north pole. The Big Bear and the Little Bear are sometimes known as the Big Dipper and the Little Dipper, because their stars that are most easily seen appear to form two dippers, or cups with long handles. The two stars that form the larger end of the Big Dipper are known as the pointer stars because they form the beginning of a straight line that leads to the North Star at the tail end of the Little Dipper.

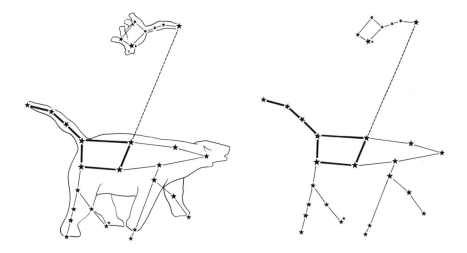

THE BIG BEAR AND THE LITTLE BEAR

Selected Bibliography

BIBLE TEXTS, VERSIONS, AND HELPS

Ancient Texts

Biblia Hebraica Stuttgartensia. 1967, 1977, 1983. Edited by K. Elliger and W. Rudolph. Stuttgart: Deutsche Bibelgesellschaft.

The Septuagint with Apocrypha: Greek and English. 1851. Edited by Lancelot C.L. Brenton. 11th printing. Grand Rapids, Michigan: Zondervan. (Cited as Septuagint.)

Septuaginta: Id est Vetus Testamentum graece iuxta LXX interpretes. 1935, 1979. Edited by Alfred Rahlfs. Stuttgart: Deutsche Bibelgesellschaft.

Modern Versions

Die Bibel in heutigem Deutsch: Die Gute Nachricht des Alten und Neuen Testaments. 1982. Stuttgart: Deutsche Bibelgesellschaft. (Cited as GECL, German Common Language Version)

The Bible: A New Translation. 1922, 1954. James Moffatt, translator. New York: Harper and Row. (Cited as Mft.)

La Bible de Jérusalem. 1984. Paris: Éditions du Cerf. (Cited as BJ.)

La Bible en français courant. 1982. Paris: Société biblique française. (Cited as FRCL, French Common Language Version.)

Dios Habla Hoy: La Biblia, Versión Popular. 1966, 1970, 1979. New York: Sociedades Bíblicas Unidas. (Cited as SPCL, Spanish Common Language Version.)

Good News Bible: The Bible in Today's English Version. 1976, 1979. New York: American Bible Society. (Cited as TEV.)

The Holy Bible. (Authorized, or King James Version). 1611. (Cited as KJV.)

The Holy Bible: New International Version. 1973, 1978, 1987. New York: New York International Bible Society. (Cited as NIV.)

The Living Bible: Paraphrased. 1971. Wheaton, Illinois: Tyndale House Publications. (Cited as LB.)

The New American Bible. 1983. New York: Thomas Nelson Publications. (Cited as NAB.)

The New English Bible. 1961, 1970. London: Oxford University Press; and Cambridge: Cambridge University Press. (Cited as NEB.)

The New Jerusalem Bible. 1985. Garden City, New York: Doubleday. (Cited as NJB.)

The Oxford Annotated Bible with the Apocrypha: Revised Standard Version. 1962, 1965. Herbert G. May and Bruce Metzger, editors. New York: Oxford University Press. (Cited as RSV.)

TANAKH: A New Translation of the Holy Scriptures According to the Traditional Hebrew Text. 1985. Philadelphia: The Jewish Publication Society. (Cited as NJV, New Jewish Version.)

Traduction œcuménique de la Bible. 1988. Paris: Société biblique française et Éditions du Cerf. (Cited as TOB.)

Lexicons, Concordances, and Other Reference Works

Barthélemy, Dominique; A.R. Hulst; Norbert Lohfink; W.D. McHardy; H.P. Rüger; and James A. Sanders. 1979. *Preliminary and Interim Report on the Hebrew Old Testament Text Project*, Volume 3, *Poetical Books*. New York: United Bibile Societies. (Cited as HOTTP.)

Brown, Francis; S.R. Driver; and Charles A. Briggs, editors. 1968. *A Hebrew and English Lexicon of the Old Testament*. London: Oxford University Press. (Cited as BDB.)

Fauna and Flora of the Bible. 1972. London: United Bible Societies.

Holladay, William L., editor. 1971. *A Concise Hebrew and Aramaic Lexicon of the Old Testament*. Leiden: E. J. Brill; and Grand Rapids, Michigan: Eerdmans.

Koehler, Ludwig, and Walter Baumgartner, editors. 1958. *Lexicon in Veteris Testamenti Libros*. Two volumes. Leiden: E. J. Brill. (Cited as K-B.)

Lisowsky, Gerhard, editor. 1958. *Konkordanz zum hebräischen Alten Testament*. Stuttgart: Württembergische Bibelanstalt.

Nelson's Complete Concordance of the Revised Standard Version. 1957. New York: Thomas Nelson.

Robinson, David, editor. 1983. *Concordance to the Good News Bible*. Swindon: The British and Foreign Bible Society.

GENERAL BIBLIOGRAPHY

Commentaries

Dhorme, Edouard. 1967. *A Commentary on the Book of Job*. H. Knight, translator. New York: Thomas Nelson.

Freehof, Solomon B. 1958. *The Book of Job, A Commentary* (The Jewish Commentary for Bible Readers). New York: Union of American Hebrew Congregations.

Gordis, Robert. 1978. *The Book of Job: Commentary, New Translation and Special Studies*. New York: Jewish Theological Seminary of America.

Habel, Norman C. 1985. *The Book of Job: A Commentary* (The Old Testament Library). Philadelphia: Westminister Press.

Pope, Marvin H., editor. 1965. *Job: Introduction, Translation, and Notes* (The Anchor Bible). Garden City, New York: Doubleday.

Rowley, Harold H. Revised edition, 1976. *The Book of Job* (The New Century Bible Commentary). Grand Rapids, Michigan: Eerdmans; and London: Marshall, Morgan, and Scott.

Tur-Sinai, Nahum H. (H. Torczyner). 1967, revised edition 1981. *The Book of Job: A New Commentary*. Jerusalem: Kiryat-Sepher.

Special Studies

Alter, Robert. 1985. *The Art of Biblical Poetry*. New York: Basic Books.

Berlin, Adele. 1985. *The Dynamics of Biblical Parallelism*. Bloomington: Indiana Universty Press.

Collins, T. 1979. *Line-Forms in Hebrew Poetry*. Rome: Biblical Institute Press.

Geller, Stephen A. 1979. *Parallelism in Early Biblical Poetry*. Missoula, Montana: Scholars Press.

Greenstein, Edward L. 1982. "How does parallelism mean?" In *A Sense of Text: The Art of Language in the Study of Biblical Liaterature*. Papers from a symposium on Literature, Language and the Study of the Bible at the Dropsie College. Winona Lake, Indiana: Eisenbrauns.

Grossberg, Daniel. 1989. *Centripetal and Centrifugal Structures in Biblical Poetry* (The Society of Biblical Literature, Monograph Series No. 39). Atlanta: Scholars Press.

Kugel, James L. 1981. *The Idea of Biblical Poetry: Parallelism and Its History.* New Haven: Yale University Press.

O'Connor, M. 1980. *Hebrew Verse Structure.* Winona Lake, Indiana: Eisenbrauns.

Watson, Wilfred G. E. 1984. *Classical Hebrew Poetry: A Guide to Its Techniques.* Journal for the Study of the Old Testament, Supplement Series 26. Sheffield, England.

Wendland, Ernst R. 1984. "Patterns of Inclusion in Job: Their Forms and Functional Significance." Paper presented at the United Bible Societies Trienniel Translation Workshop, May 15-26, at Bernhäuser Forst, Stuttgart, West Germany.

Glossary

This Glossary contains terms that are technical from an exegetical or a linguistic viewpoint. Other terms not defined here may be referred to in a Bible dictionary.

ABSTRACT refers to terms which designate the qualities and quantities (that is, the features) of objects and events but which are not objects or events themselves. For example, "red" is a quality of a number of objects but is not a thing in and of itself. Typical abstracts include "goodness," "beauty," "length," "breadth," and "time."

ACROSTIC refers to a style of writing lines, usually poetic lines, in such a way that the first letter of every line will combine with the other first letters to form the letters of the alphabet in their order, or else to form a phrase or a message.

ACTIVE. See **VOICE**.

ACTOR (AGENT) is the one who accomplishes the action in a sentence or clause, regardless of whether the grammatical construction is active or passive. In "John struck Bill" (active) and "Bill was struck by John" (passive), the actor in either case is John.

ADJECTIVE is a word which limits, describes, or qualifies a noun. In English, "red," "tall," "beautiful," and "important" are adjectives.

ADVERB is a word which limits, describes, or qualifies a verb, an adjective, or another adverb. In English, "quickly," "soon," "primarily," and "very" are adverbs.

ADVERBIAL refers to adverbs. An **ADVERBIAL PHRASE** is a phrase which functions as an adverb. See **PHRASE**.

AGENT. See **ACTOR**.

ALLITERATION is the repetition of the same sound or group of sounds in a series of words, as in "He is a genuine genius of a gentleman."

AMBIGUOUS (AMBIGUITY) describes a word or phrase which in a specific context may have two or more different meanings. For example, "Bill did not leave because John came" could mean either (1) "the coming of John prevented Bill from leaving" or (2) "the coming of John was not the cause of Bill's leaving." It is often the case that what is ambiguous in written form is not ambiguous when

788

actually spoken, since features of intonation and slight pauses usually make clear which of two or more meanings is intended. Furthermore, even in written discourse, the entire context normally serves to indicate which meaning is intended by the writer.

ANCIENT VERSIONS. See **VERSIONS.**

ANIMATE identifies objects which are regarded as alive and normally able to move voluntarily. "Man," "dog," and "fish" are animate objects, but "tree" is not.

ANTECEDENT describes a person or thing which precedes or exists prior to something or someone else. In grammar, an antecedent is the word, phrase, or clause to which a pronoun refers.

APPOSITION is the placing of two expressions together so that they both refer to the same object, event, or concept; for example, "my friend, Mr. Smith." The one expression is said to be the **APPOSITIVE** of the other.

ARAMAIC is a language that was widely used in Southwest Asia before the time of Christ. It became the common language of the Jewish people in Palestine in place of Hebrew, to which it is related.

ARTICLE is a grammatical class of words, often obligatory, which indicate whether the following word is definite or indefinite. In English the **DEFINITE ARTICLE** is "the," and the **INDEFINITE ARTICLE** is "a" or ("an").

CAUSATIVE relates to events and indicates that someone or something caused something to happen, rather than that the person or thing did it directly. In "John ran the horse," the verb "ran" is a causative, since it was not John who ran, but rather it was John who caused the horse to run.

CHIASMUS (CHIASTIC) is a reversal of words or phrases in an otherwise parallel construction. For example: "I (1) / was shapen (2) / in iniquity (3) // in sin (3) / did my mother conceive (2) / me (1)."

CLAUSE is a grammatical construction, normally consisting of a subject and a predicate. An **INDEPENDENT CLAUSE** may stand alone. The **MAIN CLAUSE** is that clause in a sentence which could stand alone as a complete sentence, but which has one or more dependent or subordinate clauses related to it. A **SUBORDINATE CLAUSE** is dependent on the main clause, but it does not form a complete sentence.

COLLECTIVE refers to a number of things (or persons) considered as a whole. In English, a collective noun is considered to be singular or plural, more or less on the basis of traditional usage; for example, "The crowd is (the people are) becoming angry."

COMMON LANGUAGE TRANSLATION is one that uses only that portion of the total resources of a language that is understood and accepted by all as good usage. Excluded are features peculiar to a dialect, substandard or vulgar language, and technical or highly literary language not understood by all.

COMPARATIVE refers to the form of an adjective or adverb that indicates that the object or event described possesses a certain quality to a greater or lesser degree than does another object or event. "Richer" and "smaller" are adjectives in the comparative degree, while "sooner" and "more quickly" are adverbs in the comparative degree. See also **SUPERLATIVE**.

CONCESSIVE means expressing a concession, that is, the allowance or admission of something which is at variance with the principal thing stated. Concession is usually expressed in English by "though" ("even though," "although"). For example, "Though the current was swift, James was able to cross the stream."

CONDITIONAL refers to a clause or phrase which expresses or implies a condition, in English usually introduced by "if."

CONDITION-CONSEQUENCE describes two parts of an expression, the one showing condition and the other the result. The parts are usually introduced by conjunctions such as "if" and "then," as in "If it will rain, then I will stay home."

CONJECTURE. See **TEXTUAL**.

CONJUNCTIONS are words which serve as connectors between words, phrases, clauses, and sentences. "And," "but," "if," and "because" are typical conjunctions in English.

CONNECTIVE is a word or phrase which connects other words, phrases, clauses, etc. See **CONJUNCTIONS**.

CONSEQUENCE is that which shows the result of a condition or event.

CONSONANTS are symbols representing those speech sounds which are produced by obstructing, blocking, or restricting the free passage of air from the lungs through the mouth. They were originally the only spoken sounds recorded in the Hebrew system of writing; **VOWELS** were added later as marks associated with the **CONSONANTS**. See also **VOWELS**.

CONSTRUCTION. See **STRUCTURE**.

CONTEXT (CONTEXTUAL) is that which precedes and/or follows any part of a discourse. For example, the context of a word or phrase in Scripture would be the other words and phrases associated with it in the sentence, paragraph, section, and even the entire book in which it occurs. The context of a term often affects its meaning, so that a word does not mean exactly the same thing in one context that it does in another context.

CONTRASTIVE expresses something opposed to or in contrast to something already stated. "But" and "however" are **CONTRASTIVE CONJUNCTIONS**.

COORDINATE structure is a phrase or clause joined to another phrase or clause, but not dependent on it. Coordinate structures are joined by such conjunctions as "and" or "but," as in "the man and the boys" or "he walked but she ran"; or they are paratactically related, as in "he walked; she ran."

COPYISTS were people who made handwritten copies of books, before the invention of printing. See **MANUSCRIPTS**.

CULTURE (**CULTURAL**) is the sum total of the beliefs, patterns of behavior, and sets of interpersonal relations of any group of people. A culture is passed on from one generation to another, but undergoes development or gradual change.

DEPENDENT CLAUSE is a grammatical construction consisting normally of a subject and predicate, which is dependent upon or embedded within some other construction. For example, "if he comes" is a dependent clause in the sentence "If he comes, we'll have to leave." See **CLAUSE**.

DIRECT ADDRESS, DIRECT DISCOURSE, DIRECT SPEECH. See **DISCOURSE**.

DISCOURSE is the connected and continuous communication of thought by means of language, whether spoken or written. The way in which the elements of a discourse are arranged is called **DISCOURSE STRUCTURE. DIRECT DISCOURSE** (or, **DIRECT ADDRES, DIRECT SPEECH**) is the reproduction of the actual words of one person quoted and included in the discourse of another person; for example, "He declared 'I will have nothing to do with this man.'" **INDIRECT DISCOURSE** (or, **INDIRECT ADDRESS, INDIRECT SPEECH**) is the reporting of the words of one person within the discourse of another person, but in an altered grammatical form rather than as an exact quotation; for example, "He said he would have nothing to do with that man."

DISTRIBUTIVE refers not to the group as a whole, but to the members of the group.

DYNAMIC EQUIVALENCE is a type of translation in which the message of the original text is so conveyed in the receptor language that the response of the receptors is (or, can be) essentially like that of the original receptors, or that the receptors can in large measure comprehend the response of the original receptors, if, as in certain languages, the differences between the two cultures are extremely great. In recent years the term **FUNCTIONAL EQUIVALENCE** has been applied to what is essentially the same kind of translation.

ELLIPSIS (plural, **ELLIPSES**) or **ELLIPTICAL EXPRESSION** refers to words or phrases normally omitted in a discourse when the sense is perfectly clear without them.

In the following sentence, the words within brackets are **ELLIPTICAL**: "If [it is] necessary [for me to do so], I will wait up all night." What is elliptical in one language may need to be expressed in another.

EMENDATION (EMEND) is the process of substituting what appears to be a better form of the text for one which is judged to be incorrect.

EMPHASIS (EMPHATIC) is the special importance given to an element in a discourse, sometimes indicated by the choice of words or by position in the sentence. For example, in "Never will I eat pork again," "Never" is given emphasis by placing it at the beginning of the sentence.

EUPHEMISM is a mild or indirect term used in the place of another term which is felt to be impolite, distasteful, or vulgar; for example, "to pass away" is a euphemism for "to die."

EXCLUSIVE first person plural excludes the person(s) addressed. That is, a speaker may use "we" to refer to himself and his companions, while specifically excluding the person(s) to whom he is speaking. See **INCLUSIVE**.

EXCLUSIVE AND INCLUSIVE LANGUAGE are terms that apply to certain uses in languages such as English, where a term that includes only a portion of a group is used to refer to the entire group. For example, "brothers" is appropriate as an **EXCLUSIVE** term if indeed the intended meaning of the text does exclude sisters; however, when "brothers" designates, for example, fellow believers who are both male and female, it is far better to use an **INCLUSIVE** expression such as "fellow Christians" or "believers." Of course, in languages where the term for "brother" already includes both male and female, there will be no such problem.

EXEGESIS (EXEGETICAL) is the process of determining the meaning of a text (or the result of this process), normally in terms of "who said what to whom under what circumstances and with what intent." A correct exegesis is indispensable before a passage can be translated correctly.

EXPLICIT refers to information which is expressed in the words of a discourse. This is in contrast to implicit information. See **IMPLICIT**.

FIGURE, FIGURE OF SPEECH, or **FIGURATIVE EXPRESSION** involves the use of words in other than their literal or ordinary sense, in order to bring out some aspect of meaning by means of comparison or association. For example, "raindrops dancing on the street," or "his speech was like thunder." **METAPHORS** and **SIMILES** are figures of speech.

FIRST PERSON. See **PERSON**.

FUTURE TENSE. See **TENSE**.

GENERIC has reference to a general class or kind of objects, events, or abstracts; it is the opposite of **SPECIFIC**. For example, the term "animal" is generic in relation to "dog," which is a specific kind of animal. However, "dog" is generic in relation to the more specific term "poodle."

GRAMMATICAL refers to **GRAMMAR**, which includes the selection and arrangement of words in phrases, clauses, and sentences.

HYPERBOLE is a figure of speech that makes use of exaggeration. That is, a deliberate overstatement is made to create a special effect. For example, "John ate tons of rice for dinner."

HYPOTHETICAL refers to something which is not recognized as a fact but which is assumed to be true to develop an argument or line of reasoning.

IDEOPHONE is a vocal expression, often one that does not fit into the usual grammatical pattern of a language, yet expresses such things as an emotion, a quality, or a movement, and may sometimes mark or emphasize a feature of discourse. Ideophones are especially common in African languages, where their use and definition vary greatly.

IDIOM, or **IDIOMATIC EXPRESSION**, is a combination of terms whose meanings cannot be understood by adding up the meanings of the parts. "To hang one's head," "to have a green thumb," and "behind the eightball" are American English idioms. Idioms almost always lose their meaning or convey a wrong meaning when translated literally from one language to another.

IMPERATIVE refers to forms of a verb which indicate commands or requests. In "Go and do likewise," the verbs "Go" and "do" are imperatives. In most languages imperatives are confined to the grammatical second person; but some languages have corresponding forms for the first and third persons. These are usually expressed in English by the use of "must" or "let"; for example, "We must not swim here!" or "They must work harder!" or "Let them eat cake!"

IMPLICIT (IMPLIED, IMPLICATION) refers to information that is not formally represented in a discourse, since it is assumed that it is already known to the receptor, or evident from the meaning of the words in question. For example, the phrase "the other son" carries with it the implicit information that there is a son in addition to the one mentioned. This is in contrast to **EXPLICIT** information, which is expressly stated in a discourse. See **EXPLICIT**.

INCLUSIVE first person plural includes both the speaker and the one(s) to whom that person is speaking. See **EXCLUSIVE**.

INDICATIVE refers to forms of a verb in which an act or condition is stated as an actual fact rather than as a potentiality, a hope, or an unrealized condition. The verb "won" in "The king won the battle" is in the indicative form.

INDIRECT ADDRESS, INDIRECT DISCOURSE, INDIRECT SPEECH. See **DISCOURSE.**

INFINITIVE is a verb form which indicates an action or state without specifying such factors as agent or time; for example, "to mark," "to sing," or "to go." It is in contrast to **FINITE VERB** form, which often distinguishes person, number, tense, mode, or aspect; for example "marked," "sung," or "will go."

INSTRUMENT (INSTRUMENTAL) is the object used in accomplishing an action. In the sentence "John opened the door with a key," the "key" is the instrument. See also **ACTOR.**

INTERPRETATION of a text is the exegesis of it. See **EXEGESIS.**

INTERROGATIVE pertains to asking a question.

IRONY (IRONIC, IRONICAL) is a sarcastic or humorous manner of discourse in which what is said is intended to express its opposite: for example, "That was a smart thing to do!" when intended to convey the meaning, "That was a stupid thing to do!"

LINGUISTIC refers to language, especially the formal structure of language.

LITERAL means the ordinary or primary meaning of a term or expression, in contrast with a figurative meaning. A **LITERAL TRANSLATION** is one which represents the exact words and word order of the source language; such a translation is frequently unnatural or awkward in the receptor language.

MANUSCRIPTS are books, documents, or letters written or copied by hand. A **SCRIBE** is one who copies a manuscript. Thousands of manuscript copies of various Old and New Testament books still exist, but none of the original manuscripts. See **TEXT.**

MASORETIC TEXT is the form of the text of the Hebrew Old Testament established by Hebrew scholars around the eighth and ninth centuries **A.D.**

METAPHOR is likening one object, event, or state to another by speaking of it as if it were the other; for example, "flowers dancing in the breeze" compares the movement of flowers with dancing. Metaphors are the most commonly used figures of speech and are often so subtle that a speaker or writer is not conscious of the fact that he or she is using figurative language. See **SIMILE.**

MODIFIER is a grammatical term referring to a word or a phrase which is used to **MODIFY** or affect the meaning of another part of the sentence, such as an adjective modifying a noun or an adverb modifying a verb.

NONFIGURATIVE. See **FIGURE, FIGURATIVE.**

NOUN is a word that names a person, place, thing, or idea, and often serves to specify a subject or topic of discussion.

OBJECT of a verb is the goal of an event or action specified by the verb. In "John hit the ball," the object of "hit" is "ball."

PARAGRAPH is a distinct segment of discourse dealing with a particular idea, and usually marked with an indentation on a new line.

PARALLEL, PARALLELISM, generally refers to some similarity in the content and/or form of a construction; for example, "The man was blind, and he could not see." The structures that correspond to each other in the two statements are said to be parallel.

PARENTHETICAL statement is a statement that interrupts a discourse by departing from its main theme. It is frequently set off by marks of parenthesis ( ).

PARTICIPLE is a verbal adjective, that is, a word which retains some of the characteristics of a verb while functioning as an adjective. In "singing children" and "painted house," "singing" and "painted" are participles.

PARTICLE is a small word whose grammatical form does not change. In English the most common particles are prepositions and conjunctions.

PASSIVE. See **VOICE**.

PAST TENSE. See **TENSE**.

PERSON, as a grammatical term, refers to the speaker, the person spoken to, or the person or thing spoken about. **FIRST PERSON** is the person(s) speaking (such as "I," "me," "my," "mine," "we," "us," "our," or "ours"). **SECOND PERSON** is the person(s) or thing(s) spoken to (such as "thou," "thee," "thy," "thine," "ye," "you," "your," or "yours"). **THIRD PERSON** is the person(s) or thing(s) spoken about (such as "he," "she," "it," "his," "her," "them," or "their"). The examples here given are all pronouns, but in many languages the verb forms have affixes which indicate first, second, or third person and also indicate whether they are **SINGULAR** or **PLURAL**.

PERSONIFY (PERSONIFICATION) is to refer to an inanimate object or an abstract idea in terms that give it a personal or a human nature; as in "Wisdom is calling out," referring to wisdom as if it were a person.

PHRASE is a grammatical construction of two or more words, but less than a complete clause or a sentence. A phrase is usually given a name according to its function in a sentence, such as "noun phrase," "verb phrase," or "prepositional phrase."

PLAY ON WORDS in a discourse is the use of the similarity in the sounds of two words to produce a special effect.

PLURAL refers to the form of a word which indicates more than one. See **SINGULAR**.

PREFIX is a part of a word which cannot stand alone and which is positioned at the beginning of the word to which it belongs; for example, "im-possible," or "re-structure."

PREPOSITION is a word (usually a **PARTICLE**) whose function is to indicate the relation of a noun or pronoun to another noun, pronoun, verb, or adjective. Some English prepositions are "for," "from," "in," "to," and "with."

PRESENT TENSE. See **TENSE**.

PRONOMINAL refers to **PRONOUNS**.

PRONOUNS are words which are used in place of nouns, such as "he," "him," "his," "she," "we," "them," "who," "which," "this," or "these."

PROSE is the ordinary form of spoken or written language, without the special forms and structure of meter and rhythm which are characteristic of poetry.

QUALIFIER (QUALIFICATION) is a term which limits the meaning of another term.

QUALIFY is to limit the meaning of a term by means of another term. For example, in "old man," the term "old" qualifies the term "man."

RECEPTOR is the person(s) receiving a message. The **RECEPTOR LANGUAGE** is the language into which a translation is made. For example, in a translation from Hebrew into German, Hebrew is the source language and German is the receptor language.

REDUNDANT (REDUNDANCY) refers to anything which is entirely predictable from the context. For example, in "John, he did it," the pronoun "he" is redundant. A feature may be redundant and yet may be important to retain in certain languages, perhaps for stylistic or for grammatical reasons.

REFERENT is the thing(s) or person(s) referred to by a pronoun, phrase, or clause.

RELATIVE CLAUSE is a dependent clause which describes the object to which it refers. In "the man whom you saw," the clause "whom you saw" is relative because it relates to and describes "man."

RELATIVE PRONOUN is a pronoun which refers to a noun in another clause, and which serves to mark the subordination of its own clause to that noun; for example, in "This is the man who came to dinner," "who" is the relative pronoun referring to "the man" in the previous clause. The subordinated clause is also called a relative clause.

RENDERING (RENDER) is the manner in which a specific passage is translated from one language to another.

RESTRUCTURE. See **STRUCTURE.**

RHETORICAL QUESTION is an expression which is put in the form of a question but which is not intended to ask for information. Rhetorical questions are usually employed for the sake of emphasis.

SARCASM (SARCASTIC) is an ironical and frequently contemptuous manner of discourse in which what is said is intended to express its opposite; for example, "What a brilliant idea!" when intended to convey the meaning, "What a ridiculous idea!" (See also **IRONY.**)

SCRIBE, SCRIBAL. See **MANUSCRIPT.**

SECOND PERSON. See **PERSON.**

SEMANTIC (SEMANTICALLY) refers to meaning. **SEMANTICS** is the study of the meaning of language forms.

SENTENCE is a grammatical construction composed of one or more clauses and capable of standing alone.

SEPTUAGINT is a translation of the Hebrew Old Testament into Greek, begun some two hundred years before Christ. It is often abbreviated as LXX.

SIMILE (pronounced SIM-i-lee) is a **FIGURE OF SPEECH** which describes one event or object by comparing it to another, using "like," "as," or some other word to mark or signal the comparison. For example, "She runs like a deer," "He is as straight as an arrow." Similes are less subtle than metaphors in that metaphors do not mark the comparison with words such as "like" or "as." See **METAPHOR.**

SINGULAR refers to the form of a word which indicates one thing or person, in contrast to **PLURAL**, which indicates more than one. See **PLURAL.**

SOURCE LANGUAGE is the language in which the original message was produced. For the Old Testament it is the Hebrew language spoken at that time.

SPECIFIC refers to the opposite of general, **GENERIC.** See **GENERIC.**

STRUCTURE is the systematic arrangement of the elements of language, including the ways in which words combine into phrases, phrases into clauses, clauses into sentences, and sentences into larger units of discourse. Because this process may be compared to the building of a house or bridge, such words as

797

STRUCTURE and CONSTRUCTION are used in reference to it. To separate and rearrange the various components of a sentence or other unit of discourse in the translation process is to RESTRUCTURE it.

STYLE is a particular or a characteristic manner in discourse. Each language has certain distinctive STYLISTIC features which cannot be reproduced literally in another language. Within any language, certain groups of speakers may have their characteristic discourse styles, and among individual speakers and writers, each has his or her own style. Various stylistic devices are used for the purpose of achieving a more pleasing style. For example, synonyms are sometimes used to avoid the monotonous repetition of the same words, or the normal order of clauses and phrases may be altered for the sake of emphasis.

SUBJECT is one of the major divisions of a clause, the other being the predicate. In "The small boy walked to school," "The small boy" is the subject. Typically the subject is a noun phrase. It should not be confused with the semantic AGENT, or ACTOR.

SUFFIX is a letter or one or more syllables added to the end of a word, to modify the meaning in some manner. For example, "-s" suffixed to "tree" changes the word from singular to plural, "trees," while "-ing" suffixed to "sing" changes the verb to a participle, "singing."

SUPERLATIVE refers to the form of an adjective or adverb that indicates that the object or event described possesses a certain quality to a greater or lesser degree than does any other object or event implicitly or explicitly specified by the content. "Most happy" and "finest" are adjectives in the superlative degree. See also COMPARATIVE.

SYNONYMS are words which are different in form but similar in meaning, such as "boy" and "lad." Expressions which have essentially the same meaning are said to be SYNONYMOUS. No two words are completely synonymous.

SYRIAC is the name of a Semitic language, a part of the Aramaic family, used in Western Asia, into which the Bible was translated at a very early date.

TENSE is usually a form of a verb which indicates time relative to a discourse or some event in a discourse. The most common forms of tense are past, present, and future.

TEXTUAL refers to the various Hebrew and Greek manuscripts of the Scriptures. A TEXTUAL READING is the form in which words occur in a particular manuscript (or group of manuscripts), especially where it differs from others. TEXTUAL EVIDENCE is the cumulative evidence for a particular reading. TEXTUAL PROBLEMS arise when it is difficult to reconcile or to account for conflicting readings. TEXTUAL VARIANTS are readings of the same passage that differ in one or more details. A CONJECTURE is a scholar's reconstruction of what the ancient text may have been, even though no manuscript exists today to support that reconstruction.

THIRD PERSON. See **PERSON.**

TRANSLATION is the reproduction in a receptor language of the closest natural equivalent of a message in the source language, first, in terms of meaning, and second, in terms of style.

TRANSLITERATE (TRANSLITERATION) is to represent in the receptor language the approximate sounds or letters of words occurring in the source language, rather than translating their meaning; for example, "Amen" from the Hebrew, or the title "Christ" from the Greek.

TRANSPOSITION (TRANSPOSE) is the act, process, or result of exchanging the relative position of two elements, substituting one for the other. For example, the adjectives in "the little laughing girl" may be transposed to "the laughing little girl."

VERBS are a grammatical class of words which express existence, action, or occurrence, such as "be," "become," "run," or "think."

VERBAL has two meanings. (1) It may refer to expressions consisting of words, sometimes in distinction to forms of communication which do not employ words ("sign language," for example). (2) It may refer to word forms which are derived from verbs. For example, "coming" and "engaged" may be called verbals, and participles are called verbal adjectives.

VERSIONS are translations. The ancient, or early, versions are translations of the Bible, or of portions of the Bible, made in early times; for example, the Greek Septuagint, the ancient Syriac, or the Ethiopic versions.

VOCATIVE indicates that a word or phrase is used for referring to a person or persons spoken to. In "Brother, please come here," the word "Brother" is a vocative.

VOICE in grammar is the relation of the action expressed by a verb to the participants in the action. In English and many other languages, the **ACTIVE VOICE** indicates that the subject performs the action ("John hit the man"), while the **PASSIVE VOICE** indicates that the subject is being acted upon ("The man was hit").

VOWELS are symbols representing the sound of the vocal cords, produced by unobstructed air passing from the lungs though the mouth. They were not originally included in the Hebrew system of writing; they were added later as marks associated with the consonants. See also **CONSONANTS.**

VULGATE is the Latin version of the Bible translated and/or edited originally by Saint Jerome. It has been traditionally the official version of the Roman Catholic Church.

WORDPLAY (PLAY ON WORDS) in a discourse is the use of the similarity in the sounds of different words to produce a special effect.

Index

This Index includes concepts, key words, and terms for which the Handbook contains a discussion useful for translators. Hebrew words that are included are listed according to transliterated English alphabetical order.

PRINTED IN THE UNITED STATES OF AMERICA